The Design Studio

Developing Technical and Creative Skills Using AutoCAD and ADT

Carolyn Gibbs

California State University—Sacramento

Fairchild Books, Inc.

New York

Director of Sales and Acquisitions: Dana Meltzer-Berkowitz

Executive Editor: Olga T. Kontzias

Acquisitions Editor: Joseph Miranda

Assistant Acquisitions Editor: Jaclyn Bergeron

Senior Development Editor: Jennifer Crane

Development Editor: Michelle Levy

Art Director: Adam B. Bohannon

Production Manager: Ginger Hillman

Senior Production Editor: Elizabeth Marotta

Assistant Development Editor: Blake Royer

Interior Design: Mary Neal Meador and Barbara Barg

Cover Design: Adam B. Bohannon

Library of Congress Catalog Card Number: 2007942715

ISBN: 978-1-56367-442-6

GST R 133004424

Printed in the United States of America

TP 12

Contents

Extended Contents

Preface

This textbook is a result of several colliding interests, all related to the advancement of student learning. The first interest is a result of the noticeable division between the CAD gurus and the computerphobes—students who continuously have a difficult time embracing the medium. Even with the adoption of CAD as a common drafting medium within practice and education, this division is still evident. This problem becomes especially apparent in the classroom. The high-learning curve required to learn and master most CAD programs continues to be overwhelming, leaving many student learners at a disadvantage in technology skill development. When looking for solutions, I realized that most textbooks explain the tools and then assume that students, through reading and practice, will become more efficient and productive in time. From my experience, I believe that CAD textbooks need to become better classroom teaching aids. They need to speak to all students regardless of learner type, from limited knowledge of the subject matter to an intermediate or advanced level.

My second interest is the importance of skill mastery. Only knowing CAD is no longer an advantage in the professional market. Fundamental principles of interior design and its space planning components are critical to drafting skill development. In a cyclical fashion, skill development is also critical to developing an advanced design vocabulary and thought process. Mastery over the software early on in the student's education is essential to the overall development of an interior designer.

My third interest relates to how CAD software could facilitate student learning of design and building vocabulary. Could the vocabulary and tools of CAD software provide a bridge to the principles and building systems of design? Could a textbook on CAD incorporate these ideas into a useful classroom aid? What positive impacts could the software bring to the traditional studio approach? These questions have been discussed for more than a decade. Have they been resolved? While it is questionable whether the architectural community has promoted the role of CAD software in reshaping design processes, anecdotal evidence has shown interior design to be undoubtedly lacking in this endeavor. Most CAD software programs are still used as drafting tools only, and most CAD textbooks remain technical manuals.

My final interest is the creative possibilities of CAD software—specifically AutoCAD and Architectural Desktop. CAD software's stereotypical role in the building design industry has always been presumed as a drafting medium only. AutoCAD as the leader within the industry has not been able to disengage itself from this primary role.

The introduction of Architectural Desktop (ADT) was an attempt to show users that it could create an integrated product that was good in the conceptual and schematic phases while it provided all the project organization and management that construction drawings require. The latest releases of ADT continue to promote a tight integration of the software into all phases of the design process—programming, conceptual, schematic, design development, contract documents, and construction administration. While not a true Building Information Modeling (BIM) program, ADT utilizes many of the features of BIM technology.

Acknowledgments

I would like to thank my support network—my friends, my colleagues, my family, my students, and Fairchild Books. Without their encouragement and assistance this book would never have found its way. Feedback offered by reviewers Sean MacNintch and Stephanie Clemons was helpful. Thanks also to my friends—Michele, Madeline, Tim, and Mithia—who were there for me when things got really tough. And a special thanks to all the students who helped contribute to the examples in the text. Finally, to my couch, who became my desk and chair, sofa and bed, and whereupon I completed most of this book.

Introduction

Technical skills development has always been a component of interior design and architectural curriculums. Its significance is usually a result of a school's overall philosophy and approach toward design. Although drawing skill development is critical to the demands of the profession in addition to creative thinking, many times CAD training is separated or downplayed in traditional studio curriculums. Many articles criticizing CAD for being taught within the design studio have done so based on the argument that students have no adeptness with digital tools and processes and are therefore hindered in design studio progress. There are just as many articles, however, that argue how computers can help with the design learning process.

This textbook obviously sides with the latter notion. It encourages the synthesis among creative skill development, (digital) drawing skill development, and practical skill development. Unlike other texts of its kind, it purposely focuses on the mastery of two specific software programs while exposing students to the various elements of design and construction practice.

The text uses Malcolm McCullough's concept of digital craft as its main driving force. Why craft? Because craft evokes images of artistry in combination with prowess. It is a term where creativity and function are collaborative partners.

There are very few textbooks on AutoCAD and Architectural Desktop tailored to beginner design students who know very little about their discipline. The textbooks that do exist stop short of extensive drawing complexity common to professional practice or advanced form manipulation. Using these textbooks tends to teach students only the basic AutoCAD skills. The concept of digital mastery applied in this textbook emphasizes CAD skill development and retention.

Purpose of the Text

CAD textbooks for students need to become better classroom teaching aids. They need to take the student from a limited knowledge base to an advanced level in a relatively short period of time. *The Design Studio* is tailored to the digital studio classroom. Its primary goals are as follows:

- To present AutoCAD and Architectural Desktop in an accessible and logical format that is technique-based and cross-referenced.
- To provide a means for students to achieve digital mastery at a quicker rate.
- To introduce beginner students to building systems and construction practice while learning to draw.
- To help students understand the significance of the synthesis between technical and creative skill development.
- To provide a guidebook that encourages good drawing practices—that is, drawing craft.

Secondary goals include the following:

- To help students become aware of the overall software strengths and limitations of AutoCAD and Architectural Desktop.
- To provide a useful classroom teaching aid that accommodates multiple learning styles.
- To advance visualization and creativity skill development in beginner and intermediate student designers.
- To motivate students to bring construction realities into the creative process.

Organization of Text and Specific Aims

The textbook is designed to be a general CAD manual and technique reference in one. Body text provides students with a thorough understanding of the topics in AutoCAD and Architectural Desktop while stepped procedures found in the Techniques to Master provide quick references to commonly used techniques and workflow processes used in digital drawing. And while each text part is sequential, students shouldn't feel the need to read the text consecutively. Instead, once students obtain a minimum of CAD skills, the textbook is designed to be cross-referenced during their progression in skill development.

To aid in this cross-referencing format, each Technique to Master is numbered to correspond to its associated figure number and chapter. For example, Technique T13.04 corresponds to Figure 13.4 in Chapter 13. Techniques also build on one another. Students are consistently directed to review foundation techniques as their learning skills advance.

Part I: Learning to Draw in 2-D with AutoCAD provides an introduction to AutoCAD and its basic commands.

Part II: Learning to Draw in 3-D with Architectural Desktop provides an introduction to 3-D modeling and the Architectural Desktop interface.

Part III: Drawing Technique Introduction to Drawing Craft and the Orthographic Drawing Types continues the development of digital skills in the context of drawing craft and efficiency.

Part IV: Linking Drawing Technique to Design Exploration provides an introduction to using the digital tools creatively.

Parts I and II of the textbook utilize the familiar, topic-based approach to present the AutoCAD and Architectural Desktop's commands and vocabulary. Its chapters summarize commands and procedures so that students become familiar with the programs. Parts I and II are also intended to be used as a reference for techniques. Both parts utilize drawing technique summaries and step-by-step demonstrations as the primary means for illustrating the CAD commands and concepts. Part II establishes the architecture behind the drawings by introducing Architectural Desktop's building objects within the context of building systems and construction practice. Chapter demonstrations and exercises help students become comfortable learning the tools of AutoCAD and ADT as well as encourage skill mastery over the topic.

Part III focuses on using the drawings as a communication tool for both presentation and construction purposes. While much of Part III is a drawing resource for the common orthographic types, it also concentrates on how the commands are used in the digital drawing/drafting process. Individual techniques from Parts I and II are referenced into workflow processes for more advanced skill development.

The drawing technique exercises in Part III concentrate on understanding how the workflow process is an important component to good drawing practice. The technique exercises for each chapter, which can be found on the accompanying CD-ROM, emphasize drawing craft development by encouraging conscientious workflow assessment. Dissecting a given drawing through analysis becomes an important learning tool in the CAD classroom and beyond.

Part IV presents the creative and exploratory side to AutoCAD and ADT. Topics on using the techniques discussed in Parts I, II, and III for advancing design development are presented. Chapters discuss various ideas for using AutoCAD and ADT creatively, including brainstorming and design alternative approaches. Design Expression Problems provide students with additional practice solving several types of creative conditions using the suggested approaches.

Key Features of the Textbook

- The textbook can be used with AutoCAD 2004 to 2007 and Architectural Desktop 2004 to 2007.
- The textbook is designed to be used within a variety of classroom settings. Each chapter can be used as a separate teaching module. It provides chapter objectives and end-of-chapter exercises.
- The accompanying CD-ROM contains chapter exercises as well as sample drawing techniques and Design Expression Problems. It also includes templates and other material to help students customize their software.
- Chapter exercises include a diversity of problem types increasing in complexity to target all levels of learners. The exercises and problem types are designed to create a ladder for learning by integrating computer skill development with design skill development. Many exercises are short, allowing students to complete them within the allocated studio time periods.
- Exercises and problem types emphasize simultaneous left- and right-brain development by combining technique-driven steps with design problems requiring creative strategies so that students learn to quickly switch between the two.
- Throughout Parts II, III, and IV, the textbook encourages further student research in the areas of the building industry by directly referencing design practice and construction materials and methods.

Part I

Learning to Draw in 2-D with AutoCAD

Getting Started: The AutoCAD User Interface

1

Objectives

This chapter introduces you to the AutoCAD software platform and the techniques and concepts surrounding its user interface. It also emphasizes the importance of understanding the various parts of the AutoCAD user interface as well as creating, opening, saving, and plotting drawing files.

Working Efficiently

As a student, you will most likely need to access your files on your laptop or home desktop computer and your classroom computer. While AutoCAD and Architectural Desktop require only CD-ROM drives, you may want to upgrade to a CD-RW or DVD-RW. Most current computer systems are sold with writable CD drives. Another option is to use USB flash drives, which provide hard disk storage that is compact and portable. Affordable drives are available in 64, 128, 256, and 512 megabyte and 1 gigabyte increments.

Box 1.1 Understanding Units of Memory

1 kilobyte (KB) = 1,000 bytes

1 MB = 1 million bytes or 1,000 KB

1 GB = 1 billion bytes or 1,000 MB

small jpeg image = 150 KB

small Adobe Illustrator file = 1 MB

1-page Microsoft Word file = 28 KB

20-page Microsoft Word file = 76 KB

small AutoCAD file = 130 KB

large AutoCAD file = 2 MB

Starting AutoCAD

Although there are several ways to start AutoCAD, the standard method is to double-click on the icon that is typically found on your desktop. Figure 1.1 shows examples of the various icons for AutoCAD and Architectural Desktop you might find on a desktop. If there is no icon on the desktop, then click the Start button and find the program under Programs; click on the program name to open it (Figure 1.2). If you have already saved an AutoCAD drawing file, then you can also open the program by double-clicking on the file itself (Figure 1.3).

When you first open AutoCAD or Architectural Desktop, both programs default to a new blank drawing (Figure 1.4). This drawing has the generic name Drawing1.dwg. While users are able to begin their own

Figure 1.1 Software icons for AutoCAD and Architectural Desktop, 2005 through 2007.

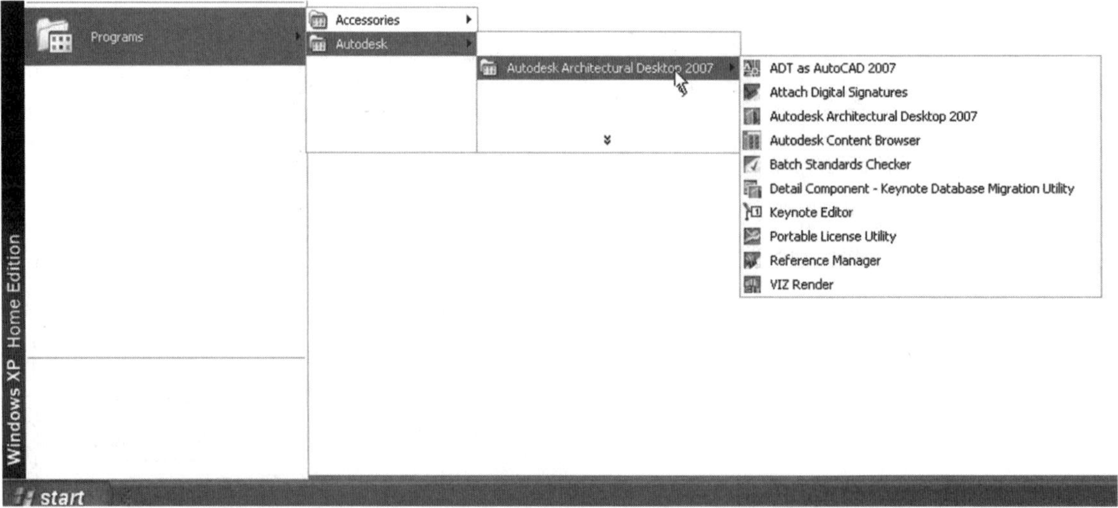

Figure 1.2 AutoCAD and Architectural Desktop programs are located in the Autodesk folder within the Microsoft Windows Start button and programs list.

Figure 1.3 The AutoCAD drawing file as shown in icon view. Open by double-clicking on it.

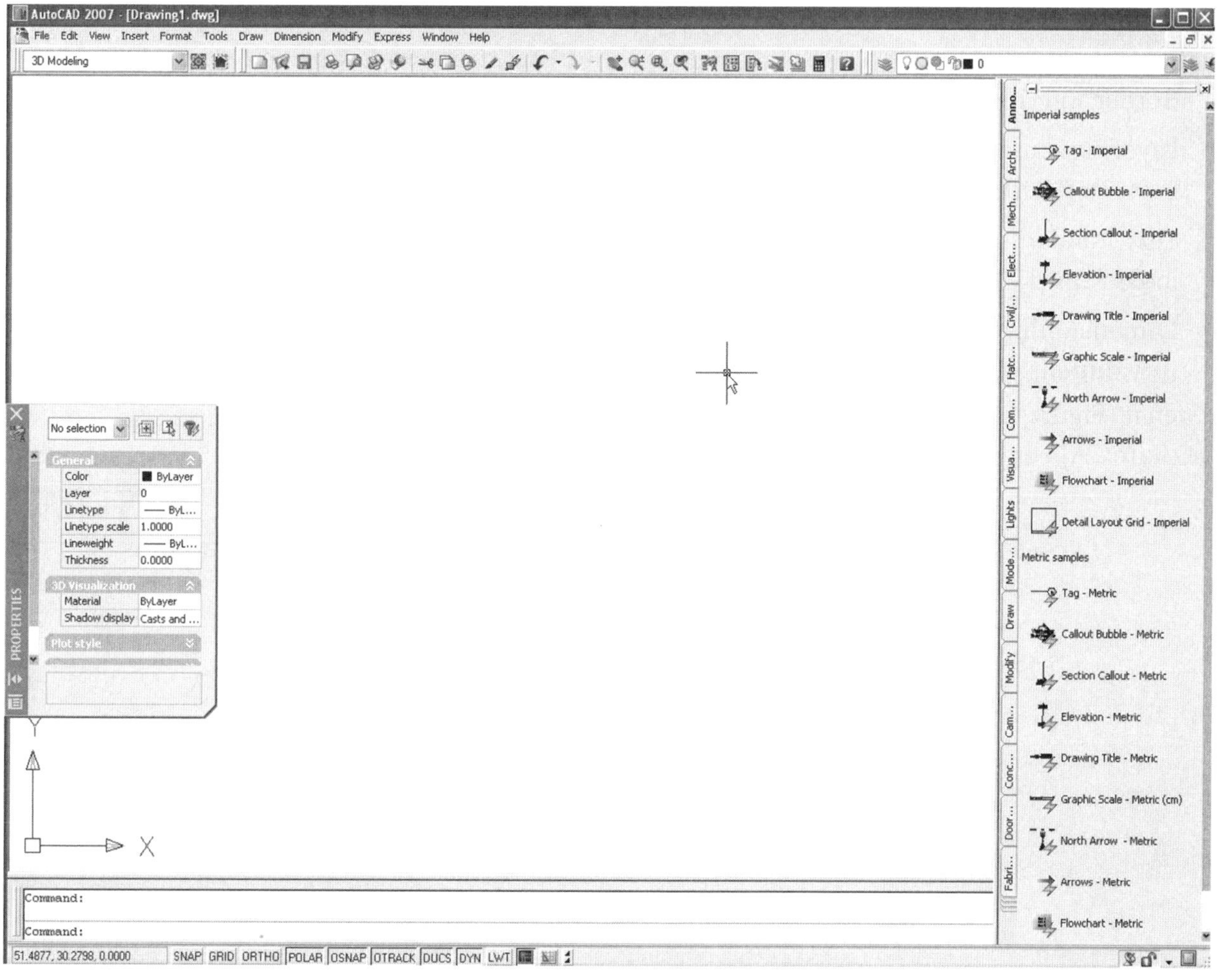

Figure 1.4 AutoCAD opens with a new unsaved drawing. When you create a new drawing, it is always temporarily named "Drawing" with a numeral suffix.

drawings using this generic blank, the settings are typically too broad for productive use. A better option is to start a new drawing using one of the many templates available (Figure 1.5). Templates use initial settings from prototype drawings. Templates are valuable because they allow users to save and reuse settings and other information that remain consistent from project to project. These settings are saved in the template file itself. Templates in design offices frequently hold the office's CAD standards, making it easier for designers and drafters to furnish drawings that adhere to common guidelines.

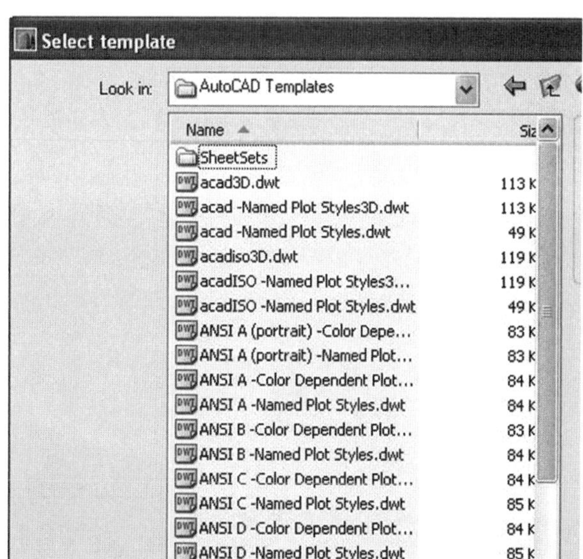

Figure 1.5 The Select Template dialogue box displays drawing templates that are a part of AutoCAD and Architectural Desktop.

Template information can include the following:

- Border and title block designs (Figure 1.6)
- Layering standards that organize the geometry within a drawing
- Text standards that establish how the text looks for various notes, titles, and so on
- Dimensioning standards that establish the way dimensions look

See Appendix A for a description of templates that are available in AutoCAD and Architectural Desktop.

To use a template, start a new drawing using the File>New menu command, or type in New at the command line. A Select Templates dialogue box appears and displays templates from which you can choose. Figure 1.7 demonstrates how users can create a new drawing by using existing AutoCAD and Architectural Desktop templates.

Figure 1.6 An example of a border design saved as a template file.

Technique to Master **T01.07** Creating New Drawings Based on a Template

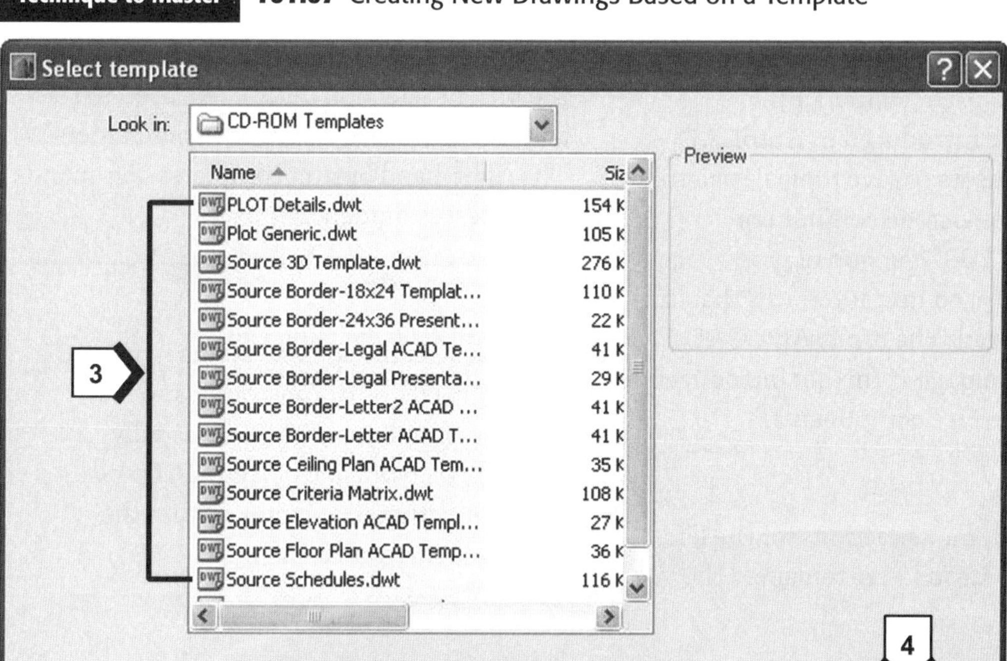

Figure 1.7 Create a new drawing by using one of the AutoCAD or Architectural Desktop templates.

1	[File menu]	Select New. The keyboard shortcut is Ctrl+N.
2	[Select Template dialogue]	At the bottom of the dialogue box, make sure File of Type reads Drawing Template (*.dwt).
3	[Select Template dialogue]	Select a template file on which to base a new drawing.
4	[Select Template dialogue]	Left-click the open button.

Note: For instructions on how to create a new drawing using a template from the CD-ROM, see Appendix B.

Box 1.2

Tip: You can change the folder locations of template files in the Options>Files tab dialogue box. To add your own customized template files or change the location of the template folder, see Appendix A.

Box 1.3

If you select the New icon, then AutoCAD starts a new drawing without giving you the choice to select a specific template.

Opening Existing Files

Users can open existing AutoCAD and Architectural Desktop files by double-clicking on the drawing file icon in any folder. However, if AutoCAD is already open, simply use the File>Open menu command or the File>Open icon located in the upper-left corner of the toolbar.

Workspaces

When you first open AutoCAD 2007, you see a dialogue box that displays choices for your initial workspace (Figure 1.8). Workspaces were introduced in AutoCAD 2006 and allow users to save toolbar, palette, and other drawing-screen component placements. The 2007 version of workspaces focuses on task-based user interfaces that can be fully customized. The topic, AutoCAD User Interface, on page 7, further introduces various user-interface components.

Learning to Use the Mouse

For the most part, mouse actions for the left- and right-hand buttons have remained the same for all types of mouse devices. Within the AutoCAD and Architectural Desktop environments, the left-hand button—called the pick or selection button—is used to start commands, select objects, or open folders. The right-hand button completes commands and accesses hidden menus.

> **Box 1.4**
> Because of the advancements in mouse design, customization of the mouse buttons and track wheels is usually performed outside of AutoCAD and Architectural Desktop—within the mouse software itself.

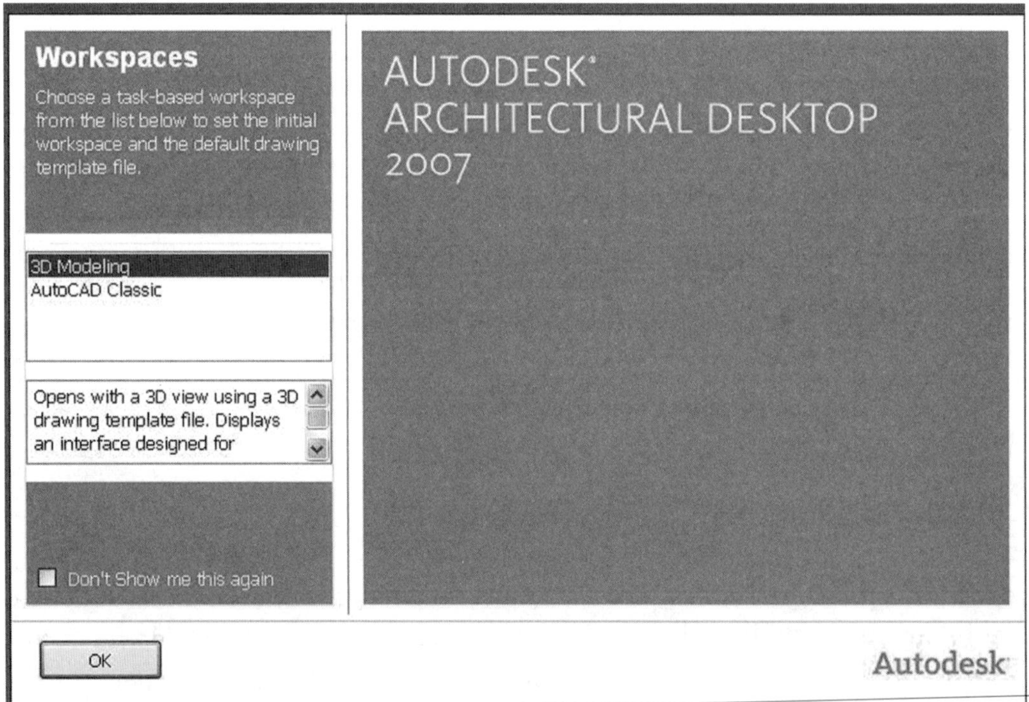

Figure 1.8 The workspace dialogue appears when you open an AutoCAD session. Check "Don't Show me this again" to hide the dialogue box in future sessions.

The AutoCAD User Interface

The AutoCAD screen is divided into various distinct areas: title bar, menu bar, drawing area, toolbars/button commands, palettes (Tools and Properties), Dashboard, status bar, Command Line, and scroll bar, as shown in Figure 1.9. Both AutoCAD and Architectural Desktop have similar user interfaces; however, this chapter focuses on AutoCAD's user interface. Differences between the two programs are discussed in Chapter 9.

Title Bar

The title bar is located at the very top of the screen and displays the application name (AutoCAD in this case) and the release date. If the drawing file is maximized, then the title bar also displays the drawing file name. As with title bars in most Microsoft Windows programs, this title bar includes three buttons at the far right. When multiple drawing files are open and maximized to the extents of the display, AutoCAD will display only the current drawing file.

Menu Bar

AutoCAD's menu bar is similar to all Microsoft Windows menu structures. It is located below the AutoCAD title bar. Left-clicking on one of the menu bar categories displays a series of cascading menus, where users can access most of AutoCAD's commands. For the most part,

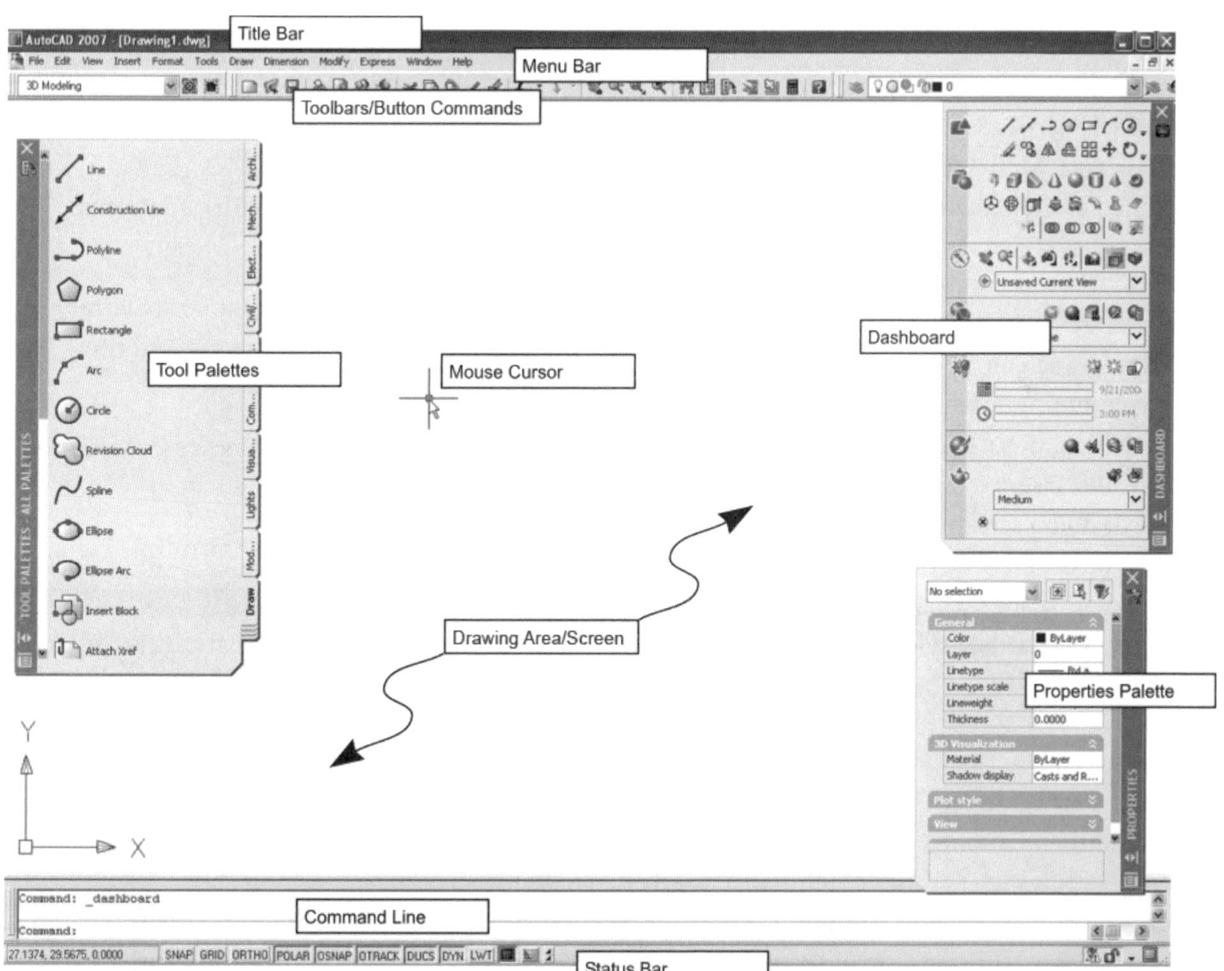

Figure 1.9 The AutoCAD user interface.

menus are divided by topic. For example, the Draw menu contains all of AutoCAD's drawing tools. Appendix C lists the various menus for AutoCAD and Architectural Desktop 2007. Because users can customize the menu bar, there may be additional menu topics that appear on various setups of AutoCAD and Architectural Desktop.

Drawing Area

The drawing area, or drawing screen, is the digital space that replaces the paper on which you would have manually drafted your work. It is the visible part of an infinite or a limitless space where you draw. You can use the zooming tools to view parts of the drawing area close up or from a distance. Chapter 2 discusses zooming in more detail. The default drawing area where you design and draw is called *model space*. The layout tab(s) located to the right of the model space tab open up the paper space drawing area. Model space and paper space are explained in more detail in Chapter 7.

Toolbars/Button Commands

Toolbars are located along the top and sides of the drawing screen. Each toolbar has buttons that have symbolic pictures called icons on them, which, in turn, call up specific AutoCAD commands. Users can place toolbars anywhere on the drawing screen in either docked or floating positions. The default AutoCAD Classic workspace opens with the following toolbars: Standards, Styles, Layers, Property, Draw, and Modify.

Palettes

Palettes were added to AutoCAD 2004. The Tool palette—just one type of available palette—allows users to save frequently used objects in icon-based environments. Tool palettes in the 2005 version of the software may contain hatches, blocks, commands, lisp routines, scripts, and drawing and raster files. Users who wish to add content to tool palettes typically save it locally (on their computers) and cannot share it with other computers (in a network).

Status Bar

The status bar area is located at the bottom of the AutoCAD screen and displays command toggles that are frequently used during the drawing process. Command toggles are used like on/off buttons. When the toggle is depressed, it is on or running. Later released versions of AutoCAD software have a series of balloon notifications displayed at the lower right-hand corner of the status bar to help users manage information that requires constant updating. Use the tray settings arrow to adjust the information that gets displayed.

> **Box 1.5 Other User Interface Shortcuts**
>
> **Ctrl+Tab** Flips among multiple opened drawing files.
>
> **Ctrl+0** Clean screen. Removes palettes, tool buttons, and so on to expand the drawing area real estate.
>
> **F2** Function key. Displays the Command Line in a full text window.
>
> **F1** Function key. Opens the online help.

One of the balloon notifications is the Communications Center, which communicates with the Autodesk website to provide up-to-date announcements, articles, and tips that are relevant to the product.

Command Line

The Command Line keeps and displays a record of your communications with AutoCAD. Users type commands and command option instructions in this window and send them to AutoCAD. AutoCAD communicates back by using a series of message prompts.

Scroll Bars

Scroll bars in AutoCAD work in the same manner they do in other Microsoft Windows applications. They move the drawing screen horizontally or vertically, allowing you to see hidden portions of the drawing area. In AutoCAD and Architectural Desktop, this action is called *panning*. Scroll bars are located at the right and bottom areas, adjacent to the drawing screen.

Viewing Your Drawings

The drawing area in AutoCAD gives users the flexibility to view one or more drawing files during their everyday workflow needs. Users are able to simultaneously view drawings at different magnification levels, and they may also view multiple drawings adjacent to one another.

Using Multiple Viewports Within a Single Drawing

When users open AutoCAD, the program displays a single drawing, called *the model space viewport.* Users can split this primary viewport into multiple viewports so they can view a drawing file at multiple magnification levels and viewing angles. Figure 1.10 shows the three model space viewports of a single floor plan drawing. The bottom viewport shows the floor plan in its entirety, the upper-left shows a close-up of the entry spaces, and the upper-right shows the workspaces. These viewports are showing three perspectives of the same drawing file.

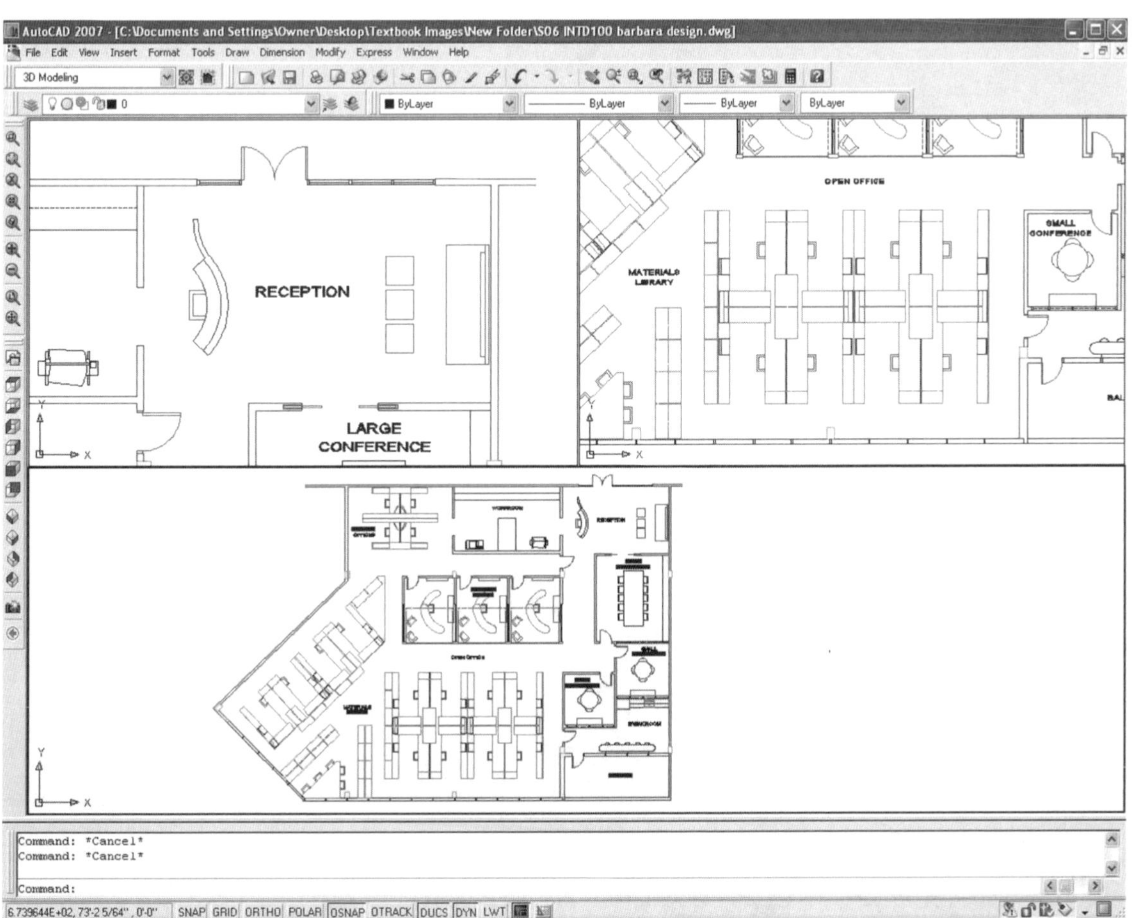

Figure 1.10 Office floor plan displayed in multiple viewports.
Student project: Office Renovation, courtesy of Barbara Rinehart.

Using Model Space Viewports in the Drawing Process

Viewports are extremely beneficial to users who need to work on three-dimensional drawings. They also come in handy when users need to work on multiple areas of a drawing simultaneously. Most intermediate to advanced users set up their drawing templates by using a combination of model space viewports to create user interfaces that give them maximum flexibility with the drawing tools. Figure 1.11 demonstrates how to create multiple viewports within a given model space viewport.

Viewing Multiple Drawings

AutoCAD gives users the ability to view multiple drawing files simultaneously, which brings added advantages for users who need to work on designs that use multiple files. Figure 1.12 illustrates how two drawings are placed side by side for simultaneous viewing. Drawing tiling is accomplished through the Tiling option in the window menu bar. The window menu bar shown in Figure 1.13 also shows a list of all drawings that are open. To switch among drawing files, select from the list. Users can also set the Taskbar system

Technique to Master **T01.11** Creating a Multiple Viewport Drawing Area

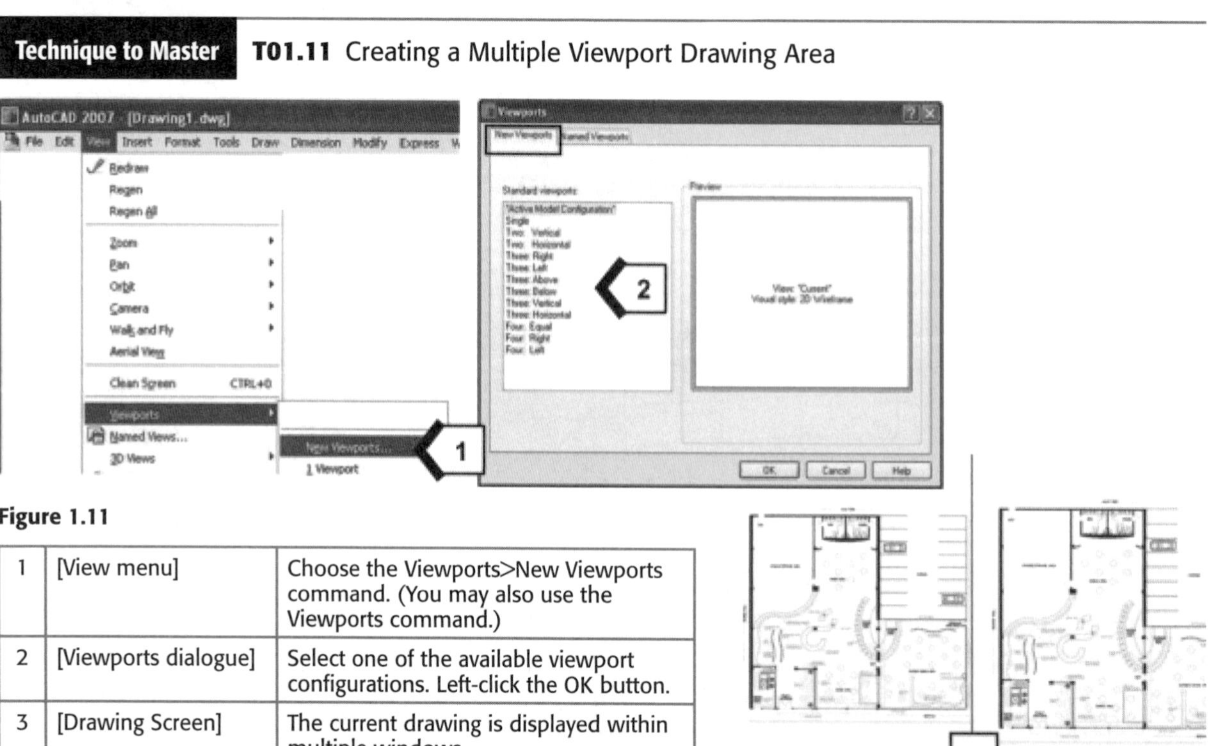

Figure 1.11

1	[View menu]	Choose the Viewports>New Viewports command. (You may also use the Viewports command.)
2	[Viewports dialogue]	Select one of the available viewport configurations. Left-click the OK button.
3	[Drawing Screen]	The current drawing is displayed within multiple windows.

Technique to Master **T01.12** Tiling Multiple Drawings

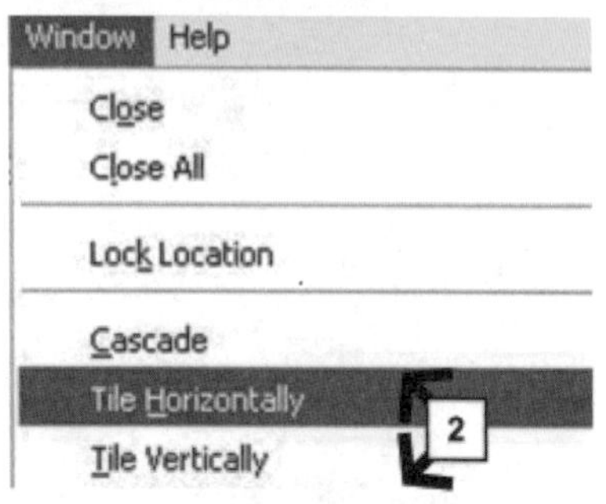

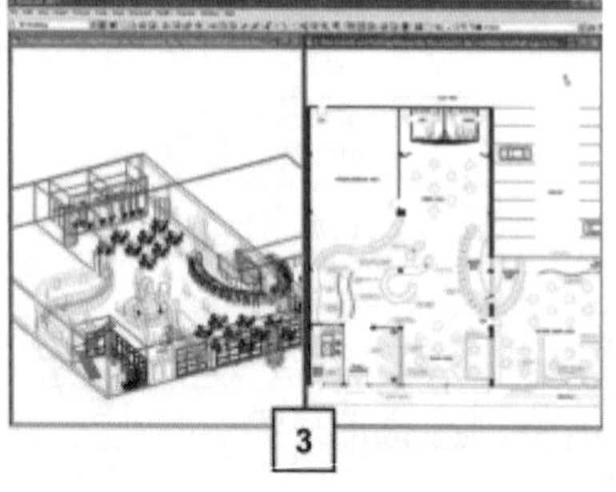

Figure 1.12

1	[File menu]	Open the two drawing files that you would like to see side by side.
2	[Window menu]	Choose the Tile Horizontally or Tile Vertically command.
3	[Drawing Screen]	Both drawing files are displayed simultaneously within the drawing area.

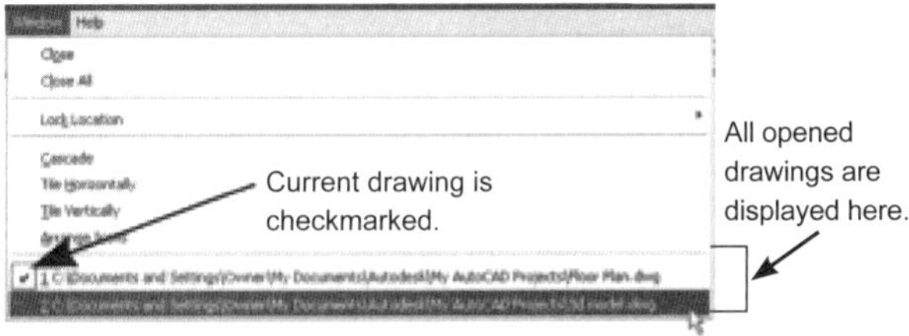

Figure 1.13 The Window menu displays all opened drawings. The checkmark designates the current drawing.

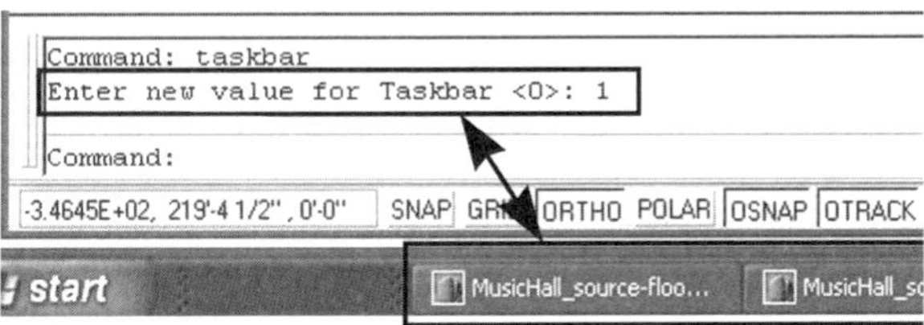

Figure 1.14 When the Taskbar system variable is set to 1, all opened drawings are displayed as separate icons on the Windows status bar.

variable to 1 so they can see each drawing file as an icon at the bottom of their computer screens (Figure 1.14).

The Design Center

The Design Center is AutoCAD's organizational file cabinet. It is a palette that combines the Windows Explorer tools with library database type functions. The Design Center can be opened by typing the command Adcenter or by using the Ctrl+2 shortcut. Since the Design Center is a palette, it has the same features (hide, close, minimize, dock, float, and so on) as other palettes in AutoCAD. Figure 1.15a–c displays the various areas of the Design Center palette.

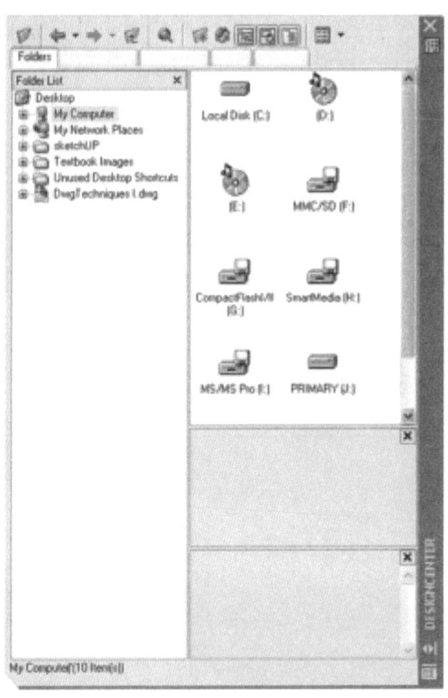

a

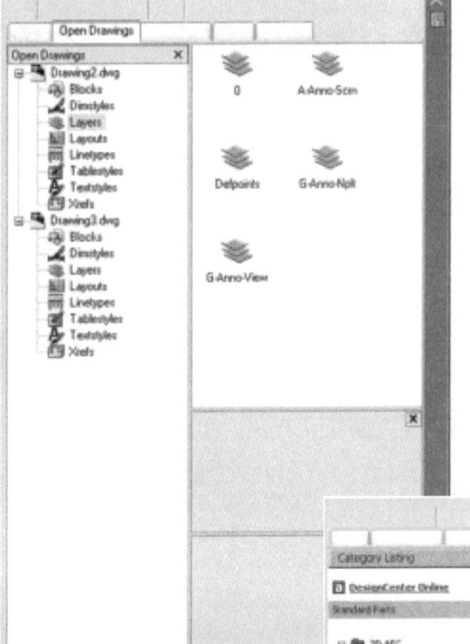

b

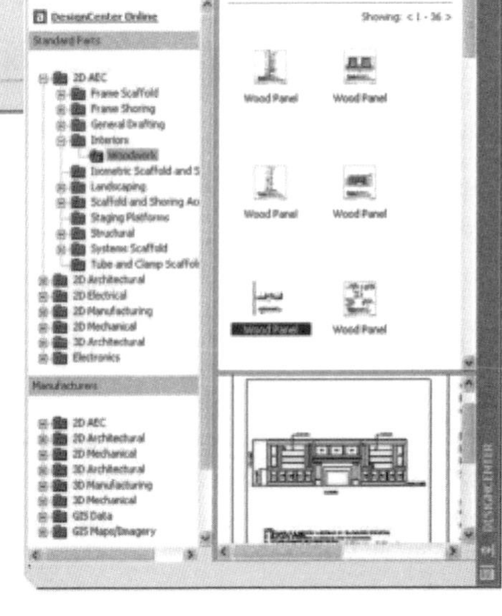

c

Figure 1.15 Getting to Know the Design Center Palette

The Folders tab. Similar to the Windows Explorer tab, the Folders tab shows the folder and subfolder tree of your computer and removable media drives. Use it to preview drawing files, hatch and linetype pattern files, and image files such as jpegs (.jpg) and bitmaps (.bmp). If you right-click on any of these files, it displays options for opening drawings, creating Tool palettes, and accessing other functions.

The Open Drawings tab. This tab displays all AutoCAD drawings that are open. Drawing content such as layers, blocks, and text styles can be easily exchanged among drawings.

DC Online tab. This tab is the gateway to countless symbols and product information from the Internet. It is organized into categories on the left and is continually updated and expanded. Additionally, product manufacturers constantly add symbols to this library. To use DC Online, your computer must be connected to the Internet.

Entering Commands in AutoCAD

The latest released versions of AutoCAD provide users with many approaches to communicate commands—they can use tool buttons, tool palettes, the Command Line, and menu commands. When AutoCAD was first released, it ran in a text-only environment; therefore, only the Menu Bar and Command Line were available. As Microsoft Windows evolved, AutoCAD was able to run in an increasingly icon-based, user-friendly environment. Today, Autodesk recognizes that everyone uses the software differently and keeps this built-in flexibility as one of its company's core values. Figure 1.16 (a–d) illustrates the different approaches to entering commands.

Commands and Command Sequences

A command refers to an order that is given to AutoCAD so that it can complete a task. The order initiates a command sequence—a series of steps that the program must follow to complete a given task. Except for dialogue box commands, every command has a required order in which AutoCAD asks for specific information so it may complete the command. During the progression of a command, AutoCAD prompts users for information it needs and waits for the response, which users either type in as an entry or supply with a mouse action. One of the fundamental skills users should strive to master during their AutoCAD training is learning what information the program needs to complete a task and knowing when this information is needed during a command's sequence. The more command sequences users memorize, the less intrusive this technology is in the design process.

Flexibility is built into the command sequence through command options. Command options

- allow users to input necessary information in a different sequence from the one required. For example, the default sequence for creating an arc is: start of arc segment, middle of arc segment, and then end of arc

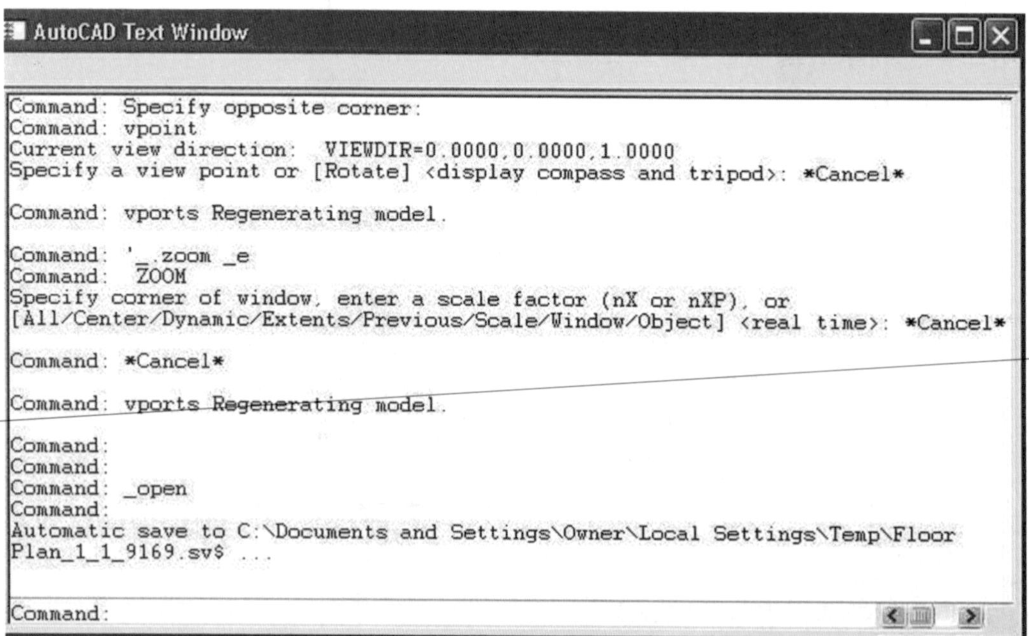

Figure 1.16a Entering AutoCAD commands—Command Line Entry.

Command Line entry refers to using the keyboard to type commands and other required information. Users can type into the command line anytime in the drawing and editing process as long as there is not a dialogue box in session.

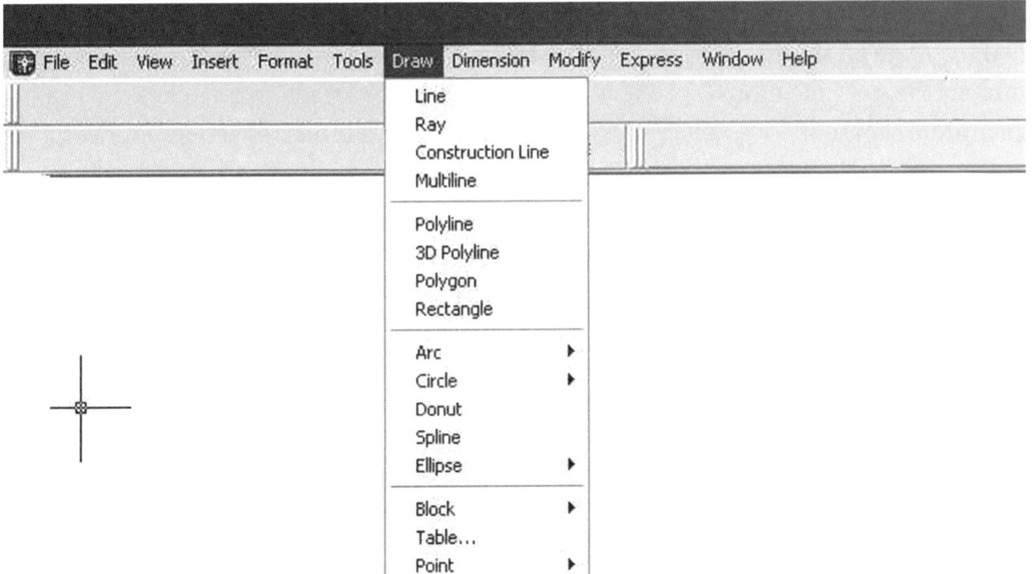

Figure 1.16b Entering AutoCAD commands—Menu Commands

Menu commands are mostly divided by topic; for example, the Draw menu contains all of AutoCAD's drawing tools.

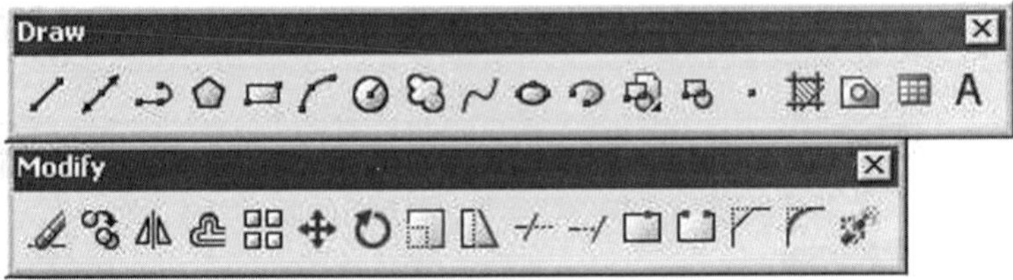

Figure 1.16c Entering AutoCAD commands—Toolbar Commands

To access toolbar commands, left-click once on the button. You can open additional toolbars by right-clicking on any AutoCAD toolbar you see on-screen.

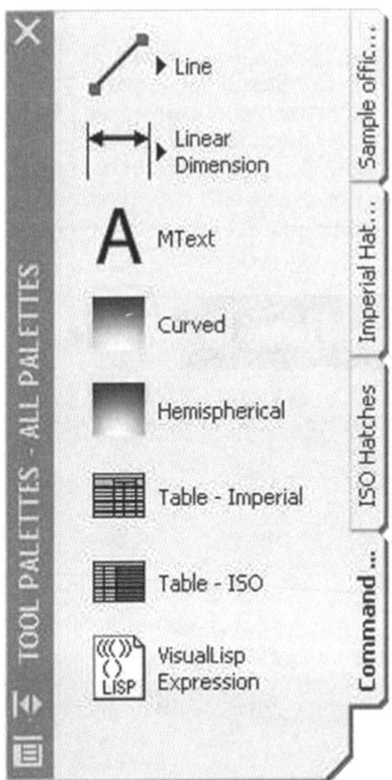

Figure 1.16d Entering AutoCAD commands—Tool Palette Commands

Tool palette commands are accessed by left-clicking once on the tool icon or name. The Tool palette is toggled on and off by using Ctrl+3. Tools located in tool palettes are able to

- run a command
- insert a symbol, an object, a pattern, or text into the existing drawing
- open a drawing file

How to use the Tool palette is explained in more detail in technique T01.18.

segment. However, there are times when you might need to create an arc by specifying the start and end segments before specifying the middle segment.

- provide additional sub-commands.

Look at Figure 1.17 to see how commands, command sequences, and command options work in AutoCAD. Figure 1.18 demonstrates how to use tool palette commands in more detail.

> **Box 1.6 Did You Know?**
> There is never a need to left-click within the Command Line area when you want to type a command or command option. AutoCAD automatically focuses the cursor whenever typed commands are used.

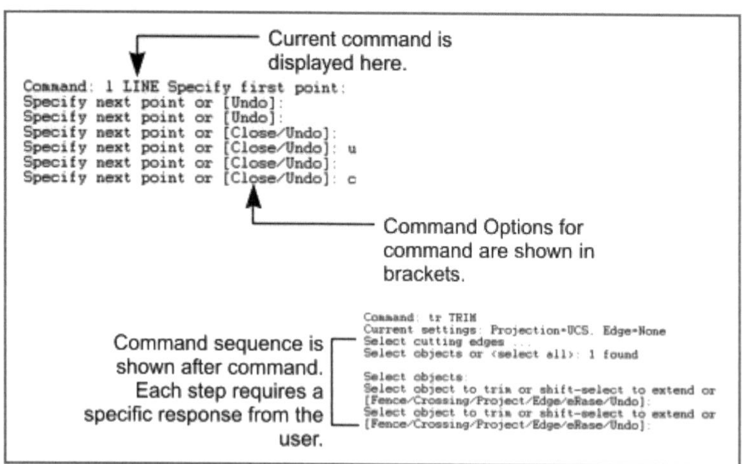

Figure 1.17 Understanding Command and Command Sequence Logic

The command sequences of the Line and Trim commands shown in the Command Line area. Notice that AutoCAD prompts for a specific location or selection (at the start of each sentence) and displays other responses that are also acceptable in brackets.

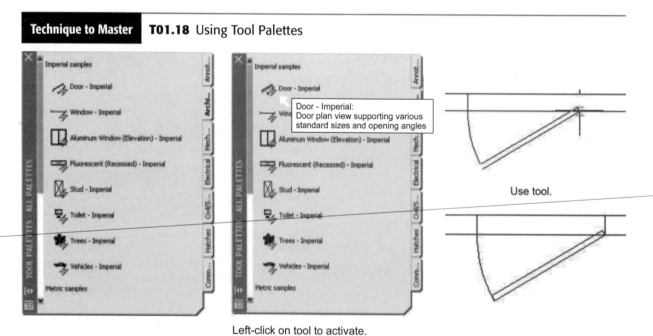

Technique to Master **T01.18** Using Tool Palettes

Door - Imperial: Door plan view supporting various standard sizes and opening angles

Use tool.

Left-click on tool to activate.

Figure 1.18

Choose the tool you want to use. Select the tool tab category, and select the tool symbol by left-clicking once on the tool.
If the tool is a symbol or pattern, place the symbol or pattern within your drawing by left-clicking once. If the tool is a command, follow the prompts displayed in the Command Line to complete the command.

Basic Output Concepts and Procedures

Output refers to the process of making a hard copy of a digital file. This section reviews the AutoCAD interface used in the output process, and essential vocabulary and concepts of output are explained.

Printers and Plotters to Output Your Work

Printers are connected to computers so software may output graphics and text onto paper. Most printers typically print to smaller pieces of paper; however, plotters are another type of output device that print to larger paper sizes (see Figure 1.19).

Figure 1.19 Example of a large format plotter.

Epson Stylus Photo 1270 ESC/P 2
EPSON Stylus Photo 1270
Adobe PDF
Adobe PDF.pc3
CSUS-1050C.pc3
CSUS-Monochrome-LaserPrinter.pc3
Default Windows System Printer.pc3

Figure 1.20a Plotting Vocabulary—The Printer/Plotter List Box

The Printer/Plotter list box displays the various printer/plotter options available.

Printing in AutoCAD

Printing from AutoCAD can be a confusing process. There are a large number of choices to make when you navigate your way through this dialogue-based command. For the most part, all the information for the Print command has remained the same on most of the released versions of AutoCAD; however, the look of the dialogue box has changed.

Plotting Vocabulary and Concepts

The Printer/Plotter Name list box (Figure 1.20a) allows you to select the type of device to which you want to print. The term *plotter* is herein used to refer to both printer and plotter devices. The number of available plotters is generally limited by the number you have attached to your computer or computer network. Left-clicking on the down arrow to the right of the list box will show you all available plotters. The plotter Properties button allows you to configure and customize the current plotter's settings.

If there is no plotter physically connected to your computer or network, then you may install and use a ghost plotter by clicking the Plot to File checkbox. It essentially allows you to print to plotters that are not connected to your computer or network. When you check Plot to File, AutoCAD creates a data file with a .plt extension and saves the file to a location you specify. The data file contains directions for how the drawing eventually prints and can be taken to a reprographics service that specializes in CAD printing.

All plotters have paper size limits as well as built-in margin limits. While not explicit, paper size limits are indicated through the Paper Size list box. It is a list that displays the various sizes to which the current plotter device can print. Additional sizes may be added through customization. Since paper sizes are always based on the chosen plotter device, it is always a good idea to choose the plotter *before* choosing the paper size.

Notice how in the list box there are standard sizes for sheets of paper that appear—some of which may be familiar. Letter, legal, and tabloid are the most popular paper sizes available for the majority of home and commercial printers. These descriptions refer to the following paper sizes: 8.5 × 11, 8.5 × 14, and 11 × 17. Plotters are used when jobs required paper sizes that are larger than 11 × 17. Typical plot widths start at 18 inches and continue up to 60 inches. Figure 1.20b shows a list of the many standard sizes available today.

Knowing paper size limits for printers and plotters is helpful when choosing the size of your drawing's borders. Remember, nothing prints outside of a paper's margin limits; therefore, paper sizes must be large enough to accommodate both the drawing's and the paper's margins.

The Plot area (Figure 1.20c) allows you to select the part of the drawing screen that you actually want to plot. These special selection commands offer four choices through the list box—selection of the display, selection through a window, selection of a saved view, and the drawing's limits.

The Plot scale area (Figure 1.20d) is where you specify the size at which the drawing will plot. (For a greater understanding of the meaning of scale, read the next section on scale and plotting, page 18.) It allows three different methods to input scale—the Fit-to-scale checkbox, Custom scale input, and Standard scale selection. The input method Fit to paper is a checkbox that is used when scaled drawings are not important. If the box is checked, AutoCAD fits the Plot area to the paper size without regard to any scale. Custom input gives you the opportunity to specify a scale ratio. The Scale list box displays a large selection of widely used plotting scales for interior design, architecture, and engineering.

Drawing orientation (Figure 1.20e) refers to the orientation of the image on the paper when it plots. Choices are portrait and landscape.

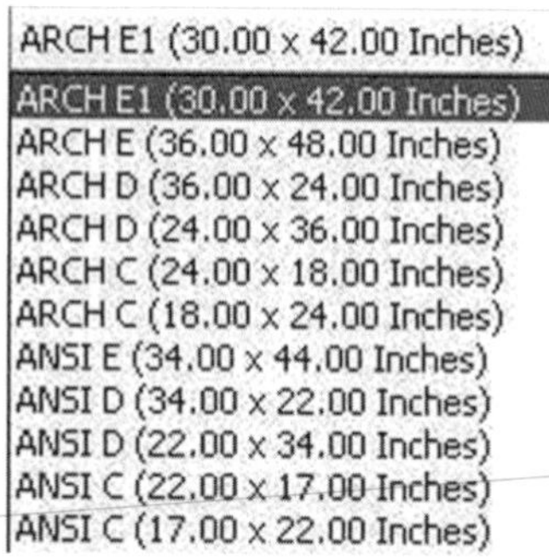

Figure 1.20b Plotting Vocabulary—Paper Sizes

The paper sizes shown in the list box are specific to the selected printer/plotter.

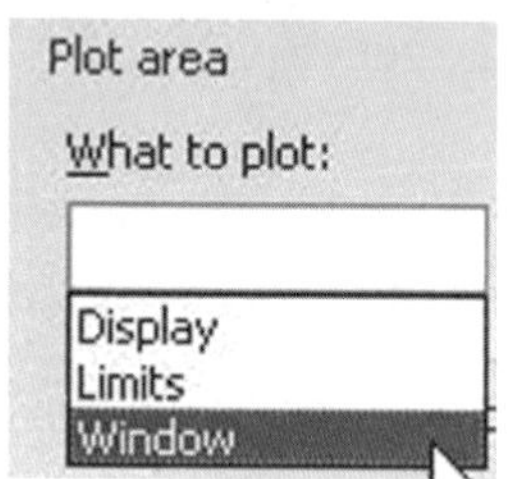

Figure 1.20c Plotting Vocabulary—Plot Area

The Plot area options within the Plot area list box let users select from three options when they select the areas of the drawing screen they want to print.

1/128" = 1'-0"
1/64" = 1'-0"
1/32" = 1'-0"
1/16" = 1'-0"
3/32" = 1'-0"
1/8" = 1'-0"
3/16" = 1'-0"
1/4" = 1'-0"
3/8" = 1'-0"
1/2" = 1'-0"

Figure 1.20d Plotting Vocabulary—Plot Scale

Preset scales are listed in the Standard Scale list box.

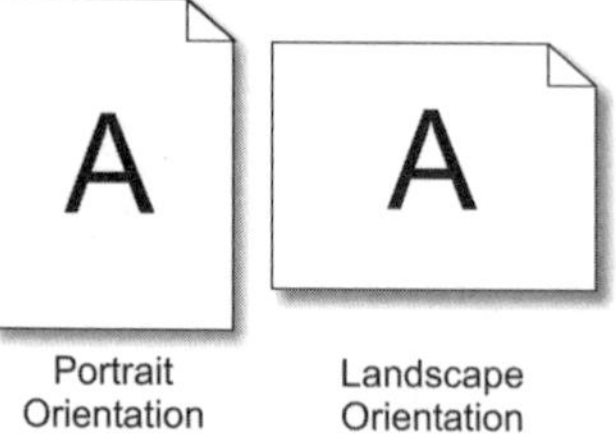

Figure 1.20e Plotting Vocabulary—Drawing Orientation

The drawing orientation options are Portrait and Landscape.

DWF Virtual Pens.ctb
Fill Patterns.ctb
Grayscale.ctb
hp1050c_full.ctb
hp1050c_half.ctb
hp1050c_temp.ctb
hp5si-fine.ctb
Monochrome - all one weight

Figure 1.20f Plotting Vocabulary—Plot Style

The Plot style option lists the available Plot style tables.

The Plot style parameter uses Plot style tables (Figure 1.20f) to control how AutoCAD communicates color, line thickness, and other line characteristics to the plotter. Color-dependent plot styles assign color to line thickness. It is the old method of plotting in AutoCAD and is still a part of many office standards today. Style-dependent plot styles assign previously set color, line thickness, and other line characteristics to a named style. The default style of Normal, found in all .stb plot style tables, plots AutoCAD geometry using the object's color and line thickness properties.

The Plotting Process

Now that you are familiar with the various plotting terminology, the workflow is illustrated in Figure 1.21. Until familiarity is established, the steps should be followed in the order given.

Technique to Master **T01.21** The Plotting Process Within the Plot dialogue box

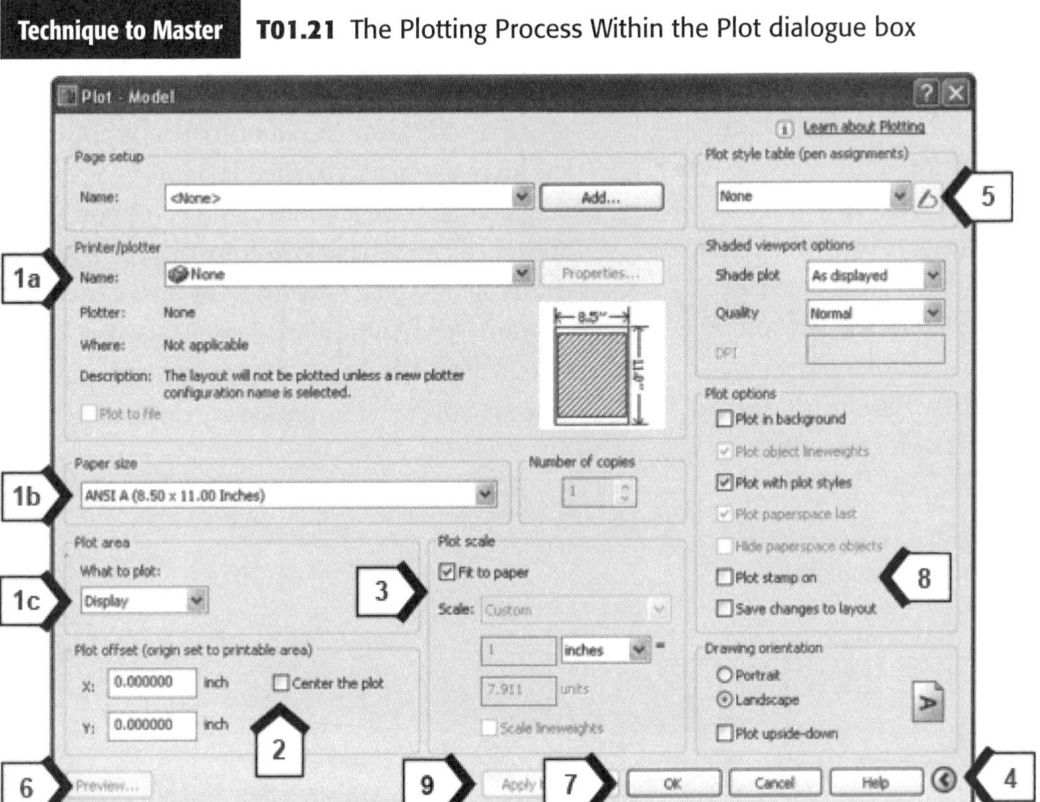

Figure 1.21

1	Choose (or verify) the plotter or printer you want to use, the paper size, and the Plot area.
2	Check the "Center the plot" checkbox.
3	Choose (or verify) the Plot scale. If the scale does not matter, check Fit to Scale. (If Plot Scale is grayed out, simply uncheck Fit to Scale.)
4	Users of versions from 2004 to 2006 should left-click the arrow at the lower-right of the dialogue box for more selections.
5	Choose (or verify) the Plot style table.
6	Full preview the Plot. (Press the Enter key to finish displaying in preview mode.)
7	Left-click on the OK button to plot.
	Optional steps include
8	Checkmark the Plot stamp on box.
9	Save the Plot settings using the Apply to Layout button.

Scale and Plotting

Drawing within AutoCAD requires users to draw in real units. For example, if you want to create a drawing that represents what the side of a chair looks like, then you would draw it at its true dimensions—width, height, and depth. However, because of its size, it would be difficult to print this chair drawing at its real units. Instead, you would need to use a ratio method to print it so that the rendition of the chair is still measurable on an 8½ × 11 sheet of paper.

When printing, if the ratio ¼" = 1'-0" is used, it means that every ¼" measured on a drawing represents 12 inches in real life (Figure 1.22). Therefore, if the height of the chair drawing is 3 feet and printed at ¼" = 1'-0", the height will measure only ¾" on paper. Try it. Measure it with a regular inch ruler (Figure 1.23). In every released version of AutoCAD, there is a location on the Plot dialogue box to specify this ratio. It's called setting the plotting scale for the drawing.

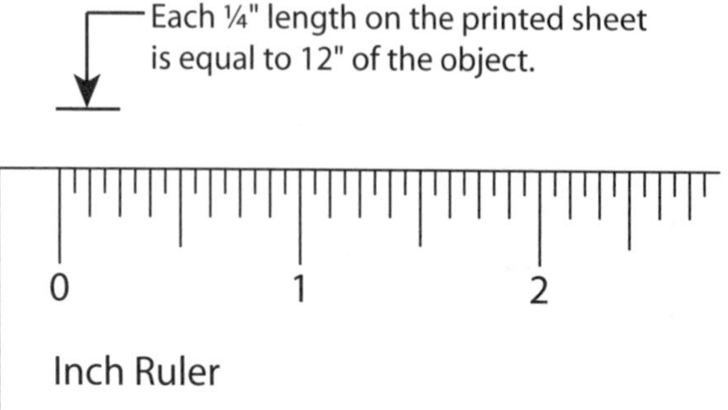

Figure 1.22 Understanding scale and scaled drawings

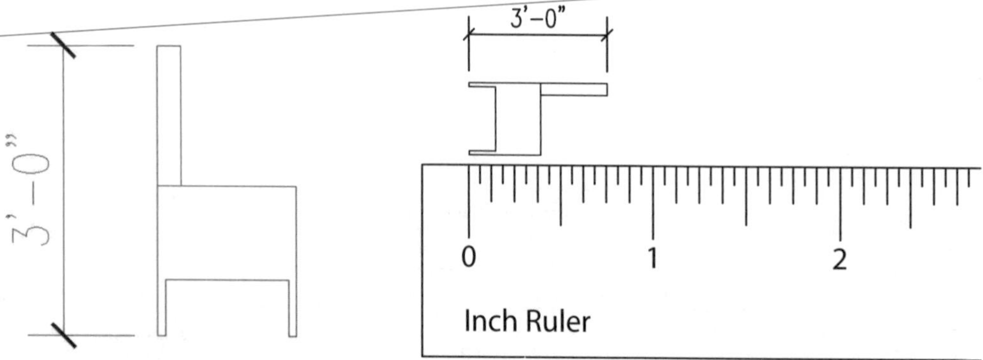

Figure 1.23 Side view of a chair as a drawing within AutoCAD. Side view of a chair after it is printed at ¼" = 1'-0".

Saving and Exiting AutoCAD

There are several ways to save and store your work sessions with AutoCAD. The following section briefly describes these options.

If you want to save changes to an existing drawing, then use the File>Save command or Save tool button to save it in its original location with its original name. It replaces the .dwg file.

If you want to save a new drawing or one that still has AutoCAD's default Drawing name, then use the File>Save command to save your drawing to a specific location using whatever new name you decide (Figure 1.24). Once saved, AutoCAD automatically appends the .dwg extension to the file name.

The File>Save As command gives you the ability to create a backup copy of a current drawing or start a new drawing based on a current opened drawing. Do not use the File>Save As command for routine saving since it can create unnecessary duplicate files.

Technique to Master **T01.24** Saving a New Drawing

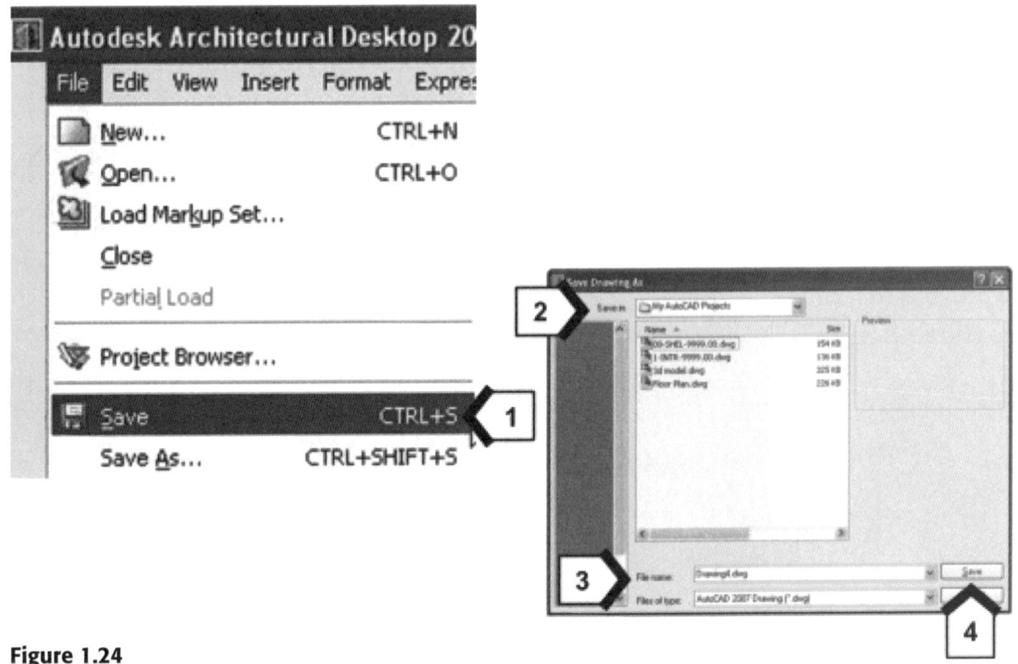

Figure 1.24

1	[File menu]	Choose the Save command or use the Ctrl+S shortcut.
2	[Save Drawing As dialogue box]	To the right of the Save in list box, use the arrow to specify the subfolder within which the drawing will be saved.
3	[Save Drawing As dialogue box]	Name the file within the File Name list box. Refer to Chapter 7 for file naming guidelines.
4	[Save Drawing As dialogue box]	Left-click on the Save button to save.

Saving Strategies

Since AutoCAD has limited automatic saving capabilities, it is a good idea to develop saving strategies when working on a project. Saving strategies refer to how you save, when you save, and where you save. These strategies help prevent erasing accidents and file corruption problems, saving you time and effort. Two main strategies are as follows:

1. Save often to prevent recent design changes from being lost because of computer crashes. Use the File>Save command (or Ctrl+S) every 5 to 10 minutes to ensure all changes made to the .dwg file are saved.
2. Save backup copies of all important drawing files within a project. After each drawing session, make two copies. Save one copy within the same media as the original drawing; save the other on an external media storage device to protect work from lost or damaged computers.

Exiting AutoCAD

Exit AutoCAD by using the File>Exit command (Ctrl+Q). Make sure you save all important design and drawing work prior to exiting or as part of the exiting process. AutoCAD always prompts you to save a drawing that has been changed in any way. Pay attention to these prompts and respond accordingly.

Chapter Exercises

Open the Chapter 01 Exercise Text.doc located on the supplementary CD-ROM to access the chapter exercises. Workspace customization and template creation exercises allow you to continue exploring AutoCAD's user interface.

Learning to Draw Precisely

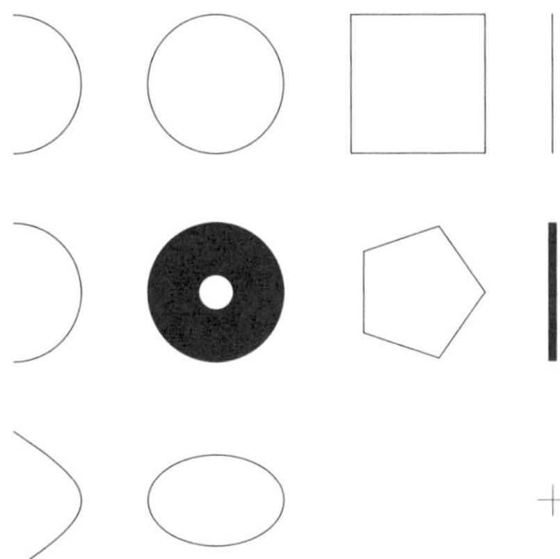

Figure 2.1 The basic shapes of AutoCAD

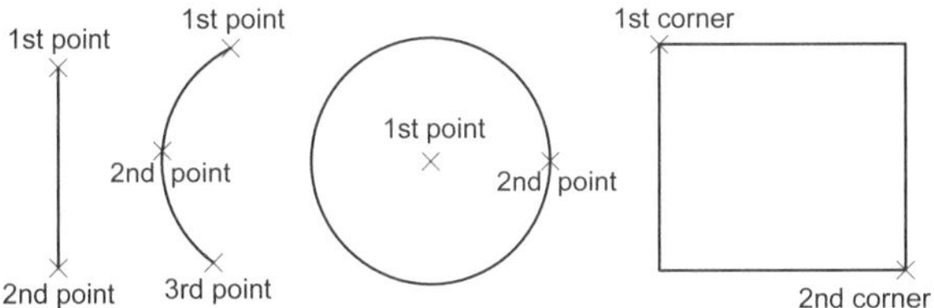

Figure 2.2 Summary of the Drawing Command Sequence (simplified)

Execute Drawing Command

1. Using any of the methods below, choose the tool with which you want to draw.

   File>Draw

   Pick one of the Draw tools on the Draw toolbar

2. [Command Line] Locate the first point for the shape. This first point will be either an endpoint, a corner, or a center on the shape.

Locate Remaining Points

3. In required order, locate the remaining points you need to draw the shape. For example, a line needs a minimum of two points. A shape appears once you place the last point.

End the Command

4. Typically, most shapes are nonrecurring—that is, once you draw one shape, you need to repeat the command to draw another one. This rule applies to all the commands you may run for any given project, except the line and polyline commands. Continue executing these commands until you stop locating points.

Objectives

This chapter describes the commands and concepts you need to begin drawing within AutoCAD. It emphasizes the importance of becoming familiar with basic 2-D drawing, editing, viewing, and precision tools. The end-of-chapter exercises provide additional practice opportunities, requiring readers to accurately draw and modify familiar architectural elements, including walls, windows, doors, and furniture in plan and elevation views.

Basic Geometric Shapes

All drawing and drafting in design starts with the basic geometric shapes, as shown in Figure 2.1. You can use basic shapes to create complex drawings. Users have the ability to draw lines, circles, and arcs in most AutoCAD software programs. In addition, users can work with points, ellipses, polygons, rectangles, doughnuts, and polylines. Figure 2.2 summarizes the drawing sequence for the basic geometric shapes, and Figure 2.3 on the next page demonstrates the command sequences required to draw each shape.

Technique to Master **T02.03** Drawing the Basic Shapes

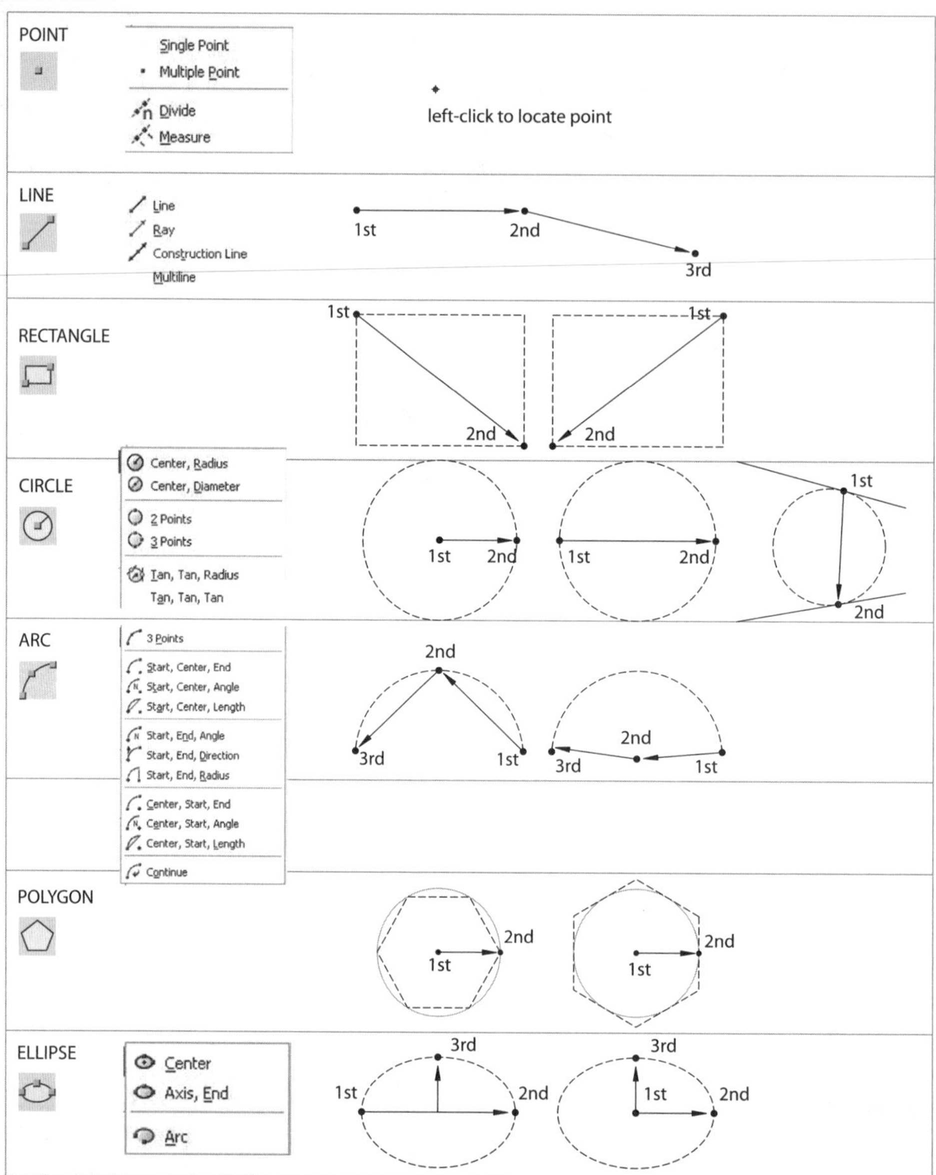

Figure 2.3

1	The Point command creates a point at any specified location of the drawing screen.	[Drawing Screen] Left-click to locate the point on the drawing screen.
2	The Line command creates a single or multiple straight line segments.	[Drawing Screen] Left-click to locate the start of the line. Left-click to locate the end of the line. This command continues to create line segments until you press the Enter key.
3	The Rectangle command creates square and rectangular shapes.	[Drawing Screen] Left-click to locate the first corner. Left-click to locate the opposite corner.
4	There are multiple methods to create a circle. The default option is shown above.	[Drawing Screen] Left-click to locate the center point. Left-click to locate the circle radius (or type in a radius).
5	You can create arcs by using various command options.	[Drawing Screen] Left-click to locate the start of the arc. Left-click to locate the second point of the arc. Left-click to locate the end of the arc.
6	The Polygon command creates triangles, pentagons, and other multisided shapes.	[Drawing Screen] Left-click to locate the center of the polygon. Left-click to locate the radius (or type in a radius).
7	The Ellipse command creates elliptical shapes by identifying two axes.	[Drawing Screen] Left-click to locate first point main axis. Left-click to locate the diameter of the main axis (or type in diameter). Left-click to locate radius of secondary axis (or type radius).

Viewing in AutoCAD

Chapter 1 introduced AutoCAD's model space drawing screen as the area where users can create their digital drawings. This drawing screen is infinite in all directions—the visible part of the drawing screen represents only a fraction of a much larger area, as shown in Figure 2.4. This visible area is magnified to an unknown percentage. When you view in AutoCAD, you are actually controlling the drawing screen's frame of reference and magnification. Think of viewing tools as a pair of binoculars or a camera with zooming capabilities. If you stand in one place, you have the ability to see into the far distance as well as to focus on small objects. You can use AutoCAD's viewing commands to enlarge the drawing screen and see more detail or reduce it to show more of a drawing. Although the size of the drawing seems to change, no change has actually occurred in the dimensions of the objects themselves. The following pages will explain the basic viewing commands in greater detail.

Viewing Commands

The essential viewing commands within AutoCAD are Zoom, Pan, Redraw, Regen, and View. The Dsviewer command is an additional viewing tool that opens a special Aerial View window. Of these commands, Zoom, Pan, and Aerial View are the tools you use to display different areas of the drawing screen at various magnifications.

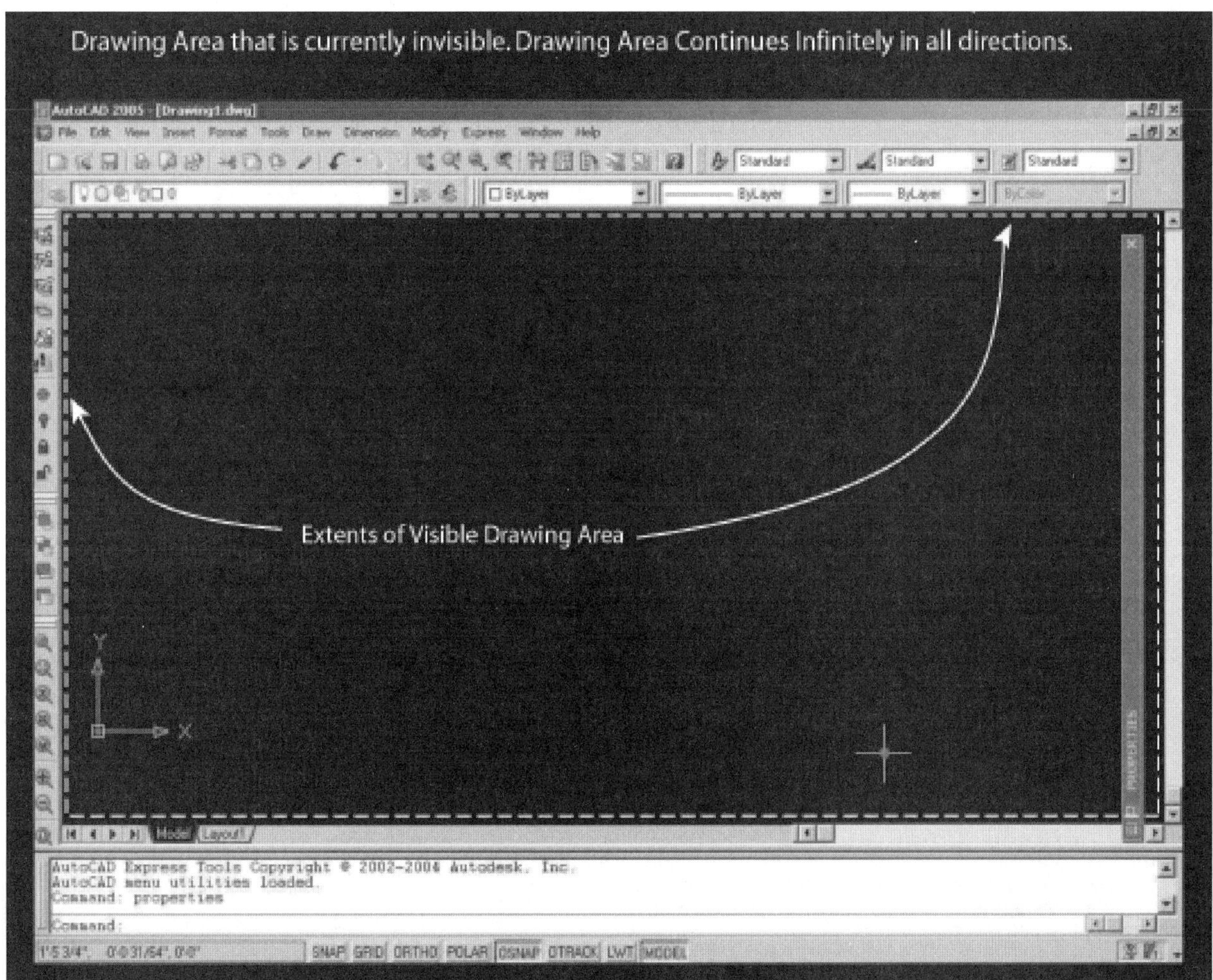

Figure 2.4 Understanding the drawing area and its relationship to the viewing tools

The Zoom command is an umbrella for the following sub-commands: All, Center, Dynamic, Extents, Left, Previous, Vmax, Window, Scale, ScaleX, and ScaleXP. There are additional tools within the Pan command that allows users to see different parts of the screen without having to change magnification. It also includes a few popular sub-commands. When you use the Pan command, you can use the Pan Left, Pan Right, Pan Up, and Pan Down sub-commands to restrict direction. You can also use the Pan Points sub-command to restrict both the direction and distance.

Redraw and Regen are screen cleanup commands that redraw and regenerate the display screen, respectively. During the regeneration process, AutoCAD recalculates all geometry within the drawing database to produce an updated image on the display area. Many times, extreme zoom magnifications require screen regeneration. These commands are also useful for getting rid of any incidental marks left over from commands such as Erase. Figure 2.5 shows essential viewing commands, and Figures 2.6 through 2.8 show additional viewing techniques.

Technique to Master **T02.05** Using Essential Viewing Commands

	The Zoom window enlarges the specified window so you can fill the drawing area.	1. [Command Line] Type Zoom, and press Enter on the keyboard. 2. [Drawing Screen] Left-click the first corner of the window. 3. [Drawing Screen] Left-click the opposite corner of the window.
	Zoom Extents lets you enlarge or reduce the drawing area magnification so that you can view all drawn objects at once.	1. [Command Line] Type Zoom, and press Enter on the keyboard. 2. [Command Line] Type E, and press Enter on the keyboard.
	Zoom All changes the drawing area magnification to the limits or current extents of the drawing, whichever is greater.	1. [Command Line] Type Zoom, and press Enter on the keyboard. 2. [Command Line] Type A, and press Enter on the keyboard.
	Zoom Previous restores the previous view magnification and framing of the drawing area.	1. [Command Line] Type Zoom, and press Enter on the keyboard. 2. [Command Line] Type P, and press Enter on the keyboard.
	Zoom Scale X lets you enlarge or reduce the drawing area magnification by a percentage that is relative to the current view. Example: 1.5 equals 150%.	1. [Command Line] Type Zoom, and press Enter on your keyboard. 2. [Command Line] Type nX (where n is the variable), and press Enter on your keyboard.
	Pan lets you keep the drawing area at the same magnification while moving around it to see other parts that are not on the visible drawing area.	1. [Command Line] Type Pan, and press Enter on your keyboard. 2. [Drawing Screen] Use the mouse to move the drawing area in any direction.
	Pan (Left, Right, Up, Down) lets you keep the drawing area at the same magnification while moving around it to see other parts that are not on the visible drawing area. While the Pan command allows you to pan in any direction at any time, the Pan Left, Pan Right, Pan Up, and Pan Down directional options restrict movement in those respective directions, allowing for additional precision.	1. [Pan Toolbar] Select the appropriate direction. 2. [Drawing Screen] Use mouse to move the drawing area in the restricted direction.
	Pan Points lets you add even more precision to the Pan command by using Pan Points. This command pans the drawing screen a specific distance.	1. [Pan toolbar] Select the Pan Points tool. 2. [Drawing Screen] Use mouse to move the drawing area a specific distance.

Figure 2.5

Technique to Master **T02.06** Zoom Window/Zoom Previous

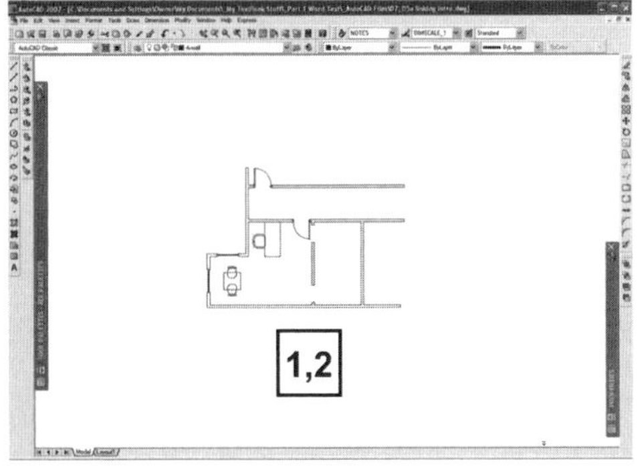

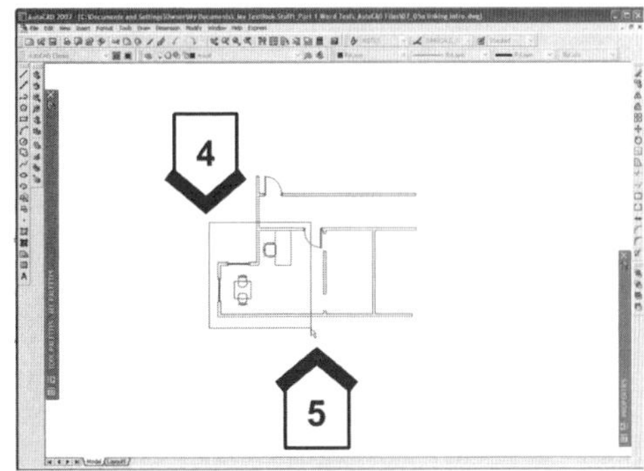

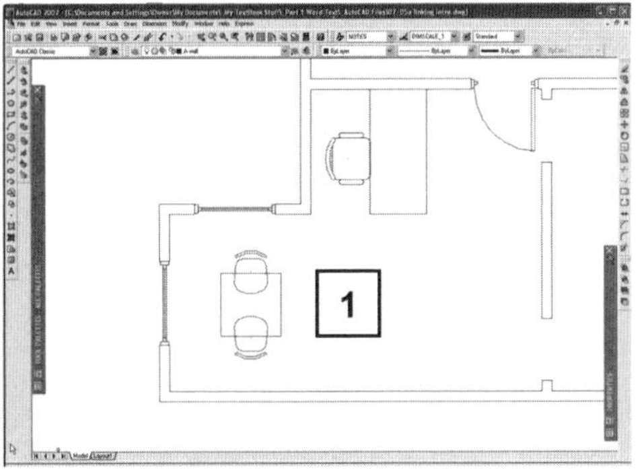

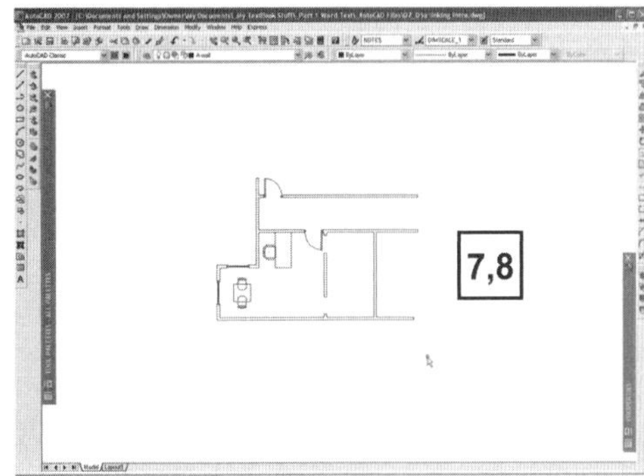

Figure 2.6

Make sure you zoom your screen to extents.		
1	[Command Line]	Type Z, and press Enter on your keyboard.
2	[Command Line]	Type E, and press Enter on your keyboard.
Zoom Window to the desired area.		
3	[Command Line]	Type Z, and press Enter on your keyboard.
4	[Drawing Screen]	Left-click the first corner of the window.
5	[Drawing Screen]	Left-click the opposite corner of the window.

Draw or make desired modifications.		
6	[Drawing Screen]	This is the area in which you work.
Zoom Previous to see all of the drawing again.		
7	[Command Line]	Type Z, and press Enter on your keyboard.
8	[Command Line]	Type P, and press Enter on your keyboard.

Viewing Transparency

In AutoCAD, the term *transparency* refers to a user's ability to use a command while another command is in progress. The most popular example of transparency is when people use the Zoom and Pan commands at the same time while drawing and editing.

> **Box 2.1**
> Note: Zoom and Pan transparency is always available unless a screen regeneration is needed.

Technique to Master **T02.07** Saving a View Position for Later Restoration

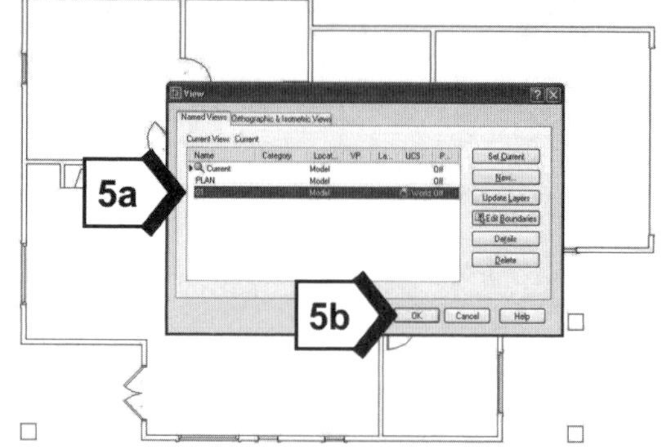

Figure 2.7

1	[Command Line]	View command, or press V for the shortcut.
2	[View dialogue box]	Left-click on the New button.
3	[New View dialogue box]	Type in a name and description for the view.
4	[New View dialogue box]	Left-click OK to save the view.
5a, 5b	[View dialogue box]	New view is displayed. Left-click OK to exit.

Technique to Master **T02.08** Using the Aerial Viewing Window

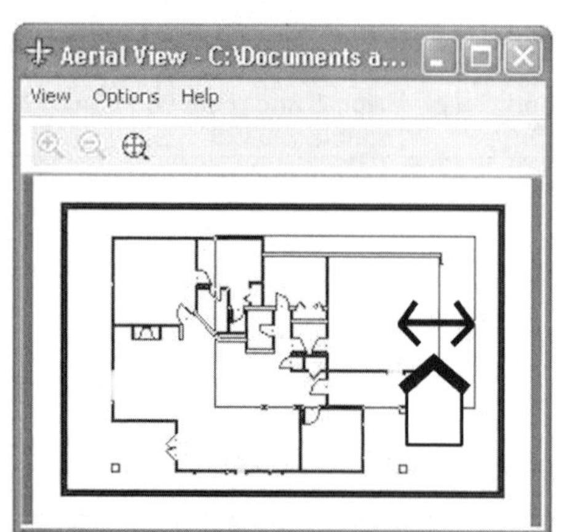

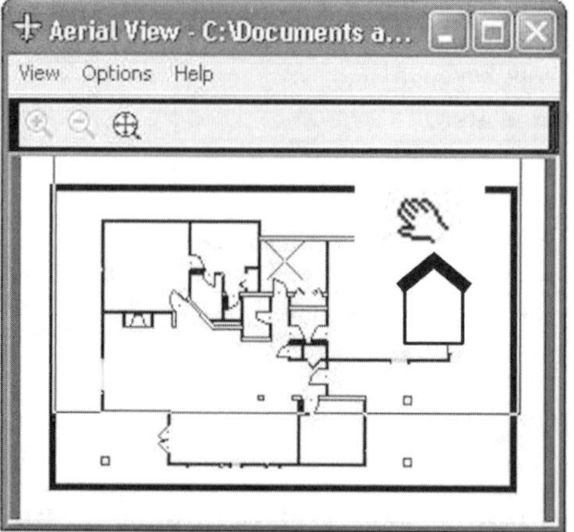

Figure 2.8 Within the Aerial View window, hold down the left mouse button while moving to make the rectangle larger or smaller. Left-click to locate and pan.

Viewing Display and Viewing Quality

The quality of geometric display is largely dependent on a few AutoCAD drawing and system variables—that is, adjustable settings in AutoCAD saved either globally or to a specific drawing file. Appendix D lists drawing and system variables that might be important to a drawing's development. Specific system variables that affect viewing display are Regenmode, Regenauto, and Viewres.

CAD and the Coordinate System

Throughout history people have documented surveys of topography, streets, and buildings by using maps. We use maps to find places and understand relationships between buildings, streets, and natural elements. Maps include superimposed grids that help distinguish the relative location of a place or feature. Each of the lines in a grid is identified in an arbitrary manner, such as A, B, C or 1, 2, 3, in essence defining coordinate locations. Coordinates are not a new invention—we use them all the time in everyday life. Think of how a street is located on a street map: The intersection of the horizontal and vertical grids usually refers to a coordinate location that helps you find the street.

This process of mapping was incorporated into computer-aided design and functions in very much the same way it does on an actual map. In AutoCAD, there is an invisible grid superimposed on the drawing screen. You can identify any location on the grid by using coordinate methods, as if you were looking at a map.

What Is a Coordinate System?

In AutoCAD, a coordinate system uses a generic grid to determine the measurement system that allows users to draw objects at their correct sizes. Coordinate systems allow users to draw and locate objects precisely. All AutoCAD programs have a generic coordinate system called *the Cartesian Coordinate System.* This type of coordinate system has no units and is infinite in all directions; think of how we currently view outer space.

In the Cartesian Coordinate System, there are three axes that define digital space, otherwise known as directional paths. The X, Y, and Z axes are each symbolic representations of directional paths (Figure 2.9). Consider the X axis to be the representation of infinite left-right directions. Consider the Y axis to be the representation of infinite forward-backward directions. Finally, consider the Z axis to be the representation of infinite up-down directions. The following is a summary:

- Look at the drawing screen. The X axis is the horizontal axis that runs from left to right. It is generally thought of as giving width to an object. Positive X is to the right, and negative X is to the left.
- The Y axis is the vertical axis that runs from top to bottom. It is generally thought of as giving depth to an object. Positive Y is above the midline, and negative Y is below.
- The Z axis is the axis that runs toward and away from you. It is generally thought of as giving height to an object. Positive Z is toward you and generally understood as the elevation of an object, and negative Z is away from you and generally thought of as the part of an object that is buried in the ground.

In AutoCAD, the coordinate system is the default way for users to view and locate points in AutoCAD. It is defined as the World Coordinate System (WCS) and is identified by the icon located at the bottom of the screen (Figure 2.10).

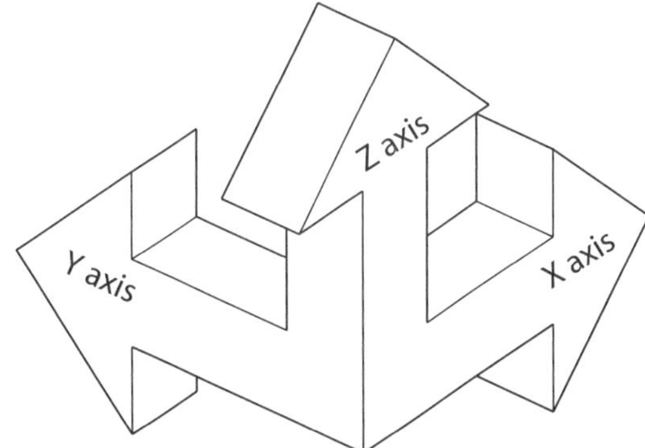

Figure 2.9 The three axes are each symbolic representations of directional paths–east/west, north/south, and up/down.

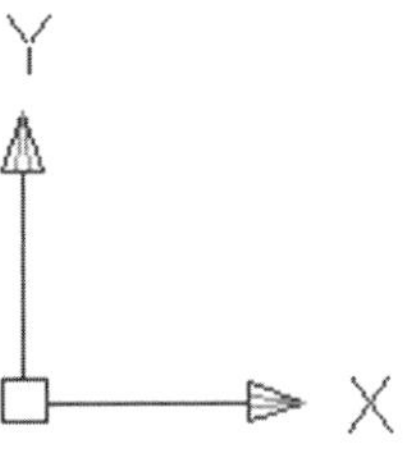

Figure 2.10 The WCS icon is located at the bottom-left corner of the drawing screen.

Locating points in digital space requires a minimum of an X and a Y value separated by a comma. In 2-D drawings, the Z value of a point can be ignored and is therefore 0 by default.

Absolute Coordinates

Absolute coordinates within the WCS are based on a coordinate origin (0,0,0). All coordinates are determined by a set distance in the positive or negative direction from the (0,0,0) location (Figure 2.11).

When specifying absolute coordinates, the correct syntax is as follows:

X value,Y value,Z value

Example: 15,12,0

Each axis value is separated by a comma. Remember, the Z value may be omitted if it is 0, as follows:

X value,Y value

Example: 15,12

Drafting with absolute coordinates in design practice is something users do very sparingly because it generally requires too much math to make it a practical drawing technique. Figure 2.12 shows a drawing that was created with absolute coordinates.

> **Box 2.2**
> Tip: If you make a mistake, use the escape key (Esc) to cancel the command.
>
> Remember to use the Enter key or space bar to end a command.
>
> The Enter key and space bar will also repeat last used commands.

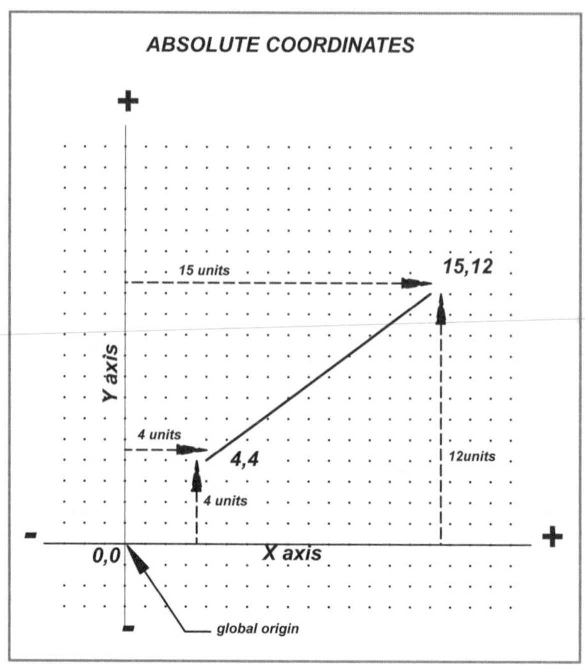

Figure 2.11 Understanding absolute coordinates

Technique to Master **T02.12** Drawing with Absolute Coordinates

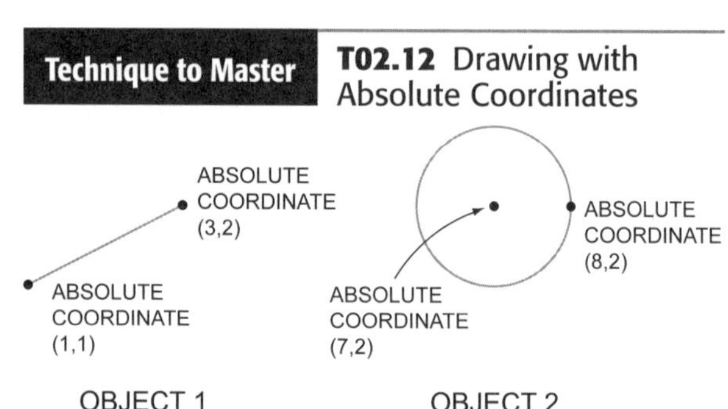

Figure 2.12

1	[Command Line]	Choose the Draw command to create a line, circle, arc, or some such shape.
2	[Command Line]	Locate the first point of a shape by typing in absolute coordinates by using the correct syntax.
3	[Command Line]	Locate the remaining points of the shape by typing in absolute coordinates by using the correct syntax.

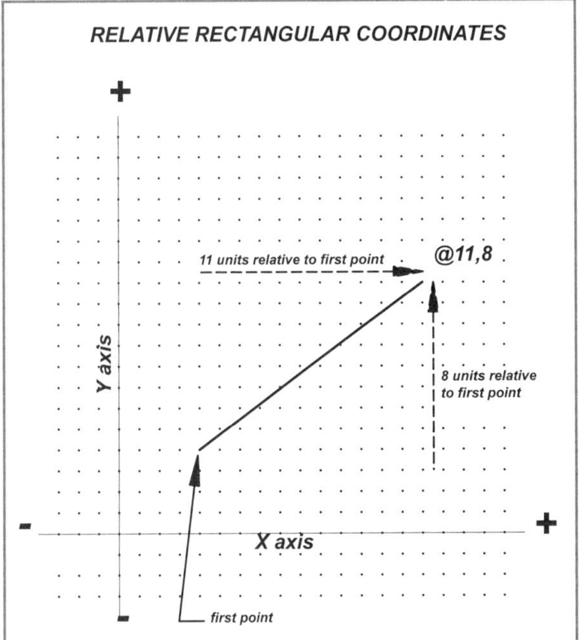

Figure 2.13 Understanding relative rectangular coordinates

Technique to Master **T02.14** Drawing with Relative Rectangular Coordinates

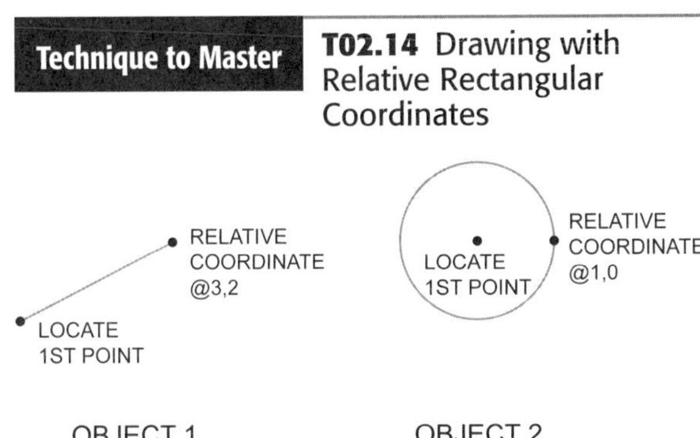

Figure 2.14 The illustration shows the coordinates for a line and circle object.

1	[Command Line]	Choose the Draw command to create a line, a circle, an arc, or some such shape.
2	[Command Line]	Locate the first point by left-clicking on any location on the screen.
3	[Drawing Screen]	Locate the next point of the shape by typing in the relative X and Y distances from the previous point. Continue locating points on the screen repeating Step 3 until a shape is completed.

Relative Coordinates

A much more efficient technique is to draw by using relative coordinates. Relative coordinates are always based on the last point entered. Relative coordinates are useful for specifying points that are at a known distance apart. One method for entering relative coordinates is to use relative rectangular coordinates (Figure 2.13).

> **Box 2.3**
> Relative coordinates have an added advantage over absolute coordinates. Since they reference the last point entered, knowledge of the actual grid location is unnecessary.

Relative Rectangular Coordinates

When specifying a relative rectangular coordinate, the correct syntax is as follows:

@X distance,Y distance,Z distance

Example: @11,8,0

The @ symbol must be used as the prefix to differentiate between an absolute coordinate and a relative coordinate. Remember, the Z distance may be omitted if it is 0, as follows:

@X distance,Y distance

Example: @11,8

Figure 2.14 shows a drawing created with relative rectangular coordinates.

> **Box 2.4**
> Note: There is no need to add the inches symbol after 11'8 in the example. AutoCAD will automatically assume you mean inches.

Relative Polar Coordinates

A different type of relative coordinate is the relative polar coordinate. Relative polar coordinates are used only when the linear distance and angle of a shape are known (Figure 2.15). Its correct syntax is as follows:

@distance<angle

Example: @4<45

Figure 2.16 shows a drawing created with relative polar coordinates.

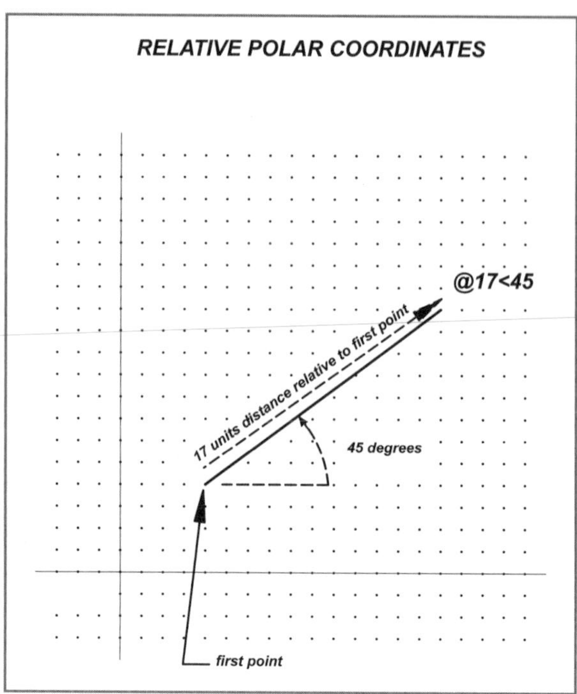

Figure 2.15 Understanding relative polar coordinates

Relative Coordinates Using Direct Distance Entry

The most widely used method to enter relative coordinates is direct distance entry in which you use the drawing aid Ortho with your mouse to specify the directional axis. Once you locate the first point on the drawing screen, locate the next point by moving the cursor in the direction you want and entering a distance with the keyboard. Remember that the Ortho drawing aid must be on for you to create horizontal and vertical lines. The following is an example:

Make sure the Ortho command toggle is ON.

[Command Line] Type Line and press Enter.

[Drawing Screen] Left-click to locate the first point anywhere on the drawing screen.

[Drawing Screen] Move the mouse toward the left.

[Command Line] Type in 4 as the distance and press Enter.

> **Box 2.5**
>
> The Ortho command is a drawing aid toggle that limits the cursor's movement to horizontal and vertical directions. It can be toggled on or off at any time in a command's sequence through the status bar button or using the function key F8.

Technique to Master **T02.16** Drawing with Relative Polar Coordinates

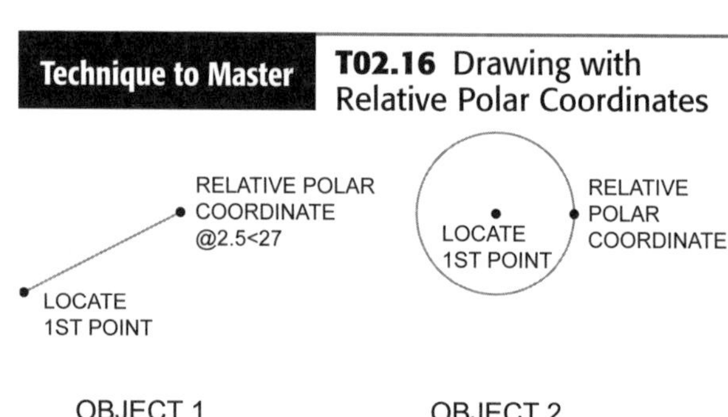

Figure 2.16

1	[Command Line]	Choose the Draw command to create a line, a circle, an arc, or some such shape.
2	[Command Line]	Locate the first point by left-clicking on any location on the drawing screen.
3	[Drawing Screen]	Locate the next point of the shape by typing in the relative angle and distance from the previous point. Continue locating points on the drawing screen repeating Step 3 until a shape is completed.

Technique to Master **T02.17** Drawing with Direct Distance Entry

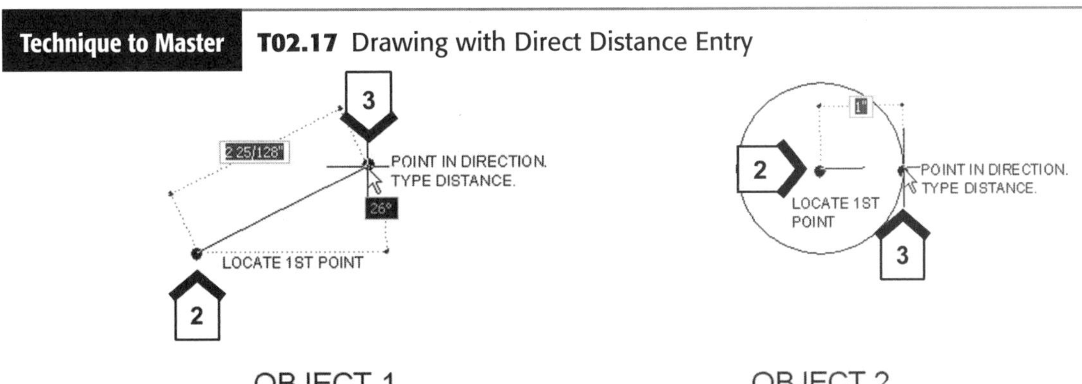

Figure 2.17

1	[Command Line]	Choose the Draw command to create a line, a circle, an arc, or some such shape.
2	[Command Line]	Locate the first point by left-clicking on any location on the screen.
3	[Drawing Screen]	Locate the next point of the shape by turning on the Ortho toggle (F8). Move your mouse in the direction where the next point will be placed, and type in the relative distance from the previous point. Continue locating points on the screen repeating Step 3 until a shape is completed.

Technique to Master **T02.18** Summary of the Drawing Command Sequence Using Precision (simplified)

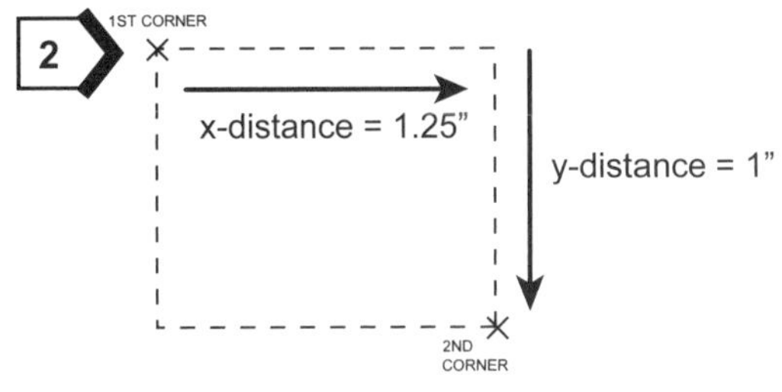

Command: rc RECTANGLE
Specify first corner point or [Chamfer/Elevation/Fillet/Thickness/Width]:
Specify other corner point or [Area/Dimensions/Rotation]: @1.25,-1 4

Figure 2.18

1	[Command Line]	Choose the Draw command to create a line, a circle, an arc, or some such shape.
2	Locate the first point on the shape.	
3	Locate the first point by clicking anywhere on the screen. This first point will either be an endpoint, a corner, or a center on the shape.	
4	In required order, locate the remaining points to complete the shape using relative coordinates.	

The technique is demonstrated in Figure 2.17. Direct distance entry is the fastest and most efficient method of drawing orthogonal lines since the full relative coordinate (@X distance,Y distance) is unnecessary.

Adding Precision When Drawing Geometric Shapes

For the most part, when you start a drawing on a blank drawing screen, you begin by locating an arbitrary point. You would then use relative coordinates to locate the remaining points of the object you are drawing. Figure 2.18 shows a drawing in which the user added precision input with relative coordinates to the drawing command sequences learned previously.

Adding Architectural Units When Specifying Coordinates

So far the text has described precision without highlighting the units that are used. AutoCAD has a very specific syntax for entering feet, inches, and fractions of inches. The syntax for specifying architectural units are as follows:

Feet are represented by the ' symbol

Inches are represented by the " symbol

Example: [Drawing Screen] Locate the first point with your mouse anywhere on the drawing screen.

[Command Line] Type @4'3,7"

You may specify fractions either in decimal or fractional format. When expressing fractions, you must place the hyphen symbol between full inches and fractional inches. The following are two examples of how to express fractions:

Example: [Drawing Screen] Locate the first point line with your mouse anywhere on the drawing screen.

[Command Line] Type @4'3.125,7

Example: [Drawing Screen] Locate the first point with your mouse anywhere on drawing screen.

[Command Line] Type @4'3-1/8,7

Adding Precision with Object Snaps

Object snaps allow you to literally snap precisely to a key point of an existing shape. As with coordinates, they allow for additional accuracy and drafting precision. Key points may be endpoints, midpoints, centers, intersections, and more. A list of frequently used object snaps and their descriptions is shown in Figure 2.19.

ENDPOINT	Snaps to the ends of lines and arcs.	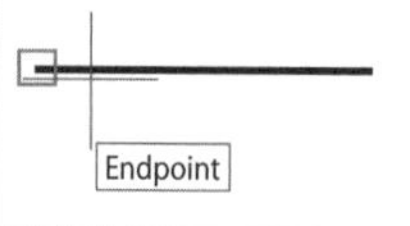
MIDPOINT	Snaps to the midpoint of lines and arcs.	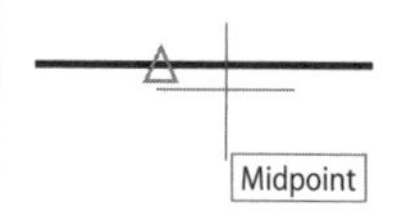
CENTER	Snaps to the center of an arc or circle.	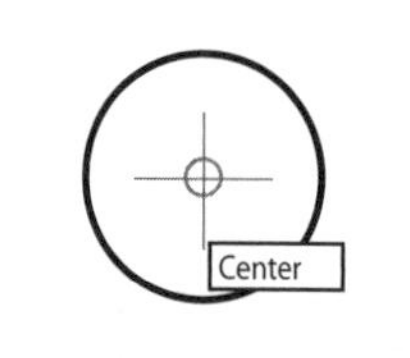
QUADRANT	Snaps to the 0, 90, 180, and 270 degree quadrants of an arc or circle.	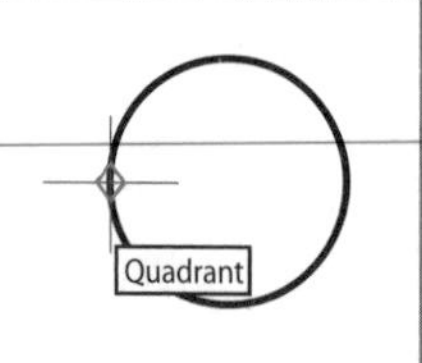
NODE	Snaps to the AutoCAD point entity.	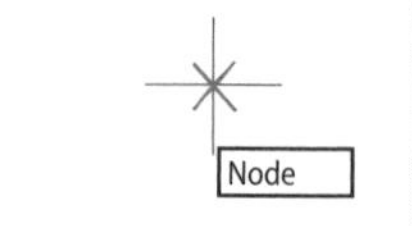
INTERSECTION	Snaps to the intersection of intersecting lines, arcs, and circles.	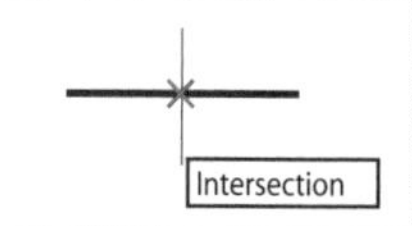
PERPENDICULAR	Snaps to the point on a line so that an angle of 90 degrees is created.	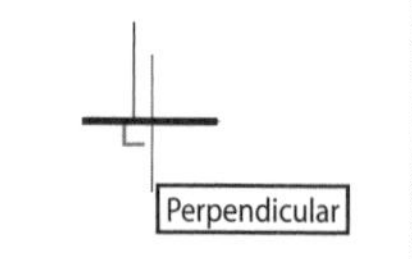
INSERT	Snaps to the intersection point of text and all block types.	
NEAREST	Snaps to the line, arc, or circle at the point specified.	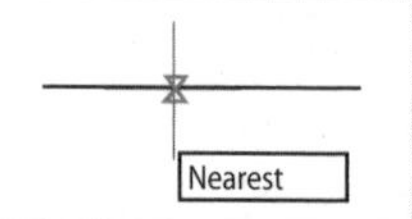

Figure 2.19 The essential object snaps

Box 2.6
Tip: Only keep the most often used objects snaps running. These might include Endpoint, Midpoint, Center, Intersection, and Extension. Objects snaps such as perpendicular that are rarely used tend to supersede other object snaps when continuously running.

Object snap drawing aids are used within a command sequence. There are a number of ways to do this, the easiest of which is to have your most frequently used object snaps on all the time. Running Osnap—where object snaps are always available for use—can be set up in the Objects Snaps tab of the Drafting Settings dialogue box (Figure 2.20) or by using the command Osnap. Check off the object snaps you want to run. At the top left, make sure to check the Object Snap On box.

Box 2.7
Shortcut: Function key F3 also toggles running Osnap on and off.

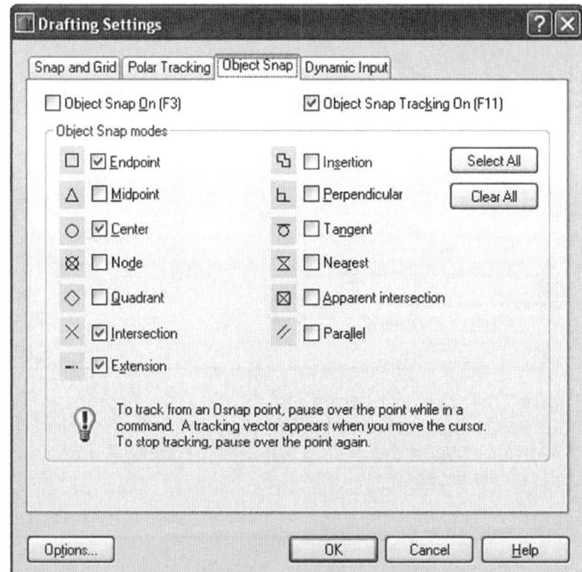

Figure 2.20 Use the Osnaps Drafting settings to toggle specific object snaps on and off.

Another method of using the object snaps drawing aids is to use an object snap only when you need it; the manual method. Manual object snaps can be implemented as follows:

- Select the bject snap from the object snap toolbar. Figure 2.21 identifies each of the object snap tools.
- Type in the Object Snap command shortcut.
- Right click to access the mouse's Object Snaps hidden menu.

Object snaps are used only within a command sequence. You can grasp how to incorporate object snaps into a command sequence by talking your way through a drawing instruction. Figure 2.22 illustrates how the instruction, "Draw a line from the endpoint of arc A to the midpoint of line B" is translated visually. The supplementary CD-ROM contains demonstrations of how to apply object snaps to a few geometrical drawing challenges.

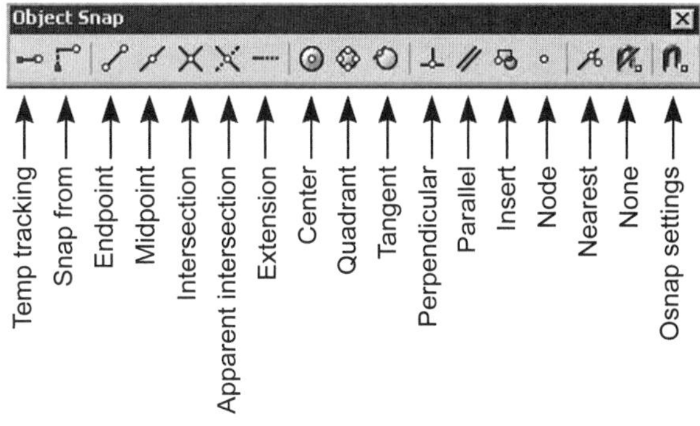

Figure 2.21 The object snaps toolbar

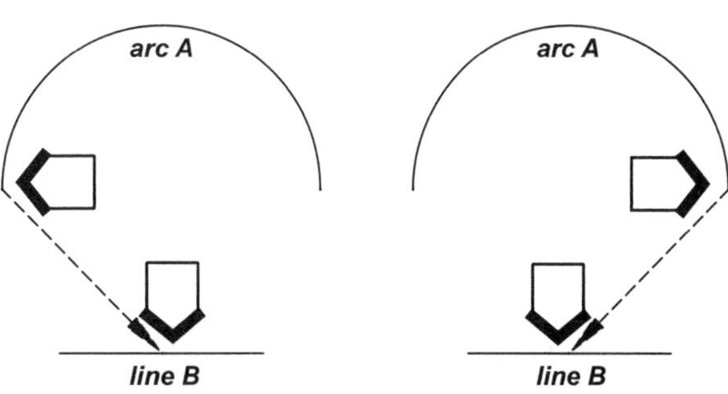

Figure 2.22 Using object snaps to draw a line that is connected to an arc

Chapter 2 Learning to Draw Precisely

Coordinate Inquiry

AutoCAD's inquiry commands give you access to the tools you need to verify the dimensional properties of your geometry. Figure 2.23 identifies the tools on the Inquiry toolbar. The inquiry commands relevant to coordinate entry are ID, Dist, and List. The following pages describe the ID and Dist command tools.

The ID command identifies the absolute X, Y, and Z values (or the coordinate location) of a specified point. The following is its command sequence:

[Command Line] ID

[Drawing Screen] Locate the desired point by using object snaps.

Using the ID command in combination with object snaps is the most appropriate method. Endpoints, midpoints, intersections, centers, and quadrants are all good choices for identifying points on geometry.

> **Box 2.8**
> Tip: When drawing three-dimensionally, the ID command is a valuable tool for identifying the Z values of points on your geometry.

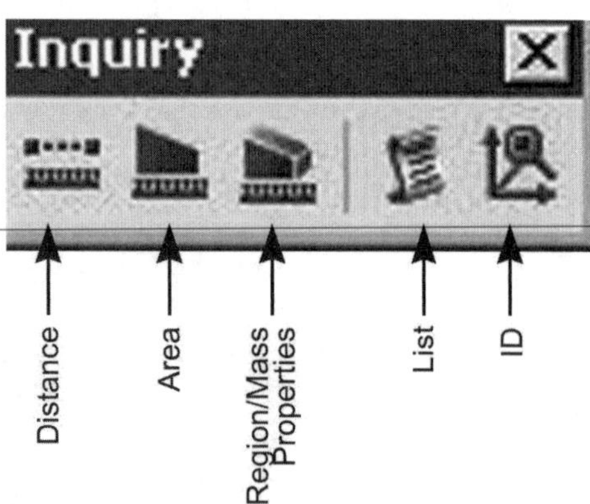

Figure 2.23 The Inquiry toolbar

The Dist command displays the distance and angle between two points. This distance is actually broken up into three measurements (Figure 2.24) in which the following holds true:

- The distance represents the direct measurement between the two points.
- The Delta X represents the horizontal measurement between the two points.
- The Delta Y represents the vertical measurement between the two points.

The Dist command is an excellent tool for finding the height, length, depth, and width of an object.

Sample Scenario

Open the drawing file called 023201.dwg on the supplementary CD-ROM. Identify the width and length of the rectangle shown using the Dist command only once.

To complete the task successfully, snap to the points A and D or B and C (Figure 2.25).

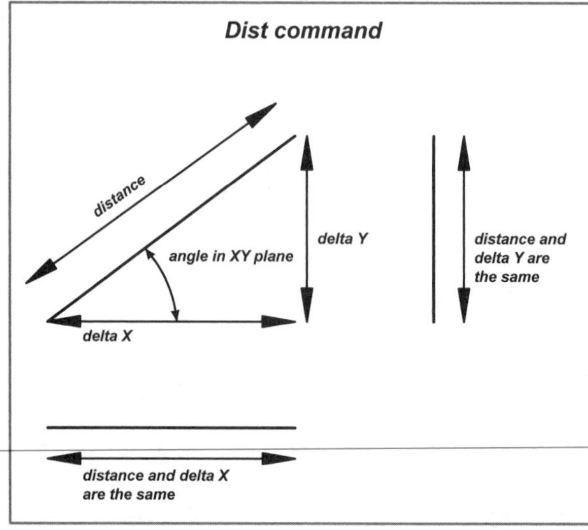

Figure 2.24 The Dist command displays the distance between two points. It responds with not only the direct distance between the points but also the Delta X and Delta Y distances.

Technique to Master **T02.25** Identifying the Width and Length of a Rectangle Using the Distance Command

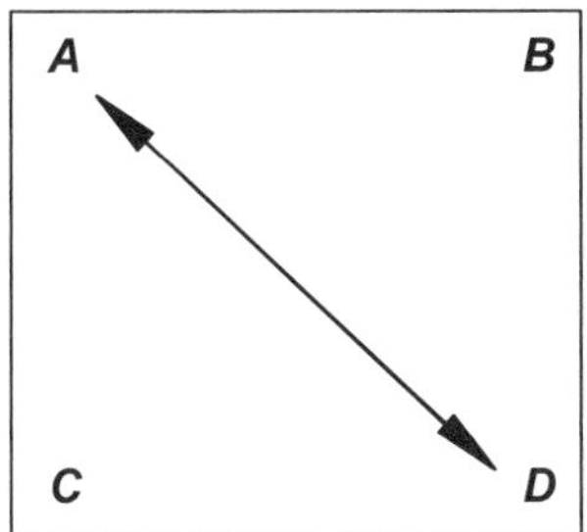

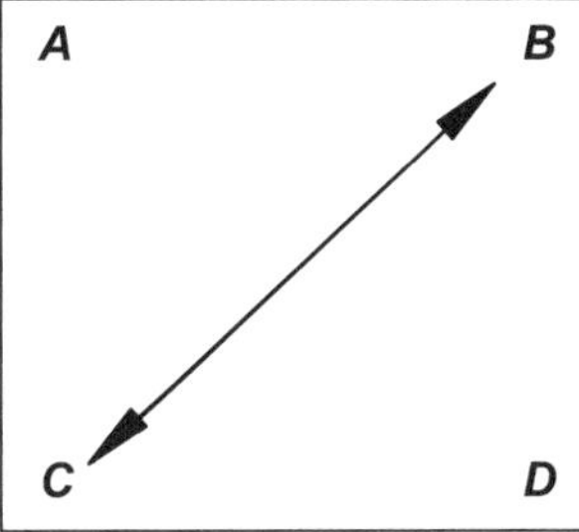

Figure 2.25 To complete the task successfully, snap to the points A and D or B and C. Look at the Delta X. The width of the rectangle is identified here. Delta Y identifies the rectangle's dimensional height.

Both point combinations result in the following information:

Using points A and D

Distance = 0'-4 3/16", Angle in XY Plane = 318, Angle from XY Plane = 0

Delta X = 0'-3 1/8", Delta Y = -0'-2 25/32", Delta Z = 0'-0"

Using points B and C

Distance = 0'-4 3/16", Angle in XY Plane = 42, Angle from XY Plane = 0

Delta X = 0'-3 1/8", Delta Y = 0'-2 25/32", Delta Z = 0'-0"

Look at the Delta X to identify the rectangle's width, and look at Delta Y to identify the rectangle's dimensional height. The Dist command can be also used to identify the radius and/or diameter for arcs and circles. Refer to the supplementary CD-ROM for an example.

Building Complexity Through the Editing Process

A design can go through many changes while you work on developing it into a functional and aesthetical solution to a design problem. As you develop any given design, you make constant modifications that necessitate changes to some or all of a project's drawings. In these types of situations, AutoCAD's editing tools prove to be much more efficient than manual drafting.

Editing refers to the process of changing existing geometry. Since you can edit only existing geometry, the editing process is closely tied to the selection tools in AutoCAD. The following section summarizes the editing process and introduces you to the editing and selection commands and command sequences in AutoCAD.

Editing in AutoCAD—An Outline of the Command Sequence

1. Invoke Modification command.
2. Select the object(s) you want to modify.
3. Continue the command sequence for the specific modification command.

The word *Select* appears in Step 2 of the above summary. Object selection refers to the process of choosing shapes and objects. One of the key housekeeping rules in the editing process is that you cannot edit anything unless you select something. In other words, all modification commands must include the selection of geometry within their command sequences.

Common Selection Methods

AutoCAD includes many selection methods. This flexibility allows for greater efficiency and accuracy in the editing process. First, there are certain selection methods that are mouse-enabled. These are the pick, window, and crossing methods. A lesson contained on the supplementary CD-ROM demonstrates the mouse-enabled selection methods.

The second method uses keyboard shortcuts that are typed in at the Select Objects prompt. These selection operators include W, C, L, P, A, R, F, and CP. A lesson contained on the CD-ROM demonstrates the more commonly used selection operators.

The Editing Tools

The editing tools within AutoCAD can be classified by their operation type. The Move, Copy, Rotate, Mirror, Scale, Offset, and Array commands make location or dimensional changes to existing objects. The Trim, Extend, Fillet, Chamfer, and Stretch commands change an object's actual shape. An overview of the commonly used editing commands can be found on the supplementary CD-ROM.

The Move and Copy Modification Commands

The Move command lets you relocate one or more selected shapes and/or objects to a new location. The Copy command lets you duplicate one or more selected shapes and/or objects and moves the duplicate to a new location. Figure 2.26 demonstrates various application techniques using the Move and Copy modification commands.

The Rotate, Mirror, and Scale Modification Commands

The Rotate command lets you rotate one or more selected shapes around a reference point. The Align command lets you align one or more selected shapes with a reference angle. The Mirror command lets you create a reflected image of one or more selected shapes using a reference line. The Scale command lets you change the dimensional size (height, width, depth) of one or more selected shapes. Figures 2.27 through 2.29 demonstrate various application techniques using these commands.

Technique to Master T02.26 The Move and Copy Modification Commands

Moving/Copying Without Precision

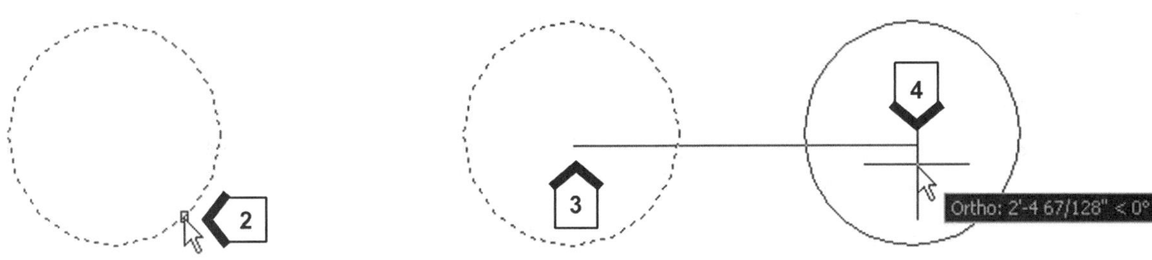
2
3
4
Ortho: 2'-4 67/128" < 0°

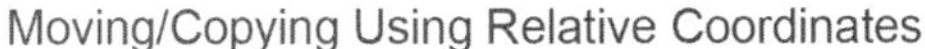

Moving/Copying Using Relative Coordinates

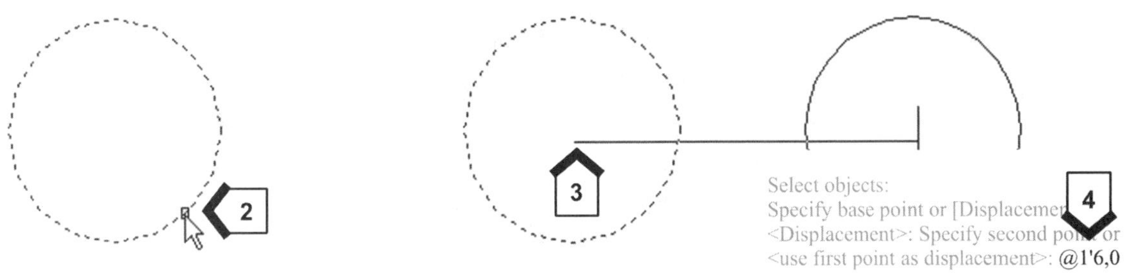
2
3
4
Select objects:
Specify base point or [Displacement]
<Displacement>: Specify second point or
<use first point as displacement>: @1'6,0

Moving/Copying Using Object Snaps

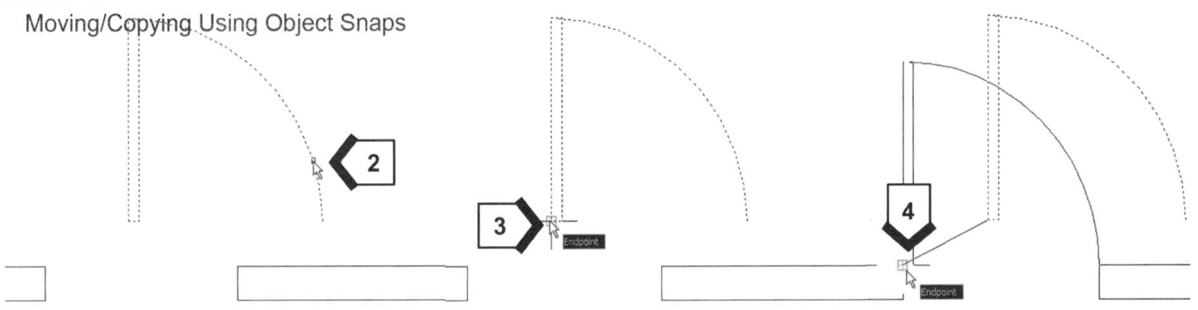
2
3
4
Endpoint
Endpoint

Figure 2.26

Moving/Copying Without Precision		
1	[Command Line]	Choose the Move or Copy command.
2	[Drawing Screen]	Select the shape(s) you want to move or copy.
3	[Drawing Screen]	Click on the screen to locate the point of reference for the shape(s).
4	[Drawing Screen]	Click on the screen to locate the new location for the shape(s).

Moving/Copying Using Relative Coordinates		
1	[Command Line]	Choose the Move or Copy command.
2	[Drawing Screen]	Select the shape(s) you want to move or copy.
3	[Drawing Screen]	Click on the screen to locate the point of reference for the shape(s).
4	[Command Line]	Use relative coordinates to specify the new location for the shape(s).

Moving/Copying Using Object Snaps		
1	[Command Line]	Choose the Move or Copy command.
2	[Drawing Screen]	Select the shape(s) you want to move or copy.
3	[Drawing Screen]	Snap to an existing key point to locate the point of reference for the shape(s).
4	[Drawing Screen]	Snap to an existing key point to locate the new location for the shape(s).

Technique to Master T02.27 The Rotate Modification Command

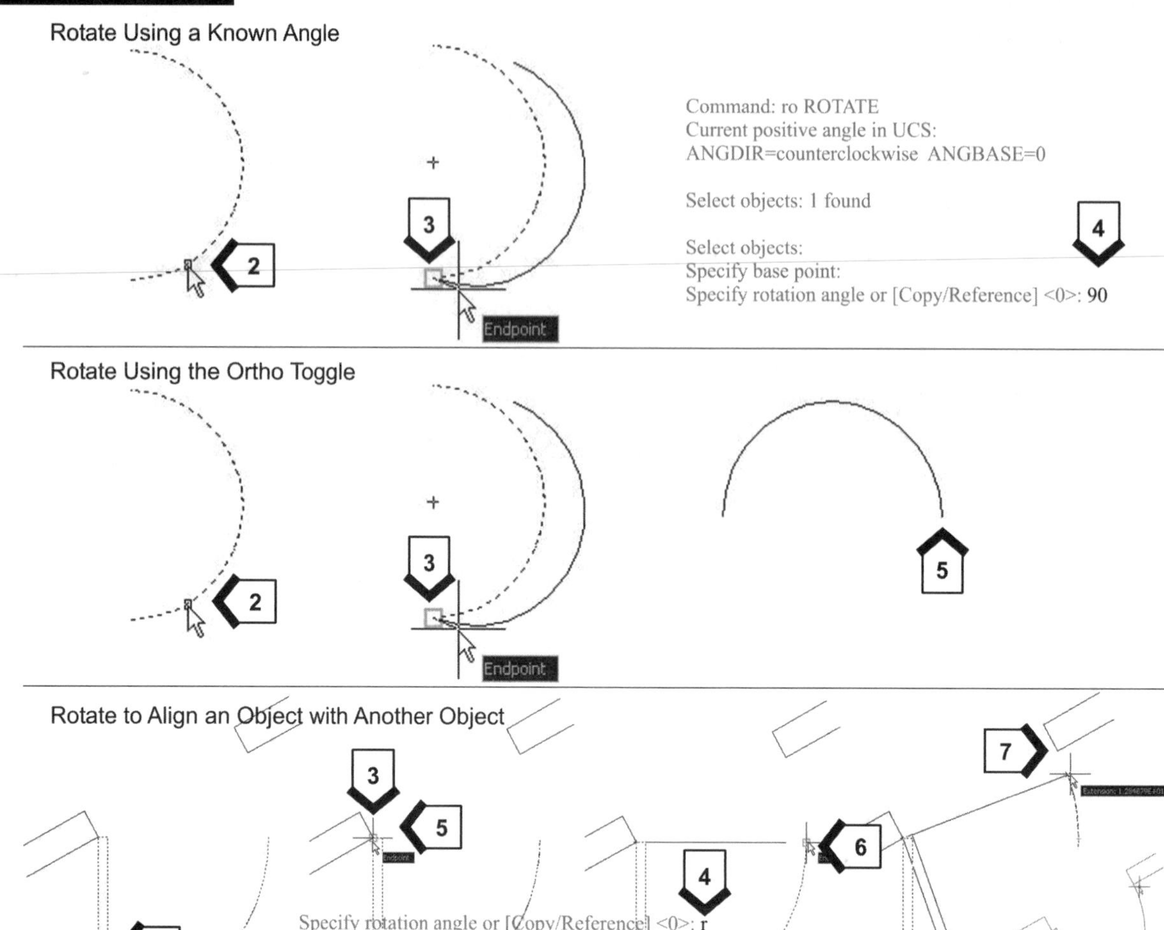

Rotate Using a Known Angle
Command: ro ROTATE
Current positive angle in UCS:
ANGDIR=counterclockwise ANGBASE=0
Select objects: 1 found
Select objects:
Specify base point:
Specify rotation angle or [Copy/Reference] <0>: 90
Endpoint
Rotate Using the Ortho Toggle
Endpoint
Rotate to Align an Object with Another Object
Specify rotation angle or [Copy/Reference] <0>: r
Specify the reference angle <0>:
Specify second point:
Specify the new angle or [Points] <0>:

Figure 2.27

Rotate Using a Known Angle		
1	[Command Line]	Type Rotate.
2	[Drawing Screen]	Select the shape(s) you want to rotate.
3	[Drawing Screen]	Using object snaps, snap to the point of reference (rotational point) for the shape(s).
4	[Command Line]	Type in an angle to specify the angle to rotate.

Rotate Using the Ortho Toggle		
1	[Command Line]	Type Rotate.
2	[Drawing Screen]	Select the shape(s) you want to rotate.
3	[Drawing Screen]	Using object snaps, snap to the point of reference (rotational point) for the shape(s).
4	Make sure Ortho is toggled on (F8 key).	
5	[Drawing Screen]	Move the mouse until the object rotates to the desired angle.

Rotate to Align an Object with Another Object		
1	[Command Line]	Type Rotate.
2	[Drawing Screen]	Select the shape(s) you want to rotate.
3	[Drawing Screen]	Using object snaps, snap to the point of reference (rotational point) for the shape(s).
4	[Command Line]	Type r, and press Enter to use the Reference command.
5	[Drawing Screen]	Using object snaps, snap to the same point of reference (rotational point).
6	[Drawing Screen]	Using object snaps, snap to the current angle of the shape(s).
7	[Drawing Screen]	Using object snaps, snap to the angle you want to align with.

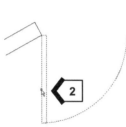

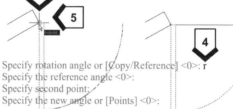

Technique to Master **T02.28** The Mirror Modification Command

Mirror Using Object Snaps and Ortho

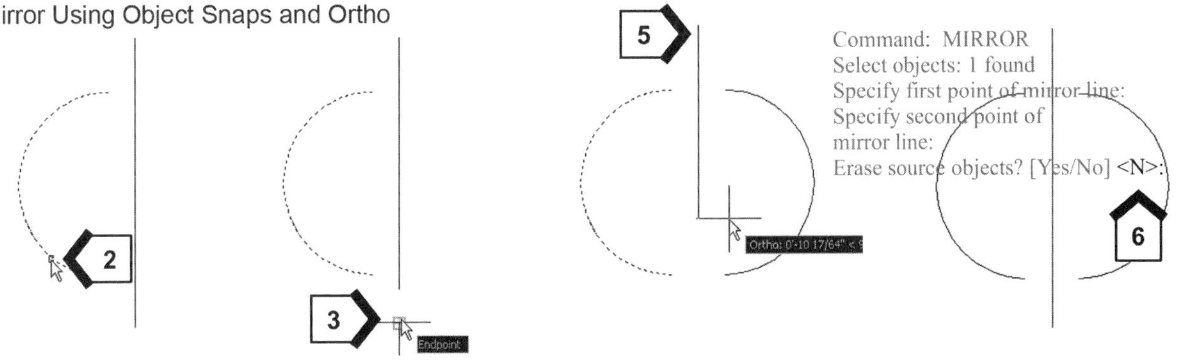

2
3
Endpoint
5
Ortho: 0'-10 17/64" < 9
Command: MIRROR
Select objects: 1 found
Specify first point of mirror line:
Specify second point of
mirror line:
Erase source objects? [Yes/No] <N>:
6

Mirror Using Ortho

2
4
Ortho: 0'-10 13/64" < 90°
3
Command: MIRROR
Select objects: 1 found
Specify first point of mirror line:
Specify second point of
mirror line:
Erase source objects? [Yes/No] <N>:
5

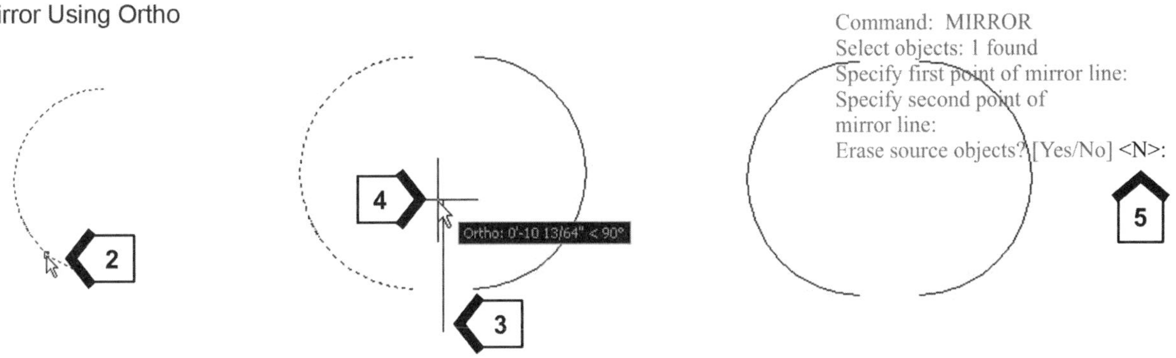

Figure 2.28

Mirror Using Object Snaps and Ortho		
1	[Command Line]	Type Mirror.
2	[Drawing Screen]	Select the shape(s) you want to mirror.
3	[Drawing Screen]	Specify the first point of the mirror line by left-clicking anywhere on the screen.
4		Make sure Ortho is toggled on (F8 key).
5	[Drawing Screen]	Specify the second point of the mirror line.
6	[Command Line]	Type Y or N to specify whether you want to keep the original object.

Mirror Using Ortho		
1	[Command Line]	Type Mirror.
2	[Drawing Screen]	Select the shape(s) you want to mirror.
3	[Drawing Screen]	Using object snaps, snap to a location on an existing object (or the first point of the mirror line).
4	[Drawing Screen]	Using object snaps, snap to a location on an existing object (or the second point of the mirror line).
5	[Command Line]	Type Y or N to specify whether you want to keep the original object.

Technique to Master **T02.29** The Scale Modification Command

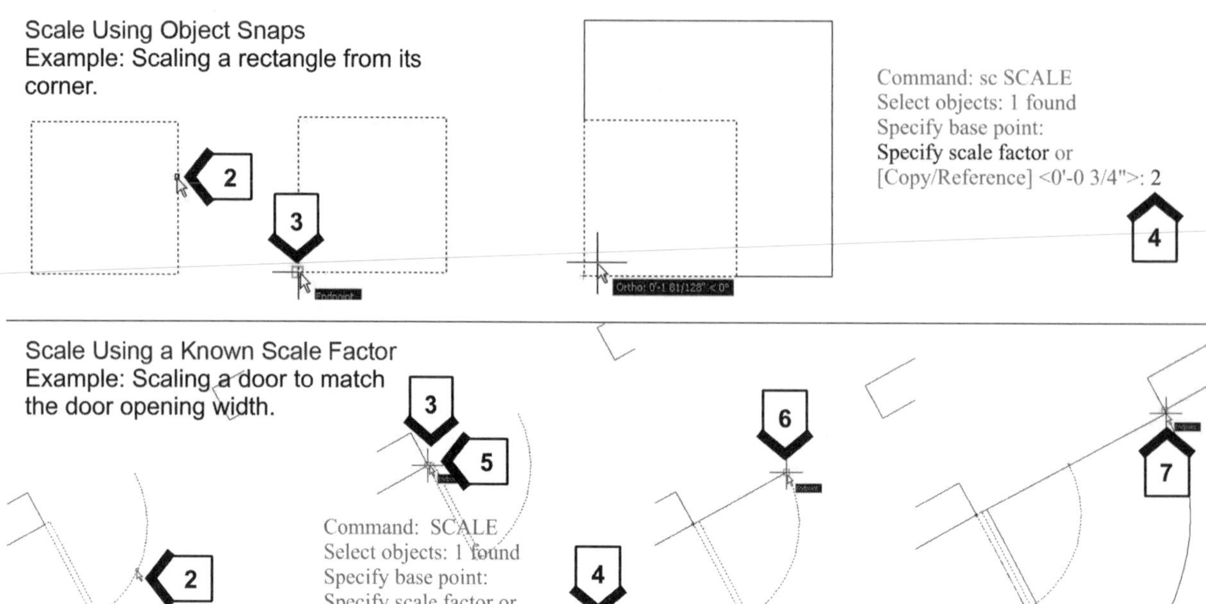

Scale Using Object Snaps
Example: Scaling a rectangle from its corner.
Command: sc SCALE
Select objects: 1 found
Specify base point:
Specify scale factor or
[Copy/Reference] <0'-0 3/4">: 2
Scale Using a Known Scale Factor
Example: Scaling a door to match the door opening width.
Command: SCALE
Select objects: 1 found
Specify base point:
Specify scale factor or
[Copy/Reference] <0'-1 1/2">: r
2
3
4
5
6
7

Figure 2.29

Scale Using Object Snaps		
1	[Command Line]	Type Scale.
2	[Drawing Screen]	Select the shape(s) you want to scale.
3	[Drawing Screen]	Using object snaps, snap to the point of scaling reference for the shape(s).
4	[Command Line]	Type in a scale factor to specify the amount of scaling.

Scale Using a Known Scale Factor		
1	[Command Line]	Type Scale.
2	[Drawing Screen]	Select the shape(s) you want to scale.
3	[Drawing Screen]	Using object snaps, snap to the point of reference for the shape(s).
4	[Command Line]	Type r, and press Enter to use the Reference command.
5	[Drawing Screen]	Using object snaps, snap to the same point of reference.
6	[Drawing Screen]	Using object snaps, snap to the scaling distance you wish to affect.
7	[Drawing Screen]	Using object snaps, snap to or type in the new distance.

The Trim and Extend Modification Commands

The Trim command lets you crop or cut off a portion of one or more selected shapes. The Extend command lets you extend one or more selected lines or arcs to a specified boundary edge. The Trim and Extend modification commands are used frequently at corners and intersections of lines that represent walls, as shown in Figure 2.30.

Technique to Master **T02.30** The Trim and Extend Modification Commands

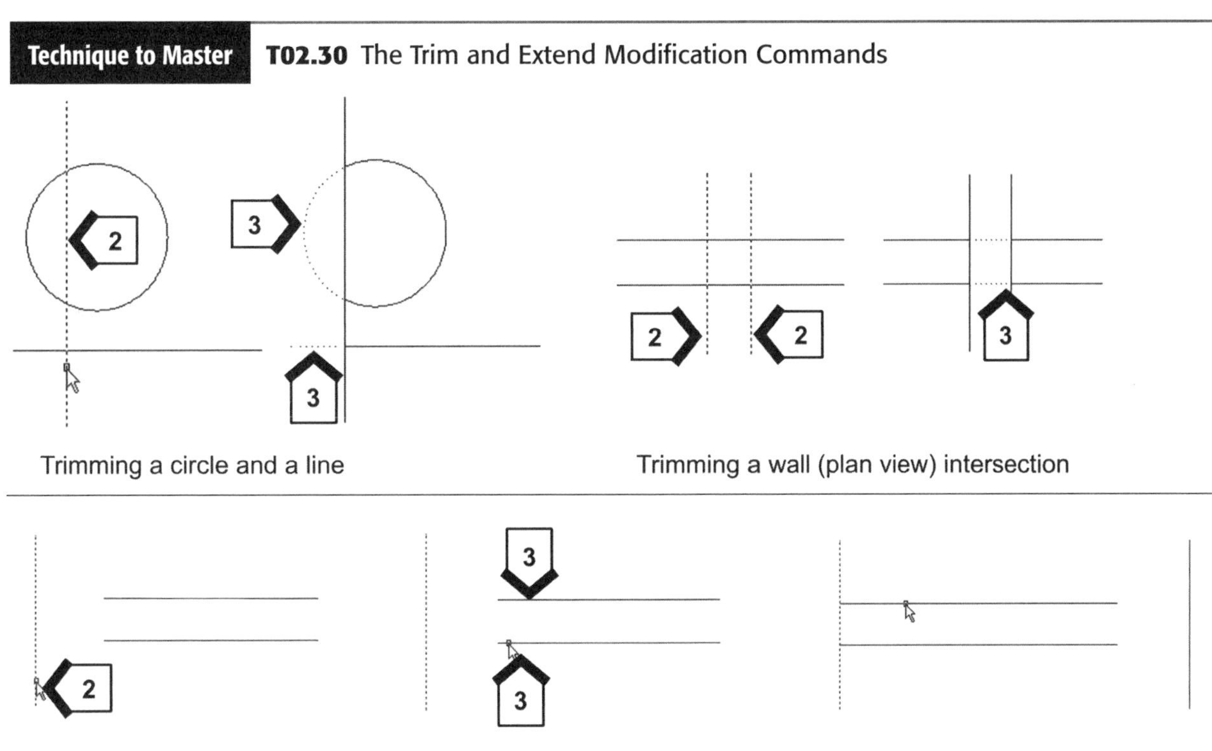

Figure 2.30

Using the Trim Command		
1	[Command Line]	Type Trim.
2	[Drawing Screen]	Select the cutting edge(s).
3	[Drawing Screen]	Using the Pick Select method, click the part of the shape that will be removed by the trim.

Using the Extend Command		
1	[Command Line]	Type Extend.
2	[Drawing Screen]	Select boundary edge(s).
3	[Drawing Screen]	Pick select the side of the shape that will be extended.

The Fillet and Chamfer Modification Commands

The Fillet command lets you create a rounded corner between two intersecting or apparently intersecting lines or arcs. The Chamfer command lets you create an angled corner between two intersecting or apparently intersecting lines or arcs. Figure 2.31 demonstrates various application techniques using these commands.

Technique to Master **T02.31** The Fillet and Chamfer Modification Commands

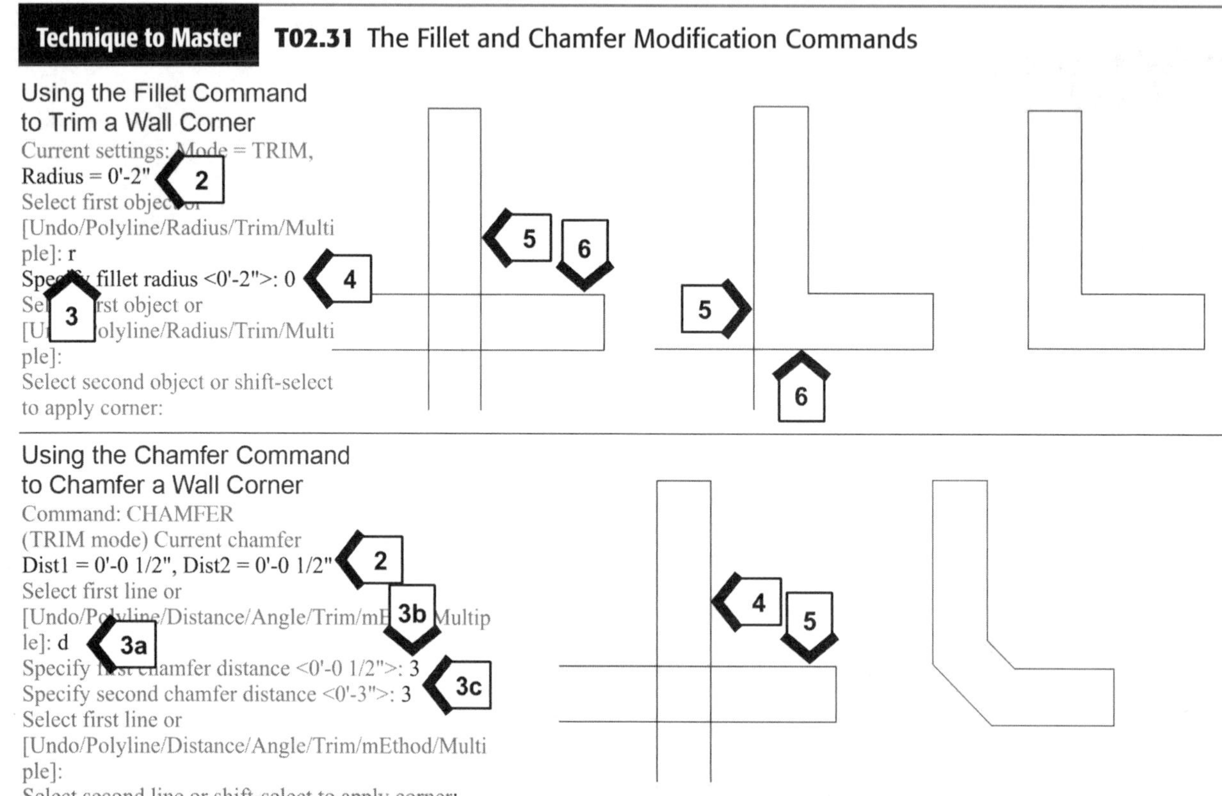

Using the Fillet Command
to Trim a Wall Corner
Current settings: Mode = TRIM,
Radius = 0'-2"
2
Select first object or
[Undo/Polyline/Radius/Trim/Multiple]: r
Specify fillet radius <0'-2">: 0
4
3
Select first object or
[Undo/Polyline/Radius/Trim/Multiple]:
Select second object or shift-select to apply corner:
5
6
5
6
Using the Chamfer Command
to Chamfer a Wall Corner
Command: CHAMFER
(TRIM mode) Current chamfer
Dist1 = 0'-0 1/2", Dist2 = 0'-0 1/2"
2
Select first line or
[Undo/Polyline/Distance/Angle/Trim/mEthod/Multiple]: d
3b
3a
Specify first chamfer distance <0'-0 1/2">: 3
Specify second chamfer distance <0'-3">: 3
3c
Select first line or
[Undo/Polyline/Distance/Angle/Trim/mEthod/Multiple]:
Select second line or shift-select to apply corner:
4
5

Figure 2.31

Using the Fillet Command		
1	[Command Line]	Type Fillet.
2	Verify radius.	Go to Step 3 if you need to change the radius.
3	[Command Line]	Type r to change the fillet radius.
4	[Command Line]	Type in a new radius value.
5	[Drawing Screen]	Pick Select the side of the first shape that will be affected by the radius.
6	[Drawing Screen]	Pick Select the side of the second shape that will be affected by the radius.

Using the Chamfer Command		
1	[Command Line]	Type Chamfer.
2	Verify distances for the chamfer.	Follow Step 3 if you need to change the distance.
3	a. [Command Line]	Type D to change the chamfer distances.
	b. [Command Line]	Type in the new chamfer distance for the first shape.
	c. [Command Line]	Type in the new chamfer distance for the second shape.
4	[Drawing Screen]	Pick Select the side of the first shape that will be affected by the chamfer.
5	[Drawing Screen]	Pick Select the side of the second shape that will be affected by the chamfer.

The Offset and Array Commands

The Offset command lets you create parallel lines and arcs, as well as concentric circles and rectangles. The Array command lets you create a rectangular array consisting of rows and columns or a polar array rotated around a common center. Figure 2.32 demonstrates various application techniques using these commands.

Technique to Master **T02.32** The Offset and Array Modification Commands

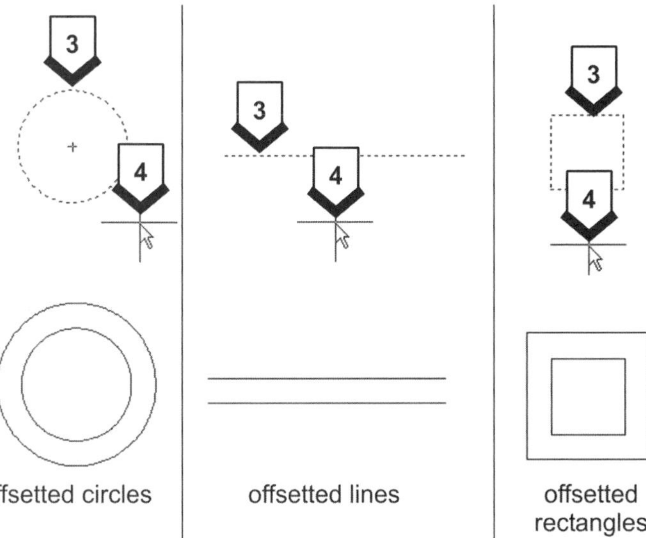

Using the Offset Command by Typing in a Distance
Command: OFFSET
Current settings: Erase source=No Layer=Source
OFFSETGAPTYPE=0
Specify offset distance or [Through/Erase/Layer] <Through>: 6
Select object to offset or [Exit/Undo] <Exit>:
Specify point on side to offset or [Exit/Multiple/Undo] <Exit>:
2
3
4
offsetted circles
offsetted lines
offsetted rectangles

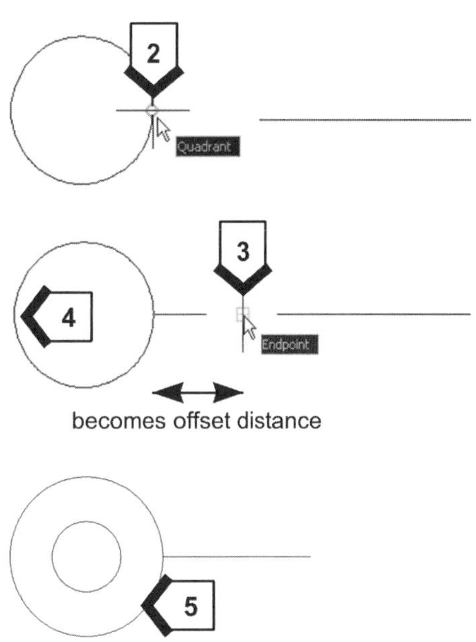

Figure 2.32

Using the Offset Command by Typing in a Distance		
1	[Command Line]	Type Offset.
2	[Command Line]	Type in the offset distance.
3	[Drawing Screen]	Select the shape(s) to offset.
4	[Drawing Screen]	Select the side to offset.

Using the Offset Through Option		
1	[Command Line]	Type Offset.
2	[Drawing Screen]	Select the first point of visual distance.
3	[Drawing Screen]	Select the second point of visual distance.
4	[Drawing Screen]	Select the shape(s) to offset.
5	[Drawing Screen]	Select the side to offset.

The Stretch Command

The Stretch command lets you modify an object by distorting it (making it longer, thinner, shorter, taller, and so on). Figure 2.33 demonstrates the Stretch modification command.

Technique to Master **T02.33** The Stretch Modification Command

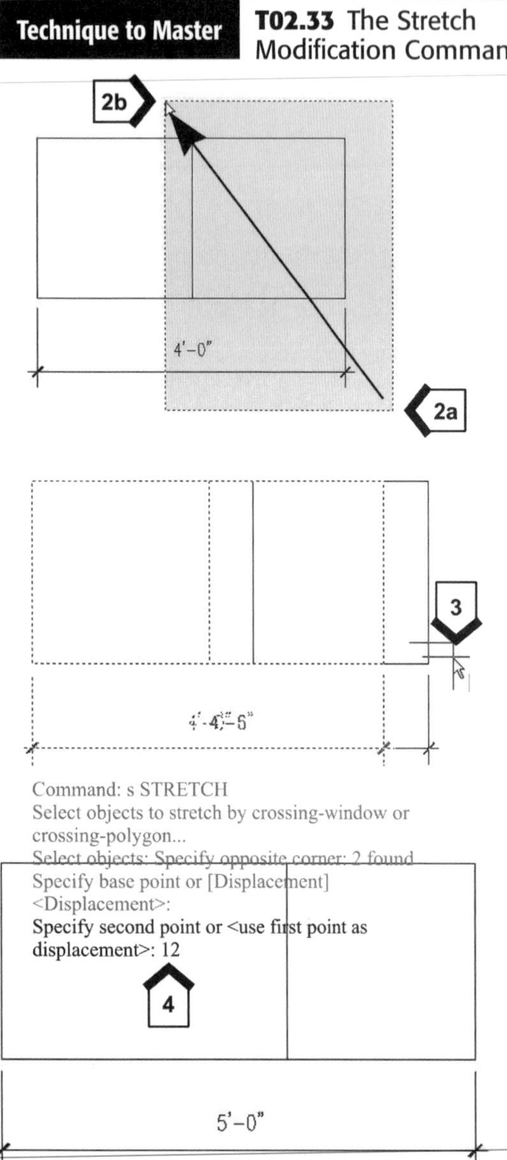
2b
2a
4'-0"
3
Command: s STRETCH
Select objects to stretch by crossing-window or crossing-polygon...
Select objects: Specify opposite corner: 2 found
Specify base point or [Displacement] <Displacement>:
Specify second point or <use first point as displacement>: 12
4
5'-0"

Figure 2.33

Using the Stretch Command		
1	[Command Line]	Type Stretch.
2a, 2b	[Drawing Screen]	Using a crossing selection, select the part of the shape(s) to stretch.
3	[Drawing Screen]	Click on the screen to locate the point of reference for the stretch.
4	[Command Line]	Use the direct distance entry to specify the amount of the stretch.

Grip Editing

Grips, also called Entity Grips, are blue squares and triangles that are located at key locations on a shape (Figure 2.34). They are used to make quick edits to shapes and text, as well as objects that are grouped together. Grips let you make basic modifications without making you type in or use any formal AutoCAD commands. Most grip manipulations allow stretching, moving, rotating, scaling, and mirroring.

For grip editing to work, the Grips system variable is set to 1 (the default setting). Notice that Grip editing cannot be used within a command sequence. Grip squares are visible only when you select a shape and have no command in progress. When selected, squares appear at the endpoints, midpoints, and/or centers of the shape(s). These special squares are unfilled and, therefore, unselected. Left-click on one of the squares to activate the grip and turn it red. The default editing process is set to Stretch. To access other editing options, press the Enter key or tap the spacebar. Figure 2.35 demonstrates the various editing options using grips.

Box 2.9

Tip: To add precision when editing objects, simply substitute the 'by clicking on screen' instruction with either a coordinate or an object snap.

Box 2.10

Tip: Grips can be used with several shapes at a time.

Box 2.11

Tip: Press and hold the Shift key while left-clicking to select additional grips.

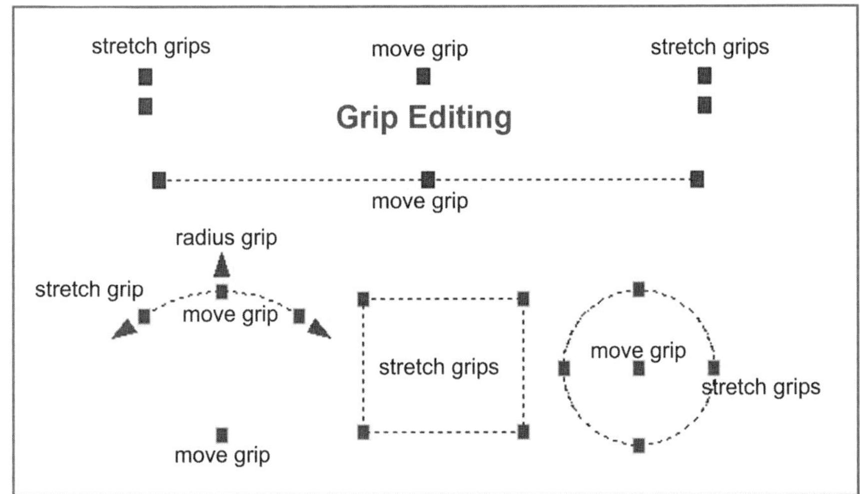

Figure 2.34 Grip locations on the basic geometric shapes

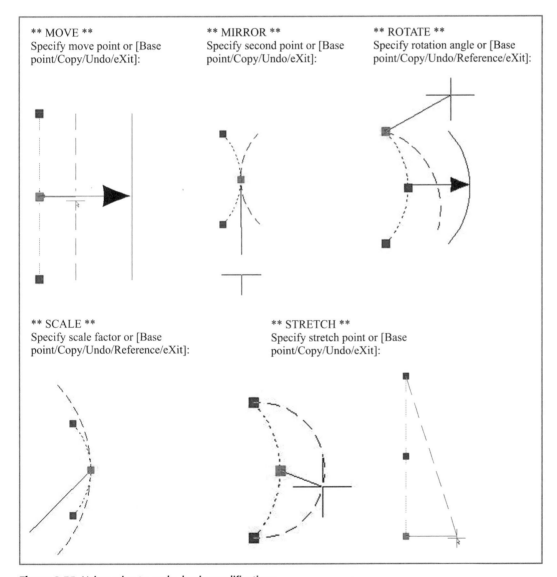

** MOVE **
Specify move point or [Base point/Copy/Undo/eXit]:

** MIRROR **
Specify second point or [Base point/Copy/Undo/eXit]:

** ROTATE **
Specify rotation angle or [Base point/Copy/Undo/Reference/eXit]:

** SCALE **
Specify scale factor or [Base point/Copy/Undo/Reference/eXit]:

** STRETCH **
Specify stretch point or [Base point/Copy/Undo/eXit]:

Figure 2.35 Using grips to make basic modifications

Figure 2.36 Building elements and their drafted representations–top, front, and side views

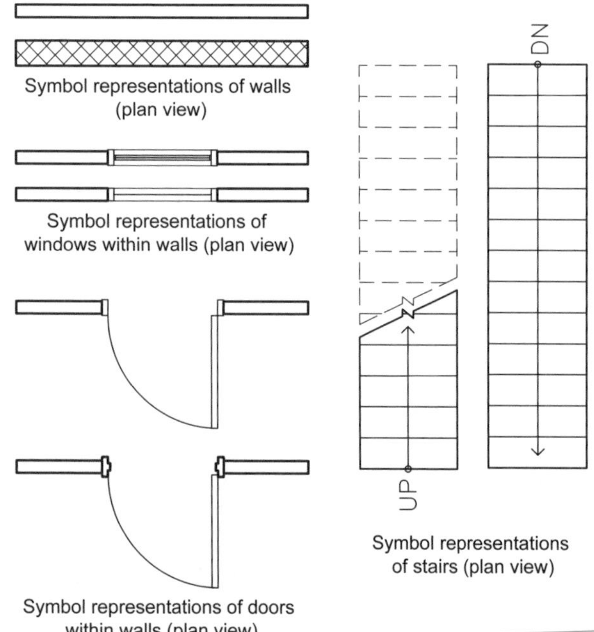

Figure 2.37 Typical symbol representations of building elements

Using the Basic Shapes to Create Object Representations

When you draw and paint, you use basic geometric shapes to create representations of the real world. Representations are drawings that look like or symbolize real-life objects. When you draft representations of objects, you use lines, arcs, and other basic shapes to distinguish the object from surrounding areas. Figure 2.36 shows some basic examples of how objects in real life can be represented with lines, arcs, and circles.

Many times symbols are used to simplify building elements that are too complicated or have too much detail. These symbols tend to generically represent their real-life counterparts. Windows, doors, and stairs are just a few of the many building elements that designers represent through symbols. Figure 2.37 shows some common building elements with their associated symbols. These standard conventions are explored in more detail in Chapter 18.

Understanding Orthographic Projections

In the design and construction disciplines, drawings communicate how a building is designed and constructed. Orthographic projections refer to the types of standard measurable views design and construction professionals use when they communicate their work. Measurable views include the top view (also known as the roof plan view), the floor plan view, the ceiling plan view, the section view, the elevation view, and the isometric view. All orthographic projections are drawn at real scale when drafted on the computer.

The Top View

The top view represents what the top of a building or an object looks like. Vertical planes are shown as single lines as if you were looking directly down on a building or an object.

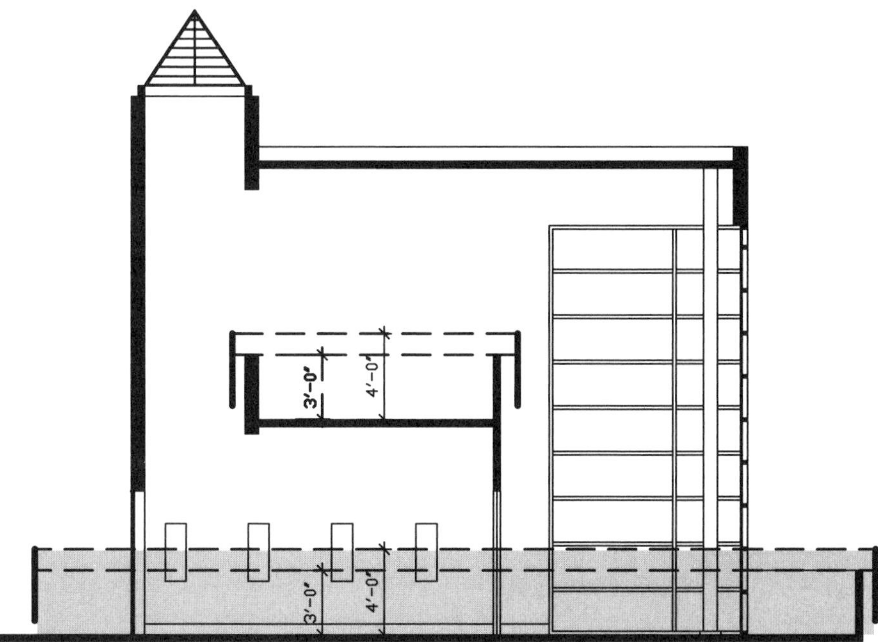

Figure 2.38 The example shows a sectional view of an artist studio. To create the floor plan for this studio, the cut plane is typically located between 3 and 4 feet above the finish floor.

The Floor Plan View

Similar to the top view, the floor plan view shows a top view of the exterior and interior for each level of a building, including all visible building systems, furniture, and equipment. Based on drawing conventions, a floor plan's cut plane is typically located between 3 and 4 feet above the finish floor (Figure 2.38). The orthographic view that results is a top view of each associated floor level. Multistory buildings have floor plans for each floor (Figure 2.39), while double-height and split-level spaces rely on the main floor to govern the entire floor's cut plane.

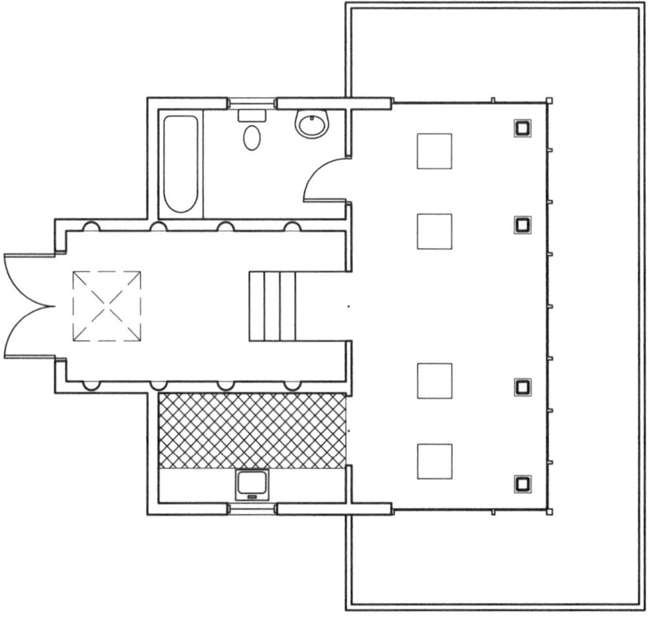

First Floor - Artist Studio

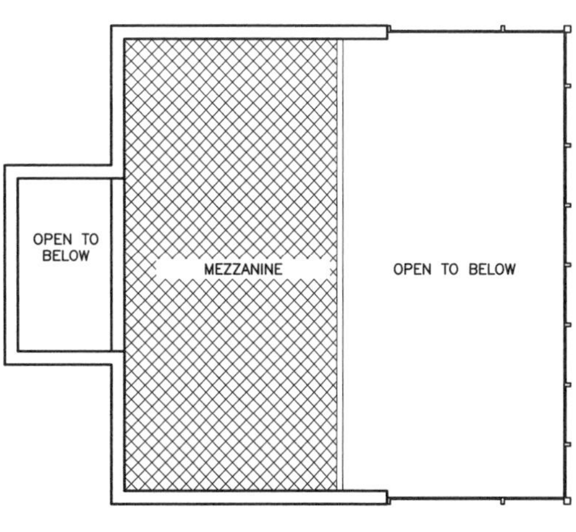

Loft - Artist Studio

Figure 2.39 Multistory buildings have floor plans for each floor.

The Ceiling View

As with floor plan views, ceiling plans show the design and positioning of building elements on the ceiling of each building level. Drawing conventions for ceiling plan cut planes are typically around 6 to 7 feet above the finished floor (Figure 2.40).

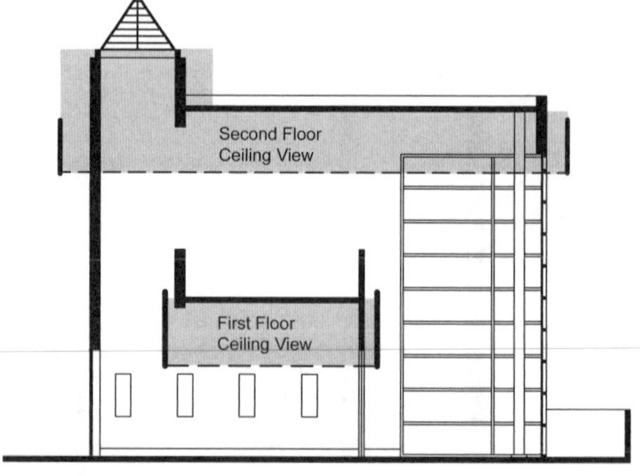

Figure 2.40 Drawing conventions for ceiling plan cut planes.

The Section View

Unique to the design and building industry are section views that provide a view through a building or an object by creating a vertical cut plane. This vertical cut plane slices through the entire building, which reveals all the elements inside (Figure 2.41).

The Elevation View

Elevations show the exterior of a building or an object from a frontal or side view. They are used in interior design to show the frontal views of casework and cabinetry as well as the detailing of a distinctive wall.

The Isometric View

Isometric views are three-dimensional views that can be measured with an architect's or engineer's scale. To create the isometric view, objects are rotated from the horizontal plane and given height.

Chapter Exercises

Open the Chapter 02 Exercise Text.doc located on the supplementary CD-ROM to access the chapter exercises. The exercises let you practice creating geometry and modifying geometry by using relative coordinates.

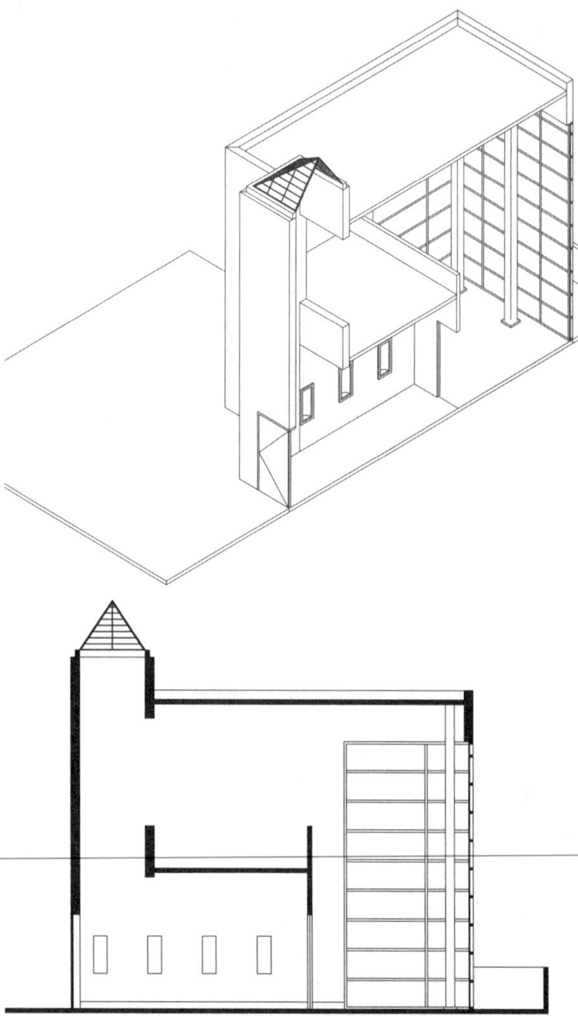

Figure 2.41 This vertical cut plane slices through the entire building, which shows all the building elements.

3 Drawing Organization and Office Standards

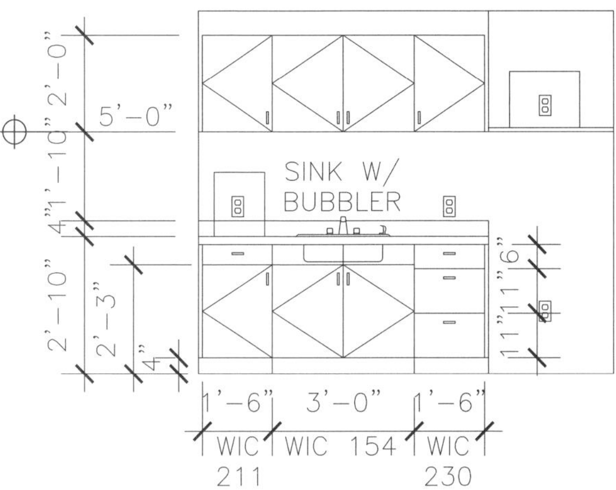

Figure 3.1 The cabinet elevations at NLA Office Renovation is also used to communicate the sizes of the wall cabinets.

Courtesy of Nacht & Lewis Architects, Sacramento, CA.

Objectives

This chapter explains the drafting conventions of the design discipline and how they are integrated within AutoCAD. It introduces drafting conventions, including layers, lineweights, and linetypes. It also examines the relevance of drafting standards to the design and drawing processes. End-of-chapter exercises give you the opportunity to practice using layers, lineweights, and linetypes in the floor plan, section, and elevation views.

Understanding Typical Drafting Conventions

Whenever a building requires construction or renovation, someone needs to design and draft it first. Drafting is treated separate from designing because it refers to dissimilar actions and skill sets. Drafting requires precision during the drawing process because its purpose is to communicate through a variety of technical drawings what you need to build and how you need to build it (Figure 3.1). Although sometimes people use the terms *drafting* and *designing* synonymously, drafting requires you to master accuracy, exactness, and detail in the drawing process. Drafting is technical, whereas designing is conceptual.

The multiple disciplines of the building industry—architecture; interior design; and structural, civil, mechanical, landscape, and electrical engineering—have created standards in an effort to facilitate communication via the drawing form among all the disciplines. They have established rules for how each ortho-graphic drawing type should be drawn. Rules of practice include orthographic drawing type, symbol, line thickness, and line style.

Chapter 2 touches on the rules of drafting conventions—the orthographic drawing type. The various building elements, equipment, and furniture in plan and elevational views shown at the end of Chapter 2 were drawn with AutoCAD's basic shapes. The objects below, however, were drawn using the same line thickness and line styling (Figure 3.2). If it were a more complicated drawing, its printout would appear illegible, and you would find it very difficult to distinguish between objects within the drawing.

Another rule in drafting conventions prompts you to use line thickness and line styling to differentiate between objects sliced by the cut plane, objects beyond the cut plane, and objects above the cut plane (Figure 3.3).

Box 3.1
Line thickness conventions are also affected by plotting scale.

Tables 3.1 and 3.2 provide helpful guides for determining line thickness conventions and their relationship to cut planes and plotting scale. Figures 3.4 and 3.5 apply the conventions to floor plan and section drawings.

Figure 3.2 This student's floor plan of the Parker House has no line thicknesses or line styling.
Courtesy of Tiffany White.

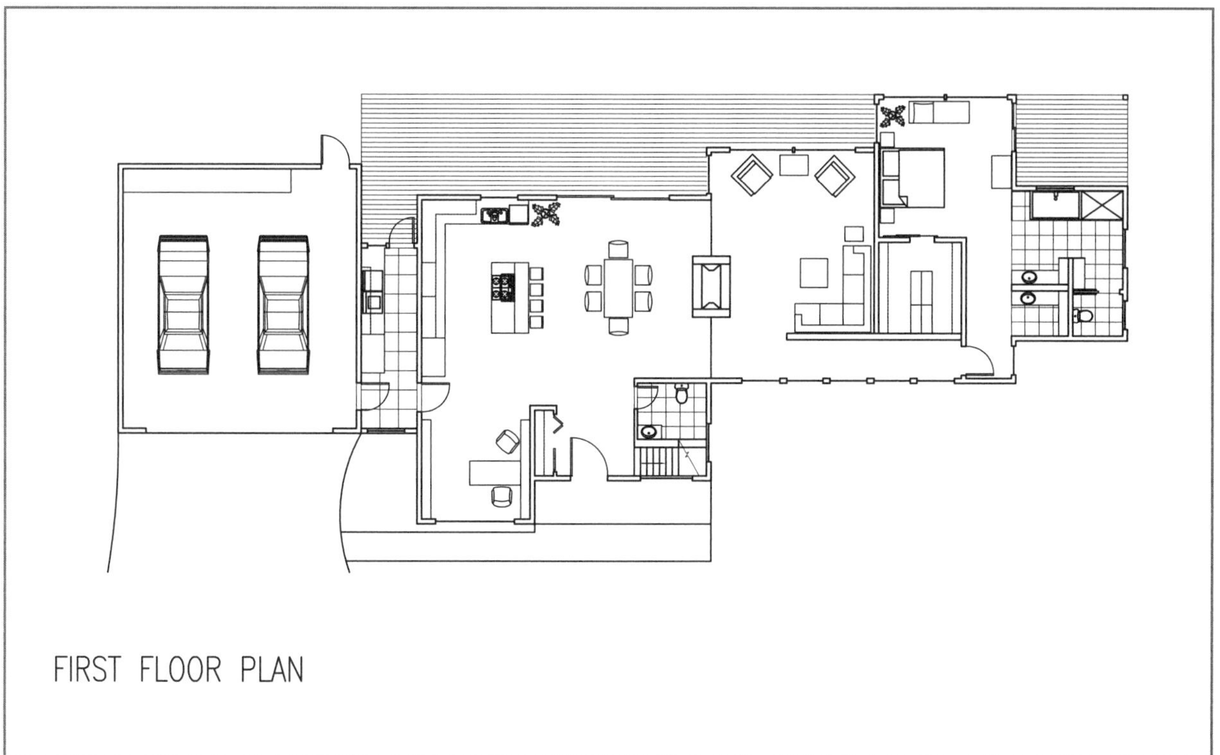

Figure 3.3 In this same floor plan of the Parker House, the student has applied line thickness and styling.
Courtesy of Tiffany White.

Table 3.1 Lineweight Conventions (Plan View)

Objects in Plan View	Scale = 1/8" = 1'-0"	Scale = 1/4" = 1'-0"
Walls and columns at cut plane	.40 mm	.70 mm
Window glazing and jamb	.40 mm	.40 mm
Walls below cut plane	.25 mm	.35 mm
Walls above cut plane	.25 mm	.35 mm
Doors, casework, appliances, fixtures	.30 mm	.40 mm
Stairs, level changes, floor slabs, toilet partitions	.15 mm	.30 mm
Furniture	.20 mm	.25 mm
Equipment	.15 mm	.25 mm
Entourage, floor patterns, railings, accessories, window sills	.09 mm	.09 mm

Table 3.2 Lineweight Conventions (Section View)

Objects in Section/Elevation View	Scale = 1/8" = 1'-0"	Scale = 1/4" = 1'-0"
Walls and columns at cut plane	.50 mm	.60 mm
Window glazing and jamb at cut plane	.40 mm	.50 mm
Walls beyond cut plane	.25 mm	.25 mm
Casework, appliances, fixtures, toilet partitions at cut plane	.40 mm	.50 mm
Casework, appliances, fixtures, toilet partitions beyond cut plane	.20 mm	.20 mm
Stairs, level changes, floor slabs at cut line	.40 mm	.50 mm
Stairs, level changes, floor slabs beyond cut line	.20 mm	.30 mm
Equipment, furniture	.15 mm	.15 mm

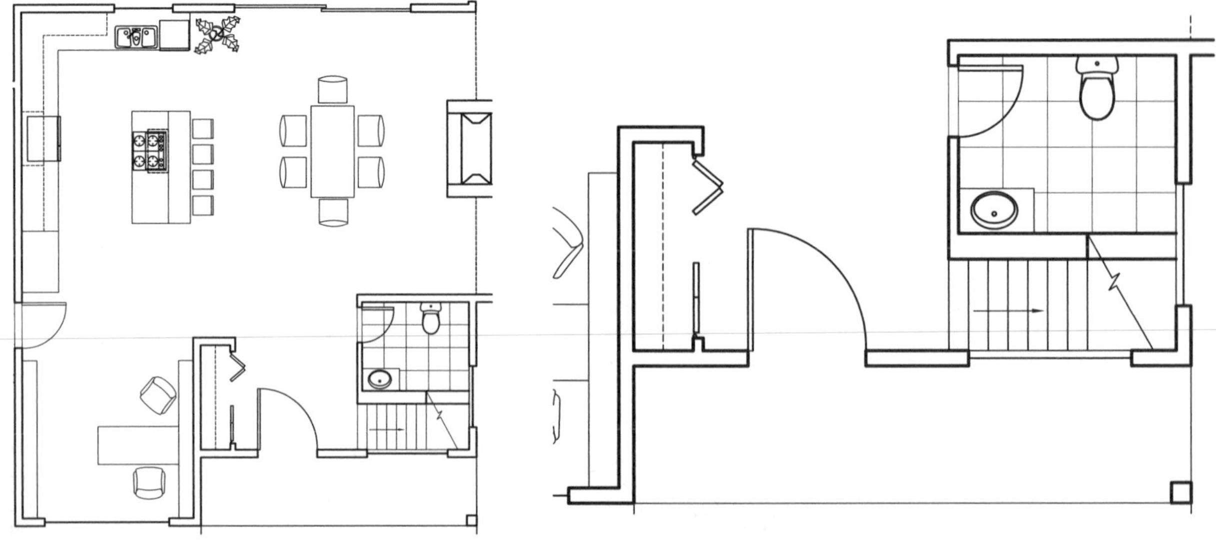

Partial Floor Plan plotted at ⅛" = 1'-0" using lineweight conventions.

Partial Floor Plan plotted at ¼" = 1'-0" using lineweight conventions.

Figure 3.4 The various plan views of the Parker House plotted at the different scales using lineweights.

Courtesy of Tiffany White.

Cross Section plotted at ⅛" = 1'-0" using lineweight conventions.

Partial Section plotted at ¼" = 1'-0" using lineweight conventions.

Figure 3.5 These section views of an office renovation project are plotted at the different scales using lineweights.

Courtesy of Tiffany White.

Objectives of Line Thickness and Line-Styling Drafting Conventions

Line thickness is referred to as lineweight in AutoCAD, and it communicates depth in drawings. In plans and sections, the lineweight of an object increases when the invisible cut plane slices it. Lineweights of objects that are further away from the imaginary cut plane decrease in thickness. Lineweight choice is also directly affected by the amount of detail within a drawing and the drawing's eventual plotting scale. Typically, a hierarchy of three or more lineweights is used in orthographic drawings, as described in Table 3.3.

Line styles are repeating patterns of lines, spaces, and dots that communicate other types of information, such as whether an object is above the cut plane, hidden from

Table 3.3 Relationships Among Lineweight, Scale, View, and Detail

Plotting Scale	1/8" = 1'-0"	1/4" = 1'-0"	1" = 1'-0"	3" = 1'-0"
Floor plans	Minimal detail; higher contrasting lineweights are needed	————	————	————
Enlarged plans	————	Medium detail; bolder lineweights; lower contrasting lineweights are apparent	Medium detail; bolder lineweights; lower contrasting lineweights are apparent	————
Plan details	————	————	High detail; bolder lineweights; lower contrasting lineweights are apparent	High detail; bolder lineweights; lower contrasting lineweights are apparent
Exterior elevations	Medium detail; higher contrasting lineweights are needed	Medium detail; bolder lineweights; lower contrasting lineweights are apparent	————	————
Interior elevations	————	Medium detail; bolder lineweights; lower contrasting lineweights are apparent	————	————
Building sections	Minimal detail; higher contrasting lineweights are needed	Medium detail; bolder lineweights; lower contrasting lineweights are apparent	————	————

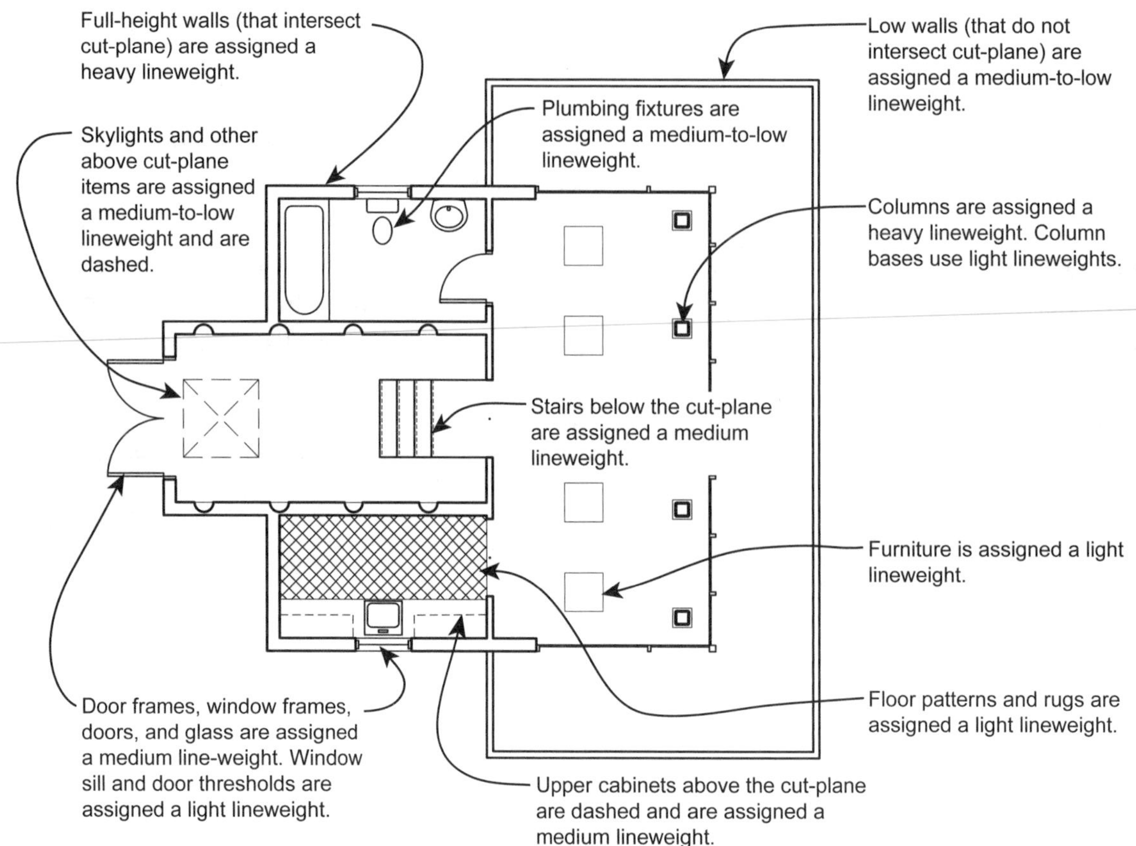

Full-height walls (that intersect cut-plane) are assigned a heavy lineweight.
Skylights and other above cut-plane items are assigned a medium-to-low lineweight and are dashed.
Plumbing fixtures are assigned a medium-to-low lineweight.
Low walls (that do not intersect cut-plane) are assigned a medium-to-low lineweight.
Columns are assigned a heavy lineweight. Column bases use light lineweights.
Stairs below the cut-plane are assigned a medium lineweight.
Furniture is assigned a light lineweight.
Floor patterns and rugs are assigned a light lineweight.
Door frames, window frames, doors, and glass are assigned a medium line-weight. Window sill and door thresholds are assigned a light lineweight.
Upper cabinets above the cut-plane are dashed and are assigned a medium lineweight.

Figure 3.6 Lineweight conventions: Dissecting the plan view

view, or centered within a space. Typical line styles that are used in orthographic drawings include the following:

- Dashed lines indicate objects that are not visible in the current view. Examples on floor plans include upper cabinets in kitchens, hanging rods in closets, skylights, ceiling fans, and roof overhangs.
- Hidden lines indicate when an object is hidden below another object. Examples on floor plans include stair risers beneath tread nosings and the part of a chair tucked under a table.
- Center lines indicate the centers of objects and are typically used when dimensioning is required.

Figure 3.6 shows how line thickness and line style are important when drawing floor plans.

The Properties of Geometric Shapes

All geometric shapes within AutoCAD have properties. While dimensional properties are automatically determined as you draw the shape, additional properties for shapes include color, linetype, lineweight, and plot style (Figure 3.7).

Color

The color property assigns a specific color to AutoCAD geometry. AutoCAD's Color Index (ACI) has 255 colors available so users can organize objects by using the color property. The seven basic colors are assigned numbers 1 through 7 and are typically used by architecture and other design offices to simplify color choices. People might find a complicated drawing with objects that are all white confusing. Users can therefore use the color property to distinguish objects from one another onscreen.

True colors and color books were added to the 2002 edition of AutoCAD, giving users more flexibility for making color presentations. The accompanying CD-ROM shows the True Color tab. Users can select colors by maneuvering in the color spectrum box until they get the desired shade or by using one of the color models: HSL or RGB. Also on the CD-ROM are the DIC Color Guide and the Color book list boxes.

Lineweight

The use of lineweights in AutoCAD is adopted directly from manual drafting. Typically used for drafting conventions, the lineweight property assigns a line thickness to geometry that is apparent when the geometry is printed. There are 24 predefined lineweights in AutoCAD, which are displayed in millimeters. The Lineweight Settings dialogue box allows you to adjust various settings for lineweight display, including units.

Figure 3.7 Examples of the color (shown in shades of gray here and in color on the CD-ROM), linetype, lineweight, and plot style properties

Box 3.2

You can access the Lineweight Settings dialogue box by using the commands Lweight and LW.

Linetype

Line styling, also known as linetype, refers to a repeating linear pattern that uses lines, points, and arcs to define a noncontinuous line. As with lineweights, linetypes were adopted directly from manual drafting. They are loaded from a linetype library and stored in the drawing's database. The Linetype Manager dialogue box lists the linetypes that are currently loaded. You can load additional linetypes from the default library, acad.lin, which is located in the AutoCAD support subfolder shown in a figure on the supplementary CD-ROM. Users can also create custom linetype libraries or download them from the Internet.

Box 3.3

Tip: The size of the dashes and blank spaces in a line type is controlled by the linetype scale also known as Ltscale. You may control linetype scales globally or on an object by object basis. Correct Ltscale settings are always based on the eventual plotting scale. Refer to Appendix J for Ltscale settings for the common plotting scales.

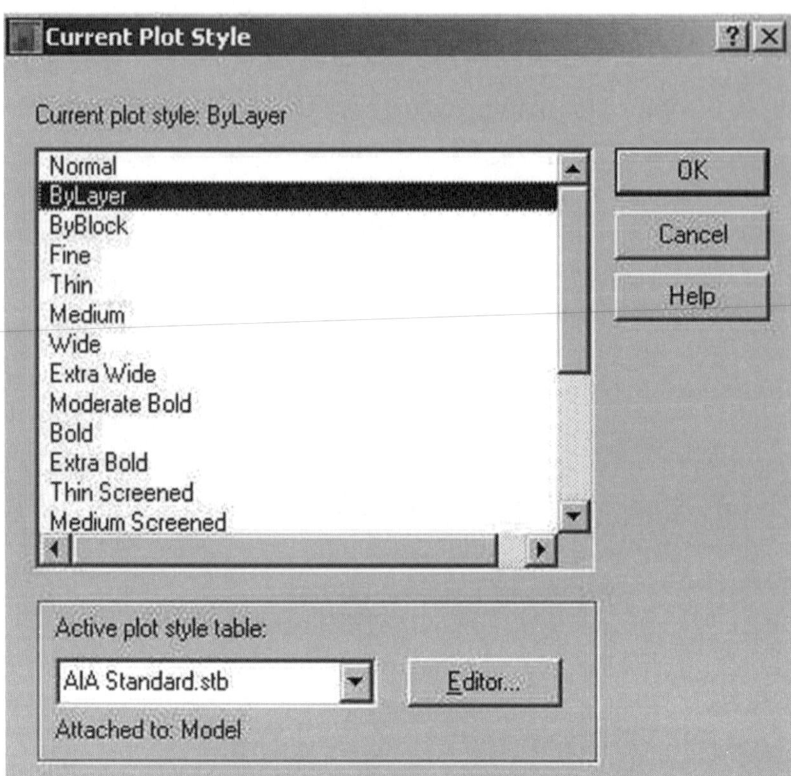

Figure 3.8 This dialogue box sets the plot style for the current drawing.

Plot Style

The plot style property uses plot style tables to configure how objects are plotted. Plot style tables are instructions for how a geometry's lineweight, color, and percentage screening should print (Figure 3.8). Plot styles are explained in more detail in Chapter 20.

An Introduction to Drawing Organization Concepts

Organizing refers to arranging. It is a process people use to make sense of the virtual world. In AutoCAD, drawings can get rather large and complex and often difficult to interpret. One of AutoCAD's organizational systems uses layers to aid drawing management.

You may be familiar with the term *layer*. In the context of digital drafting, the Layers function allows you to sort and separate geometry into logical, distinctive functions. Layers group together similar objects so users can organize their material more easily. Layer management strategies come in handy when users are viewing and plotting. When users view layers onscreen, the geometric visibility is improved. Layers also can control what is printed and how it is printed.

As with objects, layers have properties assigned to them. Colors, lineweights, and linetypes can all be associated with a layer, which makes it easier to manage similar objects. Although you can assign objects their own color, lineweight, and linetype properties, doing so proves to be inefficient. Assigning color, lineweight, and linetype properties to layers, instead of individual objects, makes for easier and quicker property assignments. For example, if you assign the color 21 and lineweight .25mm to the layer A-Door, then all lines that represent doors are immediately assigned to the layer A-Door (Figure 3.9).

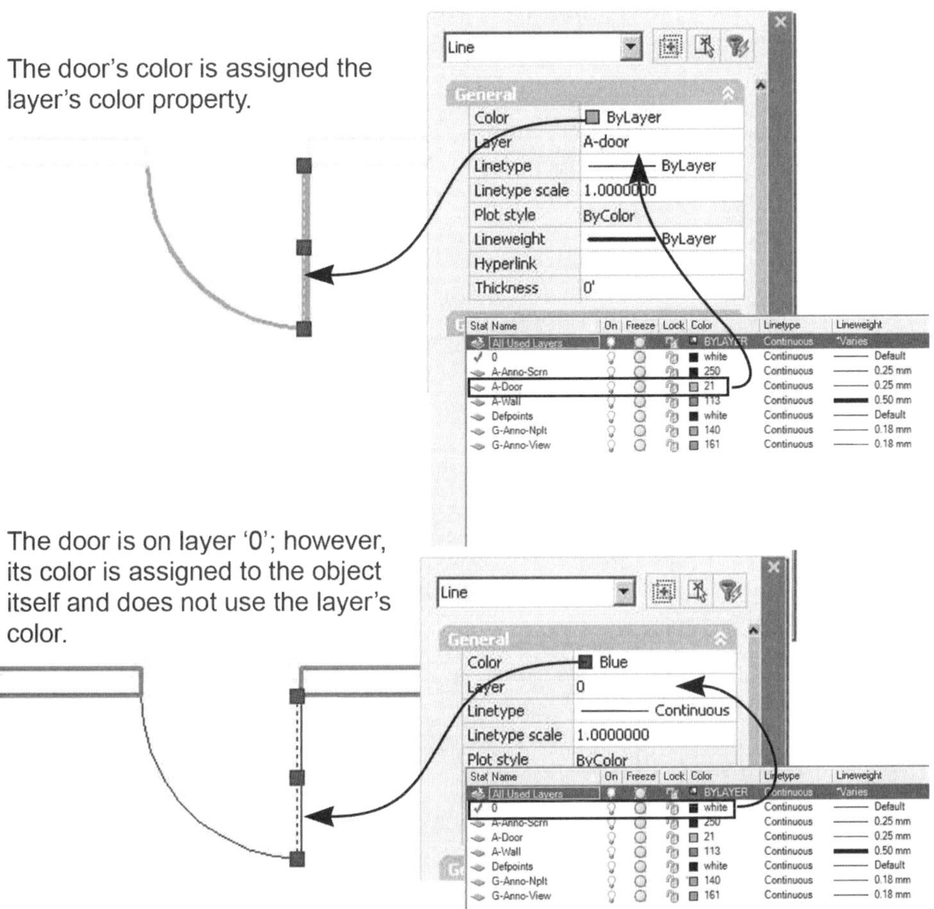

Figure 3.9 This example illustrates the differences between assigning properties by layer versus assigning them by object. (See the CD-ROM for this image in color.)

> **Box 3.4**
> An example of organization by object: All of the building's doors are changed to yellow and their lineweights are changed to .25mm.

Advantages of Using Layer Organization

- Layers allow you to assign specific names to AutoCAD's generic shapes (Figure 3.10). Meaningful layer names such as A-Wall-Exterior, A-Door, A-Window, and A-furniture help you to group and organize geometry that represent each of the above building elements.
- Layers allow you to control what is currently visible on the drawing screen. If you organize geometry by using layers, then you can temporarily turn off any layer—that is, not have it display on the drawing screen. This is helpful during drawing sessions in which your focus might shift to specific building elements.
- Instead of setting the color, linetype, and lineweight for each object, you can give layers distinctive color assignments (Figure 3.11). This system makes it easier to keep property assignments consistent throughout the various building elements.

The Layer Properties Manager has changed significantly throughout the software's evolution. Although the 2007 Layer Properties Manager looks very complicated compared with earlier versions, the options are essentially the same.

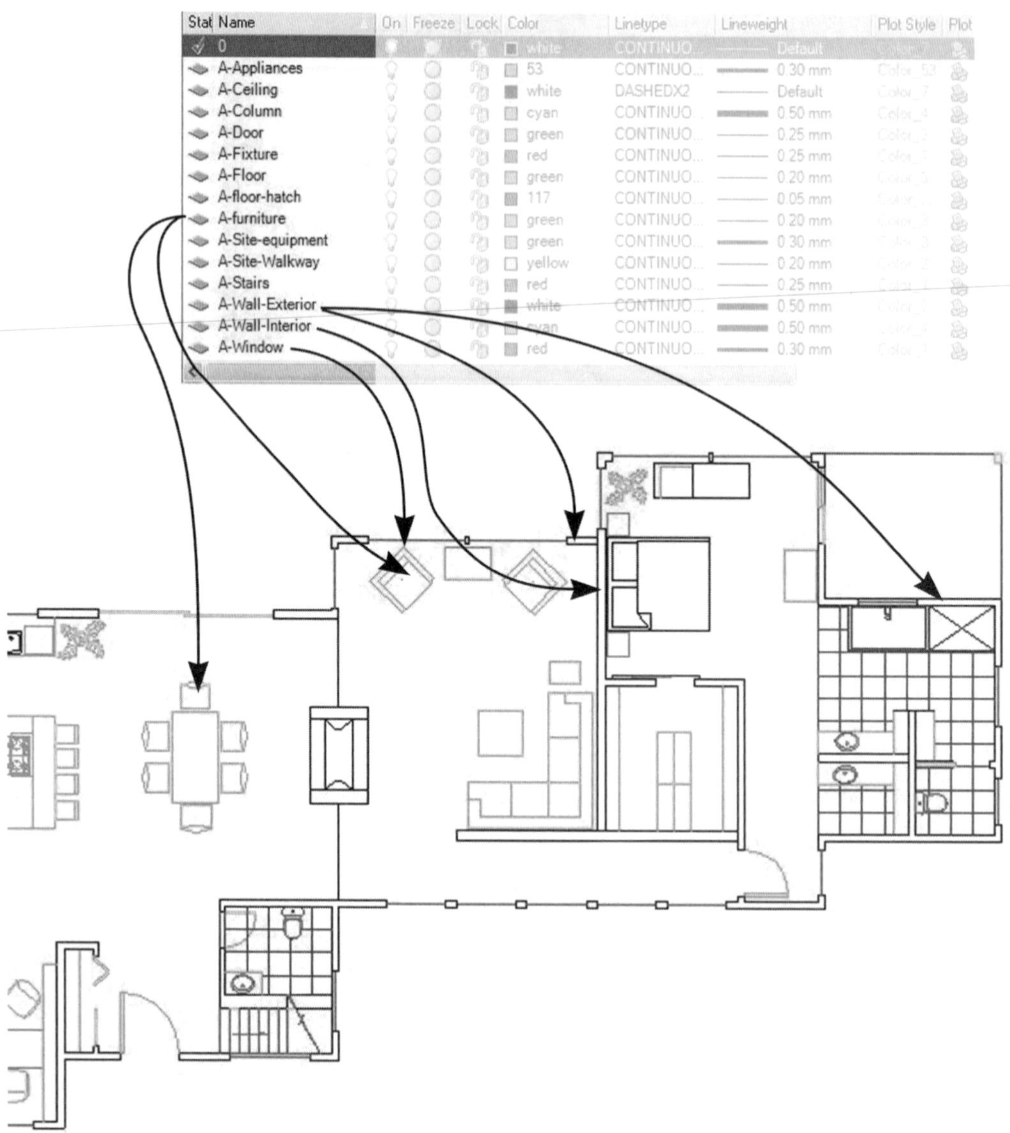

Figure 3.10 Layers allow you to assign meaningful names to AutoCAD's generic lines, arcs, and circles. In this example, layer names such as A-Wall-Exterior, A-Door, A-Window, and A-furniture are used to group and organize geometry that represent each of the corresponding building elements. (See the CD-ROM for this image in color.)

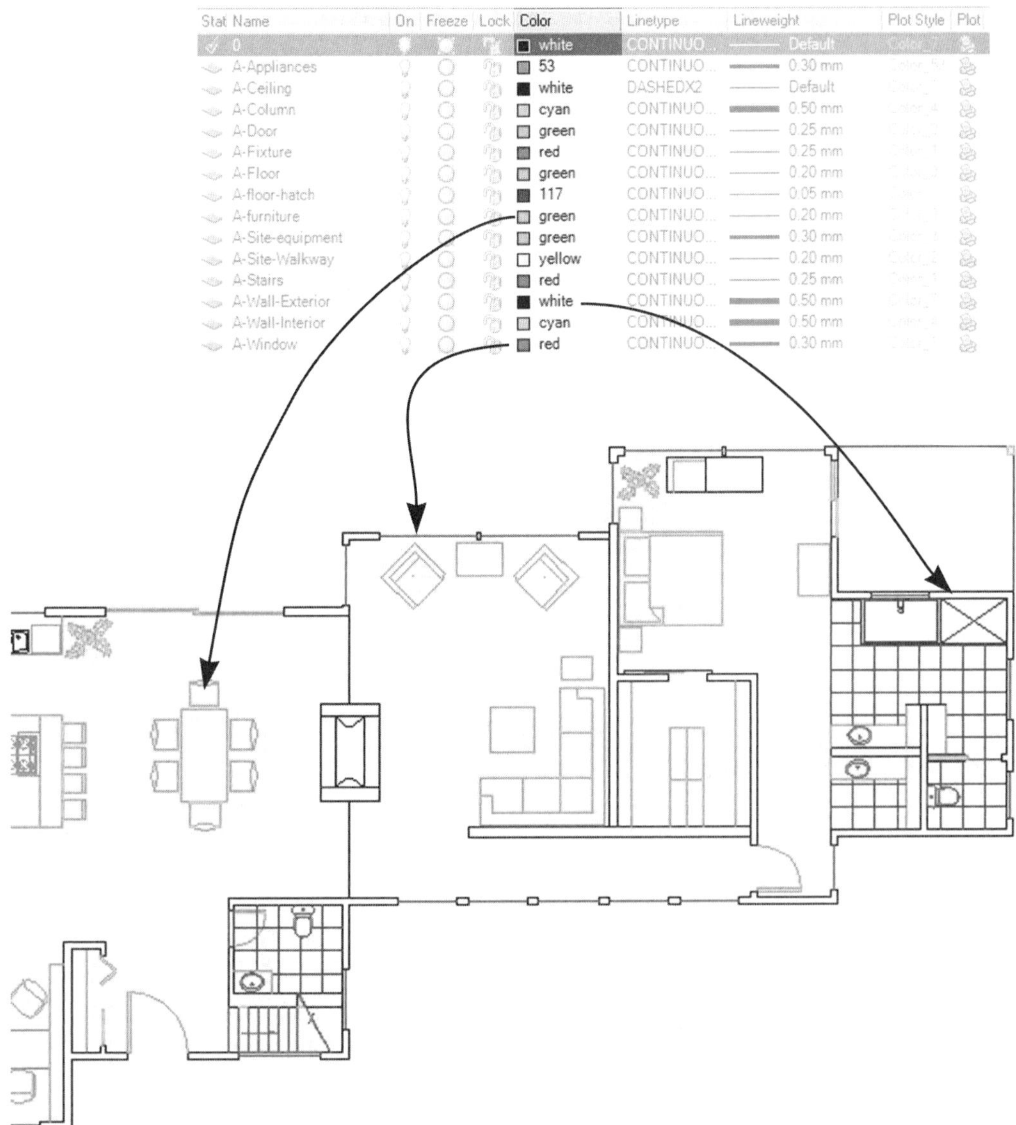

Figure 3.11 Layers with distinctive color assignments also help distinguish building elements on the drawing screen. (See the CD-ROM for this image in color.)

Understanding the Layer Properties Manager

Figure 3.12 identifies the different areas of the Layer Properties Manager, and Table 3.4 lists and describes its various properties. Essential techniques needed to master the Layer Properties Manager are demonstrated in Figures 3.13 through 3.17.

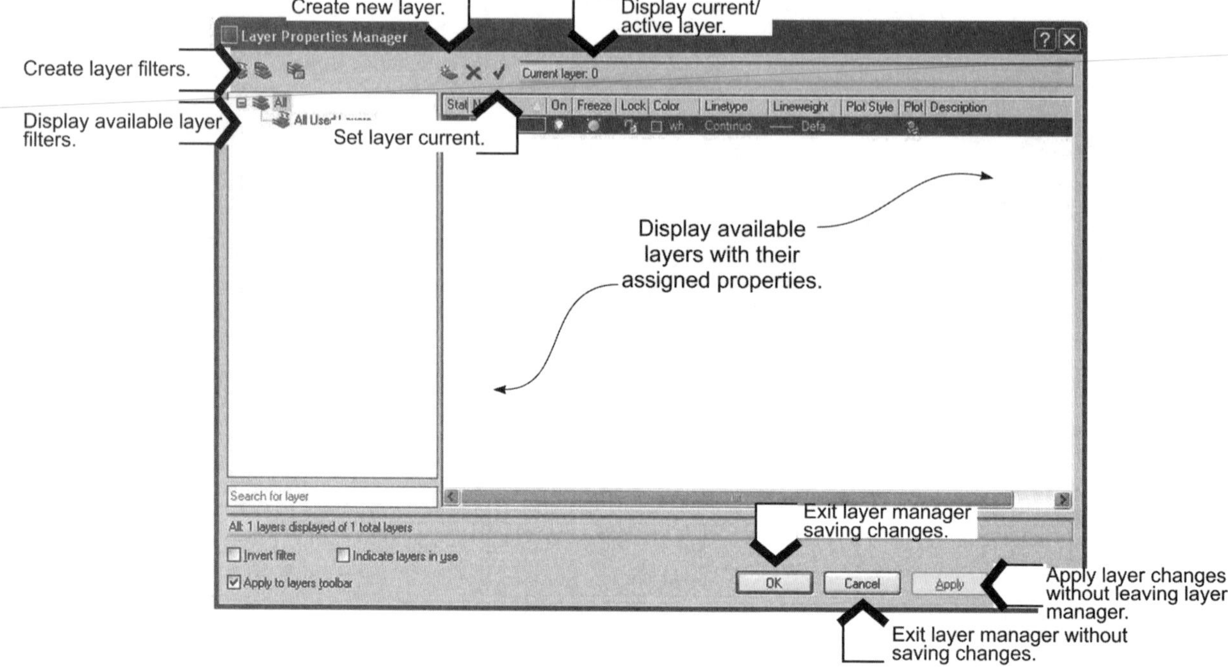

Figure 3.12 The different areas of the Layer Properties Manager

Table 3.4 Layer Manager Properties

Layer name	Assigns a meaningful name that is used to categorize objects	
On/off	Controls visibility of each layer	When off, any object on that layer becomes invisible onscreen.
Freeze/thaw	Controls visibility of each layer	When off, any object on that layer becomes invisible onscreen.
Lock/unlock	Controls ability to draw on layer	When locked, any object on that layer cannot be edited onscreen.
Color	Assigns a color to the layer	All objects assigned a color property by layer will use the layer's color.
Linetype	Assigns a linetype to the layer	All objects assigned a linetype property by layer will use the layer's linetype.
Lineweight	Assigns a lineweight to the layer	All objects assigned a lineweight property by layer will use the layer's lineweight.
Plot style	Assigns a plot style to the layer	All objects assigned a plot style property by layer will use the layer's plot style (not true for color-dependent drawing types). Plot styles and color-dependent drawing types are explained in greater detail in Chapter 20.
Plot	Controls if objects assigned to the layer are plotted	When the plotter icon has a slash through it, any object on that layer will not be plotted.

Technique to Master **T03.13** Creating Several Layers

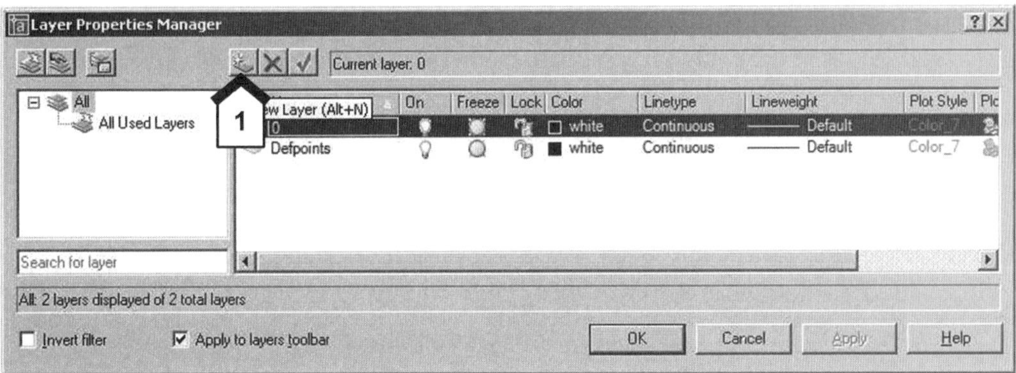

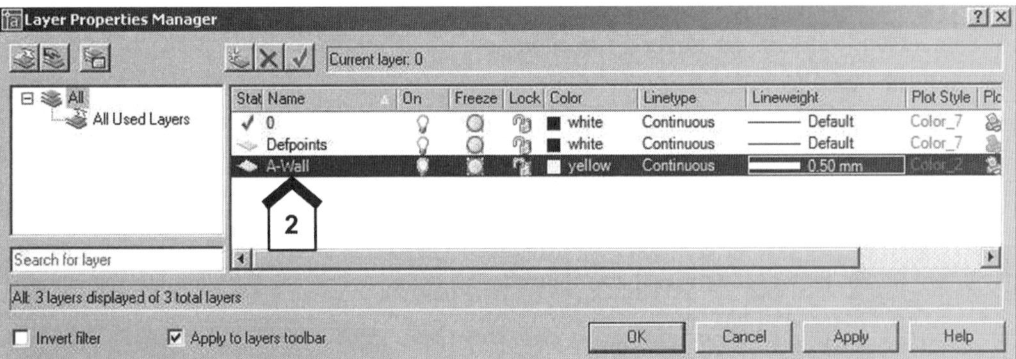

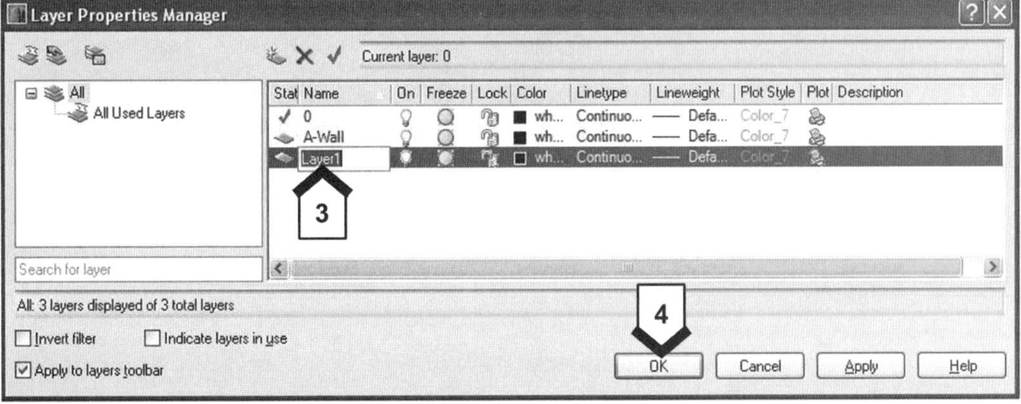

Figure 3.13

1	[Layer Properties Manager dialogue box]	Click the New button.
2	[Layer Properties Manager dialogue box]	Type the name of the layer, and add a comma to the end of the layer's name, which automatically creates another new layer that is cued up for you to type in its name.
3	[Layer Properties Manager dialogue box]	Repeat Step 2 as many times as you need to until you are finished.
4	[Layer Properties Manager dialogue box]	Left-click the OK button to close the Layer Properties Manager.

Technique to Master **T03.14** Purging Unused Layers from the Layer Properties Manager

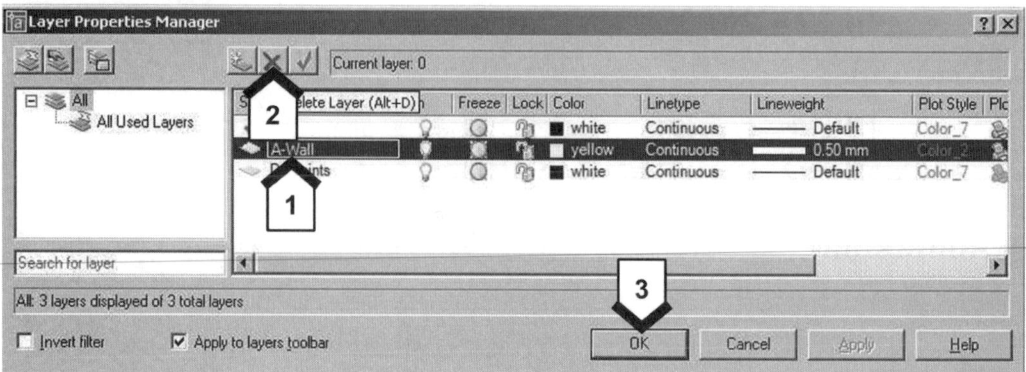

Figure 3.14

A layer is deleted only if objects are not assigned to it.		
1	[Layer Properties Manager dialogue box]	Select a layer.
2	[Layer Properties Manager dialogue box]	Left-click on the delete button.
3	[Layer Properties Manager dialogue box]	Left-click OK to exit.

Technique to Master **T03.15** Creating Layer Filters

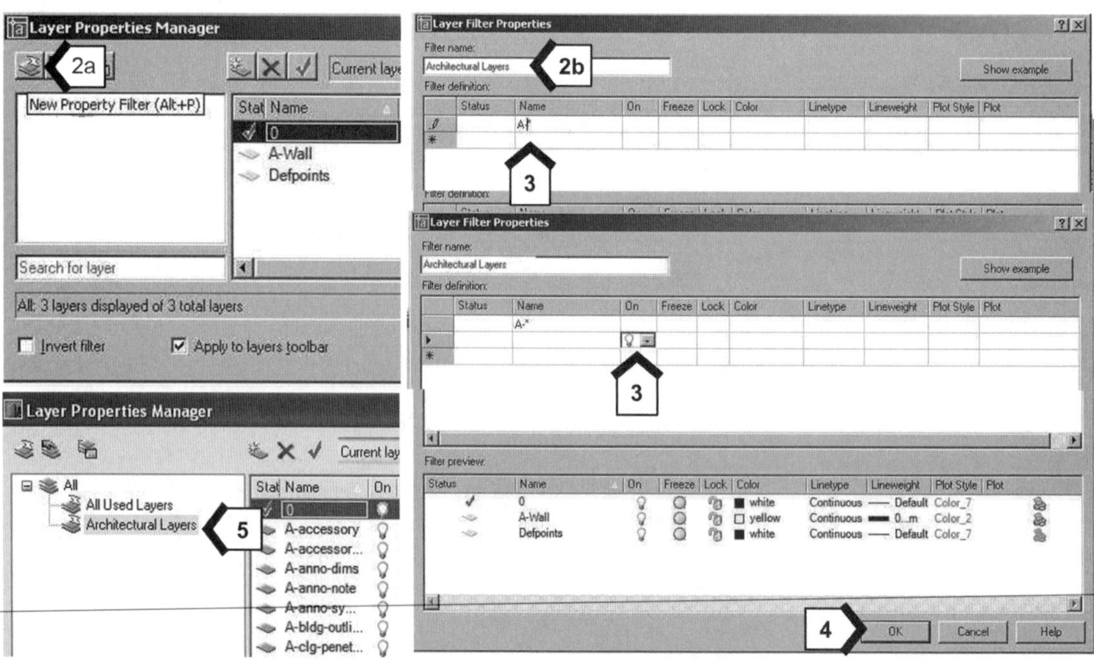

Figure 3.15

1	[Drawing Screen]	Open the Layer Properties Manager.
2a, 2b	[Layer Properties Manager dialogue box]	Left-click on the New Property Filter button, and name the filter.
3	[Layer Filters Properties dialogue box]	Add the type of filtering property. You can create multiple filters by adding additional filters for each line.
4	[Layer Filters Properties dialogue box]	Left-click OK to exit.
5	[Layer Properties Manager dialogue box]	Left-click on a filter to apply your changes.

Technique to Master **T03.16** Using Layer Filters

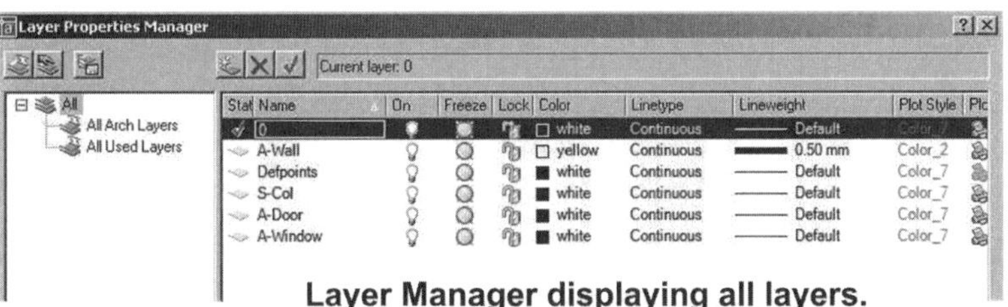

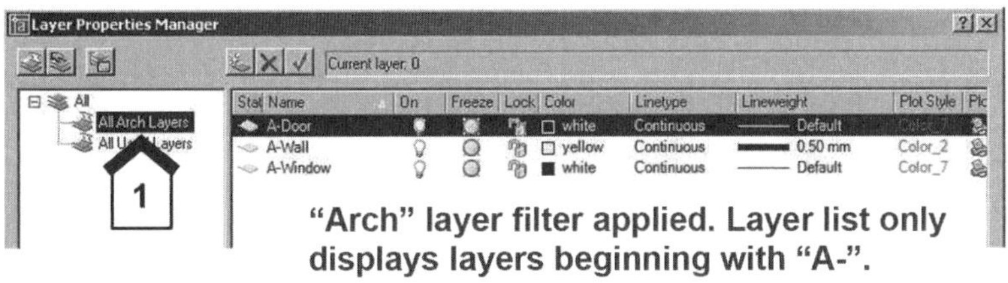

Layer Manager displaying all layers.

Layer Properties Manager
1
"Arch" layer filter applied. Layer list only displays layers beginning with "A-".

Layer Properties Manager
"Used" layer filter applied. Layer list only displays layers that have objects assigned to them.

Figure 3.16

1	[Layer Properties Manager dialogue box]	Left-click on a filter to apply it to the layer list on the right.

Technique to Master **T03.17** Making a Layer Current

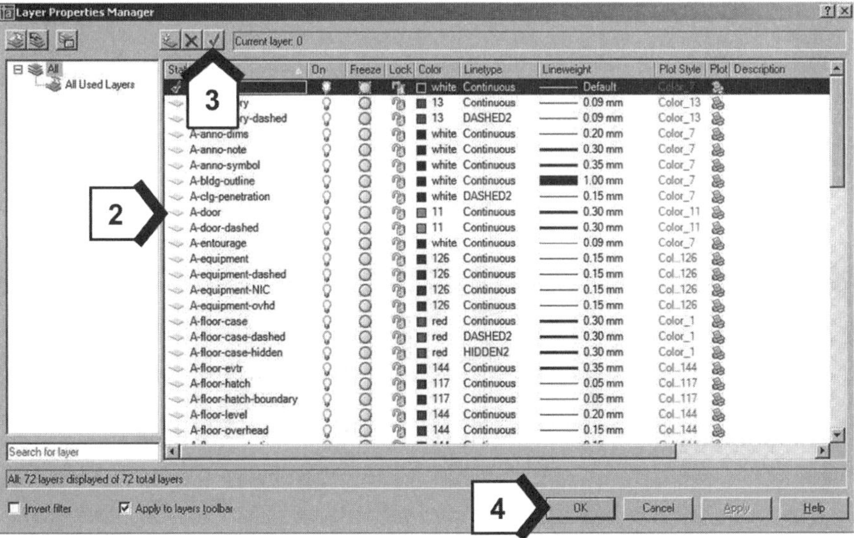

Figure 3.17

1	[Drawing Screen]	Open the Layer Properties Manager.
2	[Layer Properties Manager dialogue box]	Select a layer.
3	[Layer Properties Manager dialogue box]	Left-click on the checkmark. (Note that frozen layers cannot be current).
4	[Layer Properties Manager dialogue box]	Left-click the OK button to exit.

Using the Additional Layer Commands and Tools

The Layer Properties Manager is the primary area where most layer manipulations occur. However, there are a few other locations where you can control layer operations: the Layers toolbar, the Layers II toolbar, the Express Layer commands, and the ET:Layer toolbar; the last two apply to anyone using pre-2007 software. Combined with the Layer Properties Manager, these tools give you access to advanced techniques for when you work with layers during a drawing session.

The Layers Toolbar

The Layers toolbar has a default location just above the drawing area. Its tools include the Layer Properties Manager tool, Layer Drop-down list, Make Object's Layer Current tool, and Layer Previous tool. Figure 3.18 identifies the tools and gives a description of their functions, and Figures 3.19 through 3.21 show how to apply them.

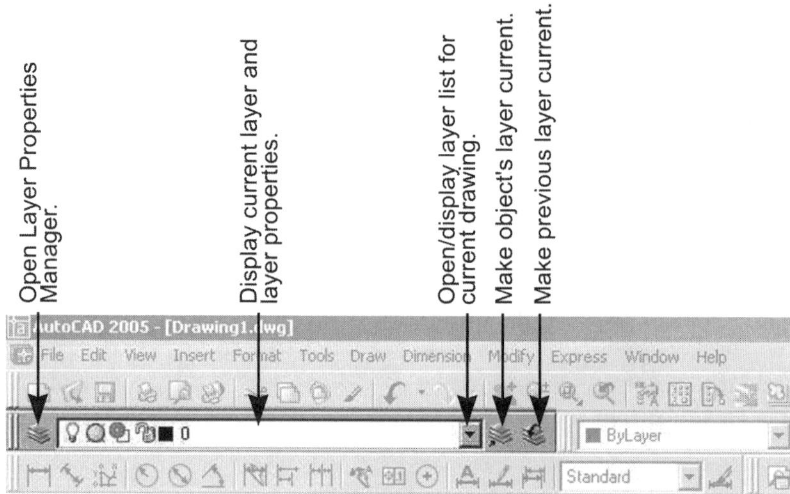

Figure 3.18 The Layers toolbar

Technique to Master **T03.19** Using the Layers Drop-Down List to Make a Layer Current

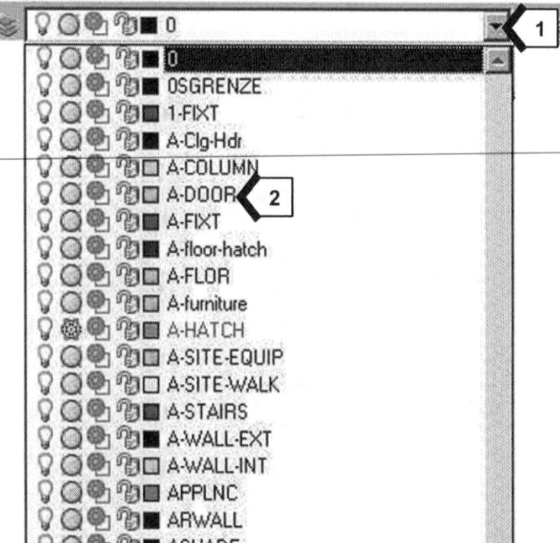

Figure 3.19 The easiest way to change the current layer is to use the Layers toolbar.

1	[Layers toolbar]	Click on the down arrow next to the layer name.
2	[Layers toolbar]	Select the layer you would like to make current.
3	[Properties toolbar]	Remember to leave the color, linetype, lineweight, and plot style setting on ByLayer.
4	[Drawing Screen]	Start drawing. All new geometry is drawn on that layer.

Technique to Master T03.20 Using the Make Object's Layer Current Tool

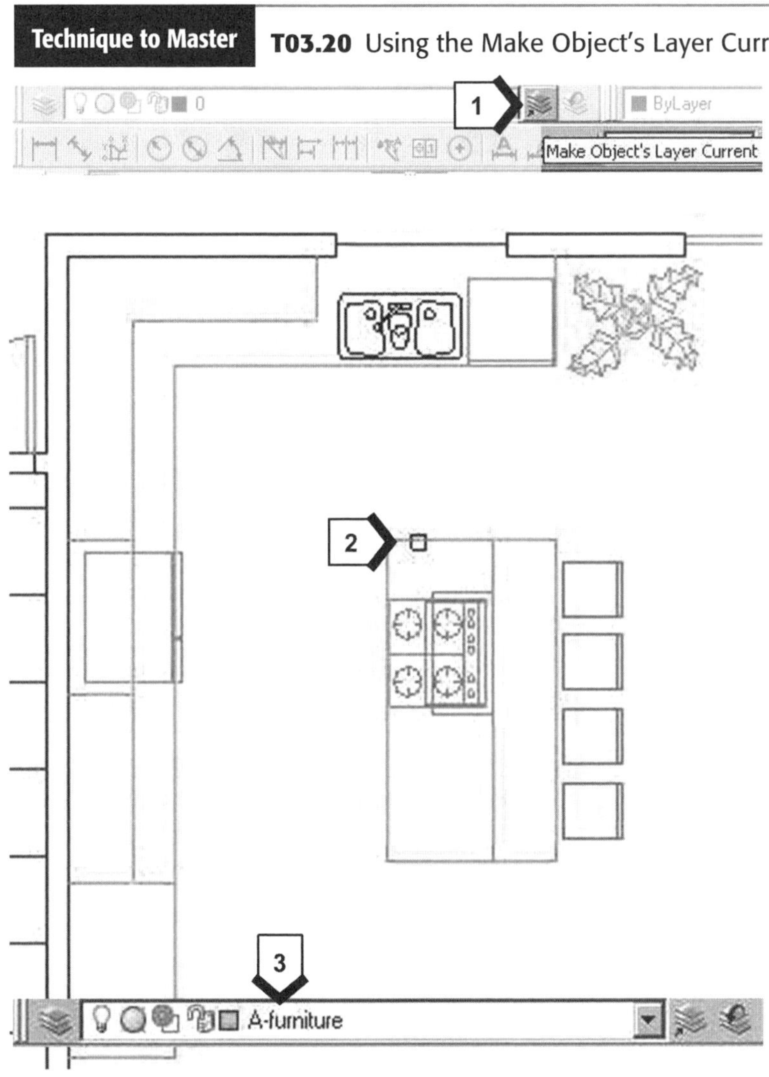

Figure 3.20 This command changes the current layer to match the layer of a selected object.

1	[Layers toolbar]	Left-click the Make Object's Layer Current command.
2	[Drawing Screen]	Left-click on the object.
3	[Layers toolbar]	Current layer changes to match the layer of the object.

Technique to Master T03.21 Using the Layer Previous Tool

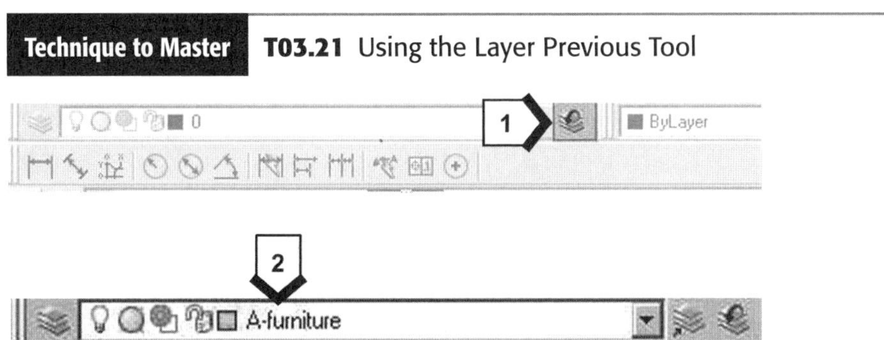

Figure 3.21 This command changes the current layer to the layer that was previously current.

1	[Layers toolbar]	Left-click the Layer Previous command.
2	[Layers toolbar]	Current layer changes to previous layer.

The Express Layer Tools

Express tools are a recently added feature in AutoCAD 2007. The Express Layer tools allow users to employ very specific commands that let them work with layers quickly and efficiently, which cuts down on the number of times users need to access the Layer Properties Manager. The tools include Layer match, Change to current layer, Layer isolate, Layer unisolate, Copy objects to a new layer, Layer walk, Layer freeze, Layer off, Layer lock, and Layer unlock. Figure 3.22 identifies the tools and gives a description of their functions, and Figures 3.23 through 3.27 show how to apply them.

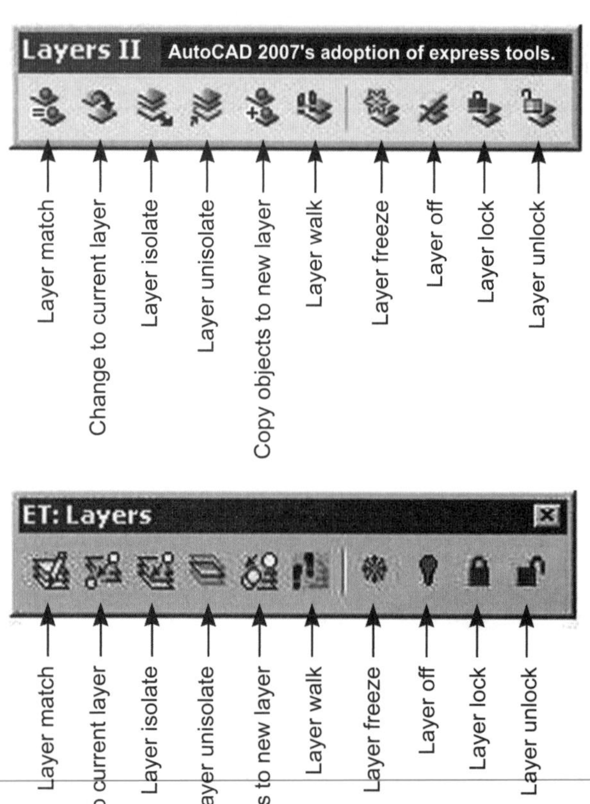

Figure 3.22 The Express Layer toolbar

Technique to Master **T03.23** Using the Layer Match Tool

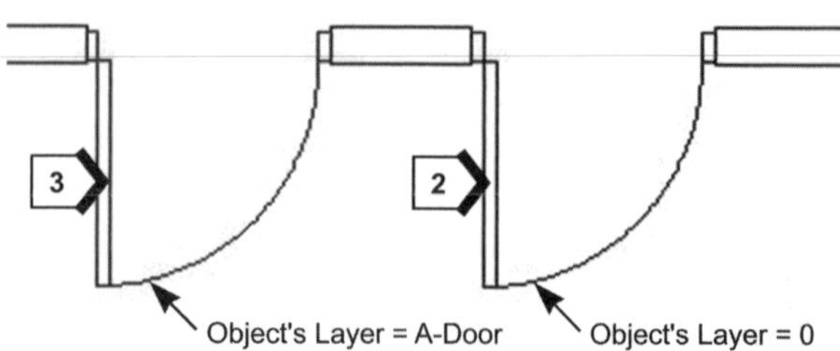

Figure 3.23 The Layer Match tool takes the layer, lineweight, linetype, and other property settings of a selected object and applies them to other objects.

1	[Drawing Screen]	Left-click on the Layer Match tool.
2	[Drawing Screen]	Left-click on the object(s) that you want to change.
3	[Drawing Screen]	Left-click on the object whose properties other objects should match.

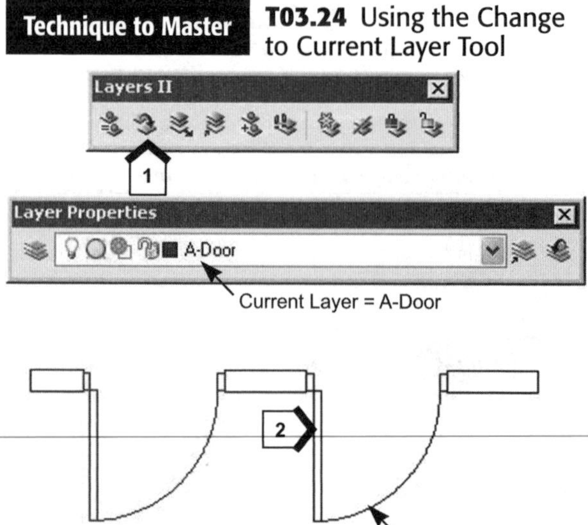

Figure 3.24 This command works the same as the Make Object's Layer Current tool (T03.20).

Technique to Master **T03.25** Using the Layer Isolate Tool

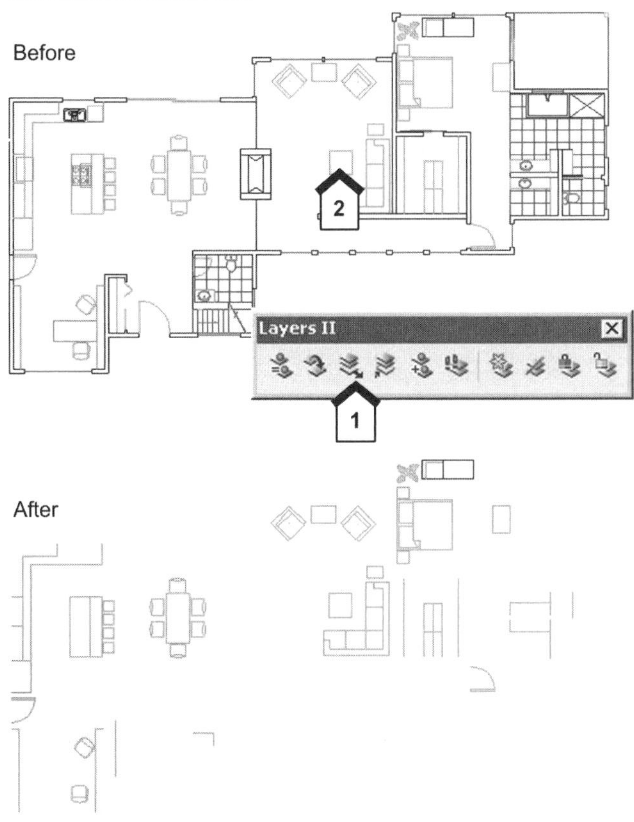

Figure 3.25 The Layer Isolate tool turns off all layers except for the layer of the object selected.

1	[Drawing Screen]	Left-click on the Layer isolate tool.
2	[Drawing Screen]	Left-click on an object whose layer you want to isolate.

Technique to Master **T03.26** Using the Layer Freeze, Layer Lock, Layer Unlock Tools

Figure 3.26 These tools freeze, lock, and/or unlock the layer of the selected object.

1	[Drawing Screen]	Left-click on the appropriate tool.
2	[Drawing Screen]	Left-click to select an object.

Technique to Master **T03.27** Using the Copy Objects to New Layer Tool

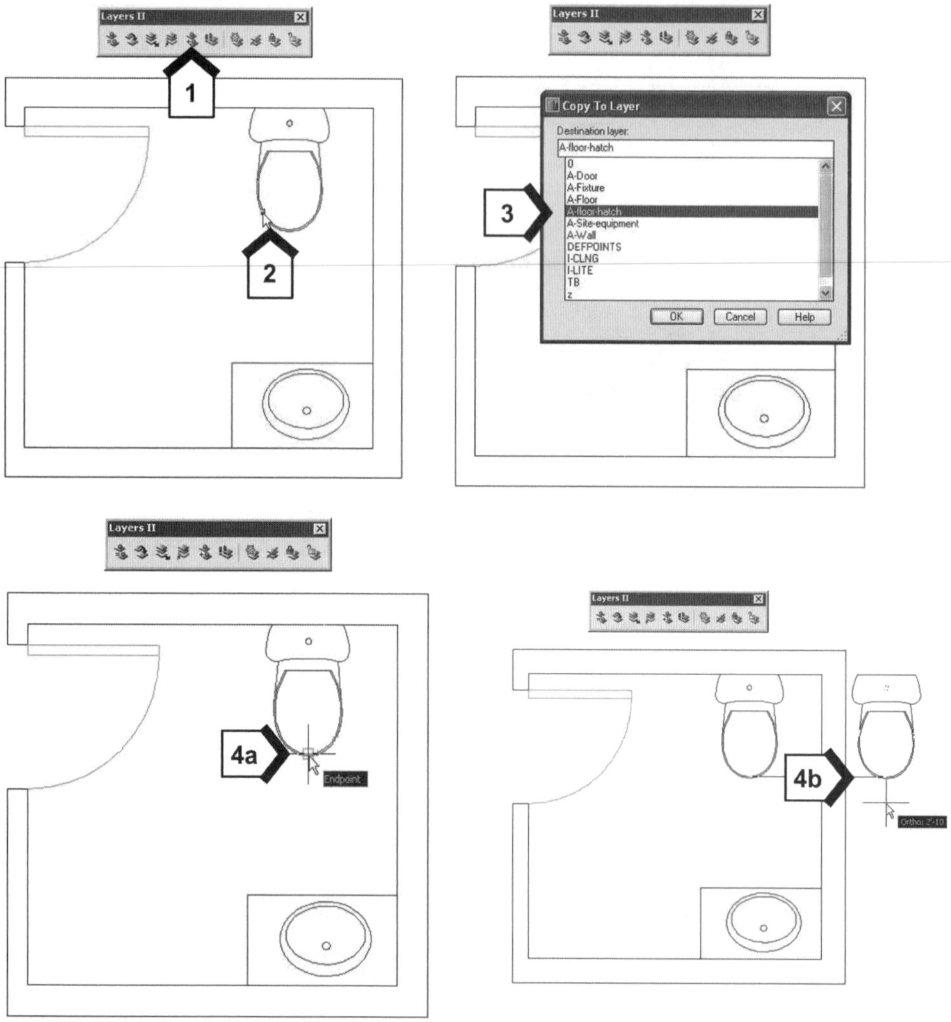

Figure 3.27 This tool duplicates the selected object and simultaneously changes the layer of the duplicated object. The example copies the toilet object so that it can be used as a boundary that floor patterns will avoid.

1	[Drawing Screen]	Left-click on the Copy Objects to New Layer tool.
2	[Drawing Screen]	Select an object.
3	[Copy to Layer Dialogue Box]	Select the layer for the duplicate object. Left-click the OK button.
4a, 4b	Notice that the duplicate object is directly on top of the original.	

Assigning Properties

The two most predominant methods of changing an object's color, lineweight, and linetype are by using the Properties palette and by using the Object Properties toolbar.

The Properties Palette

The Properties palette (Figure 3.28) is based on the original Properties dialogue box. The palette is set up as a visually organized list of properties belonging to selected geometry. The palette is toggled on and off using the keyboard shortcut Ctrl+5. When you select geometry, the Properties palette displays the name of the AutoCAD shape in the list box at the top of the dialogue, as well its current property settings. Notice that when you select more than one object, the Properties palette displays only properties that are common to the selected objects.

Most property changes, when using the Properties palette, tend to be layer and color assignments; however, dimensional property changes may also occur.

> **Box 3.5**
> Sometimes properties are grayed out, which means you have no ability to change these properties.

The Object Properties Toolbar

The Object Properties toolbar has existed within AutoCAD since toolbars were incorporated into the software. This toolbar gives you immediate access to the layer, color, linetype, and lineweight properties (Figure 3.29).

Properties and Being Current

When you draw in AutoCAD, you are always using active property assignments for layer, lineweight, linetype, color, and plot style. The active or current properties always appear in the Layers and Properties toolbars. When you change the current layer, all new objects and shapes are drawn on this layer.

Drawing Organization Standards

Standards are guidelines that give consistency to repetitively used objects in CAD. Standards also help users name and format rules for text and dimensions.

Technique to Master **T03.28** Identifying/Changing Object Properties Through the Properties Palette

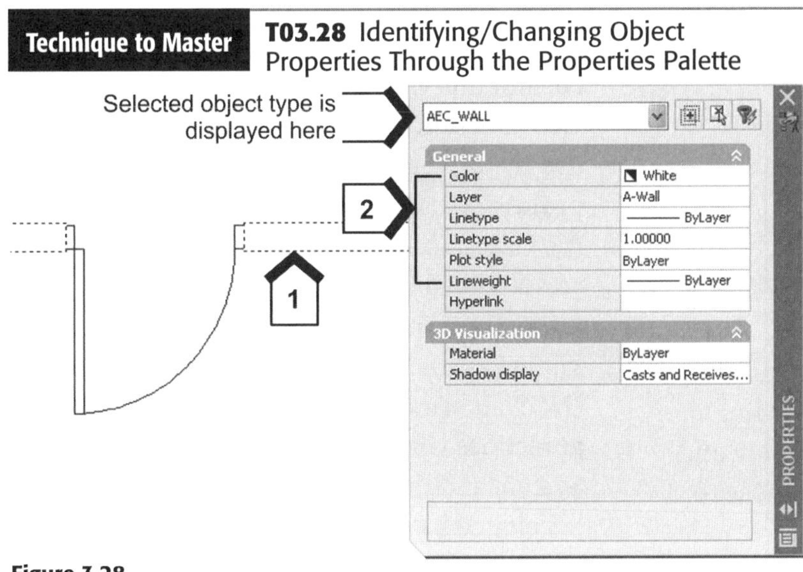

Figure 3.28

1	[Drawing Screen]	Select an object.
2	[Properties palette]	Review/change color, layer, lineweight, linetype, and/or plot style properties for the selected object.

Technique to Master **T03.29** Identifying/Changing Object Properties Through the Properties Toolbar

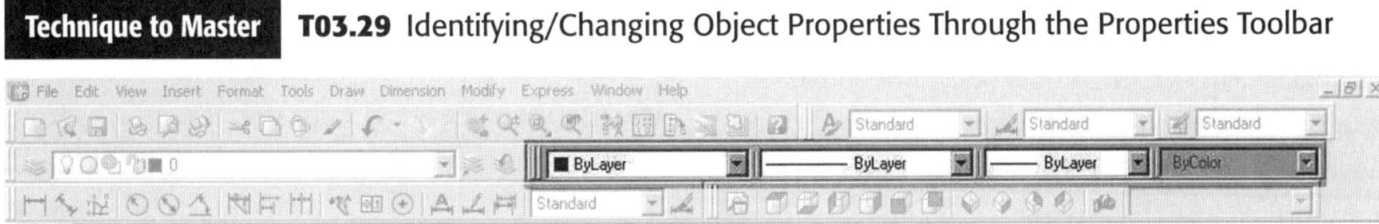

Figure 3.29

1	[Drawing Screen]	Select object.
2	[Properties toolbar]	Review/change color, layer, lineweight, and/or linetype properties for selected object.

CAD standards often refer to any naming or formatting convention or procedure that is related to a project's information. Typical standards include the following:

- Project folder and subfolder naming
- Project setup
- Individual drawing setup
- Drawing file naming
- Project plot sheet setup
- Text and dimension formatting
- Layer naming
- Lineweight and linetype conventions
- Page setups

The Importance of Professional Standards

Standards are beneficial because they allow users to accomplish the following:

- Consistency when they work on design teams
- Increased productivity since they can reuse prototypes multiple times
- Efficiency because of reduced project setup time

Every new project includes drawings that utilize similar layers to organize building elements, text and dimensioning styles, and project borders. Why would you choose to recreate this work for each project each and every time? The efficiency of using standards is beneficial not only in design offices but also in an educational setting.

Design offices benefit from using standards because consistency is maintained regardless of the number of designers working on a project; standards also keep things consistent from project to project. Employers don't need to worry about teaching the office's standard—new employees can easily read the CAD standards manual to learn how plans are executed within the particular office. Without these standards, design offices would spend valuable time and money training new employees on their methods of operation.

Students also benefit from using standards because many standards include predefined setups that they can use to create new drawings. Students don't have to waste precious time performing the repetitive setup and completion tasks required for every project. Moreover, once they are familiar with the standards manual, students can save time during the development of their projects by not having to do everything from scratch each time.

The American Institute of Architects (AIA) layer guidelines are standards that define how a layer is named as well as its color, lineweight, and linetype property assignments. These layer guidelines have been adopted and promoted by the AIA to help architects and their consultants with drawing collaborations. The Construction Specifications Institute (CSI) has also developed standards for its associated professionals. To further collaboration among the various building industries, the CSI, AIA, and National Institute of Building Sciences (NIBS) currently publish a standards book known as the *U.S. National CAD Standard (NCS)*. It brings together the AIA's layering guidelines with CSI's Uniform Drawing System and the Tri-Service plotting guidelines developed by the U.S. Department of Defense.

Chapter Exercises

Open the Chapter 03 Exercise Text.doc located on the supplementary CD-ROM to access the chapter exercises. By completing these exercises, you can practice how to use layers, lineweights, and linetypes in the floor plan, section, and elevation views. You also learn how to develop your own standards for your projects.

Blocks and Block Libraries

4

Objectives

This chapter describes block tools and the techniques associated with them within AutoCAD. It emphasizes block creation, placement, and editing techniques and also touches on additional specialty block commands. The end-of-chapter exercises focus on creating and editing blocks that are used to create many common building elements.

An Introduction to Blocks

Blocks let you join AutoCAD shapes together so you can manipulate them as one object. You can assign a descriptive name to each block you create. The block is then stored in the drawing's database under its name so that you may retrieve it later.

There are many benefits to using blocks. First, you create blocks that you intend on using repeatedly. Since many elements of floor plans and elevations tend to be reused, blocks help make the drafting process more efficient. Second, creating block libraries helps cut the time it takes to draft a project. You can easily collect and organize reusable parts of drawings from a project for future use. Third, blocks keep drawing files small. Because block definitions are counted only once in the database, they significantly reduce the amount of memory and hard disk space a drawing file uses. Finally, blocks make global design changes effortless. If you edit a block, then all instances of the block are automatically updated. You place blocks by using the Insert command. If you want to store a block outside of a current drawing's database, then you need to export the block using the Wblock command.

Block Creation and Placement

You can use all existing AutoCAD geometry to create a block. You group together the geometry by using the Block dialogue box. The created block is then stored behind-the-scenes in the current drawing file's database as block definitions. Blocks do not have to actually be placed on the drawing screen to be saved in the drawing.

Grouping Geometry into Blocks

To create a block, you first need to draw shapes and objects. Figure 4.1 demonstrates the block creation process. Table 4.1 offers some file naming guidelines for blocks.

Doors make excellent blocks, both in plan and elevation, because the graphic symbol for the various door styles looks the same—only the size of the symbol changes. Since blocks can be scaled quickly, the same symbol applies to all door widths (Figure 4.2).

Technique to Master **T04.01** The Block Creation Process

Figure 4.1 The Block command opens a dialogue box. Remember that you can complete dialogue boxes in any order.

1	[Command Line]	Type the Block command.
2	[Block Definition dialogue box]	Name the block. The name should be unique and can be up to 255 characters but cannot contain symbols.
3	[Block Definition dialogue box]	Select the geometry you want to be a part of the block.
4	[Block Definition dialogue box]	Select the base point for the block.
5	[Block Definition dialogue box]	Select how you want to treat the existing objects.
6	[Block Definition dialogue box]	Click OK to make the block.

Blocks and Block Organization

In Chapter 3, you learned about objects and their layer, color, lineweight, and linetype properties. Property types such as layers and lineweights have special conditions when they are assigned to a block's geometry. You should pay special attention to how you assign these properties to the geometry you will be using for a block. For the most part, blocks display the geometry's properties regardless of the layer on which the block is inserted. However, there are some exceptions, and they are illustrated in Table 4.2.

The Block's Base Point

The block's base point is the location that becomes its datum point (also called insertion point) during placement. You should always keep in mind this relationship when you are determining the base point location. You should always use object snaps to locate base points precisely. For example, when you place a door within a wall, the inside of the door's frame (hinge side) is usually located 4" to 6"

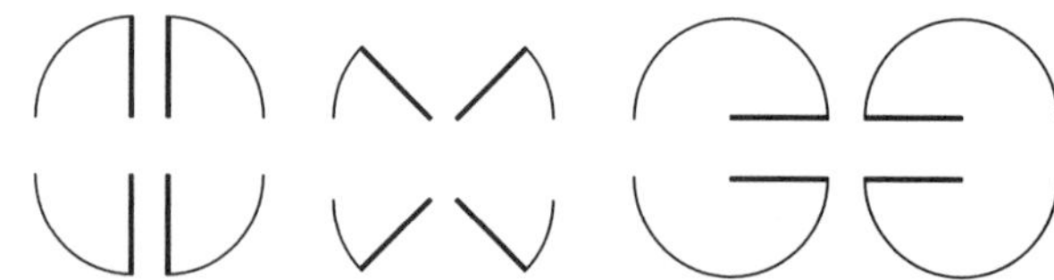

Figure 4.2 Door symbols with 90 degree, 45 degree, and 180 degree swings. The conventional symbols for doors in plan view. The arc shows the door's angle of swing.

Table 4.1 File Naming Conventions

Symbol Type	Plan View	Front View	Side View	Section View
Non-scalable door	Door_3ft_plan	Door_7ft_elev	———	———
Scalable door	DoorScalable_1unit_plan	DoorScalable_1unit_elev	———	———
Stove	Stove_30x38_plan	Stove_30x38_elev	Stove_30x38_side	———
Room name symbol-scalable	RoomName_scalable	———	———	———
Lower cabinets	———	CabinetsLower_elev	CabinetsLower_side	CabinetsLower_section

Table 4.2 Blocks and Properties

Rule	The Assigned Properties of the Geometry Before Block Is Made	Visual Example of Assigned Properties Before Block Is Made	How the Block Looks After Insertion on Layer Furniture
Any geometry drawn on a layer other than layer zero (0) with properties set to Bylayer will inherit the properties of the layer on which the geometry is drawn.	Geometry shown is on layer equipment with the following assigned properties: Color = Bylayer Lineweight = Bylayer Linetype = Bylayer		
Any geometry drawn on layer zero (0) with properties set to Bylayer will inherit the properties of the block's layer.	Geometry shown is on layer 0 with the following assigned properties: Color = Bylayer Lineweight = Bylayer Linetype = Bylayer	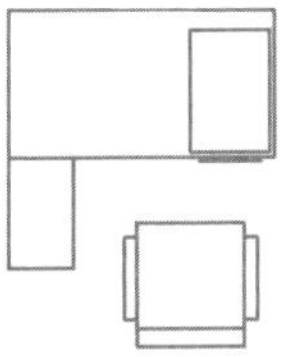	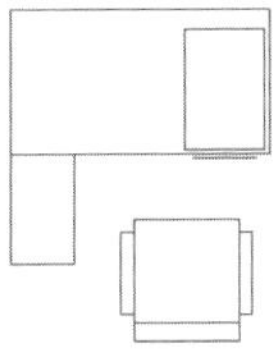
Any geometry with properties set to Byblock will inherit the properties of the block.	Geometry shown is on layer 0 with the following assigned properties: Color = Byblock Lineweight = Byblock Linetype = Byblock	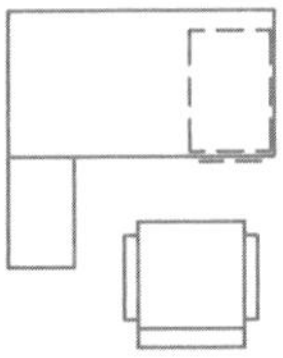	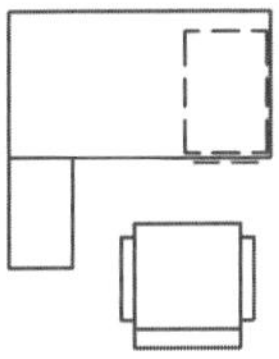
Any geometry drawn on layer zero (0) with properties individually set will display the properties of the individual objects.	Geometry shown is on layer 0 with the following assigned properties: Color = red Lineweight = .35mm Linetype = continuous	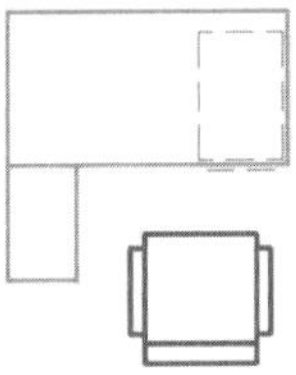	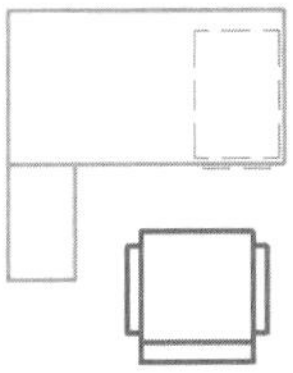

away from the wall corner. Although centering doors within rooms is also standard practice, it is best to locate the door's base point at the door hinge (Figure 4.3).

Blocks are also useful when you need to draw representations of kitchen appliances and bathroom fixtures. It is best to position the base points at the backs of the appliances or fixtures because appliances and fixtures are usually dimensioned at midpoints in construction drawings (Figure 4.4). Figure 4.5 illustrates some additional common plan symbols with their respective base points.

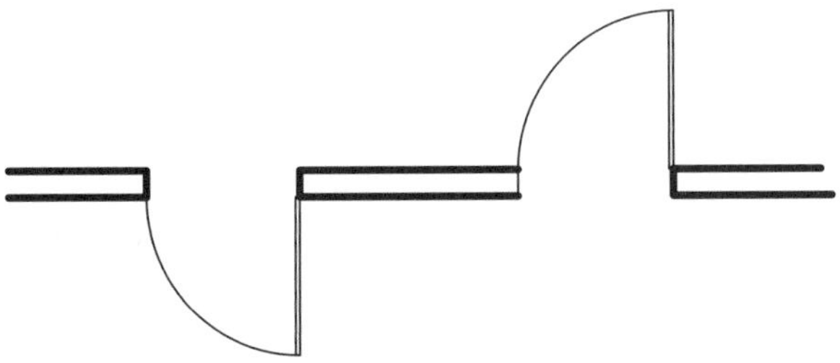

Figure 4.3 Door swing suggested base points are based on the door being inserted at the hinge point.

> **Box 4.1**
> Tip: When properly placed, base points speed up the drafting process because they represent how the block will be inserted in the drawing. If the insertion point of a door is at its door hinge, then inserting the door at wall jambs becomes very efficient.

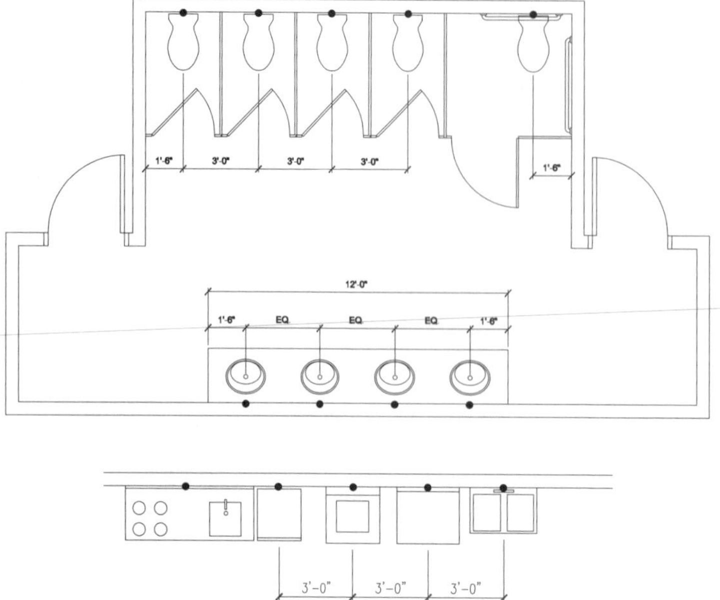

Figure 4.4 Appliances and fixtures are typically dimensioned from center to center. Suggested base points are therefore at the midpoint at the back of the equipment. (Base points shown as large dots.)

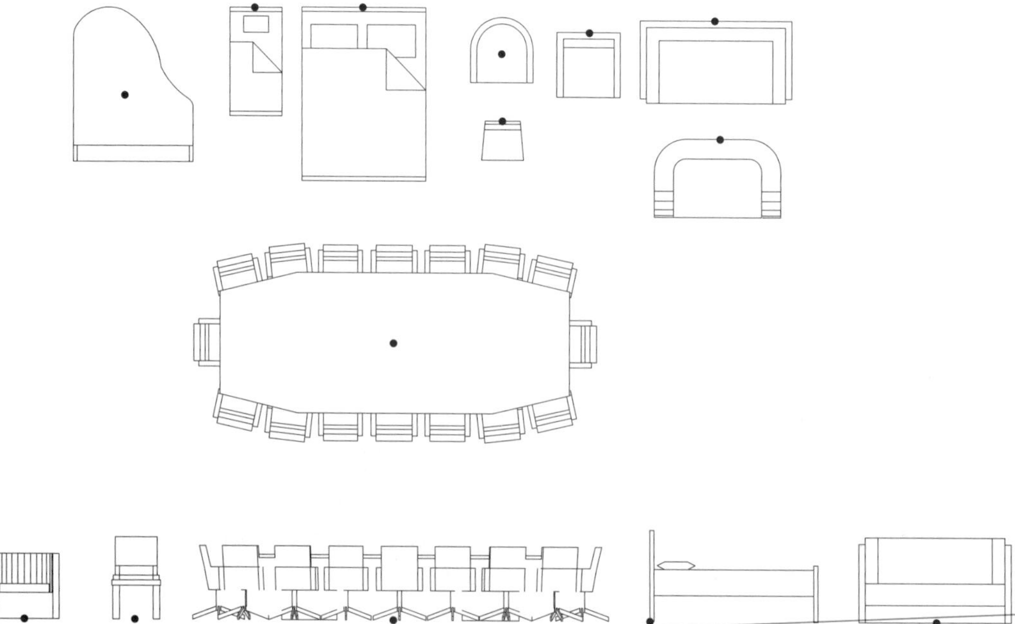

Figure 4.5 Common plan and elevation symbols with suggested base points (shown as large dots).

Block Changes in AutoCAD 2006

The process of using blocks in AutoCAD 2006 became more flexible and intelligent. Being able to use dynamic blocks lets you use automatic scaling and block variations within one block definition. Automatic scaling allows you to insert scale-dependent symbols without having to make any calculations. Block variations allow you to build dimensional and design variations directly into the same block definition. Figures 4.6 through 4.8 demonstrate a few common uses of dynamic blocks.

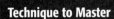

Technique to Master T04.06 Creating Adjustable Size Dynamic Blocks

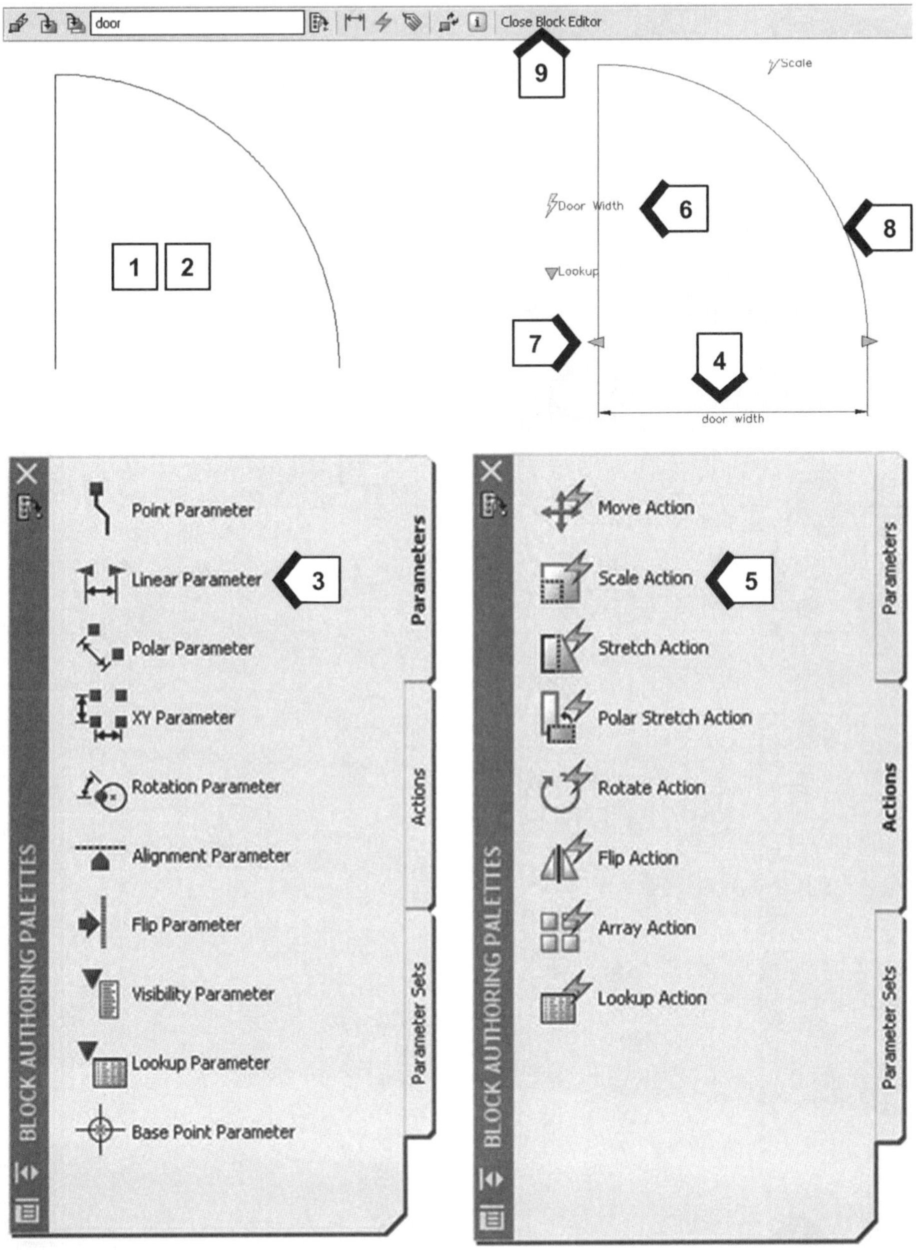

Figure 4.6

1	[Drawing Screen]	Draw a representation of a symbol.
2	[Block dialogue box]	Create block. See Technique T04.01 to review identification of options. Before completing the block creation process, click Open in Block Editor.
3	[Block Editor Mode>Block Authoring palette>Parameters]	Select Linear Parameter.
4	[Drawing Screen]	Specify start and endpoint of linear parameter type on block.
5	[Block Editor Mode>Block Authoring palette>Actions]	Select Scale Action.
6	[Drawing Screen]	Select parameter to set up relationship.
7	[Drawing Screen]	Set reference point for action.
8	[Drawing Screen]	Select objects that will be affected by scale.
9	Close Block Editor to save changes.	

Technique to Master **T04.07** Creating a Dynamic Block with Multiple Insertion Points

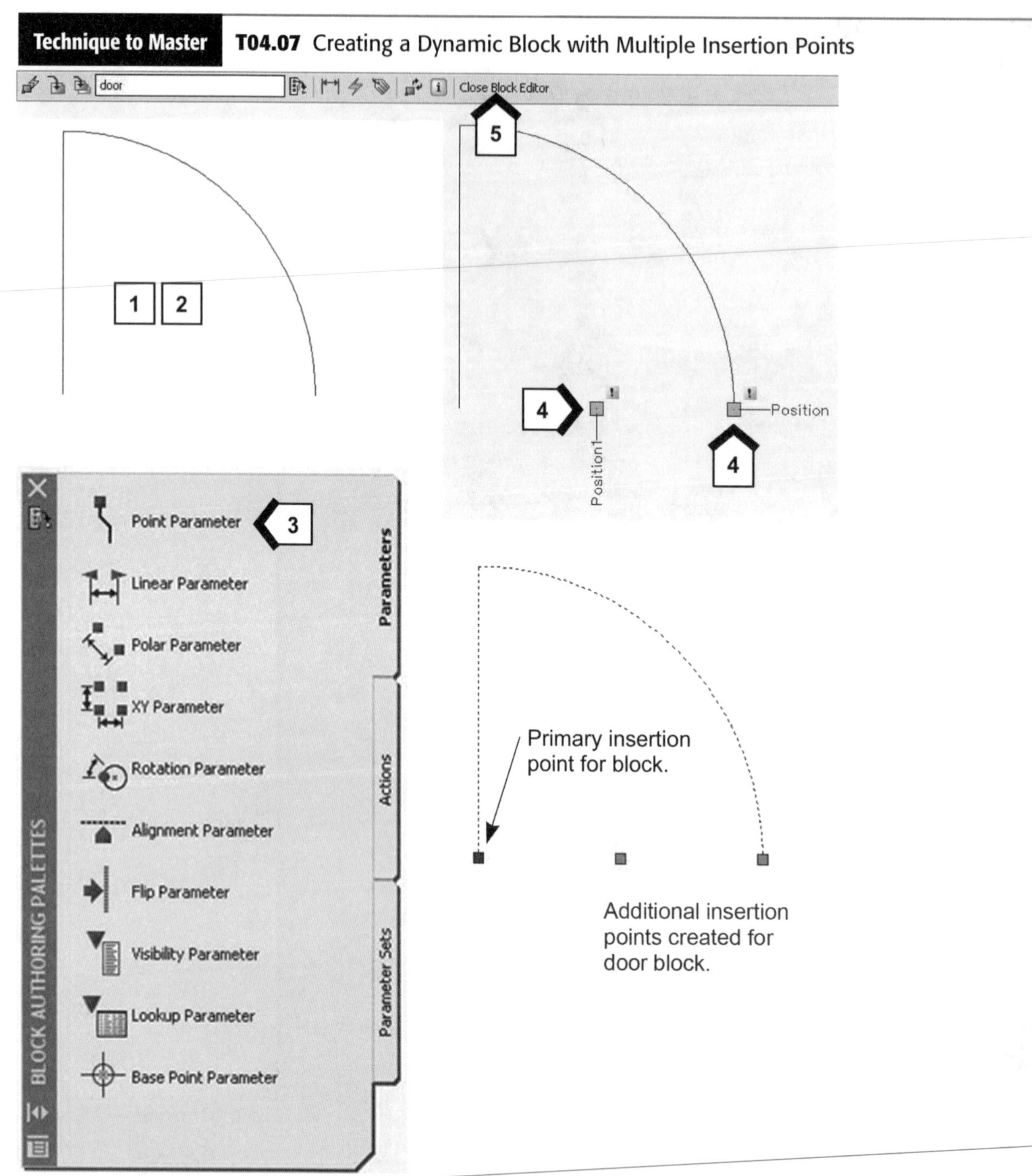

Figure 4.7

1	[Drawing Screen]	Draw a representation of a symbol.
2	[Block dialogue box]	Create block. See Technique T04.01 to review identification of options. Before completing the block creation process, click Open in Block Editor.
3	[Block Editor Mode>Block Authoring palette>Parameters]	Select Point Parameter.
4	[Drawing Screen]	Locate a point parameter wherever you want additional insertion points.
5	Close Block Editor to save changes.	

Technique to Master **T04.08** Adding Visibility States to Different Parts of a Dynamic Block

Figure 4.8

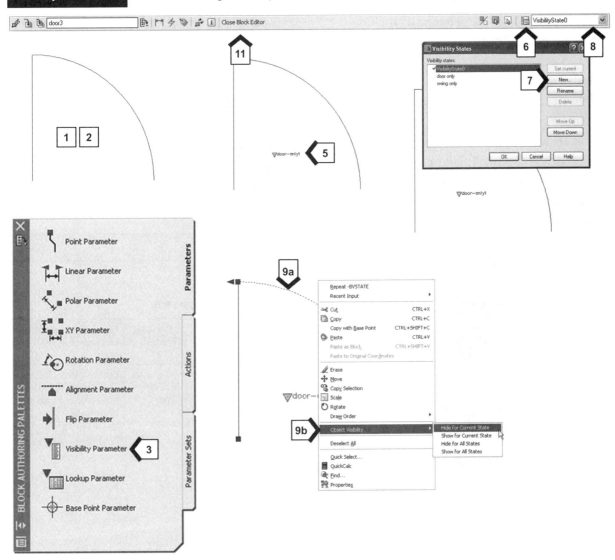

1	[Drawing Screen]	Draw a representation of a symbol.
2	[Block dialogue box]	Create block. See Technique T04.01 to review identification of options. Before completing the block creation process, click Open in Block Editor.
3	[Block Editor Mode>Block Authoring palette> Parameters]	Select Visibility Parameter.
4	[Command Line]	Type N, and press Enter to name the visibility parameter.
5	[Drawing Screen]	Specify the location for the visibility parameter.
6	[Block Editor Mode>Tool palette]	Select Manage Visibility States tool.
7	[Block Editor Mode>Visibility States dialogue box]	Select New button to create visibility states. Do not worry about hiding objects yet.
8	[Block Editor Mode>Tool palette]	Set one of the newly created visibility states to current.
9a, 9b	[Drawing Screen]	Select objects to hide for current visibility state, right-click, and choose Object Visibility>Hide for Current State.
10	Repeat until all visibility states are correct.	
11	Close Block Editor to save changes.	

Scalable Versus Non-Scalable Blocks

Scalable blocks refer to blocks that can have several size variations and typically include doors and windows in the plan and elevation views. Blocks that are not typically scaled include kitchen appliances and bath fixtures, accessories, and equipment. You should always use a generic unit when creating scalable blocks so you are able to use the same block for all the size variations. Figure 4.9 demonstrates how to create a door block that is scalable. Use the dimensional specifications for the object to create non-scalable blocks (Figure 4.10).

Wblocks and Block Organization

The Wblock command lets you save selected objects, block definitions, or both into their own individual drawing files. It is one of the methods used to export existing blocks for block libraries. The Wblock command uses a dialogue box format (Figure 4.11).

> **Box 4.2**
> Tip: Use the Wblock command to export all symbols that you might need to reuse in future projects.

Technique to Master **T04.09** Creating Scalable Blocks

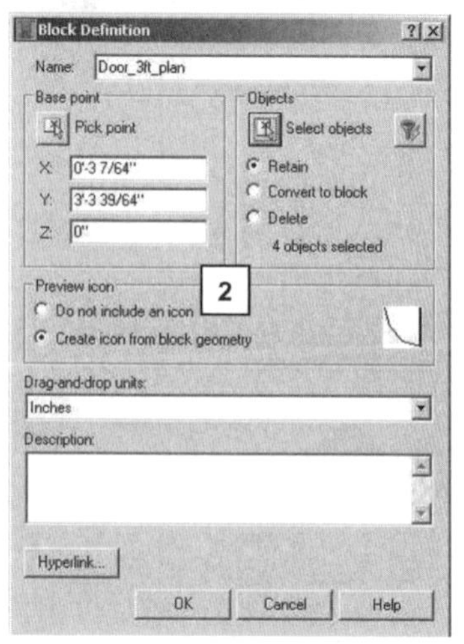

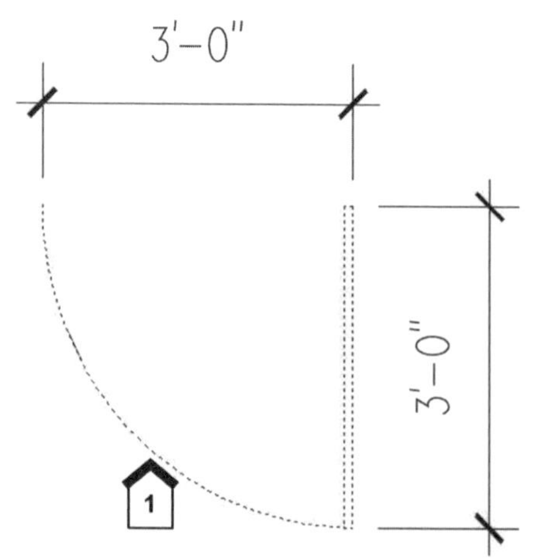

Figure 4.9

1	[Drawing Screen]	Draw representation of symbol at real scale (1:1).
2	[Block dialogue box]	Create block. Refer to Technique T04.01 to review identification of options.

Technique to Master **T04.10** Creating Non-Scalable Blocks

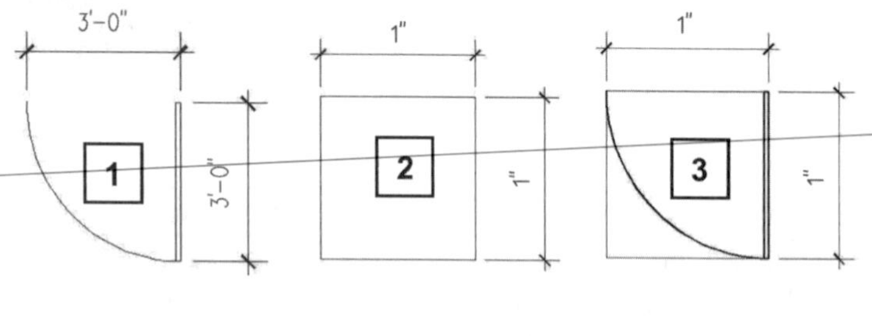

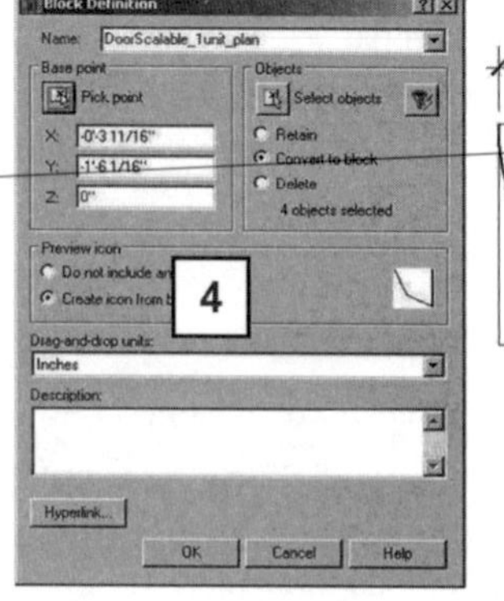

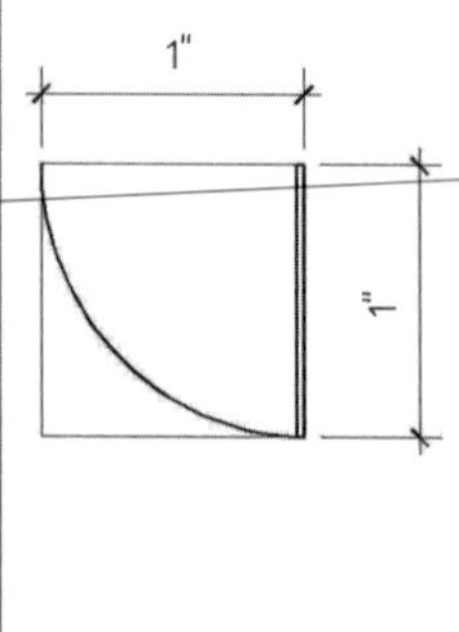

Figure 4.10

1	[Drawing Screen]	Draw representation of symbol at real scale 1:1.
2	[Drawing Screen]	Draw a 1" × 1" rectangle.
3	[Drawing Screen]	Scale door to fit within 1" × 1" rectangle.
4	[Block dialogue box]	Create block. See Technique T04.01 to review identification of options.

Technique to Master **T04.11** Using the Wblock Command

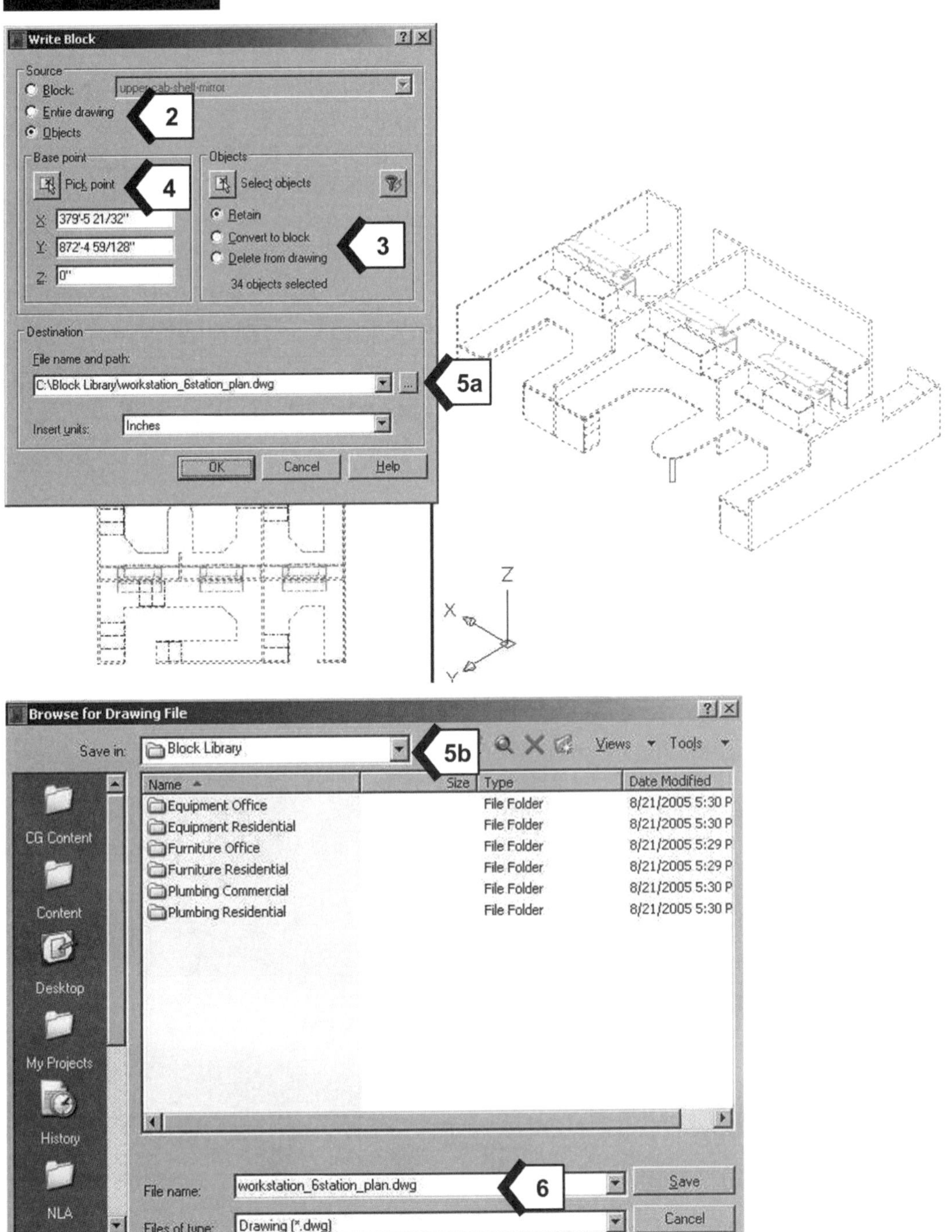

Figure 4.11 The command Wblock opens a dialogue box. Remember that you can complete dialogue box commands in any order.

1	[Command Line]	Type the Wblock command.
2	[Write Block dialogue box>Source option]	Choose the objects to export—refer to Technique T04.12 for selection options.
3	[Write Block dialogue box>Objects option]	Select what you want to do with your selection after the block is made.
4	[Write Block dialogue box>Base point option]	Select the base point of the block.
5a, 5b	[Write Block dialogue box]	Choose the location for the exported objects.
6	[Write Block dialogue box]	Type a distinctive name for the block.

There are three different source options you can use to create or export a block: exporting a block within the current drawing's database, exporting the entire drawing, or exporting selected geometry from the drawing. If you need to export a block that already exists in the current drawing's database, choose Block as the source option. If you would like to export all objects that are visible on the drawing screen, choose Entire drawing as the source option. If you need to export selected geometry, choose the Object source button and then use the Select Objects button to complete the selection. Figure 4.12 shows examples of all three source options.

Setting Up Your Own Block Library

The best reason to set up block libraries is so that you can save symbols while working on a project for future use. There are two methods for setting up block libraries, the easiest of which is to set up a traditional folder structure on your hard drive or flash drive. (The flash drive allows you to access your blocks from multiple locations where AutoCAD is loaded.) Each folder categorizes the symbol type. Each drawing file within a folder represents a block. The second method is to create a Tool palette block library where each tab categorizes the symbol type (Figure 4.13). The one thing to keep in mind is that it is difficult to transport Tool palettes; therefore, it will be problematic to access your Tool palettes from more than one computer. It is best to choose the method that fits your personal approach and use it consistently.

Technique to Master **T04.12** Using the Block Exporting Options

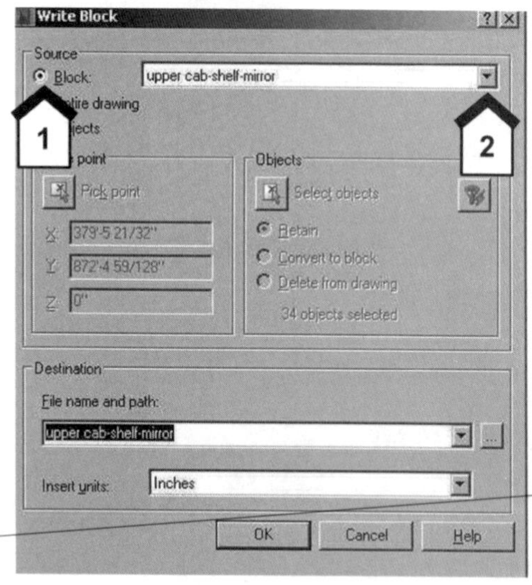

Figure 4.12

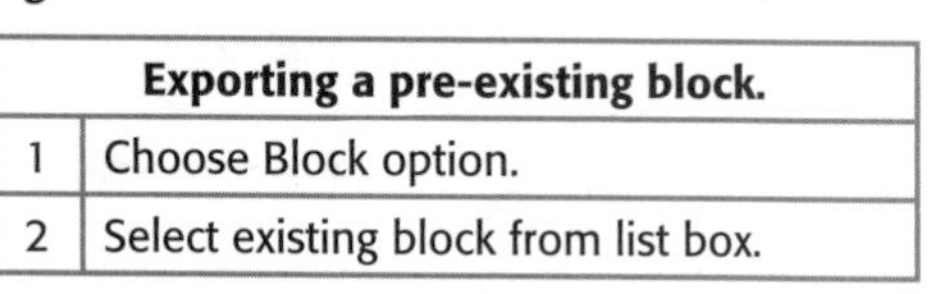

Exporting a pre-existing block.	
1	Choose Block option.
2	Select existing block from list box.

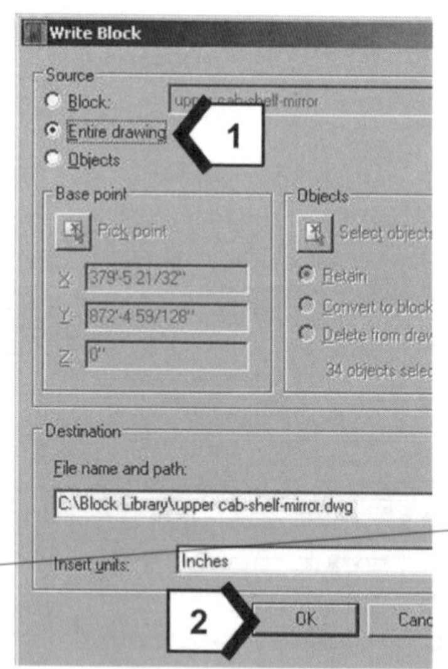

Exporting an entire drawing.	
1	Choose the Entire drawing option.
2	Click OK to export entire drawing.

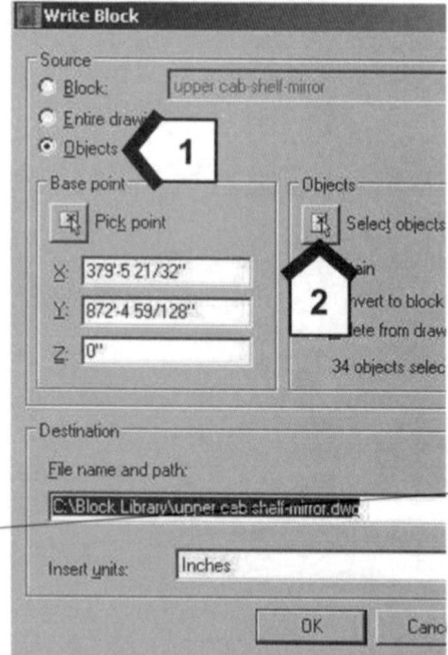

Exporting an object selection set.	
1	Choose Objects option.
2	Left-click Select Objects button.
3	Select objects to export and press Enter.

Technique to Master **T04.13** Setting up Tool Palette Block Libraries

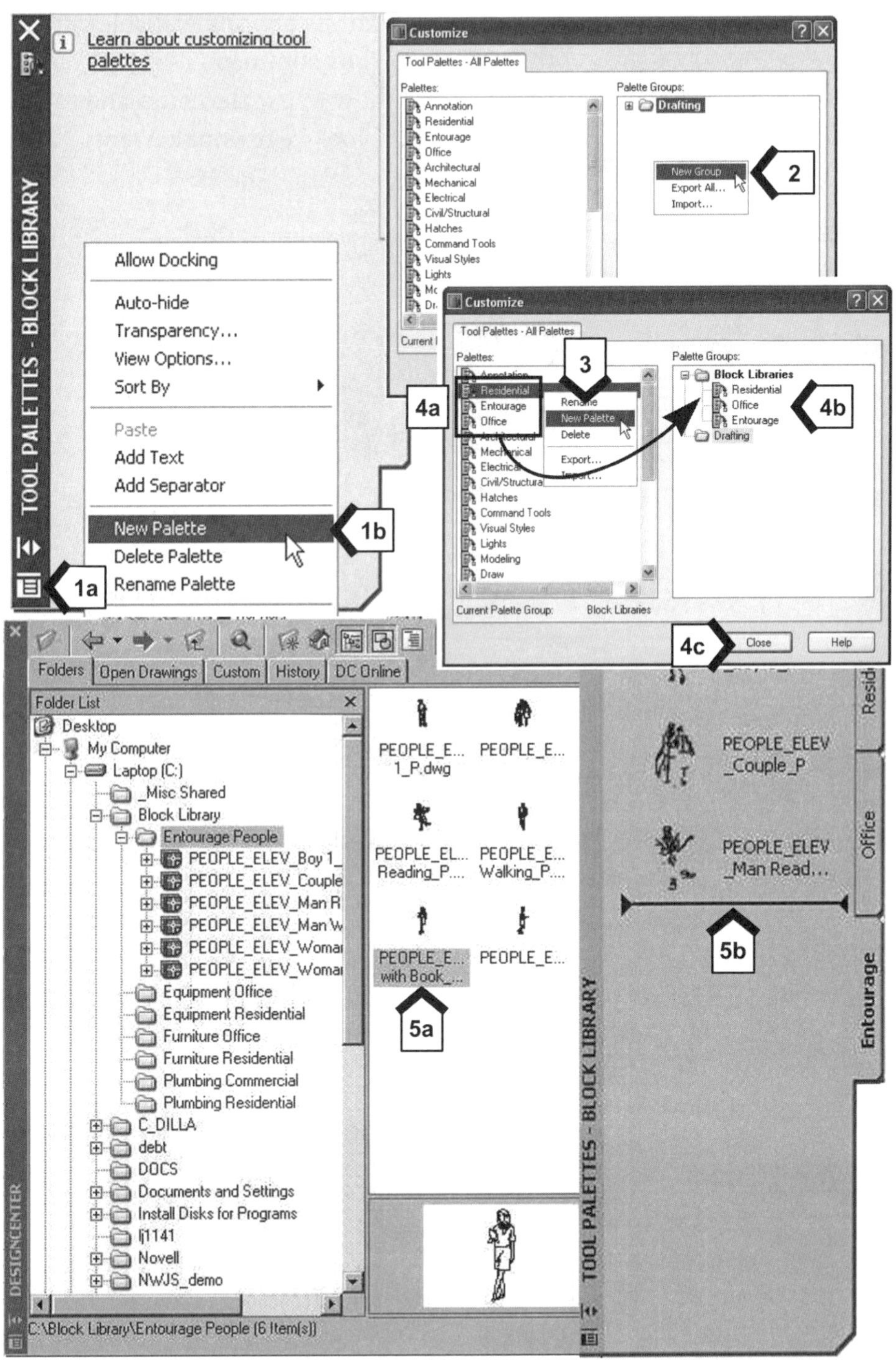

Figure 4.13

1a, 1b	[Tool palette]	Create a new palette group by left-clicking on the properties button and choosing the New Palette command.
2	[Customize dialogue box]	Create new palette group by right-clicking in the blank area under Palette Groups and choosing New Group. Name the palette group.
3	[Customize dialogue box]	Create palette categories for each symbol type by right-clicking in the blank area under Palettes and choosing New Palette. Name the palette.
4a, 4b, 4c	[Customize dialogue box]	Drag newly created palettes to the palette group. Left-click on the Close button.
5a, 5b	Drag existing blocks to appropriate tabbed areas.	

Block Insertion

When you place blocks into a drawing, you use a range of methods that depend on how you stored the block. If you stored the block in the current drawing, then you can use the Insert dialogue box command to place the block. You can also use this command if you stored the block in a folder library. Figure 4.14 identifies the various options available in the Insert dialogue box command. Figure 4.15 demonstrates how to use the command to insert existing blocks into your current

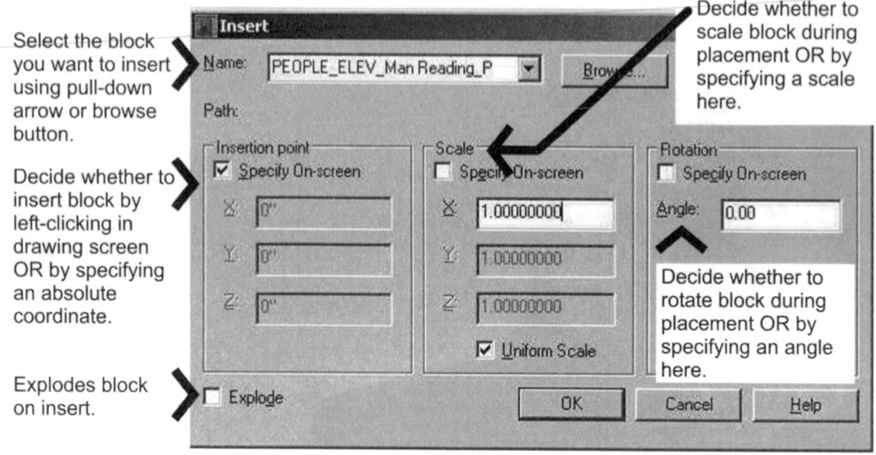

Select the block you want to insert using pull-down arrow or browse button.
Decide whether to insert block by left-clicking in drawing screen OR by specifying an absolute coordinate.
Explodes block on insert.
Decide whether to scale block during placement OR by specifying a scale here.
Decide whether to rotate block during placement OR by specifying an angle here.

Figure 4.14 The Insert dialogue box command

Technique to Master **T04.15** Using the Insert Command

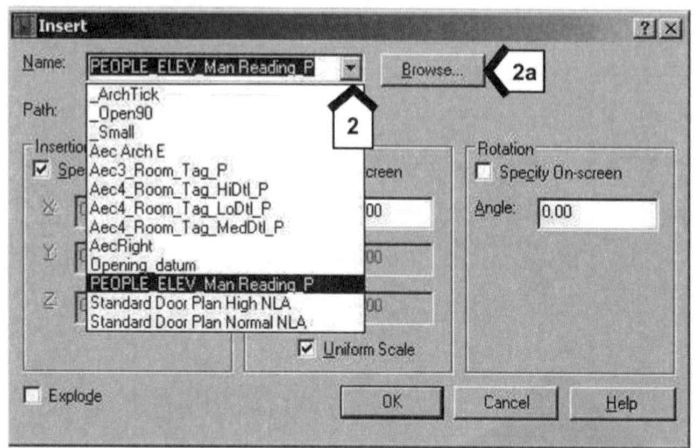

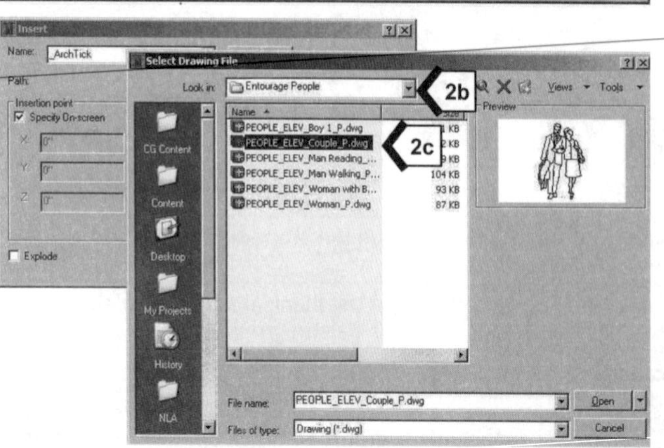

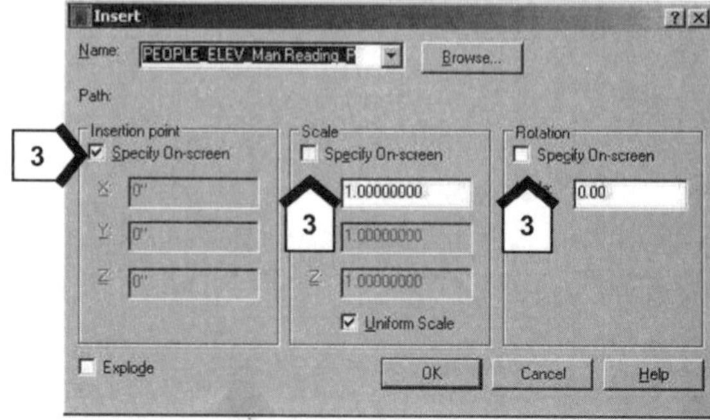

Figure 4.15

1	[Command Line]	~~Type the Insert command.~~
2a 2b 2c	[Insert dialogue box>Name option]	Choose the block you need to insert. You can select blocks from the current drawing's database from the internal list box. You can access blocks located outside of the drawing database by using the Browse button.
3	The options at the bottom of the dialogue box let you either type in a value in the box or specify the value during the placement process. Decide which of the insertion, scale, and rotation options you will specify on-screen by checking them off.	
4	Click OK, and insert the block in the desired location on-screen.	

drawing session. You need to follow a different technique, which is shown in Figure 4.16, to insert a Tool palette block. Figures 4.17 and 4.18 show how you can insert blocks from the DC Online and Design Center libraries.

Technique to Master **T04.16** Inserting a Tool Palette Block

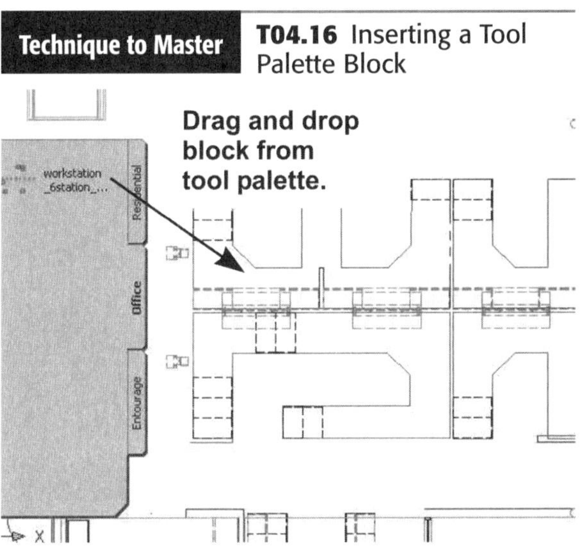

Figure 4.16

1	[Tool Palette]	Left-click on the Block icon and drag it to the drawing screen.
2	[Drawing Screen]	Specify the location for the block within the drawing.

Technique to Master **T04.18** Inserting a Design Center Block

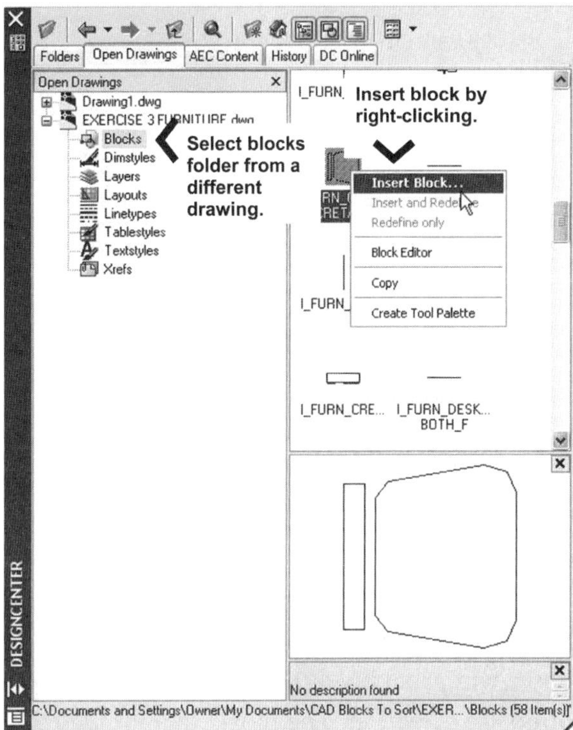

Figure 4.18

1	Open the Design Center.	
2	Locate the desired block.	
3	Right-click on the block and choose the Insert command.	
4	[Drawing Screen]	Specify the location for the block within the drawing.

Technique to Master **T04.17** Inserting a DC Online Block

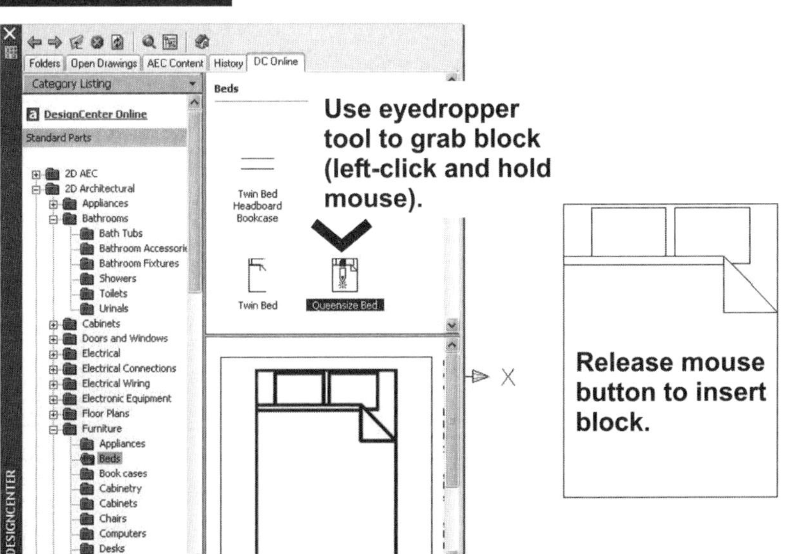

Figure 4.17

1	Open the Design Center. Left-click on the DC Online tab.
2	Locate the desired block.
3	Left-click and hold the cursor over the block so you can drag it to the drawing screen. Release the mouse to insert the block.

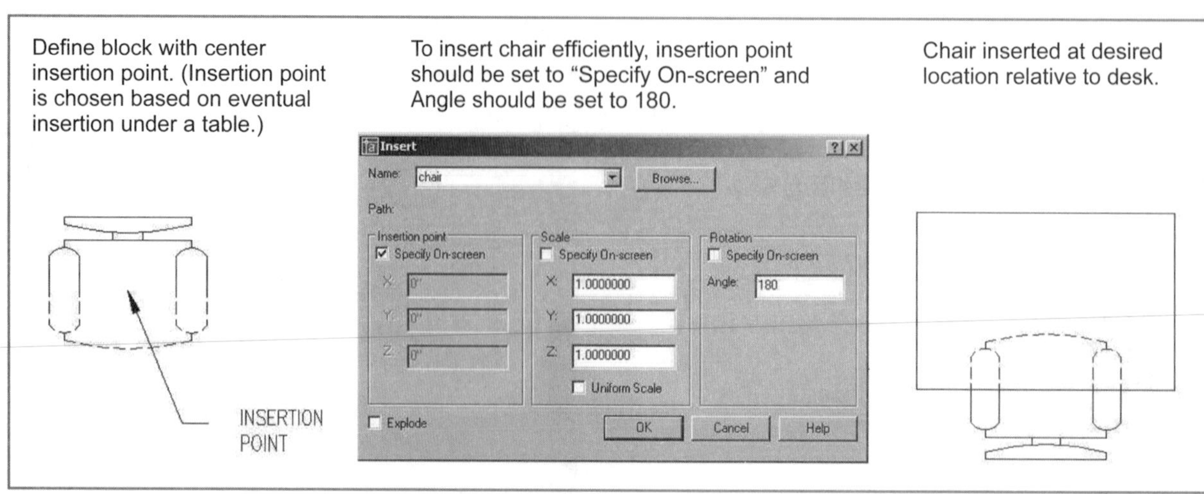
Define block with center insertion point. (Insertion point is chosen based on eventual insertion under a table.)
INSERTION POINT
To insert chair efficiently, insertion point should be set to "Specify On-screen" and Angle should be set to 180.
Insert
Name: chair
Browse...
Path:
Insertion point
Specify On-screen
Scale
Specify On-screen
X: 1.0000000
Y: 1.0000000
Z: 1.0000000
Uniform Scale
Rotation
Specify On-screen
Angle: 180
Explode
OK
Cancel
Help
Chair inserted at desired location relative to desk.

Figure 4.19 Using the Insert command efficiently

For maximum drawing efficiency, try placing blocks by using as few steps as possible. For example, Figure 4.19 shows a chair block that was created with the seat facing downward that needs to be positioned in the opposite direction. The most efficient way to accomplish this task is to access the Insert command's dialogue box so you can set the Insertion Point to Specify On-screen and type 180 into the Angle box. Look at Chapter 4 on the CD-ROM to visualize how to set the correct parameters and get practice using the Insert command.

Block Editing

Sometimes it is necessary to edit existing blocks. For example, you may need to add or remove details from a block to accommodate a developing design. The typical block editing tools include the Explode command, the Block Editor, and the Refedit command. Additional tools are also available in the Express menu's Blocks area.

The Explode Command

When you explode blocks, they return to their original individual geometry—that is to say, the individual line, arc, and circle pieces that made up the block. The command sequence is as follows:

[Command Line] Type Explode.

[Drawing Screen] Select the block you wish to explode.

Once you explode a block, it loses all its ties to the database's block definition, which means that it is impossible to automatically update exploded blocks.

> **Box 4.3**
> Tip: If you accidentally explode a block, then use the Undo command to revert geometry back to its block definition.

The Block Editor and the Refedit Command

The advantage of using blocks becomes most apparent when edits are necessary. Block edits are applied to all instances of the block in the current drawing to match the change. Two methods for editing blocks are manual redefinition and in-place block editing.

Manual Redefinition

Manual redefinition refers to the process of exploding a block, editing the geometry, and then recreating the block. The new version of the block definition is saved over the old by using the same name as the original block definition. In earlier versions of the software, this method of block editing was the only one available; it still works well today.

In-Place Editing

The Refedit command allows you to edit a block in its current position without having to explode it. During in-place reference editing mode, you can only manipulate the block's geometry. The Refedit toolbar appears when you are in the reference editing mode (Figure 4.20). Figure 4.21 demonstrates the Refedit command.

The Block Editor, and the subsequent addition of dynamic blocks, is a relatively new feature of AutoCAD. The Block Editor lets you add and edit dynamic behavior within a block definition. However, you can also use it to make physical modifications—from simple to complex—to an existing block definition.

Specialty Block Commands

There are many other commands that let you create, use, and modify blocks flexibly. The following pages introduce some of the commands that beginners frequently use.

The Measure and Divide Commands

The Measure command places a block at specified distances along a selected object. This command lets you array blocks along an object quickly (Figure 4.22). The Divide command places a block at equal distances along a selected object. Wall-mounted lighting (wall sconces) as well as electrical-outlet placements are excellent examples of using the Divide command in your day-to-day drawing (Figure 4.23).

Figure 4.20 The Refedit toolbar

Technique to Master **T04.21** Editing Blocks Using the Refedit Command

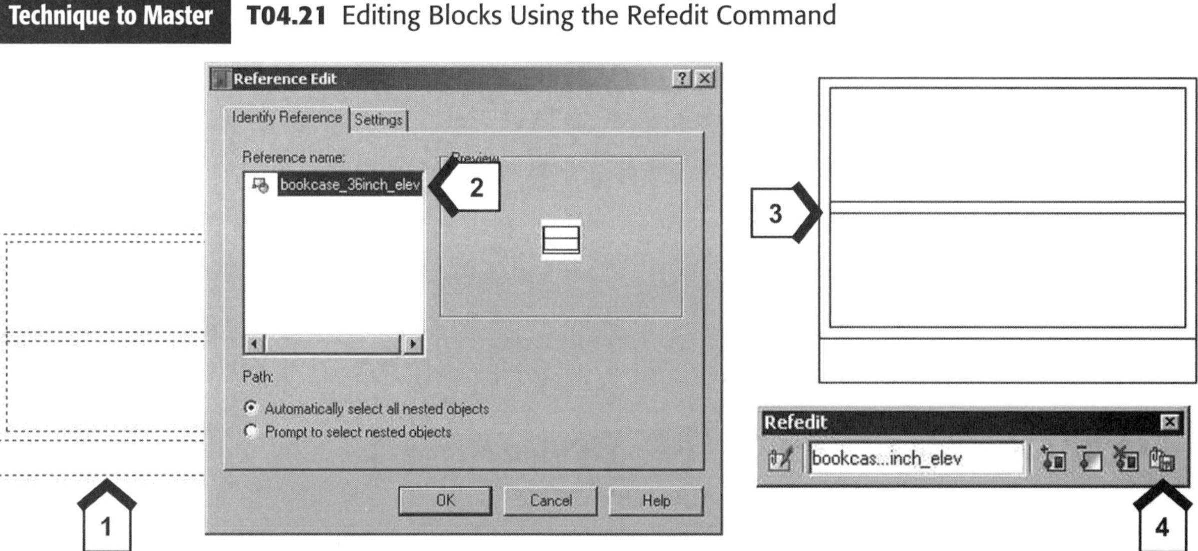

Figure 4.21

1	[Drawing Screen]	Select the block and right-click to choose Edit Block In-place
2	[Reference Edit dialogue box]	Select the name of block you want to edit. (Note that multiple blocks will display if there is block nesting.)
3	[Drawing Screen]	Make the desired changes to the block lines.
4	[RefEdit toolbar]	Save changes.

Technique to Master **T04.22** Using the Measure Command

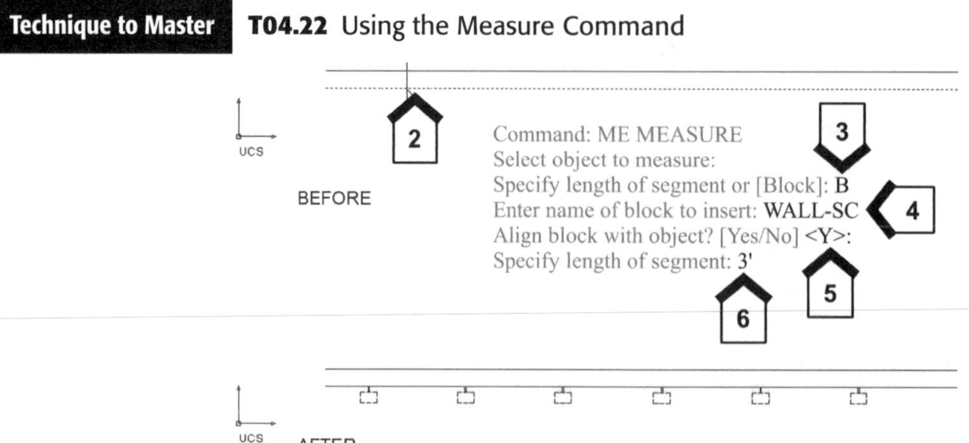

Command: ME MEASURE
Select object to measure:
Specify length of segment or [Block]: B
Enter name of block to insert: WALL-SC
Align block with object? [Yes/No] <Y>:
Specify length of segment: 3'
BEFORE
AFTER
UCS
2
3
4
5
6

Figure 4.22

1	[Command Line]	Type the Measure command.
2	[Drawing Screen]	Select the line, arc, spline, circle, ellipse, or polyline to which you want to apply measure.
3	[Command Line]	Type B and press Enter to insert blocks instead of points.
4	[Command Line]	Type in the name of the block.
5	[Command Line]	Choose Yes to align with object or No for 0 rotation.
6	[Command Line]	Type in the measured distance.

Technique to Master **T04.23** Using the Divide Command

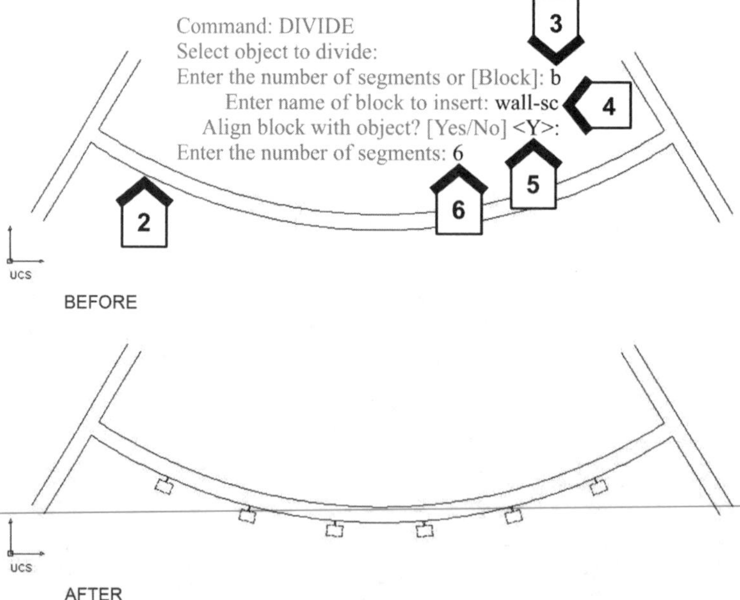

Command: DIVIDE
Select object to divide:
Enter the number of segments or [Block]: b
Enter name of block to insert: wall-sc
Align block with object? [Yes/No] <Y>:
Enter the number of segments: 6
BEFORE
AFTER
UCS
2
3
4
5
6

Figure 4.23

1	[Command Line]	Type the Divide command.
2	[Drawing Screen]	Select the line, arc, spline, circle, ellipse, or polyline to which you want to apply the Divide command.
3	[Command Line]	Type b and press Enter to insert blocks instead of points.
4	[Command Line]	Type in the name of the block.
5	[Command Line]	Choose Yes to align with object or No for 0 rotation.
6	[Command Line]	Type in the number of spaces you want between the blocks.

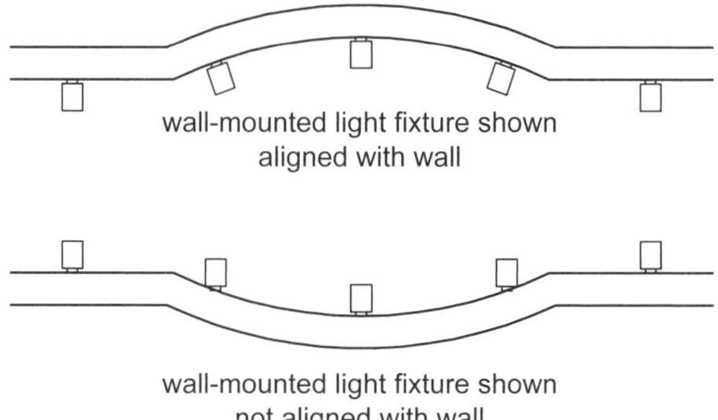

Figure 4.24 Both the Measure and Divide commands give you the ability to rotate the block as you place it so that it maintains a perpendicular relationship to its selected object.

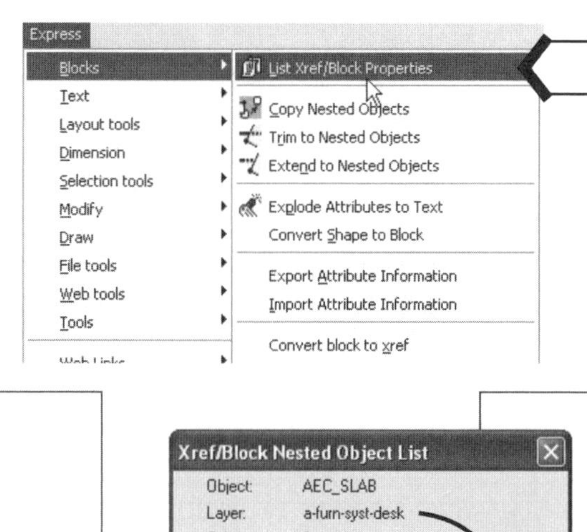

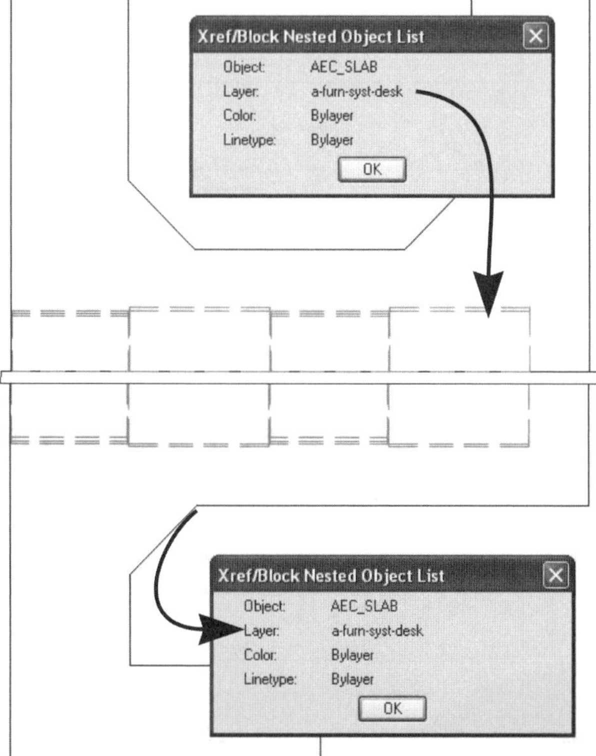

Figure 4.25 The Xlist command lists the layer, color, and linetype properties of a selected object within the block definition.

The benefit of the Measure and Divide commands is best understood when you need to array a block along any nonlinear object. Both commands let you accomplish the task quickly and accurately, without having to make additional mathematical calculations. Moreover, both commands let you rotate a block so that it maintains a perpendicular relationship to its selected object (Figure 4.24).

Specialty Block Commands from the Express Tools

Found in the Express>Block menu, these specialty block commands help you identify block properties and switch block definitions.

List Xref/Block Properties

The Xlist command lists the layer, color, and linetype properties of a selected object within the block definition (Figure 4.25). To use the Xlist command, select one object within a block.

Replace Block with Another Block

The Blockreplace command replaces one block definition with another. This command is useful when quick replacements of repetitive blocks are necessary (Figure 4.26). Figure 4.27 demonstrates how to employ the technique.

Chapter Exercises

Open the Chapter 04 Exercise Text.doc located on the CD-ROM and access the chapter exercises. The exercises let you create and edit blocks used for many common building elements. You can also practice using blocks in floor plans, ceiling plans, and elevations, and you can practice advanced block manipulations by using the specialty block commands.

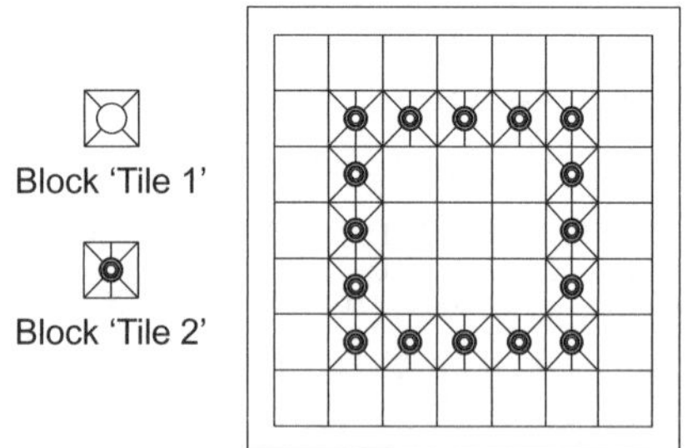

Block 'Tile 2' inserted in floor plan.

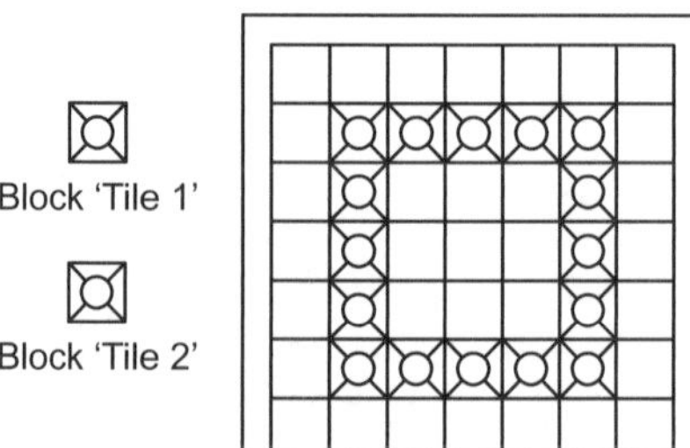

Block 'Tile 1' replaces 'Tile 2'.

Figure 4.26 The Blockreplace command replaces one block definition with another.

Technique to Master T04.27 Using the Blockreplace Command

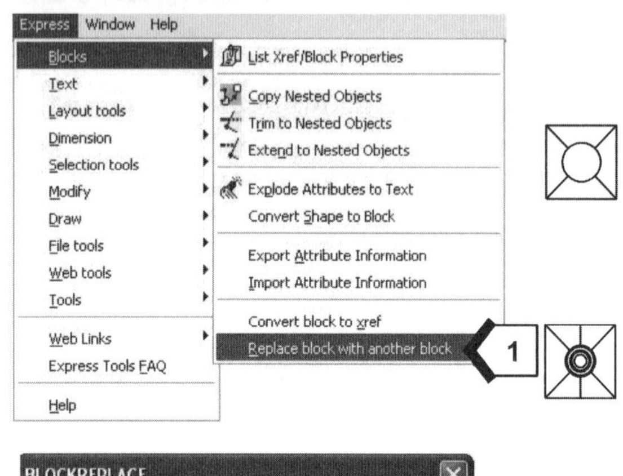

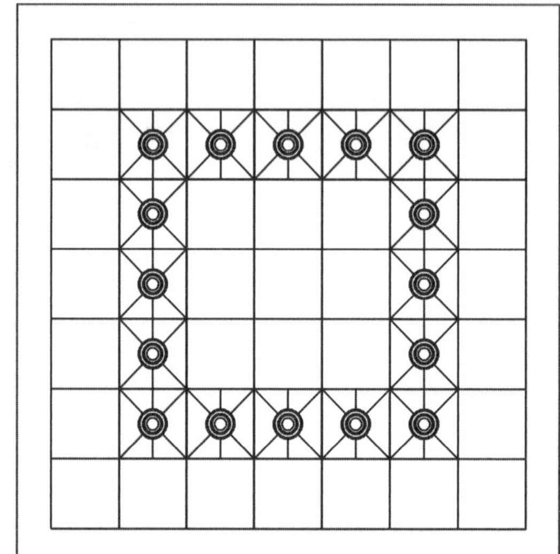

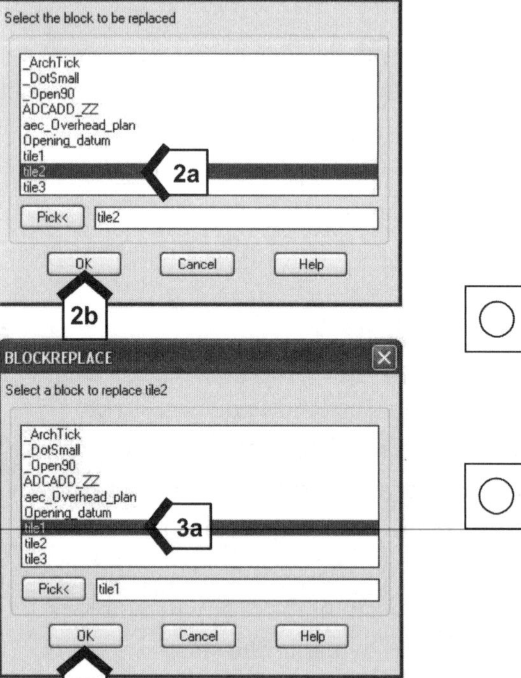

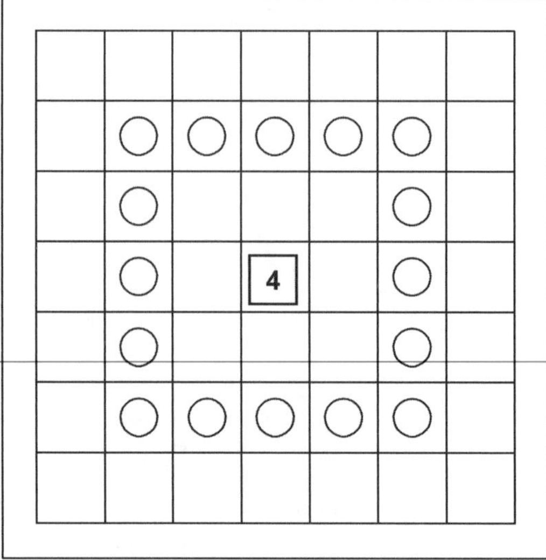

Figure 4.27

1	[Express menu]	Replace block with another block command.
2	[Blockreplace dialogue box]	Select the block you want to replace and click OK.
3	[Blockreplace dialogue box]	Select the replacement block and click OK.
4	The block is replaced in all locations on the drawing screen.	

Hatching and Patterning

5

Objectives

This chapter introduces you to the tools, commands, vocabulary, and techniques used to create patterns and the pattern boundaries within AutoCAD. It focuses on efficient workflow procedures for placing hatches, editing hatches and hatch boundaries, and saving customized hatches as tools. The chapter also emphasizes advanced hatch editing techniques. The end-of-chapter exercises let you practice using the hatching and polyline tools.

Hatching and Patterning

A hatch represents a repeating pattern of lines, arcs, circles, and more. Patterns can be as simple as a series of parallel lines and as complex as a parquet wood floor pattern. When you hatch in AutoCAD, it means you fill a selected area with a hatch or solid color. As with blocks, you may group together geometry that defines the hatch as a single component. Interior designers and architects use hatches in many applications of the design process. Hatches represent floor textures and tiled joints in floor plans. You use hatching techniques in elevations for exterior plaster, siding, and brick applications. You can also use hatches in sections and details to symbolize materials. For the most part, hatches symbolize real-life material textures and material joints.

The Hatch Dialogue Box

The Hatch command is used to create all hatching, solid fills, and gradients in AutoCAD. Similar to the Block command, it is also a dialogue box. Within this dialogue box, AutoCAD divides the hatch-making selections into two types. The user-defined hatch type is used to create parallel lines and crosshatching (Figure 5.1a). The predefined hatch type is a collection of approximately 70 various patterns created by the makers of AutoCAD. Look at Figure 5.1b to see a few of hatches. Appendix H identifies a selection of commonly used patterns in interior design and architecture.

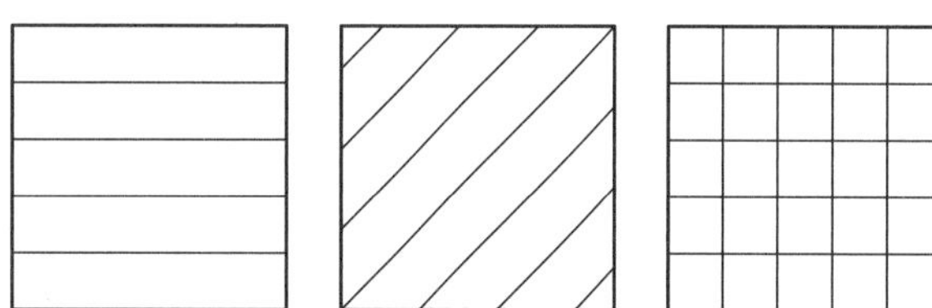

Figure 5.1a Examples of user-defined hatch types in AutoCAD

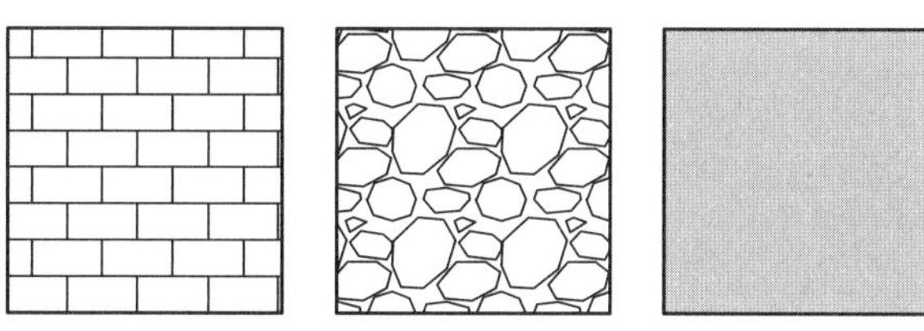

Figure 5.1b Examples of predefined hatch types in AutoCAD

Although the Hatch dialogue box has changed throughout the past few editions of AutoCAD, mainly due to added improvements and functionality, its core command options have remained the same.

Because each hatch type has specific properties that define how it is drawn, the options change depending on the hatch type you choose. User-defined hatch options create parallel and perpendicular lines at a set distance (Figure 5.2a). These options include all the components necessary to make simple parallel lines—spacing, angle, and double. Since predefined hatches are hatches that are predesigned, options for this hatch type include only swatch, angle, and scale (Figure 5.2b).

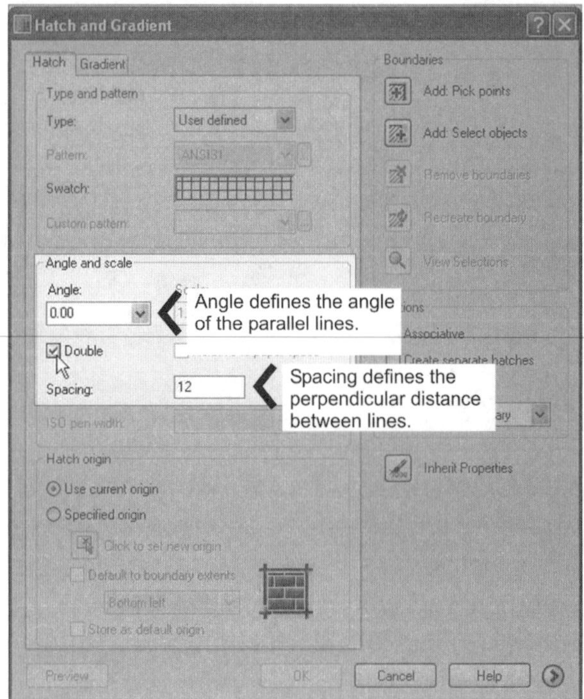

Figure 5.2a Understanding the user-defined hatch type's options

Options for the User-Defined Hatch

The Spacing option defines the distance between the parallel lines of the hatch while the Angle option controls the angle of placement on the drawing screen (Figure 5.3a). The Double checkbox option creates crosshatches by showing additional parallel lines at 90 degrees to the original angle (Figure 5.3b).

> **Box 5.1**
> Keep in mind that the hatch angle is always relative to the axis of the current User Coordinate System (UCS). (See Chapter 8 for more information.)

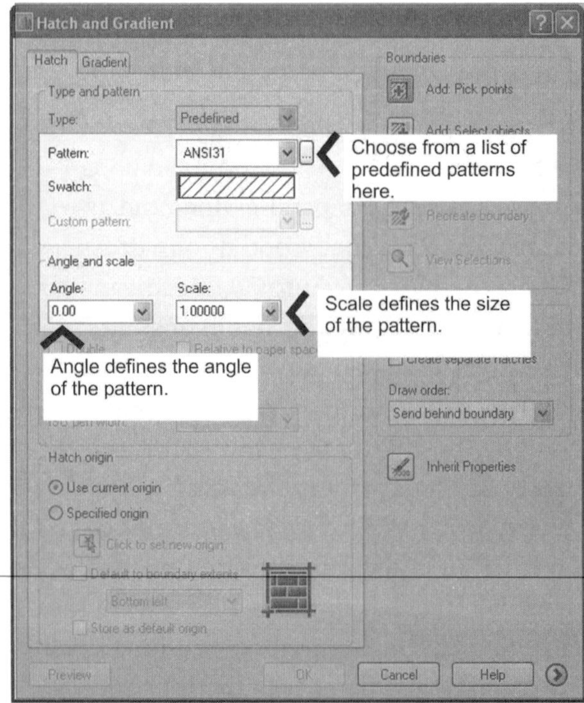

Figure 5.2b Understanding the predefined pattern type's options

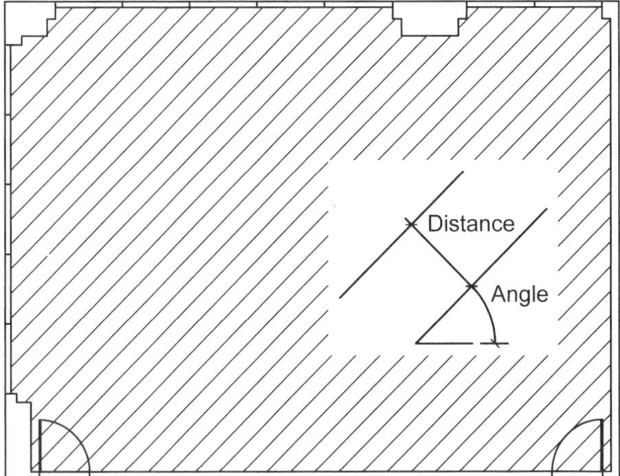

Figure 5.3a The spacing and angle of the user-defined hatch sets the distance between parallel lines and the angle of the parallel lines.

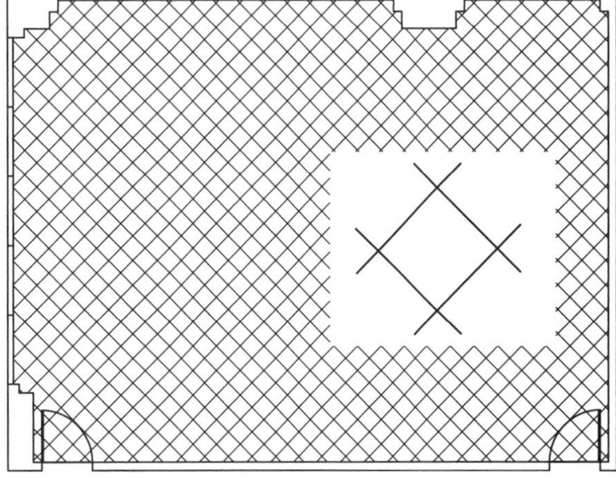

Figure 5.3b The double checkbox option in the user-defined hatch duplicates the spacing and angle of the parallel lines to create a crosshatch.

Options for the Predefined Hatch

Use the Pattern drop-down list to choose one of the available patterns that are defined in the acad.pat file found in the AutoCAD support folder. Left-clicking on the down arrow or ellipses button opens the Hatch Pattern Palette (Figure 5.3c). A swatch of the currently selected hatch or color sample appears as a result.

The Hatch Pattern Palette is the visual representation of the hatches defined in acad.pat. There are four tabs—ANSI, ISO, Other Predefined, and Custom. The majority of hatch selections come from the Other Predefined tab. The Custom tab displays patterns from other .pat files.

Box 5.2

Tip: To import hatch patterns from other .pat files, copy the file(s) to the AutoCAD support folder. The list of patterns appear in the Custom tab of the Hatch Pattern Palette.

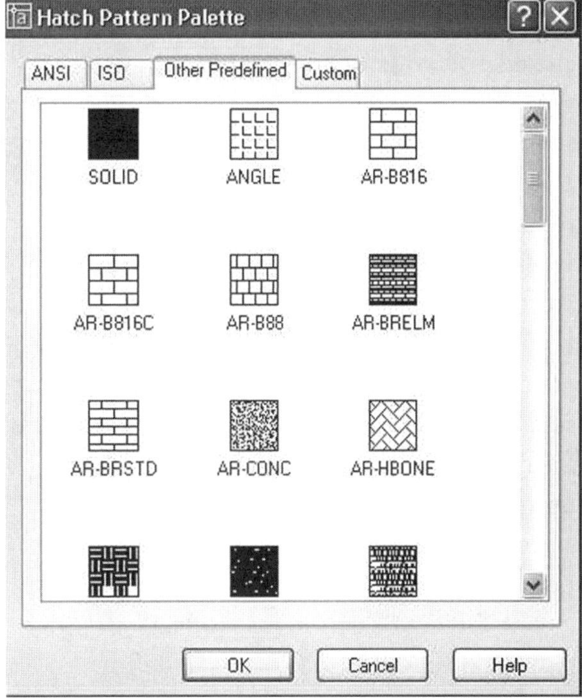

Figure 5.3c AutoCAD's predefined pattern library

The Scale option refers to how large the pattern is drawn onscreen (Figure 5.4). Since many predefined patterns have been created with no relationship to the actual size of building materials, oftentimes we must determine scale through a trial-and-error process. Chapter 18 discusses hatching scale and its relation to building materials in more detail.

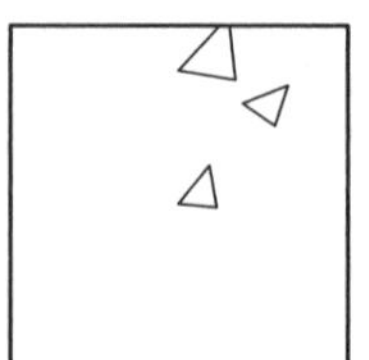
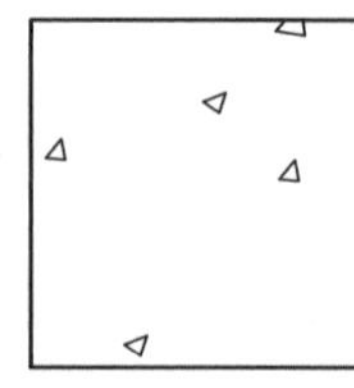
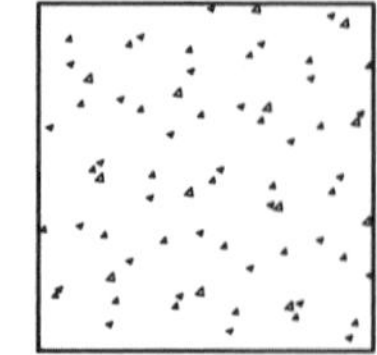

Figure 5.4 Various scaling factors of the hatch AR-CONC. The left is set at a scale of 0.5, the middle at a scale of 0.25, and the right at a scale of 0.05.

Selecting the Area the Hatch Occupies (The Hatch Boundary)

After you make decisions about a hatch and its associated options, you need to specify a hatch boundary. The hatch boundary always refers to the area the hatch occupies. Hatch boundaries can be existing geometry, such as a closed polygonal shape, or rooms in floor plans that have well-defined boundaries, such as the wall's perimeter. Hatch boundaries can also be created to provide a closed, temporary region for the hatch to occupy.

The Pick Point Selection method lets AutoCAD attempt to define a boundary automatically by using existing surrounding geometry (Figure 5.5). To use this method, select any point *within* your desired boundary area. AutoCAD highlights the resulting boundary by using dashed lines. During selection, you can choose additional pick points to have multiple boundary selections.

The Object Selection method lets AutoCAD use existing shapes to define the hatch boundary (Figure 5.6). To use this method, select one or more closed objects.

Technique to Master **T05.05** Using the Pick Point Selection Method to Select Hatch Boundaries

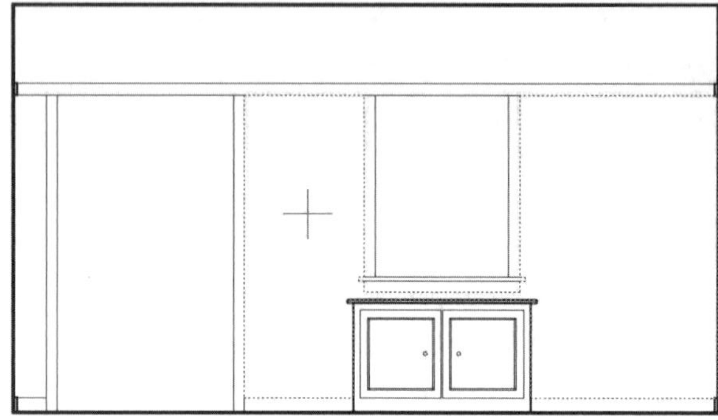

Figure 5.5

1	[Drawing Screen]	Left-click inside an area to let AutoCAD find the boundary.

Technique to Master **T05.06** Using the Select Objects Selection Method to Select Hatch Boundaries

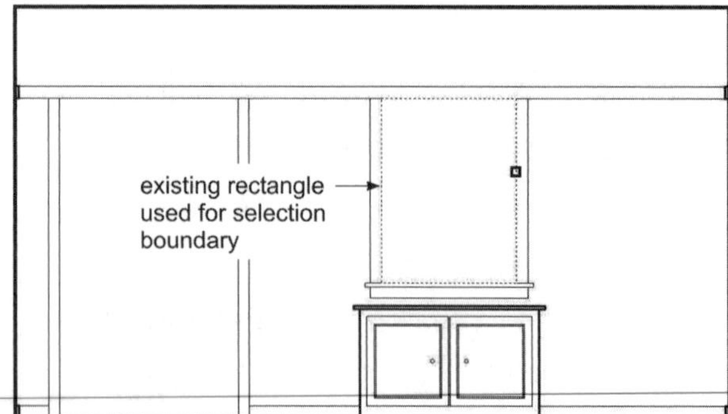

Figure 5.6

1	[Drawing Screen]	Select a closed rectangle or polygon.

Using the Hatch Dialogue Box

Figures 5.7 and 5.8 illustrate the steps you follow to create user-defined and predefined hatch types, respectively.

Technique to Master **T05.07** Creating User-Defined Hatches

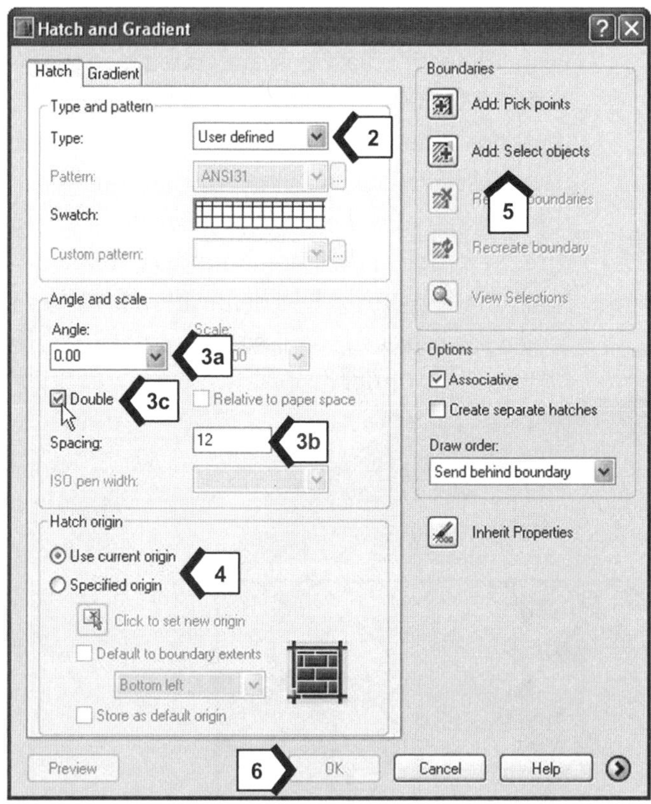

Figure 5.7

1	Use the Hatch command.	
2	[Hatch and Gradient dialogue box]	Change the Hatch Type to User defined.
3a 3b 3c	[Hatch and Gradient dialogue box]	Specify the Angle and Spacing parameters. Check off Double if you desire crosshatching.
4	[Hatch and Gradient dialogue box]	Specify the Hatch origin if you are working with 2006 or 2007 software versions.
5	[Hatch and Gradient dialogue box]	Select Hatch Boundaries by using Add Pick points or Add Select objects.
6	[Hatch and Gradient dialogue box]	Left-click OK to complete the command.

Technique to Master **T05.08** Creating Predefined Hatches

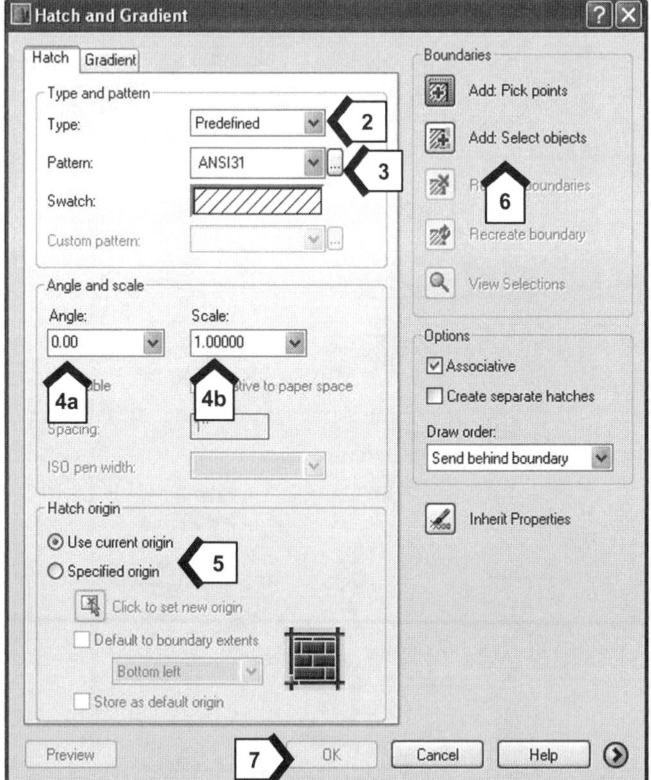

Figure 5.8

1	Access the Hatch command.	
2	[Hatch and Gradient dialogue box]	Change the Hatch Type to Predefined.
3	[Hatch and Gradient dialogue box]	Select the Pattern or Swatch type.
4a 4b	[Hatch and Gradient dialogue box]	Select the Angle and Scale for pattern.
5	[Hatch and Gradient dialogue box]	Specify the Hatch origin if you are working with 2006 or 2007 software versions.
6	[Hatch and Gradient dialogue box]	Select the Hatch Boundary using Add Pick points or Add Select objects.
7	[Hatch and Gradient dialogue box]	Left-click OK to complete the command.

Other Helpful Hatch Options

Use the Inherit Properties button in the Hatch and Gradient dialogue box when you need to match the properties of an existing hatch pattern. This hatch option is valuable when you need to duplicate a hatch whose spacing, scale, and/or pattern type cannot be determined (Figure 5.9).

Associative hatches link the pattern to its associated boundaries. When boundaries change shape, the hatches reflect the change automatically. Non-associative hatches are independent of their boundaries.

The Island Detection option gives AutoCAD instructions on how to treat nested boundaries by using an Island display style (Figure 5.10). Island detection has been integrated into the AutoCAD 2006 edition's primary selection methods. The default Island display style is the normal style where the outermost boundary is the boundary for the hatch pattern. Boundaries directly inside of the outer boundary create holes in the pattern. This delineation is repeated with each successive boundary.

The Draw Order drop-down list is an option that was added to AutoCAD 2005. It allows

Technique to Master **T05.09** Using Inherit Properties to Hatch New Areas

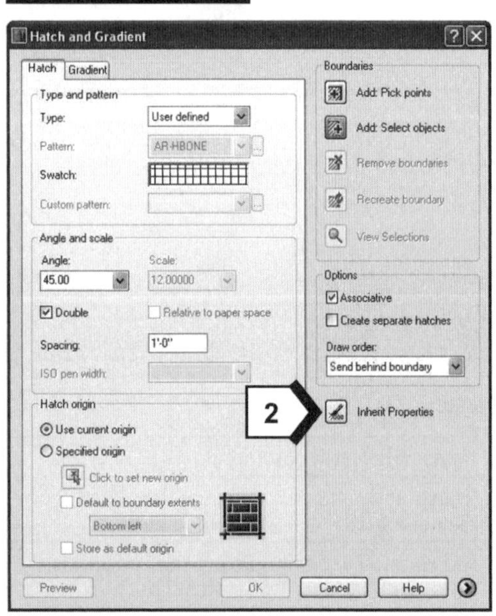

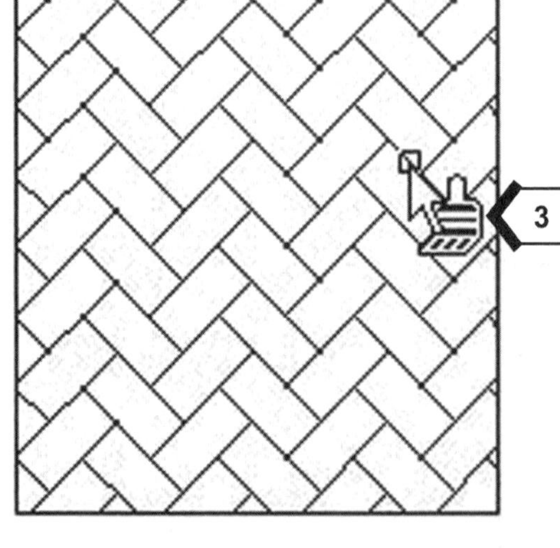

Figure 5.9

1	Use the Hatch command.	
2	[Hatch and Gradient dialogue box]	Select the Inherit Properties button.
3	[Drawing Screen]	Select the existing hatch within the drawing that you want to replicate. Press Enter to complete the selection.
4	[Hatch and Gradient dialogue box]	Select the hatch boundary by using Add Pick points or Add Select objects.
5	[Hatch and Gradient dialogue box]	Left-click OK to complete the command.

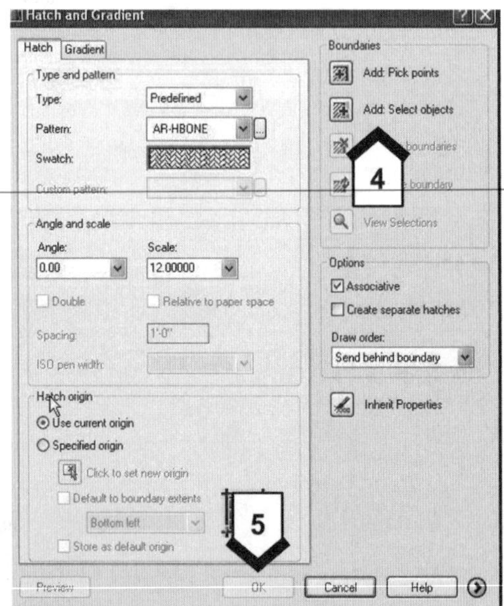

you to place hatches behind or in front of other objects in the drawing (Figure 5.11). Options include Do not assign, Send to back, Bring to front, Send behind boundary, and Bring in front of boundary. Draw Order within AutoCAD becomes important when there are objects that need to be in front of hatched areas.

When you create hatches, their default origin point coincides with the drawing's global origin. This point is not always practical when you are trying to align floor and ceiling patterns to a particular room. Prior to AutoCAD 2006, the Snapbase system variable allowed you to adjust this origin point before using the hatching procedure, as demonstrated in Figure 5.12. However, in AutoCAD 2006, you can adjust hatch alignment easily within the Hatch dialogue box. Figure 5.13 identifies the options available for defining the hatch origin.

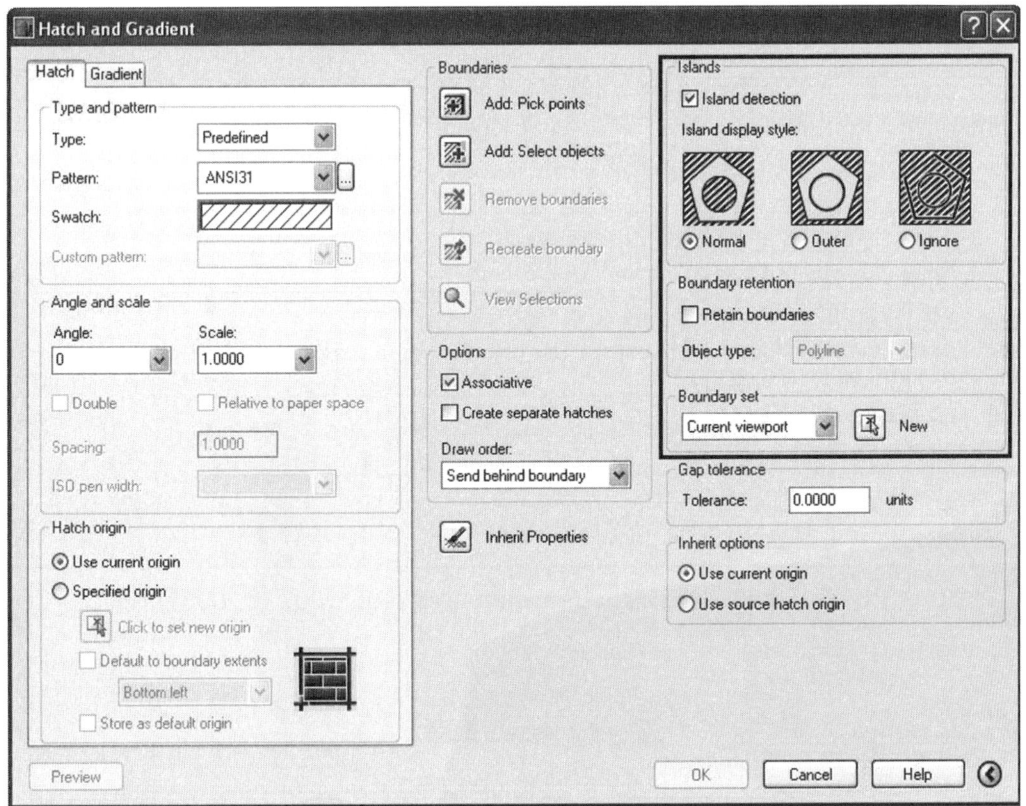

Figure 5.10 The Island detection dialogue box

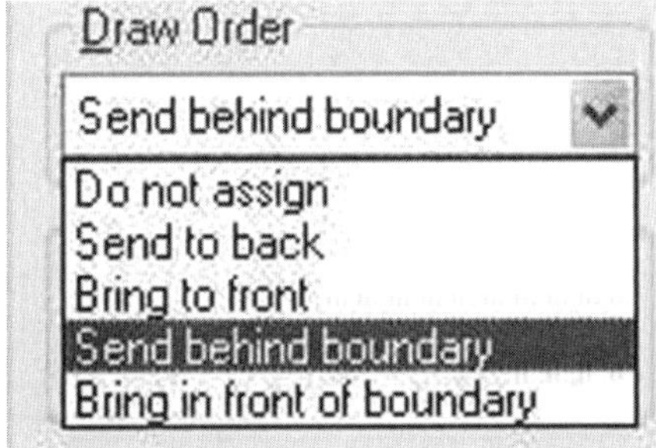

Figure 5.11 The Draw Order options

Technique to Master T05.12 Setting the Hatch Origin Prior to AutoCAD 2006

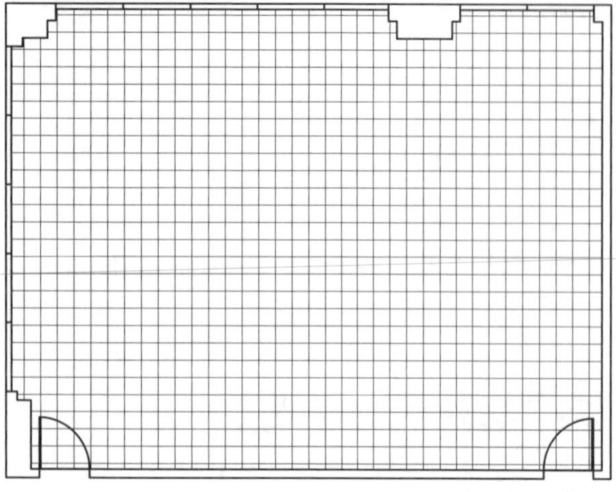

Floor pattern centered within room above,

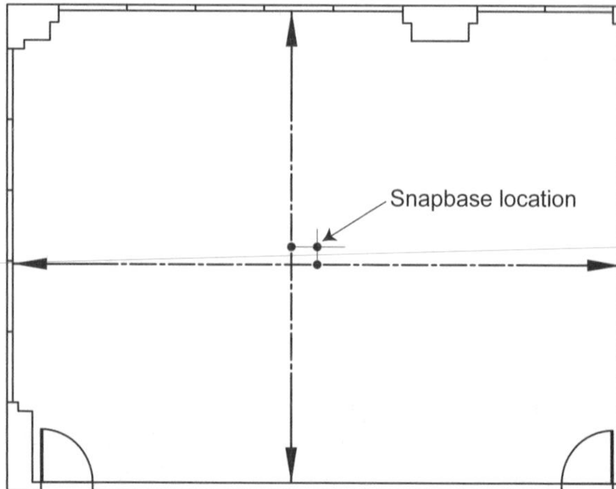

Snapbase location is specified at the midpoints of the length and width of the room.

Figure 5.12

Centering a hatch within a space		
1	[Drawing Screen]	Draw a temporary diagonal line through the room.
2	[Command Line]	Use the Snapbase command.
3	[Drawing Screen]	Specify the origin for the hatch pattern. Use object snaps to snap to the midpoint of the diagonal line.
4	[Drawing Screen]	Erase the temporary line.
5	Use the Hatch command to hatch the area.	

Technique to Master T05.13 Setting the Hatch Origin Using AutoCAD 2006, 2007, or 2008

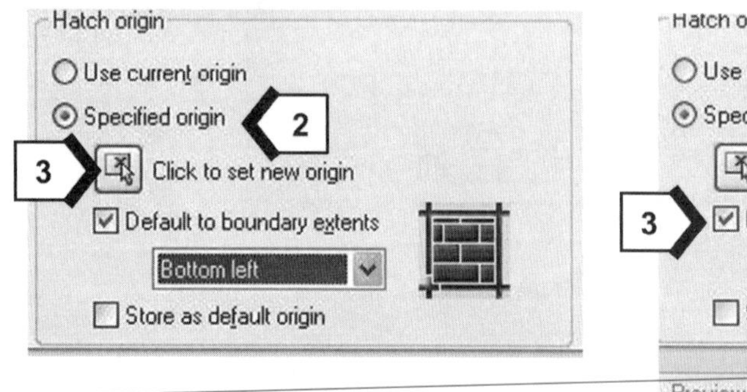

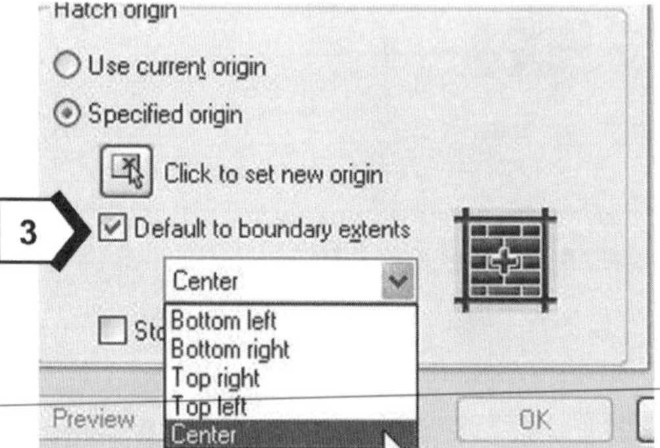

Figure 5.13

1	Use the Hatch command.	
2	[Hatch and Gradient dialogue box]	Select Specified origin button.
3	[Hatch and Gradient dialogue box]	Either left-click on Click to set new origin button or check off Default to boundary extents.

Polylines

A polyline is a shape made up of one or more connected segments. These segments share common vertex points and can be a combination of lines and arcs. Polylines are selected and manipulated as a single shape and can be open or closed (Figure 5.14).

The commands associated with polylines include the Pline, Pedit, Explode (see Chapter 4), and Boundary commands. First, you can create polylines by using the Pline and Boundary commands. Second, you can convert existing lines and arcs to polylines by using the Pedit command. Finally, you can use the Explode command to convert a polyline back into its individual line and arc segments.

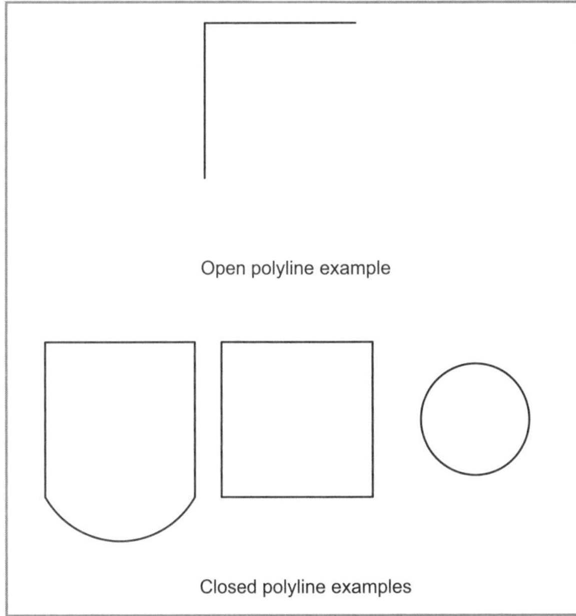

Figure 5.14 Open versus closed polylines

The Pline Command

Because the Pline command includes many command options, it can sometimes be a little intimidating. The following is a list of regularly used options and their respective descriptions:

- The Close command creates a segment between the last located point and the first located point, which closes the polyline.
- The Undo command erases the last drawn segment.
- The Arc command creates arc segments within the polyline.
- The Width command changes the width of the next line segment. AutoCAD prompts for both the starting width and ending width of the line or arc segment.

Figures 5.15 through 5.18 demonstrate basic techniques for how to use the Polyline command.

Technique to Master **T05.15** Creating a Polyline with Multiple Line Segments

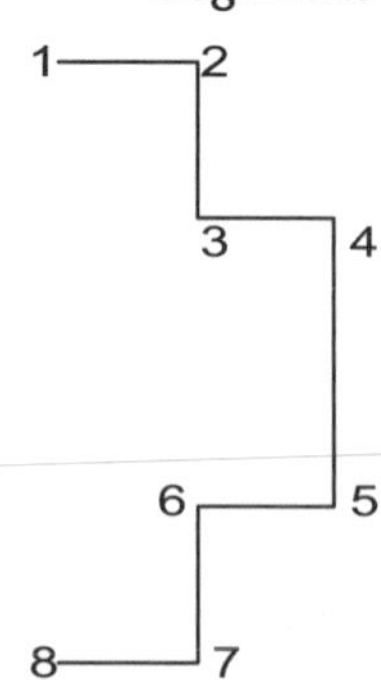

Figure 5.15

1	[Command Line]	Type Pline.
2	[Drawing Screen]	Locate the first point for the polyline.
3	[Drawing Screen]	Locate the second point for the polyline.
4	[Drawing Screen]	Keep locating points.
5	Press Enter to complete the command.	

Technique to Master **T05.16** Creating a Closed Polyline with Multiple Line Segments

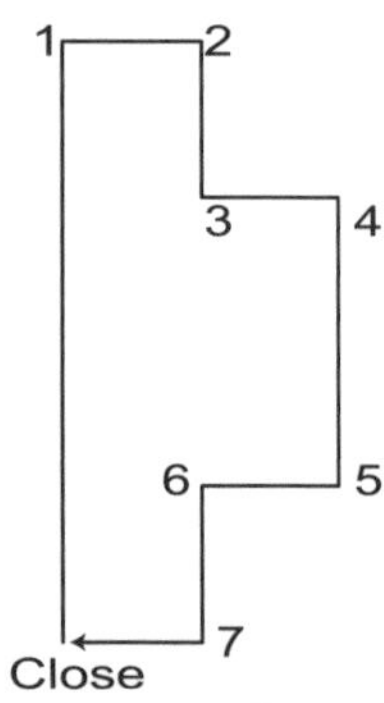

Figure 5.16

1	[Command Line]	Type Pline.
2	[Drawing Screen]	Locate the first point for the polyline.
3	[Drawing Screen]	Locate the second point for the polyline.
4	[Drawing Screen]	Keep locating points.
5	[Command Line]	Type C and press Enter to close polyline.

Technique to Master **T05.17** Creating a Closed Polyline with Both Line and Arc Segments

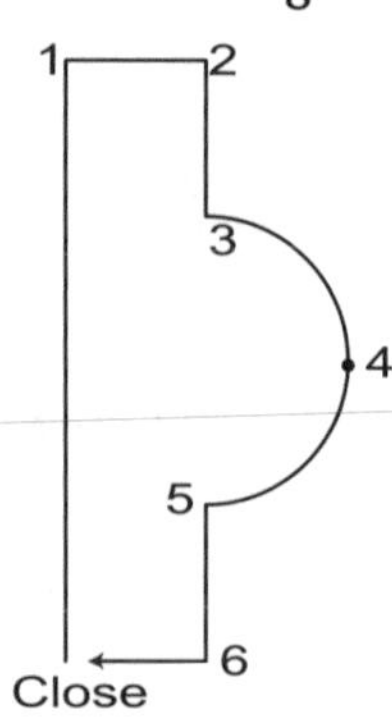

Figure 5.17

1	[Command Line]	Type Pline.
2	[Drawing Screen]	Locate the first point of the line segment.
3	[Drawing Screen]	Locate the second point of the line segment.
4	[Command Line]	Type A and press Enter to change to draw arcs.
5	[Command Line]	Type S and press Enter to locate the second point of the arc (the arc's midpoint).
6	[Drawing Screen]	Locate the second point of the arc segment.
7	[Drawing Screen]	Locate the end of the arc segment.
8	[Command Line]	Type L and press Enter to switch back to drawing straight segments.
9	[Drawing Screen]	Locate the first point of the line segment.
10	[Drawing Screen]	Locate the second point of the line segment.
11	[Command Line]	Type C and press Enter to close the polyline.

Technique to Master	**T05.18** Creating an Arrow with a Polyline

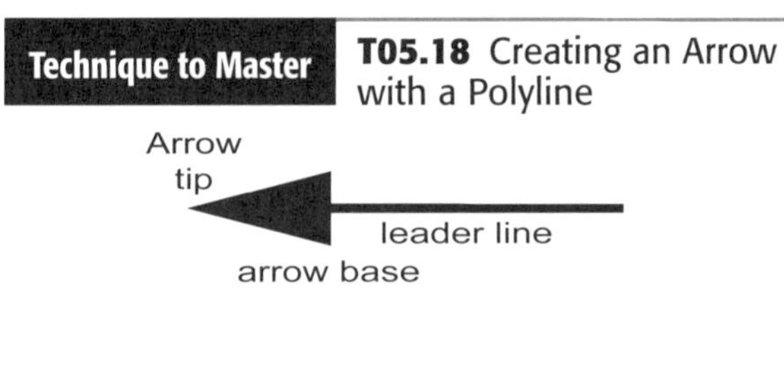

Figure 5.18

1	[Command Line]	Type Pline.
2	[Drawing Screen]	Locate the arrow tip.
3	[Command Line]	Type W and press Enter to change the line thickness of the next segment.
4	[Command Line]	Type 0 and press Enter to keep the start width at 0.
5	[Command Line]	Type $^1/_8$ and press Enter to change the end width to $^1/_8$".
6	[Drawing Screen]	Using Direct Distance Entry, locate the arrow base .25″ away.
7	[Command Line]	Type W and press Enter to change the line thickness of the next segment.
8	[Command Line]	Type 0 and press Enter to change the start width to 0.
9	[Command Line]	Type 0 and press Enter to change the end width to 0.
10	[Drawing Screen]	Using Direct Distance Entry, locate the leader end 1″ away.
11	[Command Line]	Press Enter to complete the command.

The Pedit Command

The Pedit command lets you convert existing AutoCAD shapes into polylines. Lines and arc segments whose endpoints meet can all be changed to polyline entities, as demonstrated in Figures 5.19. and 5.20. You cannot convert circles, and also keep in mind that rectangles and polygons are already closed polyline entities. The following is a list of Pedit command options and their respective descriptions:

- The Close option creates a new segment that closes an open polyline.
- The Join option joins line and arc segments to create a multisegmented polyline.
- The Width option changes the width of the selected line segments.
- The Edit Vertex option provides additional options to add or delete polyline vertices.
- The Fit option uses existing polyline vertices to convert polyline segments into arc curves.
- The Spline option uses existing polyline vertices to convert polyline segments into Spline curves.

> **Box 5.3**
> In AutoCAD, Splines are smooth, nonuniform curves you can create by using a series of points.

Technique to Master T05.19 Creating a Polyline with the Pedit Command

Command: pedit
Select polyline or [Multiple]:
Object selected is not a polyline
Do you want to turn it into one? <Y> 3
Enter an option [Close/Join/Width/Edit vertex/Fit/Spline/Decurve/Ltype gen/Undo]:**J** 4
Select objects: Specify opposite corner:
4 found
3 segments added to polyline

2

5

Closed Polyline

Figure 5.19 Create a polyline with the Pedit command by using shapes that have touching endpoints.

1	[Command Line]	Type Pedit.
2	[Drawing Screen]	Select objects using a Pick Selection.
3	[Command Line]	Type Y and press Enter to convert an object into a polyline.
4	[Command Line]	Type J and press Enter to access the Join command.
5	[Drawing Screen]	Select all of the objects you wish to join together. Use a Window or Crossing Selection for efficiency. Refer to techniques T02.34 or T02.35.
6	[Command Line]	Press Enter to complete the command.

Technique to Master T05.20 Creating a Polyline with the Pedit Command

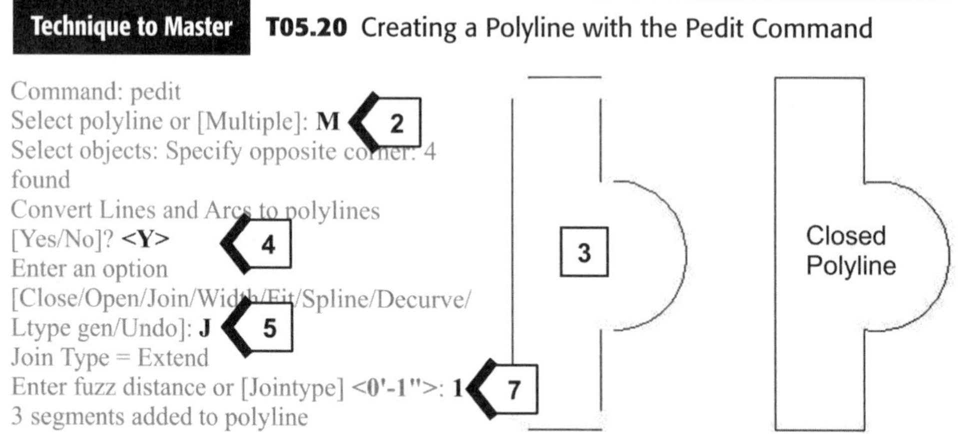

Command: pedit
Select polyline or [Multiple]: M
2
Select objects: Specify opposite corner: 4 found
Convert Lines and Arcs to polylines [Yes/No]? <Y>
4
Enter an option [Close/Open/Join/Width/Fit/Spline/Decurve/Ltype gen/Undo]: J
5
Join Type = Extend
Enter fuzz distance or [Jointype] <0'-1">: 1
7
3 segments added to polyline
3
Closed Polyline

Figure 5.20 Create a polyline with the Pedit command by using shapes that do not have touching endpoints.

1	[Command Line]	Type Pedit.
2	[Command Line]	Type M and press Enter to activate the Multiple command.
3	[Drawing Screen]	Select all the objects you want to join together.
4	[Command Line]	Type Y and press Enter to convert objects into polylines.
5	[Command Line]	Type J and press Enter to invoke the Join command.
6	AutoCAD displays how it will attempt to join the shapes.	
7	[Command Line]	Type 1 and press Enter to enter fuzz distance.
8	[Command Line]	Press Enter to complete the command.

Technique to Master **T05.21** Create a Polyline with the Boundary Command

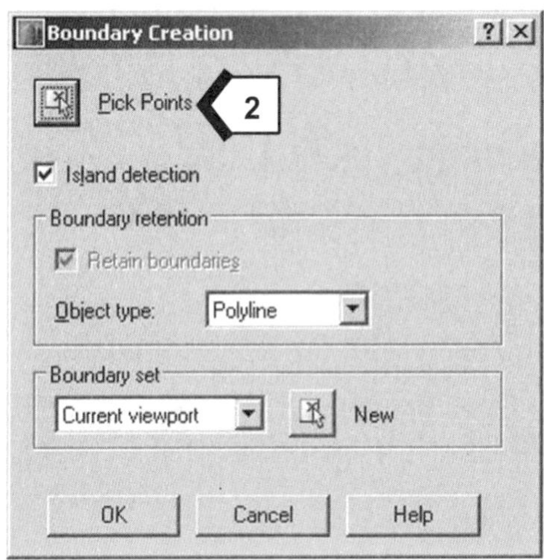

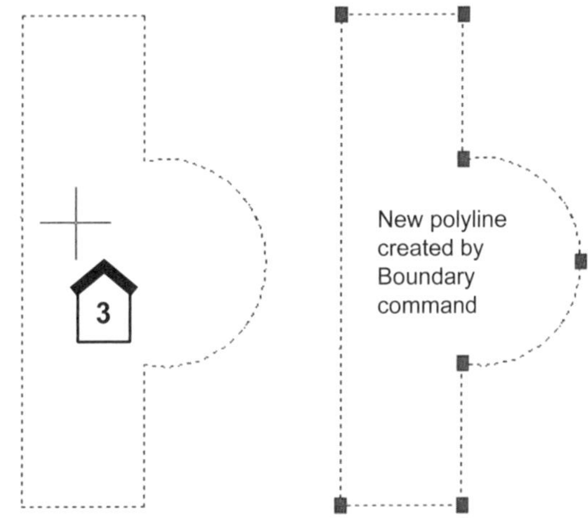

Figure 5.21

1	[Command Line]	Type Boundary.
2	[Boundary dialogue box]	Left-click on the Pick Points button.
3	[Drawing Screen]	Click into the area to have AutoCAD sense the boundaries.
4	[Command Line]	Press Enter to complete the command.

The Boundary Command

The Boundary command creates closed polylines from existing surrounding geometry by using a Pick Point selection method (Figure 5.21).

Hatching by Using Polylines for Hatch Boundaries

The following workflow process promotes the use of polylines as hatch boundaries. Several times during the design process, room size and shapes are changed or reconfigured due to design development. Establishing room boundaries by using polylines makes hatch updating faster and more efficient in the long run.

This method entails creating a closed boundary for each space that requires a hatch pattern. When you create hatches, the hatches become associated with the polyline boundary. All changes to the hatch boundary are immediately reflected by the hatches' extents. The following paragraphs describe the workflow process in more detail.

When you create the hatch boundary for each room, space, or floor area, do so by using the following Techniques to Master: T05.16, T05.17, T05.19, or T05.20. Make sure you place boundaries on their own unique, non-plotting layer. An example might be the A-hatch-boundary layer.

If you set the hatch origin using AutoCAD 2005 or earlier editions, then use the Snapbase command (Refer to Technique T05.12). Set the appropriate hatching layer to Current in the Properties toolbar. Examples may include A-wall-hatch, A-floor-hatch, A-pattern (Refer to Technique T03.17). Use the Hatch command to create the hatch or solid fill. Do the following within the Hatch dialogue box:

1. Select the hatch type: Predefined or User-defined. If you choose Predefined, then also choose the pattern type. If you choose User defined, then specify the spacing for the lines. Check off the Double box if you want a crosshatch.
2. Select the hatch boundary as well as any boundary holes by using the Add Select objects button.

3. Change the angle and scale settings as necessary to achieve your desired results.
4. Under Options, check off the Associative box.
5. Specify the Hatch origin if you are using AutoCAD 2006 or 2007.
6. Preview your hatch. If the hatch is not visible, then verify the hatch's scale. Hatches that are too dense do not display.
7. Use the Escape key to modify any of the hatching parameters or the Enter key to accept the hatch. To correct hatch scaling problems, increase the scale factor by typing in a value. (Ignore the scale selections available to you.) You should size hatch patterns realistically to match the material you are replicating. Read Chapter 18 for more details on this subject.

Hatching Without Polyline Boundaries

(Also Known as Hatching When You Are in a Hurry)

Sometimes time constraints make it impossible for you to create boundaries for every hatch pattern you need to complete. The Add Pick points selection is a quicker way to create hatches. Figures 5.22 and 5.23 illustrate the workflow process.

Technique to Master **T05.22** Hatching Without Polyline Boundaries—Wall Fills

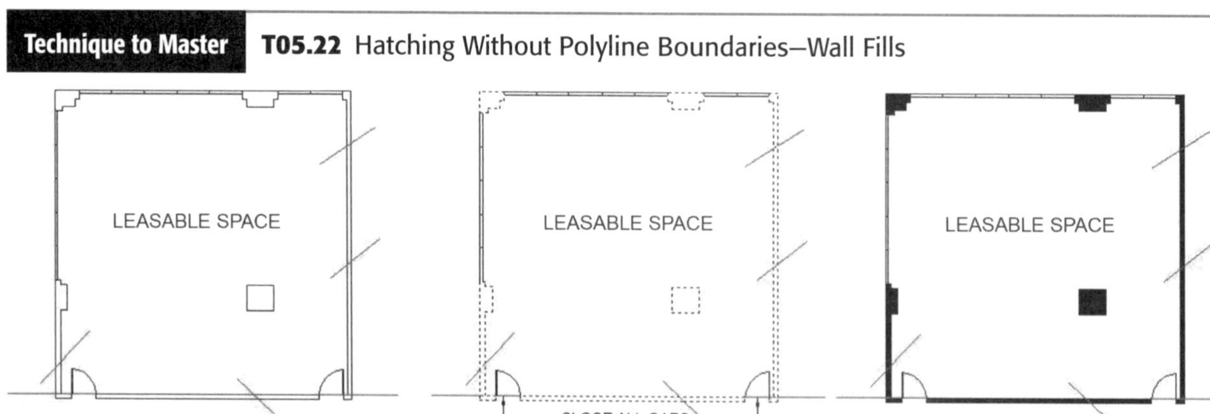

Figure 5.22

1	Divide wall areas into smaller sections. Use temporary lines and arcs to close off these areas.
2	Hatch wall boundaries using Point Acquisition.
3	Erase temporary lines.

Technique to Master **T05.23** Hatching Without Polyline Boundaries—Floor Patterns

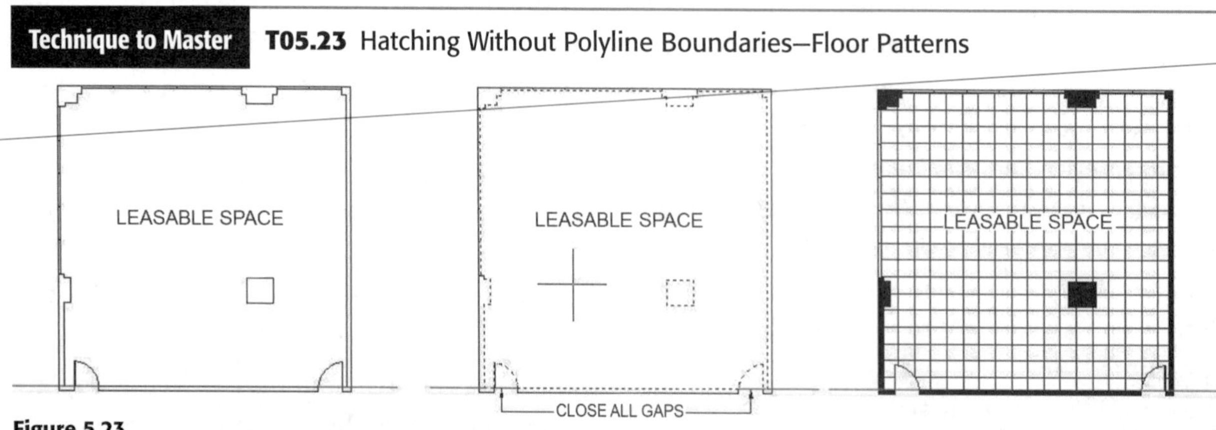

Figure 5.23

1	Temporarily close off areas of a room or space so that AutoCAD can automatically find a boundary.
2	Hatch room using Point Acquisition.

Setting Up for Point Acquisition

Rooms, spaces, and floor areas that do not have defined boundaries need to be temporarily closed. You can divide walls that will be filled (poche) into smaller sections. Just use temporary lines and arcs to close off these areas. Don't forget to use the Properties toolbar to set the appropriate hatching layer to Current. Examples may include A-wall-hatch, A-floor-hatch, A-pattern (Refer to Technique T03.17).

Hatching with Point Acquisition

Use the Hatch command to create the hatch or solid fill. Do the following within the Hatch and Gradient dialogue box:

1. Select the hatch type: Predefined or User defined.
2. Use the Add Pick oints button to select the hatch boundary. The Add Pick Points button takes you to the AutoCAD drawing screen. To have AutoCAD find the boundary, left-click within the area that you want to hatch. You may continue clicking additional areas as appropriate. If AutoCAD cannot find a boundary, a warning alerts you. Before you can successfully hatch your area, you need to either fix any gaps or set the gap tolerance to a higher value (Figure 5.24).
3. Change the angle and scale settings as necessary to achieve your desired results.
4. Uncheck the Associative box.
5. Preview your hatch. If the hatch is not visible, then verify the hatch's scale. Hatches that are too dense do not display.
6. Use the Escape key to modify any of the hatching parameters or the Enter key to accept the hatch. To correct hatch scaling problems, increase the scale factor by typing in a value. (Ignore the scale selections available to you.) You should size hatch patterns realistically to match the material you are replicating. Read Chapter 18 for more details on this subject.
7. Erase the temporary lines.

Technique to Master **T05.24** Gap Tolerance Option in AutoCAD 2006 and Later

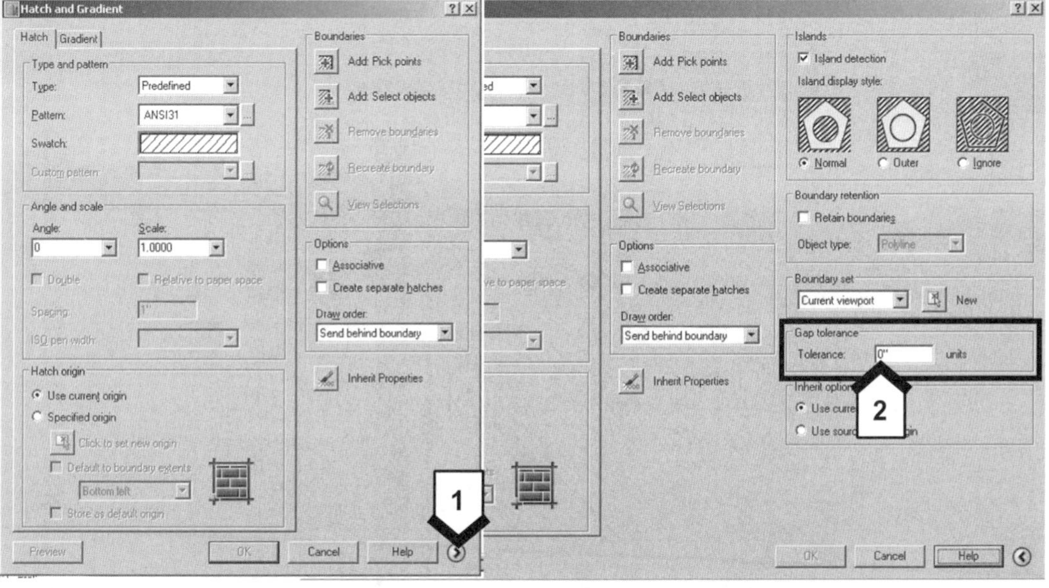

Figure 5.24 The Gap tolerance command option lets you hatch gaps in areas. The default value is set to no tolerance (0). You may set gap tolerance values to up to 5,000 units.

1	To locate the gap tolerance options, left-click on the more sign.
2	Gap tolerance is located at the lower right area of the screen.

Hatching Using the Hatch Tools on the Tool Palette

Tool palettes have become a very resourceful location for saving customized pattern configurations, including the hatch type, scaling, and angle. Figure 5.25 demonstrates how to use hatch tools that are saved within a tool palette.

Figure 5.26 shows how you can build your own customized hatch tools library.

Editing Hatches

Hatch-editing demands for beginner drafters tend to be limited to changing existing properties, trimming existing hatches, and creating holes in hatches.

Technique to Master **T05.25** Hatching Using the Tool Palette

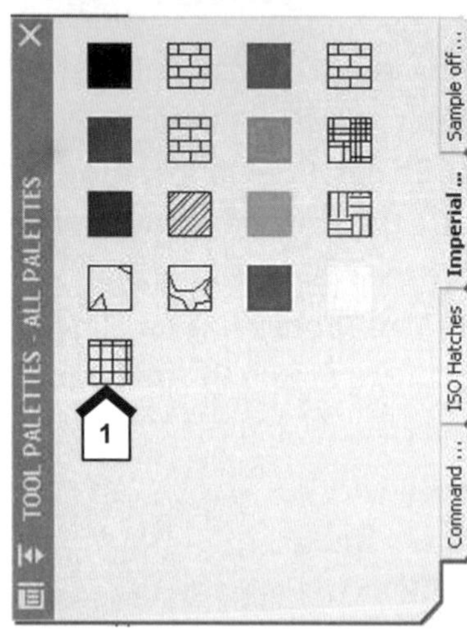

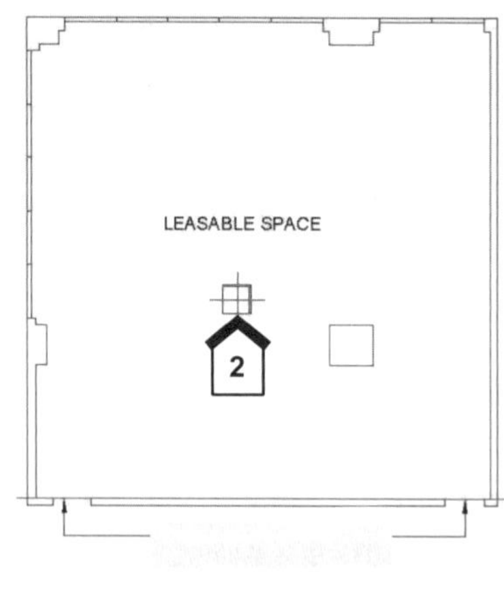

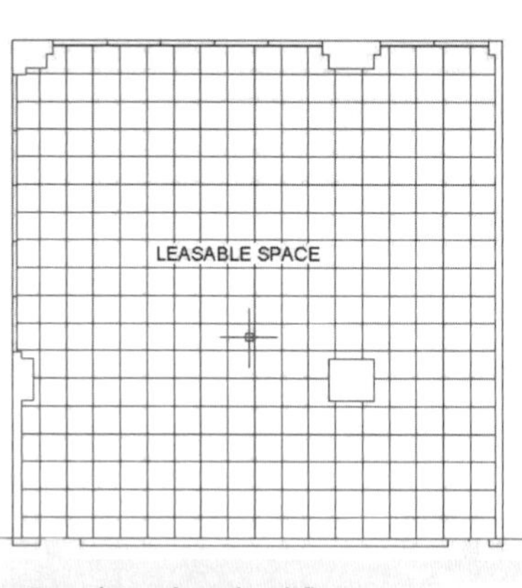

Resulting hatched floor pattern.

Figure 5.25

1	[Tool palette]	Left-click on the Hatch tool.
2	[Drawing Screen]	Left-click into a closed room or space.

Technique to Master **T05.26** Adding Customized Hatches to Tool Palettes

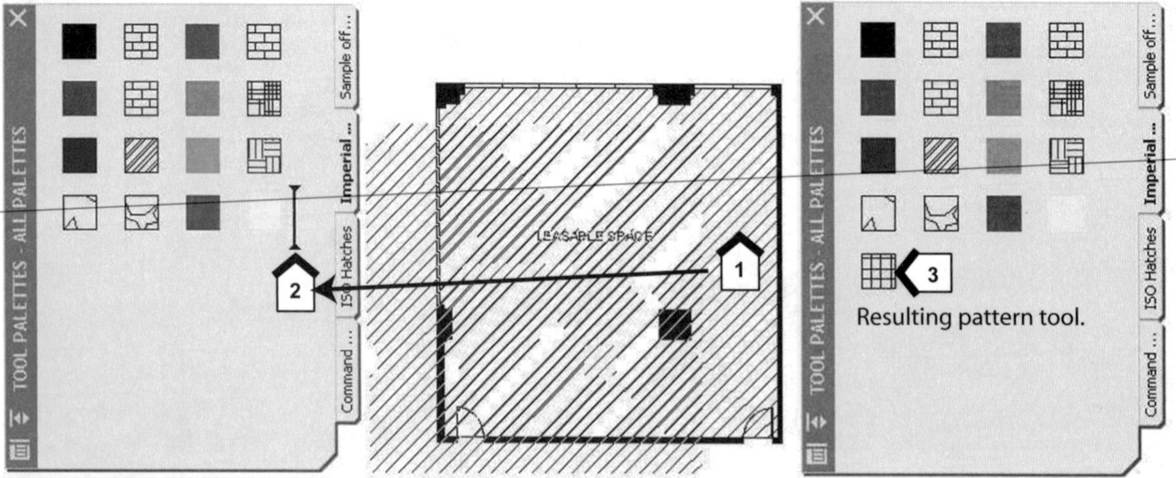

Figure 5.26

1	[Drawing Screen]	Select the hatch at the edge and drag it to the Tool palette.
2	[Tool palette]	Drop it into the Tool palette.

The Hatchedit Command

The Hatchedit command changes the properties of existing hatches. The dialogue box for this command is very similar to the Hatch command's dialogue box. You can adjust all hatch property options by using the Hatchedit command. Most boundary adjustments, however, tend to be made during grip editing. Figure 5.27 shows the grip-editing techniques you use to modify existing hatch boundaries.

Trimming Hatches

The ability to trim hatches is a relatively new feature introduced in AutoCAD 2005. You can use any basic shape as the boundary for the hatch by using the Trim command you learned in Chapter 2. The floor pattern in Figure 5.28 has been trimmed around a desk symbol.

Creating Holes in Hatches

Create holes in hatches during the hatch procedure by selecting the boundaries that represent holes after you define the pattern boundary (Figure 5.29).

Technique to Master **T05.27** Editing Hatch Boundaries with Grips

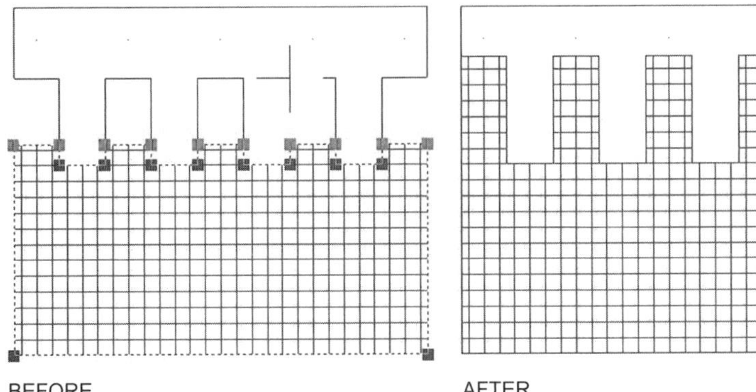
BEFORE
AFTER

Figure 5.27

1	Select hatch boundary and highlight grip points. Grip stretching is used to elongate boundary.
2	Result of grip editing. Notice that the hatch is associative. Because associative hatches are linked to their boundaries, the hatch always reflects the shape changes made by the hatch boundary.

Technique to Master **T05.28** Using the Trim Command on Hatches

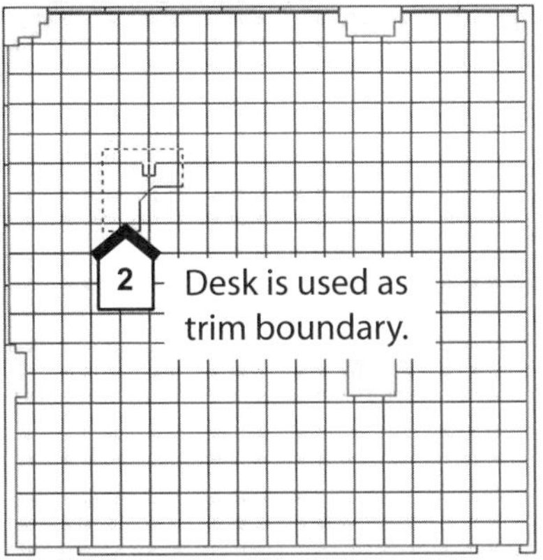
2
Desk is used as trim boundary.

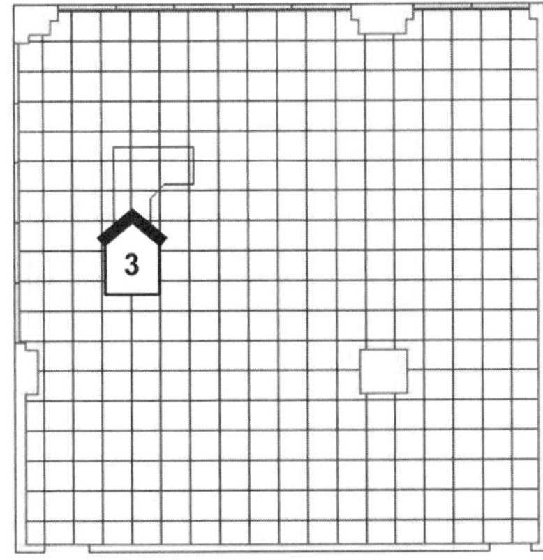
3

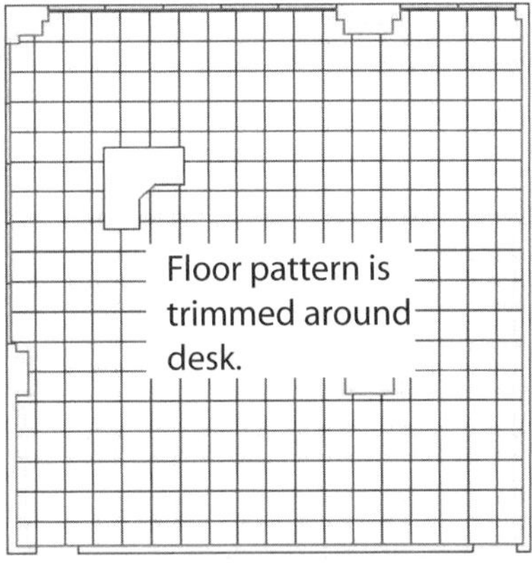
Floor pattern is trimmed around desk.

Figure 5.28

1	Use the Trim command.	
2	[Drawing Screen]	Select trim cutting edge(s).
3	[Drawing Screen]	Select hatch at the area to remove.

Technique to Master **T05.29** Creating Holes in Hatches Using Object Selection

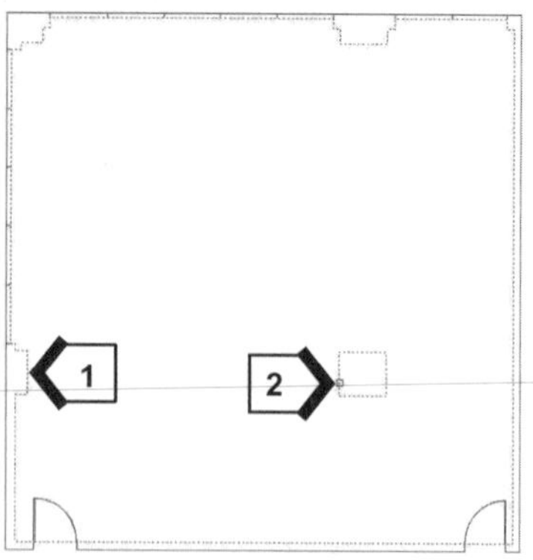

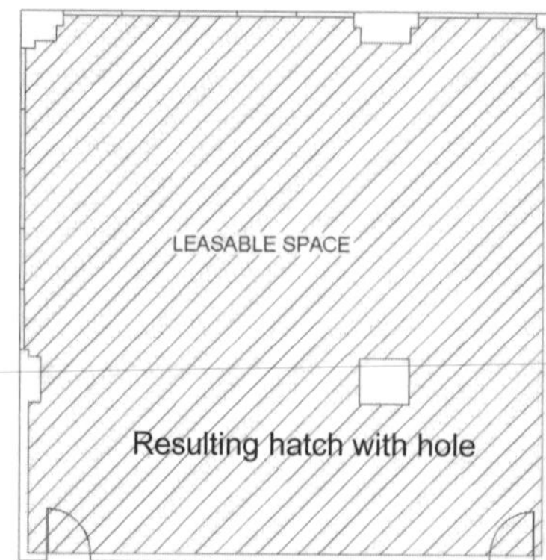

Figure 5.29

1	[Drawing Screen]	Select boundary area first.
2	[Drawing Screen]	Select hole(s) next.

Technique to Master **T05.30** Adding Vertices to an Existing Polyline Boundary.

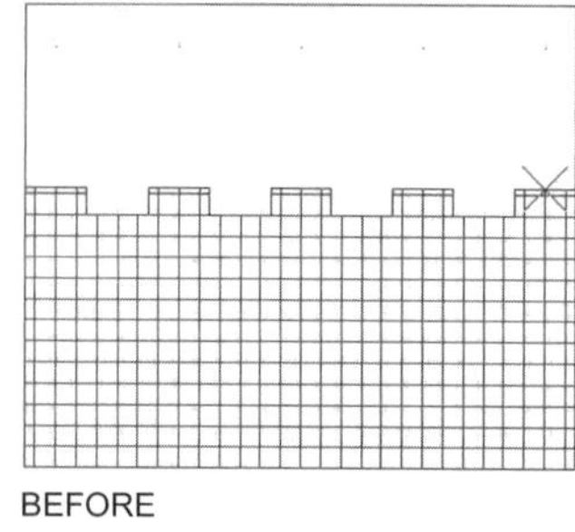
BEFORE

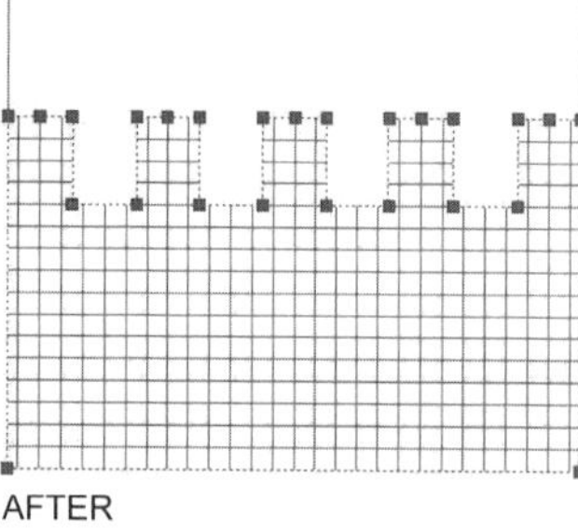
AFTER

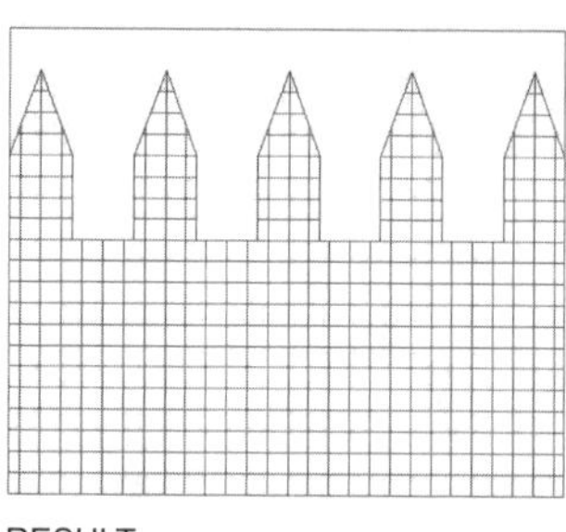
RESULT

Figure 5.30

1	Edit the trim boundary with the Pedit command by using the Edit Vertex command option. The X symbol locates the current position of the vertex.
2	It shows vertices added to the midpoints.
3	Move midpoint vertices by using grip editing to create points. Notice the hatch updates conform to the new boundary.

Snapping to Hatches

The ability to use object snaps to snap to existing hatch patterns is a drawing variable that you can set up in AutoCAD's Options dialogue box under the Drafting tab. Refer to Appendix D.

Advanced Polyline Construction and Editing

Vertex editing refers to the process of adding more vertices to an existing polyline to create additional corners. Figure 5.30 demonstrates how to use the Pedit command for Vertex Editing.

Chapter Exercises

Open the Chapter 5 folder located on the CD-ROM and access the chapter exercises. The exercises let you practice how to use the hatching and polyline tools to create floor patterns and ceiling materials.

Text, Annotation, and Dimensioning

6

Objectives

This chapter introduces you to the text and dimension tools within AutoCAD and demonstrates the conventional usage of text and dimensions within drawings. It also explains the relevance of text and dimensions within the design process, and places emphasis on proper annotation and dimensioning, scaling, and placement techniques. The end-of-chapter exercises let you get additional practice creating and editing text.

Understanding Annotations in Design

Sometimes you cannot rely on graphics alone to convey all the necessary information required to communicate your design intent. Therefore, you must use annotations to complete it. Annotation refers to labeling and notes you may add to drawings to communicate information that you cannot show in graphical form. Some objectives of annotations include:

- Notes to the contractors and subcontractors to help fabricate and construct the design
- Notes to the client (or professor) to help communicate design intentions
- Symbol notes that reference legends to keep drawings legible by reducing the amount of actual text within the drawing
- Notes to limit drawing detail

Examples of annotations include dimensioning, identification symbols, notes, titling, and leaders. Figure 6.1 shows examples of annotation.

Text is an important component of annotations in drawings. For drawings to be understood and considered as a drawing set, text should be legible, consistent, and straightforward.

Annotation Types

As already stated, you may use annotations in both working and presentation drawings to include information that is not readily apparent in graphic form. The typical annotations are described below.

- Project titles and other project information, which may include information that repeats on each sheet of a project, similar to the running heads of a newspaper or book
- The design firm's name and location help to identify the owners of the drawing sheets
- The date and job number. The date usually represents the submission date at the end of a design phase. The job number is unique to each project and is used in the office to track a project's profits or losses.
- Sheet titles provide a descriptive heading for the types of drawings found on the sheet.
- Drawing sheet numbers organize each sheet numerically within a project set. Sheet numbers make it easy to locate a specific drawing within a large set of drawings.
- Total sheets. Since a project contains multiple drawing sheets, each sheet identifies the total amount of sheets within a project to help safeguard against missing sheets.

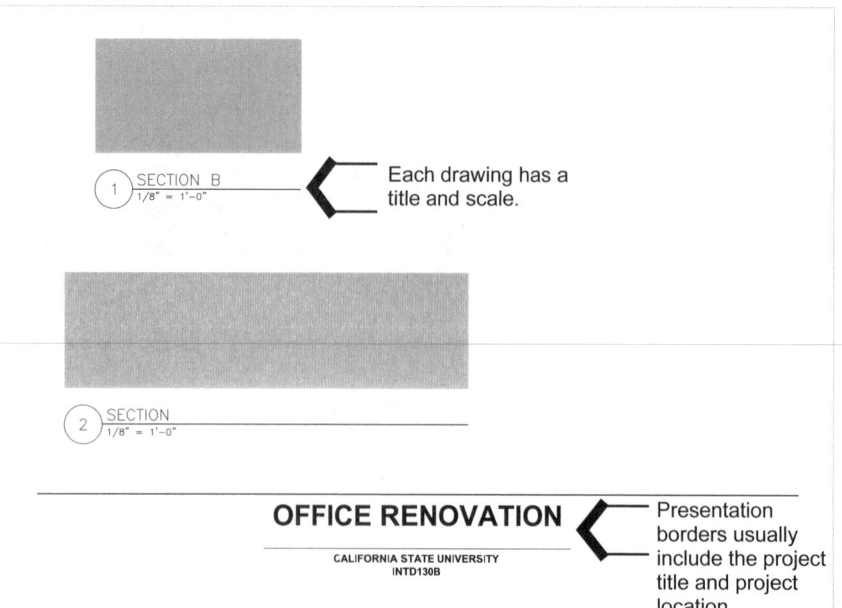

Figure 6.1a Examples of annotations used in student presentation drawings. Each drawing is identified with a title and scale directly below it.

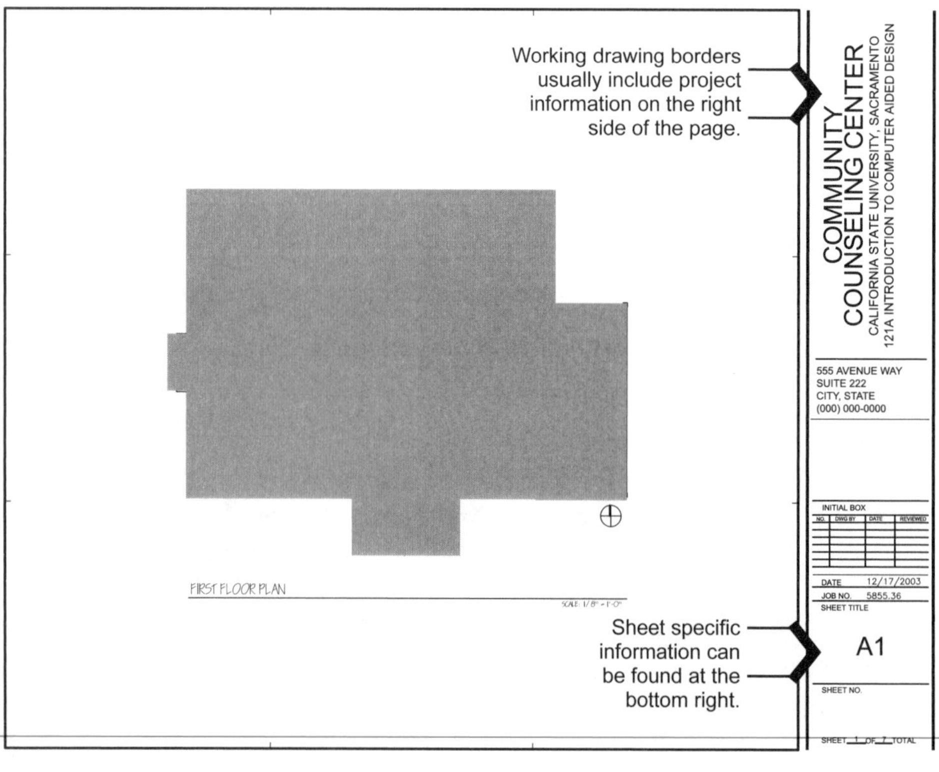

Figure 6.1b Examples of annotations used in student presentation drawings. All drawing sheets include a border, also called a title block. Information about the project and designer is noted within the border.

- Drawing titles and drawing scales are used to communicate the title and scale for each drawing located on a sheet. Multiple drawings on one sheet are usually numbered so that references to each drawing are possible.
- General notes and keynotes are typically placed along the left or right side of a drawing, away from the drawing itself. General notes provide directions that are not object-specific. Keynotes reference a specific area on a drawing and are used to associate the note to the area it references.

- Leader notes are a part of the drawing and add additional information to the item they reference.
- Annotation tags, also known as identification tags, are used to identify a particular building component or space within the design. You can use tags to provide individual identification to an object or a room or to assign it a type. Typical identification symbols include the following:
  —Room name and room number tags, which identify the room or space
  —Window and door tags, which provide a way to type and number each door and window in the building design
  —Furniture and equipment tags that link each furniture and equipment item with a schedule that identifies their manufacturer and other related information
  —Finish tags, which provide information about a room wall, a floor, and ceiling finishes
  —Wall tags, which provide information about the construction of the identified wall
  —Elevation tags, which include floor and ceiling finish tags typically found on section and elevation drawings. They are used to identify the height (elevation) of a horizontal floor or ceiling surface.
  —Legends are placed on the sides of drawings and help to reference various symbols found on the floor and ceiling plans to their respective product or material finish. Floor finish and ceiling legends are widely used legend types in both working and presentation drawings.
- Callouts. Since most design projects consist of more than one drawing sheet, callouts were created to reference one drawing to another drawing. Most callouts are located on floor plans, which provide references to any section, elevation, and detail drawings located on other drawings.

All of the annotation types listed thus far have specific text size and formatting requirements. Many of these requirements come from individual office standards. See Appendix I for a sample of annotation and callout symbols scaled for 1/8" and 1/4" plotting.

Controlling Text Height in Model Space

Remember that floor plans and elevations are drawn at real scale, that is, walls that are 6 inches wide are drawn within AutoCAD as 6 inches wide. If this same rule is applied to text, however, it would display much too small in comparison with the rooms and building objects surrounding it. This is because the heights of all text and dimensions need to be adjusted for eventual plotting.

This relationship refers to the ratio between the drawing's text size and the eventual printed/plotted text size. For you to place text or dimensions at the correct height and scale within a drawing, you must know the eventual plotting scale of the drawing. In other words, for you to place the room labels at the appropriate size on the floor plan shown, you must decide whether the floor plan will be printed at 1/4" = 1'-0" or 1/8" = 1'-0" or 3/16" = 1'-0". Each of these selections creates a different AutoCAD text height for the room labels. Notice however, that although the scale of the drawings changes when printed, the text height remains consistent as shown in Figure 6.2.

Calculating Text Sizes

To create room names to approximate an eighth of an inch in height when printed at 1/4" = 1'-0", the text size in AutoCAD will need to be 6 inches:

X * 12 * Y = AutoCAD text height;

where X is the height of the eventual plotted text;

and Y represents the plot scale's denominator.

1/8 * 12 * 4 = 6 inches

You would therefore size all room names and notes within AutoCAD to 6 inches to plot correctly at 1/4 scale. Table 6.1 shows the text heights in relation to their plotted scale and text size.

Choosing Your Text Size for the Different Annotation Types

As seen in Appendix I, each of the annotation types has specific text size and formatting requirements. While these requirements are generally directed by the specific CAD standards of design firms, some basic guidelines can be used for determining how text should print. In general, standard sizes for the different annotation types are as follows:

- Notes: 3/32" to 1/8".
- Legend or note titles: 3/32" to 3/16".
- Drawing titles: 3/16" to 3/8".
- Drawing scale: 1/8".
- Sheet titles: no larger than 3/4" and should reduce in size from title to subtitle to topic. (For example, 3/4" title, 3/8" subtitle, and 3/16" info in border that is not as important.)

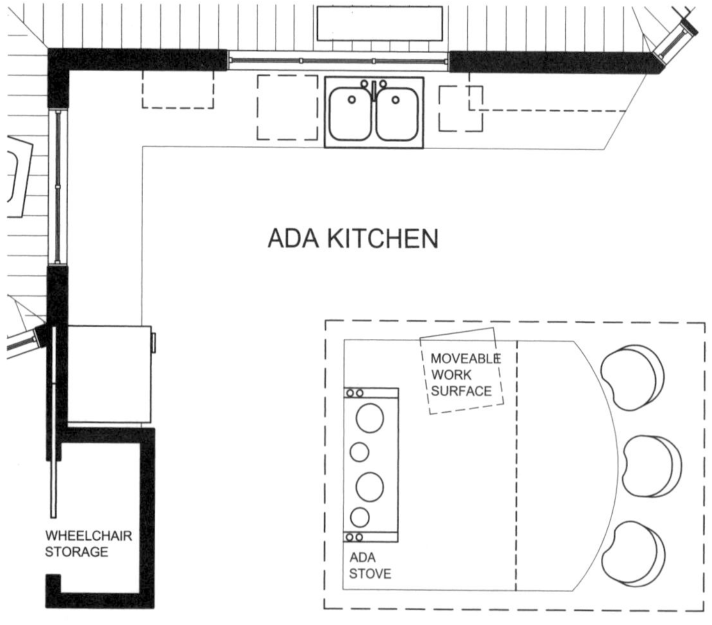

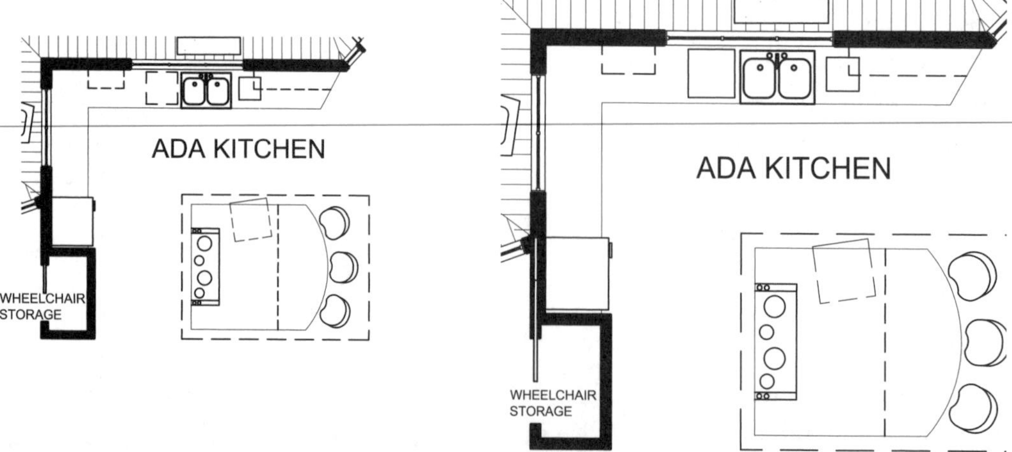

Figure 6.2 Controlling the text height in model space

Table 6.1 Model Space Text Height Scaling

Output Plotted Scale	Text Height in Model Space for 1/16" (text style)	Text Height in Model Space for 3/32" (text style)	Text Height in Model Space for 1/8"	Text Height in Model Space for 3/16" (text style)	Text Height in Model Space for 1/4"	Text Height in Model Space for 3/8"
1/32" = 1'-0"	2'-0"	3'-0"	4'-0"	6'-0"	8'-0"	12'-0"
1/16" = 1'-0"	1'-0"	1'-6"	2'-0"	3'-0"	4'-0"	6'-0"
1/8" = 1'-0"	6"	9"	1'-0"	1'-6"	2'-0"	3'-0"
1/4" = 1'-0"	3"	4.5"	6"	9"	1'-0"	1'-6"
3/8" = 1'-0"	2"	3"	4"	6"	8"	12"
1/2" = 1'-0"	1.5"	2.25"	3"	4.5"	6"	9"
1" = 1'-0"	3/4"	1.125"	1.5"	2.25"	3"	4.5"
3/4" = 1'-0"	1"	1.5"	2"	3"	4"	6"
1 1/2" = 1'-0"	1/2"	.75"	1"	1.5"	2"	3"
3" = 1'-0"	1/4"	3/8"	1/2"	3/4"	1"	1.5"
6" = 1'-0"	1/8"	3/16"	1/4"	3/8"	1/2"	3/4"

Text in AutoCAD

To create annotation within AutoCAD, you primarily use the text tools. The paragraphs that follow introduce the text types and properties and their creation and editing methods.

Types of Text

Mtext and Dtext are two text types that exist in current versions of AutoCAD. Mtext text is AutoCAD's version of paragraph text, that is, text that wraps within a specified column width. Dtext, AutoCAD's old method of text entry, is used for single-line text entry.

Mtext

Paragraph text is now the default text type used in AutoCAD. The Mtext command lets users create an invisible box that determines how text wraps around the drawing. The Mtext command is a dialogue-driven command. Figure 6.3 displays the various parts of the Mtext dialogue box, including the formatting toolbar, ruler, and editing area.

Dtext

Use the Dtext command for single-line text entry. It is command-line driven, as illustrated in Figure 6.4. Figure 6.5 demonstrates Mtext placement.

Text Properties

In addition to the general properties standard to all AutoCAD geometry (layer, lineweight, linetype, and so on), there are additional properties unique to text objects. These properties can be divided into two groups—the properties that are saved within a text style and the properties that are modified independently of style.

Properties Saved in Text Styles

Text styles are similar to those you can set up within any word processing program. Their main purpose is to provide consistency in text appearance throughout a drawing. Text style properties include font type, font style, text height, text slant, and text width.

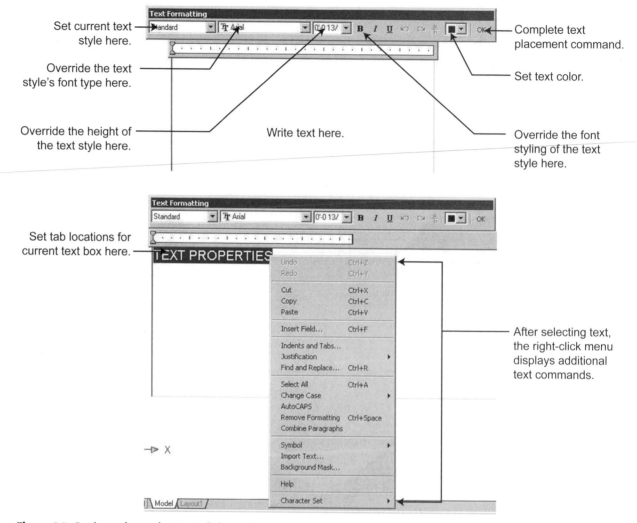

Set current text style here.

Override the text style's font type here.

Override the height of the text style here.

Write text here.

Complete text placement command.

Set text color.

Override the font styling of the text style here.

Text Formatting

Standard | Arial | 0'-0 13/ | B I U | OK

Set tab locations for current text box here.

TEXT PROPERTIES

Undo Ctrl+Z
Redo Ctrl+Y
Cut Ctrl+X
Copy Ctrl+C
Paste Ctrl+V
Insert Field... Ctrl+F
Indents and Tabs...
Justification
Find and Replace... Ctrl+R
Select All Ctrl+A
Change Case
AutoCAPS
Remove Formatting Ctrl+Space
Combine Paragraphs
Symbol
Import Text...
Background Mask...
Help
Character Set

After selecting text, the right-click menu displays additional text commands.

Model / Layout1

Figure 6.3 Getting to know the Mtext dialogue box

Technique to Master **T06.04** Placing Single-Line Text

Command: DTEXT
Current text style: "RomanS" Text height: 0'-0 3/32"
Specify start point of text or [Justify/Style]:
Specify height <0'-0 3/32">: 1/8"
Specify rotation angle of text <0.00>: 0

3

4 PLACED DTEXT PLACED DTEXT
second line

Figure 6.4

1	[Command Line]	Use the Dtext command.
2	[Drawing Screen]	Locate the start point. The start or insertion point always becomes the justification point. Since the default justification when placing text is left, the start point will be the left side of the text.
3	[Command Line]	AutoCAD prompts you to determine the text style, text height, and rotation.
4	[Drawing Screen]	Type in text. You can place text on multiple lines by pressing Enter.

Technique to Master **T06.05** Placing Multi-line Text

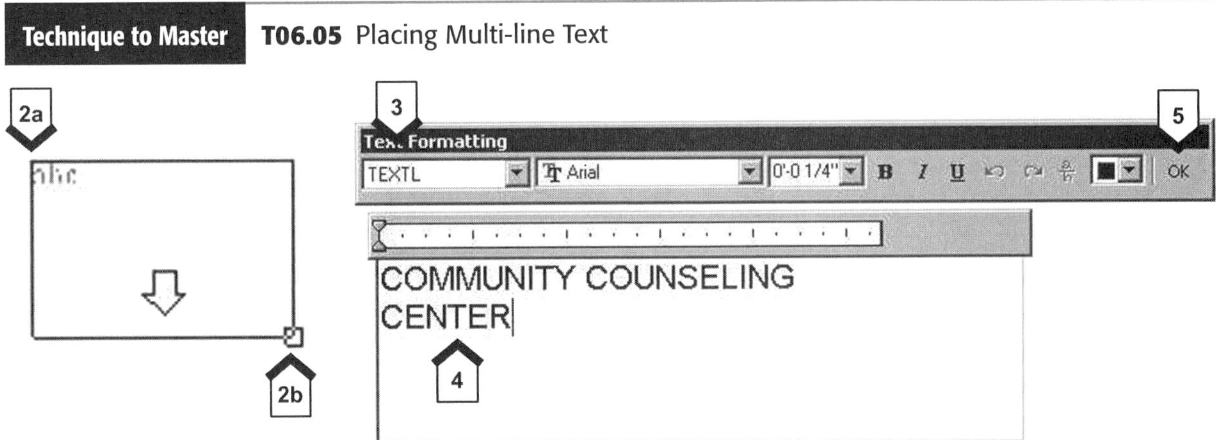

Figure 6.5

1	[Command Line]	Use the text command.
2a, 2b	[Drawing Screen]	Specify the rectangle, by determining the first corner and the opposite corner, for the text box.
3	[Mtext dialogue box]	Select the appropriate text style.
4	[Mtext dialogue box]	Type in the desired text.
5	[Mtext dialogue box]	Left-click OK to complete the command.

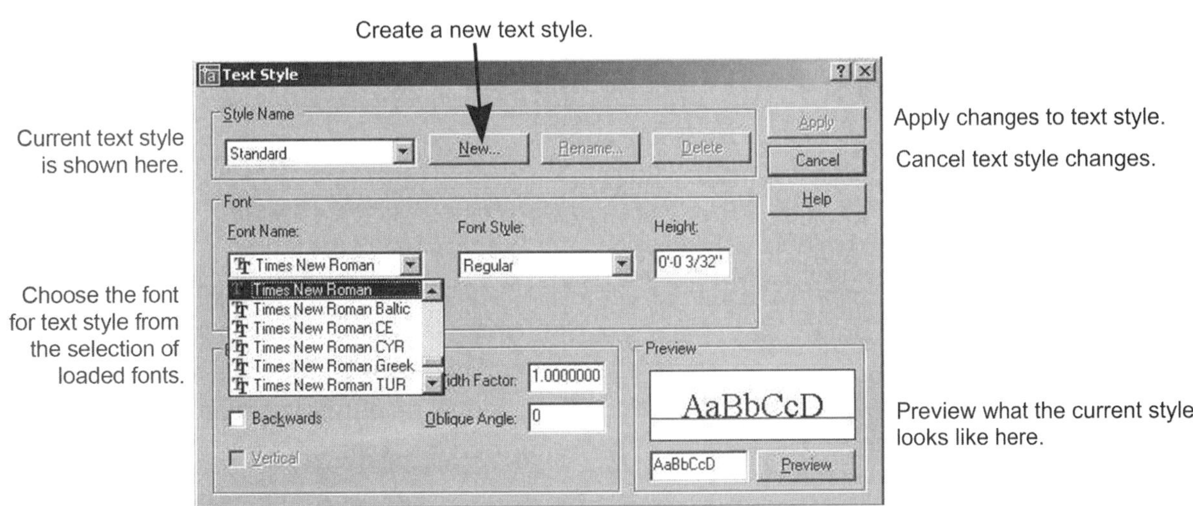

Figure 6.6 Getting to know the Text Style dialogue box

There are four text properties you can save in text styles. Set up text styles through the Text Style command's dialogue box. Figure 6.6 shows the various parts of the Text Style dialogue box, and Figure 6.7 demonstrates the style creation process.

Property: Font Name

Select the font for the text style. There are two types of fonts used to create text within AutoCAD. TrueType fonts are the familiar fonts found within the PC Windows environment. AutoCAD's own font definitions are available and visible only within the program. AutoCAD definitions have a slight advantage over TrueType fonts because they display and print very quickly. However, TrueType fonts tend to look better and always print smoothly. Unlike AutoCAD's font definitions, TrueType fonts ignore lineweights.

Technique to Master **T06.07** Creating Text Styles

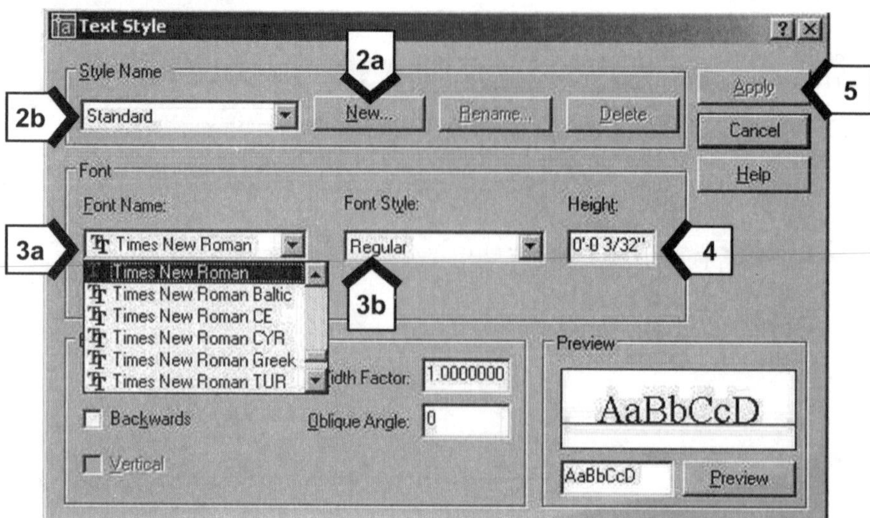

Figure 6.7

1	[Command Line]	Access the Style command, or type ST and press Enter.
2a, 2b	[Text Style dialogue box]	Click the New button to create a new style or choose an existing style from the arrow drop-down menu.
3a, 3b	[Text Style dialogue box]	Select the Font Name and Font Style.
4	[Text Style dialogue box]	Set the text height. See Table 6.1 to determine proper text height value.
5	[Text Style dialogue box]	Apply changes. Close the dialogue box.

Property: Font Style

Font style refers to the ability to bold or italicize a font. You can use this property only for TrueType fonts.

Property: Height

The text style property Height allows you to define both fixed height text styles and variable height text styles. Create variable height text styles by leaving the text height at 0"; they are best used for dimension text styles.

Property: Width Factor

The width factor allows you to selectively compress or expand the initial font definition's width. Experiment with different width factors, for example, 1 and 1.5 to visualize the results.

Properties Accessed Through the Properties Palette

The Properties palette displays additional text properties that are modified independently of text style. They include justification, direction, width, height, rotation, background mask, and line spacing.

Property: Justification

Text justification refers to its alignment. You can set this while determining text placement or afterward through the Properties palette. Justification options for Mtext include the following: TL (top left), TC (top center), TR (top right), ML (middle left), MC (middle center), MR (middle right), BL (bottom left), BC (bottom center), and BR (bottom right) (Figure 6.8).

Figure 6.8 The Justification property

Figure 6.9 The Align Justification property

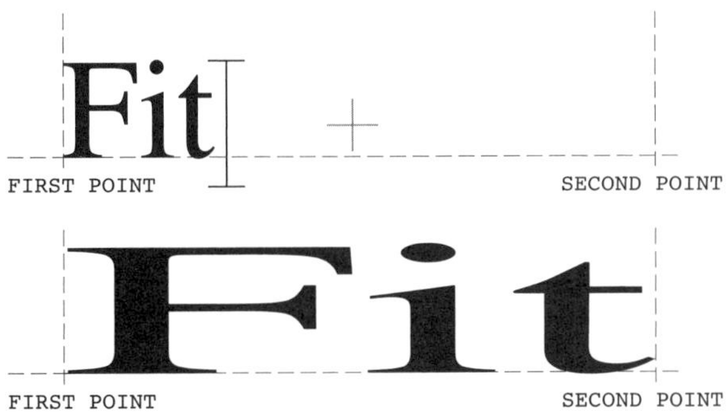

Figure 6.10 The Fit Justification property

Additional justification options are available for Dtext and include the following:

Align aligns and scales the text to fit between two specified points (Figure 6.9)

Fit adjusts the width factor of the text to fit between two specified points (Figure 6.10)

Center centers the text horizontally

Middle centers the text horizontally and vertically

Right right justifies the text

Editing Text

Text modifications include changes to the text itself as well as its formatting and paragraph size.

Modifying the Text Box Using Grips

Left-click on any existing multi-line text and notice the grip point at each corner of the paragraph text object. You can control the width of the text box by clicking and dragging the grip points or by using the Properties palette's width value.

Modifying Text Properties Using the Properties Palette

Figure 6.11a identifies the text properties that can be modified through the Properties palette. These include the text style, justification, direction, width, height, rotation, background mask, and line spacing properties.

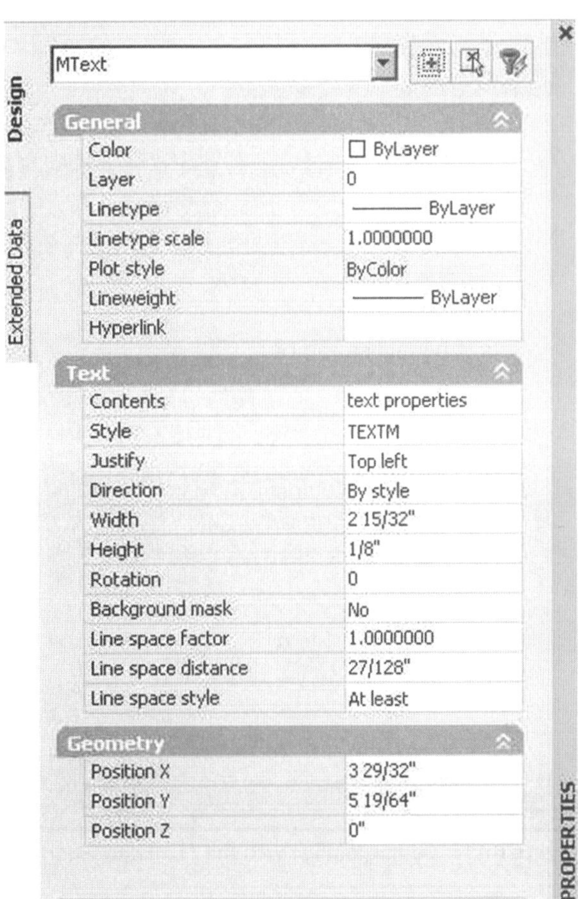

Figure 6.11a Set text properties for selected text object in the Properties Palette.

The Text Editor Shortcut Menu

You can edit text content by double-clicking on existing placed text.

> **Box 6.1**
> When you double-click on any text, it opens the Mtext Editor; the actual AutoCAD text editing command is Ddeditor the shortcut ED.

Additional text command options and properties are available through the text editor's right-click menu (see Figure 6.11b). Valuable right-click commands include text-justification changes, text symbol access, text-importing commands, and more.

Using the Text Tools in Common Drawing Applications

Figures 6.12 through 6.16 apply the concepts and techniques you've learned to a variety of common drawing problems, including creating project titles for title blocks, abbreviation tables, and annotation callouts.

Specialty Text Commands

There are many additional text-related commands that are useful during the drawing process, including Spell, Symbol, Find and Replace, Qtext, and Import Text. With the exception of the Spell and Qtext commands, most text-related specialty commands are found in the Mtext Editor's right-click menu.

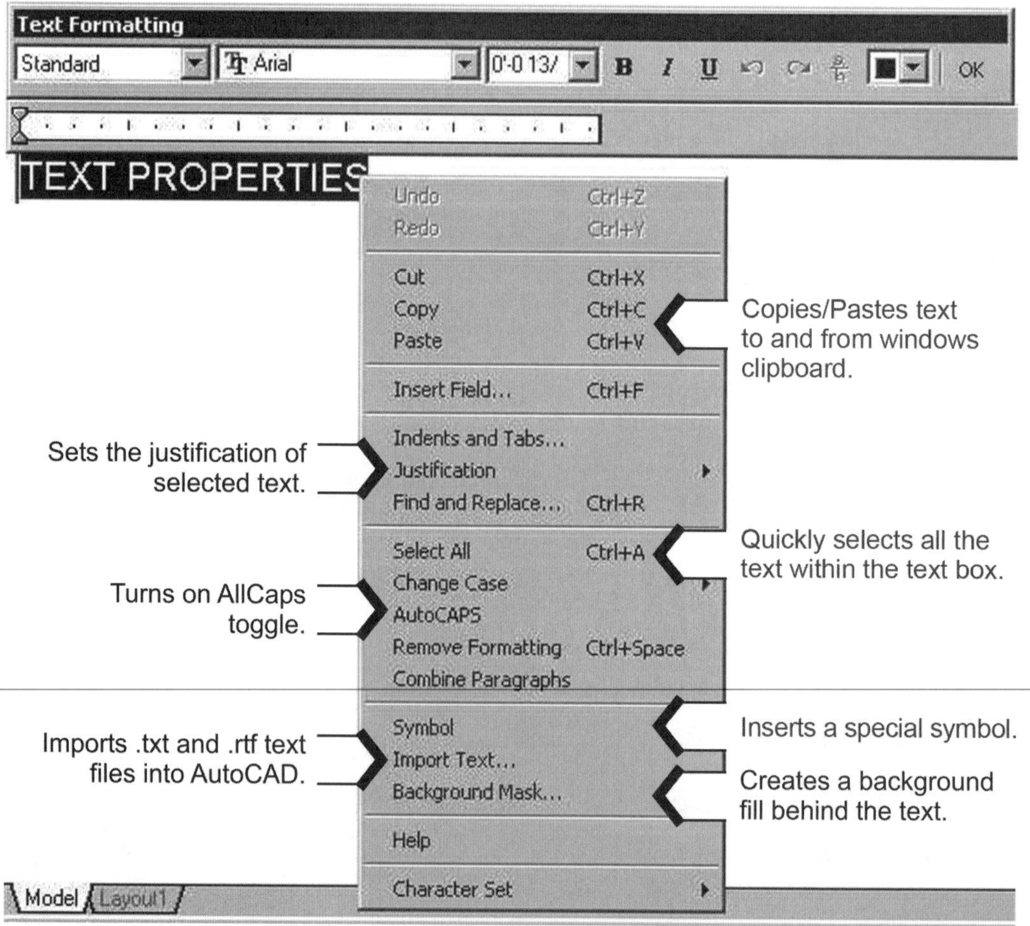

Figure 6.11b Getting familiar with the Text Editor shortcut menu

T06.12 Creating a Project Title for Title Blocks

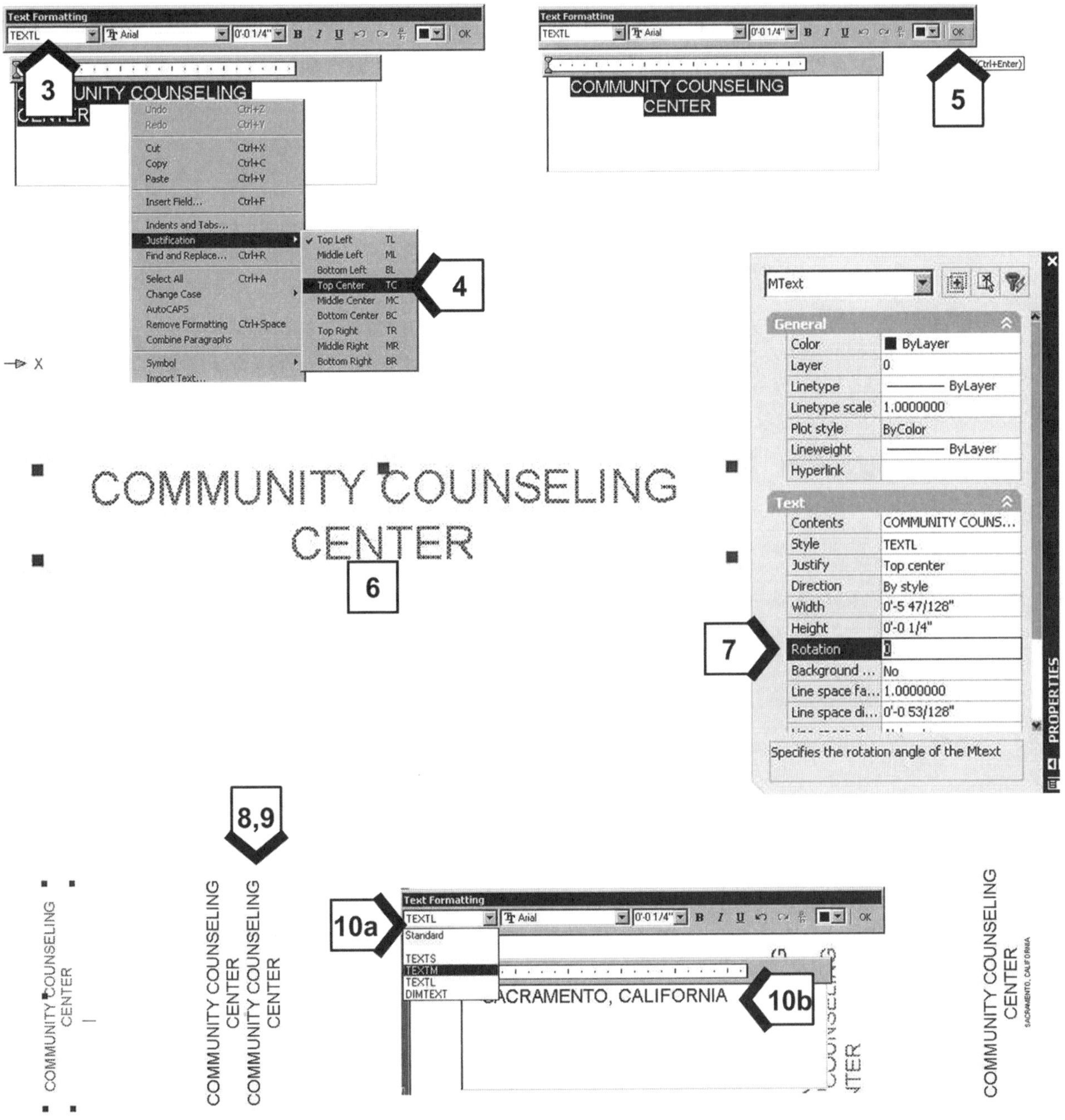

Figure 6.12

1	Create the title block text styles using Technique T06.07.	
2	Create multi-line text using Technique T06.05.	
3	[Mtext Editor]	Select the text and set to correct text style.
4	[Mtext Editor]	Select text then right-click and change the justification to Top Center.
5	[Mtext Editor]	Click OK to exit Mtext Editor.
6	[Drawing Screen]	Select text.
7	[Properties palette]	Rotate text 90 degrees.
8	[Drawing Screen]	Copy text and make sure Ortho toggle is on.
9	[Drawing Screen]	Double-click on copied text.
10a, 10b	[Mtext Editor]	Select text and change Text Style to Textm. Modify text to read location of project.

Technique to Master **T06.13** Aligning Multi-line Text Objects

GENERAL NOTES

1. CONTRACTOR SHALL BE RESPONSIBLE FOR ALL APPLICABLE CODES AND REGULATIONS.

2. DO NOT SCALE DRAWINGS, WRITTEN DIMENSIONS TAKE PRECEDENCE. OVER SCALE. SHOULD ANY DISCREPANCIES OCCUR, NOTIFY ARCHITECT BEFORE PROCEEDING WITH WORK.

3. CONTRACTOR SHALL FIELD VERIFY ALL DIMENSIONS AND EXISTING CONDITIONS AT THE SITE AND SHALL REPORT ANY DISCREPANCIES IN WRITING TO THE ARCHITECT PRIOR TO SUBMITTALS.

4. SPECIFIC ITEMS NOTED TO BE VERIFIED OR FIELD VERIFIED ARE REQUIRED TO BE VERIFIED PRIOR TO ORDERING MATERIALS OR PROCEEDING WITH THE WORK.

GENERAL NOTES

1. CONTRACTOR SHALL BE RESPONSIBLE FOR ALL APPLICABLE CODES AND REGULATIONS.

2. DO NOT SCALE DRAWINGS, WRITTEN DIMENSIONS TAKE PRECEDENCE. OVER SCALE. SHOULD ANY DISCREPANCIES OCCUR, NOTIFY ARCHITECT BEFORE PROCEEDING WITH WORK.

3. CONTRACTOR SHALL FIELD VERIFY ALL DIMENSIONS AND EXISTING CONDITIONS AT THE SITE AND SHALL REPORT ANY DISCREPANCIES IN WRITING TO THE ARCHITECT PRIOR TO SUBMITTALS.

4. SPECIFIC ITEMS NOTED TO BE VERIFIED OR FIELD VERIFIED ARE REQUIRED TO BE VERIFIED PRIOR TO ORDERING MATERIALS OR PROCEEDING WITH THE WORK.

Insert

GENERAL NOTES

1. CONTRACTOR SHALL BE RESPONSIBLE FOR ALL APPLICABLE CODES AND REGULATIONS.

2. DO NOT SCALE DRAWINGS, WRITTEN DIMENSIONS TAKE PRECEDENCE. OVER SCALE. SHOULD ANY DISCREPANCIES OCCUR, NOTIFY ARCHITECT BEFORE PROCEEDING WITH WORK.

3. CONTRACTOR SHALL FIELD VERIFY ALL DIMENSIONS AND EXISTING CONDITIONS AT THE SITE AND SHALL REPORT ANY DISCREPANCIES IN WRITING TO THE ARCHITECT PRIOR TO SUBMITTALS.

4. SPECIFIC ITEMS NOTED TO BE VERIFIED OR FIELD VERIFIED ARE REQUIRED TO BE VERIFIED PRIOR TO ORDERING MATERIALS OR PROCEEDING WITH THE WORK.

Perpendicular

GENERAL NOTES

CONTRACTOR SHALL BE RESPONSIBLE FOR ALL APPLICABLE CODES AND REGULATIONS.

2. DO NOT SCALE DRAWINGS, WRITTEN DIMENSIONS TAKE PRECEDENCE. OVER SCALE. SHOULD ANY DISCREPANCIES OCCUR, NOTIFY ARCHITECT BEFORE PROCEEDING WITH WORK.

3. CONTRACTOR SHALL FIELD VERIFY ALL DIMENSIONS AND EXISTING CONDITIONS AT THE SITE AND SHALL REPORT ANY DISCREPANCIES IN WRITING TO THE ARCHITECT PRIOR TO SUBMITTALS.

4. SPECIFIC ITEMS NOTED TO BE VERIFIED OR FIELD VERIFIED ARE REQUIRED TO BE VERIFIED PRIOR TO ORDERING MATERIALS OR PROCEEDING WITH THE WORK.

1. CONTRACTOR SHALL BE RESPONSIBLE FOR ALL APPLICABLE CODES AND REGULATIONS.

2. DO NOT SCALE DRAWINGS, WRITTEN DIMENSIONS TAKE PRECEDENCE. OVER SCALE. SHOULD ANY DISCREPANCIES OCCUR, NOTIFY ARCHITECT BEFORE PROCEEDING WITH WORK.

3. CONTRACTOR SHALL FIELD VERIFY ALL DIMENSIONS AND EXISTING CONDITIONS AT THE SITE AND SHALL REPORT ANY DISCREPANCIES IN WRITING TO THE ARCHITECT PRIOR TO SUBMITTALS.

4. SPECIFIC ITEMS NOTED TO BE VERIFIED OR FIELD VERIFIED ARE REQUIRED TO BE VERIFIED PRIOR TO ORDERING MATERIALS OR PROCEEDING WITH THE WORK.

GENERAL NOTES

1. CONTRACTOR SHALL BE RESPONSIBLE FOR ALL APPLICABLE CODES AND REGULATIONS.

2. DO NOT SCALE DRAWINGS, WRITTEN DIMENSIONS TAKE PRECEDENCE. OVER SCALE. SHOULD ANY DISCREPANCIES OCCUR, NOTIFY ARCHITECT BEFORE PROCEEDING WITH WORK.

3. CONTRACTOR SHALL FIELD VERIFY ALL DIMENSIONS AND EXISTING CONDITIONS AT THE SITE AND SHALL REPORT ANY DISCREPANCIES IN WRITING TO THE ARCHITECT PRIOR TO SUBMITTALS.

4. SPECIFIC ITEMS NOTED TO BE VERIFIED OR FIELD VERIFIED ARE REQUIRED TO BE VERIFIED PRIOR TO ORDERING MATERIALS OR PROCEEDING WITH THE WORK.

Figure 6.13

1	[Drawing Screen]	Create text using the Dtext (single-line text) or Mtext (multi-line text) commands.
2	[Drawing Screen]	Draw a temporary construction line that represents vertical alignment.
3a, 3b	[Drawing Screen]	Move the first text object to the construction line. Use Object Snap Insertion to snap to each text object's insertion point. Then use the Perpendicular snap to snap to the vertical line.
4	[Drawing Screen]	Repeat for each text object.

Technique to Master **T06.14** Creating a Presentation Title Block

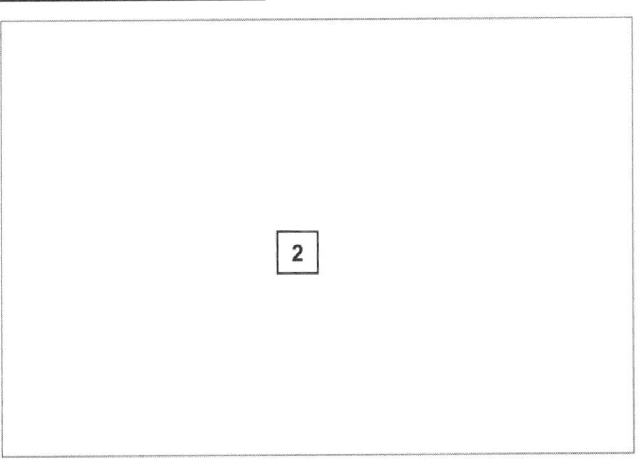

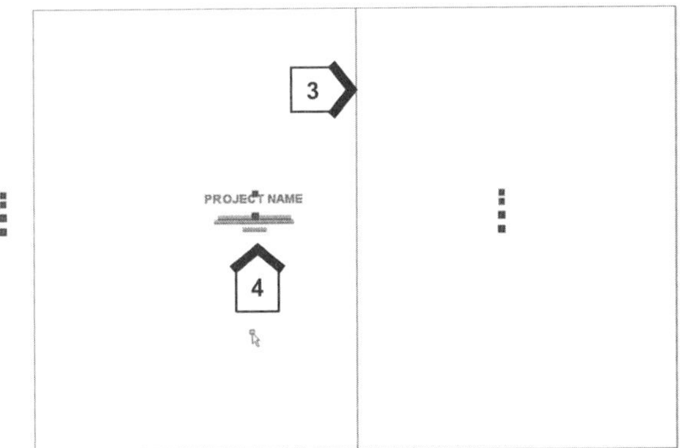

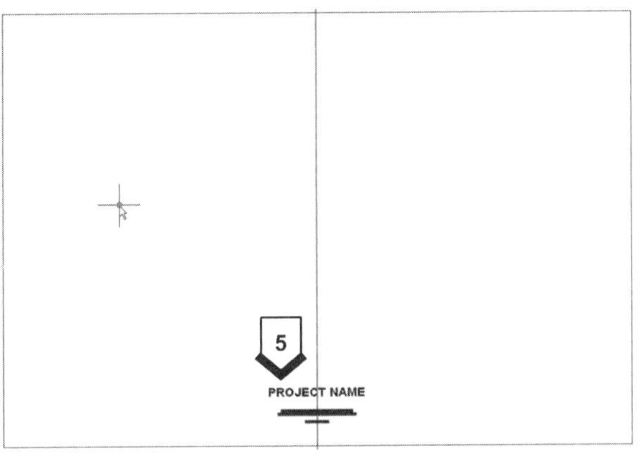

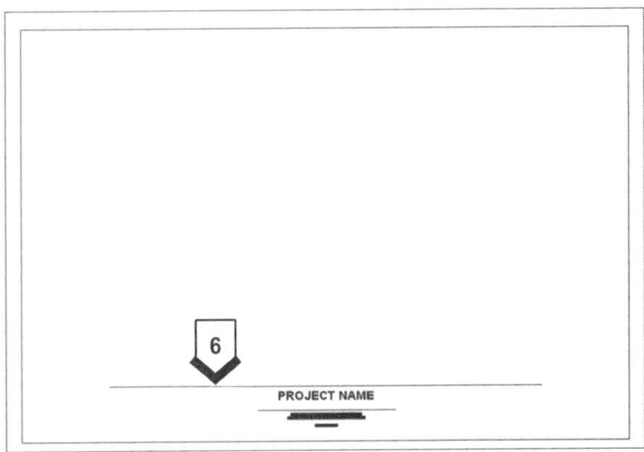

Figure 6.14

1	Use the recommended text sizes for the different text objects. Refer to Table 6.1 on page 111.	
2	[Drawing Screen]	Create a rectangle that represents the paper border.
3	[Drawing Screen]	Draw a temporary construction line at the midpoint of the rectangle.
4	[Drawing Screen]	Center justify the project title and location.
5	[Drawing Screen]	Center align text to sheet border.
6	[Drawing Screen]	Create lines between project title and location for compositional clarity.

Technique to Master **T06.15** Creating an Abbreviations Legend with Mtext

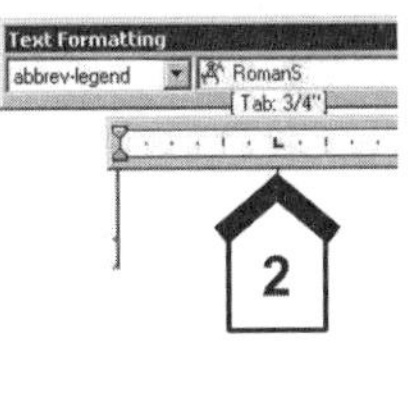

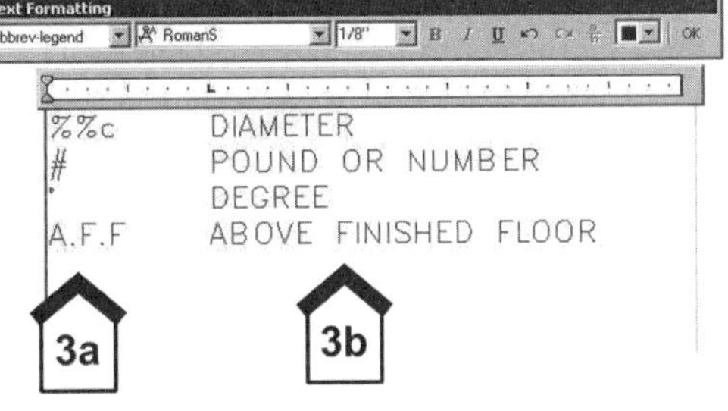

ABBREVIATIONS

∅	DIAMETER
#	POUND OR NUMBER
°	DEGREE
A.F.F	ABOVE FINISHED FLOOR

4

Figure 6.15

1	[Drawing Screen]	Create text using the Mtext (multi-line text) command. Refer to Technique T06.05.
2	[Mtext Editor]	Left-click on the tab ruler to place a tab location for the second column.
3a, 3b	[Mtext Editor]	Type the abbreviated word in the first column. Type the full word or phrase in the second column.
4	The resulting abbreviation list is shown.	

Technique to Master **T06.16** Creating Annotation Symbols Using Block Attributes

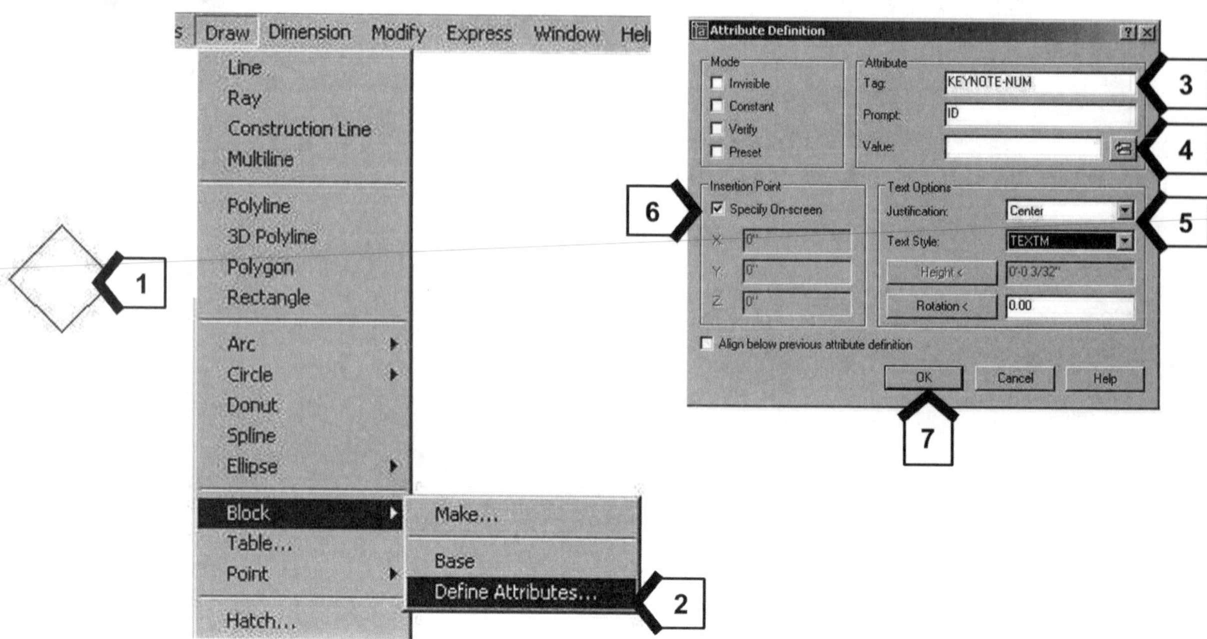

Figure 6.16

1	[Drawing Screen]	Create the geometry part of a symbol.
2	[Command Line]	Type ATTDEF and press Enter to create attribute text, or use Menu command.
3	[Attribute Definition dialogue box]	Name the attribute.
4	[Attribute Definition dialogue box]	If a default value is desired, type in the Value box.
5	[Attribute Definition dialogue box]	Specify the text style, justification, and rotation for the attribute.
6	[Attribute Definition dialogue box]	Check the Specify On-screen box.
7	[Attribute Definition dialogue box]	Click OK to exit.
8	[Drawing Screen]	Place the attribute text centered on the geometry by using object snaps. Repeat the attribute definition and placement for all the text lines you need.
9	[Drawing Screen]	Create the block. Refer to Techniques T04.09 and T04.10 to review block-creation procedures. When you select the objects for the block, select the attribute text individually in the order you want to see it.
10	The resulting Keynote symbol is shown.	

> **Box 6.2**
> Notice the amount and variety of additional commands available through the Mtext Editor's right-click menu. Most of these commands are easy to use and self-explanatory.

Spell-Checker

Similar to most word processing spell-checkers, the Spell command in AutoCAD is a simple spell-check program. If it finds misspelled words, AutoCAD tries to correct them through a dialogue box.

> **Box 6.3**
> The Spell command is also available in the Tools menu. The shortcut is SP.

To spell-check all the text in a drawing file, type in the word *all* when AutoCAD prompts you for a selection set.

Special Characters

There are about twenty special characters available in AutoCAD, including the degree symbol, the plus/minus symbol, and the diameter symbol, and you can access them through the Mtext Editor's right-click menu. When you access the Mtext Editor, you may insert symbols into paragraph text by simply selecting the symbols' names (Figure 6.17).

Find and Replace Command

The Find and Replace command lets you search for specified text strings and replace them with other text strings.

Qtext

Text objects take up a lot of memory, especially when the drawing is heavy on the text. Text-heavy drawings slow down your ability to process commands dramatically. Screen regeneration, screen redraws, zooms, and pans are all affected by slower processing (review Viewing in AutoCAD in Chapter 2). The Qtextmode system variable improves screen display speeds by temporarily changing text into rectangles (Figure 6.18).

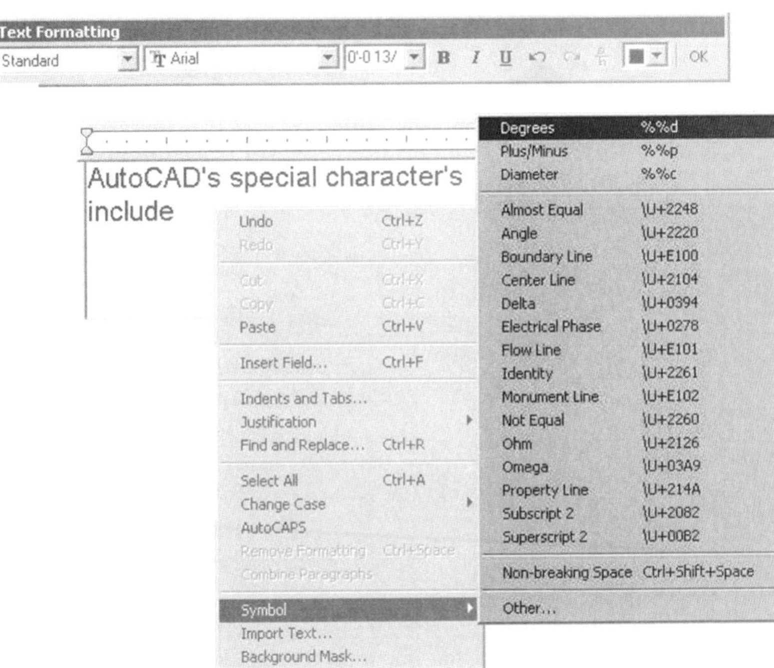

Figure 6.17 AutoCAD's special characters

HERE IS AUTOCAD TEXT AS IT WOULD NORMALLY SHOW IN A DRAWING. IF A DRAWING INCLUDES A LOT OF TEXT OBJECTS, THE DRAWING BECOMES SLOW AND UNMANAGEABLE. TO SPEED UP THE DRAWING SESSION, QTEXT TEMPORARILY CHANGES THE TEXT TO SQUARES.

Figure 6.18 The Qtextmode system variable improves screen display speeds by temporarily changing text into rectangles.

Importing Text from Other Software

Text from Microsoft Word or other word processing software can be imported into AutoCAD's Mtext Editor as demonstrated in Figure 6.19. The text, however, must first be converted to .txt or .rtf file types for AutoCAD to recognize the import. You can usually accomplish this conversion by using the Save As feature of most word-processing software.

Labeling with Leaders

Leaders are used to identify or clarify a visual element within a drawing. You will often see leaders in drawings identifying various elements (Figure 6.20). They are a combination of lines, terminuses, and text, and you can invoke them by typing the Qleader command or using the Dimension toolbar's Qleader tool (Figure 6.21).

> **Box 6.4**
> When placing leaders, make sure the terminus touches the object it identifies.

Dimensioning and Dimension Styles

While leaders are used to identify components within a drawing, dimensions communicate sizes and locations of building components. The basic AutoCAD dimensioning tools and how dimensions are properly placed on drawings are discussed in the paragraphs that follow.

Technique to Master **T06.19** Importing Text from Other Software

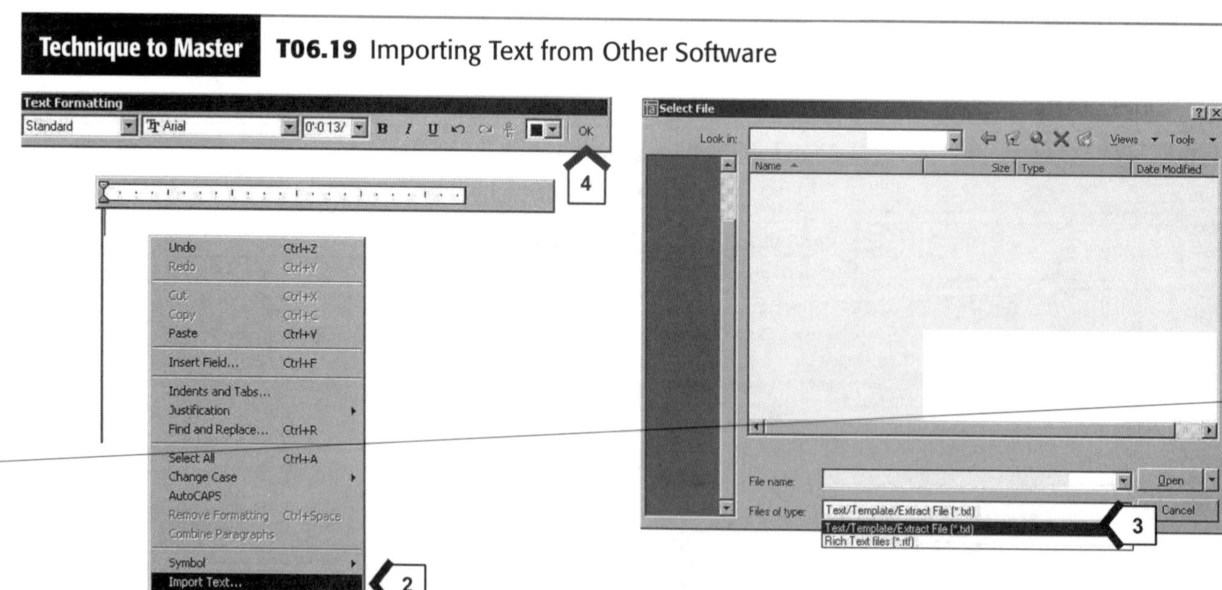

Figure 6.19

1	Access the Mtext command.	
2	[Mtext Editor dialogue box]	Right-click within the writing area and choose the Import Text command.
3	[Select File dialogue box]	Select .txt file or .rtf file to import. Note that you must convert .doc files before text importing can be successful.
4	[Mtext Editor]	Click OK to exit editor.

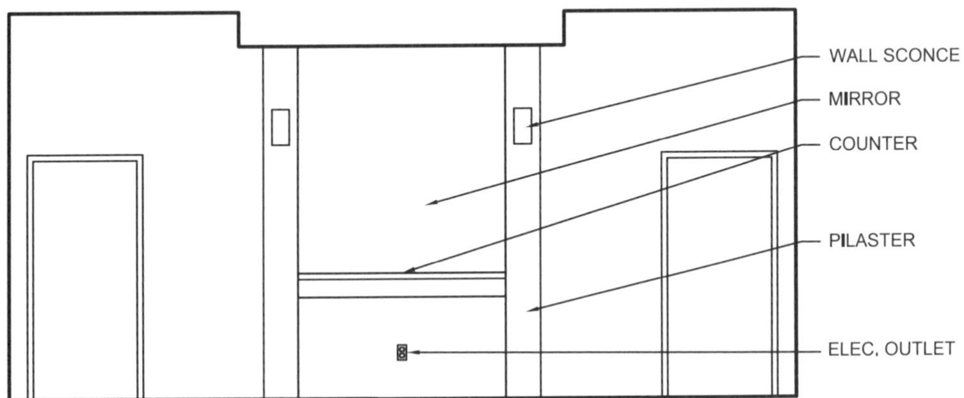

Figure 6.20 Examples of leaders in notes

Technique to Master **T06.21** Using Qleaders

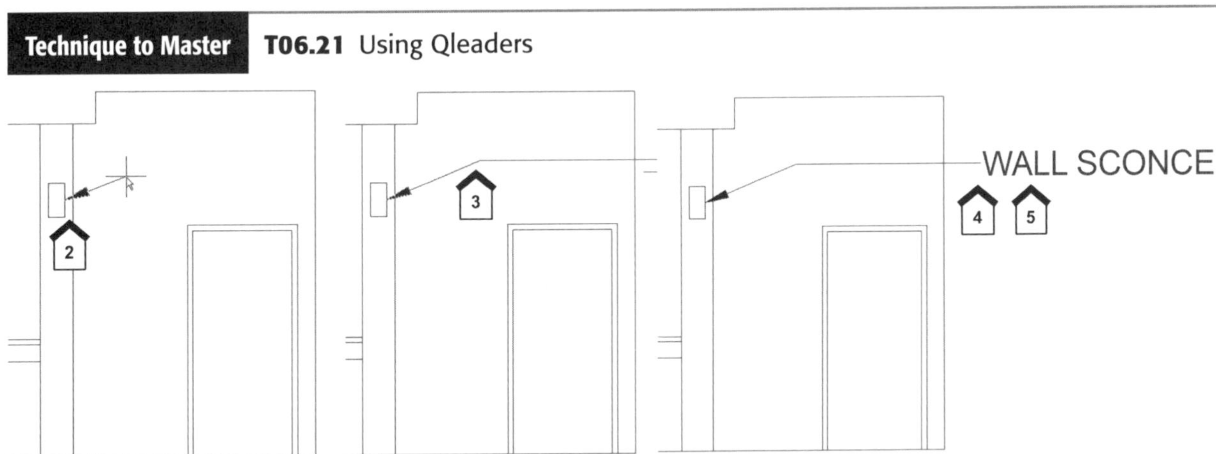

Figure 6.21

1	Access the Qleader command.	
2	[Drawing Screen]	Locate the first point of leader. This represents the arrow tip.
3	[Drawing Screen]	Locate the second point, which represents the end of diagonal part of the leader line.
4	[Drawing Screen]	With Ortho toggled on, locate the third point of the leader that creates the horizontal line.
5	[Drawing Screen]	Write the leader text.

The Dimension Types

AutoCAD includes six basic dimension types that provide the means to dimension linear and curved elements. These include the Linear, Aligned, Arc Length, Radius, Diameter, and Angular dimension types. The Baseline and Continue dimensioning tools offer additional flexibility to linear dimensions.

Linear Dimensions Linear dimensions measure the horizontal or vertical distance between two points.

Aligned Dimensions Similar to a Linear dimension, the Aligned dimension measures the parallel distance between two points.

Arc Length Dimensions The Arc length dimension measures the actual length of the curve in any arc segment.

Radius Dimensions Use this dimension tool to identify the radius of an arc or a circle.

Diameter Dimensions Similar to the Radius dimension tool, this tool measures the diameter of an arc or a circle.

Angular Dimensions This tool identifies the degree angle between two lines that are not parallel.

Baseline Dimensions Use Baseline dimensions to create multiple dimension strings that originate from the same start point.

Continue Dimensions Continue dimensions create a series of dimension strings that are placed end to end.

The Dimensioning Tools

The dimensioning commands can be found in the Dimension menu and Dimension toolbar (Figure 6.22). Dimension types are identified in Figure 6.23.

The Elements of a Dimension

Similar to text styles, dimension settings are saved formatting instructions for how a dimension looks. These settings make continuity between two or among more dimension objects consistent. All dimension settings are saved to a dimension style using the Dimstyle command. Some of the settings include the display of arrowheads, the location of extension lines, and the style of text that will be used. Dimensions, in general, look very similar to one another. Most dimensions include the following components shown in Figure 6.24. These components are described in more detail in the paragraphs that follow. Notice the display of each of these components can be altered within the dimension style.

The Dimension Text

The dimension text gives you the actual measurement or distance you have indicated. AutoCAD automatically computes the distance for you. Dimension text sits above the dimension line in architectural applications.

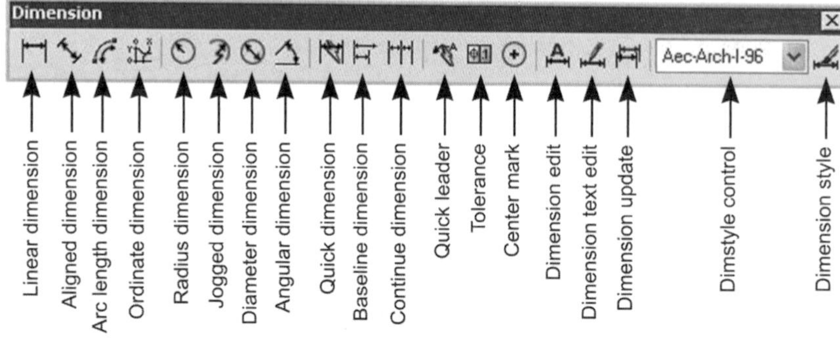

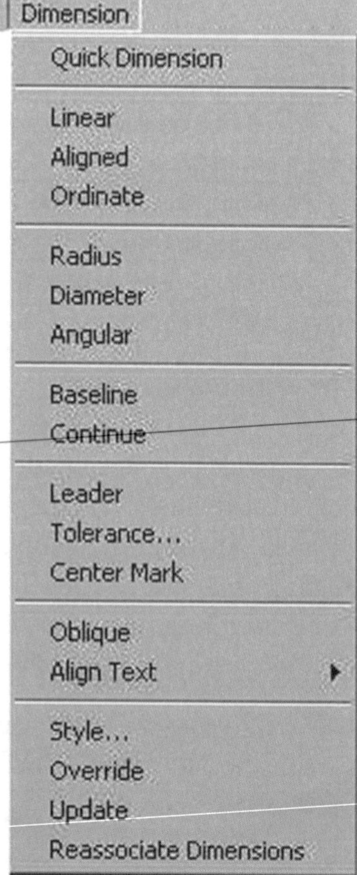

Figure 6.22 Getting to know the dimension toolbar and menu

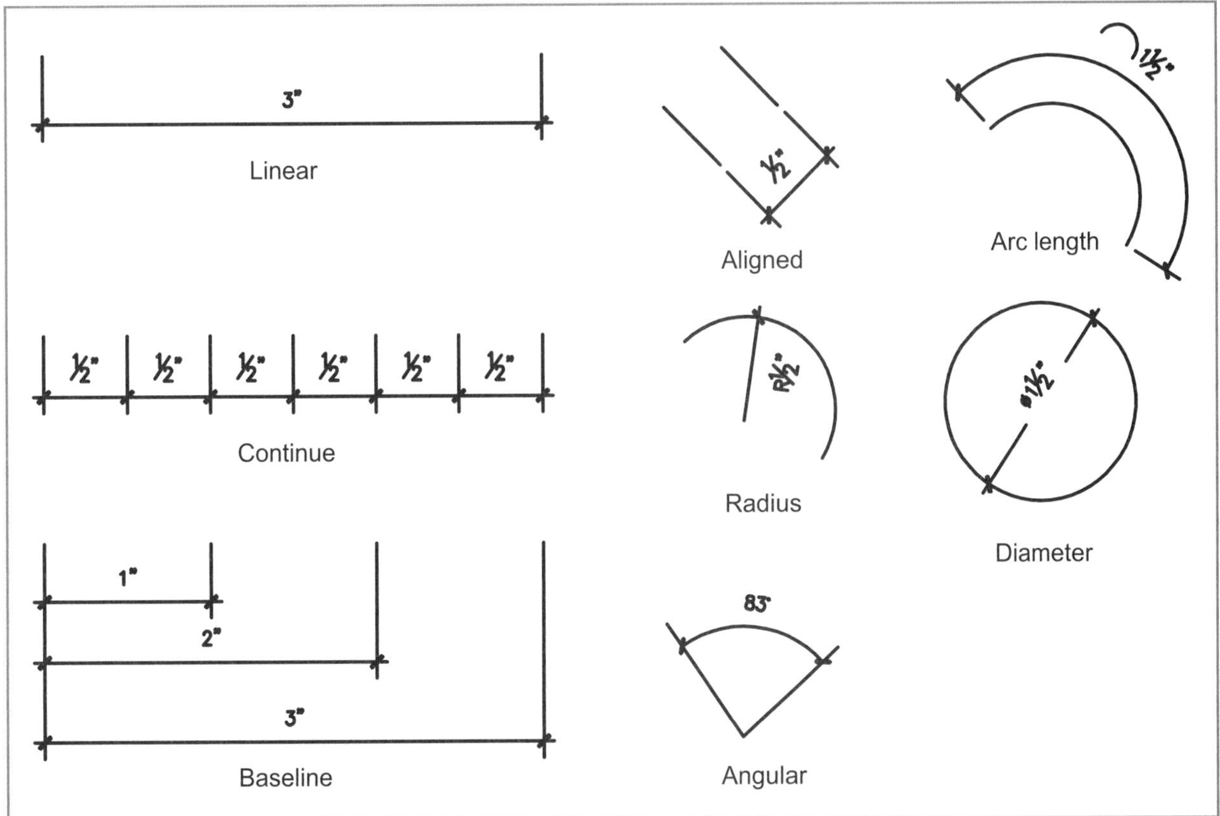

Figure 6.23 The dimension types

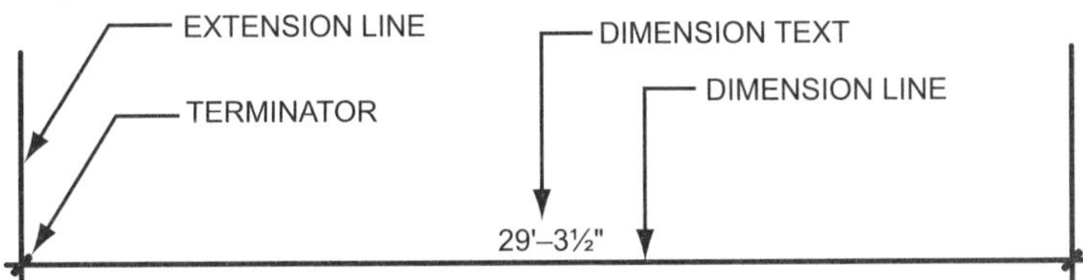

Figure 6.24 The elements of a dimension

The Dimension Line

This line connects the dimension text to the extension lines.

The Extension Lines

Extension lines indicate the limits of the measured area and intersect with the dimension line.

The Terminator Symbol

The terminator marks the point at which the dimension line intersects with the extension line. Terminator symbols are tick marks in most architectural applications.

A Look Behind the Scenes of a Dimension Style

Dimension styles are created and modified using the Dimension Style Manager, shown in Figure 6.25. The Dimension Style Manager saves the following information:

- Extension lines; dimension lines; and terminator shape, size, lineweight, and color
- Dimension text color, size, and placement
- The type of units of the dimension, including how the measurement is rounded off

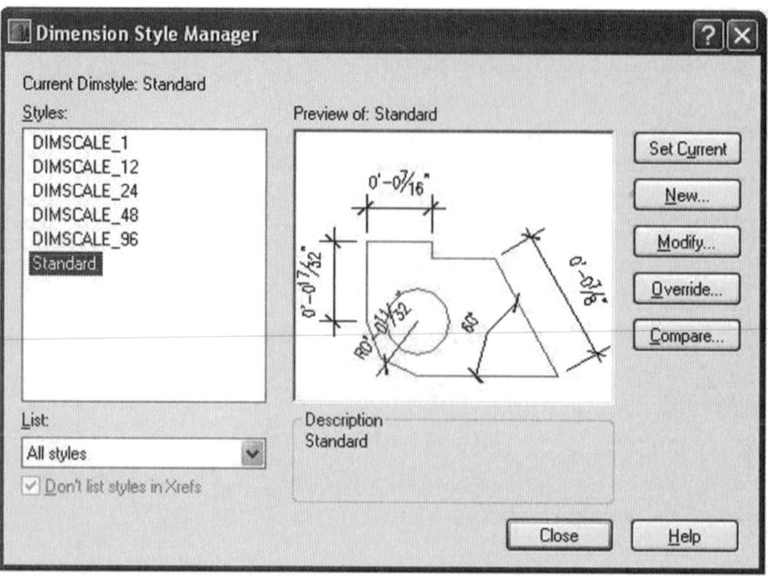

Figure 6.25 AutoCAD's Dimension Style Manager

Explore the Lines, Symbols and Arrows, Text, Fit, and Primary Units tabs of the Standard dimension style. Modifications that are made to a dimension style also update all existing placed dimensions created with that style.

Dimensioning Properly

Within floor plans, contractors not only need to know how large components are but also where an item is located. This is the primary purpose of dimensioning drawings. The following tips offer some guidelines toward learning how to properly add dimensions to drawings.

> **Box 6.5**
> The guidelines listed only provide an introduction to proper dimensioning technique. The best way to continue to learn is to look at several example floor plan, section, and elevation construction drawings.

In general:

1. Try to add dimensions with as few dimension strings as possible. On the CD-ROM you can find an illustration of the difference between an excessively dimensioned drawing and an appropriately dimensioned drawing.
2. Avoid repetitive dimensioning. It will confuse contractors and ultimately cause mistakes.
3. When dimensioning a drawing, always leave room for error. Along a dimension string, leave one dimension out to allow for building construction tolerances.
4. When dimensioning floor plans, dimension consistently with respect to where a measurement starts on a material or an assembly. If one wall is dimensioned to the face of a stud, then all walls (of that type) should be dimensioned to the same face unless there are building-code clearance issues to address (Figure 6.26).
5. When dimensioning floor plans, dimension the floor plan exterior using a hierarchical technique (Figure 6.27). Always dimension the overall length and width of

the building for new building designs. These dimensions should be the outermost dimensions. In addition, dimension all changes in building shapes such as wall jogs. Dimension locations of exterior doors and windows or other minor important building elements.

6. When dimensioning floor plans, always dimension column locations from center to center.
7. When dimensioning the floor plan interior, dimension all interior wall locations and lengths (Figure 6.28). If an interior wall has already been located with an exterior dimension, do not dimension again. Place dimensions of walls where they are easy to see on the floor plan.
8. When dimensioning the floor plan interior, dimension all door and window locations that are not 4" to 6" from a wall corner. Doors and windows that are centered on a wall should have the Equal or EQ dimensioning text associated with it.
9. When dimensioning the floor plan interior, do not dimension sizes of doors or windows. This information is communicated through a schedule.
10. When dimensioning the floor plan interior, dimension the location of all major fixed equipment. Do not dimension the size of the equipment; this information is also given through a schedule.

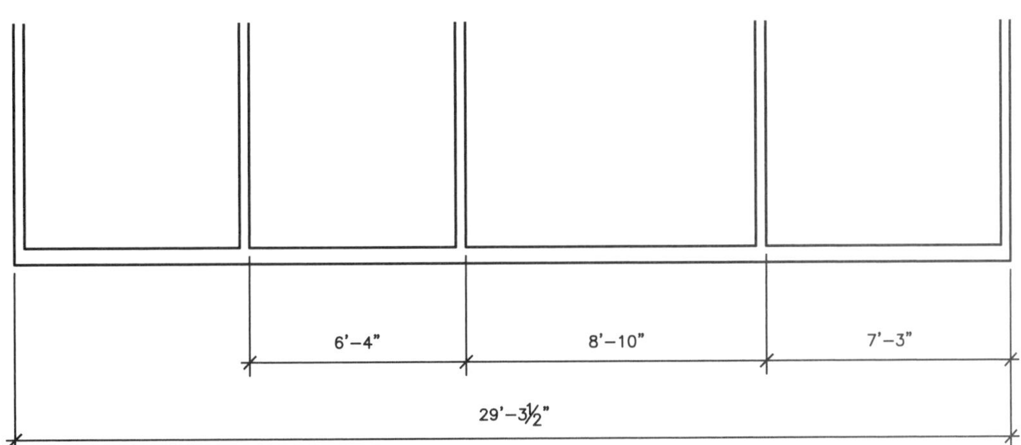

Figure 6.26 Dimensioning floor plans with the same side rule. Dimension consistently with respect to where a measurement starts on a material or assembly.

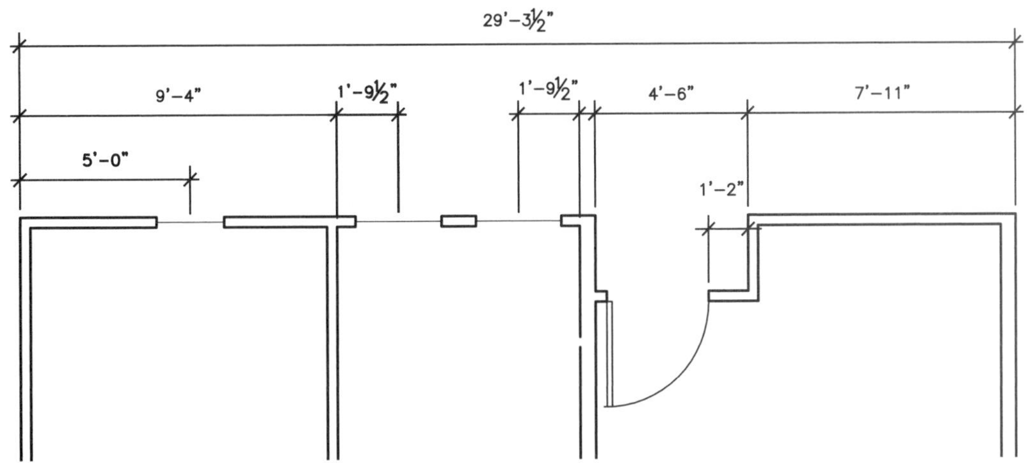

Figure 6.27 Dimension the floor plan exterior using a hierarchical technique.

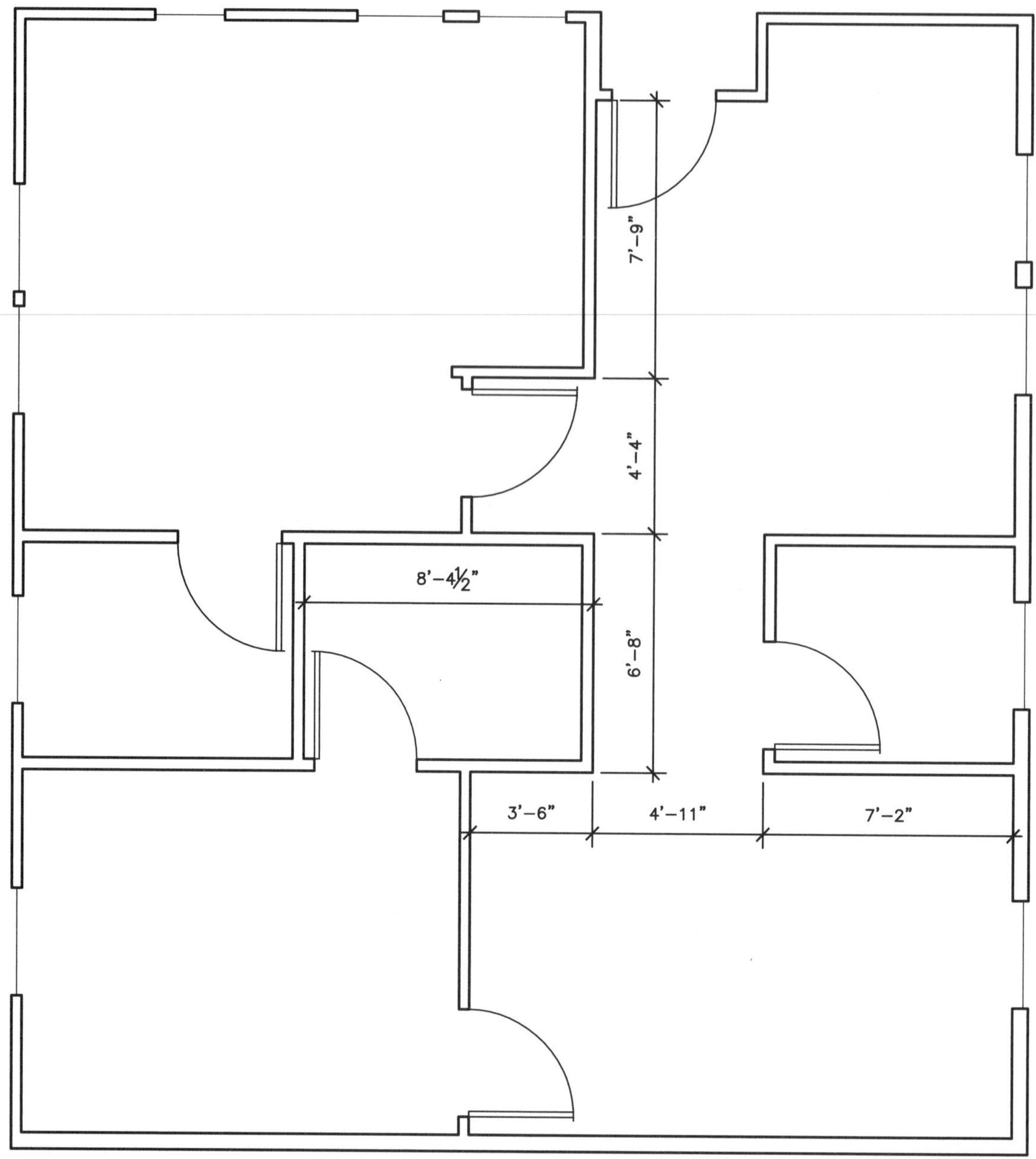

Figure 6.28 Dimension all interior wall locations and lengths.

Using AutoCAD's Dimensioning Tools—The Dimensioning Process

Figure 6.29 demonstrates the dimensioning process using AutoCAD's dimensioning tools.

Editing Dimensions

Dimension editing refers to the ability to edit the location and extents of the dimension itself, the appearance of the dimension, and the text information shown in the dimension. Dimension location editing is accomplished using AutoCAD grips while dimension appearance and text overrides can be changed through the Properties palette.

Technique to Master **T06.29** The Dimensioning Process

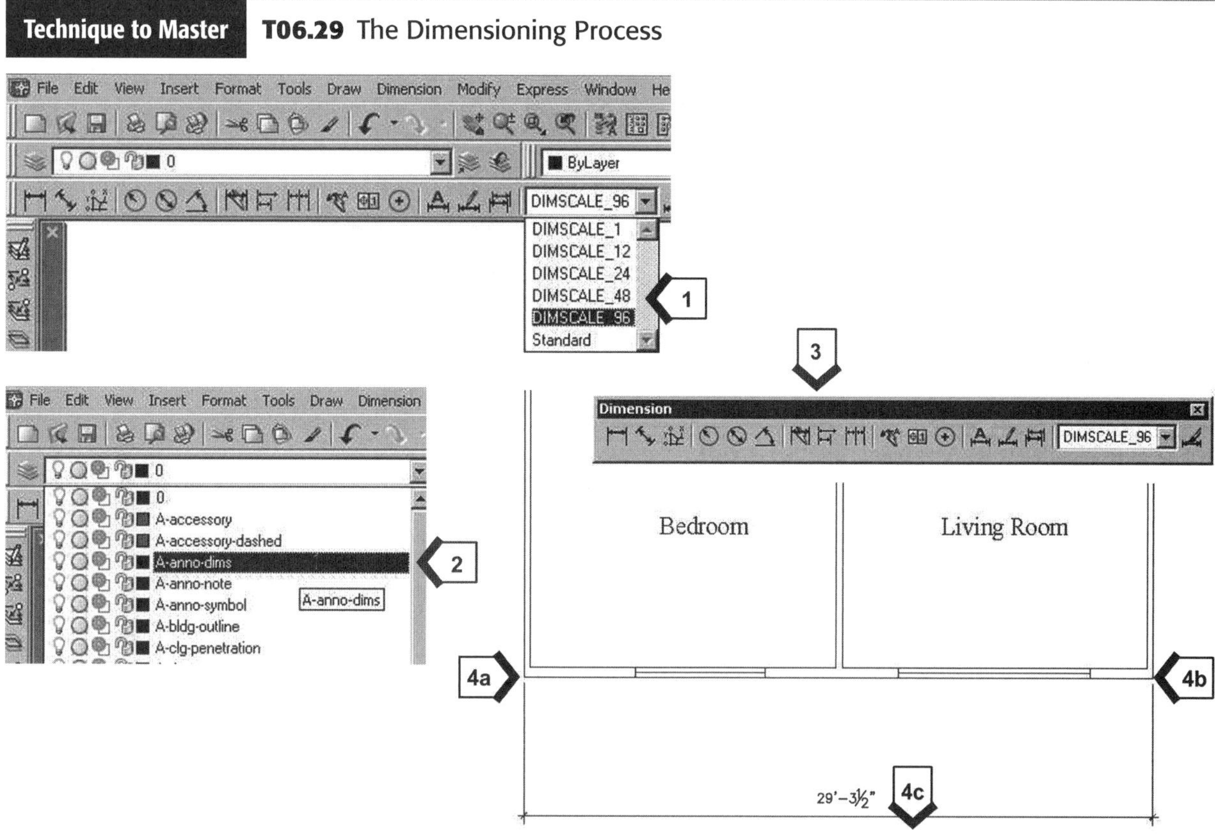

Figure 6.29

1	[Styles toolbar]	Select the appropriate dimension style. Select the dimension style from the Styles or Dimension toolbars. The appropriate dimension style always relates to the eventual plotting scale. Use the AutoCAD Scaling Table in Appendix J. Remember you always need to set text heights and terminus size in relation to the eventual plotting scale.
2	[Layer Properties toolbar]	Make the dimensioning layer current (Refer to Technique T03.17). Create a layer if the appropriate layer doesn't exist (Refer to Technique T03.13). The AIA layer standard is A-anno-dims, or use A-dimension with a lineweight of .20 mm.
3	[Drawing Screen]	Dimension in model space. Use the Dimension toolbar or the menu to access the appropriate dimensioning commands.
4a 4b 4c	[Drawing Screen]	To place a dimension object: a. Snap to the endpoint, intersection, or center to locate the first point of the dimension. b. Snap to the endpoint, intersection, or center to locate the second point of the dimension. c. Pull the dimension line away from the drawing geometry. Left-click to place.

Editing Dimensions with Grips

Grip locations occur at the extension line ends, the intersection of the extension lines and dimension line, and the text location. Each grip location can be moved or stretched and will affect the dimension component on which it is located. Figure 6.30 illustrates how each grip affects the editing of the dimension.

Editing Dimensions with the Properties Palette

Figure 6.31 identifies the various properties of a dimension that can be edited through the Properties palette.

> **Box 6.6**
> The Ddedit command also lets you edit text within a dimension.

Technique to Master **T06.30** Editing Dimensions with Grips

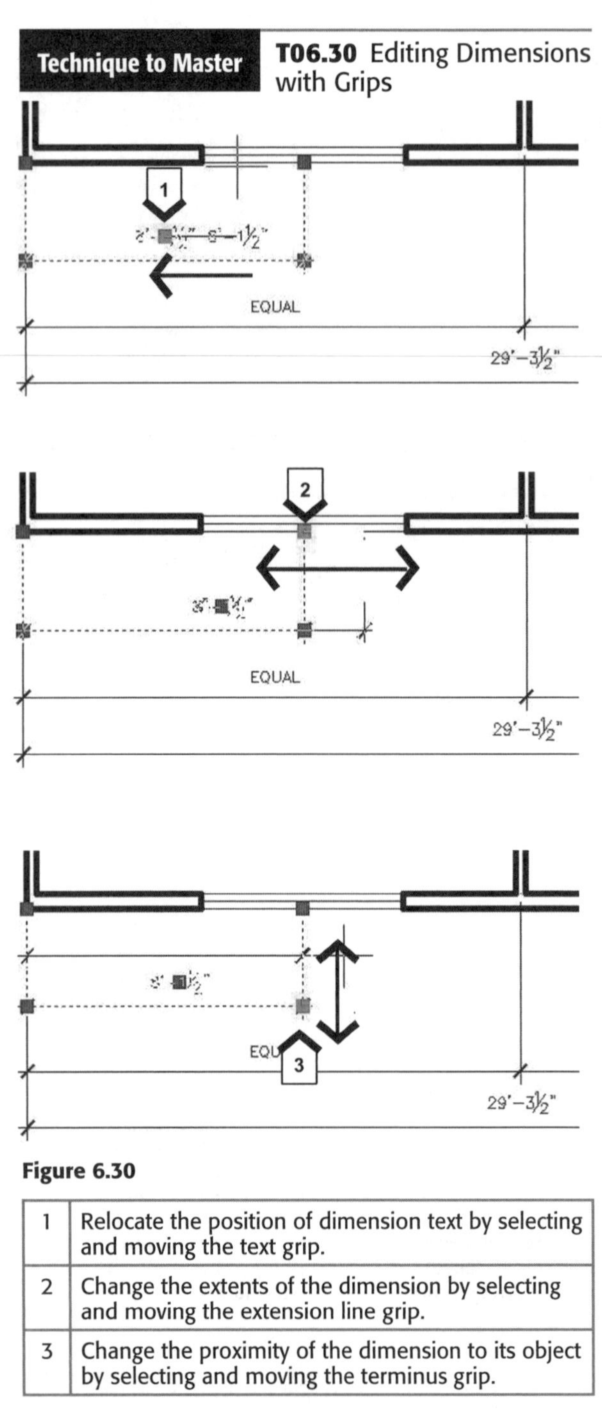

Figure 6.30

1	Relocate the position of dimension text by selecting and moving the text grip.
2	Change the extents of the dimension by selecting and moving the extension line grip.
3	Change the proximity of the dimension to its object by selecting and moving the terminus grip.

Chapter Exercises

Open the Chapter 6 folder located on the CD-ROM and access the chapter exercises. The exercises let you practice the following:

- Creating and editing text for room labels, keynotes, and drawing and border titles.
- Setting up text styles for the above text types.
- Dimensioning floor plans and elevations.

Technique to Master **T06.31** Editing Dimensions with the Properties Palette

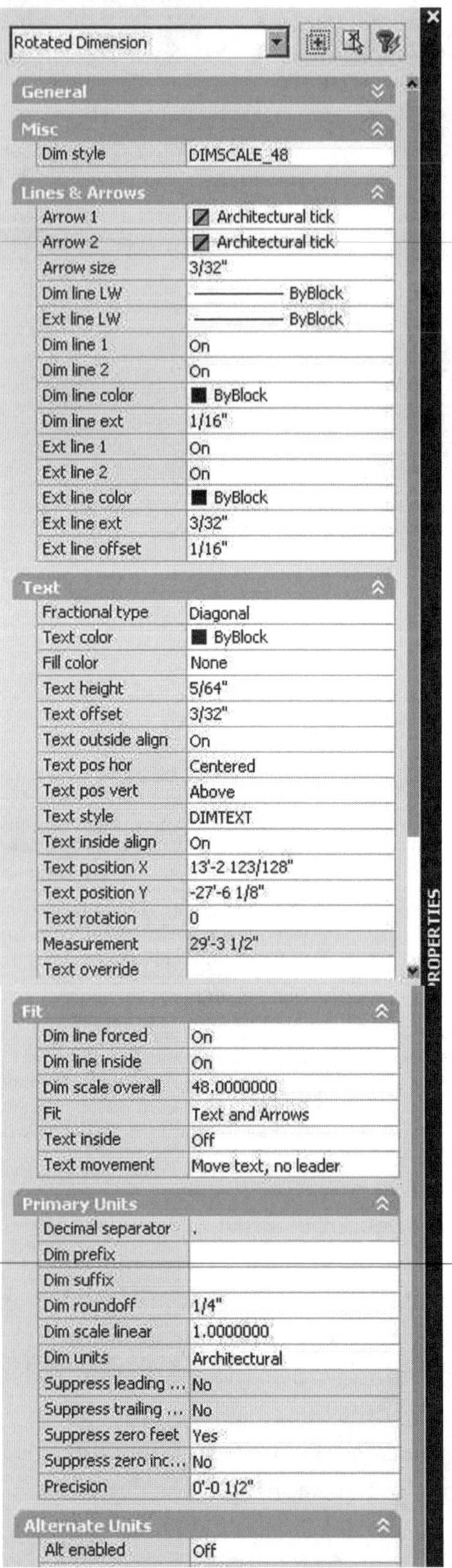

Figure 6.31 All dimension properties are listed in the Properties palette. The properties can be individually modified here.

Project Organization Concepts in AutoCAD

7

Objectives

This chapter introduces you to project organization concepts. It discusses the relevance of file organization and file-naming consistency. It places emphasis on proper file management techniques used to name, organize, and set up plot sheets for drawing files. The end-of-chapter exercises let you get some additional practice using linking (or Xref for short) and paper and model space concepts and techniques to draw second and third floors of buildings, ceiling plans, and elevations as well as set up plot sheets.

Working with Multiple Files Within a Project

Project organization refers to the organizational strategy you should use to manage all the digital files related to one project. For example, if you were a student working on an office redesign project whose submission requirements called for floor plans, ceiling plans, elevations, sections, and schedules, you, or any beginner CAD student, might be tempted to draw all of the requirements in one drawing (Figure 7.1). However, there are several reasons why doing so is not an appropriate method to accomplish this task.

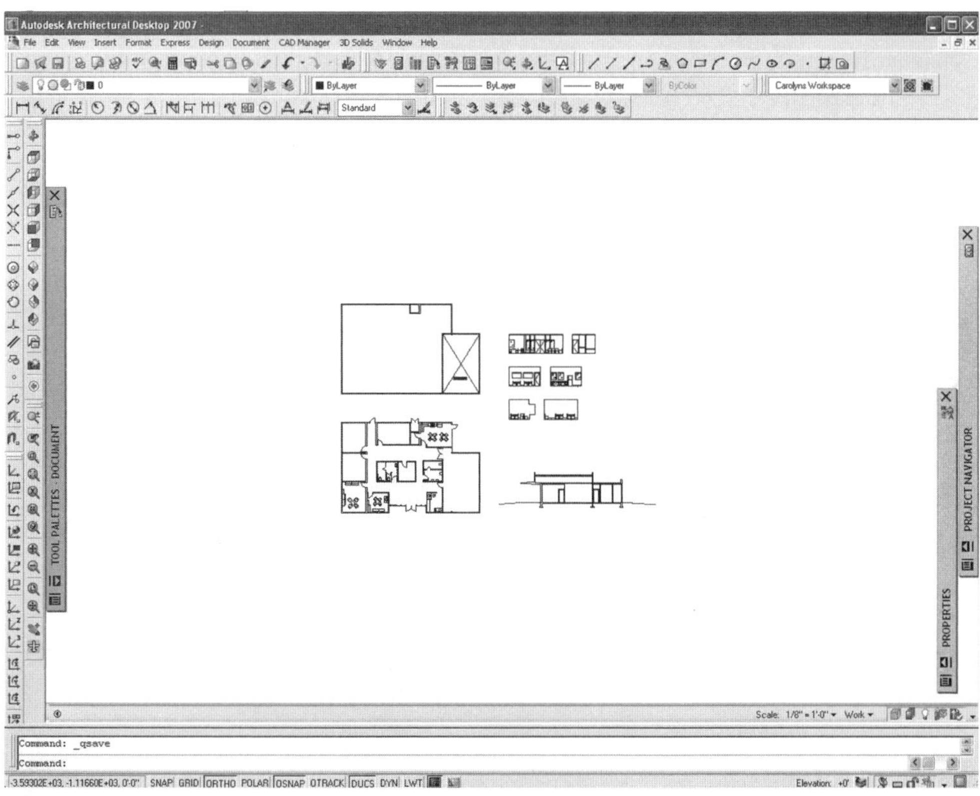

Figure 7.1 Example of an incorrectly set up design project

- First, if the project is large and contains a lot of detail and complex elements, the drawing file size will be enormous. This makes it difficult for you to manage it during the design's development. Any zooming or screen redraws will be slow and cumbersome.
- Second, coordinating between multiple floors and between ceiling and floor plans becomes extremely difficult and makes you prone to making mistakes. Since the drawings cannot be overlaid on top of one another, it makes it difficult for you to confirm that critical design alignments, such as stairs, elevators, and window placements that need to be consistent from floor to floor, are maintained.
- Finally, single drawing project management is ineffective when you have to work in teams. In the real world, there are typically two or more people working on one design project. If all the drawings were located within one drawing file, it would make it impossible for everyone to collaborate.

Certainly one of the first important parts of project organization is learning to use multiple files to design and draw a project. Multiple file project organization is the only method used in design firms today.

How Multiple File Drawing Management Works

You have seen the student office redesign project presented in Figure 7.1, but a more efficient approach to creating a project in AutoCAD is to draw each orthographic drawing in separate .dwg files. See Figure 7.2 for what the resulting file structure might end up looking like.

During the design and drawing of any project—whether it be a schematic presentation of an interior renovation or contract drawings for a new residence—multiple drawing file management lets you organize a project so that all drawings are legible and consistent. Using this method, drawings are placed into separate .dwg files with very specific naming conventions so that drawing retrieval is efficient, easy, and well organized. See Figure 7.3 for an example of this folder and file organization.

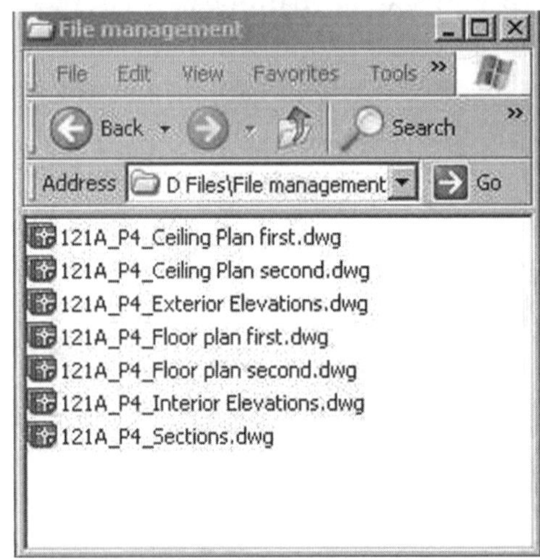

Figure 7.2 Multiple file organization: example of a drawing file structure

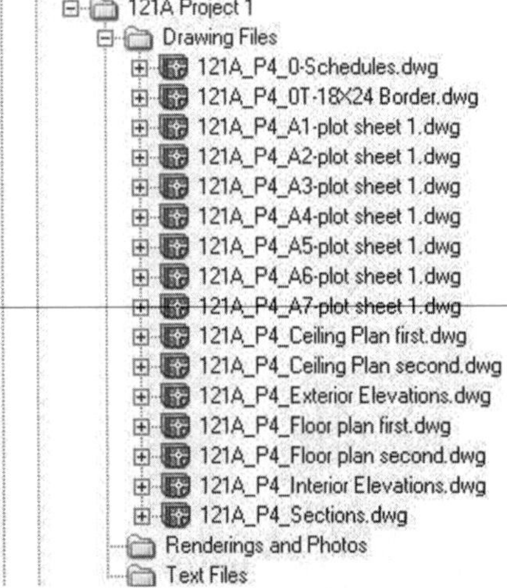

Figure 7.3 Multiple file organization: example of project folder and file structure

Managing Drawing Files for a Project

The second most important part of project organization is the naming convention you use for individual drawing files. Most file-naming conventions within design firms include a project number (that ties to accounting and project billing) and an abbreviated shortcut as a drawing identifier. Figure 7.4 shows an example of a file naming standard used in design offices.

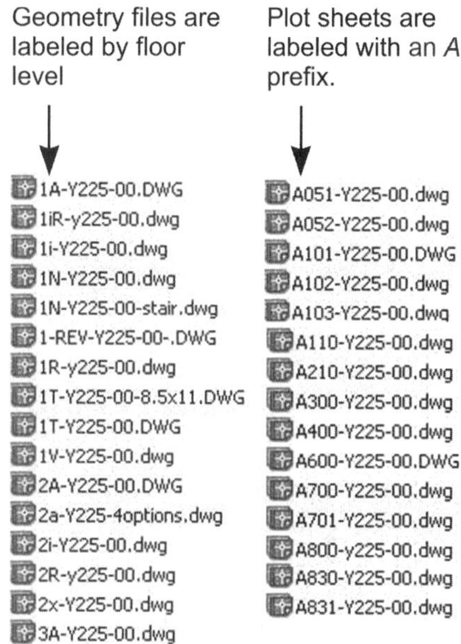

Figure 7.4 Multiple file organization: example of a design office's folder and file naming standards

Drawing with Multiple File Management

You might ask how coordination occurs using the multiple file management process. The secret is AutoCAD's .dwg linking capabilities. Linking one drawing to another drawing allows you to see any or all parts of the link so that one drawing is based on another (Figure 7.5).

Visualize the following scenario:

The problem: The first floor plan of an office renovation project has been designed and drawn. The second floor plan is ready to be drawn.

The solution: Link the file floorplan1.dwg into a new drawing file. Save the new drawing file as floorplan2.dwg. Draw the second floor using the first floor as an underlay.

The problem: Both floor plans (floors 1 and 2) have been drawn in separate drawing files. The section is ready to be drawn for the office renovation.

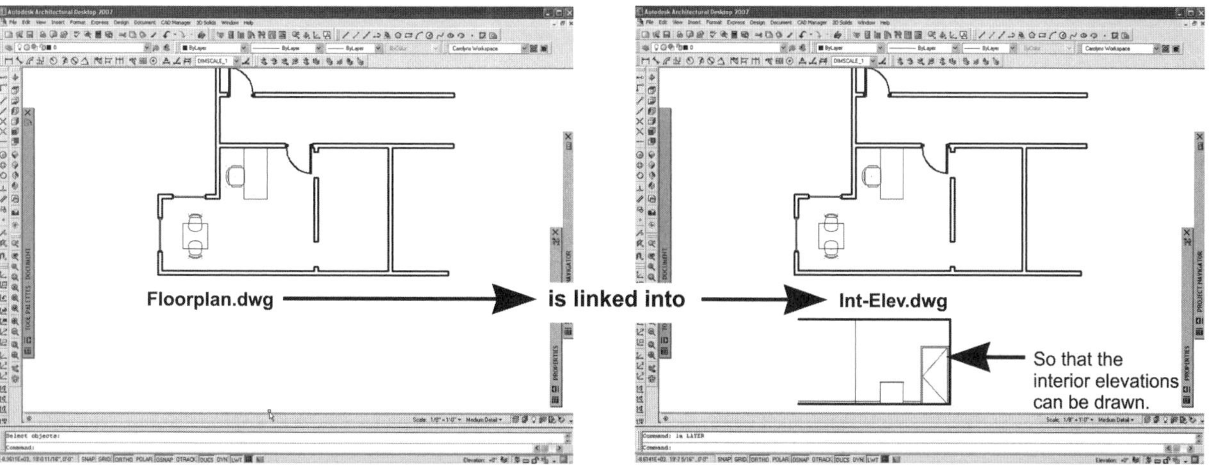

Figure 7.5 When you want to create a new drawing based on an existing drawing, follow this example. First, link a simple floor plan (Floorplan.dwg) to a new drawing. Save the new drawing as Int-Elev.dwg. Now you can draw the interior elevations for the floor plan in their own .dwg files and still use the floor plan as reference.

The solution: Link the files floorplan1.dwg and floorplan2.dwg into a new drawing. Align the links vertically. Save the new drawing file as Section.dwg. Extend temporary lines from the floor plans to create the building section (Figure 7.6). These examples illustrate just a few of the concepts of file linking.

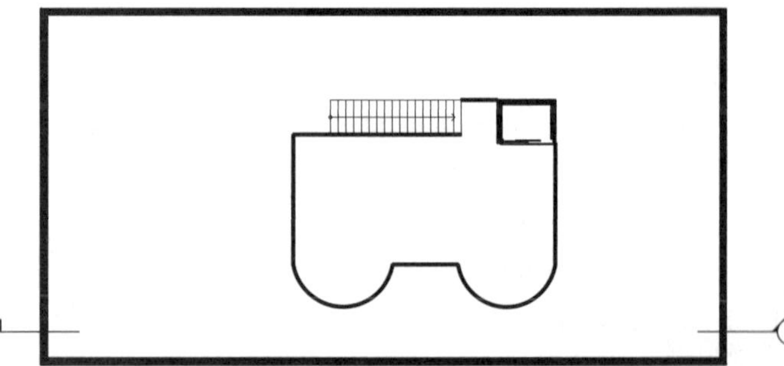

Understanding File-Linking Concepts

As you've read, there are several important reasons for using file linking in the development of a design project. First, during the start of a project when drawings are in their origin, file linking allows you to use one drawing as a basis for another drawing. As the design develops, file linking helps you coordinate the drawings. Finally, when you are ready to print your drawings, file linking allows you to compose plot sheets (Figure 7.7).

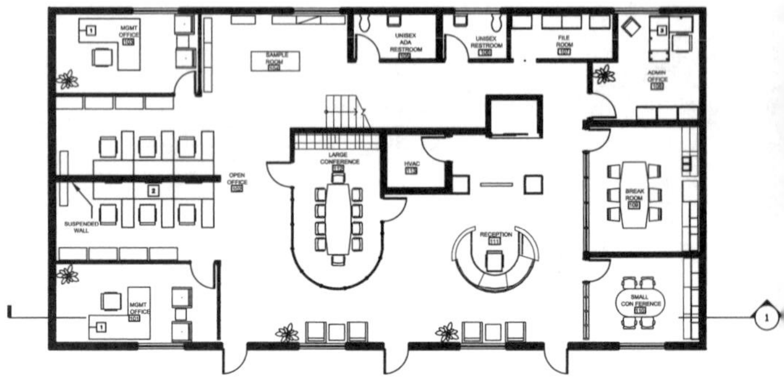

Linking Drawings in AutoCAD—External References

An external reference is an AutoCAD drawing that has been linked to another AutoCAD drawing. Since you can link any drawing file, any drawing file can become an external

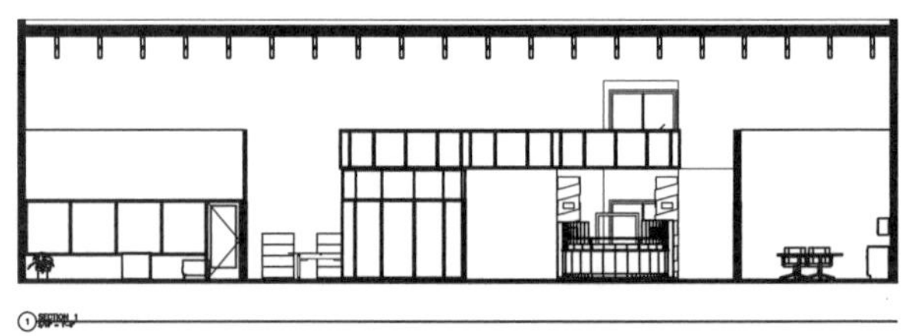

Figure 7.6 This student project for an office renovation shows a completed building section drawing created by using Xref-linking concepts to link the first and second floor plans.

Courtesy of Tiffany White.

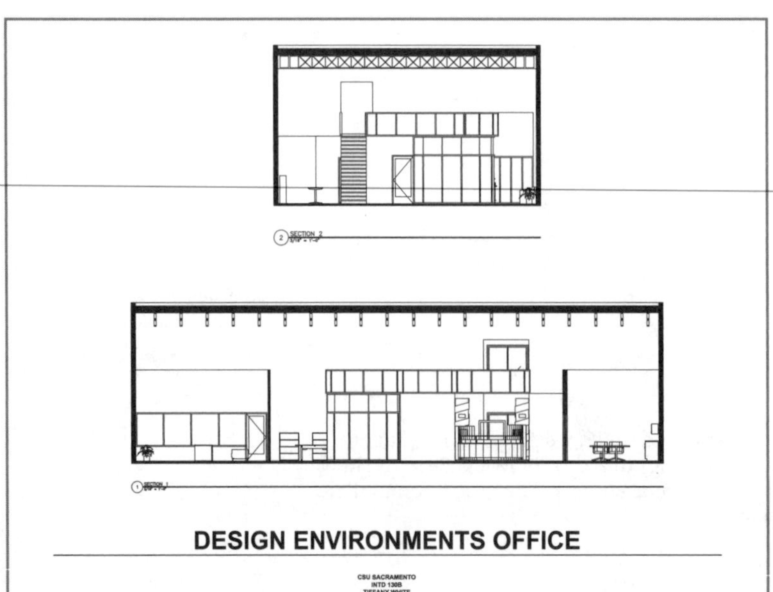

Figure 7.7 In this office renovation student project, a plot sheet is created by linking the project title block and the project's sections into a new drawing saved as Plotsheet-A3.dwg.

Courtesy of Tiffany White.

reference. A drawing may have several external references—that is, several drawings may be linked into one drawing. If you want to link files in AutoCAD, you must do so through the External References palette. When a drawing file is linked to another drawing, it is defined as an external reference (Xref for short). You may open the External References palette by using the Xref command.

> **Box 7.1**
> The External References palette is new to AutoCAD 2007. Previous versions of AutoCAD allowed users to attach and detach file links through a dialogue box.

> **Box 7.2**
> Because Xrefs are links to original .dwg files, any changes to the original drawing file are automatically reflected in the Xref.

The External References Palette

The External References palette not only displays the status of each Xref you attach but also incorporates all Xref-related commands, including commands to link (attach) new drawings and unlink (detach) currently linked drawings. Figure 7.8 identifies the various areas of the AutoCAD 2007 External Reference palette as well as its predecessor, the Xref Manager.

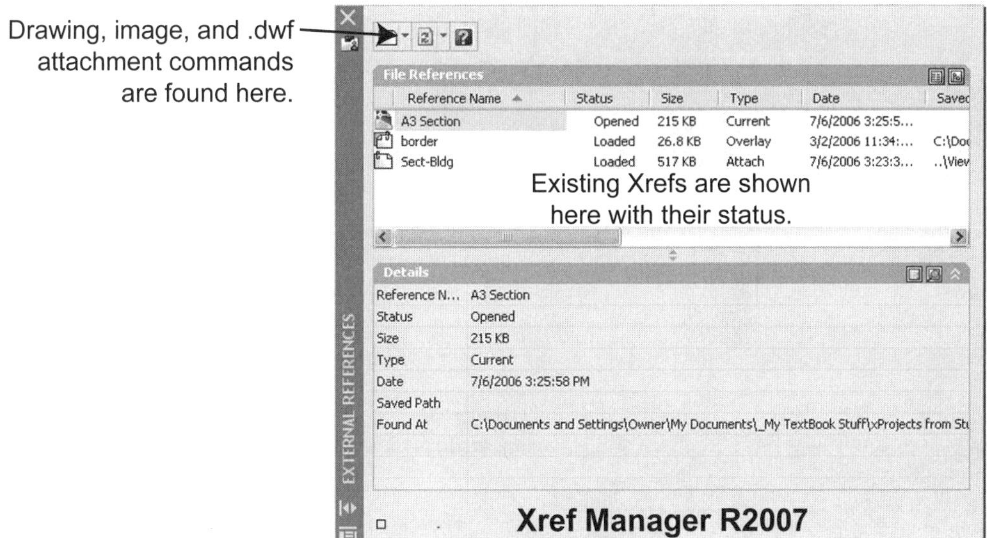

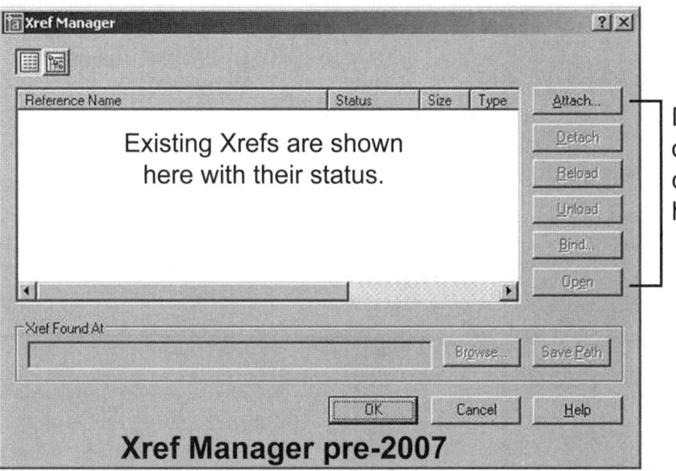

Figure 7.8 Getting to know the Xref Manager

Attaching and Detaching Xrefs

Link drawing files by using the Attach button. Once you select a drawing file to attach, you will see a dialogue box that gives you options to adjust the reference type, insertion point, scaling, and rotation. Figure 7.9 demonstrates the file-linking process.

> **Box 7.3**
> When you attach Xrefs, it's better to set the Path type to No Path if you are using multiple computers during the design of a project.

Detaching Xrefs refers to the procedure of removing an existing attached drawing. To accomplish this procedure, right-click the Xref and choose the Detach command from the displayed menu.

> **Box 7.4**
> When you detach a Xref, AutoCAD removes all copies of the Xref within the current drawing.

T07.09 Attaching Xrefs

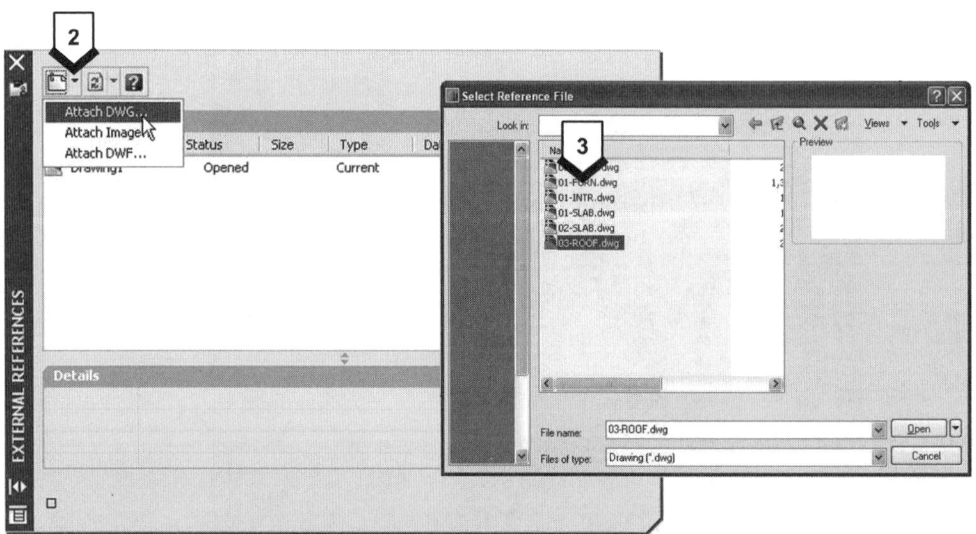

Figure 7.9

1	[Command Line]	Use the Xref command.
2	[External References palette]	Left-click the Attach button.
3	[Select Reference file dialogue box]	Select the drawing file to link.
4	[External Reference dialogue box]	Determine reference type, path type, insertion point, scale, and rotation.
5	[External Reference dialogue box]	Click OK when you're done.

Technique to Master **T07.10** Unloading and Reloading Xrefs

Figure 7.10

1	[Command Line]	Use the Xref command.
2	[External Reference palette]	Left-click to select existing Xref. Right-click and choose the Unload or Reload command.

Unloading and Reloading Xrefs

The Unload and Reload commands within the External Reference palette controls the visibility of a linked drawing. When you unload a linked drawing, the Xref is still linked but temporarily invisible. When you reload a Xref, it becomes visible on the drawing screen again. The locations of these commands are shown in Figure 7.10.

Xref Behavior

Because of the nature of the linking mechanism, Xrefs are unique AutoCAD entities that have special behavioral and property characteristics. For example, drawings that include Xrefs must always maintain connections to the original drawing referenced. This is because every time you open a drawing file that includes Xrefs. Autocad looks for each of the original drawings to be able to update the Xrefs.

Broken Links

There are times when a drawing cannot find an external reference that was previously linked. The status column tn the External References palette will read "Not Found" (Figure 7.11). If drawings are not found, it is usually because they've been moved from their original locations. To fix this situation, you need to identify the correct path for the Xref by clicking on the browse button within the External References palette (see Figure 7.12).

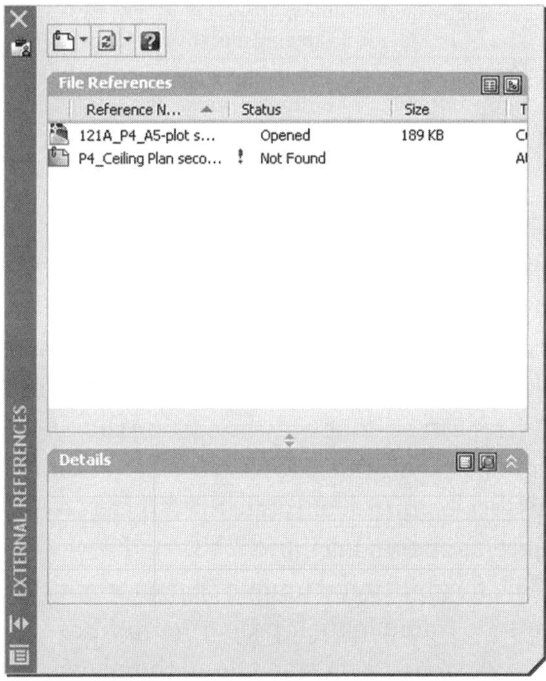

Figure 7.11 A Xref whose link has been broken displays a exclamation and "Not Found" label in the External References palette.

Technique to Master **T07.12** Changing a Xref's Path

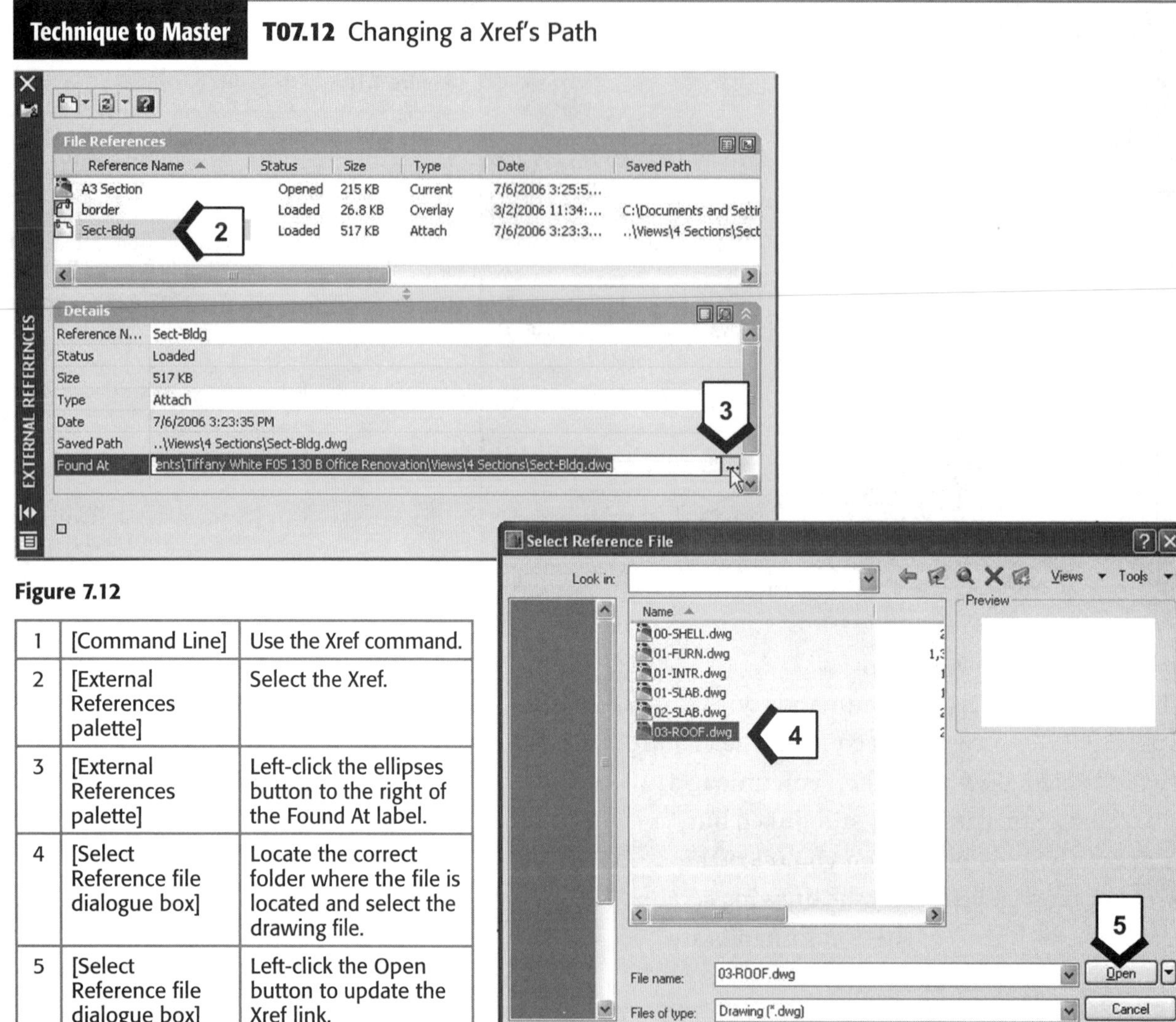

Figure 7.12

1	[Command Line]	Use the Xref command.
2	[External References palette]	Select the Xref.
3	[External References palette]	Left-click the ellipses button to the right of the Found At label.
4	[Select Reference file dialogue box]	Locate the correct folder where the file is located and select the drawing file.
5	[Select Reference file dialogue box]	Left-click the Open button to update the Xref link.

Modifying Xrefs

When you link a drawing file to another drawing, the Xref behaves very similar to a block in that it is displayed and selected as one object. Modifications to the geometry within the Xref can be done only by editing the original drawing file. However, you can move, copy, scale, mirror, or rotate the Xref as one object, as shown in Figure 7.13.

The flexibility and unique characteristics of Xrefs are found in their property modifications. Attached Xrefs include all their layer, text style, and dimension style definitions (Figure 7.14). This is useful since operations such as layer freezing and/or layer color and lineweight changes can be isolated to the Xref only. Figure 7.15 demonstrates this usefulness by using a floor plan to create a ceiling plan drawing. The floor plan drawing is Xrefed into the ceiling plan drawing. By using the Xref's autonomous layers, you freeze the doors, furniture, and casework layers. You can then add ceiling headers and ceiling patterns to complete the ceiling plan drawing.

Xrefs can also be clipped to temporarily hide portions of the drawing—which comes in handy for projects since it is useful for setting up interior elevations. Clipped areas of plans and sections also provide great backgrounds that create details in construction drawings. Figure 7.16 demonstrates the Xref-clipping command.

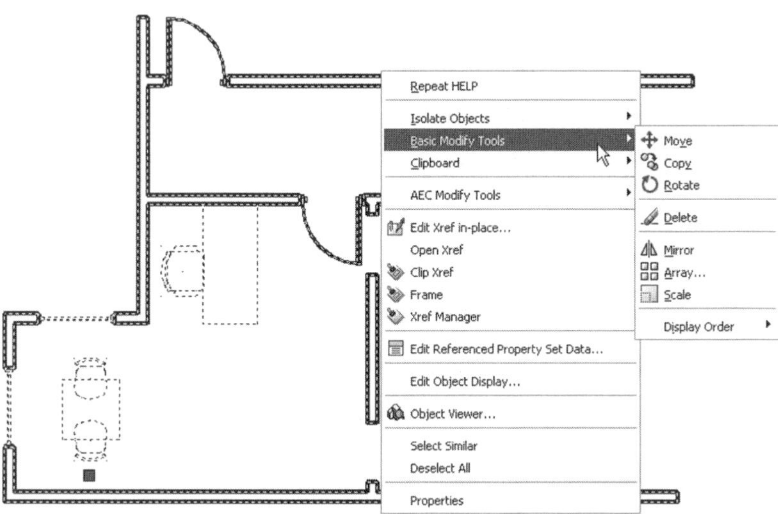

Figure 7.13 A Xref that is selected behaves as one object. It can be moved, copied, scaled, mirrored, and rotated similar to an AutoCAD block.

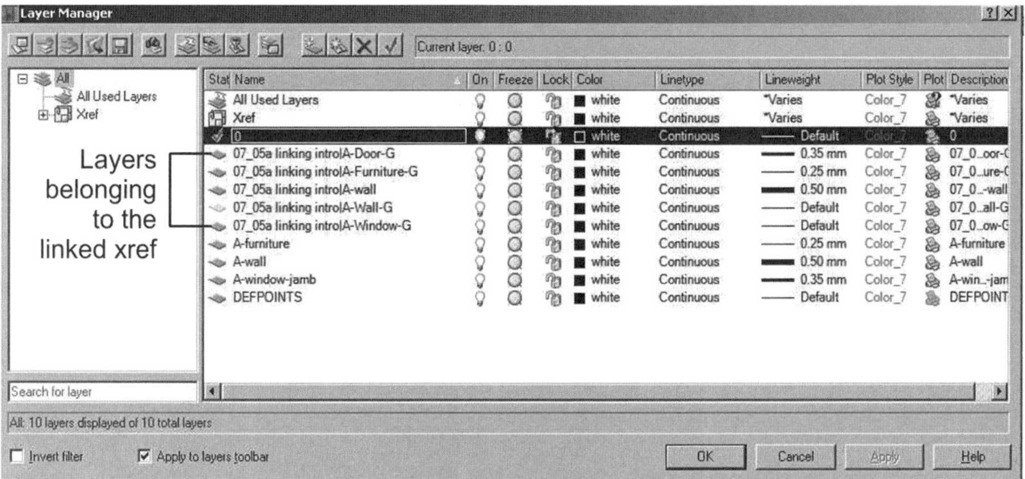

Figure 7.14 Attached Xrefs bring in all of their layer, text-style, and dimension-style definitions.

> **Box 7.5**
> Xref clipping does not affect the original drawing. It simply hides a portion of the linked file.

The Two Spaces of AutoCAD

The bottom of the AutoCAD screen displays two tabs that were identified in Chapter 1—the Model and Layout tabs (Figure 7.17). So far the Model tab has been the primary location for all your drawing exercises. Now the Layout tab will be explained in more detail, including its relationship to the Model tab.

Model Space and Paper Space

In the earlier releases of AutoCAD, the only method for setting up a drawing and its title block border was through one drawing environment—model space. The title block for a project was Xrefed into each floor plan, section, and elevation .dwg file and scaled up proportionally to create the plot sheet. This method, while effective for plot sheets containing identically scaled drawings, results in problems for plot sheets that contain details at different scales.

To solve the problem, AutoCAD created a second drawing environment for borders and other title block related information. This

Technique to Master T07.15 Using a Floor Plan to Create a Ceiling Plan with Xrefs

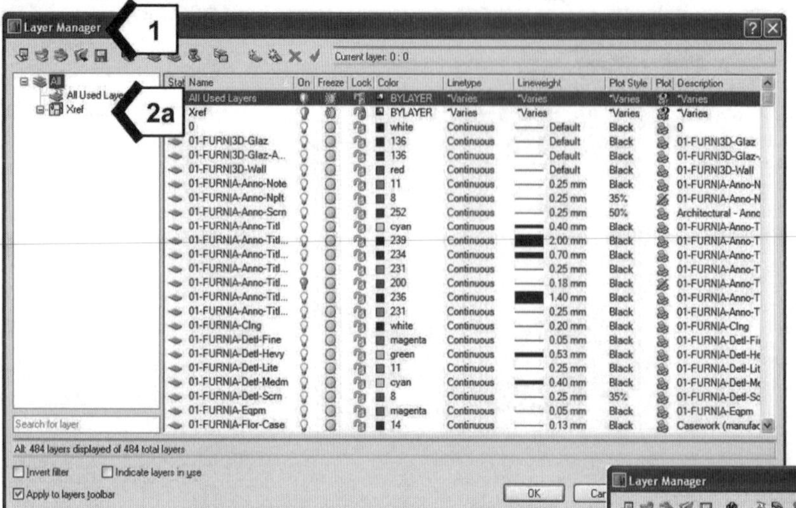

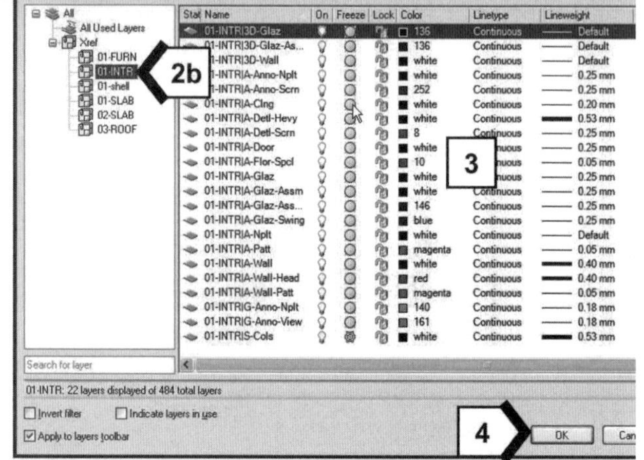

Figure 7.15

1	Use the Layer Manager.	
2a 2b	[Layer Manager]	Within the left pane of the Layer Manager, click on the plus sign next to the word Xrefs. Locate the desired Xref.
3	[Layer Manager]	Within the right pane of the Layer Manager, modify the layer visibility, lineweight, and color properties of the Xref layers as desired. Ceiling plans do not show doors, furniture, and floor patterns; therefore, these layers would be frozen.
4	[Layer Manager]	Left-click OK to complete the command.

Technique to Master T07.16 Clipping Xrefs

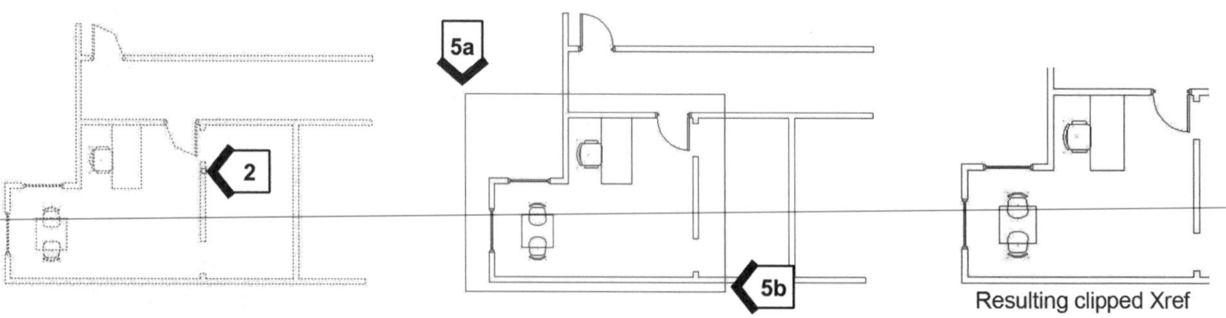

Figure 7.16

1	[Command Line]	Type XCLIP and press Enter.
2	[Drawing Screen]	Select the Xref to clip.
3	[Command Line]	Type N and press Enter to create a new clipping boundary.
4	[Command Line]	Type R and press Enter to specify shape of clipping boundary; use polygonal for a multisided shape.
5a, 5b	[Drawing Screen]	Specify the first corner and the opposite corner to create clipping rectangle.

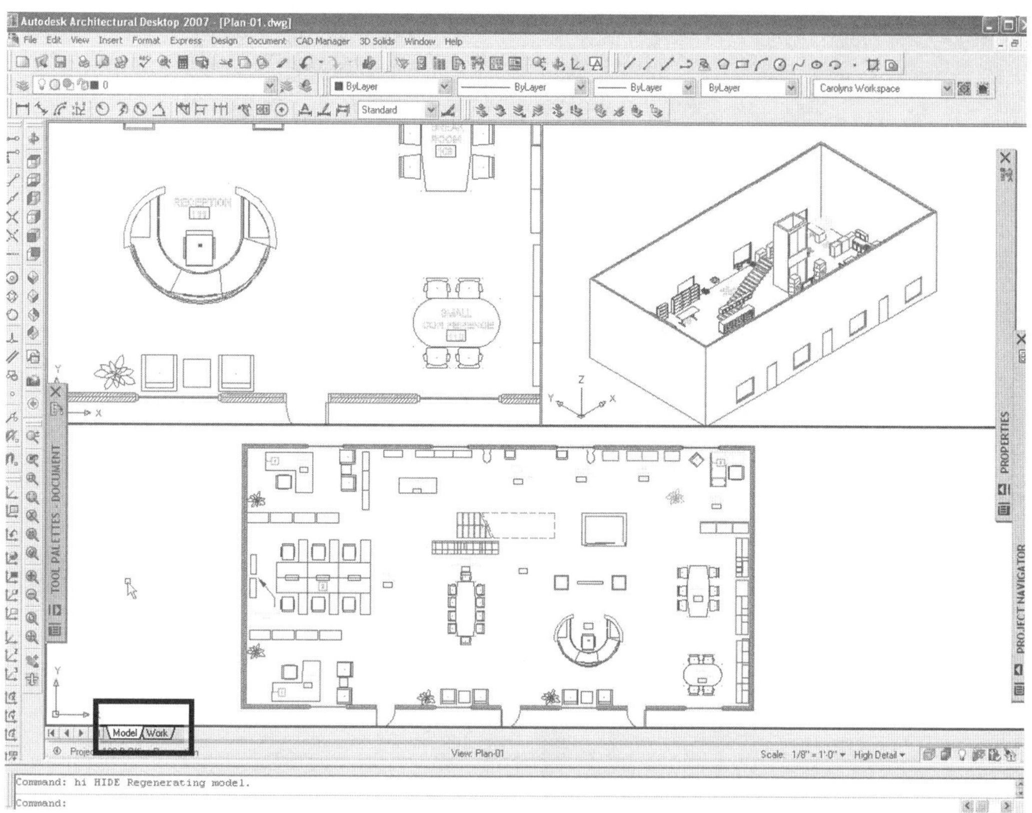

Figure 7.17 The Model and Layout tabs are located at the bottom of the screen near the status bar.

second drafting environment was named "paper space." Paper space is analogous to the pre-made vellum title blocks to which drafters would tape their drawings. The original drafting environment became model space because of its three-dimensional design capabilities.

The Design Versus the Border

Currently, model space is the space where you draw the geometry of your design. It is typically the default drawing environment you see when starting a new AutoCAD drawing session. Paper space is the space where you set up and print plot sheets.

The primary benefit of the separation of border from design geometry is the ability of both types of information to remain at their true dimensional characteristics, that is, 18 by 24 size paper is drawn at 18 × 24 inches instead of being scaled up to accommodate the plotting ratio problem. Additional benefits include the following:

- Multiple views of a design model can be set up in paper space at different scales.
- Plotting from paper space is always full scale (a 1:1 ratio). Annotation, when placed in paper space, is also always at full scale.

Today, the paper space environment is found in each Layout tab to the right of the Model tab. Each drawing file can contain multiple layouts, which allows to set up multiple plotting sheets (Figure 7.18). Figure 7.19 demonstrates how to set up borders within paper space.

> **Box 7.6**
>
> Although you can create multiple layouts in one drawing (.dwg) file, AutoCAD advocates using a single layout for each drawing file. This practice is consistent with the multiple file organization concept discussed earlier.

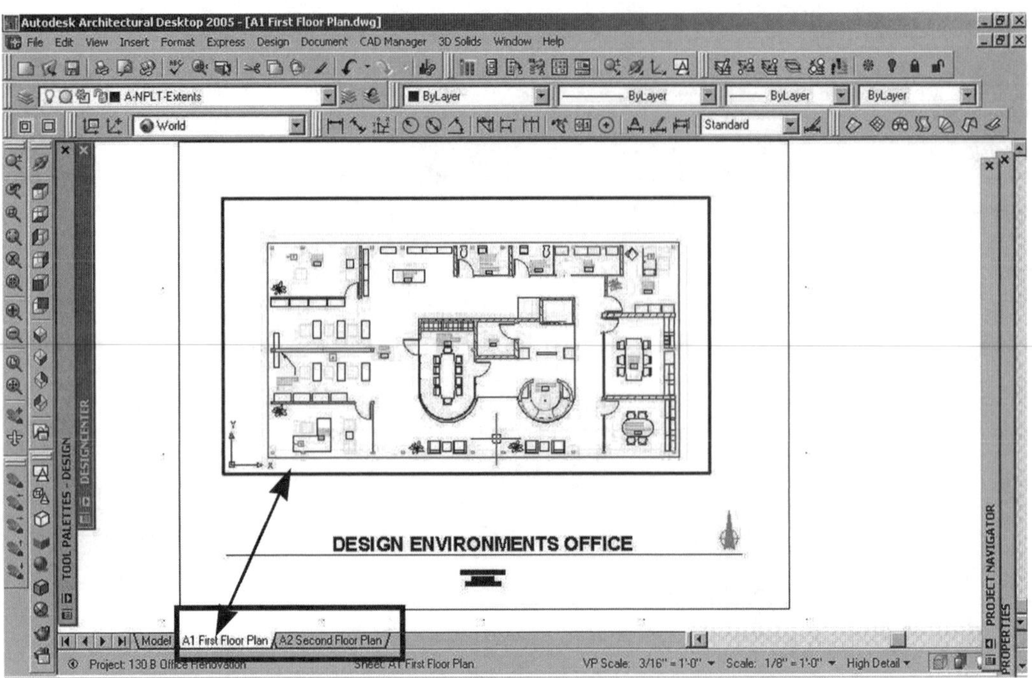

Figure 7.18 Student project for an office renovation showing the paper space drawing area
Courtesy of Tiffany White.

> **Box 7.7**
> All information that is drawn in paper space is drawn at real scale. If you were to create a 24" × 36" rectangle that represents a sheet of paper in paper space, you would use its actual dimensions. Text is also drawn at the same height at which it will eventually print.

Paper Space Viewports

You might be wondering how paper space sees model space geometry. It is through the use of special geometric shapes called viewports. Viewports are shapes that display specific views of the model space geometry. The viewport assigns a specific scale to the contents displayed, allowing you to compose each plot sheet with differently scaled drawings (Figure 7.20). The typical viewport shape is a rectangle, but viewports can be designated any shape. Paper space viewports carry the same editing characteristics as many other entities. You can copy, move, stretch, and overlap them, just to name a few. Think of a viewport as a one-way window between two rooms—similar to one-way mirrors used by law enforcement. If the window is opened, a physical connection is established between the two rooms. In other words, if you open the window you could touch something within the adjacent room. When the window is closed, however, all physical contact is lost. Only visual contact with the room remains.

In the analogy above, the room with the one-way window represents paper space. The window (viewport) creates the aperture to the model space drawing (Figure 7.21). Paper space viewports have the added advantage of allowing you to still work in model space while in paper space. In the analogy above, the window opens and allows physical contact between the rooms. You can open viewports by double-clicking within any viewport. When a viewport is open, it allows you to draw and manipulate any geometry located in model space. Therefore, using viewports in paper space becomes an efficient method to modify model space geometry. Close the viewport by double-clicking outside of the viewport.

T07.19 Xref a Border into Paper Space

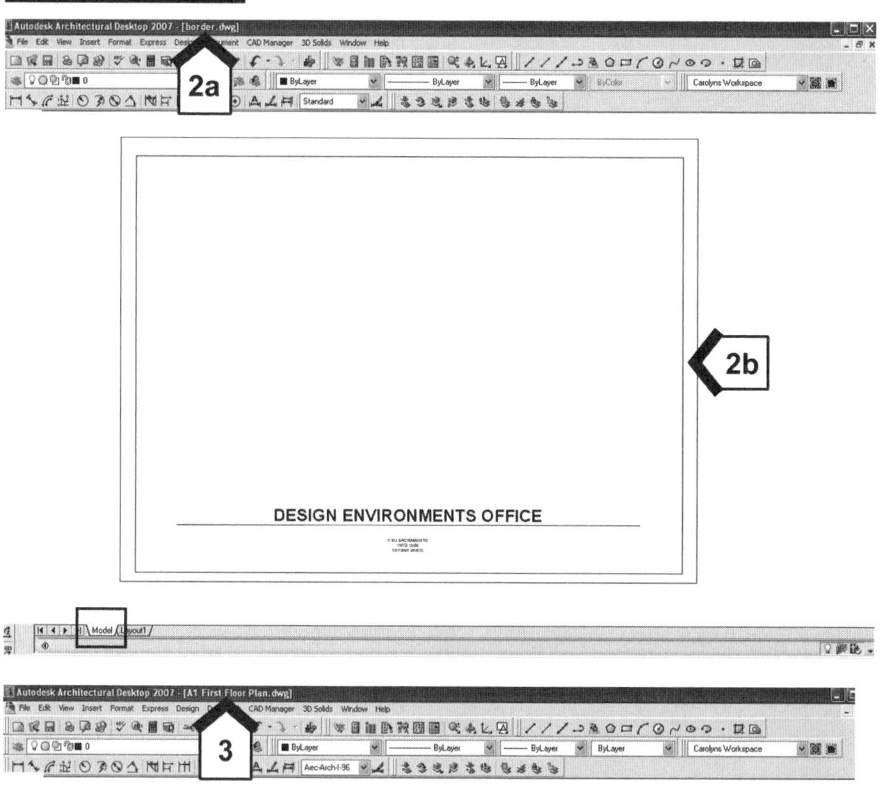

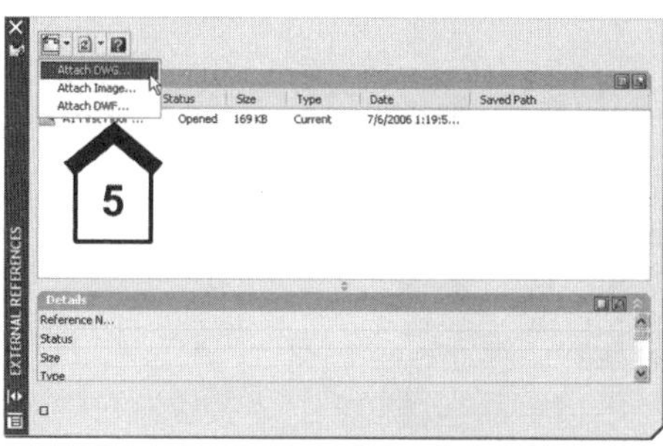

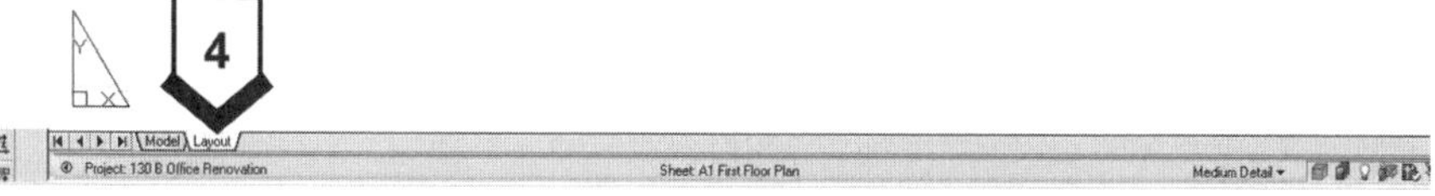

Figure 7.19

1	Create a new drawing where the border design will be drawn.	
2a, 2b	Save drawing as border.dwg. Create a title block (refer to Technique T06.24).	
3	Create a new drawing for plot sheet. Save the drawing.	
4	[AutoCAD Status bar]	Left-click the Layout tab.
5	[Paper Space Drawing Screen]	Using the Attach command, Xref border.dwg into plot sheet (refer to Technique T07.09).

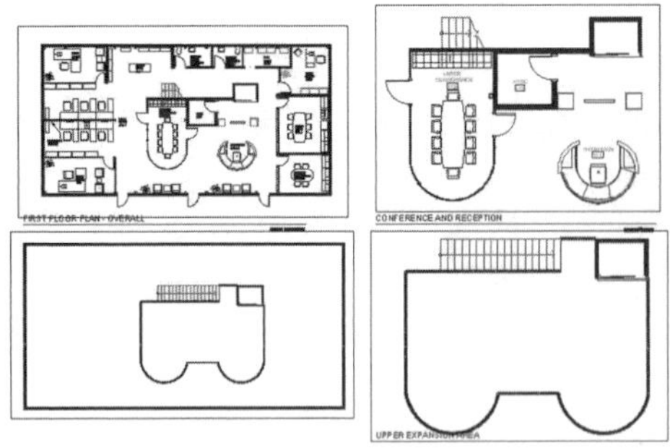

Figure 7.20 The viewport assigns a specific scale to the contents displayed allowing each plot sheet to be composed with differently scaled drawings. This example of a student project for an office renovation shows the lower and upper floor plans at different scales.

Courtesy of Tiffany White.

The Viewport Toolbar

Figure 7.22 explains the various tools in the Viewports toolbar.

Working with Viewports–Workflow Process

A viewport is best utilized for setting up plot sheets for printing. One primary purpose is to provide a window to the model space's design. Setting up viewports may seem confusing at first so the steps are summarized in the list that follows.

1. To see a drawing in model space, you must draw or reference a design in model space.
2. Create a viewport in paper space.

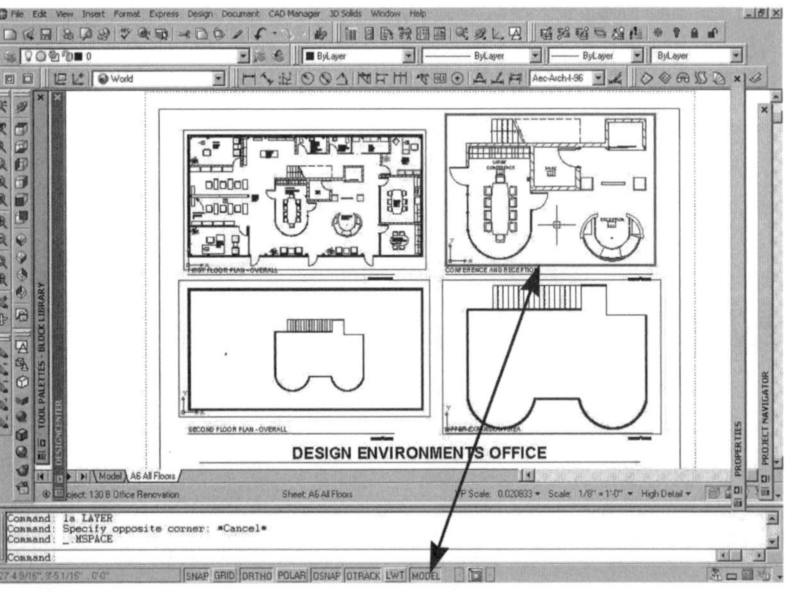

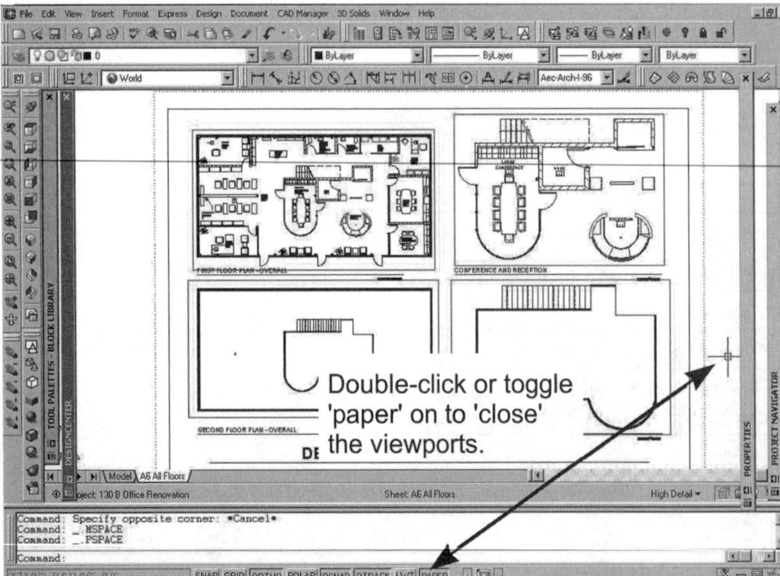

Figure 7.21 The window (viewport) creates the aperture to the model space drawing. Double-clicking the viewport allows you to zoom, pan, and/or modify the contents of model space.

3. Set the scale of the viewport so that it plots correctly.
4. Use the Pan command in model space to compose the drawing within the viewport.
5. Additionally, you can resize the viewport to accommodate the extent of the drawing.

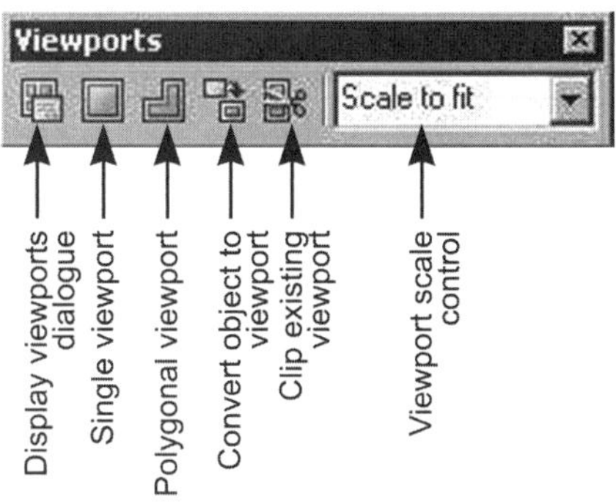

Figure 7.22 The Viewports toolbar

6. Lock the viewport to prevent unintentional scaling.

Repeat this process for additional viewports. Figures 7.23 and 7.24 demonstrate the techniques.

Scaling Viewports

Set the scale of the information within the viewport by using the viewport scaling property. The Standard Scale property displays selections for many of the standard architectural plotting scales. By choosing a scale, you adjust the zoom percentage within the viewport to that scale. If a scale is not available in the standard scale list box, use the Custom Scale property to type in the scaling ratio.

Technique to Master **T07.23** Creating and Scaling Viewports

Figure 7.23

1	[AutoCAD Status bar]	Left-click on any of the layout tabs to enter paper space.
2	[View menu]	Use the Single Viewport tool button of the Viewports toolbar or the View menu Viewports>1 Viewport to create the rectangular or polygonal viewport. Draw the viewport by specifying two points.
3	[Paper Space Drawing Screen]	Select viewport by left-clicking once on the viewport border.
4	[Properties Palette]	With the viewport selected, set the scale of the viewport. You may also set the scale using the toolbar's Scale drop-down menu.
5	Press the Escape key to deselect viewport.	

Technique to Master **T07.24** Composing the Model Space View/Locking the Viewport

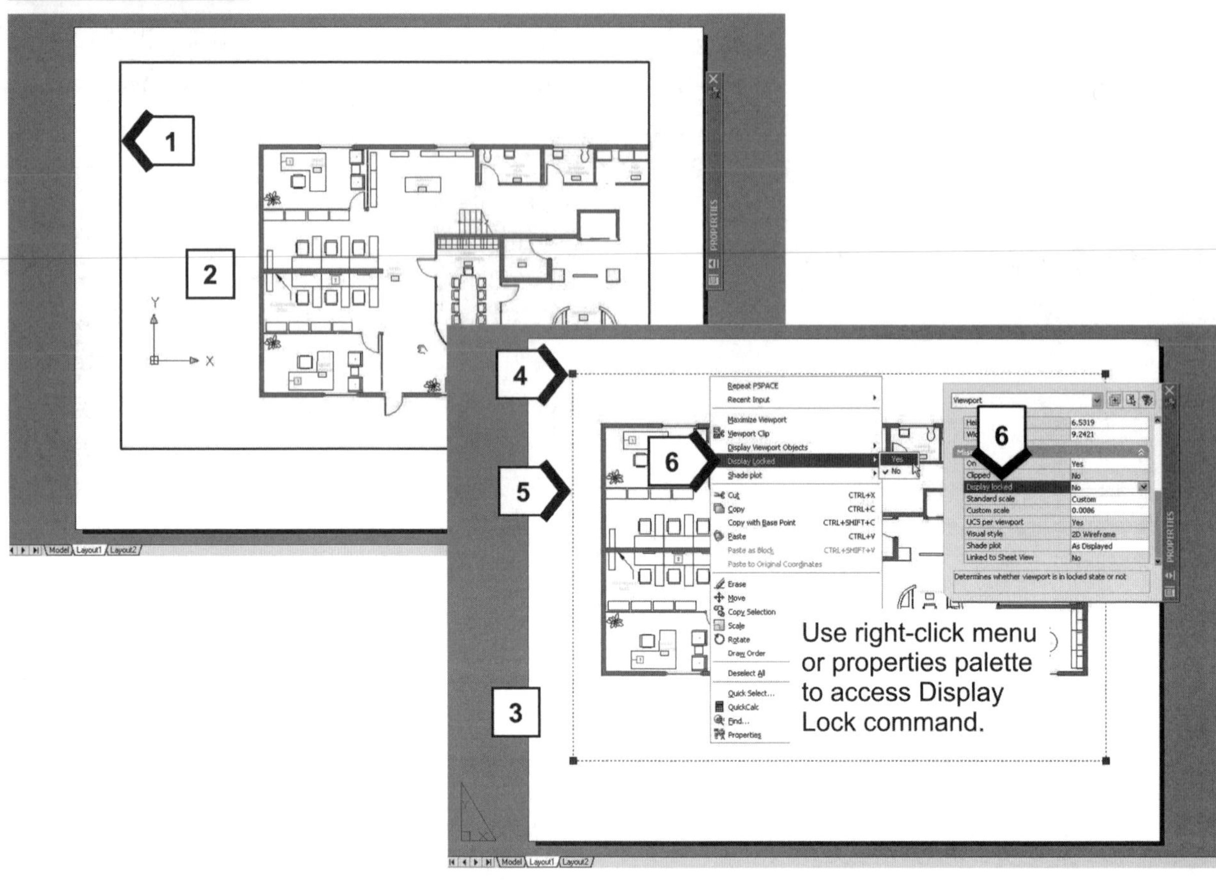
1
2
3
4
5
6
6
Use right-click menu or properties palette to access Display Lock command.

Figure 7.24

1	Use Technique T07.23 to create and scale viewport.	
2	[Paper Space Drawing Screen]	Double-click into an existing viewport. Use the Pan command to adjust the viewport's composition. Do not use any of the other Zoom commands, or they will unintentionally change the scale.
3	[Paper Space Drawing Screen]	Double-click outside of the viewport.
4	[Paper Space Drawing Screen]	Left-click on the viewport border to select the viewport. Use the blue grip squares to fine-tune the size of the viewport.
5	[Paper Space Drawing Screen]	Use the Move command to fine-tune the location of the viewport.
6	[Properties palette]	Select the viewport so you can set the Display Locked property to Yes. This prevents future accidental viewport zooming.

Box 7.8

Remember that if you use the zoom tools within a viewport after setting a scale, you lose the scaling value you assigned to the viewport. Locking the viewport after a scale has been assigned prevents this from happening.

Moving Between Model Space and Paper Space (Layout)

The Model/Paper toggle on the status bar is another way to switch between model space and paper space (Figure 7.25). With Model toggled on (by double-clicking *in* the viewport), you can use the Pan command to easily control the geometry displayed through the viewport window. With Paper toggled on (double-clicking *outside* of the viewport), you can select and modify the viewport object through grips or the Properties palette.

Additional Viewport Properties

The Standard scale and Custom scale are two of several unique properties of viewports that are controlled through the Properties palette. To view or edit these properties, left-click to select the viewport and scroll to the bottom of the Properties palette where Misc is visible (Figure 7.26). The additional properties are summarized in the paragraphs that follow.

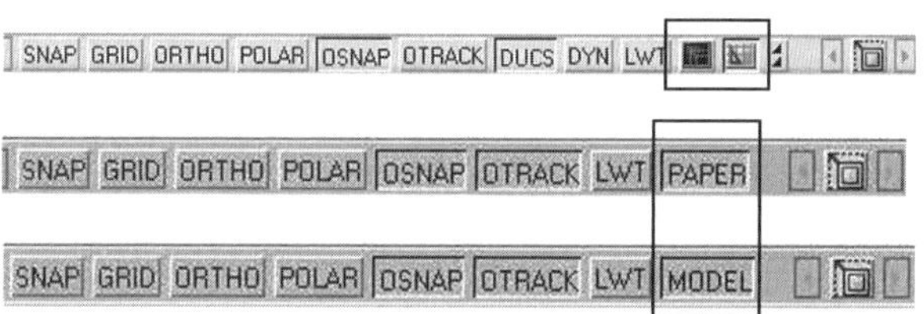

Figure 7.25 The Model/Paper toggle on the status bar is another way to switch between model space and paper space.

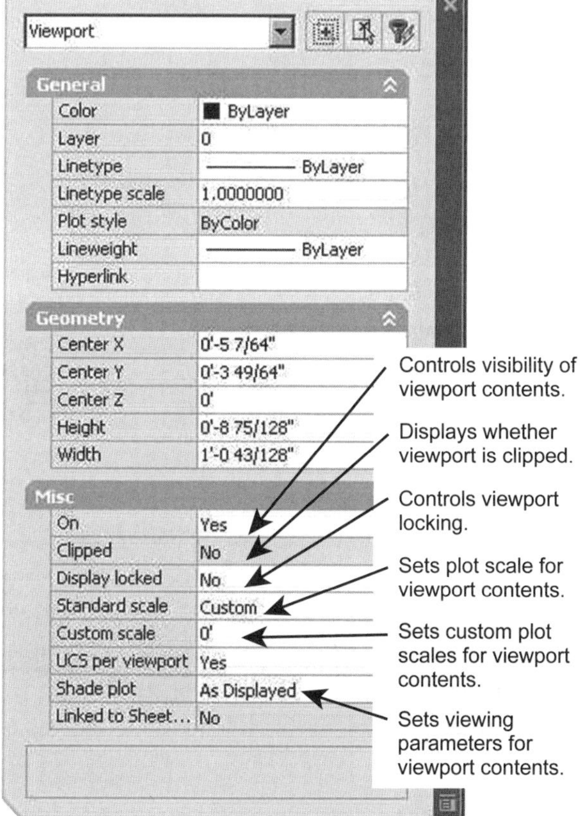

Figure 7.26 Getting to know viewport properties

Hiding the Viewports Contents

The On property is an on/off toggle that controls the visibility of the viewport's contents. When a viewport is off, the contents of the viewport are not visible and screen regeneration is much faster.

Viewport Clipping

Similar to an Xref, a viewport can be clipped to a nonrectangular shape. Figure 7.27 demonstrates this technique.

Locking the Viewport's Magnification

Once you scale and compose a viewport, the viewport locking property prevents accidental changes such as zooming from occurring.

Viewport Techniques

Figures 7.28 through 7.31 demonstrate several additional viewport techniques relevant to plot sheet preparation.

Setting Up a Drawing for Presentation and Plotting

This chapter has introduced you to all of the key ingredients necessary for setting up drawings for printing and plotting. File-management guidelines were introduced at the beginning of the chapter with a focus placed on multiple-file project organization. The file-linking concepts and the two distinct working environments were also discussed. All of the above concepts and techniques come together in the plot sheet setup process.

Creating plot sheets refers to the process where floor plan, section, elevation, and detail drawings are composed within a border (also called a title block). The resulting plot sheet is then ready to be printed. Many design firm standards separate their plot sheets from their design files by using multiple-file project organization techniques. Plot sheet .dwgs simply become the mechanism to link the design drawings to the border.

Technique to Master **T07.27** Viewport Clipping

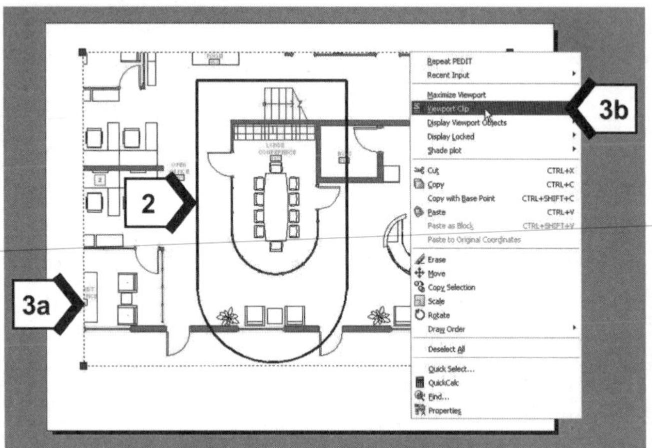

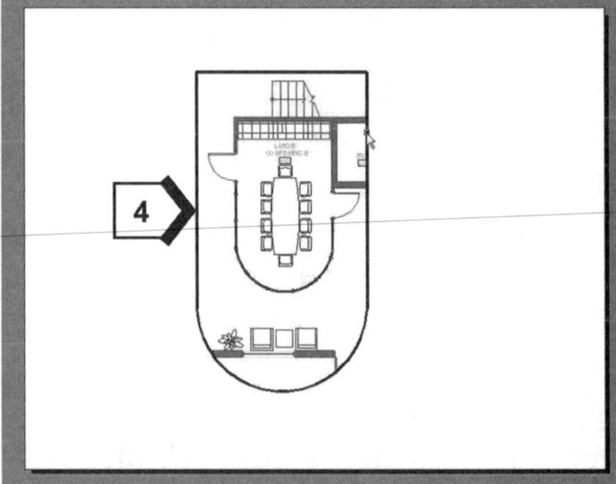

Figure 7.27

1	[AutoCAD Status bar]	Left-click on the Layout tab (or Work tab) to enter paper space.
2	[Paper Space Drawing Screen]	Draw closed polyline to define the new viewport boundary.
3	[Paper Space Drawing Screen]	Select viewport and right-click to choose the Viewport Clip command.
4	[Paper Space Drawing Screen]	Select closed shape.

Technique to Master **T07.28** Setting up Multiple New Viewports

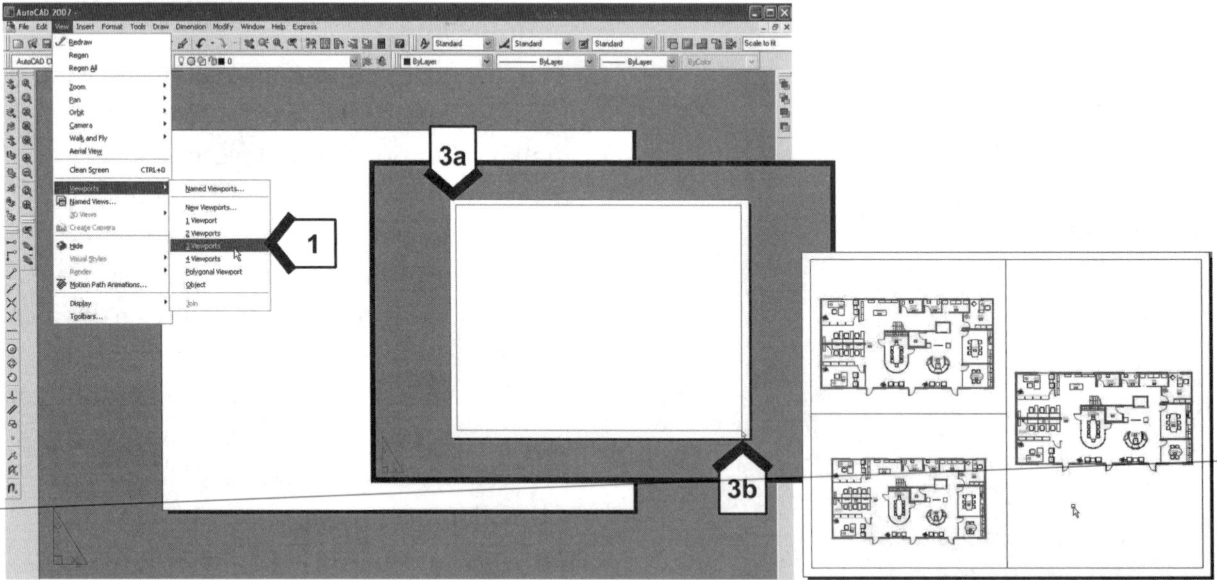

Figure 7.28

1	[View Menu]	Choose the number of viewports you want to create through the View>Viewports menus.
2	[Command Line]	Type your choice for viewport arrangement.
3a, 3b	[Drawing Screen]	Specify the boundary corners for viewport arrangement.

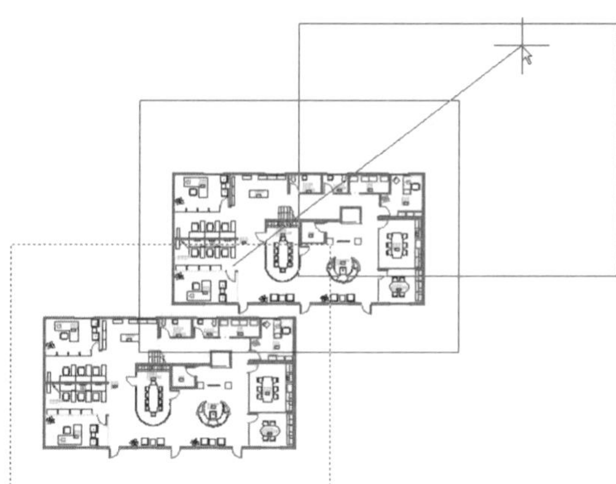

Technique to Master T07.29 Setting up Multiple Viewports by Copying

Figure 7.29

1	The contents of viewport duplicates may be invisible by default. To turn the viewport on, select the viewport, right-click, and use the on/off toggle under Display Viewport Objects.	
2	[Paper Space Drawing Screen]	Use the Copy command to copy existing viewports.

Courtesy of Tiffany White.

Technique to Master T07.30 Aligning Information Within Multiple Viewports in Layout View

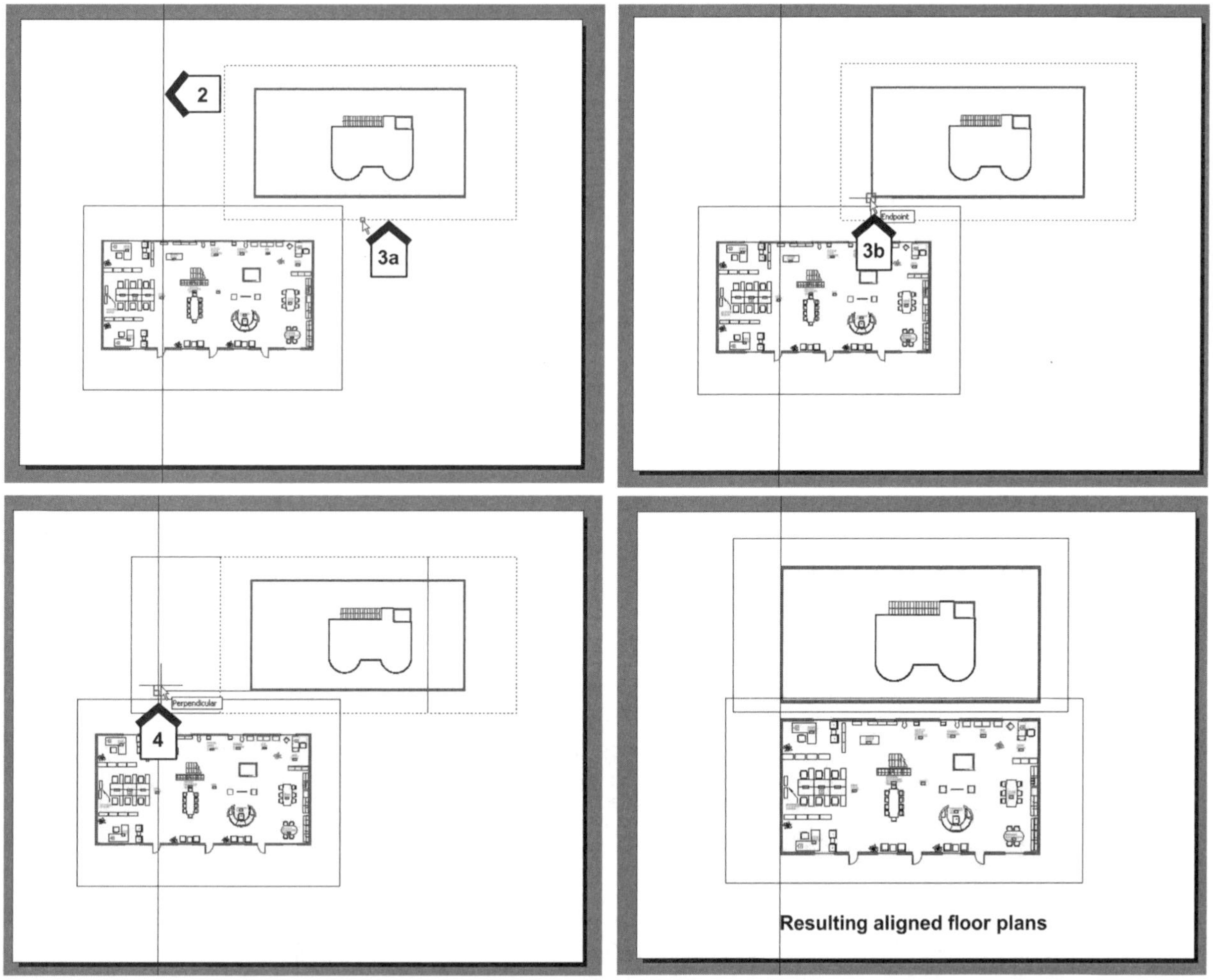

Figure 7.30 This technique is great for aligning multiple plan drawings on a plot sheet.

1	[AutoCAD Status bar]	Left-click on the Layout tab (or Work tab) to enter paper space.
2	[Paper Space Drawing Screen]	Create a temporary construction line using the Xline command at the point of alignment.
3	[Paper Space Drawing Screen]	Use the Move command to move viewport(s). Use object snaps to snap to a point within the viewport for the Move command's base point.
4	[Paper Space Drawing Screen]	Use the perpendicular object snap to align with the construction line.

Technique to Master T07.31 Converting an Object to a Viewport

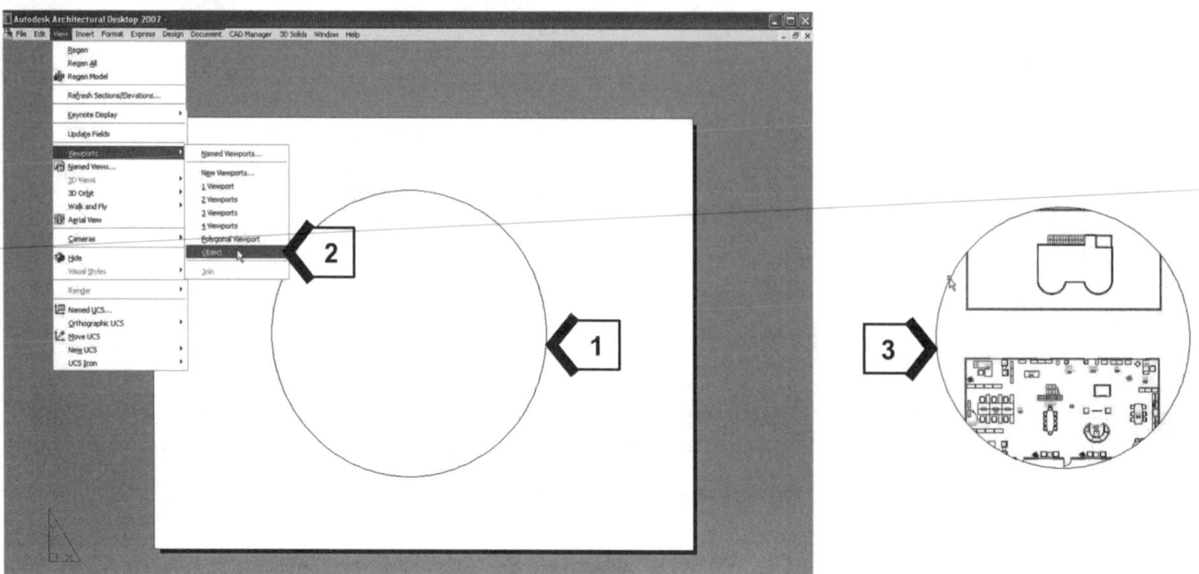

Figure 7.31

1	[Drawing Screen]	Create a closed polyline, circle, and/or rectangle.
2	[View menu]	Go to View>Viewports>Object to choose the Object command.
3	[Drawing Screen]	Select created object.

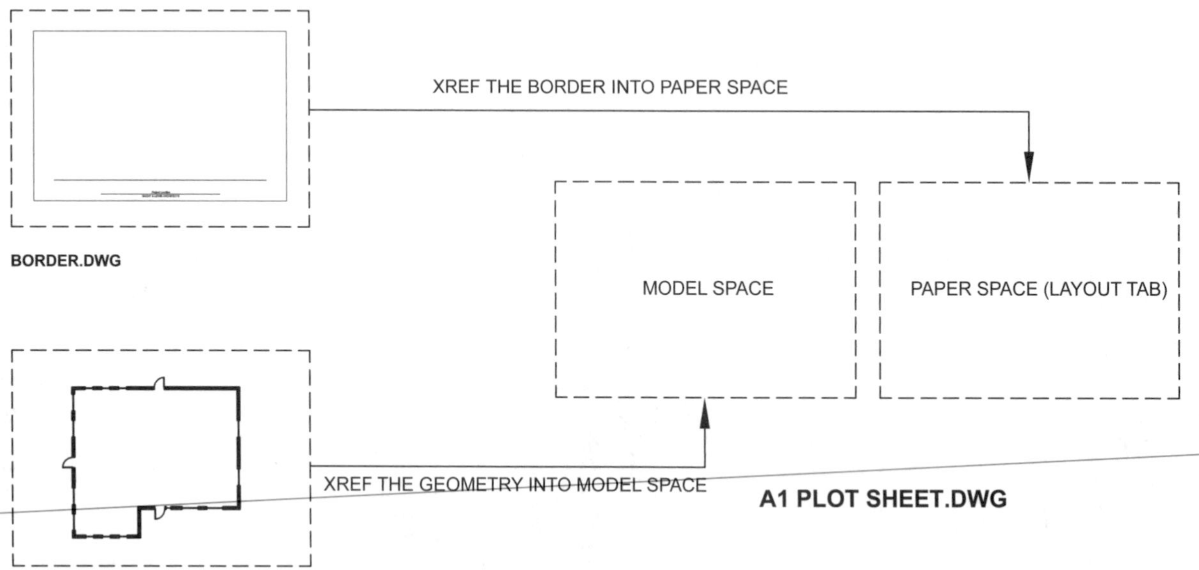

Figure 7.32 The diagram illustrates how the plot sheet A1 PLOT SHEET.dwg is created. First—in model space—the floor plan of the design (floor plan.dwg) is linked into the plot sheet. Second—in paper space—the border drawing file (border.dwg) is linked. A viewport window is then created with the appropriate scale assigned.

The diagram in Figure 7.32 illustrates how file organization, drawing linking, and the two drawing environments come together to create plot sheets. This procedure is repeated using the same border as diagrammed in Figure 7.33. Figure 7.34 demonstrates plot sheet setup.

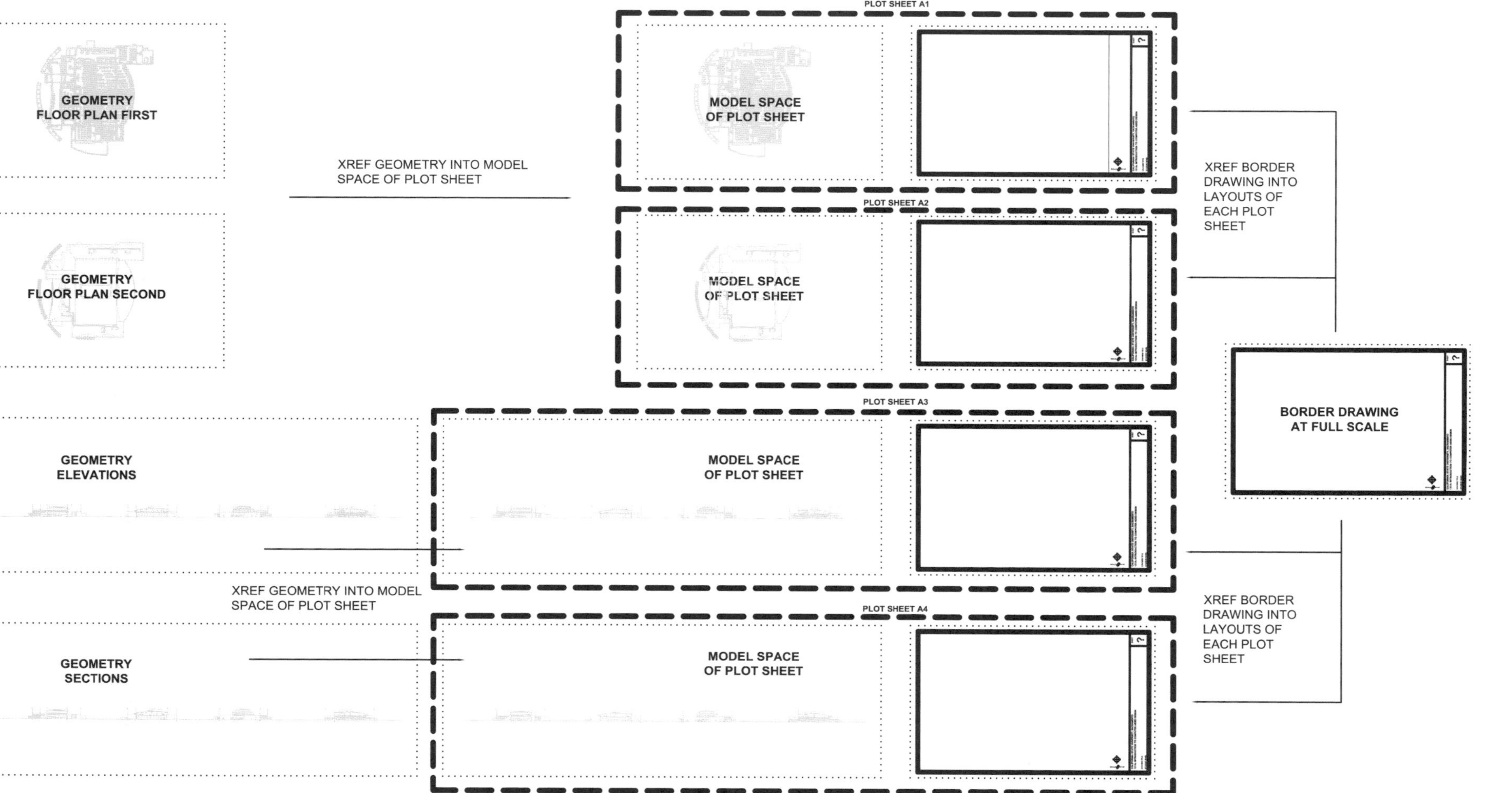

Figure 7.33 The diagram illustrates how several plot sheets within a project are set up by using the same border file. A new drawing file is created for each plot sheet. The project's orthographic drawings are then Xrefed into the model space of these files. The border drawing is Xrefed into the layout (paper space) of each of these plot sheet files.

Technique to Master T07.34 Creating Plot Sheets Without the Sheet Set Manager

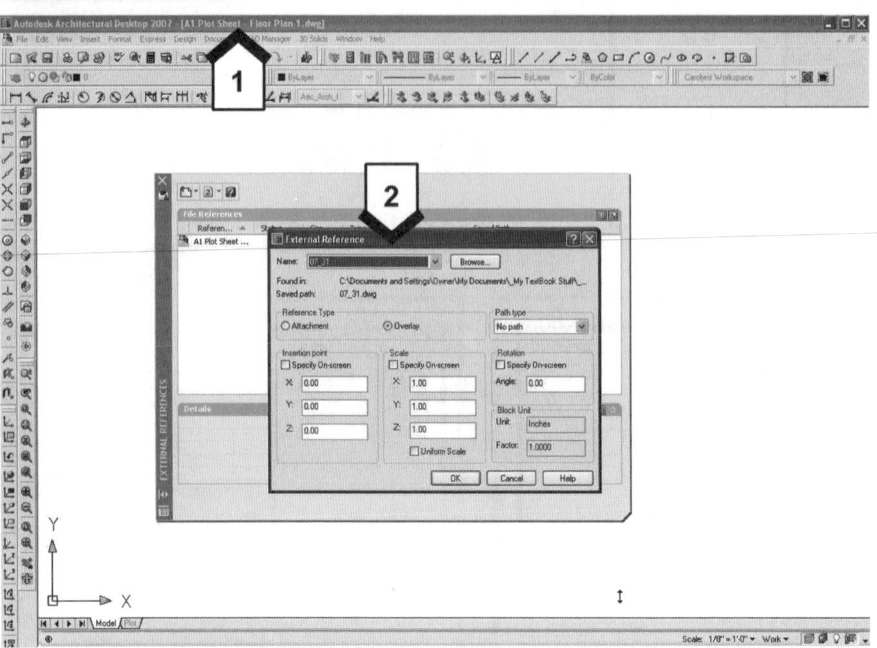

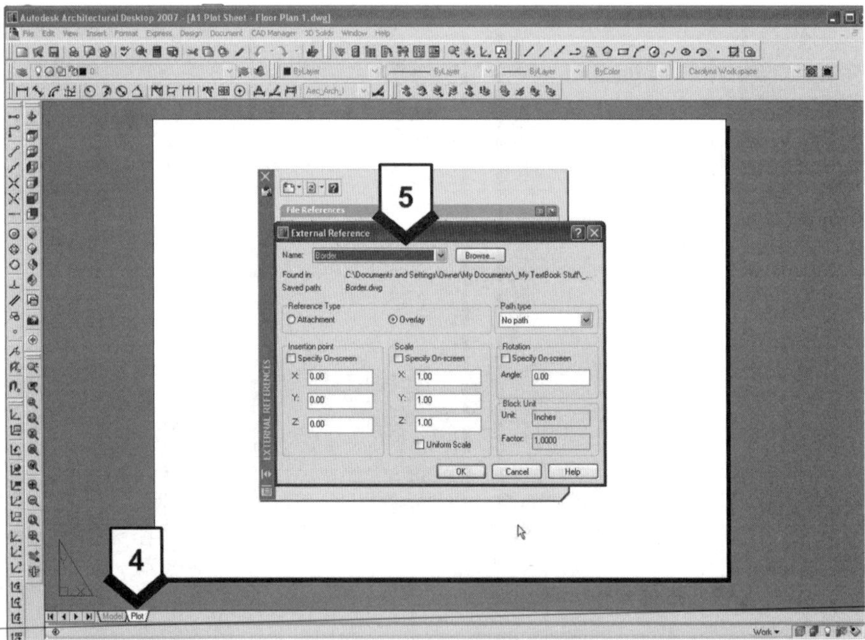

Figure 7.34

1	Create a new drawing for the plot sheet. Save drawing file as A? Plot Sheet.dwg, where the question mark represents a number within the sheet set.	
2	[Model Space Drawing Screen]	Xref design geometry at full scale (either the floor plan or section or elevation). Refer to Technique T07.09.
3	[Model Space Drawing Screen]	Use the Zoom Extents command if geometry does not appear immediately within the drawing area.
4	[AutoCAD Status bar]	Left-click on Layout tab (or Work tab) to enter paper space.
5	[Paper Space Drawing Screen]	Xref border.dwg at full scale. Refer to Technique T07.19.

(continued)

Technique to Master **T07.34** Creating Plot Sheets Without the Sheet Set Manager (cont.)

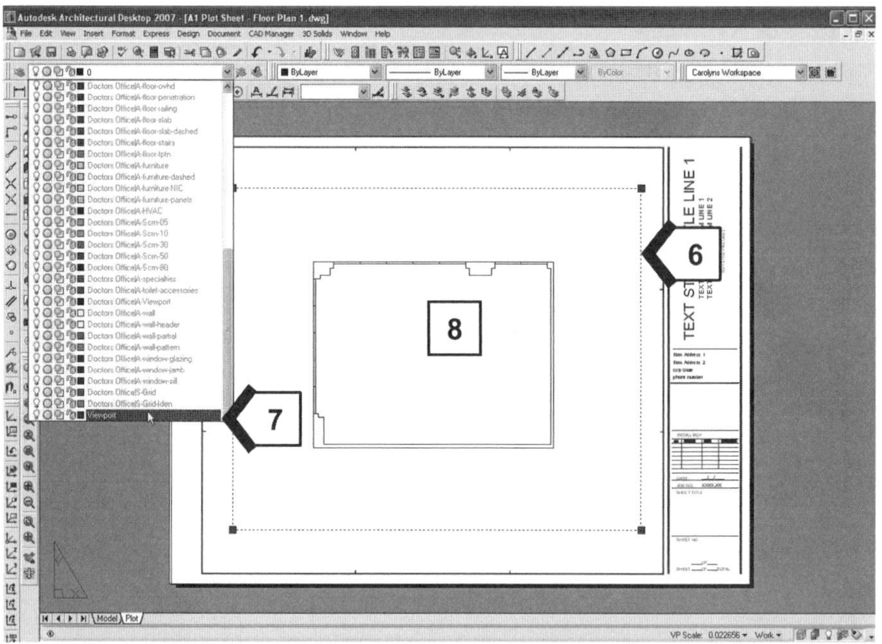

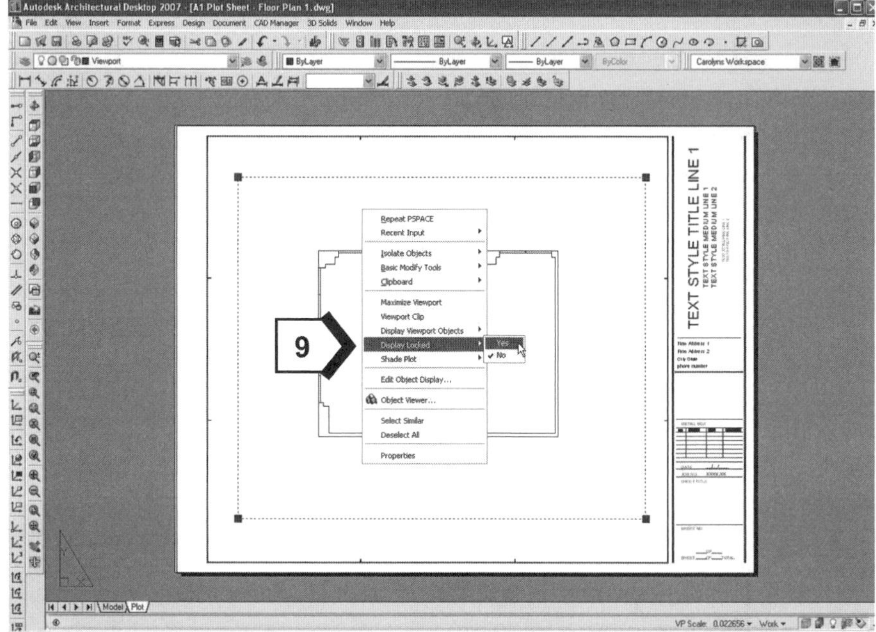

Figure 7.34 (continued)

6	[Paper Space Drawing Screen]	Create a viewport. Refer to Technique T07.23.
7	[Paper Space Drawing Screen]	Change viewport layer to A-viewport or any nonplotting layer. Refer to Technique T03.26.
8	[Paper Space Drawing Screen]	Compose model space view within the viewport. Refer to Technique T07.24.
9	[Paper Space Drawing Screen]	Lock the viewport.

AutoCAD Sheet Set Manager

AutoCAD's sheet set manager automates the process of assembling plot sheets as described in the previous section. You can open the Sheet Set Manager tool palette by using the shortcut Ctrl+4 or through the tool button on the Standard toolbar (Figure 7.35). Figure 7.36 shows the palette before a project folder has been specified. To use the Sheet Set Manager, use the New Sheet Set command found in the drop-down list at the top of the dialogue box. Figures on the supplementary CD-ROM demonstrate how to use the Sheet Set Manager to create and save plot sheets for a project.

Chapter Exercises

Open the Chapter 7 folder located on the supplementary CD-ROM to access the end-of-chapter exercises. These exercises let you get additional practice using linking (Xref) and paper space/model space concepts and techniques to draw second and third floors of buildings, ceiling plans, and elevations and to set up plot sheets.

Figure 7.35 The Sheet Set Manager tool is located in the Standard toolbar.

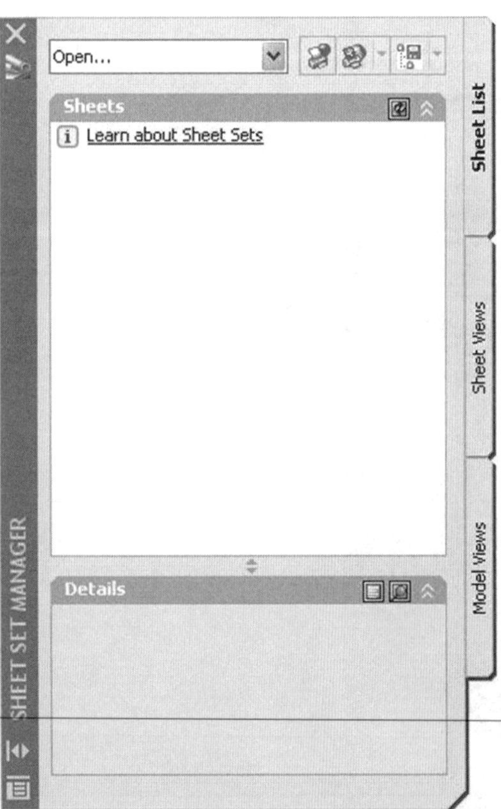

Figure 7.36 The Sheet Set Manager palette before a project has been specified

Part II

Learning to Draw in 3-D with Architectural Desktop

Introduction to the Third Dimension

8

Objectives

This chapter introduces you to the third dimension and thus touches on the various methods of 3-D modeling within the AutoCAD and Architectural Desktop drawing environments. It emphasizes the basic 3-D drawing tools and the viewing techniques used for displaying objects three-dimensionally. The end-of-chapter exercises give you the opportunity to get additional practice with modeling and viewing the basic geometric shapes.

The Addition of the Z-Axis

When you draw in 3-D, you represent all the dimensional characteristics of an object: width, depth, and height. The height characteristic of the object is the third dimension, represented by the Z-axis within AutoCAD.

Incorporating the Z-Axis

Chapter 2 introduced the default coordinate system used in AutoCAD and Architectural Desktop: the world coordinate system, or WCS. Figure 8.1 illustrates its icon symbol in plan and 3-D views. The three different directional axes of the WCS were also introduced in Chapter 2. The X-axis was related to the east/west direction; the Y-axis related to the north/south direction. The Z-axis is analogous to the upward direction (pointing toward the sky) and the downward direction (pointing toward the Earth's core). The Z-axis not only locates points at different elevations but also gives objects height. The 0 height plane is typically assigned to the ground plane, as shown in Figure 8.2. With the WCS as the current coordinate system, all geometry is typically drawn on this 0 height elevation plane. To get a better understanding of how the third dimension is used, the next section discusses the world coordinate system (WCS) and user coordinate system (UCS) in further detail.

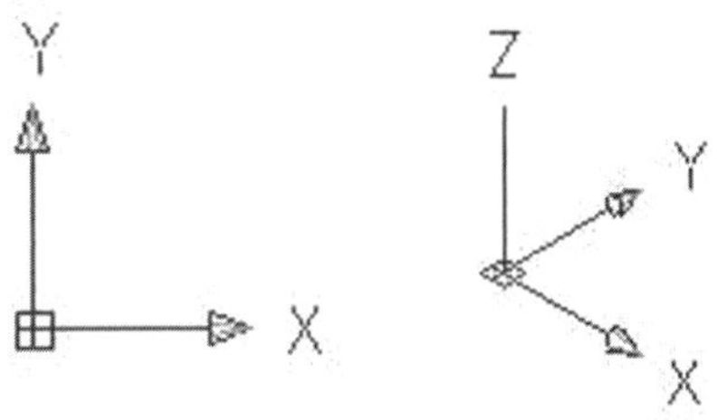

Figure 8.1 The World Coordinate System (WCS), plan symbol and 3-D symbol

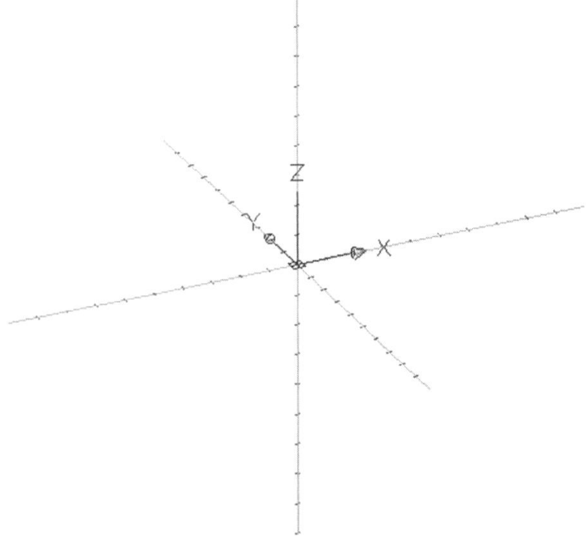

Figure 8.2 The WCS icon related to an imaginary grid. Notice that the origin of the WCS icon is located at the intersection of the three axes. The location at this intersection is also known as coordinate 0,0,0.

The UCS Command and 3-D

Whenever the default XYZ orientation is changed, the WCS turns into a UCS. Changing the WCS sets up a temporary working plane (the UCS) on which you can draw objects more efficiently.

The purpose of the most common WCS changes is to aid in object rotations. In the WCS, object rotations can occur only on the Z-axis, as shown in Figure 8.3a. For non-z-axis object rotations to occur, the xyz-axis orientation must change (Figure 8.3b).

Temporary UCS rotations are particularly handy when you need to extrude two-dimensional shapes. All two-dimensional objects that are given height (called extrusions) can extend only in the positive or negative Z directions (Figure 8.4a). By rotating the WCS, extrusions can occur in any direction (Figure 8.4b).

> **Box 8.1**
>
> The Ortho command is tied to the current UCS and restricts movement in the directions of the current x- and y-axis.

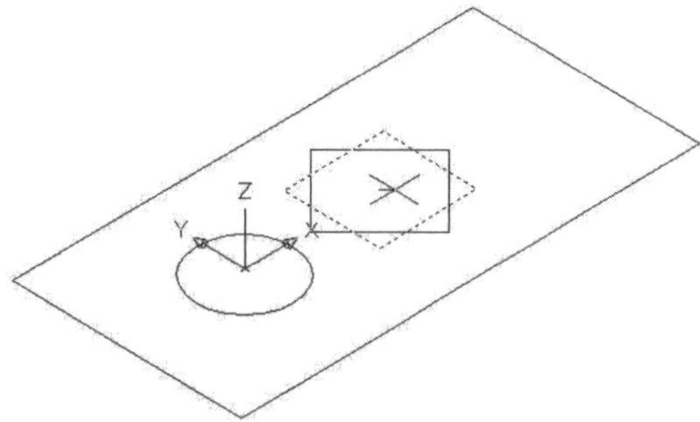

Figure 8.3a Rotating the WCS to accomplish object rotations: notice the default WCS with the Z direction pointed upward allows for only horizontal rotations.

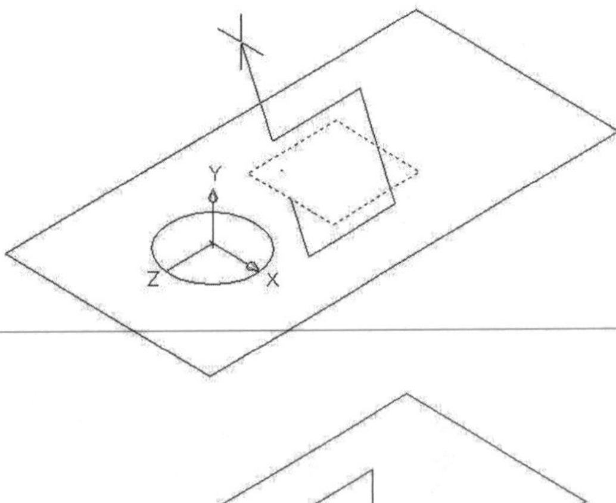

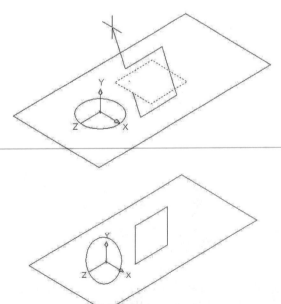

Figure 8.3b Rotating the WCS to accomplish object rotations: the temporary UCS changes the Z direction where the Z-axis points to allow for nonplanar object rotations.

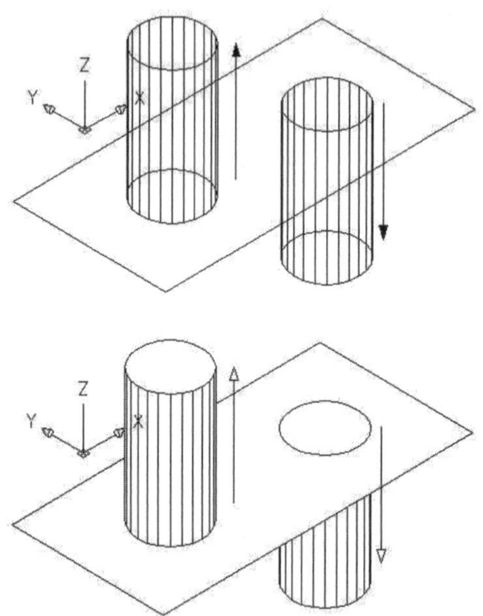

Figure 8.4a 3-D extrusions and their relationship to the WCS/UCS: With the default WCS, you can extrude a circle upward and downward by giving it a thickness value to create a cylinder. This illustration shows both wireframe and hidden line views.

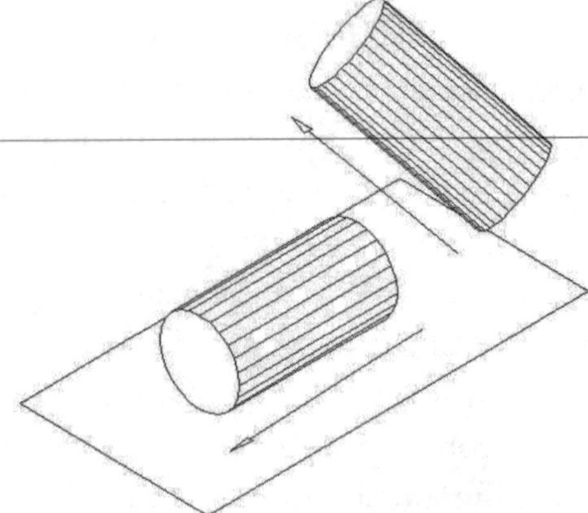

Figure 8.4b 3-D extrusions and their relationship to the WCS/UCS: When you rotate the WCS to various angles, you can extrude the circle in other directions to create the cylinder.

Temporarily Changing the WCS (UCS Rotation Techniques)

There are several methods for rotating and realigning the WCS. You can accomplish simple rotations through the UCS toolbar (Figure 8.5). Furthermore, you can align with existing objects by using either the UCS>Object option (Figure 8.6) or through the UCS>3-point option of the UCS command (see Figure 8.7)

Once you rotate the UCS, use the Plan command to align the view window with the UCS rotation (Figure 8.8). You can save this temporary UCS for future use through the Dducs command (Figure 8.9).

> **Box 8.2**
> To return the UCS to the default WCS, use the UCS>World command.

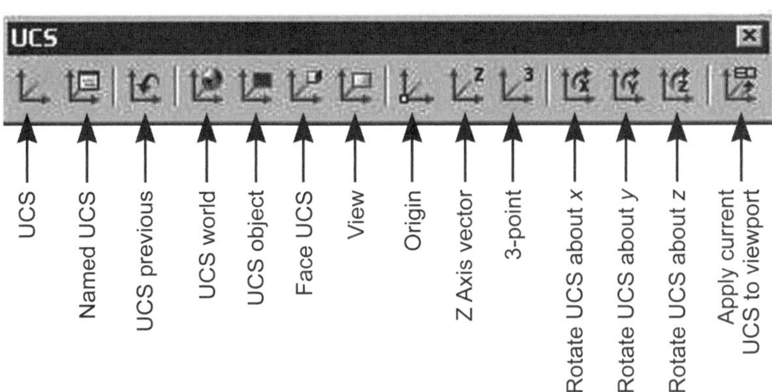

Figure 8.5 The UCS toolbar

Technique to Master **T08.06** Aligning the WCS with an Object's Surface

```
Command: UCS
Current UCS name: *NO NAME*
Enter an option [New/Move/orthoGraphic/Prev/Restore/Save/Del/Apply/?/World]
<World>: ob
Select object to align UCS:
```

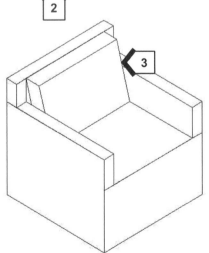

2

3

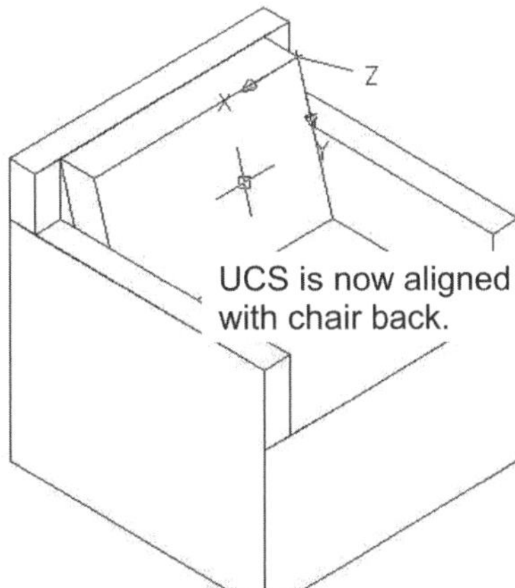

Figure 8.6

1	[Command Line]	Type UCS, and press Enter.
2	[Command Line]	Type ob, and press Enter.
3	[Drawing Screen]	Select the object you want UCS to align with.

Technique to Master **T08.07** Rotating the UCS Using the 3-Point Option

```
Command: UCS
Current UCS name: *WORLD*
Enter an option [New/Move/orthoGraphic/Prev/Restore/Save/Del/Apply/?/World]
<World>: 3p
Specify new origin point <0,0,0>:
Specify point on positive portion of X-axis
Specify point on positive-Y portion of the UCS XY plane
```

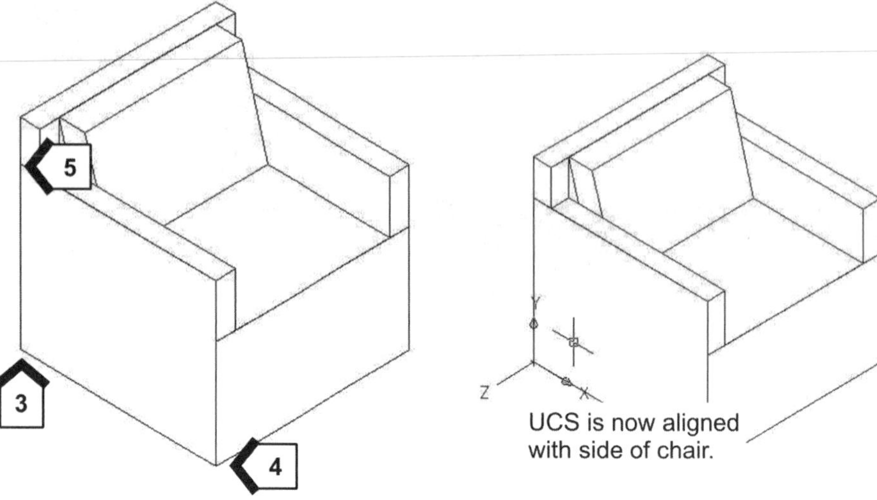

Figure 8.7

1	[Command Line]	Type UCS, and press Enter.
2	[Command Line]	Type 3p, and press Enter.
3	[Drawing Screen]	Specify the location for the new UCS origin.
4	[Drawing Screen]	Specify the point from the origin that will be the positive x-axis direction.
5	[Drawing Screen]	Specify the point from the origin that will be the positive y-axis direction.

Technique to Master **T08.08** Aligning the View with the Current UCS

Command: PLAN
Enter an option [Current ucs/Ucs/World] <Current>:
Regenerating model.

Figure 8.8

1	[Command Line]	Type PLAN, and press Enter.
2	[Command Line]	Type Current, and press Enter.

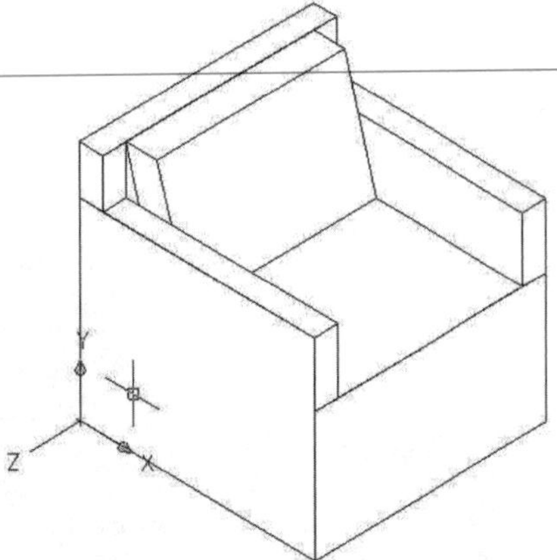

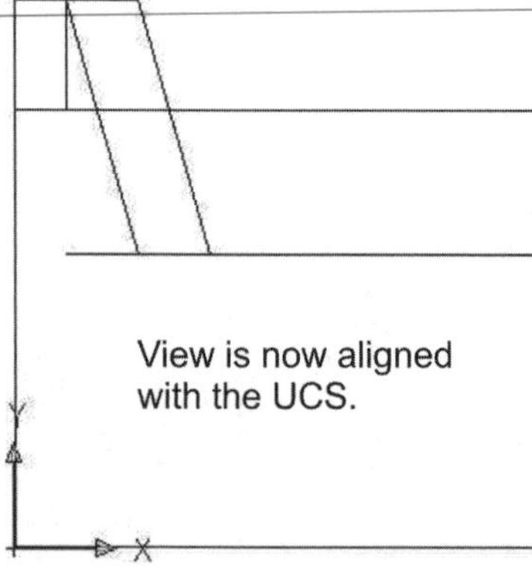

T08.09 Saving a Temporary UCS for Future Retrieval

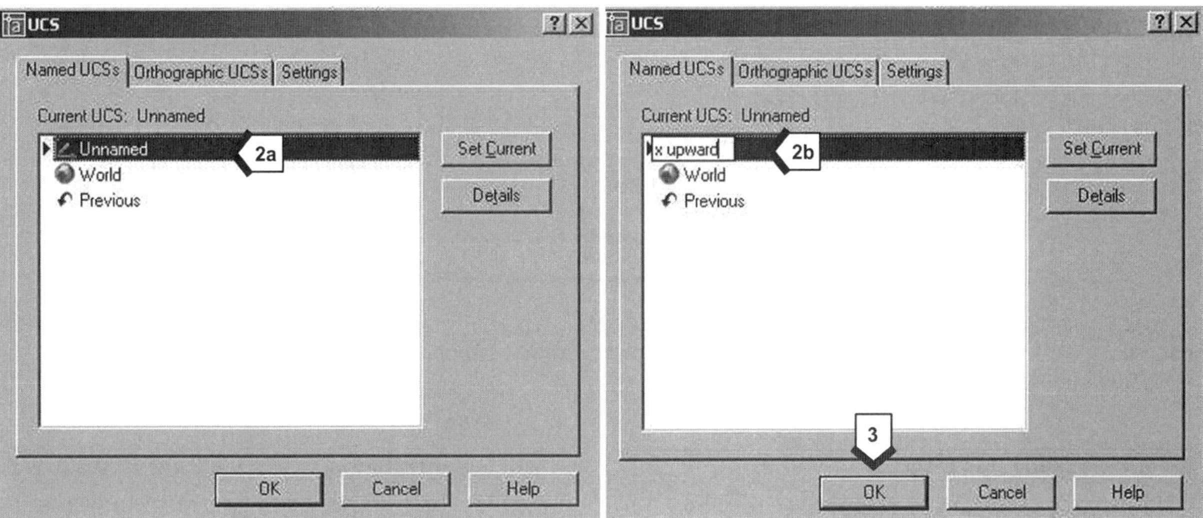

Figure 8.9

1	[Command Line]	Type DDUCS, and press Enter.
2a, 2b	[UCS dialogue box]	Double-click on the unnamed UCS, and rename it.
3	Click OK to save it.	

The WCS/UCS Icon

By default the WCS/UCS icon is shown in the lower left-hand corner. The Dducsicon dialogue command contains settings to relocate the position where the icon is displayed on-screen as well as settings to turn off its display (Figure 8.10).

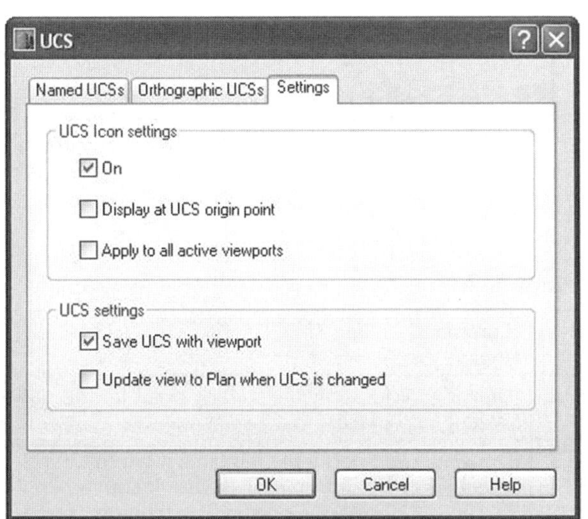

Figure 8.10 The UCS Settings dialogue box

The 3-D Object Types

All CAD programs use one or more of the three approaches to creating three-dimensional objects. The paragraphs that follow briefly summarize AutoCAD's three-dimensional modeling tools before introducing Architectural Desktop.

AutoCAD uses two primary modeling approaches (which have been available since the tenth release): surface and solid modeling. Surface modeling uses zero thickness planes that describe the different sides of a three-dimensional object. Objects built with surface-modeling techniques are hollow. The tools to create them include extrusions, 3-D faces, regions, and meshes. In the solid modeling approach, objects are not hollow and have additional dimensional properties of volume and density.

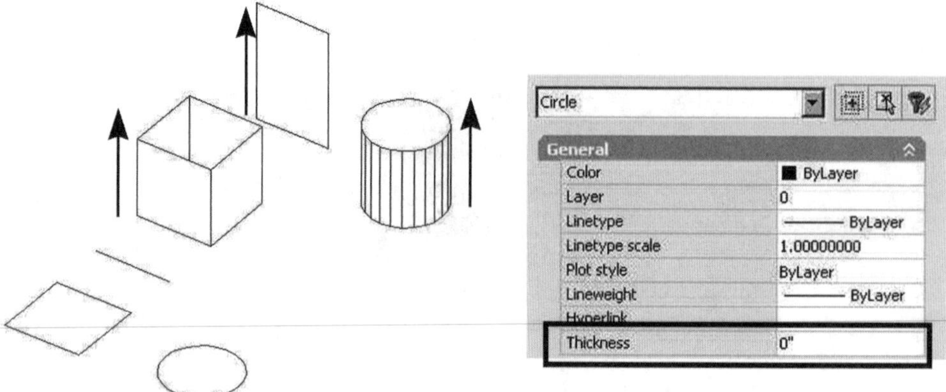

Figure 8.11 2-D object extrusions using the thickness property: extrude 2-D objects by changing the thickness property to a value other than 0".

Extrusions from 2-D Objects

3-D extrusions in AutoCAD are created by giving existing 2-D objects a thickness value (see Figure 8.11). You can change an object's thickness through the properties palette. When you give thickness to 2-D lines, they become planes; similarly, when you add thickness to circles, they become cylinders, and when you do so to rectangles, they become open boxes. Essentially, by using the thickness value, you can create simple three-dimensional objects quickly.

> **Box 8.3**
> While the Thickness property is still available in current releases of AutoCAD, most three-dimensional models do not use this property since surface and solid modeling are more practical.

3-D Faces and Surface Meshes

If you want to create 3-D faces, you can do so by manually specifying points (corners) of the surface. You need a minimum of three points to create a surface. If you use four points, then you will create a rectangular surface. Figure 8.12 demonstrates the technique.

Surface meshes use 3-D Faces to create a complex surface that usually approximates a curve (see Figure 8.13). Although it is made up of multiple 3-D Faces, surface meshes behave as a single object. The size of surface mesh rectangles are controlled by the Surftab1 and Surftab2 variables—variables that specify a cell size by defining the number of columns and rows within the mesh. There are several kinds of meshes, including Rulesurf meshes and Revsurf meshes, as shown in Figure 8.14.

Technique to Master **T08.12** Creating a 3-D Face to Provide the Top for the Box

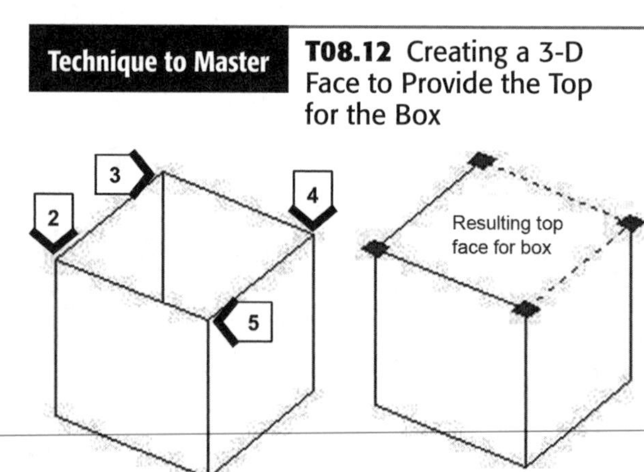

Figure 8.12

1	[Command Line]	Type 3f.
2	[Drawing Screen]	Specify the starting point for the face.
3 4 5	[Drawing Screen]	Specify the remaining two to three points in a clockwise or counter-clockwise order. Three points create a triangular face; four points create a rectangular face.

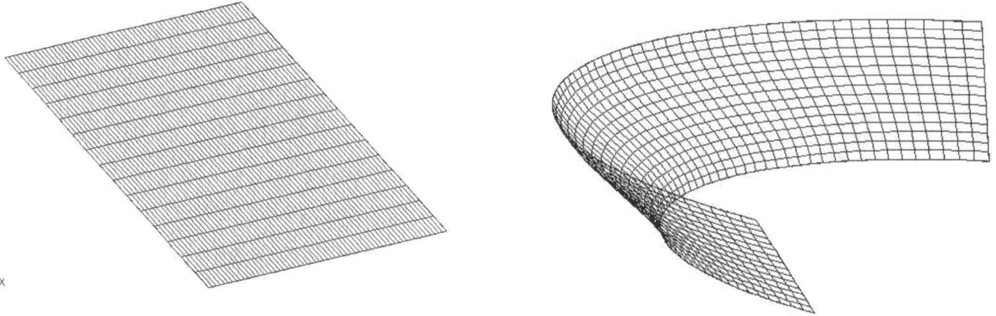

Figure 8.13 Surface meshes use 3-D Faces to create a complex surface that usually approximates a curve. Example shows two surface meshes—a flat mesh and a curved mesh.

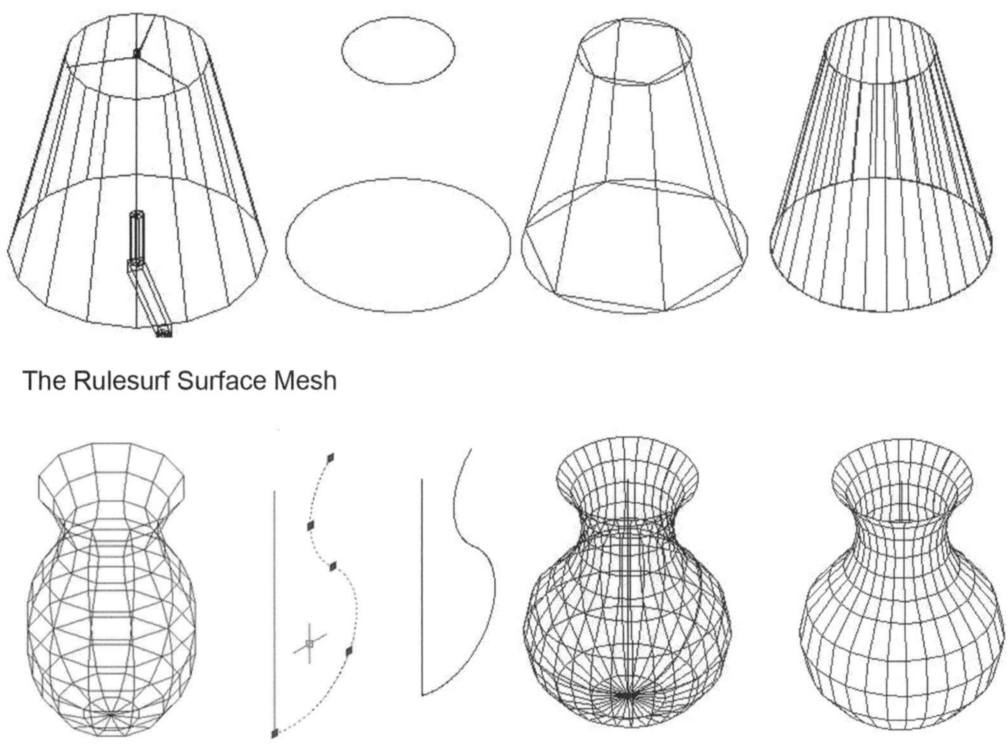

Figure 8.14 Other surface meshes include the Rulesurf mesh and Revsurf mesh, shown in this example of a lamp shade and vase, created with these two surface meshes, respectively.

Creating Complex Surfaces with Surface Modeling

By using a combination of axis rotation and 2-D extrusion, you can create many complex objects. Complex objects are drawn by using a combination of mesh types, 3-D faces, and 2-D extrusions (Figure 8.15).

> **Box 8.4**
>
> The 2007 edition includes all the surface mesh types that are now available in the solid modeling tools and that have become much more intuitive with these tools.

Solid Models

Solid model objects differ from three-dimensional surfaces because they carry the same physical attributes of an actual solid object. Solid model objects are often used to create objects used in engineering so that additional analysis can be performed. You will find, however, that adding solid model objects to your tool kit gives you additional modeling and editing commands that are not readily available in Architectural Desktop's component command set. Chapter 10 shows you how to use solid model objects within the Architectural Desktop interface.

The basic solid model object types include the cube, cone, cylinder, sphere, solid torus, and wedge (Figure 8.16). Each of these objects (including solid model extrusions) can be combined to create more complex geometry through the Boolean functions Extrude, Revolve, Union, Subtract, Intersect, Slice, Imprint, Separate, and Shell. Figure 8.17 shows examples of each of the above functions.

3-D Improvements in AutoCAD 2007

AutoCAD 2007 brought a host of new improvements to its 3-D tools and interface. The 3-D Modeling Workspace includes a new palette, the Dashboard, which provides easy access to all of AutoCAD's 3-D tools, including its viewing, lighting, materials, and rendering tools. The section that follows introduces the Dashboard and the new 3-D creation and modification tools added to AutoCAD 2007.

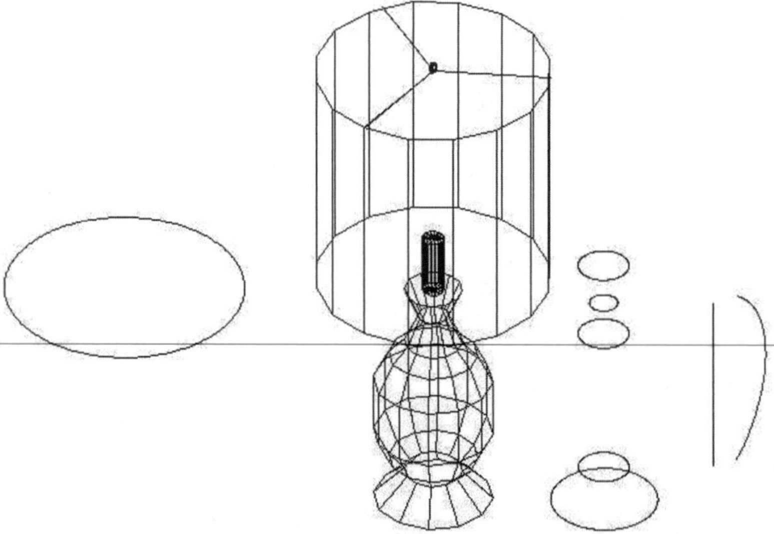

Figure 8.15 Combining the extrusion and surface-modeling techniques to create complex objects

3D Solids

Polysolid
Box
Wedge
Cone
Sphere
Cylinder
Torus
Pyramid
Helix
Planar Surface

Convert to 3D Solids

Extrude
Revolve
Sweep
Loft
Union
Subtract
Intersect
Slice
Section
Thicken
Convert to Solid

Faces
Edges

Imprint
Clean
Separate
Shell
Check
Setup

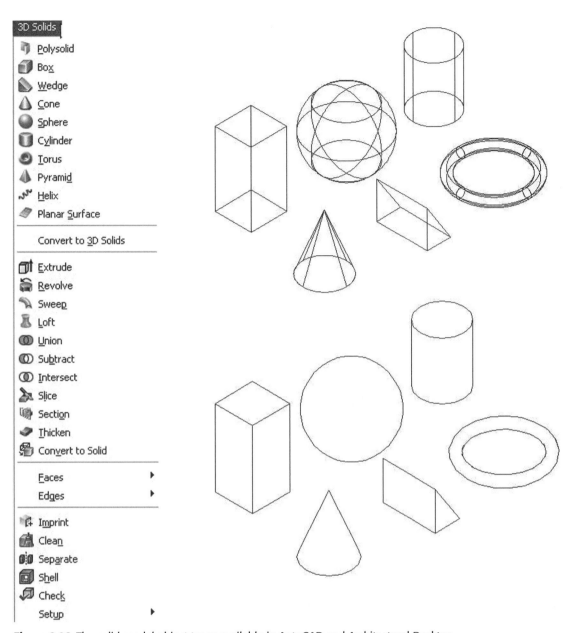

Figure 8.16 The solid model object types available in AutoCAD and Architectural Desktop

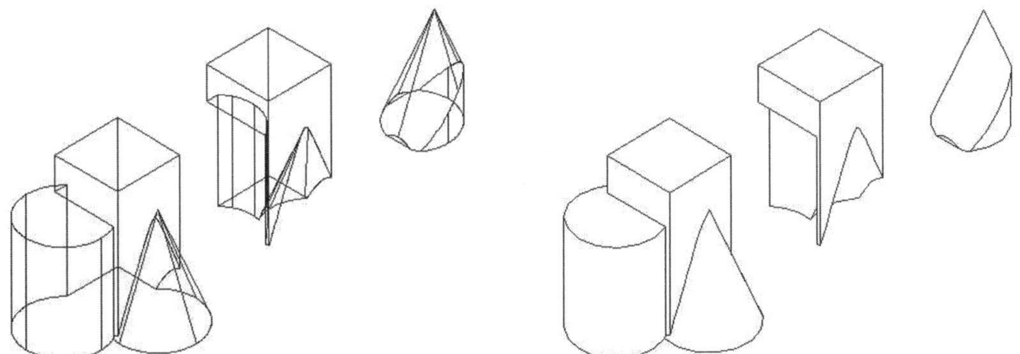

Figure 8.17 The Boolean functions of Extrude, Revolve, Union, Subtract, Intersect, Slice, Imprint, Separate, and Shell shown in the wireframe view on the left and hidden line view on the right.

The Dashboard Palette

Figure 8.18 identifies the assorted areas of the Dashboard palette. Notice that the tools are grouped into categories called control panels. They include the 2-D Draw, 3-D Make, 3-D Navigate, Visual Style, Light, Materials, and Render control panels. You can expand each control panel to display additional tools within that category (Figure 8.19).

> **Box 8.5**
> The Material, Light, and Render tools are not discussed within this text. Refer to AutoCAD's online help to learn about rendering in AutoCAD.

The tools within each control panel are used in the same way as any tool on the Tool palette, that is, by left-clicking to access the command. Explore each of the 3-D Make tools.

The 3-D Tools Added to 2007

AutoCAD 2007 makes it much easier to create and edit 3-D objects. Figures 8.20 through 8.25 demonstrate how to create 3-D objects with these new additions.

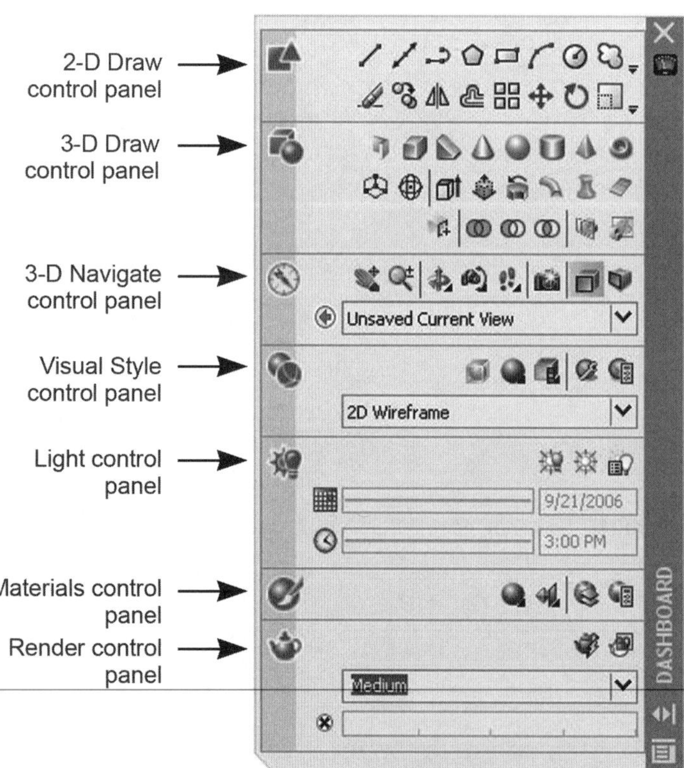

Figure 8.18 The Dashboard palette is a new addition to AutoCAD 2007; it has all the tools necessary to create, modify, view, and render AutoCAD 3-D objects.

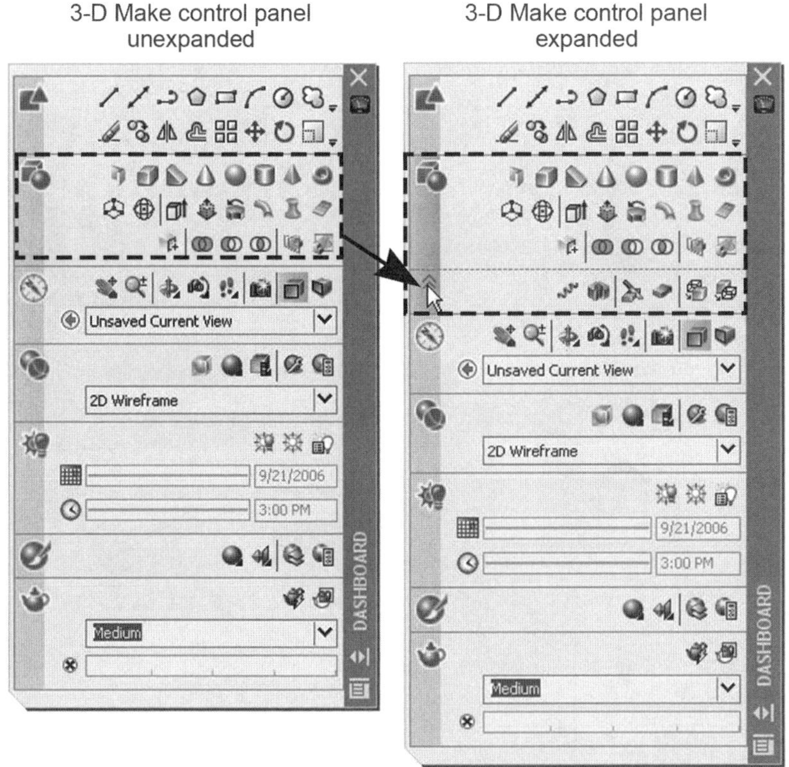

Figure 8.19 Each control panel within the Dashboard palette can be expanded to display additional tools.

Technique to Master **T08.20** Creating a Polysolid by Specifying Points

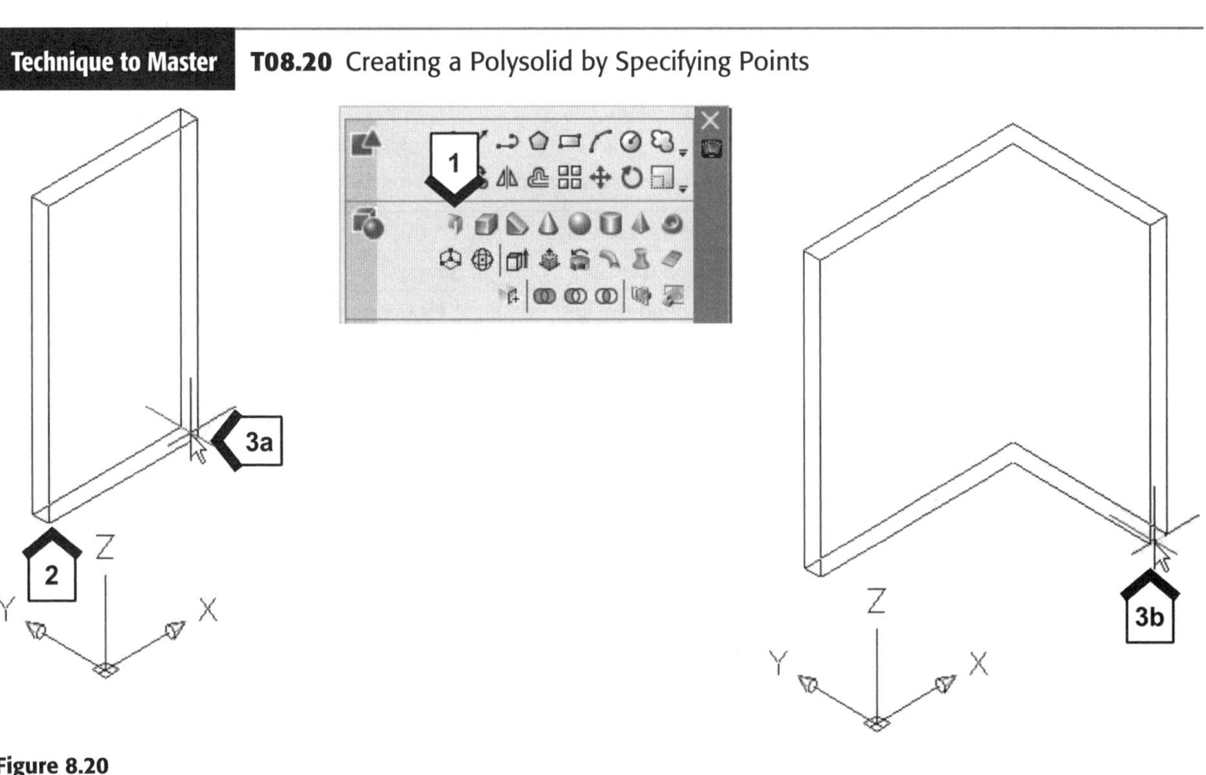

Figure 8.20

1	[Command Line]	Access the Polysolid tool on the Dashboard palette.
2	[Drawing Screen]	Locate the start point for the polysolid.
3a, 3b	[Drawing Screen]	Continue locating points until the polysolid shape is complete.

Technique to Master **T08.21** Creating a Polysolid by Selecting Objects

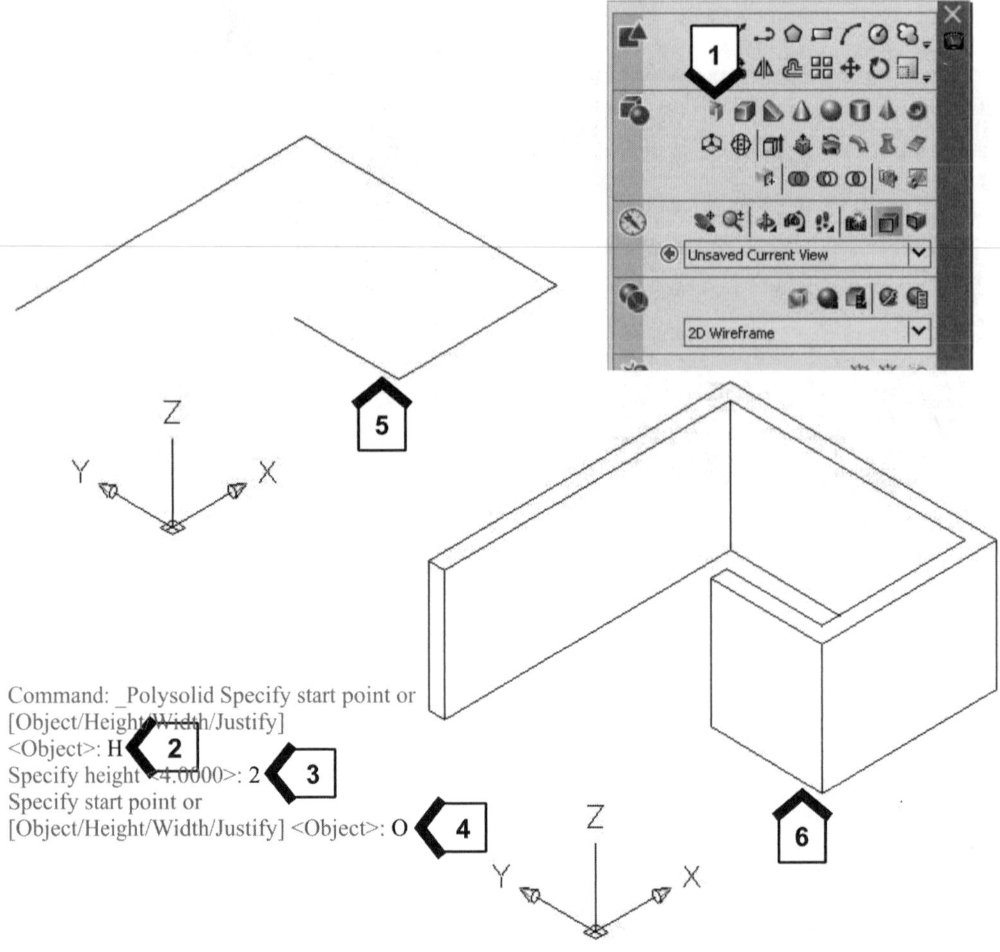
1
Unsaved Current View
2D Wireframe
5
Z
Y
X
Command: _Polysolid Specify start point or
[Object/Height/Width/Justify]
<Object>: H
2
Specify height <4.0000>: 2
3
Specify start point or
[Object/Height/Width/Justify] <Object>: O
4
6

Figure 8.21 Any existing line, arc, circle, or polyline can be used to create a polysolid.

1	[Command Line]	Access the Polysolid tool on the Dashboard palette.
2	[Command Line]	Type H to specify Height option.
3	[Command Line]	Type in the desired height for the polysolid.
4	[Command Line]	Type O to specify Object option.
5	[Drawing Screen]	Select the object you want to change into a polysolid.
6	[Drawing Screen]	The polysolid is created from linework.

Technique to Master **T08.22** Creating a Helix

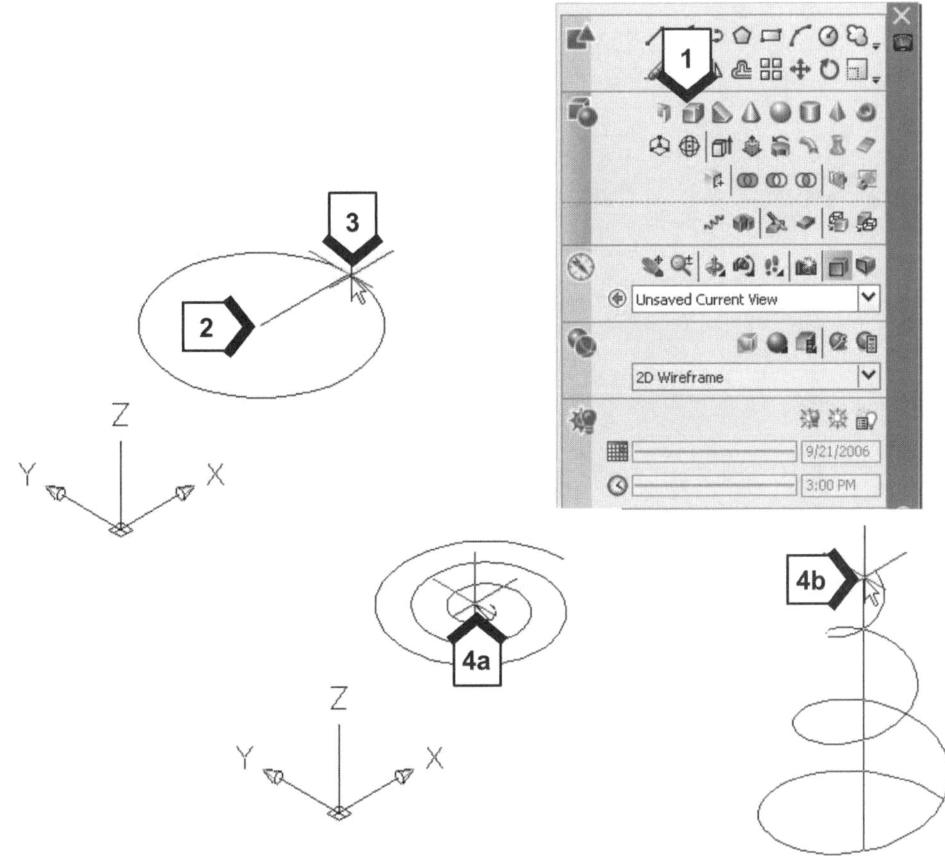

Figure 8.22

1	[Command Line]	Access the Helix tool on the Dashboard palette.
2	[Drawing Screen]	Locate the center point for the bottom part of the helix.
3	[Drawing Screen]	Locate the radius for the bottom part of the helix. (This may be specified by typing in a radius value in the Command Line.)
4a, 4b	[Command Line]	Specify the helix height by either locating two points on the drawing screen or typing in a height value.

Technique to Master **T08.23** Using the Sweep Tool

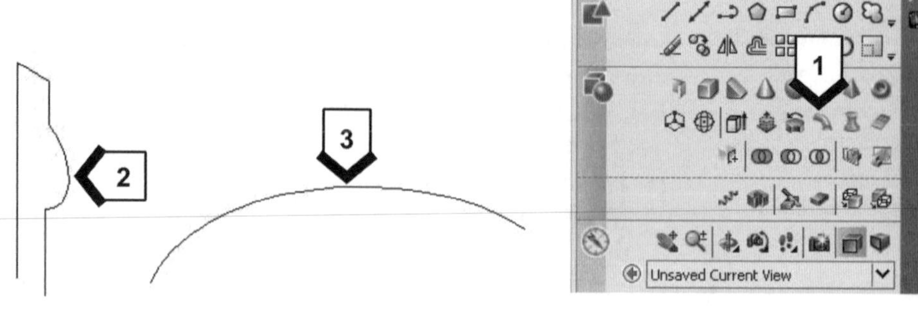

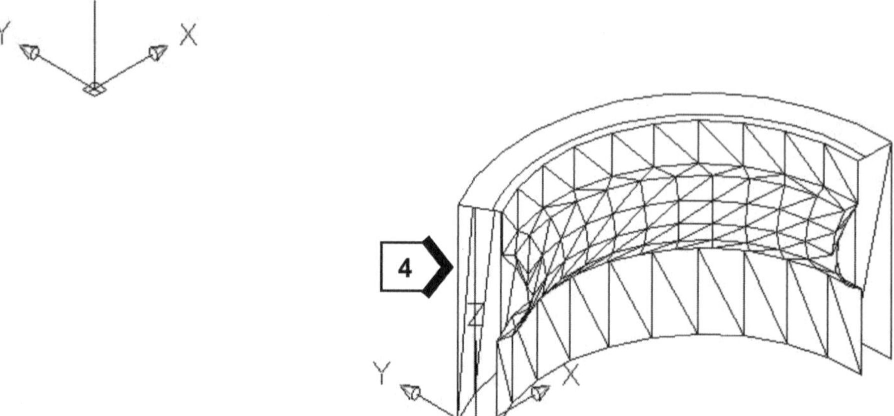

Figure 8.23

1	[Command Line]	Access the Sweep tool on the Dashboard palette.
2	[Drawing Screen]	Select the 2-D object to use for the sweep.
3	[Drawing Screen]	Select the sweep path.
4	[Drawing Screen]	Completed the sweep created from linework.

Technique to Master **T08.24** Using the Loft Tool

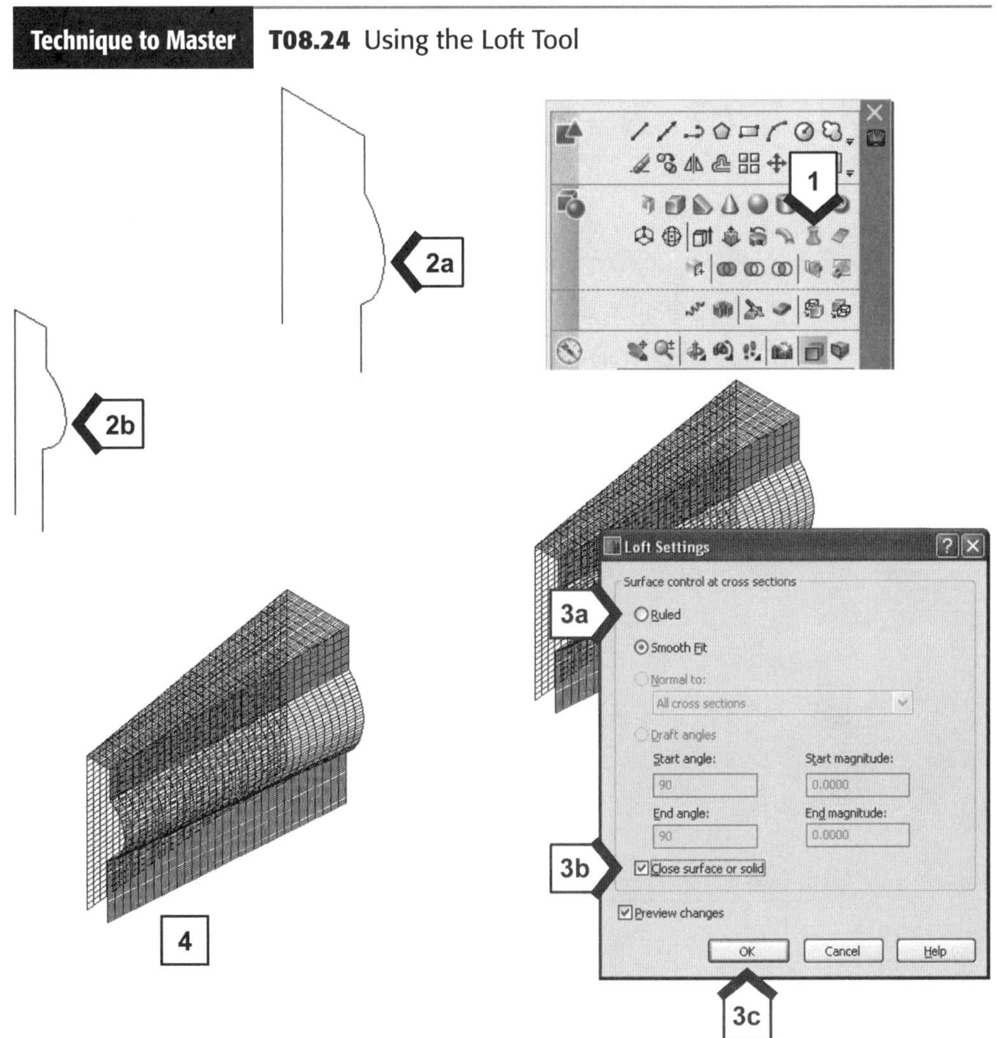

Figure 8.24

1	[Command Line]	Access the Loft tool on the Dashboard palette.
2a, 2b	[Drawing Screen]	Select the two open polylines, lines, and/or arcs that represent the profile or cross-section of the loft.
3a, 3b, 3c	[Loft Settings Dialogue]	Specify how the objects will loft.
4	[Drawing Screen]	Completed loft object created from linework.

Technique to Master **T08.25** Using the Slice Tool

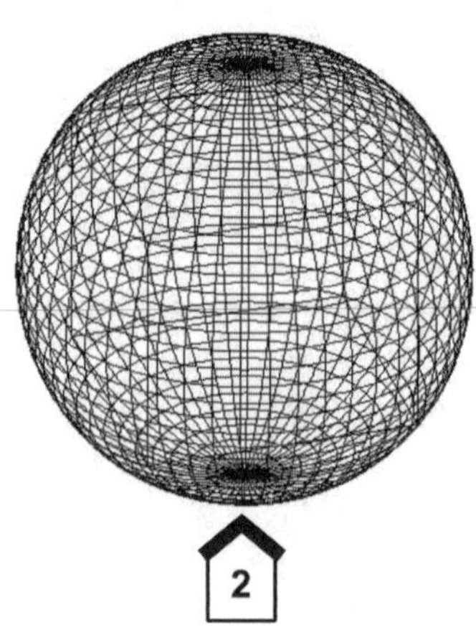

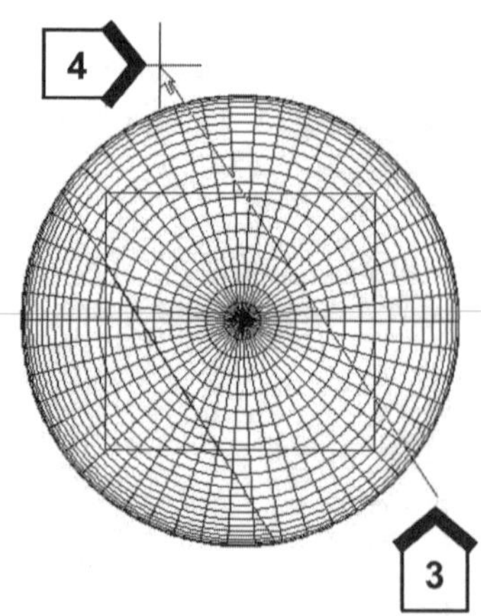

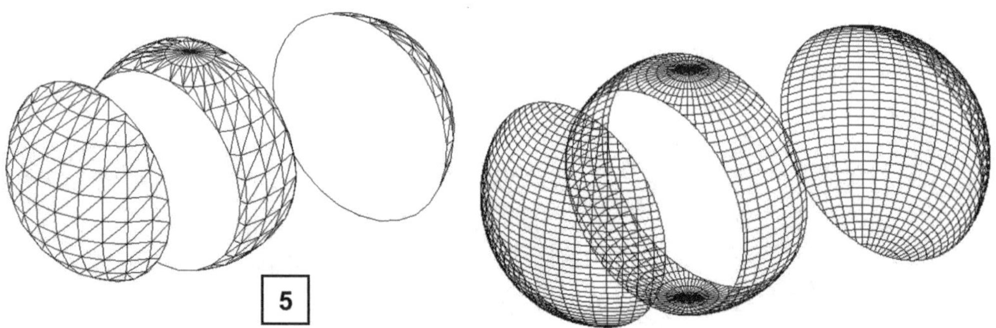

Figure 8.25

1	[Command Line]	Access the Slice tool on the Dashboard palette.
2	[Drawing Screen]	Select the 3-D objects to slice.
3	[Drawing Screen]	Specify the first slice point on the 3-D object.
4	[Drawing Screen]	Specify the second slice point on the 3-D object.
5	[Command Line]	Type B and press Enter to keep both sides of the 3-D object.

Modifying 3-D Objects

Modification to AutoCAD 3-D objects has been simplified in the 2007 release. Objects can now be edited with special grip locations using a push/pull technique. Each part of an object—its edges, faces, or vertices—can all be selected and modified using this technique. Figures 8.26 through 8.29 demonstrate the various 3-D object modification techniques.

Technique to Master **T08.26** Selecting and Modifying the Subobjects (Faces, Edges, and Vertices) of a 3-D Object

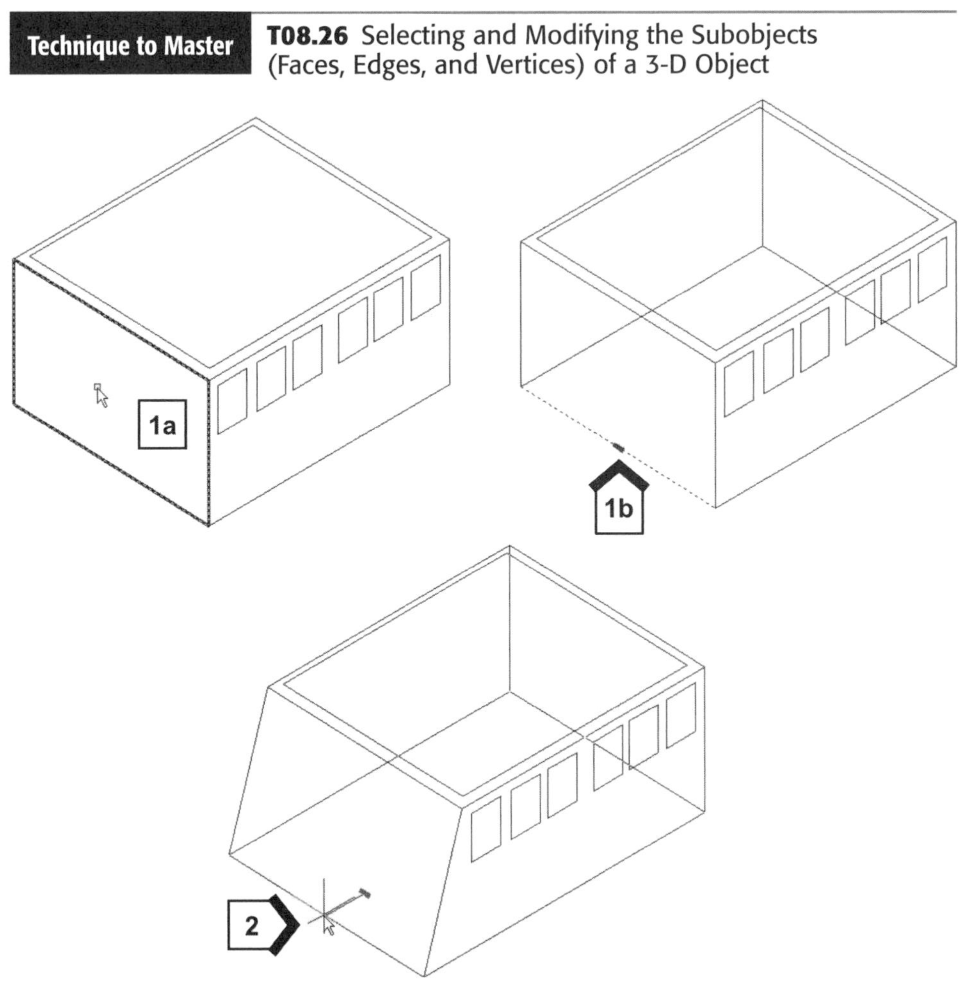

Figure 8.26

1a, 1b	Press the Ctrl key to select the subobjects.
2	Press Shift + Ctrl to deselect the subobjects.
3	Left-click and hold down the mouse button while dragging to modify.

Technique to Master **T08.27** Using the Grip Tools to Modify the Subobjects (Faces, Edges, and Vertices) of a 3-D Object

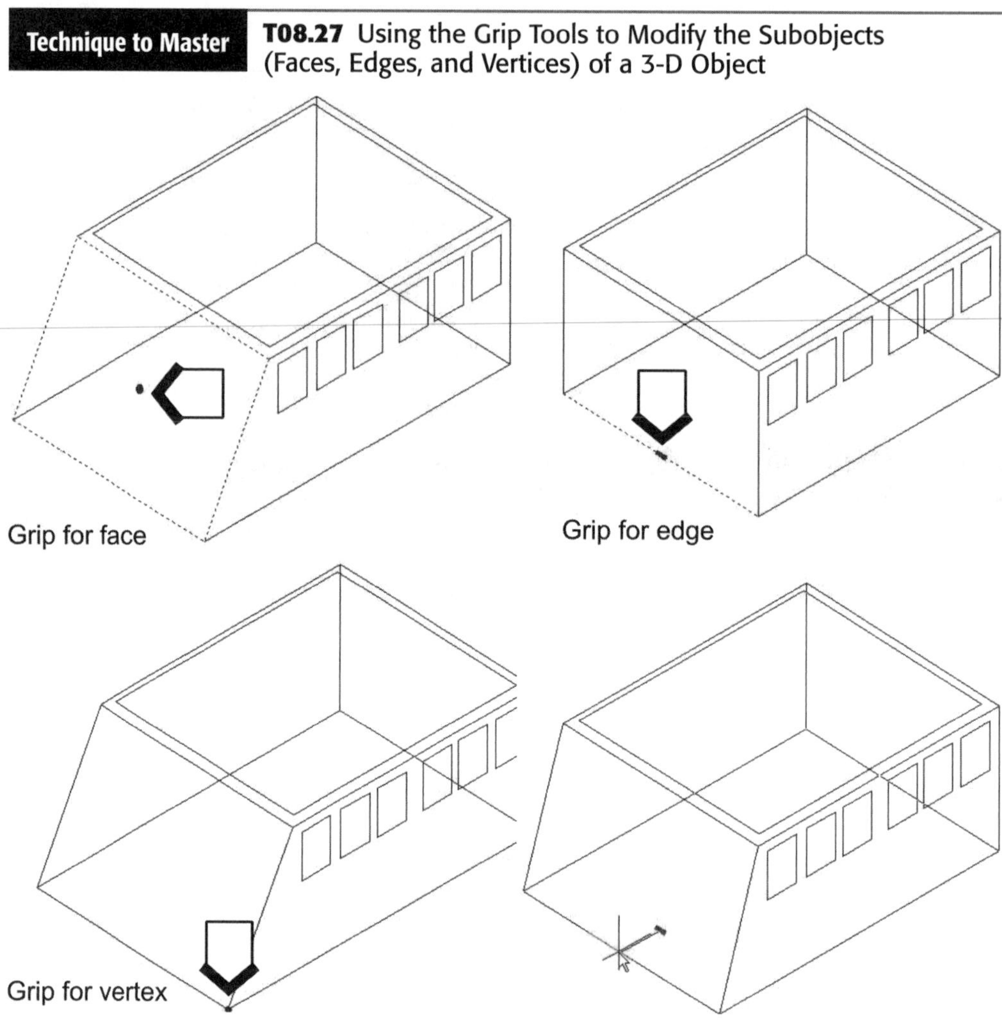

Figure 8.27

For each grip type shown (face, edge, or vertex):		
1	[Drawing Screen]	Left-click the 3-D object to display the object's grips.
2	Use the Ctrl key to select an individual edge, face, or vertex (corner) on the 3-D object.	
3	Left-click on the displayed grip to modify (as you drag your mouse, you can press the Ctrl key to cycle between modification options).	

Technique to Master **T08.28** Adding Faces to an Existing 3-D Object Using the Imprint Tool

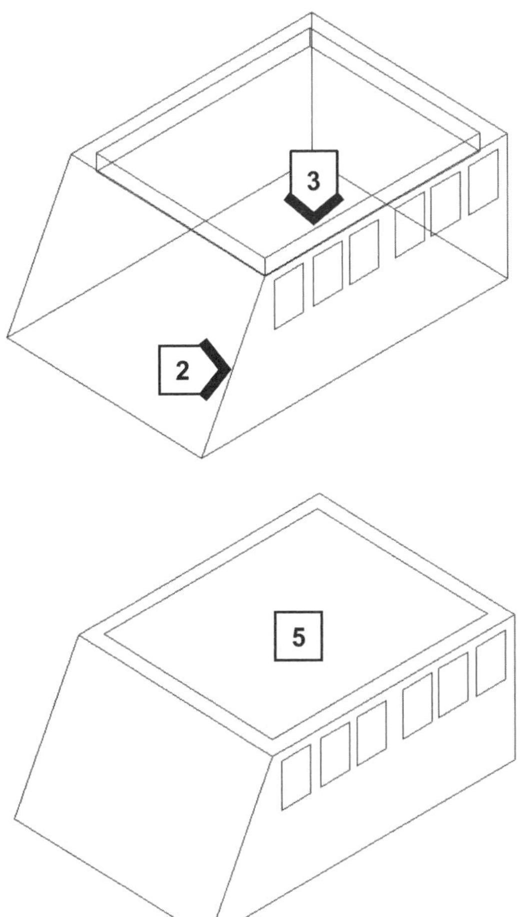

Figure 8.28

1	[Command Line]	Access the Imprint tool on the Dashboard palette.
2	[Drawing Screen]	Select a 3-D object.
3	[Drawing Screen]	Select any 2-D or 3-D object to imprint onto 3-D object.
4	[Command Line]	Type Y and press Enter to erase the source object.
5	Completed face.	

Technique to Master **T08.29** Using the Presspull tool to Push or Pull Faces of a 3-D Object

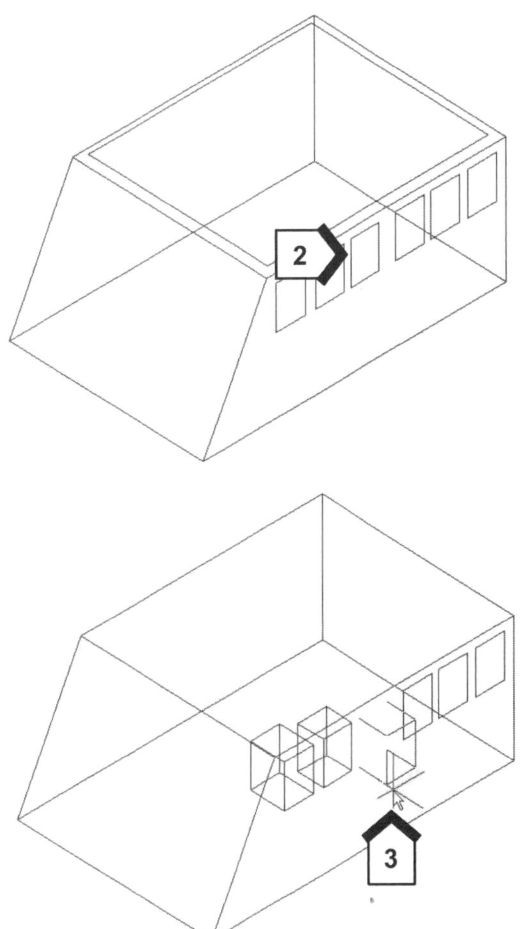

Figure 8.29

1	[Command Line]	Access the Presspull tool on the Dashboard palette.
2	[Drawing Screen]	Left-click inside a closed boundary.
3	[Drawing Screen]	Move the mouse to extrude object inward or outward.

ADT's Object-Oriented Geometry

Architectural Desktop uses object-oriented geometry, that is, three-dimensional objects that represent real-life objects (Figure 8.30). Object-oriented objects are the present and future of CAD three-dimensional software. They offer manufacturers the opportunity to produce their products three-dimensionally so that they can be easily imported into a variety of CAD programs. Chapters 9 through 16 introduce you to the object-oriented geometry of Architectural Desktop.

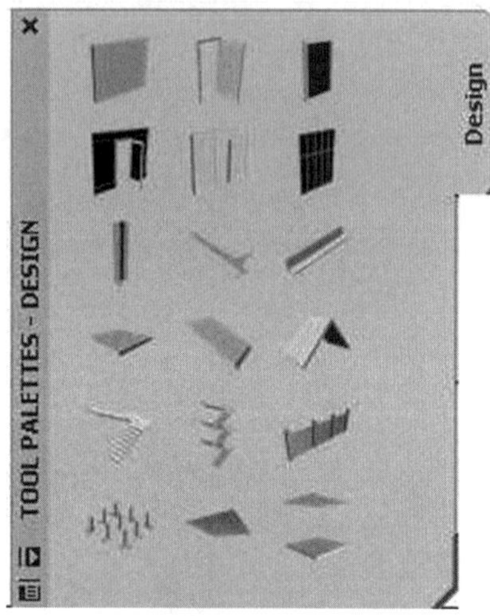

Figure 8.30 Architectural Desktop's object-oriented design objects

Viewing Display and 3-D

When drawing three-dimensionally, you will need tools to view your drawing in ways other than the plan view. Learning fast viewing techniques is another important skill in achieving digital craft and dexterity. In the three-dimensional world, efficient viewing techniques become even more critical since drawings tend to get large and complicated very quickly. This topic introduces the most commonly used three-dimensional viewing methods in AutoCAD and ADT.

Viewing Three-dimensionally

Usually when starting a new drawing the default view is the plan view, also known as the top view. To draw three-dimensionally, you need to see your design three-dimensionally (Figure 8.31). The tools to accomplish this are described in the sections that follow.

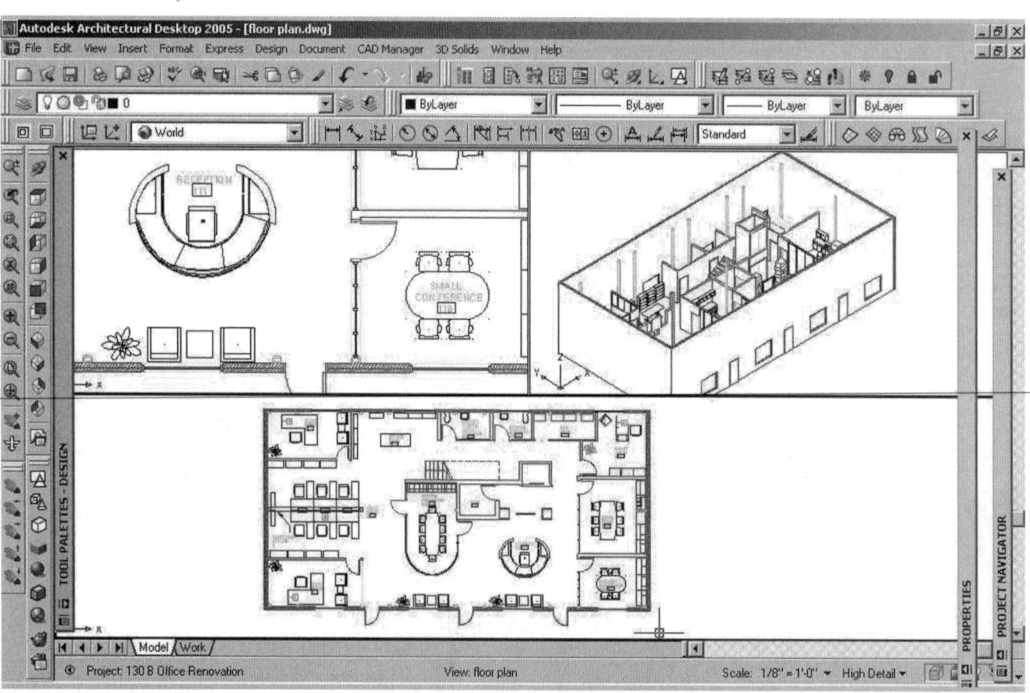

Figure 8.31 Viewing the design using multiple view orientations

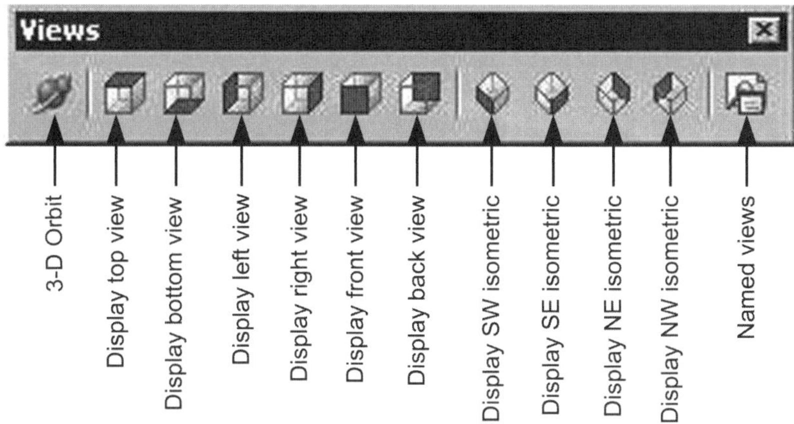

Figure 8.32 The View toolbar

Viewing in Isometric Using the Preset View Settings

Since many designers like to draw and visualize a design in isometric, the View toolbar provides easy access to six preset orthographic views, including four isometric views (Figure 8.32). The isometric views are preset to azimuth angles 45, 135, 225, and 315. All four views use an altitude viewing angle of approximately 35 degrees from horizontal.

Viewing in Isometric with the Ddvpoint Command

The Ddvpoint dialogue box gives you the flexibility to visually set your own azimuth and altitude viewing angles to create the three-dimensional viewing angle. Viewing angles can be set relative to the WCS or relative to the current UCS (Figure 8.33).

> **Box 8.6**
> The Ddvpoint command can also be found in the View menu's 3-D Views>Viewpoint Presets option.

Using 3-D Orbit to Create Perspective Views

The 3-D Orbit command tool provides dynamic 3-D rotation and viewing without the need for screen regeneration. This is a fairly new Autodesk improvement and is advantageous when needing to quickly circumnavigate around a model.

While the primary 3-D Orbit tool can be found on the Navigate toolbar, additional dynamic viewing tools are available through the 3-D Orbit toolbar. Figures 8.34 through 8.36 demonstrate various techniques for using the orbit tools.

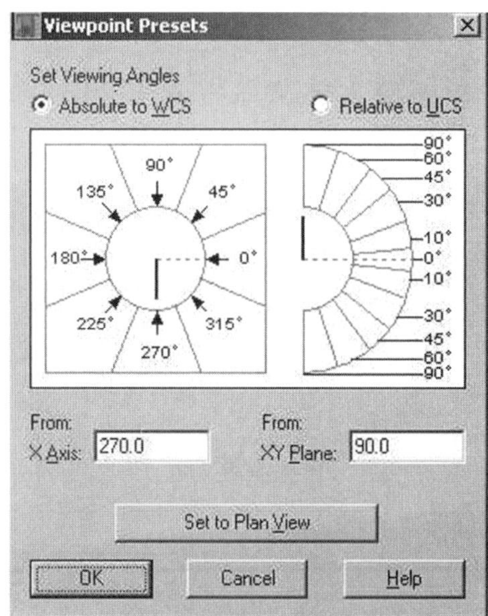

Figure 8.33 The Viewpoint presets dialogue box; to set the viewpoint angle, left-click an azimuth and altitude angle. Left-click the OK button to apply.

Technique to Master **T08.34** Understanding the Orbit Tool

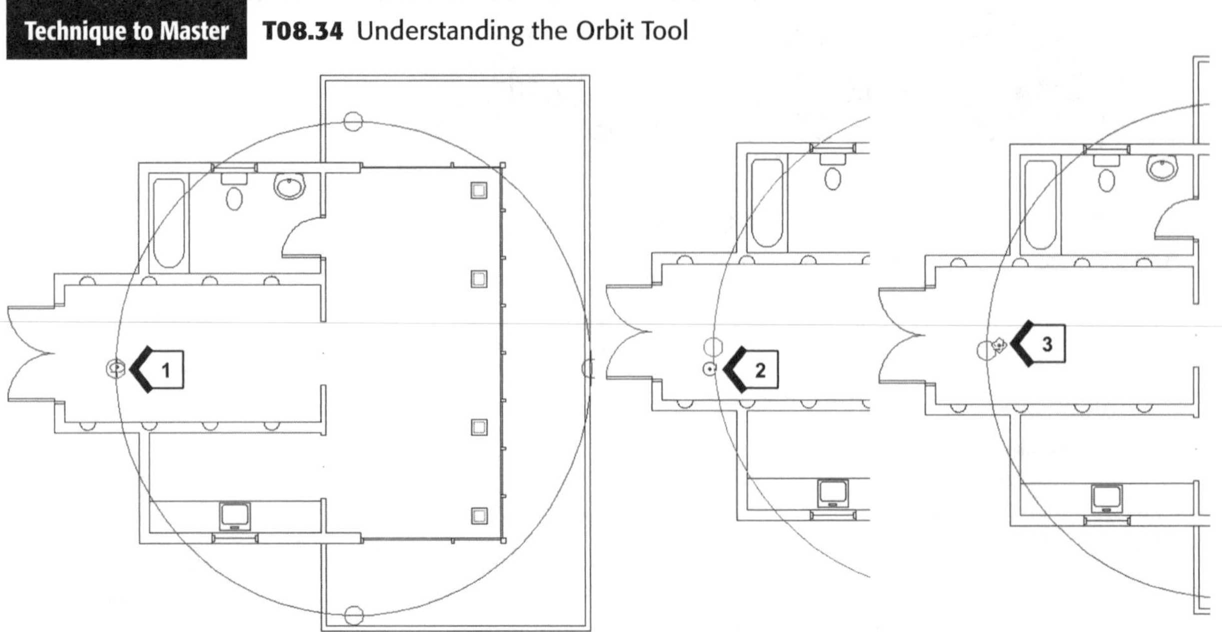

Figure 8.34 When the main tool, 3-D Orbit, is accessed, a large circle appears—called an arcball—with smaller circles at its north, south, east, and west quadrants. Left-click, hold, and drag the mouse within the main circle to rotate the screen into a three-dimensional image. This first click becomes the center of rotation. Clicking (and holding) within any of the smaller quadrant areas produces a panning orbit.

Technique to Master **T08.35** Orbiting from Plan to Isometric View

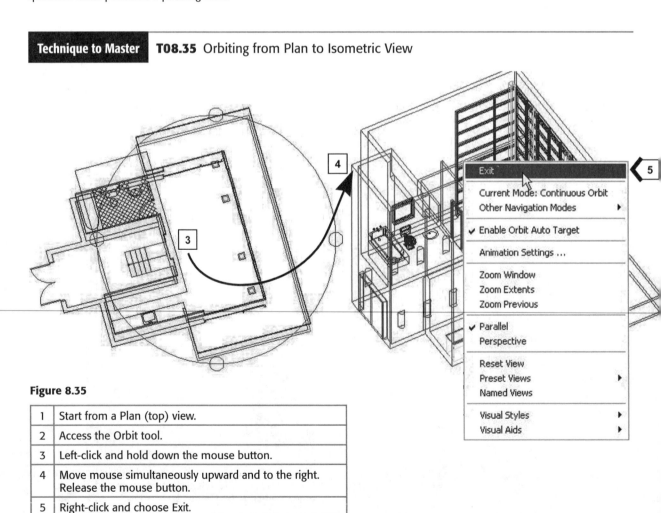

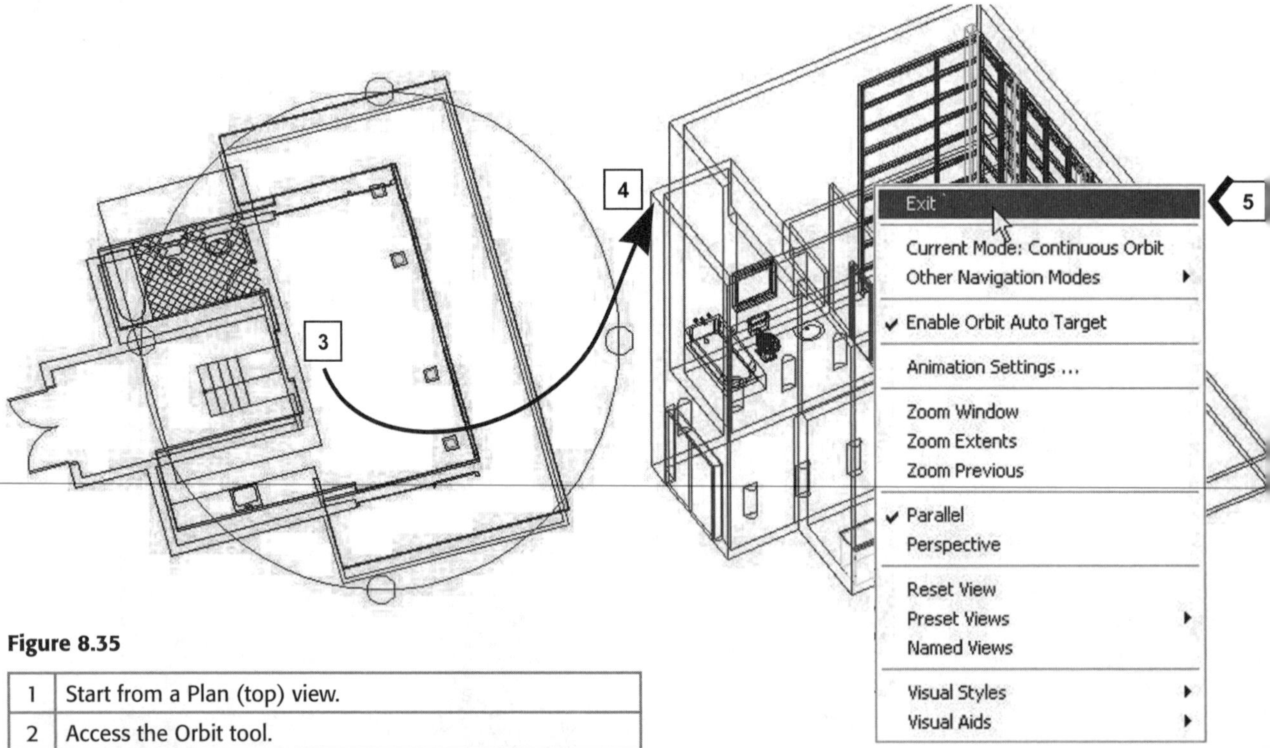

Figure 8.35

1	Start from a Plan (top) view.
2	Access the Orbit tool.
3	Left-click and hold down the mouse button.
4	Move mouse simultaneously upward and to the right. Release the mouse button.
5	Right-click and choose Exit.

Technique to Master **T08.36** Orbiting Panning

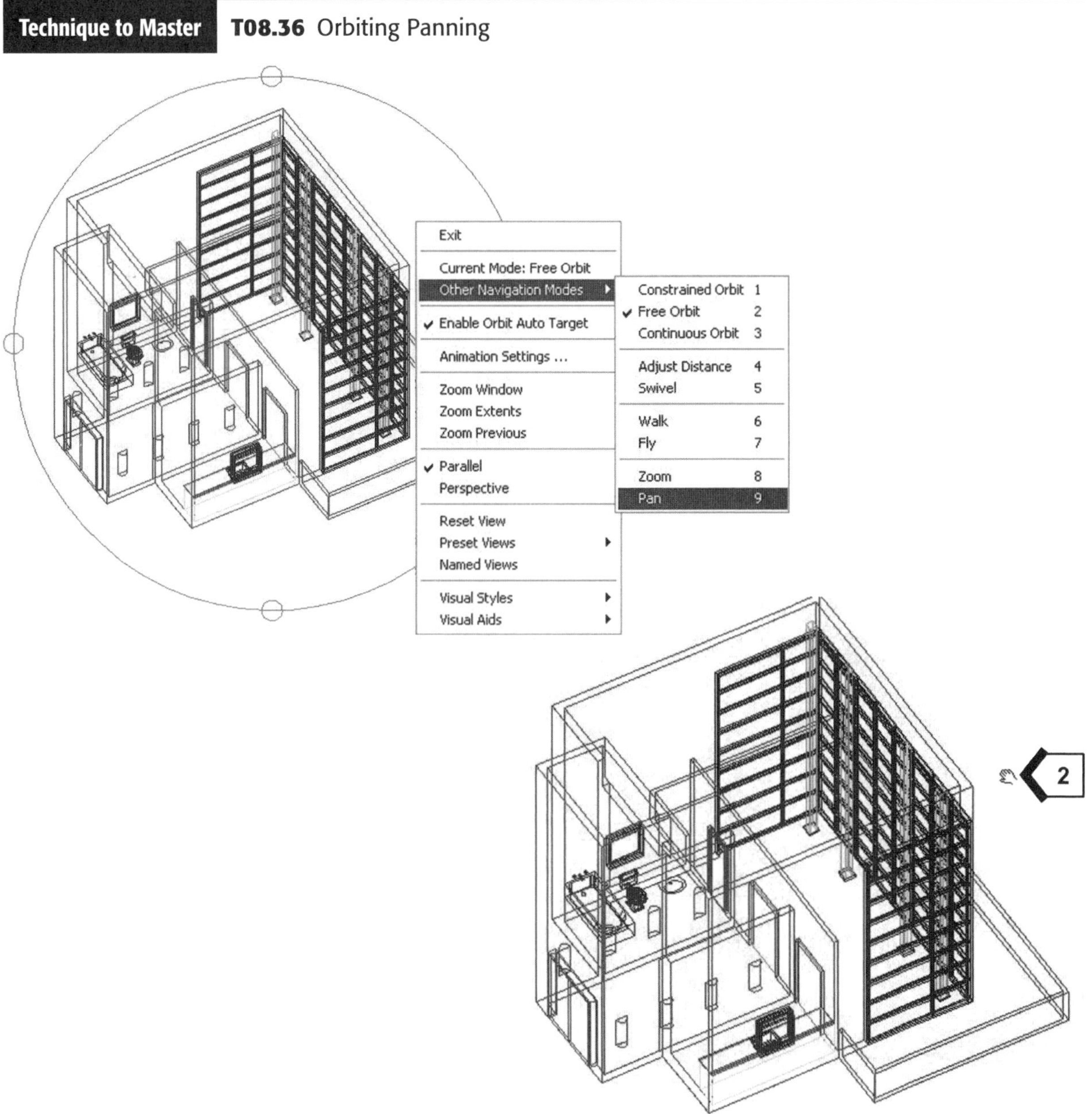

Figure 8.36 With Orbit command running, type 9. Orbit's current mode changes to Pan, and the hand symbol appears (see #2). (The Pan command is also available through the right-click menu).

Viewing Using the Object Viewer

The object viewer tool is another three-dimensional viewing tool. Similar to the orbit tool, it is interactive and does not require regeneration. The object viewer tool is available through the right-click menu (see Figure 8.37 on page 180).

Technique to Master **T08.37** Using the Object Viewer

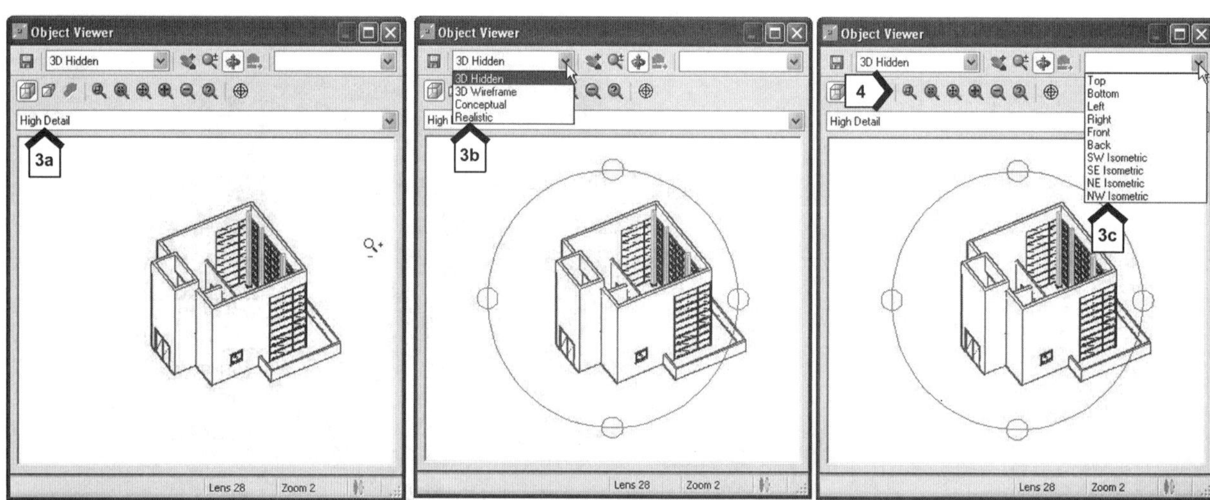

Figure 8.37

1	Open Object Viewer (without selection, right-click on the drawing screen).	
2	[Drawing Screen]	Select the object(s) to view in isolation.
3a, 3b, 3c	[Object Viewer Dialogue Box]	Select Visual Style, View Control, and Display Configuration.
4	[Object Viewer Dialogue Box]	Use Orbit, Pan, and/or Zoom buttons for additional viewing manipulation options.

Chapter Exercises

Open the Chapter 8 folder located on the CD-ROM to access the chapter exercises. Exercises are designed to reinforce your knowledge of using basic geometric shapes to create common building elements and allow you to practice using three-dimensional viewing tools.

Getting Started with ADT

9

Objectives

This chapter builds on the project organization concepts of Chapter 7. It introduces the tools and techniques used for project design and project organization in Architectural Desktop, including Architectural Desktop's user interface and display concepts.

What is ADT?

Architectural Desktop (ADT) is an object-based CAD product. It uses intelligent objects (such as walls, windows, and doors) to create the most often used components of a virtual building model. ADT is distinct from other object-oriented CAD software because it incorporates many of the characteristics of building information modeling (BIM) into its foundation. Together, the object-based components along with BIM create design objects that carry information pertinent to the object (Figure 9.1).

> **Box 9.1**
> Architectural Desktop is not considered a true BIM program because changes to schedules, sections, or elevations do not update the virtual model.

An example of this information for a door might include its door size (height and width), its door type (solid core or metal), its door thickness, and its door frame characteristics. This door might also have glass windows (called lites) within it. All of these defining characteristics are attached to this object door (Figure 9.2). In traditional CAD, none of these characteristics would be available; doors are simply two lines and an arc, and no further information is provided.

Whenever a software program is complicated, it takes time to understand and apply it to complex projects. ADT is not an easy software program to master. It requires users to have time and patience to understand all of the various concepts underlying its complex structure. The complexity of ADT, however, is not in its commands or techniques but rather in the procedural nature of these techniques. Many of the techniques have numerous commands and command options that users must complete in a required order. Therefore, it is difficult for users to memorize techniques and their sequences, which means there is a greater risk for making mistakes. Once you accept Architectural Desktop's procedural nature, it will ease your frustrations as well as your learning curve. In addition, keeping technique notes and troubleshooting logs will help to minimize repeated aggravations and keep you encouraged.

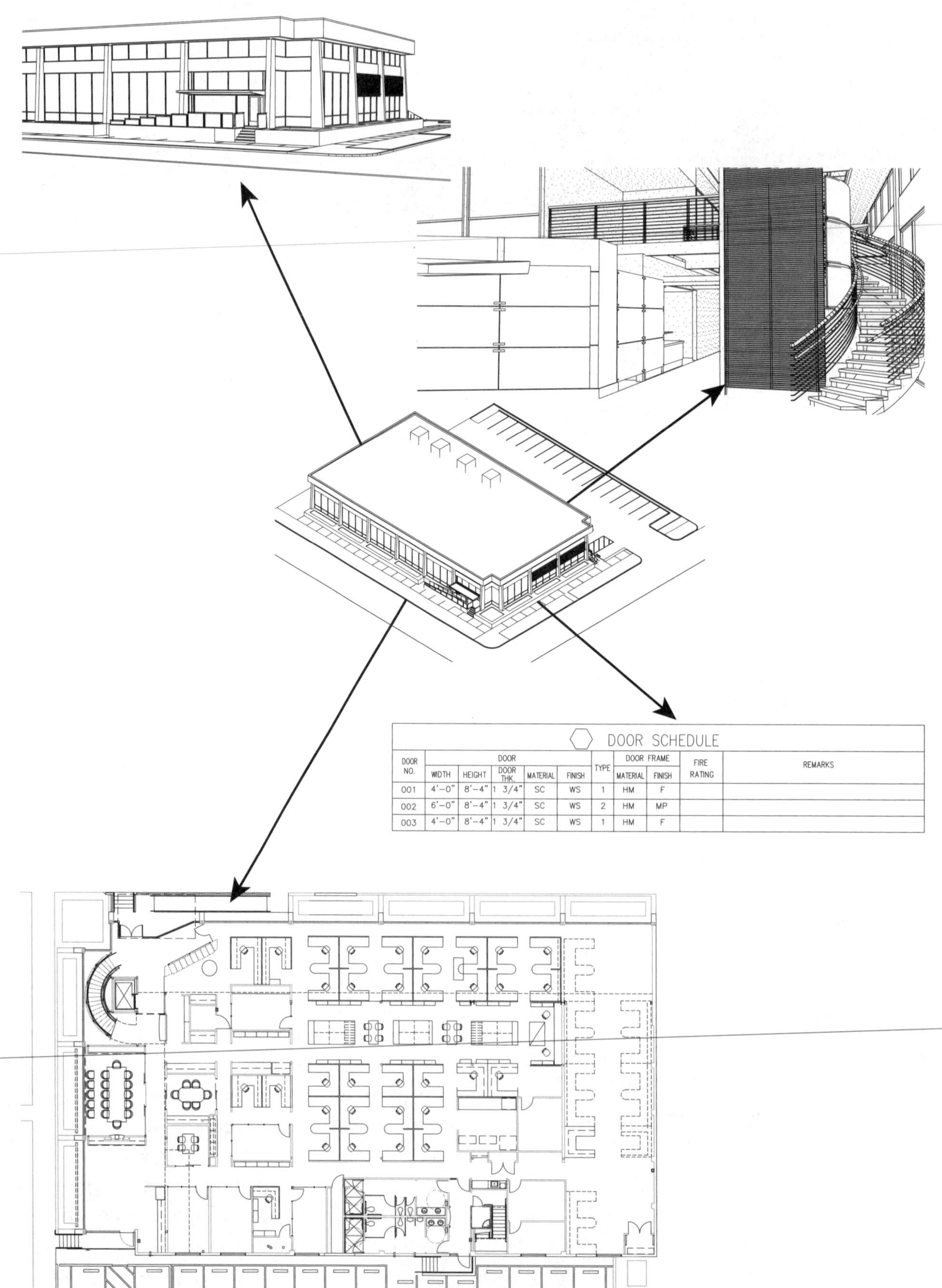

DOOR SCHEDULE

DOOR NO.	DOOR					TYPE	DOOR FRAME		FIRE RATING	REMARKS
	WIDTH	HEIGHT	DOOR THK.	MATERIAL	FINISH		MATERIAL	FINISH		
001	4'–0"	8'–4"	1 3/4"	SC	WS	1	HM	F		
002	6'–0"	8'–4"	1 3/4"	SC	WS	2	HM	MP		
003	4'–0"	8'–4"	1 3/4"	SC	WS	1	HM	F		

Figure 9.1 The characteristics of building information modeling

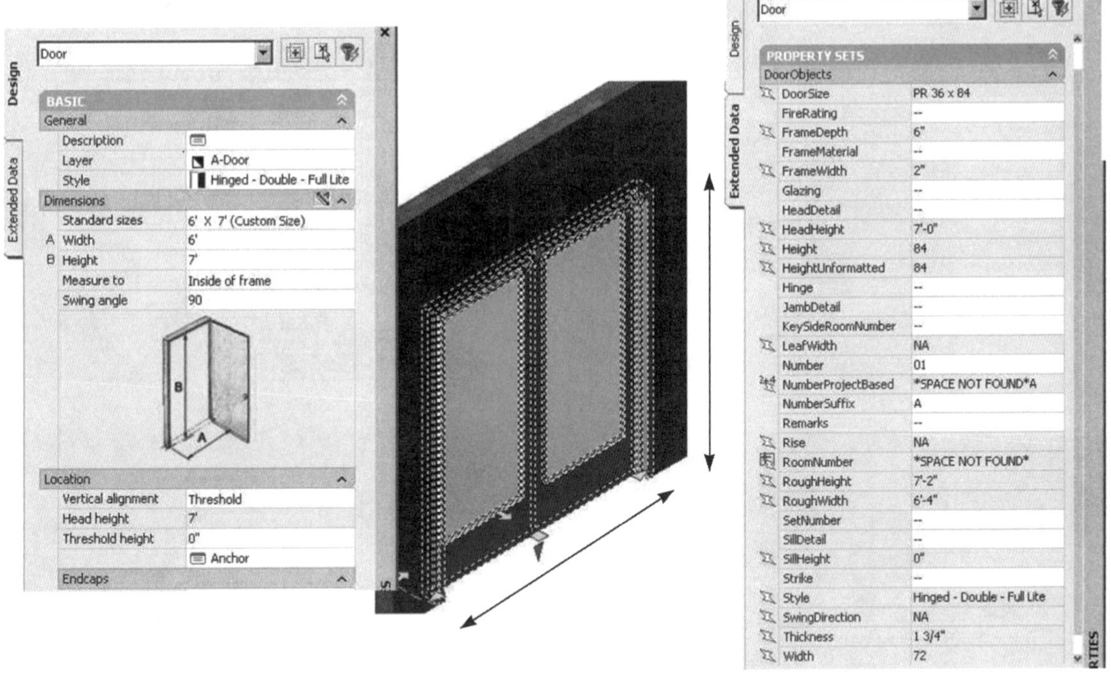

Figure 9.2 Door properties saved in the ADT database include both dimensional properties and manufacturer information.

AutoCAD is built into Architectural Desktop. This means that all of the commands and procedures that you learned in Part I of this text can be incorporated into the drawing process within ADT. This chapter explains the logic and concepts underlying the ADT interface. It also provides a quick look at Architectural Desktop's design and organization tools.

Drawing and Display in ADT

Architectural Desktop's uniqueness can be seen both in the types of objects used to design with as well as how the program displays those objects. This topic introduces object-oriented design and its system of display.

Object-Oriented Design

Object-oriented design refers to the identifiable objects you use to design projects. Objects are broken up into categories because they share common attributes. Walls, for example, are vertical planes made up of various materials with different thicknesses. All walls, however, share certain common attributes that make it convenient to group them together as one object type. The attributes that make each wall distinct (wall materials, wall thicknesses, and so forth) are broken into subgroups in ADT through the use of Styles in the Style Manager window (Figure 9.3).

ADT objects use object types that correspond to real building components. These include walls, windows, doors, openings, window assemblies, curtain walls, stairs, railings, roofs, slabs, and structural columns, beams, and braces (Figure 9.4). Because these objects represent real building components, each object type has its own set of behaviors that directly relates to the component it is imitating. Becoming proficient in ADT begins with understanding the capabilities and limitations of these objects. Other building components such as furniture, fixtures, and equipment must either be created from the generic ADT objects or borrowed from a library of premade objects (Figure 9.5).

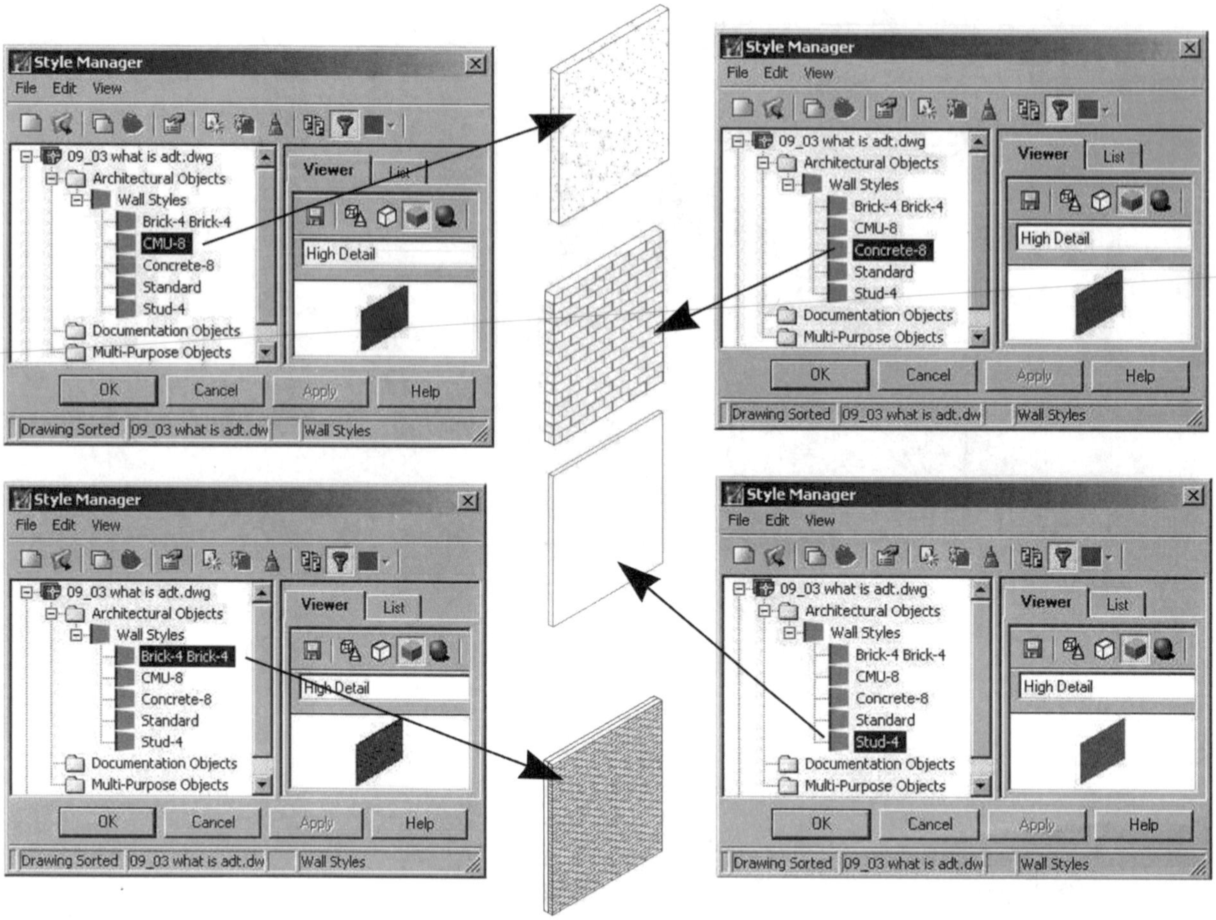

Figure 9.3 The example shows four different wall styles—a brick wall style, a concrete wall style, a concrete masonry unit (cmu) wall style, and a metal stud wall style. Each style differentiates the wall's assembly.

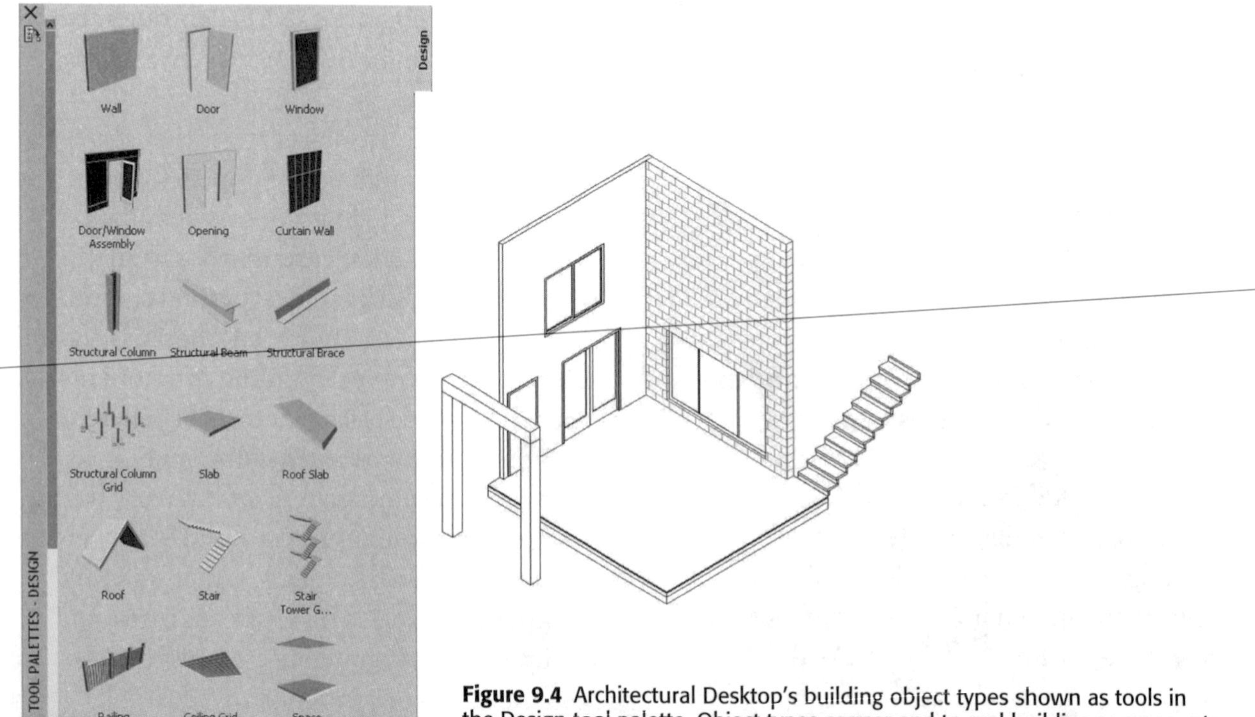

Figure 9.4 Architectural Desktop's building object types shown as tools in the Design tool palette. Object types correspond to real building components. These include walls, windows, doors, openings, window assemblies, curtain walls, stairs, railings, roofs, slabs, and structural columns, beams, and braces.

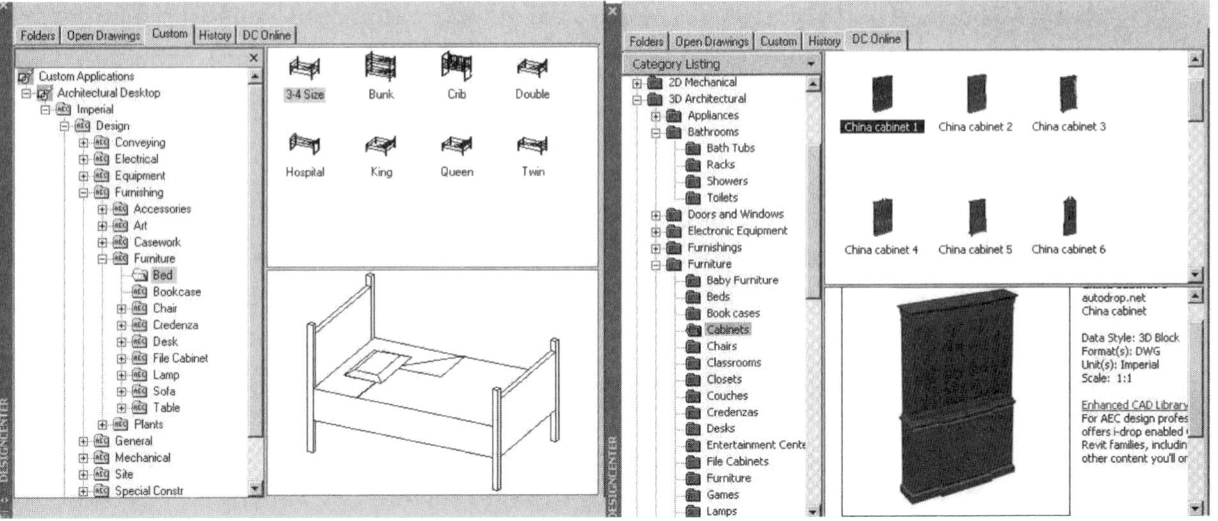

Figure 9.5 Premade symbols and building objects can be found in the Design Center's AEC Content or DC Online.

ADT Display Logic

Learning architectural drafting requires that you learn the rules for creating the conventional orthographic drawings types of floor plan, section, elevation, and ceiling plan. In each of these orthographic views, you learn that each drawing type has established rules for when and how an object is drawn. A ceiling plan, for example, does not include doors. ADT incorporates these established rules automatically into the software. Since each object is drawn only once, three-dimensionally, these rules are incorporated through the use of Display Representations. This display matrix can be understood as a checklist that dictates which views the object will be shown in as well as how the object will be shown (Figure 9.6). The built-in ADT views include floor plan, ceiling plan, elevation, section, and model; however, other custom views and rules can be easily established. Figure 9.7 shows how the drawing of a

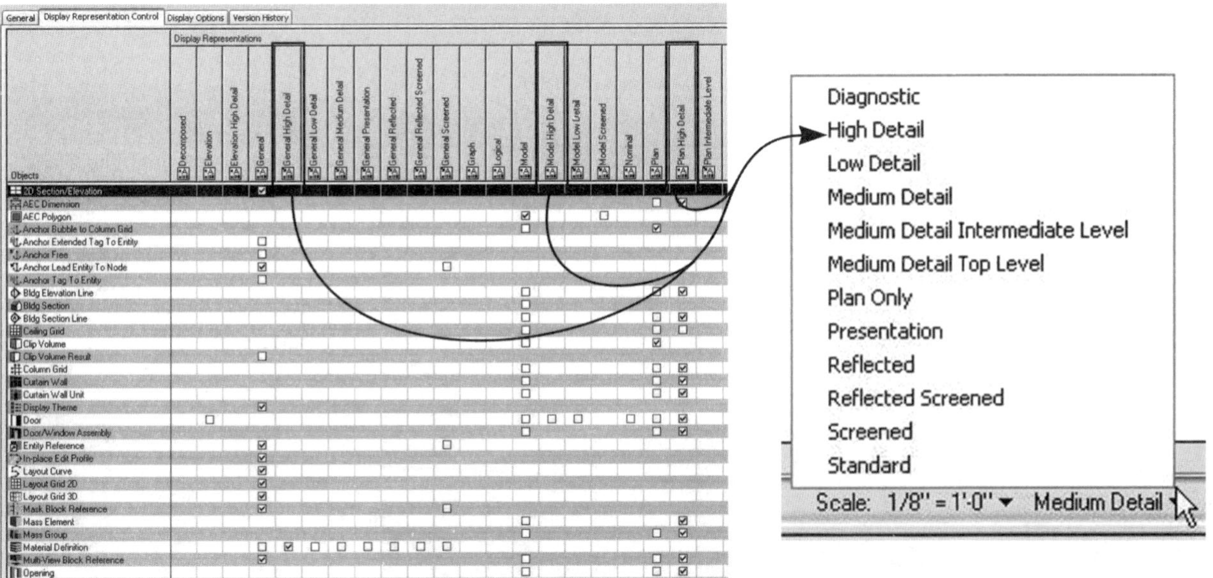

Figure 9.6 The Display Matrix saves rules for how ADT will create floorplans, reflected ceiling plans, sections, and more. These rules are by default based on the conventions for the typical orthographic view types.

wall, window, and door object is changed based on the display representation.

Notice that the level of detail an object displays is also controlled through Display Representations. Many objects in ADT are made up of multiple components. A window, for example, has a frame component, a mullion component, and a glass component. Through Display Representations, the properties (i.e., layer, lineweight, color, and so on) of each component, in most situations, can be controlled (Figure 9.8). Although Display Representations automate visibility correctly for most objects, layer management is still necessary in some working and plotting operations.

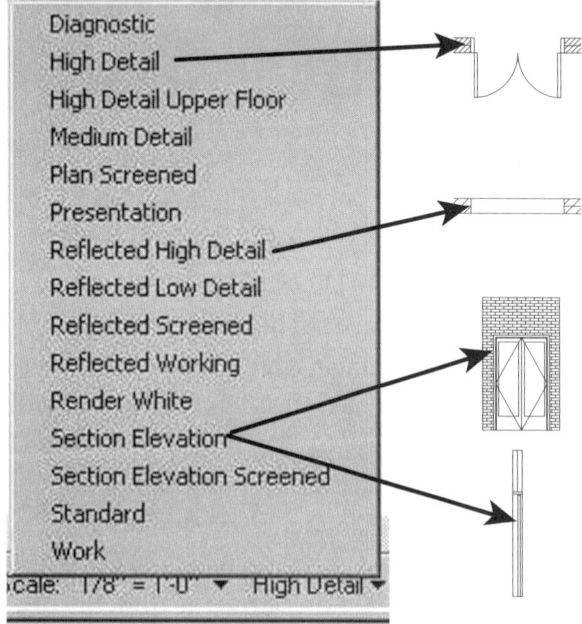

Figure 9.7 The Display Representation list box changes the display of building objects.

Display Representation rules form the foundation for the draw once principle. Floor plans, ceiling plans, elevations, and sections can be quickly generated from the virtual (three-dimensional) building model. Display Representations also allow for flexibility through custom tailoring.

Understanding Styles

The use of Styles in ADT allows you to customize building components to suit the design situation at hand. The concept can be explained through the analogy to architectural styles in history. As a student, you've learned about the different styles throughout European history. A column's form and detailing, for example, would identify whether the column is of the Corinthian or Doric historic style. ADT uses styles in a similar way. Most objects have a style property attached to allow for differences in appearance, material, detailing, or a combination of the three. The style property groups these characteristics into a named subcategory.

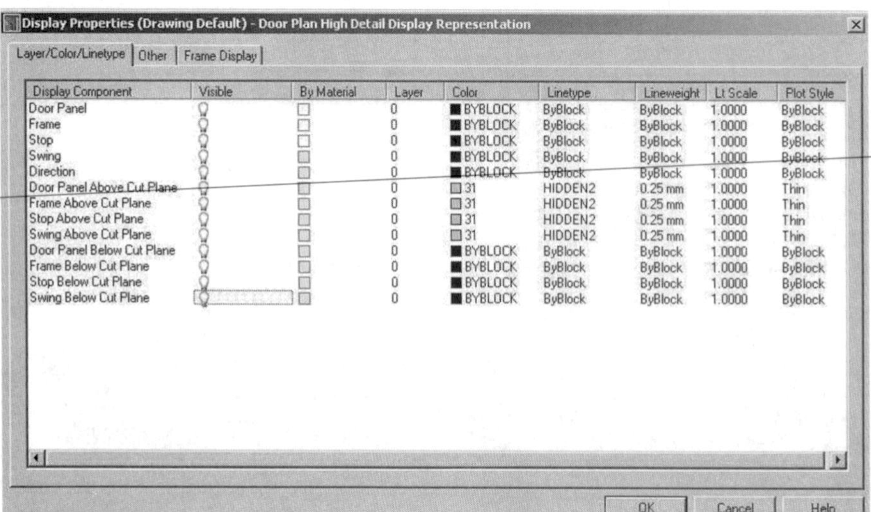

Display Properties (Drawing Default) - Door Plan High Detail Display Representation

Layer/Color/Linetype | Other | Frame Display

Display Component	Visible	By Material	Layer	Color	Linetype	Lineweight	Lt Scale	Plot Style
Door Panel			0	BYBLOCK	ByBlock	ByBlock	1.0000	ByBlock
Frame			0	BYBLOCK	ByBlock	ByBlock	1.0000	ByBlock
Stop			0	BYBLOCK	ByBlock	ByBlock	1.0000	ByBlock
Swing			0	BYBLOCK	ByBlock	ByBlock	1.0000	ByBlock
Direction			0	BYBLOCK	ByBlock	ByBlock	1.0000	ByBlock
Door Panel Above Cut Plane			0	31	HIDDEN2	0.25 mm	1.0000	Thin
Frame Above Cut Plane			0	31	HIDDEN2	0.25 mm	1.0000	Thin
Stop Above Cut Plane			0	31	HIDDEN2	0.25 mm	1.0000	Thin
Swing Above Cut Plane			0	31	HIDDEN2	0.25 mm	1.0000	Thin
Door Panel Below Cut Plane			0	BYBLOCK	ByBlock	ByBlock	1.0000	ByBlock
Frame Below Cut Plane			0	BYBLOCK	ByBlock	ByBlock	1.0000	ByBlock
Stop Below Cut Plane			0	BYBLOCK	ByBlock	ByBlock	1.0000	ByBlock
Swing Below Cut Plane			0	BYBLOCK	ByBlock	ByBlock	1.0000	ByBlock

OK | Cancel | Help

Figure 9.8 Component visibility, layer, lineweight, and color of objects can be controlled through the Display Properties for an object. This dialogue is very similar to AutoCAD's Layer Manager. To the right of each component are toggles to control the component's visibility, layer, lineweight, and color.

Adding Detail to Refine Drawings

Complete and detailed information is rarely known at the early stages of the design process, and design changes occur frequently. It, therefore, becomes important to establish efficient procedures and techniques to anticipate change. Architectural Desktop encourages a procedure that starts by using generic conceptual objects that are later converted into building objects and then further refined with styles as new information becomes known. Chapters 18 and 19 go into further detail on this subject.

Differences in the ADT User Interface

While the drawing area in Architectural Desktop is the same as in AutoCAD, the surrounding menus, palettes, toolbars, and status bar areas have significant differences. At first, the ADT user interface as a whole may seem foreign to you. This topic identifies some of the key differences in user interface to familiarize you with your work environment. Figure 9.9 identifies each of the areas discussed in the paragraphs that follow.

Drawing Status Bar

Autodesk has integrated project management capabilities within ADT. Although Architectural Desktop's project management concepts are formally introduced at the end of this chapter, let's look at how these capabilities have affected the user interface. When an ADT project is current and a drawing within the project is opened, the drawing's status bar shows the current project's name, drawing name, and drawing category.

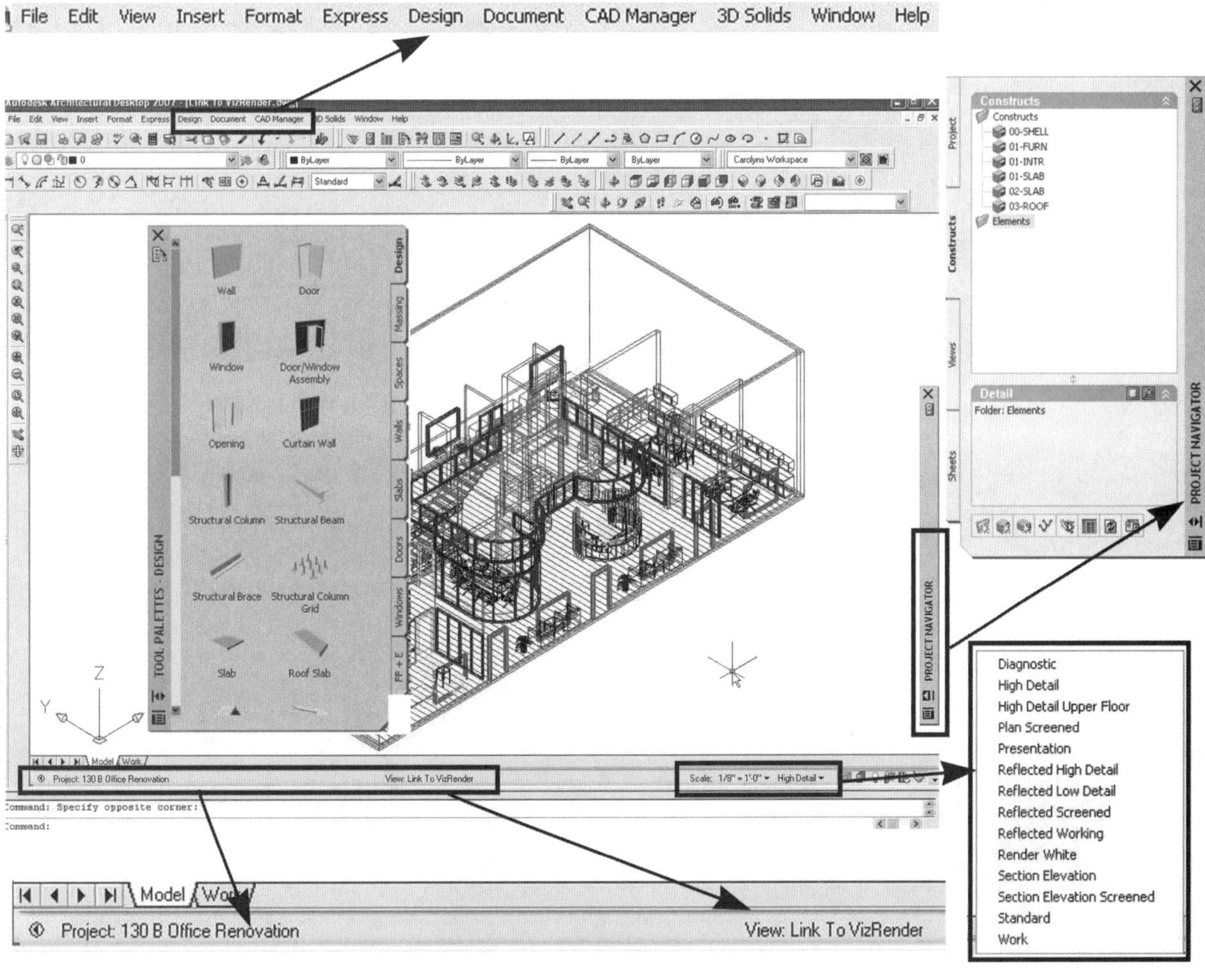

Figure 9.9 Differences in the Architectural Desktop User Interface

Other drawing status differences include the following:

- *Open Drawing menu* provides quick access to drawing setup and drawing properties, as well as plotting and publishing commands for the current drawing.
- *Scale menu* invokes the AecDwgScaleSetup command, which sets the drawing scale for the current drawing.
- *Display Configuration menu* changes the display configuration for the current drawing.
- Additional toggles such as surface hatching, layer key styles, and object hiding are included in the program.

ADT Menu Bars

If you are a current user of AutoCAD, then you'll notice significant menu bar differences between AutoCAD and ADT. First, ADT specific commands have been integrated into all of AutoCAD's menus. Second, you will notice the addition of four new menus: the Format Design, Document, and CAD Manager menus (Figure 9.10). These menus contain most of the ADT-specific tools for drawing and annotation.

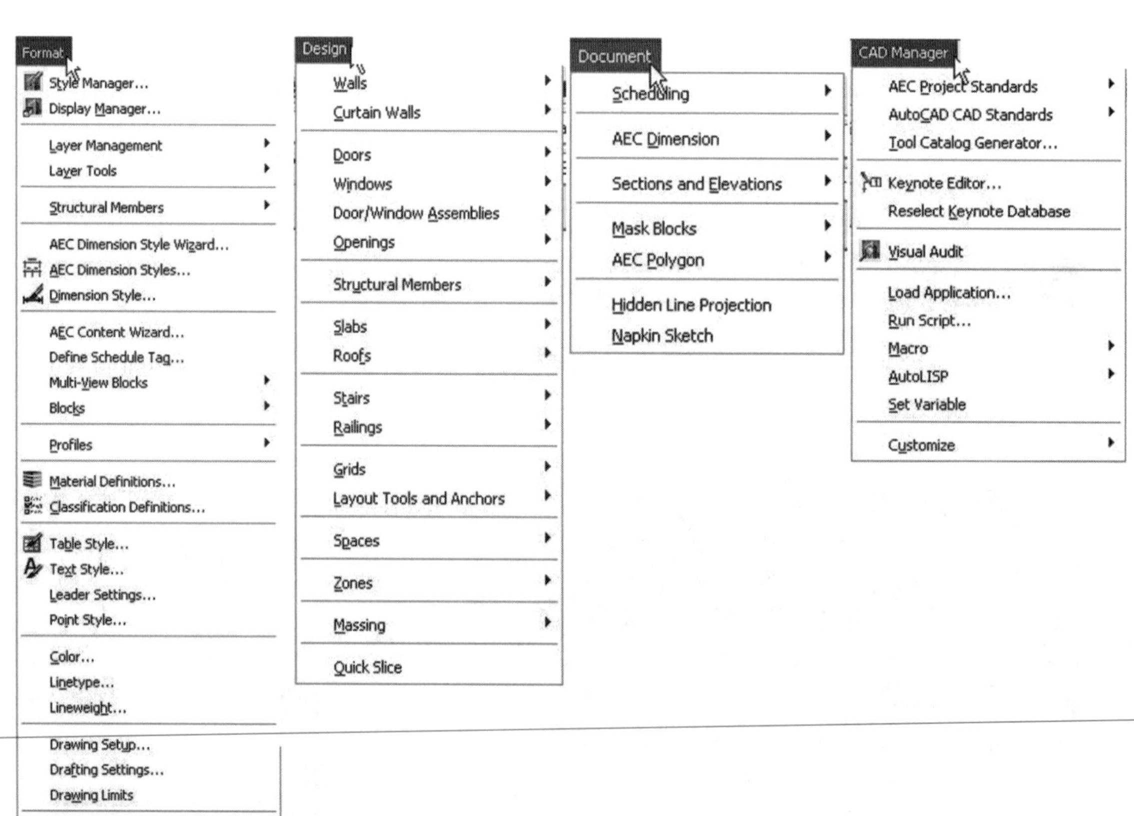

Figure 9.10 The additional ADT menus

Palettes

Another significant difference between the AutoCAD and ADT environments are the additional Tool palette groups: Design, Document, and Detailing. These palettes provide quick access to most ADT specific commands and command options.

Figure 9.11 identifies the variety of tabbed palette categories, including the hidden menu options available through the Properties button. Chapters 9 through 16 give you the opportunity to become familiar with using these Tool palette groups.

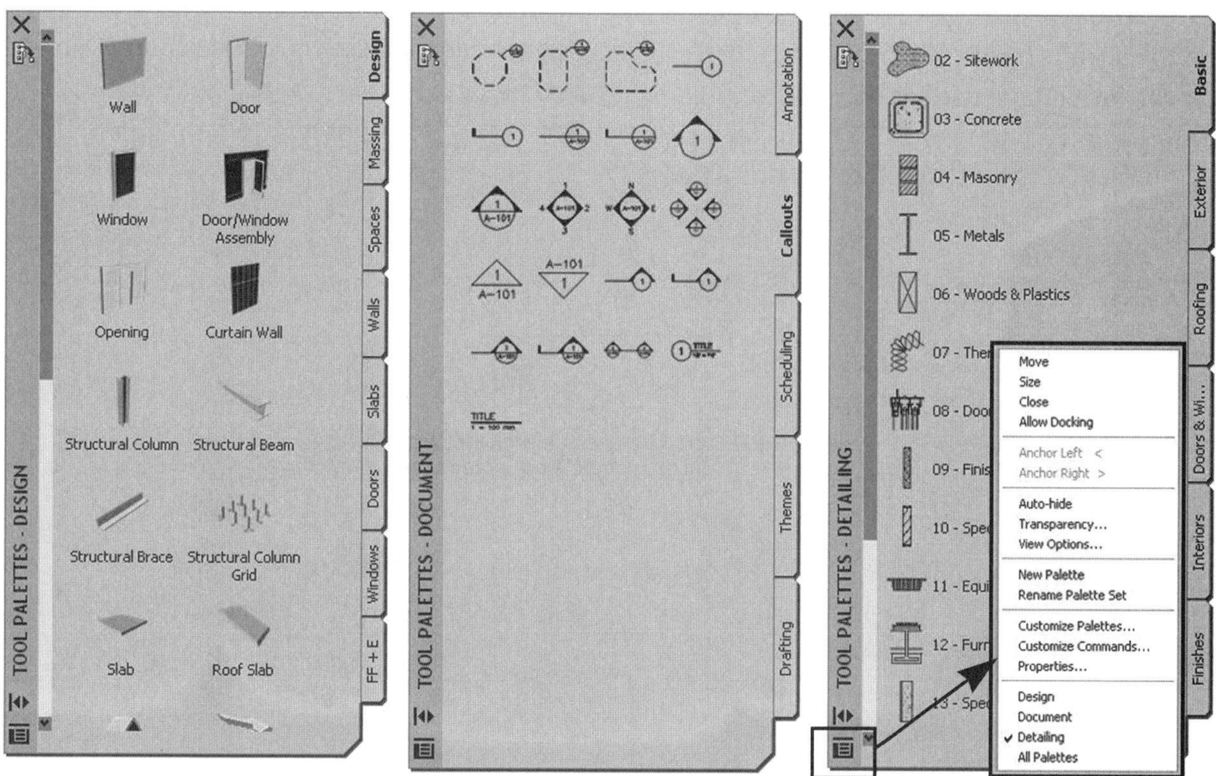

Figure 9.11 The additional ADT tool palettes—design, document, and detailing.

The Design tool palette provides all the drawing tools needed to draw the objects representing building elements. The main Design tabs are all the generic architectural objects; that is, they have no material or stylistic features attached to them. The additional tabs provide the preset, style-based architectural objects.

The Document tool palette provides all the text, dimension, and symbol callouts needed to annotate your drawings.

The Detailing tool palette provides additional 2-D components to quickly create details for construction documentation.

The Tool palette also has its own menu that contains additional commands for creating and customizing the palette.

Design Center

Architectural Desktop also has a built-in block organizer accessible through the Design Center palette. The AEC Content library has hundreds of stored geometry that can be used in drawings. The content stored in this library is a special kind of block called an AEC Content block.

The AEC Content folder structure is organized into two main groups: content used for design such as furniture and plumbing fixture blocks and content used for documentation such as room name tags and section callout symbols. For blocks to be placed in this library, they must be exported using the AEC Content Wizard. Figure 9.12 identifies the areas of the AEC Content tab.

The Content Browser

The Content Browser is another type of organizational library in ADT. The Content Browser is unique because it not only stores symbols and blocks but also object styles and commands that have specific properties and settings attached to it. Figure 9.13 identifies the areas of the Content Browser.

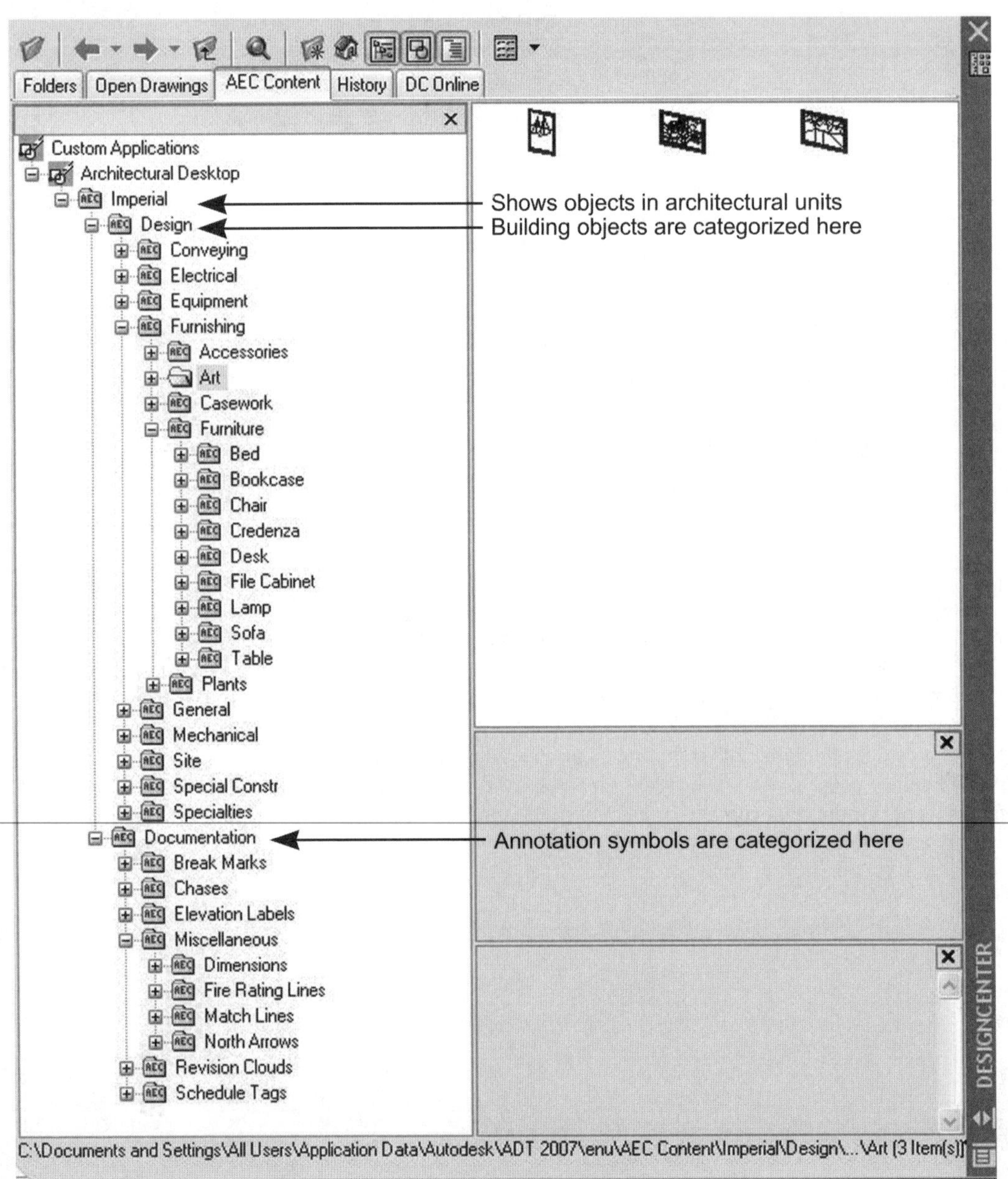

Figure 9.12 The areas of the AEC Content tab in Design Center

Symbols, blocks, and styles from the Content Browser are imported into current drawings using i-drop technology. I-drop technology allows you to quickly drag-and-drop any content simply by pressing the left mouse button while it's over the content until the i-dropper symbol fills. When the i-dropper is filled, move your mouse to your drawing screen and release the button.

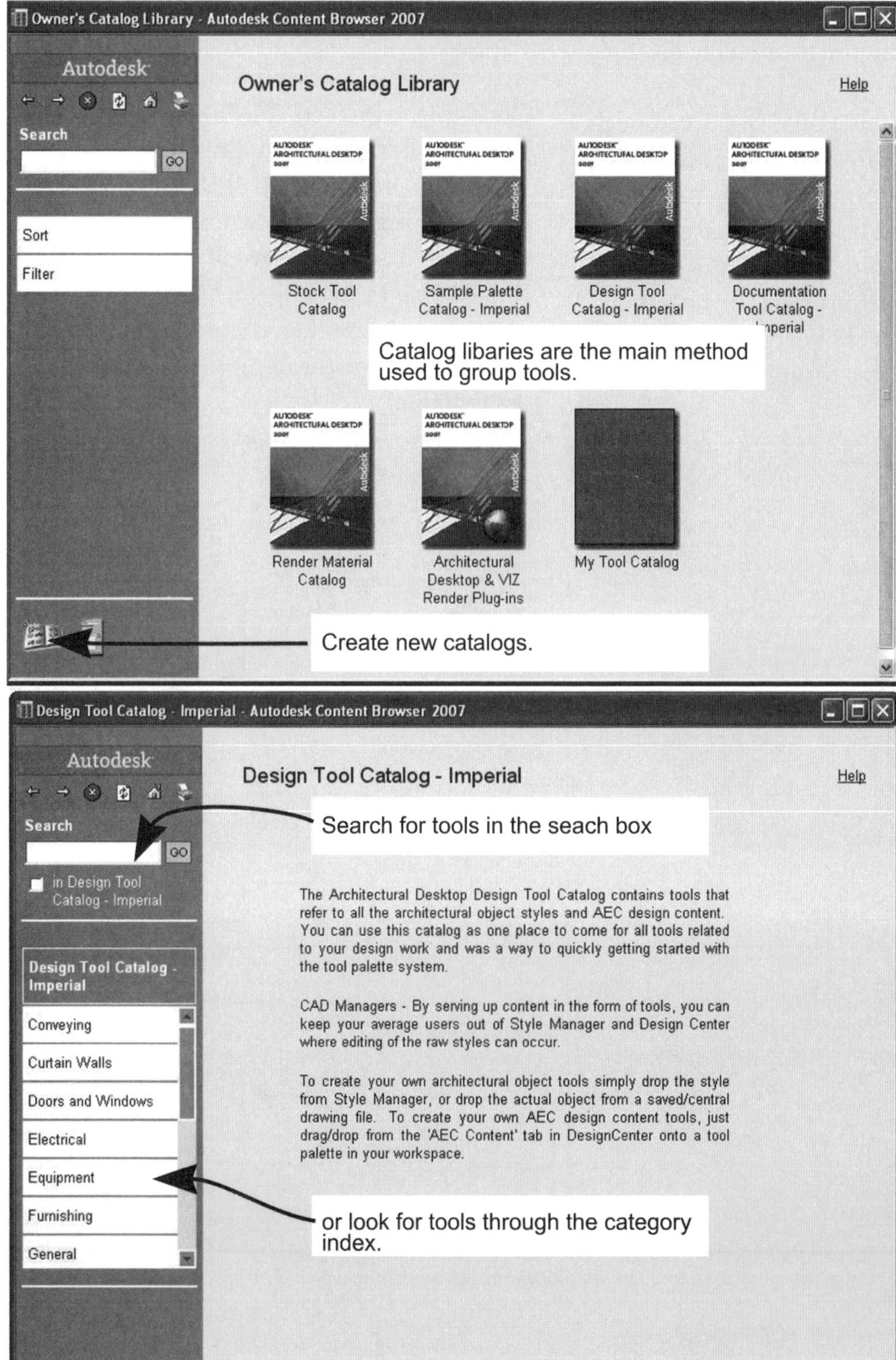

Figure 9.13 The areas of the Content Browser

Project Organization Concepts in ADT

As you will recall from Chapter 7, project organization refers to your organizational strategy for managing all the digital files related to a project. It focused on the use of multiple drawing (.dwg) files to draw a project. It also introduced you to file-linking concepts and techniques to bring the multiple files together for project coordination and project output. Architectural Desktop models much of its project organization procedures and concepts after this conventional and well-established process. It sets up a four-category system of drawing file types; each category has a distinct role in the project organization process. These categories of drawings include drawings that are used to build the virtual model; drawings used to view critical plans, sections, and elevations of the virtual model; and drawings that are used to plot views of the model. ADT then automates the file-linking operations between the category types (Figure 9.14).

Project Organization Vocabulary

Architectural Desktop's project organization starts with a Project. The Project represents a theoretical space (or building) that is then drawn three-dimensionally in ADT. This three-dimensional model (called a virtual model) is made from several .dwg files that are linked together. Orthographic views of the virtual model are then composed and plotted to communicate the design to clients and contractors.

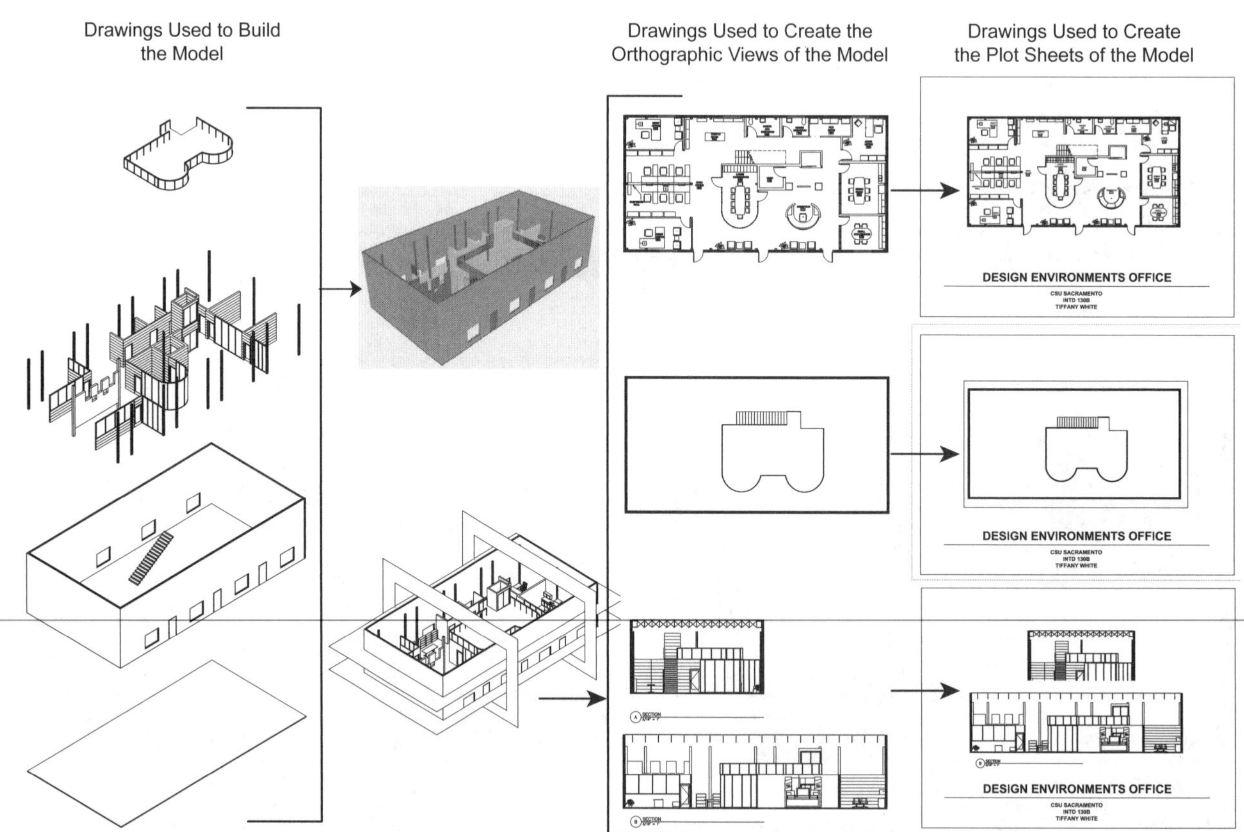

Figure 9.14 Architectural Desktop's project organization uses four categories of .dwg types to build the virtual design model. Drawings used to build the model include two of the types: constructs and elements.

Office renovation student project courtesy of Tiffany White.

An ADT Project is displayed as a folder where all the .dwg files of the project are stored. This folder is usually found on your hard drive or other media storage location. In addition to the drawing files, other file types are used behind the scenes to store project database information. These include the following:

Apj file Stores project properties including where to find the project's drawing templates, project tools, and project bulletin board.

Dst file Stores plot sheet sets and other information relating to the plotting or publishing of a project.

Xml files Every drawing (.dwg file) has an associated Xml file. Xml files contain the database of information that is linked to the associated drawing files.

> **Box 9.2**
> Make sure the .xml files remain with their associated .dwg files. The .xml file saves the database information for its associated drawing.

Project Levels

Establishing the number of levels and their floor-to-floor heights is one of the first steps toward setting up a project. Levels represent the floor levels of a building (Figure 9.15). In addition to the main floors, basements and roofs are also considered levels. Setting the appropriate levels for a project helps to automate the View creation process. When levels are correctly set, ADT automatically places each construct at the accurate Z-elevation during the View creation process.

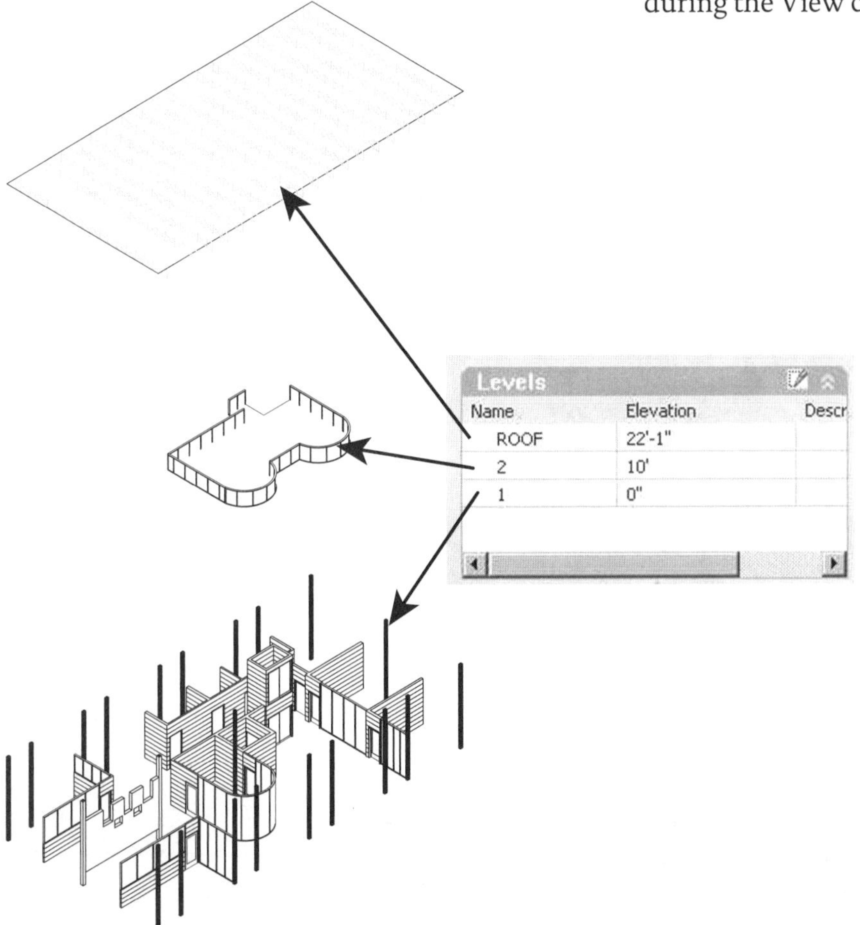

Levels
Name
Elevation
Descr
ROOF
22'-1"
2
10'
1
0"

Figure 9.15 Architectural Desktop's project organization uses levels to define the number of floors of the virtual model. The first-floor interior is placed at elevation 0 (Z = 0'-0") based on the levels setting. The roof is automatically placed at elevation 22'-1" based on the levels setting.

Office renovation student project courtesy of Tiffany White.

Constructs

The virtual model is built in Construct drawings. While the whole virtual model may be drawn within one Construct drawing, using multiple Constructs help to make file sizes easier to manage. Figure 9.16 shows an example of using multiple Constructs to draw an office design.

Elements

Element drawing files are similar to AutoCAD blocks in that they are reusable pieces of the building model, that is, elevator lobby cores, stair cores, repeatable furniture layouts, and more. Element drawings are referenced into Constructs through a simple drag-and-drop process.

Views

Views use Display Representations to create the conventional orthographic drawing types of floor, section, elevation, and ceiling plans. Each View drawing is a horizontal or vertical slice of the virtual model (Figure 9.17). ADT automatically references the correct constructs according to their location within the building model to create the correct view slice.

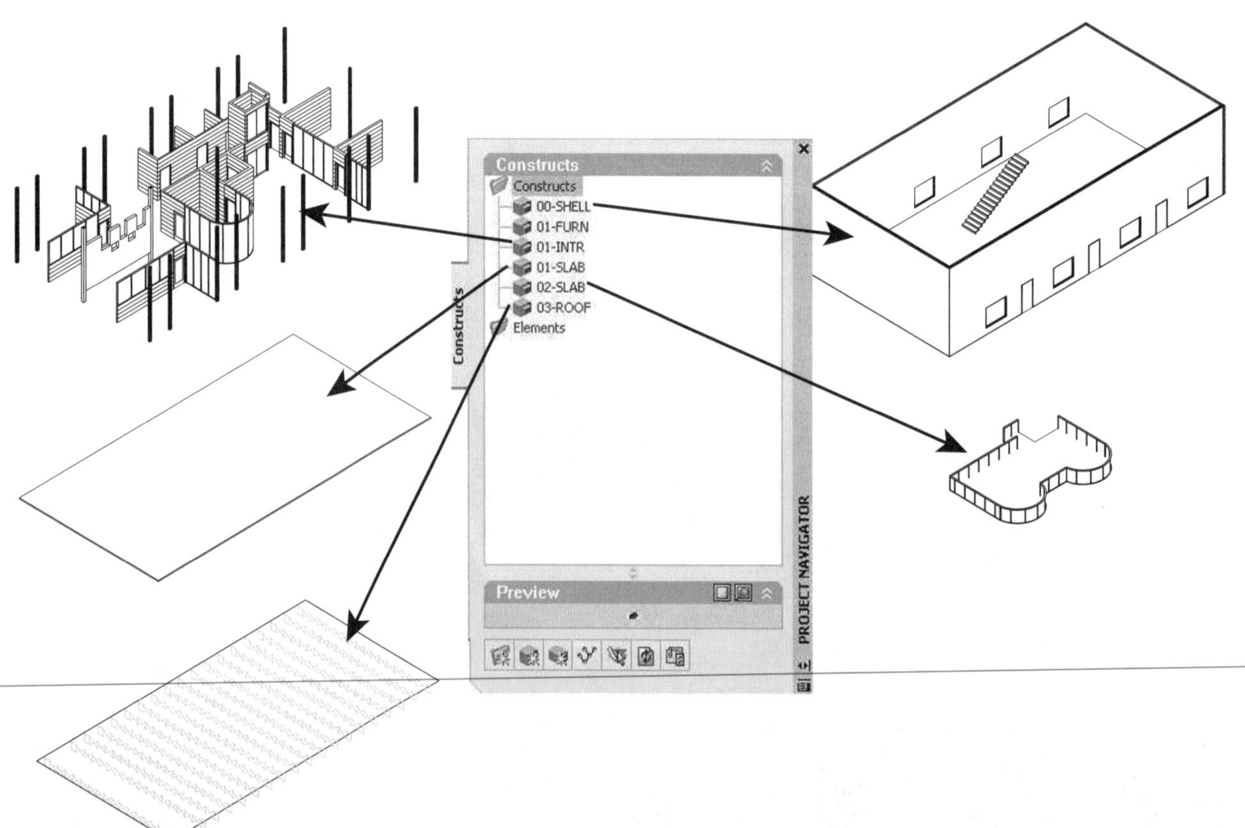

Figure 9.16 Construct drawings (.dwg files) break up the virtual model into manageable files.
Office renovation student project courtesy of Tiffany White.

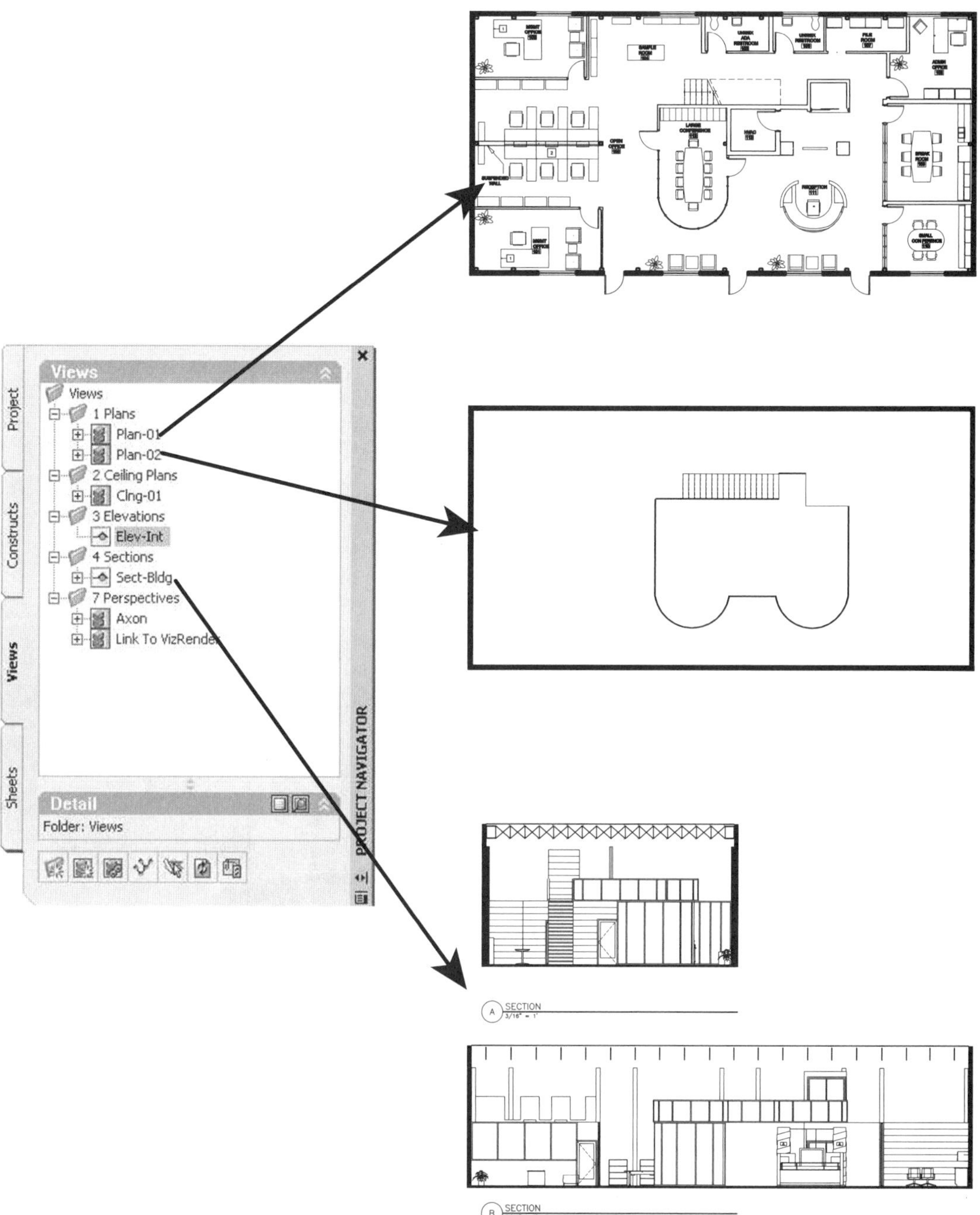

Figure 9.17 View drawings create the conventional orthographic drawings types of floorplan, section, elevation, ceiling plan, and so on. Each orthographic view type is separated into individual View drawings.

Office renovation student project courtesy of Tiffany White.

Sheets

Plot sheets make the individual drawing sheets ready for plotting. See Figure 9.18. Sheets are paper space layouts set up with a border. They show one or more sheet views (through viewports). Sheet Subsets are folder structures within the project navigator that help organize the plot sheets.

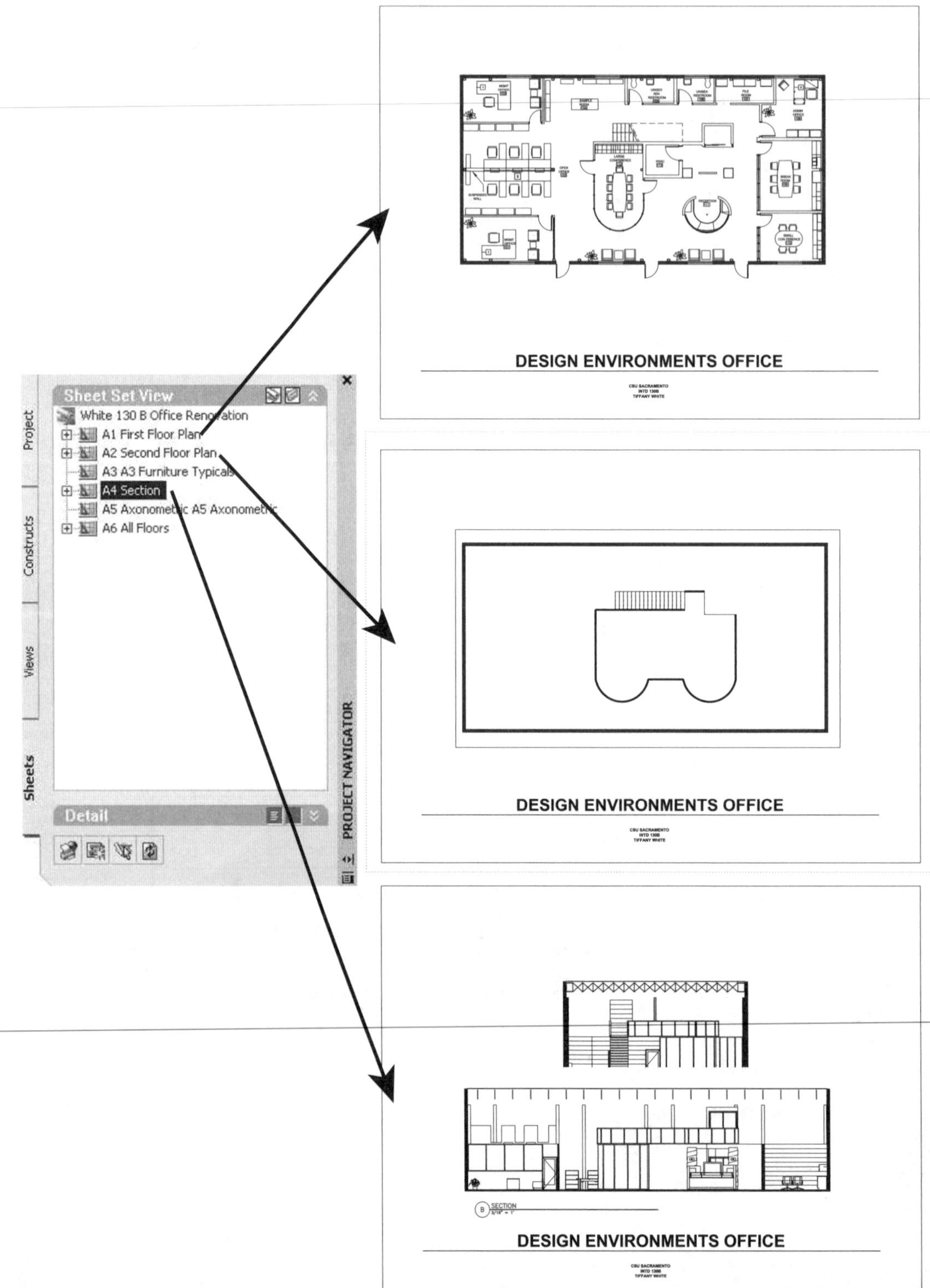

Figure 9.18 Sheets (also known as plot sheets) prepare View drawings so you can output them on a printer or plotter. In this illustration, three plot sheets are created for the project.

Office renovation student project courtesy of Tiffany White.

The Project Browser

Projects in ADT are created using the Project Browser. It is a dialogue box that can be opened through the File menu. The Project Browser's primary functions are to change the active or current project, change a project's properties and templates, and create new projects. Figure 9.19 illustrates the various parts of the Project Browser. Figure 9.20 demonstrates how to create a new project using the Project Browser.

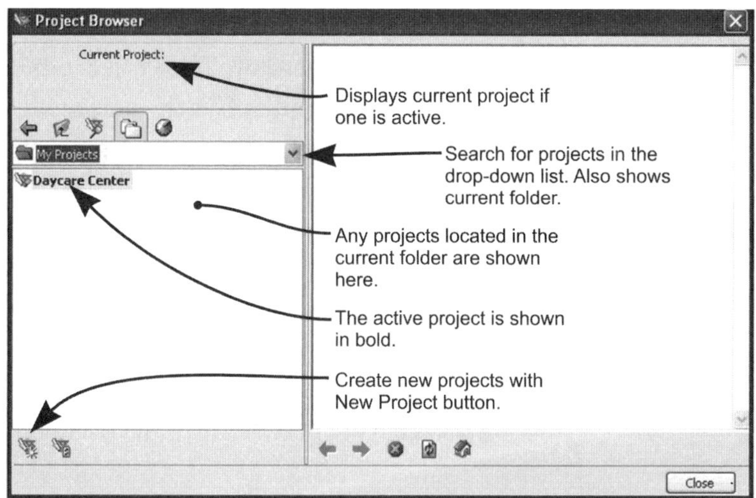

Figure 9.19 The project browser

Technique to Master **T09.20** Creating a New Project

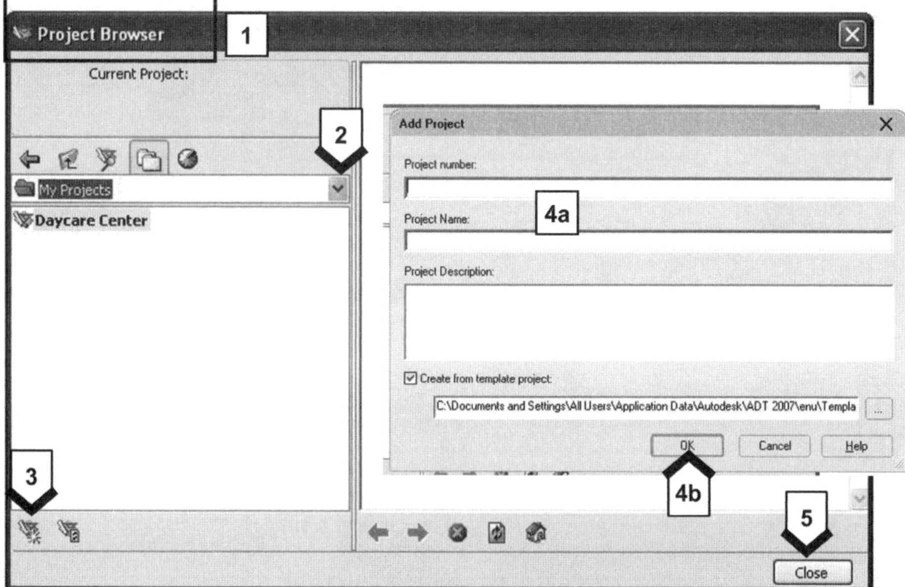

Figure 9.20

1	[File Menu>Project Browser]	Open the Project Browser.
2	[Project Browser dialogue box]	Using the Browse Project button, locate the folder to place the project within.
3	[Project Browser dialogue box]	Click the New Project button.
4a, 4b	[Add Project dialogue box]	Fill in the Project number, Project Name, and Project Description boxes. Note that the Project Name is the shortened name that will become the title of the folder where your drawings are saved. The Project Description is the long title that can be linked to your border sheets.
5	[Project Browser dialogue box]	Close the Project Browser. The Project Browser must be closed to continue.

Making an Existing Project Active

A project is active or current when it appears in bold black letters.

Changing the Properties of a Project

Figure 9.21 demonstrates how to change the properties of an existing project after a project has been created.

The Project Navigator

The Project Navigator is the main palette used in Architectural Desktop's project organization toolset. Functions of the Project Navigator include creating new drawings that are part of the current project, opening existing drawings that are part of the current project, and organizing drawing types.

> **Box 9.3**
> Use the Project Navigator to create, modify, and xref any project drawing files.

The Project Navigator is divided into four tabs: the Project tab, the Constructs tab, the Views tab, and the Sheets tab. The Project tab of the Project Navigator displays the name and description of the current project. It is also where you set your building levels and divisions. Figure 9.22 identifies the areas of this tab. Drawings are created and opened from the Constructs, Views, and Sheets tabs. Figure 9.23 identifies the various areas of these tabs.

Notice that the Project Navigator only shows drawing files that are part of the project. This is

Technique to Master **T09.21** Changing the Properties of a Project

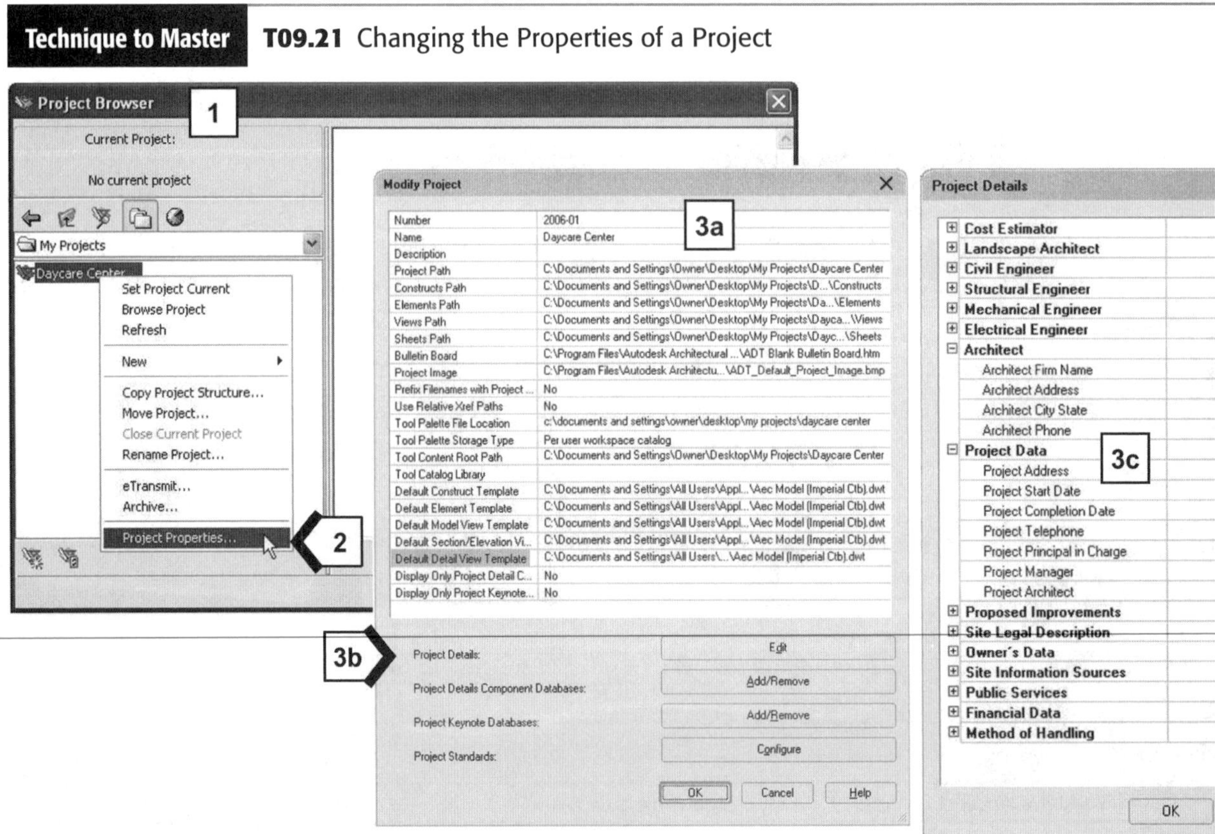

Figure 9.21

1	[File Menu>Project Browser]	Open the Project Browser.
2	[Project Browser dialogue box]	Locate the project, right-click, and choose Project Properties.
3a, 3b, 3c	[Modify Project dialogue box]	Project name, number, description, and template paths can be modified at the top of the dialogue box. Other project-oriented details can be adjusted from the Project Details button.

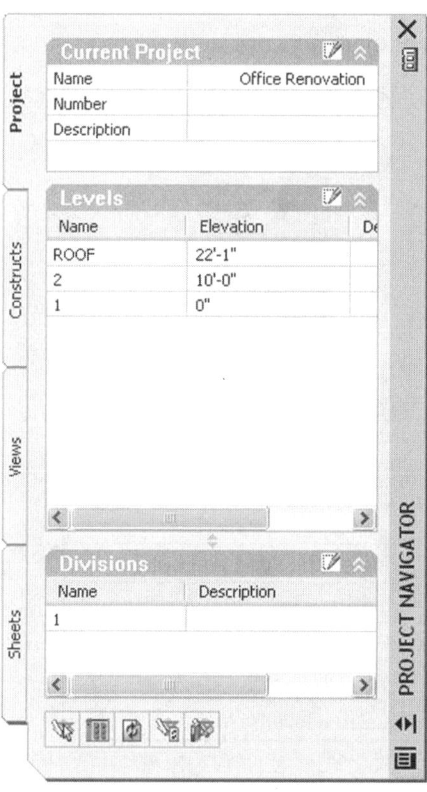

Figure 9.22 The Project Navigator palette. The Project tab displays the active project as well as its building levels and divisions.

a critical difference between using the Project Navigator to open drawings and using the File>Open command. Because a drawing that is included within a Project should always be opened through the Project Navigator, switching between Projects using the Project Browser becomes a necessary day-to-day action.

> **Box 9.4**
> If you want to use nonproject drawing files, import them into the project first.

Creating a New Project: The Workflow Process

Although complex, the Project Navigator is a powerful tool to use for project creation and project organization. Its benefits to a project far outweigh its minor difficulties. First, it helps you learn and practice project organization. Second, it makes putting a virtual model together very quick and painless. Learning to design with the Project Navigator is outlined in the next section and demonstrated in Figures 9.24 through 9.27.

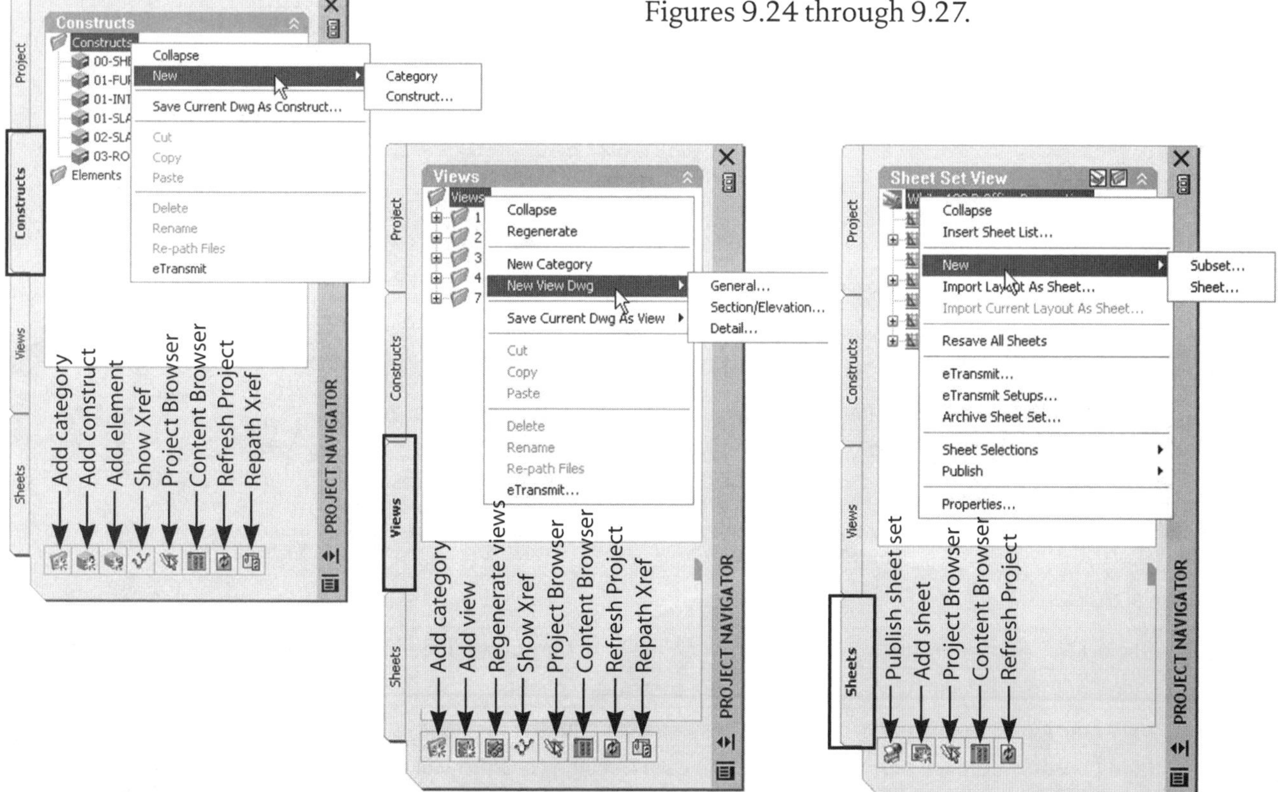

Figure 9.23 The Constructs, Views, and Sheets tabs of the Project Navigator palette

Technique to Master T09.24 Setting Up Building Levels for the New Project

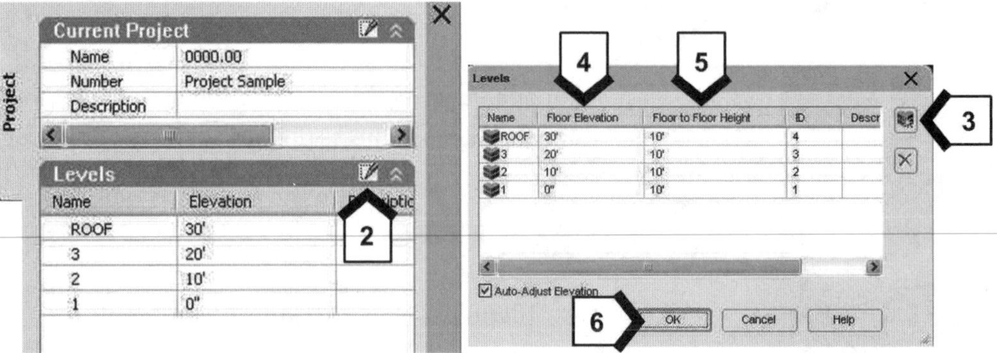

Figure 9.24

1	Open the Project Navigator (Ctrl + 5).	
2	[Project Navigator>Project Tab]	Set up the levels for the Project by left-clicking on the Edit Level button.
3	[Add Levels dialogue box]	Click on the New Level button. Click OK to finish.
4	[Add Levels dialogue box]	Define the level's current floor height.
5	[Add Levels dialogue box]	Define the level's floor to floor height.
6	[Add Levels dialogue box]	Repeat as necessary. (Remember the roof is also a level!)

Technique to Master T09.25 Creating Construct Drawings

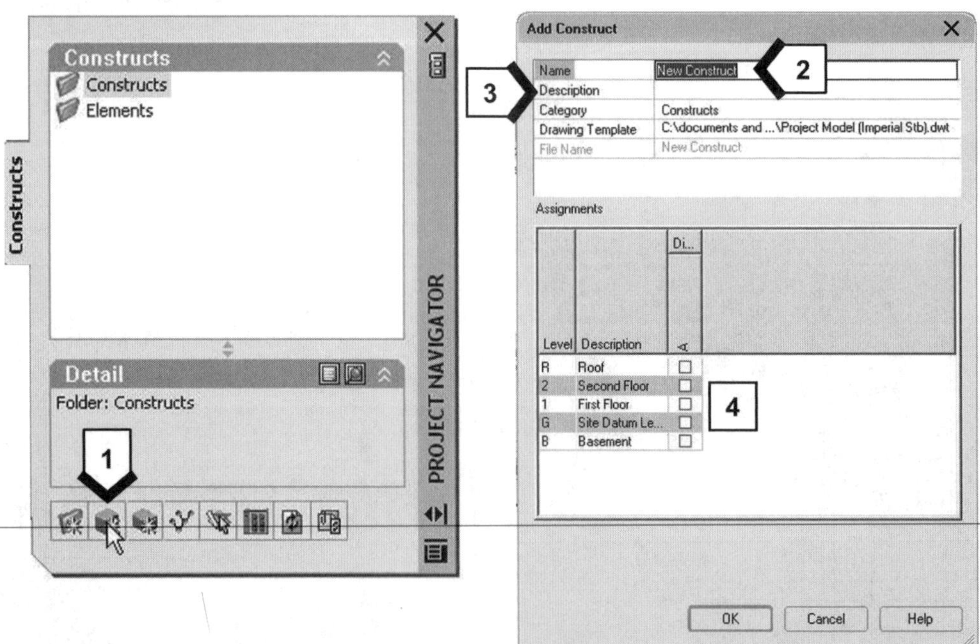

Figure 9.25

1	[Project Navigator>Constructs tab]	Left-click on the New Construct button located at the bottom of the palette.
2	[Add Construct dialogue box]	Name the construct.
3	[Add Construct dialogue box]	Type in a description for the construct.
4	[Add Construct dialogue box]	Check off each level the construct will affect. For example, the building shell construct will affect all levels while the floor-2 furniture construct will affect only level 2. Click OK to finish.
5	Repeat Steps 1 through 4 until all constructs have been made.	

Technique to Master **T09.26** Creating Plan View Drawings

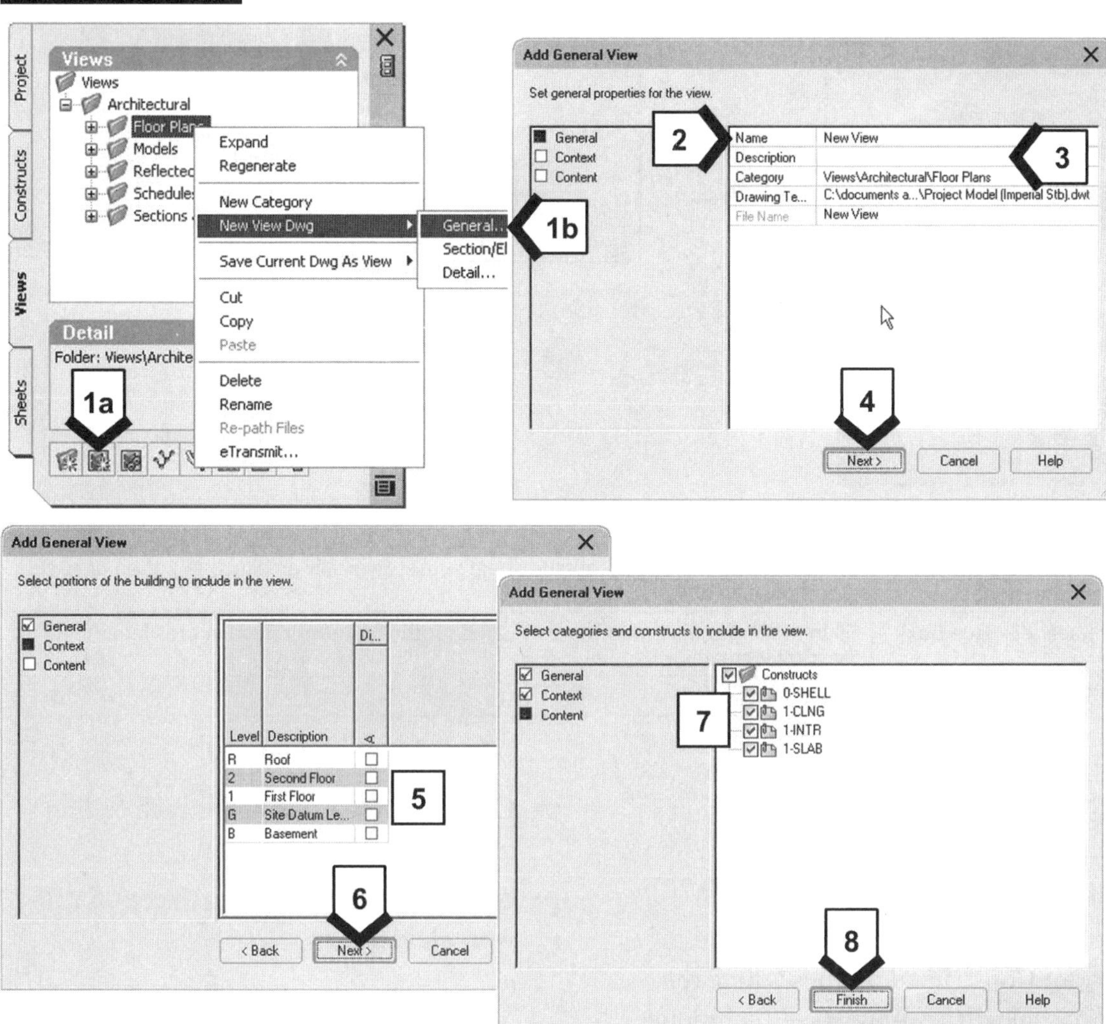

Figure 9.26

1a, 1b	[Project Navigator Palette>Views tab]	Select New View Dwg tool button. Choose General View.
2	[Add General View dialogue box]	Name the View drawing.
3	[Add General View dialogue box]	Type in the description.
4	[Add General View dialogue box]	Click Next.
5	[Add General View dialogue box]	Check off the appropriate level(s).
6	[Add General View dialogue box]	Click Next.
7	[Add General View dialogue box]	Uncheck all constructs that should not appear in this view.
8	[Add General View dialogue box]	Click Finish.

Technique to Master **T09.27** Setting Up Plot Sheets with the Project Navigator

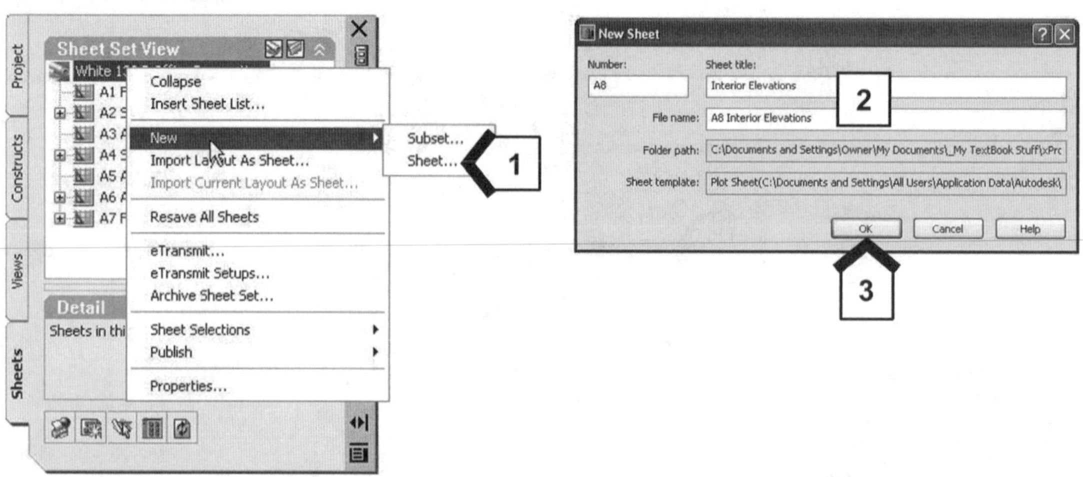

Figure 9.27

1	[Project Navigator Palette>Sheets tab]	Left-click to select the appropriate sheet subset (typically architectural), then right-click and choose New>Sheet.
2	[New Sheet dialogue box]	Fill in the appropriate number and name for the plot sheet. Type in the filename for the .dwg it creates.
3	[New Sheet dialogue box]	Select OK.

Overall Workflow Process

1. With the Project tab current, set the building levels for the project (see Technique T09.24).
2. With the Constructs tab current, create the various Construct drawings where the virtual model will be drawn (see Technique T09.25).
   - Create a Construct drawing for the building's exterior walls, doors, and windows.
   - Create a Construct drawing for each floor level's interior building elements: walls, windows, doors, and more.
   - Create a Construct drawing for the roof.
3. With the Views tab current, create the conventional orthographic views for communicating the project (see Technique T09.26).
   - Create a View drawing for each floor plan, including the roof plan.
   - Create a View drawing for each ceiling plan.
   - Create one View drawing to contain all your elevations.
   - Create one View drawing to contain all your sections.
   - Create a View drawing for the building model that will be rendered.
4. With the Sheets tab current, create the plot sheets to print/plot the project (see Technique T09.27).

Chapter Exercises

Open the Chapter 9 folder located on the CD-ROM to access the exercises for this chapter. Exercises let you practice setting up hypothetical projects using the Project Browser and Project Navigator.

Basic 3-D Shapes in ADT

10

Objectives

This chapter introduces the ADT mass element and mass group objects as versatile tools to use when starting your building model. It describes the tools and techniques related to mass elements and mass groups that assist in form development while showing the versatility of the tools. The end-of-chapter exercises allow you to apply techniques to create complex building mass models and common furniture and lighting objects.

The Basic Mass Elements

Autodesk probably had conceptual designing in mind when the company created mass elements: generic, three-dimensional shapes that have no relation to any building elements in real life. During the conceptual and schematic phases, mass elements provide the three-dimensional building blocks for massing studies when details of a building are not typically known (Figure 10.1). During the design development stage and beyond, mass

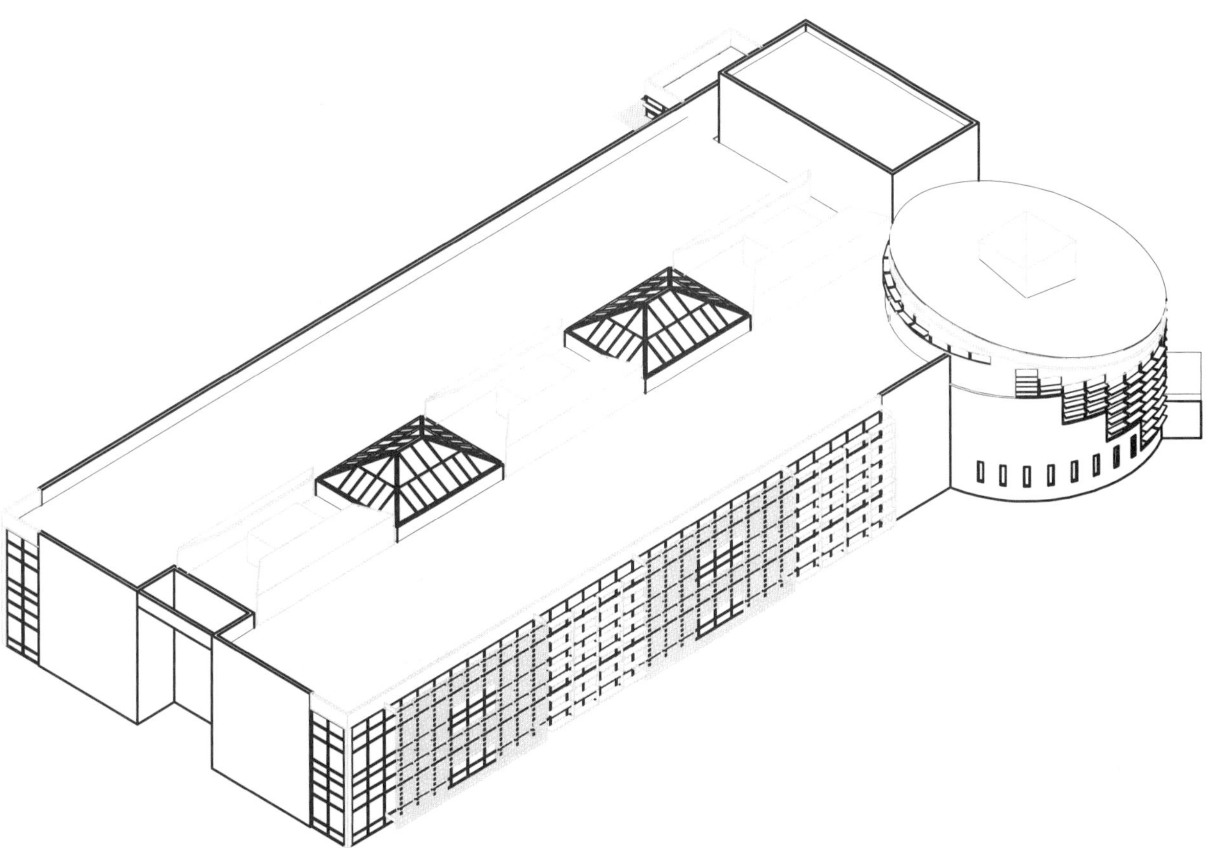

Figure 10.1 In the conceptual stage, mass elements provide the 3-D building blocks for creating exterior and interior massing studies.

3-D model courtesy of Nach & Lewis architects.

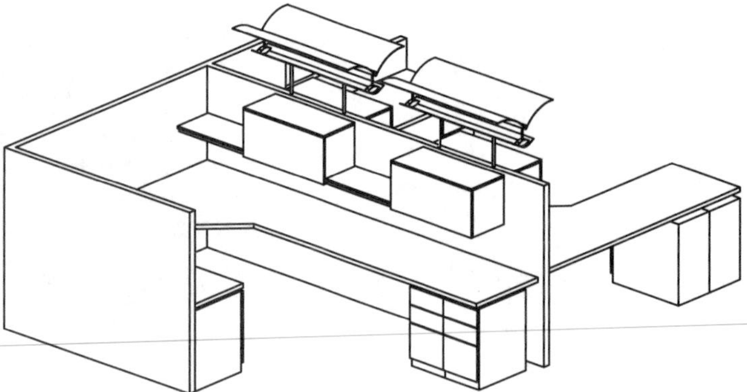

Figure 10.2 Mass elements and mass groups are used for furniture, equipment, and other specialty objects.

elements become very useful for building furniture, casework, and other building elements that are not part of the ADT library. Mass elements and mass groups are often used to create furniture, equipment, and other specialty objects. Figure 10.2 shows a workstation and lighting fixture built from mass elements.

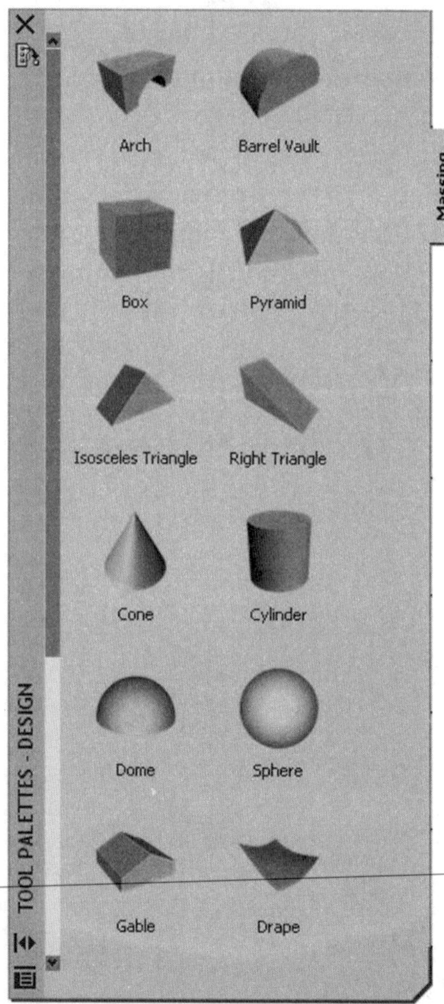

Figure 10.3 The Mass Elements Tool palette and its twelve basic shapes

Mass Element Types

The standard library of mass element objects is made up of twelve basic shapes. They are the Arch, Barrel Vault, Box, Cone, Cylinder, Dome, Drape, Gable, Pyramid, Isosceles Triangle, Right Triangle, and Sphere (Figure 10.3). Users may create all the basic shapes by entering their dimensional properties of width, depth, and height into the Properties palette or specifying them on-screen. Dimensional properties of the objects vary based on their shapes (Figure 10.4). There are many times that some of the dimensional properties are grayed out or fixed at the time of creation. Editing these grayed out areas can typically occur after placement. Figure 10.5 illustrates the steps to create a mass element.

You may also create nonstandard mass element shapes by using extruded geometry. With this method, you first create profiles of the shape using 2-D geometry and then extrude it into a mass element object.

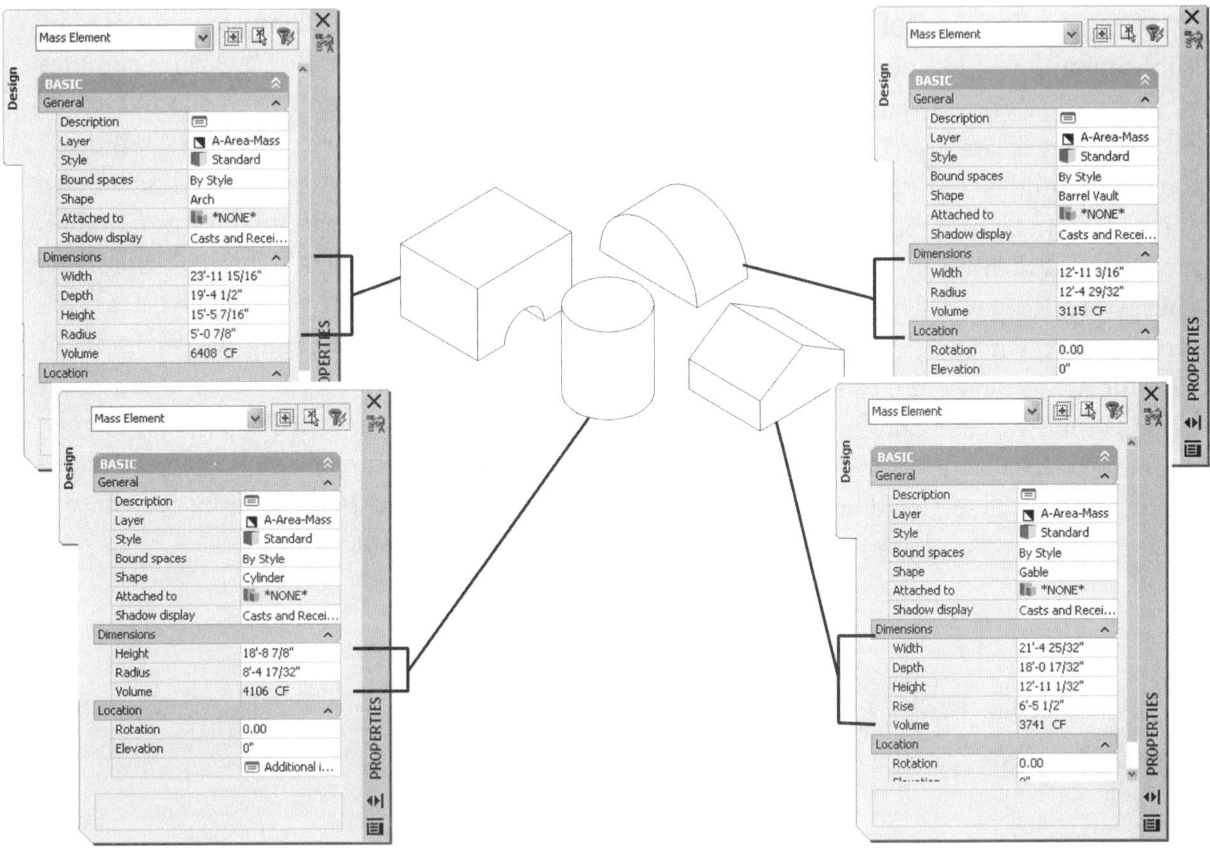

Figure 10.4 The Dimensional Properties of the twelve mass element types vary based on shape.

Technique to Master **T10.05** Placing a Mass Element

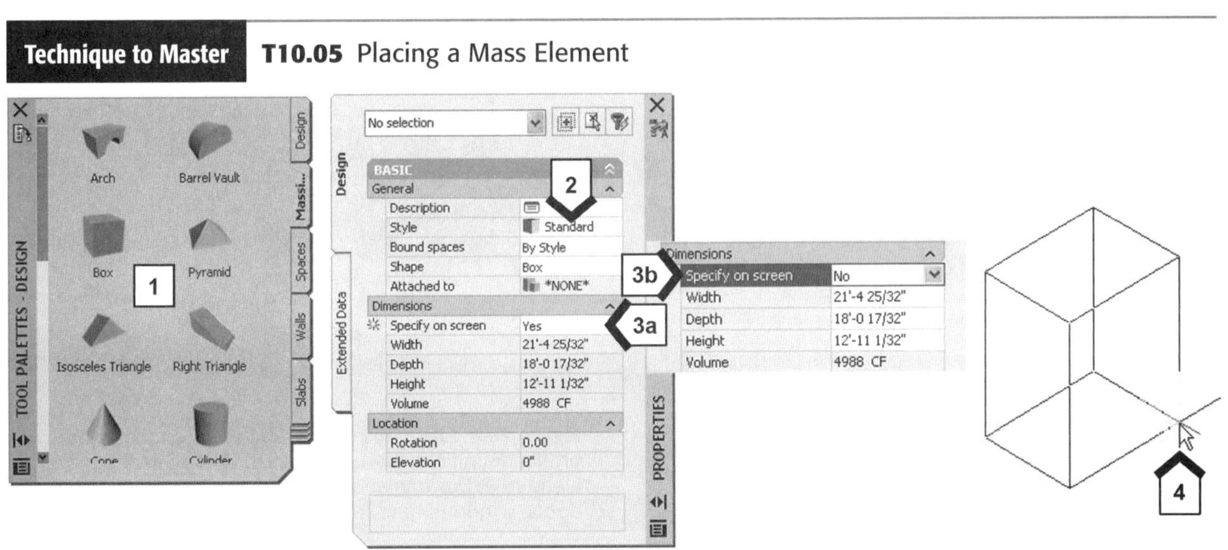

Figure 10.5

1	[Mass Element Tool Palette]	Select the appropriate massing tool.
2	[Properties palette]	Choose the style of the mass element.
3a, 3b	[Properties palette]	Specify the width, height, and other appropriate dimensional properties for the mass element. (You may also opt to draw the mass element on-screen, specifying width, depth, and height as you draw.)
4	[Drawing Screen]	Specify the insertion point of the mass element.
5	[Drawing Screen]	Specify the rotation angle.
6	[Command Line]	Press Enter to complete command.

Profiles and Profile Definitions

Profile definitions add a powerful advantage to Architectural Desktop's customization abilities. They create user-friendly customization opportunities to the basic ADT building objects. You must be familiar with polylines to create a profile definition, and polyline editing is necessary. Review polylines in Chapter 5 to refresh your memory.

Profile definitions—also called profiles—use one or more closed polylines to customize the shape of ADT objects. You can use the closed polylines as sectional profiles, elevational profiles, or plan-based extrusions (Figure 10.6). Profile definitions are used in many different scenarios in ADT. Examples include mass element extrusions and revolutions, wall sweeps, custom doors, windows, and frames. A single closed polyline will typically represent the solid portion of the object when extruded. When multiple closed polylines are used, the inner polylines typically represent holes (Figure 10.7). In doors and windows, however, these inner polylines represent glass surfaces. Figure 10.8 shows just a sampling of these various applications. Figures 10.9 and 10.10 demonstrate how to create profile definitions in ADT.

Figure 10.6 Closed polylines are converted to profile definitions where they can be used as sectional profiles, elevational profiles, or plan-based extrusions.

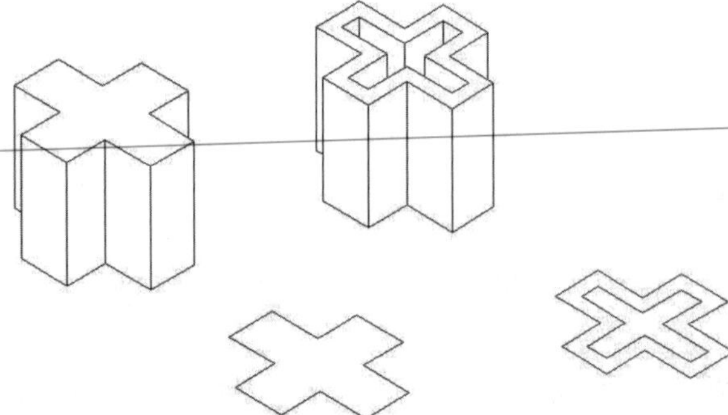

Figure 10.7 Profile definitions may be defined using one closed polyline or may have multiple closed polylines. When multiple closed polylines are used, the inner polylines typically represent holes.

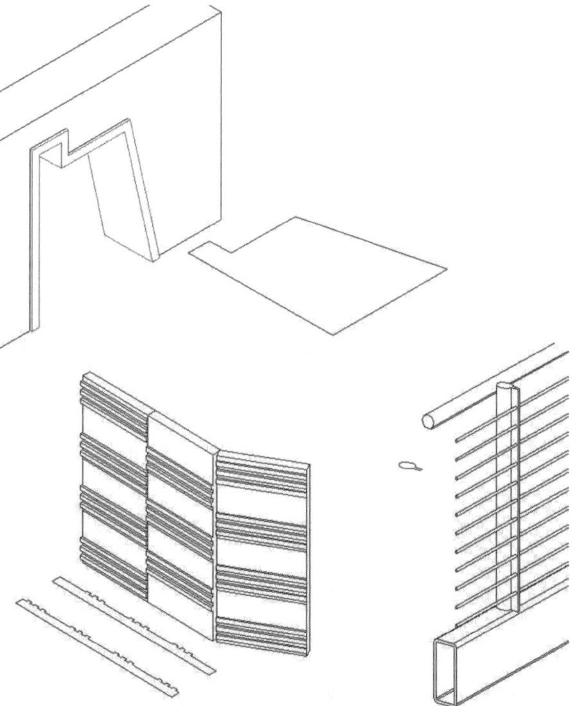

Figure 10.8 Examples of the different scenarios where profile definitions are used in ADT. These include mass element extrusions and revolutions, wall sweeps, custom doors, windows, and frames.

Technique to Master T10.09 Creating a Profile Definition Using a Single Polyline

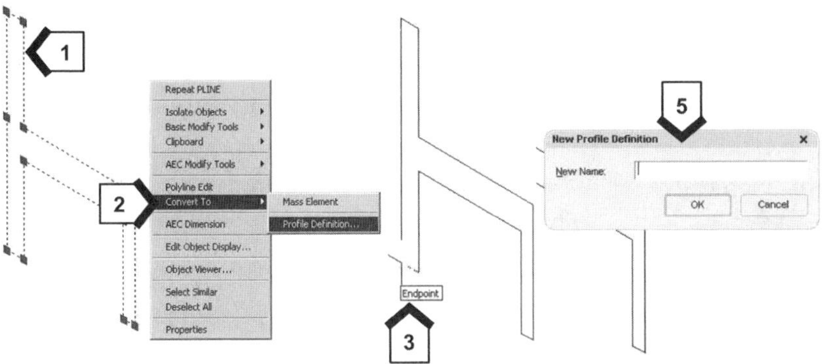

Figure 10.9

1	[Drawing Screen]	Draw a closed polyline.
2	[Drawing Screen]	Select the polyline, right-click, and choose Convert To>Profile Definition.
3	[Drawing Screen]	Locate the insertion point for the profile. Locate the insertion points of elevational and sectional profiles at what is considered the bottom of the object.
4	[Command Line]	Type N and press Enter to create a new profile.
5	[New Profile Definition dialogue]	Name the profile definition.

Technique to Master T10.10 Creating the Profile Definition Using Multiple Polylines

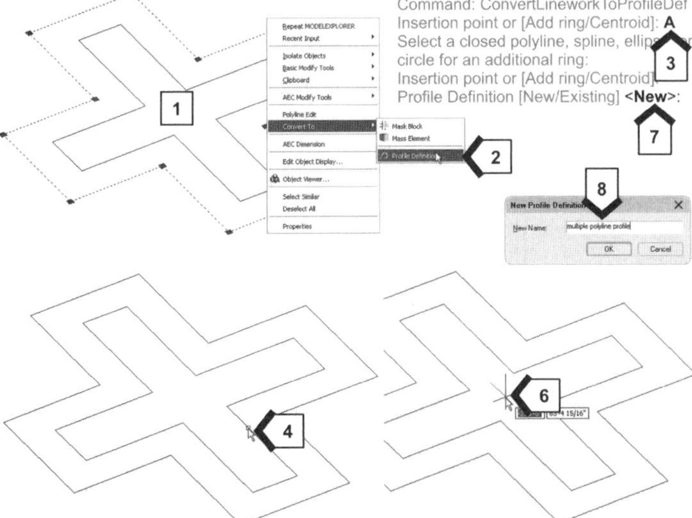

Figure 10.10

1	[Drawing Screen]	Draw closed polylines.
2	[Drawing Screen]	Select the outer closed polyline, right-click, and choose Convert To>Profile Definition.
3	[Command Line]	Type A and press Enter to switch to the Add ring command option.
4	[Drawing Screen]	Choose the second polyline.
5	Continue repeating Steps 3 and 4 until all polylines are selected.	
6	[Drawing Screen]	Locate the insertion point for the profile. Locate the insertion points of elevational and sectional profiles at what is considered the bottom of the object.
7	[Command Line]	Type <New> and press Enter to create new profile.
8	[New Profile Definition dialogue box]	Name the profile definition.

Creating Mass Elements with Profiles

The shortcut technique for creating a mass element based on a profile is to use the Convert To>Mass Element hidden menu command. Without first converting to a profile definition, you can quickly extrude a closed polyline into a mass element with the technique, as outlined in Figure 10.11.

Mass Elements That Use Profile Definitions

There are three mass element creation tools that are not shape specific. The Extrusion, Revolution, and Drape tools all create molded mass elements that are based on profile definitions. The tools are located at the bottom of the Design Tool palette's Massing tab.

Creating Mass Elements Using the Extrusion Tool

The Extrusion tool creates a mass element using a closed polyline or profile definition. The profile is extruded by giving it height in the z-axis. Figure 10.12 illustrates the steps.

Creating Mass Elements Using the Revolution Tool

The Revolution Tool creates a mass element by revolving a closed polyline or profile definition along an axis (Figure 10.13). Revolution extrusions are great for creating any profile-based circular object, such as vases and bowls.

Technique to Master **T10.11** Creating Mass Elements Using Profiles

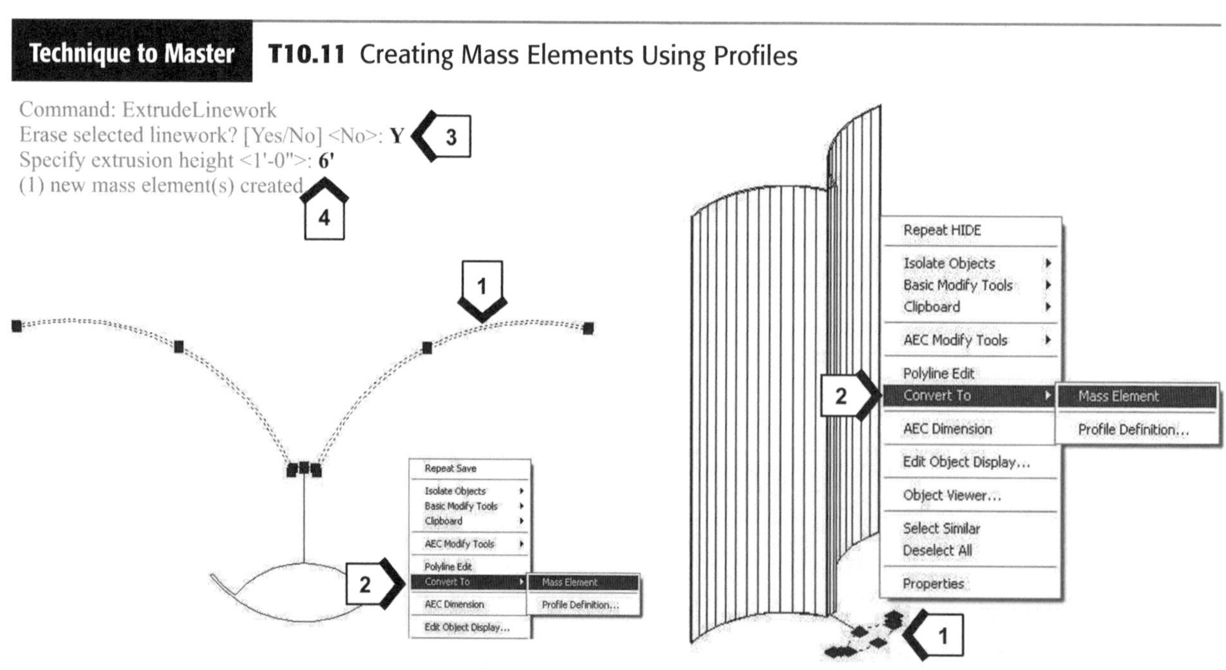

Figure 10.11

1	[Drawing Screen]	Draw a closed polyline.
2	[Drawing Screen]	Select a closed polyline, right-click, and choose Convert To>Mass Element.
3	[Command Line]	Type Y and press Enter to choose to erase original polyline.
4	[Command Line]	Type in the extrusion length.
5	Polyline profile is converted to a mass element. Select the mass element.	
6	[Properties palette]	Change the mass element to the appropriate mass element style.

Technique to Master T10.12 Creating a Mass Element Using the Extrusion Tool

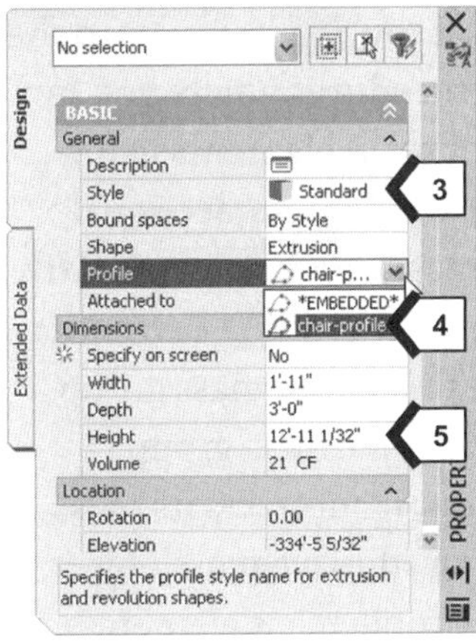

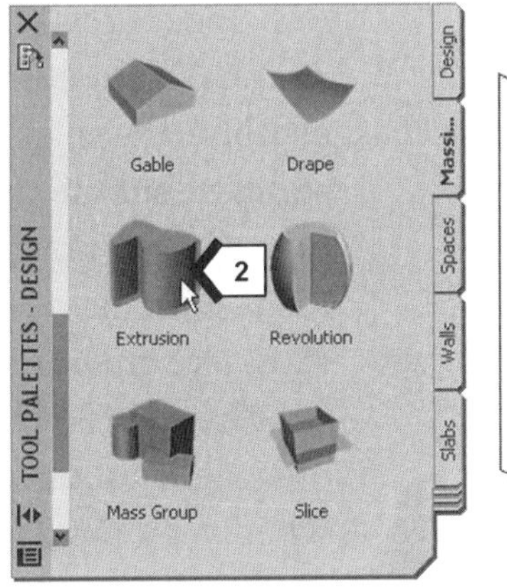

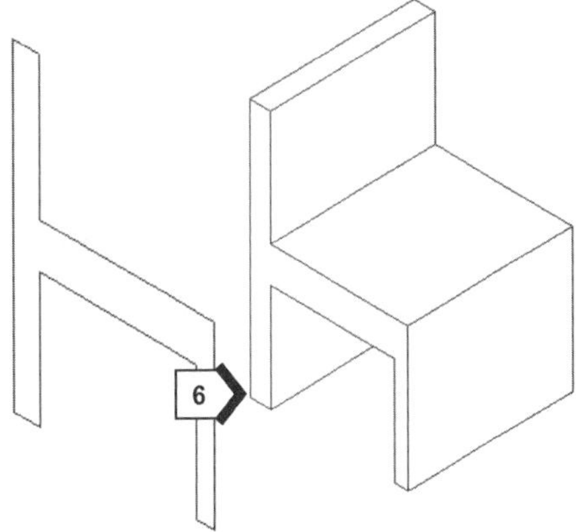

Figure 10.12

1	A profile definition must exist before completing the command. See Technique T10.09.	
2	[Mass Element Tool palette]	Select the Extrusion Massing tool.
3	[Properties palette]	Choose the style of the mass element.
4	Properties palette]	Choose the profile definition for extrusion.
5	[Properties palette]	Specify the width, height, and other appropriate dimensional properties for the mass element. (You may also opt to draw the mass element on-screen, specifying width, depth, and height as you draw.)
6	[Drawing Screen]	Locate the insertion point for the mass element.

Technique to Master T10.13 Creating a Mass Element Using the Revolution Tool

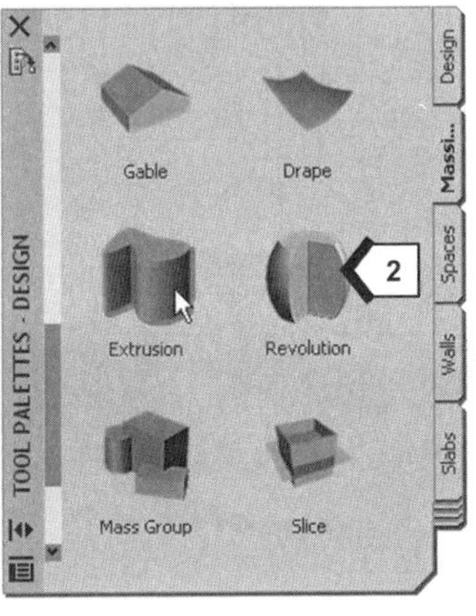

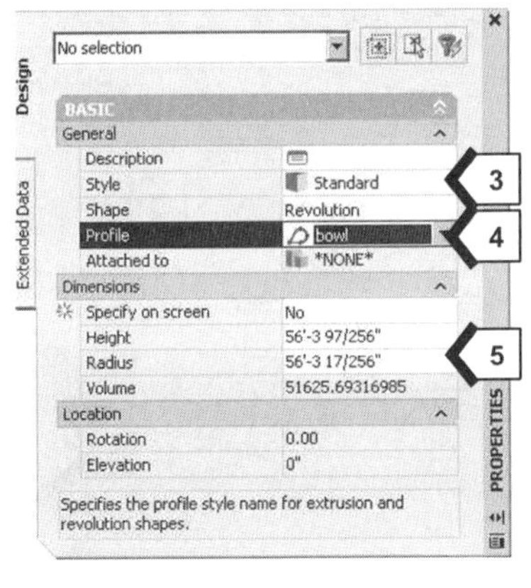

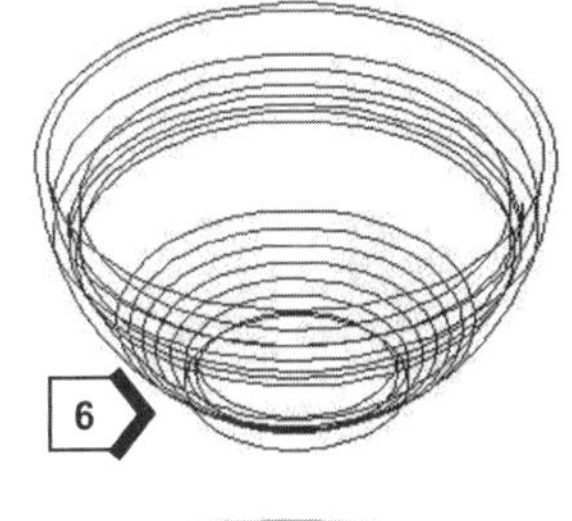

Figure 10.13

1	A profile definition must exist before completing the command. See Technique T10.09.	
2	[Mass Element Tool palette]	Select the Revolution Massing tool.
3	[Properties palette]	Choose the style of the mass element.
4	[Properties palette]	Choose the profile definition for revolution.
5	[Properties palette]	Specify the width, height, and other appropriate dimensional properties for the mass element. (You may opt to draw the mass element on-screen, specifying width, depth, and height as you draw.)
6	[Drawing Screen]	Locate insertion point for mass element.

Creating Mass Elements Using the Drape Tool

The Drape tool is useful for landscape terrain or any freeform modeling. The tool creates a mass element from polylines and AEC polygons that are located at different elevations. During the creation process, the resolution or detail within the terrain is determined by the user-specified rectangular mesh. Smaller mesh sizes will allow for more detailed contouring. Figure 10.14 illustrates these steps.

> **Box 10.1**
> An AEC polygon is a unique type of closed 2-D object that adds additional flexibility to ADT objects. AEC polygons are primarily used for customizing doors, windows, door/window assemblies, and curtain walls.

Mass Groups

Mass Groups are used to group mass elements into one object. Mass Groups are similar to the AutoCAD Boolean procedures where you can combine the shapes of mass elements using additive, subtractive, and/or intersectional operations. Though mass groups are primarily made with mass elements, any ADT volumetric object can be used to create a mass group.

When a mass element within a group operates by subtraction, it subtracts its mass wherever it overlaps an additive mass object. Figure 10.15a uses a simple mass element box and a cylinder to represent a perforated metal panel (Figure 10.15b). The cylinder is placed to intersect with the box and arrayed to represent the holes. When creating the mass group, the operation of the box is set to

Technique to Master **T10.14** Creating a Mass Element Using the Drape Tool

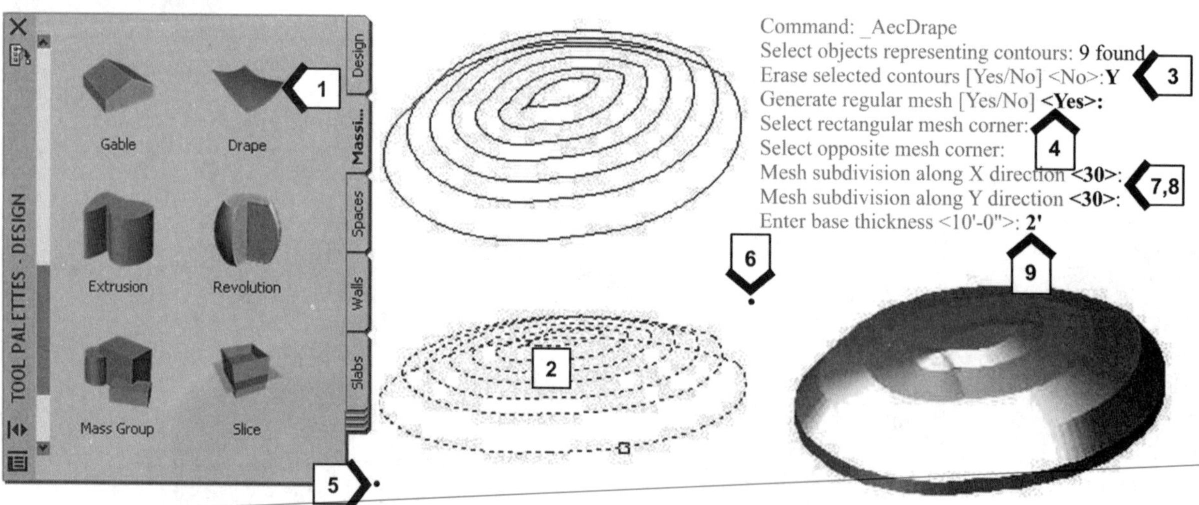
Gable
Drape
Extrusion
Revolution
Mass Group
Slice
TOOL PALETTES - DESIGN
Design
Massi...
Spaces
Walls
Slabs
Command: _AecDrape
Select objects representing contours: 9 found
Erase selected contours [Yes/No] <No>:Y
Generate regular mesh [Yes/No] <Yes>:
Select rectangular mesh corner:
Select opposite mesh corner:
Mesh subdivision along X direction <30>:
Mesh subdivision along Y direction <30>:
Enter base thickness <10'-0">: 2'
1
2
3
4
5
6
7,8
9

Figure 10.14 Polylines and AEC Polygons can be used as contours for the Drape tool.

1	[Mass Element Tool palette]	Select the Drape Massing tool.
2	[Drawing Screen]	Select contours.
3	[Command Line]	Type Y and press Enter to erase original contours.
4	[Command Line]	Type <Yes> and press Enter to generate regular mesh.
5	[Drawing Screen]	Specify the first corner of rectangular mesh.
6	[Drawing Screen]	Specify the opposite corner of rectangular mesh.
7	[Command Line]	Type in the number of mesh subdivisions for x direction.
8	[Command Line]	Type in the number of mesh subdivisions for y direction.
9	[Command Line]	Type in the base thickness.

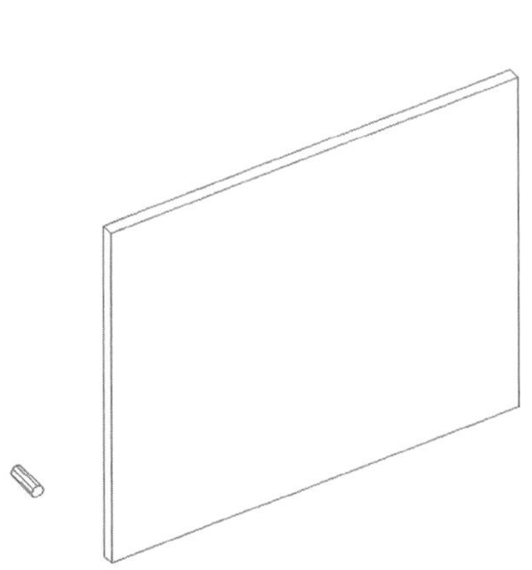

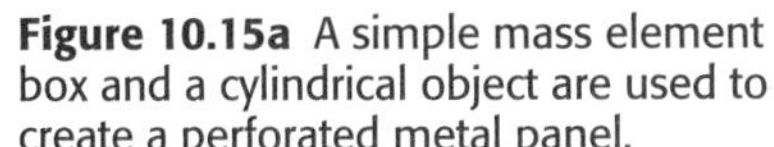

Figure 10.15a A simple mass element box and a cylindrical object are used to create a perforated metal panel.

Figure 10.15b Example of a perforated metal panel that the ADT object is based on

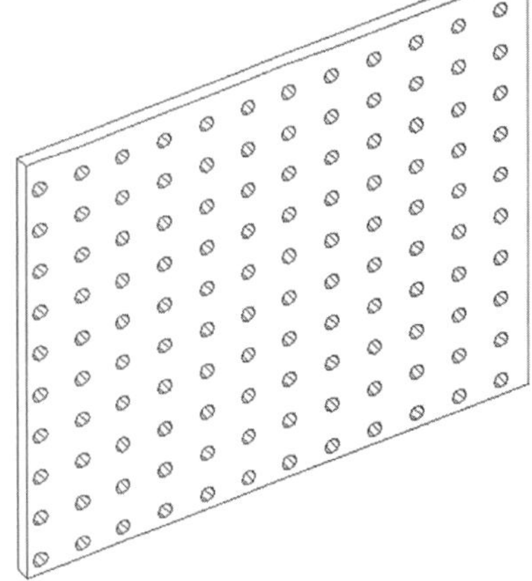

Figure 10.15c The cylinders create the holes in the mass element box, creating the perforations in the ADT box.

additive while the cylinders are set to subtractive. The cylinders create the holes in the mass element box, thereby creating the perforations (Figure 10.15c).

Creating the Mass Group

When you first create a mass group, all the mass elements that make up the mass group are additive by default. After you make the mass group, you can change the Boolean operation of any attached mass element to subtraction or intersection. Figure 10.16 demonstrates how to create the mass group, while Figure 10.17 demonstrates changing the operation of a mass element after it has been attached to a mass group. Editing of existing mass groups is demonstrated in Figure 10.18.

Technique to Master **T10.16** Creating the Mass Group

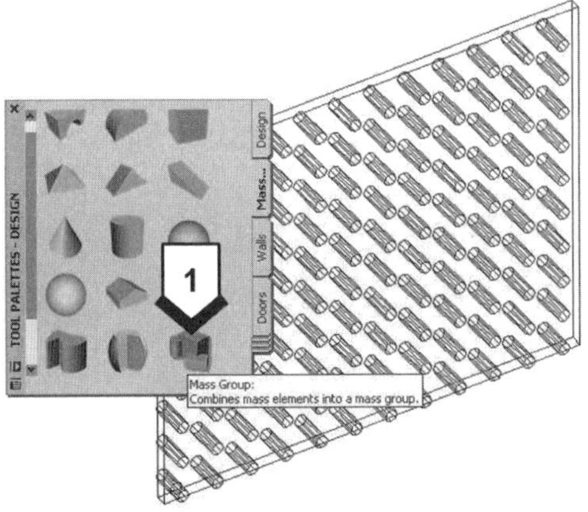

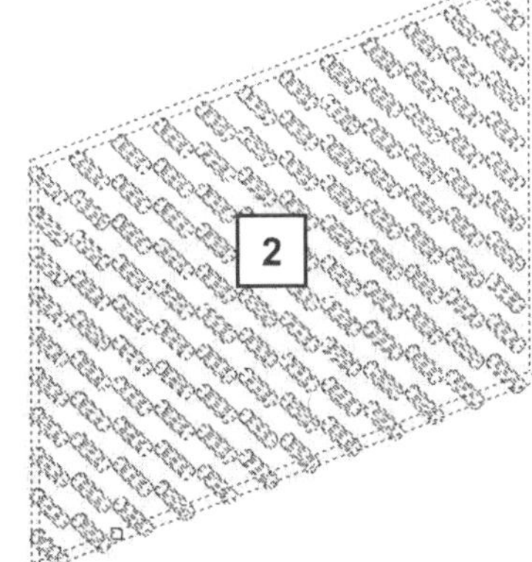

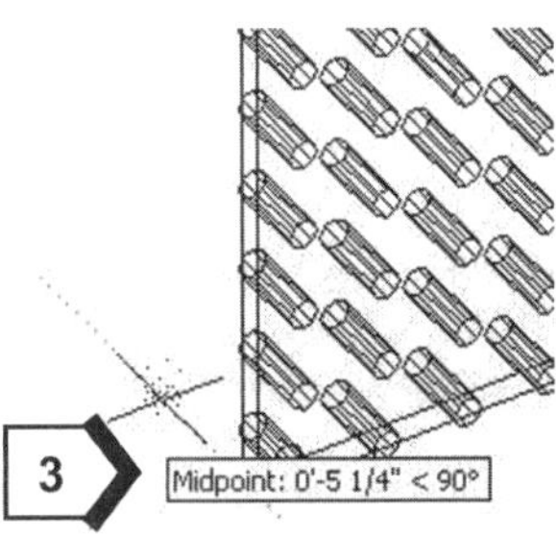

Figure 10.16

1	[Massing Tool palette]	Select the Mass Group tool.
2	[Drawing Screen]	Select the mass elements to attach to the group.
3	[Drawing Screen]	Position the Mass Group icon somewhere near the mass elements. (Note: The mass group icon disappears.)

Technique to Master **T10.17** Changing the Operation of a Mass Element Within a Mass Group

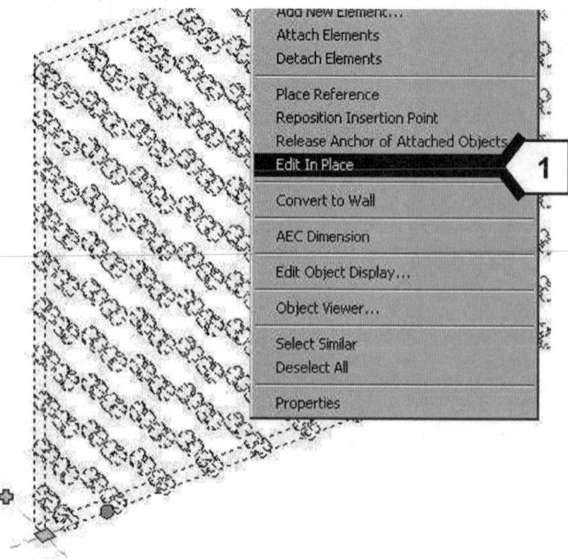

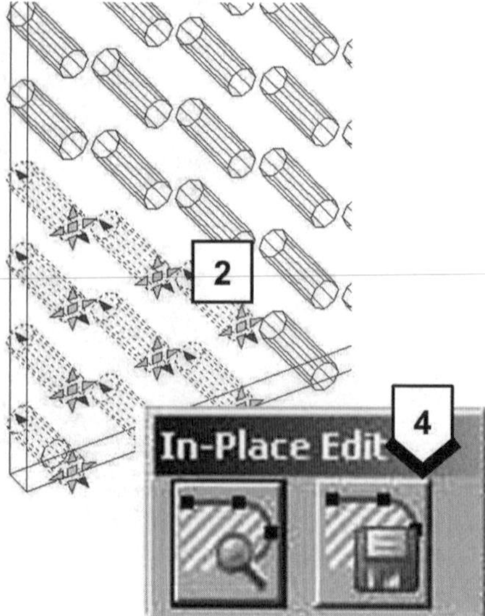

Figure 10.17 To change the mass element's operation to subtractive or intersection:

1	[Drawing Screen]	Right-click on the Mass Group and choose Edit In Place. (The individual mass elements are now visible and can be selected individually.)
2	[Drawing Screen]	Select the mass element to change.
3	[Properties palette> Basic>Operation]	Change the operation to Subtract or Intersect.
4	[In Place Edit floating toolbar]	Select the Save Changes tool button.

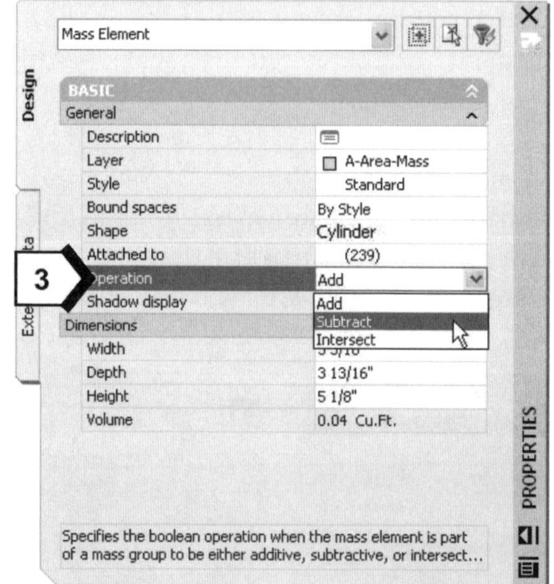

Technique to Master T10.18 Making Mass Element Modifications After They Have Been Grouped

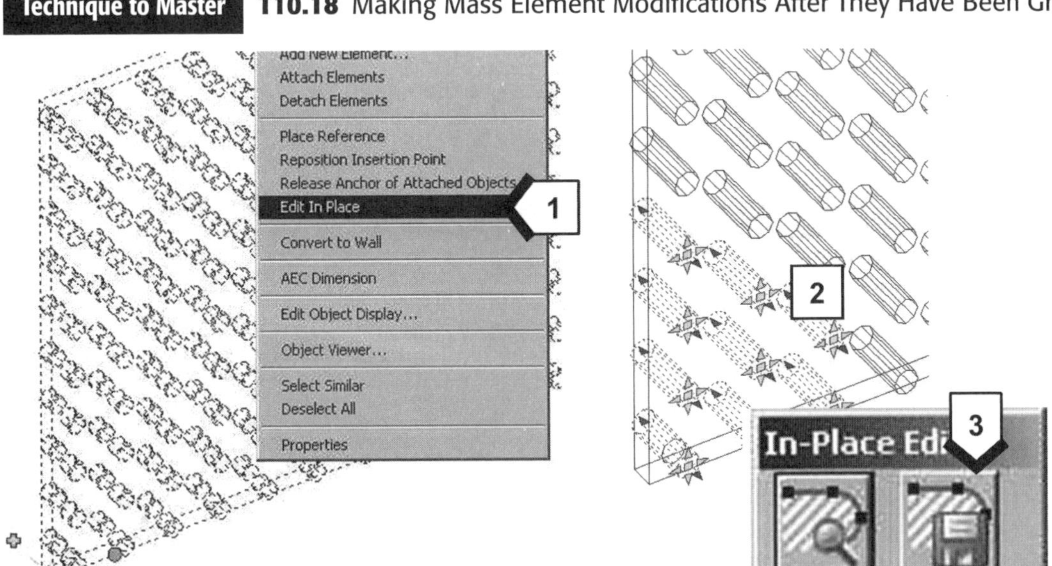

Figure 10.18

1	[Drawing Screen]	Right-click on the Mass Group and choose Edit In Place. (The individual mass elements are now visible and can be selected individually.)
2	[Drawing Screen]	Modify desired mass element(s). (See Technique T12.05 for property modifications.)
3	[In Place Edit floating toolbar]	Select the Save Changes tool button.

Using the Mass Modeler

The Model Explorer provides an easy interface to manipulate mass groups and the three-dimensional objects that make up the group. It can be accessed by right-clicking any selected mass group (Figure 10.19).

The Model Explorer dialogue box shows the menu and toolbars at the top. It also shows a two-pane dialogue box—the left pane displaying the tree view of all open drawings and the right pane showing a preview of the selected mass group. Figure 10.20 illustrates the various areas of the Model Explorer.

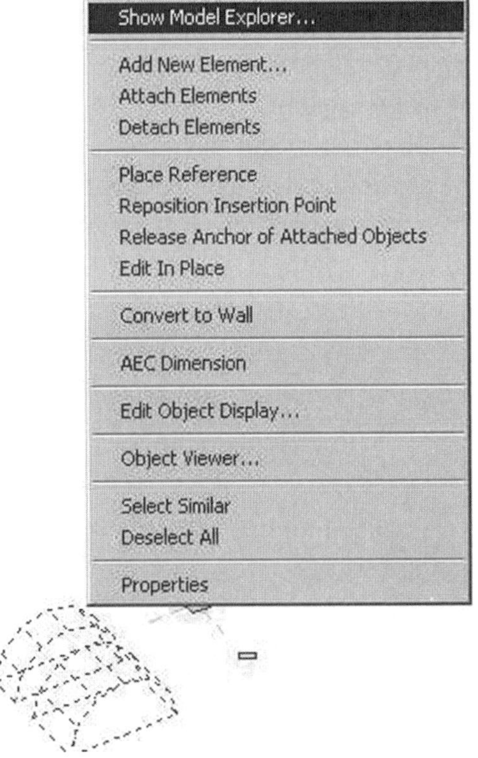

Figure 10.19 Accessing the Model Explorer window

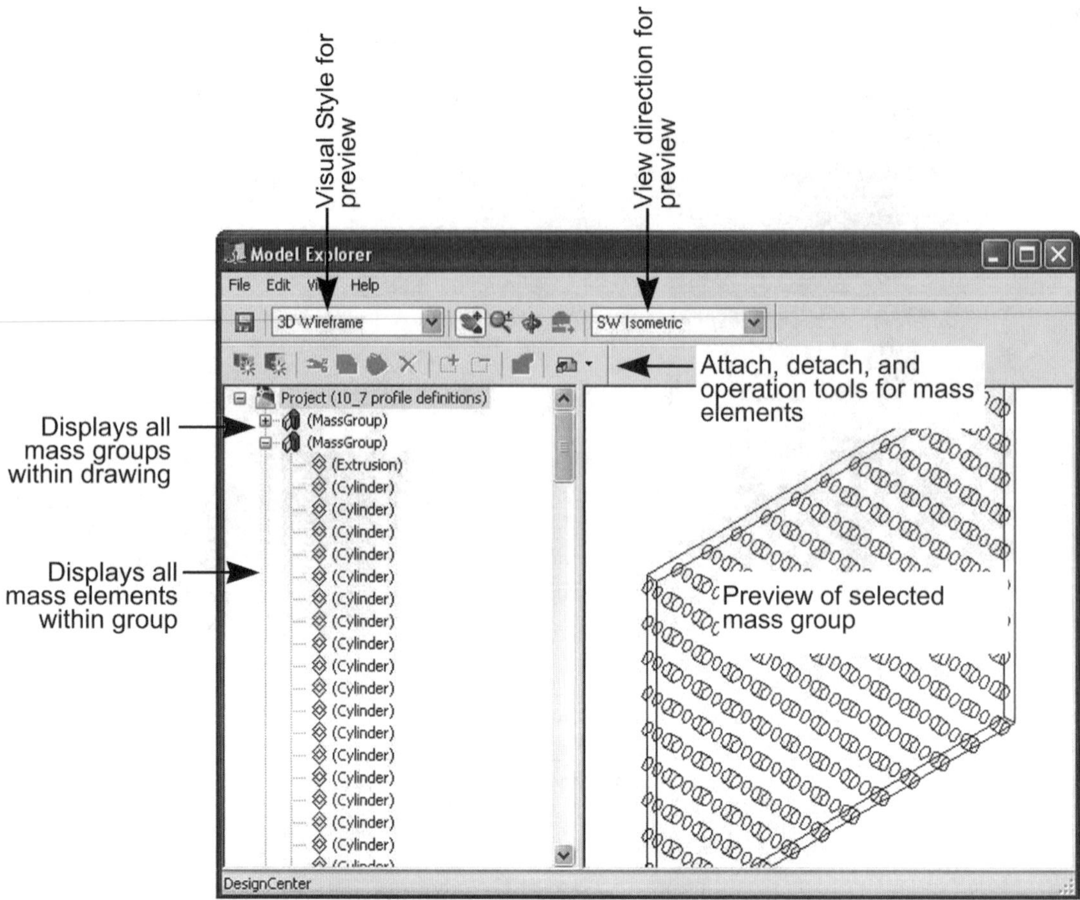

Figure 10.20 Getting to know the Model Explorer

Attaching and Detaching Elements Within the Model Explorer

The Model Explorer's right-click menu shows options to attach and detach elements from the selected mass group. This is illustrated in Figure 10.21.

Changing the Operations of Mass Elements Within the Model Explorer

The Model Explorer's right-click menu also shows options for changing the operation of a mass element. Remember that when mass elements are originally attached to a mass group, the operation defaults to additive. To change the operation, right-click on any selected mass element and choose Operation.

Technique to Master **T10.21** Attaching and Detaching Elements Within the Model Explorer

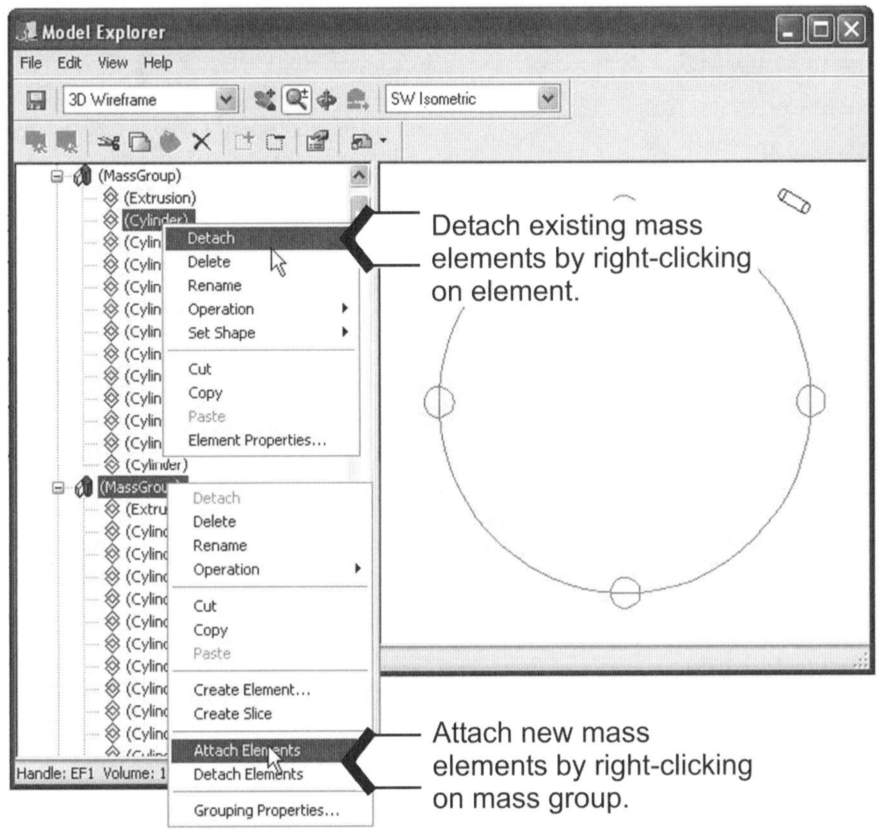

Figure 10.21

1	Open the Model Explorer.	
2	[Model Explorer dialogue box]	Select an existing mass element, right-click, and choose Detach.
	OR	
3	[Model Explorer dialogue box]	Right-click on the mass group icon and choose Attach Elements.
4	[Drawing Screen]	Choose the mass element to attach.

Converting Other Objects to Mass Elements

Any of the AutoCAD solids, as described in Chapter 8, can also be converted to a mass element. This technique is convenient when the mass element shapes and extrusions are inadequate. Figure 10.22 shows a tapered AutoCAD solid. This shape is much easier to create using an AutoCAD solid rather than a mass element. Other AutoCAD 2007 3-D creation tools like the helix, loft, and torus expand the mass element toolset when converted.

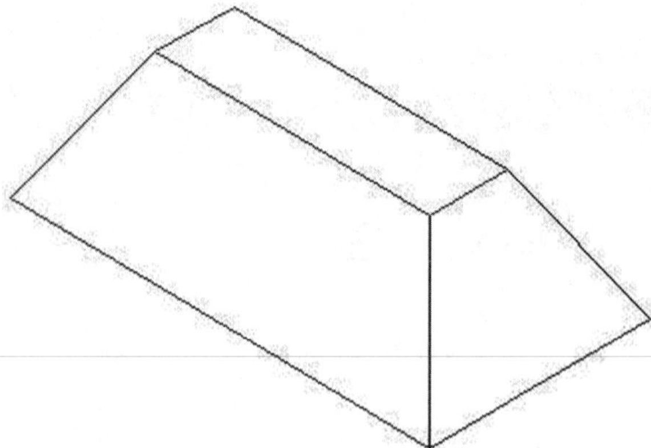

Figure 10.22 A tapered rectangle is much easier to create in AutoCAD using the AutoCAD solid creation tools. The solid is then converted to a mass element.

Chapter Exercises

Open the Chapter 10 folder located on the CD-ROM to access the exercises for this chapter. Exercises allow you to apply techniques to create complex building mass models and common furniture and lighting objects.

Drawing in ADT: Walls, Windows, Doors, and Openings 11

Objectives

This chapter introduces the wall, window, door, and opening objects. It emphasizes the importance of learning and using the various properties of these objects as well as how to place them accurately. The chapter provides demonstrations on how you can execute these procedures properly. The end-of-chapter exercises let you apply these techniques to simple space-planning problems.

Walls Systems and Wall Assemblies

A building starts with an envelope that separates the inside from the outside. Walls are an integral role in defining this envelope. Frances Ching says, "Walls are the vertical constructions of a building that enclose, separate, and protect its interior spaces" (*Building Construction Illustrated,* Ching, 2000). In building design and construction, walls are categorized by material and by function. Wall materials include homogeneous materials such as concrete and brick or composite wall assemblies made up of several materials. Wall function refers to the wall's primary duties within the building. Exterior walls protect the insides of buildings from the outside elements of nature. Each part of the exterior wall assembly has a purpose that helps to manage the amount of moisture, air, sound, and light that enters the building. Interior wall systems are used to divide the building into distinctive rooms and spaces. They are also the primary means for providing visual and acoustic privacy. Walls are also used as conduits that channel water, electricity, and communications to the different areas of the building.

An Introduction to Walls in ADT

The previous section introduced you to some of the typical wall assemblies used in building design and construction today. The ADT wall objects are designed to represent these various vertical assemblies used in buildings, and, therefore, by default, these objects have vertical orientations that relate to the world coordinate system (WCS), which you learned about in Chapter 2. The ADT wall object is also one of the more complicated tools in Architectural Desktop because it assumes many similar behaviors as its real-life counterpart. This section introduces you to the Wall tool and its many unique properties.

A Quick Look at the Wall Object

Wall objects have many attributes (also called properties) that directly influence wall placement, editing, and interaction. Knowing how the different attributes interrelate with one another becomes invaluable. Figure 11.1 illustrates the many attributes that make up the AEC wall object defined in Table 11.1.

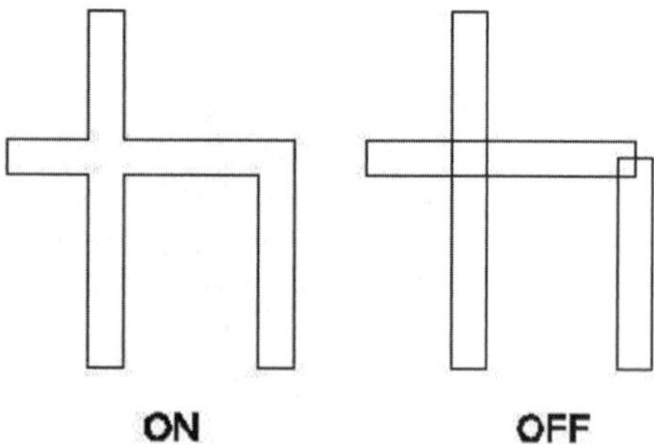

Figure 11.1a The Cleanup ON/OFF property

Figure 11.1b The Cleanup Group property

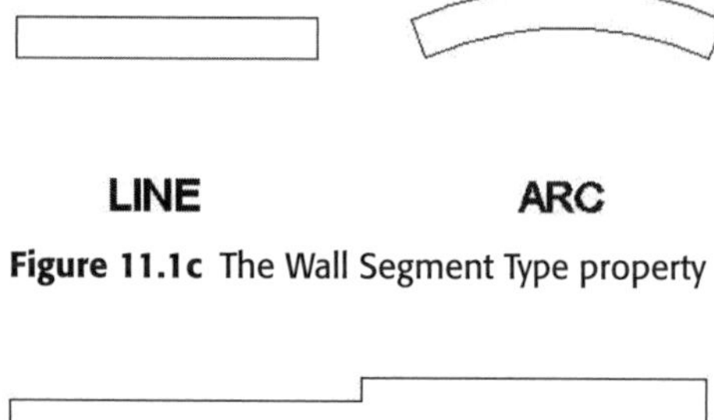

Figure 11.1c The Wall Segment Type property

6 in wall

12 in wall

Figure 11.1d The Wall Width property

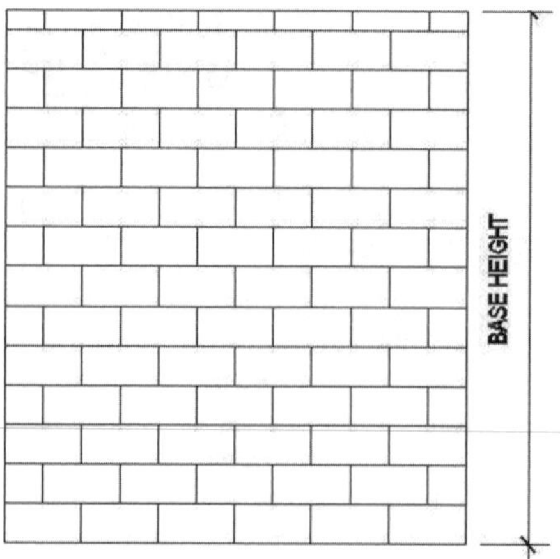

Figure 11.1e The Base Height property

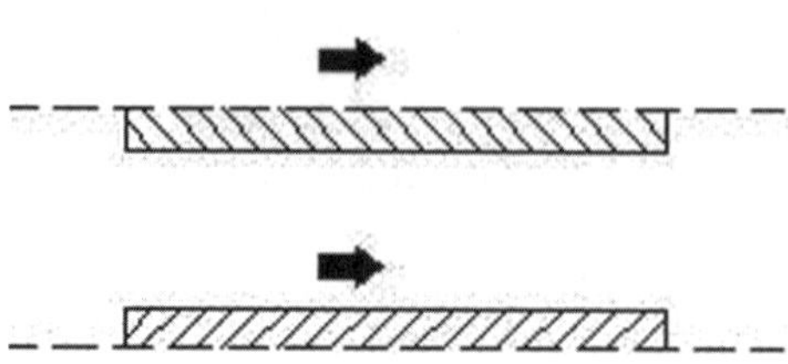

Figure 11.1f The Wall Justification property

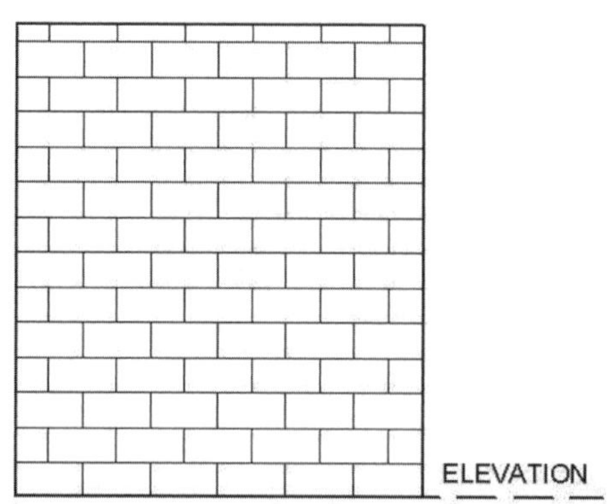

Figure 11.1g The Wall Elevation property

Table 11.1 Understanding ADT Wall Objects and the Properties

Wall Property	Property Description and Function	Property Effects
Wall style	Use to differentiate how a wall looks. Each style can represent a different wall assembly, that is, cmu, brick, metal stud, and so on. Controls the appearance of the wall in plan, elevation, section, and 3-D. It can control how the ends of the wall look, as well as the kinds of hatches that are applied.	Can control wall width
Cleanup ON/ OFF toggle	Use to toggle the wall's cleanup property. Is assigned individually to walls to determine if wall will clean up with other walls.	If off, it disables all other cleanup properties.
Wall Cleanup group definition	Manages how walls clean up with one another. Wall with the same Cleanup group definition will attempt to clean up with one another.	The Cleanup group definition will affect all cleanup properties of the walls in question.
Segment Type	Specifies whether the wall is straight or curved	Dimensional properties of the wall segment change based on whether the wall is straight or curved.
Width	Specifies the total width of the wall segment	The width is only changeable when wall styles are designed with a variable width component.
Base Height	Specify how high the wall is—that is, 16-foot-tall wall, 4-foot-tall wall. Note the base height is not always synonymous with the top of wall.	
Justification	Determines the direction of the wall. Analogous to text justification, wall justifications can be set to right, center, left, or baseline. The wall's grip points will occur at this justification line. To determine which side of a wall is left or right, the left side of a wall is always determined by the side the directional arrow is located.	When a wall style includes more than one component, wall justification determines on which side the components will be placed.
Elevation	Determines where the bottom of the wall sits in elevation by setting the z-axis location for the bottom of the wall.	
Cleanup Radius	The radial distance that a wall looks to clean up with another wall. Helps to fix wall conditions that do not easily clean up.	The cleanup radius affects all cleanup properties of the walls in question.

ADT wall objects relate to wall assemblies and construction practices in real life. First, differing wall assemblies are represented in ADT through the use of wall styles and wall components. Wall styles (Figure 11.2) not only categorize the differing wall assemblies but also control the wall's appearance in plan, elevation, section, and 3-D views. Representing wall systems with multiple materials is possible through the use of wall components that are assigned within each wall style (Figure 11.3). These components are placed side by side, each representing a material used to construct the wall. Components can include brick, concrete

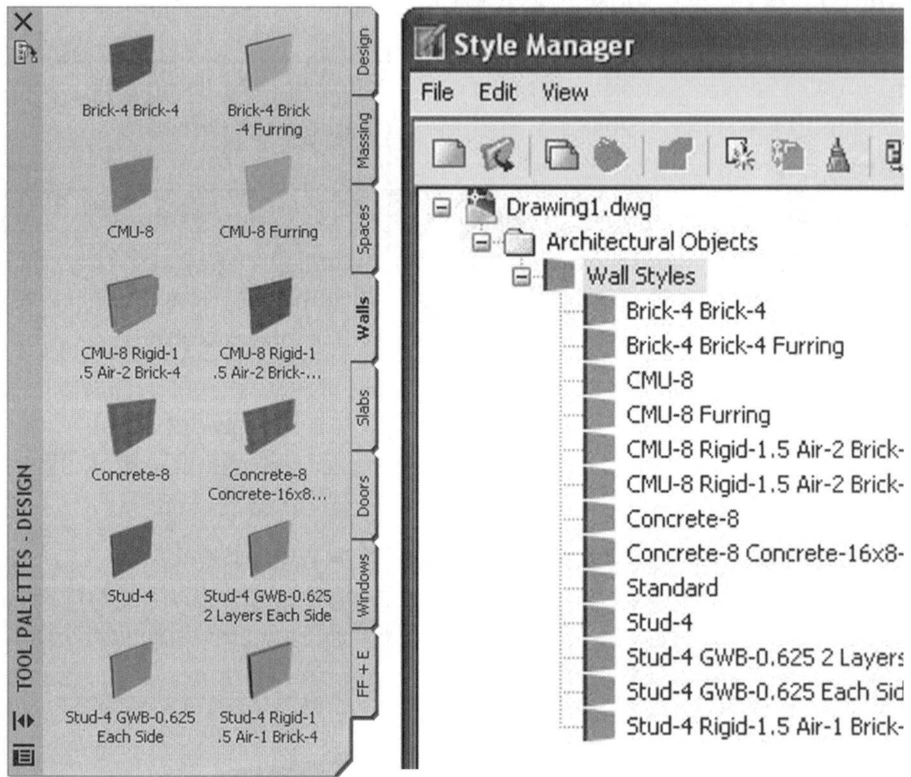

Figure 11.2 Wall styles categorize walls and control the appearance in plan, elevation, section, and 3-D views.

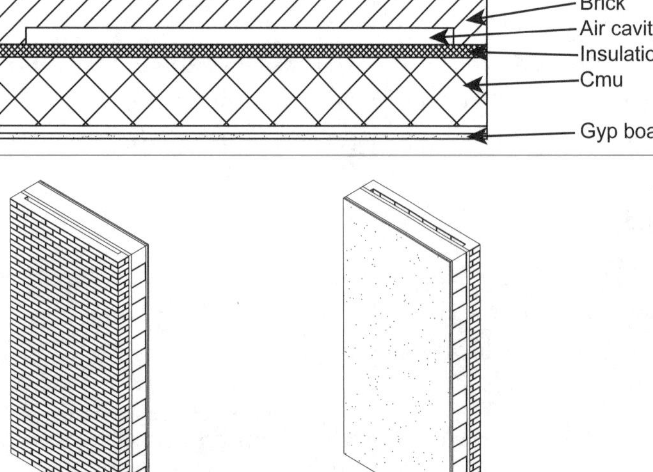

Figure 11.3 Wall systems with multiple materials are possible through the use of wall components.

masonry unit (cmu), concrete, studs, air gaps, and insulation, as well as other representations. Second, wall properties represent the physical attributes of the wall assembly and are assigned individually to each wall. Some of the more familiar properties include wall width, length, height, and shape. Wall properties can be assigned before, during, or after wall placement. Figure 11.4 illustrates the basic properties distinctive to the individual AEC wall object. Third, Wall Cleanup tools are used to direct how walls are trimmed when they intersect with one another. Finally, anchoring mechanisms are applied to provide the special link between walls and the door, window, and opening objects.

Wall Placement (Drawing with the Wall Object)

Wall objects are drawn using a variety of tools and commands in ADT. The WallAdd tool and command is probably the most widely used.

> **Box 11.1**
> Notice that the WallAdd command keeps on drawing wall segments until the command is properly completed or canceled.

Typically during the wall-placement process, the most important wall properties to verify are Wall Style, Wall Width, Wall Height, and Wall Justification. A good habit is to change these properties to the configuration you want before drawing the wall on-screen. For consistent results, ADT recommends drawing walls in a clockwise direction using a consistently set justification. The basic summary of steps is outlined in Figure 11.5. Figures 11.6 through 11.12 demonstrate various methods for placing walls.

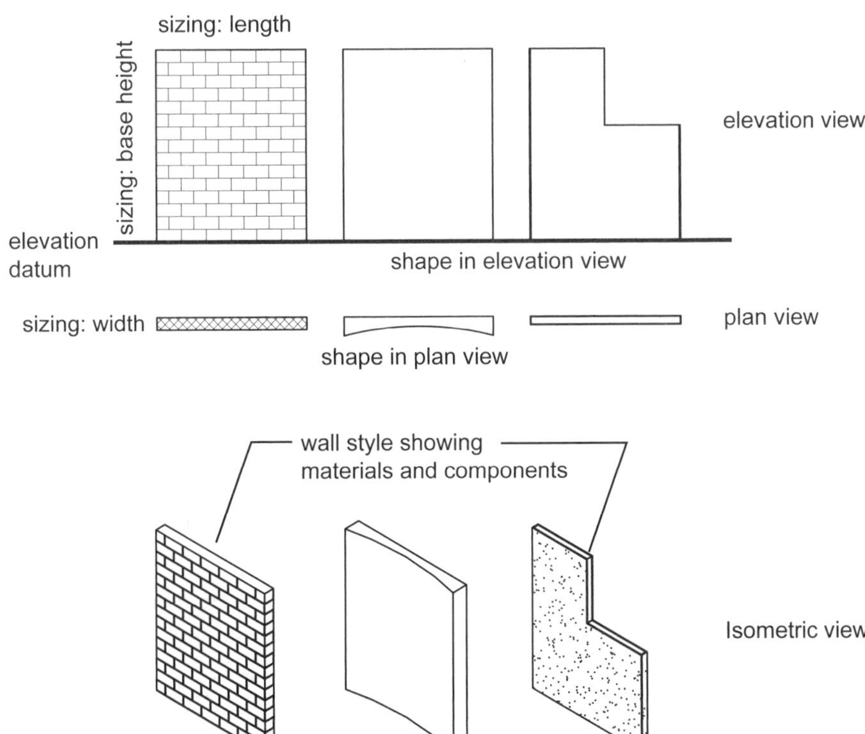

Figure 11.4 A closer look at the properties of individual walls

Technique to Master **T11.05** Summary of the Wall Placement Command Sequence (simplified): Drawing Walls

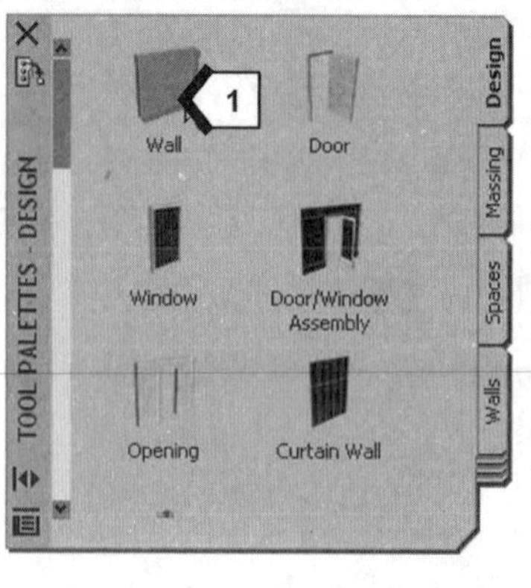

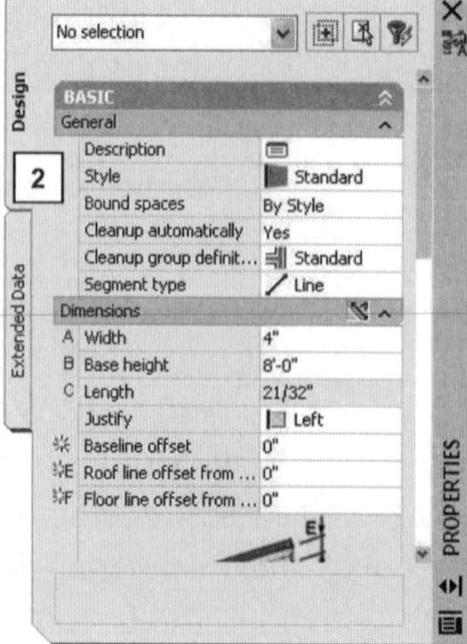

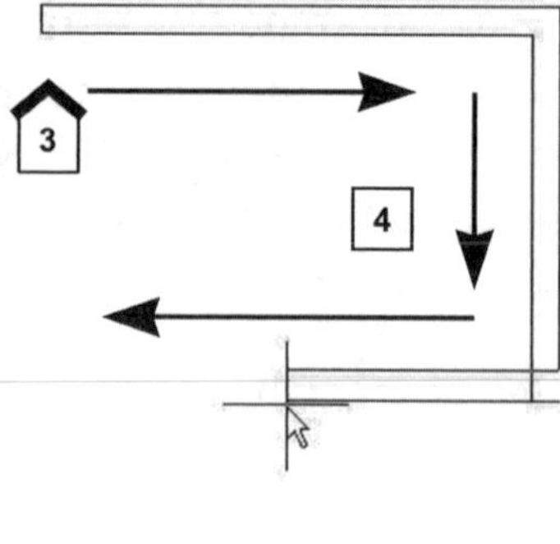

Figure 11.5

1	[Command Line]	Execute the Wall Command by using the Tool palette or WallAdd command.
2	[Properties palette > Design Tab]	Verify/Review/Update the following property information. a. Wall Style b. Wall Width (if the wall style lets you have a changeable width) c. Wall Height d. Wall Justification (use baseline whenever possible) e. Cleanup group definition f. Cleanup radius (typically set it to either 0 or the width of the wall)
3	[Drawing Screen]	Locate the beginning of the wall segment.
4	[Drawing Screen]	Begin drawing wall(s) in a clockwise direction.
5	Locate the end of the wall segment.	
6	Continue placing wall segments. Complete the wall command by pressing Enter or using the OrthoClose or Close options.	

Box 11.2

The way you place the wall determines the wall's directions. ADT recommends a clockwise direction as much as possible. This is easily accomplished for exterior walls but becomes more complicated when working with interior walls.

Box 11.3

Tip: The settings of wall properties are retained from the last time you placed a wall. Remember that some of the wall tools have their properties preset, so it is a good idea to always double-check before placing a wall.

Box 11.4

Tip: The NOD object snap snaps to the justification endpoints of walls.

Box 11.5

To create an elliptical wall, set the drawing variable Pellipse to 1. Ellipses will now be drawn as polylines. Draw the ellipse and then convert it to a wall.

Technique to Master **T11.06** Placing Walls with the WallAdd tool

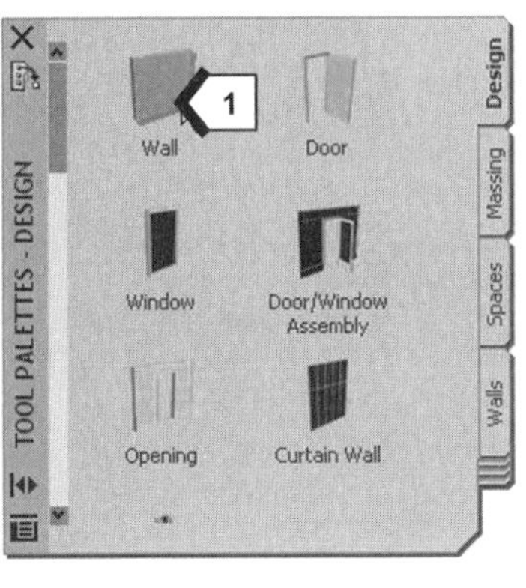
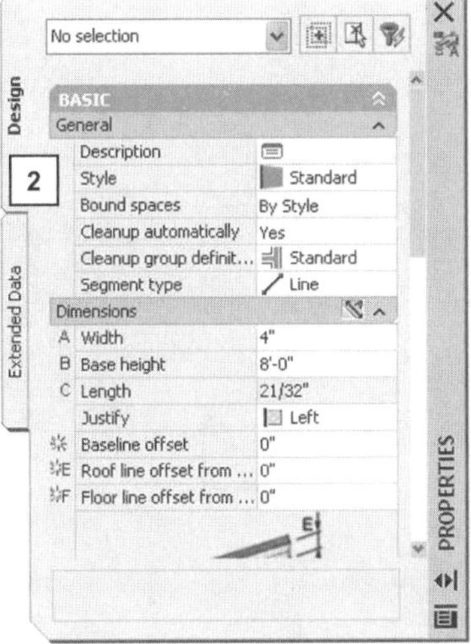
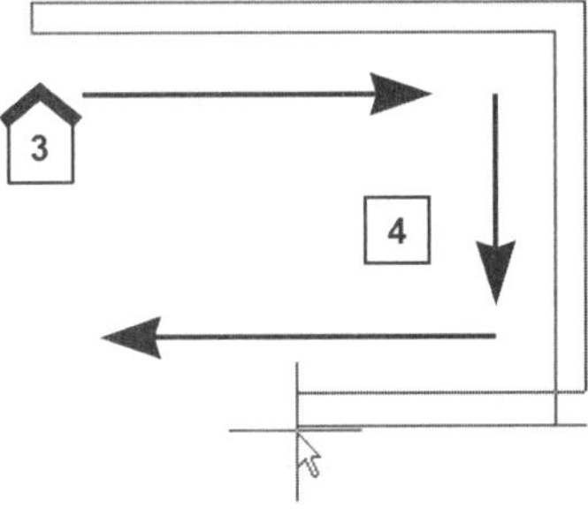

Figure 11.6

1	[Design Tool palette>Design tab]	Select the Wall tool.
2	[Properties palette>Design tab]	Verify/update the following wall properties: a. Wall Style b. Wall Width c. Wall Height d. Wall Justification e. Cleanup group definition
3	[Drawing Screen]	Begin the wall by specifying the wall start. Continue specifying points for additional wall segments.
4	Complete the wall command by pressing Enter.	

Technique to Master **T11.07** Placing Curved Walls

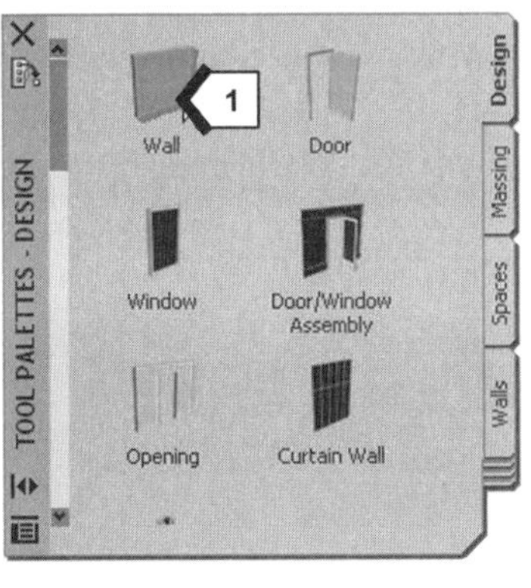
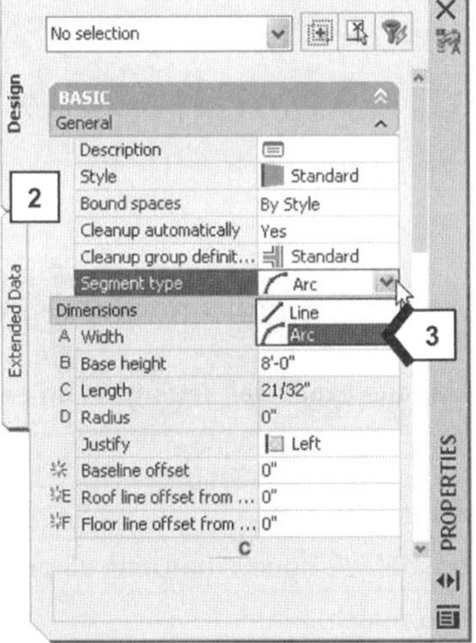
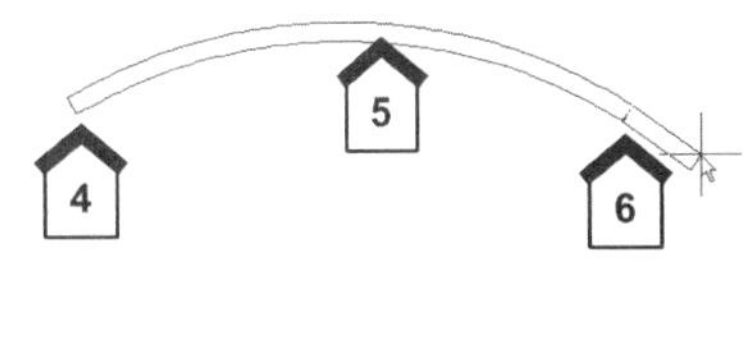

Figure 11.7

1	[Command Line]	Execute the Wall Command or select the Wall tool.
2	[Properties palette>Design tab]	Verify the wall properties.
3	[Properties palette>Design tab]	Choose ARC for Segment type.
4	[Drawing Screen]	Begin the curved wall by locating the first point of the wall segment.
5	[Drawing Screen]	Locate the midpoint of the curved wall segment.
6	[Drawing Screen]	Locate the end of the curved wall segment.

Technique to Master T11.08 Placing Walls Through the Add Selected Command

Figure 11.8 This command will place a new wall using the exact wall settings of an existing wall.

1	[Drawing Screen]	Select existing wall, right-click, and choose Add Selected.
2	[Drawing Screen]	Begin locating points for the new wall segment.

Technique to Master T11.09 Placing Walls Using the Match Option of the WallAdd Command

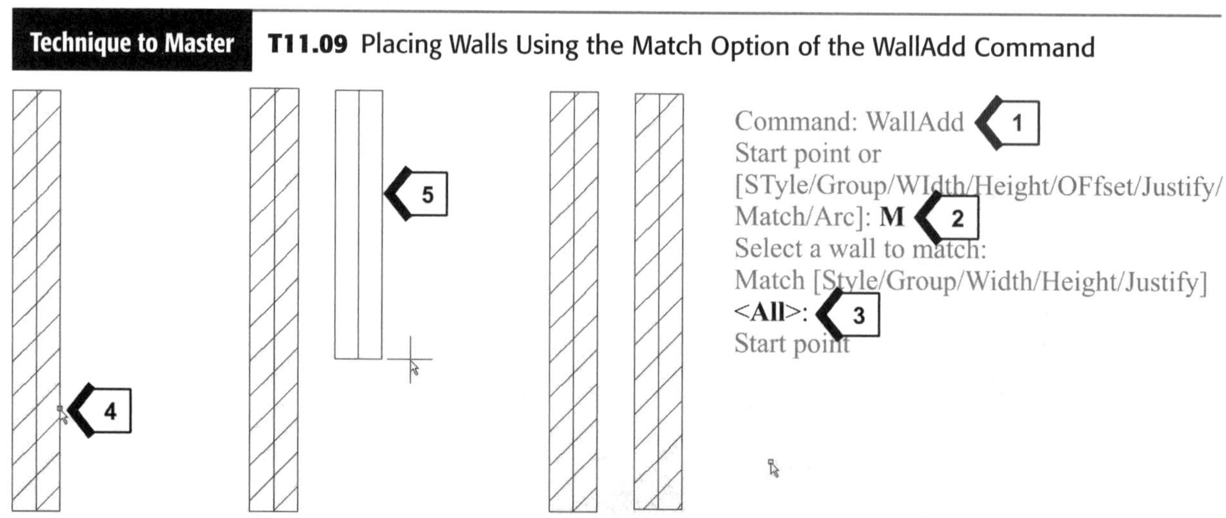

Command: WallAdd 1
Start point or
[STyle/Group/WIdth/Height/OFfset/Justify/
Match/Arc]: M 2
Select a wall to match:
Match [Style/Group/Width/Height/Justify]
<All>: 3
Start point
4
5

Figure 11.9 This command will place a new wall using the exact wall settings of an existing wall.

1	[Command Line]	Execute the WallAdd command.
2	[Command Line]	Type M for the command option Match.
3	[Command Line]	Press Enter to accept the default option matching all properties.
4	[Drawing Screen]	Select the existing wall to match.
5	[Drawing Screen]	Begin drawing the new wall.

Technique to Master **T11.10** Creating Walls from Linework

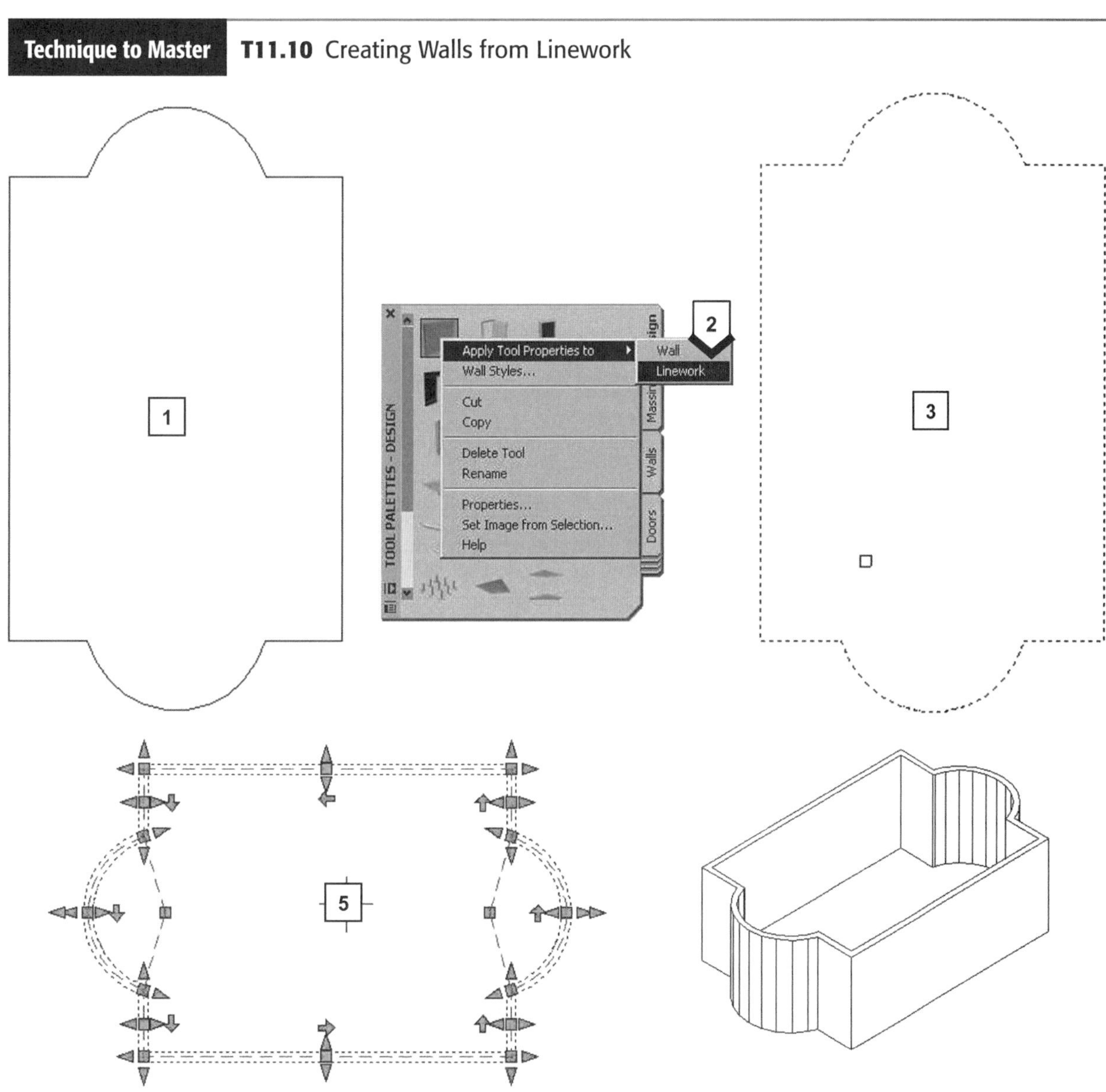

Figure 11.10 This command converts AutoCAD lines, polylines, arcs, and circles into wall objects. Remember that the start and end points of the AutoCAD entities will directly relate to the wall's direction when it is converted.

1	[Drawing Screen]	Draw 2-D linework.
2	[Design Tool palette>Design tab]	Right-click on the wall tool and choose Apply Tool Properties to>Linework.
3	[Drawing Screen]	Select Linework to convert.
4	[Command Line]	Decide whether to keep or delete the original linework.
5	[Drawing Screen]	Select newly created walls.
6	[Properties palette>Design tab]	Verify/change properties as appropriate.

Technique to Master T11.11 Placing Walls Using the Close Option

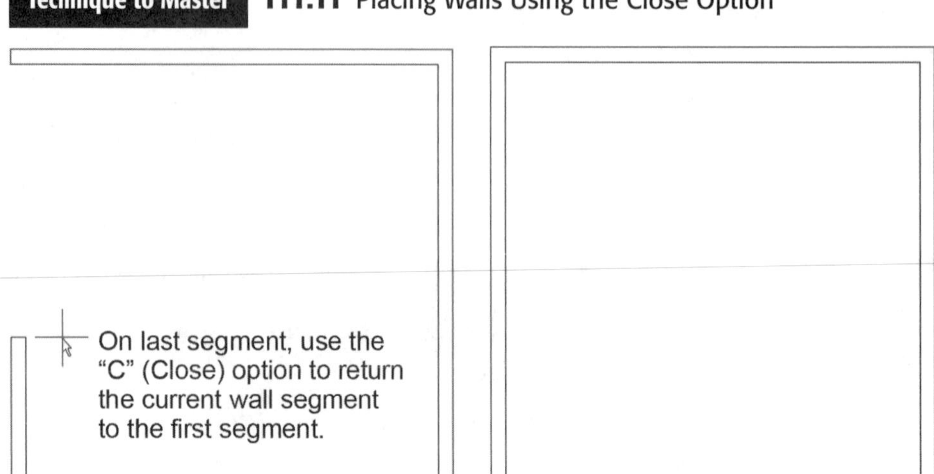

On last segment, use the
“C” (Close) option to return
the current wall segment
to the first segment.

Figure 11.11 This option of the WallAdd command closes a series of wall segments back to the first segment.

1	[Command Line]	Execute the Wall Command.
2	[Properties palette>Design tab]	Change/verify the properties for the new walls.
3	[Drawing Screen]	Locate two or more wall segments.
4	[Command Line]	Type C and press Enter to close and end the Wall command.

Technique to Master T11.12 Placing Walls Using the OrthoClose Option

After second segment,
use the “OR” (Ortho Close)
option to complete the
rectangular form.

Figure 11.12 This command option will complete a rectangular or square shape after two wall segments are placed.

1	[Command Line]	Execute the Wall Command.
2	[Properties palette>Design tab]	Change/verify the properties for the new walls.
3	[Drawing Screen]	Locate two or more wall segments.
4	[Command Line]	Type OR and press Enter.
5	[Drawing Screen]	Left-click in the direction for the rectangular close.

Understanding Wall Cleanup

Wall cleanup refers to controlling how multiple walls join and cross with others at corners and intersections. In ADT there are several wall properties, cleanup commands, and vocabulary that affect how walls interact with one another.

The primary properties include wall cleanup group, the cleanup radius, and component priority. Table 11.2 provides an overview of the properties, commands, and vocabulary related to wall cleanup. Figure 11.13 illustrates these properties.

Table 11.2

Name	Description
Wall Cleanup group definition	Assigned to an individual wall. Walls on the same Cleanup group definition attempt to clean up where they intersect. Walls that belong to different cleanup groups will not clean up. Cleanup group definitions also manage how walls in referenced drawings clean up with walls in the host drawing.
Cleanup ON/OFF toggle	All walls with the toggle assigned to NO will not attempt to clean up with other walls. Keep this toggled to YES as a default.
Wall component priority	Wall components with the same priority number will attempt to clean up with one another. See Table 13.2 for a list of ADT's component priority numbers.
Wall cleanup radius	The cleanup radius is the radial distance a wall extends to clean up with another wall. Cleanups for walls can be set individually at wall ends and intersections. If the cleanup radius is zero, wall graphlines must meet exactly to clean up.

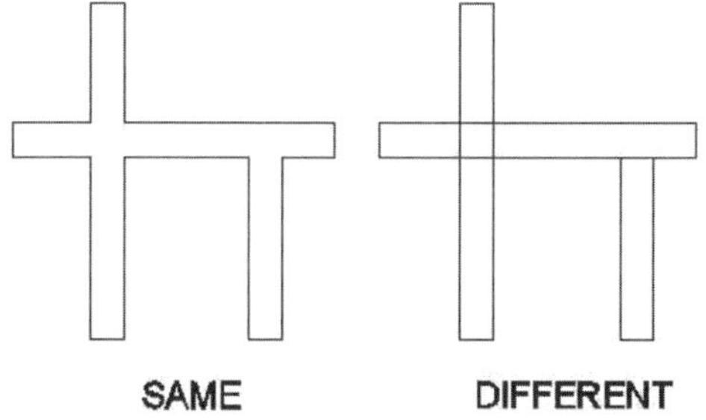

Figure 11.13a The Cleanup Group property

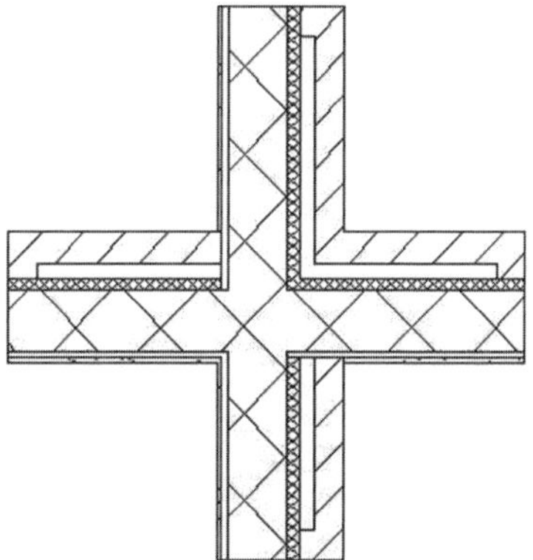

Figure 11.13c The Wall Component Priority property

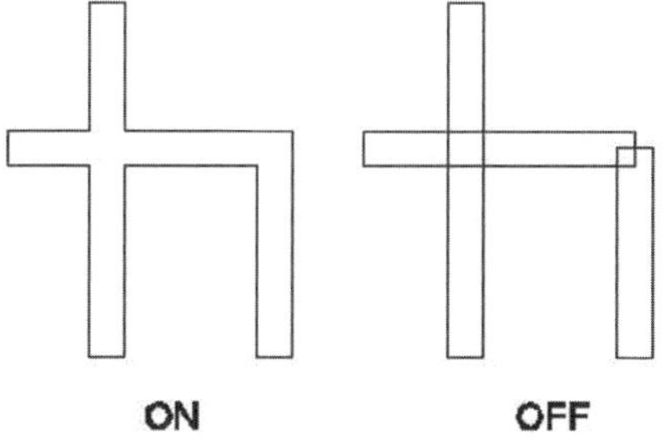

Figure 11.13b The Cleanup ON/OFF property

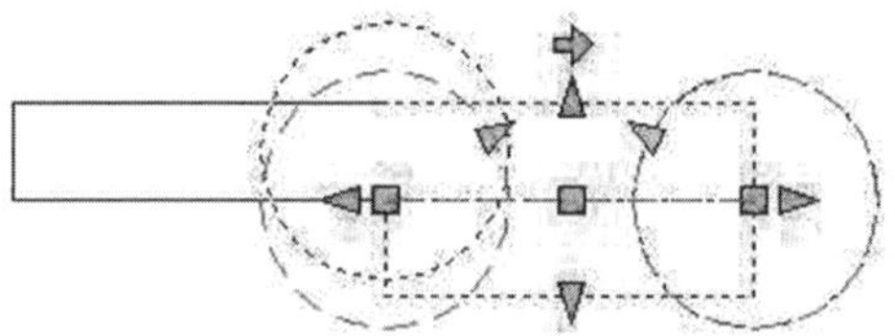

Figure 11.13d The Wall Cleanup Radius property

Chapter 11 Drawing in ADT: Walls, Windows, Doors, and Openings

Controlling Wall Cleanup

Consistent successful wall cleanup not only comes through understanding the basic rules for cleanup but also understanding how each of the cleanup attributes relates to one another as shown in Figure 11.14.

General Rules for Successful Wall Cleanup

Successful automatic cleanup between walls and/or individual wall components occurs when the following is true:

- Walls share the same wall cleanup definition.
- Walls are on the same elevation (See CD-ROM and T13.27 for how to handle variable floor lines).
- Walls are all drawn in model space.
- Wall graphlines meet exactly, or the cleanup circle of one wall overlaps the graphline of another wall. Remember that when determining wall cleanup, the largest of the two cleanup radii is used.
- There is only one wall occupying the same place. Make sure you don't accidentally have one or more walls overlapping one another.

The following are some tips for controlling wall cleanup during wall placement.

- Use good drafting habits. In AutoCAD, 2-D lines that represent walls had to meet exactly. Keep using this technique when drawing walls. It promotes good digital craftsmanship.

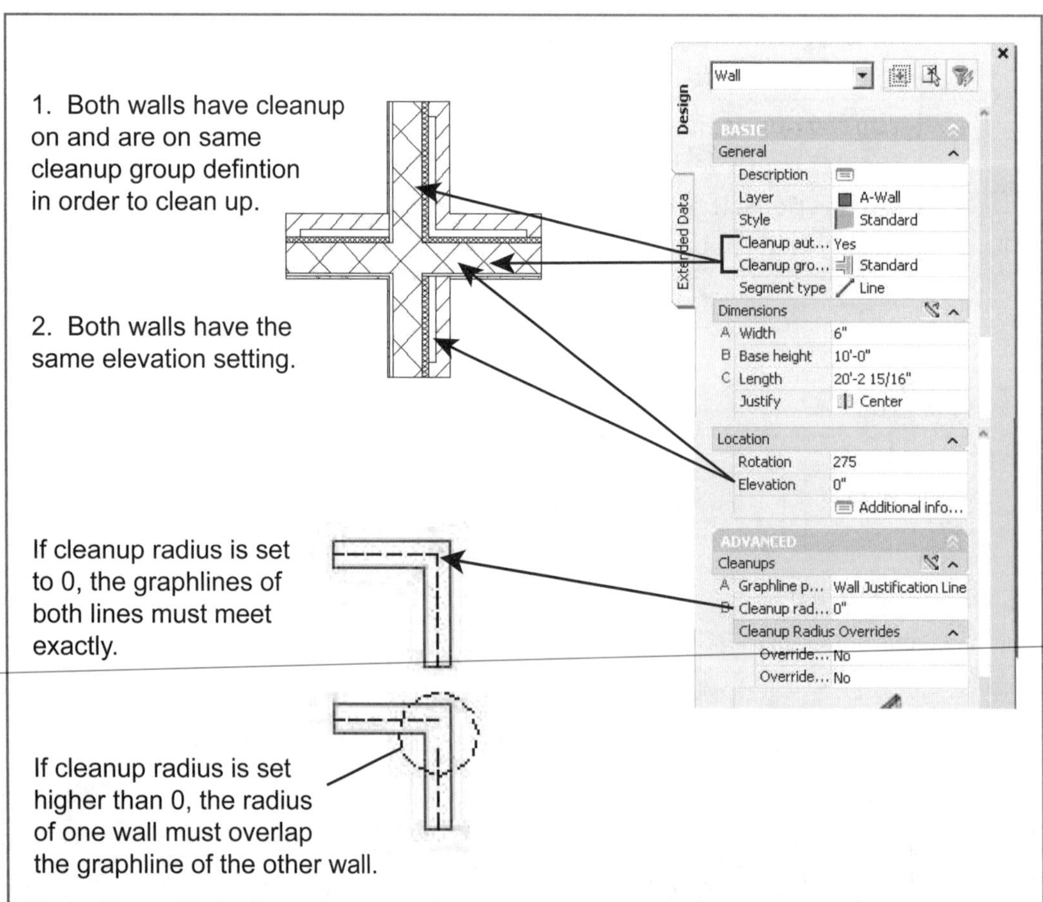

Figure 11.14 Hierarchy of how each of the cleanup attributes relates to one another will help during complex wall cleanups.

- Toggle the Wall Graph Display to ON when placing walls (Figure 11.15). The Wall Graph Display shows how the graphline of each wall meets or intersects.
- Make sure the graphline coincides with the justification line; the graphline is typically set to coincide with the justification line. Although this setting can be changed, it is suggested that you leave it in its default setting.

> **Box 11.6**
> Having coincident justification lines and graph lines will eliminate wall cleanup problems caused by using editing commands to trim and extend walls. Editing commands always use the justification line to clean up walls while the Autosnap New Wall Baselines option and cleanup radius use the graph line. If the justification line and graph line are not coincident, it could cause a lot of problems.

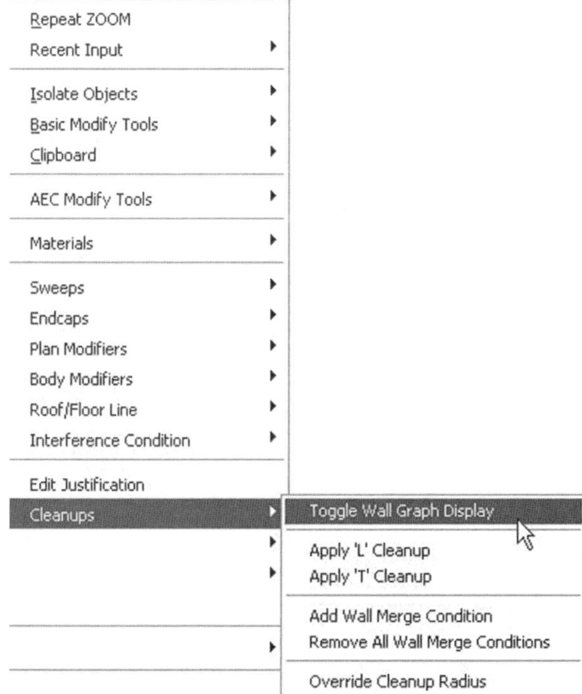

Figure 11.15 The Cleanups menu is displayed after selecting a wall and right-clicking.

- The rule of thumb for setting the wall cleanup radius is to set the cleanup radius to zero. This forces accurate drawing habits—endpoint to endpoint. As an alternate solution only, adjust the cleanup radius to equal to half of the wall width.
- Use the Autosnap New Wall Baselines setting found in the AEC Object Settings tab of the Options dialogue. It assists with the wall-drawing process by automatically snapping to wall corner and wall-T conditions.

Wall Defect Markers

When walls do not clean up properly, a small red circular symbol appears. This wall defect marker typically indicates that something is preventing wall cleanup (Figure 11.16). The following list offers some helpful trouble-shooting advice for wall cleanup problems.

- Toggle the wall Graph Display to ON to visually see how walls are interacting with other walls. (Note: Cleanup circles do not display in this view for walls with a cleanup radius of 0).
- Try overriding the cleanup radius of one end of the wall segment (Figure 11.17). If the cleanup problem is at one end of a wall segment, first try to override the cleanup radius for the segment end that is problematic. This can be accomplished either through the properties palette or visually on-screen.

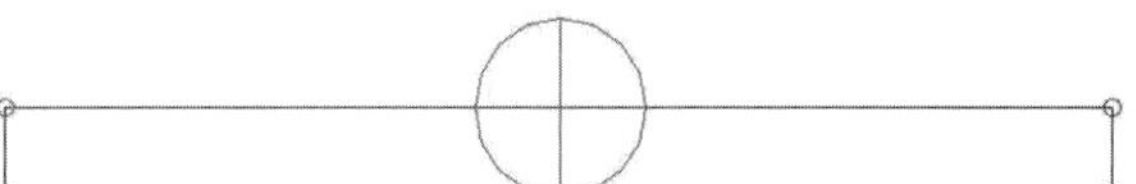

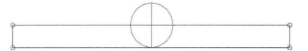

Figure 11.16 The wall defect marker typically indicates two (or more) walls are having difficulty cleaning up with each other.

Technique to Master **T11.17** Using the Cleanup Grip in the Wall Graph Display

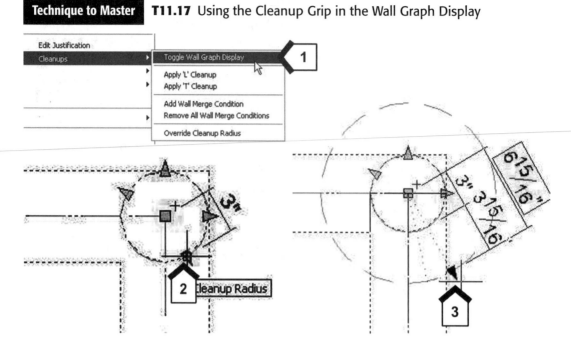

Figure 11.17

1	[Drawing Screen]	Select wall, right-click, and choose Cleanups>Toggle Wall Graph Display.
2	[Drawing Screen]	Left-click on the Cleanup Radius grip at the wall end in question.
3	[Drawing Screen]	Move the mouse (or type in the value) to increase the cleanup's circle radius.
4	[Drawing Screen]	Use the Escape key to deselect the wall.

- Try adjusting the cleanup radius of the entire wall using the Properties palette (Figure 11.18). Cleanup problems that are at an intersection will need each wall's cleanup radius adjusted. If the cleanup radius is set to zero, incrementally increase the radius until the problem is solved. If the radius is set to a value larger than the wall segment's width or length, incrementally decrease the radius value.
- Cleanup problems within wall components will need their component priorities adjusted. See Chapter 13 for a more detailed discussion.
- Cleanup between xrefs are usually a result of the Cleanup group definitions setting (Figure 11.19).

T11.18 Adjusting the Cleanup Radius of the Entire Wall Using the Properties Palette

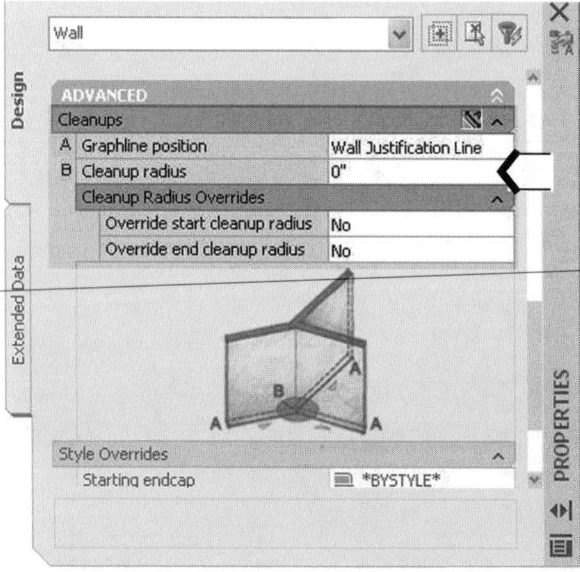

Figure 11.18

1	[Drawing Screen]	Select a wall.
2	[Properties palette> Design tab>Advanced]	Type in the new value for the cleanup radius.

Technique to Master **T11.19** Cleaning up Walls Between Xrefs

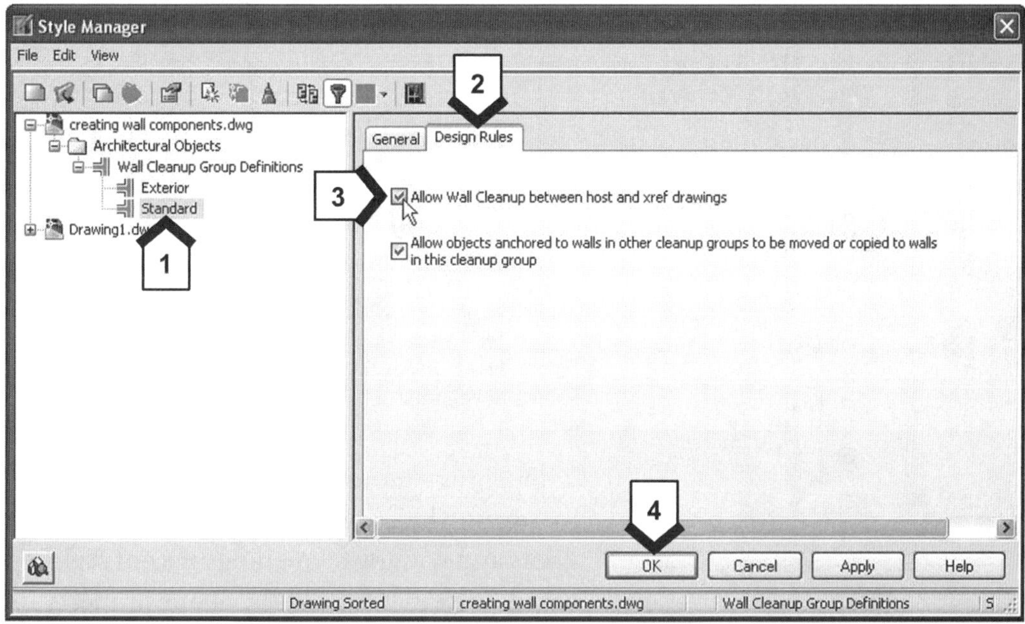

Figure 11.19 Wall cleanup between Xrefs must be toggled on through each of the cleanup group definition styles in each drawing file.

1	[Design Menu>Walls]	Access the Cleanup group definitions command.
2	[Wall Cleanup Group Definitions Style Manager]	Left-click on the Design Rules tab.
3	[Wall Cleanup Group Definitions Style Manager]	Check Allow cleanup between host and xref drawings on.
4	[Wall Cleanup Group Definitions Style Manager]	Left-click OK to complete command.

Windows, Doors, and Openings in ADT

The door, window, and opening objects in ADT interact with walls. Because of this interaction, walls are automatically edited and trimmed when these objects are placed within them. Both the door and window objects use styles to control how they look in plan, elevation, and three-dimensional views.

Doors

The ADT door object is used to represent door assemblies in buildings. Door assemblies typically include the door, the door's frame, and the door's threshold. While dimensional sizing of the frame and threshold is saved through the door style, the actual door width and door height is controlled through the Properties palette. Figure 11.20 shows the prebuilt door styles available through the Design Tool palette. Notice the naming convention of the door styles, which helps to organize and classify each door by interior and exterior application as well as by material and look.

Windows

The window object represents window assemblies in buildings. It consists of the window, window glass, window frame, and the hardware that makes it operable. Similar to the door object, the window object defines its glass and frame dimensional sizing within the window style. How the window looks is also controlled by the window style. During

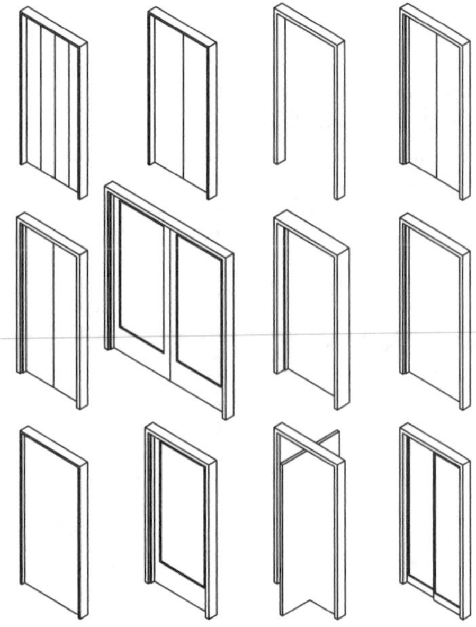

Style	Description
Bifold - Double	Double bifold doors
Bifold - Single	Single bifold door
Cased Opening	Cased opening
Hinged - Double	Double hinged door
Hinged - Double - Exterior	Double exterior door
Hinged - Double - Full Lite	Double full glass door
Hinged - Single	Single hinged door
Hinged - Single - Exterior	Single exterior door
Hinged - Single - Full Lite	Single full glass door
Overhead - Sectional	Overhead door
Pocket - Single	Single pocket door
Revolving - Simple	Simple revolving door
Sliding - Double - Full Lite	Double sliding door
Standard	

Figure 11.20 The ADT prebuilt door styles available through the Design tool palette

placement, window width, height, and location are controlled through the Properties palette. There are several preset window styles that are available through the Design Tool palette, as shown in Figure 11.21.

Openings

The opening object is used to represent unframed wall penetrations.

> **Box 11.7**
> Use openings instead of trimming walls because openings automatically create headers above the opening, and thus reducing two steps to one.

Figure 11.21 The ADT prebuilt window styles available through the Design Tool palette

Openings automatically interact with walls by creating holes within the wall. Unlike doors and windows, openings are not style-based. Instead, they use the Shape property in combination with its dimensional properties to determine the shape and size of the opening in the wall (Figure 11.22).

> **Box 11.8**
> Tip: If the opening is cased, that is, framed without a door or window, use the Case Opening Door or Cased Window Style.

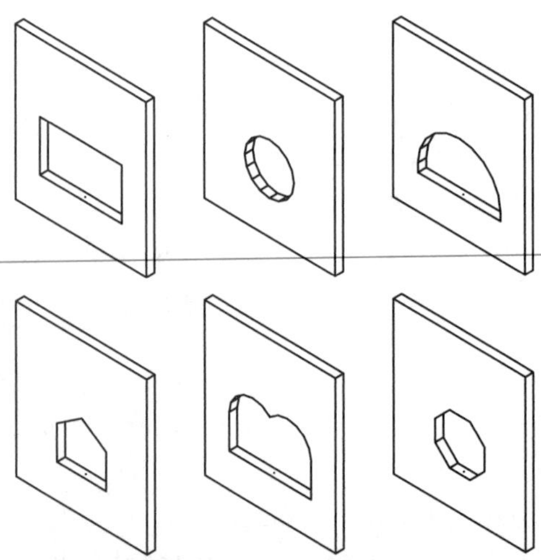

Figure 11.22 Openings are not style-based but instead use the Shape property in combination with dimensional properties to determine shape and size.

Object Anchoring

ADT uses a technique that constrains the door, window, and opening objects to specific locations within a wall. Object anchoring in ADT is a method of binding one object to another so that links are created between the two. This is an automatic procedure that takes place during door, window, and opening placement.

In addition, when a door, a window, or an opening is anchored to a wall, a hole is automatically created to accept the object. While doors, windows, and openings can be placed within the drawing without it being anchored to a wall, the holes are not created in the wall (Figure 11.23).

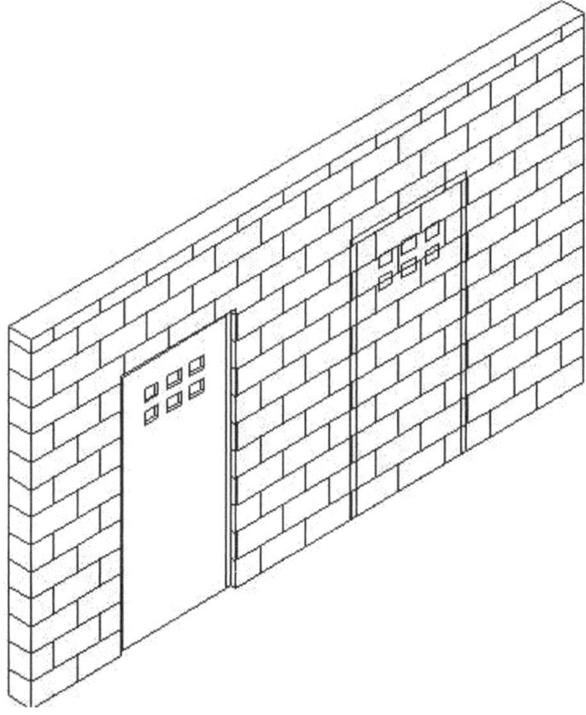

Figure 11.23 The wall anchoring concept is demonstrated by the two doors placed in the wall. The left door shows the door anchored to the wall. The wall, therefore, creates a hole the size of the door automatically. The right door shows a door that is placed without using the automatic anchoring. Notice that the wall does not respond to the door's placement.

> **Box 11.9**
> To place doors or windows on the drawing screen without anchoring them to a wall, use the Enter key after selecting the Door or Window tool.

The Properties of Doors, Windows, and Openings

The properties associated with walls have comparable properties with the door, window, and opening objects. Similar to wall properties, these objects have dimensional properties that define the width and height. The style property of doors and windows are also used to define how the object looks. Figures 11.24a, 11.24b, and 11.24c identify these properties using the Properties palettes. Unique to the door, window, and opening object are the properties within the Location category—that is, properties that help control where the object is placed within the wall.

Understanding the Position Along Wall Property

The Position Along Wall property allows you to anticipate accurate placement of door, window, and opening objects by typing in a value in the Properties palette before actual placement. The Position Along Wall property along with its associated Automatic Offset property will automatically set the distance of the door, window, or opening object based on this setting.

> **Box 11.10**
> The practical relevance of this feature can be linked to the industry standard of placing doors at a distance of 4' to 6" from the wall.

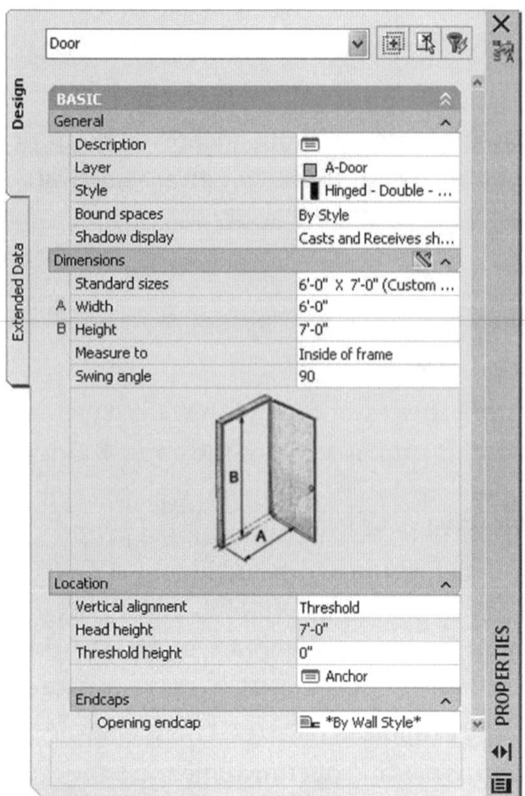

Figure 11.24a The Properties palette for door object types

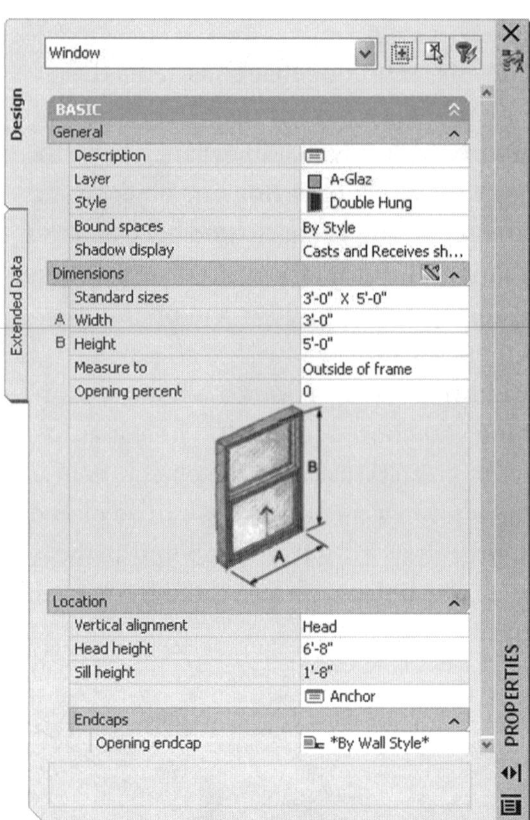

Figure 11.24b The Properties palette for window object types

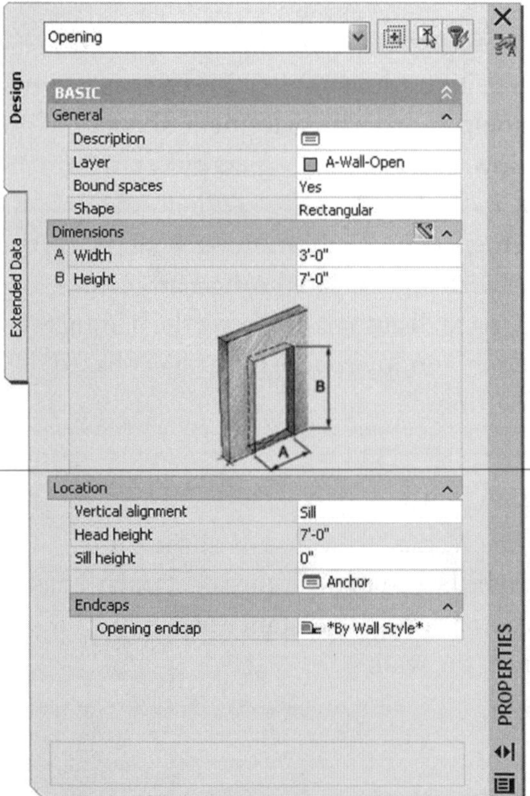

Figure 11.24c The Properties palette for opening object types

If you want to locate a door, a window, or an opening object at a specific distance from a room corner, select the Offset/Center option for Position Along Wall. Next, enter the distance next to the Automatic Offset property. If you want to locate the door, window, or opening object at the center of a wall within a room, select the Offset/Center option for Position Along Wall; notice no additional offset value is needed. The last option—unconstrained—allows you to place the object directly on the drawing screen without the above constraints. Figure 11.25 demonstrates each of the above techniques.

Vertical Alignment

The vertical alignment property uses the threshold height or head height of a door, a window, or an opening to locate the bottom or top of the object (Figure 11.26).

Technique to Master **T11.25** The Position Along Wall Property—Offset/center Versus Unconstrained

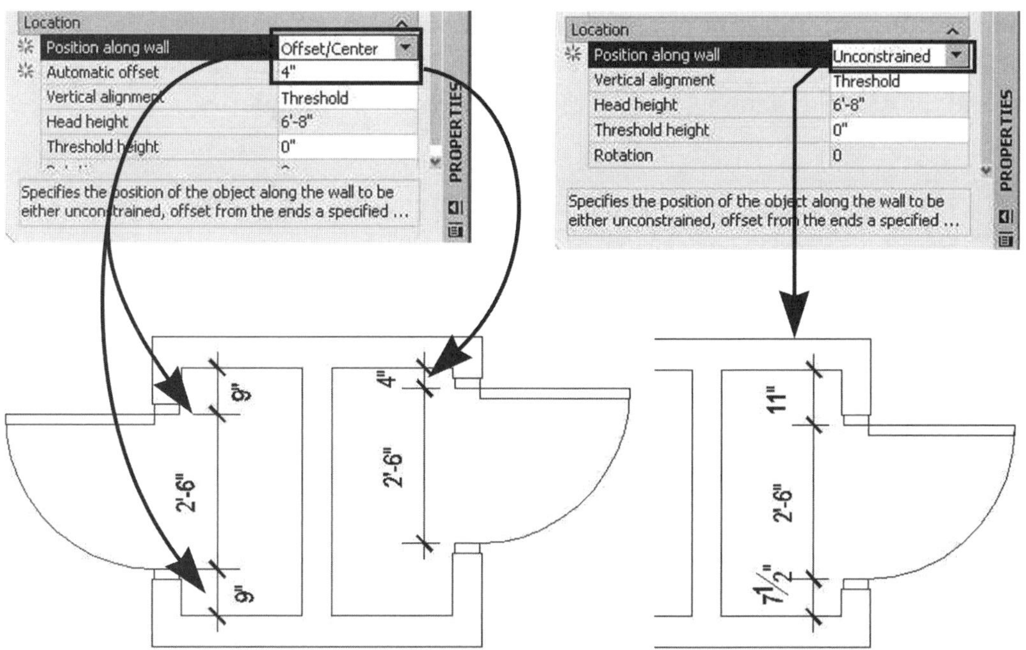

Figure 11.25

To position the object at a specific distance from a wall's corner, select Offset/center, enter a value for the automatic offset, and move your mouse near the corner during placement.

To position the object centered within a room, select Offset/center for position along wall, and move the mouse near the center of the wall during placement.

To position the object anywhere along the wall, select Unconstrained next to position along wall.

Technique to Master **T11.26** Understanding Vertical Alignment for Doors, Windows, and Openings

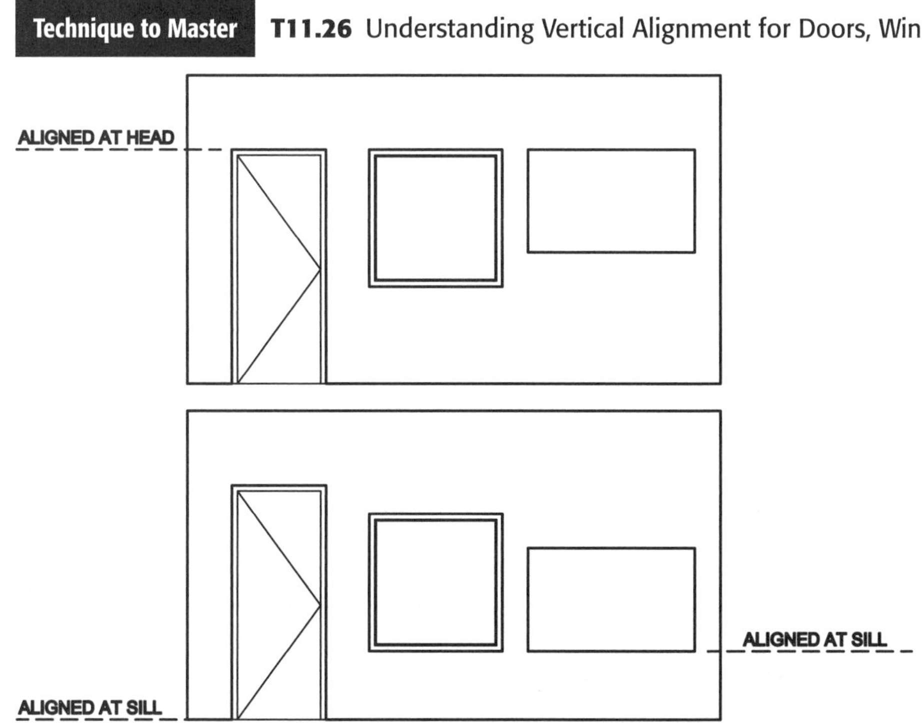

Figure 11.26 Note how alignment properties relate to the door, window, and opening objects.

Placing Doors, Windows, and Openings Within a Wall

Door, window, and opening objects are best placed without using objects snaps. The Properties palette and the use of dynamic dimensions provide the best way to accurately control placement. Figure 11.27 provides a simplified summary of the placement process. Figures 11.28 and 11.29 demonstrate additional placement techniques.

Technique to Master **T11.27** Summary of the Drawing Command Sequence (Simplified)—Placing a Door, Window, or Opening Within a Wall

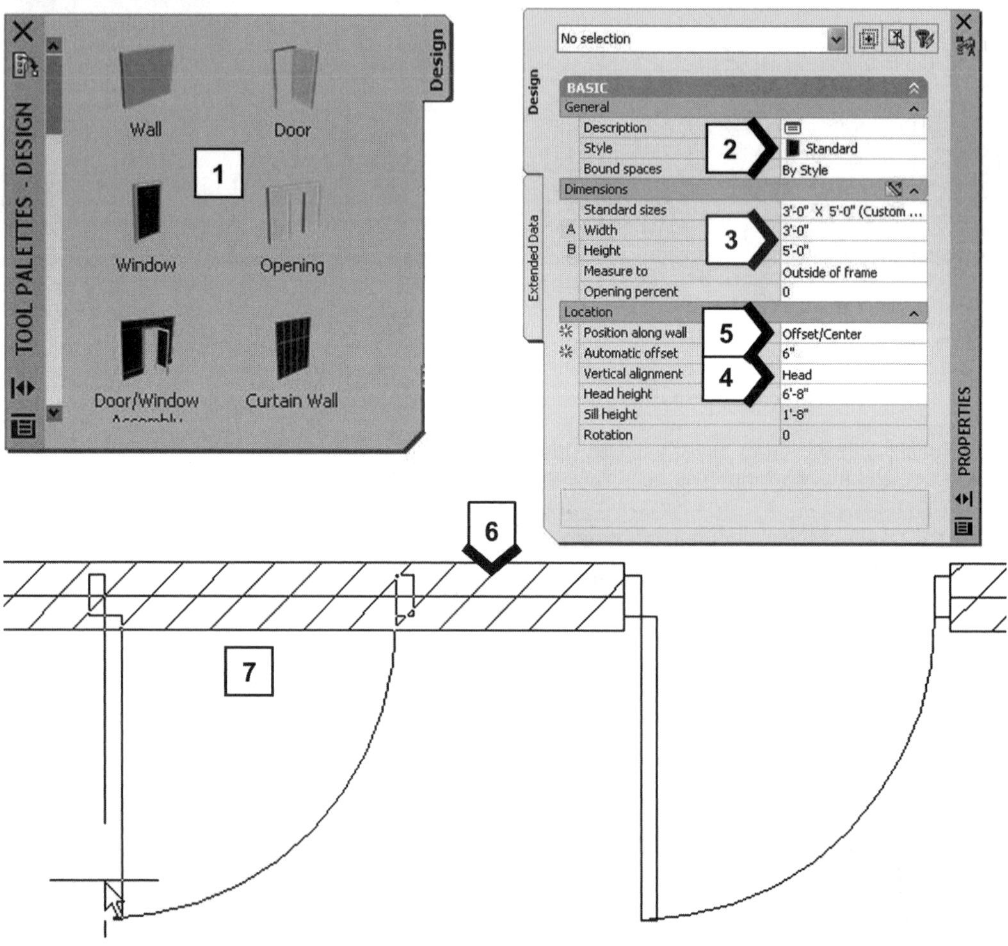

Figure 11.27

1	Execute Door, Window, or Opening Command using the Tool palette, Design menu, or Command Line (DoorAdd, WindowAdd, or OpeningAdd).	
2	[Properties palette > Design tab]	Verify/update the object's style.
3	[Properties palette > Design tab]	Verify/update the object's size (width and height) and Measure to property (for door and windows).
4	[Properties palette > Design tab]	Verify/update the object's Vertical alignment. Align door, window, or opening vertically using head or sill height (see Technique T11.26).
5	[Properties palette > Design tab]	Choose positioning method (see Technique T11.25).
6	[Drawing Screen]	Select existing wall where door, window, or opening will be placed.
7	[Drawing Screen]	Left-click to place. Enter to complete command or continue placing additional objects by left-clicking.

Technique to Master T11.28 Placing Door, Window, or Opening in Reference to Another Object

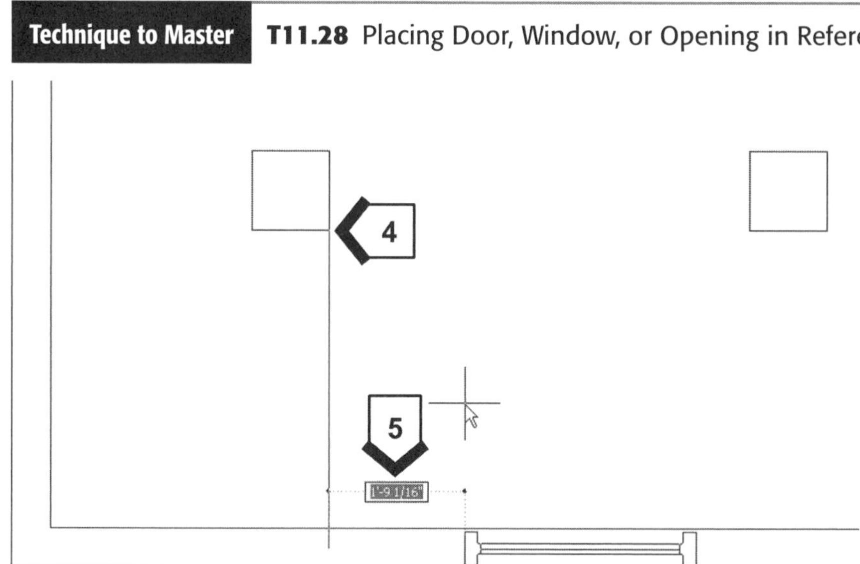

Figure 11.28 Use the Reference point command option to locate a door, window, or opening in reference to another object in the building model.

1	Execute Door, Window, or Opening command using the Tool palette, Design menu, or Command Line (Type DoorAdd, WindowAdd, or OpeningAdd).	
2	Complete Steps 2 through 7 of Technique T11.27.	
3	[Command Line]	Type RE and press Enter for Reference To command option.
4	[Drawing Screen]	Snap to point on the reference object.
5	[Drawing Screen]	Use dynamic dimensions to type relative distance.

Technique to Master T11.29 Changing the Door, Window, or Opening Insertion Point from End to Center

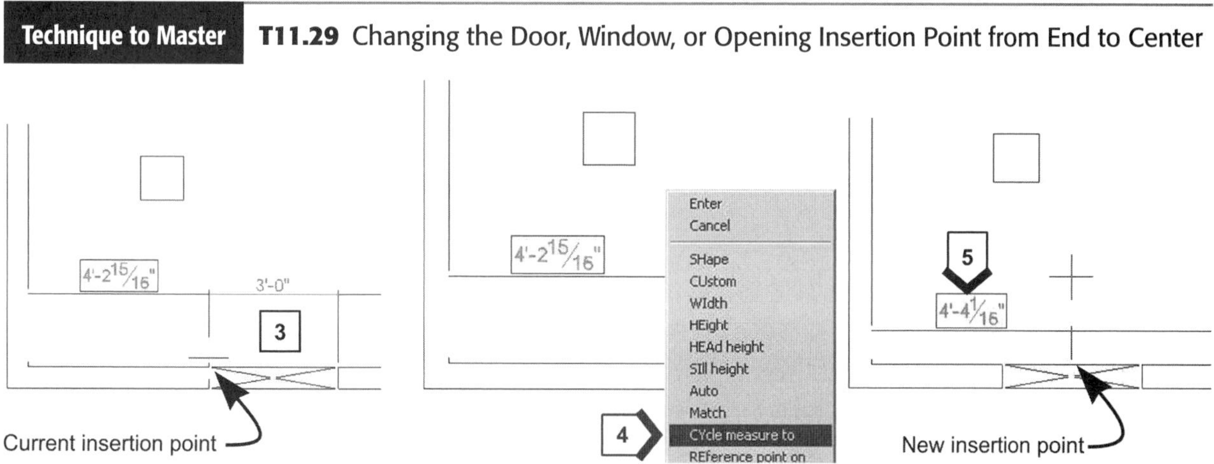

Figure 11.29 Typically, the insertion point for doors, windows, and openings is along the frame end of the object. This can be changed during object placement.

1	[Command Line]	Execute the Door, Window, or Opening Command using the Tool palette, Design menu, or Command Line (Type DoorAdd, WindowAdd, or OpeningAdd).
2	Complete Steps 2 through 7 of Technique T11.27.	
3	[Drawing Screen]	Left-click to place.
4	[Drawing Screen]	Right-click to access the Cycle measure to command toggle. Toggle this option until your desired insertion point is current.
5	[Drawing Screen]	Place the object using dynamic dimensions.

Chapter Exercises

Open the Chapter 11 folder located on the CD-ROM to access the exercises for this chapter that allow you to practice using the wall, window, door, and opening objects on simple one- and two-story space-planning problems.

Basic Modifications

12

Objectives

This chapter shows you how to edit and modify features of the ADT wall, window, door, and opening objects. It emphasizes the property differences among object types. Demonstrations within the chapter illustrate the various modification techniques. The end-of-chapter exercises let you practice how to edit and modify wall, window, door, opening, and mass element modifications using the techniques herein.

Modifying the Properties of ADT Objects

Property modifications refer to changing one or more properties of an ADT object. These can include but are not limited to dimensional, location, and style-based properties that are particular to an object. Though most property modifications are completed using the Properties palette, dimensional and location-based modifications can also be accomplished using grips.

Chapter 11 introduced many of the ADT object properties assignable to walls, doors, windows, and openings. This chapter builds on that discussion by demonstrating the various techniques for modifying the properties of existing ADT objects.

Using the Properties Palette for Object Modifications

There are two tabs on the Properties palette. The first tab, the Design tab, is where most of property modifications occur (Figure 12.1).

The second tab, the Extended Data tab, is used for ADT's database features. When a database is attached to an object, it holds additional information for that object. There are several uses for database information acquired from placed ADT objects, including material estimating, quantity take-offs, and the assorted schedules created in construction drawings.

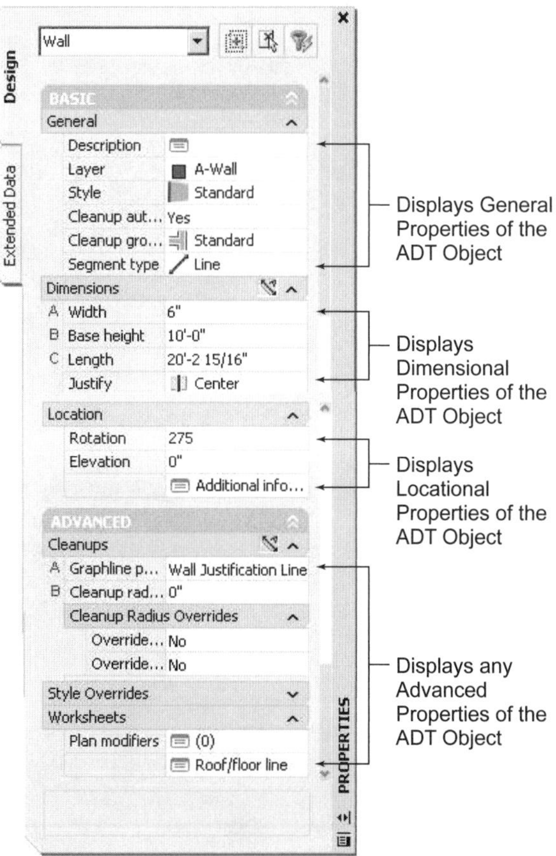

Figure 12.1 The design tab is where most property modifications take place.

The Properties palette lists only an object's property if the object is selected. You should notice that the properties that are listed for an object are distinctive to the object type. When more than one object of similar type—for example, two or more walls—are selected, the Properties palette shows the properties that are similar to the objects. Figure 12.2 shows what the Properties palette looks like when two walls with different widths and styles are selected.

When differing ADT objects are selected, the Properties palette shows only limited properties for the objects with the word **VARIES** listed.

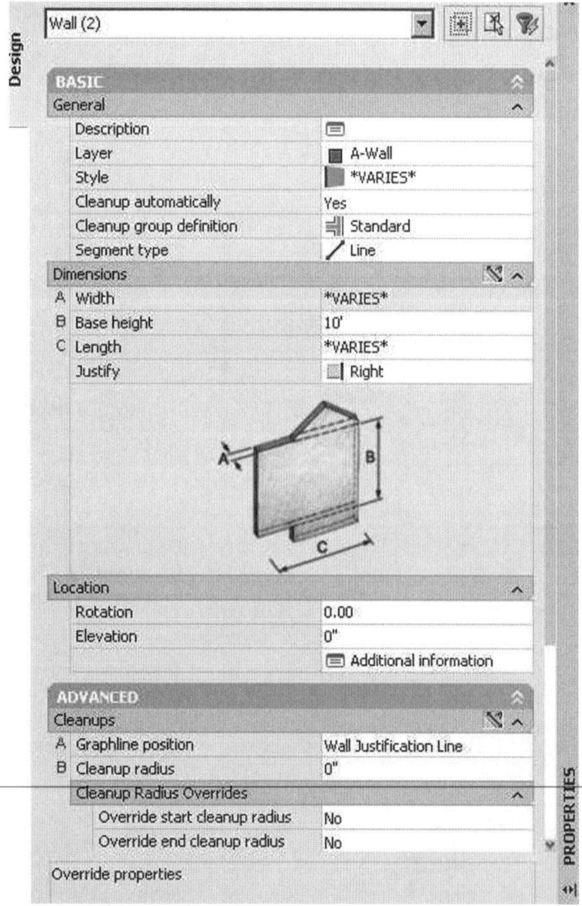

Figure 12.2 The Properties palette when two of the same objects are selected

Changing Object Properties with the Properties Palette

Figure 12.3 identifies each property in the Properties palette for the wall, window, door, opening, and mass element objects. Changing object properties with the Properties palette is straightforward. Selecting an object and left-clicking into any nongrayed field allows you to edit its individual properties.

Editing Through Grips

Grips are located at explicit locations on ADT objects to allow for immediate visual modifications. The ADT grip editing works the same as its AutoCAD counterpart. When you select a grip, it becomes active. Unlike AutoCAD grips, however, each ADT grip is assigned a specific function. Review the Chapter 2 section on grips for a more detailed introduction to grips.

Using Grips to Edit Walls

Grip modifications on a wall include wall length, wall width (if the style allows), wall base height, wall location, and top of wall nodes. The CD-ROM illustrates these grip modifiers for the wall object. Demonstrated in this chapter are techniques for moving and stretching walls with grips.

> **Box 12.1**
> When used with dynamic dimensions, grip modifications are very efficient methods to perform most of your dimensional and location editing.

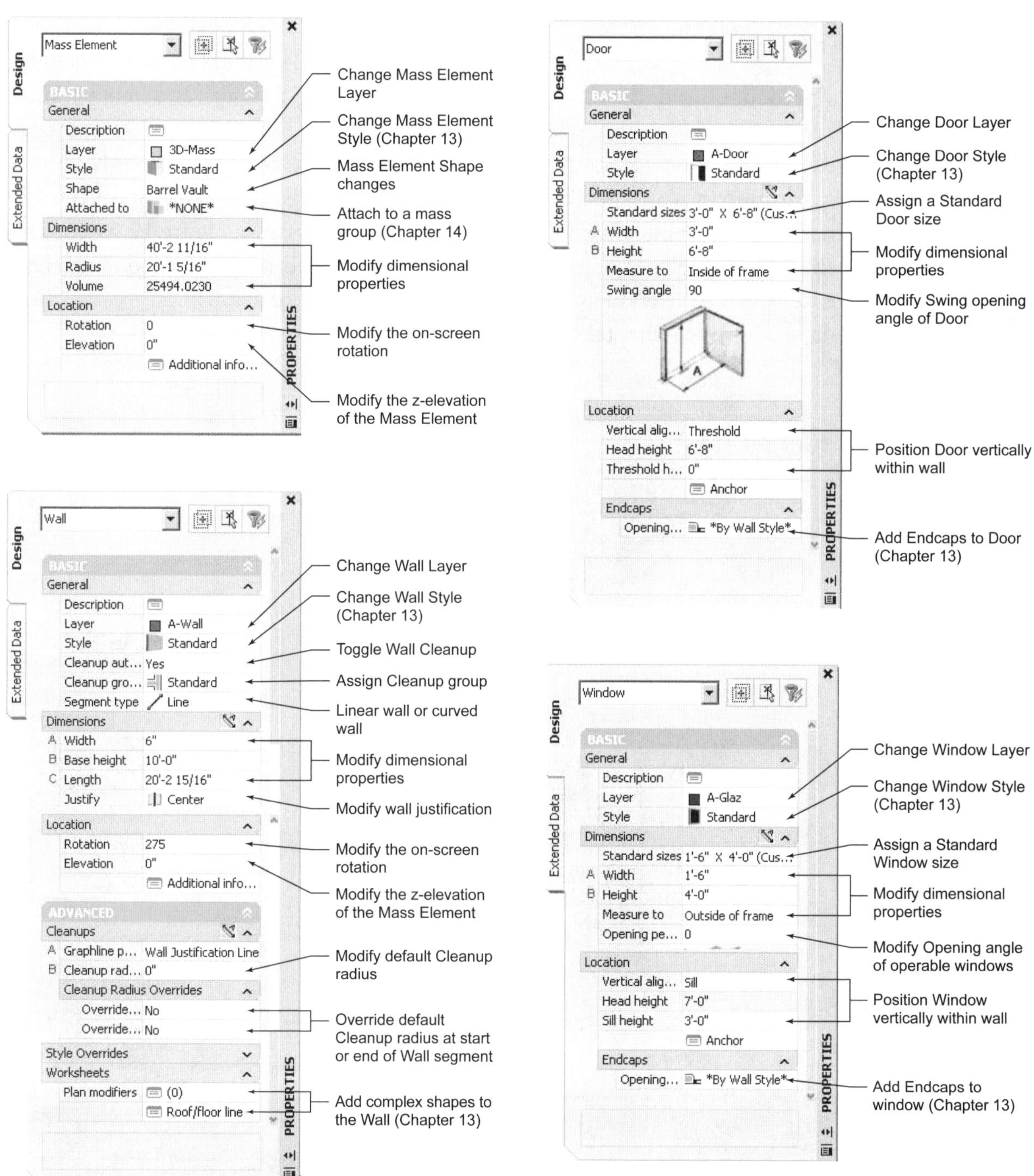

Figure 12.3a–d Getting to Know: The Properties palette Design tab displays properties for Mass Elements, Walls, Doors, Windows, and Openings.

Using Grips to Edit Doors, Windows, and Openings

The grip modifications for doors, windows, and openings are very similar. They include dimensional changes (width and height) and location changes. Swing directions are specific to movable doors and windows, while hinge placements are specific only to the door object. The following pages discuss the different grip modifiers for these objects (also see Chapter 12 folder on CD-ROM).

Using Grips to Edit Mass Elements

Grip modifications for mass elements include general, dimensional (width and height), and location changes (Figure 12.4). Mass elements created by extruded closed polylines have additional edge grips that allow for other types of editing features. Figure 12.5 demonstrates the three additional edges-edit modes for mass element extrusions.

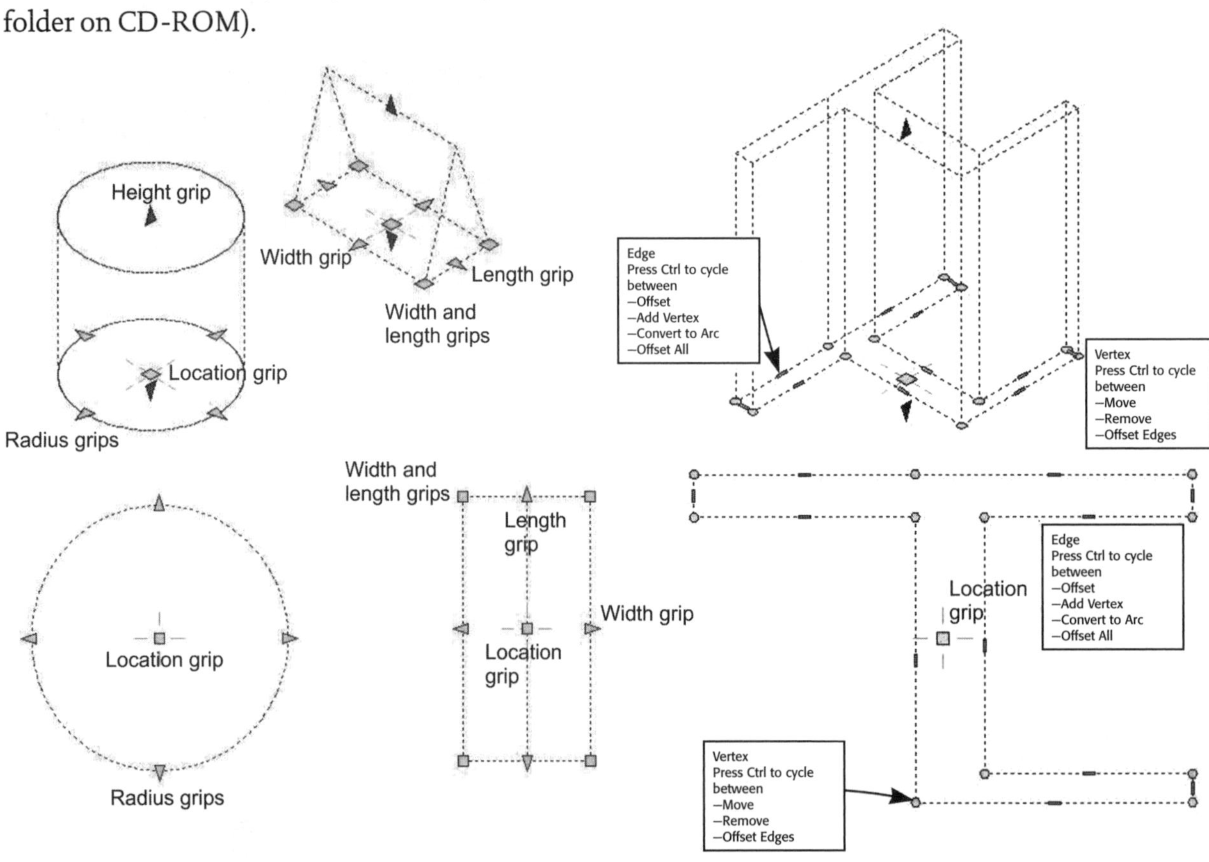

Figure 12.4 The specific functions for each grip on mass objects

Technique to Master **T12.05** Using the Additional Edge-Edit Modes for Mass Element Extrusions

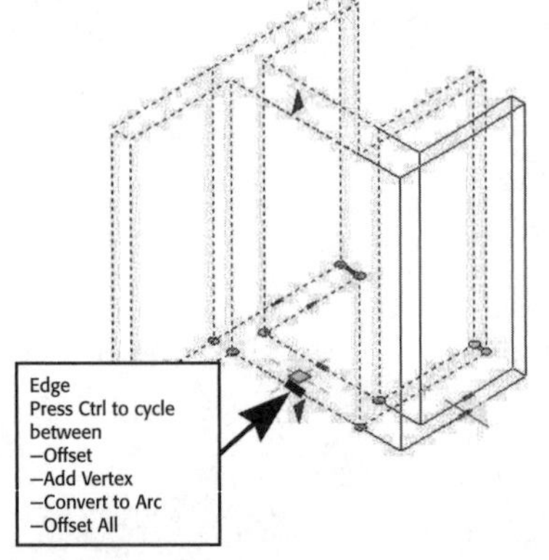

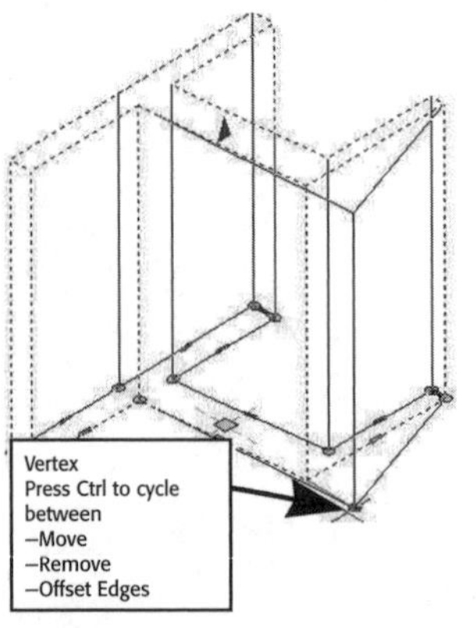

Figure 12.5

Circle grips will adjust mass element corners. Press the Ctrl key once to cycle between moving the vertex, deleting the vertex, or offsetting the edges adjacent to the vertex.
Edge grips will adjust the mass element's selected edge. Press the Ctrl key once to cycle between moving the edge, adding a vertex, converting the straight edge to a curved edge, or offsetting all edges inward or outward.

Specialty Editing Commands for ADT Objects

Most of ADT's building objects include special commands that are specific to the object type. These commands are generally located by selecting the object and right-clicking to show the object's hidden menu. This section introduces the specialty commands for walls, doors, windows, and mass elements.

Specialty AEC Editing Commands Available to All Objects

The tool and menu commands that follow are available to all objects through the right-click menu.

Basic Modify Tools

Under the Basic Modify Tools menu, you will find a shortcut to the most often used AutoCAD modification commands—Move, Copy, Rotate, Delete, Mirror, Array, and Scale. Refer to Chapter 2 to review procedures for using these commands.

> **Box 12.2**
> Clipboard tools work the same in any software application. Select the object or objects that you want to copy or cut from the drawing screen, choose the Ctrl+C or Ctrl+X, and switch to a different drawing to paste the objects with Ctrl+V.

Clipboard Tools

The Clipboard Tools menu provides access to the Cut, Copy, and Paste commands that are familiar to all Windows-based computer applications.

AEC Modify Tools

The AEC Modify tools are new commands that give users additional flexibility to edit ADT objects. Each of the AEC Modify tools—Array, Reposition From, Space Evenly, and Center—are all tools to help quickly implement everyday drawing situations. The Array tool's visual interface allows you to specify the array distance and array count directly on the drawing screen while previewing the results of the command. This tool becomes an efficient tool for placing repetitive objects, including structural elements like beams and trusses (Figure 12.6). The Reposition From command quickly relocates an object by specifying a reference point and a new relative distance. As shown in Figure 12.7, this tool is a much more efficient method to relocate furniture and equipment in a floor plan. Figure 12.8 demonstrates the drawing of a structural truss using the Space Evenly tool. This tool spaces in a specified distance any selected objects evenly with one another. Finally, the Center tool centers a selected object in a space with a specified distance. Figure 12.9 shows how you can quickly relocate the credenza without having to draw construction lines.

> **Box 12.3**
> When you need to use the AutoCAD modification commands—Move, Copy, Array—try to substitute AEC Modify Tools whenever possible.

Technique to Master T12.06 Using the AEC Modify Tools>Array Command

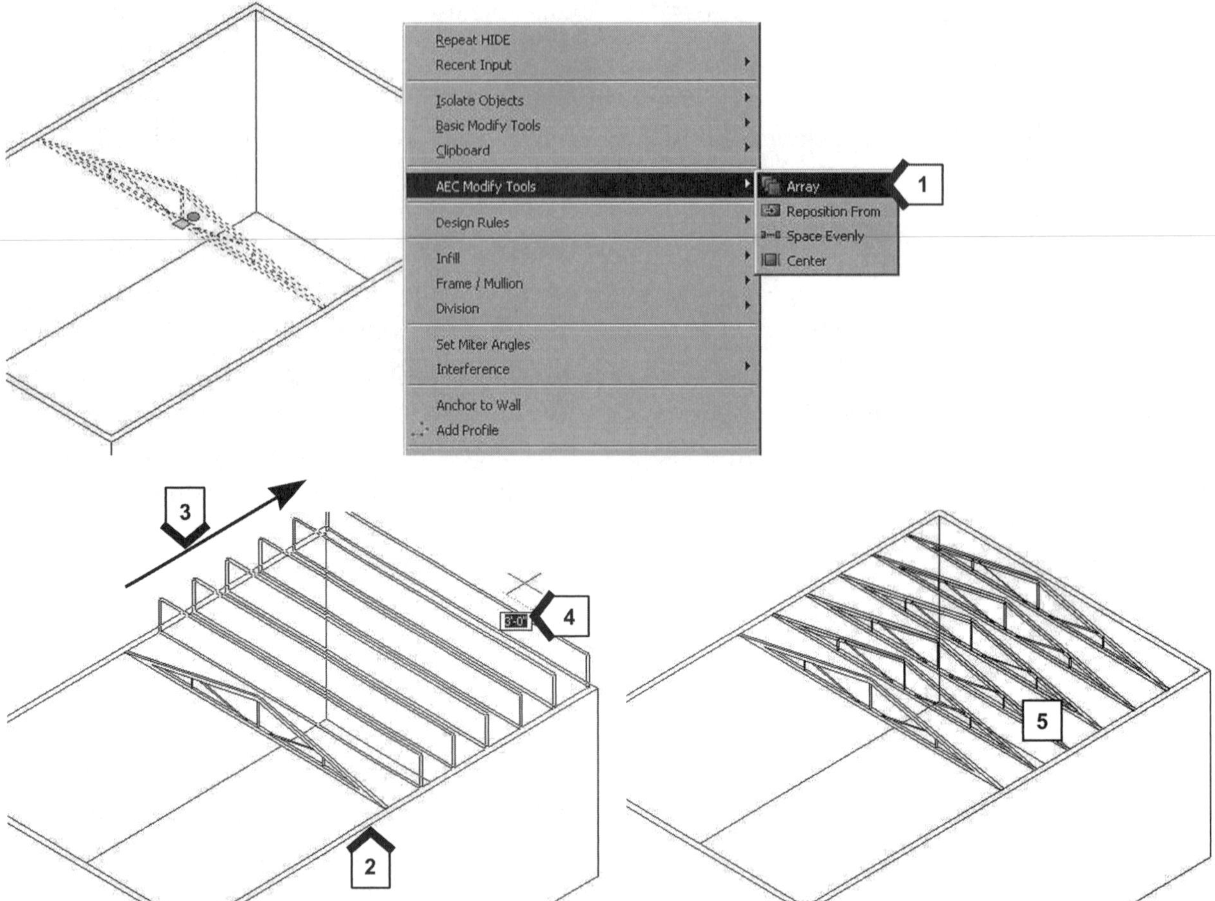

Figure 12.6

1	[Right-click menu]	Execute AEC Modify Tools>Array command.
2	[Drawing Screen]	Select the edge from which to array.
3	[Drawing Screen]	Move mouse in the direction of array. The farther the mouse is from the starting edge, the greater the overall clear distance.
4	[Command Line]	Type in array distance.
5	[Drawing Screen]	Left-click to complete array.
6	Object moves the specified distance from the reference point.	

Technique to Master T12.07 Using the AEC Modify Reposition From Command

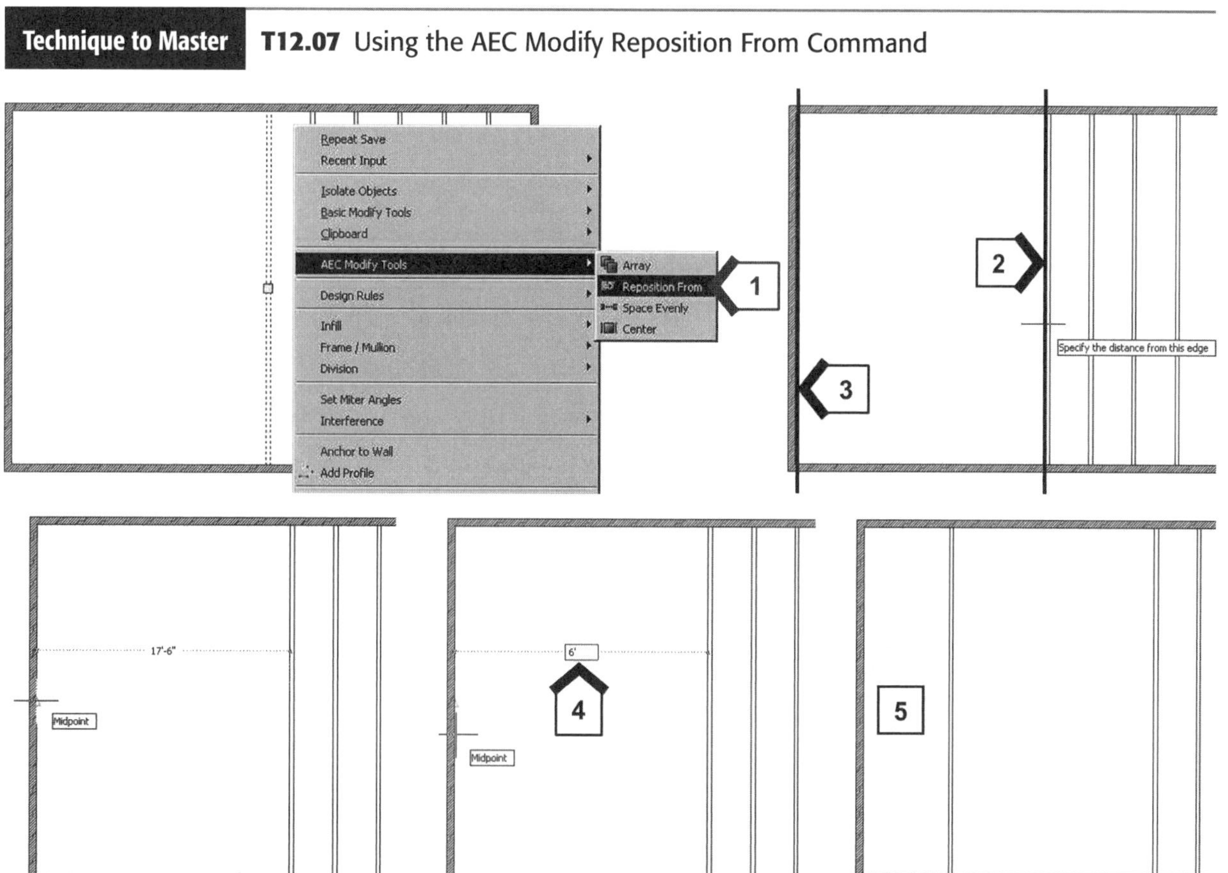

Figure 12.7 The illustration shows how a wood ceiling beam (plan view) could be easily relocated using the AEC Reposition From command. The current location of the left-most beam is 17'-6" from the left wall. Using the AEC Reposition From command, the beam-to-wall distance can be quickly changed to 6'-0".

1	[Right-click menu]	Execute AEC Reposition From command.
2	[Drawing Screen]	Select first reference edge; this would be the left surface of the beam.
3	[Drawing Screen]	Select the second reference edge; this would be the right surface of the wall.
4	[Command Line]	Type in the new distance between reference edges.
5	[Drawing Screen]	Newly relocated beam will appear.

Technique to Master **T12.08** Using the AEC Modify Space Evenly Command

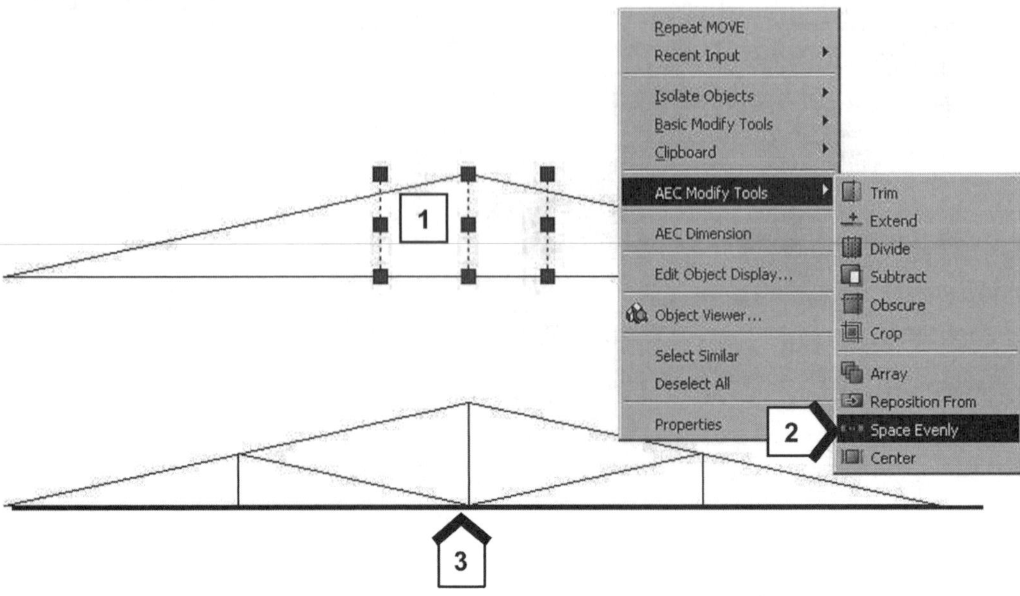

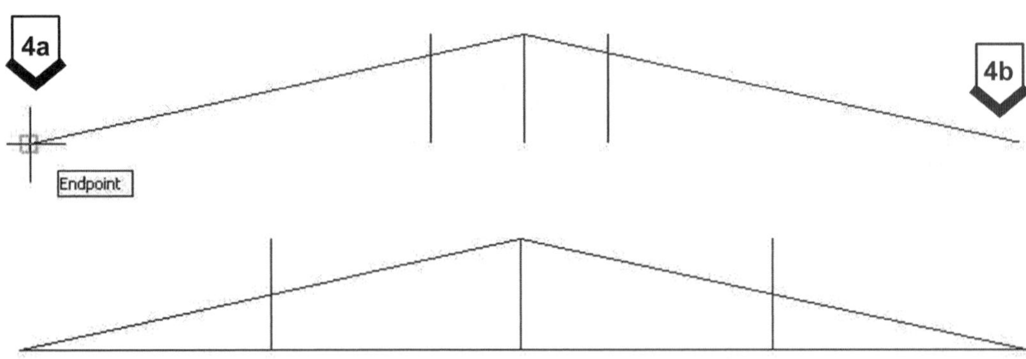

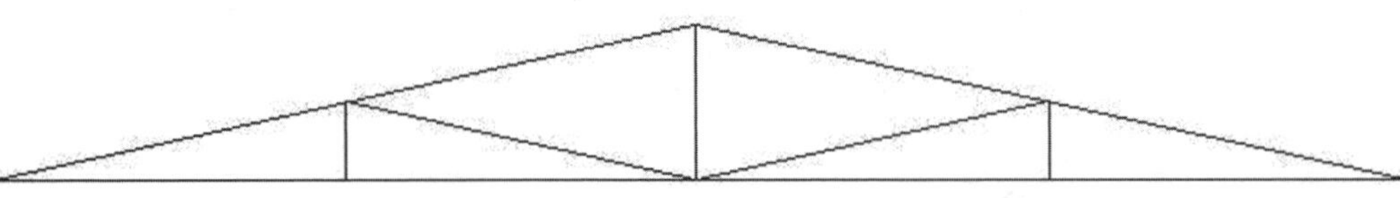

Figure 12.8

1	[Drawing Screen]	Select objects to space evenly.
2	[Drawing Screen]	Right-click on the object. Select AEC Modify Tools>Space Evenly.
3	[Drawing Screen]	Specify the axis along which objects will be spaced.
4a, 4b	[Drawing Screen]	Specify by snapping to two points—the distance the objects will be evenly spaced within.

Technique to Master **T12.09** Using the AEC Modify Center Command

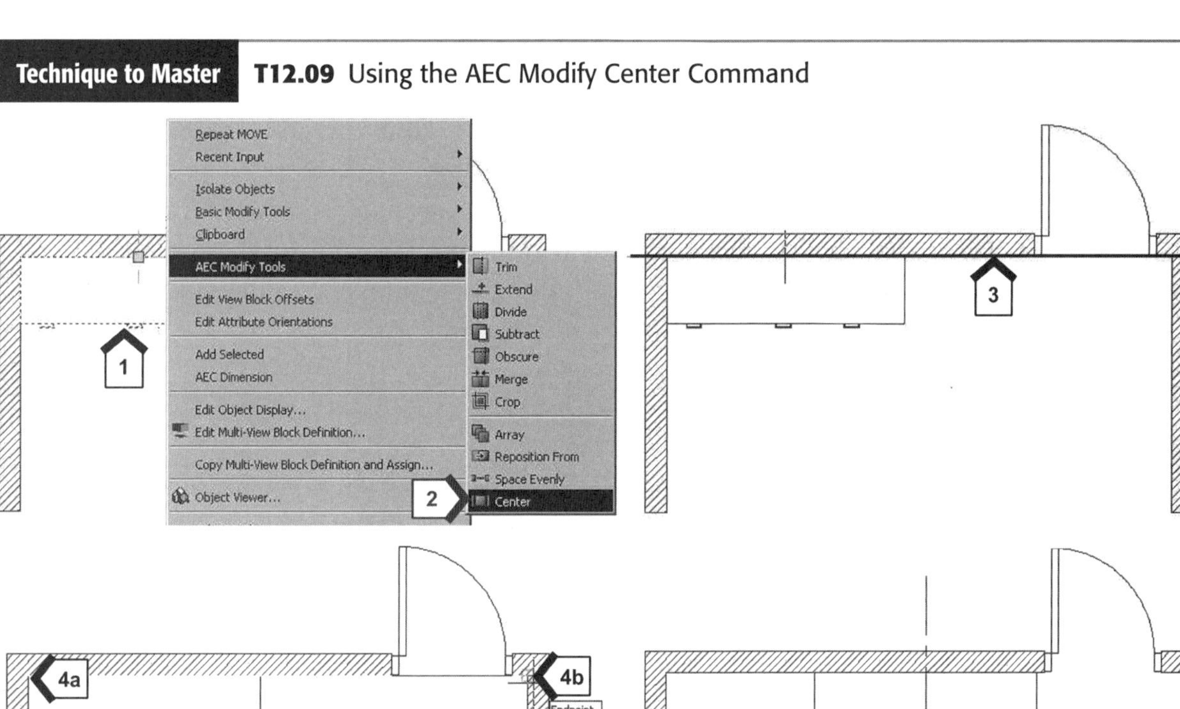

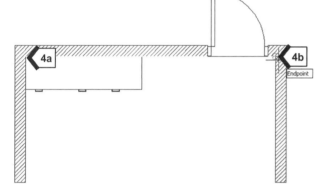

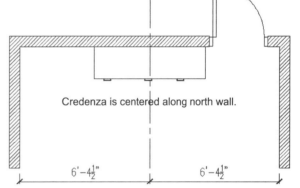

Figure 12.9

1	[Drawing Screen]	Select objects to center.
2	[Drawing Screen]	Right-click on the object. Select AEC Modify Tools>Center.
3	[Drawing Screen]	Specify the axis along which objects will be centered.
4a, 4b	[Drawing Screen]	Specify by snapping to two points—the distance the objects will be centered within.

Add Selected

The Add Selected menu command is another command that is common to all ADT objects. It is used as a sort of match properties tool. For example, this command allows you to draw a wall object with the same properties of an existing wall object. Simply select the wall, right-click, and choose Add Selected to begin drawing new walls. All resulting new walls have the exact same properties as the initial wall. This command works similarly for any of the ADT objects.

> **Box 12.4**
> The Add Selected command removes the step of continuously changing the Properties palette when placing different styles and sizes of an ADT object.

Specialty Wall Commands

The right-click menu of the wall object probably includes the largest selection of specialty commands compared with the other ADT objects. This topic introduces some of the more commonly used commands.

Modifying a Wall's Direction

The WallReverse command reverses the justification of a wall. If a wall is right-justified, it becomes left-justified and vice versa. If a wall has more than one component, then the wall is mirrored. The WallReverse command has two options: In Place and Baseline. The In Place option reverses the wall direction but retains the location of the justification line (Figure 12.10a), while the Baseline option moves the justification that results in moving the wall (Figure 12.10b). The WallReverse command is particularly useful when solving cleanup problems of walls with multiple components.

Specialty Trim Commands for Cleaning Up Walls

Typical cleanups between walls include corners (L-cleanups) and perpendicular relationships (T-cleanups). The WallCleanupT and WallCleanupL commands provide quick trimming commands for these types of cleanups. Figure 12.11 illustrates the command sequence.

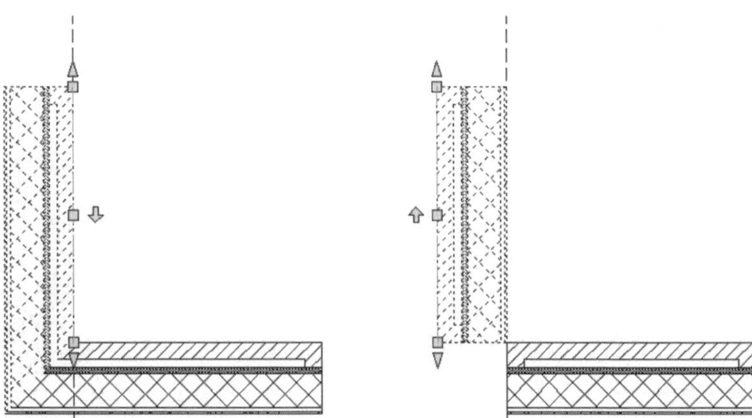

Figure 12.10a The InPlace option reverses direction but retains wall position.

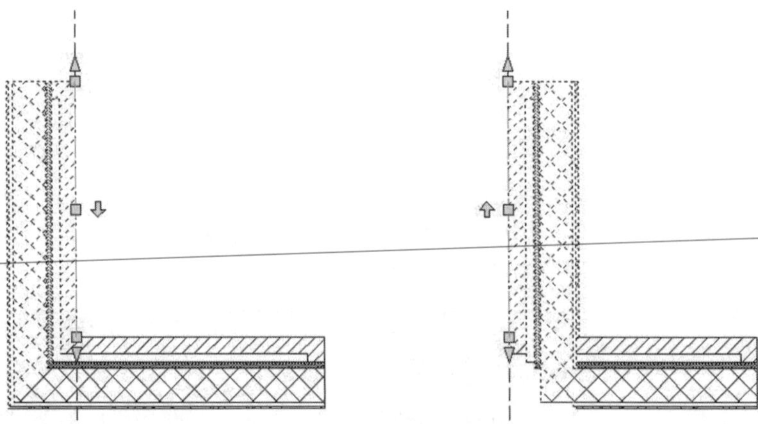

Figure 12.10b With the Baseline option, the justification line moves and the wall shifts.

Technique to Master **T12.11** Wall Cleanup with the L and T Cleanup Commands

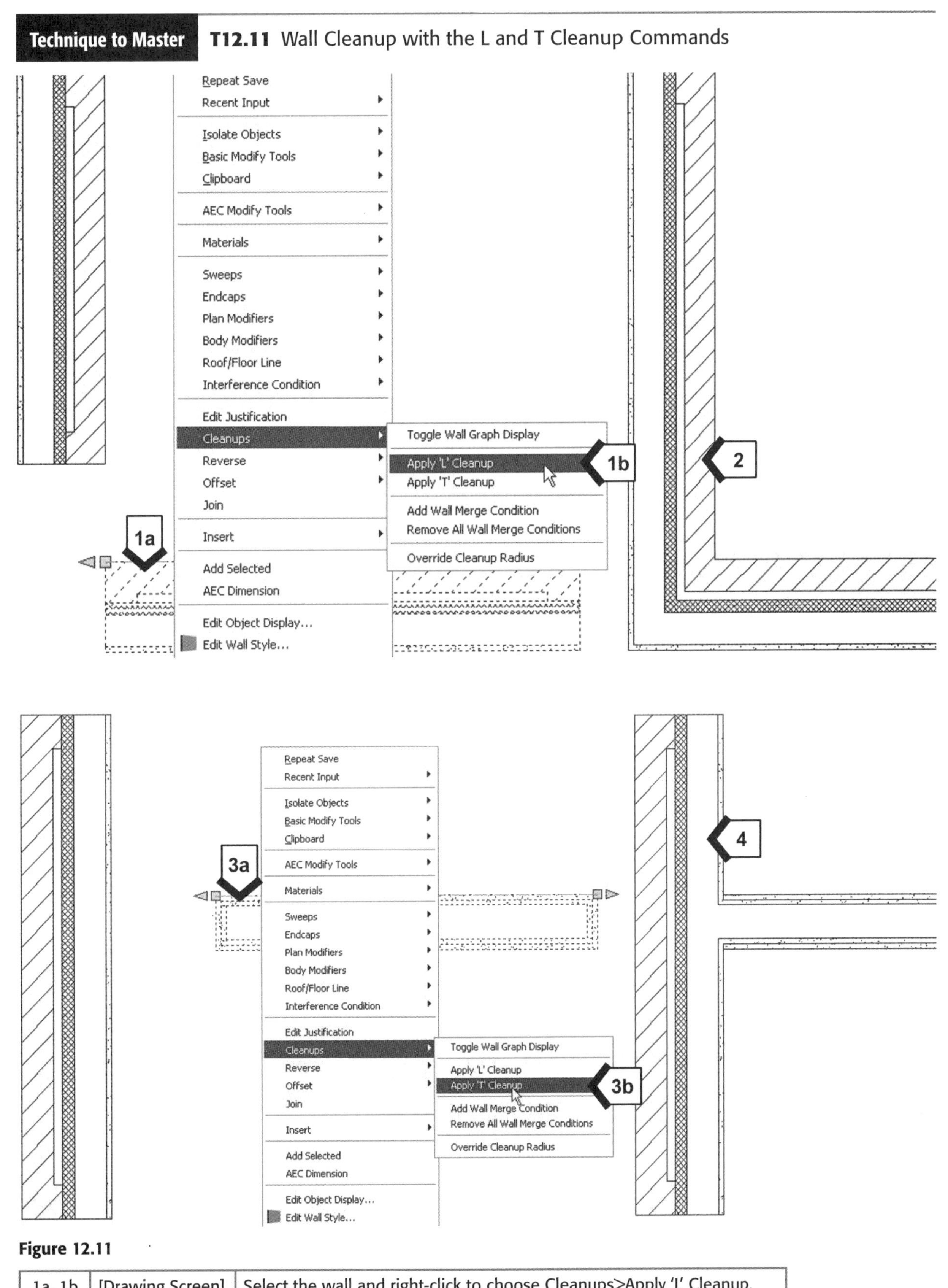

Figure 12.11

1a, 1b	[Drawing Screen]	Select the wall and right-click to choose Cleanups>Apply 'L' Cleanup.
2	[Drawing Screen]	Select the second wall.
3a, 3b	[Drawing Screen]	Select the wall and right-click to choose Cleanups>Apply 'T' Cleanup.
4	[Drawing Screen]	Select the second wall.

Merging Walls

The WallMergeAdd command is useful for when you need to add pilasters and other wall depths intermittently to different areas of a wall. This command is reversible through the WallMergeRemove command. Figure 12.12 illustrates the technique.

Wall Commands to Help the Space Planning Process

The WallOffsetCopy, WallOffsetMove, and WallOffsetSet are specialty wall commands that are very useful when space planning floor areas. The WallOffsetCopy command lets you create additional copies of an existing wall at an offset distance that is specified; it is a valuable command for when you need to copy walls at specified clear distances. In a similar way, the WallOffsetMove command lets you move an existing wall at specified distance in the parallel direction. The WallOffsetSet command lets you change the distance between two surfaces to a new specified distance. Figures 12.13 through 12.15 demonstrate the three commands.

> **Box 12.5**
> Make sure the Dynamic Distance drawing aid is toggled ON when using any of the WallOffset tools.

Technique to Master **T12.12** Building Up a Wall with Wall Merge

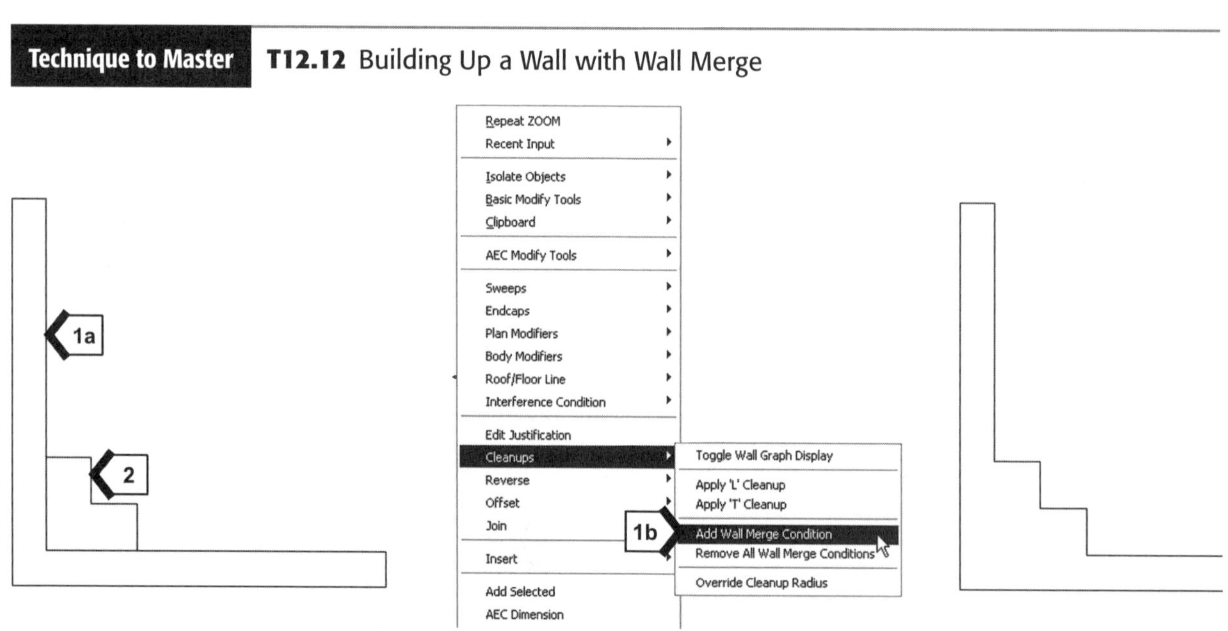

Figure 12.12

Two or more walls need to be adjacent to each other for the wall merge to be successful.		
1	[Drawing Screen]	Select the primary wall and right-click to choose Cleanups>Add Wall Merge Condition command.
2	[Drawing Screen]	Select the adjacent wall.

Technique to Master T12.13 Using the WallOffsetCopy Command

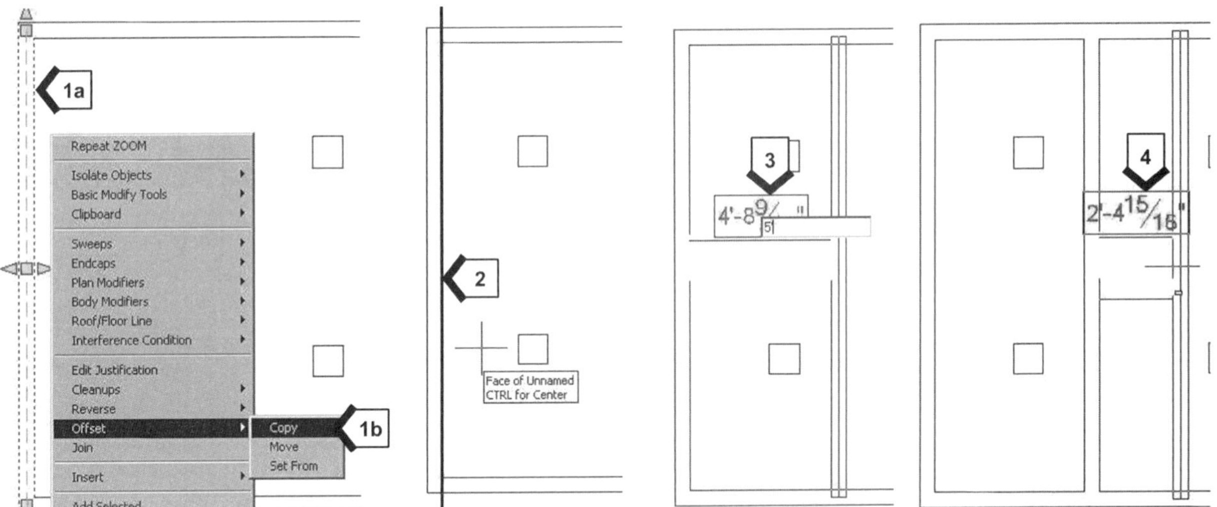

Figure 12.13

1a, 1b	[Drawing Screen]	Select the wall to copy, right-click, and choose Offset>Copy command.
2	[Drawing Screen]	Specify wall's left or right edge for the reference point.
3	[Drawing Screen]	Specify the offset distance.
4	[Drawing Screen]	Additional walls can be added. Each new wall is offset from the face or center of the wall you added before it. (You can specify a different offset distance each time you add another wall.)
5	Press Enter to complete the command.	

Technique to Master T12.14 Using the WallOffsetMove Command

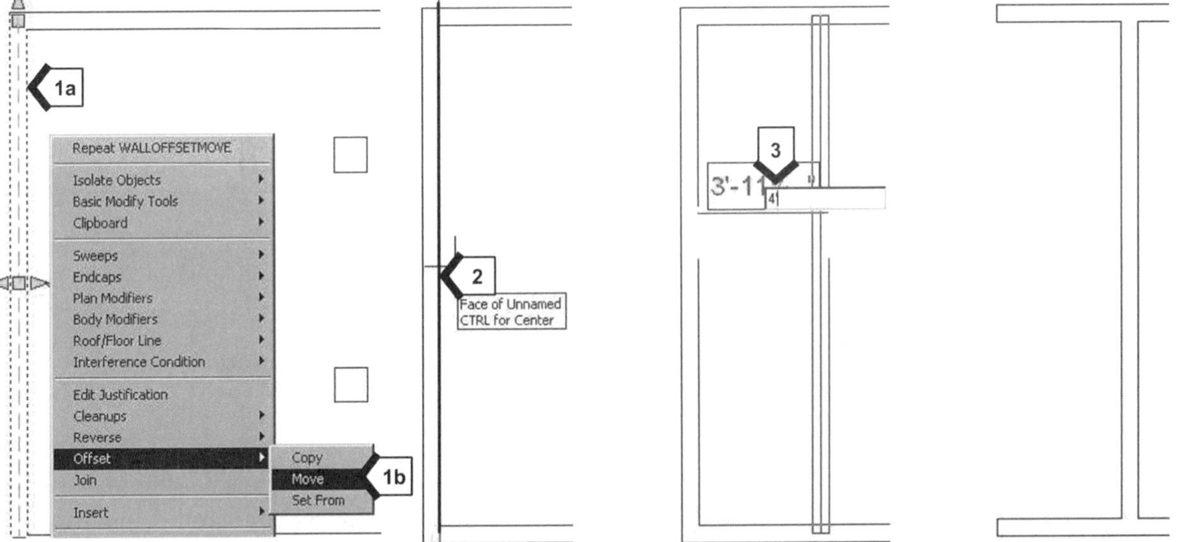

Figure 12.14

1a, 1b	[Drawing Screen]	Select wall to move, right-click, and choose the Offset>Move command.
2	[Drawing Screen]	Specify the reference line (wall's left, right, or center justification)
3	[Drawing Screen]	Specify the offset distance.
4	Press Enter to complete the command.	

Technique to Master **T12.15** Using the WallOffsetSet Command

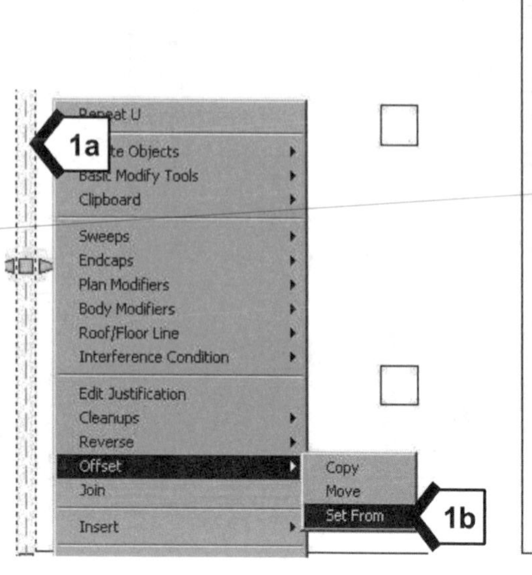

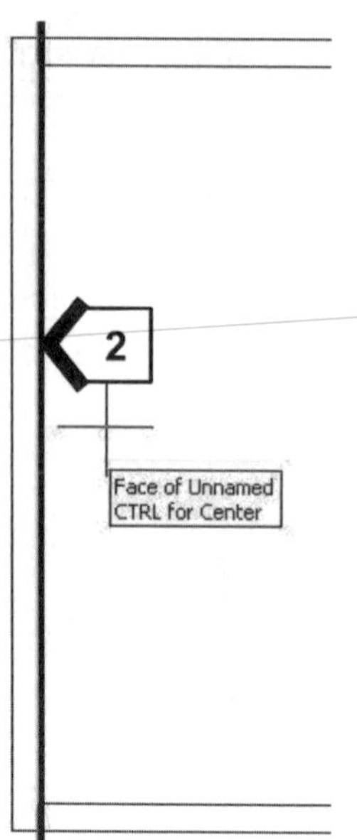

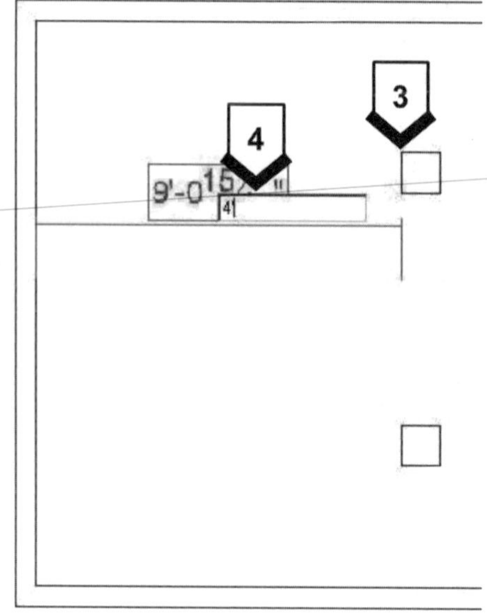

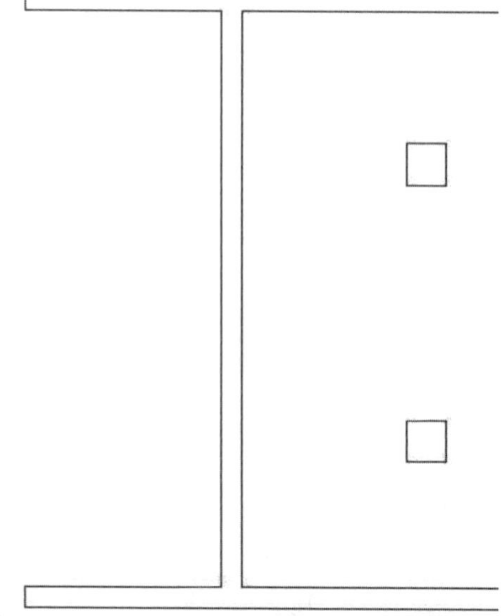

Figure 12.15

1a, 1b	[Drawing Screen]	Select the wall, right-click, and choose Offset>Set From.
2	[Drawing Screen]	Specify the reference line (wall's left, right, or center justification)
3	[Drawing Screen]	Specify the location of the second reference point.
4	[Command Line]	Type in new distance.

Joining Walls

The WallJoin command lets you join two walls into one wall segment. When walls are joined together, the second wall adopts all the properties of the first wall, including wall height, cleanup radius, wall modifiers, and so on. The rules that establish whether two walls join are as follows:

- Wall segments must have the same justification and graphlines and be touching at one end. Curved walls must also share the same center and have the same radius.
- Wall styles, wall widths, and cleanup groups must be the same.

Figure 12.16 demonstrates the Join command.

Specialty Door and Window Commands

The Reposition Along Wall and Reposition Within Wall commands are two specialty commands that help you relocate doors, windows, and openings within a wall with high levels of precision (Figure 12.17). The Reposition Along Wall command lets you

Technique to Master T12.16 Using the Join Command

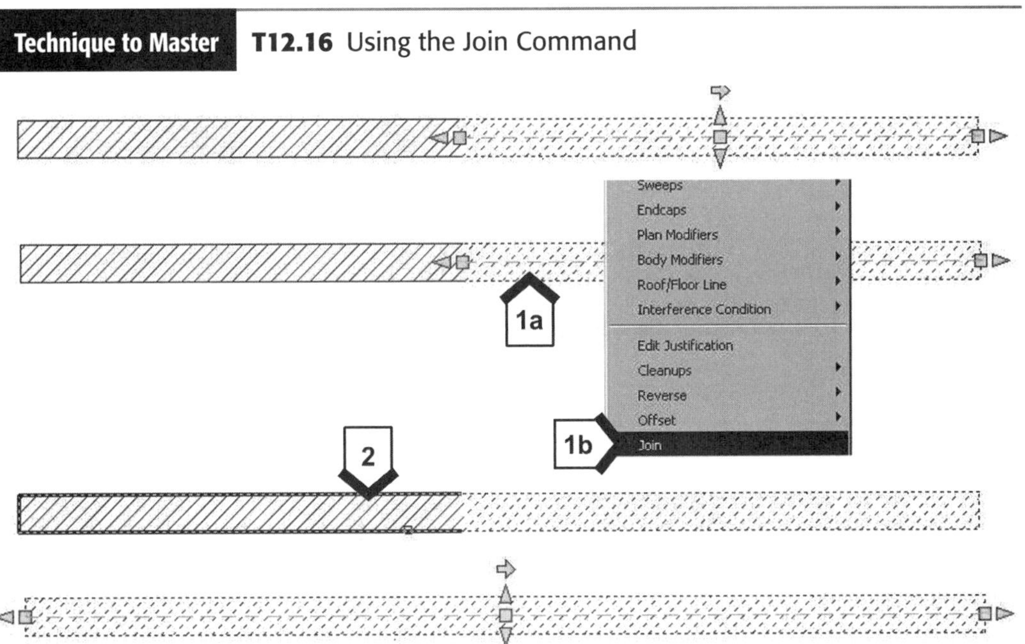

Figure 12.16

1a, 1b	[Drawing Screen]	Select the first wall, right click, and choose the Join command.
2	[Drawing Screen]	Select the second wall.

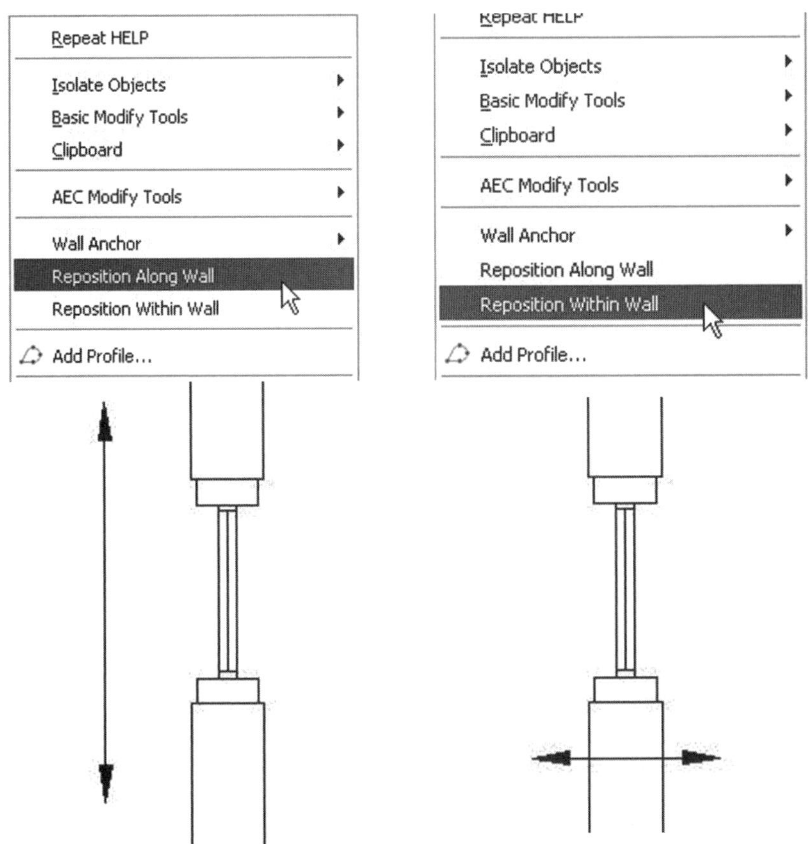

Figure 12.17 Specialty commands help relocate doors, windows, and openings within a wall with high levels of precision.

Technique to Master **T12.18** Using the Reposition Within Wall Command

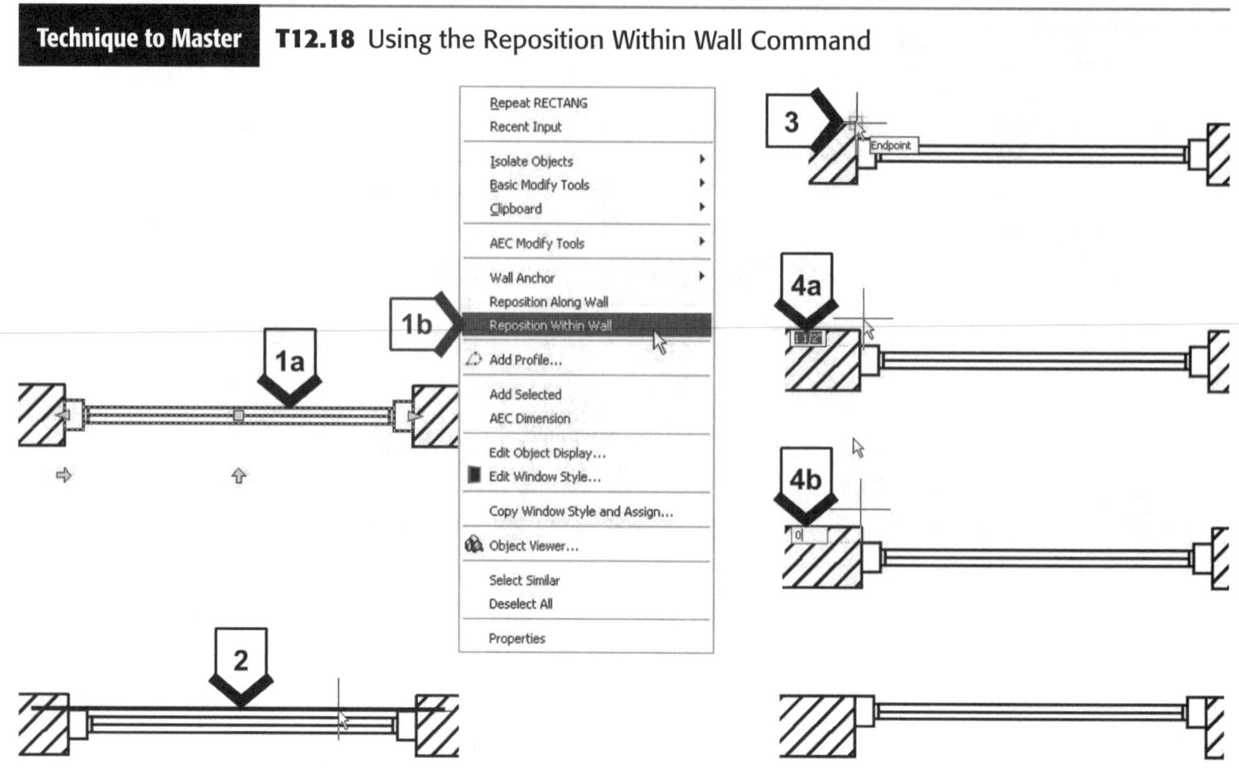

Figure 12.18

1a, 1b	[Drawing Screen]	Select a door or window, right-click, and choose the Reposition Within Wall command.
2	[Drawing Screen]	Specify the reference line on the door or window (left, right, or center of frame).
3	[Drawing Screen]	Specify the location of the second reference point.
4a, 4b	[Command Line]	(The current distance between the reference points is shown.) Type in the new distance.

move the door or window a specified distance along the wall. The Reposition Within Wall command lets you move the door or window forward or backward within the wall. Figure 12.18 demonstrates how to use the Reposition Within Wall command.

Specialty Mass Element and Mass Group Commands

Mass elements and mass group objects also have specialty commands that tend to focus around conversion tools and surface editing. Surface editing tools include the MassElementDivide, MassElementTrim, and the MassElementFaceDivide commands. The MassElementDivide command lets you divide a mass element by specifying a division plane. The MassElementTrim command lets you trim a section of a mass element by specifying a trim plane. The MassElementFaceDivide command lets you divide up a selected surface of a mass element. Figures 12.19 through 12.21 demonstrate how to use these commands. The conversion tools convert mass elements and mass groups into other types of ADT objects.

Technique to Master T12.19 Using the Split by Plane (MassElementDivide) Command

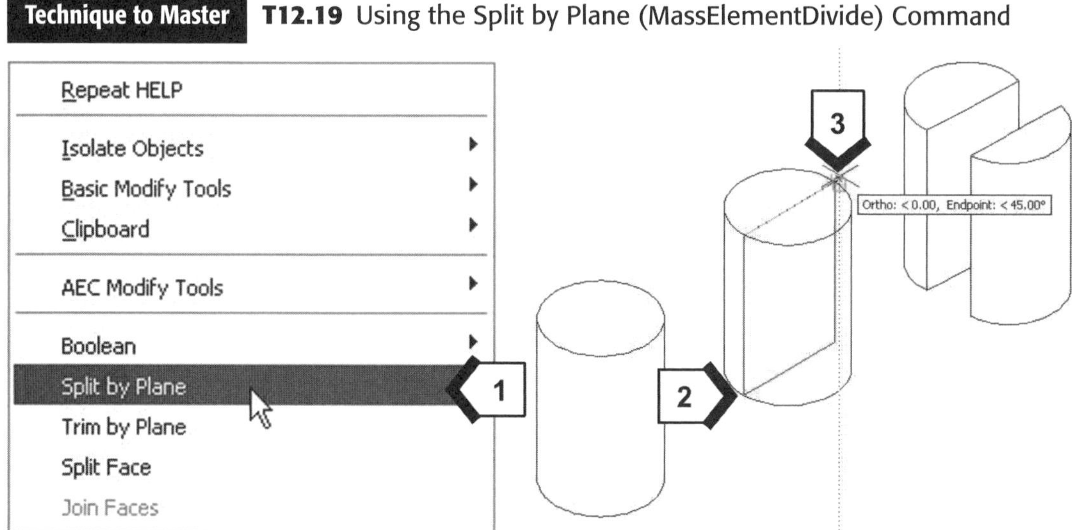

Figure 12.19 The plane that will divide the mass element is created by specifying two points.

1	[Drawing Screen]	Select the mass element, right-click, and choose Split by Plane.
2	[Drawing Screen]	Using object snaps, specify plane start point.
3	[Drawing Screen]	Using object snaps, specify plane endpoint.

Technique to Master T12.20 Using the Trim by Plane (MassElementTrim) Command

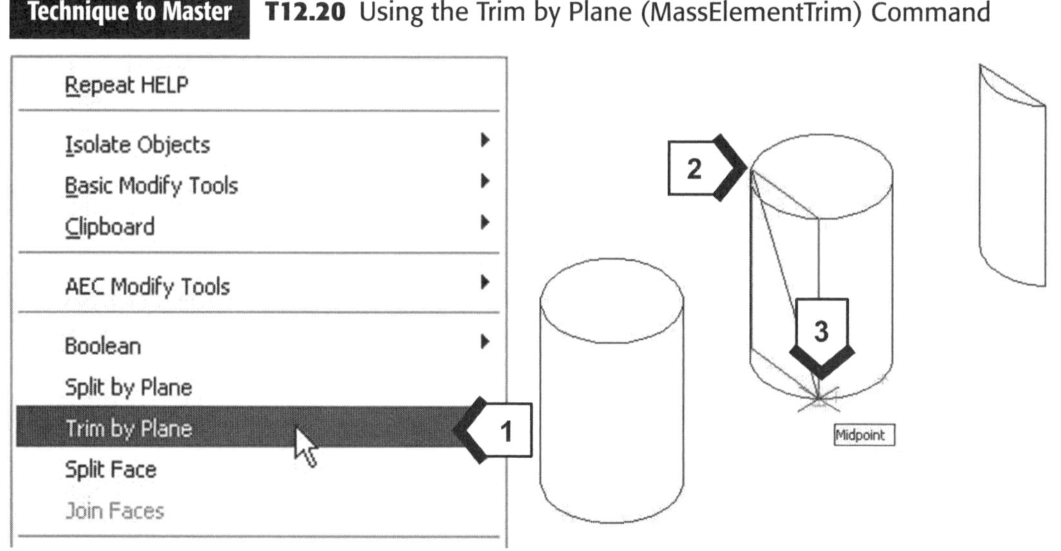

Figure 12.20 The plane that will trim the mass element is created by specifying two points.

1	[Drawing Screen]	Select mass element, right-click, and choose Trim by Plane.
2	[Drawing Screen]	Using object snaps, specify plane start point.
3	[Drawing Screen]	Using object snaps, specify plane endpoint.
4	[Drawing Screen]	Select the side of the mass element to remove.

Technique to Master **T12.21** Using the Split Face (MassElementFaceDivide) Command

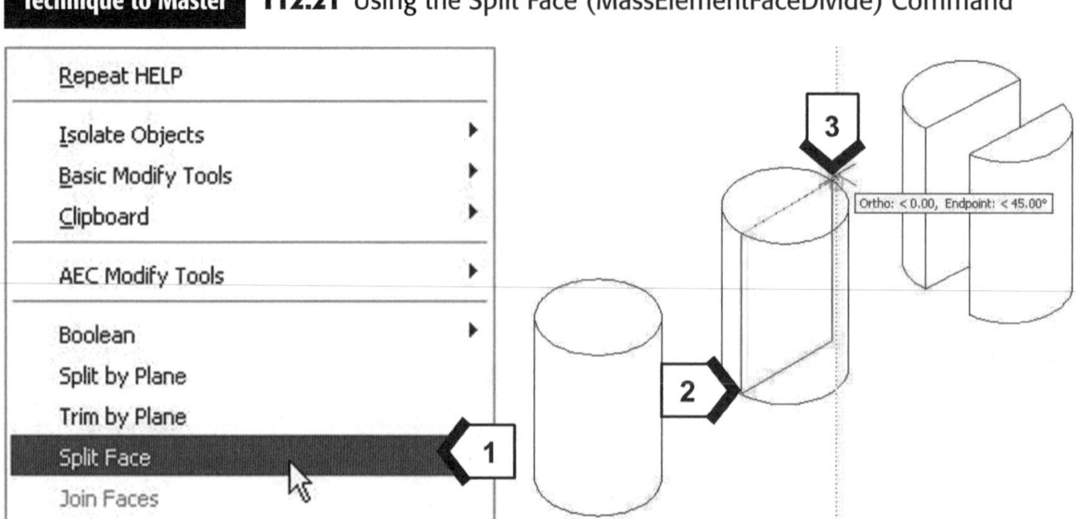

Figure 12.21 Splitting the face of a mass element requires specifying a minimum of two points.

1	[Drawing Screen]	Select mass element, right-click, and choose Split Face.
2	[Drawing Screen]	Select the first point on the face to be split.
3	[Drawing Screen]	Select the second point on the face to be split.

Chapter Exercises

Open the Chapter 12 folder located on the CD-ROM to access the exercises for this chapter. They let you practice how to make property, grip, and other modifications on wall, window, door, opening, and mass element objects.

Adding Complexity: Customizing the Main Components

13

Objectives

This chapter expands on ADT wall, window, door, opening, and mass element objects, and therefore, emphasizes customizations to walls, windows, doors, openings, and mass elements through the use of styles and object modifiers.

ADT Customization

Keeping objects simple during the conceptual and schematic stages allows you to quickly build up a three-dimensional model for massing studies. However, as a design develops, added detail helps show the appropriateness and constructability of design decisions. This chapter introduces you to the ADT commands and techniques used to add complexity, detail, and realism to your building model.

ADT Styles

Styles in ADT are analogous to the historical styles of art and architecture. Most objects have a style property that is used to define subclasses of the object. All ADT objects that use styles have a default style called Standard. This style is the most generic representation of the object. During the initial design stages when details of a design are still unknown, the Standard style is a great choice to use because, as evidenced by the name, it does not have specific characteristics. As the design progresses, however, creating and using additional styles add complexity to ADT objects. Styles not only help to assign hatching surfaces and material textures to ADT objects but also often define what the object looks like (Figure 13.1).

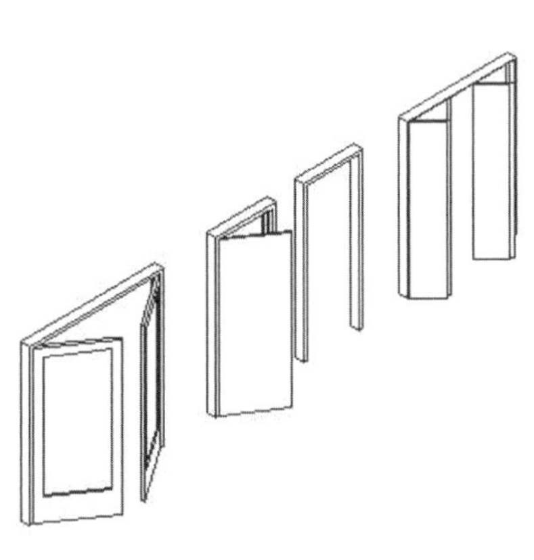

Figure 13.1 Styles not only help you to assign hatching surfaces and material textures to ADT objects but also often define what the object looks like. In this example, four different door styles are defined to create four distinct door types.

The Style Manager is the dialogue box used to create and edit styles for any style-based object. It is also where you transfer styles between drawings. You can open the Style Manager through a variety of methods. To display the list of styles for all object types within the current drawing, open the Style Manager through the Format menu (Figure 13.2). To list only a specific object style, use the individual object's Style Manager found in the Design menu or Design Tool palette (Figure 13.3).

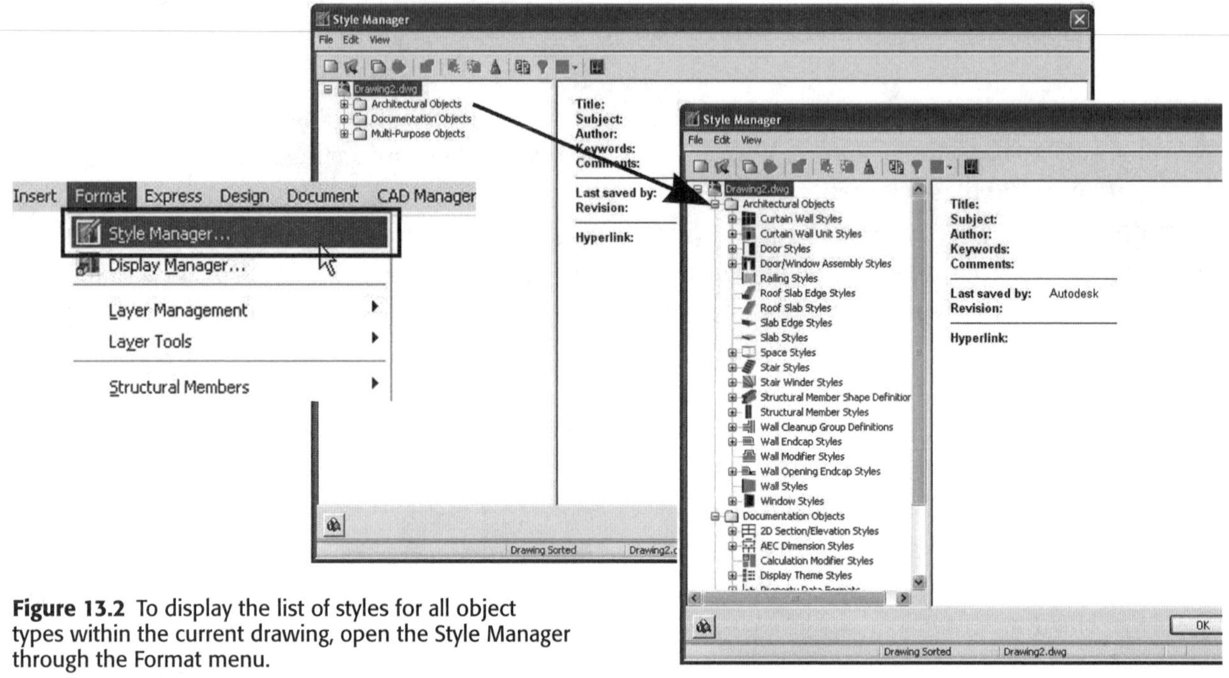

Figure 13.2 To display the list of styles for all object types within the current drawing, open the Style Manager through the Format menu.

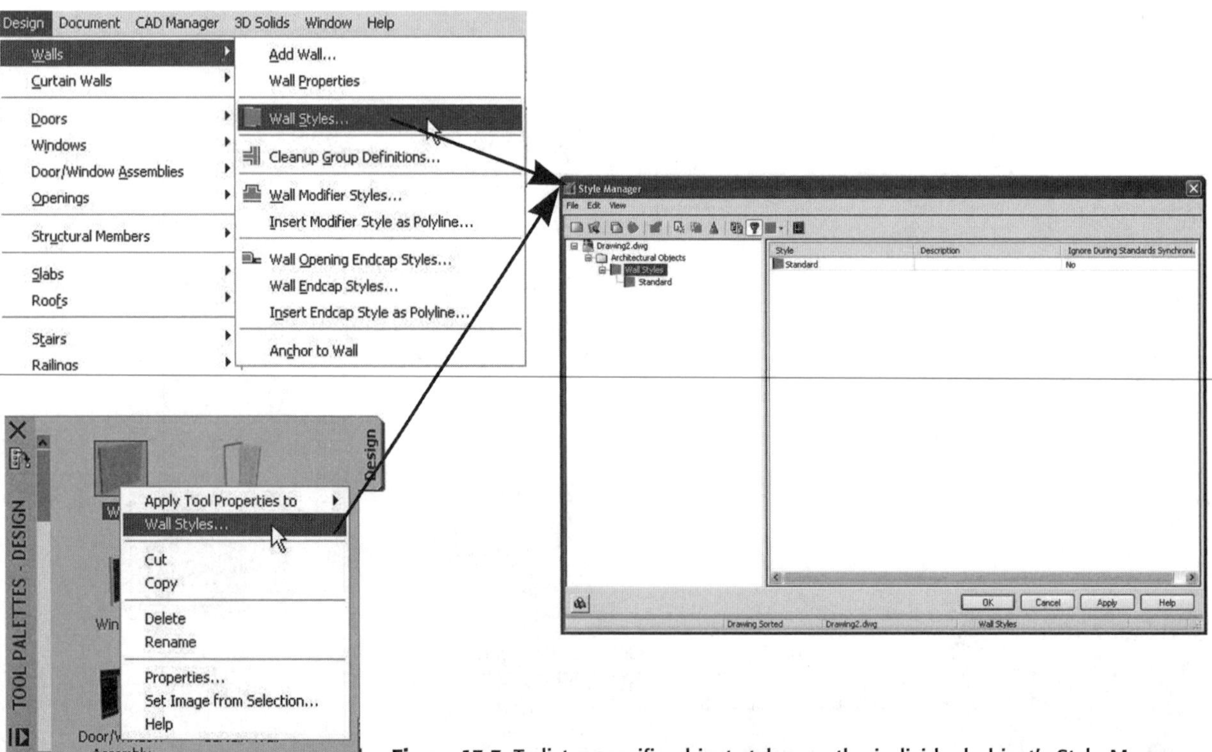

Figure 13.3 To list a specific object style, use the individual object's Style Manager found in the Design Menu or Design Tool palette.

When the Style Manager is opened, it displays a dialogue box that is divided into three areas. Figure 13.4 identifies the relevant parts of these areas. Individual style properties are categorized into tabbed areas within the right pane. Left-clicking on any of these tabs will display additional properties specific to the object type's style.

Existing Styles

Default ADT templates have only the Standard style defined. However, ADT has a collection of pre-made styles for all of the style-based objects included with the software. You may import these styles from the Design Tool palette, the Content Browser Library, or other drawing files. Figure 13.5 demonstrates how to use the Style Manager to transfer styles between drawings. Figure 13.6 provides guidance on finding the styles within the Content Browser Library.

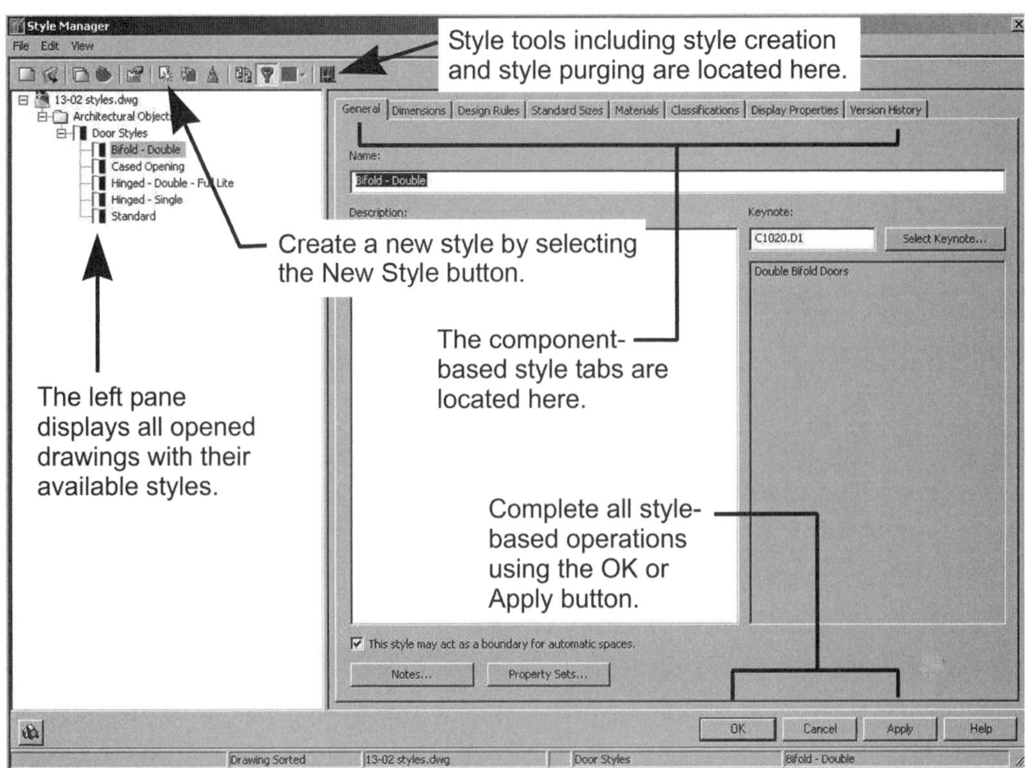
Style tools including style creation and style purging are located here.
Create a new style by selecting the New Style button.
The component-based style tabs are located here.
The left pane displays all opened drawings with their available styles.
Complete all style-based operations using the OK or Apply button.

Figure 13.4 When the Style Manager is opened, it displays a dialogue box that is divided into three areas.

Technique to Master T13.05 Transferring Styles Between Drawings (Importing/Exporting)

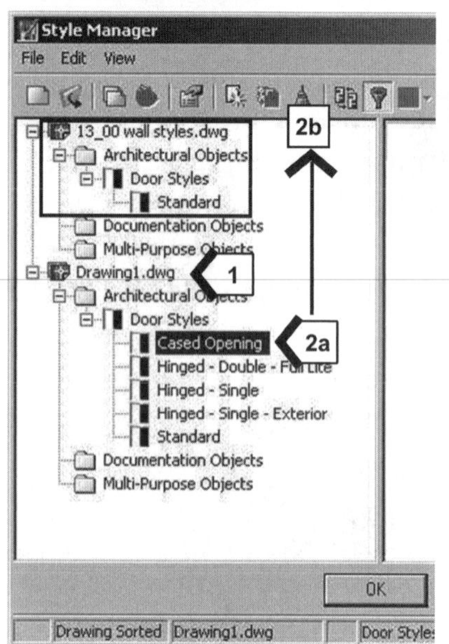

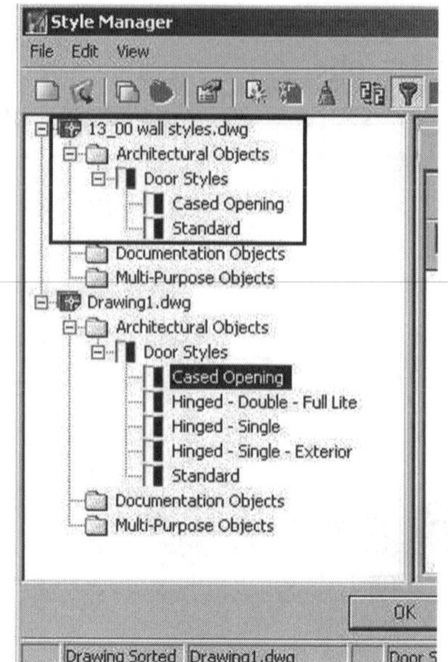

Figure 13.5

1	[Format menu> Style Manager]	In the Style Manager, open the drawing that you want to use to import/export styles.
2a 2b	[Style Manager]	In the left pane, left-click on the style you want to transfer. Keep the mouse held down, and drag and drop the style from one drawing to another.

Technique to Master T13.06 Importing Styles from the Content Browser

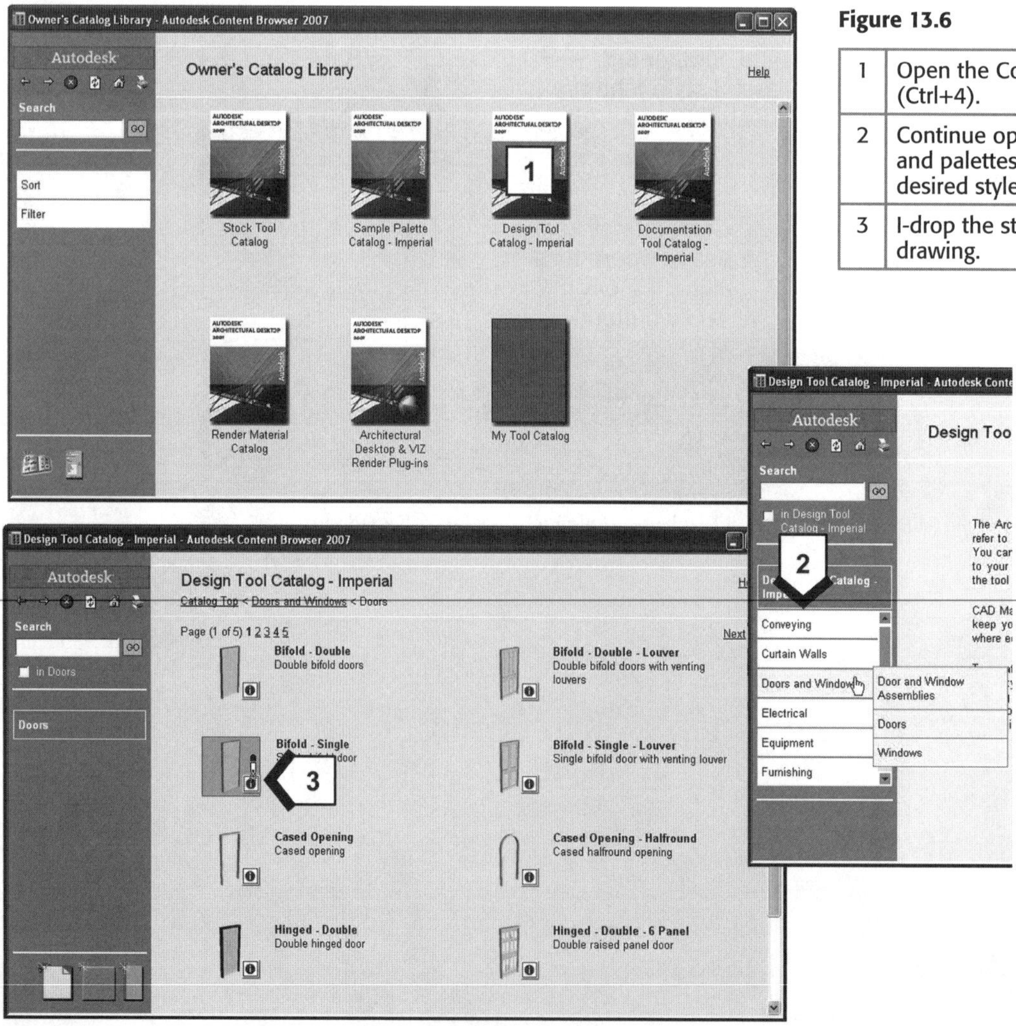

Figure 13.6

1	Open the Content Browser (Ctrl+4).
2	Continue opening catalogs and palettes until you find the desired style.
3	I-drop the style into the current drawing.

The Design Tool palette shows predefined styles for the wall, window, and door object types. Notice that the initial stylistic differences include type—for example, the window types are subdivided into awning, casement, glider, picture, and more. (Figure 13.7).

Editing an Existing Style

Editing the various style-based settings occurs through the Style Manager. To view the settings for an existing style, left-click on the style in the left pane of the Style Manager. In the right pane, cycle through each of the Style Property tabs, editing individual properties as necessary.

Creating New Styles

In the Style Manager, create a new style using the New Style tool icon located at the top of the Style Manager dialogue box. Figure 13.8 lists the file-naming examples that ADT uses in its style naming. It is advantageous to keep your style-naming conventions consistent.

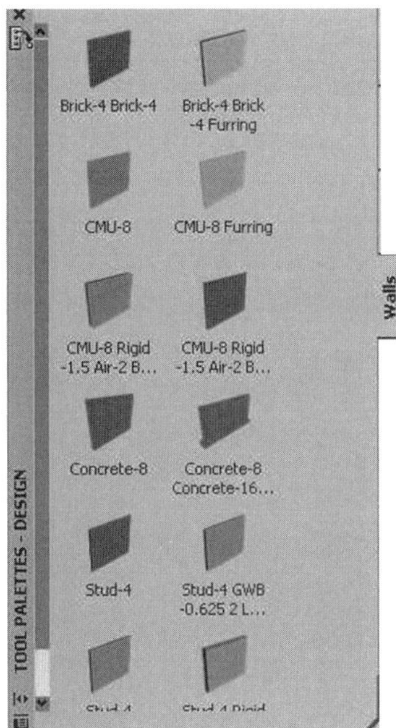

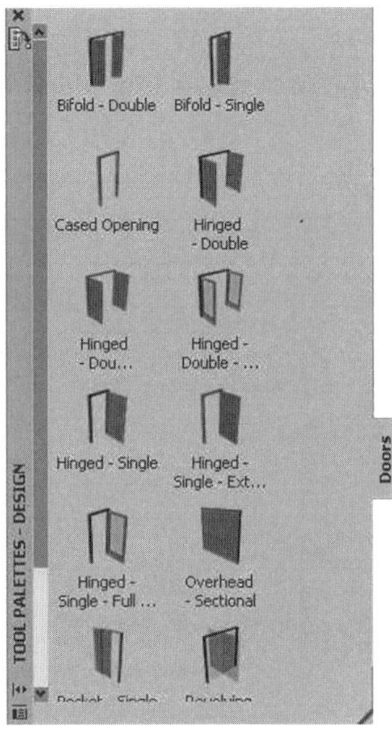

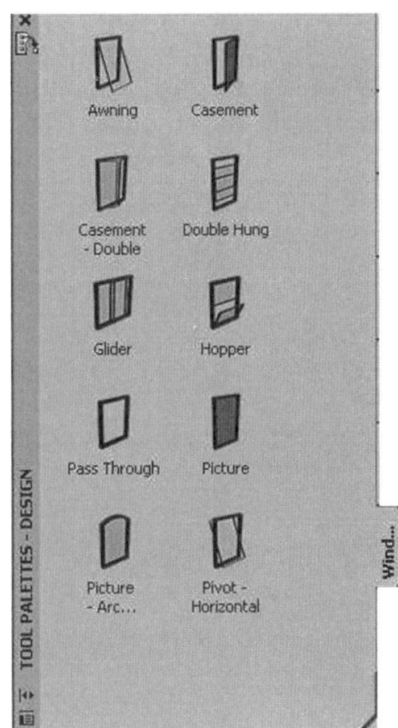

Figure 13.7 The Design Tool palette shows predefined styles for the wall, window, and door object types. Notice that the initial stylistic differences include type; that is, the window types are subcategorized into awning, casement, glider, picture, and so on.

Style	Description
Brick-4 Brick-4	4" Brick and 4" Brick Wall
Brick-4 Brick-4 Furring	4" Brick and 4" Brick Wall with 2" Furring
CMU-8	8" CMU Wall (Nominal)
CMU-8 Furring	8" CMU Wall
CMU-8 Rigid-1.5 Air-2 Brick-4	8" CMU Wall
CMU-8 Rigid-1.5 Air-2 Brick-4 Fur...	8" CMU Wall
Concrete-8	8" Concrete
Concrete-8 Concrete-16x8-footing	8" Concrete
Standard	
Stud-4	4" Stud Ptn.
Stud-4 GWB-0.625 2 Layers Each...	4" Stud Ptn.
Stud-4 GWB-0.625 Each Side	4" Stud Ptn.
Stud-4 Rigid-1.5 Air-1 Brick-4	4" Stud Cavit

Style	Description
Bifold - Double	Double bifold doors
Bifold - Single	Single bifold door
Cased Opening	Cased opening
Hinged - Double	Double hinged
Hinged - Double - Exterior	Double exterio
Hinged - Double - Full Lite	Double full glas
Hinged - Single	Single hinged c
Hinged - Single - Exterior	Single exterior
Hinged - Single - Full Lite	Single full glass
Overhead - Sectional	Overhead door
Pocket - Single	Single pocket c
Revolving - Simple	Simple revolvin
Standard	

Style	Description
Awning	Single Awning
Casement	Single Casement
Casement - Double	Double Casement
Double Hung	Double Hung
Glider	Gliding
Hopper	Single Hopper
Pass Through	Rectangular Pass Through
Picture	Rectangular Picture
Picture - Arched	Arched Picture
Pivot - Horizontal	Horizontal Pivot
Standard	

Figure 13.8 File-naming examples that ADT uses for its styles

Creating a New Style Based on an Existing Style

To create a new style that is based on an existing style, use the CopyAndAssignStyle command (found in the object's right-click menu) or Copy/Paste tools within the Style Manager.

The CopyAndAssignStyle command is accessed through any selected object's right-click menu. The style of the selected object is duplicated and the Style Manager automatically opens for editing (Figure 13.9). The Copy/Paste procedure within the Style Manager is illustrated in Figure 13.10.

> **Box 13.1**
> Notice that when the CopyAndAssign Style command is used, the duplicated style is named the same as its original adding a number in parenthesis to the end of the name.

Technique to Master **T13.09** Using the CopyAndAssignStyle Command to Create a New Style Based on an Existing Style

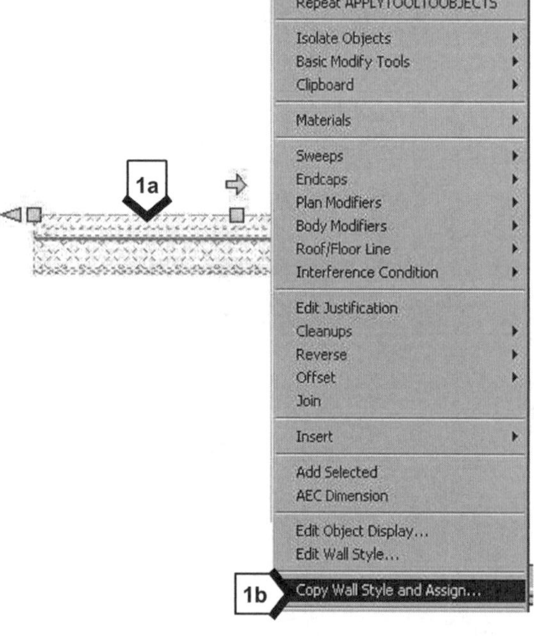

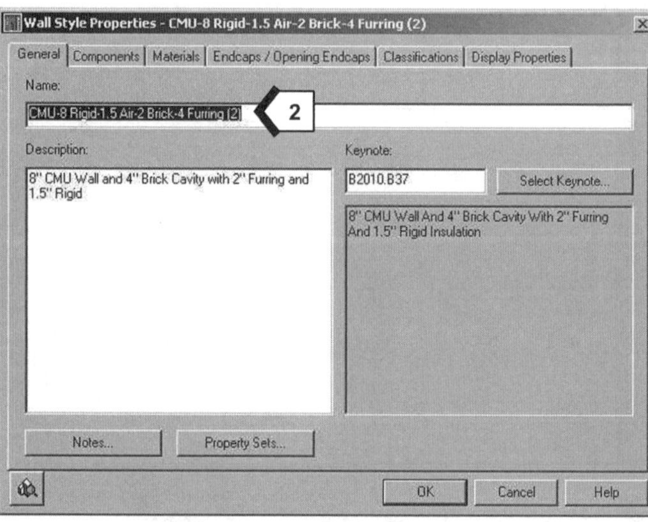

Figure 13.9

1a, 1b	[Drawing Screen]	Select an object whose style assignment you want to duplicate. Right-click and choose the CopyAndAssignStyle command.
2	[Object's Style Manager>General tab]	Rename the style.

Technique to Master **T13.10** Creating a New Style Using Copy/Paste Within the Style Manager

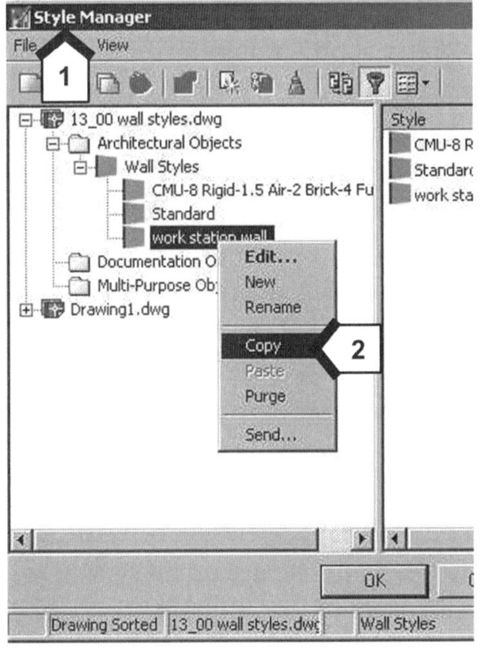

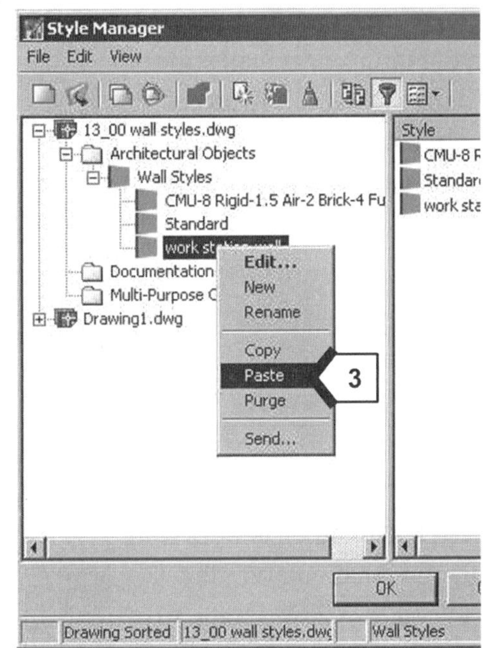

Figure 13.10

1	Open the Style Manager.	
2	[Style Manager]	Left-click on the style, then right-click and choose the Copy command.
3	[Style Manager]	Left-click on the style again, then right-click and choose the Paste command.
4	[Style Manager]	The object style is duplicated. Rename the duplicated version of the style.
5	[Style Manager]	Edit the duplicated style to make any necessary changes.

Creating Object Specific Styles

The following section focuses on style creation specific to walls, windows, doors, and mass objects.

Wall Styles

The Standard wall style appears as only two lines. It has no materials or hatching assigned to it, and its property width is changeable (Figure 13.11). You might start with this wall style at the beginning of a design project. As the design progresses, however, added detail might be needed to evaluate the constructability of your design intentions. This next section explores the complexity of creating wall styles that use multiple components.

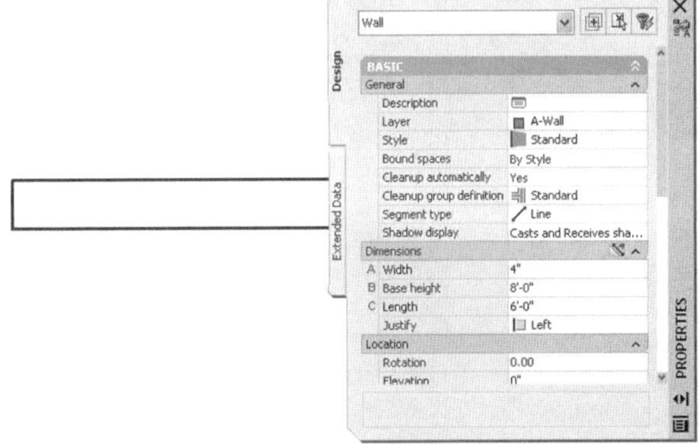

Figure 13.11 The Standard wall style appears as only two lines. It has no materials or hatching assigned to it, and its property width is changeable.

Building Your Own Wall Assemblies (Wall Styles)

In Chapter 11, you had a chance to practice placing walls; the next step is to learn to create wall styles. When defining a new wall style, the first step is to define the wall's individual components. To help you become familiar with the component, material, and display tabs, draw two walls.

> **Box 13.2**
> Remember, wall styles allow for the creation of different types of wall systems.

First, create and name the brick veneer wall style. It is recommended that you remain consistent with ADT's file-naming standards shown earlier this chapter. In the left pane of the Style Manager, left-click on the Brick Veneer style; in the right pane of the Style Manager, left-click on the Component Tab (Figure 13.12).

Understanding the Components Tab

The components of a wall refer to the individual materials that make up the wall system. For every material (including air spaces) that is a part of a wall assembly, a component is created to represent that material. All ADT wall components have an identifiable name and number, a priority number, a component width, and a location. These properties are described in Table 13.1. Wall components may go the full height of the wall or only remain partial height. Figure 13.13 identifies where each of these properties are located within the component pane.

Each wall component's location is always related to a baseline, also referred to as the datum line of a wall. The datum line is where you begin offsetting the components to create the component width (Figure 13.14).

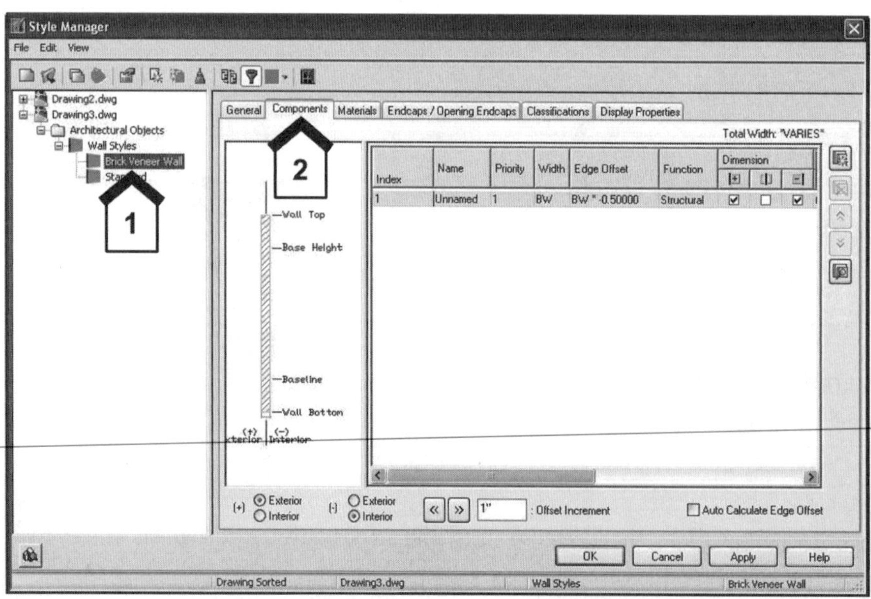

Figure 13.12 The Component tab of the newly created brick veneer wall

Table 13.1 Understanding the Properties of Components

Settings for Each Component	Description of Setting
Index	A unique random number that becomes the identifier for the component
Name	A short descriptive name for the component
Priority	Priorities are another layer of wall cleanup. Components with the same priority will clean up to each other. Lower priority values take precedence over higher values.
Width	Determines the width of the component. Widths that are specified as BW allows the component's width to change during wall placement.
Edge offset	The distance of the component from the baseline
Function	Categorizes the component as structural or nonstructural. For example, the wood stud component within a wall definition would be considered structural while the gyp-board finish would not.
Dimension	Sets the method for dimensioning the component. Note: Choices include dimension inside, dimension center, and dimension outside.
Bottom elevation	Sets component's bottom elevation
Top elevation	Sets component's top elevation

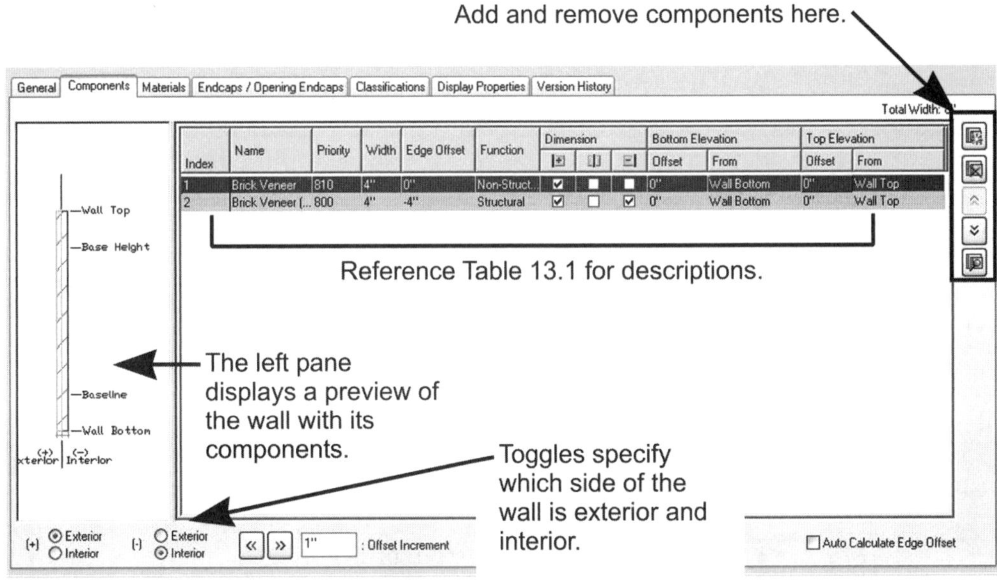

Figure 13.13 The various areas of the Component tab in the Wall Styles dialogue

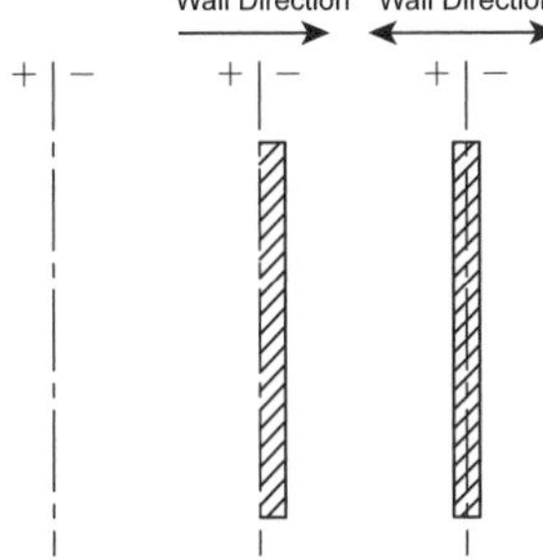

Figure 13.14 Each component's location is always related to a baseline, also referred as the datum line of wall. The datum line is the area from where you begin offsetting the components.

Cleanup Between Wall Components

Cleanup between wall components is determined by the priority number that a component is set to. Wall components that have the same priority number will clean up while components with differing values will not. The lower priority numbers have precedence over higher values (Figure 13.15). When creating a wall style, be attentive to the priority numbers set for each component. Whenever possible, try to match ADT's default priority list shown in Table 13.2.

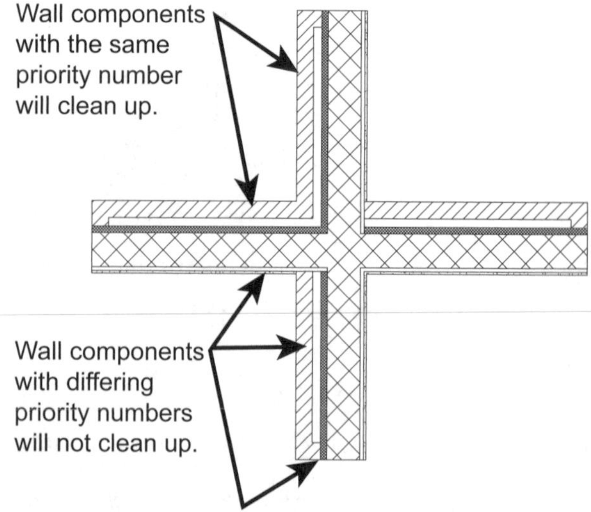
Wall components with the same priority number will clean up.
Wall components with differing priority numbers will not clean up.

Figure 13.15 Wall components that have the same priority number clean up while components with differing values do not. The lower priority numbers have precedence over higher values.

Creating the Brick Veneer Wall

Brick veneer wall systems are a popular choice in both residential and commercial design applications. Brick homes are popular because they are low maintenance, bug-resistant, and energy efficient. Appendix L lists some references to learn more about masonry design and construction. Figure 13.16 shows a section through a system that uses 3⁵⁄₈" brick veneer

Table 13.2 The Wall Component Priorities

Component Index	ADT Default Priority (Additional Recommended Priorities Are Set in Italics)	Component Index	ADT Default Priority (Additional Recommended Priorities Are Set in Italics)
Air gap	700	Concrete (footing)	200
Air gap (brick/brick)	805	Glass	1200
Air gap (cmu/cmu)	305	GWB	1200
Air gap (stud/stud)	505	GWB (X)	1200, 1210, 1220, 1230
Brick	800		
Brick veneer	810	Insulation (cmu/brick, stud/brick)	600
Bulkhead	1800		
Casework-backsplash	2030	*Metal panel*	*1000*
Casework-base	2010	Precast panel	400
Casework-counter	2020	*Rigid insulation (brick)*	*404*
Casework-upper	2000	*Siding*	*900*
cmu	300	Stucco	1100
cmu veneer	350	Stud	500
Concrete	200	Toilet partition	3000

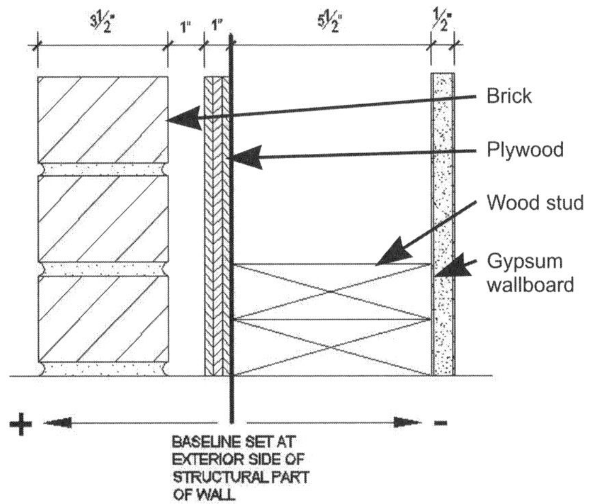

Figure 13.16 Example section through a brick veneer wall system that uses $3\frac{5}{8}$" brick veneer with a 1" airspace, sheathing, and wood studs.

with a 1" airspace, sheathing, and wood studs. This system is mostly used in residential applications because of its wood structure. The airspace is used to allow water that penetrates the brick masonry to drain easily to the ground. Masonry ties anchor the veneer to the wood studs. Plywood sheathing along with the wood studs create the structural envelope. On the inside, gypsum board is usually used (painted) to provide the finished wall surface. Figure 13.17 demonstrates creating the components for the brick veneer wall system.

Technique to Master **T13.17** Creating the Components for the Brick Veneer Wall System

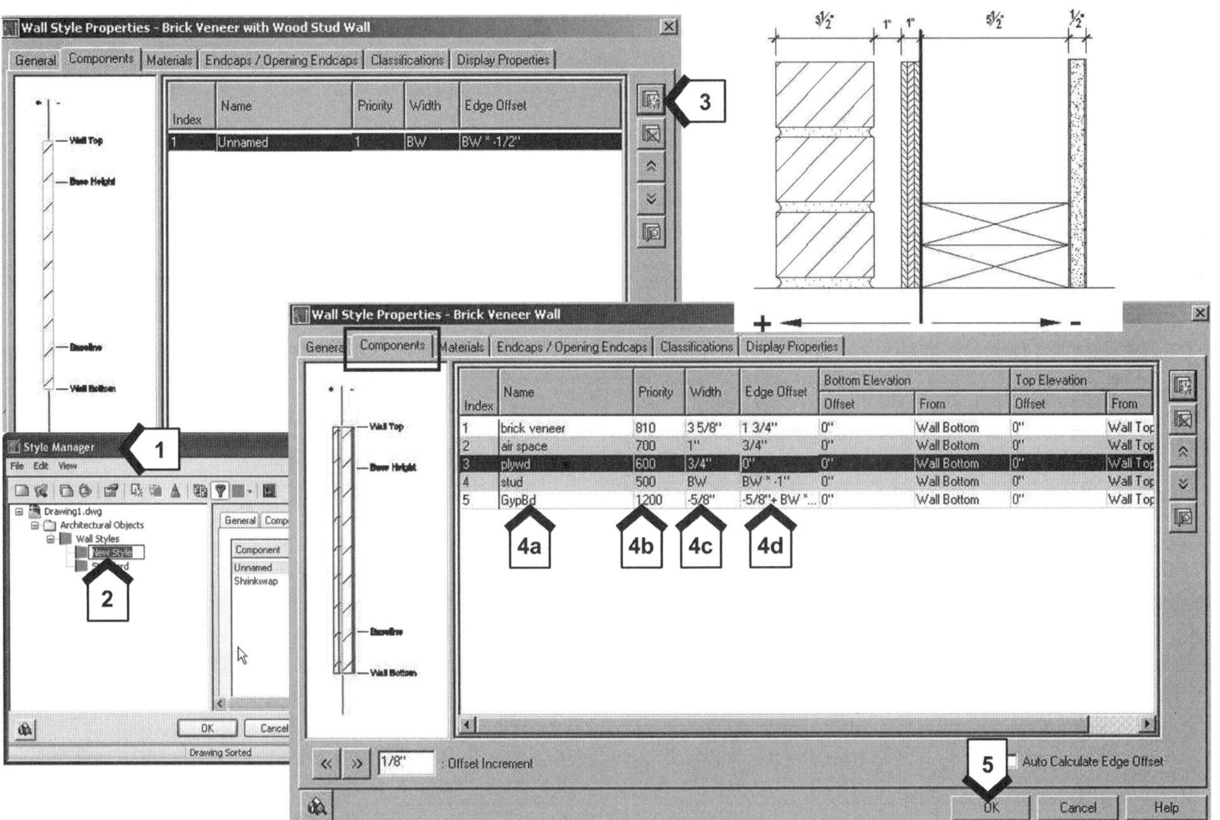

Figure 13.17

1	Open the Wall Style Manager.	
2	[Wall Style Manager]	Create a new wall style and name it.
3	[Wall Style Manager> Components tab]	Create the individual components that make up the brick veneer wall system by adding each component using the Add Component button.
4a, 4b, 4c, 4d	[Wall Style Manager> Components tab]	Name each component, and assign priorities, width, and edge offsets. Use the illustration above for guidance.
5	[Wall Style Manager]	Click OK to complete the command.

After the components of the wall are created, they must be assigned materials and display properties. Rendering materials can be quickly assigned to each wall component through the Materials tab. See the topic "Materials, Display Properties, and the ADT Objects" at the end of this chapter for a more in-depth understanding of material definitions and object display. Figure 13.18 demonstrates how to assign a material definition to each wall component. Figure 13.19 demonstrates the procedure for controlling how the components display in plan, ceiling, section, and elevation views.

Technique to Master **T13.18** Assigning Material Definitions to the Wall Components

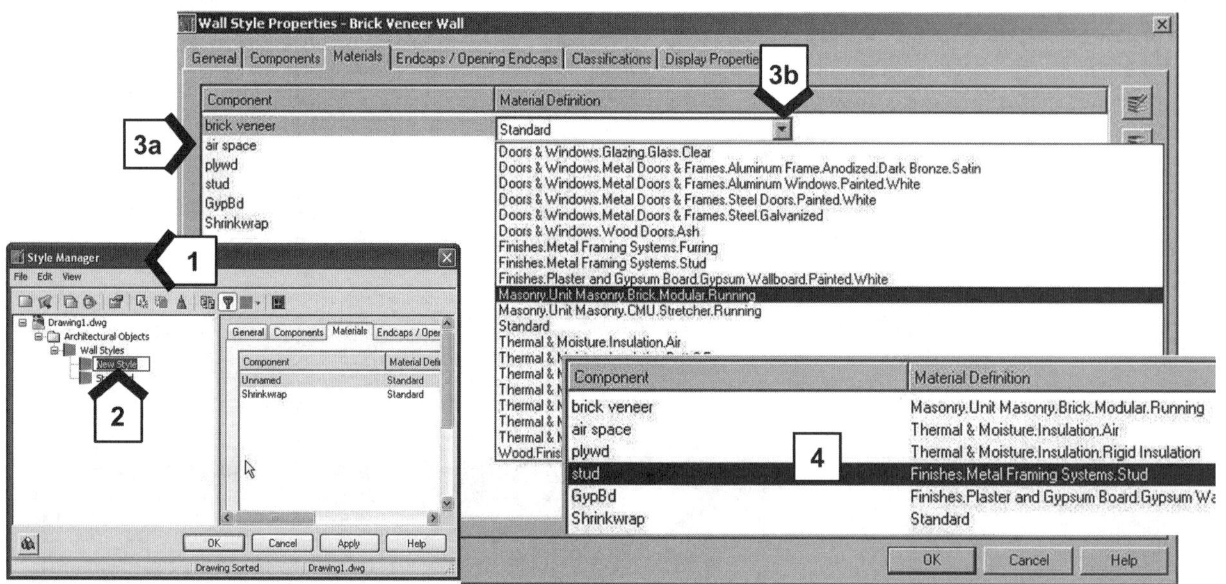

Figure 13.18

1	Open the Wall Style Manager.	
2	[Wall Style Manager]	In left pane, select an existing wall style (or create a new style).
3a, 3b	[Wall Style Manager> Materials tab]	Assign a material definition for each component. If desired materials definitions do not exist, either import existing material definitions from the Content Browser (see Technique T13.59) or create a new material definition.
4	[Wall Style Manager> Materials tab]	Example of all wall components assigned appropriate material definitions.

Technique to Master **T13.19** Controlling How the Wall Components Appear in Plan, Ceiling, and Section/Elevation Views

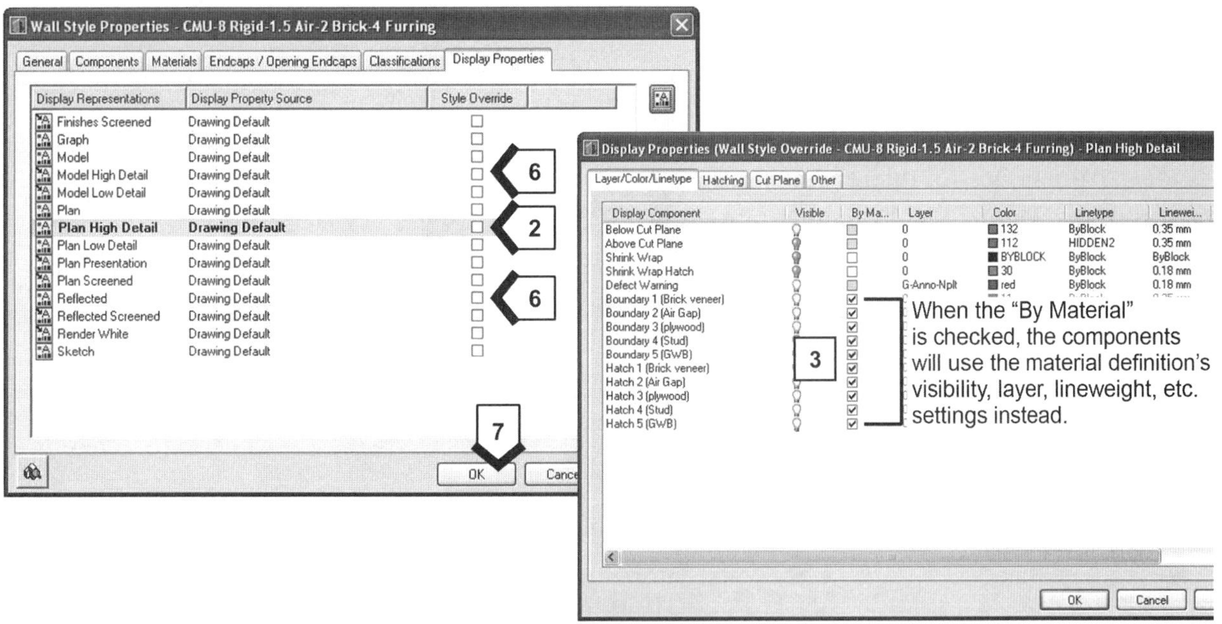

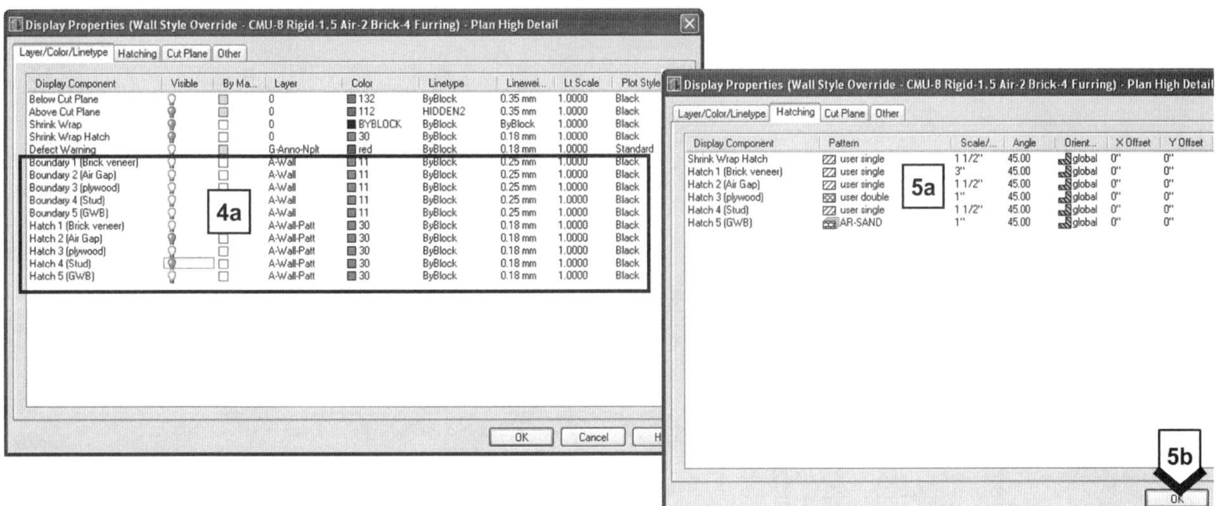

Figure 13.19

The following technique overrides the default wall display for the selected wall style.		
1	Open the Wall Style.	
2	[Wall Style>Display Properties tab]	Check the box next to Plan High Detail to open the Display Properties for the Plan View of the wall style. (If it's already checked, select Display Representation and left-click on the Edit Display Properties button.)
3	[Wall Style>Display Properties>Wall Style Override>Layer tab]	Notice that by default the components use the material definition's settings. Uncheck to have the component's visibility, layer, lineweight, and so on controlled through the wall style instead.
4	[Wall Style>Display Properties>Wall Style Override>Layer tab]	For each component and component hatch, adjust the visibility, layer, lineweight, and plotstyle settings.
5a, 5b	[Wall Style>Display Properties>Wall Style Override>Hatching tab]	For each component where appropriate, choose a hatch pattern and hatch scaling. Choose OK to apply changes.
6	[Wall Style>Display Properties tab]	Repeat for the Model and Reflected Display Representations.
7	[Wall Style>Display Properties tab]	Choose OK to apply changes.

Creating a Plaster Wall System

Used frequently in the Western United States for both residential and commercial applications, this wall system is made up of the plaster system, exterior sheathing, and the metal or wood stud structure (Figure 13.20). Refer to Appendix L for references on plaster wall systems. Figure 13.21 demonstrates how the wall system is represented as wall components within a wall style.

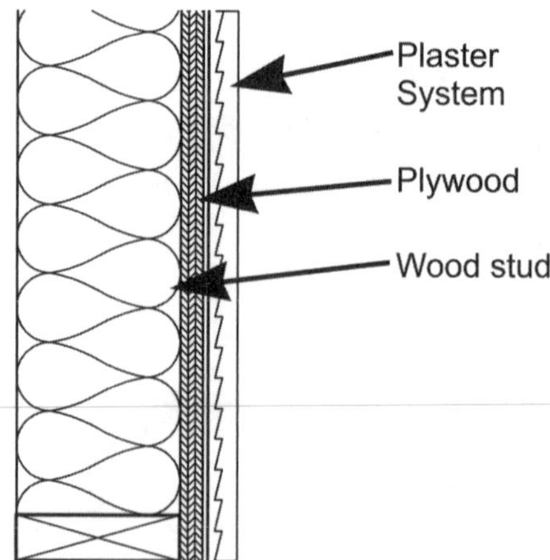

Figure 13.20 Example section through a plaster wall system that uses plaster, sheathing, and wood studs

Technique to Master **T13.21** Creating the Components for the Plaster Wall System

Figure 13.21

1	Open the Wall Style Manager.	
2	[Wall Style Manager]	Create a new wall style and name it.
3	[Wall Style Manager> Components tab]	Create the individual components that make up the brick veneer wall system by adding each component using the Add Component button.
4	[Wall Style Manager> Components tab]	Name each component, and assign priorities, width, and edge offsets. Use the illustration above for guidance.
5	[Wall Style Manager]	Click OK to complete the command.

Door and Window Styles

There are more than 25 door and window styles available in ADT through the Design palette. Additional door and window styles can be easily created when these existing styles are not enough. This topic emphasizes style creation specific to the door and window objects.

The Style Manager for door and window objects looks very similar to the Style Manager of other ADT objects. There are tabs—General, Materials, Classifications, and Display Properties—that appear in all style-based ADT objects. You will notice that the door and window Style Manager also includes Dimensions, Design Rules, and Standard Sizes.

The Dimensions tab sets the dimensions for the door or window frame, stop, and glazing (Figure 13.22a).

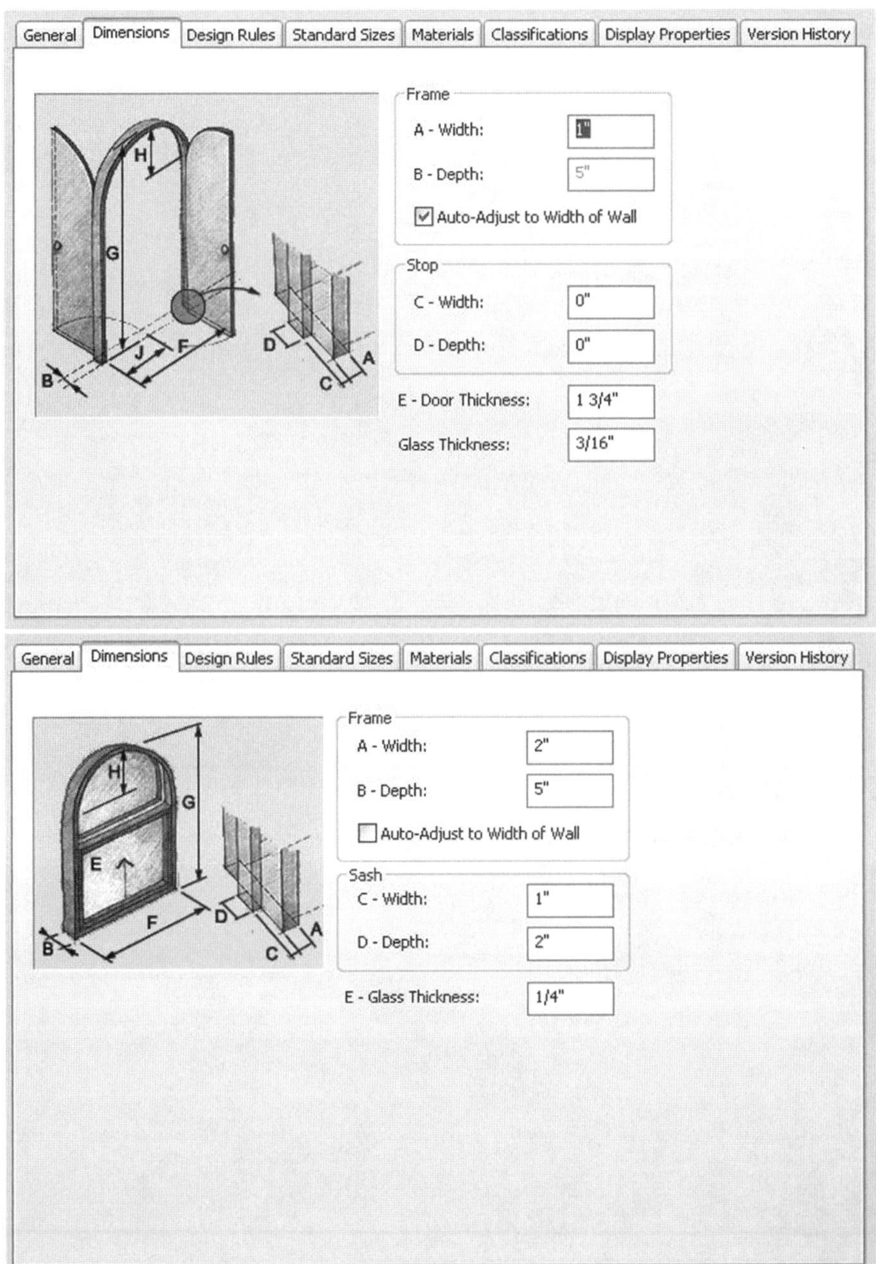

Figure 13.22a The Dimensions tab sets the dimensions for the door or window frame, stop, and glazing.

The Design Rules tab shows the available door (or window) types and also defines their shapes (Figure 13.22b). Besides the default rectangular shape, doors have five additional shape possibilities and windows have 12 additional shapes. When you need unique shapes, you can use a profile definition. (Refer to Chapter 10 to review profile definitions, concepts, and techniques).

In the Standard Size tab, you can establish standard width and height sizes for the style (see Figure 13.22c).

Chapter 13 files on the CD-ROM demonstrate the procedure for creating two door and two window examples that are relevant to many residential and commercial design applications.

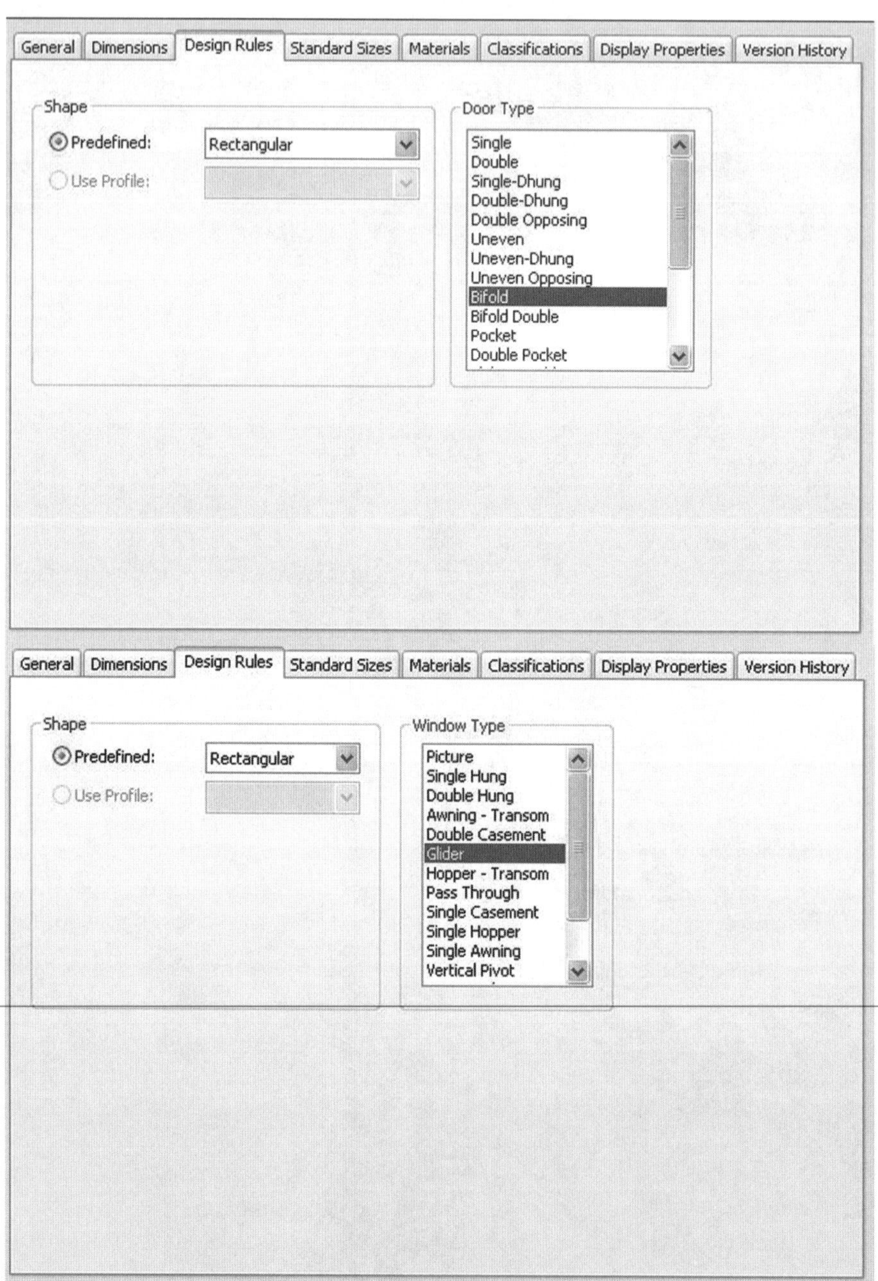

Figure 13.22b The Design Rules tab shows the available door (or window) types and also defines their shapes.

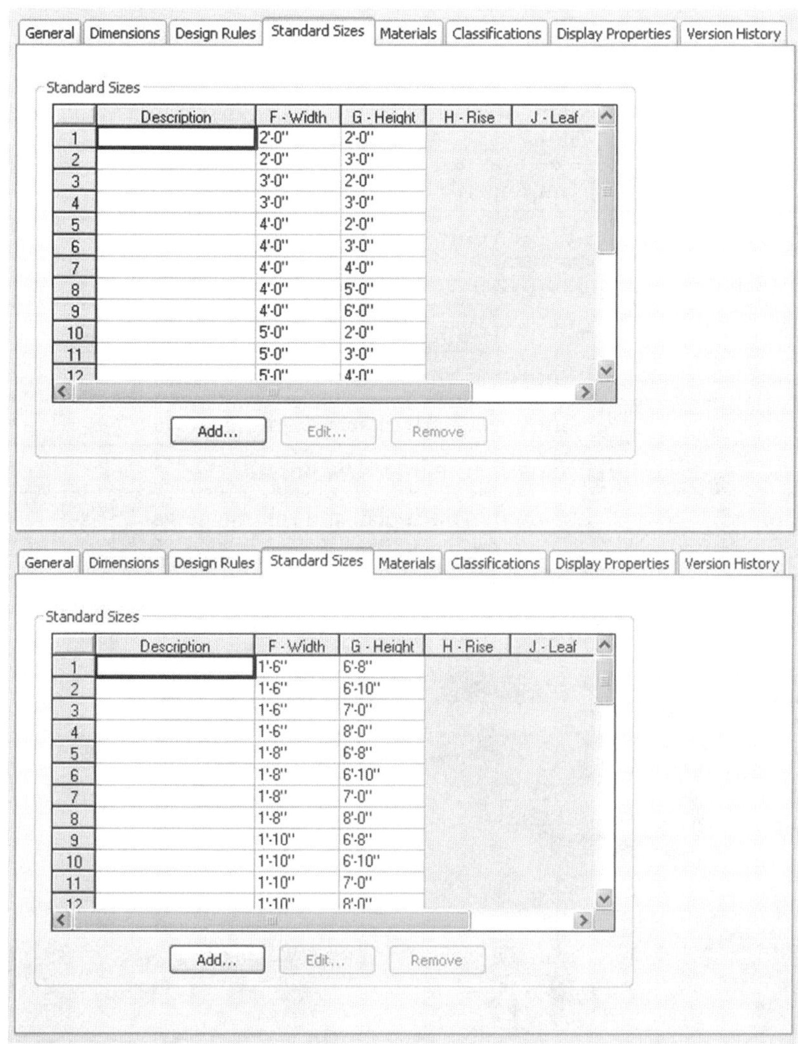

Figure 13.22c In the Standard Size tab, standard width and height sizes can be established for the style.

Mass Element Styles

Since mass elements and mass groups are used to create any building object that isn't part of the ADT library, the mass element styles are multifunctional. First, mass element styles are used to categorize building element types. A storefront canopy made with mass elements should have a different style from a file cabinet or light fixture. Second, mass element styles are used to assign rendering materials. The mass element style called file cabinet-black metal might have the black metal material assigned to it, while the mass element style called file cabinet-gray metal might have the gray metal material assigned to it. Finally, mass element styles are used for the correct display of objects in plan view. For example, built-in upper cabinets should be dashed in plan view—therefore, the mass element style should reflect this in its Display Properties. Table 13.3 lists possible uses for mass elements and mass groups. Figure 13.23 provides a summary of steps to create a mass element style. At the end of the chapter, there is a discussion on tips for using mass elements for furniture, casework, and light fixtures, including setting up the materials and display properties for these various style conditions.

Table 13.3 Style Tips for Mass Elements

The following represents a list of possible uses for mass elements and mass groups. It also shows how style differentiation of mass elements helps to control mass element display for the specific type.	
Mass elements used for furniture	Shown only in plan view
Mass elements for lower casework and cabinetry	Shown only in plan view
Mass elements for upper casework and cabinetry	Shown in both plan and ceiling views
Mass elements for equipment below counters	Shown only in plan view, with a hidden line
Mass elements for upper shelving	Shown in both plan and ceiling views
Mass elements for light sconces	Shown in both plan and ceiling views
Mass elements for ceiling light fixtures	Shown in ceiling view only
Mass elements for canopies and sunscreens	Shown in both plan and ceiling views

Technique to Master **T13.23** Creating Mass Element Styles

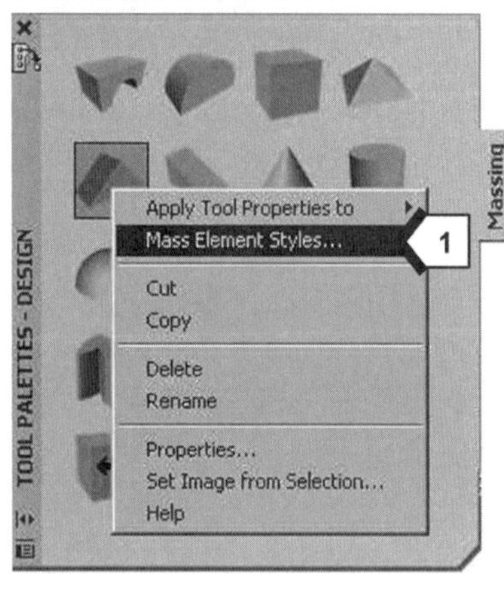

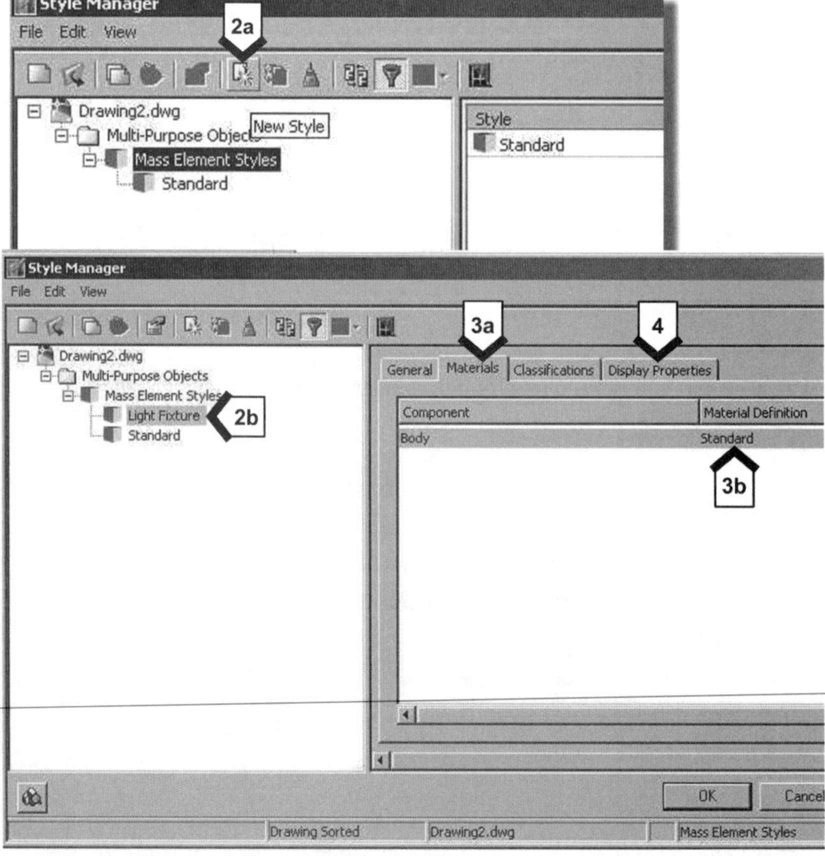

Figure 13.23

1	[Design Tool palette>Massing tab]	Right-click on any mass element primitive, and choose the Mass Element Styles command.
2a, 2b	[Massing Style Manager]	Click on the new button to add a new mass element style and name it.
3a, 3b	[Massing Style Manager>Materials tab]	Assign appropriate material to the mass element style. Review the section on material definitions in this chapter.
4	[Massing Style Manager>Display Properties tab]	Verify/change display properties for the mass element style.

Creating Custom Wall Shapes

Once you have created your basic wall types (wall styles), more advanced customization is possible through other types of specialty wall commands.

Roof/Floor Line

The Roof/floor line wall modifier creates complex elevational wall shapes. Examples of Roof/floor line modifications include stepped-shaped and gable-shaped wall elevations. Similar to polyline vertex editing discussed in Chapter 5, vertices are used to create new corners on the wall's elevation (Figure 13.24). You can access the Roof/floor line modifier dialogue box by first selecting a wall and then left-clicking the Roof/floor line property in the Properties palette (Figure 13.25a). Roof/floor line modifications can also be made directly on-screen using the wall's hidden menu command (Figure 13.25b).

The dialogue for Roof/floor line modifications defaults to the roof-line editing mode. Use the buttons identified in Figure 13.26 to toggle between roof editing and floor editing. Figures 13.27 and 13.28 illustrate how to use the Vertex Editing dialogue. Chapter 13 files on the CD-ROM demonstrate roof and floor line editing to create four common wall shapes. Figure 13.29 shows you the technique for creating a workstation wall.

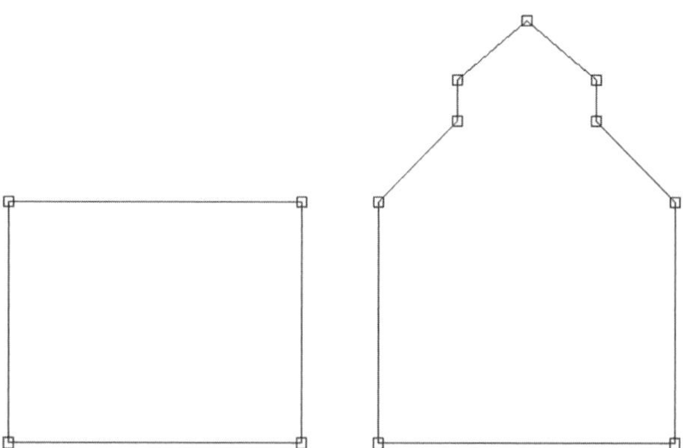

Figure 13.24 Vertices are used to create new corners on the wall's elevation.

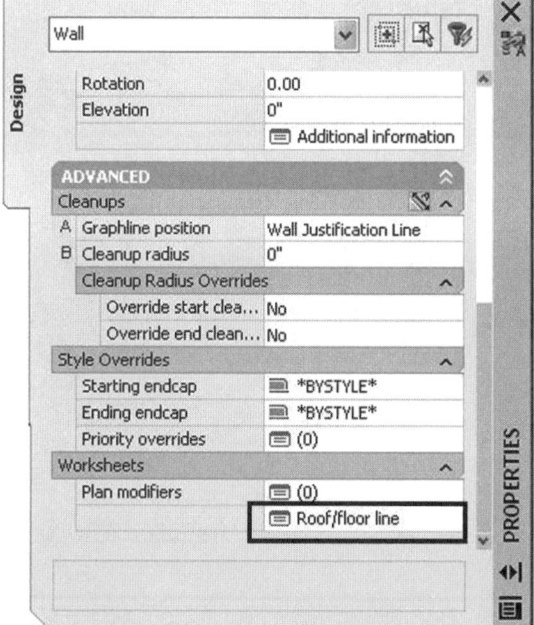

Figure 13.25a The Roof/floor line modifier dialogue box can be accessed through the Wall Properties palette.

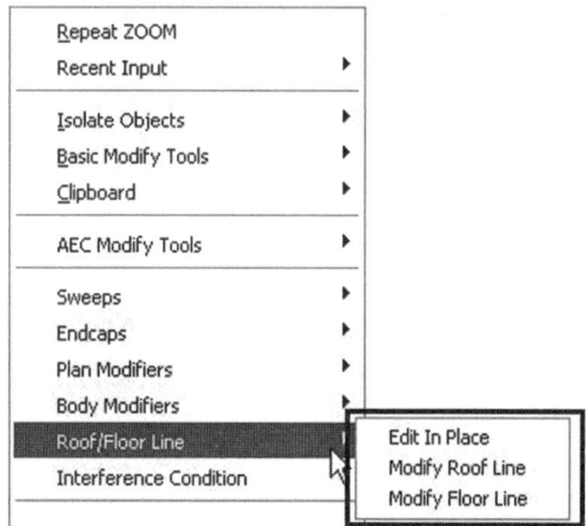

Figure 13.25b The Roof/floor line modifier dialogue box can be accessed through the wall's right-click menu.

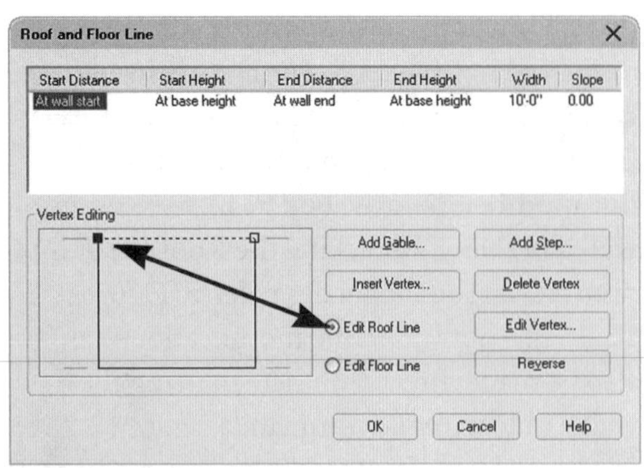
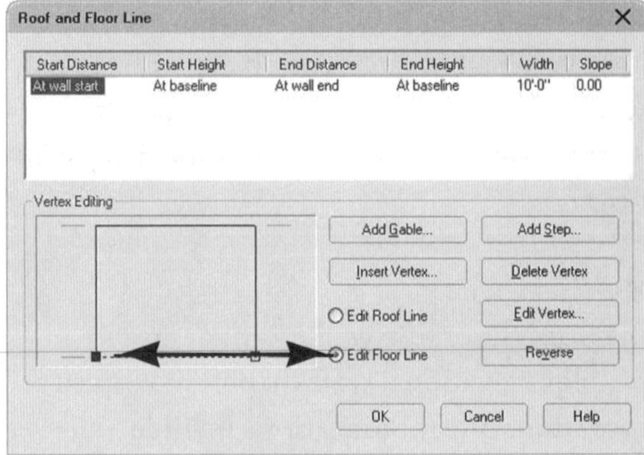

Figure 13.26 Use the Edit Roof Line and Edit Floor Line buttons to toggle between roof-editing and floor-editing modes.

Technique to Master **T13.27** Editing the Location of Existing Vertices of a Wall Elevation

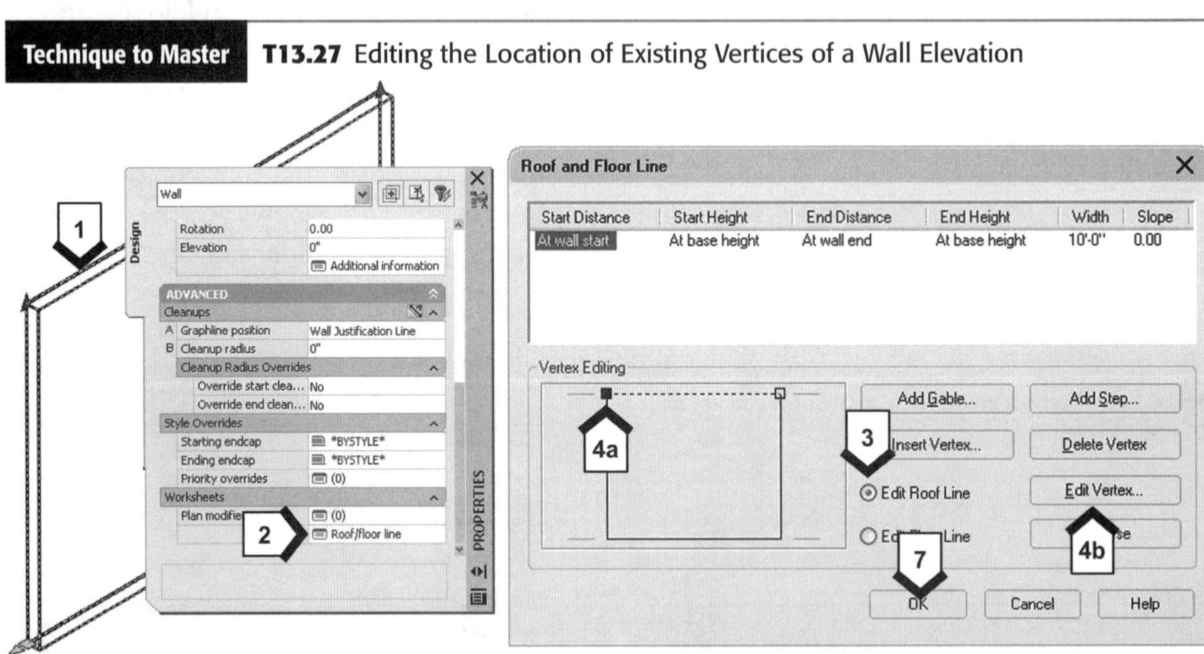

Figure 13.27

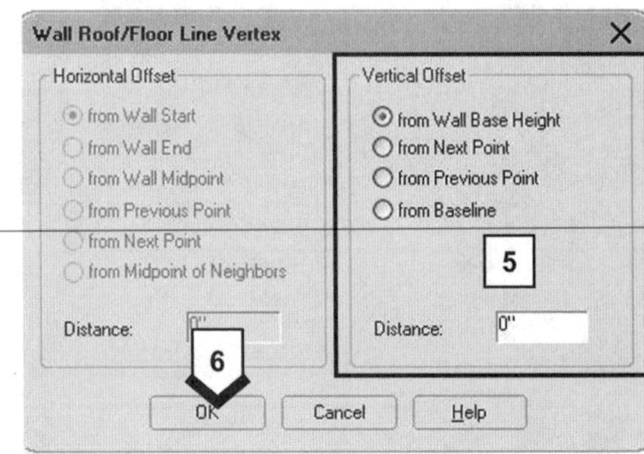

1	[Drawing Screen]	Select an existing wall.
2	[Properties palette]	Use the Properties palette to open the Roof/floor line modifier.
3	[Roof and Floor Line dialogue box]	Select appropriate roof or floor editing button.
4a, 4b	[Roof and Floor Line dialogue box]	Select an existing vertex to edit, then left-click on the edit button.
5	[Wall Roof/Floor Line Vertex dialogue box]	Set the vertical offset reference point and offset distance for the selected vertex. The right side shows options to relocate the vertex vertically along the wall's height.
6	[Wall Roof/Floor Line Vertex dialogue box]	Click OK to exit.
7	[Roof and Floor Line dialogue box]	Click OK to complete the command.

Technique to Master **T13.28** Adding New Vertices to a Wall Elevation

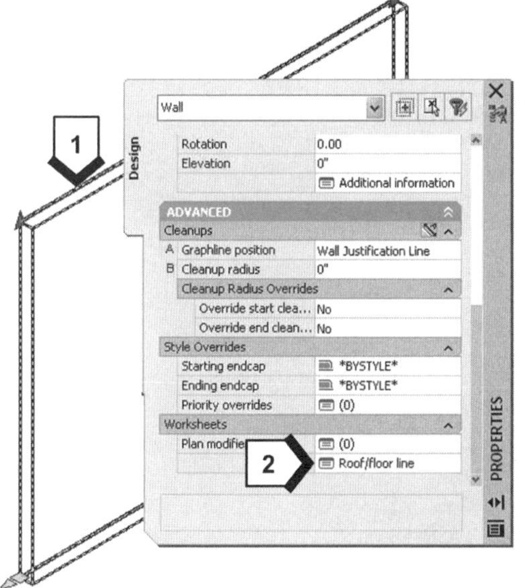

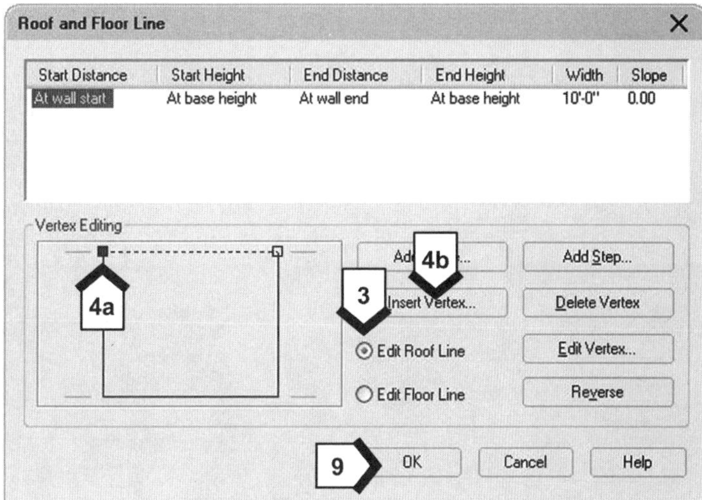

Figure 13.28

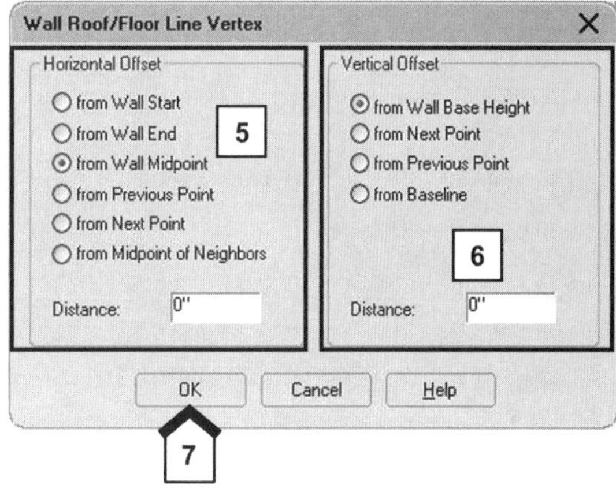

Select an appropriate roof or floor editing button.		
1	[Drawing Screen]	Select an existing wall.
2	[Properties palette]	Use the Properties palette to open Roof/floor line modifier.
3	[Roof and Floor Line dialogue box]	Select appropriate roof or floor editing button.
4	[Roof and Floor Line dialogue box]	Select an existing vertex, then left-click on the insert vertex button. Remember, new vertices must always be added to the right of an existing vertex.
5	[Wall Roof/Floor Line Vertex dialogue box]	Set the horizontal offset reference point and offset distance for the selected vertex. The left side shows options to relocate the vertex horizontally along the wall's length.
6	[Wall Roof/Floor Line Vertex dialogue box]	Set the vertical offset reference point and offset the distance for the selected vertex. The right side shows options to relocate the vertex vertically along the wall's height.
7	[Wall Roof/Floor Line Vertex dialogue box]	Click OK to exit.
8	[Roof and Floor Line dialogue box]	Continue adding vertices until the desired shape is completed.
9	[Roof and Floor Line dialogue box]	Click Ok to complete command.

Technique to Master **T13.29** Creating a Workstation Wall

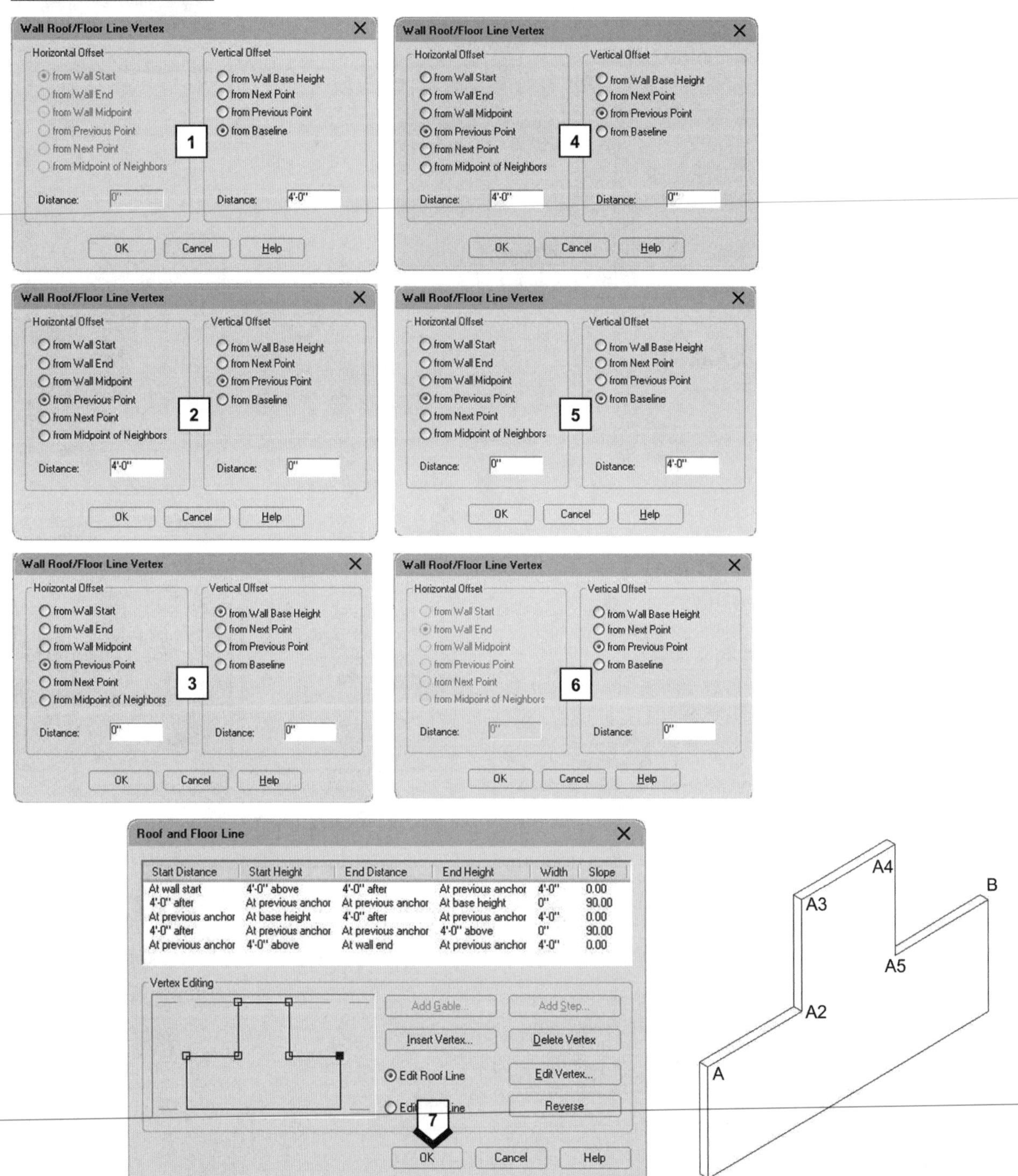

Figure 13.29

1	[Wall Roof/Floor Line Vertex dialogue box]	Edit vertex A using the illustrated parameters.
2	[Wall Roof/Floor Line Vertex dialogue box]	Insert vertex A2 using the illustrated parameters.
3	[Wall Roof/Floor Line Vertex dialogue box]	Insert vertex A3 using the illustrated parameters.
4	[Wall Roof/Floor Line Vertex dialogue box]	Insert vertex A4 using the illustrated parameters.
5	[Wall Roof/Floor Line Vertex dialogue box]	Insert vertex A5 using the illustrated parameters.
6	[Wall Roof/Floor Line Vertex dialogue box]	Edit vertex B using the illustrated parameters.
7	[Roof and Floor Line dialogue box]	Click OK to complete workstation wall.

Plan Modifiers

Plan modifiers create wall protrusions by extruding a 2-D shape along the wall height (Figure 13.30). Plan modifiers make excellent wainscots, ribbed wall surfaces, and corrugated wall panels. They add additional thickness to the wall at defined areas. The easiest method for creating plan modifiers is to first create a 2-D polyline that becomes the modifier. Note that the created polyline must remain an open polyline and must be drawn at the location of the wall (Figure 13.31). Figure 13.32 demonstrates the technique for creating a ribbed wall.

Plan modifiers can be full or partial height extrusions. They can start at the baseline of the wall and extend upward or start at the top of the wall and extend downward. See the Chapter 13 folder on the CD-ROM to learn to create a wood-paneled wainscot using plan modifiers.

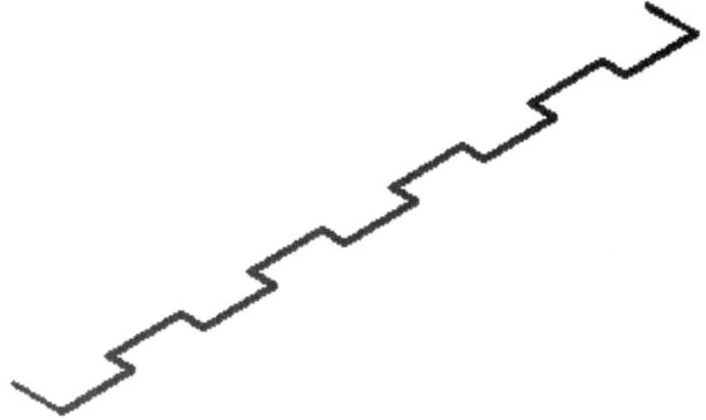

Figure 13.31 Use a 2-D polyline for the plan modifier. Note that the created polyline must remain an open polyline and must be drawn at the location of the wall.

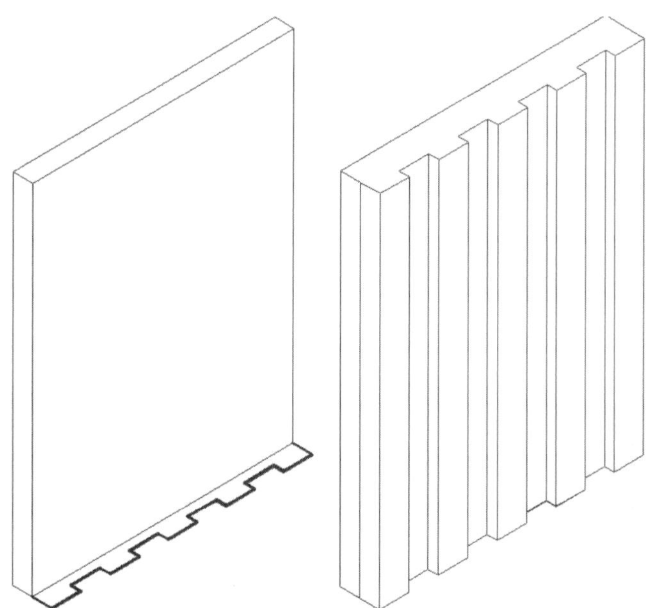

Figure 13.30 Plan modifiers create wall protrusions by extruding a 2-D shape along the wall height.

Technique to Master **T13.32** Creating and Assigning a Plan Modifier to an Existing Wall

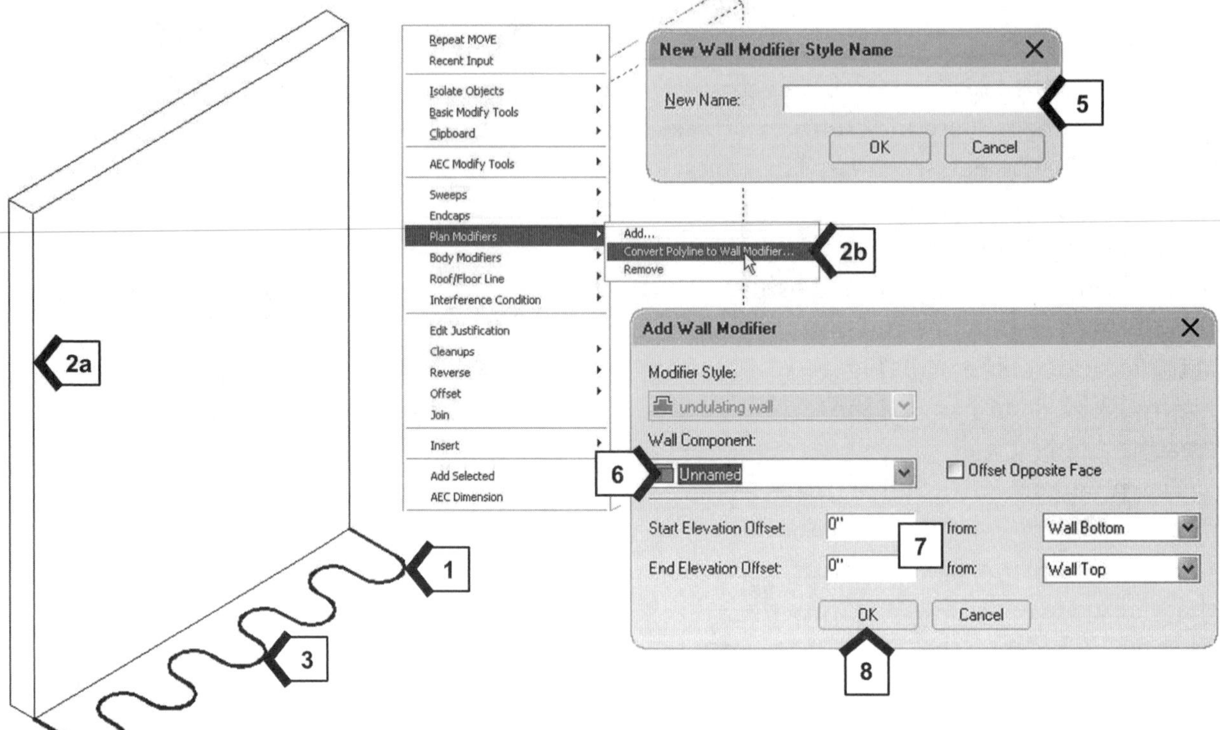

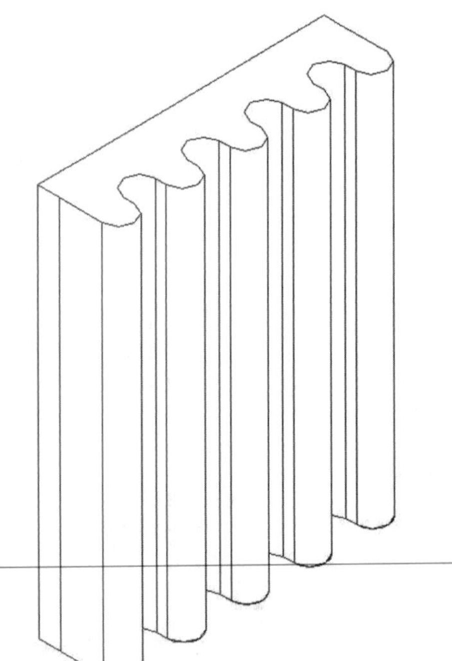

Figure 13.32

1	[Drawing Screen]	Draw a polyline at the location of the wall. (The polyline must be open and must start and end at the surface of the wall)
2a, 2b	[Drawing Screen]	Select the wall to which you want to attach the modifier, right-click, and choose Plan Modifier>Convert Polyline to Wall Modifier.
3	[Drawing Screen]	Select the polyline.
4	[Command Line]	Type Y (Yes) to erase original polyline or N (No) to keep the polyline in the drawing.
5	[New Wall Modifier Style Name dialogue box]	Name the wall Modifier Style. Click OK to apply name.
6	[Add Wall Modifier dialogue box]	Specify the wall component to which the wall modifier will be applied.
7	[Add Wall Modifier dialogue box]	Specify the wall modifier's sill height and head height. By default the wall modifier will run from floor to ceiling.
8	[Add Wall Modifier dialogue box]	Click OK to apply wall modifier.

Sweeps

Wall sweeps change the sectional profile of a wall. Irregularly shaped wall widths, such as canted walls, are perfect examples of wall sweeps (Figure 13.33). Wall sweeps use profile definitions to create the sectional profile of a wall. (Refer to Chapter 10 to review profile definition concepts and techniques.) Figure 13.34 demonstrates how to apply a wall sweep to an existing wall. Figure 13.35 creates a bar design using wall sweeps, and Figure 13.36 uses a wall sweep to create a wall cornice.

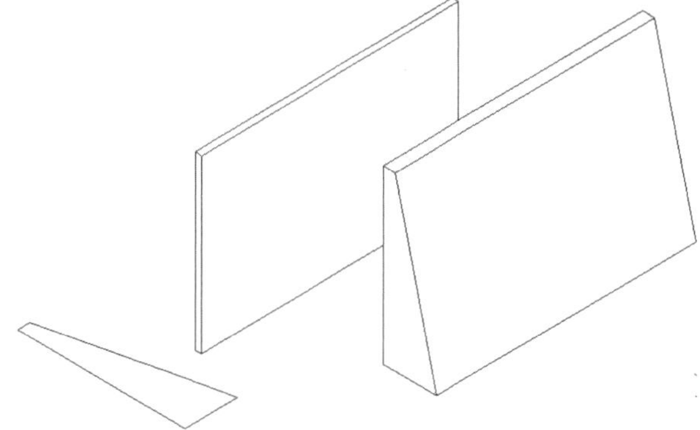

Figure 13.33 Wall sweeps changes the sectional profile of a wall. Irregularly shaped wall widths like canted walls are perfect examples of wall sweeps.

Technique to Master **T13.34** Creating and Assigning a Wall Sweep to an Existing Wall

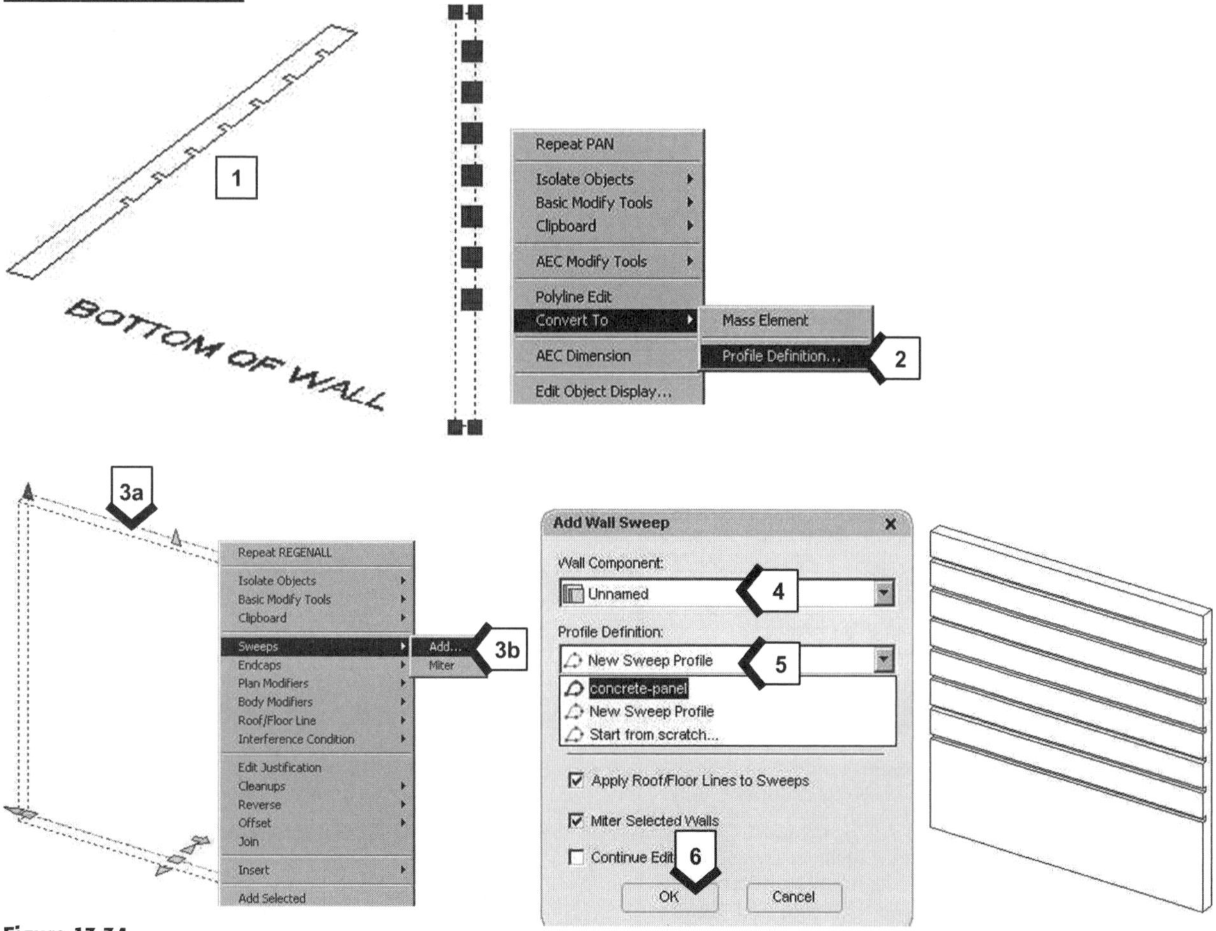

Figure 13.34

1	[Drawing Screen]	Draw a closed polyline that represents the wall's sectional profile.
2	[Drawing Screen]	Create a profile definition using the closed polyline. Refer to Technique T10.09.
3a, 3b	[Drawing Screen]	Choose a wall and right-click to access Sweeps>Add command.
4	[Add Wall Sweep dialogue box]	If the wall has more than one component, specify the component to which the wall sweep will be applied.
5	[Add Wall Sweep dialogue box]	Select the correct profile definition.
6	[Add Wall Sweep dialogue box]	Click OK to apply wall sweep.

Technique to Master T13.35 Creating a Custom Bar Base Using a Wall Sweep

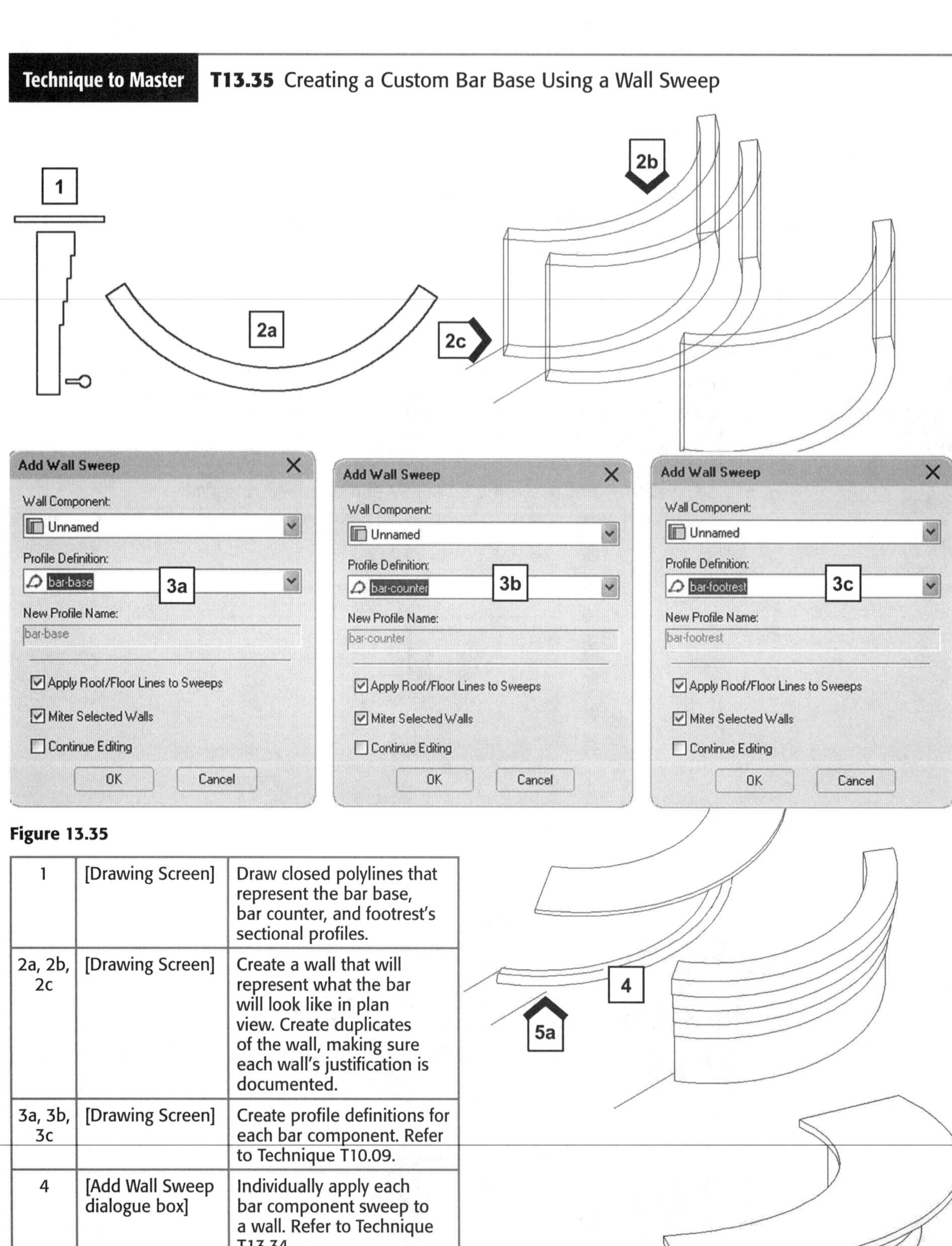

Figure 13.35

1	[Drawing Screen]	Draw closed polylines that represent the bar base, bar counter, and footrest's sectional profiles.
2a, 2b, 2c	[Drawing Screen]	Create a wall that will represent what the bar will look like in plan view. Create duplicates of the wall, making sure each wall's justification is documented.
3a, 3b, 3c	[Drawing Screen]	Create profile definitions for each bar component. Refer to Technique T10.09.
4	[Add Wall Sweep dialogue box]	Individually apply each bar component sweep to a wall. Refer to Technique T13.34.
5a, 5b	[Drawing Screen]	Using insertion points, assemble the bar.

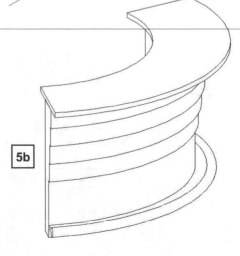

Technique to Master **T13.36** Creating Crown Molding Using a Wall Sweep

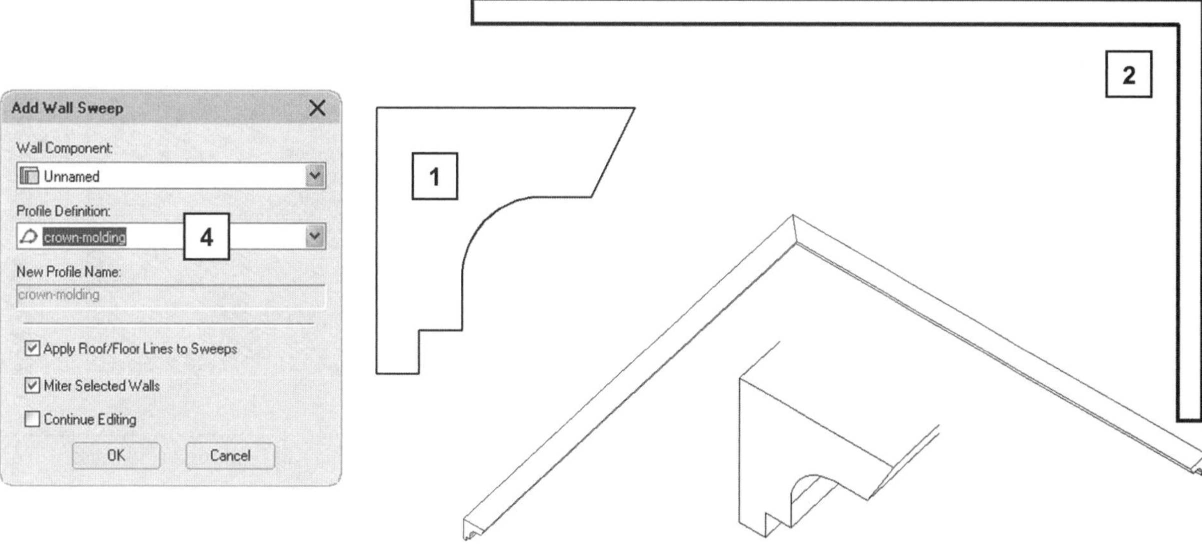

Figure 13.36

1	[Drawing Screen]	Draw closed polyline that represents the crown molding's sectional profiles.
2	[Drawing Screen]	Create the walls to which the crown molding sweep will be applied.
3	[Drawing Screen]	Create the profile definition for the molding. Refer to Technique T10.09.
4	[Add Wall Sweep Dialogueue]	Create the wall sweep by applying the profile definition. Refer to Technique T13.34.

Wall Interferences

There are many times when furniture and equipment are designed to be recessed or semi-recessed within a wall. Wall interference modifiers provide one option for creating the needed cutouts in walls. Before using this command, it is necessary to first create an object to be used as a cutout, an opening, or an add-on by using mass elements and mass groups. Figure 13.37 demonstrates how to apply interference conditions to an existing wall. Figure 13.38 demonstrates how to create the cutout in a wall so a bookcase can be recessed.

Box 13.3

Interference Conditions must always maintain a touching relationship with the wall for the interference to apply.

Technique to Master T13.37 Creating and Assigning an Interference Condition to an Existing Wall

Figure 13.37

1	[Drawing Screen]	Create the object to be used as a cutout, opening, or add-on. This can be done using mass elements and mass groups.
2	[Drawing Screen]	Place the object in the precise location that you want to use it. Interference Conditions must always involve touching the wall for the interference to apply.
3	[Drawing Screen]	Draw object(s). Locate object(s) in relation to wall.
4	[Drawing Screen]	Choose wall, right-click, and choose Interference Condition> Add.
5	[Drawing Screen]	Select the object(s) used as interferences.
6	[Command Line]	Type either A (for an Additive interference), S (for a Subtractive interference), or I (to Ignore).

Technique to Master T13.38 Insetting a Bookcase into an Existing Wall

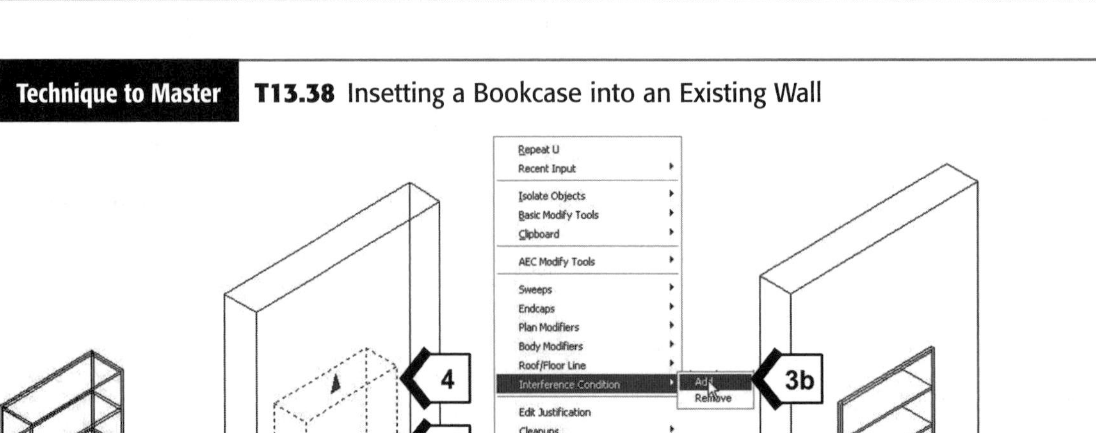

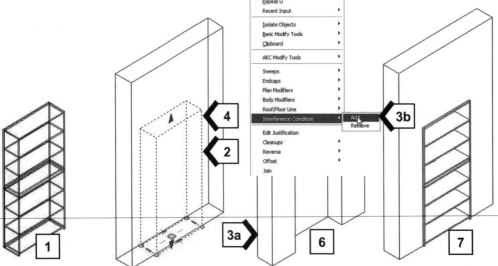

Figure 13.38a

1	[Drawing Screen]	Draw bookcase using mass elements.
2	[Drawing Screen]	Draw solid mass element (that will become subtractive interference) within wall.
3a, 3b	[Drawing Screen]	Choose wall, right-click, and choose the Interference Condition> Add command.
4	[Drawing Screen]	Select the object(s) used as interferences.
5	[Command Line]	Type S (for a Subtractive interference).
6	[Drawing Screen]	Freeze (using layer control) the mass element that represents subtractive interference.
7	[Drawing Screen]	Move the bookcase to desired location within wall.

Figure 13.38b Example of a bookcase inset into a wall (shown on the right).

Body Modifiers

Body Modifiers add or subtract objects from a wall (Figure 13.39). Wall reveals and wall joints in walls are excellent examples of Body Modifier applications (Figure 13.40). With Body Modifiers, you have the option of deleting your modifier object. All AEC objects may be used as objects to add or subtract. Figure 13.41 demonstrates how to apply Body Modifiers to an existing wall. Figure 13.42 creates a wood-paneled wall, and Figure 13.43 uses Body Modifiers to clean up acute walls that would normally not clean up well.

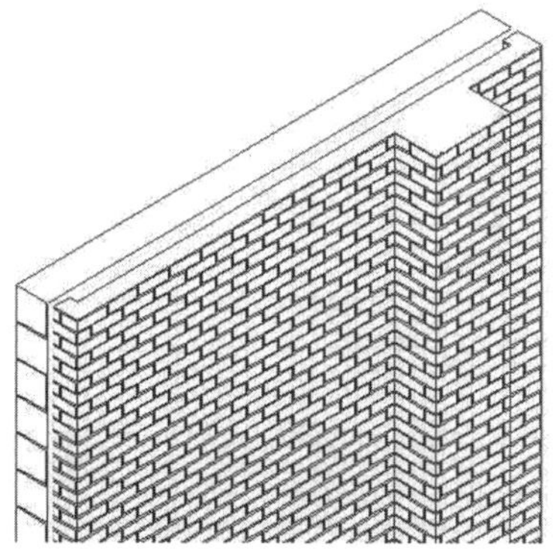

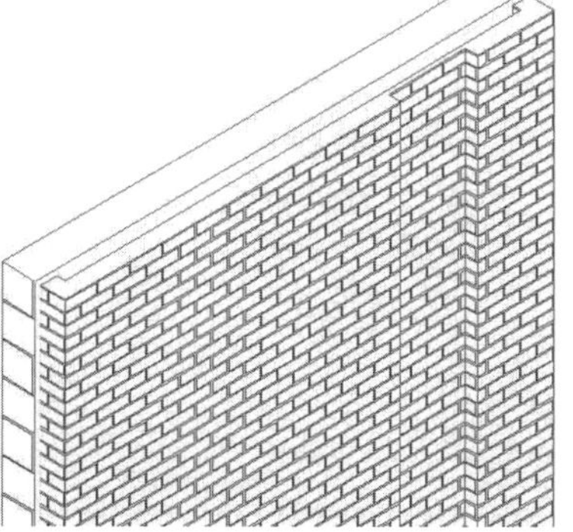

Figure 13.39 Body Modifiers add or subtract objects from a wall. Reveals and joints in walls are excellent examples of Body Modifier applications.

Figure 13.40 Wall reveals and wall joints in walls are excellent examples of Body Modifier applications.

Technique to Master T13.41 Creating and Assigning a Body Modifier to an Existing Wall

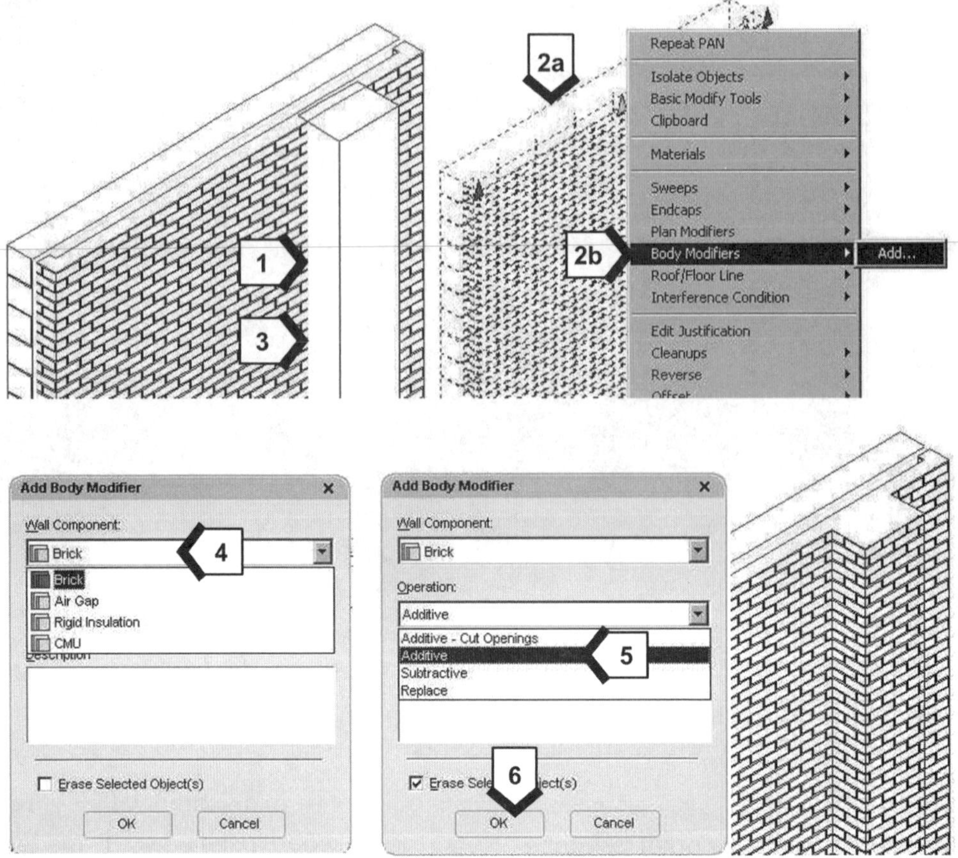

Figure 13.41

1	[Drawing Screen]	Place the object at the precise location on the wall.
2a, 2b	[Drawing Screen]	Choose the wall, right-click, and choose Body Modifier>Add.
3	[Drawing Screen]	Select the object(s) used as Body Modifiers.
4	[Add Body Modifier dialogue box]	Select the appropriate wall component to which the Body Modifier will be applied.
5	[Add Body Modifier dialogue box]	Select the operation. Subtractive will cut openings in the wall, while Additive will add the object and make it part of the wall.
6	[Add Body Modifier dialogue box]	Click OK to apply the Body Modifier.

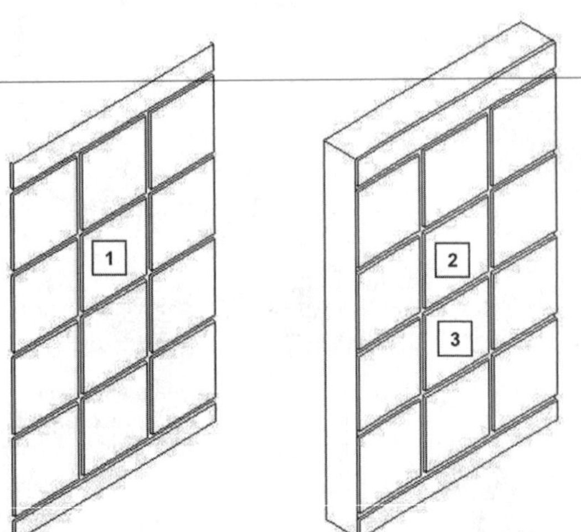

Technique to Master T13.42 Creating a Wood-Paneled Wall Using Body Modifiers

Figure 13.42

1	[Drawing Screen]	Create mass elements to represent the individual panels of the wall.
2	[Drawing Screen]	Place the mass elements at their precise locations on the wall.
3	[Drawing Screen]	Apply Body Modifiers to the wall.

Technique to Master **T13.43** Cleaning Up Wall Problems with Body Modifiers

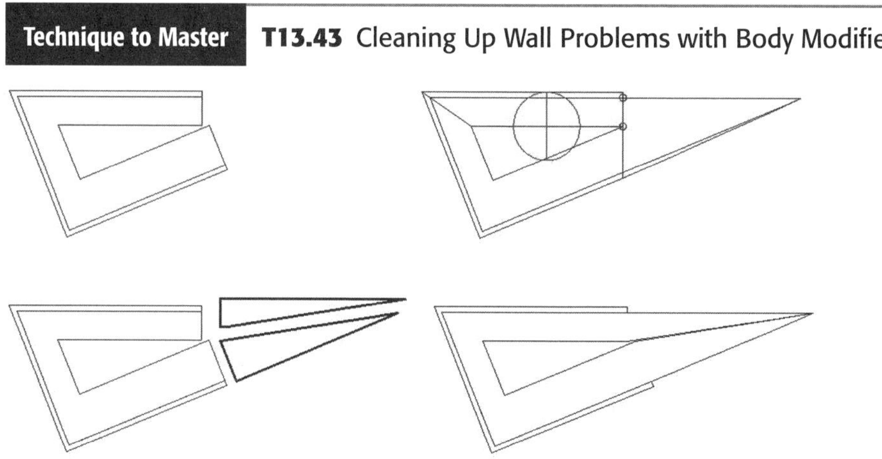

Figure 13.43 Sometimes wall cleanups are difficult between acute angles. Wall problems result from trying to fillet these types of walls together. Body Modifiers can help solve these types of cleanup problems.

1	[Drawing Screen]	Create closed polylines for each wall component and then convert each to mass elements.
2	[Drawing Screen]	Place the mass elements at their precise locations along the wall.
3	[Drawing Screen]	Apply Body Modifiers to each wall component.

Removing Applied Modifiers

Plan Modifiers, Body Modifiers, and Interference Conditions all can be removed from a wall once applied. The Properties palette for the selected wall shows the types of modifiers applied (Figure 13.44). Left-click the field to open the Modifier dialogue box.

Figure 13.45 illustrates how to remove an existing modifier.

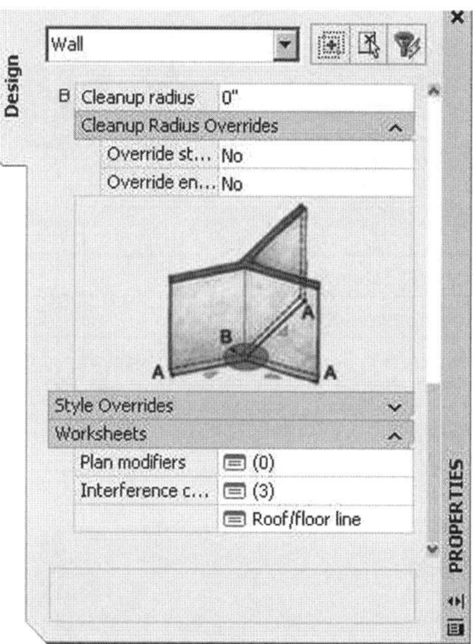

Figure 13.44 The Properties palette for the selected wall shows the type and quantity of modifiers that have been applied.

Technique to Master **T13.45** Removing an Existing Modifier

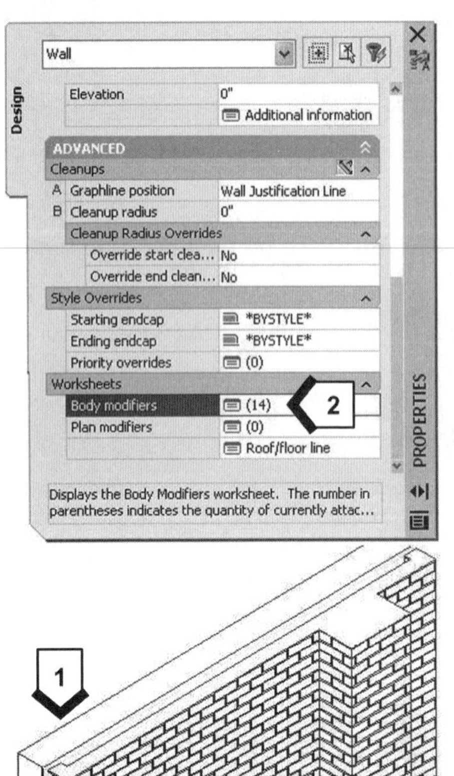

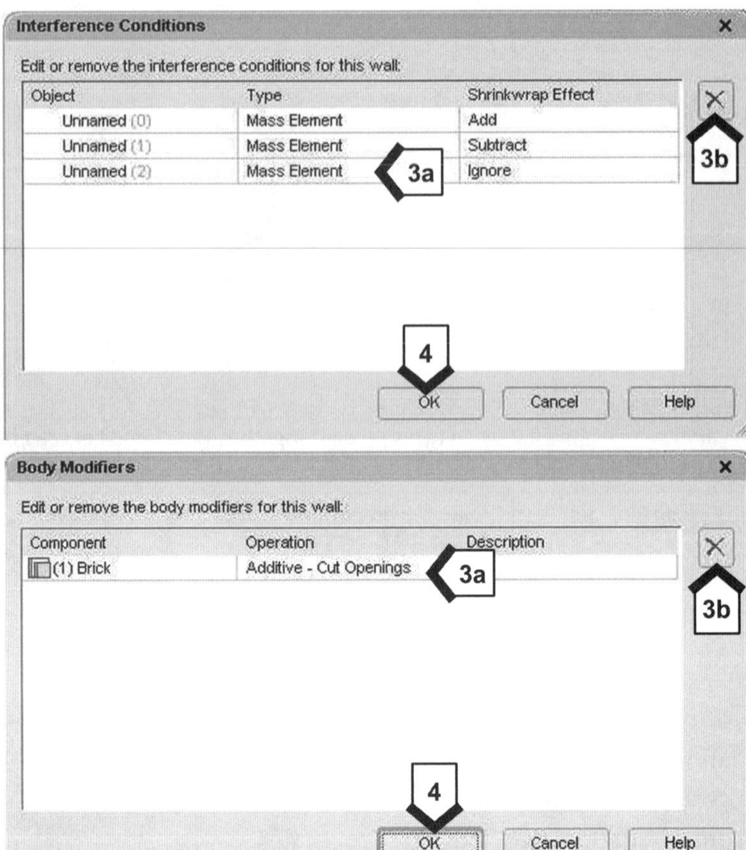

Figure 13.45

1	[Drawing Screen]	Select a wall that has a Body Modifier or an Interference Condition.
2	[Properties palette]	Click on an area that displays the modifier.
3a, 3b	[Interference Condition or Body Modifier dialogue box]	Left-click on the modifier and then click on the delete button.
4	[Interference Condition or Body Modifier dialogue box]	Click OK to complete the command.

Creating Custom Openings

You can also use profile definitions to create the elevational-shaped openings. Figure 13.46 creates a uniquely designed wall opening by using profile definitions.

Technique to Master **T13.46** Creating Custom Shaped Openings

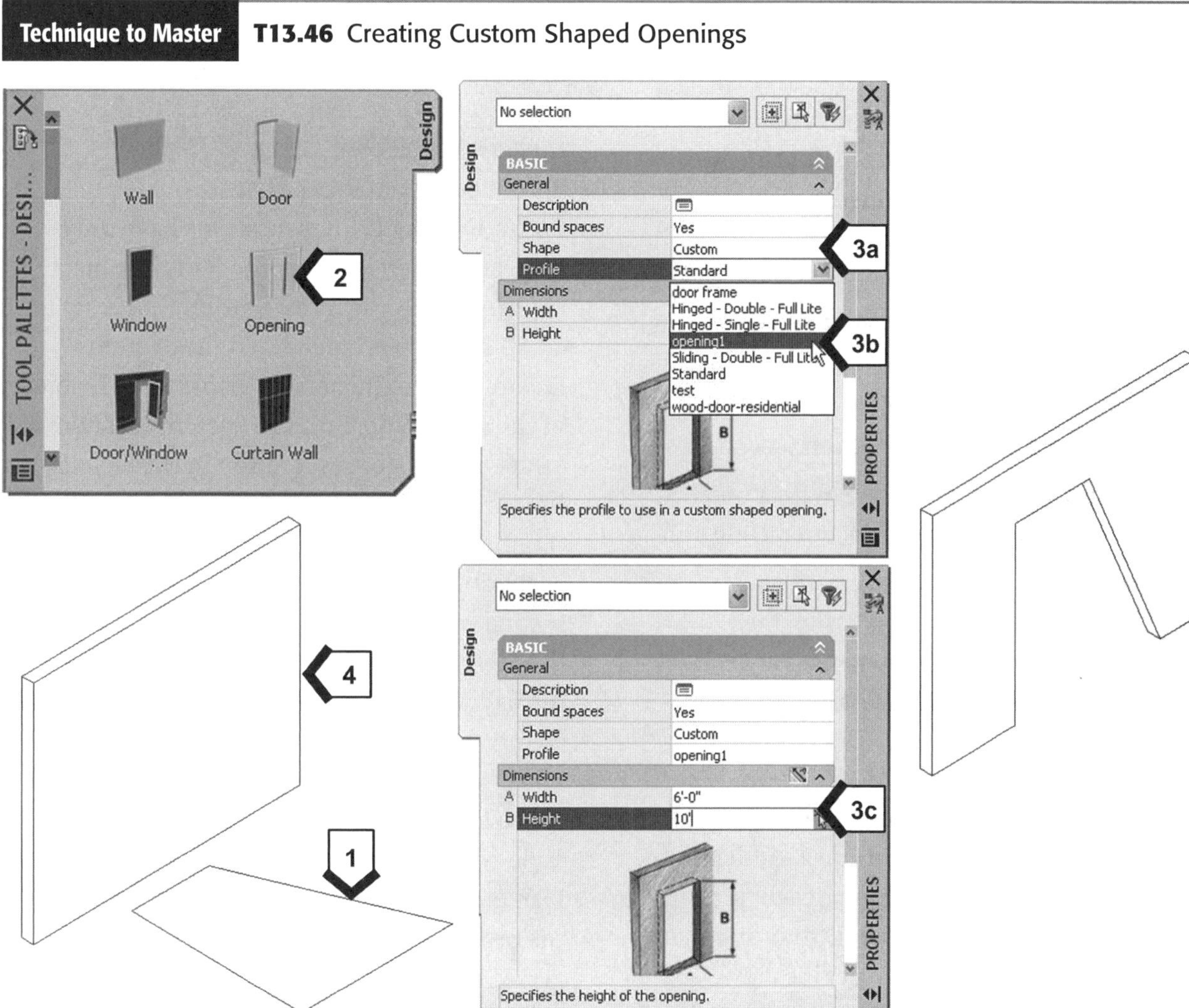

Figure 13.46

1	[Drawing Screen]	Draw the shape that will become shape for custom opening. Convert 2-D shape into profile definition. Refer to Technique T10.09.
2	[Design Tool palette]	Select the Opening tool.
3a, 3b, 3c	[Properties palette]	Next to shape, specify Custom. Next to Profile, select appropriate profile definition. Specify the width and height of opening.
4	[Drawing Screen]	Left-click on wall, and left-click again to locate opening.

Understanding How Objects Display in ADT—The Display System Structure

Chapter 9 introduced the Display System in ADT and how it relates to the way objects are shown on the drawing screen. You learned that the Display System can be understood as a complex matrix or checklist that dictates which views an object is displayed, as well as how it will be displayed. This matrix uses rules that are based on the conventions of orthographic drawing and are, for the most part, automatically embedded.

The Display System's primary responsibilities include the following:

- Providing the ADT objects with a means to display automatically and correctly in the various orthographic views, including floor and ceiling plan and elevation views.
- Providing the ADT objects with a mechanism to show or hide object detailing and hatching.

To help clarify the display labyrinth, descriptions with visual diagrams are provided in the pages that follow.

The Display Representations

Each ADT object type includes several predefined display representations that determine how it is viewed. Think of a display representation as a 2-D or 3-D drawing that represents the object for a specific view. Although users don't tie these predefined display representations to a specific orthographic view, they have these preconceived views in mind when making each of them.

Display Representations not only control how the object is viewed but also the amount of detail that is displayed for the object. The two left dialogue boxes in Figure 13.47 show the Plan High-Detail Display Representation for a wall and door. It shows that all of the components and their hatches are visible. In contrast, notice that the Plan Low-Detail Display Representation (the right dialogue boxes) has these components turned off.

In addition to visibility, Display Representations for the object types also control the properties that each of the components get assigned. Display Properties for objects are discussed further in the next section.

Display Representations and Their Relationship to Object Styles

So far, Display Representations have only been addressed in the context of the object type. A Display Representation that is set for an object type is considered the System Default and is the default display for all objects of the same type. Edit the System Defaults for each Display Representation in the Display Properties tab for the selected object (Figure 13.48).

Because most objects are style-based, the second level of Display Representations is through Style Overrides. At this level, the display properties of the System Default can be changed for a specific style condition. Figure 13.49 shows style overrides in place for three of the Display Representations in the brick wall style—Plan High Detail, Plan Low Detail, and Plan Presentation. Figure 13.50 demonstrates the procedure for creating style overrides.

Box 13.4

Reasons for creating style overrides might include turning on the display of hatch patterns in plan view (for a brick wall, for example) or changing the hatch pattern type for a specific wall style (cmu walls use a crosshatch, while brick walls use a simple hatch).

High-Detail Representation—Wall

Display Properties (Drawing Default) - Plan High Detail

Layer/Color/Linetype | Hatching | Cut Plane | Other

Display Component	Layer	Color	Linetype	Lineweight
Below Cut Plane	0	132	ByBlock	0.35 mm
Above Cut Plane	0	112	HIDDEN2	0.35 mm
Shrink Wrap	0	BYBLOCK	ByBlock	ByBlock
Shrink Wrap Hatch	0	30	ByBlock	0.18 mm
Defect Warning	G-Anno-Nplt	red	ByBlock	0.18 mm
Boundary 1	0	11	ByBlock	0.25 mm
Boundary 2	0	11	ByBlock	0.25 mm
Boundary 3	0	11	ByBlock	0.25 mm
Boundary 4	0	11	ByBlock	0.25 mm
Boundary 5	0	11		
Boundary 6	0	11		
Boundary 7	0	11		
Boundary 8	0	11		
Boundary 9	0	11		
Boundary 10	0	11		
Boundary 11	0	11		
Boundary 12	0	11		
Boundary 13	0	11		
Boundary 14	0	11		
Boundary 15	0	11		
Boundary 16	0	11		
Boundary 17	0	11		
Boundary 18	0	11		
Boundary 19	0	11		
Boundary 20	0	11		
Hatch 1	0	30		
Hatch 2	0	30		
Hatch 3	0	30		
Hatch 4	0	30		
Hatch 5	0	30		

Low-Detail Representation—Wall

Display Properties (Drawing Default) - Plan Low Detail

Layer/Color/Linetype | Hatching | Cut Plane | Other

Display Component	Layer	Color	Linetype	Lineweight
Below Cut Plane	0	132	ByBlock	0.35 mm
Above Cut Plane	0	112	HIDDEN2	0.35 mm
Shrink Wrap	0	BYBLOCK	ByBlock	ByBlock
Shrink Wrap Hatch	0	30	ByBlock	0.18 mm
Defect Warning	G-Anno-Nplt	red	ByBlock	0.18 mm
Boundary 1	0	11	ByBlock	0.25 mm
Boundary 2	0	11	ByBlock	0.25 mm
Boundary 3	0	11	ByBlock	0.25 mm
Boundary 4	0	11	ByBlock	0.25 mm
Boundary 5	0	11	ByBlock	0.25 mm
Boundary 6	0	11	ByBlock	0.25 mm
Boundary 7	0	11	ByBlock	0.25 mm
Boundary 8	0	11	ByBlock	0.25 mm
Boundary 9	0	11	ByBlock	0.25 mm
Boundary 10	0	11	ByBlock	0.25 mm
Boundary 11	0	11	ByBlock	0.25 mm
Boundary 12	0	11	ByBlock	0.25 mm
Boundary 13	0	11	ByBlock	0.25 mm
Boundary 14	0	11	ByBlock	0.25 mm
Boundary 15	0	11	ByBlock	0.25 mm
Boundary 16	0	11	ByBlock	0.25 mm
Boundary 17	0	11	ByBlock	0.25 mm
Boundary 18	0	11	ByBlock	0.25 mm
Boundary 19	0	11	ByBlock	0.25 mm
Boundary 20	0	11	ByBlock	0.25 mm
Hatch 1	0	30	ByBlock	0.18 mm
Hatch 2	0	30	ByBlock	0.18 mm
Hatch 3	0	30	ByBlock	0.18 mm
Hatch 4	0	30	ByBlock	0.18 mm
Hatch 5	0	30	ByBlock	0.18 mm

OK Cancel Help

High-Detail Representation—Door

Low-Detail Representation—Door

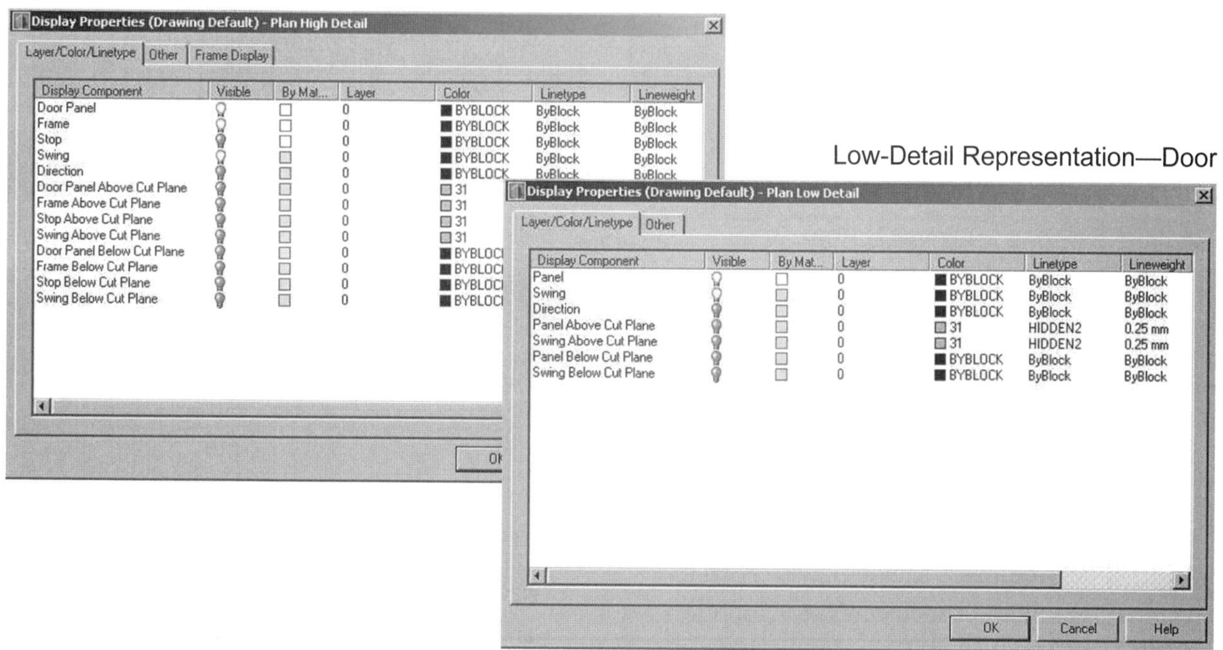

Figure 13.47 The Plan High-Detail and Low-Detail Display Representations for a wall and door.

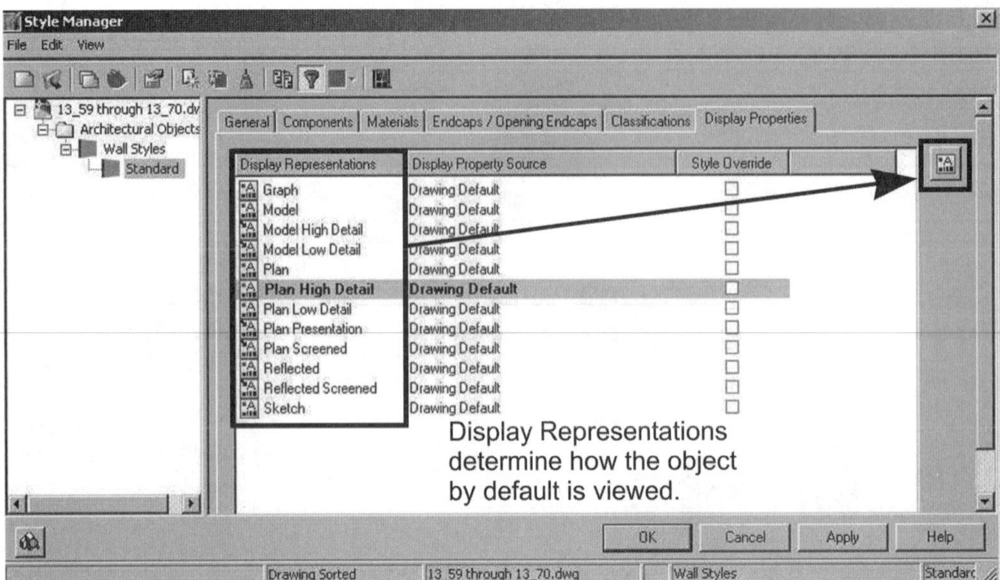

Figure 13.48 Set up office layering, line-weight, and line-style standards in the System Display Representations in the Display Manager.

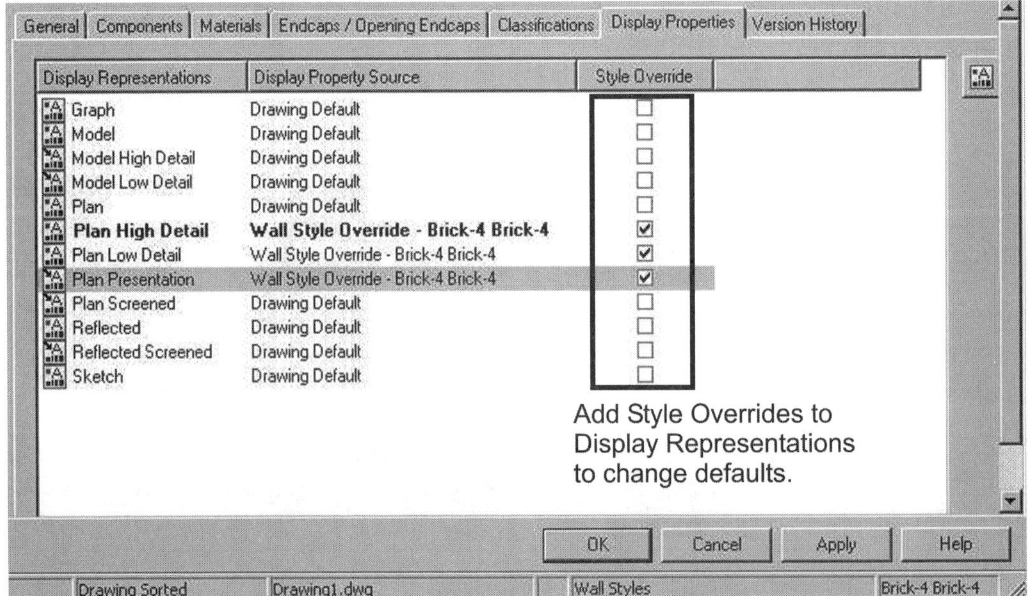

Figure 13.49 The second level of Display Representations uses Style Overrides. At this level, the display properties of the System Default can be changed for a specific style condition. The dialogue box shows style overrides in place for three of the Display Representations in the brick wall style—Plan High Detail, Plan Low Detail, and Plan Presentation.

The third level is through an Object Override. Similar to a Style Override, an Object Override alters the display to both the System Default and the Style Override. These overrides apply only to the selected object. Figure 13.51 demonstrates the procedure for creating object overrides.

Technique to Master T13.50 Creating Style Overrides

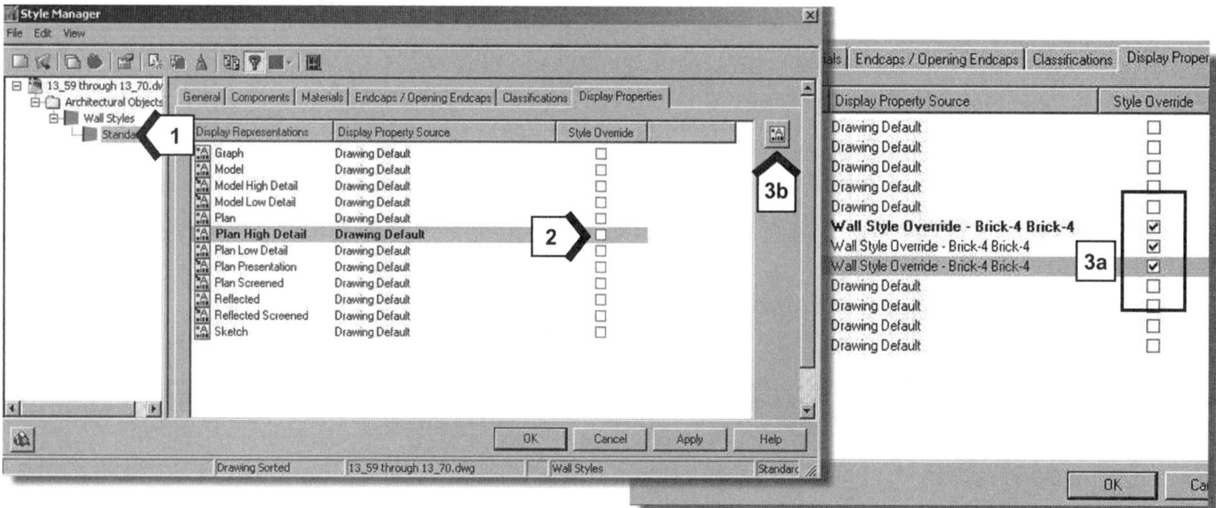

Figure 13.50

1	Open Style Manager for object.	
2	[Style Manager]	In left pane, select style.
3a, 3b	[Style Manager> Display Properties]	Check the box next to the Display Representation. The Display Properties Style Override dialogue box will appear.
4	[Style Manager> Display Properties]	If the Display Representation is already checked, select the Edit Display Properties button instead.

Technique to Master T13.51 Creating Object Overrides

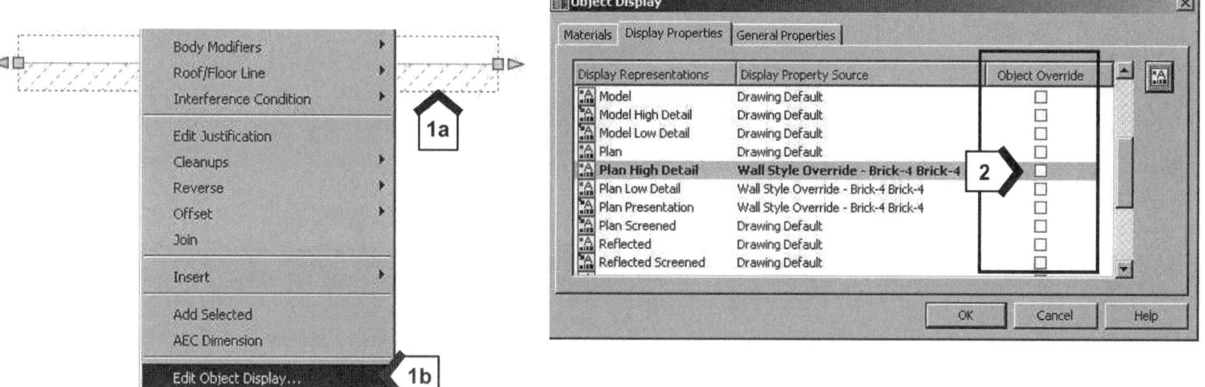

Figure 13.51

1a, 1b	[Drawing Screen]	Select an object, right-click, and choose the Edit Object Display command.
2	[Object Display dialogue box]	Check box next to the Display Representation. The Display Properties Object Override dialogue box will appear.

Display Sets

If the Display Representations provide control over each object type, the Display Set uses these representations to bring all of the object types together. Each Display Set essentially defines an orthographic view (though other types of three-dimensional views are grouped into the Model Display Set). Based on the orthographic view type, the Display Set will decide which Display Representation is most appropriate for the object type. Figure 13.52 visually illustrates the concept.

Since there are several orthographic view types (Floor Plan, Ceiling Plan, Section, Elevation) and several variations of the levels of detail in that view type (Presentation Plans, Higher Detailed Plans, Lower Detailed Plans), multiple Display Sets are used in ADT's Display System matrix.

Name	Description
Model	3D display turned on for all AEC objects
Model High Detail	
Model Low Detail	
Model Presentation	3D display turned on for all AEC objects
Plan	Medium display detail
Plan Diagnostic	Sketch, graph and diagnostic display configuration for troubleshooting AEC geometry, 2D.
Plan High Detail	High display detail
Plan Intermediate Level	Medium display detail for use at intermediate level of stairs
Plan Low Detail	Low display detail
Plan Presentation	Presentation display style
Plan Screened	All AEC objects shown with a screened effect
Plan Top Level	Medium display detail for use at top level of stairs
Reflected	Reflected display for plots
Reflected Screened	For working in reflected ceiling plans, not intended for plotting
Section_Elev	Controls the display of AEC objects in sections and elevations

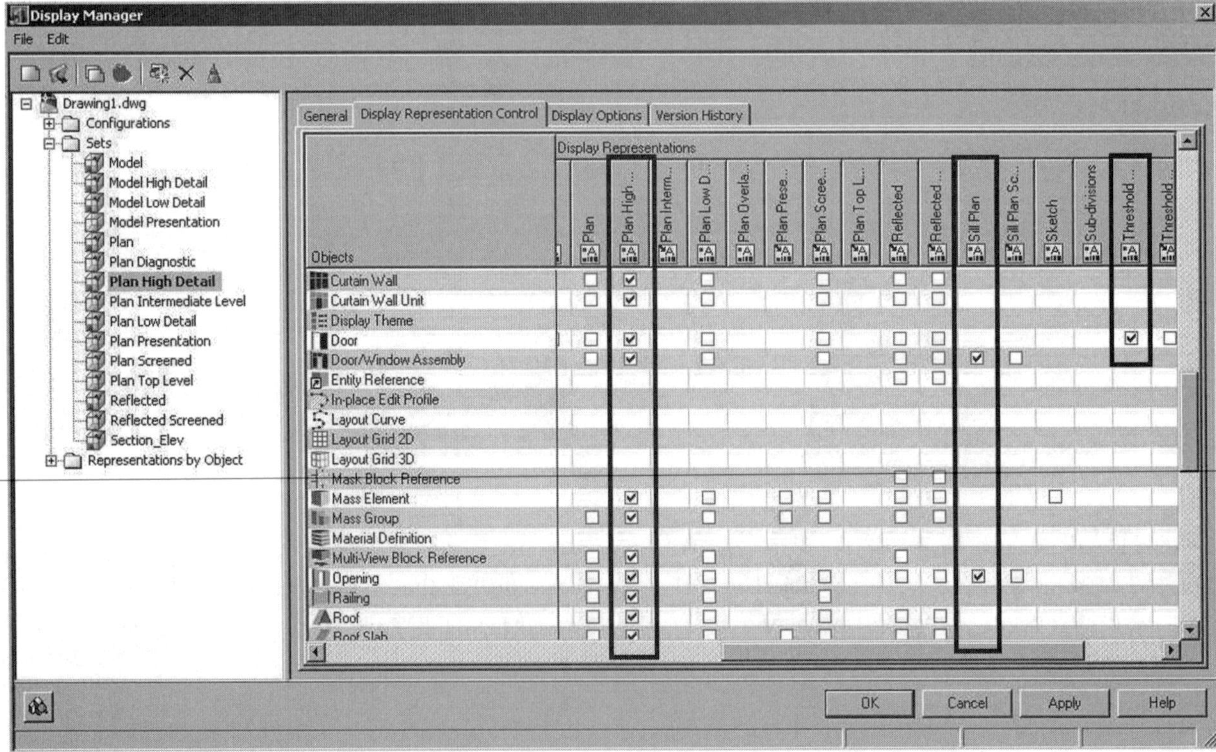

Figure 13.52 The Display Sets essentially define an orthographic view, then use the Display Representations to bring together all of the object types.

The Display Configuration

The Display Configuration is the most visible part of the Display System matrix. It groups the Display Sets into like categories to allow for quick display changes (Figure 13.53). ADT 2007 ships with 12 predefined Display Configurations. Figure 13.54 shows the Display Sets and Display Representations tied to each of these Display Configurations.

Display Configurations and Their Relationship to Viewports

Each model space and paper space viewport is set to a Display Configuration. Multiple model space viewports all use the same Display Configuration.

Materials, Display Properties, and the ADT Objects

Material Definitions are a relatively new addition to the ADT family of objects (Figure 13.55). Material Definitions are, however, not physical objects. They instead represent a collection of Display Representations to define how a specific material looks when displayed in any of the plan, section, elevation, or rendered views. Notice that material definitions also include rendering materials.

In the previous topic, you've probably noticed that most Object Display Representations have a box under a column named By Materials. When checked, the layer, line weight, line type, and plot style properties of each component in the display representation is transferred to the material assignment. Figure 13.56 illustrates this relationship.

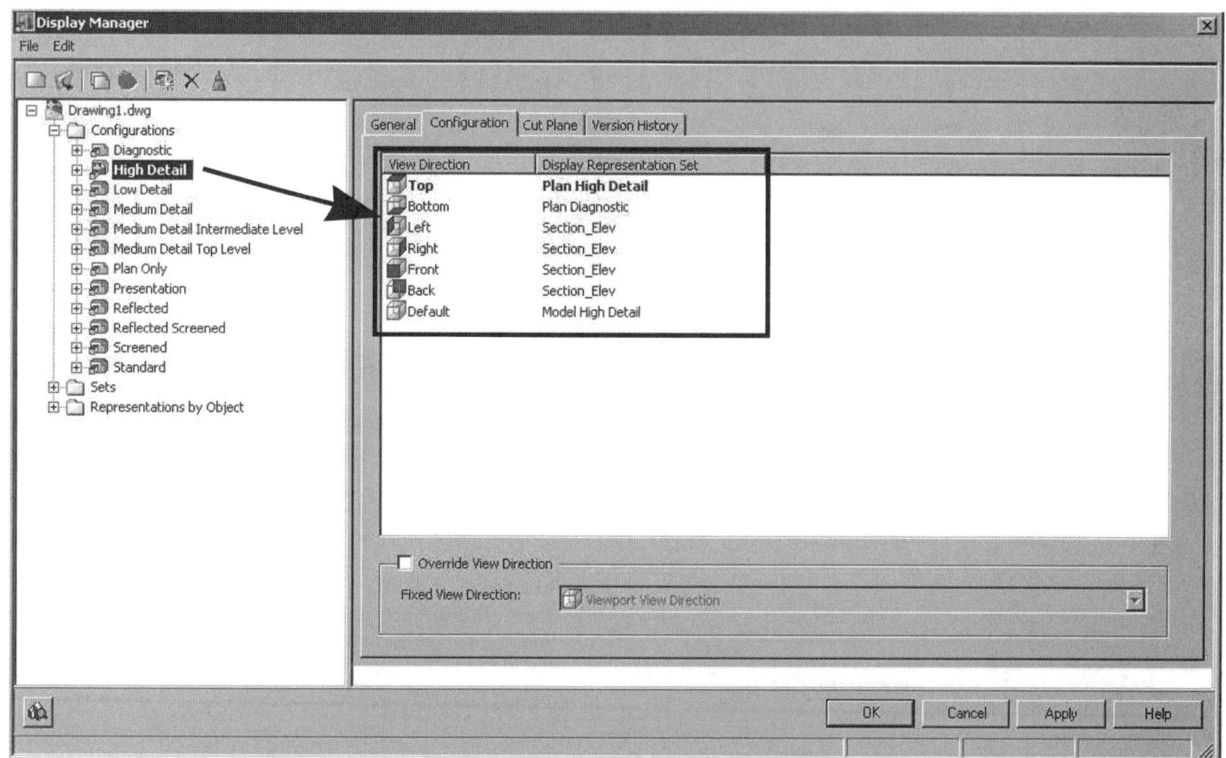

Figure 13.53 Display Configurations group the Display Sets into like categories to allow for quick display changes.

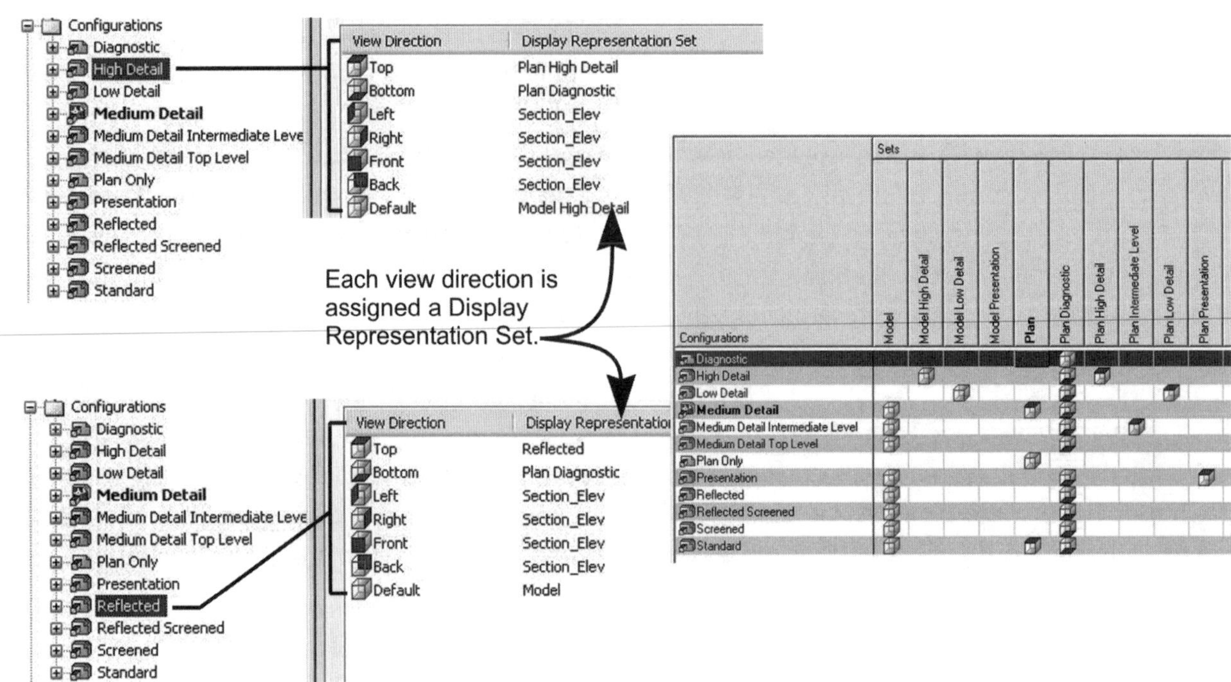

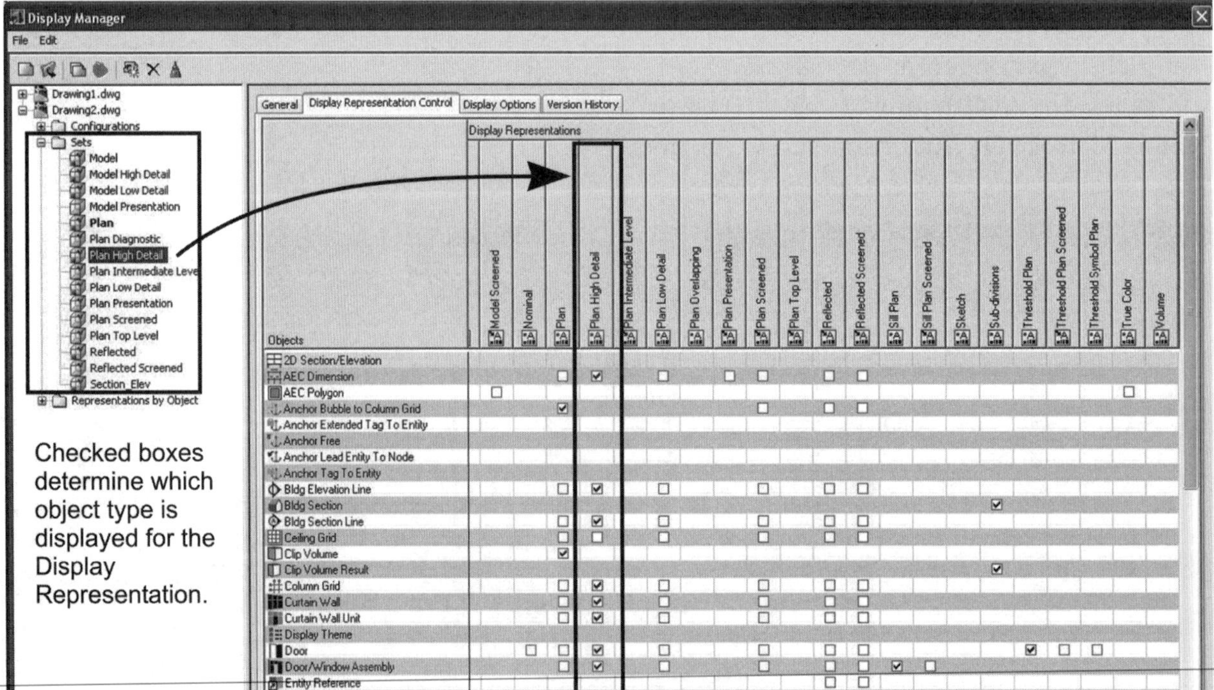

Figure 13.54 How the Display Sets and Display Representations are tied to the Display Configurations

Figure 13.55 Material Definitions represent a collection of Display Representations to define how a specific material looks when displayed in any of the plan, section, elevation, or rendered views.

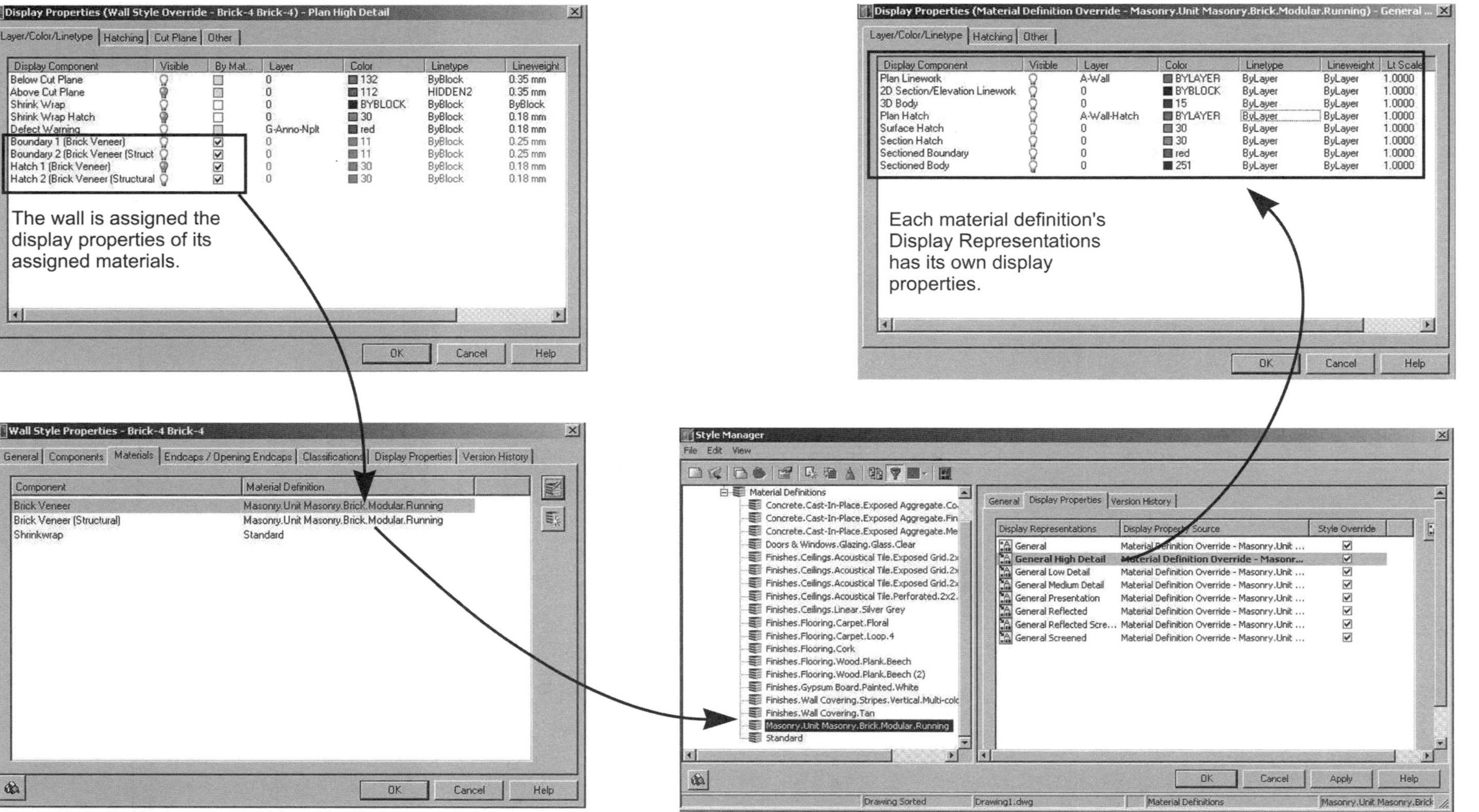

Figure 13.56 When the By Materials box is checked, the layer, lineweight, linetype, and plot style properties of each component in the display representation are transferred to the material assignment.

Using Material Definitions instead of the object type's Display Representations helps to standardize and simplify the appearance of all objects. At the same time, it sets up all of your rendering materials for the project. Figure 13.57 identifies the different areas of the Material Definition Style. Figure 13.58 shows some examples of materials found in the ADT Content Browser and their Display Properties attached to these materials. Figure 13.59 demonstrates how to import Content Browser materials. Refer to Chapter 9 to review Content Browser concepts and techniques.

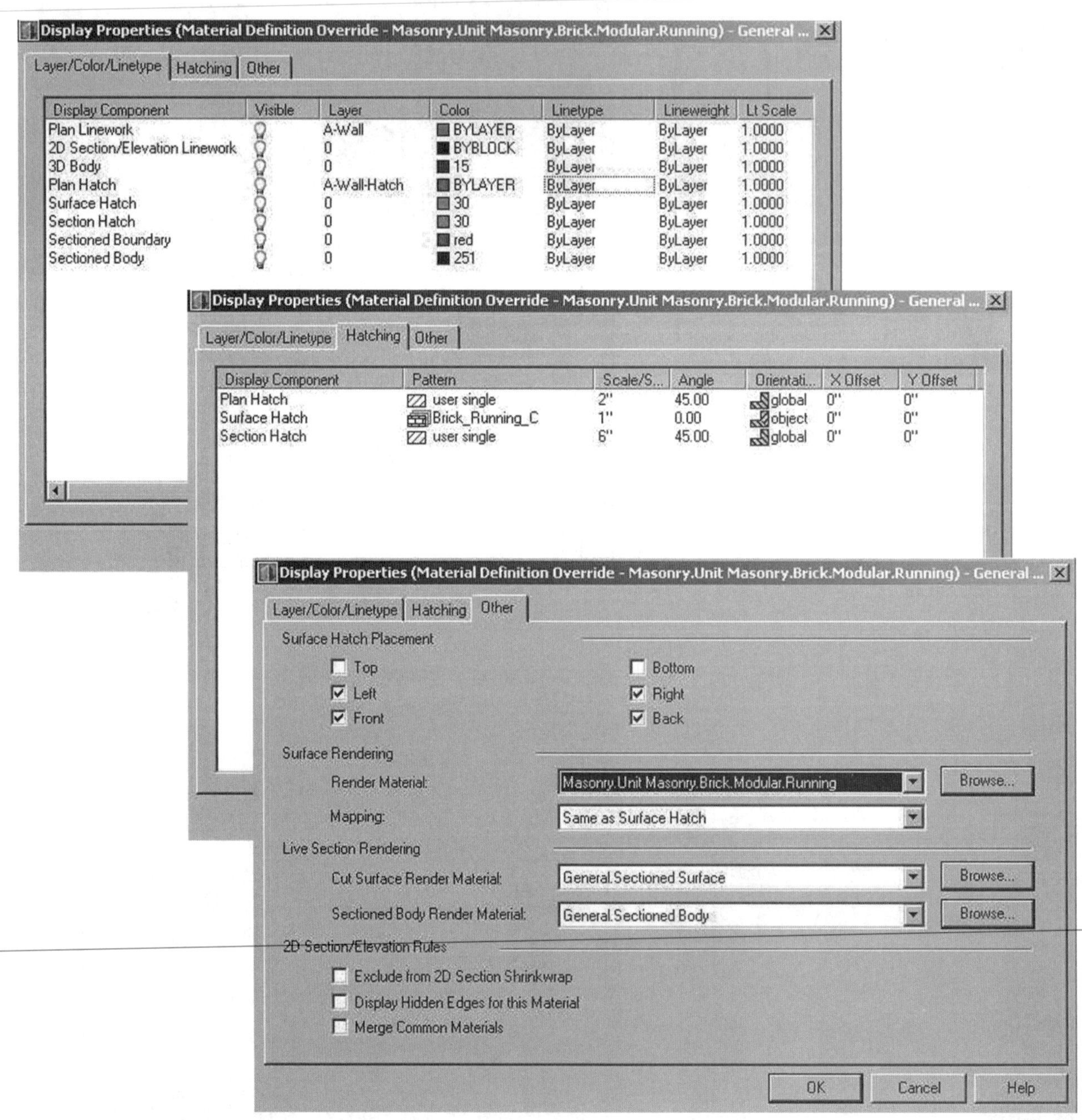

Figure 13.57 The areas of the Material Definition Style

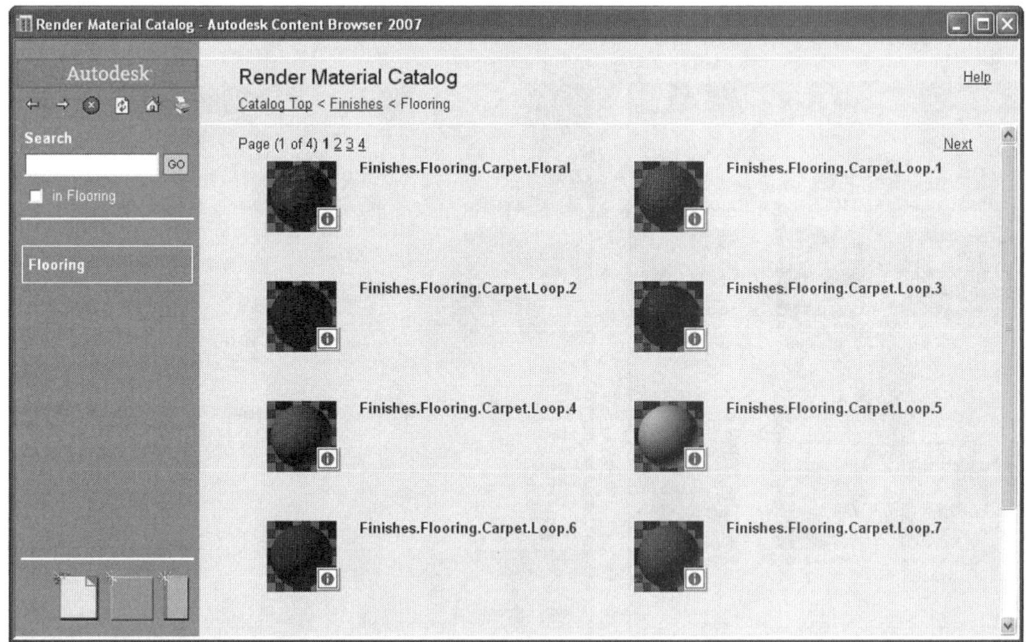

Figure 13.58 Examples of existing materials found in the Content Browser Library

Using Mass Elements for Furniture, Casework, and Other Types of Equipment

Figures found in the Chapter 13 folder of the CD-ROM demonstrate various design examples for using mass elements and mass groups to create other types of furniture, casework, and equipment not available in the Design Center and Content Browser Libraries. These examples require the use of mass element styles and material definitions and display representation manipulations.

> **Box 13.5**
>
> If you want to create a material to use only for mass elements or mass groups, you should name it accordingly. For example, if the materials have specific names, such as Mass Element-Concrete Column or Mass Group-Cable Shaft, you can simplify the organization of your material definitions.

The following is a summary of the workflow process:

1. Create the furniture, casework, appliance, or other equipment type using one or more mass elements. Refer to Techniques T10.05, T10.11, T10.12, T10.13, and T10.14 to review mass element creation.
2. Set the appropriate styles for each mass element so that it displays correctly in plan view. For example, built-in upper cabinets should be dashed in plan view; therefore, the mass element style should reflect dashed lines. Refer to Technique T13.23 and Appendix M for mass element style creation techniques.
3. Create mass groups where appropriate for Boolean type operations on mass elements. Refer to Techniques T10.16, T10.17, and T10.18.
4. Assign appropriate layer to each mass element and/or mass group (Refer to Techniques T03.17 and T03.19).

Technique to Master **T13.59** Importing Content Browser Materials

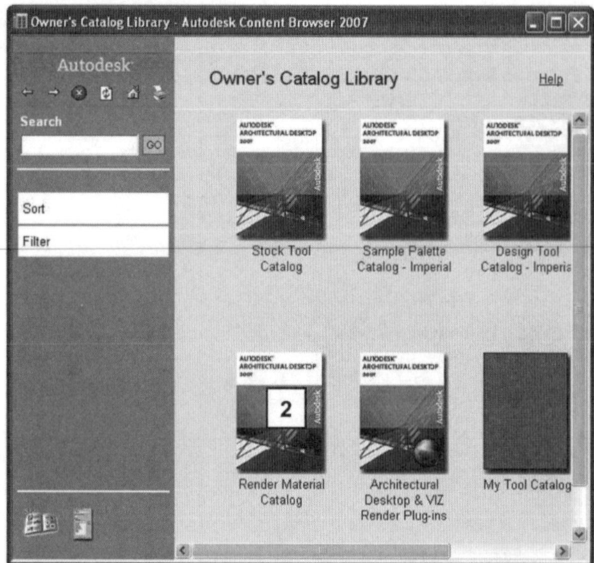

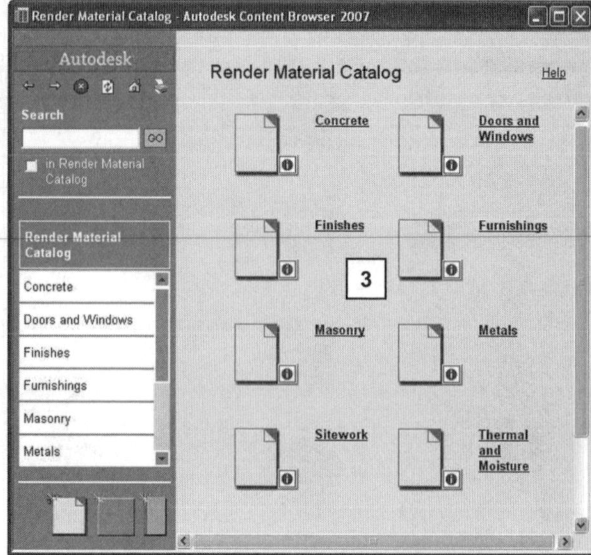

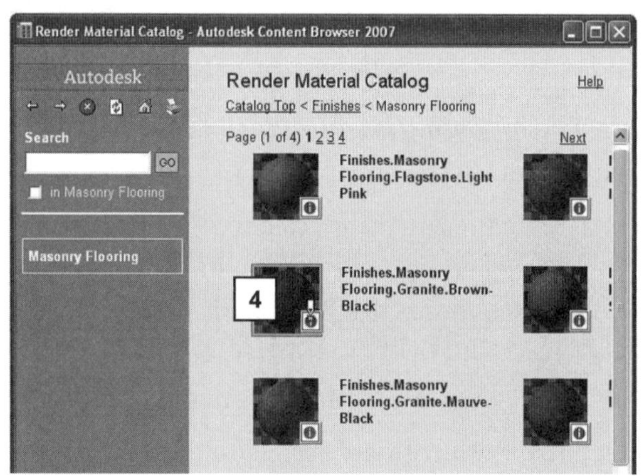

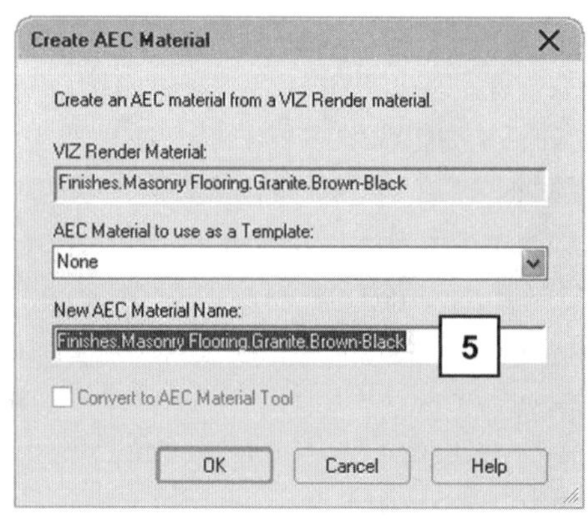

Figure 13.59

1	Open the Content Browser.	
2	[Content Browser dialogue box]	Left-click on Render Material Catalog.
3	[Content Browser dialogue box> Render Material Catalog]	Continue opening palettes until desired render materials are found.
4	[Content Browser dialogue box> Render Material Catalog]	Use the eyedropper tool to import material into current drawing.
5	[Create AEC Material dialogue box]	Name material.

Chapter Exercises

Open the Chapter 13 folder located on the CD-ROM to access the exercises for this chapter. The exercises let you practice how to create complex walls, windows, doors, openings, and mass elements using the Style Manager as well as object specific modification tools.

Creating Curtain Wall and Storefront Systems

14

Objectives

This chapter introduces the ADT curtain wall and door/window assembly objects. It places emphasis on understanding the various components of these objects as well as their accurate creation and placement. Techniques within the chapter illustrate the proper execution of curtain wall and door/window assembly procedures. The end-of-chapter exercises allow you to apply these techniques to several curtain wall and door/window assembly design problems.

Curtain Walls and Door/Window Assemblies in ADT

Curtain walls in the design and building construction industries are glazed wall systems that are used as exterior building skins. They are made up of frame, mullion, and infill components. They are designed to attach to a building's structural system as well as span multiple floors. Although today's curtain wall systems are built with aluminum extruded frame and mullions, the first curtain walls used steel. Early examples of steel curtain wall construction include the Bauhaus in Dessau and SOM's Lever House in New York City (Figure 14.1). Aluminum frame and mullions gained in popularity because of the unlimited shape possibilities.

Figure 14.1 Early example of steel curtain wall construction: SOM's Lever House in New York City.

Curtain walls are usually synonymous with skyscrapers where the infill is typically a mirrored glazing. Curtain wall infill is, in many cases, glass but can also include composite metal panels, doors, stone veneer panels, and translucent insulation panels, to name a few (Figure 14.2). The glass is typically 1/8" or 1/4" thick but can be up to 1" thick if the glass is within an insulated system.

Figure 14.2 Example of a curtain wall and two types of infill panels

Because of the popularity of skyscraper construction around the world, designers have pushed the envelope of what is possible when designing curtain walls and door/window assemblies. Inspiration can be seen in any large city. A number of architects are likewise taking new approaches in the design and application of curtain walls. Appendix N provides a list of architects to research to encourage innovative thinking in this area.

Similar to curtain walls, storefronts are also glazed systems made up of frame, mullions, and infill but instead are supported by an exterior or interior wall. Storefronts were historically designed to enlarge window displays for shop owners to show off the merchandise within their stores. Typical storefronts include signage as well as the display window system. Today, storefront systems have expanded into the commercial and residential realm—providing greater light and view access to these spaces (Figure 14.3). Storefront systems are equivalent to the door/window assemblies in ADT.

The ADT Objects That Represent Curtain Walls and Door/Window Assemblies

As with all ADT style-based objects, curtain walls and door/window assemblies also start with a default style of Standard.

ADT's Curtain Wall Object

Curtain wall objects share similar traits to the ADT wall object. The wall object and curtain walls both have baselines, base heights, and justifications. You can also make custom adjustments to its floor and roof lines, as with the wall object (see Techniques T13.27 and T13.28 in Chapter 13 for floor and roof line modifications in walls). Doors and windows also can be inserted into curtain walls, but the technique is a little more complicated than just clicking on the curtain wall. Figure 14.4 correlates the properties of the curtain wall with its representation.

ADT's Door/Window Assembly Object

Door/window assemblies are a hybrid between ADT's curtain wall object and window object. Similar to the curtain wall object, door/window assemblies are made up of the

Figure 14.3 Storefront systems are used at the base of many commercial and retail buildings.

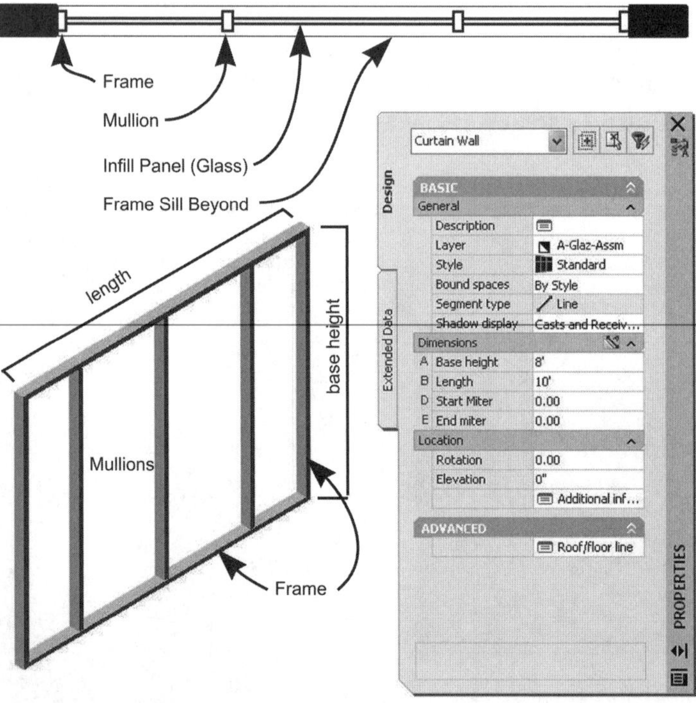

Figure 14.4 Getting to know the properties of the curtain wall object

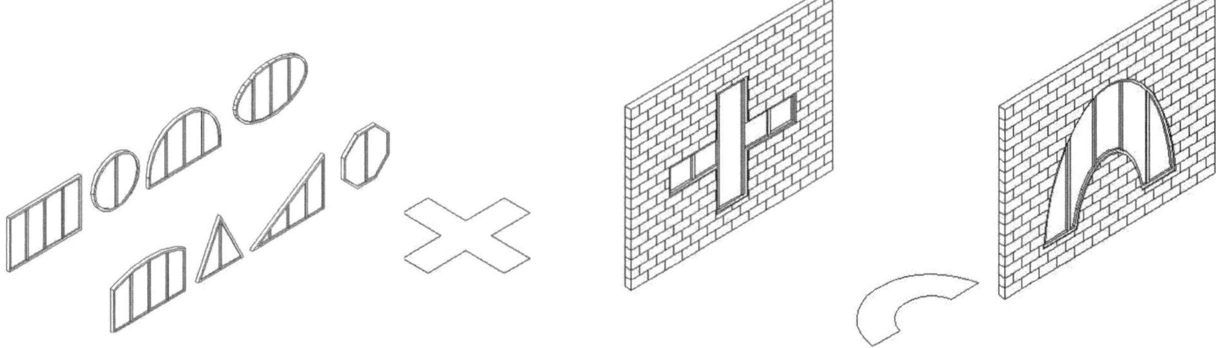

Figure 14.5 Door/window assemblies have overall shapes that can be based on profile definitions.

same components of frame, mullion, and infill. Style creation for these assemblies resembles the same procedure for creating curtain wall styles. Beyond this the similarity ends. Door/window assemblies are placed exactly like door or window objects—that is, within an existing wall with its head or sill location specified. Also, like window objects, a door/window assembly's overall shape is defined through the style. Although rectangular is the default, door/window assemblies can have shapes that are circular or arched. They can also be based on a custom shape created with a profile definition. Figure 14.5 shows examples from the library of predefined shapes as well as a few shapes based on profiles. Figure 14.6 correlates the properties of the door/window assembly with its representation.

The Components That Make Up a Curtain Wall (CW) and Door/Window Assembly (WA) Object

In ADT, the components that make up the curtain wall (also called CW) and the door/window assembly (also called WA) object are the same. These components include the infill, frame, and mullions, as shown in Figure 14.7.

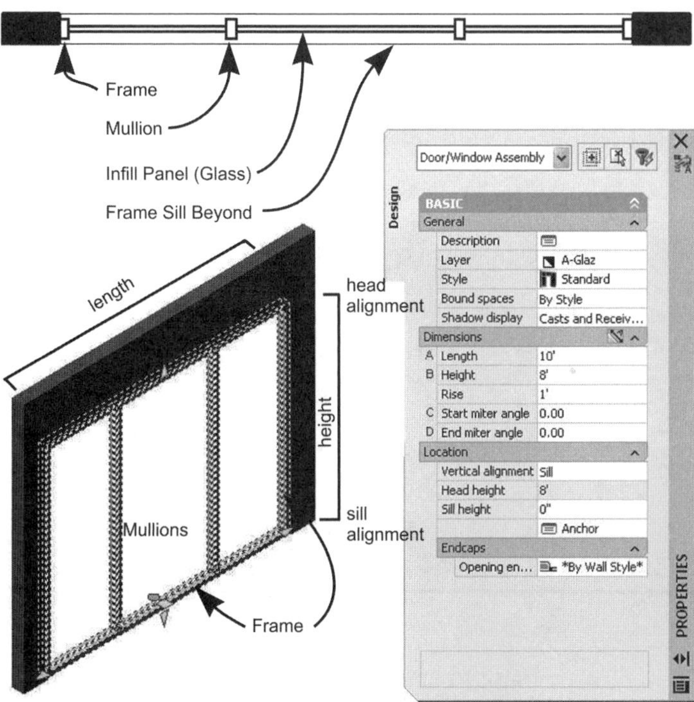

Figure 14.6 Getting to know the properties of the door/window assembly object

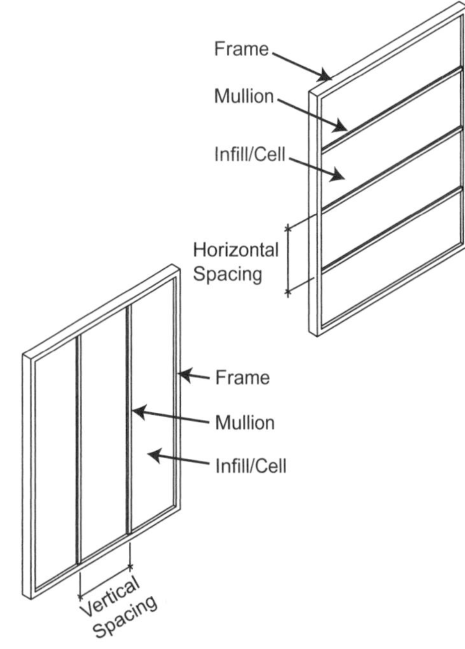

Figure 14.7 The components include the infill, frame, and mullions. In addition, the division component is an invisible component used to space the mullions of the CW or WA.

In addition, the division component is an invisible one that is used to space the mullions of the CW or WA.

Divisions

Divisions are used to define the orientation and spacing for the bays of the CW or WA. One or more of these divisions are then set to a grid that delineates the spacing of the horizontal and vertical mullions (Figure 14.8). Division orientation can only be set to a single direction—horizontal or vertical, but not both. To combine horizontally oriented and vertically oriented divisions, a technique called grid nesting must be used. Grid nesting will be discussed in further detail later in the chapter.

Infill

Infills are the panels located in between the frame and mullions. This infill is by default assumed to be glass; however, other panel material can also be used. Figure 14.9 shows a door/window assembly that uses three different infill types—door, window, and metal-panel infill.

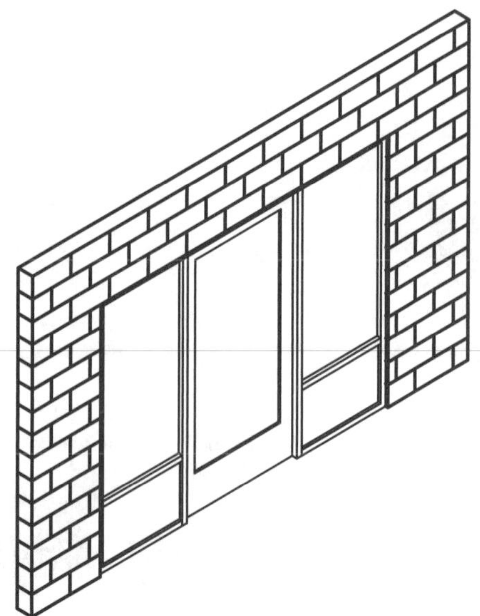

Figure 14.9 Door/window assembly using three infill types—glass, metal panel, and a door

The Frame

The Frame is located at the perimeter, surrounding the CW and WA system. The overall size of the frame is defined in the Properties palettes using the Base Height and Length properties. Today, frames are typically made out of extruded aluminum and are close to rectangular in shape. Figure 14.10 provides an example of aluminum-extruded frame component used in curtain wall and storefront system construction.

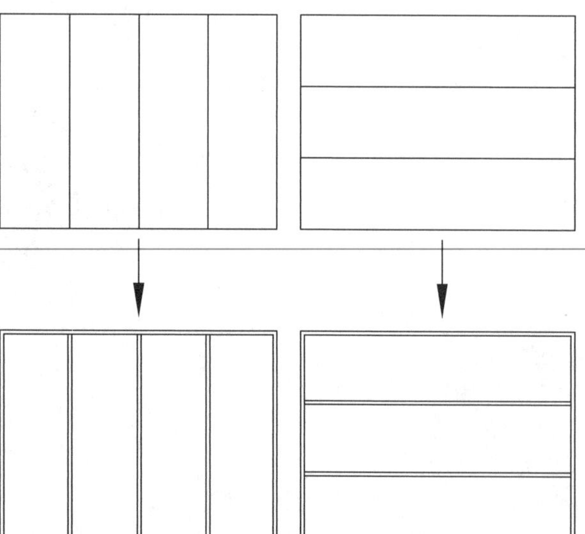

Figure 14.8 The Division component defines a specific orientation and spacing for the bays of the CW or WA. The orientation of each division can be set only to horizontal or vertical, but not both.

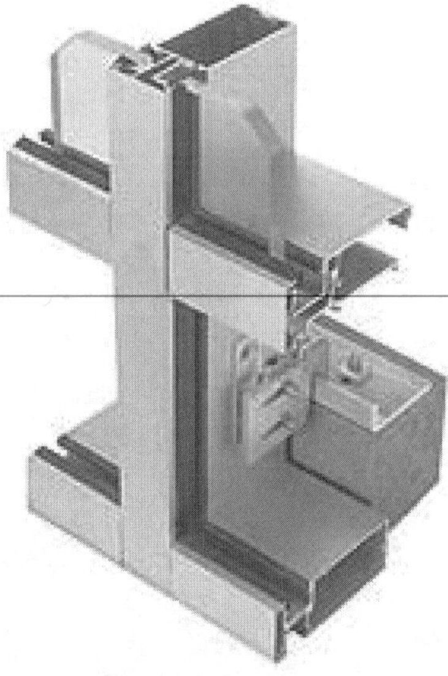

Figure 14.10 The Frame component is located at the perimeter of the CW and WA system and is a rectangular extruded aluminum profile.

Courtesy of Sota Glazing, Inc.

Mullions

Mullions are the interior framework that divides the panes of glass within the overall frame (Figure 14.11). When used creatively, mullions provide the composition and visual interest to the glazing system. It also helps connect the glazing system to other aspects of the building's order (Figure 14.12). Now that you have some familiarity with the CW and WA object types, you are ready for the next topic, which introduces the CW and WA tools and techniques for accurate placement.

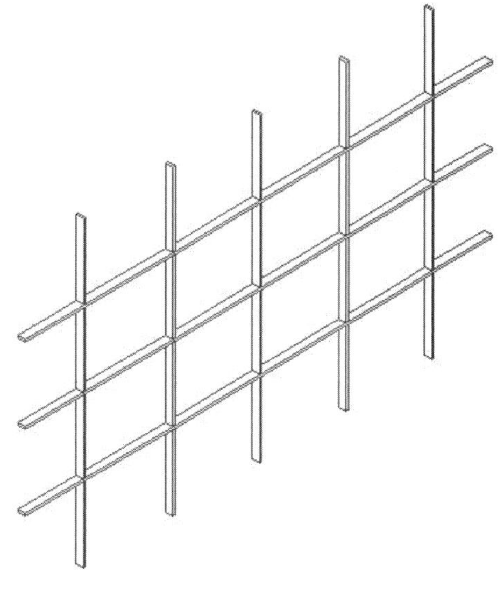

Figure 14.11 Mullions are the interior framework that divides up the panes of glass within the frame.

The Curtain Wall and Door/Window Assembly Tools

The Command Line instructions for placing curtain walls or door/window assemblies are CurtainWallAdd and DoorWinAssemblyAdd, respectively. As with most ADT commands, tools to create these objects can also be found in other locations. The Design menu at the top of the ADT screen as well as the Design Tool palette are probably the most often used methods for using these commands. Figure 14.13 displays the curtain wall and door/window assembly commands found in the Design Tool palette and the Design menu areas.

Curtain Wall Placement (Drawing with the Curtain Wall Object)

Placing curtain wall objects is exactly like placing walls: You specify a start and end point. This command also continues to prompt for additional points until the Enter key ends the command. Figure 14.14 demonstrates the curtain wall placement process.

> **Box 14.1**
>
> As with walls, curtain walls can be straight or curved or a combination of the two. Dissimilar to walls, curtain walls are always center justified.

Figure 14.12 When used creatively, mullions provide visual interest and connect the glazing to other aspects of the building's order.

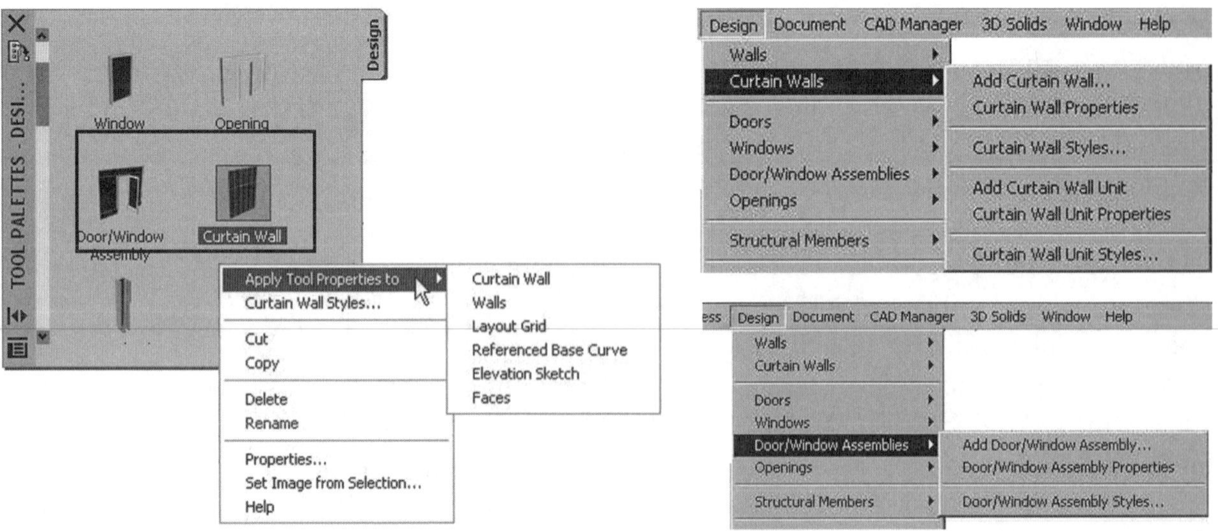

Figure 14.13 Finding the curtain wall and door/window assembly tools and their specialty commands

Technique to Master

T14.14 Placing a Straight or Curved Curtain Wall Using the Add Curtain Wall Tool

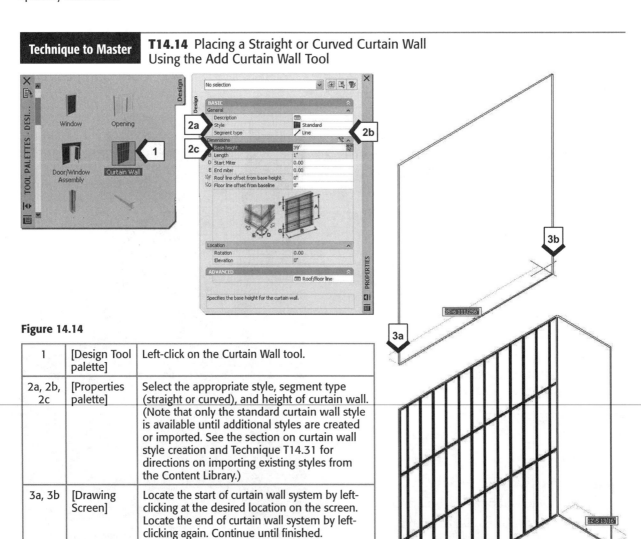

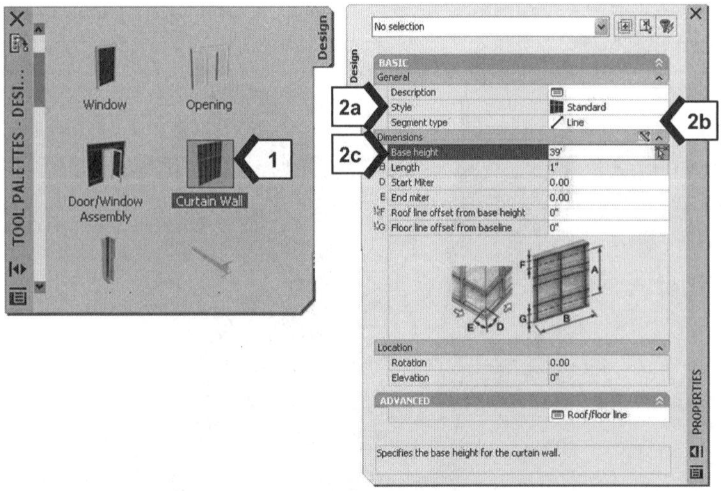

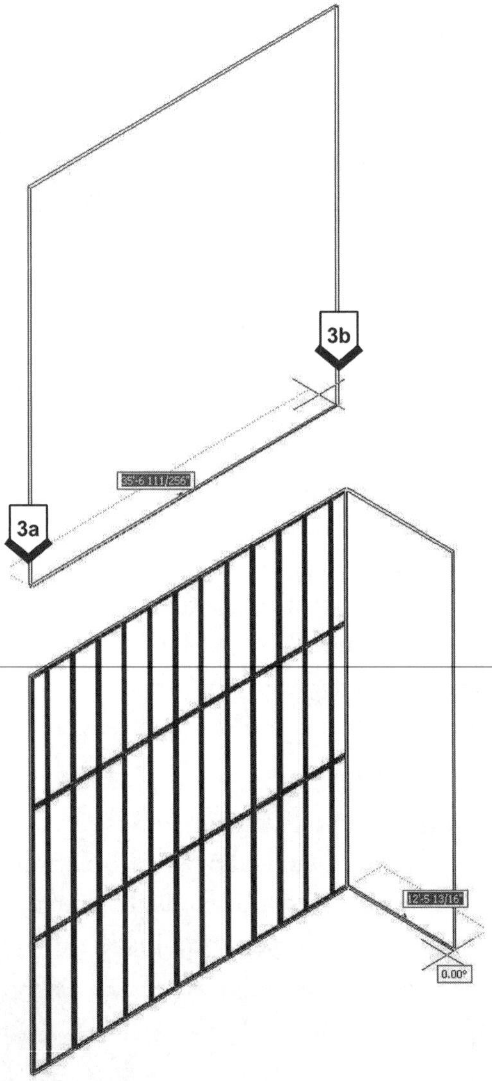

Figure 14.14

1	[Design Tool palette]	Left-click on the Curtain Wall tool.
2a, 2b, 2c	[Properties palette]	Select the appropriate style, segment type (straight or curved), and height of curtain wall. (Note that only the standard curtain wall style is available until additional styles are created or imported. See the section on curtain wall style creation and Technique T14.31 for directions on importing existing styles from the Content Library.)
3a, 3b	[Drawing Screen]	Locate the start of curtain wall system by left-clicking at the desired location on the screen. Locate the end of curtain wall system by left-clicking again. Continue until finished.

Sometimes the path of the curtain wall may be complicated—made up of a series of line and arc segments. A secondary method for placing curtain walls uses 2-D lines, arcs, rectangles, circles, and polylines as a reference for how the curtain wall meets the ground. This method has many benefits, including the ability to automatically update curtain walls if the reference curve changes. Any length or shape change to the reference curve automatically updates the curtain wall to which it is attached. Figure 14.15 demonstrates placing a curtain wall using a reference base curve.

Technique to Master **T14.15** Placing a Curtain Wall by Referencing a Base Curve

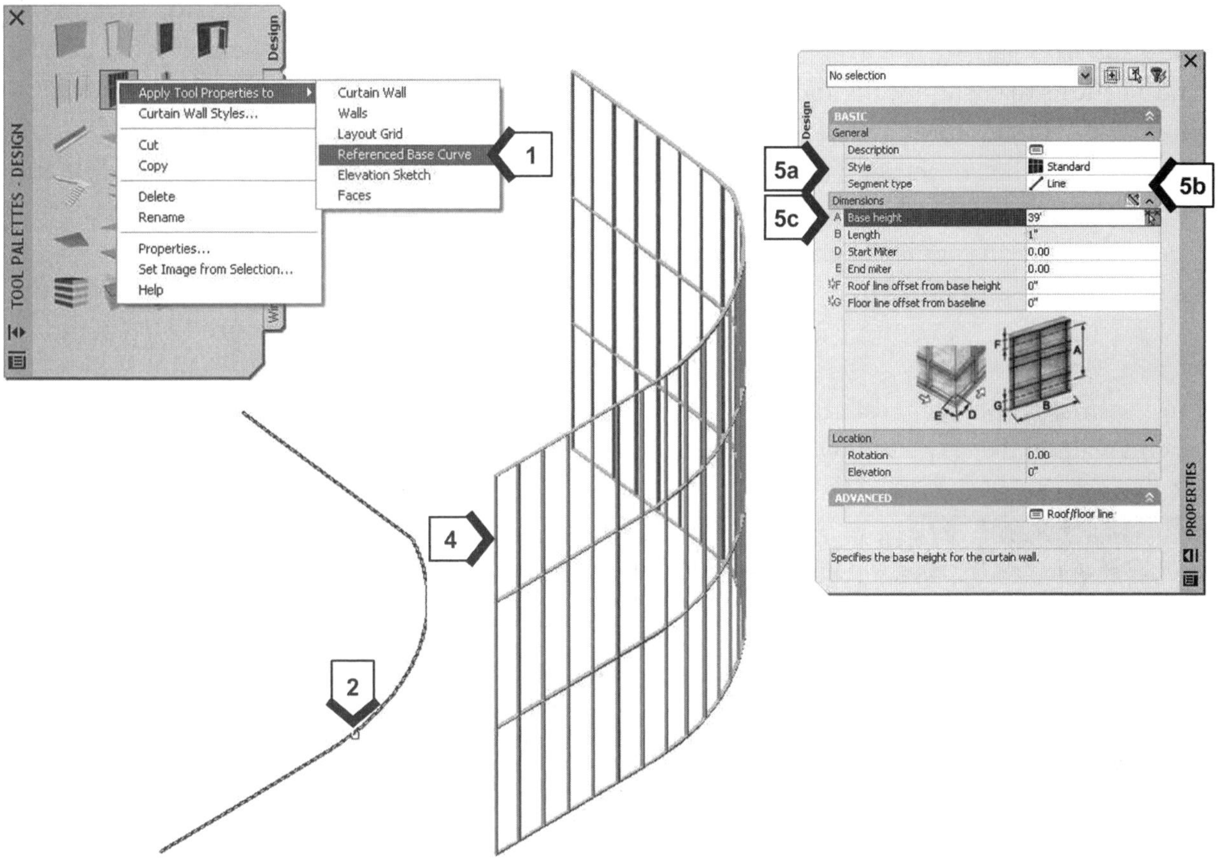

Figure 14.15

1	[Design Tool palette]	Right-click on the Curtain Wall tool to display hidden menu. Left-click on Apply Tool Properties To>Referenced Base Curve command.
2	[Drawing Screen]	Select a single line, arc, rectangle, or circle that the curtain wall object will reference. (Polylines produce unexpected results.) Only one object may be selected at a time.
3	Repeat Steps 1 and 2 until curtain wall is complete.	
4	[Drawing Screen]	Select newly created curtain wall objects.
5a, 5b, 5c	[Properties palette]	Adjust curtain style, base height, and mitering if necessary. (Note that only the standard curtain wall style is available until additional styles are created or imported. See the section on curtain wall style creation and technique T14.31 for directions on importing existing styles from the Content Library.)

Placing a Door/Window Assembly Within a Wall (Drawing with the Door/Window Assembly Object)

You place door/window assemblies by anchoring them to an existing wall. This is similar to how a door or window is placed in ADT. You'll notice that door/window assemblies are also center justified. Figure 14.16 demonstrates the door/window assemby placement process.

Curtain Wall and Door/Window Assembly Modifications

Modifications to curtain walls and door/window assemblies on an individual basis are made through the Properties palette, grip, and specialty commands available to these object types. This section provides a brief outline of the more useful properties.

Property Modifications

The essential property modifications of curtain walls and door/window assemblies include general-, dimensional-, and location-based properties. Figure 14.17 illustrates some of the properties that are relevant to the CW and WA placement process. Changing object properties with the properties palette is straightforward. By left-clicking into any non-grayed field, individual properties of the CW or WA are easily modified.

Matching the Properties of a Curtain Wall Tool

Property modifications to existing curtain wall and door/window assemblies can also be accomplished through tool-specific match commands. Using a library made up of curtain walls and door/window assemblies, style and property matching can be applied to any existing CW or WA object through the ApplyToolToObjects command located in the tool's right-click menu. Figure 14.18 demonstrates the technique.

Technique to Master **T14.16** Placing a Door/Window Assembly Using the Add Door/Window Assembly Tool

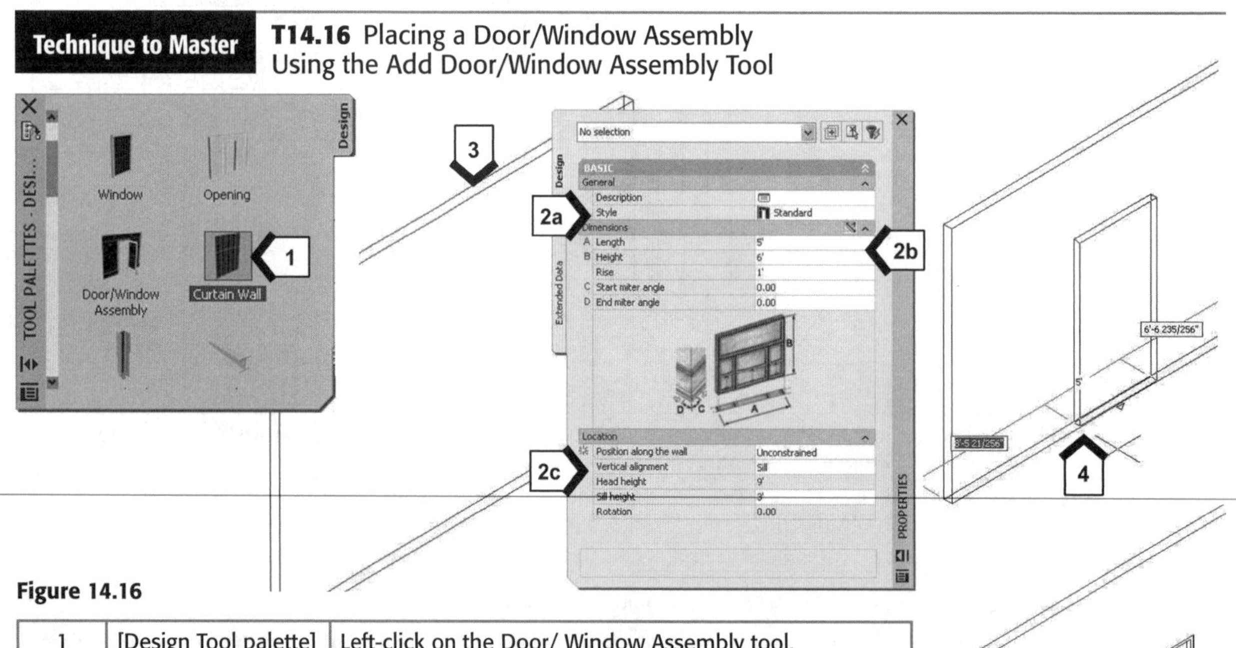

Figure 14.16

1	[Design Tool palette]	Left-click on the Door/ Window Assembly tool.
2a, 2b, 2c	[Properties palette]	Select the appropriate style, length, height, vertical alignment, and sill or head location. (Note that only the standard curtain wall style is available until additional styles are created or imported. See the section on curtain wall style creation and Technique T14.31 for directions on importing existing styles from the Content Library.)
3	[Drawing Screen]	Select the wall that the WA will be placed in.
4	[Drawing Screen]	Left-click to locate the WA system within the wall.

Technique to Master T14.17 Modifying a Curtain Wall or Door/Window Assembly Using the Properties Palette

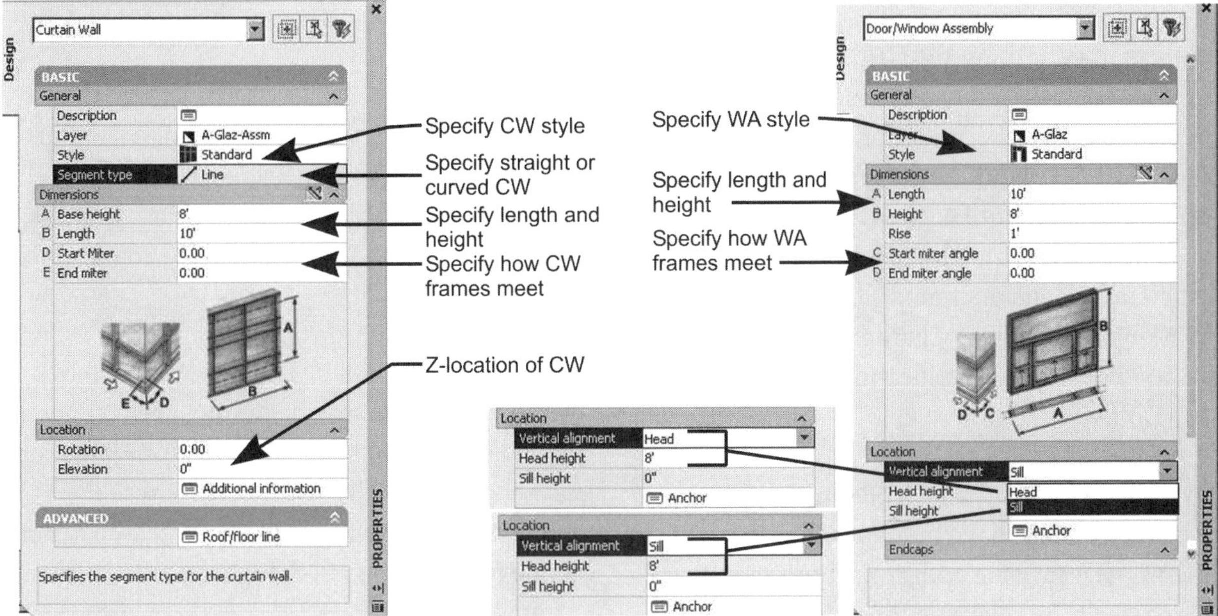

Figure 14.17 Grayed out areas designate properties that cannot be changed.

Technique to Master T14.18 Modifying an Existing Curtain Wall or Door/Window Assembly Using the ApplyToolToObjects Command

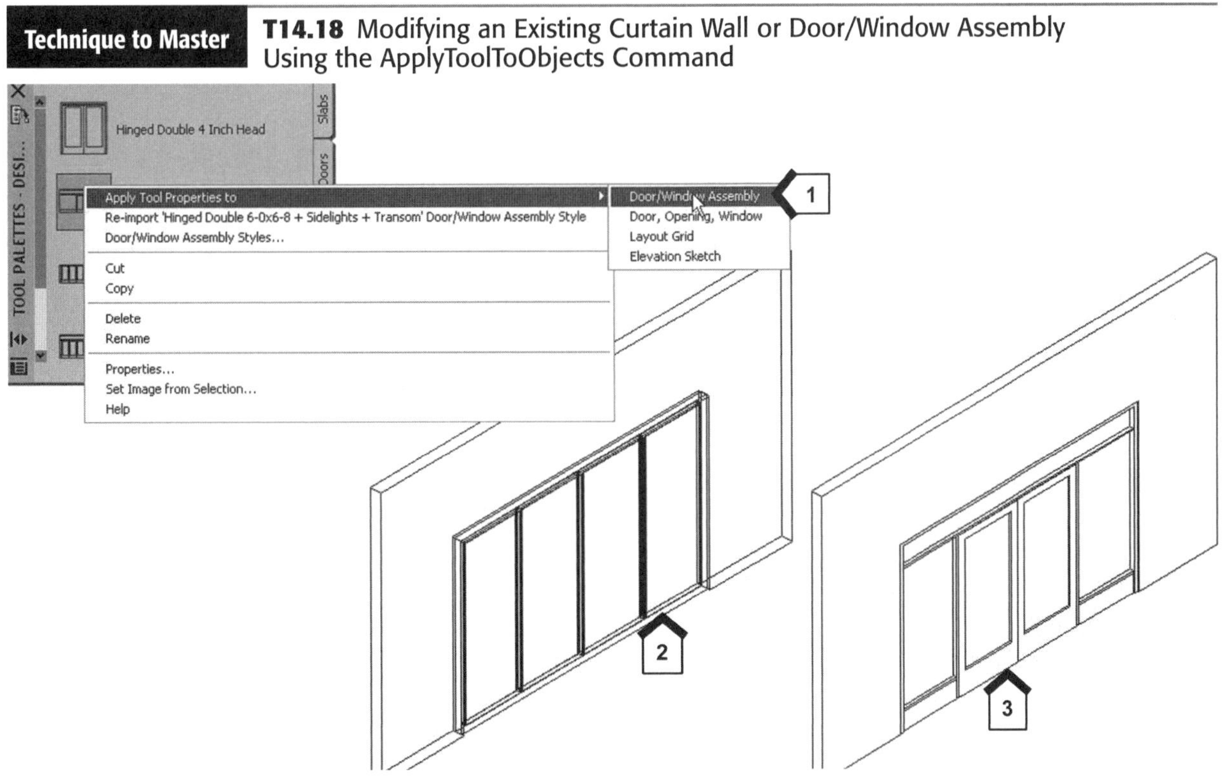

Figure 14.18

1	[Design Tool palette]	Right-click on desired tool then choose Apply Tool Properties to>Curtain Wall (or door/window assembly)
2	[Drawing Screen]	Select all curtain walls (or door/window assemblies) to change. Finish selection by pressing Enter on the keyboard.
3	The selected curtain walls (or door/window assemblies) now have the same properties as the tool.	

CW and WA Grip Editing

Chapter 2 first introduced grip usage as a means for easy visual modifications of the objects in your drawing. Grip modifications on the CW and WA objects include location, length, base height, and roof/floor line edits. Figure 14.19 identifies the grip points for this object type. Figure 14.20 reviews the use of grips with dynamic dimensions to perform efficient dimensional modifications on CW or WA objects. Refer to Chapter 2 and Chapter 12 to review grip modifications for other ADT objects.

Specialty Modification Commands

All ADT objects have hidden right-click menus that provide additional tool-specific commands. By selecting the object, then right-clicking, you can access the hidden menu containing these specialty commands. Some of the more useful commands are summarized in the paragraphs that follow.

Reverse

The Reverse Direction grip reverses the start and end points of the selected curtain wall. This is helpful for nonuniform curtain walls when specific alignments must be maintained (Figure 14.21).

Set Miter Angles

Mitering refers to the beveling of two edges so that they may join correctly. Mitering does not occur automatically at corners between curtain walls or window assemblies—a miter angle must be specified. Figure 14.22 demonstrates the technique.

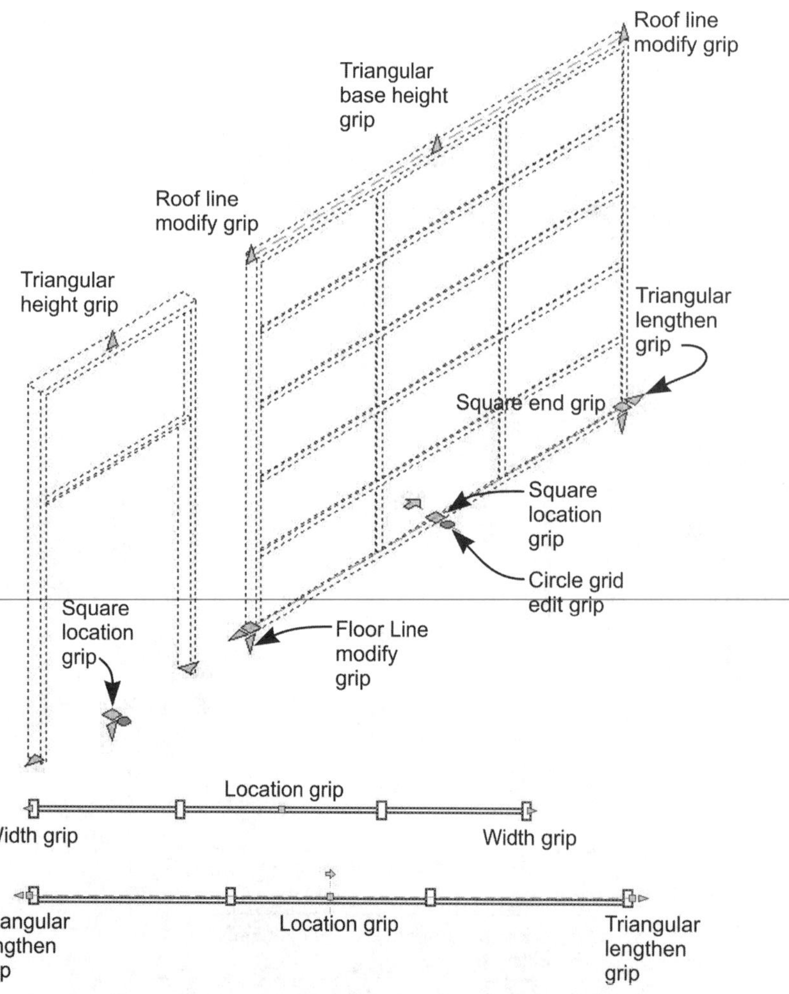

Figure 14.19 Grips for the curtain wall and door/window assembly objects

Technique to Master **T14.20** Using Grips with Dynamic Dimensions to Perform Efficient Dimensional Modifications on CW or WA Objects

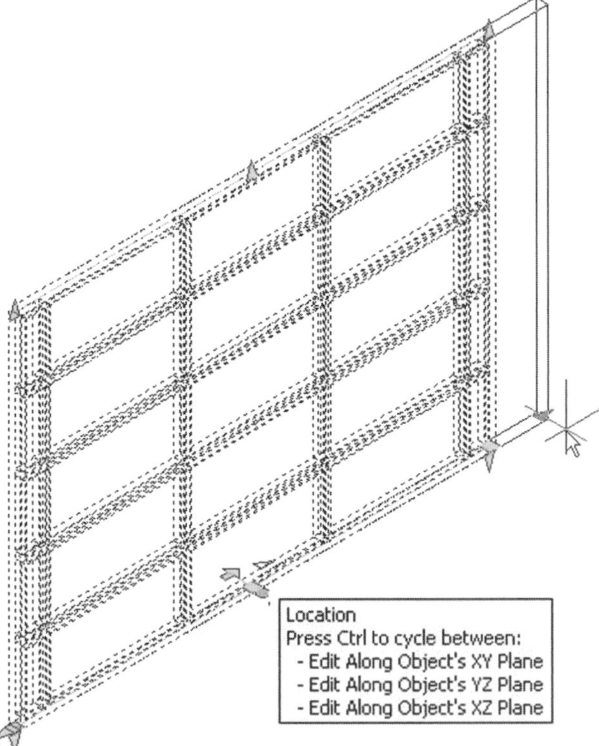

Figure 14.20

Using the CTRL key with the location grip allows you to cycle between three different methods of restricting positioning movement.
The center grip triangles at the top and bottom are used for changes in the overall base height and baseline, respectively. Grip triangles located at the corners are used to relocate corner heights.

Figure 14.21 The Reverse Direction grip reverses the start and end points of the selected curtain wall.

Technique to Master **T14.22** Modifying Curtain Wall Corners Using Set Miter Angles

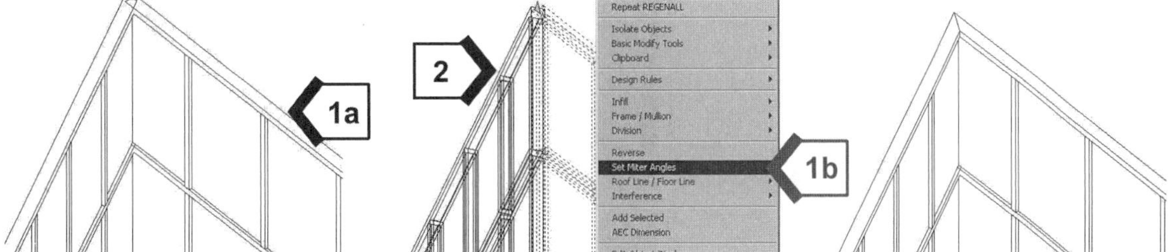

Figure 14.22

1a, 1b	[Drawing Screen]	Select first curtain wall (or door/window assembly). Right-click to access hidden menu and choose Set Miter Angles.
2	[Drawing Screen]	Select second curtain wall (or door/window assembly) to miter to.

Roof Line/Floor Line Modifications

As you may recall from Chapter 13, examples of Roof/floor line modifications included stepped walls and wall-shaped gables. Roof/floor line modifications can also be applied to curtain walls by employing the same techniques used to create the complex wall shapes. Vertices that are synonymous with corners are added and/or edited to create shapes that are nonrectangular (Figure 14.23). Chapter 13 demonstrated the roof/floor line editing dialogue method for editing wall shapes. Figure 14.24 demonstrates how to edit the roof and floor lines of curtain walls using an alternative method. Figure 14.25 uses a polyline to create a T-shaped curtain wall.

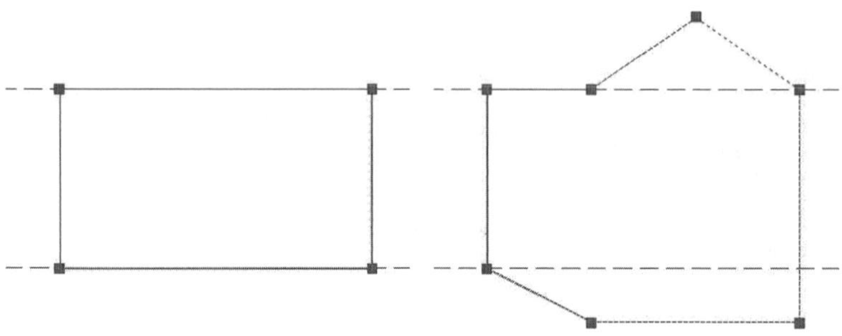

Figure 14.23 Roof/floor line curtain wall modifications employ the same techniques used to create the complex wall shapes. Vertices that are synonymous with corners are added and/or edited to create shapes that are nonrectangular.

Technique to Master **T14.24** Changing the Roof Line's Shape by Projecting to a Polyline

Figure 14.24

1	[Drawing Screen]	Draw polyline shape. Make sure the polyline is an open shape and starts and ends at the curtain wall head.
2a, 2b	[Drawing Screen]	Select curtain wall. Right-click to access hidden menu and choose Modify Roof Line.
3	Type P (to project roof line to polyline).	
4	Select polyline.	

Technique to Master T14.25 Changing the Floor Line's Shape by Projecting to a Polyline

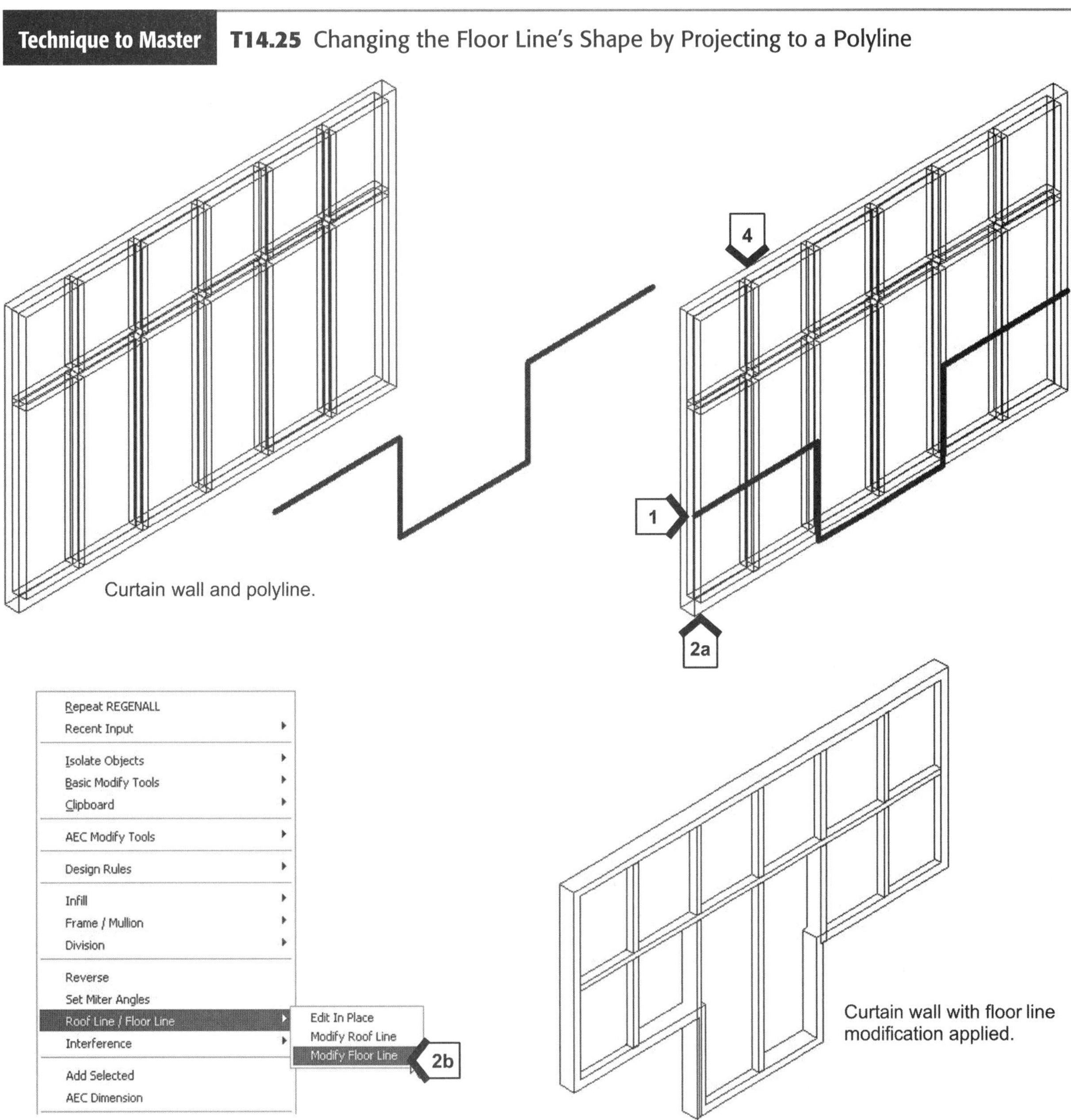

Figure 14.25

1	[Drawing Screen]	Draw a polyline at an elevation below the existing wall.
2a, 2b	[Drawing Screen]	Select wall, right-click, and choose Roof/Floor Line>Modify Floor Line command.
3	[Command Line]	Type P and hit Enter to project to the polyline.
4	[Drawing Screen]	Select the polyline.
5	Hit Enter to complete command.	

Adding Interferences to Curtain Walls and Door/Window Assemblies

Interferences use ADT objects to create cutouts in other ADT objects. Although any object may be used, mass elements, mass groups, and structural elements are the objects most often used as interferences. Figure 14.26 demonstrates the procedure.

> **Box 14.2**
>
> Before invoking the GridAssemblyInterferenceAdd command, place the interference object so that it maintains a touching relationship with the curtain wall or door/window assembly.

Technique to Master **T14.26** Adding and Removing an Interference to a Curtain Wall or Door/Window Assembly

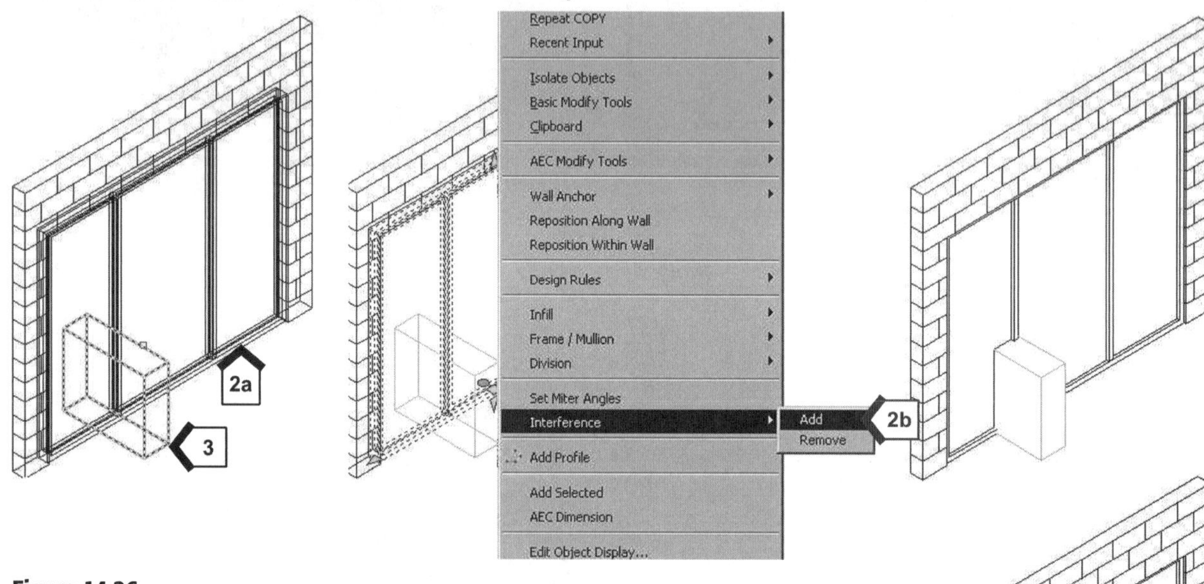

Figure 14.26

1	The interference object must continue to touch the curtain wall or door/window assembly for the command to work successfully.	
2a, 2b	[Drawing Screen]	Select the curtain wall or door/window assembly, right-click to access hidden menu, and choose the Interference>Add command. (To remove an existing interference, choose the Interference>Remove command.)
3	[Drawing Screen]	Select all objects that will create the interference. Hit Enter to finish the selection. (If you are removing an interference, select objects to remove. Removal command is completed at this point.)
4	[Command Line]	Respond to "Apply to infill?" with Yes or No.
5	[Command Line]	Respond to "Apply to frames?" with Yes or No.
6	[Command Line]	Respond to "Apply to mullions?" with Yes or No.
7	If command is successful, the following note will display of the command line: "1 object(s) added as interference."	

Curtain Wall and Door/Window Assembly Styles

Chapter 13 introduced you to the use of styles. Curtain walls and door/window assemblies also use styles. These styles are unique because in addition to controlling visibility, lineweight, hatching surfaces, and rendering textures, these styles also determine how the curtain wall and door/window assembly looks (Figure 14.27).

The default style called Standard differs from Standard styles in other ADT objects because there are already predefined division orientations and spacing. Using this Standard style during the conceptual stages of a design, therefore, might produce unexpected results since these preset division orientations and spacing might not be what you are looking for (Figure 14.28).

A Review of the Style Manager Dialogue Box

The Style Manager is the dialogue box used to create and edit styles for any of the style-based objects. Access the curtain wall or door/window assembly Style Manager by right-clicking on the appropriate tool within the Design Tool palette (Figure 14.29).

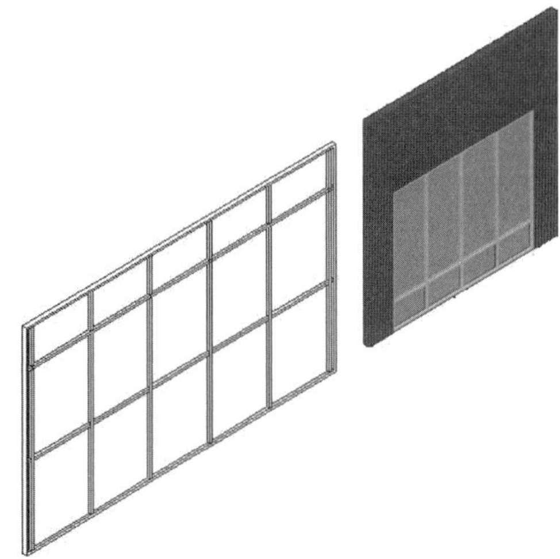

Figure 14.27 Curtain wall and door/window assembly styles control component visibility, lineweight, hatching and rendering textures, as well as how the curtain wall and door/window assembly looks.

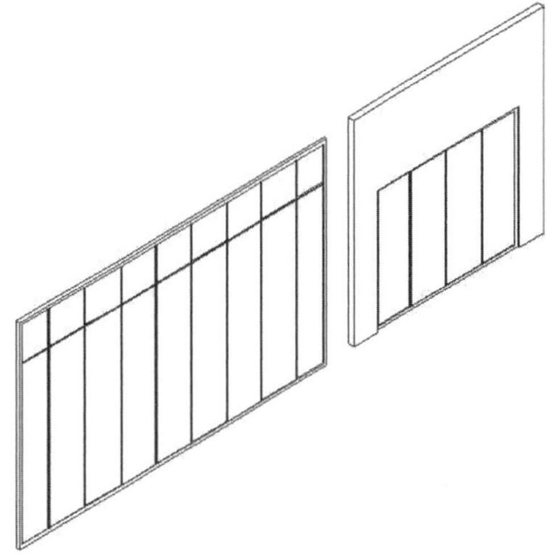

Figure 14.28 Using the Standard style during the conceptual stages of the design process may produce unwanted results since division orientations and spacing need to be unique.

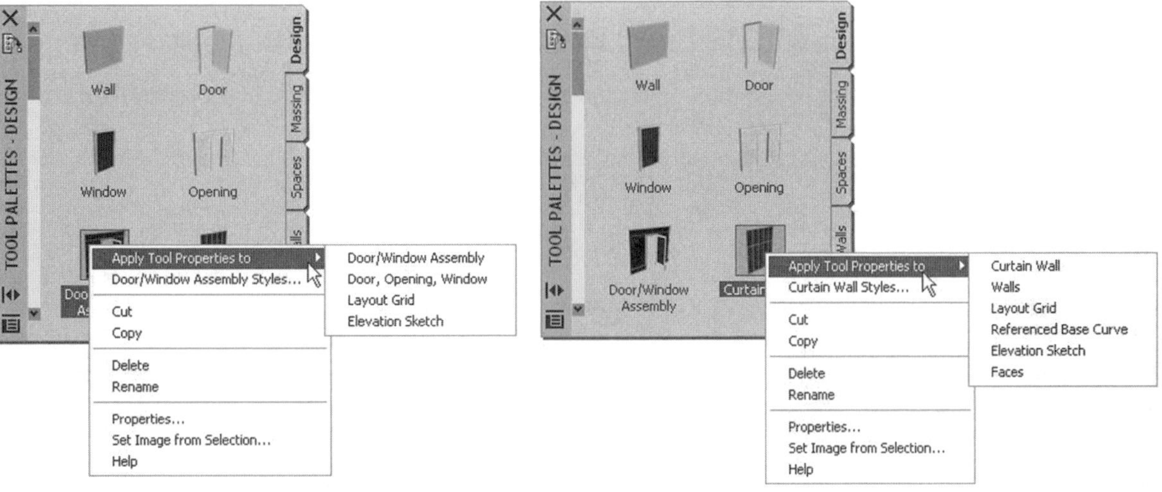

Figure 14.29 Access the curtain wall or door/window assembly style manager by right-clicking on the appropriate tool within the Design Tool palette.

When first opened, the Style Manager displays a dialogue box that is divided into three areas. Refer to Chapter 13 to review the relevant parts of these areas. The individual style properties are categorized into tabbed areas. Various tabs of the Style Manager are unique to curtain walls and door/window assemblies.

Importing Existing Curtain Wall and Door/Window Assembly Styles

The Content Browser Library contains more than 120 door/window styles and more than 10 curtain wall styles to use. A few examples are shown in Figure 14.30. Figure 14.31 demonstrates how to find and import these styles into the current drawing.

Creating New Styles

A new curtain wall or door/window assembly style is created using the Style Manager for the respective object type. Creating a new style requires the definition of the CW and WA components.

Creating the Component Definitions

Component definitions refer to the various elements that make up the eventual curtain wall. CW and WA systems will always have at least one definition for each of its component types; however, there are instances where several definitions for a type are needed. Figure 14.32 illustrates this concept. In this figure, the storefront system shows a bottom frame that is different from the top and sides. It also shows three types of infill—glass infill, metal panel infill, and a door infill. To create the above storefront system, the six component definitions identified in Table 14.1 would need to be created.

> **Box 14.3**
> Component definitions that are defined in one curtain wall or door/window assembly style cannot be transferred to other curtain wall or door/window assembly styles.

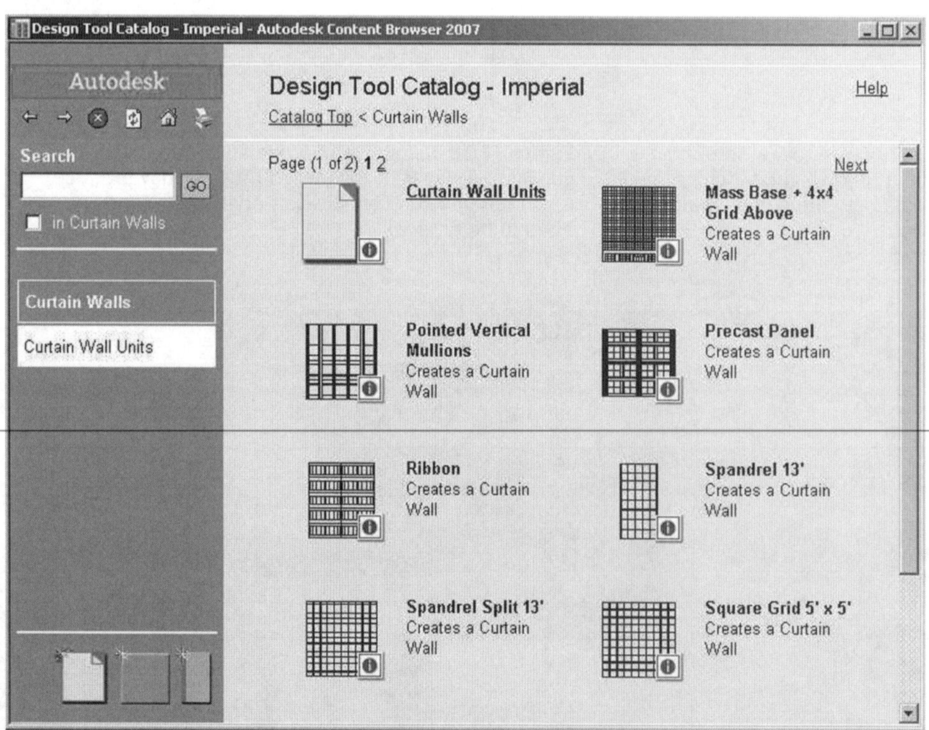

Figure 14.30 Examples of the Content Browser's Library of door/window styles and curtain wall styles

Technique to Master **T14.31** Importing an Existing Curtain Wall or Door/Window Assembly from the AEC Content Browser Library

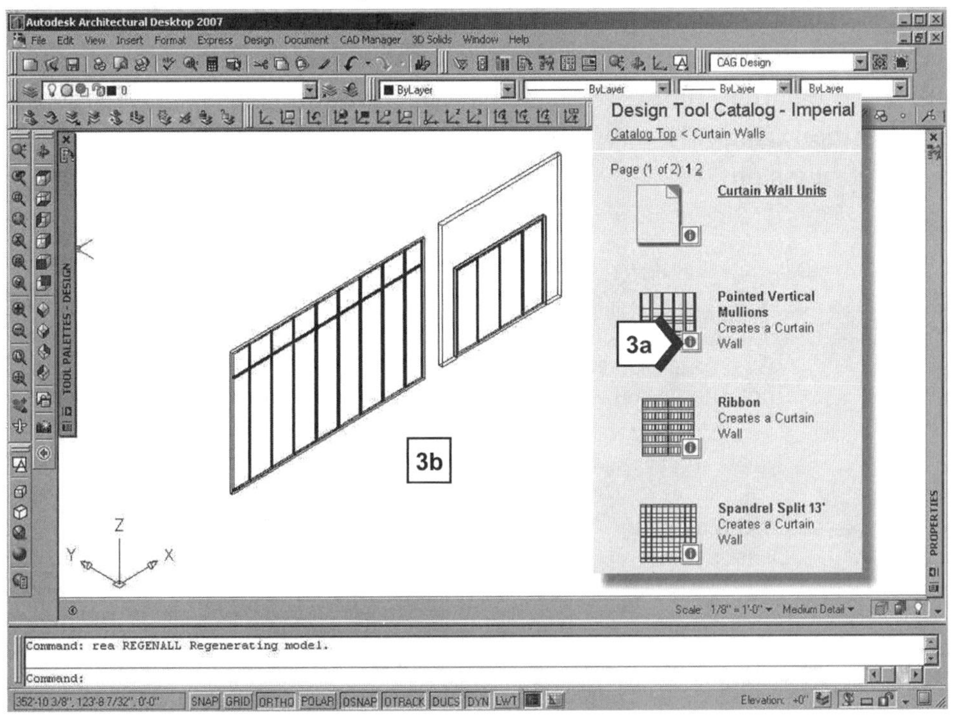

Figure 14.31

1	Open the Content Browser Library (Ctrl+4).	
2	[Content Browser Library]	Left-click on Design Tool Catalog.
3	[Content Browser Library>Design Tool Catalog]	At left-pane, click on Curtain Walls category.
4	[Content Browser Library>Design Tool Catalog>Curtain Walls]	Using the eyedropper tool, left-click and hold over curtain wall then move to drawing screen and release mouse.

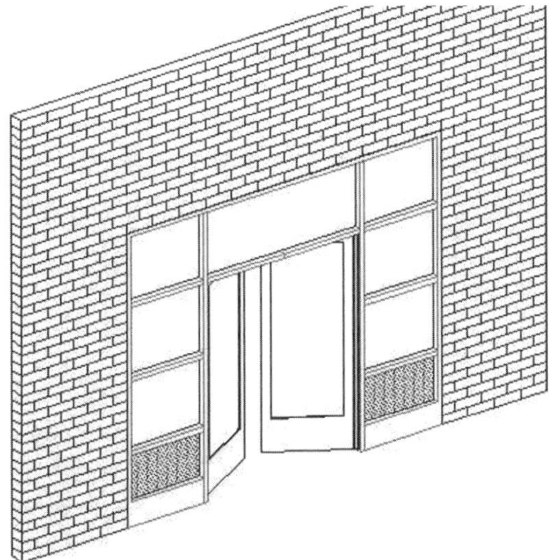

Figure 14.32 This storefront system shows a bottom frame that is different from the top and sides. It also shows three types of infill: glass infill, metal-panel infill, and a door infill.

Table 14.1 Component Definitions

Component Type	Descriptive Name	Profile Dimensions	Applied To
Frame	Frame-main	3" wide/high × 7" deep rectangle	top and sides
Frame	Frame-bottom	10" wide/high × 7" deep rectangle	bottom
Infill	Infill-door	(choose style of door)	

Creating Division Definitions

The division definition defines the spacing between mullions from edge of frame to center of mullion and center of mullion to center of mullion. Figure 14.33 identifies the key areas of the division definition window. Figure 14.34 demonstrates the division definition creation process.

Creating Frame Definitions

The frame is located on the outer edge of the curtain wall or door/window assembly. Its definition delineates what the profile of the frame looks like—its dimensional profile as well as its relation to other components. By default, frame definitions in ADT are rectangular in shape. Its specific measurements are

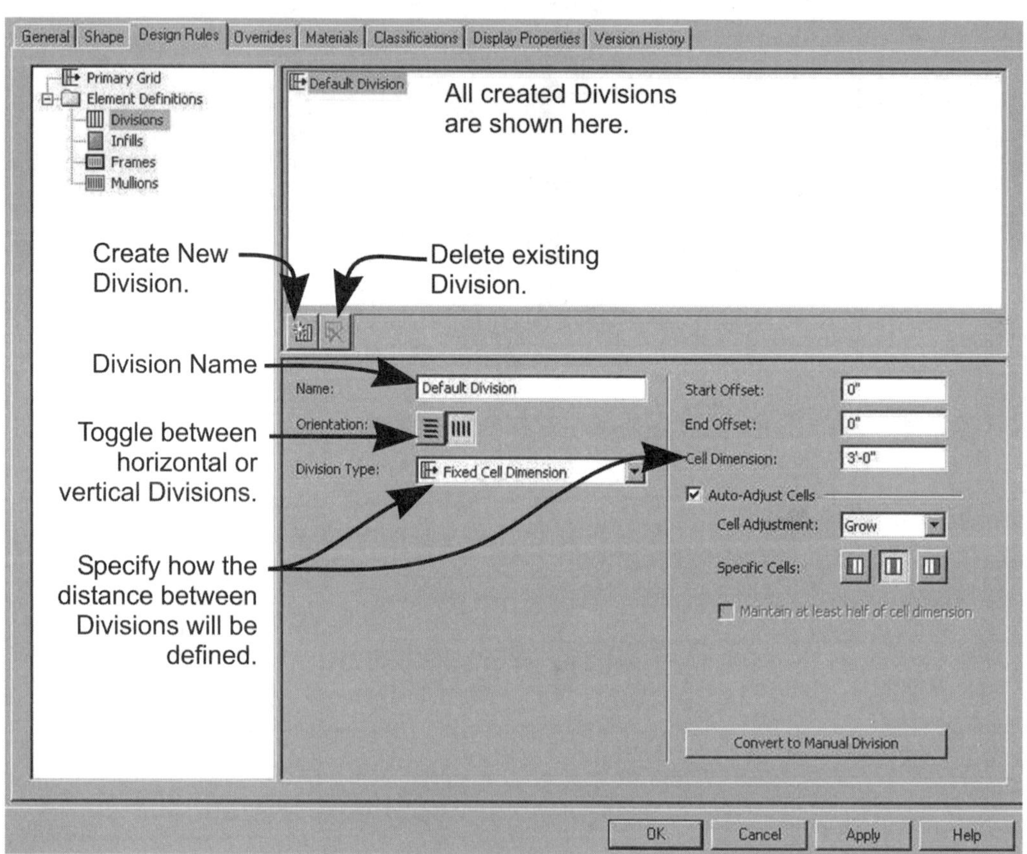

Figure 14.33 The key areas of the division definition window

Technique to Master **T14.34** Creating Division Definitions

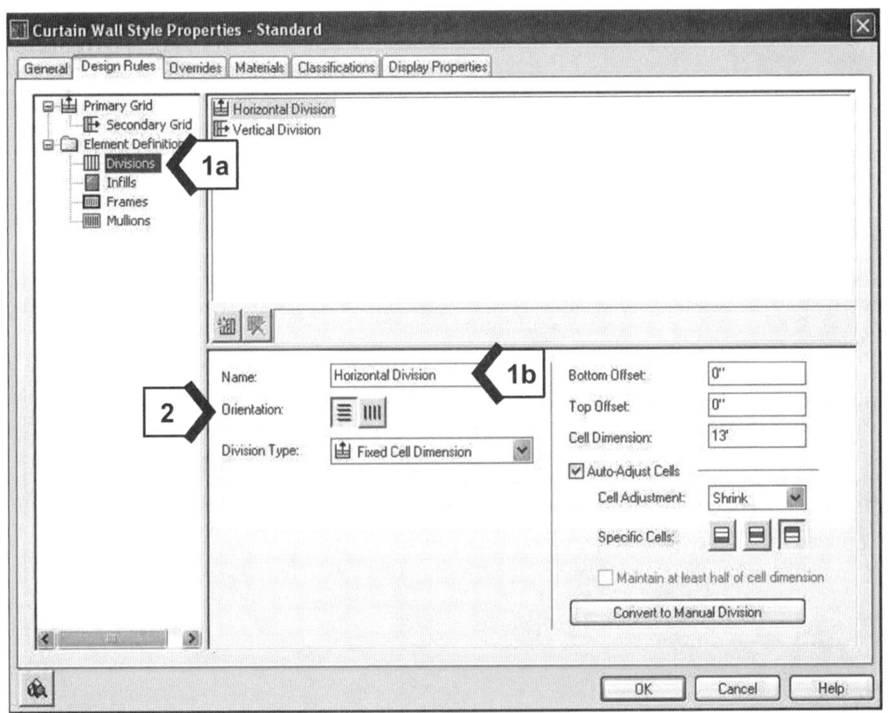

Figure 14.34 Divisions are created by first left-clicking on the Divisions Definition and then adding or editing in the lower dialogue area.

1a 1b	[Curtain Wall Style Manager> Design Rules tab]	In the left pane, select Divisions. In the right pane (middle area), left click the Add New button. Name the Division.
2	[Curtain Wall Style Manager> Design Rules tab]	Choose the Division's orientation.
3a 3b 3c	[Curtain Wall Style Manager> Design Rules tab]	Choose Division Spacing Type. Choices for creating Division Spacing are as follows: a. Fixed Cell Dimension: the spacing between grid lines is given a fixed distance. Specify the distance in the field next to cell dimension. b. Fixed Number of Cells: the Division spacing is determined by dividing the length or height into the number specified next to number of cells. c. Manual: allows you to manually add grid lines and specify the offset value for each gridline added. (For horizontal divisions, it is usually more helpful to consistently specify the offset value from the grid bottom, that is, bottom of the WA or CW.)

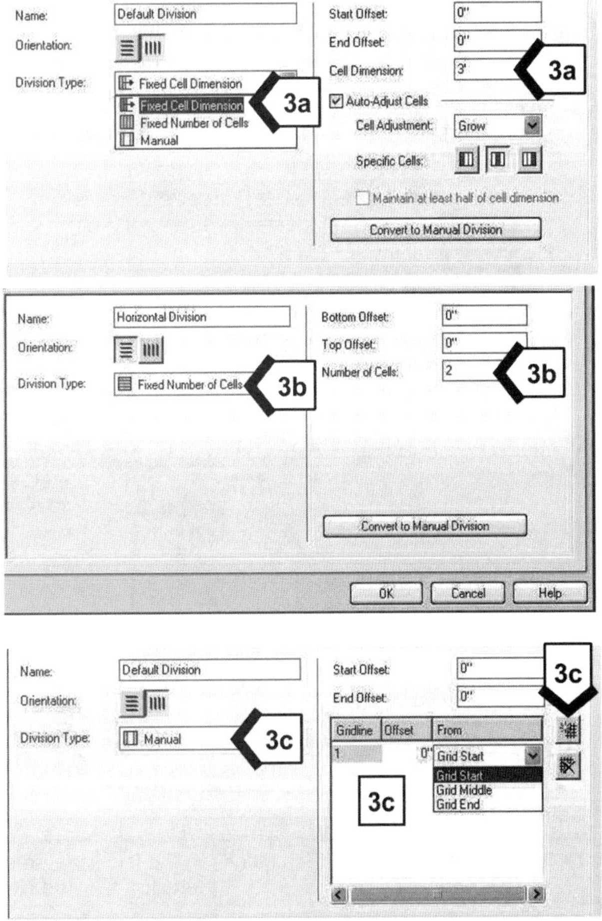

specified in the width and depth boxes. Frame definitions, however, can also be customized shapes through the use of profile definitions. Figure 14.35 identifies the key areas of the frame definition window. Figure 14.36 demonstrates the frame definition creation process.

Creating Mullion Definitions

Mullions are the interior framework that divides up the panes of infill within the frame. Like the frame definition, the mullion definition delineates what the profile looks like—its dimensional profile as well as its relation to

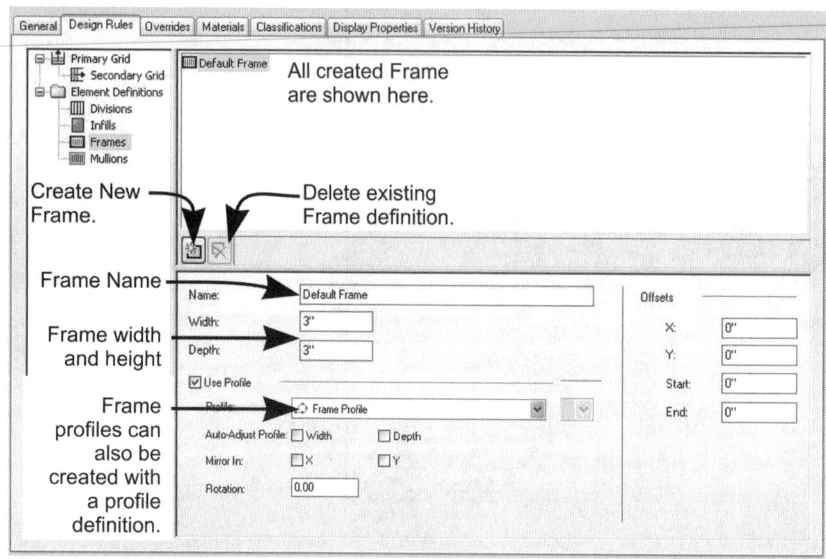

Figure 14.35 The key areas of the frame definition window

Technique to Master **T14.36** Creating Frame Definitions

Figure 14.36

1a, 1b	[Curtain Wall Style Manager> Design Rules tab]	In the left pane, select Frames. In the right pane (middle area), left-click the Add New button. Name the Frame.
2	[Curtain Wall Style Manager> Design Rules tab]	Type in the width and depth for the frame.

other components. Mullions are also by default rectangular in shape. Other shapes are applied through the use of profile definitions. Figure 14.37 identifies the key areas of the mullion definition window. Figure 14.38 demonstrates the mullion definition creation process.

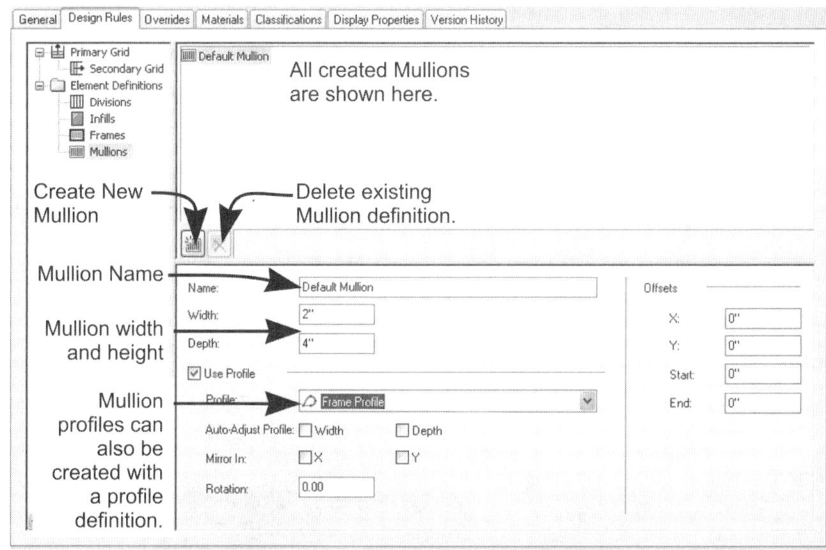

Figure 14.37 The key areas of the mullion definition window

Technique to Master **T14.38** Creating Mullion Definitions

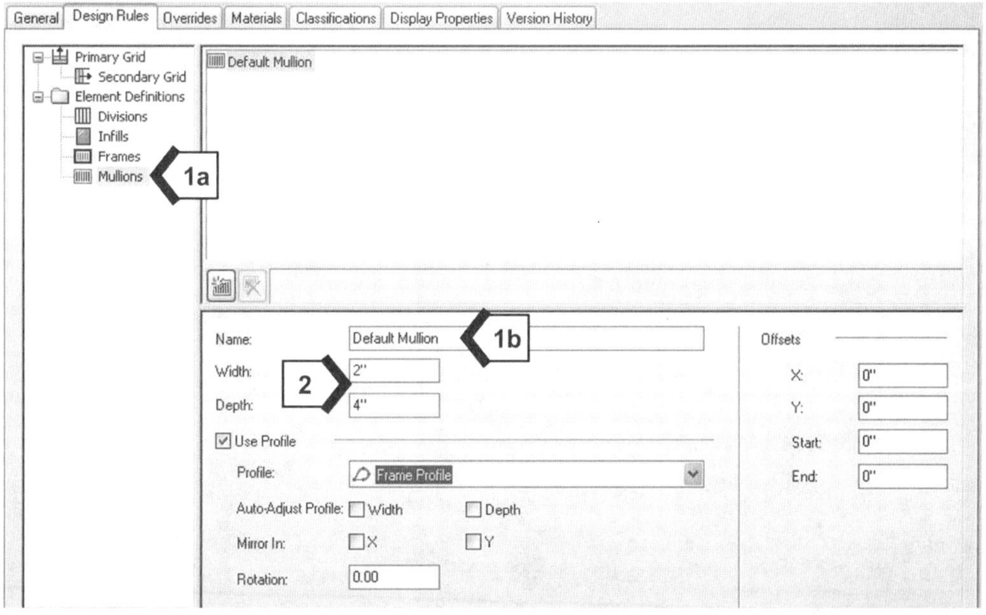

Figure 14.38

1a, 1b	[Curtain Wall Style Manager> Design Rules tab]	In the left pane, select Mullions. In the right pane (middle area), left-click the Add New button. Name the Mullion.
2	[Curtain Wall Style Manager> Design Rules tab]	Type in the width and depth for the mullion.

Using Profile Definitions for Frame or Mullion Definitions

Profile definitions, introduced in Chapter 10, create user-friendly customization opportunities to enhance the basic ADT building objects. Use a profile definition for the frame or mullion to introduce shapes that are not rectangular. Figure 14.39 demonstrates the procedure.

Creating Infill Definitions

Infills are the panes of material located between the mullions and frame components. Figure 14.40 identifies the key areas of the infill definition window. Notice that the default infill definition uses an Infill Type called Simple Panel. This default definition is a generic plane with a thickness that is specified in the Panel Thickness text box. It is usually associated with a glass material; however, any material can be assigned (see the section on assigning materials to the curtain wall and door/window assembly components).

Any door style, window style, door/window assembly style, curtain wall unit style, or AEC polygon can be used as infill definitions (Figure 14.41). Let's take the storefront example used earlier. Figure 14.42

Technique to Master **T14.39** Defining Nonrectangular Frames and Mullions

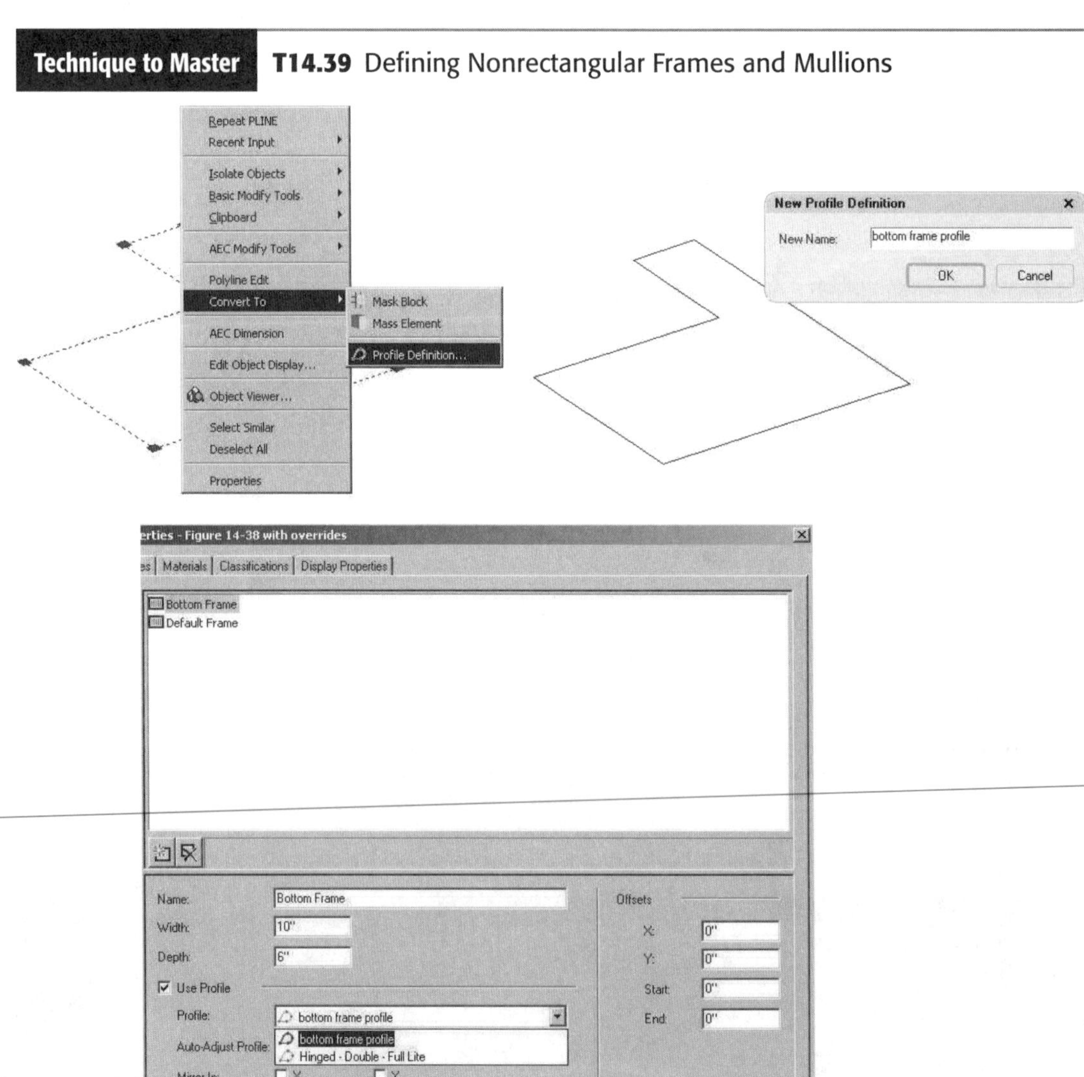

Figure 14.39 Nonrectangular frames and mullions are created by assigning profile definitions to the frame or mullion definition.

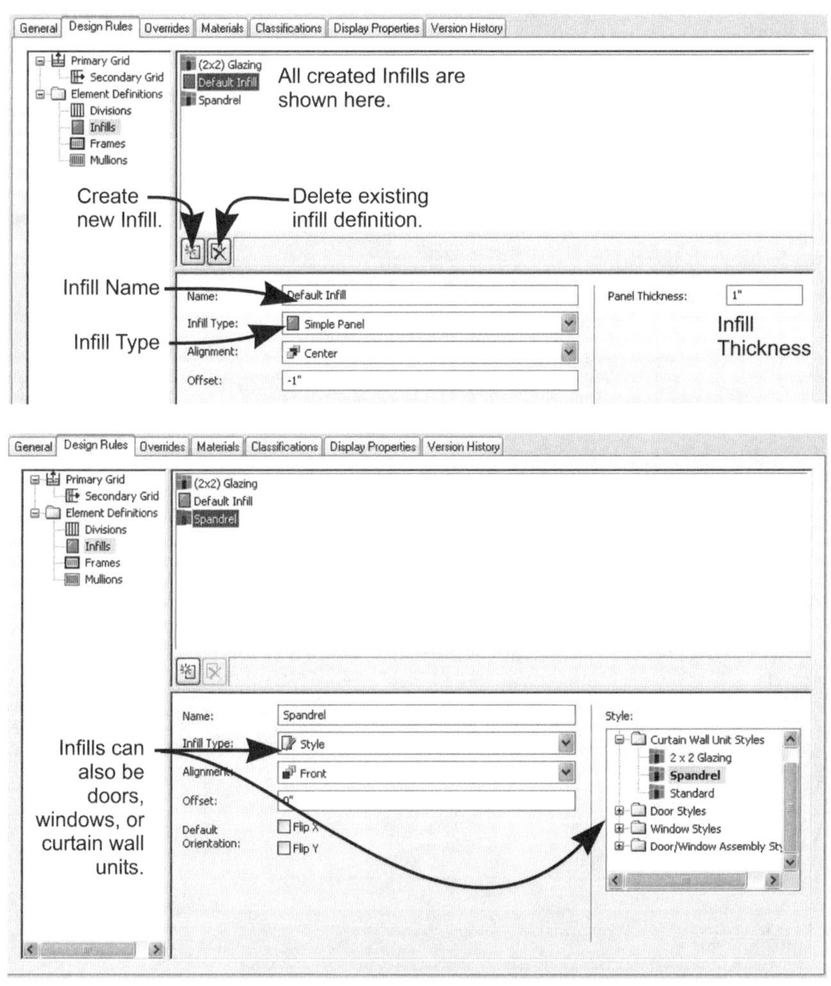

Figure 14.40 The key areas of the infill definition window

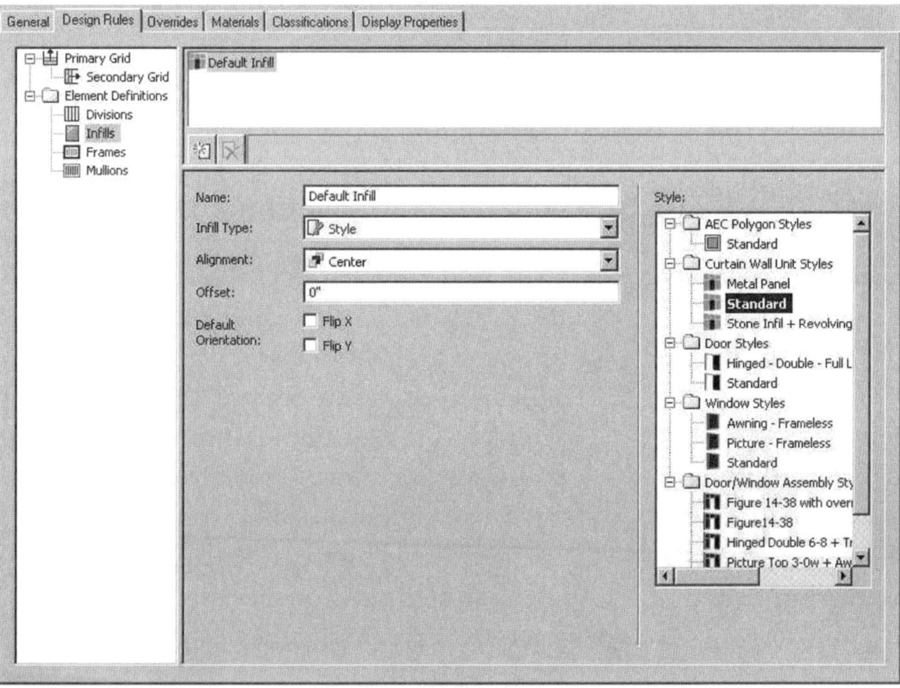

Figure 14.41 Any door style, window style, door/window assembly style, curtain wall unit style, or AEC polygon can be used as infill definitions.

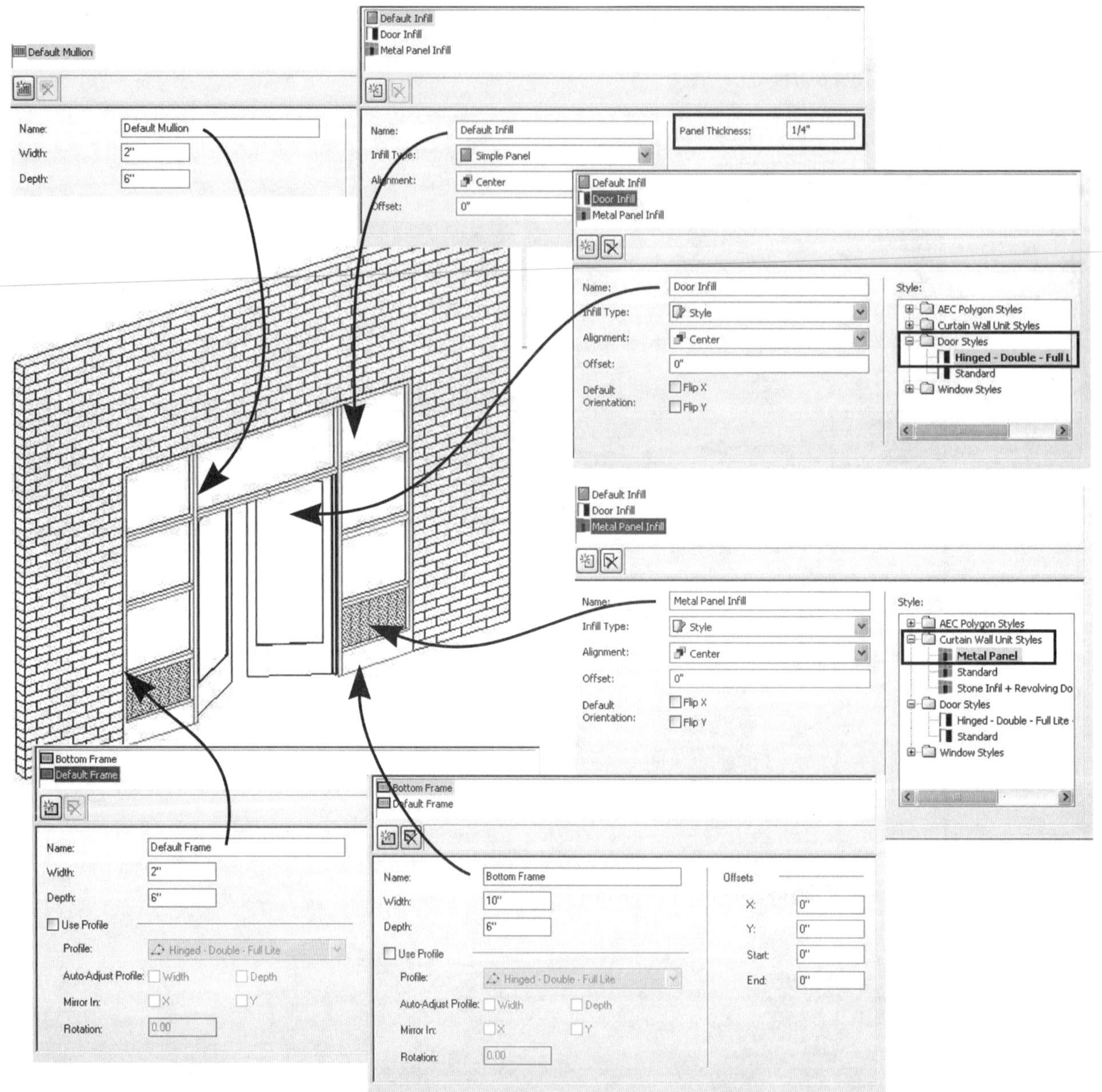

Figure 14.42 The frame, mullion, and infill needed to complete the storefront design.

illustrates the three infill definitions needed to complete the storefront design.

In addition to specifying the Infill Type and Panel Thickness, alignment and offset options are also available. These options control the relationship of the infill to its surrounding mullion and/or frame. Figure 14.43 illustrates this concept. Figure 14.44 demonstrates the infill definition creation process.

Assigning the Division, Infill, Frame, and Mullion Definitions to the Grid

Although the definitions for division, frame, mullion, and infill are defined, they still need to be assigned to a specific location on the curtain wall or door/window assembly. Curtain wall and door/window assembly component are assigned within the Style Manager's Design Rules tab or directly on-screen using assignment overrides. Assignment overrides are discussed in Chapter 15.

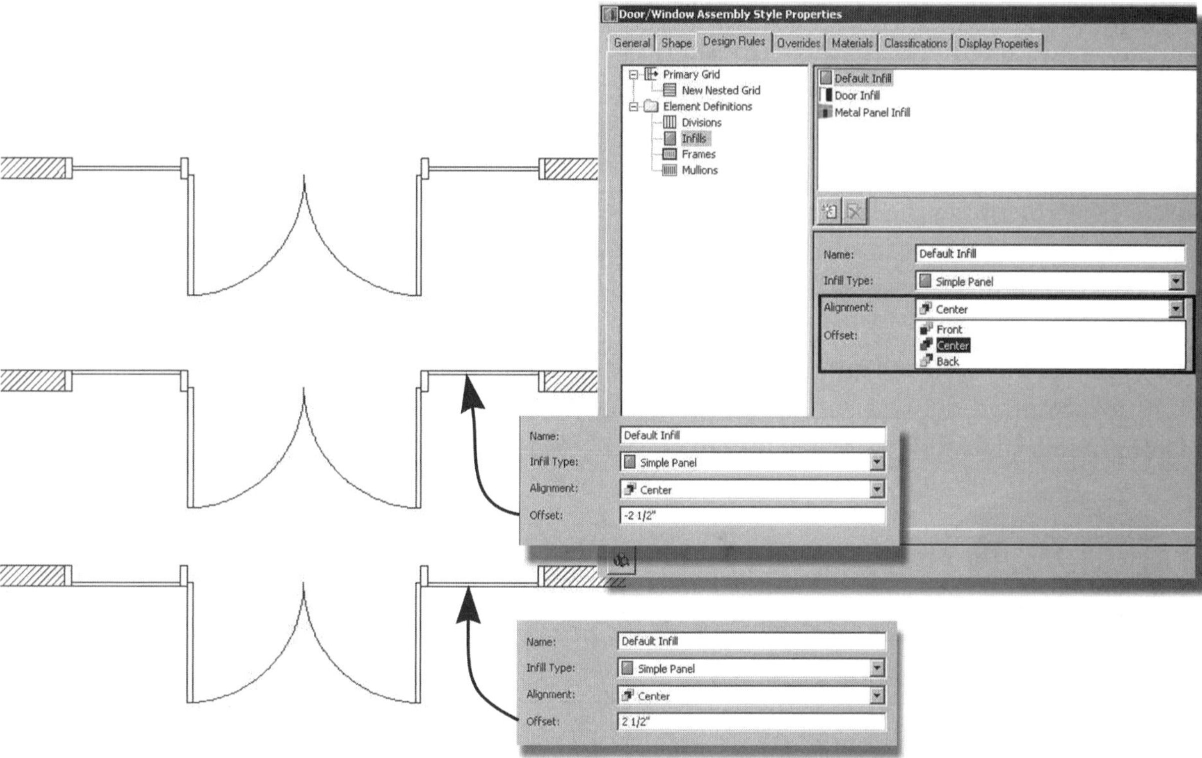

Figure 14.43 Infill Type and Panel Thickness control the relationship of the infill to its surrounding mullion and/or frame.

Technique to Master **T14.44** Creating Infill Definitions

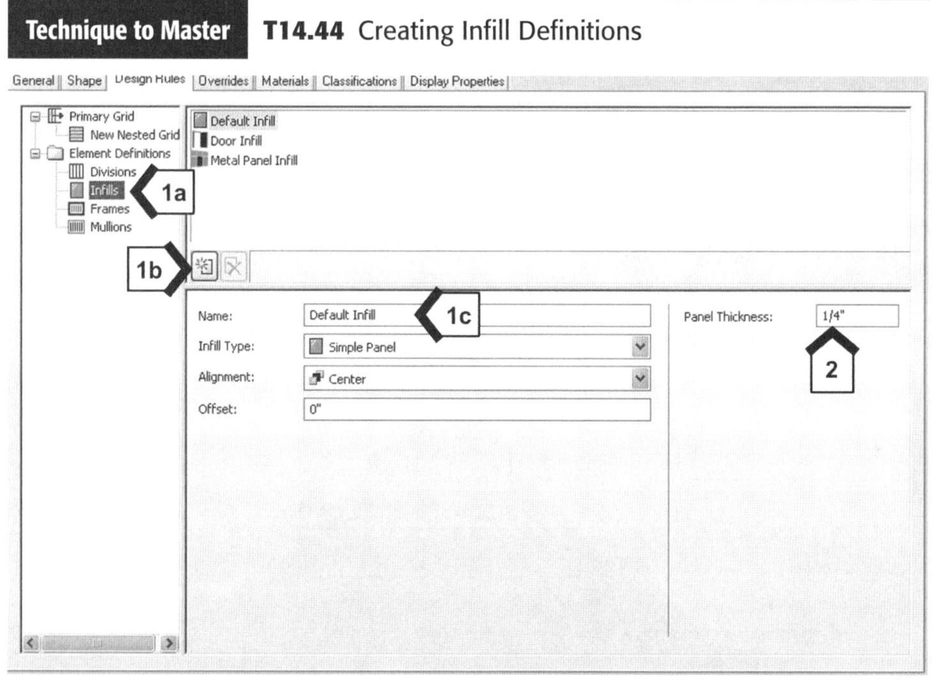

Figure 14.44

1a, 1b, 1c	[Curtain Wall Style Manager> Design Rules tab]	In the left pane, select Infills. In the right pane (middle area), left-click the Add New button. Name the Infill.
2	[Curtain Wall Style Manager> Design Rules tab]	Type in the infill Panel Thickness.

Component assignments are completed by selecting a grid and then assigning a division, frame, mullion, and infill to the grid. A grid may use multiple frame, mullion, and infill definitions, but only one division definition. Figure 14.45 identifies the key areas for assigning components.

Grid Nesting

Since a grid can be assigned only one division definition, multiple division definitions must be used for curtain walls or door/window assemblies with mullions in more than one orientation. Grid Nesting refers to combining two or more grid systems (Figure 14.46).

Establishing a Secondary Grid (Creating the Grid Nesting)

To assign the second division, Grid Nesting must be established. Figure 14.47 illustrates the procedure to create a Secondary Grid system that is nested within the Primary Grid system.

Technique to Master **T14.45** Assigning the Definitions to the Grid

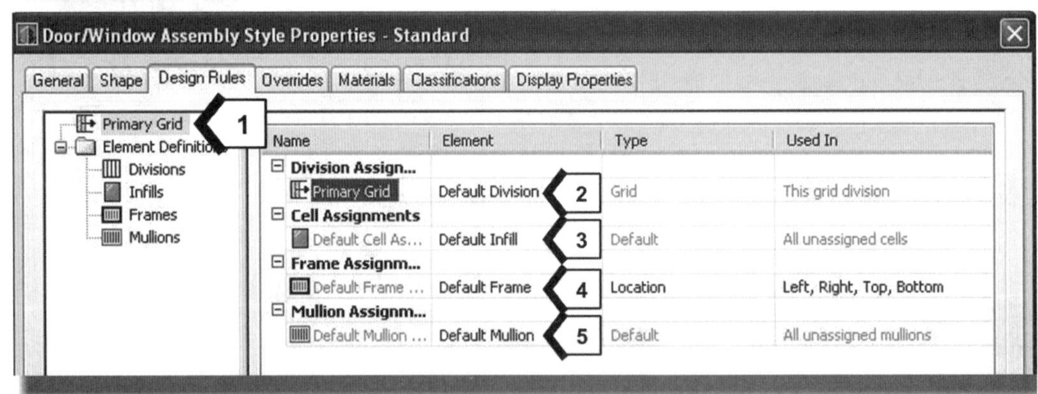

Figure 14.45

[Curtain Wall Style Manager> Design Rules tab]	In the left pane, select Primary Grid. In the right pane (upper area), assign the element definition to the division, cell, frame, and mullion assignments. If there is only one definition for the element, it will automatically use the default.

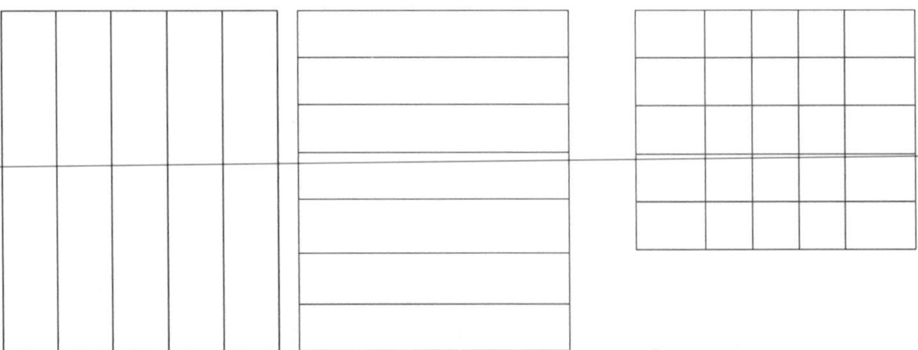

Figure 14.46 Grid Nesting refers to combining two or more grid systems.

Technique to Master T14.47 Creating a Secondary Grid System (Grid Nesting)

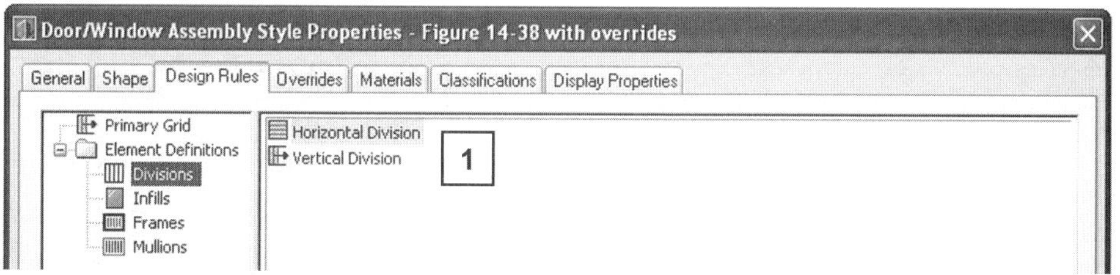

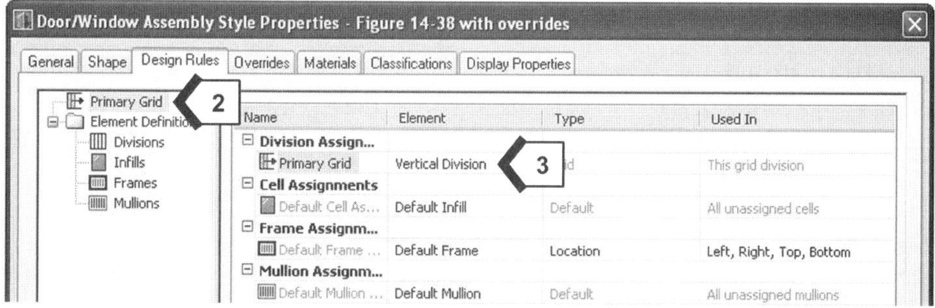

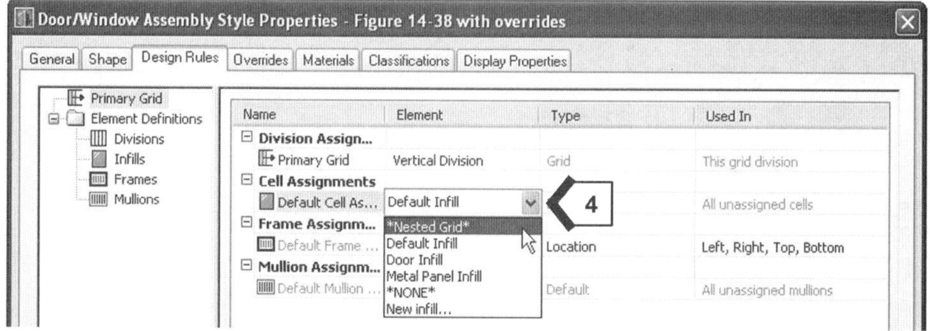

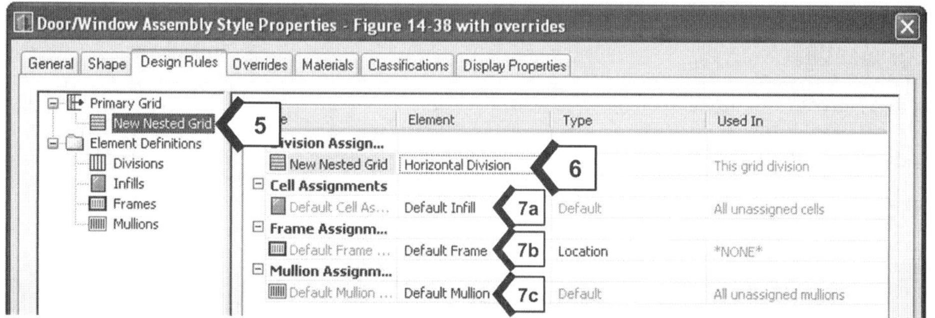

Figure 14.47

1	More than one division assignment must be created to accomplish Grid Nesting successfully.	
2	[Curtain Wall Style Manager> Design Rules tab]	Select the Primary Grid located on the left panel.
3	[Curtain Wall Style Manager> Design Rules tab]	In right pane, under Division Assignments, assign the Primary Grid a division.
4	[Curtain Wall Style Manager> Design Rules tab]	In right pane, under Cell Assignments, assign the Default Cell Assignment to Nested Grid.
5	[Curtain Wall Style Manager> Design Rules tab]	In left pane, select New Nested Grid. (You can rename this if you like.)
6	[Curtain Wall Style Manager> Design Rules tab]	In right pane, under Division Assignments, assign the secondary division.
7a, 7b, 7c	[Curtain Wall Style Manager> Design Rules tab]	Change the cell, frame, and mullion assignments as necessary for Secondary Grid.

Creating a Curtain Wall or Door/Window Assembly Style—The Workflow Process

The workflow process is summarized as follows:

1. Open the Style Manager for the appropriate object type—that is, the curtain wall style manager for curtain walls or the door/window assembly style manager for door/window assemblies.
2. Use the New Style button to create a new style, then name the style. Remember to try to keep style naming consistent.
3. For door/window assemblies only: In the right pane, left-click on the Shape tab. Choose the overall shape for the door/window assembly from the Predefined list box (Figure 14.48a). If a complex shape is desired, first create a profile definition (refer to Technique T10.09), then choose the Use Profile button (Figure 14.48b).

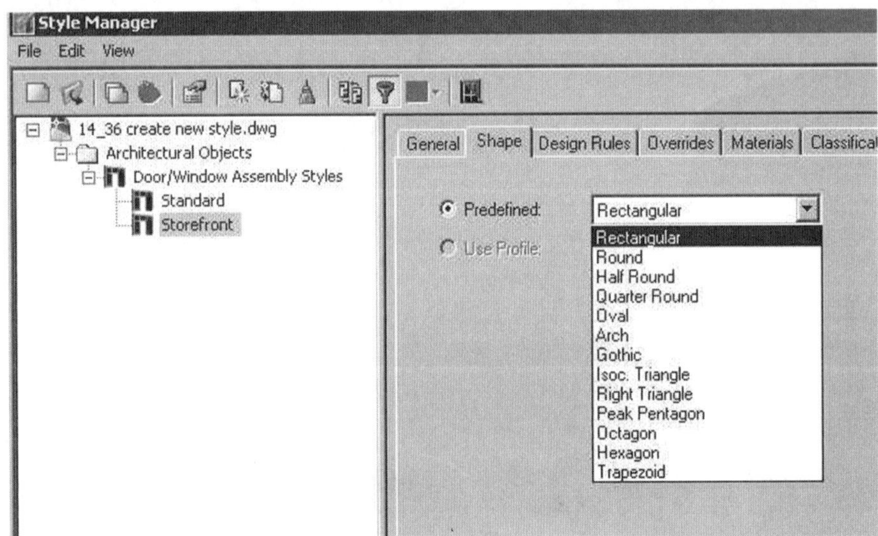

Figure 14.48a Choose the overall shape for the door/window assembly from the Predefined list box.

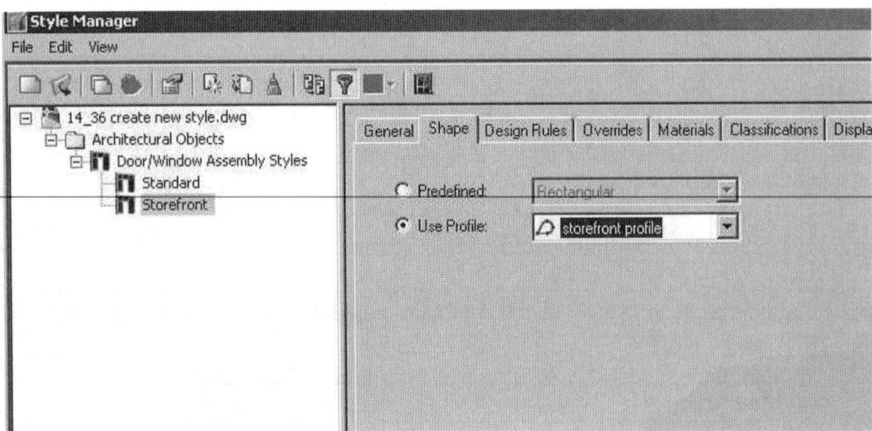

Figure 14.48b Use the Profile button to use profile definitions for overall shapes.

4. In the right pane, left-click on the Design Rules tab. This is where you describe how the curtain wall or door/window assembly will look. In this tab you will
   a. Create all division definitions—refer to Technique T14.34.
   b. Create all infill definitions—refer to Technique T14.44.
   c. Create all frame definitions—refer to Technique T14.36.
   d. Create all mullion definitions—refer to Technique T14.38.

   After the definitions are created, they must be assigned to specific locations on the curtain wall or door/window assembly object. ADT automatically assigns all default definitions, but you may want to reassign one or more of these.
   e. Set the desired division to the primary grid—refer to Technique T14.45.
   f. If a second division is needed, establish Grid Nesting—refer to Technique T14.47.
5. In the right pane, left-click on the Materials tab. Choose the rendering material for each of the CW or WA components.
6. In the right pane, left-click on the Display Properties tab. Make any additional display changes to the style—refer to Chapter 13 for a review of this subject matter.
7. Mullions, infill, and/or frame definition assignments can also be overridden through the drawing screen. Refer to Techniques T15.06 through T15.09. To save overrides back to the style, refer to Technique T15.10.

Controlling Curtain Wall and Door/Window Assembly Display in Plan View

Cut planes are used in ADT to determine how objects display in floor plan and ceiling plan views. Cut planes are assigned in the Display Configuration and apply to all objects in the virtual model (refer to Chapter 13 to review Display Configurations). Individual ADT objects, however, can override global cut planes as well as have multiple cut planes.

Why Use Multiple Cut Planes?

Out of the box, curtain walls and door/window assemblies are displayed as shown in Figure 14.49a. However, if the curtain wall or door/window assembly is located above or below the display's cut plane, it will not show in plan view (Figure 14.49b). To remedy the display problem, additional cut planes need to be added to the style's display properties as demonstrated in Figure 14.50.

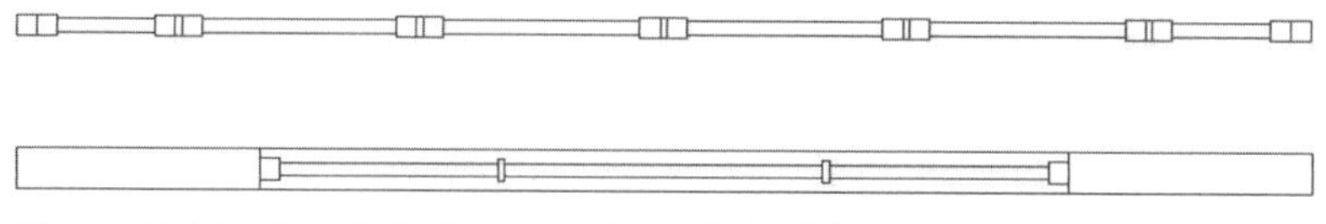

Figure 14.49a Out of the box, curtain walls and door/window assemblies are displayed as shown above.

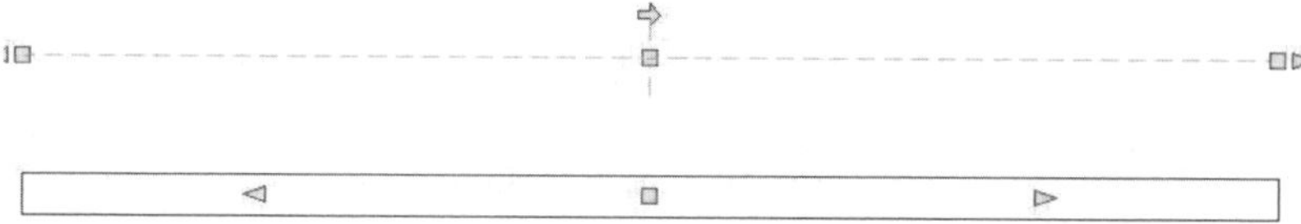

Figure 14.49b If the curtain wall or door/window assembly is located above or below the display's cut plane, by default it will not show in the plan view.

Technique to Master **T14.50** Adding Additional Cut Planes

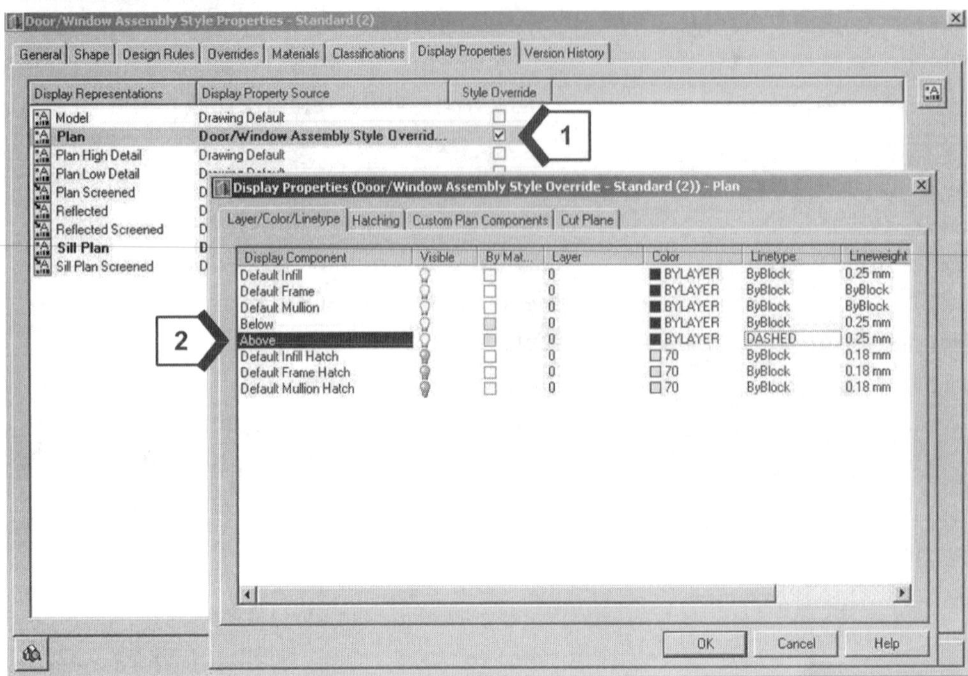

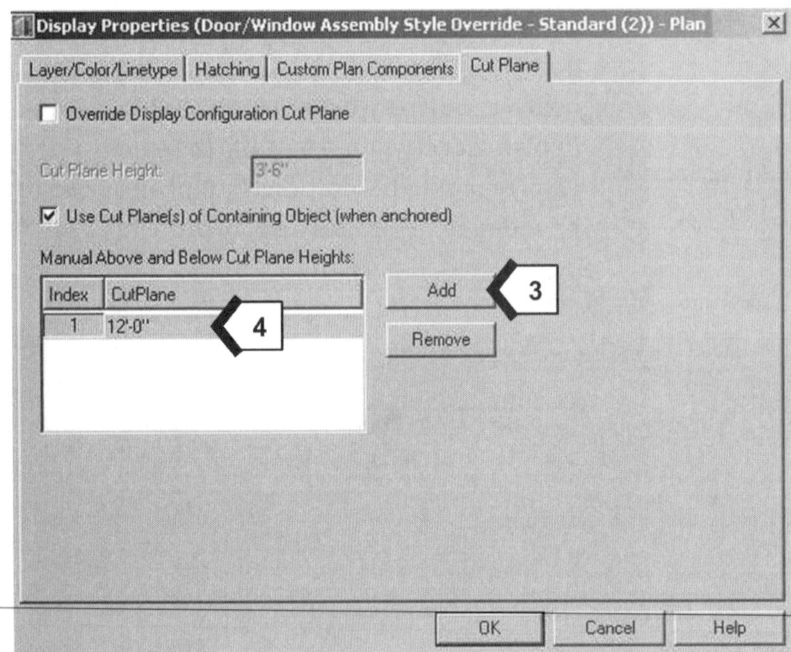

Figure 14.50 Additional cut planes for curtain wall and door/window assembly styles can be added through the Style Manager's High-Detail Display Representation's Cut Plane tab. Make sure style overrides are used when making changes to Display Properties of objects.

1	[Style Manager>Display Properties tab]	If unchecked, checkmark the box next to the desired Display Representation. If already checked, click on Properties button at upper right.
2	[Style Manager>Display Properties Override dialogue box]	Make sure the "Above" Display Component is visible.
3	[Style Manager>Display Properties Override dialogue box>Cut Plane tab]	Left-click the Add button.
4	[Style Manager>Display Properties Override dialogue box>Cut Plane tab]	Type in the additional cut plane height.

Alternative Methods to Create Curtain Wall and Door/Window Assembly Styles

So far you've learned how to create curtain wall and door/window assembly styles through the Style Manager alone. This topic introduces three additional methods.

Creating a New Curtain Wall or Door/Window Assembly Style That Is Based on an Existing Style

Using the CopyAndAssignStyle command located in the curtain wall or door/window assembly's right-click menu will duplicate the style of the selected CW or WA (Figure 14.51). The Style Manager automatically opens so that additional style editing can take place.

Creating Curtain Wall or Door/Window Assemblies by Converting Line-work

Sometimes the curtain wall or door/window assembly contains curves and is too complex to create through the Style Manager. A 2-D line sketch of what the curtain wall or door/window assembly looks like in elevation can be easily converted to the above mentioned object. Start with drawing the overall shape of the CW or WA. This should be drawn in plan view with the height of the CW or WA drawn along the y-axis. The lines that define the overall shape will be converted to the CW or WA frame. Next draw the lines or arcs that represent the locations of mullions within the CW or WA. The sketch is now ready to be converted (Figure 14.52). Figure 14.53 demonstrates the conversion process.

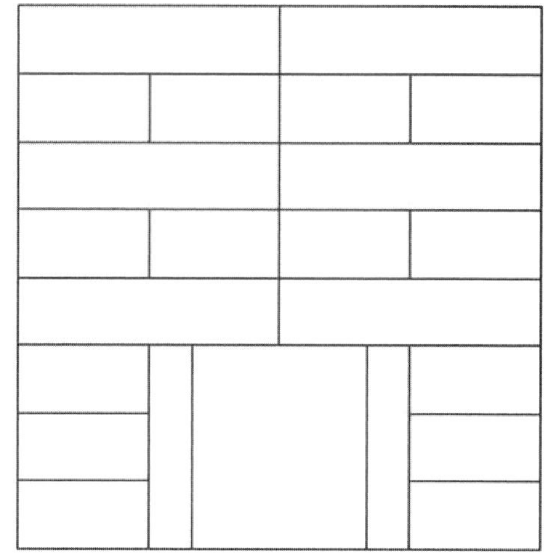

Figure 14.52 A line sketch ready to be converted to a curtain wall or door/window assembly

Whenever an elevation sketch is converted to a curtain wall or door/window assembly, the style is automatically set to Standard. Infill, mullion, and frame definitions use the Standard style's dimensions. Although the converted CW or WA is assigned the Standard style, the object cannot be used repeatedly until it is saved to its own style name (refer to Technique T15.10).

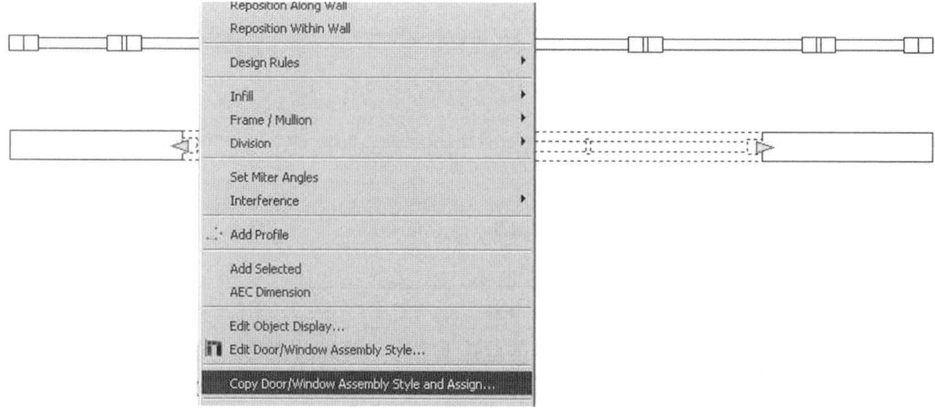

Figure 14.51 Duplicate an existing style by using the CopyAndAssignStyle command.

Technique to Master **T14.53** Creating Curtain Wall or Door/Window Assembly Styles by Converting Line-work

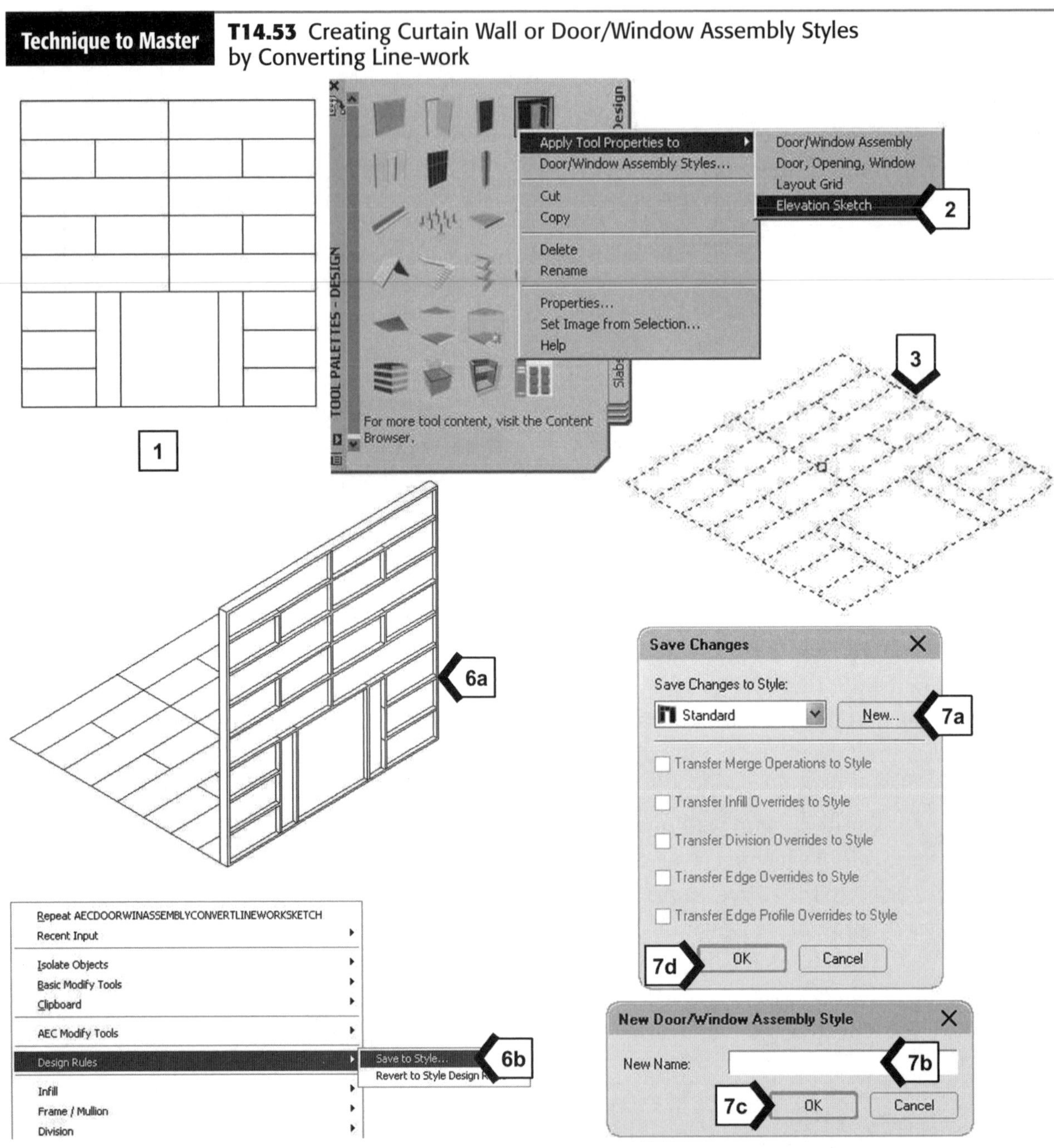

Figure 14.53

1	[Drawing Screen]	In plan view (WCS) create the custom grid using lines, arcs, circles, and polylines. Lines cannot overlap one another. Lines must meet.
2	[Design Tool palette]	Right-click on the Curtain Wall or Window Assembly tool, then left-click and choose the Apply Tool Properties to>Elevation Sketch command.
3	[Drawing Screen]	Select the custom grid you have drawn.
4	[Command Line]	Hit Enter to accept default baseline.
5	[Command Line]	Type Y and hit Enter to erase the layout grid. To have the layout grid remain after the curtain wall is created, type N.
6a, 6b	[Drawing Screen]	Select CW or WA, right-click, and choose the Design Rules>Save to Style command.
7a, 7b, 7c, 7d	[Save Changes dialogue box]	Click on New button to create a new CW or WA style. Name the style.
8	[Style Manager]	Edit the CW or WA style. (Most likely the frame and mullion widths and depths are incorrect, as well as the infill thickness.)

Creating a Curtain Wall by Converting Surfaces of Mass Elements, Mass Groups, and/or AutoCAD Surfaces

ADT was designed to mirror the design process—taking a design idea from programming to conceptual massing all the way to the final construction documents. To aid in the transition from conceptual massing to schematic design, commands such as the CurtainWallToolToFaces were created. The command will convert faces of existing AutoCAD surfaces, ADT mass elements, or mass groups to a specified curtain wall style. Figure 14.54 illustrates this technique.

Technique to Master **T14.54** Creating a Curtain Wall by Converting Surfaces of Mass Elements, Mass Groups, and/or AutoCAD Surfaces

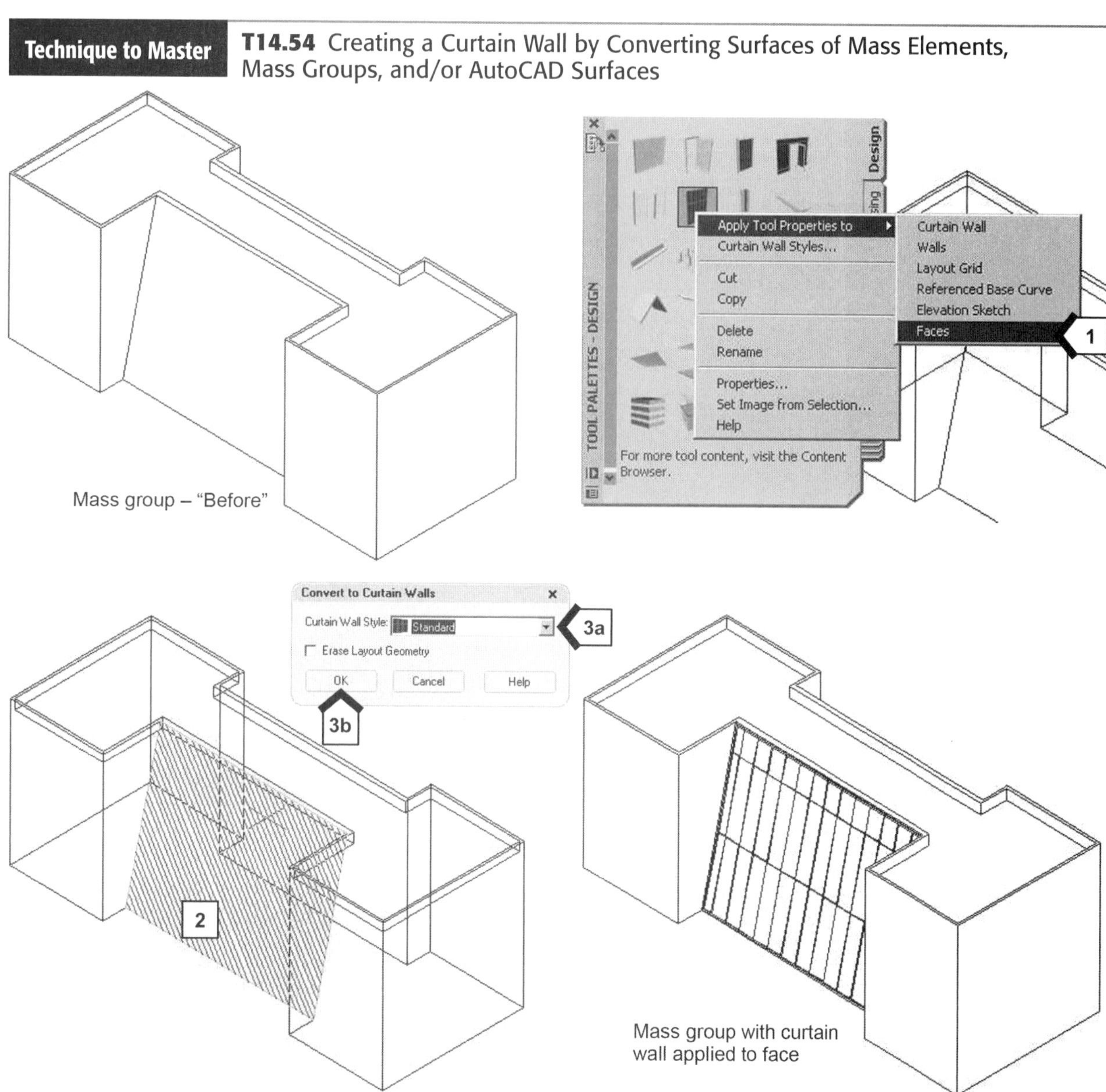

Figure 14.54

1	[Design Tool palette]	Right-click on Curtain Wall tool and choose Apply Tool Properties to>Faces.
2	[Drawing Screen]	Select face of mass element, mass group, or surface.
3a, 3b	[Convert to Curtain Wall dialogue box]	Select curtain wall style to assign to new curtain wall.

Chapter Exercises

Open the Chapter 14 folder located on the CD-ROM to access the exercises related to this chapter. The exercises allow you to practice creating, placing, and modifying curtain wall and door/window assemblies.

Adding Complexity: Curtain Wall and Door/Window Assembly Style Overrides

15

Objectives

This chapter expands on the previous chapter's introduction to curtain walls and door/window assembly objects. It introduces concepts and vocabulary underlying advanced curtain wall and door/window assembly modifications. Techniques within the chapter illustrate efficient execution of advanced curtain wall and door/window assembly procedures. The end-of-chapter exercises let you apply these techniques to advanced curtain wall and door/window assembly technique problems.

Curtain Wall and Door/Window Assembly Style Overrides

In the previous chapter, you were introduced to the curtain wall and door/window assembly objects and their individual components. You also learned how these components are delineated and assigned through the Style Manager. This chapter focuses on assigning definitions from the drawing screen. Drawing screen component assignments essentially reassign the style-based component. The technique is referred to as *assignment overrides* or *style overriding.*

This chapter introduces you to the override types and their application. The chapter also touches on creative design uses for curtain walls and door/window assemblies.

Reasons for Style Overrides

As a technique, style overrides are mostly used for special conditions, quick visual feedback, and design changes related to curtain wall and door/window assemblies. A single door in a curtain wall assembly, for example, might be considered a special condition since it is only placed in one specific part of the curtain wall. In this condition, it is easier and more efficient to assign the door directly by selecting the infill panel on the drawing screen. Trying to accomplish this through the Style Manager tends to be unwieldy (Figure 15.1).

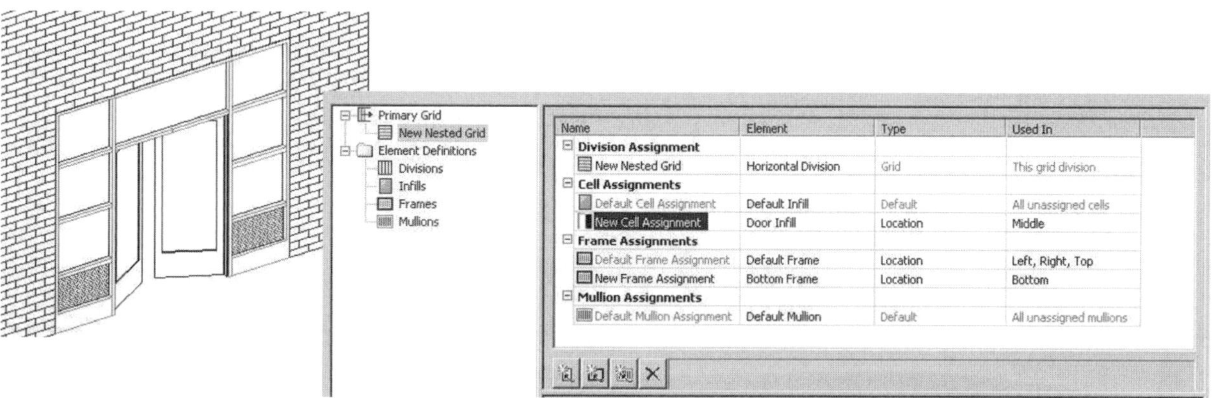

Figure 15.1 A single door in a curtain wall assembly, for example, might be considered a special condition since it is placed only in one specific part of the curtain wall. It would, therefore, be easier and more efficient to assign the door directly on the drawing screen. Trying to accomplish this through the Style Manager tends to be unwieldy.

Types of Style Overrides

Curtain wall and door/window assembly style overrides include removal overrides, replacement overrides, and merge overrides. Removal overrides remove a frame or mullion segment from the specified curtain wall (Figure 15.2). Replacement overrides replace frame, mullion, or infill definitions with a new definition (Figure 15.3). Merge overrides join two or more infill panels so that they are one by removing the mullion that separates them (Figure 15.4).

> **Box 15.1**
> Style overrides assigned to a curtain wall or door/window assembly are saved only to the individual object. They can, however, be transferred to the existing style or saved as a new style.

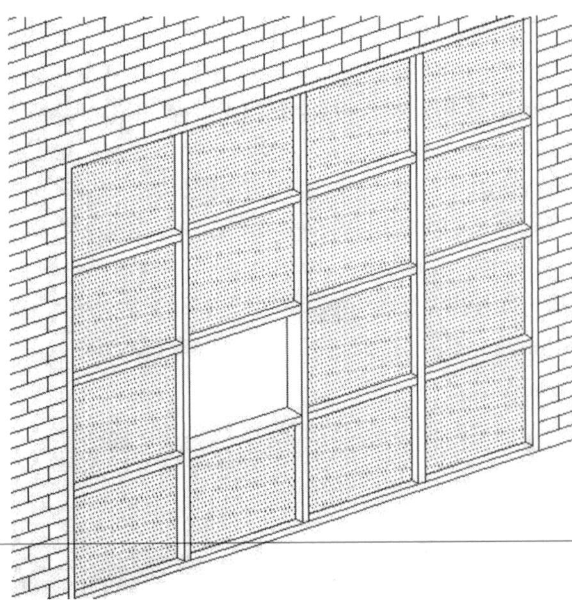

Figure 15.2 Removal overrides remove an infill, a frame segment, or a mullion segment from the specified curtain wall. This example illustrates an infill removal.

Figure 15.3 Replacement overrides replace Frame, Mullion, or Infill Definitions with a new definition. The example shows several horizontal mullions being replaced with wider substitutes.

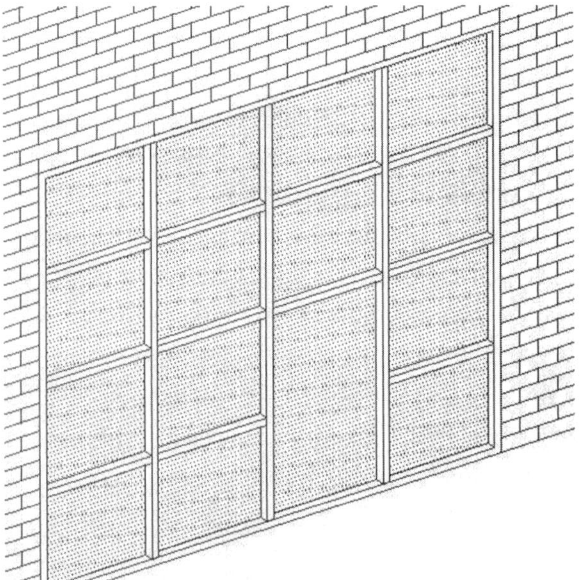

Figure 15.4 Merge overrides join two or more infill panels so that they are one. The example shows two infill panels merging to form one.

Merges

Design applications for merge overrides include merging cells together to accommodate door insertions and/or compositional transformations of the original grid system.

Replacements

Design applications for replacements overrides include door insertions and replacement of default infill panels with other types of panel material.

Creating Override Choices Within the Curtain Wall or Door/Window Assembly Style Manager

For a Frame, a Mullion, or an Infill Definition to be overridden, a second choice must be available and exist within the style as a definition. For example, if you wanted to create a style override that adds a door to an existing curtain wall style, the door must exist as its own definition within that style (Figure 15.5). Refer to Techniques T14.36, T14.38, and T14.44 for a review of component definition creation.

Cell Merges

Merge overrides join two or more infill panels so that they are one—removing the mullion that separates them. This is useful for window combining to achieve larger panes of infill. Figure 15.6 demonstrates how to create a style override through cell merging.

Cell Replacements

Cell replacements substitute the default infill definition with a new definition. Overriding the default glass infill with a door infill is a typical application of this technique. Figure 15.7 demonstrates how to create a style override for a cell definition.

Frame or Mullion Replacements

Frame/mullion replacements substitute the default Frame or Mullion Definition with a new definition. Figure 15.8 demonstrates how to override Frame and Mullion Definitions by changing the bottom frame of the storefront to a wider frame width using the Bottom Frame Definition.

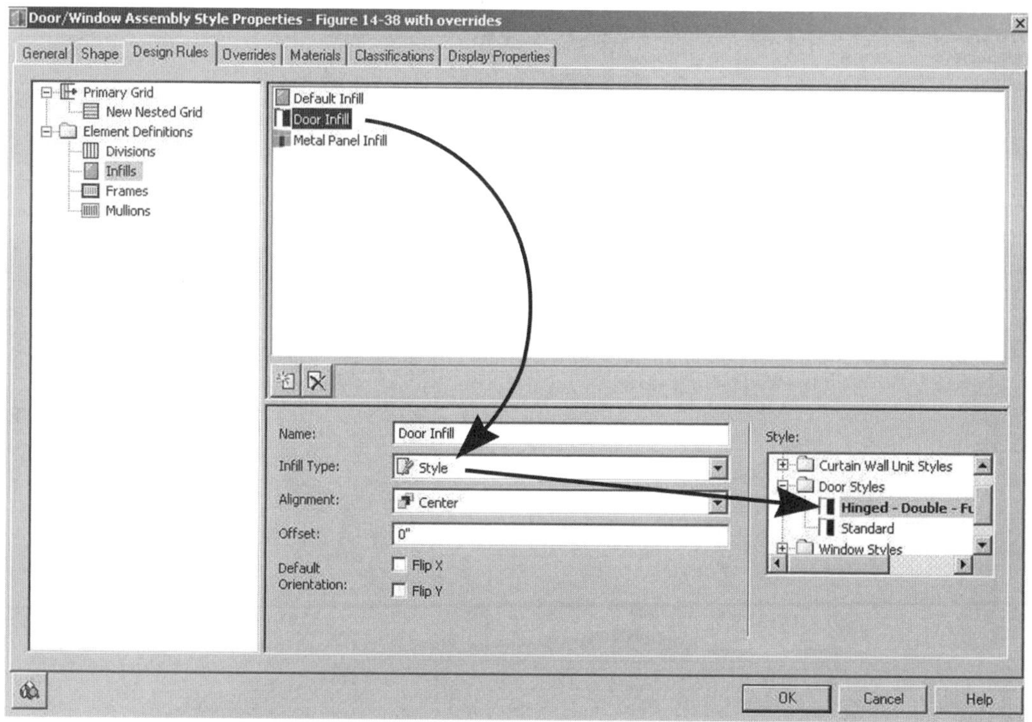

Figure 15.5 To create a style override that adds a door to an existing curtain wall style, the door must exist as its own definition within that style.

Technique to Master T15.06 Using Overrides to Merge Infills (Cell Merges)

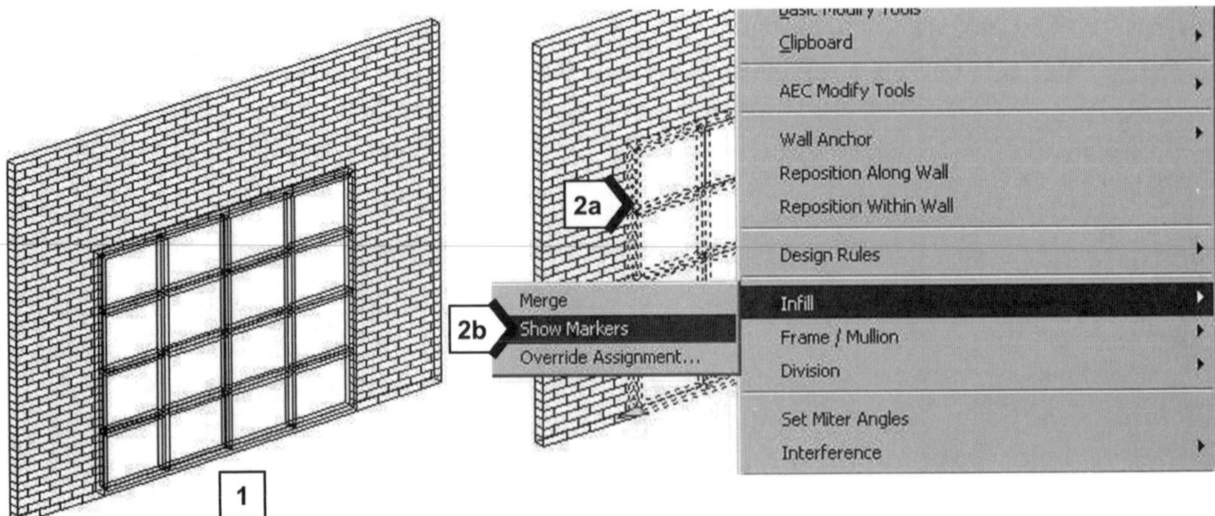

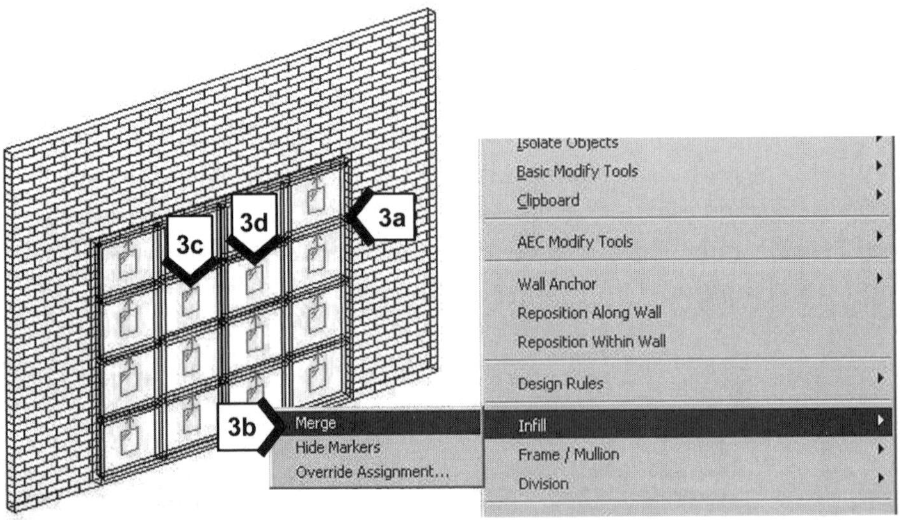

Figure 15.6

1	[Drawing Screen]	View the CW or WA in axonometric or elevation view.
2a, 2b	[Drawing Screen]	Select the CW or WA. Right-click then choose Infill>Show Markers.
3a, 3b, 3c, 3d	[Drawing Screen]	Select the CW or WA. Right-click and choose Infill>Merge. Select the Cell Markers that indicate the cells you want to merge.

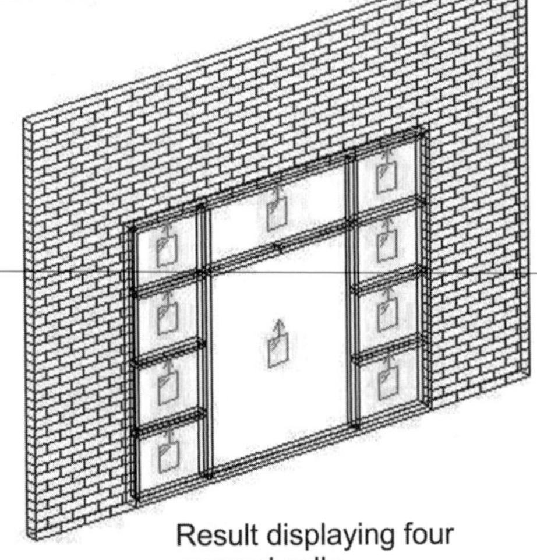

Result displaying four merged cells.

Technique to Master **T15.07** Overriding Infill (Cell Replacements)

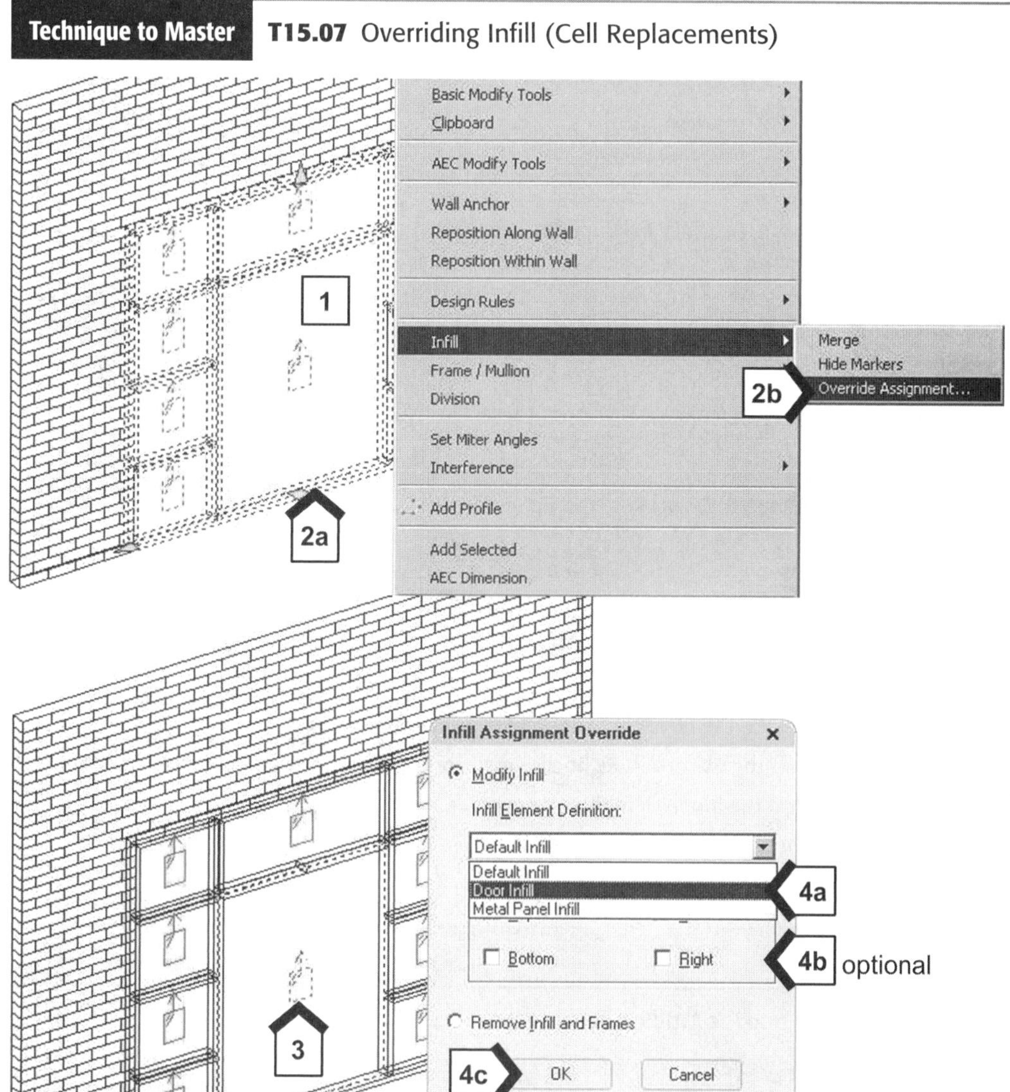

Figure 15.7 This technique requires that there be at least two or more infill elements defined in the Curtain Wall or Door/Window Assembly Style. Refer to Techniques T14.44 and T14.45.

1	[Drawing Screen]	View the CW or WA in axonometric or elevation view. Make sure Cell Markers are displayed.
2a, 2b	[Drawing Screen]	Select the CW or WA. Right-click then choose the Infill>Override Assignment command.
3	[Drawing Screen]	Select the Cell Marker that indicates the infill you want to override.
4a, 4b, 4c	[Infill Assignment Override Dialog]	Choose the new infill assignment. (If placing a door, make sure the bottom frame is removed.) Click OK.
5	If you want to save this merged override to the CW or WA style, see Technique T15.10.	

Technique to Master T15.08 Using Overrides to Replace an Existing Frame or Mullion

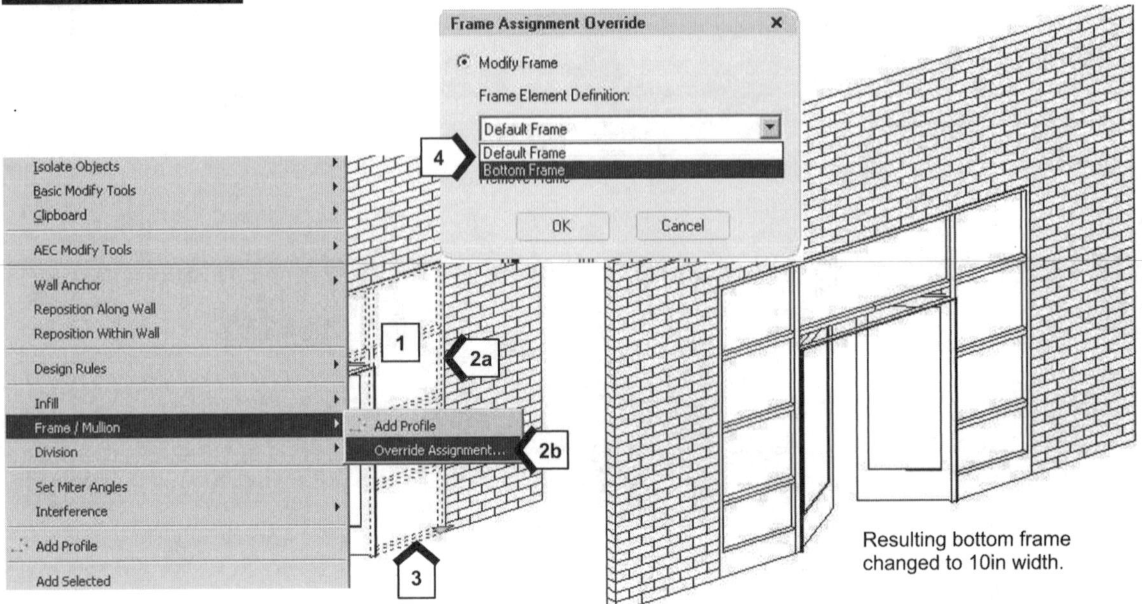

Figure 15.8

1	[Drawing Screen]	View the CW or WA in axonometric or elevation view.
2a, 2b	[Drawing Screen]	Select the CW or WA. Right-click then choose Frame/Mullion>Override Assignment.
3	[Drawing Screen]	Select the frame or mullion to override.
4	[Frame/Mullion Assignment Override dialogue box]	Choose the new frame (or mullion) assignment.
5	If you want to save the override to the CW or WA style, see Technique T15.10.	

Technique to Master T15.09 Frame and/or Mullion Removals

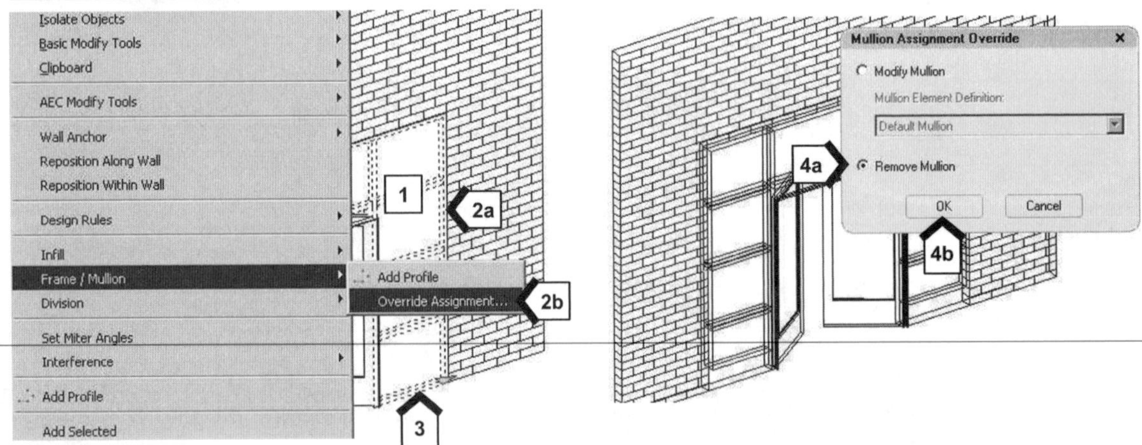

Figure 15.9

1	[Drawing Screen]	View the CW or WA in axonometric or elevation view.
2a, 2b	[Drawing Screen]	Select the CW or WA. Right-click then choose the Frame/Mullion> Override Assignment command.
3	[Drawing Screen]	Select the frame or mullion to remove.
4a, 4b	[Frame/Mullion Assignment Override dialogue box]	Choose the Remove Mullion (or Frame) button. Click OK.
5	If you want to save the override to the CW or WA style, see Technique T15.10.	

Frame or Mullion Removals

Figure 15.9 demonstrates how to remove a frame or mullion from an existing placed curtain wall or door/window assembly.

Saving Overrides Back to the Curtain Wall or Door/Window Assembly Style

An override is applied only to the individual CW or WA object. If you desire the override to become part of the style, additional steps must be performed (Figure 15.10).

Technique to Master **T15.10** Saving the Override Back to the CW or WA Style

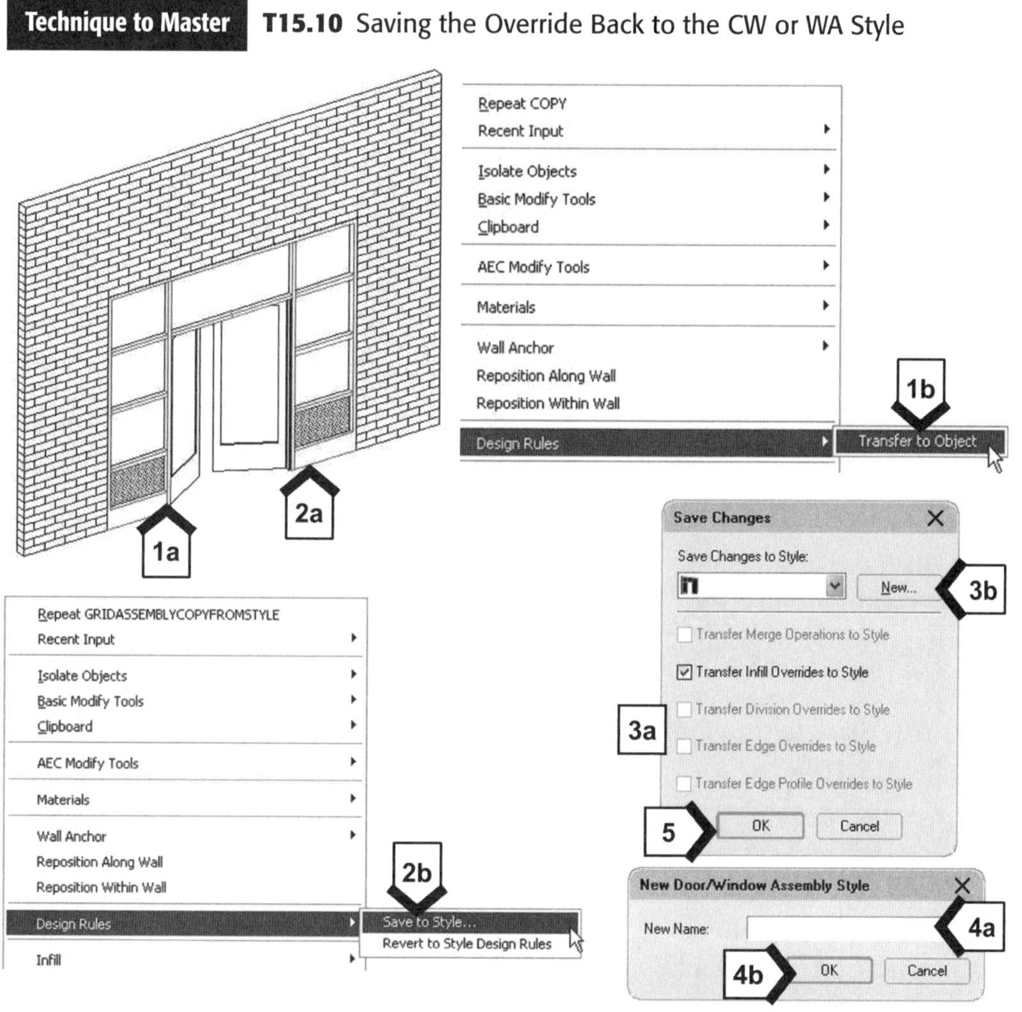

Figure 15.10

1a, 1b	[Drawing Screen]	Select the CW or WA, right-click and choose Design Rules>Transfer to Object.
2a, 2b	[Drawing Screen]	Select the CW or WA again, right-click and choose Design Rules>Save to Style.
3a, 3b	[Save Changes dialogue box]	Check all available boxes. Left-click on New button to save changes to a new style; otherwise, select an existing style from the drop-down list.
4a, 4b	[New Door/Window Assembly (or Curtain Wall) Style dialogue box]	Name the new style. Alternatively, you can save the style override(s) over the old style using the style name in the drop-down list.
5	[Save Changes dialogue box]	Click OK to save overrides to style.

Performing the Override

Style overrides are assigned to individual curtain walls and door/window assemblies. The workflow process is outlined in detail at the end of the section.

Summary of the Workflow Process

1. Open the Style Manager for the existing CW or WA style.
2. If the type of override is a replacement override, create additional Frame, Mullion, or Infill Definitions that will eventually become the replacement.
3. Save and exit the Style Manager.
4. Select the CW or WA to override and perform the desired replacement, removal, and/or merge.
   - For frame, mullion, or infill replacement overrides refer to Techniques T15.07 and T15.08.
   - For frame, mullion, or infill removal overrides, refer to Technique T15.09.
   - For infill panel merges (cell merging), refer to Technique T15.06.
5. Save the style override(s) back to the exiting style using Technique T15.10.

Curtain Wall Units

The ADT curtain wall unit object was added to simplify curtain wall and window assembly construction. A curtain wall unit object looks exactly like a curtain wall and is made up of the same components. Style creation procedures are also exactly the same. While a curtain wall unit can be placed on the drawing screen individually, its primary role is to aid in the creation of complex division arrangements within curtain walls and door/window assemblies.

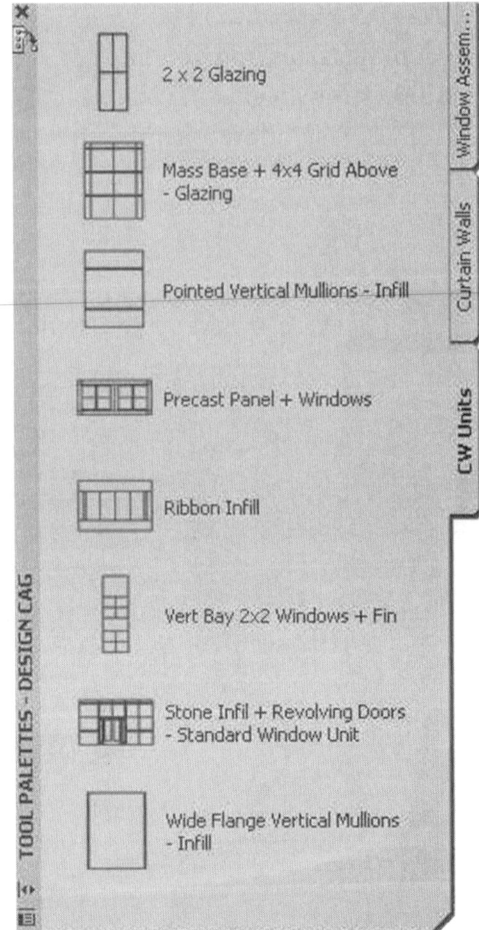

Figure 15.11 As saved styles, the various curtain wall unit styles can be stored in a library for easy access.

Curtain wall units are excellent candidates to use for saving infill panel types. As saved styles, the various curtain wall unit styles can be stored in a library for easy access. Figure 15.11 illustrates one example of this use. Figure 15.12 illustrates the curtain wall unit creation process, while Figure 15.13 demonstrates adding curtain wall unit styles to CW and WA styles.

> **Box 15.2**
> Infill panel examples include metal, concrete, stone veneer, translucent glass, mirrored glass, and insulated glass, to name a few.

Technique to Master	**T15.12** Creating a Curtain Wall Unit Style

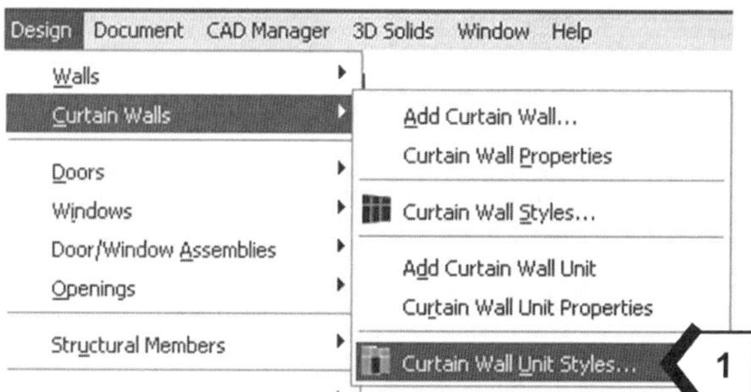

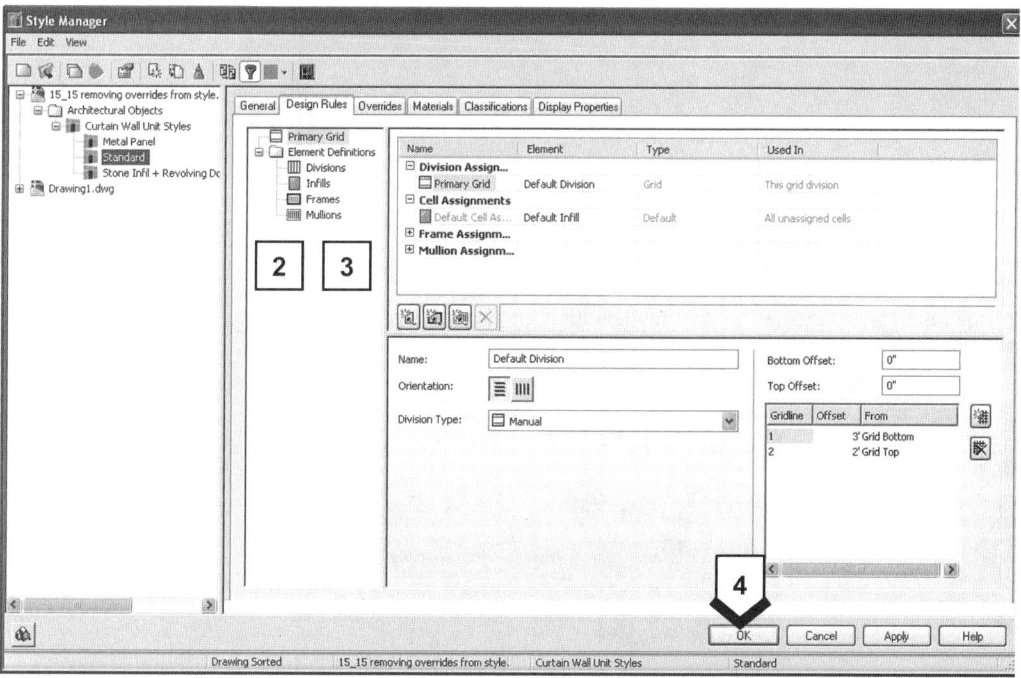

Figure 15.12

1	[Design>Curtain Walls>Curtain Wall Unit Styles.]	Use the Curtain Wall Unit Styles command.
2	[Style Manager>Design Rules]	Define Division, Frame, Mullion, and Infill elements. Refer to Techniques T14.34, T14.36, T14.38, and T14.44.
3	[Style Manager>Design Rules]	Assign definitions to the Curtain Wall Unit Grid. Refer to Techniques T14.45 and T14.47.
4	[Style Manager>Design Rules]	Left-click OK to create Curtain Wall Unit style.

Editing Curtain Wall Units

Curtain wall units can be edited using the same techniques as curtain walls. Refer to Techniques T14.17 and T14.20 to review these types of modification techniques.

Viewing and/or Removing Overrides

Overrides that are saved to the style are removed through the Style Manager's Overrides tab (Figure 15.14). The Advanced tab of the Properties palette gives access to overrides that are individual to the curtain wall or door/window assembly and not saved to a style (Figure 15.15).

Technique to Master T15.13 Adding a Curtain Wall Unit to a CW or WA Style

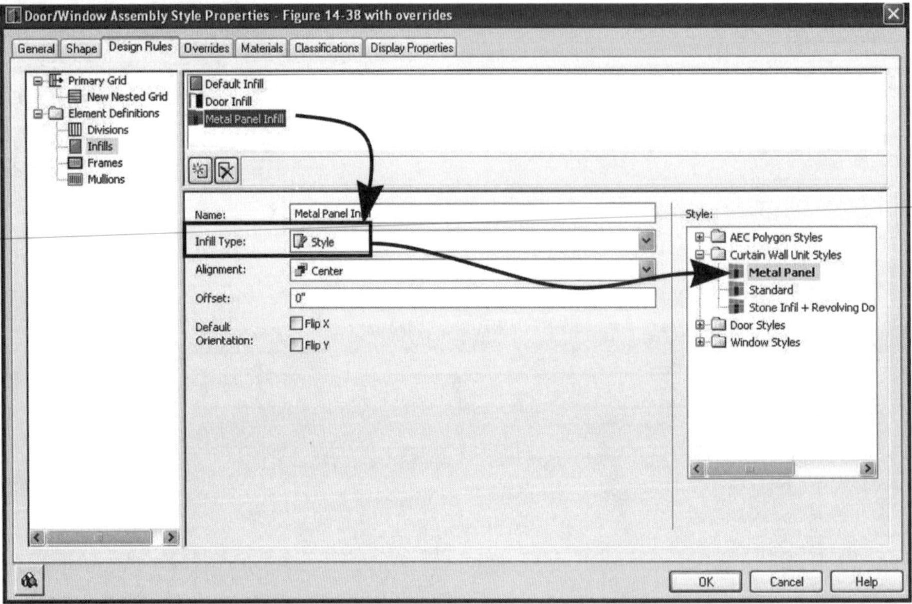

Figure 15.13 Curtain wall units can be defined as an infill definition for either Curtain walls or Door/window assemblies.

Technique to Master T15.14 Removing Overrides That Are Saved to a Style

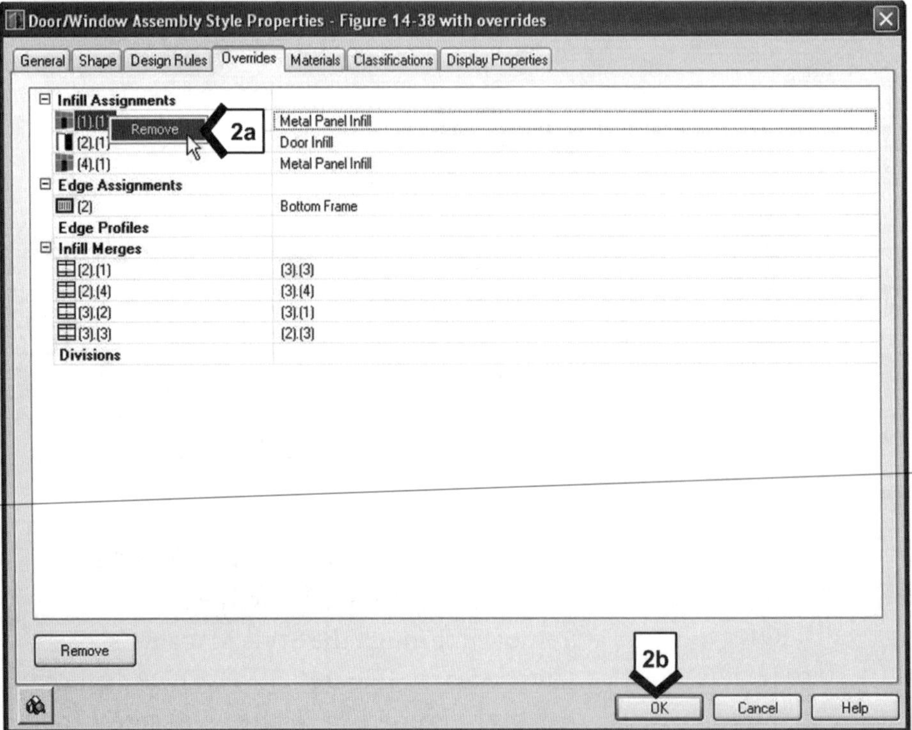

Figure 15.14

1	Open Style Manager for Curtain Wall or Door/Window Assembly style.	
2a, 2b	[Style Manager>Overrides tab]	Select override, right-click, and choose Remove. Left-click OK.

Technique to Master **T15.15** Removing Overrides That Are Not Saved to a Style

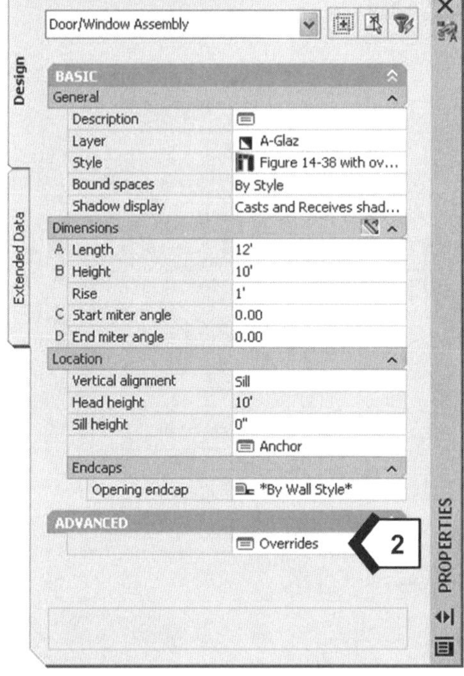

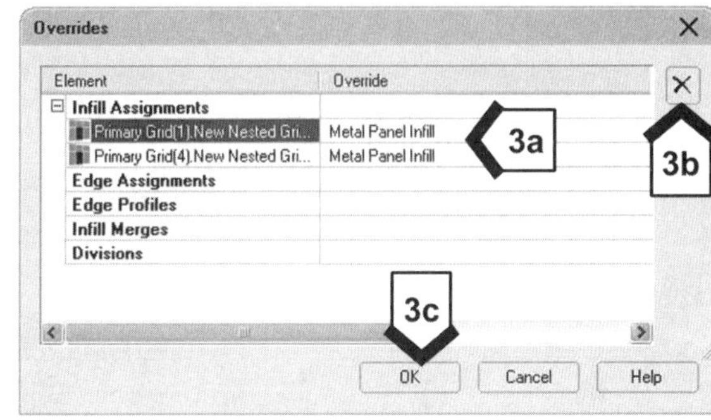

Figure 15.15

1	[Drawing Screen]	Select curtain wall or door/window assembly with override assigned.
2	[Properties palette]	Click on Overrides area.
3a 3b 3c	[Overrides dialogue box]	Click Override to remove. Click Remove button. Click OK to apply removal.

Examples of Curtain Walls and Door/Window Assemblies and How They Are Created

Chapter 15 files on the CD-ROM demonstrate the creation of three common storefront and curtain wall designs. Remember that there are always several ways to get to a desired end product—these are just a few suggested procedures.

Unique Approaches to Using the Curtain Wall Object in Design Practice

While curtain wall objects were obviously created for glazed wall systems, many other types of objects are perfect candidates because of the unique grid feature. When used creatively, curtain walls and curtain wall units can efficiently solve many other types of design and drawing challenges. Figures 15.16 through 15.19 on the following pages are just a sample of the design possibilities for curtain walls and curtain wall unit objects.

Chapter Exercises

Open the Chapter 15 folder located on the CD-ROM to access the exercises related to this chapter. Completing these exercises helps you practice the advanced curtain wall and door/window assembly techniques within sample design applications.

Technique to Master **T15.16** Using a Curtain Wall to Create Wall Control Joints

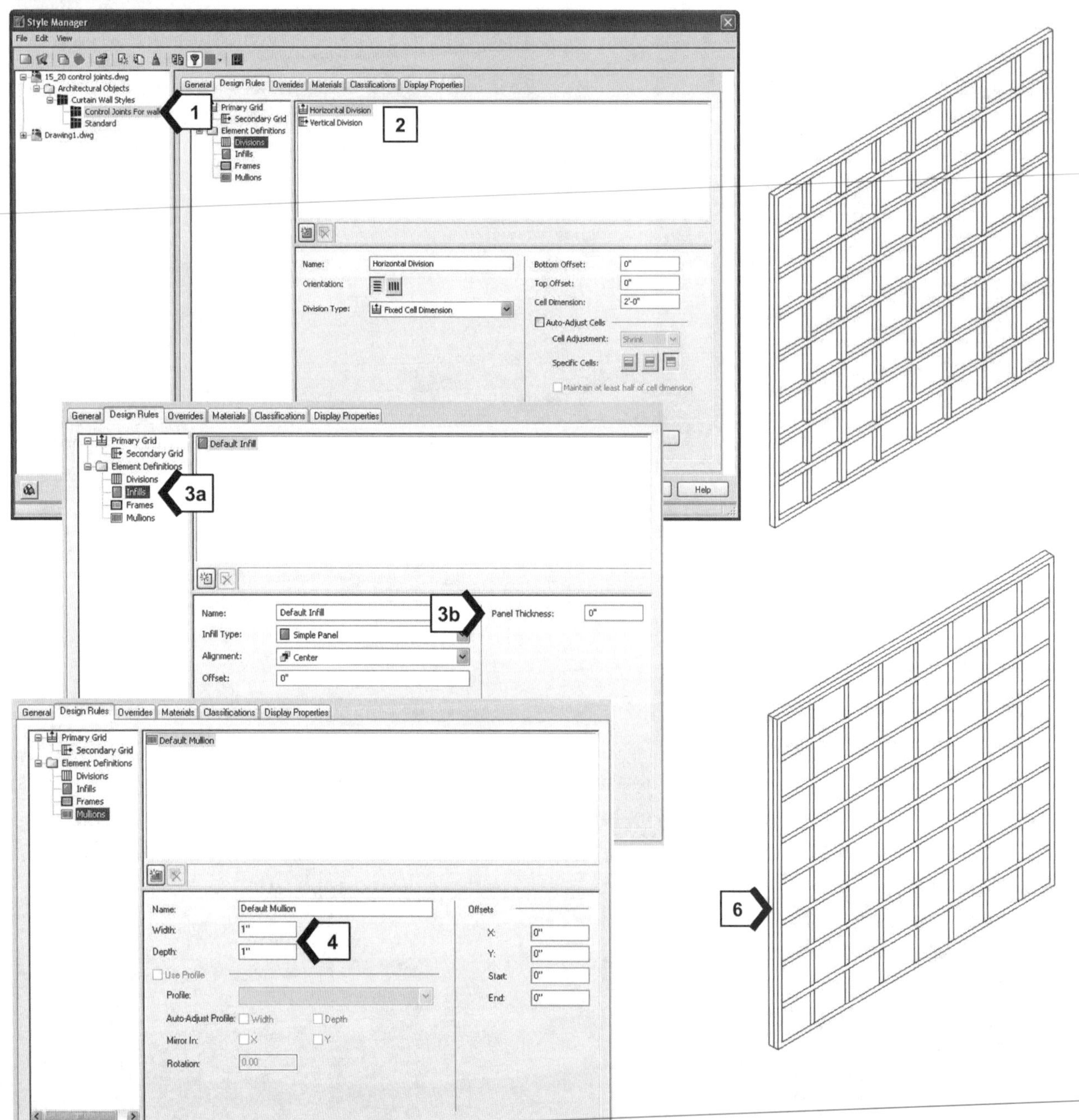

Figure 15.16a

1	[Curtain Wall Style Manager]	Create a new curtain wall style.
2	[Curtain Wall Style Manager> Design Rules tab]	Create the division assignments for the curtain wall. The divisions will represent the spacing for the vertical and/or horizontal control joints.
3a, 3b	[Curtain Wall Style Manager> Design Rules tab]	Set the infill panel thickness to 0.
4	[Curtain Wall Style Manager> Design Rules tab]	Specify the frame and mullion's width and height. They must have the same values.
5	[Curtain Wall Style Manager> Design Rules tab]	Click OK to create style.
6	[Drawing Screen]	Draw curtain wall and locate directly over wall.

(continued)

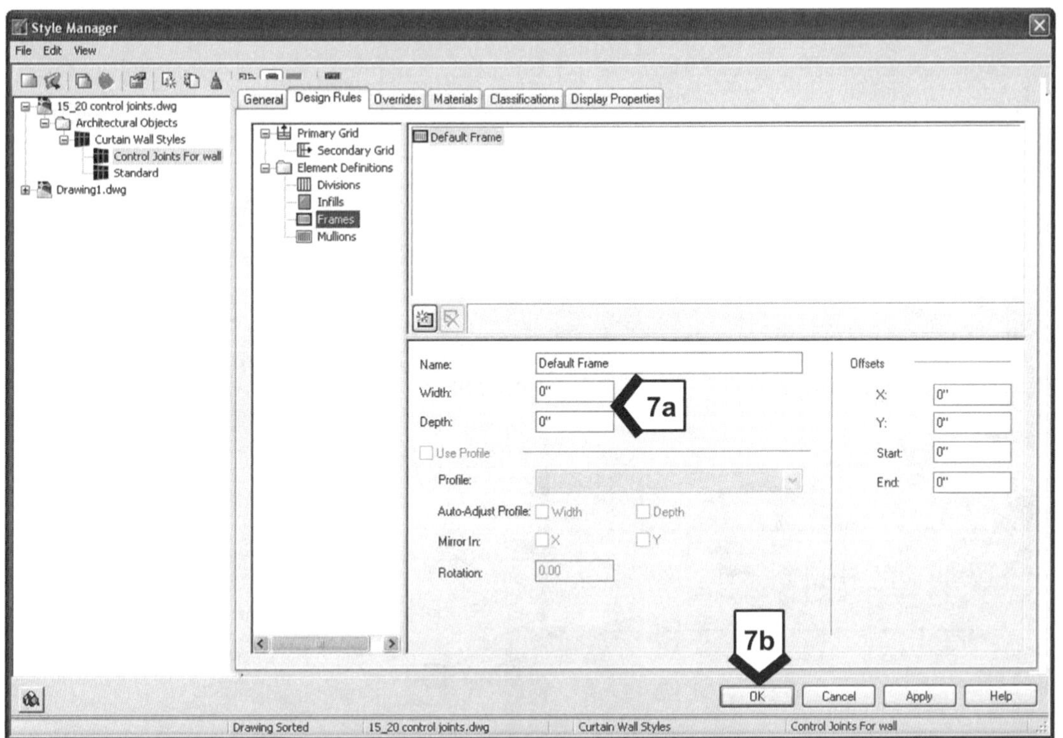

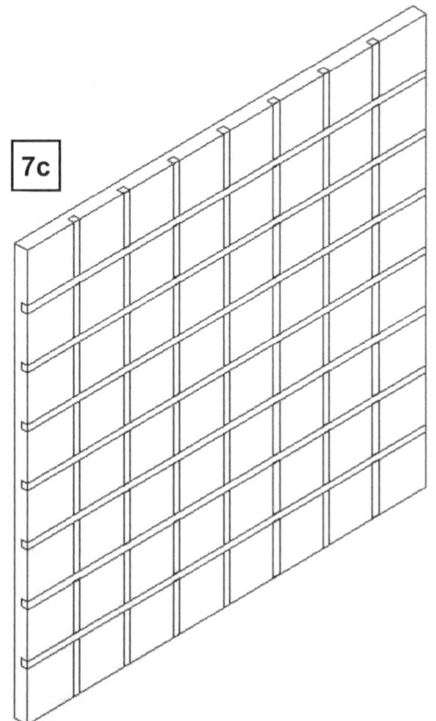

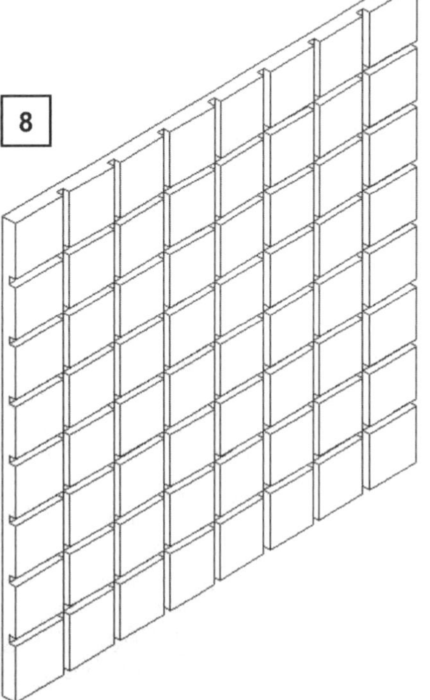

Figure 15.16b

7a, 7b, 7c	[Curtain Wall Style Manager> Design Rules tab]	Modify curtain wall frame definition by changing the frame width and height to 0. Left-click OK to apply changes.
8	[Drawing Screen]	Use curtain wall as interference condition or body modifier for specified wall. Refer to Techniques T13.37 and T13.41.

Technique to Master **T15.17** Using a Curtain Wall to Create Suspended Ceilings

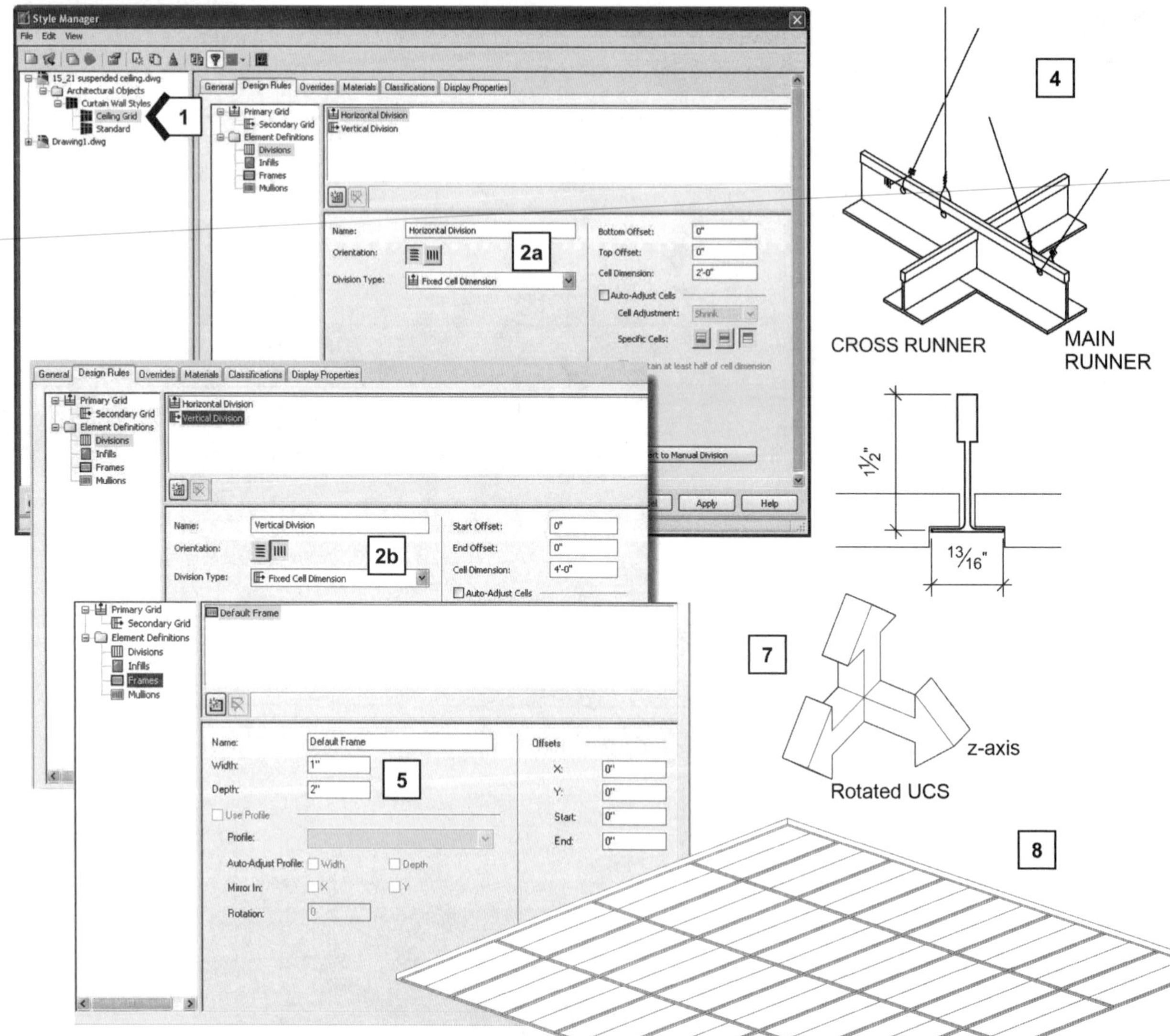

Figure 15.17 The following technique demonstrates how to set up and use a curtain wall style for a traditional 2 by 4 suspended acoustical grid. This technique can easily be modified for other types of ceiling grid systems.

1	[Curtain Wall Style Manager]	Create a new curtain wall style.
2a, 2b	[Curtain Wall Style Manager> Design Rules tab]	Create the vertical and horizontal division assignments for the curtain wall style. The horizontal division will use a fixed cell dimension of 2'-0". The vertical division will use a fixed cell dimension of 4'-0".
3	[Curtain Wall Style Manager> Design Rules tab]	Set the infill panel thickness to 1".
4	Most suspended ceilings have T-shaped metal runners that hold the acoustical tile in place. Since only the underside of the runners are seen, the runners can be generically defined as rectangles in your curtain wall style. Alternately, if sections of the drawing will eventually be cut, accurate runner profiles can be created with profile definitions.	
5	[Curtain Wall Style Manager> Design Rules tab]	Specify the frame and mullion's width and height (approximately 1" × ½").
6	[Curtain Wall Style Manager> Design Rules tab]	Click OK to create style.
7	[Drawing Screen]	Rotate UCS so that the positive z-axis is relocated to where the positive x-axis or positive y-axis is. Refer to Techniques T08.07 and T08.08.
8	[Drawing Screen]	Draw curtain wall.

Technique to Master **T15.18** Using a Curtain Wall to Create Skylights

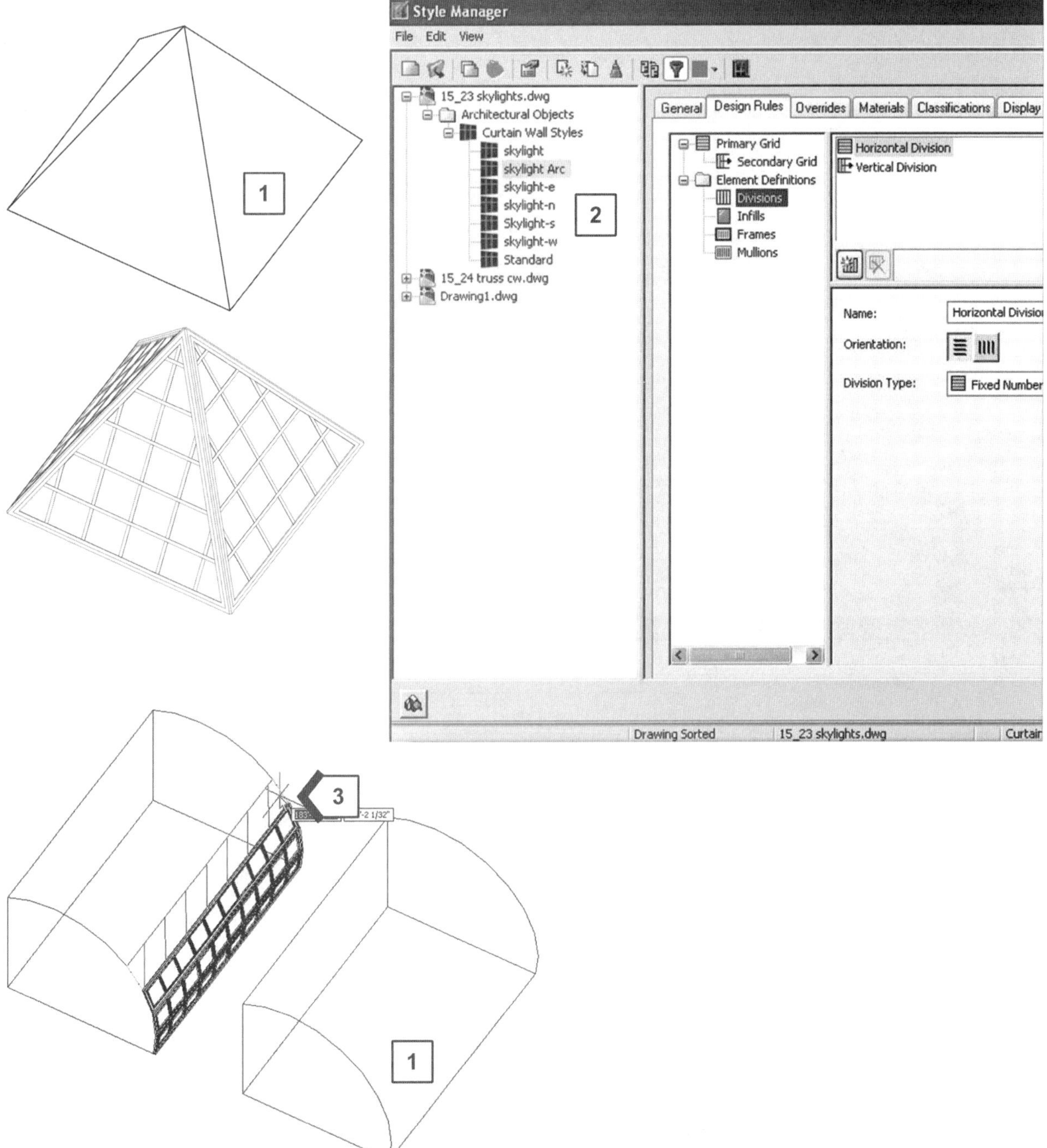

Figure 15.18 This technique uses a mass element or AutoCAD solid to create the general three-dimensional shape of the skylight. The faces of the three-dimensional shape are then converted to curtain walls.

1	[Drawing Screen]	Use an AutoCAD solid primitive, ADT mass element, or ADT mass group to create the skylight's shape. Refer to Chapters 8 and 10 to review these topics.
2	[Curtain Wall Style Manager]	Create curtain wall styles to represent each face of the skylight.
3	Using Technique T14.54, convert each face to a curtain wall. Remember that curved objects are made up of several (faceted) surfaces.	

Technique to Master **T15.19** Using a Curtain Wall to Create Roof/Floor Trusses

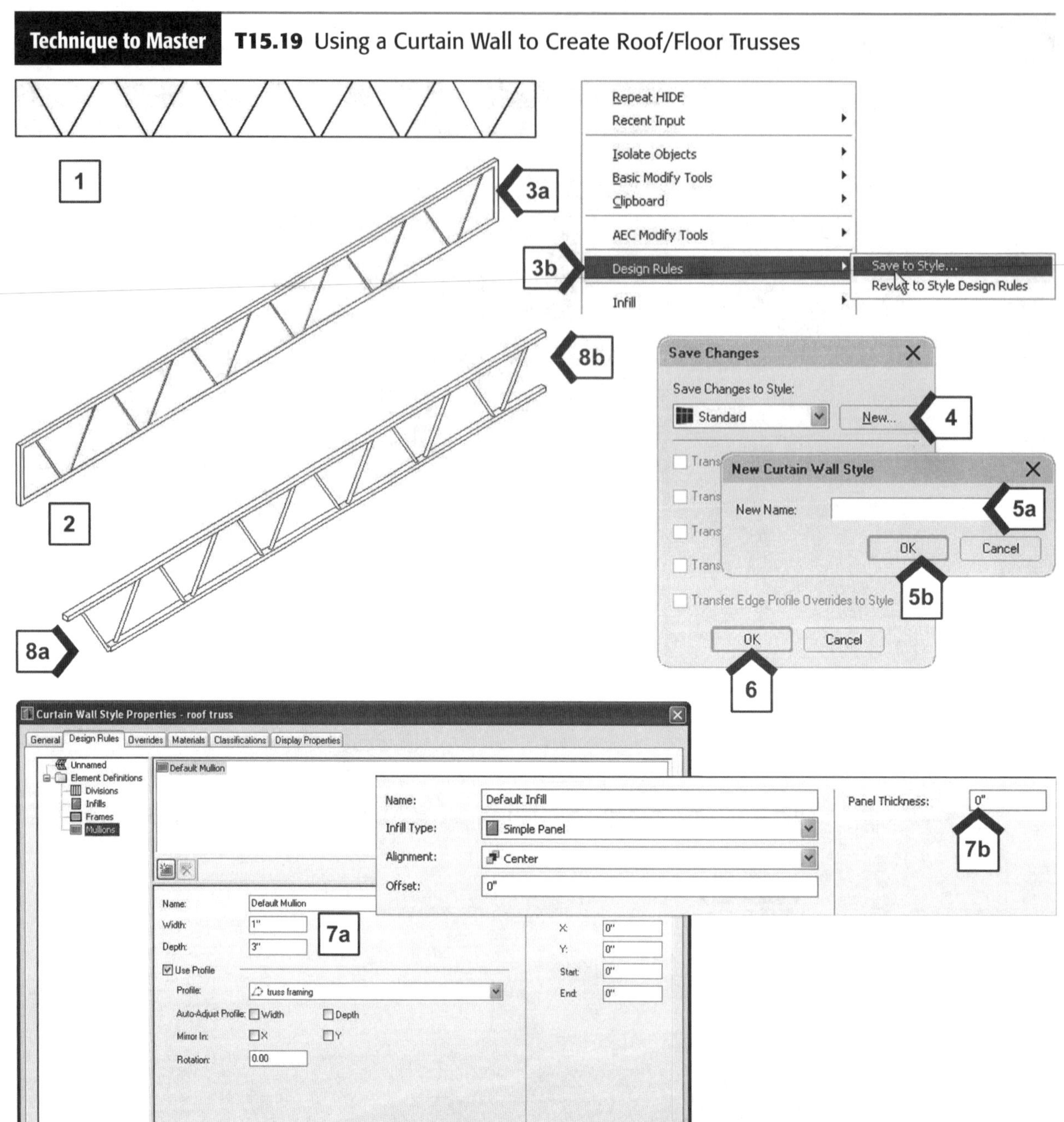

Figure 15.19 This technique creates wood trusses by converting linework to curtain walls.

1	[Drawing Screen]	Draw the wood truss as a series of lines. Remember the outside boundary represents the curtain wall frame while the inside lines represent the curtain wall mullions.
2	[Drawing Screen]	Convert linework to curtain wall. Refer to Technique T14.53.
3a, 3b	[Drawing Screen]	Select curtain wall, right-click, and choose Design Rules>Save to Style.
4	[Save Changes dialogue box]	Left-click New to create new curtain wall style.
5a, 5b	[New Curtain Wall Style dialogue box]	Name the style, and left-click OK.
6	[Save Changes dialogue box]	Left-click OK to save style.
7a, 7b	[Curtain Wall Style Manager]	Edit the frame and mullion size and profile. Use profile definitions for nonrectangular mullion profiles that will represent the truss web. The infill panel thickness should be set to 0".
8a, 8b	[Drawing Screen]	Using frame removal overrides, remove the end frames. Refer to Technique T15.09.
9	[Drawing Screen]	Save the override back to the style. Refer to Technique T15.10.

A Brief Overview of Other ADT Components

16

Objectives

This chapter introduces the roof, slab, stair, railing, and structural ADT objects. It places an emphasis on creating and placing style-based objects to correspond to the building systems they represent. Previous knowledge of the Architectural Desktop interface and logic is necessary to complete the chapter successfully.

Roofs

Roofs provide protection from rain and snow and play a significant part of the exterior skin of a building (Figure 16.1). Roof forms are tied to strong symbolic imagery in U.S. residential design and construction. Most so-called traditional housing styles and methods of construction were brought from Europe during the period of U.S. settlement and then adapted to the geography and climate—evidence of which can be seen in the many residential roof forms around us today.

Most interior designers will never actually design or draw a roof plan in their professional careers; however, understanding how a roof plan is drawn is critical to any interior designer's education. Knowing how sloped roofs work and how they are drawn will help you to understand building construction overall. This section introduces you to the roof shapes that are common to residential design in ADT, as well as roofing vocabulary important to beginning and intermediate interior design students.

Figure 16.1 Roofs play a significant part of the exterior skin of a building.

Roof Terminology

Renovating residential and commercial projects requires interior design students to have some knowledge of roof systems. Therefore, knowledge of roof vocabulary is essential to learning about roofs. Figure 16.2 gives an overview of the more common roof terminology that every beginning design student should acquire.

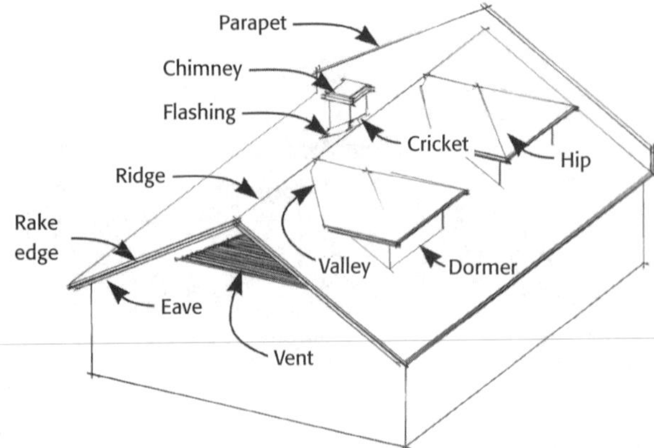

Figure 16.2 Common roofing terminology

Important Concepts in Roof Design

Roof design refers to the design of the roof form and shape, as well as the roof system. Most roof forms originate from four shapes. Figure 16.3 shows the four basic roof shapes in axonometric, plan, and elevation views. These basic shapes can be combined into more complex roof variations (Figure 16.4).

Roof slope selection is often made by considering three factors—climate and weather, roofing material choices, and aesthetics.

> **Box 16.1**
> The roof slope refers to the steepness of the roof surface. This steepness is expressed in two ways: as a ratio of rise to run or as an angle.

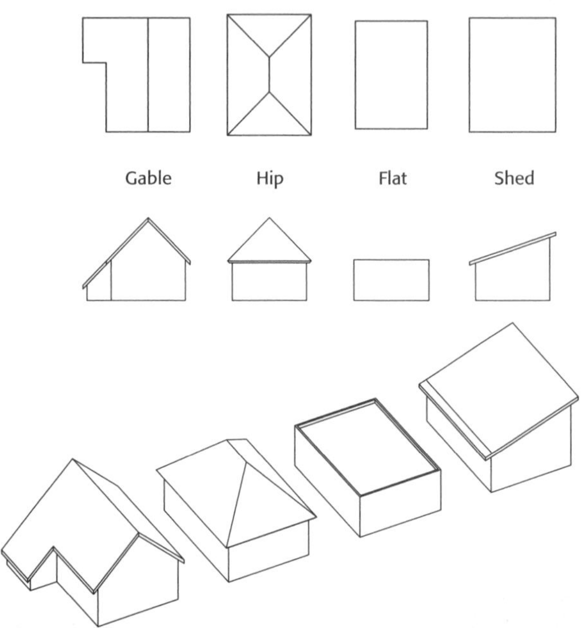

Figure 16.3 The four basic roof shapes

As a protective system, a roof must be able to perform within its local climate. Appropriate choices of slope and materials ensure that rain or snow are never allowed to sit on the roof or enter the building.

Roof systems refer to the materials used to create its insulating and waterproofing characteristics. The topmost part of a roofing system is regarded as the roofing material. There is currently a large selection of roofing materials available for sloped roof design, including asphalt shingle, fiberglass shingle, clay or concrete roofing tile, and corrugated or seam-metal roofing.

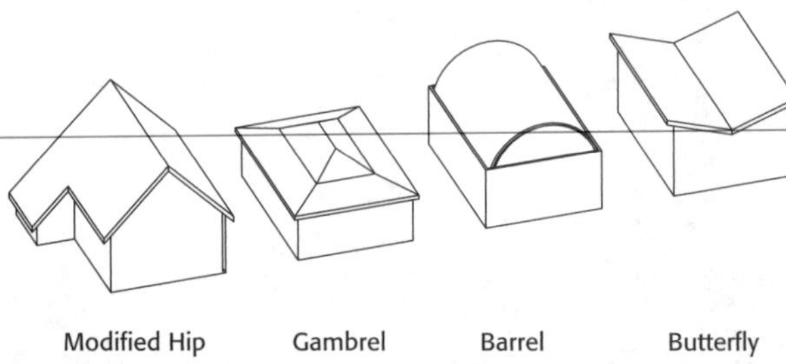

Figure 16.4 The four basic roof shapes can combine into more complex roof form variations.

Roof Structure/Framing

Typical residential roof framing uses a rafter/joist or truss system. Placement of roof framing is commonly shown in a framing plan where each single line represents the center of a rafter or truss (Figure 16.5). Figure 16.6 shows framing plans for two common roof types.

The ADT Roof Object

The ADT roof object is a single object that represents the whole roof system. Its primary use is to draw all sloped roof forms (Figure 16.7). Because of the limitations of command options associated with roof objects, additional modifications of these objects is difficult. Autodesk, therefore, recommends using roof objects only to generate a complex sloped roof structure quickly. If additional intricacy and/or modifications are necessary, it is recommended that the roof object be converted into individual roof slabs.

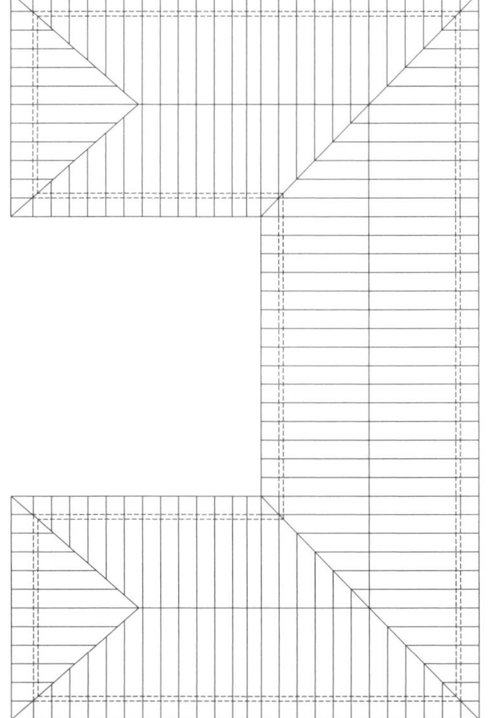

Figure 16.5 Example of a framing plan for a U-shaped hip roof

Characteristics of the ADT Roof Object

Because roof objects include the whole roof form, there is the possibility that a roof can have several slabs set at varying angles. Each articulated sloped thickness (slab) includes a top and bottom surface and the edges that connect the top to the bottom. Modifications to these sloped slabs and the edges that connect them can take place on an individual basis.

> **Box 16.2**
>
> At the conceptual or schematic phase, roof objects can be created to represent the whole roof system, including its rafter framing. As the design develops, you may need to draw exposed rafters to show the necessary detail within the roof system.

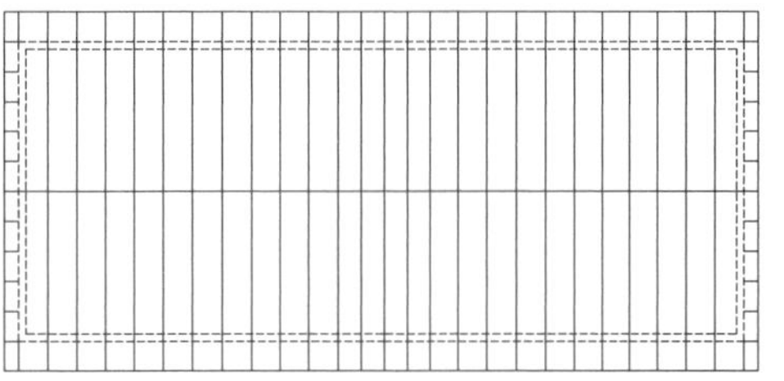

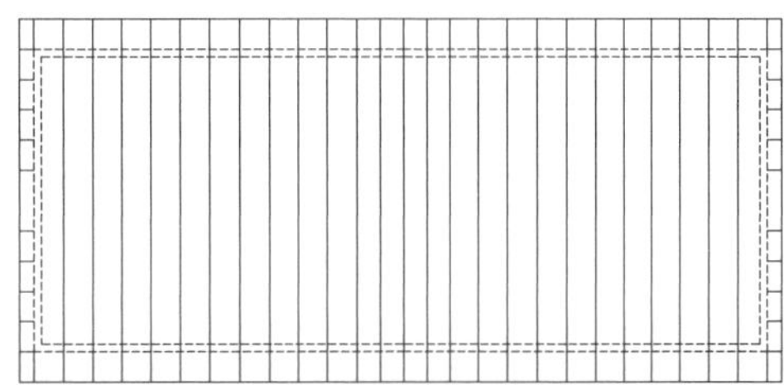

Figure 16.6 Example of a framing plan for a gable and a shed roof

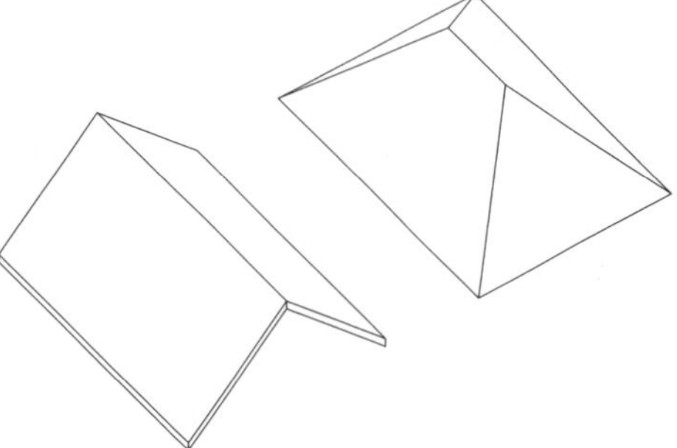

Figure 16.7 ADT's roof object

Placing a Roof Object

There are three methods used to place a roof object. If using the RoofSlabAdd tool, ADT prompts users to place the roof object by specifying each corner of the roof. Alternatively, roof objects can be created by converting polylines or selecting wall boundaries.

Placing Hip Roofs

Since hip roofs are sloped on all sides, only eave conditions are created when placing the hip roof. Figure 16.8 demonstrates how to use the RoofSlabAdd tool to create a rectangular hip roof form.

Placing Gable Roofs

When placing a gable roof, ADT requires you to specify the edges that will become the rake edges. Figure 16.9 demonstrates how to use the RoofSlabAdd tool to create a rectangular gable roof form.

Technique to Master **T16.08** Placing a Rectangular-shaped Hip Roof by Specifying Points

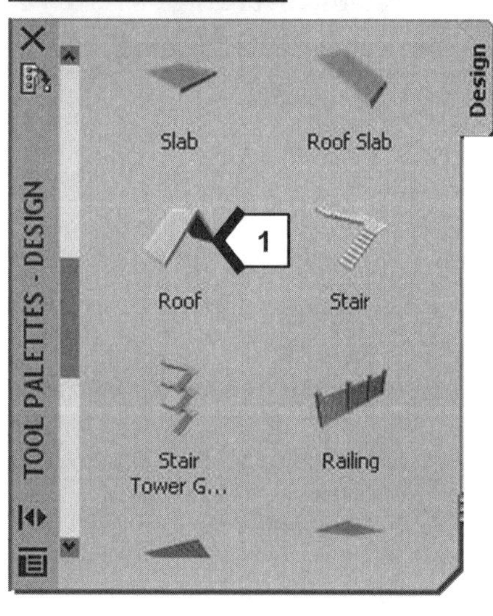

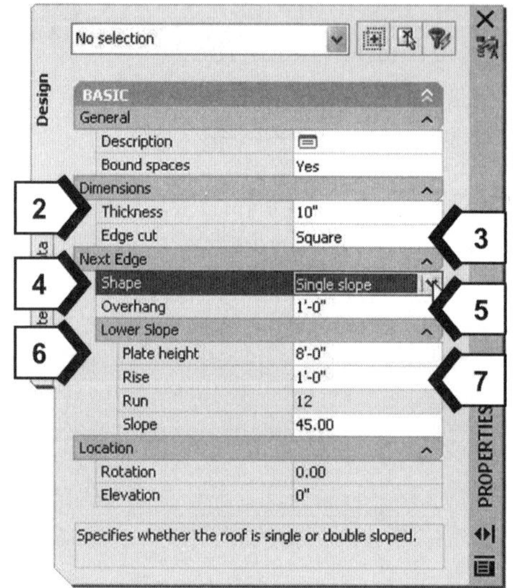

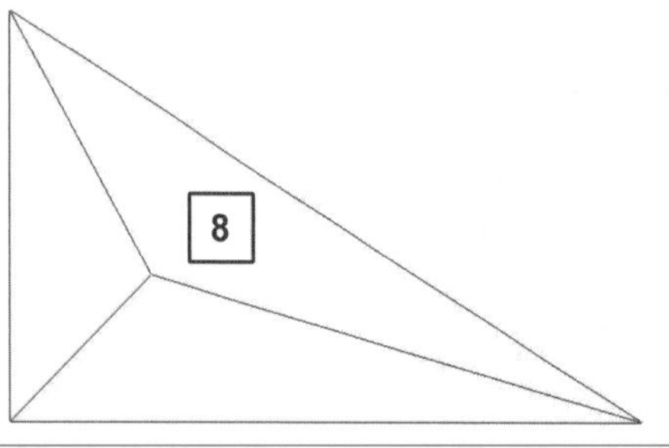

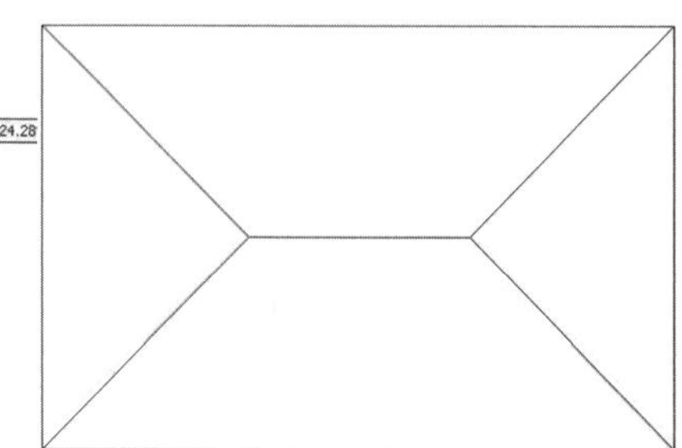

Figure 16.8

1	[Design Tool palette]	Start the Roof Object command.
2	[Properties palette>Thickness]	Type in the roof thickness.
3	[Properties palette>Edge cut]	Select the edge cut condition.
4	[Properties palette>Shape]	Select Single slope.
5	[Properties palette>Overhang]	Type in the Overhang distance beyond walls.
6	[Properties palette>Plate height]	Type in the Plate height.
7	[Properties palette>Rise]	Type in the Rise distance or alternatively the Slope angle for roof object.
8	[Drawing Screen]	Specify the four corner points that will define the plan view rectangle of the hip roof.
9	[Command Line]	Hit Enter to complete the command.

Technique to Master **T16.09** Placing a Rectangular-Shaped Gable Roof by Specifying Points

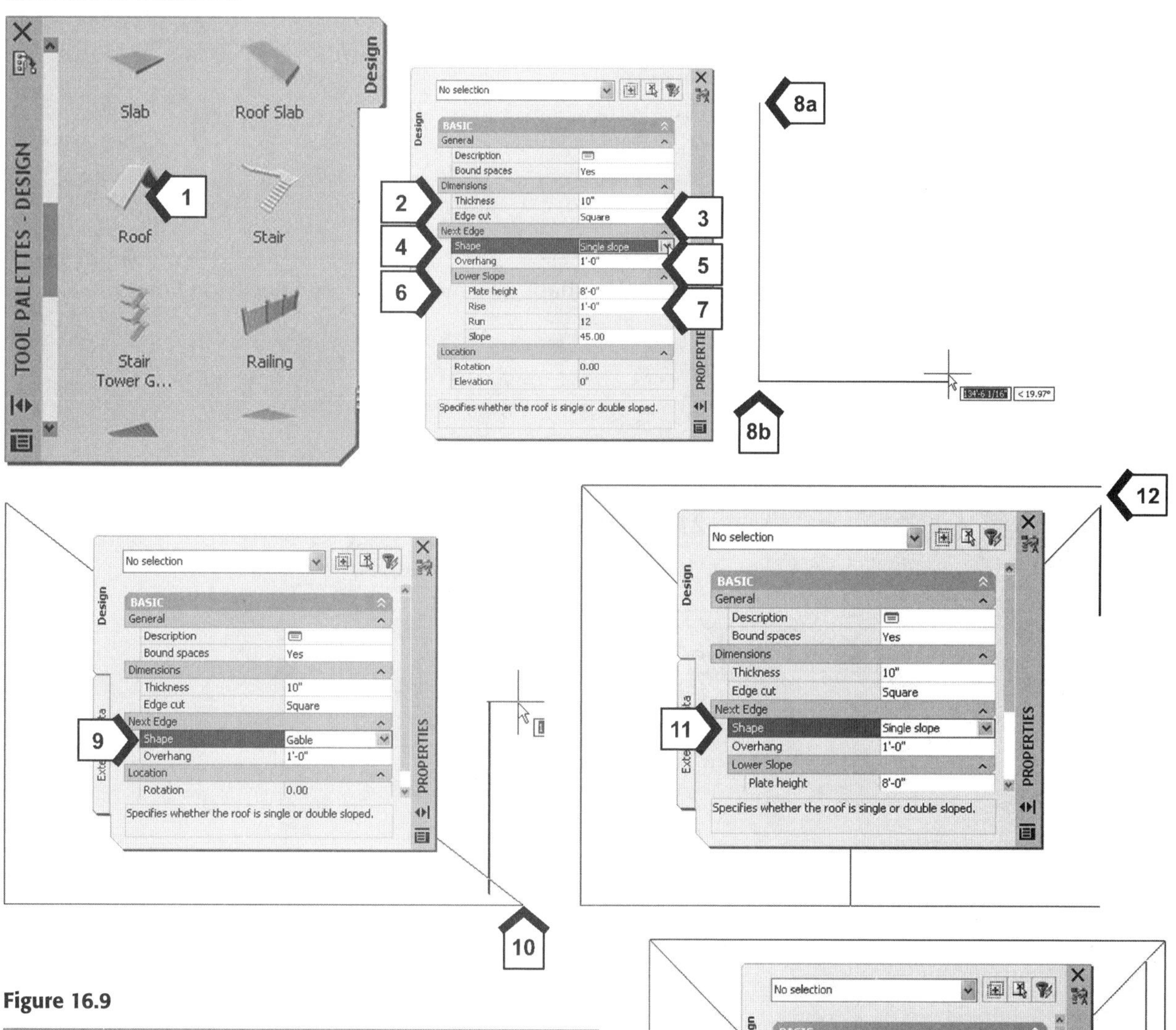

Figure 16.9

1	[Design Tool palette]	Start the Roof Object command.
2	[Properties palette> Thickness]	Type in the Thickness.
3	[Properties palette> Edge cut]	Select the Edge condition.
4	[Properties palette>Shape]	Select Single slope.
5	[Properties palette> Overhang]	Type in the Overhang distance beyond walls.
6	[Properties palette>Plate height]	Type in the Plate height.
7	[Properties palette>Rise]	Type in the Rise distance or alternatively the Slope angle for roof object.
8a, 8b	[Drawing Screen]	Specify the first two points that will define the first eave edge.
9	[Properties palette>Shape]	Specify Gable.
10	[Drawing Screen]	Specify the third point that will define the first rake edge.
11	[Properties palette>Shape]	Specify Single slope.
12	[Drawing Screen]	Specify the fourth point to complete roof object.
13	[Properties palette>Shape]	Specify Gable.
14	[Command Line]	Hit Enter to complete the command.

Placing Gambrel Roofs (Also Known as Double Slope Roofs)

Gambrel roofs have two slope conditions—the upper and lower—at all eave conditions. Figure 16.10 demonstrates how to use the RoofSlabAdd tool to create a rectangular gambrel roof form.

Technique to Master **T16.10** Placing a Rectangular-Shaped Gambrel Roof by Specifying Points

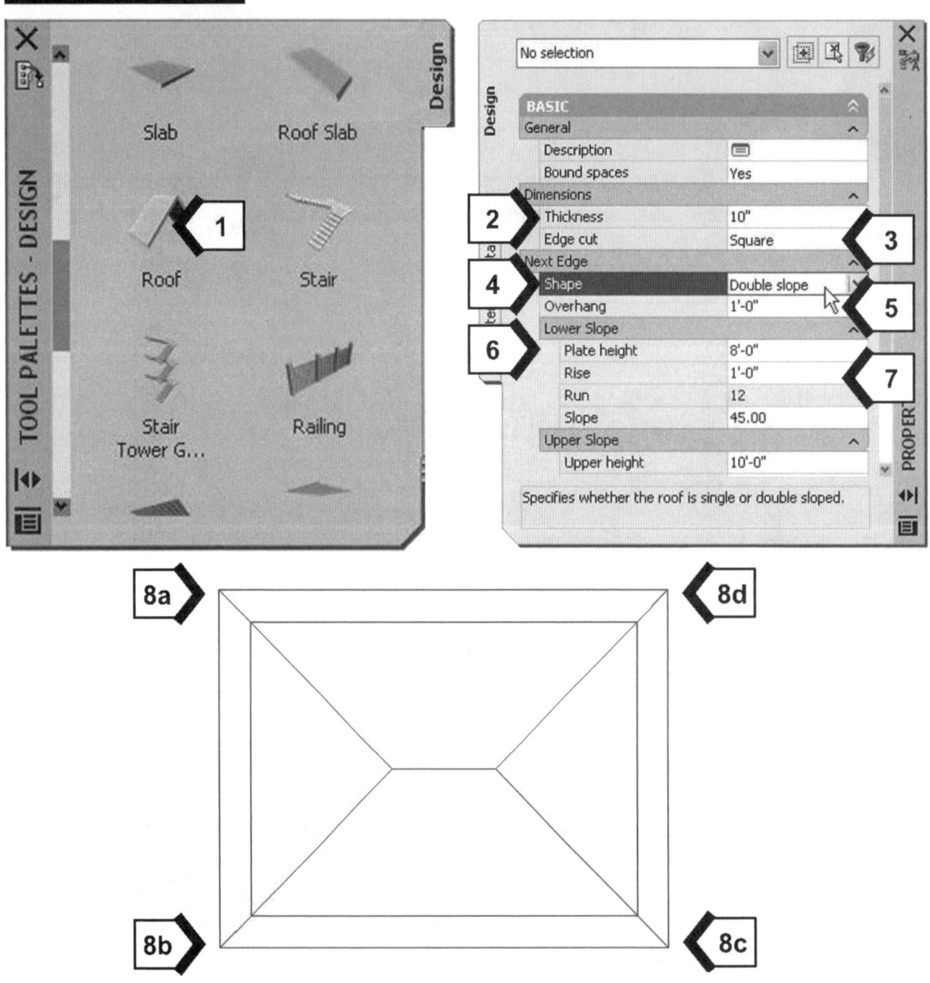

Figure 16.10

1	[Design Tool palette]	Start Roof Object command.
2	[Properties palette>Thickness]	Type in the Thickness.
3	[Properties palette>Edge cut]	Select the edge condition.
4	[Properties palette>Shape]	Select Double slope.
5	[Properties palette>Overhang]	Type in the Overhang distance beyond walls.
6	[Properties palette>Plate height]	Type in the Plate height.
7	[Properties palette>Lower Slope>Rise]	Type in the Rise distance or alternatively the Slope angle for roof object.
8a, 8b, 8c, 8d	[Drawing Screen]	Specify the four corner points that will define the plan view rectangle of the hip roof.
9	[Command Line]	Hit Enter to complete the command.

Placing Roof Objects by Converting Linework

Figures 16.11 through 16.13 demonstrate gable, hip, and gambrel roof placement using the Linework and Walls command available through the Roof tool's right-click menu.

Creating Roof Dormers

Adding roof dormers requires you to convert the roof objects to roof slabs first. Figure 16.14 illustrates one procedure for adding roof dormers to an existing roof form.

Technique to Master **T16.11** Converting Line Work to Create a Nonrectangular Hip Roof

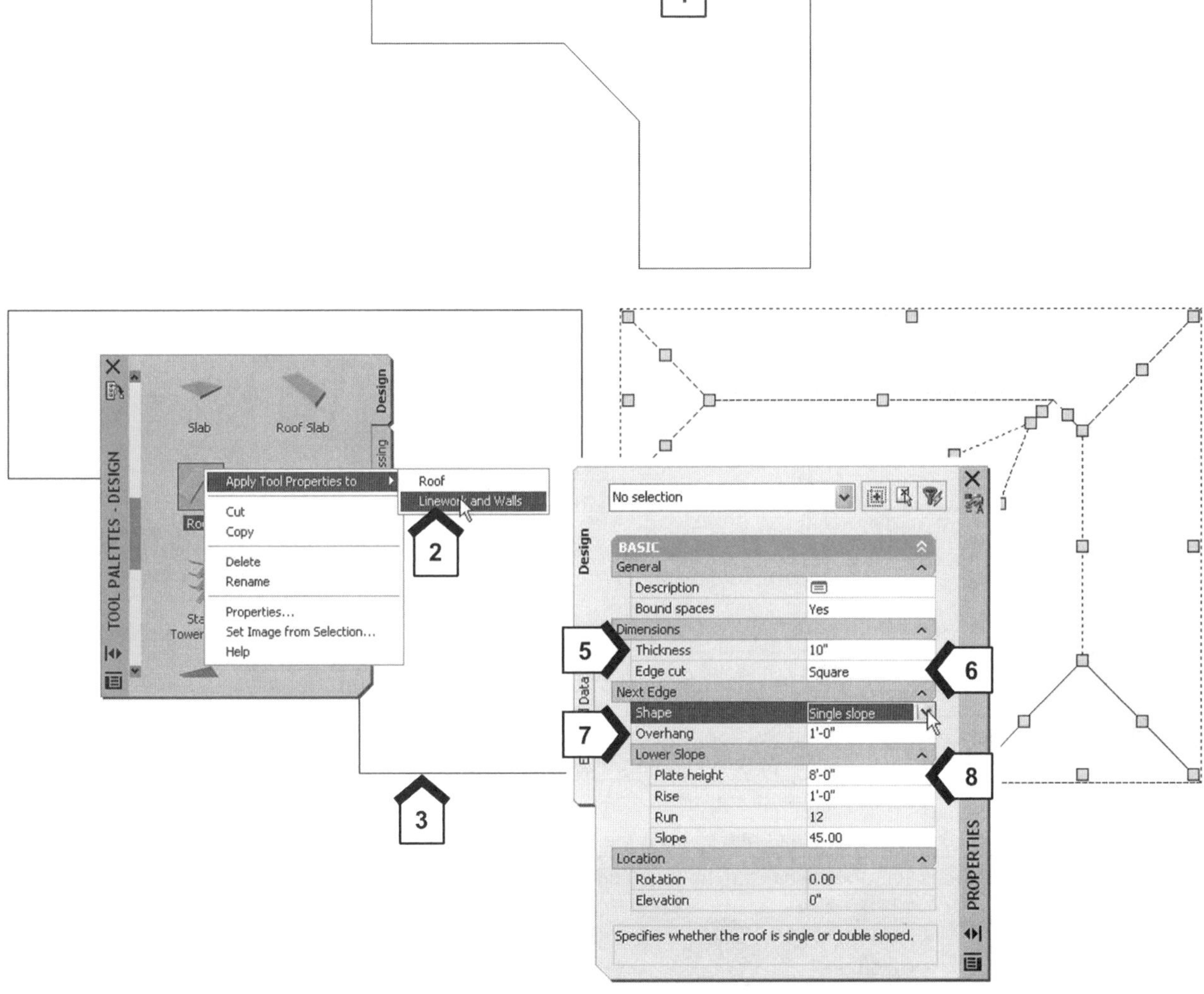

Figure 16.11

1	[Drawing Screen]	Draw a plan outline of a roof shape using a polyline.
2	[Design Tool palette>Roof Tool]	Right-click on the Roof Tool, and choose Apply Tool Properties to>Linework and Walls.
3	[Drawing Screen]	Select polyline to convert.
4	[Command Line]	Type N and hit Enter to keep the polyline.
5	[Properties palette>Thickness]	Type in the Thickness.
6	[Properties palette>Edge cut]	Select the edge condition.
7	[Properties palette>Overhang]	Type in the Overhang distance beyond walls.
8	[Properties palette>Plate height]	Type in the Plate height.

Technique to Master **T16.12** Converting Line Work to Create a Nonrectangular Gable Roof

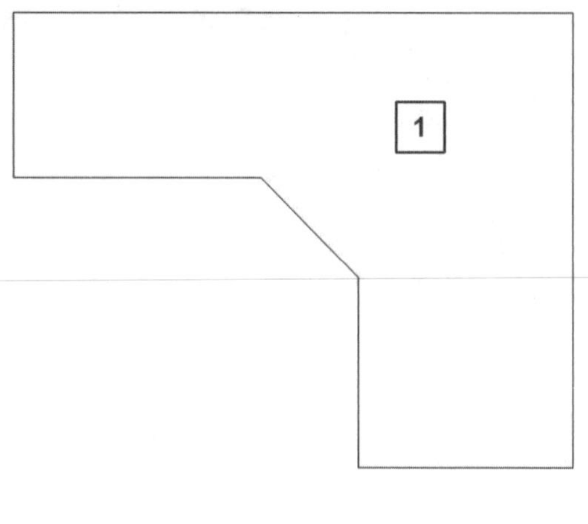

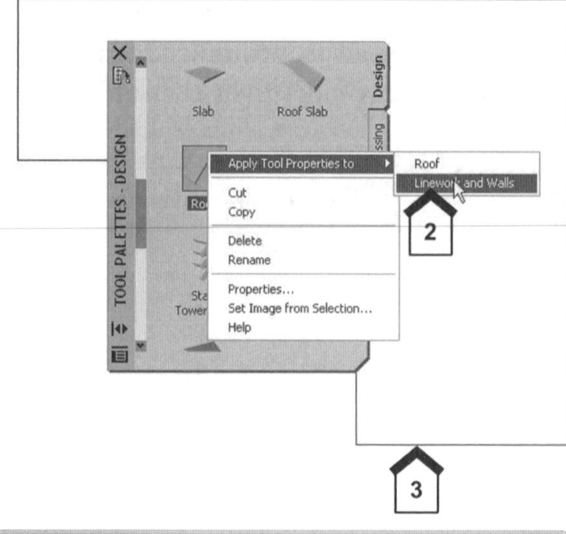

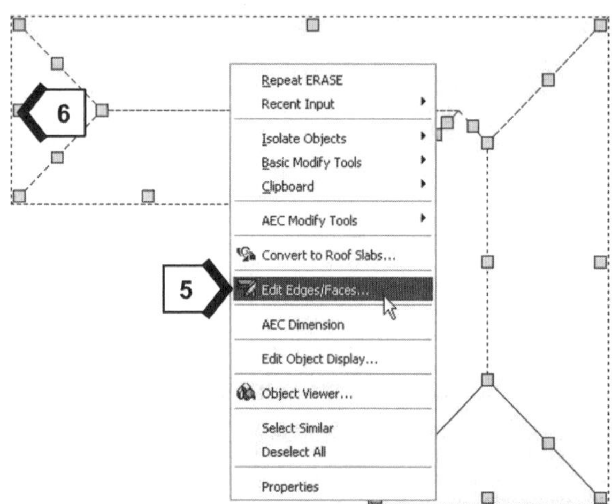

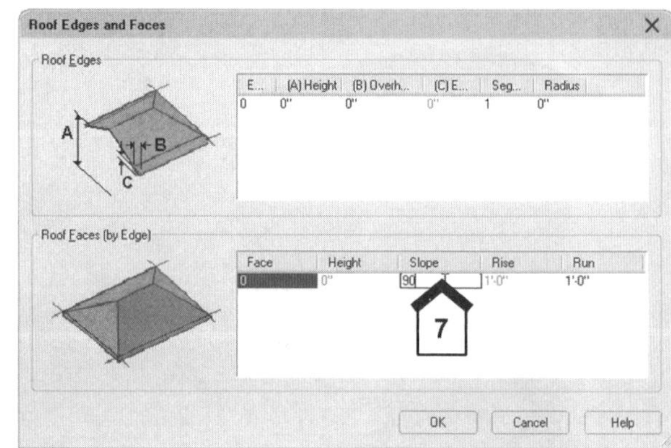

Figure 16.12

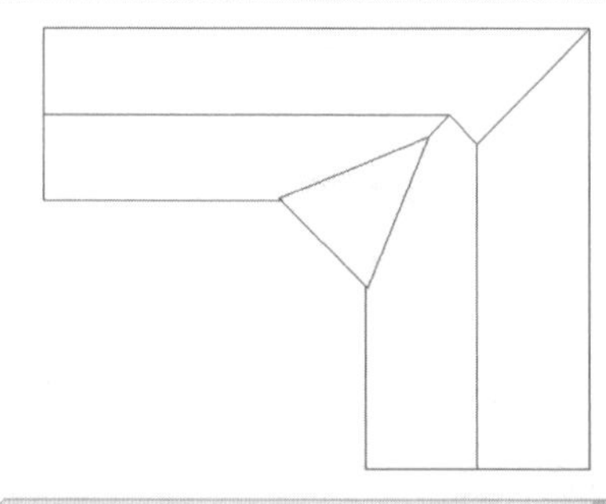

1	[Drawing Screen]	Draw a plan outline of a roof shape using a polyline.
2	[Design Tool palette> Roof Tool]	Right-click on the Roof Tool and choose Apply Tool Properties to>Linework and Walls.
3	[Drawing Screen]	Select polyline to convert.
4	[Command Line]	Type N and hit Enter to keep the polyline.
5	[Drawing Screen]	Select roof object, right-click, and choose Edit Edges/Faces.
6	[Drawing Screen]	Left-click (select) edge that will become rake condition.
7	[Roof Edge and Faces dialogue box]	Change slope angle to 90 degrees.
8	Repeat instructions 5 through 7 to complete gable roof.	
9	[Drawing Screen]	Select Roof object.
10	[Properties palette> Thickness]	Type in the Thickness.
11	[Properties palette> Edge cut]	Select the edge condition.
12	[Properties palette> Overhang]	Type in the Overhang distance beyond walls.
13	[Properties palette> Plate height]	Type in the Plate height.

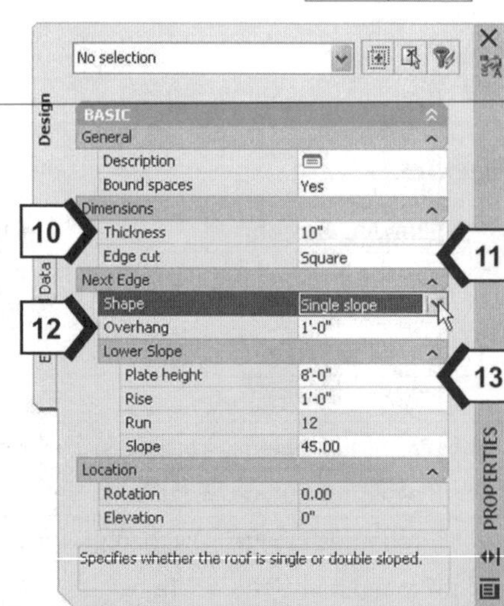

Technique to Master **T16.13** Converting Line Work to Create a Nonrectangular Gambrel Roof

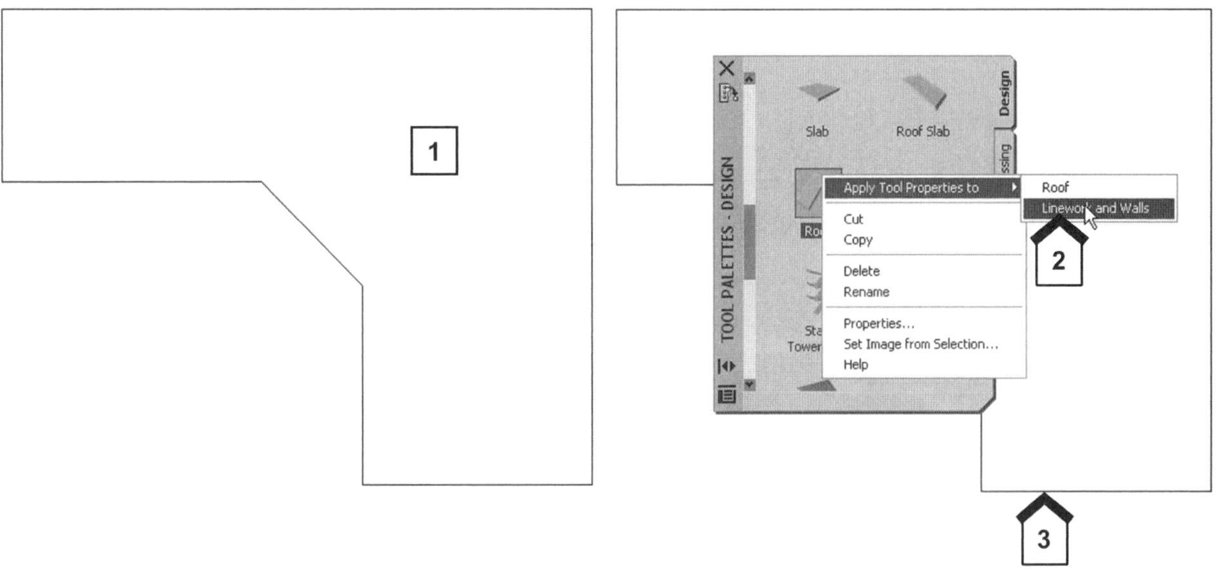

Figure 16.13

1	[Drawing Screen]	Draw a plan outline of a roof shape using a polyline.
2	[Design Tool palette>Roof Tool]	Right-click on the Roof Tool and choose Apply Tool Properties to> Linework and Walls.
3	[Drawing Screen]	Select polyline to convert.
4	[Command Line]	Type N and hit Enter to keep the polyline.
5	[Properties palette> Thickness]	Type in the roof thickness.
6	[Properties palette> Edge cut]	Select the edge condition.
7	[Properties palette> Shape]	Select Double slope.
8	[Properties palette> Overhang]	Type in the Overhang distance beyond walls.
9	[Properties palette> Lower Slope>Plate height]	Type in the Plate height for Lower Slope (refer to the section on roof vocabulary in this chapter for definition of plate height).
10	[Properties palette> Lower Slope>Rise]	Type in the Rise distance, or alternatively, the slope angle for Roof object.
11	[Properties palette> Upper Slope>Upper height]	Type in the Plate height for Upper Slope.
12	[Properties palette> Upper Slope>Rise]	Type in the Rise distance, or alternatively, the slope angle for Roof object.

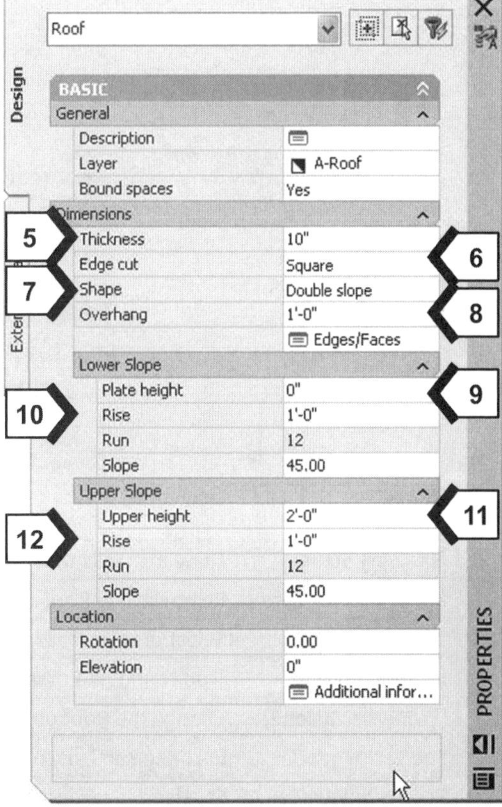

Technique to Master T16.14 Creating a Roof Dormer (Gable or Hip)

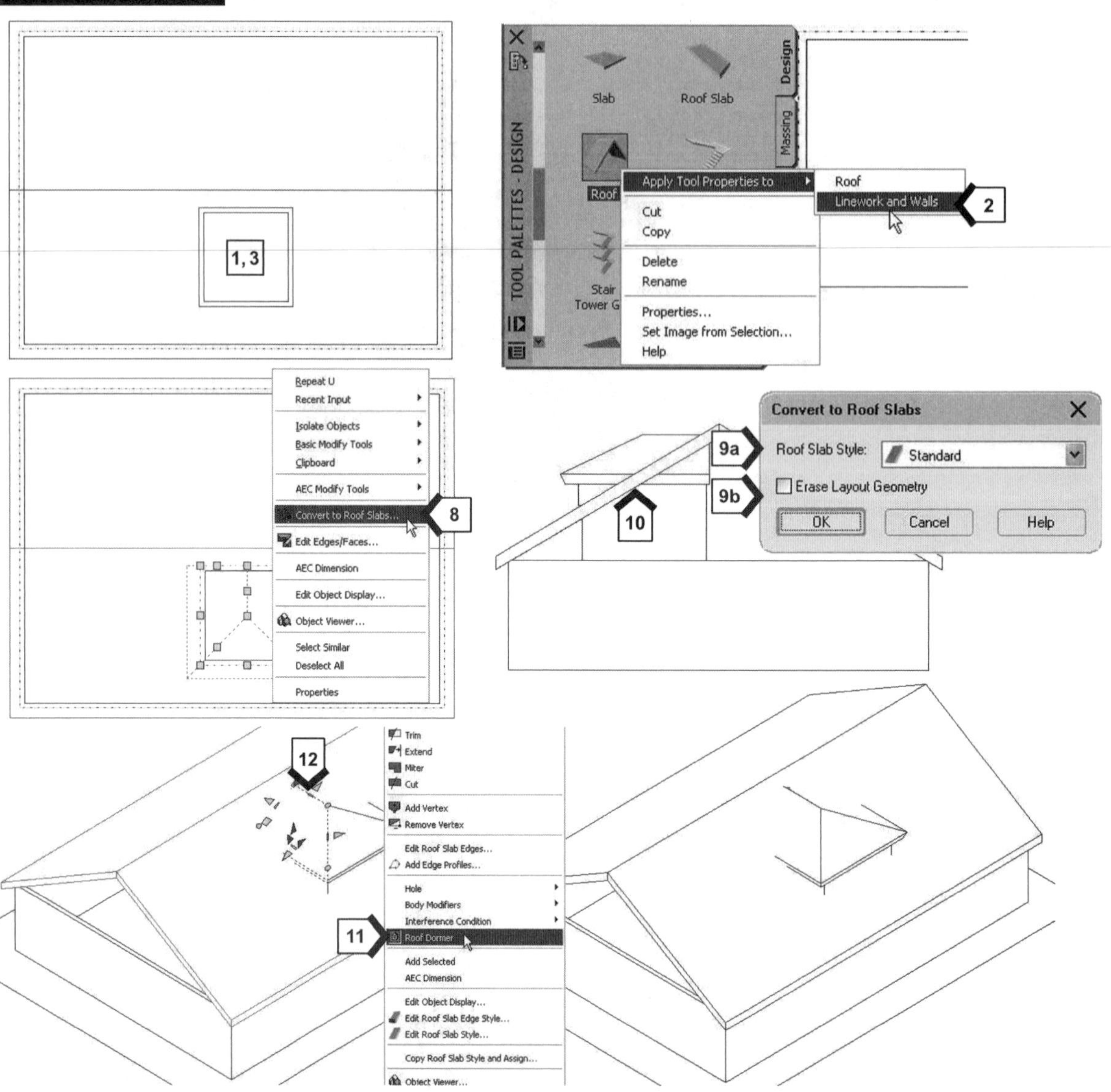

Figure 16.14

1	[Drawing Screen]	Draw the walls that the dormer will sit on.
2	[Design Tool palette]	Right-click on Roof object and choose Apply Tool Properties to>Linework and Walls
3	[Drawing Screen]	Select dormer walls to convert to roof object.
4	[Command Line]	Type N and hit Enter to keep layout geometry. (Keep the dormer walls.)
5	[Properties palette]	Change the Roof object to the desired slope.
6	See Technique T16.09 to change an existing hip roof to a gable roof.	
7	See Technique T16.16 to selectively adjust overhangs on specific edges.	
8	[Drawing Screen]	Select the main Roof object and Dormer Roof object. Right-click, choose Convert to Roof Slabs.
9a 9b	[Convert to Roof Slabs dialogue box]	Select the Ro of Slab Style. Check the Erase Layout Geometry button.
10	[Drawing Screen]	Change to a side view. Analyze dormer/main roof relationship. Dormer roof slabs as well as three of the dormer walls must overlap main roof slab.
11	[Drawing Screen]	Change to an axon view (make sure your UCS is set to world view). Select main roof slab. Right-click and choose the Roof Dormer command.
12	[Drawing Screen]	Only select the walls and roof dormer slabs that intersect the main roof slab.

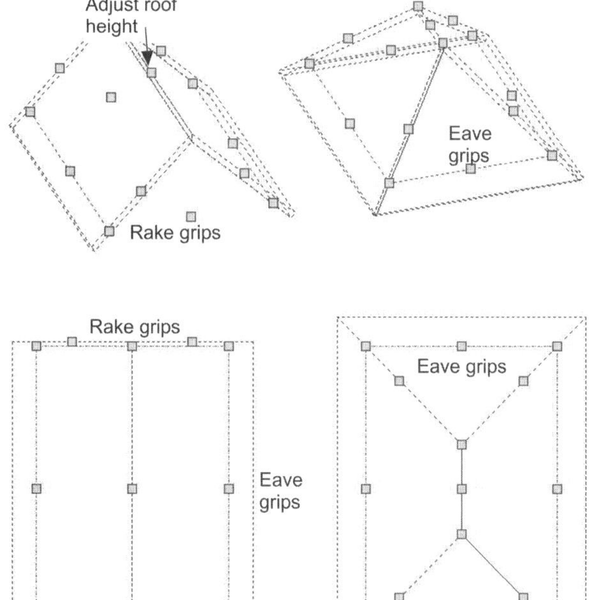

Figure 16.15 Grip points for roof objects

Modifying Roof Objects

Individual object modifications to roof objects are made through the Property palette, Grip, and Specialty commands available to this object type. Figures 16.15 and 16.16 illustrate the Grip and Edit Edges/Faces tools.

Customizing Roof Objects

Once the final roof shape is achieved, convert the Roof object to individual roof slabs to perform other types of advanced modifications.

Technique to Master **T16.16** Edit Edges/Faces

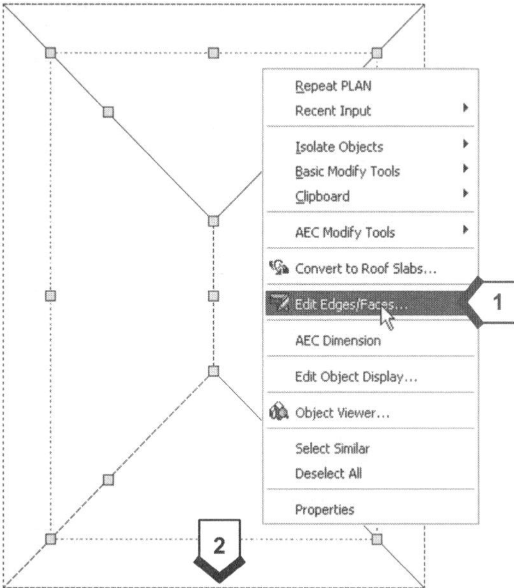

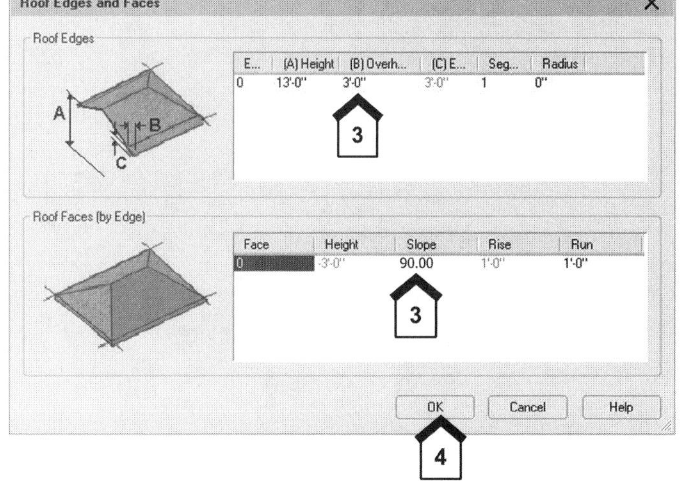

Figure 16.16

1	[Drawing Screen]	Select the roof then right-click and choose Edit Edges/Faces command.
2	[Drawing Screen]	Select the roof edge(s) to edit. Press Enter to complete the selection.
3	[Roof Edges and Faces dialogue box]	Change any edge or face properties. (To change a hip roof to a gable, set the face slope to 90.)
4	[Roof Edges and Faces dialogue box]	Click OK to complete the command.

Slabs and Roof Slabs

The ADT slab and roof slab objects are used to represent the floor and roof systems of the virtual model. Slabs and roof slab objects share common properties and behave in the same manner. They are defined by their top and bottom surfaces and their edge conditions. An added feature in ADT 2007 is the ability to identify the individual components of a slab and roof slab system.

Placing Slabs

The command line instructions for placing a slab or roof slab are SlabAdd and RoofSlabAdd. All of the slab and roof slab commands are identified in an illustration on the CD-ROM. There are three slab placement methods—locating points on-screen to specify the slab's corners, converting polylines to slab objects, and using existing walls to specify the slab's perimeters. Figures 16.17 through 16.19 demonstrate these techniques.

Technique to Master **T16.17** Placing a Slab by Specifying the Slab Corners

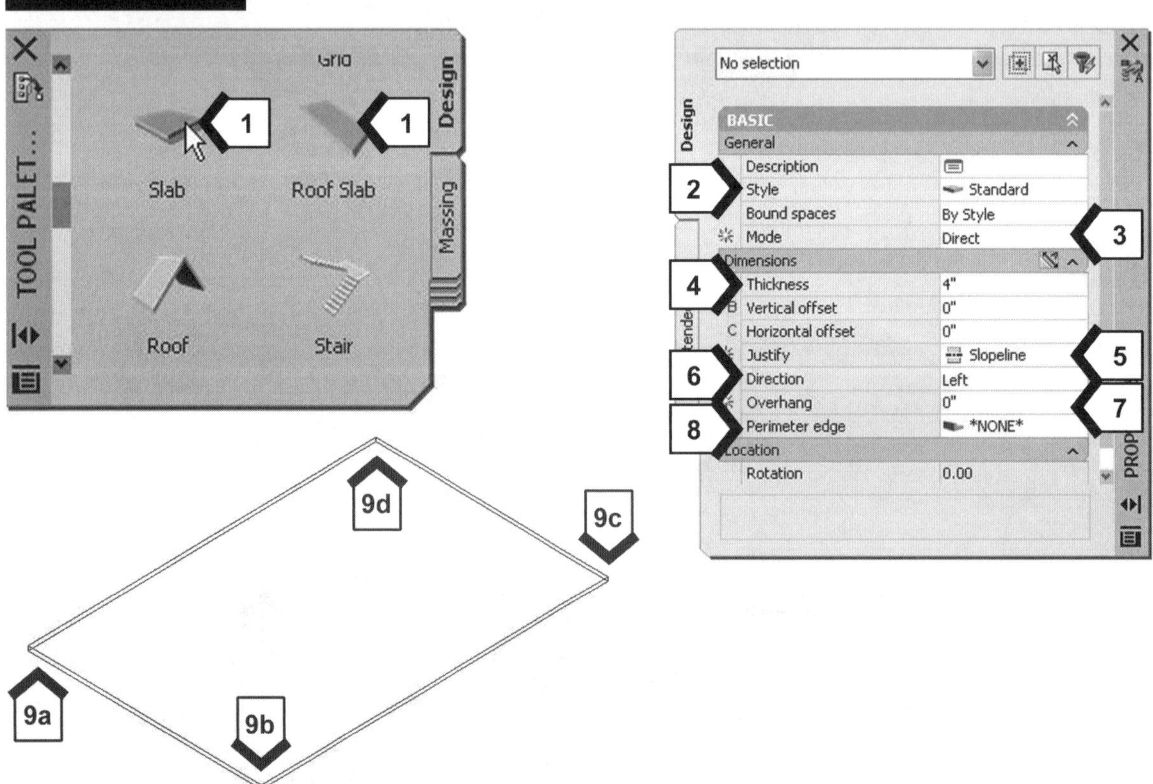

Figure 16.17

1	[Design Tool palette]	Start the Slab or Roof Slab command.
2	[Properties palette>Style]	Select the slab style.
3	[Properties palette>Mode]	Select the slab placement mode.
4	[Properties palette>Thickness]	Type in the slab thickness.
5	[Properties palette>Justification]	Select the slab justification.
6	[Properties palette>Direction]	Select the slab direction.
7	[Properties palette>Overhangs]	Type the overhang distance.
8	[Properties palette>Perimeter edge]	If using customized edge condition, select the Perimeter edge style.
9a, 9b, 9c, 9d	[Drawing Screen]	Specify the corner points that will define the plan shape of the slab or roof slab.
10	[Command Line]	Hit Enter to complete the command.

Technique to Master T16.18 Creating Slabs by Converting Linework

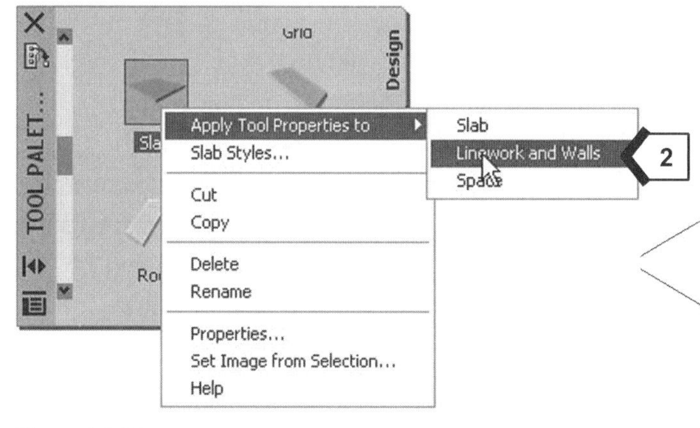

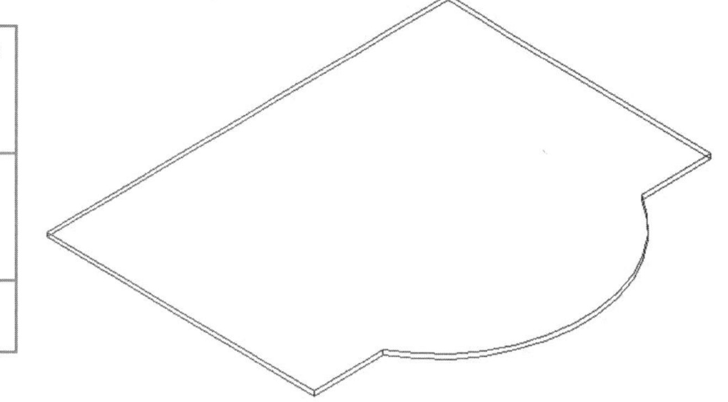

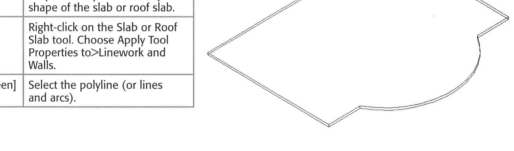

Figure 16.18

1	[Drawing Screen]	Use polyline (or a series of lines and arcs) to create a closed shape that represents the plan shape of the slab or roof slab.
2	[Design Tool palette]	Right-click on the Slab or Roof Slab tool. Choose Apply Tool Properties to>Linework and Walls.
3	[Drawing Screen]	Select the polyline (or lines and arcs).

Technique to Master T16.19 Creating Slabs by Converting Walls

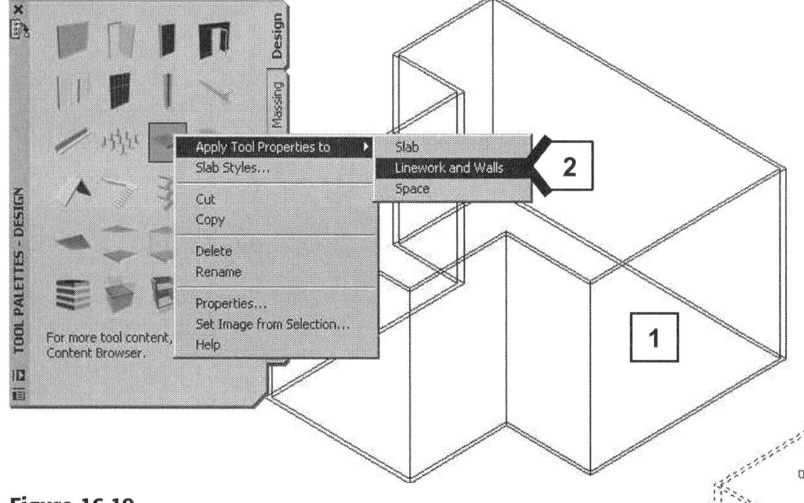

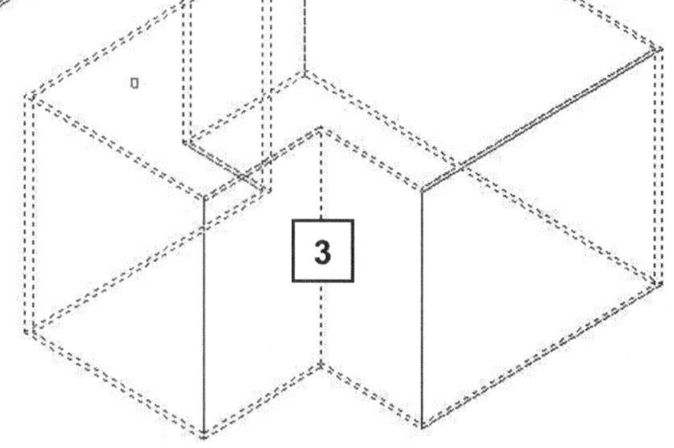

Figure 16.19

1	[Drawing Screen]	Draw walls to create a closed shape that represents the plan shape of the slab or roof slab.
2	[Design Tool palette]	Right-click on Slab or Roof Slab tool. Choose Apply Tool Properties to> Linework and Walls
3	[Drawing Screen]	Select walls.

Modify and Add Complexity to the Slab and Roof Slab Objects

Figures 16.20 through 16.23 demonstrate the Property palette and Grip tools specific to the slab object types. Additional specialty commands are introduced below.

Trim and Extend

Both slab and roof slab objects use command-specific trim and extend tools for complex editing not possible through grips. These commands use polylines, walls, or other slabs as cutting or extending planes. Slab trims remove the part of the slab that is no longer needed. While the SlabTrim command sequence is essentially the same as its AutoCAD equivalent, the SlabExtend command instead prompts you to select the edges that will be extended. Figures 16.24 and 16.25 demonstrate the two slab-editing commands.

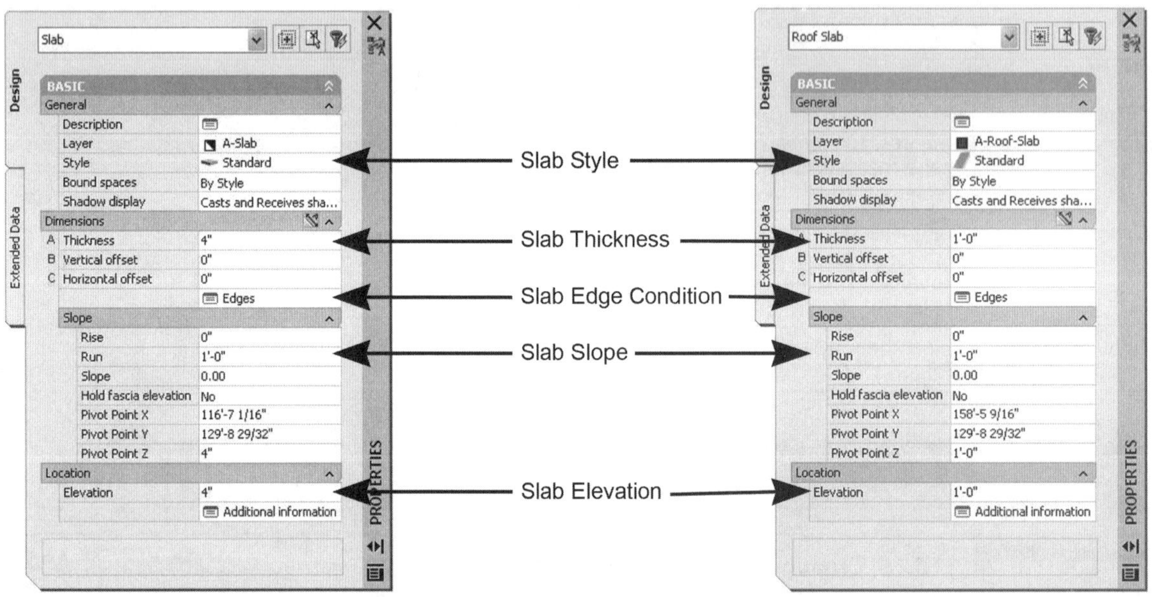

Figure 16.20 Properties of the slab and roof slab objects

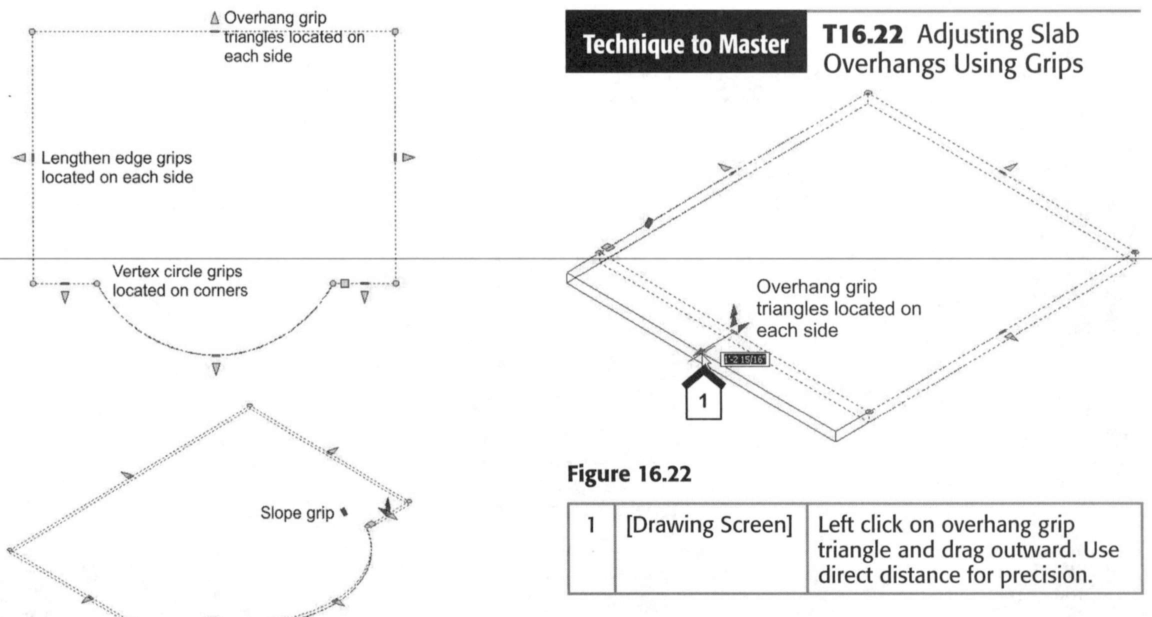

Figure 16.21 Grip points for slab and roof slab objects

T16.22 Adjusting Slab Overhangs Using Grips

Figure 16.22

1	[Drawing Screen]	Left click on overhang grip triangle and drag outward. Use direct distance for precision.

Technique to Master T16.23 Adding a Vertex to a Slab

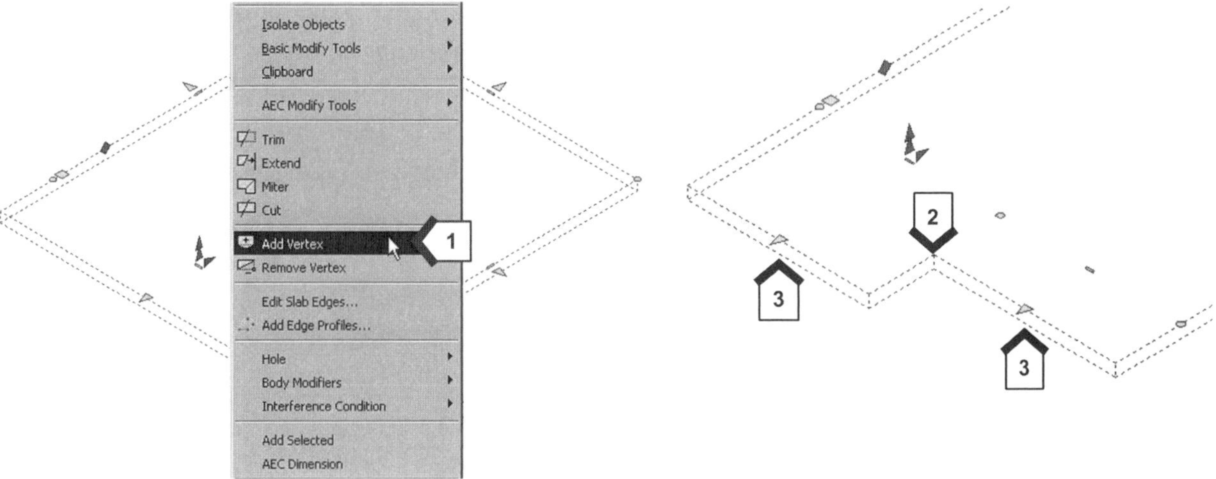

Figure 16.23

1	[Drawing Screen]	Select a slab, right-click, and choose Add Vertex.
2	[Drawing Screen]	Specify a point on the slab for the new vertex.
3	[Drawing Screen]	Added vertex creates two edges that can be manipulated individually.

Technique to Master T16.24 Trimming Slabs and Roof Slabs

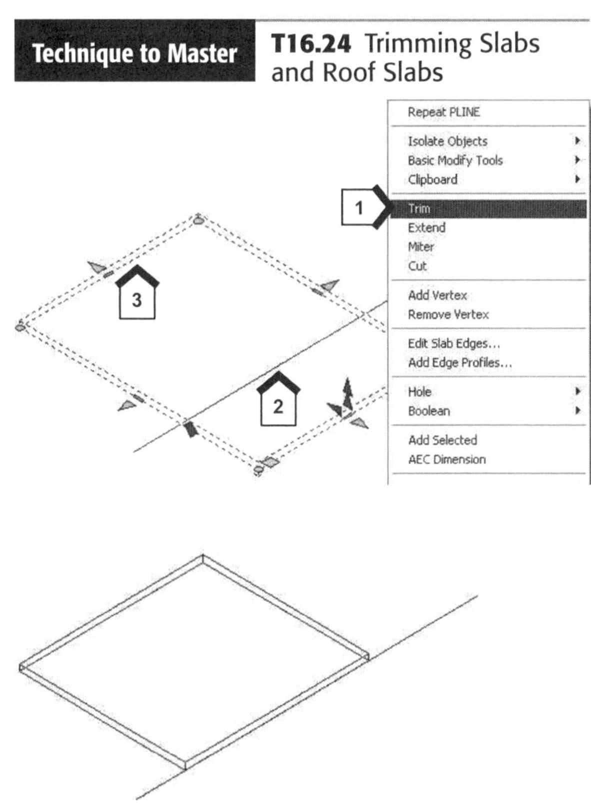

Figure 16.24

1	[Drawing Screen]	Select slab, right-click, and choose Trim.
2	[Drawing Screen]	Select cutting plane.
3	[Drawing Screen]	Select slab at side that will be kept.

Technique to Master T16.25 Extending Slabs and Roof Slabs

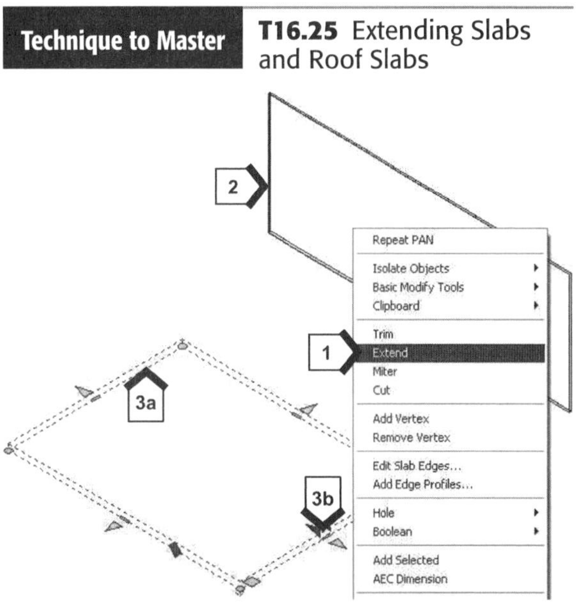

Figure 16.25

1	[Drawing Screen]	Select the slab, right-click, and choose Extend.
2	[Drawing Screen]	Select the wall to extend to.
3a 3b	[Drawing Screen]	Select the edges (perpendicular to wall) that will be extended.

Cutting

Slab cuts break a slab into multiple pieces. The command requires you to intersect 3-D objects or polylines as cutting planes for the slab cut to succeed. If walls and slabs are used, the slab cut must coincide with the wall or slab surface. If open polylines are used, the start and end of the polyline must intersect the slab's edge (Figure 16.26). Figure 16.27 demonstrates this command.

Mitering

The mitering command automatically extends or trims two slab edges to form a mitered corner. Slabs do not need to overlap; the edges, however, must be nonparallel for the command to be successful. Figures 16.28 and 16.29 demonstrate the two command options by mitering roof slabs together.

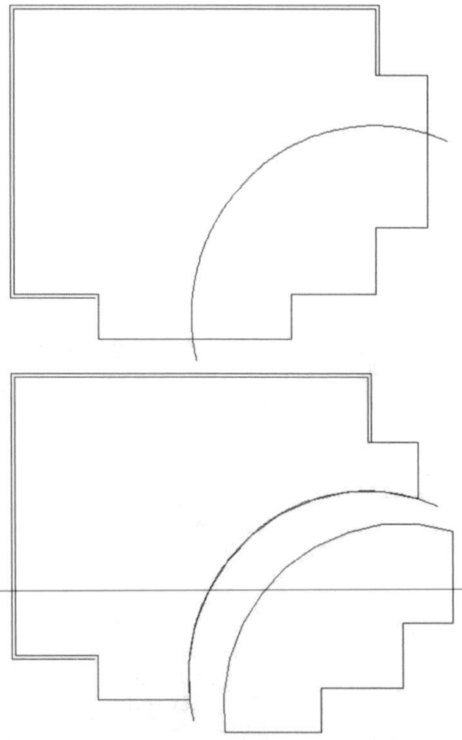

Figure 16.26 If open polylines are used as cutting planes, the start and end of the polyline must intersect the slab's edges.

> **Box 16.3**
>
> A slab may only be mitered once using the miter edge command option. Autodesk recommends creating overlapping slab conditions to accomplish additional miters on the same slab.

Technique to Master **T16.27** Cutting Slabs and Roof Slabs

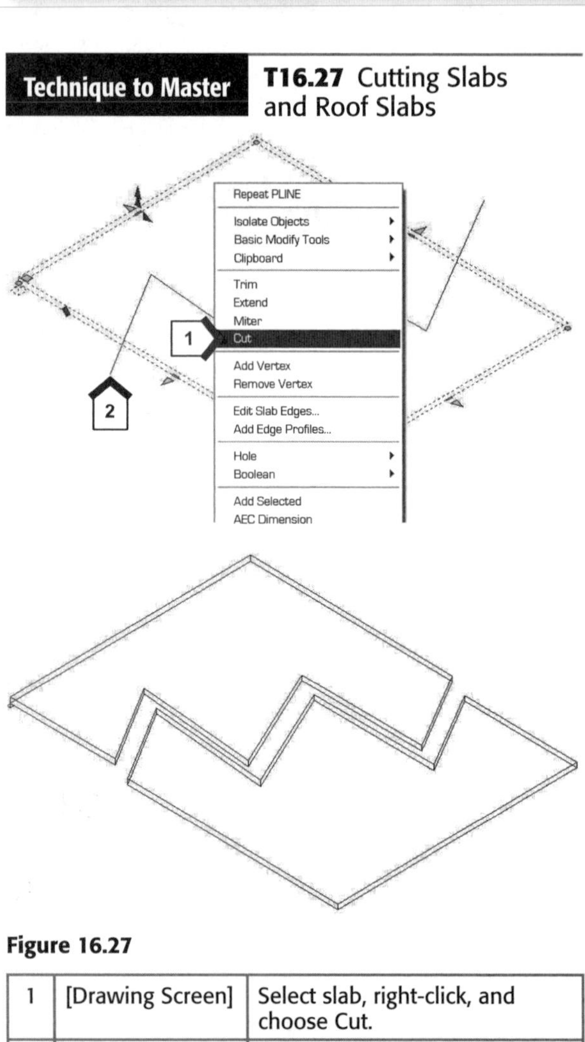

Figure 16.27

1	[Drawing Screen]	Select slab, right-click, and choose Cut.
2	[Drawing Screen]	Select cutting polyline or connected AEC objects.

Technique to Master **T16.28** Mitering Overlapping Slabs and Roof Slabs

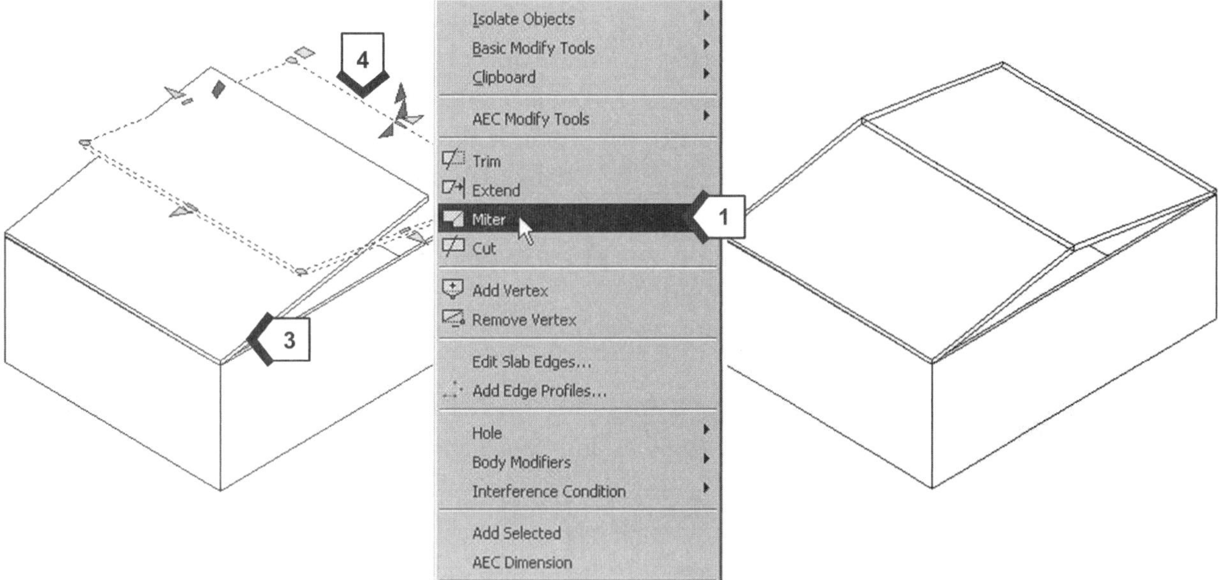

Figure 16.28

1	[Drawing Screen]	Select slab, right-click, and choose the Miter command.
2	[Command Line]	Select intersection and hit Enter.
3	[Drawing Screen]	Select the first roof slab at the side that will be kept.
4	[Drawing Screen]	Select the second roof slab at the side that will be kept.

Technique to Master **T16.29** Mitering Nonoverlapping Slabs and Roof Slabs

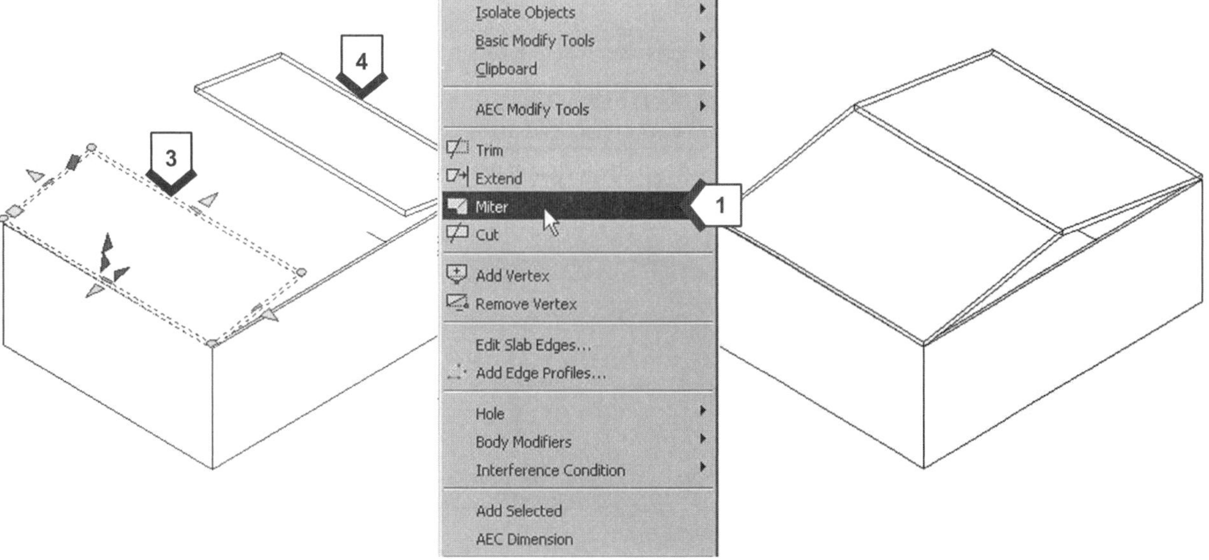

Figure 16.29

1	[Drawing Screen]	Select slab, right-click, and choose the Miter command.
2	[Command Line]	Select Edges and hit Enter.
3	[Drawing Screen]	Select the first roof slab.
4	[Drawing Screen]	Select the second roof slab.

Add Holes

The SlabAddHole command is used to produce penetrations in slab and roof slab objects. Similar to slab cuts, any 3-D object or closed polyline may be used to define the shape and size of the hole. While 3-D objects must form intersecting relationships, closed polylines can remain at any elevation for the command to be successful. When the hole is created, new vertices and edges are added and can be edited like any other vertex or edge (Figure 16.30).

Interference Conditions and Body Modifiers in Slabs and Roof Slabs

Interference conditions and body modifiers use 3-D objects to add or subtract mass from a slab (Figure 16.31). Common uses might include the creation of single-side sloped slabs, slab thickness alterations, and/or perimeter modifications. Figures 16.32 and 16.33 demonstrate the two commands.

Technique to Master **T16.30** Adding Holes to Slabs and Roof Slabs

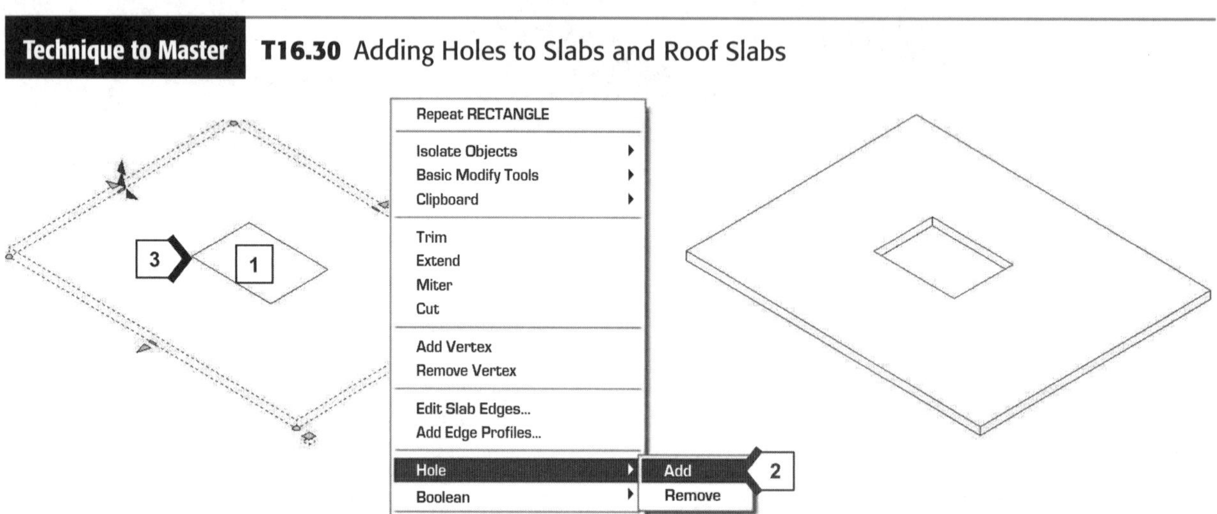

Figure 16.30

1	[Drawing Screen]	Draw polyline(s) or ADT object to represent location for slab hole.
2	[Drawing Screen]	Select slab, right-click, then choose Hole>Add.
3	[Drawing Screen]	Select the closed polyline or 3-D object, and press Enter.
4	[Command Line]	Choose No and hit Enter to keep the layout geometry.

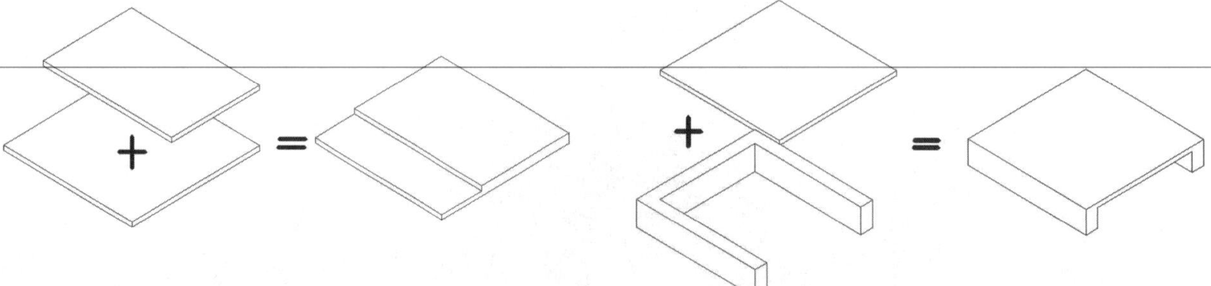

Figure 16.31 Interference conditions and body modifiers use 3-D objects to add mass or subtract mass from a slab.

Technique to Master T16.32 Adding Interference Conditions to Slabs and Roof Slabs

Figure 16.32

1	[Drawing Screen]	Draw object(s) to represent additive or subtractive objects for slab.
2	[Drawing Screen]	Select slab, right-click, then choose Interference Condition>Add.
3	[Drawing Screen]	Select the 3-D object(s), and press Enter.
4	[Command Line]	Specify whether 3-D object(s) will create a Boolean additive or subtractive condition.

Technique to Master T16.33 Adding Body Modifiers to Slabs and Roof Slabs

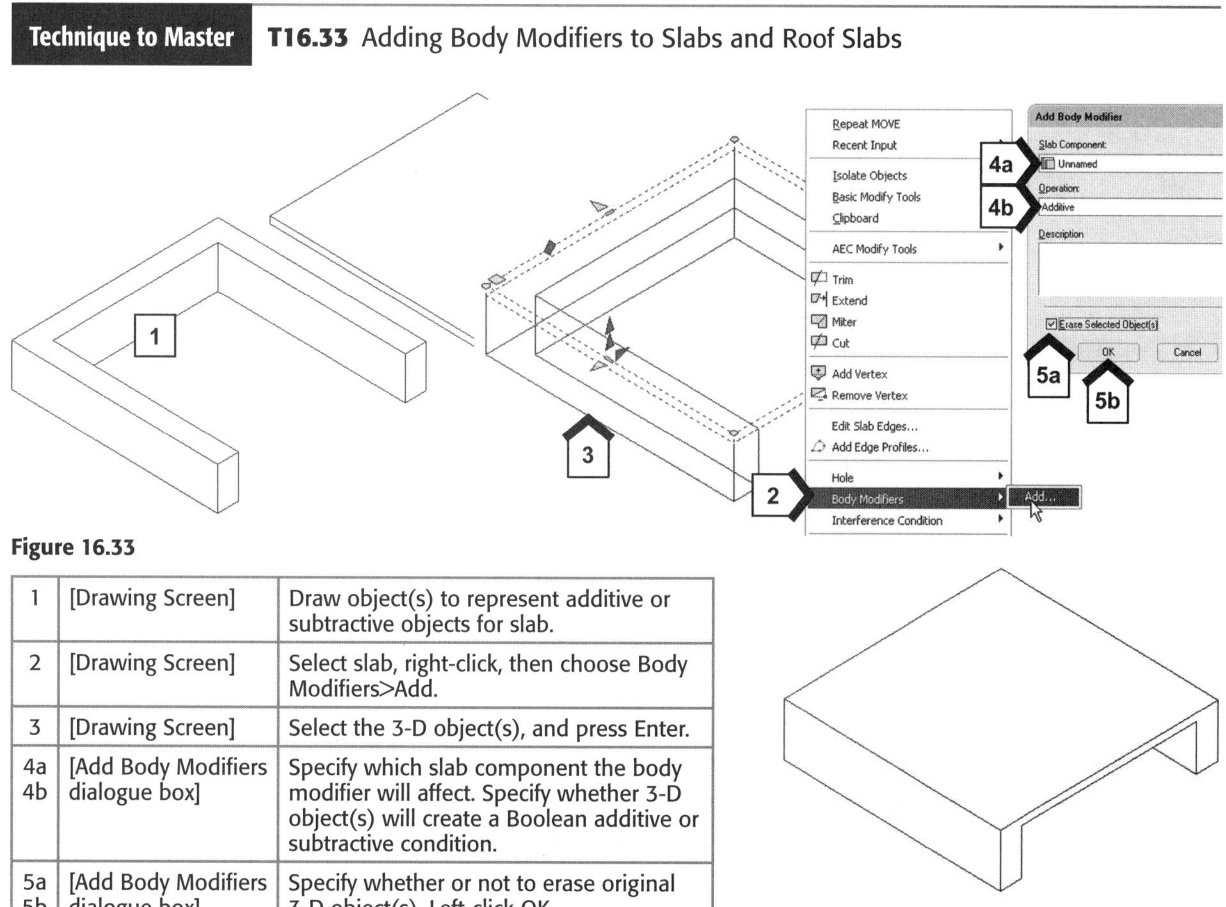

Figure 16.33

1	[Drawing Screen]	Draw object(s) to represent additive or subtractive objects for slab.
2	[Drawing Screen]	Select slab, right-click, then choose Body Modifiers>Add.
3	[Drawing Screen]	Select the 3-D object(s), and press Enter.
4a 4b	[Add Body Modifiers dialogue box]	Specify which slab component the body modifier will affect. Specify whether 3-D object(s) will create a Boolean additive or subtractive condition.
5a 5b	[Add Body Modifiers dialogue box]	Specify whether or not to erase original 3-D object(s). Left-click OK.

Other Slab-related Editing Techniques

Figure 16.34 demonstrates roof slab clipping.

Slab Styles

In Chapter 13 you learned that styles control visibility, lineweight, and surface rendering and patterns of an ADT object. Styles in the slab and roof slab objects are also used to create distinctive floor and roof systems that correlate to the systems used in building construction. Similar to wall styles, these slab and roof slab styles uses components to create slab assemblies with multiple materials.

Various tabs of the Style Manager that are unique to slab and roof slab objects. Review Techniques T13.09 and T13.10 for additional style manager operations and style creation procedures. Figures 16.35 through 16.38 illustrate how styles are created for two examples of floor and roof systems.

> **Box 16.4**
> Slab styles that represent floor and roof systems can be created with or without the subframing.

Import Existing Slab and Roof Slab Styles

Many typical floor and roof systems have already been created as styles in ADT 2007. They can be easily found in the Design Tool palette or Content Browser Library.

Technique to Master **T16.34** Clipping Roof Slabs

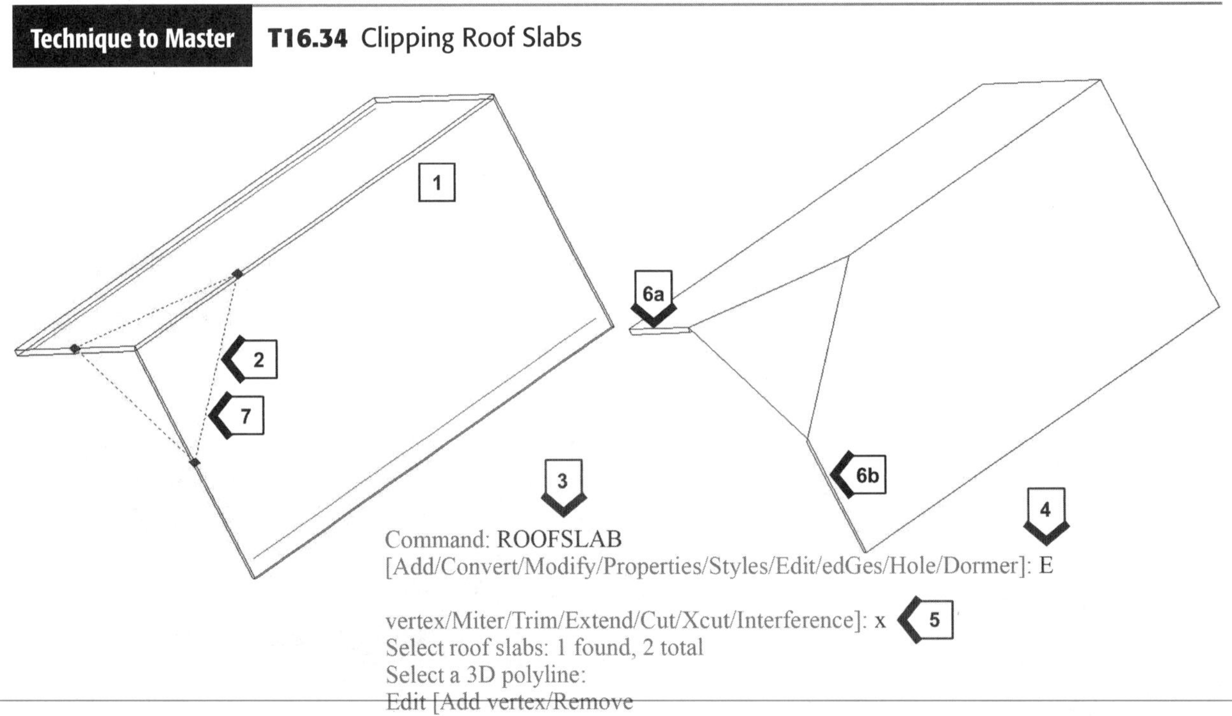

1
6a
2
7
3
6b
4
Command: ROOFSLAB
[Add/Convert/Modify/Properties/Styles/Edit/edGes/Hole/Dormer]: E
vertex/Miter/Trim/Extend/Cut/Xcut/Interference]: x
5
Select roof slabs: 1 found, 2 total
Select a 3D polyline:
Edit [Add vertex/Remove
vertex/Miter/Trim/Extend/Cut/Xcut/Interference]:

Figure 16.34 To add additional slabs at various angles to a gable or hip roof, use the roof slab clip tool.

1	[Drawing Screen]	Draw roof slabs.
2	[Drawing Screen]	Draw a 3-D polyline to represent a new slab condition that will intersect with existing slabs.
3	[Command Line]	Choose ROOFSLAB and hit enter.
4	[Command Line]	Type E and press Enter to edit.
5	[Command Line]	Type x and press Enter to trim existing roof slabs around polyline.
6a, 6b	[Drawing Screen]	Select roof slabs.
7	[Drawing Screen]	Select 3-D polyline.
8	[Command Line]	Press Enter to complete the command.

Technique to Master T16.35 Creating the Components for the Wood Floor System

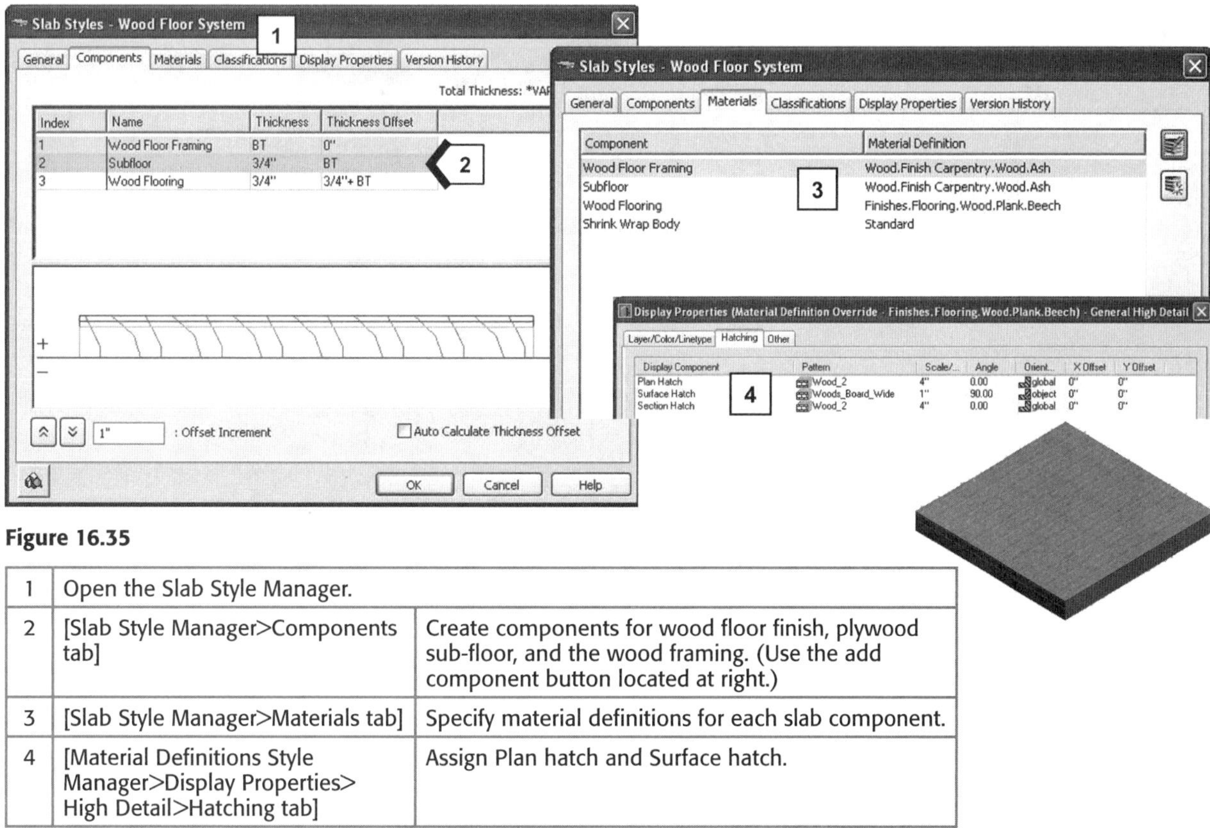

Figure 16.35

1	Open the Slab Style Manager.	
2	[Slab Style Manager>Components tab]	Create components for wood floor finish, plywood sub-floor, and the wood framing. (Use the add component button located at right.)
3	[Slab Style Manager>Materials tab]	Specify material definitions for each slab component.
4	[Material Definitions Style Manager>Display Properties> High Detail>Hatching tab]	Assign Plan hatch and Surface hatch.

Technique to Master T16.36 Creating the Components for the Concrete Floor System

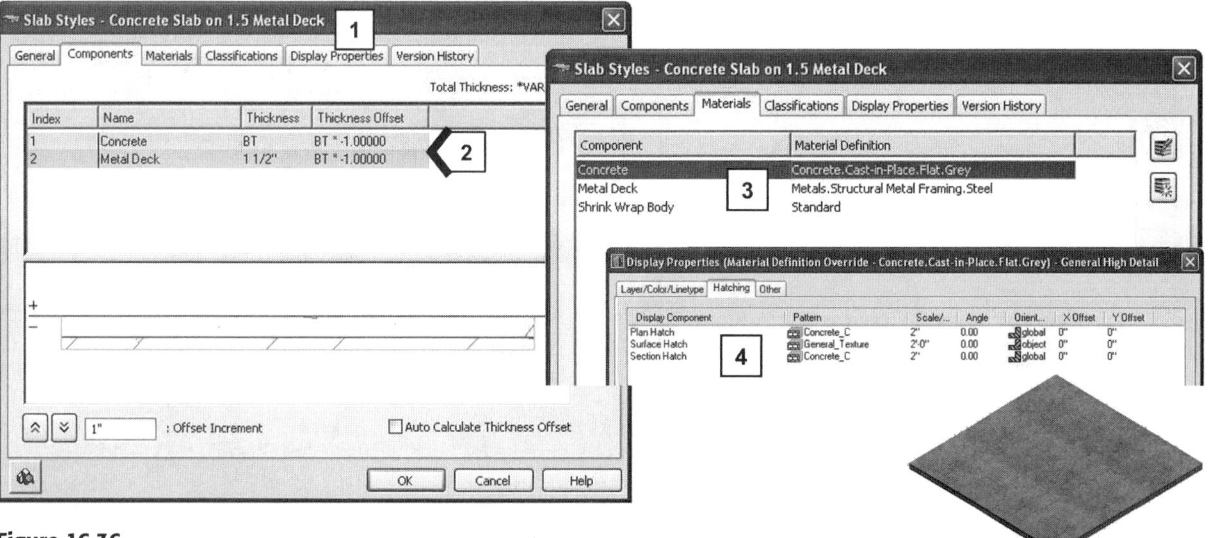

Figure 16.36

1	Open the Slab Style Manager.	
2	[Slab Style Manager>Components tab]	Create components for concrete floor and the metal deck framing.
3	[Slab Style Manager>Materials tab]	Specify material definitions for each slab component.
4	[Material Definitions Style Manager>Display Properties> High Detail>Hatching Tab]	Assign Plan hatch and Surface hatch.

Technique to Master **T16.37** Creating the Components for the Metal Roofing System

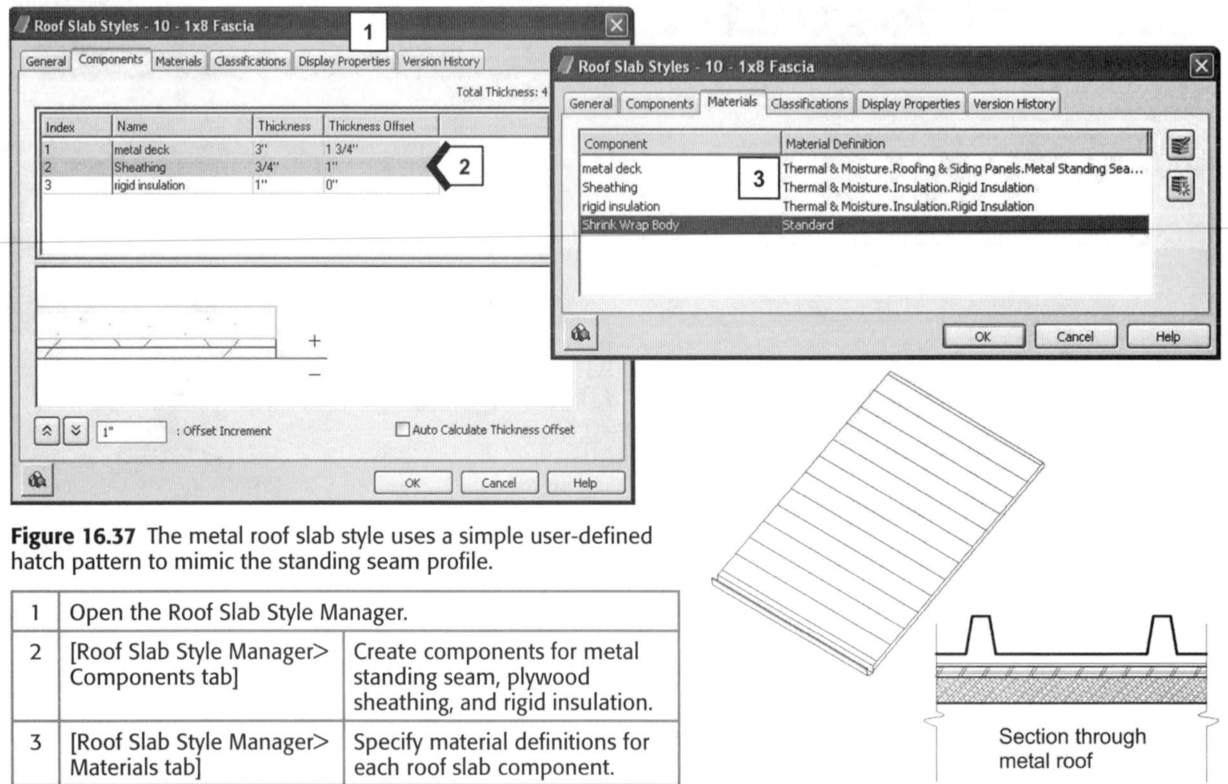

Figure 16.37 The metal roof slab style uses a simple user-defined hatch pattern to mimic the standing seam profile.

1	Open the Roof Slab Style Manager.	
2	[Roof Slab Style Manager> Components tab]	Create components for metal standing seam, plywood sheathing, and rigid insulation.
3	[Roof Slab Style Manager> Materials tab]	Specify material definitions for each roof slab component.

Technique to Master **T16.38** Creating the Components for the Shingle Roof System

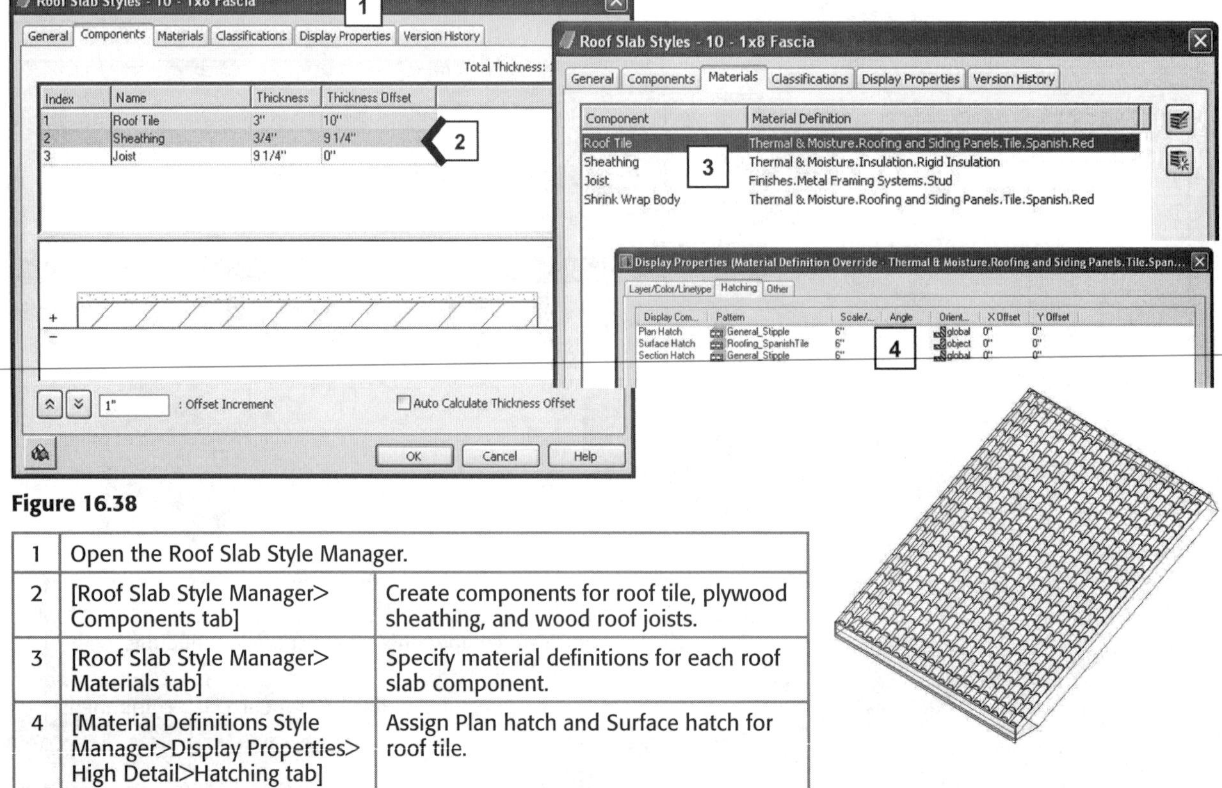

Figure 16.38

1	Open the Roof Slab Style Manager.	
2	[Roof Slab Style Manager> Components tab]	Create components for roof tile, plywood sheathing, and wood roof joists.
3	[Roof Slab Style Manager> Materials tab]	Specify material definitions for each roof slab component.
4	[Material Definitions Style Manager>Display Properties> High Detail>Hatching tab]	Assign Plan hatch and Surface hatch for roof tile.

Slab Edge Styles

Slab object types by default have simple squared or plumbed edges that connect the top and bottom surfaces of the object. Slab edge styles allow you to add additional detail to a slab by defining fascia and/or soffit profiles. Common applications for floor systems include concrete slab footing conditions, wood rim joist and blocking conditions, as well as flashing conditions (Figure 16.39). Common roof edges include penetration headers, gutters, and the various eave and rake edge detailing (Figure 16.40). Slab and roof slab edge styles use profile definitions to introduce shapes that are not rectangular. Figures 16.41 and 16.42 demonstrate the procedures.

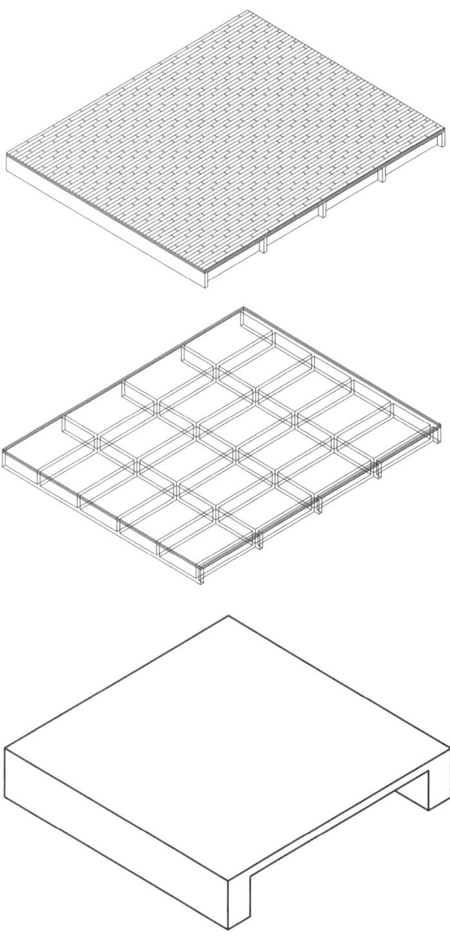

Figure 16.39 Common applications for floor systems include concrete slab footing conditions, wood rim joist and blocking conditions, and flashing conditions.

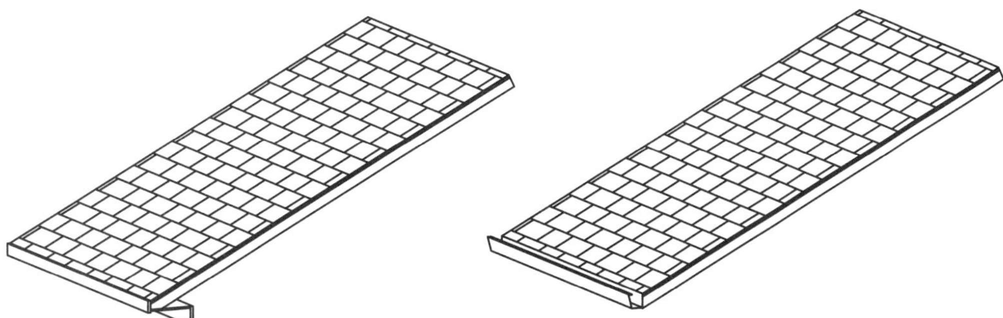

Figure 16.40 Common roof edges include penetration headers, gutters, and the various eave and rake edge detailing.

Technique to Master **T16.41** Changing the Edge Style of an Existing Slab or Roof Style

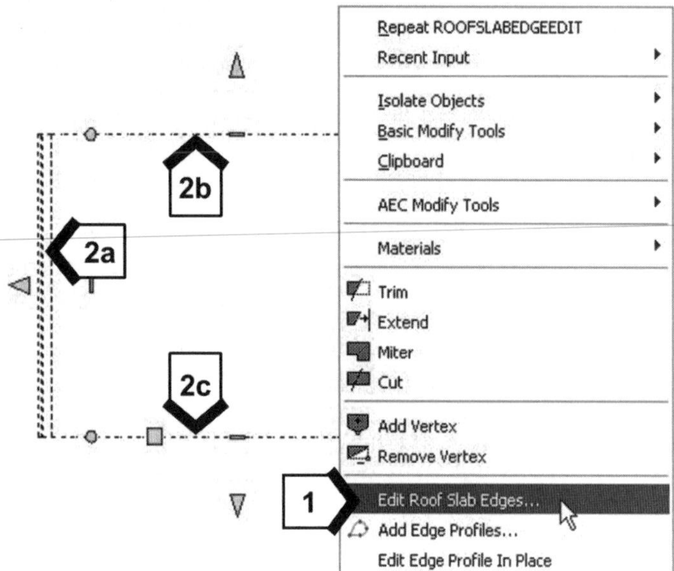

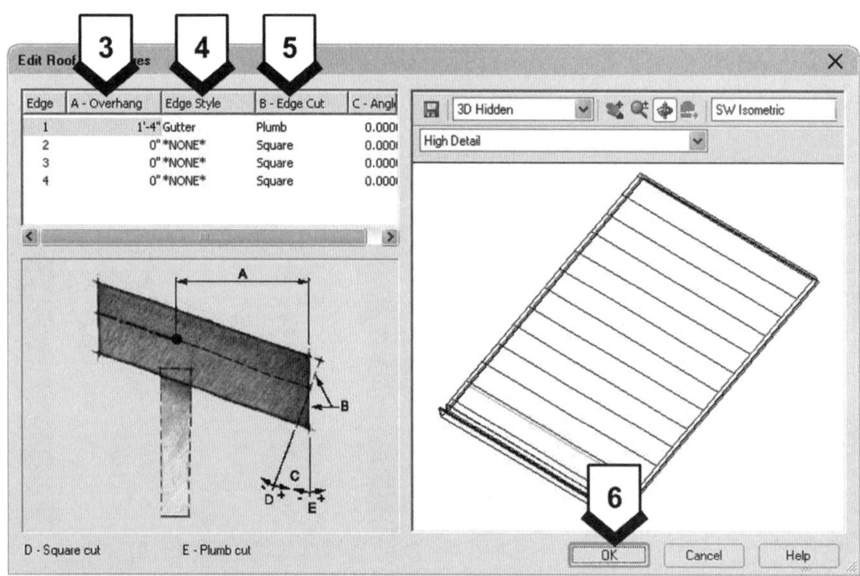

Figure 16.41

1	[Drawing Screen]	Select slab or roof slab, right-click, and choose Edit Roof Slab Edges.
2a, 2b, 2c	[Drawing Screen]	Select the all edges of the slab or roof slab that need modification.
3	[Edit Roof Slab Edges dialogue box]	For each edge, verify/change Overhang.
4	[Edit Roof Slab Edges dialogue box]	For each edge, verify/change Edge Style.
5	[Edit Roof Slab Edges dialogue box]	For each edge, verify/change Edge Cut.
6	[Edit Roof Slab Edges dialogue box]	Left-click OK to complete the command.

Technique to Master

T16.42 Creating and Applying Profile Definitions for Slab and Roof Slab Edge Conditions

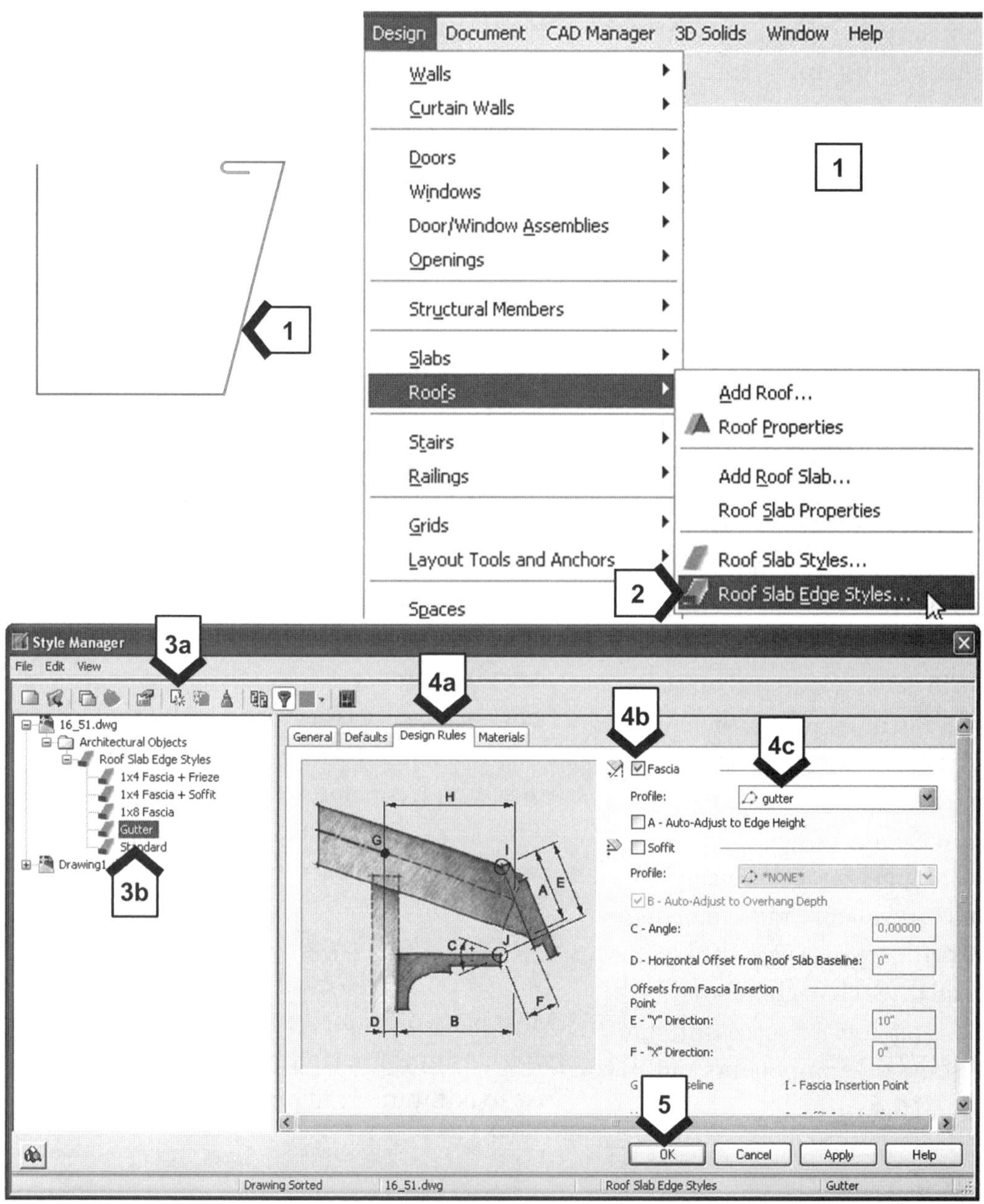

Figure 16.42

1	[Drawing Screen]	Create a closed polyline to represent edge profile. Create a profile definition from polyline (refer to Techniques T10.09 and T10.10).
2	[Design Menu>Slabs (or Roofs)>Slab Edge Styles]	Open the Roof Slab Edge Styles.
3a, 3b	[Roof Slab Edge Style Manager>left pane]	Create new edge style and name appropriately.
4a, 4b, 4c	[Roof Slab Edge Style Manager>Design Rules tab]	Apply profile definition to either the fascia or soffit slab condition.
5	[Roof Slab Edge Style Manager>Design Rules tab]	Left-click OK to complete the command.

Stairs

Stairs are one of the major parts of egress systems for all multistory building types. As with most building system components, safety standards require the design of stairs be regulated by state and local building codes. Because of the complexity of parameters that exist in stair design today, stairs tend to be a difficult subject to learn for many beginning interior design students. This topic provides students with an introduction to understanding stair systems. It introduces the various stair types, the individual elements that make up a stair, and the code regulations that relate to the ADT stair object. While this section does give examples of regulatory requirements, students should be aware that codes vary from state to state and city to city. It is always critical to research and become familiar with the regulatory requirements in effect where you practice. Additional information on drawing conventions for stairs in plan, elevation, and section views is discussed in Chapters 18 and 19.

There are times when the design of stairs seems like a constant juggling act between aesthetic appearance, regulatory requirements, and available square footage. A successful stair system integrates all three characteristics effectively. The first step toward successful stair design is to understand the components and terminology (Figure 16.43).

Stair Appearance—Types

There are essentially five main types of stair layouts that are used in stair design. They include the straight stair, the L-shaped stair, the U-shaped stair, the O-shaped stair, and the circular stair. All of these types have variations among them—that is, straight stairs can be broken with landings, U-shaped stairs can be split, L-shaped stairs can transform into T-shaped, and more (Figure 16.44).

Deciding which stair type to use, for the most part, depends on the amount of space that is available for vertical circulation. Certain stair types, such as the U-shaped and the circular shape, require a large footprint area and take up a lot of space, while other stair types, such as the straight and L-shaped, tend use space much more efficiently.

Stair Appearance—Materials

Stair appearance is also affected by the materials of the stair. Most stairs are constructed from wood, concrete, metal, or a combination of the three. Figure 16.45 illustrates a few example stairs using wood and concrete.

The Regulatory Requirements That Affect Stair Design

Most parts of a stair are affected by codes. Stair width minimum, landing width minimum, rise maximum, tread minimum, tread/riser

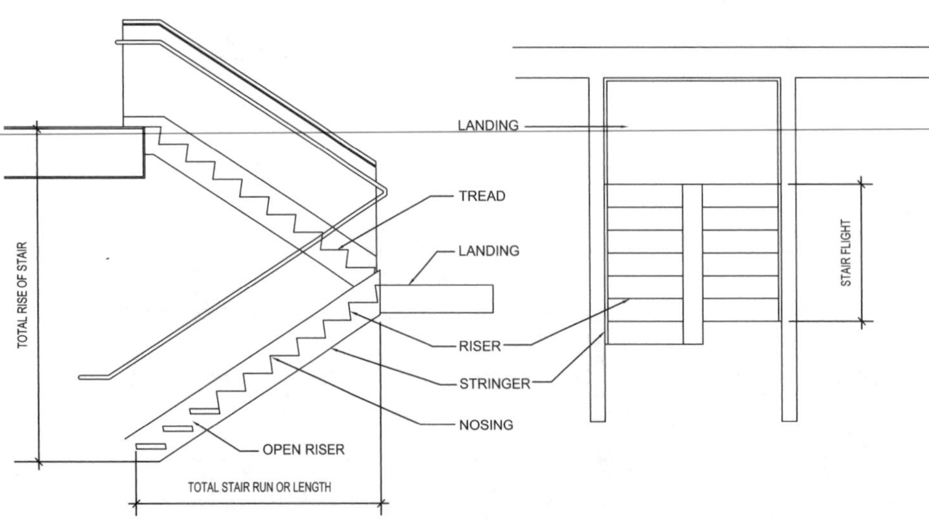

Figure 16.43 Common stair terminology

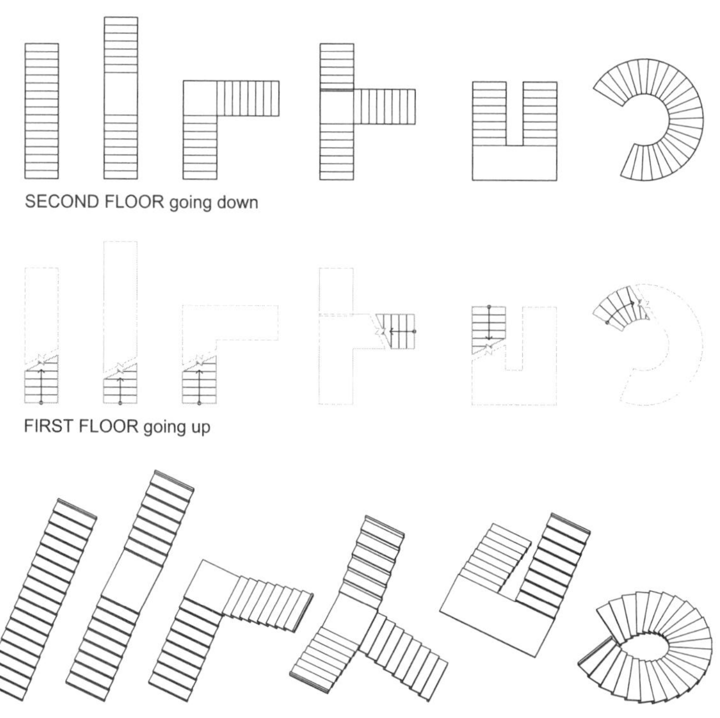

Figure 16.44 Stair types

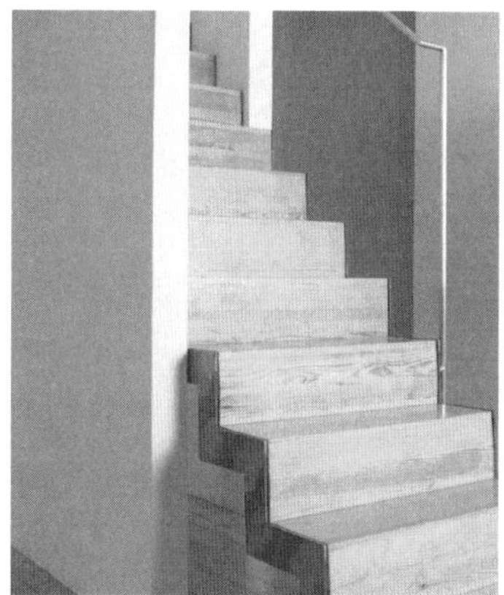

Figure 16.45 Some examples of wood and concrete stair designs

proportion, and headroom clearance are just a few of the critical dimensional limits in place for the design of stairs. Regulations for residential stairs differ from those for commercial stairs. In addition, most code regulations also categorize commercial stairs into two groups—egress and nonegress. While Figure 16.46 illustrates some of the widely accepted minimums and maximums in regulatory requirements today, it is important to carry out your own research for appropriate compliance.

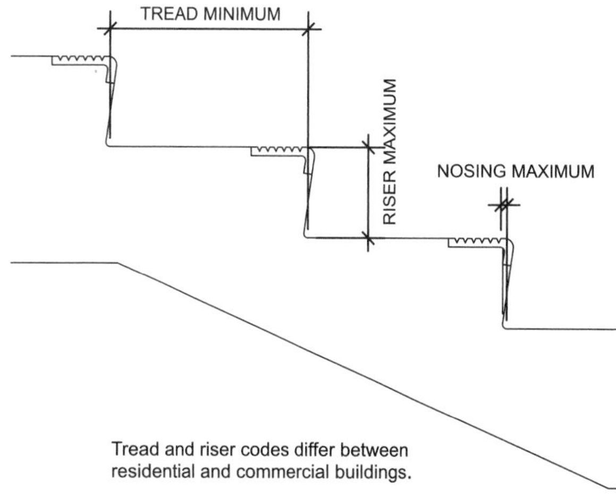

Figure 16.46 Some of the widely accepted minimums and maximums in regulatory requirements today

Placing Stairs

The placement of an ADT stair on-screen requires the selection of its shape, style, turn-type, and dimensions. With the release of ADT 2007, there have been a few improvements to the ADT stair object. The most notable improvement is the ability to convert linework into stair objects.

A visual summary of the various stair commands and command options can be found in Chapter 16 of the CD-ROM. Figures 16.47 through 16.51 demonstrate the placement process for four typical stair types and a concrete ramp. Figures 16.52 and 16.53 introduce the 2007 improvements by converting linework to create custom stairs.

Technique to Master **T16.47** Placing a Straight Stair

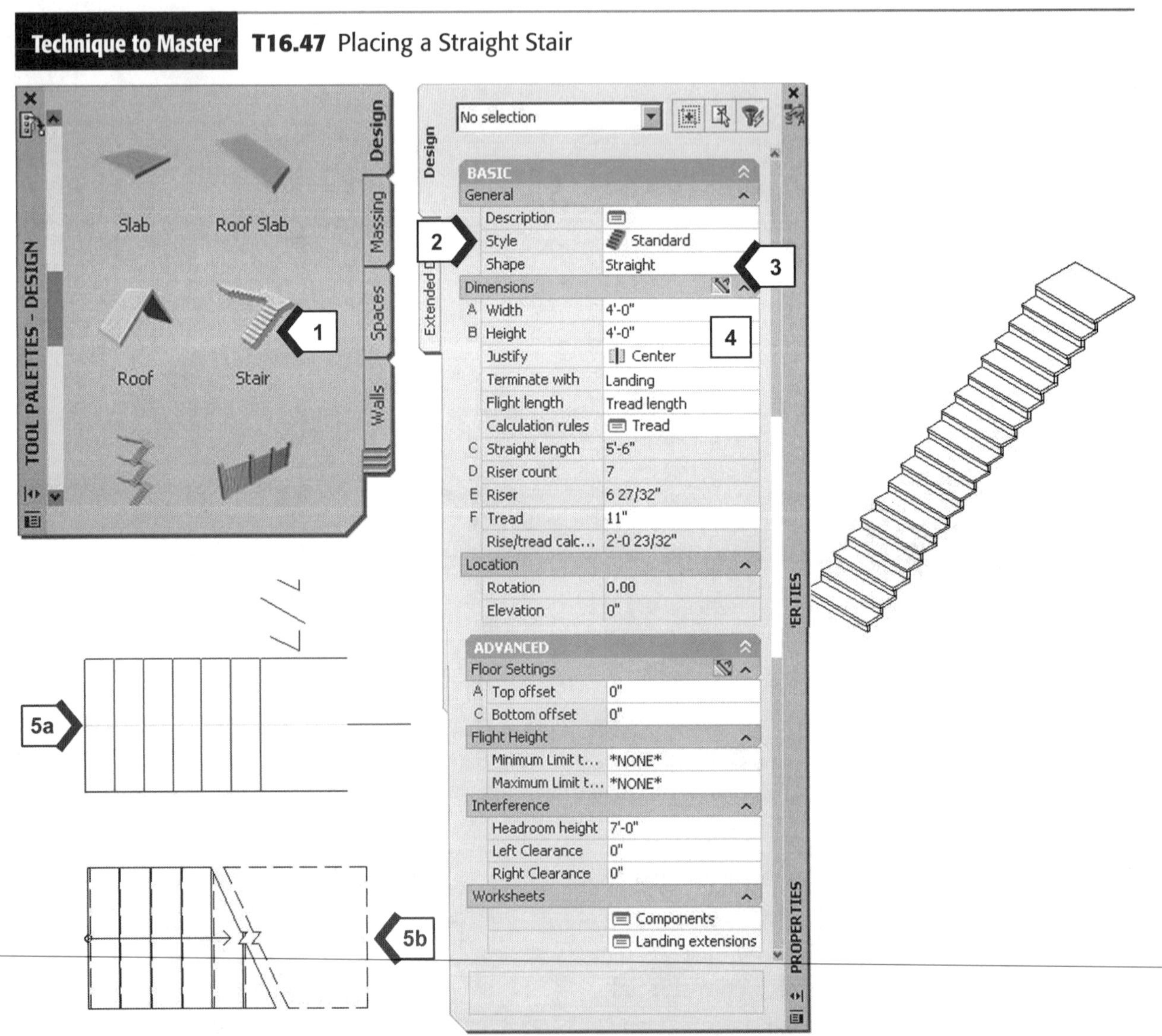

Figure 16.47 Note: When drawing a straight stair, ADT automatically calculates the length of the stair, so it is best to overdraw the stair length.

1	[Design Tool palette]	Left-click on the Stair tool.
2	[Properties palette>General]	Select the appropriate stair style.
3	[Properties palette>General]	For Shape, select Straight.
4	[Properties palette> Dimensions]	Change the stair width, height, justification, termination, and tread width to the correct dimensions.
5a, 5b	[Drawing Screen]	Draw the stair based on two points: first point is stair start, and second point is stair end.

Technique to Master **T16.48** Placing a U-shaped Stair

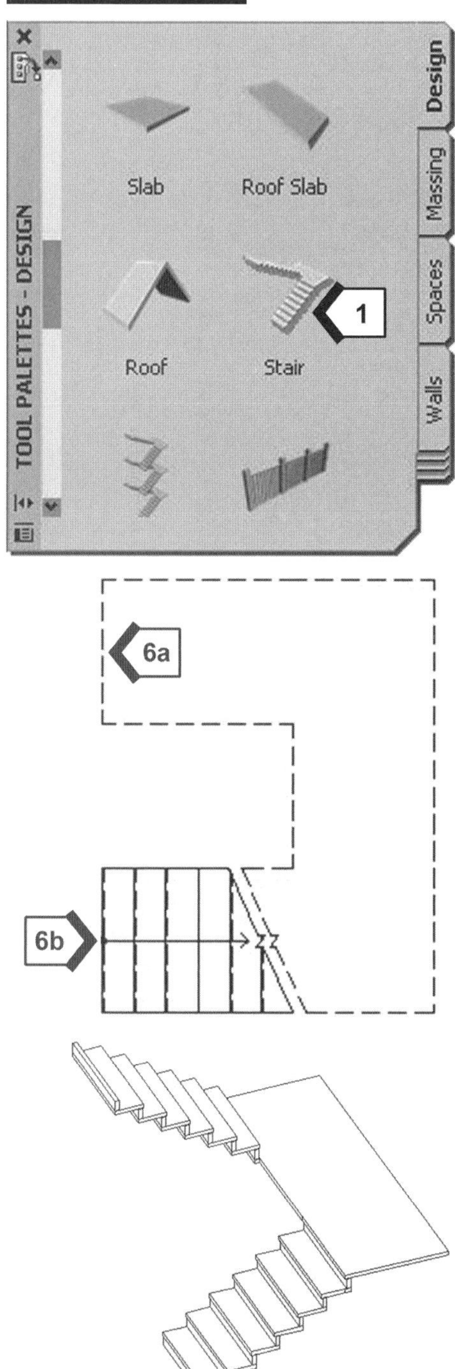

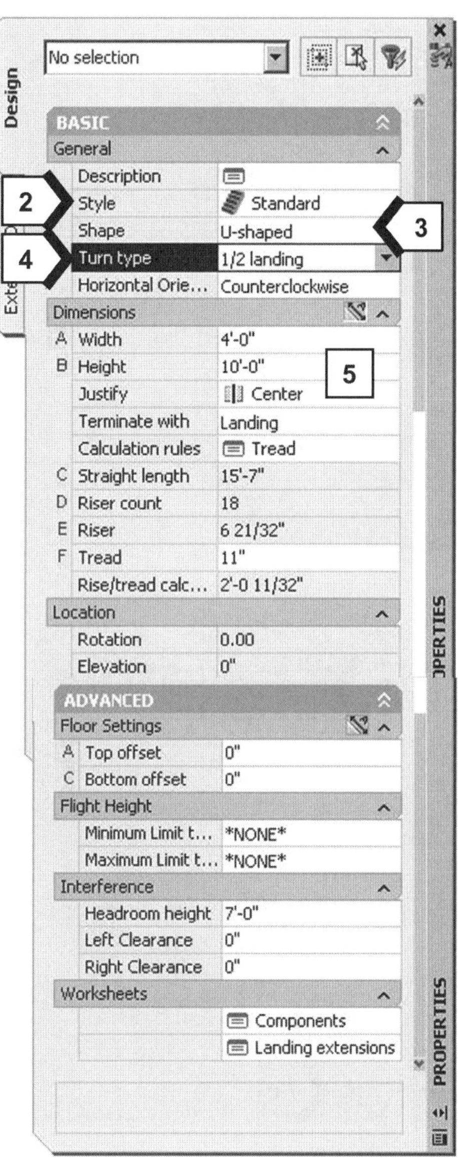

Figure 16.48

1	[Design Tool palette]	Left-click on the Stair tool.
2	[Properties palette>General]	Select the appropriate stair style.
3	[Properties palette>General]	For Shape, select U-shaped.
4	[Properties palette>General]	For Turn type, select $^1/_2$ landing to create a U-shaped stair or $^1/_2$ turn to create a L-shaped stair.
5	[Properties palette>Dimensions]	Change the stair width, height, justification, termination, and tread width to the correct dimensions.
6a, 6b	[Drawing Screen]	Specify the stair flight's start point and endpoint.

Technique to Master **T16.49** Placing a Multi-landing Stair

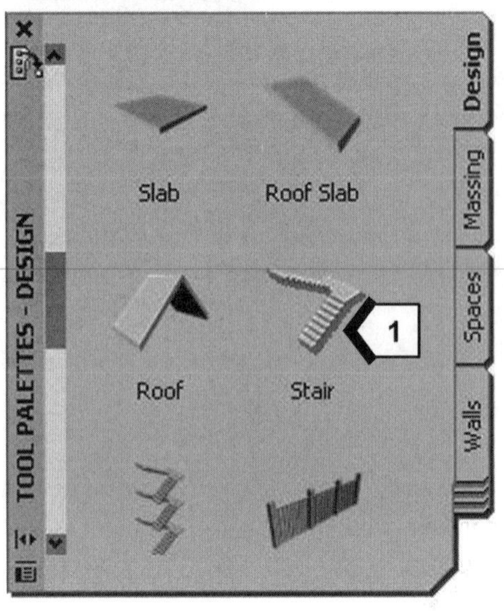

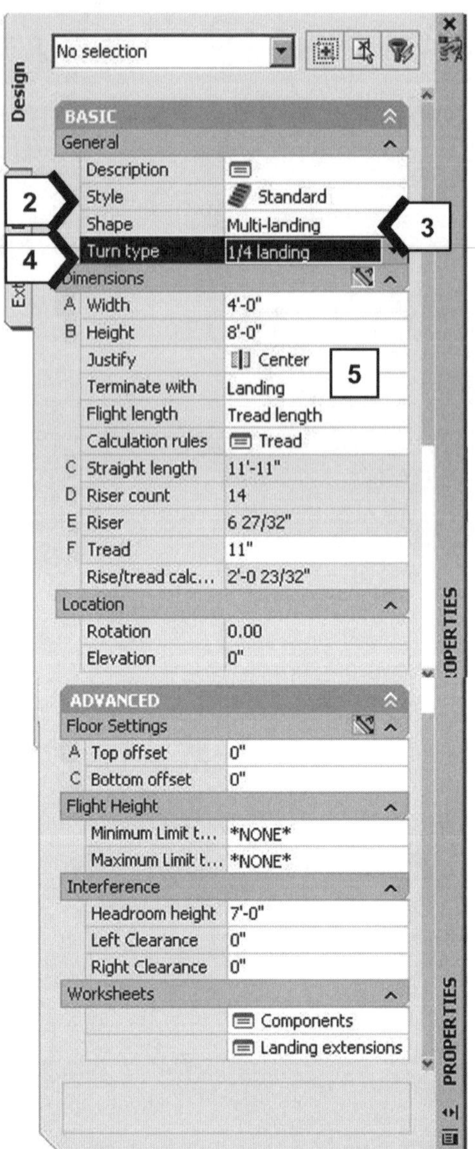

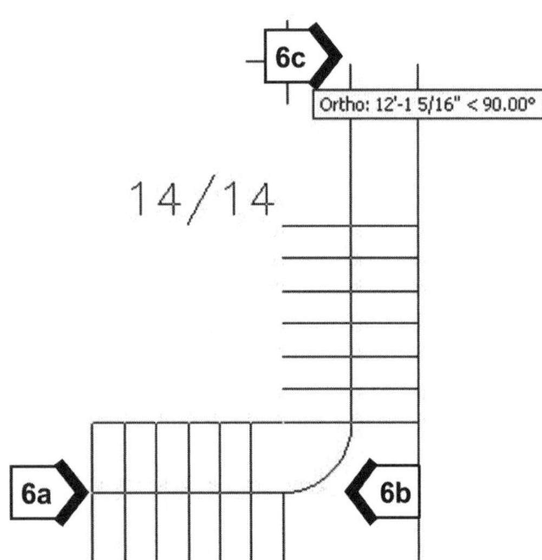

Figure 16.49

1	[Design Tool palette]	Left-click on the Stair tool.
2	[Properties palette>General]	Select the appropriate stair style.
3	[Properties palette>General]	For Shape, select Multi-landing.
4	[Properties palette>General]	For Turn Type, select $^1/_2$ landing, $^1/_2$ turn, $^1/_4$ landing, or $^1/_4$ turn.
5	[Properties palette>Dimensions]	Change the stair width, height, justification, termination, and tread width to the correct dimensions.
6a, 6b, 6c	[Drawing Screen]	Specify the stair flight's start point and endpoint. Continue flight start and endpoints until stair termination.

Technique to Master **T16.50** Placing a Curved Stair

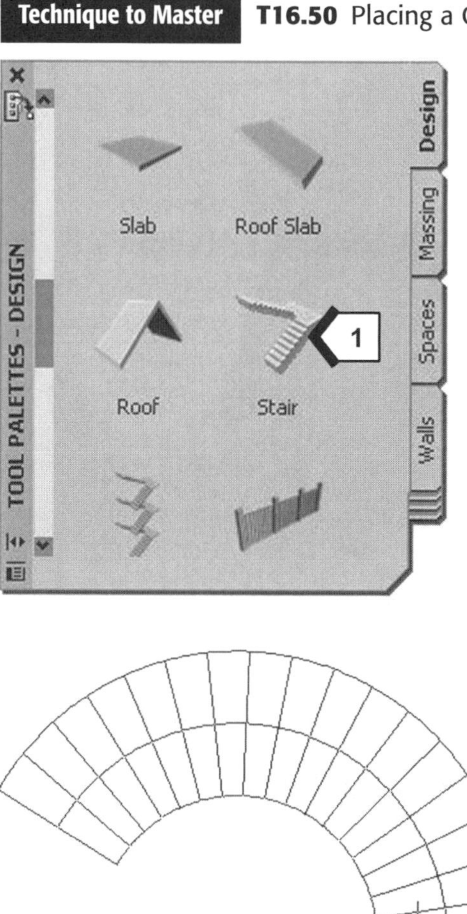

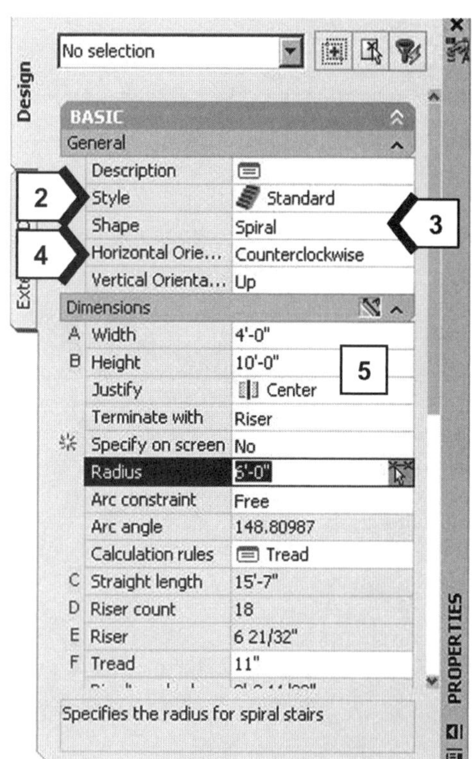

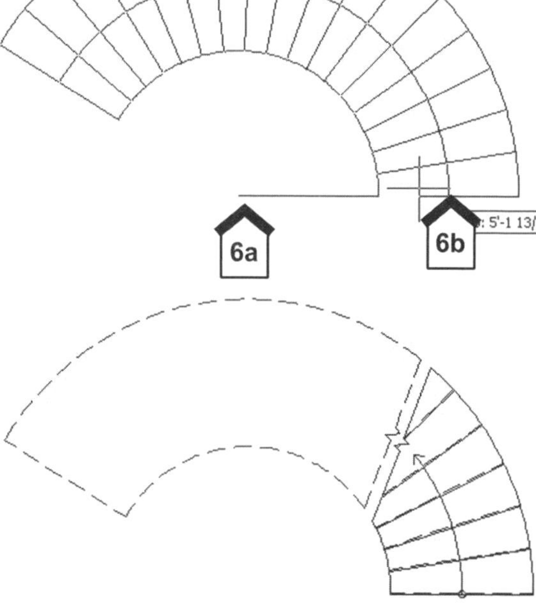

Figure 16.50

1	[Design Tool palette]	Left-click on the Stair tool.
2	[Properties palette>General]	Select the appropriate stair style.
3	[Properties palette>General]	For Shape, select Spiral.
4	[Properties palette>General]	For Horizontal Orientation, select Clockwise or Counterclockwise.
5	[Properties palette>Dimensions]	Change the stair width, height, justification, termination, and tread width to the correct dimensions.
6a, 6b	[Drawing Screen]	Specify the stair's center point and then radius.

Technique to Master **T16.51** Placing a Concrete Ramp

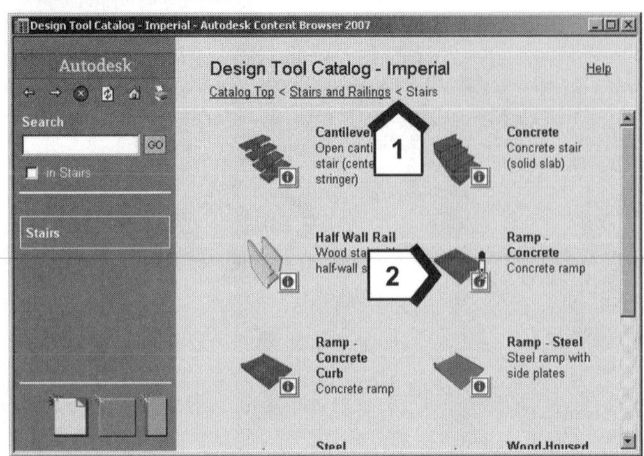

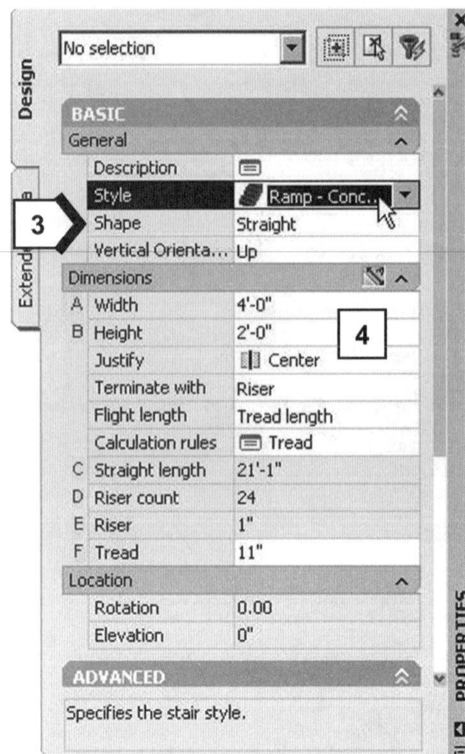

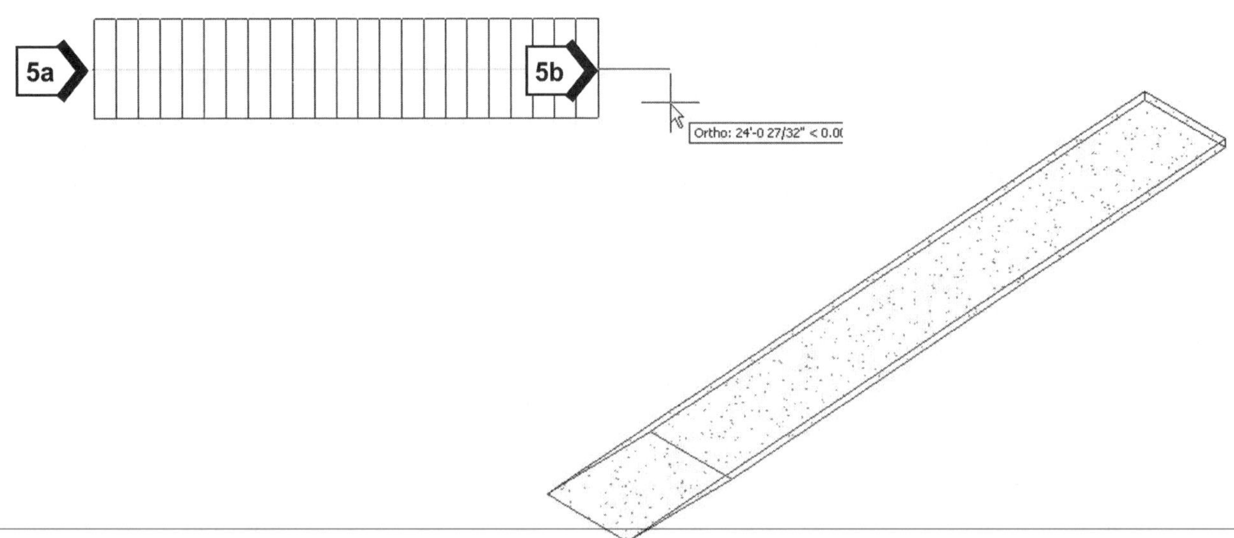

Figure 16.51

1	[Content Browser palette]	Open Design Tool Catalog and find Stair Styles.
2	[Content Browser palette>Stairs and Railings>Stairs]	Use the Eyedropper tool to import the ramp style into current drawing.
3	[Properties palette]	Specify ramp shape.
4	[Properties palette]	Specify ramp's width, height, and justification.
5a, 5b	[Drawing Screen]	Specify the ramp's start point and endpoint. Continue flight start and endpoints until ramp termination.

Technique to Master **T16.52** Creating a Custom Stair by Converting Linework

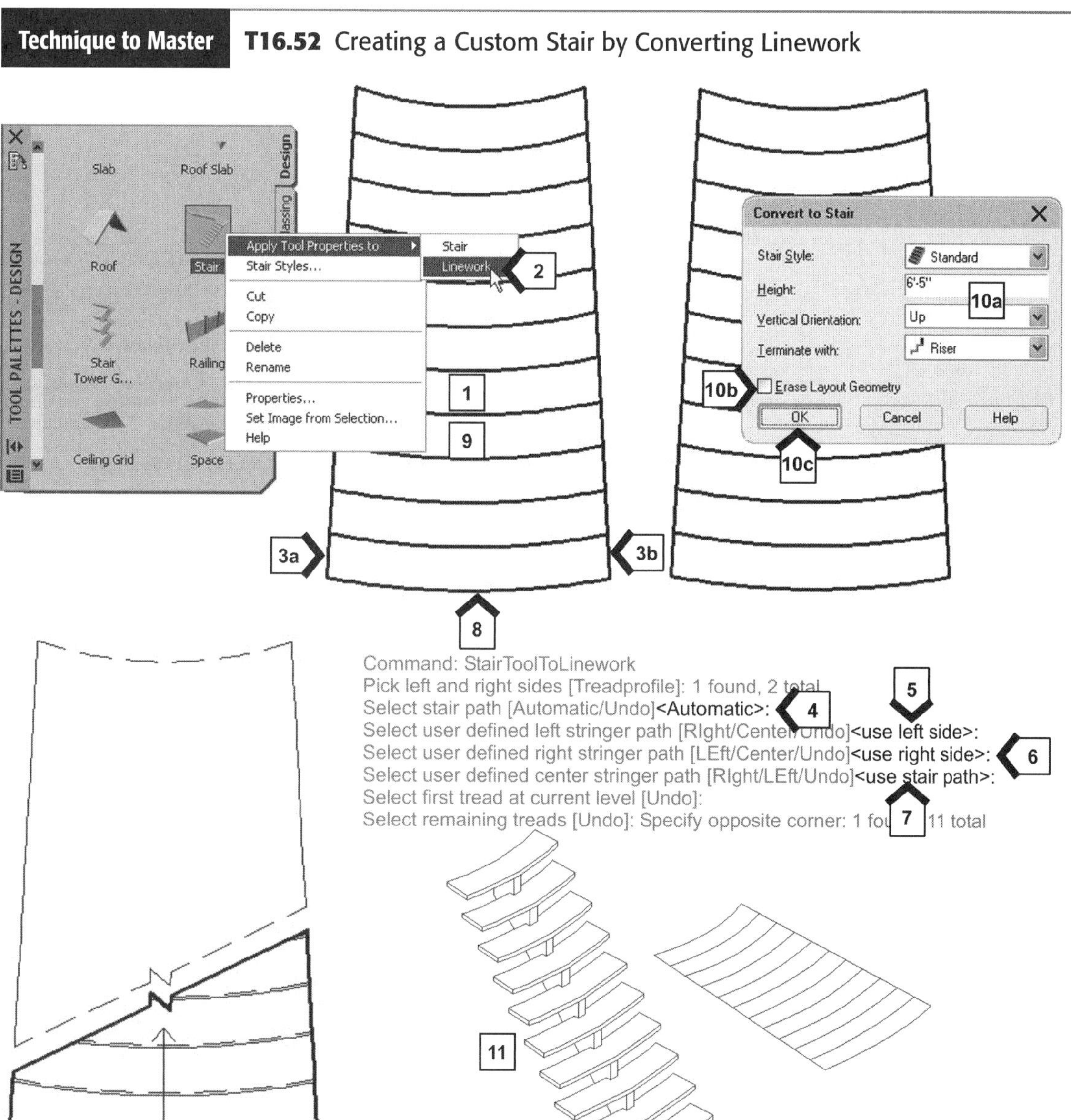

Figure 16.52

1	[Drawing Screen]	Draw linework to represent stair in plan view.
2	[Design Tool palette>Stair tool]	Right-click on the Stair tool and choose Apply Tool Properties to>Linework.
3a, 3b	[Drawing Screen]	Pick the lines/arcs/polylines that represent the left and right sides of the stair treads. Press Enter to complete the selection.
4	[Command Line]	Type <Automatic> and hit Enter to have ADT automatically find stair path.
5	[Command Line]	Hit Enter to use default setting <use left side>.
6	[Command Line]	Hit Enter to use default setting <use right side>.
7	[Command Line]	Hit Enter to use default setting <use stair path>.
8	[Drawing Screen]	Select the first tread of the current level.
9	[Drawing Screen]	Select the remaining treads in order. Hit Enter to complete selection.
10a 10b 10c	[Convert to Stair dialogue box]	Specify Stair Style, Height, Vertical Orientation, and Termination with method. Remember that stair height is based on floor-to-floor height and codes limiting riser height. Decide whether to erase original linework. Press OK.
11	Make any further adjustments to the stair's design using grips (Techniques T16.61 and T16.62) or the Style Manager tabs for stairs (Figure 16.54).	

T16.53 Creating a Custom Stair by Using Tread Profiles

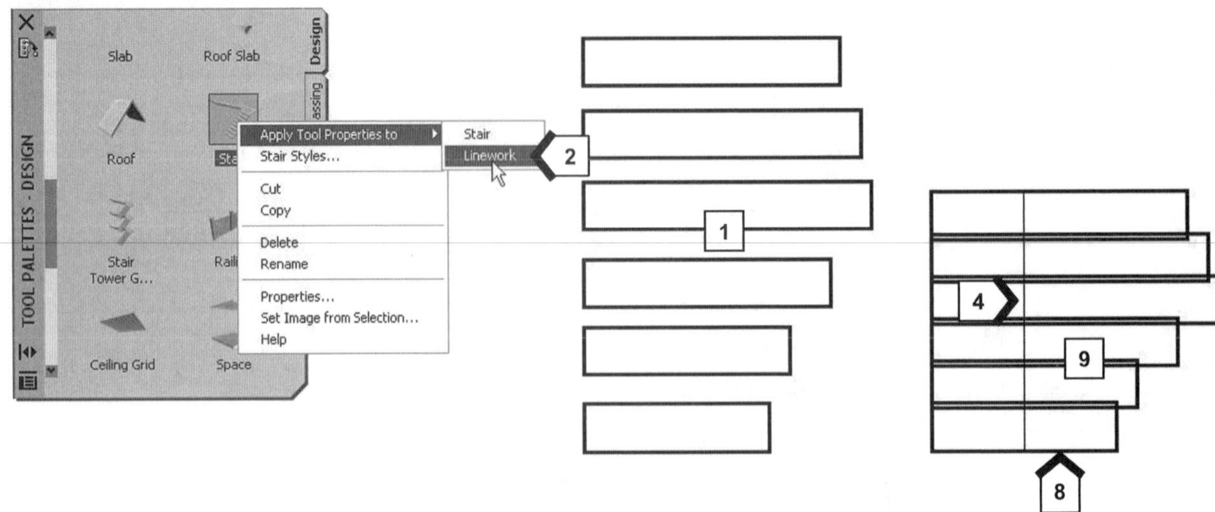

Command: StairToolToLinework
Pick left and right sides [Treadprofile]: T 3
5
Select user defined left stringer path [RIght/Center/Undo]<use left side>:
Select user defined right stringer path [LEft/Center/Undo]<use right side>: 6
Select user defined center stringer path [RIght/LEft/Undo]<use stair path>:
Select first tread at current level [Undo]:
Select remaining treads [Undo]: Specify opposite corner: 1 fo 7 11 total

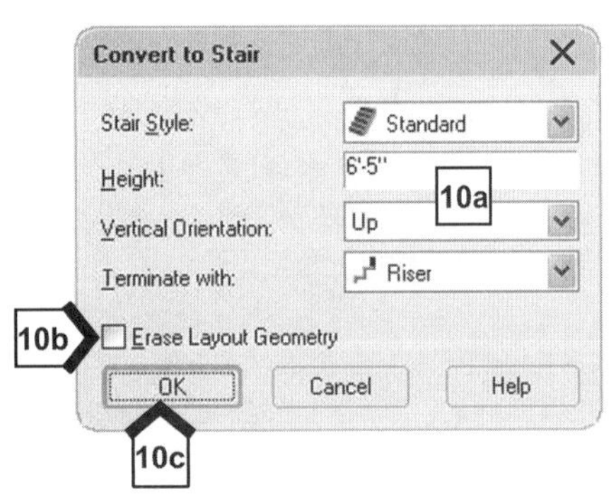

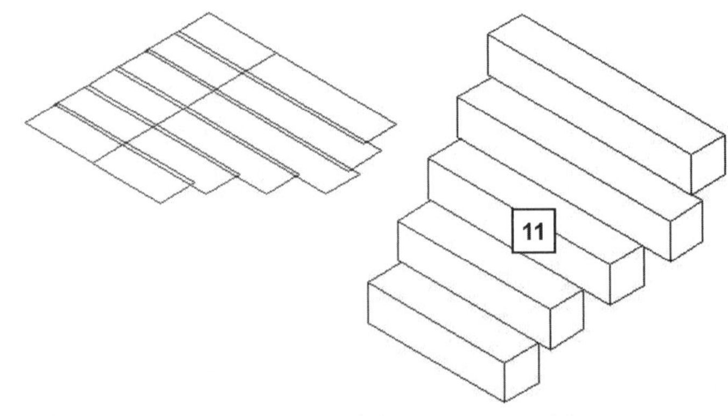

Figure 16.53

1	[Drawing Screen]	Draw closed polylines to represent stair treads in plan view.
2	[Design Tool palette>Stair tool]	Right-click on Stair tool and choose Apply Tool Properties to>Linework.
3	[Command Line]	Type T then press Enter to use the Treadprofile command option.
4	[Drawing Screen]	Select the polyline, line, or arc segment that represents the stair path.
5	[Command Line]	Press Enter to use the default setting <use left side>.
6	[Command Line]	Press Enter to use the default setting <use right side>.
7	[Command Line]	Press Enter to use the default setting <use stair path>.
8	[Drawing Screen]	Select the first tread of the current level.
9	[Drawing Screen]	Select the remaining treads in order. Press Enter to complete selection.
10a, 10b 10c	[Convert to Stair dialogue box]	Specify Stair Style, Height, Vertical Orientation, and Termination with method. Remember that stair height is based on floor-to-floor height and codes limiting riser height. Decide whether to erase the original linework. Press OK.
11	Make any further adjustments to the stair's design using grips (Techniques T16.61 and T16.62) or the Style Manager tabs for stairs (Figure 16.54).	

Stair Styles

Like most other ADT objects, the stair's object style is used to control the dimensional and material properties of its subcomponents. This includes all aspects of a stair's design, including its stringer, tread, riser, and landing. In addition, the regulatory requirements are also controlled through the Style Manager. Figure 16.54 illustrates the distinct areas of the Design Rules, Stringers, Components, and Landing Extensions tabs.

Getting Stairs to Display Properly in Plan View

Prior to ADT 2007, the drawing conventions in plan view for ADT stair objects were not correctly shown. This has been corrected in release 2007 through changes in the display representations. Figure 16.55 identifies these differences. Figures 16.56 through 16.59 demonstrate how to control the various display information pertinent to stair plan conventions.

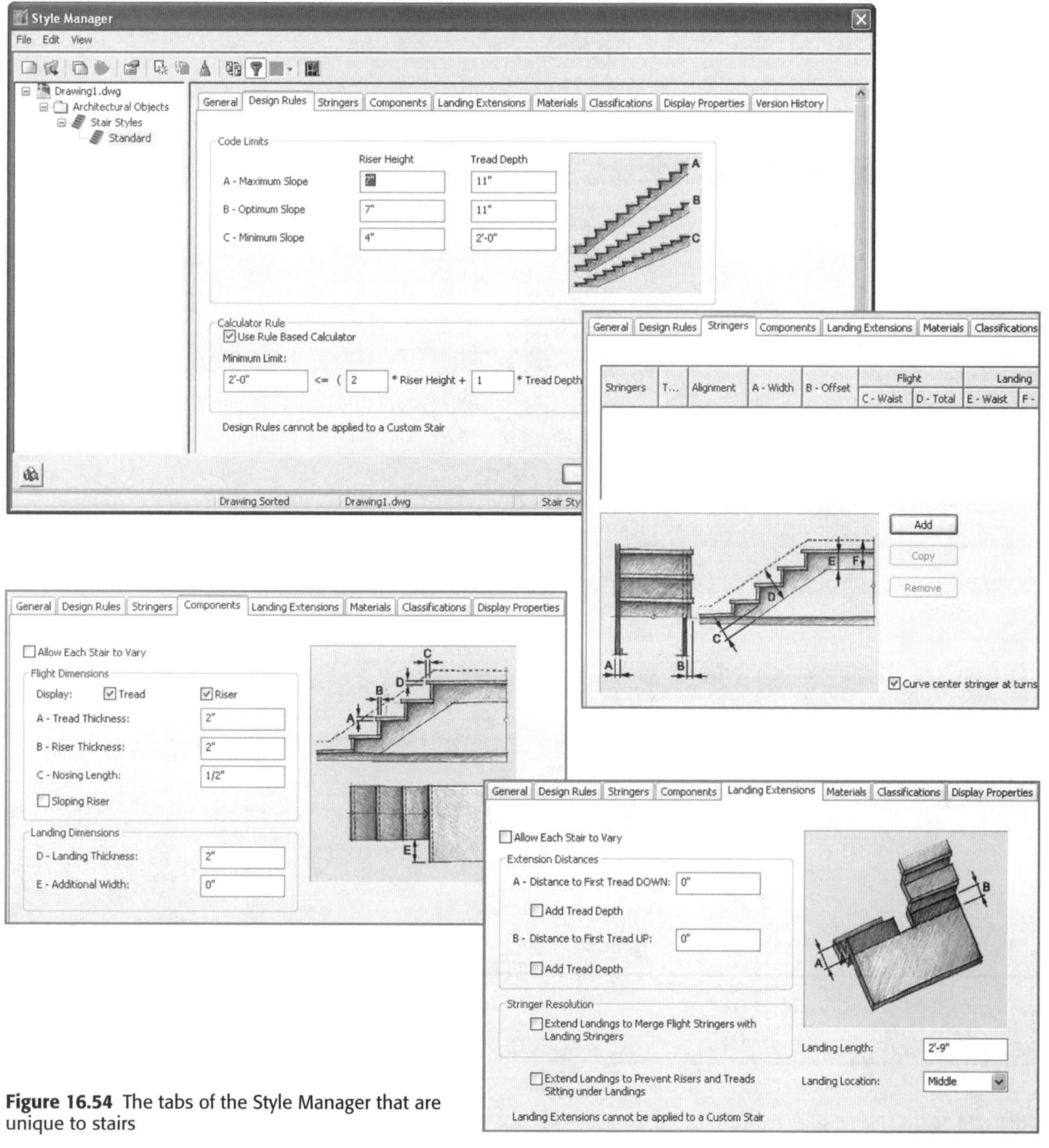

Figure 16.54 The tabs of the Style Manager that are unique to stairs

pre-AutoCad 2007

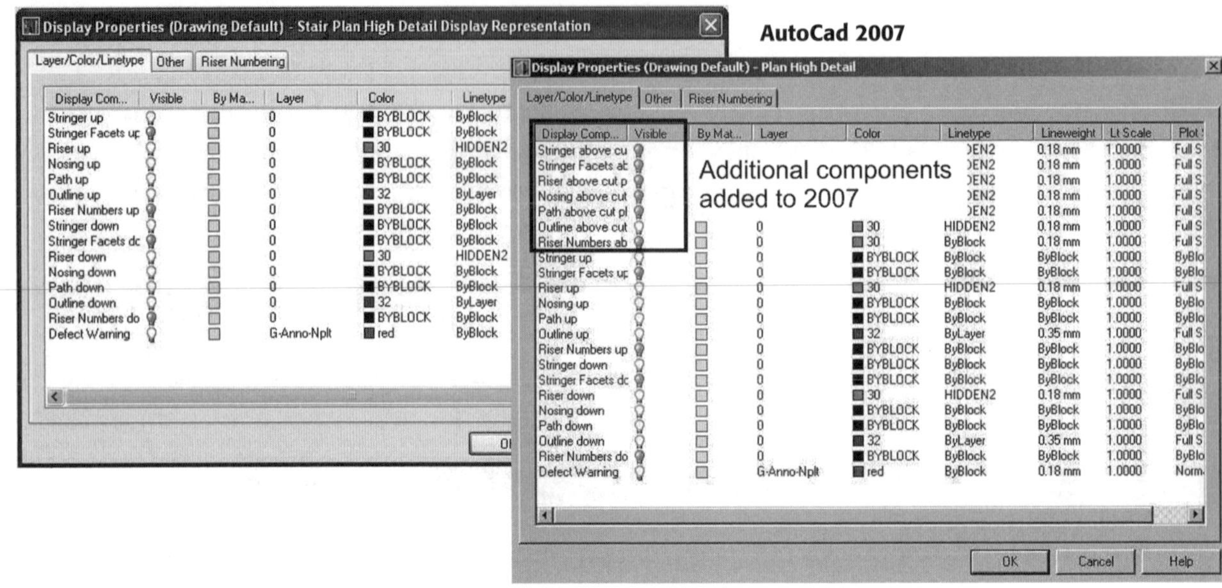

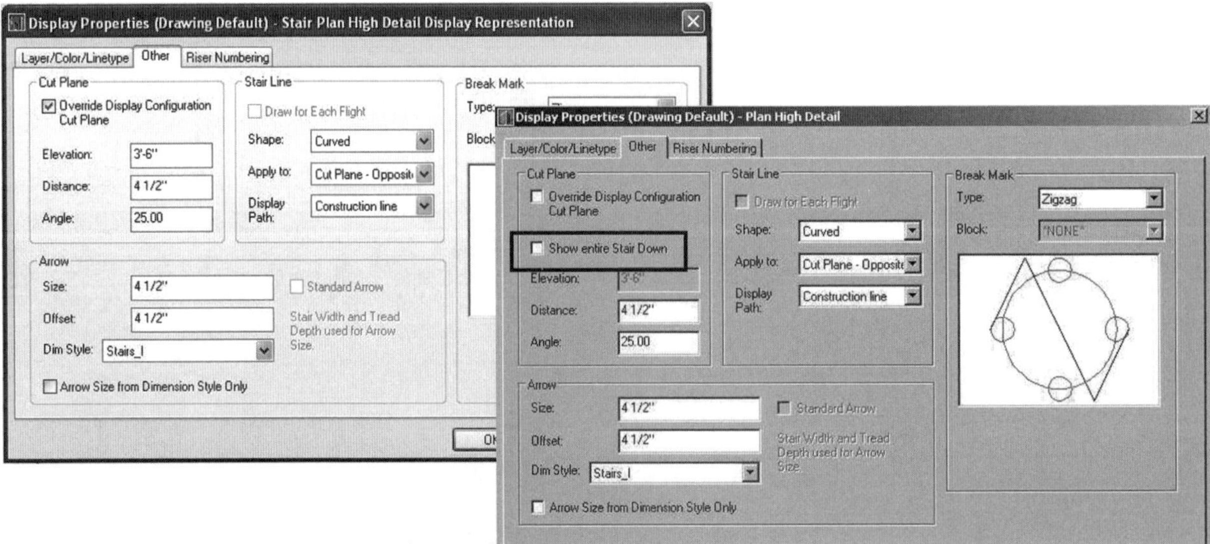

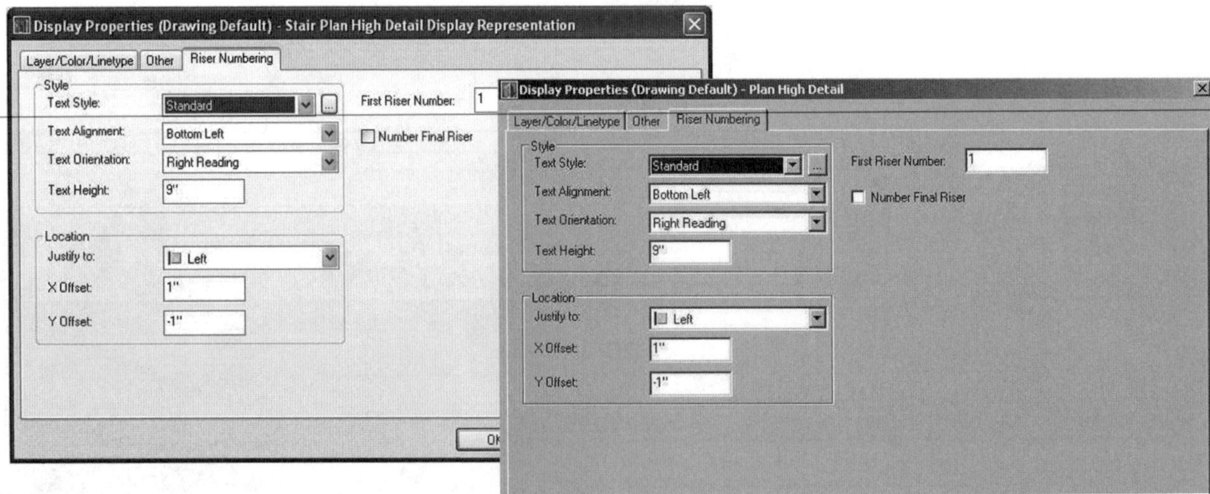

Figure 16.55 The Plan display representations for stairs—ADT 2007 versus pre-ADT 2007

Technique to Master **T16.56** Adjusting the Look of the Stair in Plan View

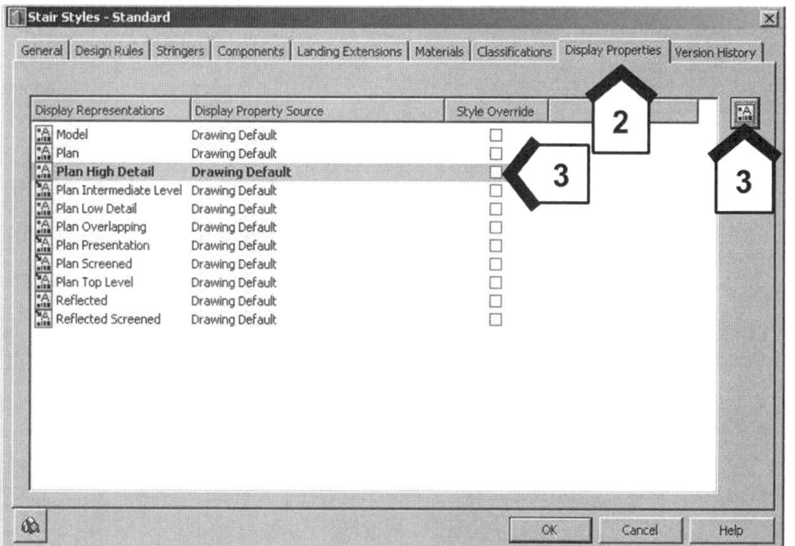

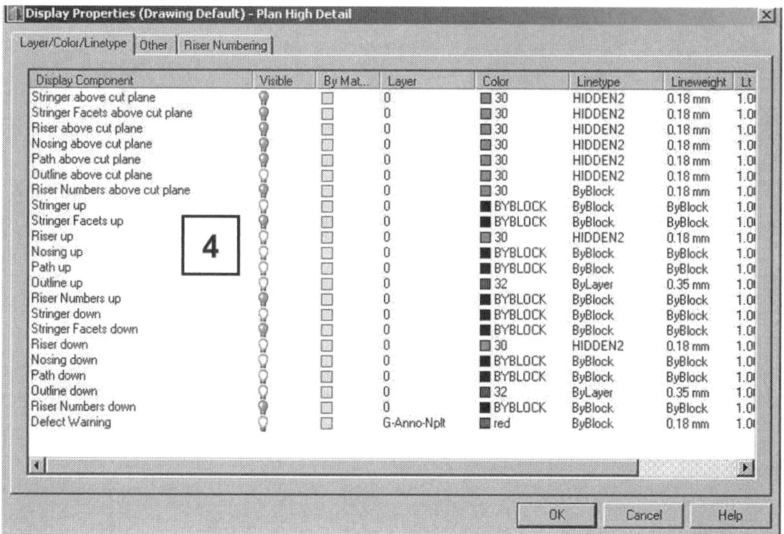

Figure 16.56

Open the Stair Style Manager.		
1	[Stair Style Manager>Left pane]	Select the desired stair style or create a new style.
2	[Stair Style Manager>Right pane]	Left-click on the Display Properties tab.
3	[Stair Style Manager>Display Properties tab]	If unchecked, select Style Override button for Plan High Detail. If Style Override is already checked, select Plan High Detail, and left-click on the Edit Display Properties button.
4	[Stair Style Manager>Display Properties Tab>Layer/Color/Linetype tab]	Adjust visibility, layer, lineweight, and linetype settings for each of the stair display components.

Technique to Master **T16.57** Setting Up Automatic Stair Riser Numbering

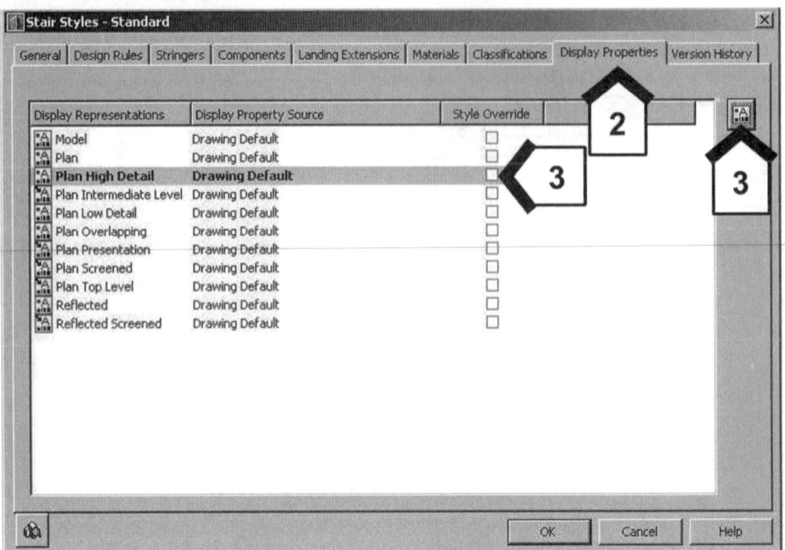

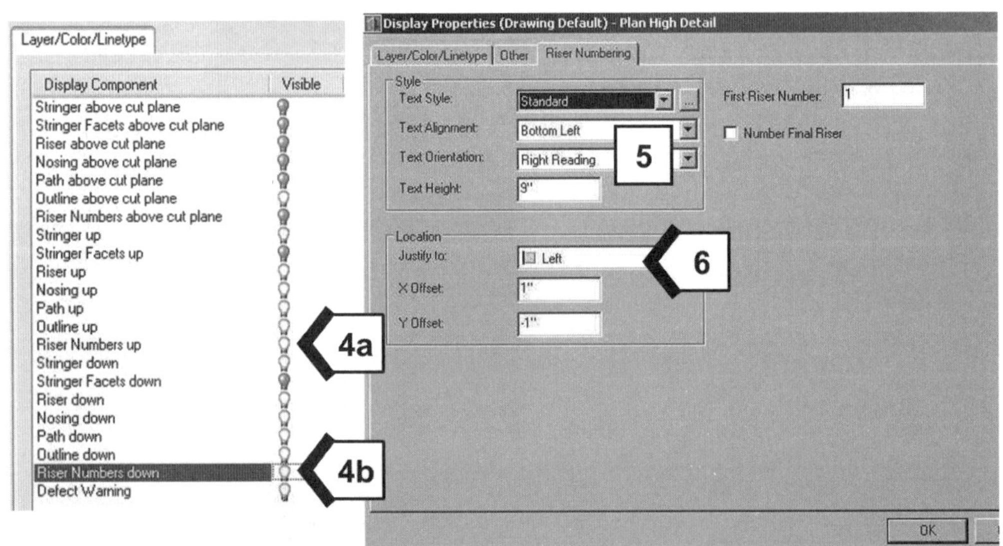

Figure 16.57

1	[Stair Style Manager>Left pane]	Select the desired stair style or create a new style.
2	[Stair Style Manager>Right pane]	Left-click on the Display Properties tab.
3	[Stair Style Manager>Display Properties tab]	If unchecked, select the Style Override button for Plan High Detail. If Style Override is already checked, select Plan High Detail, and left-click on the Edit Display Properties button.
4a, 4b	[Stair Style Manager>Display Properties tab>Layer/Color/Linetype tab]	Make sure the Display Component>Riser Numbers up and Riser Numbers down visibility component is turned on.
5	[Stair Style Manager>Display Properties tab>Riser Numbering tab]	Adjust text style, alignment, and text height for numbering each riser.
6	[Stair Style Manager>Display Properties tab>Riser Numbering tab]	Adjust the location for riser numbering text.

Technique to Master **T16.58** Changing the Cut Plane of Your Stair Style

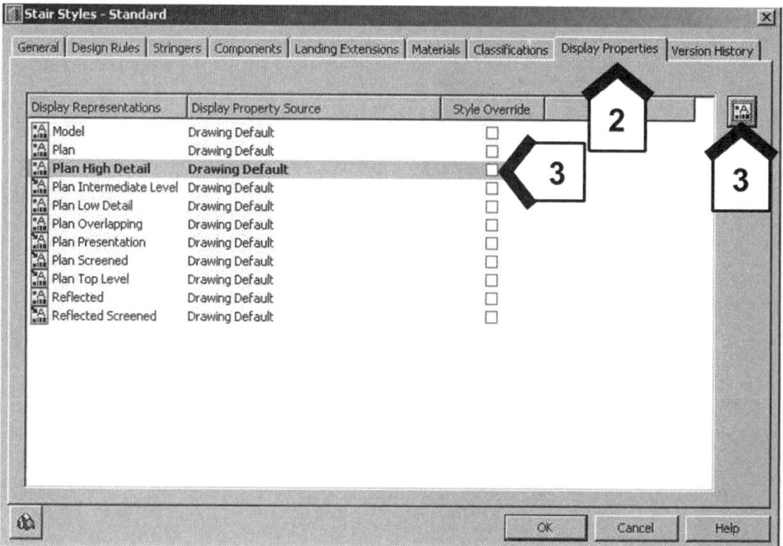

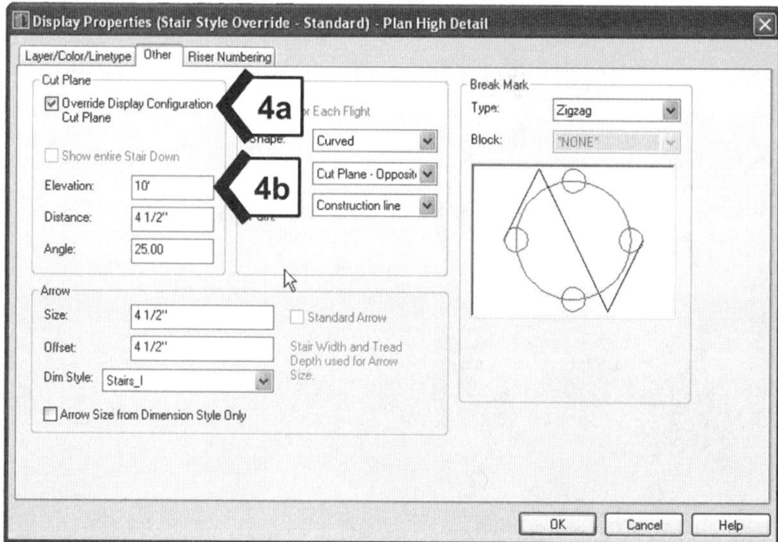

Figure 16.58

1	[Stair Style Manager>Left pane]	Select the desired stair style or create a new style.
2	[Stair Style Manager>Right pane]	Left-click on the Display Properties tab.
3	[Stair Style Manager>Display Properties tab]	If unchecked, select the Style Override button for Plan High Detail. If Style Override is already checked, select Plan High Detail, and left-click on the Edit Display Properties button.
4	[Stair Style Manager>Display Properties tab>Other tab]	Check Override Display Configuration Cut Plane. Change Elevation to the desired new cut plane height.

Technique to Master **T16.59** Adjusting the Look of the Stair Break Mark and Path Leader

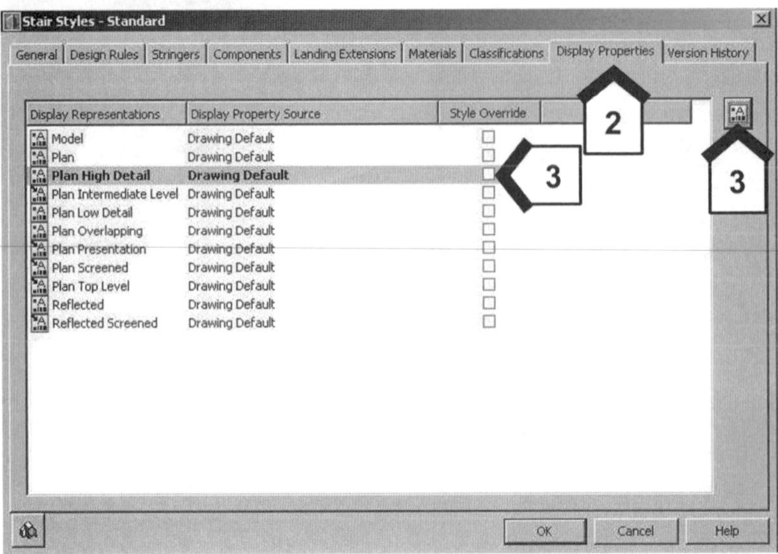

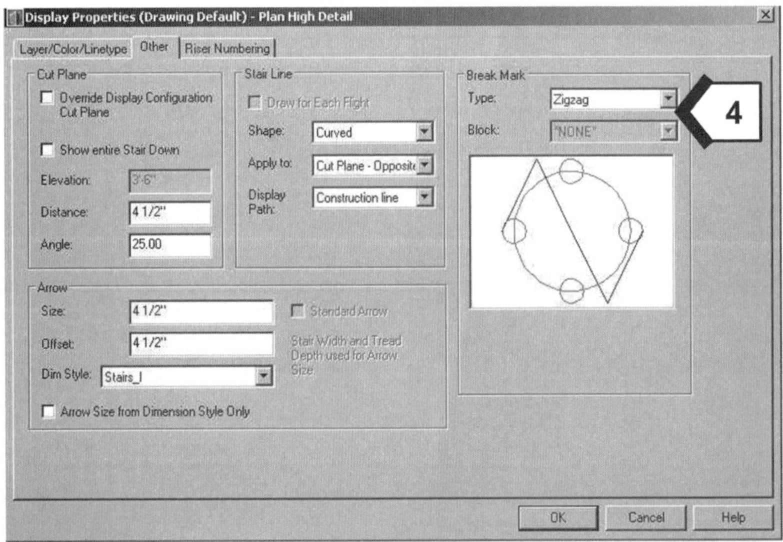

Figure 16.59

1	[Stair Style Manager>Left pane]	Select the desired stair style or create a new style.
2	[Stair Style Manager>Right pane]	Left-click on the Display Properties tab.
3	[Stair Style Manager>Display Properties tab]	If unchecked, select the Style Override button for Plan High Detail. If Style Override is already checked, select Plan High Detail, and left-click on the Edit Display Properties button.
4	[Stair Style Manager>Display Properties tab>Other tab]	Choose Break Mark type from drop-down list or use custom drawn block.

Modifying Stair Objects

Individual object modifications to stair objects are made through the Properties palette and Grip and Specialty commands available to this object type. Figure 16.60 reviews each of the modifiable properties located in the Properties palette. Notice that the modifiable properties differ between stairs that are created through converting linework and stairs that are created through the conventional placement process. This could be an important consideration in stair placement/creation decisions. Also, notice that some of the properties shown in the Properties palette are style-based, and better control might be provided through the Style Manager.

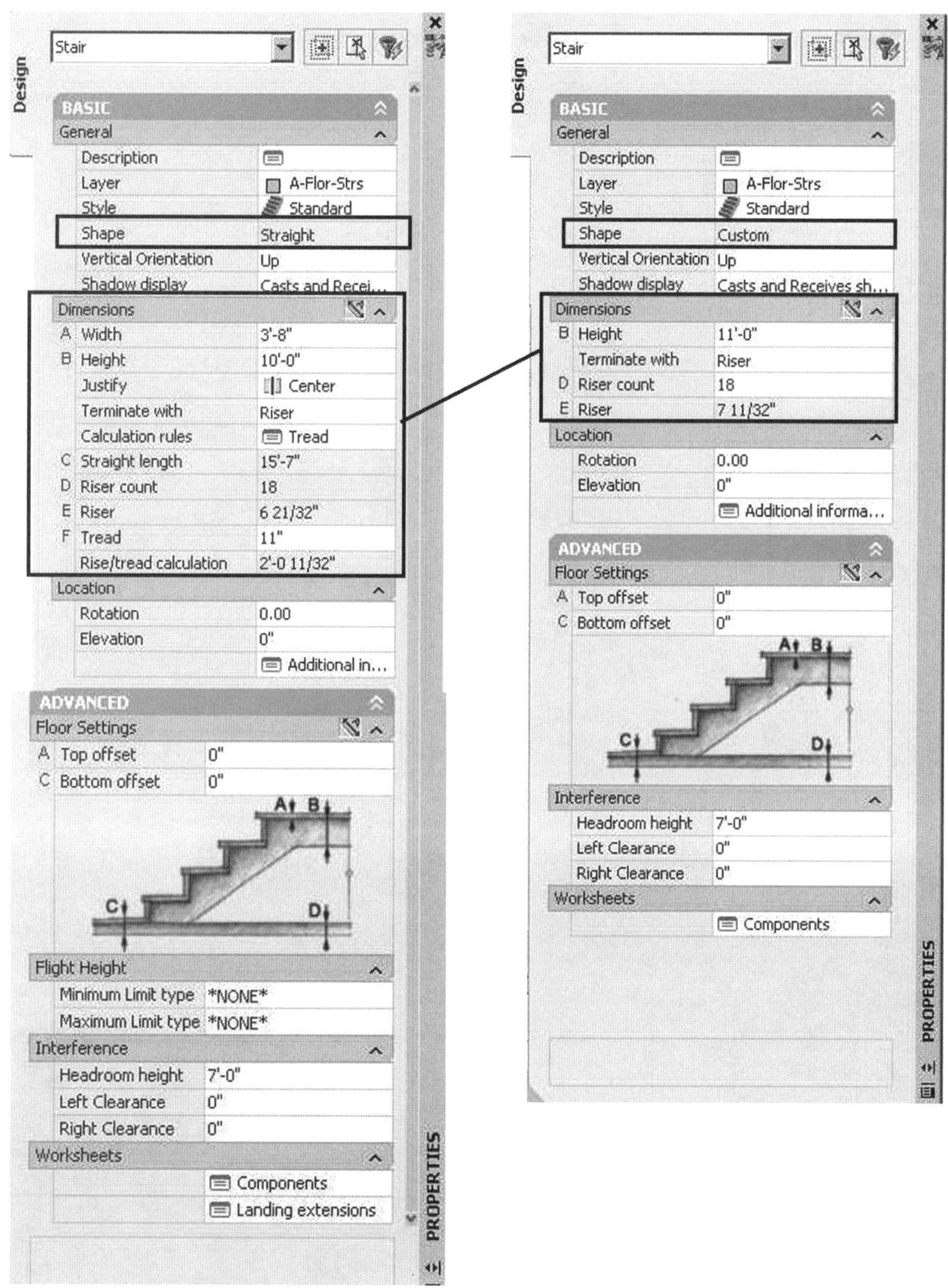

Figure 16.60 Properties of stair objects

Stair edge conditions refer to the shape at the stair sides. ADT provides many tools to customize the shape and appearance of stair flight edges—the simplest method uses the grips modification techniques learned from previous chapters. Figure 16.61 demonstrates these edge modification techniques.

Specialty Modification Commands

Other modifications to stairs occur through the specialty commands that are accessed through the stair object's right-click menu. These are summarized in the pages that follow.

Another method to create advanced edge customizations can be accomplished through the Customize Edge command. This command

Technique to Master **T16.61** Adjusting the Edge Conditions of a Stair and Stair Landing Using Grips

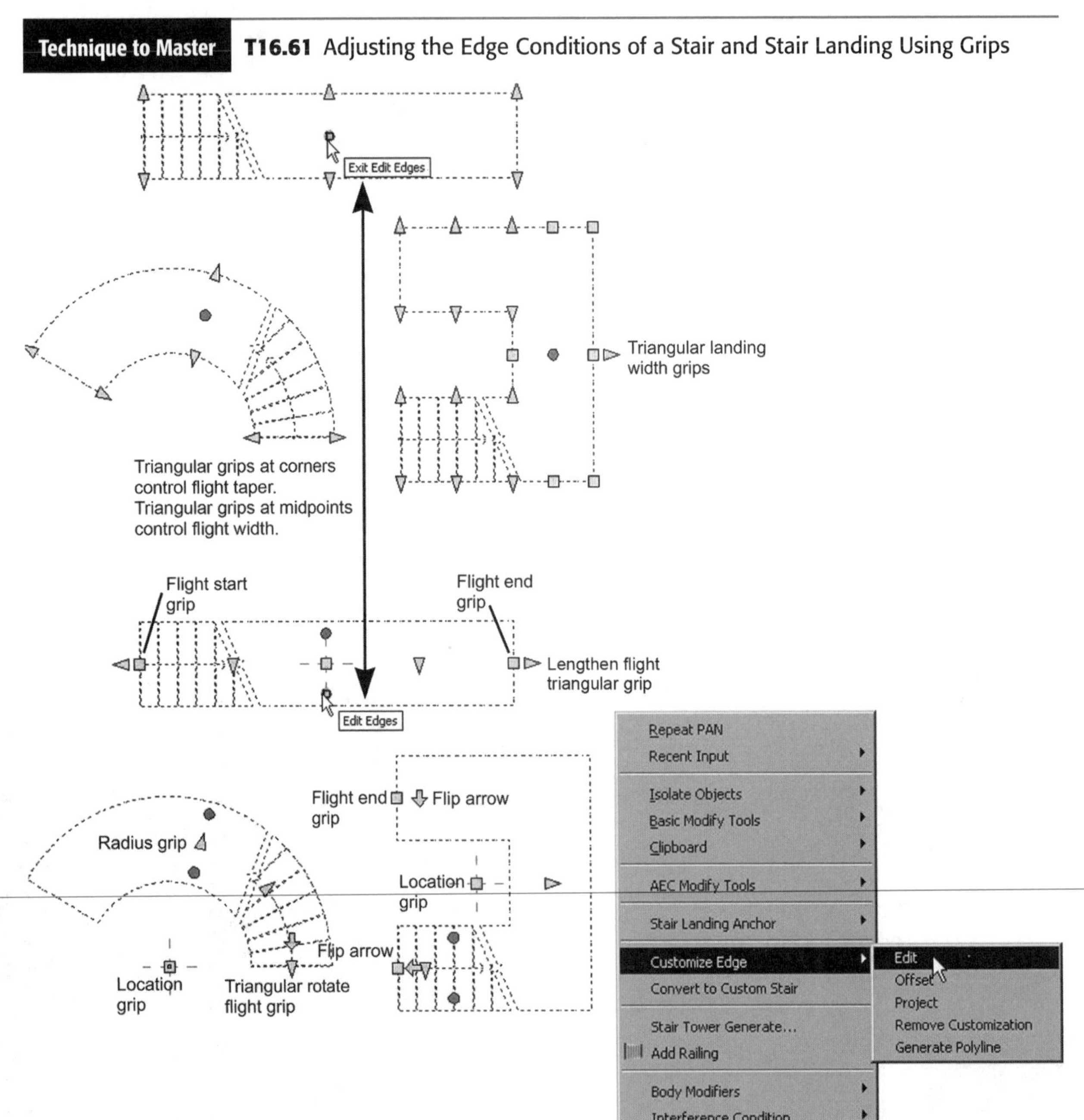

Figure 16.61 Stair edge conditions can be altered by turning on Edit Edges Mode. Use grip toggle or right-click for the Customize Edge>Edit command.

Technique to Master **T16.62** Creating a Customized Stair Edge Condition

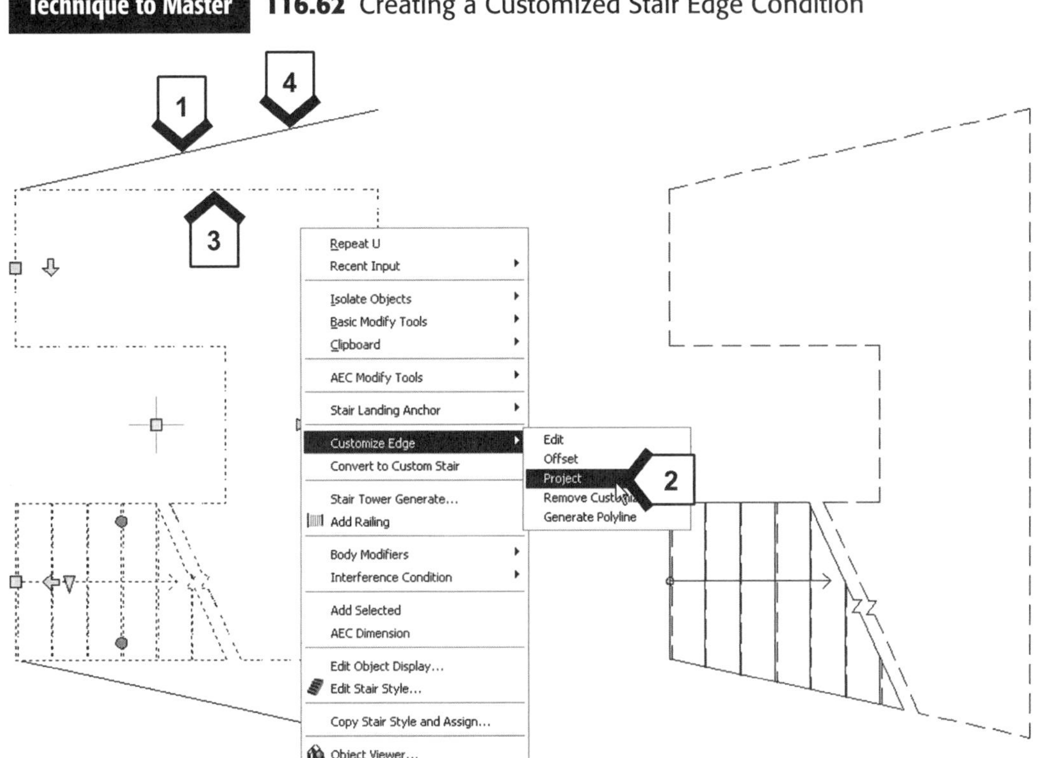

Figure 16.62 This technique uses the projection method to project stair edges to existing polylines or AEC objects.

1	[Drawing Screen]	Draw a polyline or use an existing AEC object for stair edge to conform to.
2	[Drawing Screen]	Select stair, right-click, and choose Customize Edge>Project.
3	[Drawing Screen]	Select the edge of stair that will be projected.
4	[Drawing Screen]	Select a polyline or an AEC object.
5	Repeat steps as necessary to complete stair.	

extends a stair flight's edge to any polyline, solid, or AEC object. Figure 16.62 demonstrates the technique.

The Convert to Custom Stair command converts a stair made with the stair tool to a custom stair.

Multistory buildings with repetitive stair flights can use the Stair Tower Generate command to create the stair tower (Figure 16.63). The stair tower generator only works when used within a project (see Chapter 9's "Project Organization Concepts in ADT") since it uses the project's levels. Figure 16.64 demonstrates how to create a stair tower using an existing stair. Chapter 19 provides additional project organizational guidance in the use of stair towers within a project.

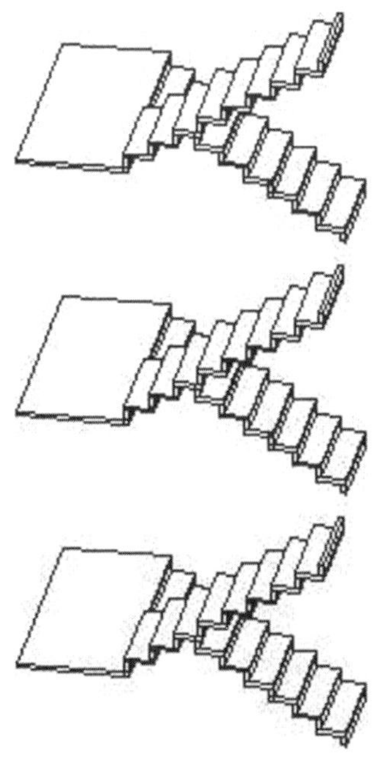

Figure 16.63 Using stair towers

Technique to Master **T16.64** Setting up Stair Towers

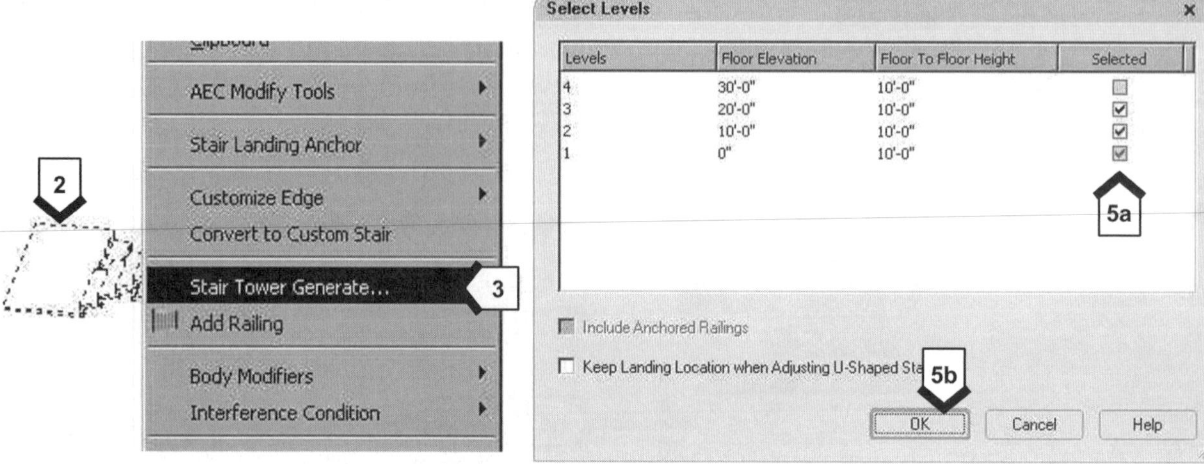

Figure 16.64 For the Stair Tower Generate command to work, the current drawing must be part of a project that has multiple levels set up. Refer to Chapter 9 to review ADT's project organization commands and techniques.

1	Open Construct drawing where stair tower will be drawn.	
2	[Drawing Screen]	Draw stair.
3	[Drawing Screen]	Select stair, right-click, and choose Stair Tower Generate.
4	[Drawing Screen]	Select any railings and slabs that will also be replicated for each floor.
5a, 5b	[Select Levels dialogue box]	Check each floor level to which the stair will be copied. Click OK to complete the command.

The Add Railing command applies a railing object to the selected stair object. Railings are introduced in the next section.

Body modifiers and interference conditions use 3-D objects to add or subtract mass from stair objects. Both commands provide additional methods for stair edge customizations. Learn more about modifying stairs on the CD-ROM.

Railings

Railings refer to the handrails and guardrails that are used with stairs, ramps, and balconies. Handrails provide a helping hand to get you up and down stairs; guardrails are a protective device to prevent you from falling (Figure 16.65). Figure 16.66 illustrates the various vocabulary terms that are necessary to understand railing design.

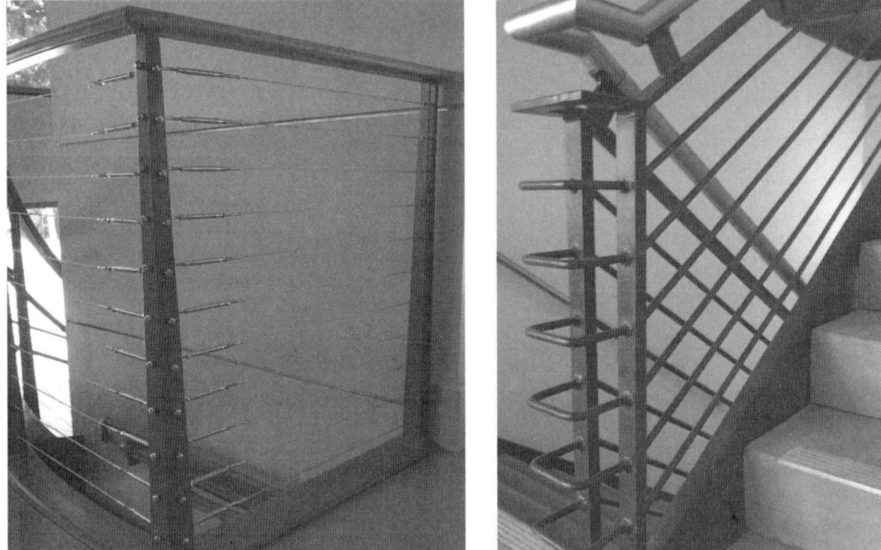

Figure 16.65 Examples of handrails and guardrails

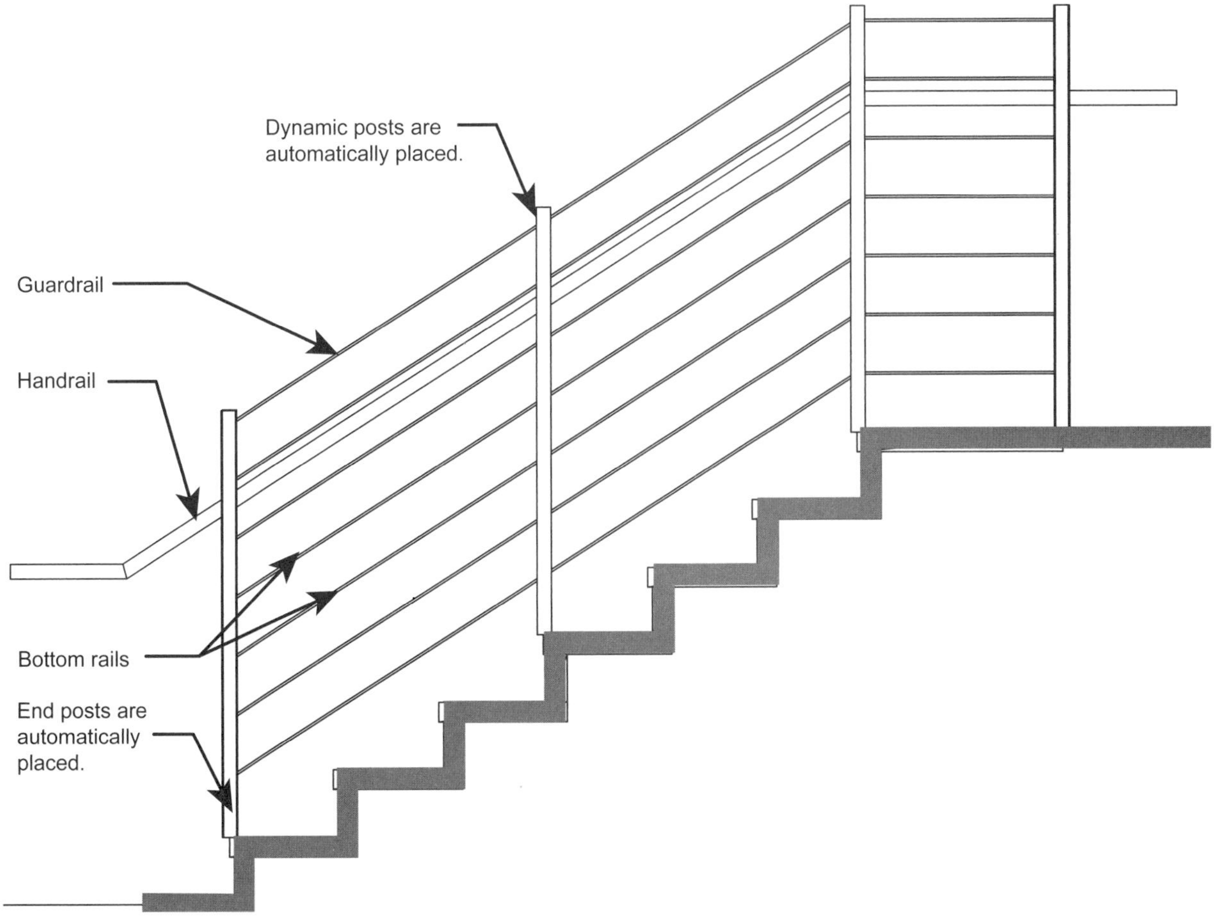

Dynamic posts are automatically placed.

Guardrail

Handrail

Bottom rails

End posts are automatically placed.

Figure 16.66 Railing vocabulary

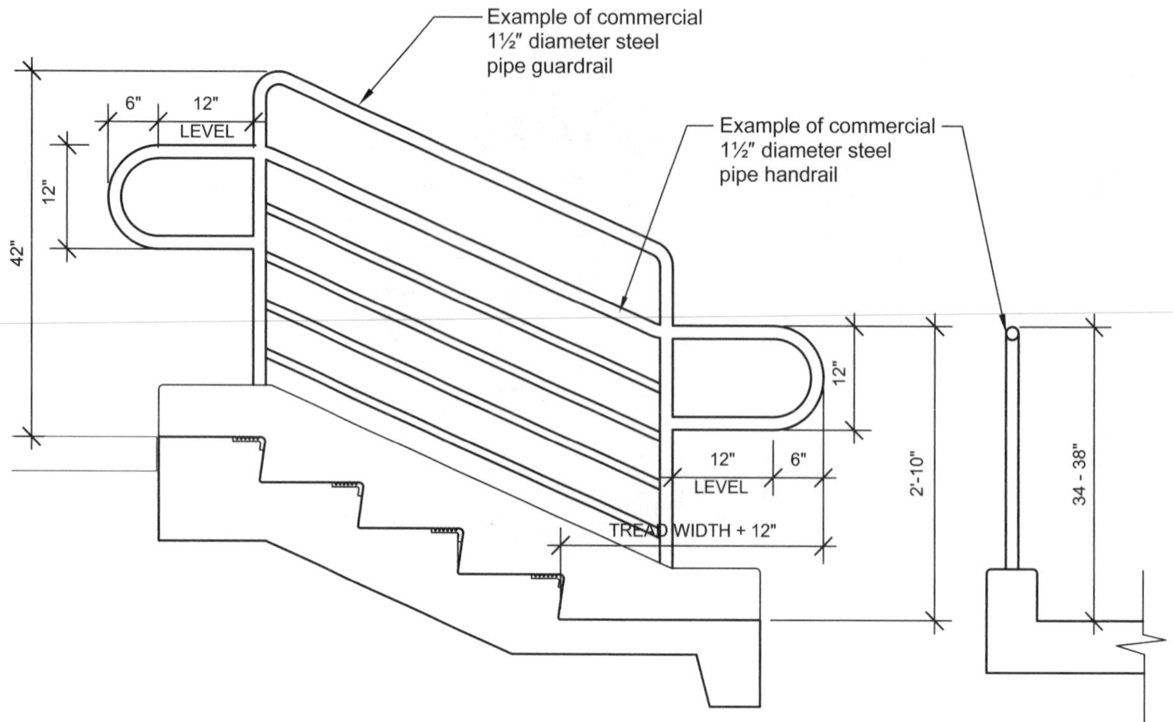

Figure 16.67 Railing parameters regulated by code

Railing Design

Many of handrails and guardrails that are commercially installed are premanufactured. However, custom designed railings are also a large part of the market. Glass, metal, and wood are all common materials used.

As a design technique, handrails and guardrails are used to reinforce the expressiveness of custom-designed stairs. Safety precautions, however, require that all handrails and guardrails be regulated. The more common regulations are illustrated in Figure 16.67. Because these regulations tend to differ between residential and commercial applications, additional research is always recommended.

Existing ADT Railing Styles

There are several existing railing styles available in the Content Browser Library. The handrail and guardrail styles found in this library are very useful for the egress stair types.

Creating New Railing Styles

Railing styles control appearance, size, location, and materials of all railing subcomponents. This also includes its regulatory heights, minimums, and maximums. The Style Manager areas include Rail Locations, Post Locations, Components, and Extensions tabs.

Placing Railings

Railings (both handrail and guardrail) can be placed with or without the ADT stair object. Railings that are not attached to stairs, however, are very difficult to place at sloped angles. Figures 16.68 and 16.69 demonstrate railing placement using the two methods.

Technique to Master T16.68 Placing a Railing (No Stair Attachment)

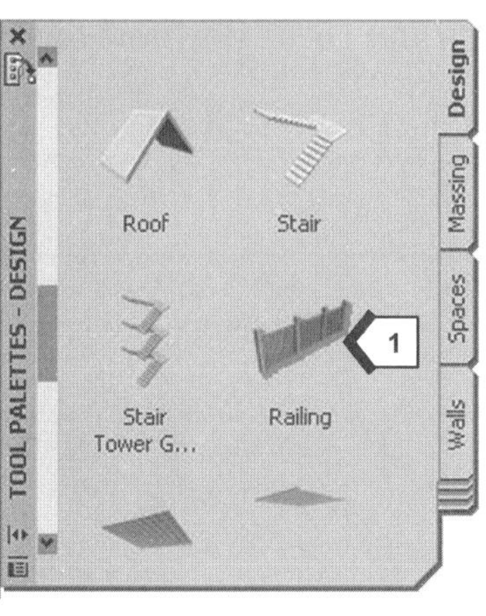

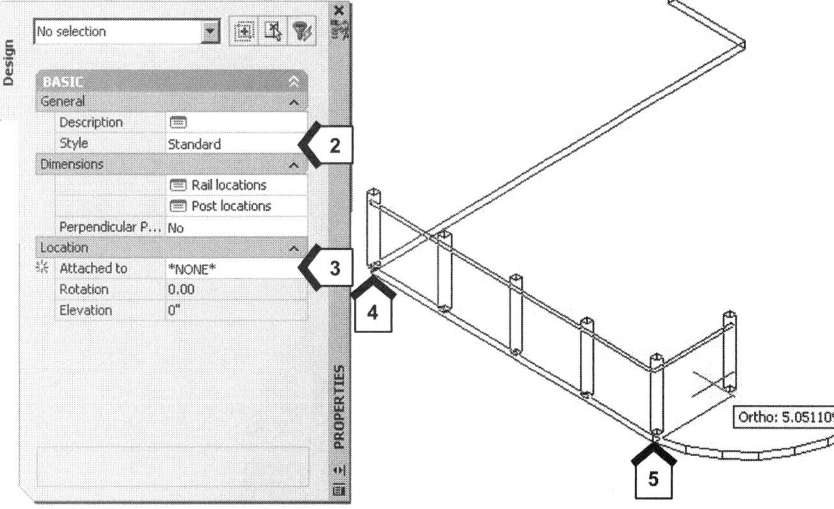

Figure 16.68

1	[Design Tool palette>Railing tool]	Left-click on the Railing tool.
2	[Properties palette>Style]	Specify the railing style.
3	[Properties palette>Attached to]	Change the attachment type to *NONE*.
4	[Drawing Screen]	Locate the start of the railing.
5	[Drawing Screen]	Keep locating start and endpoints for railing segments.

Technique to Master T16.69 Placing a Railing Attached to Stairs

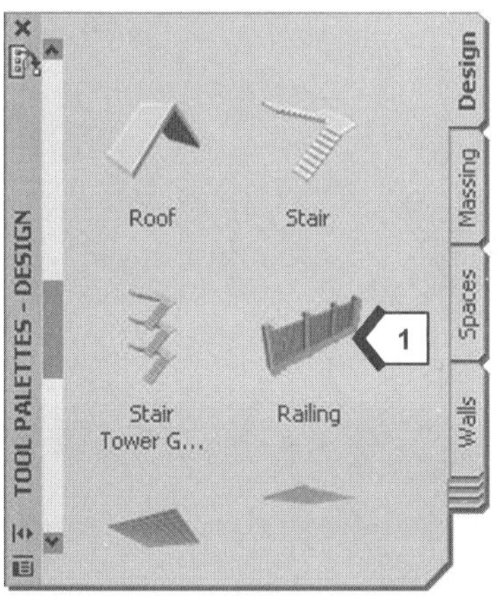

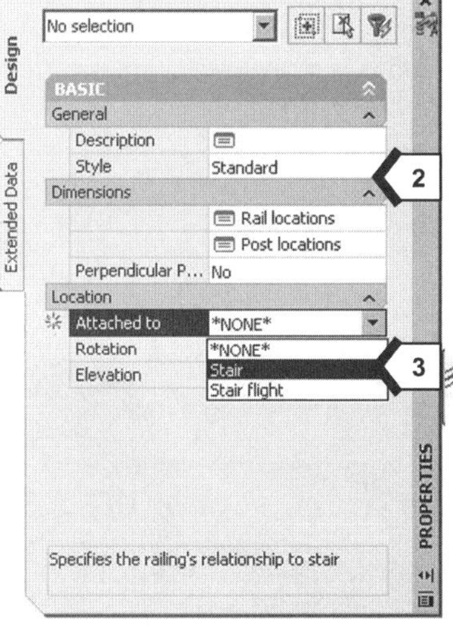

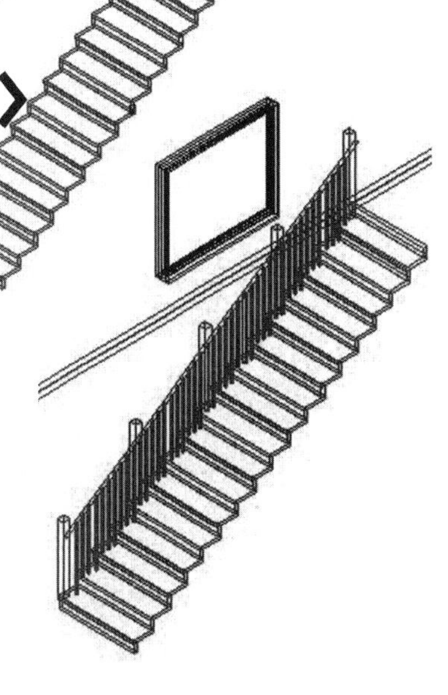

Figure 16.69

1	[Design Tool palette>Railing tool]	Left-click on the Railing tool.
2	[Properties palette>Style]	Specify the railing style.
3	[Properties palette>Attached to]	Change the attachment type to Stair or Stair flight.
4	[Drawing Screen]	Select the stair at side for railing placement.

Post Placement Changes

After you place a railing, you get access to the right-click menu, which provides additional tools to control placement of fixed and dynamic posts in railings. These include adding posts, removing or hiding existing posts, and redistributing the locations of posts. Figures 16.70 and 16.71 illustrate each of the commands.

T16.70 Adding a Post in an Existing Railing

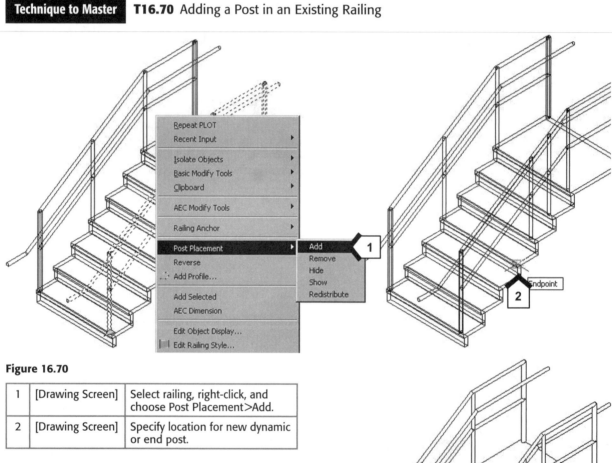

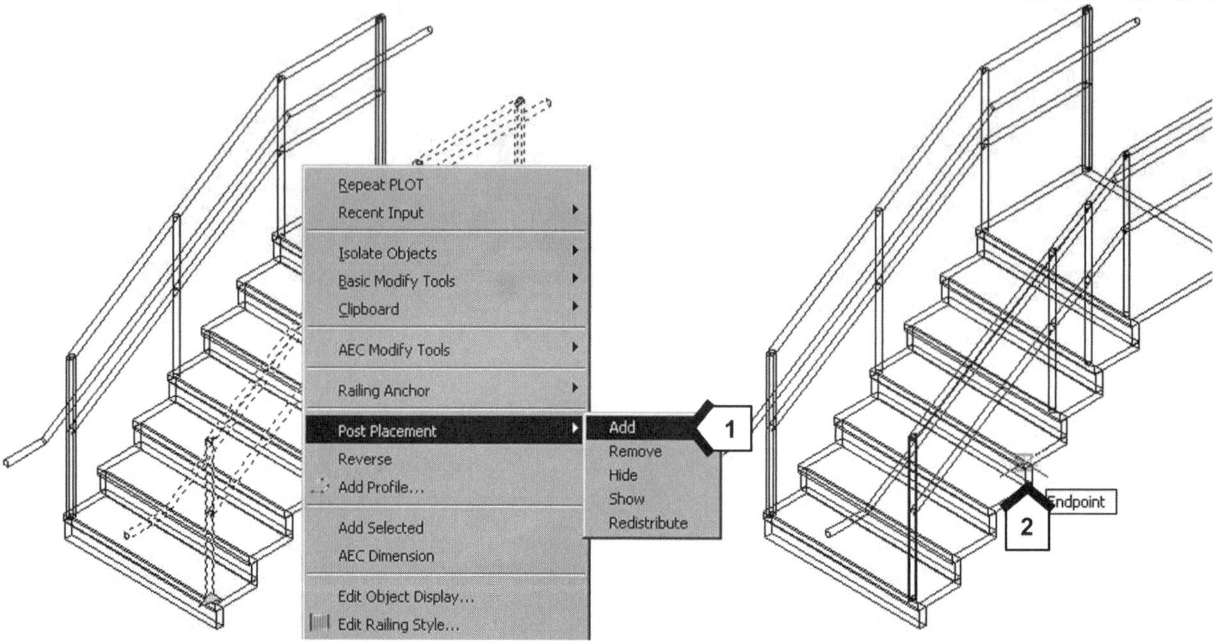

Figure 16.70

1	[Drawing Screen]	Select railing, right-click, and choose Post Placement>Add.
2	[Drawing Screen]	Specify location for new dynamic or end post.

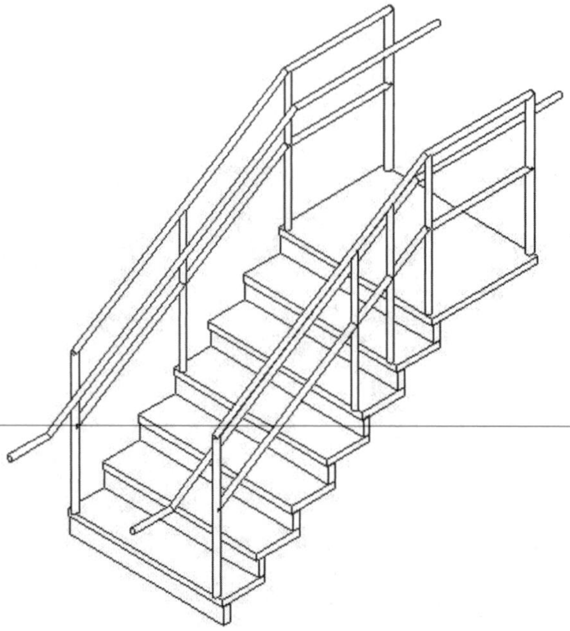

Technique to Master **T16.71** Redistributing Posts in an Existing Railing

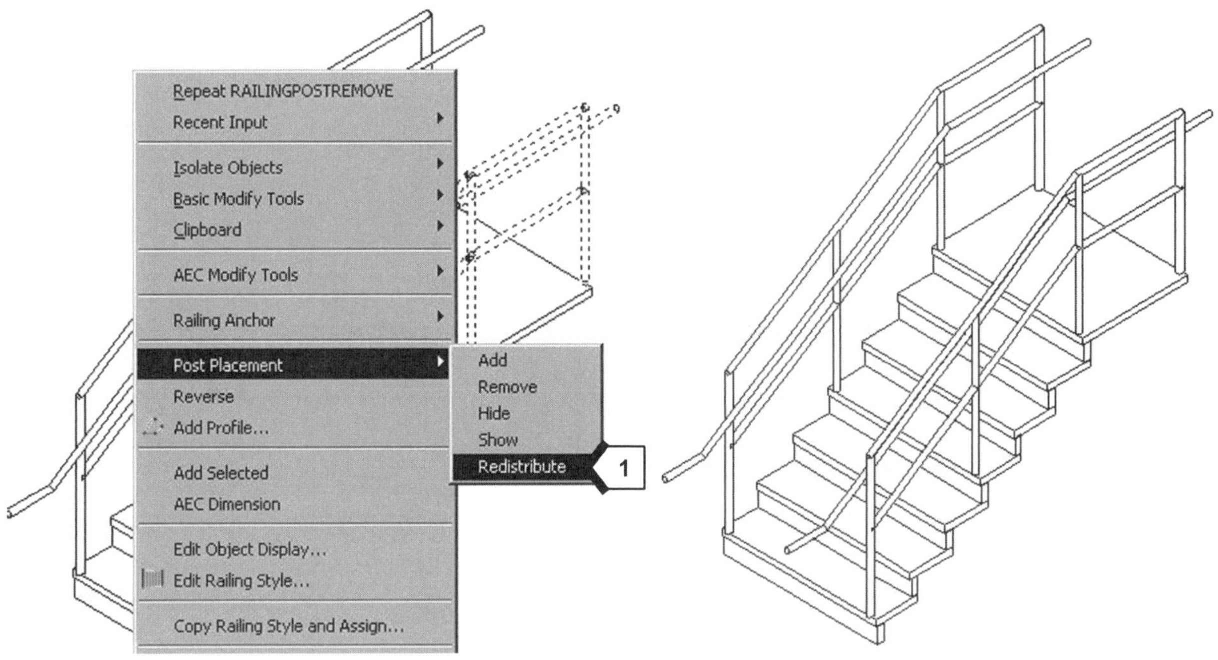

Figure 16.71

1	[Drawing Screen]	Select railing, right-click, and choose Post Placement>Redistribute.

Using Profile Definitions with Railings

Custom handrails and guardrails are made through the use of profile definitions and custom blocks. Some examples can be seen in Figure 16.72. Profiles and custom blocks can be added to the railing style or the individual railing object. Figures 16.73 through 16.76 illustrate the various techniques.

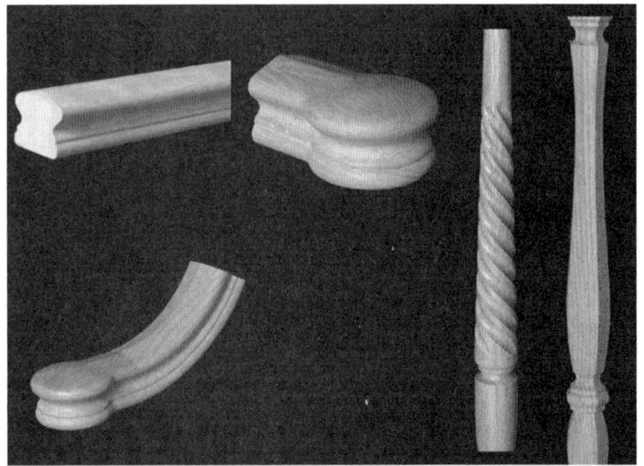

Figure 16.72 Examples of handrail, post, and baluster profiles.

Courtesy of Stair Smiths, www.stairsmiths.com

Technique to Master **T16.73** Adding a Profile to an Existing Railing Component

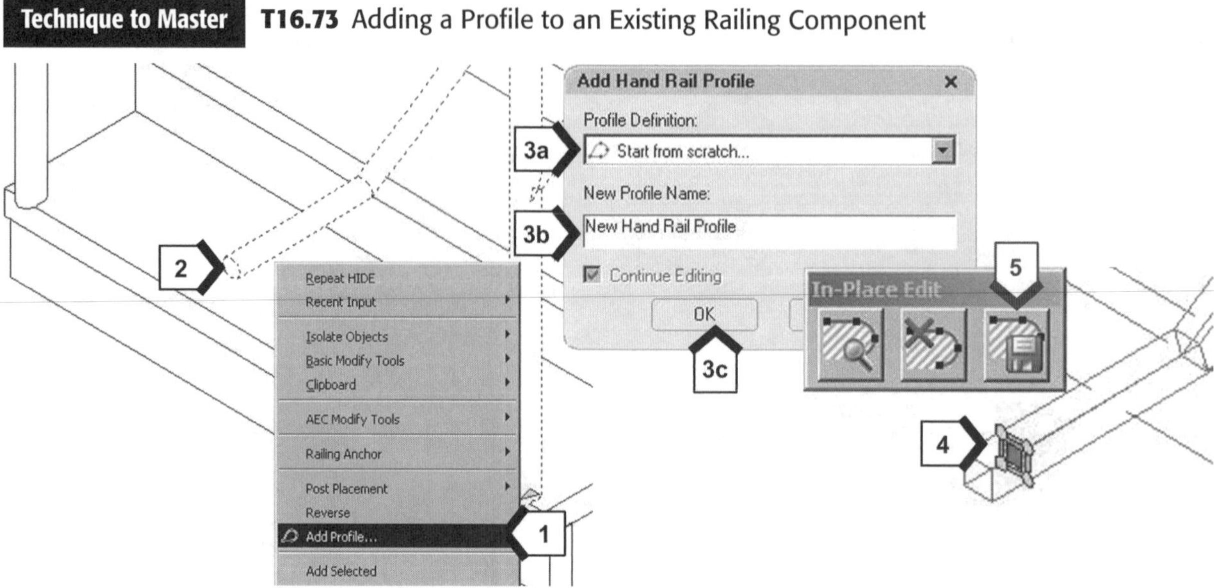

Figure 16.73

1	[Drawing Screen]	Select railing, right-click, and choose Add Profile.
2	[Drawing Screen]	Select railing component to edit.
3a, 3b, 3c	[Add Hand Rail Profile dialogue box]	If profile definition is already created, select profile. If new profile, select Start from scratch. If new, name the profile. Click OK.
4	[Drawing Screen]	Edit profile of railing component.
5	[In-Place Edit toolbar]	Save changes.

Technique to Master **T16.74** Adding a Profile to a Railing Style

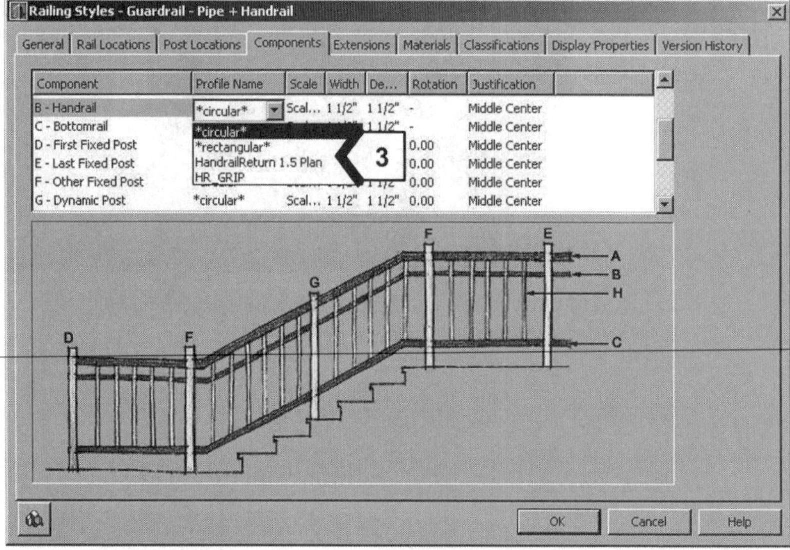

Figure 16.74 You must first create a profile definition before you can assign it to the railing component.

1	Open Railing Style Manager.	
2	[Railing Style Manager>Left pane]	Left-click on the desired style.
3	[Railing Style Manager> Components tab]	Specify the Profile Definition of the desired railing component under the Profile Name column.

Technique to Master **T16.75** Editing an Existing Railing Profile On-Screen

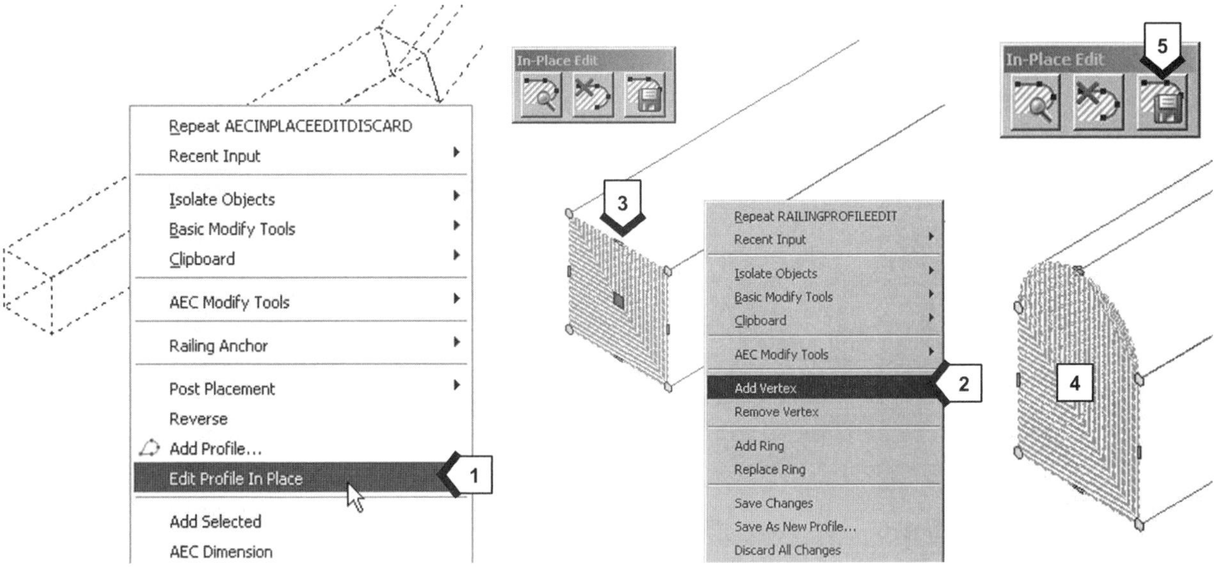

Figure 16.75

1	[Drawing Screen]	Select railing, right-click, and choose Edit Profile In Place.
2	[Drawing Screen]	Right-click and choose Add Vertex to add additional vertices to profile.
3	[Drawing Screen]	Specify location for new vertex (optional).
4	[Drawing Screen]	Modify profile using edge and vertex grips.
5	[In-Place Edit toolbar]	Save changes.

Technique to Master T16.76 Adding Custom Blocks to Railing Styles

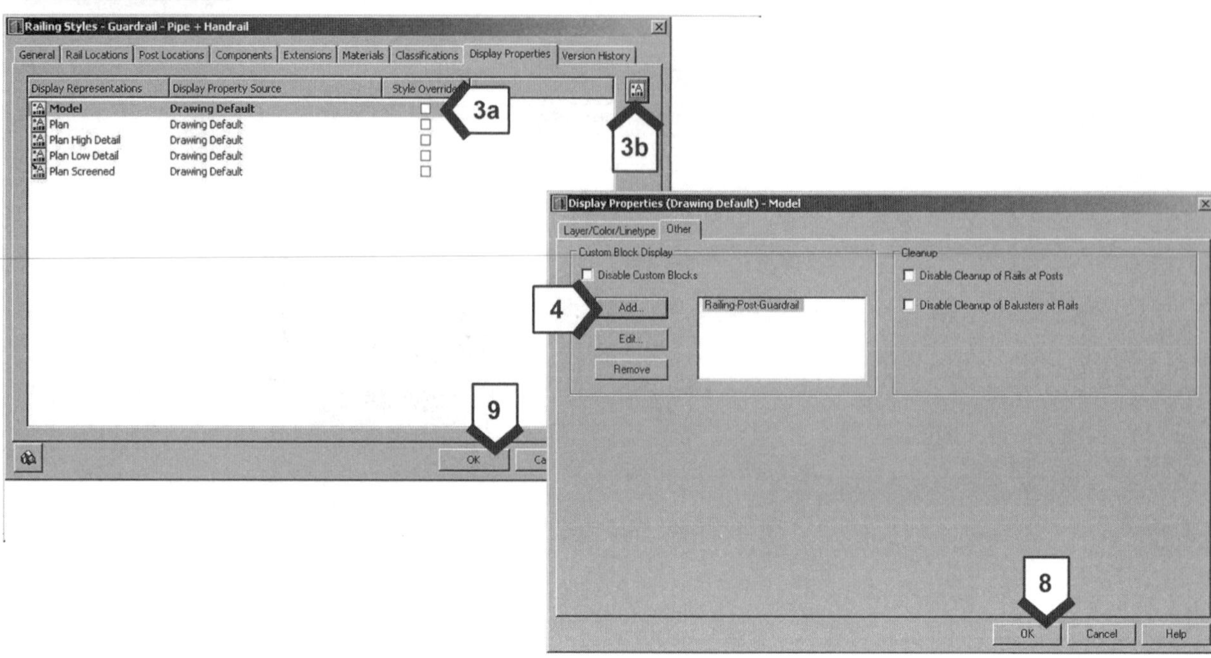

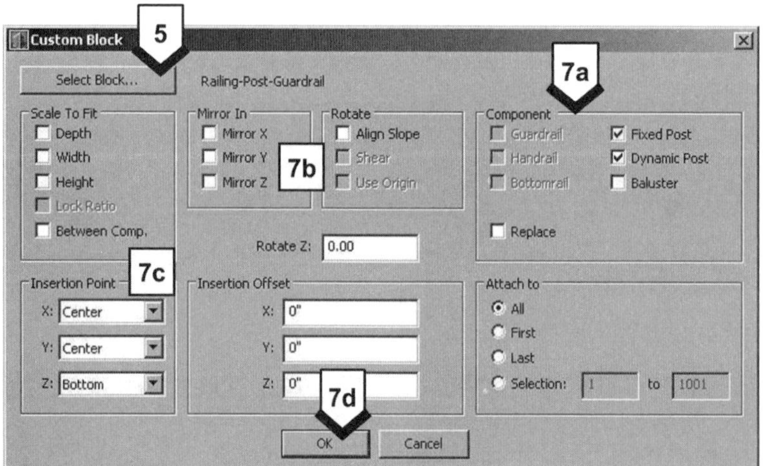

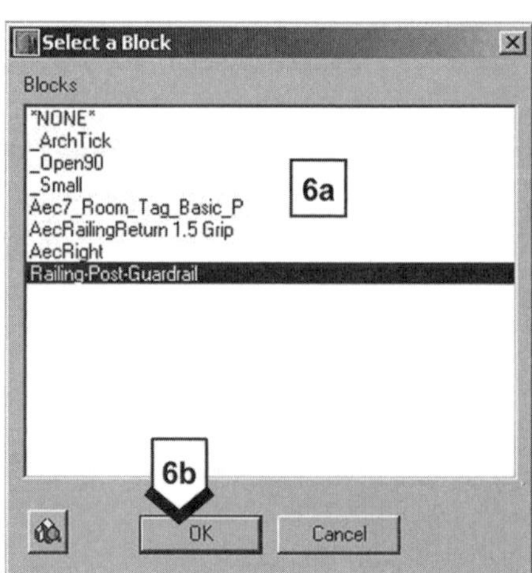

Figure 16.76

1	Open Railing Style Manager.	
2	[Railing Style Manager>Left pane]	Left-click on the desired style.
3a, 3b	[Railing Style Manager>Display Properties tab]	If unchecked, check the Style Override button for Model display representation. If Style Override is already checked, select Model and left-click on Edit Display Properties button.
4	[Railing Style Manager>Other tab]	Left-click the Add button.
5	[Railing Style Manager>Custom Block dialogue box]	Left-click the Select Block button.
6a, 6b	[Railing Style Manager>Select a Block dialogue box]	Select desired block for railing component. Click OK.
7a, 7b, 7c, 7d	[Railing Style Manager>Custom Block dialogue box]	Specify railing component that block will replace. Specify insertion point, scaling, and rotation parameters for block. Click OK.
8	[Railing Style Manager>Other tab]	Click OK.
9	[Railing Style Manager>Display Properties tab]	Click OK.

Structural Components

Since the subject of structural systems is considerable, for the purposes of this book the discussion is limited to a brief introduction to the structural object types in ADT.

ADT has three structural object types—the column, brace, and beam. These three types are representative of the various column, beam, and bracing systems used in buildings today. The column object is used for all vertical structural components; the beam—all horizontal components. Structural systems like trusses and joists are combined into the beam in ADT. The bracing object is used to represent any diagonal bracing system.

All structural object types in ADT essentially use extruded 2-D profiles to create the 3-D structural member. The extrusions can be along a linear or nonlinear path to create the appropriate 3-D object (see CD-ROM for illustration). Since, for the most part, structural members are standardized, ADT includes a catalog of predefined shapes and materials. If the desired structural member is not found within the catalog, a wizard is available to create additional structural profiles.

Any structural members imported from the catalog or created through the wizard are saved as structural styles. Once a structural member profile is saved as a style, it can be used to create any structural member type: column, beam, or brace (Figure 16.77).

The Structural Member Catalog

The structural member catalog is a collection of standardized structural shapes and materials that coincide with many wood, concrete, and steel profiles used in construction. On the left pane, the catalog is divided into three material subgroups. All concrete structural members including precast and cast-in-place members are grouped together. Steel shapes as well as timber framing make up the other two subgroups. Following material, the catalog is divided into the various profiles standard to each material type. Steel, for example, is made in tubular, circular, and L-shaped profiles.

Figure 16.78 identifies the various areas of the structural member catalog. Figure 16.79 demonstrates how to create a style from a profile selection.

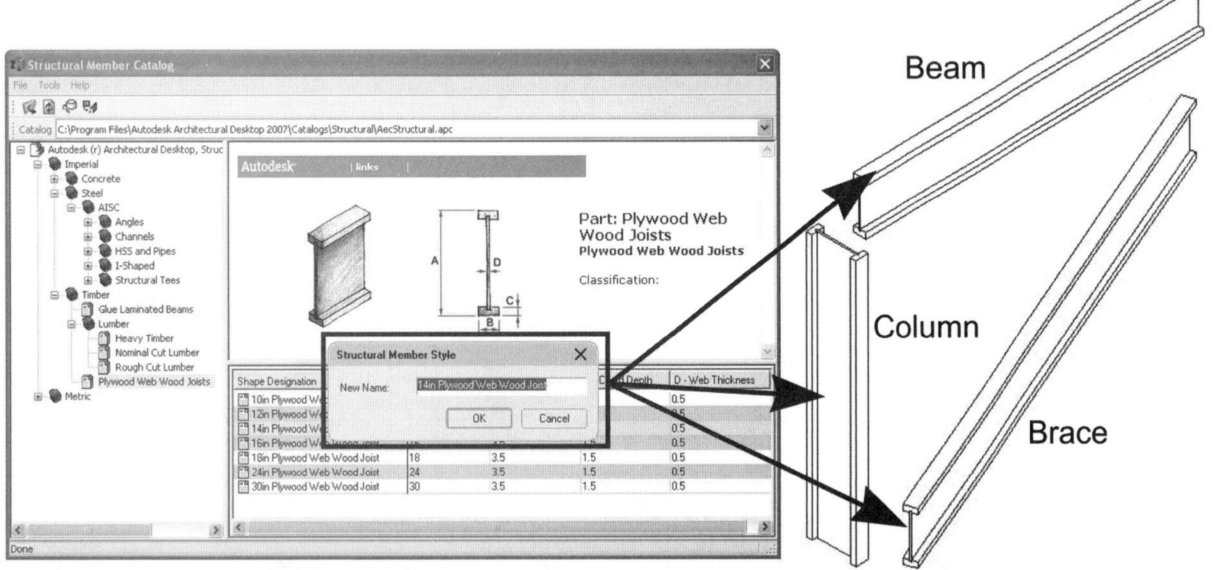

Figure 16.77 Once a structural member profile is saved as a style, it can be used to create any structural member type: column, beam, or brace.

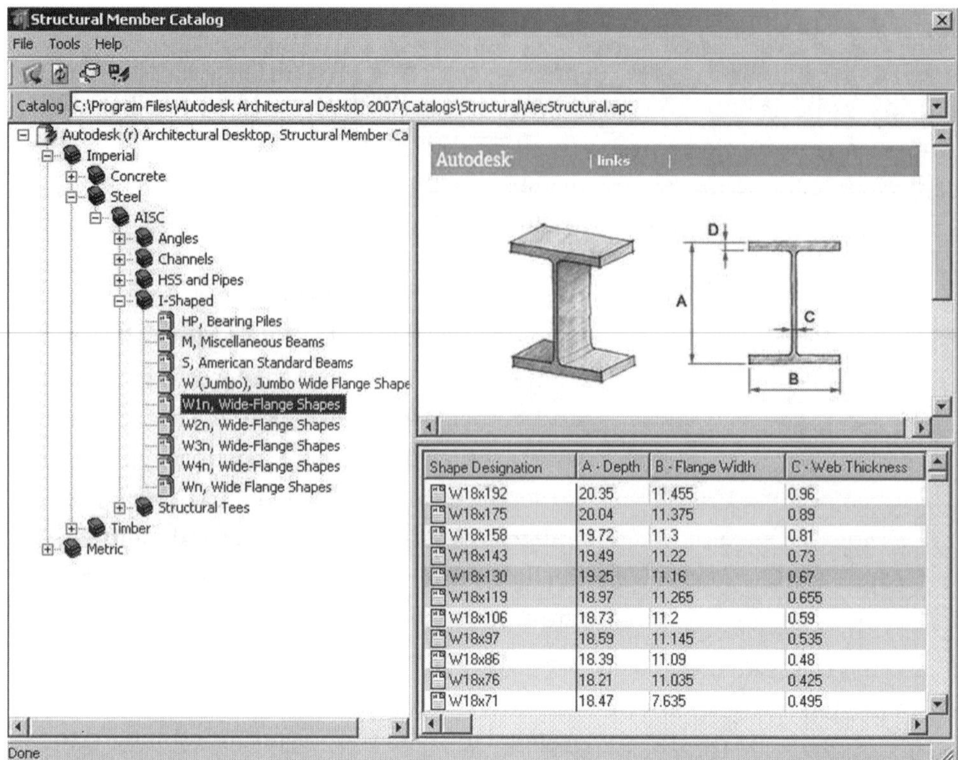

Figure 16.78 The structural member catalog

Technique to Master **T16.79** Creating a Style from the Structural Member Catalog

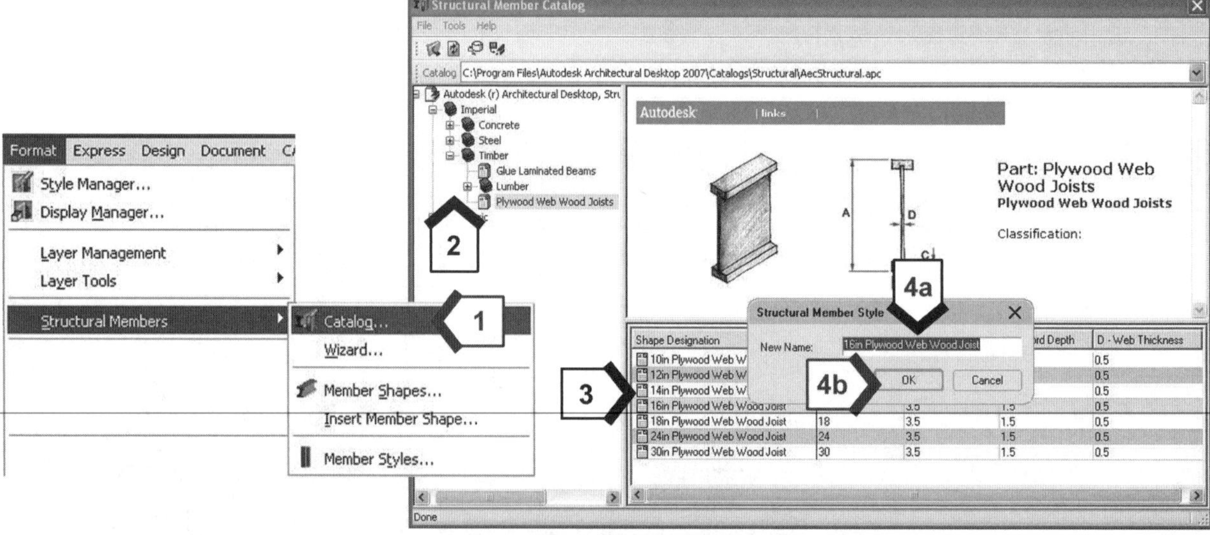

Figure 16.79

1	[Format Menu>Structural Members> Catalog]	Open the Structural Member Catalog.
2	[Structural Member Catalog]	Left click on plus signs to expand folders. Locate the structural member by material first, then type.
3	[Structural Member Catalog]	Locate structural member and double-click on it.
4a, 4b	[Structural Member Catalog> Structural Member Style dialogue box]	Rename the style, if desired. Click OK to add structural style.

Create Nonstandard Structural Members

Nonstandard structural members refer to structural members that are not prefabricated. Instead, these structural profiles must be custom-engineered using drawings from structural consultants (Figure 16.80). In ADT, there are three methods to create custom structural profiles.

The Structural Wizard

The structural wizard creates nonstandard structural members from user-specified measurements. The first step in the automated process is to choose a structural profile type. These types coincide with the available profiles in the structural member catalog. The wizard then prompts for the measurements for the selected profile. Figure 16.81 demonstrates how to create a structural style using the wizard.

Create Custom Profiles Through the Member Shape Definition Styles

The AecsMemberShape command creates custom profiles for structural member styles to use. Figure 16.82 demonstrates how to use the Member Shape Manager and then apply the Member Definition to a Structural Style.

Customize the Start and End Shapes Through the Structural Member Style Manager

Single and multicomponent structural members can be created through the member style manager. Figures 16.83 and 16.84 demonstrates the use of multicomponent structural members to create tapered steel beams and composite columns.

Place Columns, Beams, and Braces

Once structural styles are created, they can be placed with the column, beam, or brace structural tools found on the Design Tool palette. Figures 16.85 through 16.87 demonstrate the placement process using these tools.

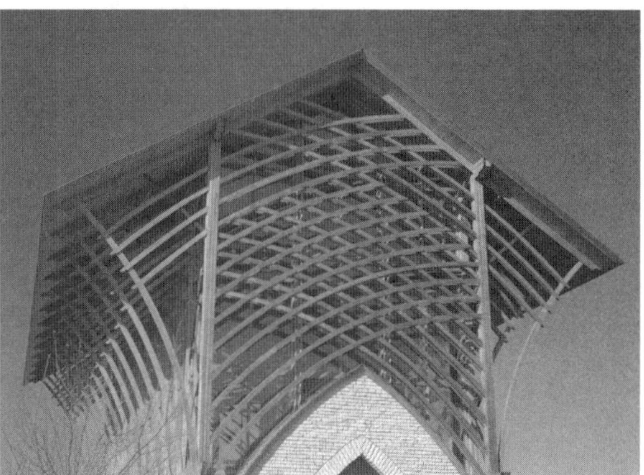

Figure 16.80 Nonstandard structural members must be custom-engineered using drawings from structural consultants.

Technique to Master **T16.81** Creating a Style Using the Wizard

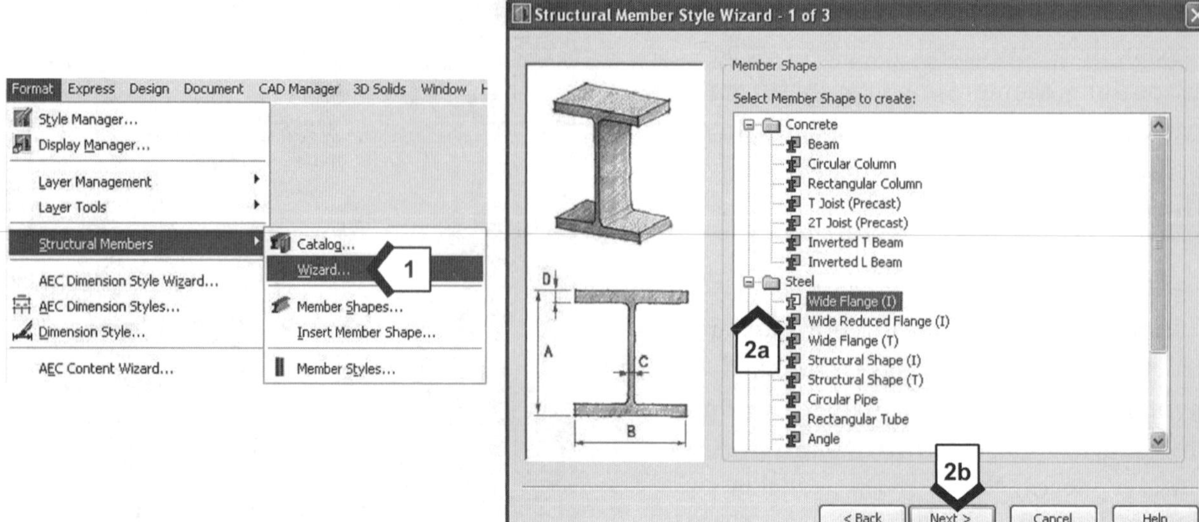

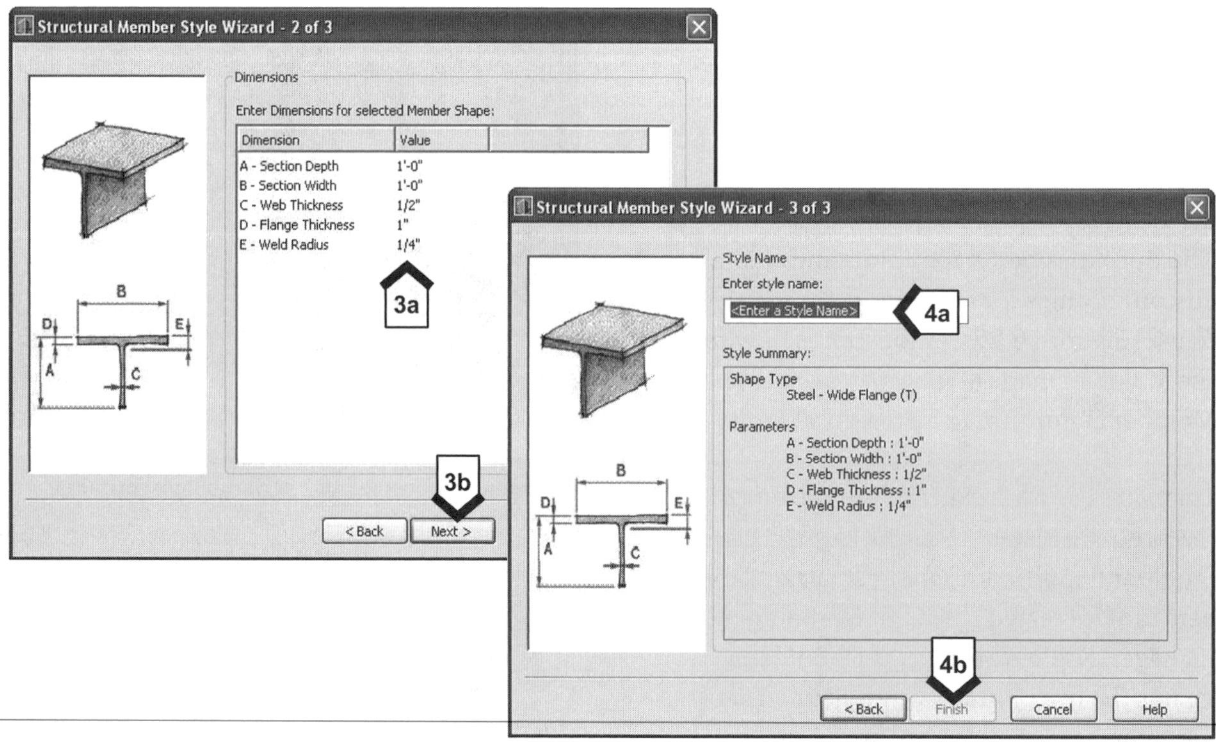

Figure 16.81

1	[Format Menu>Structural Members>Catalog]	Open the Structural Member Wizard.
2a, 2b	[Structural Member Style Wizard]	Left-click on plus signs to expand folders. Locate structural member by material first, then type. Click Next.
3a, 3b	[Structural Member Style Wizard]	Specify dimensional values for structural member shape. Click Next.
4a, 4b	[Structural Member Style Wizard]	Name the style. Click Finish.

Technique to Master **T16.82** Creating and Applying Member Shape Definition Styles

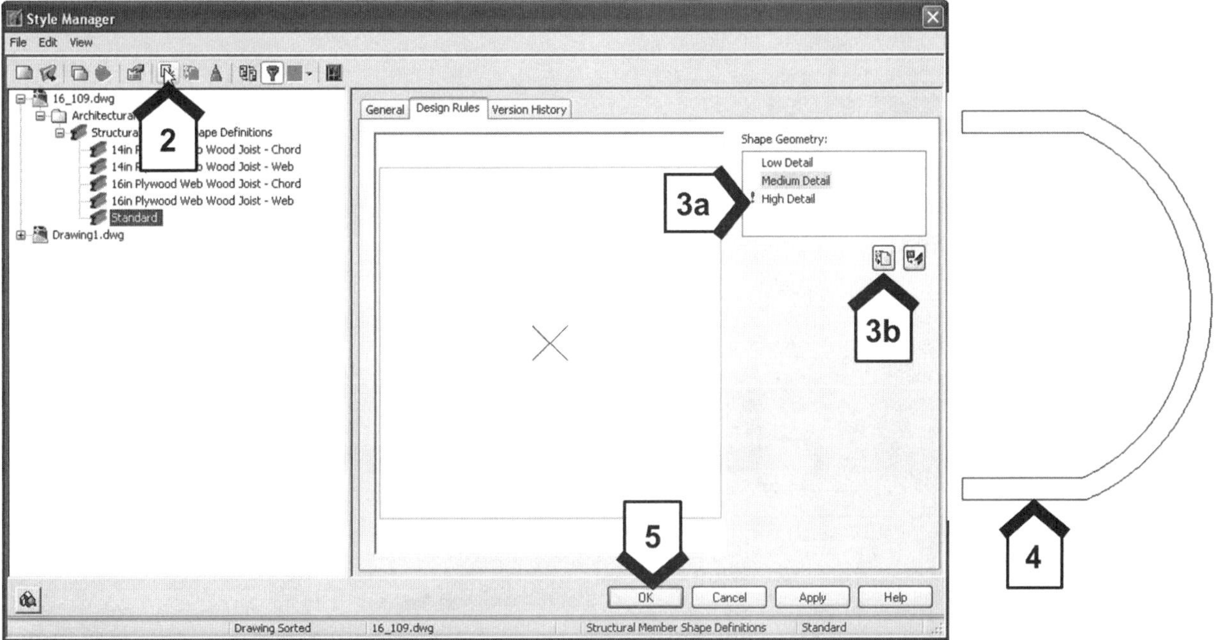

Figure 16.82

1	[Format Menu>Structural Members>Member Shapes]	Open the Member Shapes Style Manager.
2	[Member Shapes Style Manager]	Create new shape.
3a, 3b	[Member Shapes Style Manager]	Select style. In the right-pane, select High Detail, then left-click on the Specify Rings for High Detail button.
4	[Drawing Screen]	Select polyline for member shape profile.
5	[Member Shapes Style Manager]	Click OK to complete the command.

Technique to Master **T16.83** Creating a Tapered Steel Beam

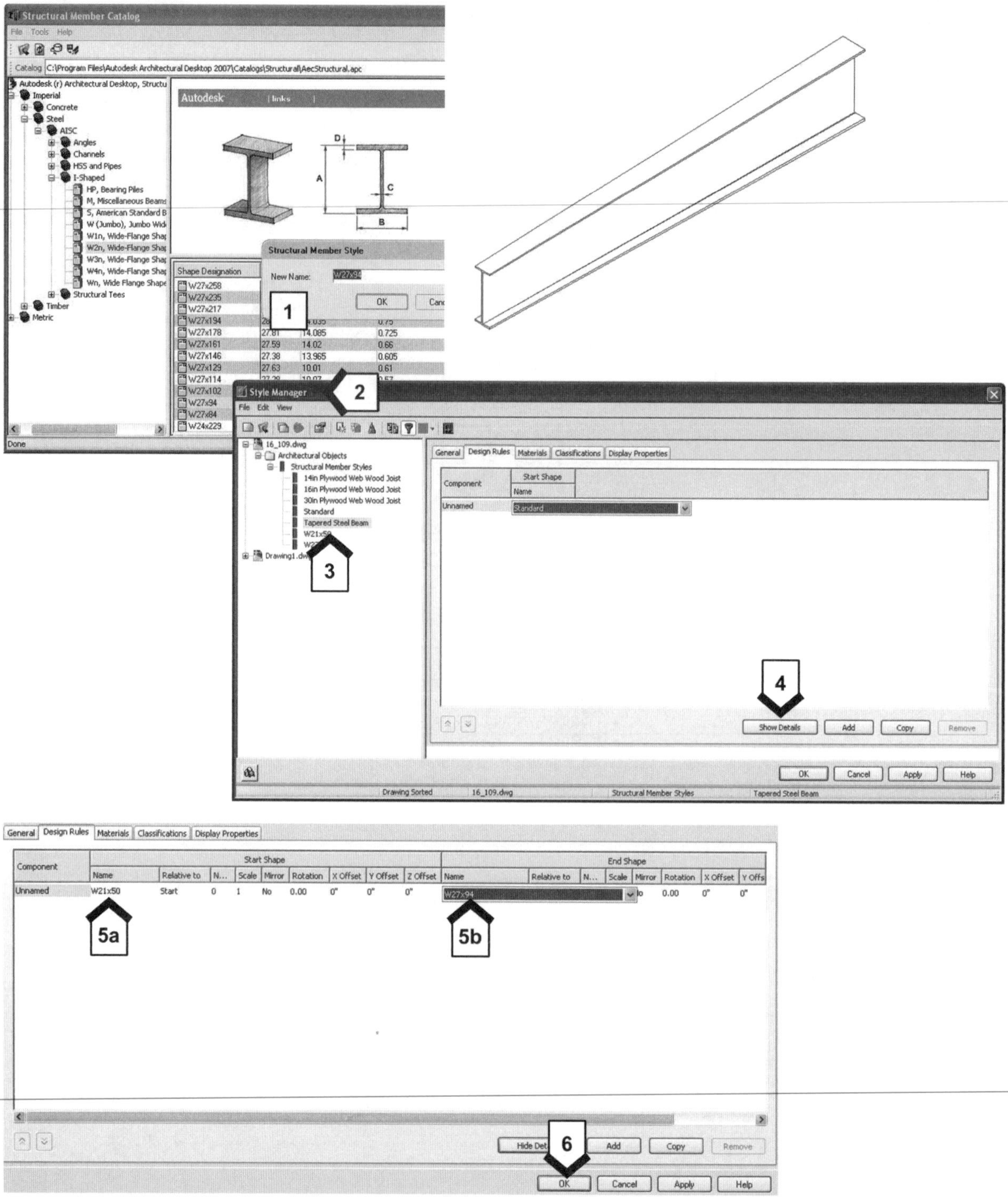

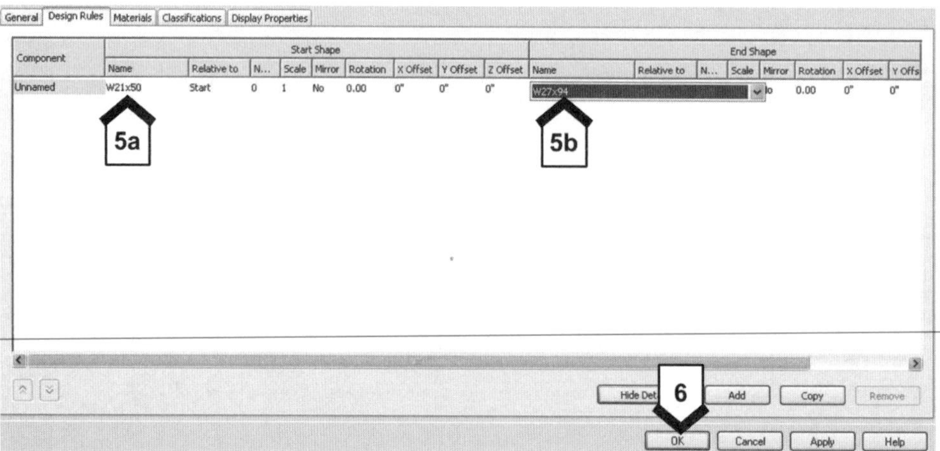

Figure 16.83

1	[Structural Member Catalog]	Create structural member styles for each size profile.
2	Open Structural Member Style Manager.	
3	[Structural Member Style Manager]	Create a new style. Select style.
4	[Structural Member Style Manager>Design Rules tab]	In right pane, left-click on Show Details button.
5a, 5b	[Structural Member Style Manager>Design Rules tab]	Specify Start Shape profile and End Shape profile.
6	[Structural Member Style Manager>Design Rules tab]	Click OK to complete the command.

Technique to Master **T16.84** Creating Composite Columns

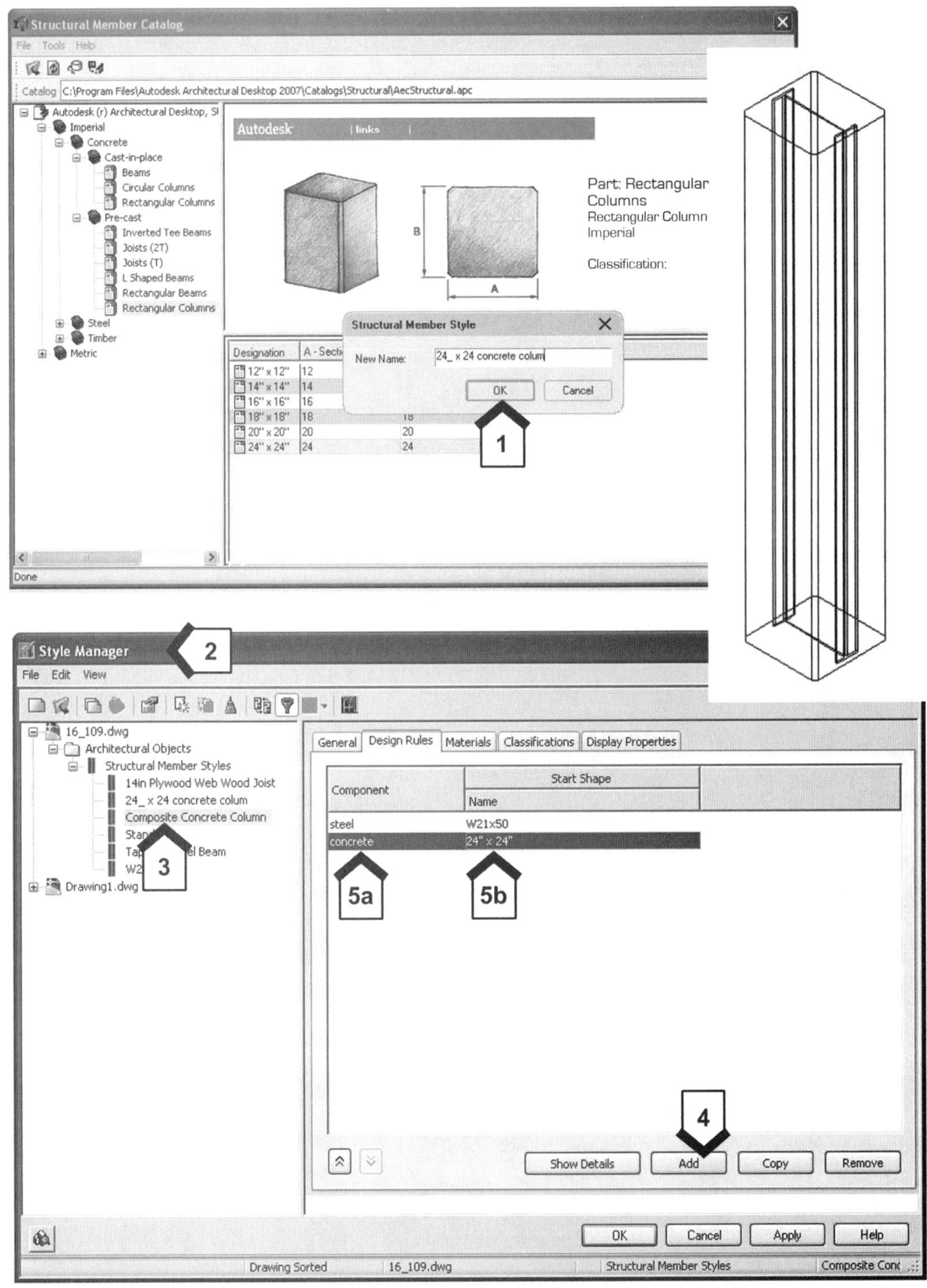

Figure 16.84

1	[Structural Member Catalog]	Create structural member styles for each size column profile.
2	Open Structural Member Style Manager.	
3	[Structural Member Style Manager]	Create a new style. Select style.
4	[Structural Member Style Manager>Design Rules tab]	In right pane, left-click on Add button.
5a, 5b	[Structural Member Style Manager>Design Rules tab]	Specify Start Shape profile for steel and concrete profiles.
6	[Structural Member Style Manager>Design Rules tab]	Click OK to complete the command.

Technique to Master T16.85 Placing a Structural Column

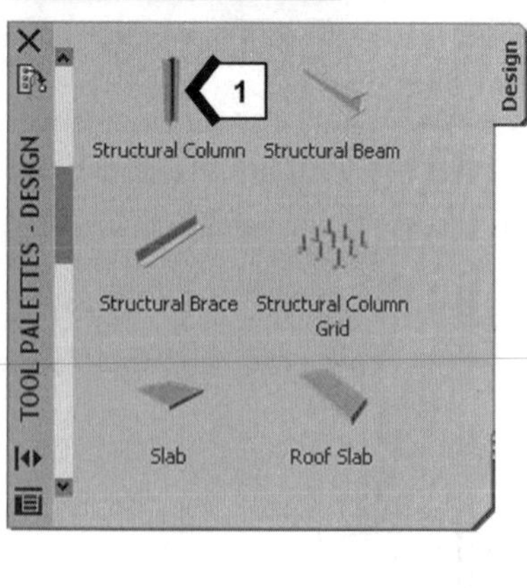

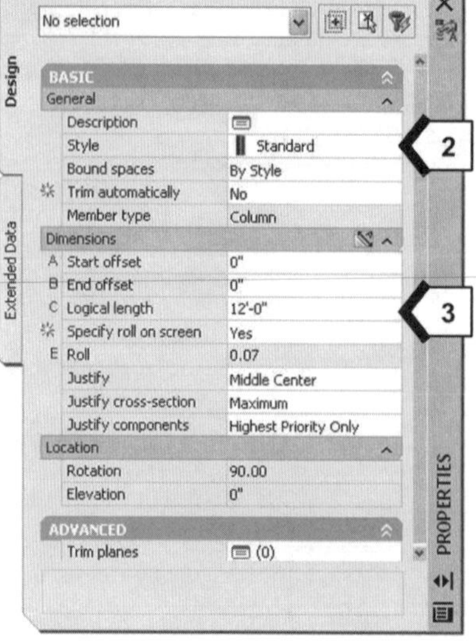

Figure 16.85 Column profiles that are nonrectangular must first be created as a style. Refer to Techniques T16.79 and T16.81.

1	[Design Tool palette]	Left-click on the Structural Column tool.
2	[Properties palette]	Specify column style.
3	[Properties palette]	Specify column length.
4	[Drawing Screen]	Place column.

Technique to Master T16.86 Placing a Structural Beam

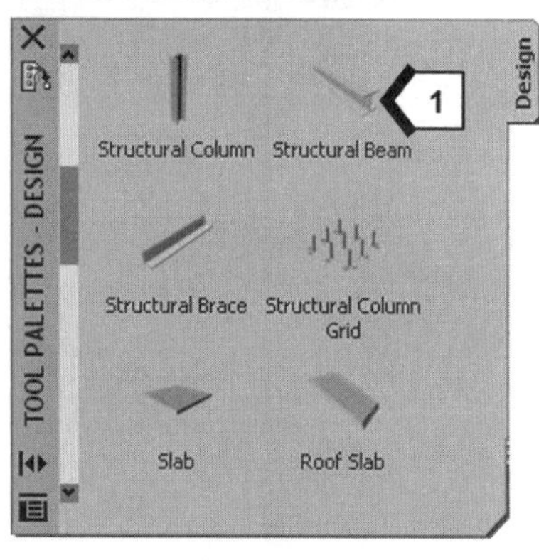

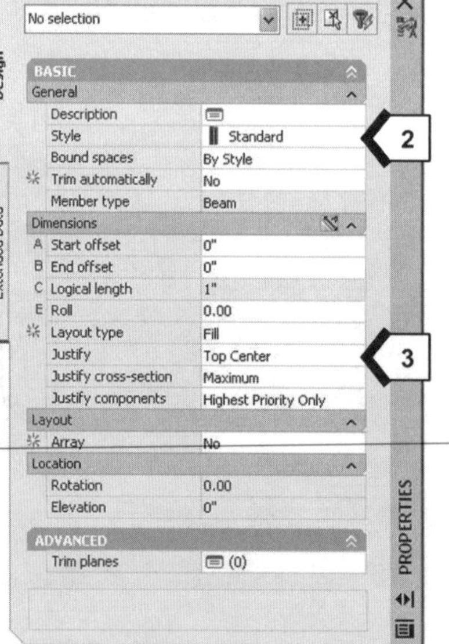

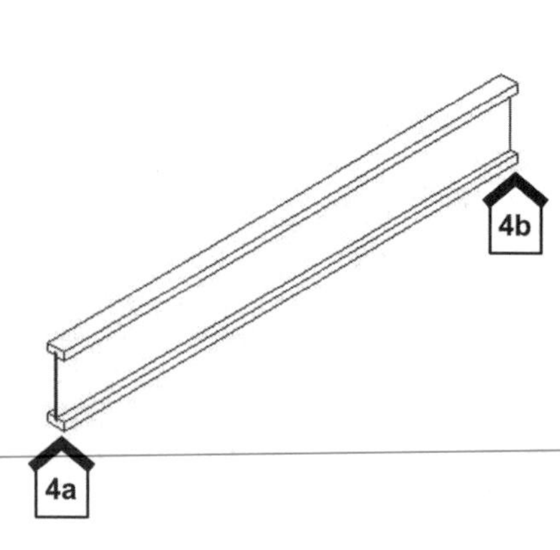

Figure 16.86 Beam profiles that are nonrectangular must first be created as a style. Refer to Techniques T16.79 and T16.81.

1	[Design Tool palette]	Left-click on Structural Beam tool.
2	[Properties palette]	Specify beam style.
3	[Properties palette]	Specify beam justification.
4a, 4b	[Drawing Screen]	Place beam by specifying start and endpoints.

Technique to Master **T16.87** Placing a Structural Member to Follow a Path

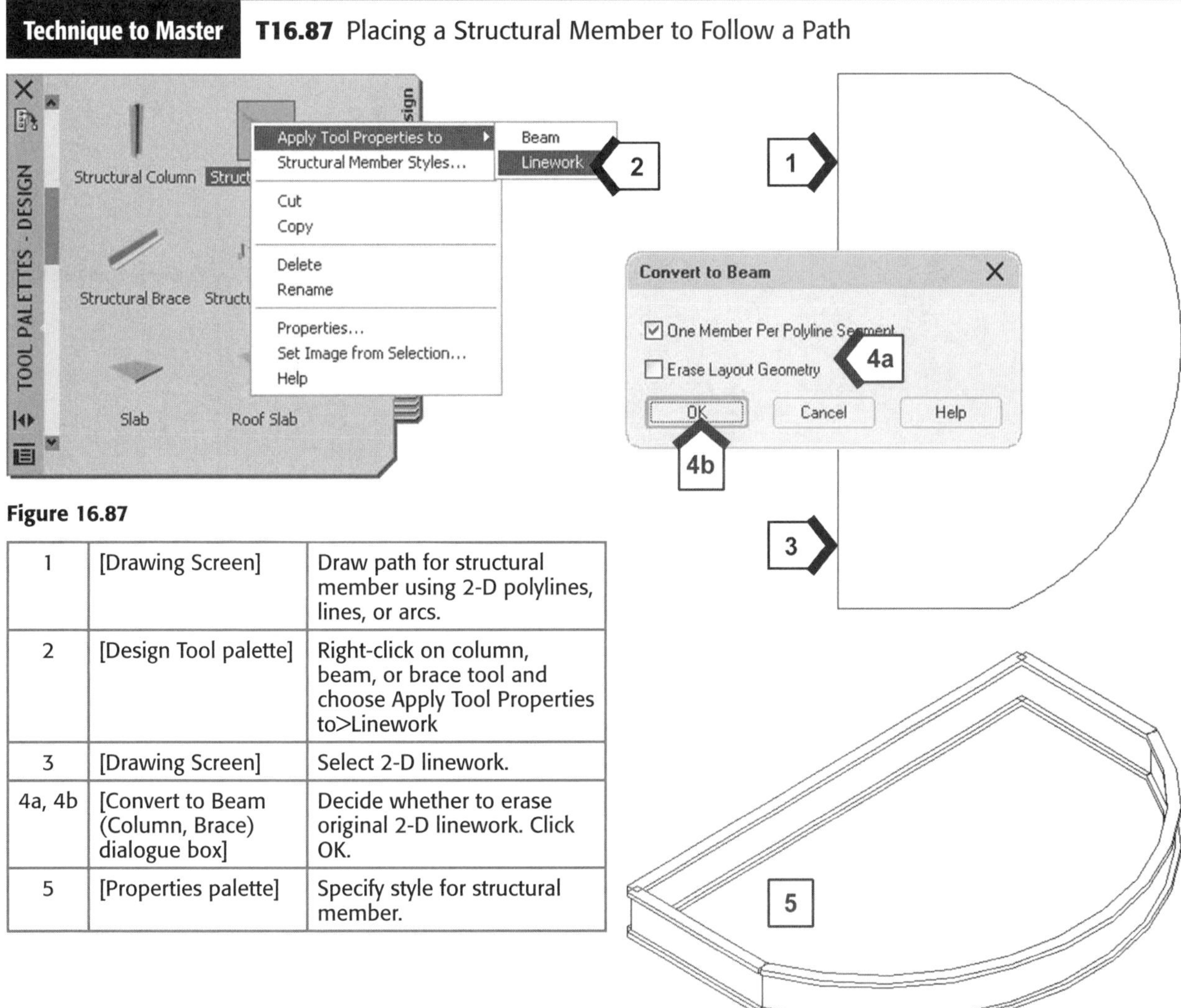

Figure 16.87

1	[Drawing Screen]	Draw path for structural member using 2-D polylines, lines, or arcs.
2	[Design Tool palette]	Right-click on column, beam, or brace tool and choose Apply Tool Properties to>Linework
3	[Drawing Screen]	Select 2-D linework.
4a, 4b	[Convert to Beam (Column, Brace) dialogue box]	Decide whether to erase original 2-D linework. Click OK.
5	[Properties palette]	Specify style for structural member.

Space Objects

Prior to ADT 2007, space objects were objects that defined a three-dimensional volume of space and its finish floor and ceiling thicknesses. Space objects provided the means to link room areas and room finish surfaces to each room within a building. The styles for space objects helped to manage room-size minimums and maximums during the space-planning process.

The space object has dramatically changed in ADT 2007. Autodesk has merged the space boundary and area objects into the space object (Figure 16.88). With the merging of functions, space objects are more flexible and powerful than ever before. This topic is an introduction to the space object.

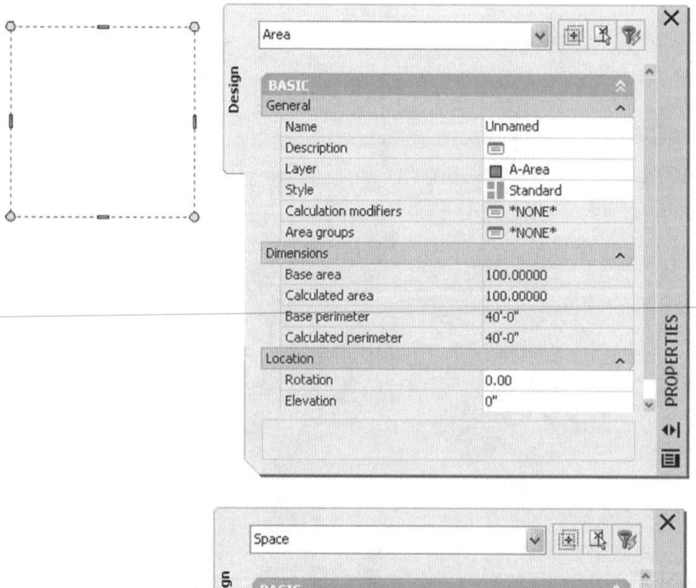

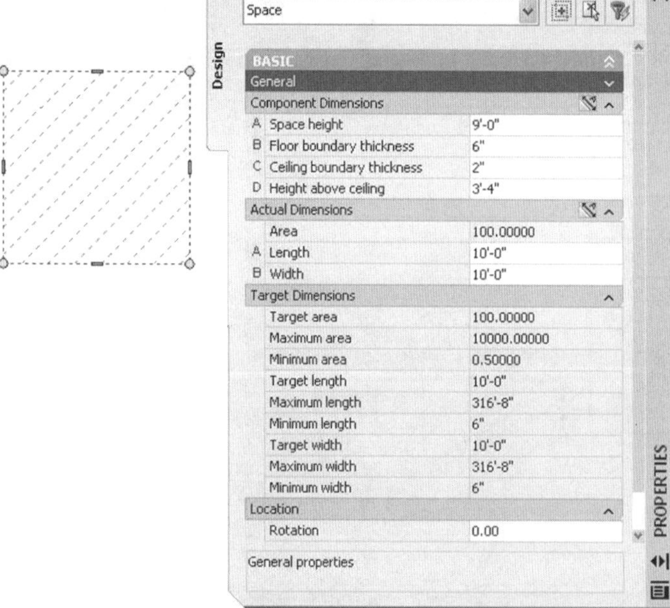

Figure 16.88 The space object in ADT 2007 has merged with the space boundary and area objects.

The Space Object Types

Space objects in 2007 now have three geometry types—the 2-D space type, the 3-D extrusion type, and the 3-D freeform type. The 2-D space objects are excellent for creating two-dimensional area, zonal, and block diagrams. They are a simplified version of the pre-2007 space object (Figure 16.89a). The 3-D extrusion space object provides further delineation of the space by including ceiling and floor finish thicknesses imbedded within the object (Figure 16.89b). Freeform space objects add flexibility to the extrusion space type since they can associate elaborately shaped spaces to their existing boundary walls (Figure 16.89c).

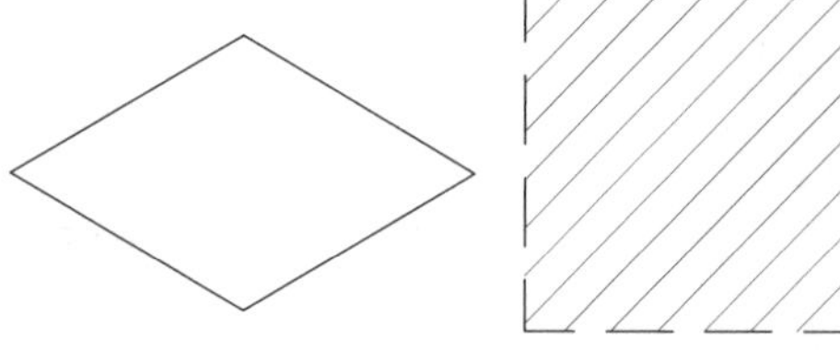

Figure 16.89a The 2-D space objects are excellent for creating two-dimensional area, zonal, and block diagrams.

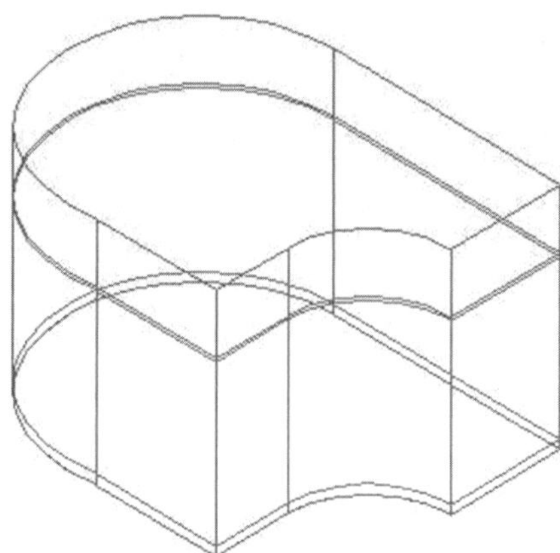

Figure 16.89b 3-D extrusion space objects provide further delineation of the space by including ceiling and floor finish thicknesses imbedded within the object.

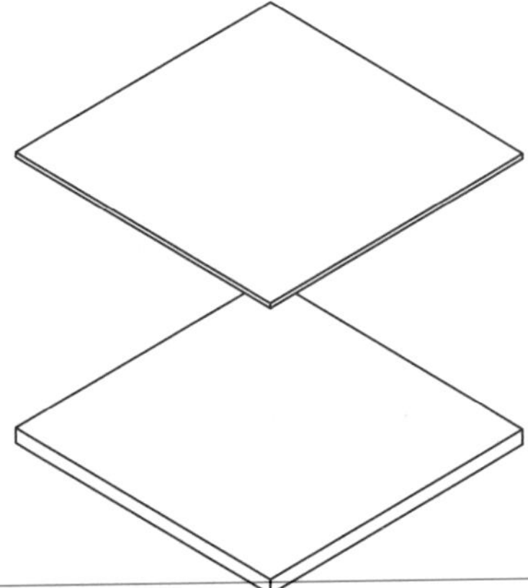

Figure 16.89c Freeform space objects can associate elaborately shaped spaces to their existing boundary walls.

A Brief Look at the Properties of the Space Object

Space objects in ADT 2007 have the ability to be either two-dimensional shapes or three-dimensional extrusions. Two-dimensional space objects have only a limited number of properties. They include style, name, offset boundary, length, and width. In addition to the properties linked to the 2-D space objects, 3-D space objects also include the ceiling height, floor and ceiling thicknesses, as well as floor and ceiling plenum dimensions.

Understanding Space Styles

Space styles can be used for a variety of purposes within the design process. In the programming stage, space styles can aid in the categorization of space types—that is, management offices, conference rooms, toilet rooms, and more. Within this categorization, square footage rules can be created—that is, all management offices cannot exceed 150 square feet. Space styles in ADT 2007 also help to calculate the gross, net, and usable spaces within a building.

> **Box 16.5**
>
> Gross-square footage refers to the overall area of a buildings footprint—level by level. Net square footage excludes wall thicknesses and columns. Usable space is even more specific; it excludes corridors and toilet rooms from its area calculations.

Finally, in the presentation stages of the design process, space styles are used to link material finishes to the ceiling and floor surfaces (Figure 16.90).

Placing a Space Object

Space objects are placed by specifying points directly on-screen, by converting AutoCAD linework, or by using existing ADT objects. If using the SpaceAdd tool, ADT prompts you to place the space object by specifying each corner of the space. Figures 16.91 through 16.93 demonstrate space object placement using each of the above options.

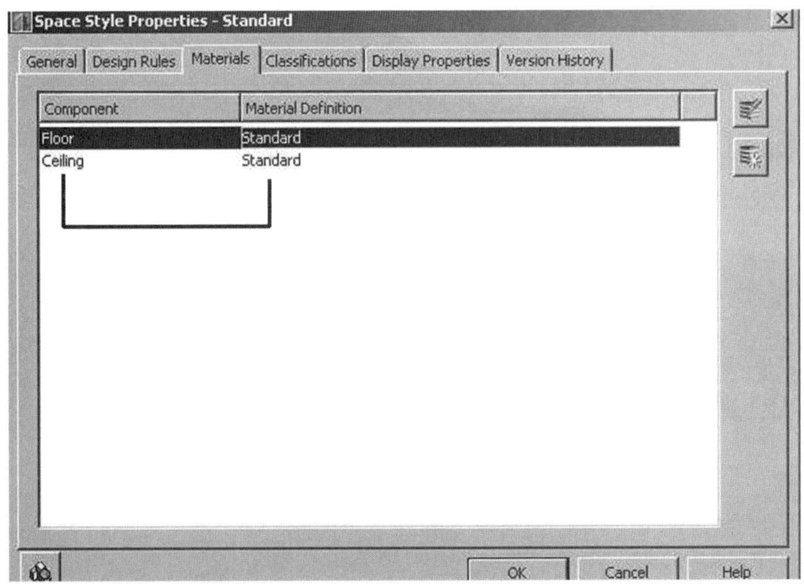

Figure 16.90 In the presentation stages of the design process, space styles can be used to link material finishes to the ceiling and floor surfaces.

Technique to Master **T16.91** Placing a Space Object by Specifying Points Directly On-screen

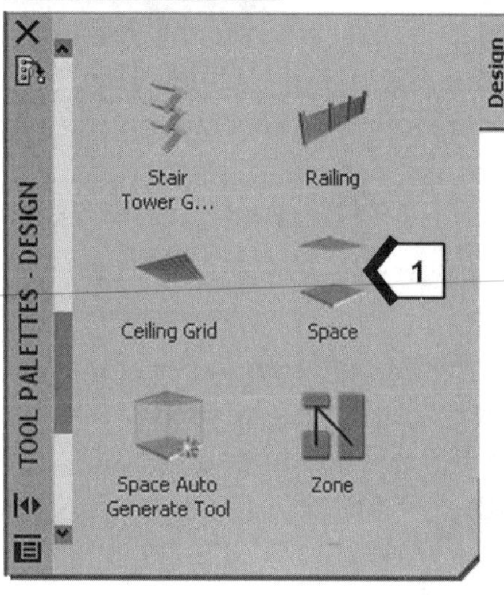

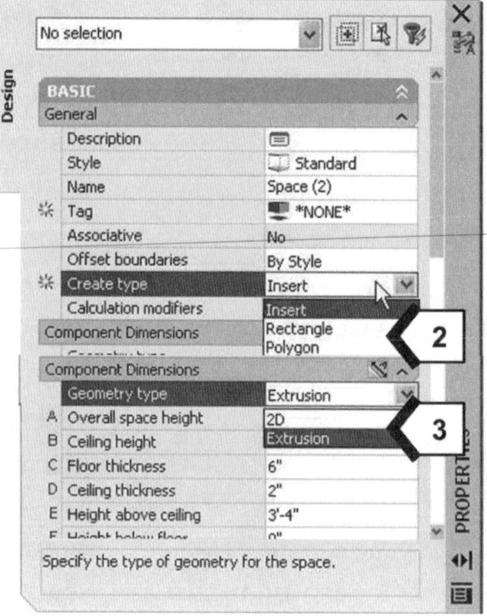

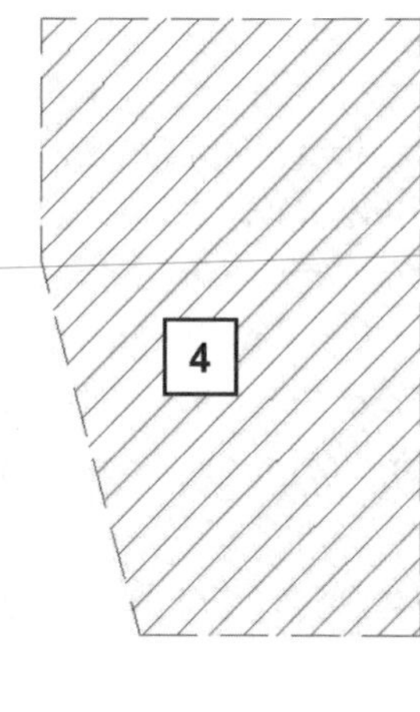

Figure 16.91

1	[Design Tool palette]	Select the Space tool.
2	[Properties palette>Create type]	Specify rectangle or polygon.
3	[Properties palette>Geometry type]	Specify the space type.
4	[Drawing Screen]	Begin drawing space object using a series of points to define the closed space boundary.

Technique to Master **T16.92** Placing a Space Object by Converting AutoCAD Linework

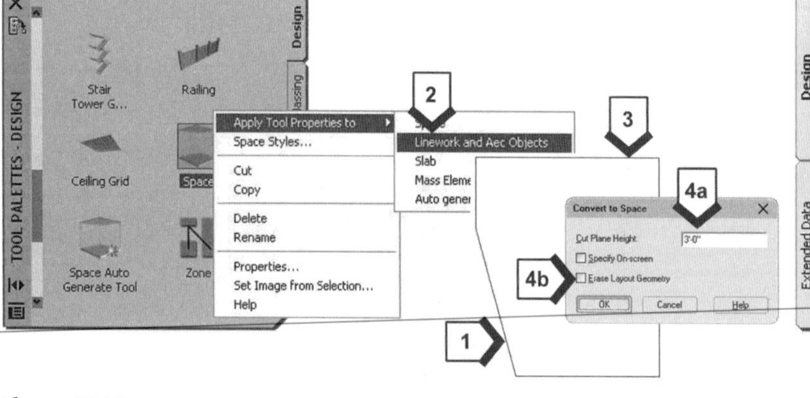

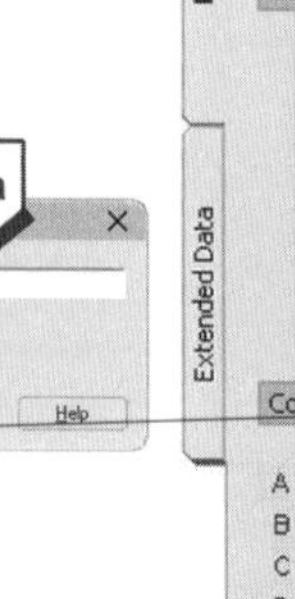

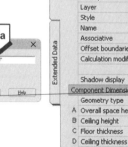

Figure 16.92

1	[Drawing Screen]	Draw closed rectangular or polygonal shape(s).
2	[Design Tool palette]	Select space tool, right-click, and choose the Apply Tool Properties to>Linework and AEC Objects.
3	[Drawing Screen]	Select closed rectangular or polygonal shape(s).
4a, 4b	[Convert to Space dialogue box]	Specify cut plane for space object. Specify whether or not to erase original polygon.
5	[Properties palette]	Change/verify the space style, space name, and space geometry type as well as component dimensions.

Technique to Master T16.93 Placing a Space Object by Using Existing ADT Objects

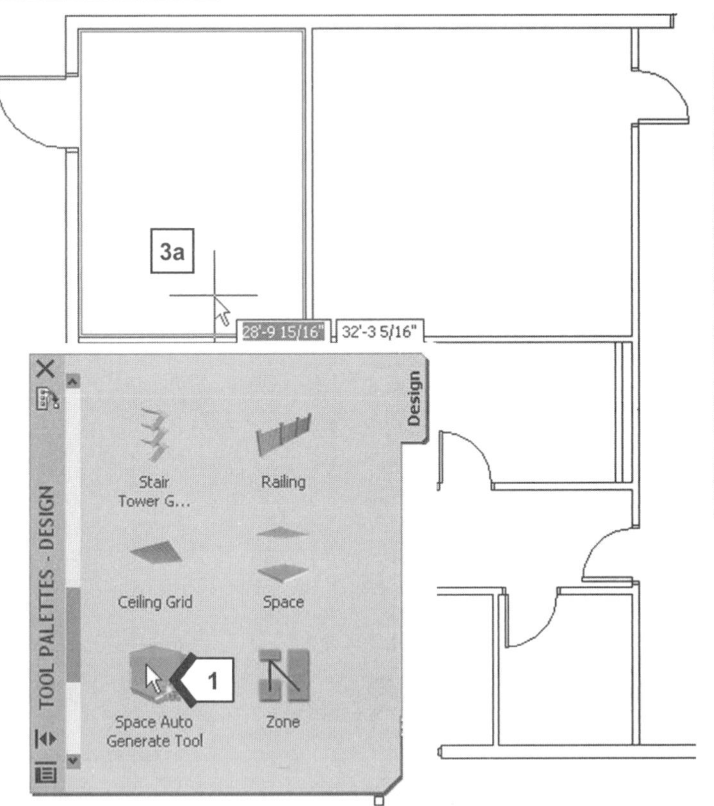

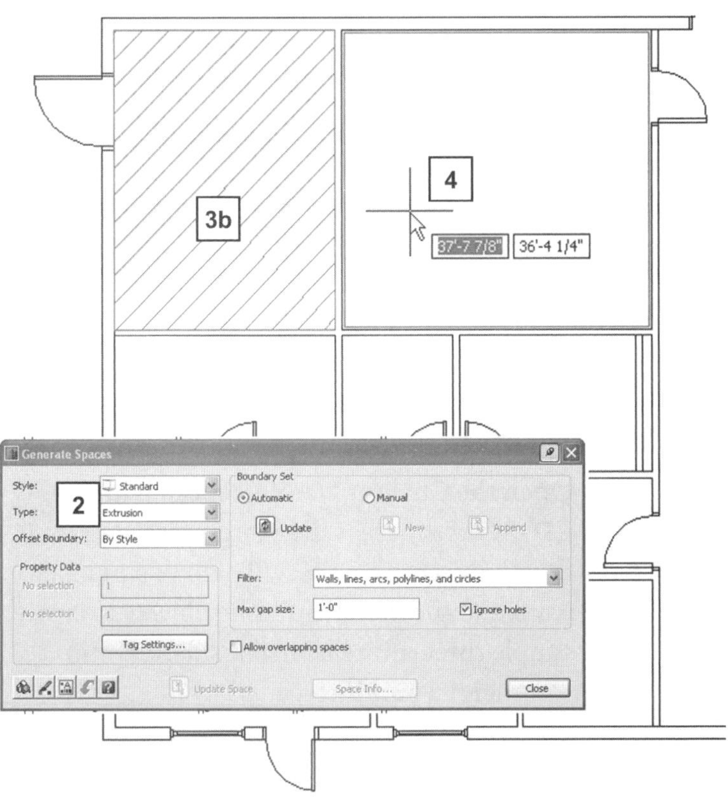

Figure 16.93

1	[Design Tool palette]	Select Space Auto Generate Tool.
2	[Generate Spaces dialogue box]	Specify space style and space type.
3a 3b	[Drawing Screen]	With cursor, hover over rooms with defined enclosures. The room should display a red rectangle or polygon to indicate space boundary. Left-click to place space object.
4	[Drawing Screen]	Repeat Step 3 until all spaces have been defined.

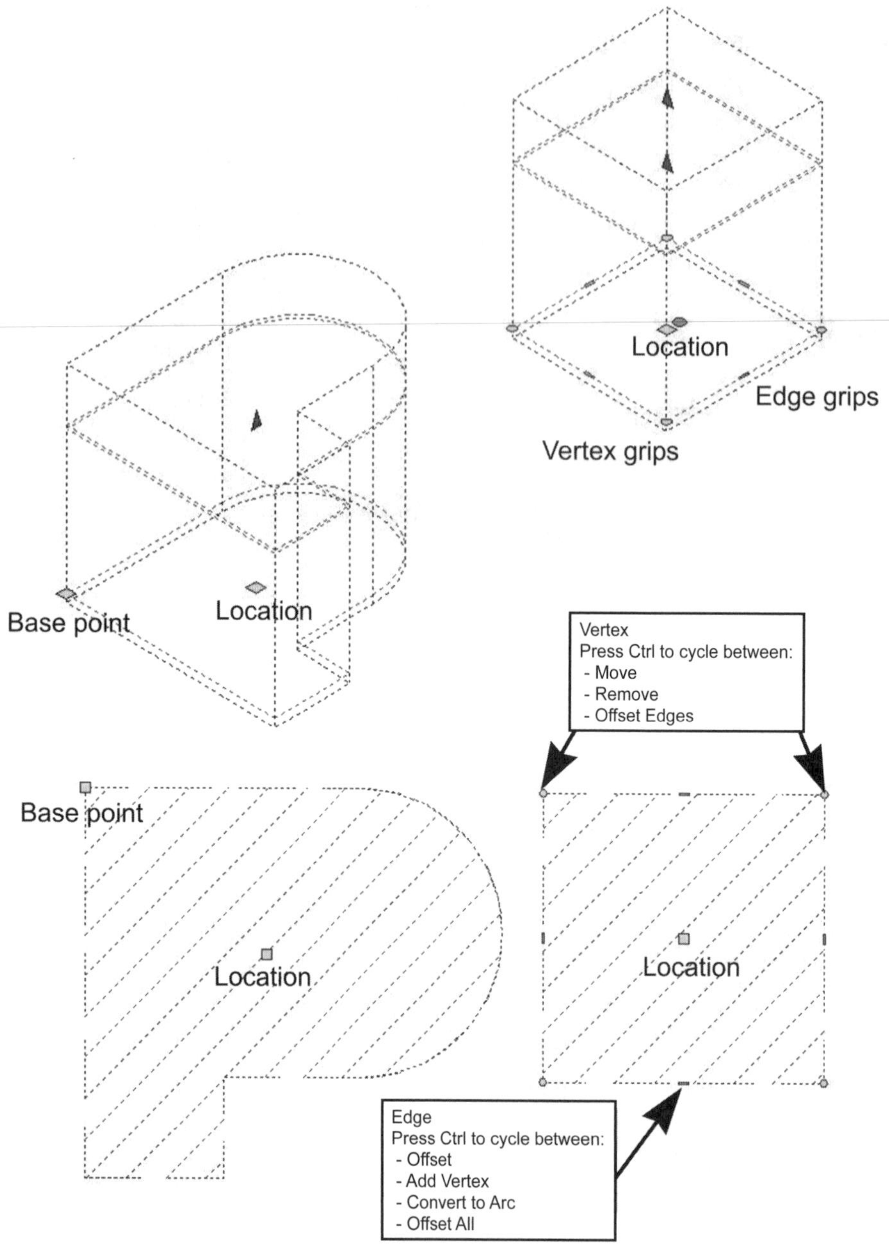

Figure 16.94 Grip points for space objects

Modify Space Objects

The specialty commands are found through a space object's right-click menu. Figure 16.94 illustrates each of the grip points for the three space types.

Chapter Exercises

Open the Chapter 16 folder located on the CD-ROM to access the exercises related to this chapter. Exercises will help you practice using the additional building objects to create simple three-dimensional residential and commercial buildings.

Part III

Drawing Technique

Drawing Craft 17

Objectives

This chapter introduces you to the concept and practice of drawing craft within the digital context. It emphasizes the importance of computer skill development through the lens of digital craftsmanship. It discusses the various characteristics that define digital craft. It also focuses on helping students understand the importance of digital craft within their design and drawing processes, as well as their professional development. Exercise scenarios within the chapter cultivate an increased understanding of the topics.

Drawing Craft

> In digital production, craft refers to the condition where people apply standard technological means to unanticipated or indescribable ends. Works of computer animation, geometric modeling and spatial databases get "crafted" when experts use limited software capacities resourcefully, imaginatively, and in compensation for the inadequacies of prepackaged, hard-coded operations. As a verb, "to craft" seemingly means to participate skillfully in some small-scale process. This implies several things. First, it affirms that the results of involved work still surpass the results of detached work. To craft is to care (*Abstracting Craft: The Practiced Digital Hand,* McCullough 1998).

This chapter introduces the concept and practice of drawing craft within the digital realm. Digital drawing craft, a concept inferred from Malcolm McCullough's *Abstracting Craft: The Practiced Digital Hand,* advocates for a change in attitude and outlook about the relationship of the designer to the software tools the designer uses. It also advocates the importance of digital mastery since the computer now plays such as huge role in the design and drawing process. The chapter makes the argument that digital drawing craft occurs when all the skills—technical, visual, and creative—are practiced and developed simultaneously.

There are seven distinct areas of focus that help to define digital drawing craft. While at times you may find it difficult to separate these areas, the goal of doing so is to help you identify the distinct areas of focus in most need of development. The areas of focus are listed below.

- Knowing what to draw
- Knowing how to draw
- Knowing how much to draw
- Knowing and applying the drawing conventions
- Drawing efficiently
- Drawing with confidence
- Drawing with passion
- Drawing output

Know What to Draw

Knowing what to draw is a critical area of drawing craft and plays a crucial role in creating good drawings. It means recognizing that various elements of drawings are not all alike and that information presented in one drawing might not be appropriate for another. In the author's experience, beginning students all too often overlook decisions regarding what to draw. Beginning students, because of their lack of experience, unduly rely on drawing conventions when completing project submission requirements. As a result, many digital drawings look formulaic and incomplete (Figure 17.1). Alternatively, there is also an inclination to overdraw. Despite its eventual plotted scale, every knob, latch, and curtain is represented in an effort to make the drawings as realistic as possible (Figure 17.2). In each of these scenarios, the students fail to understand the significance of information relevance.

This failure to recognize the significance of information relevance is most likely a failure for beginners to understand the significance of each established drawing type. Having the knowledge to make decisions on what to draw can come only from this understanding. In general, understanding the drawing type means the following:

- Knowing the objectives of each drawing type
- Understanding the drawing's role as part of a larger communication system
- Understanding each object's role in relation to the drawing
- Knowing the audience for the drawing
- Knowing the best output scale and size for the drawing

On the surface, this awareness might seem inconsequential. Nevertheless, successful drawings show an innate materialization of all of the above attributes.

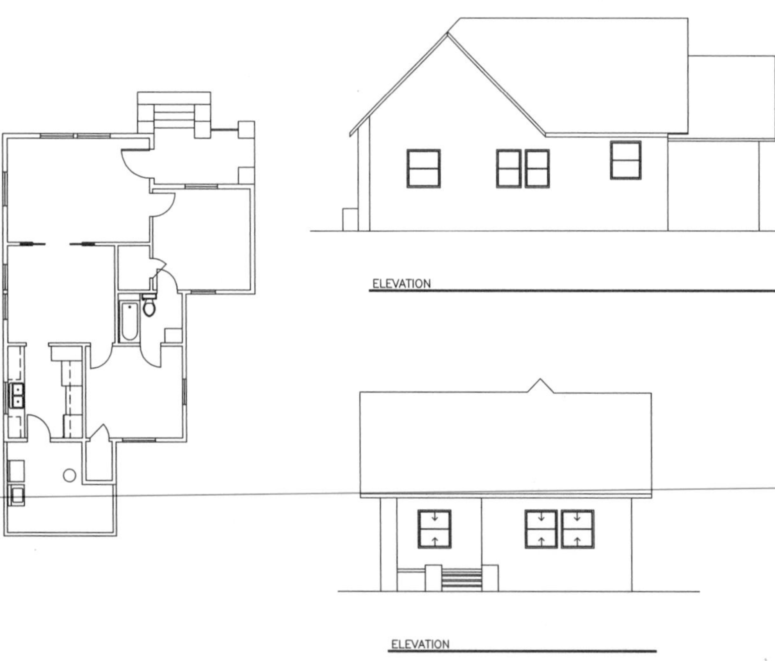

Figure 17.1 Beginner students who complete project submission requirements rely heavily on drawing conventions; therefore, many of their digital drawings look formulaic and incomplete.

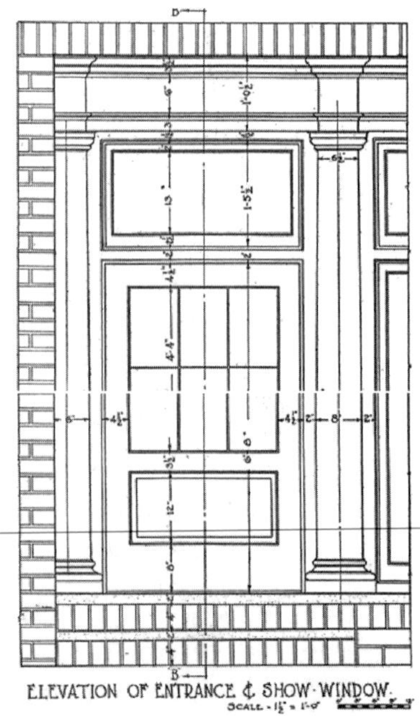

Figure 17.2 Despite its eventual plotted scale, every knob, latch, and curtain is represented in an effort to make the drawings as realistic as possible.

Box 17.1

Interior elevations are used to communicate how a wall will look. You would draw an interior elevation for a room only if the wall shows special building elements that cannot be communicated well with floor plans. Interior elevations that show only doors and windows do not communicate additional information. Examples of good interior elevation room choices include walls of toilet rooms, walls with custom casework, and kitchen walls because they usually need to communicate fixture and accessory locations as well as cabinetry appearance.

Know the Advantages and Objectives of the Drawing Type

Each orthographic drawing type carries its own advantages and disadvantages for communicating information. For example, floor plans cannot convey the height of objects while interior elevations cannot convey room sizes. While many of these might seem obvious, recognition of a drawing's advantages along with its responsibilities will always provide a yardstick to guide decisions of what to draw.

Understand the Drawing's Role as Part of a Larger Communication System

Drawings throughout the design process play several roles. At various stages of the design process, drawings can be used to explore and develop ideas, sell or market ideas, or communicate the evolution of an idea (Figure 17.3). In most cases, different drawing techniques and conventions are utilized that are specific to each role. Knowing what to draw closely correlates to the roles of each drawing within the specific design phase.

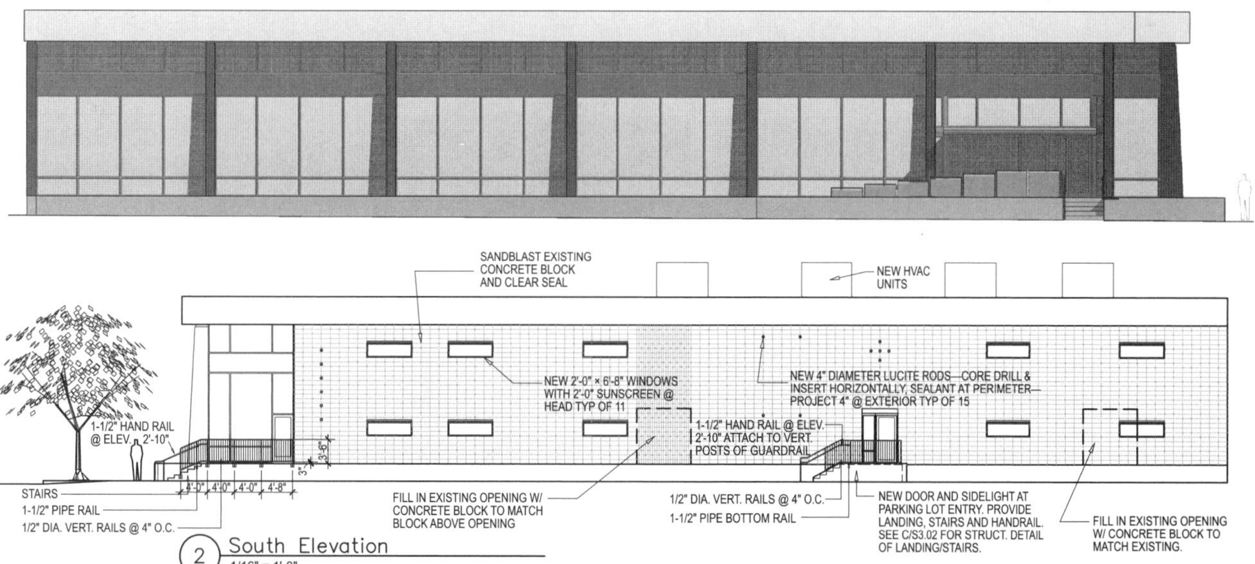

Figure 17.3 The top drawing is used for marketing material, and the bottom drawing communicates how the building is constructed.

Exterior Elevations: NLA Office Renovation, courtesy of Nacht & Lewis Architects, Sacramento, CA.

Understand Each Object's Role in Relation to the Drawing

A more formidable task is ranking objects within the drawing. An excellent practice to adopt is to prioritize each object in relation to the drawing's role and audience. By doing so, you will begin to develop the evaluative skills necessary for determining the correct information to draw (Figure 17.4).

Know the Audience for the Drawing

Linked to the drawing's role is the audience for which the drawing is intended. In professional practice, drawings communicate essential design and construction information to multiple audiences. Each audience type—contractors, clients, and/or peer reviewers—requires different types of information. Determining what information is needed for the audience type will also help to determine what to draw.

Know the Output Scale and Size of the Drawing

Plotting scale influences drawing craft in a number of ways. Knowing a drawing's plotting scale *before* the drawing is complete has a significant effect on what you draw and how much you draw. Smaller scaled drawings like 1/16 scale require less information and are used primarily to present an overall picture of a design (Figure 17.5). These drawings always refer to more detailed drawings. Standard scales between 1/8 and 1/4 provide a general view of the relationships between all elements of the design (Figure 17.6). Depending on the type of drawing and its audience, drawings plotted at these scales may have limited amounts of detail. Scales that are more than 1/4"=1'-0" are typically detailed and purposeful.

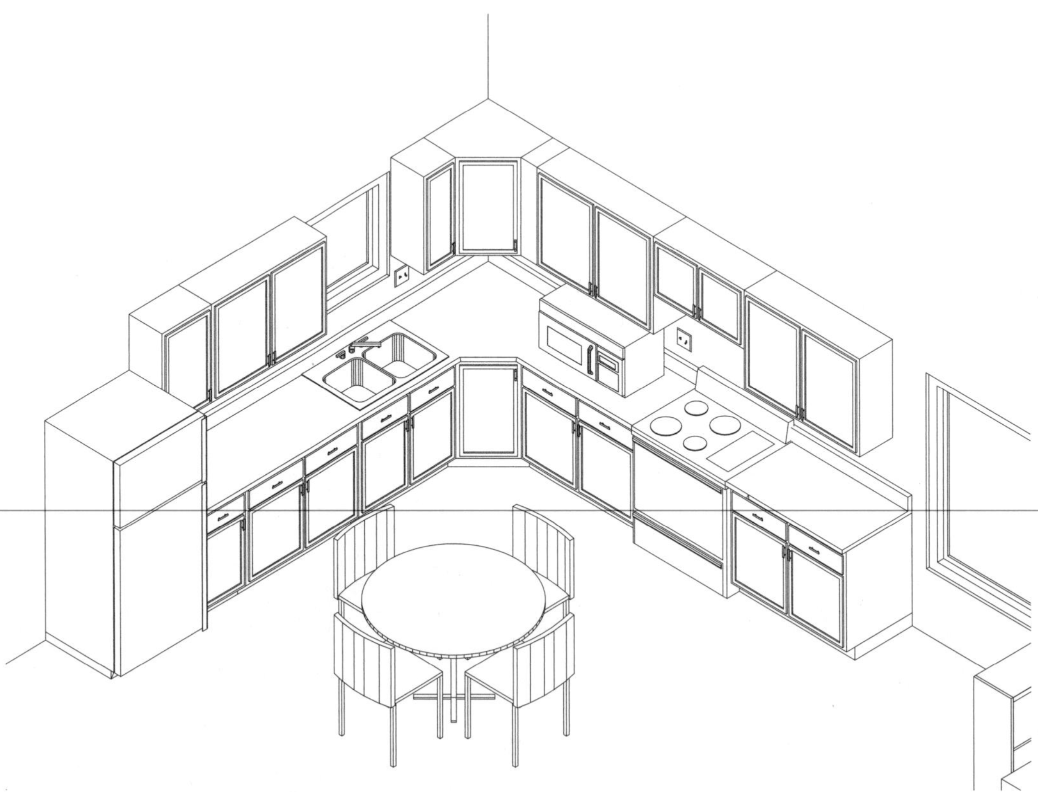

Figure 17.4 In the example, the interior elevation drawing is used for communicating the location and sizes of prebuilt cabinet sections.

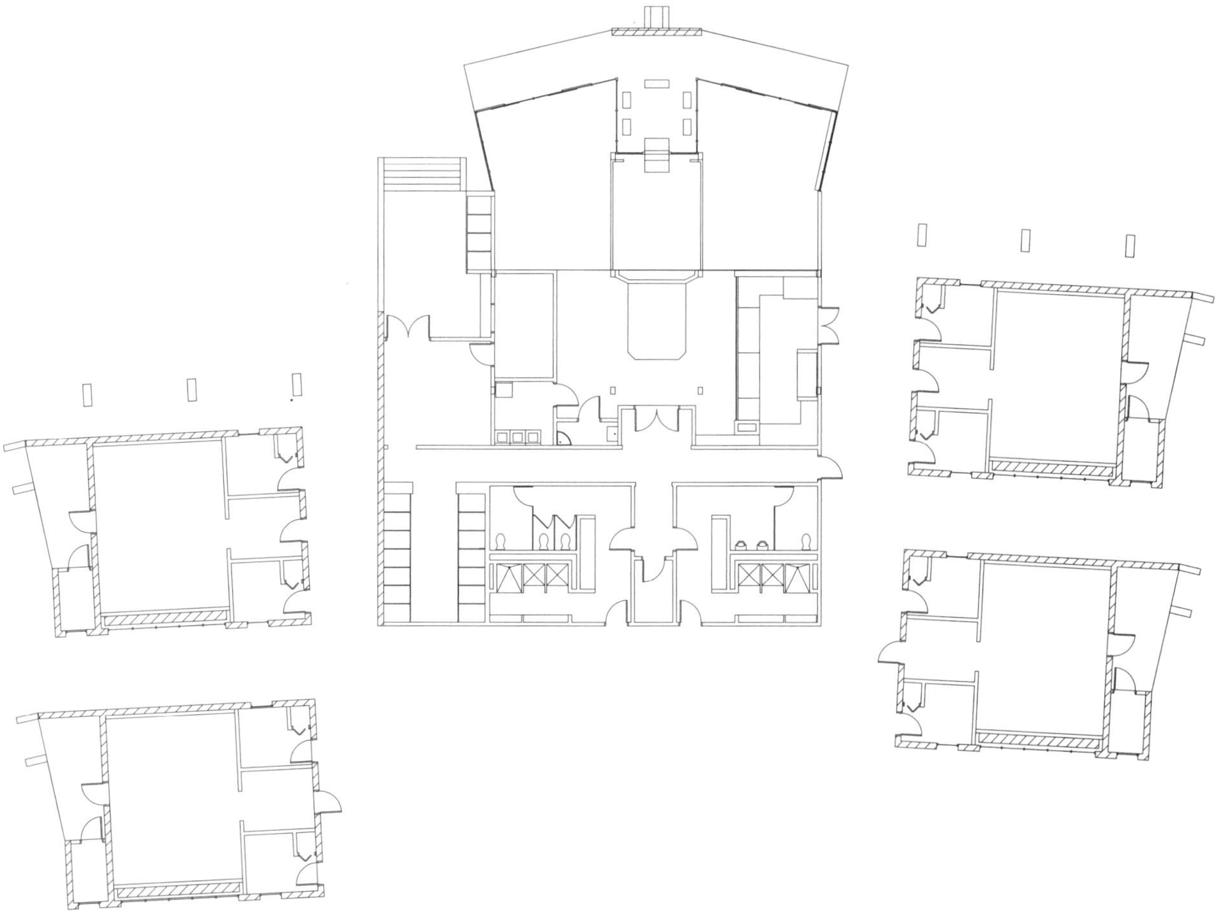

Figure 17.5 Smaller scaled drawings such as 1/16 scale require less information and are used primarily to present an overall picture of a design. This sample floor plan shows how all of the buildings for the project relate to one another on the site.

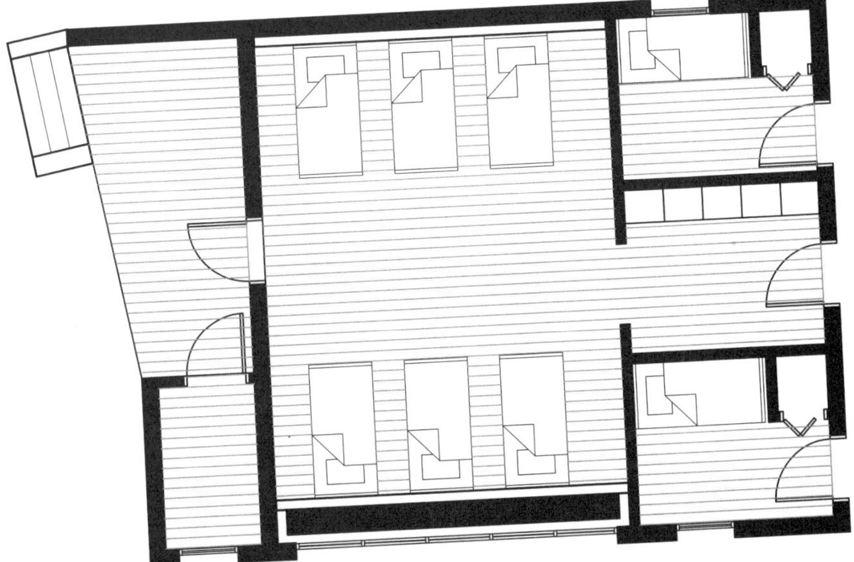

Figure 17.6 Standard scales between 1/8 and 1/4 provide a general view of the relationships among all elements of the design. This sample floor plan shows the individual building—its walls, windows, doors, and furniture placements.

For the most part, projects given to students within the design studio context include required scales as part of their submission requirements. You, however, should be aware that drawing scale plays a large role in how designs are communicated. While beginning with the standard scales is good practice, you should always question whether the selected scale is an appropriate fit for thoroughly communicating design intentions.

Scenario #1

You are on vacation at the site of the famous Leaning Tower of Pisa. Without access to any type of camera, what orthographic drawing type (as well as the drawing information) would you draw to convince a person (who has never visited or seen pictures) of its three unique features? Be very specific. Note your reasons for choosing these features.

Scenario #2

You are a home owner. You've hired a professional to build a custom bathroom vanity where the sink and sink counter are at a different level from the rest of the vanity counter. You only have the time to create one drawing that explains the design and its installation method. What information is most relevant for the professional to do his or her job properly? What factors were used as the basis of your decision? What other drawings might you include if you could?

Scenario #3

How could the drawing in Figure 17.7 be changed to only show the information needed to communicate your design idea to your client?

Know How to Draw

Another significant characteristic of drawing craft focuses on the act of drawing itself since it plays such a fundamental role in how interior designers communicate. Drawings—both presentation and construction—need to be consistent, accurate, and legible. Specific to this text's focus, knowing how to draw thus refers to knowing how to use the digital tools and techniques to accurately represent objects and building systems.

Combined with knowing AutoCAD's and Architectural Desktop's tools and techniques, visualization is an essential characteristic of learning how to draw. Visualization is the ability to create a mental image and then selectively draw the characteristics of an object that create a graphic resemblance (Figure 17.8). Because learning to draw is so closely tied to a student's visualization skills, many experts agree that they cannot be separated.

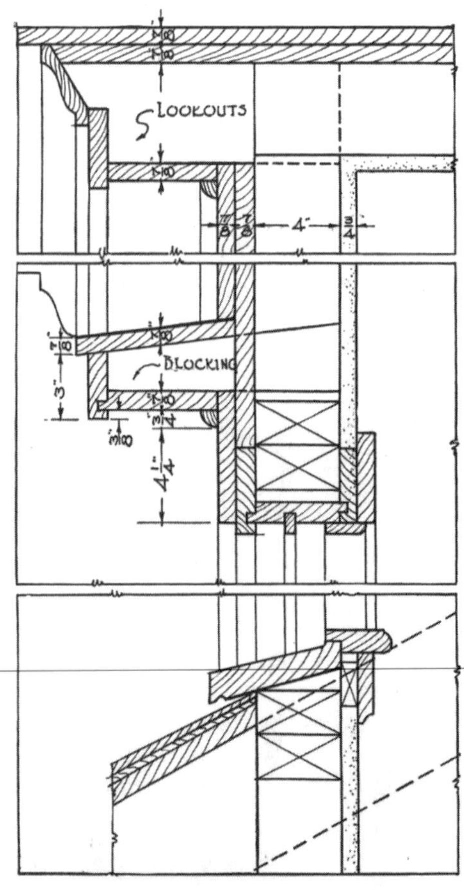

Figure 17.7 How could this drawing be changed to show only the information needed to communicate your design idea to your client?

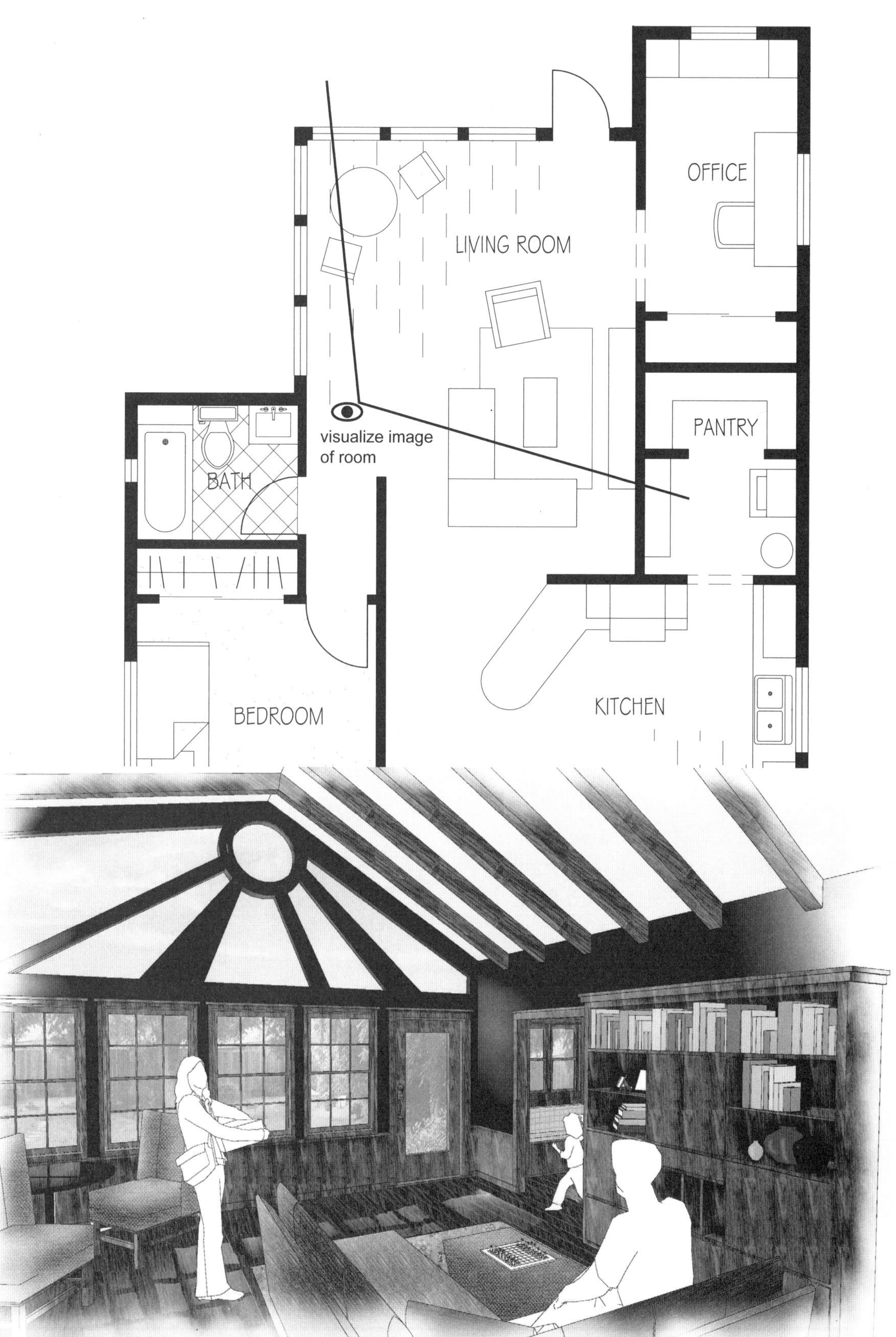

Figure 17.8 Visualization is the ability to see and then draw specific characteristics of an object. The example shows how a perspective can be imagined and then drawn from a floor plan using the skill of visualization.

Student Project: Smith House Renovation, courtesy of Brianna Bennett.

Learning to draw requires practice. Currently most digital drawing occurs during the development of design projects within the studio setting. However, digital mastery requires practice beyond the studio project. As a beginning student, make computer drawing a part of your daily routine. It is useful to use the analogy of the artist sketchbook where unstructured drawings are created regularly to develop the artist's ability to see better (Figure 17.9).

With the adoption of daily drawing and visualization development drills, digital mastery can be achieved quickly; the usual reliance on the creativity and complexity of studio projects for skill development is not needed.

This idea is not unique. Skillful practice can be found in many disciplines where skill development and retention are critical to success. It is especially evident in disciplines where the mind-body connection is crucial. If you look at the science of sports training today, coaches establish regimented training sessions centered on skill improvement and retention. Professionals and serious amateurs alike are required to perform daily drills before the main body of the practice begins. The belief in skill mastery through repetition and focused technique exercises is one of the main premises within this field.

Figure 17.9 Artists use sketchbooks to jot down ideas and to develop their visualization skills.

Scenario #4

Without any visual or written assistance (the actual objects or photographs and drawings of the objects), draw the following familiar residential objects in plan and/or elevation. Try to be precise with their dimensional properties.

- A wood double French door
- A double-hung window
- An armoire

Scenario #5

Can you detect the eight visualization mistakes in the floor plan in Figure 17.10? Use the isometric to aid in finding the mistakes in the floor plan.

Know How Much to Draw

Reality in the drawing process is represented differently, depending on the type of drawing and the use of the drawing. Presentation drawings tend to generalize reality, while construction drawings tend toward a graphic representation that communicates build ability.

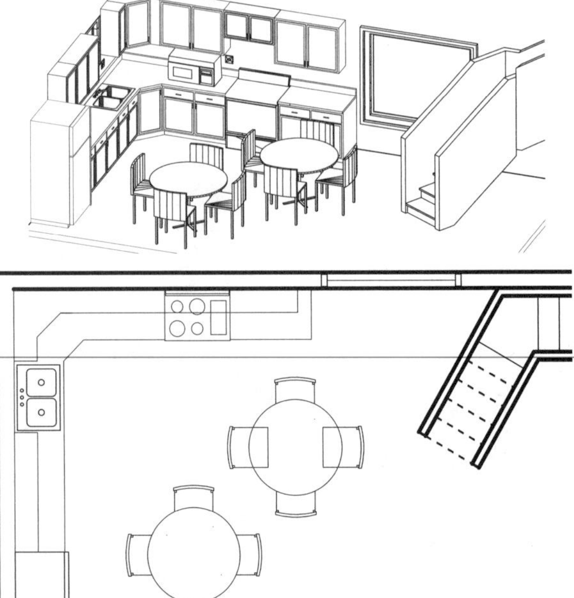

Figure 17.10 Finding drawing and visualization mistakes in a floor plan

Coincident with knowing how to draw is knowing how much to draw. This is the ability to discern the amount of detailing necessary for the object and/or the drawing's purpose.

Let's look at an example presentation perspective used to depict the atmosphere and architecture of a space. The perspective in Figure 17.11 shows very little detail and inadequately reveals the desired information about the space. Figure 17.12, however, communicates knowledge about the individual building elements and their respective finishes, which in turn communicates spatial atmosphere. On the other extreme, too much detail runs the danger of diluting the message, as well as creating drawing illegibility.

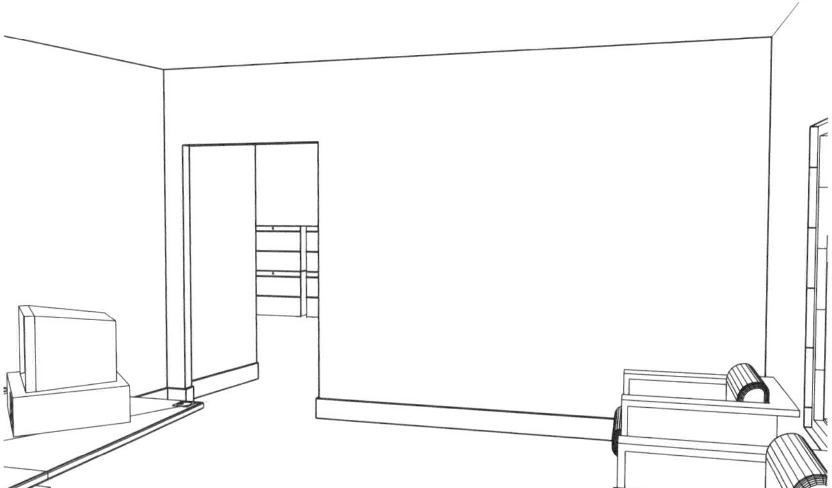

Figure 17.11 This perspective shows very little detail and inadequately reveals the desired information about the space.

Figure 17.12 This perspective communicates knowledge about the individual building elements and their respective finishes, which in turn communicates spatial atmosphere.
Student Project: Smith House Renovation, courtesy of Andrea Pabon.

As a beginning student, you might find it helpful to consciously map out the reason for and amount of detailing used in each drawing. With time and experience, you will find that knowing how much to draw will become as ingrained as the act of drawing itself. Listed below are some tips and strategies to help develop this area of drawing craft. Chapter 18 also goes into further detail about specific drawing types.

In general, use drawing detail to do the following:

- Indicate that the object is important to the drawing's overall purpose
- Make an object identifiable
- Show the stylistic characteristics of an object
- Show material and finish characteristics of an object
- Articulate connections between building systems and/or dissimilar materials

As beginner students, you tend to produce multiple plots to find the right amount of detail. Less wasteful approaches include the following:

1. Use drawing conventions and company standards to get a beginning sense of the amount of detail necessary for the scale you are thinking of.
2. Refer to visual handbooks that provide a good database of visual examples.
3. Always be willing to experiment—especially with presentation drawings. Graphic information is not always best presented by staying within the realm of convention.
4. Always draft using lineweights and linestyles. Do not wait until the drawing is complete to apply line conventions. They are a crucial part of determining how to draw.
5. Save paper! Only print out the portion of the drawing where there is a question regarding detail or legibility. Always print first drafts to the .pdf format to locate glaring lineweight and detail issues.

Scenario #6

What would be the best plotting scales for drawing 170401.dwg found on the CD-ROM?

Scenario #7

What audience might this drawing be targeted for? What information could be deleted or not shown because of its irrelevance?

Scenario #8

Given the objects in drawing 170402.dwg found on the CD-ROM, what information would you add or delete to make the objects all drawn consistently in importance?

Know and Apply the Drawing Conventions

Because drawing is one of the primary means to communicate design ideas, it requires a developed language that can be understood across all of the design disciplines. Drawing conventions provide the common language that allows the shared understanding of information within these disciplines. Drawing conventions also contribute to the meaning within drawings. Experienced professionals are easily able to read the spatial qualities of a design simply by reading its drawings. Each convention is a visual clue to how the drawn objects translate to real space.

Among other qualifications, a designer must memorize of all the standard drawing, drafting, and symbol conventions used for each orthographic type. This memorization process should start at the very beginning of a designer's education. Chapters 18 through 20 provide checklists for these conventions to start your learning process.

Some Typical Functions of Drawing/Drafting Conventions

- Establish scale, proportion, and dimensions so that buildings can be evaluated and constructed.
- Establish symbols to differentiate and identify parts of a building.
- Establish common views so that buildings can be evaluated and constructed.
- Establish methods for evaluating a building quantitatively and qualitatively.

Scenario #9

Identify the function of each drawing and symbol convention used in Figure 17.13.

Drawing Efficiently

Drawing efficiently refers to the ability to quickly and proficiently complete a drawing or drafting task. In the context of this book, drawing efficiently means using the digital tools and techniques in a productive manner. It is important to recognize that knowing how and what to draw does not automatically imply drawing proficiency. It is a characteristic that originates through a combination of tool dexterity and visualization development.

Since a large part of drawing efficiency incorporates cognitive operations, to improve the way you approach computer-aided design, you should first carefully think through techniques and scenarios before tackling them in drawing form. Scenarios #10 and #11 follow.

Scenario #10

Figure 17.14 shows before and after drawings. Given the center lines for a dining room table and a block definition chair, create the dining room placement set with the most efficient method available using AutoCAD. Before trying to complete the drawing task on-screen, first write down the sequence of steps that are needed to accomplish the task.

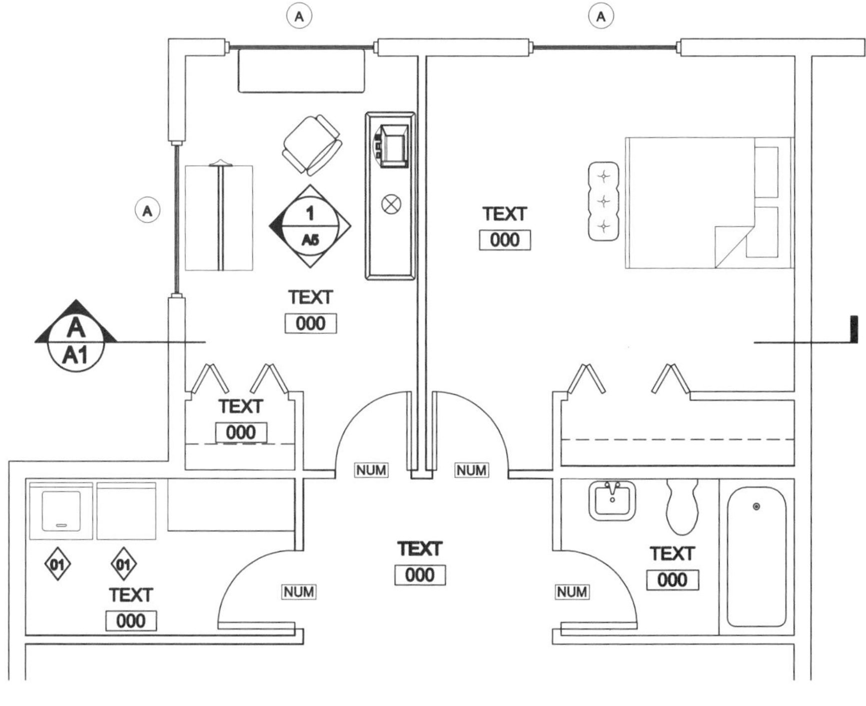

Figure 17.13 Drawing showing common symbols

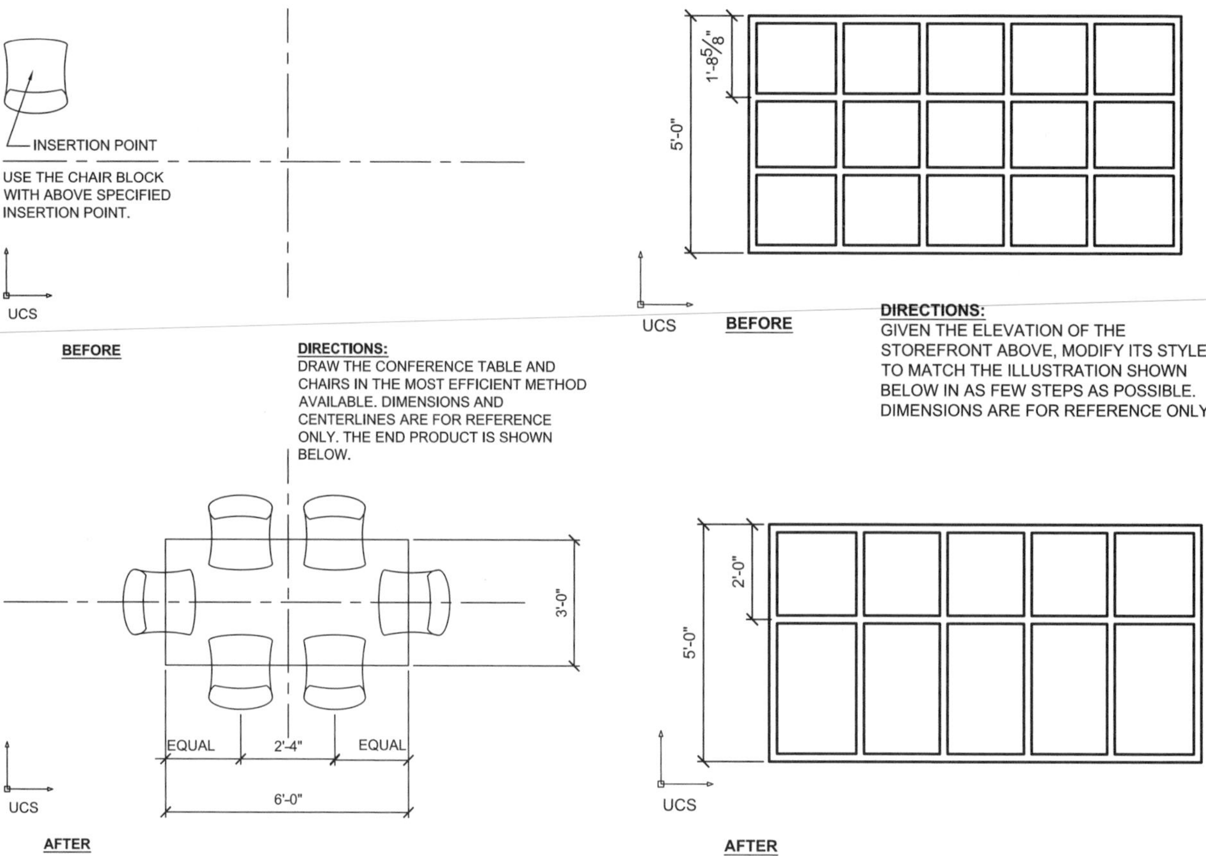

Figure 17.14 Creating a dining room placement set using AutoCAD

Figure 17.15 Modifying a storefront elevation

Scenario #11

Figure 17.15 shows before and after drawings. Given the elevation of a storefront system before, revise the design of the storefront system to match the after illustration. Write down the sequence of steps that are needed to accomplish the task before trying to complete it on-screen.

Draw with Confidence

Drawing confidence is significant to drawing craft because it incorporates the self-assurance of knowing any drawing challenge can be undertaken with a minimum of frustration. Drawings created with self-assurance always emanate. Even digital drawings reveal the skill and confidence of their maker. While a substantial part comes from experience, drawing confidence can still be greatly improved through motivation and perseverance. Once digital mastery is achieved, you can move beyond the conventional limits of what CAD can do and develop alternative design methodologies.

Drawing with Passion

A final key component of drawing craft is the passion one puts into the drawing process. Passion is the emotional bond that is created with a project and the drawings that come out of the project. It continually motivates you to explore design possibilities and solve design challenges. It brings intensity and expressiveness to all drawing types.

Passion is not a skill like the other areas of drawing craft. However, it can be cultivated as much as any skill. Cultivating passion in the drawing process means finding the mechanisms of drawing that bring enjoyment and inspiration and using these mechanisms to sustain you through each project of a lifelong career.

Drawing Techniques I: Approaches to 2-D Drawing/Drafting Craft

18

Objectives

This chapter builds on your knowledge of the practice of digital drawing craft by concentrating on the main orthographic drawings used to communicate design intentions. The lesson ties the various characteristics of digital craft to the elements of each drawing type, including floor plans, ceiling plans, roof plans, and sections and elevations. Exercise scenarios within the chapter cultivate an increased understanding of each of the orthographic view types. End-of-chapter exercises provide practice in drawing the five orthographic view types.

Drawing Craft in Floor Plans

In new construction, architectural floor plans typically show the overall size of the building, its setbacks, as well as the window and door locations for that level (Figure 18.1). If there are columns and/or structural bracing, they are also shown along with a structural grid (Figure 18.2). Both new and renovation projects on the interior show placement of interior walls, stairs, doors, windows, casework, and sometimes furniture and equipment (Figure 18.3).

Drawing Floor Plans Efficiently

Now that you have become familiar with the basics of floor plan constructions, its time to incorporate efficient drawing practices into your arsenal. Depending on how a project is started, the floor plan drawing sequence can have many variations. If you begin a project manually, then at some point you essentially draft it digitally within the computer. As a drafting exercise, start drawing the areas of the plan that are directing the overall design idea (Figure 18.4). Figure 18.5 illustrates one example for laying out floor plans.

Know How Much to Draw: The Relationship of Scale to Drawing Craft in Floor Plans

As introduced in Chapters 1 and 17, plotting scale has a significant impact on the amount of detail that is drawn in floor plans. In professional practice, plotting scales for floor plans have been standardized within each discipline. Typically, the size of the project is a common indicator of the appropriate plotting scale for a floor plan.

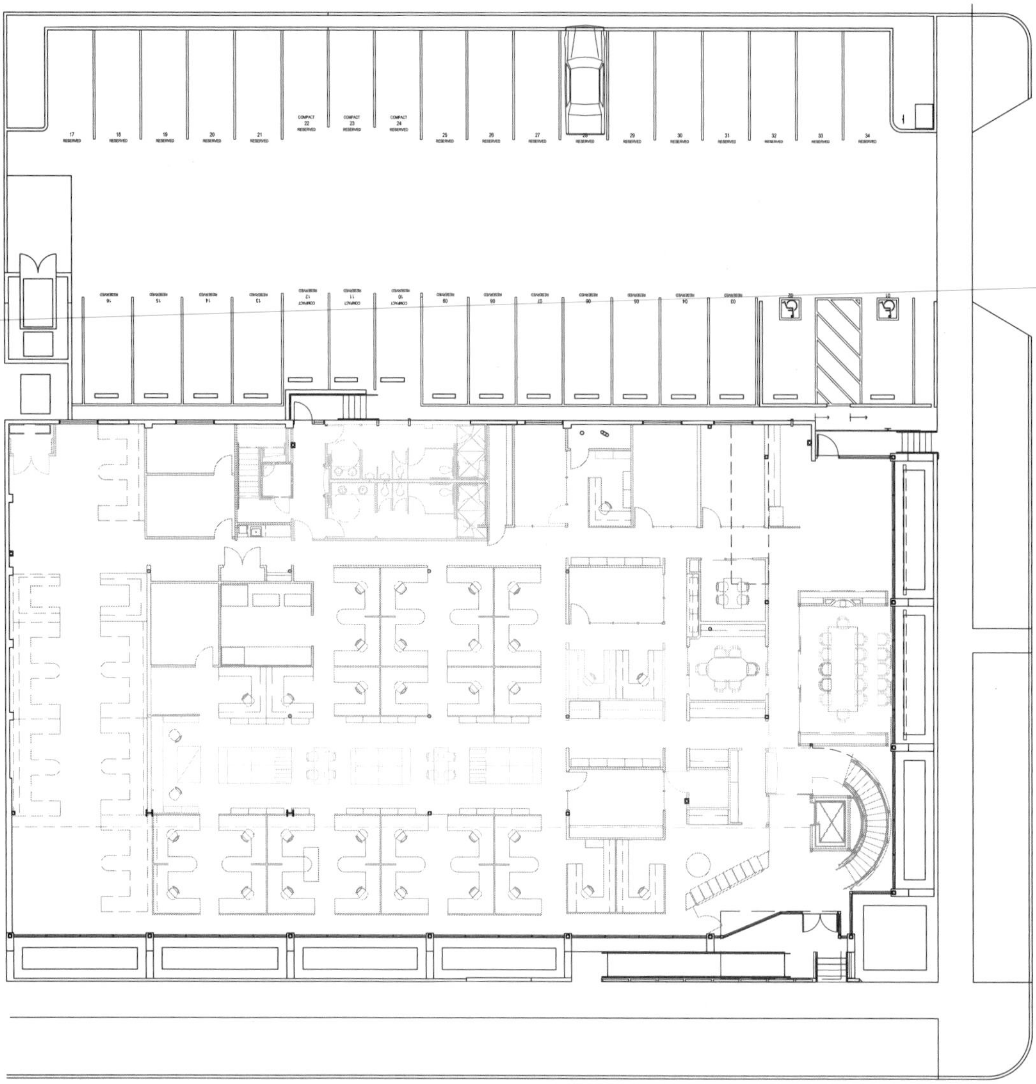

Figure 18.1 In new construction, the exterior building, including its setbacks, doors, windows, and adjoining site work is shown.

Drawing: First Floor Plan. NLA Office Renovation, courtesy of Nacht & Lewis Architects, Sacramento, CA.

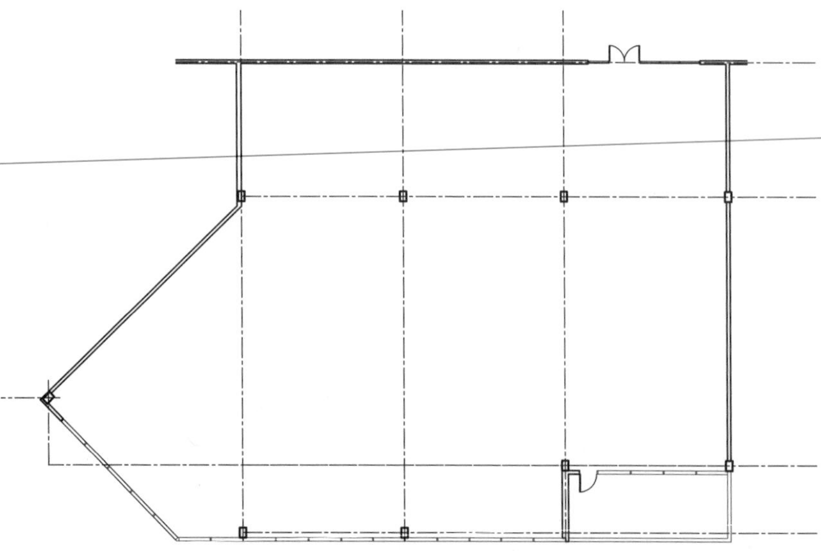

Figure 18.2 If columns and bracing are used, they are also shown in floor plans.

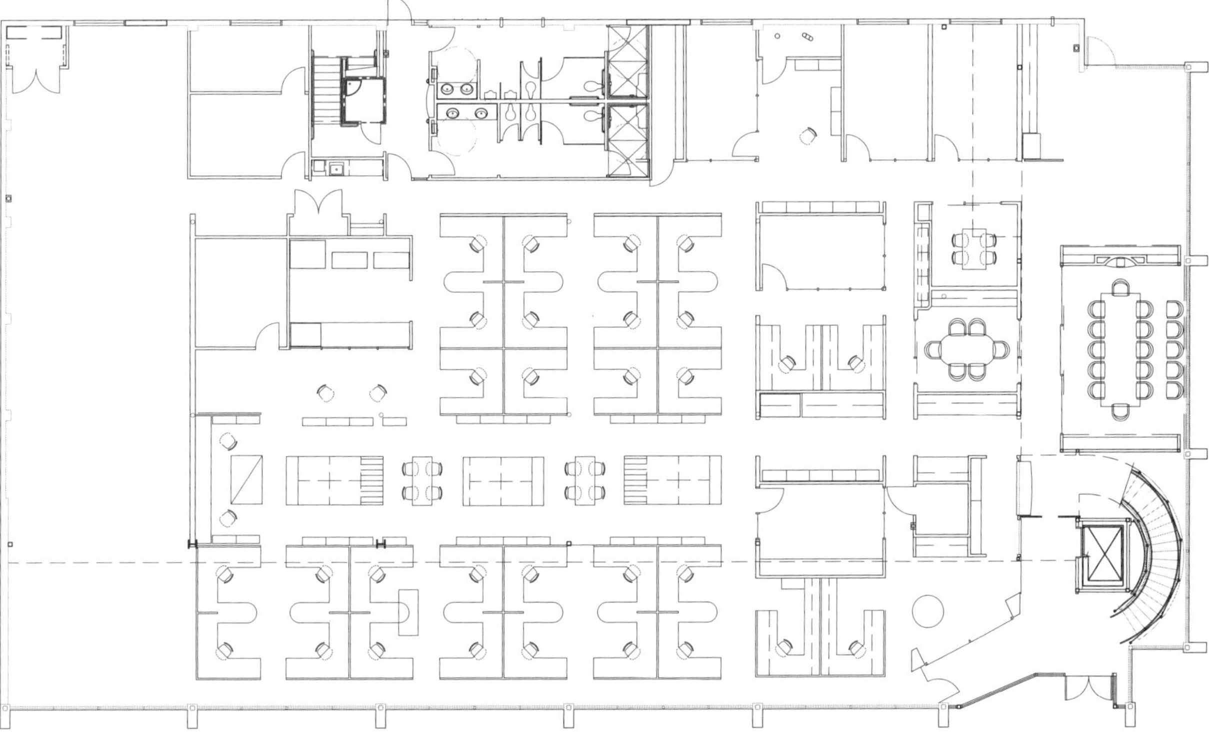

Figure 18.3 In new or renovation construction, floor plans show interior walls, stairs, doors, windows, casework, and sometimes furniture and equipment.

Drawing: First Floor Plan. NLA Office Renovation, courtesy of Nacht & Lewis Architects, Sacramento, CA.

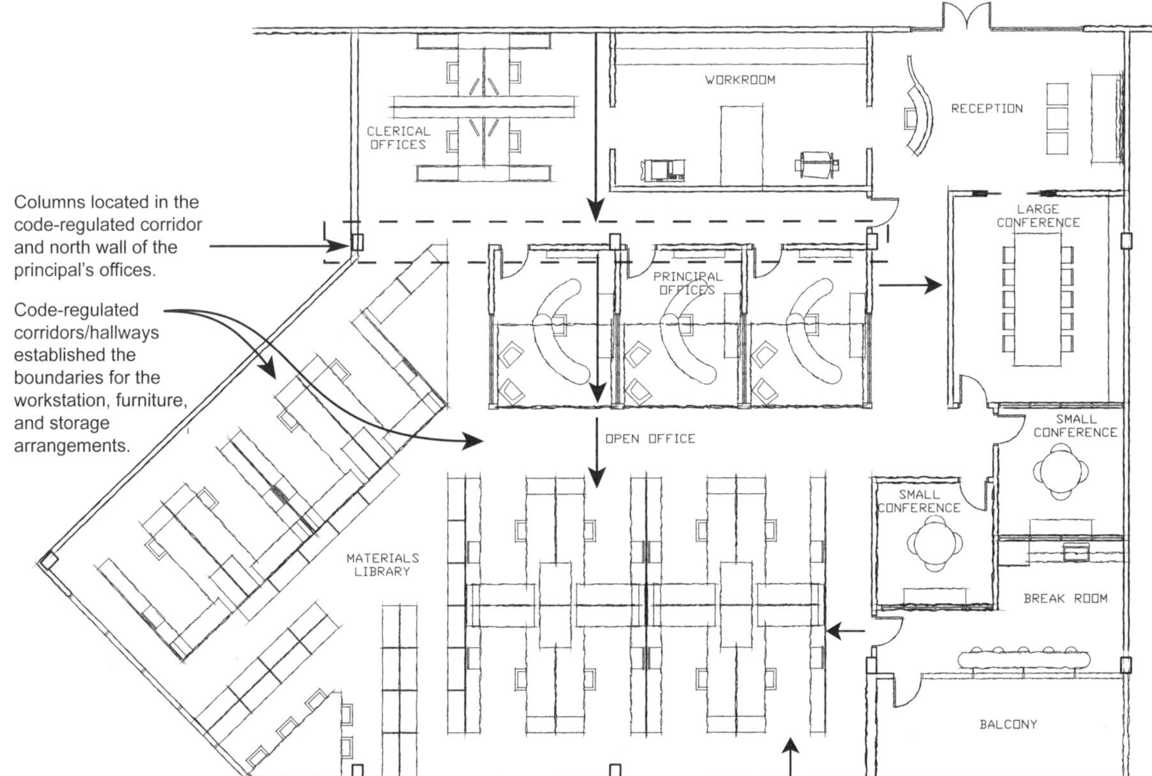
Columns located in the code-regulated corridor and north wall of the principal's offices.
Code-regulated corridors/hallways established the boundaries for the workstation, furniture, and storage arrangements.
WORKROOM
RECEPTION
CLERICAL OFFICES
LARGE CONFERENCE
PRINCIPAL OFFICES
OPEN OFFICE
SMALL CONFERENCE
SMALL CONFERENCE
MATERIALS LIBRARY
BREAK ROOM
BALCONY

Figure 18.4 When transferring an existing design to CAD, begin with the dimensions or areas that are driving the design. The example student project shows that besides the exterior boundaries, the existing column locations as well as the code regulated corridors are driving the placement of the principal offices, conference rooms, and open office workstations.

Student Project: Office Renovation, courtesy of Barbara Rinehart.

Technique to Master **T18.05** Laying Out an Existing Building with AutoCAD

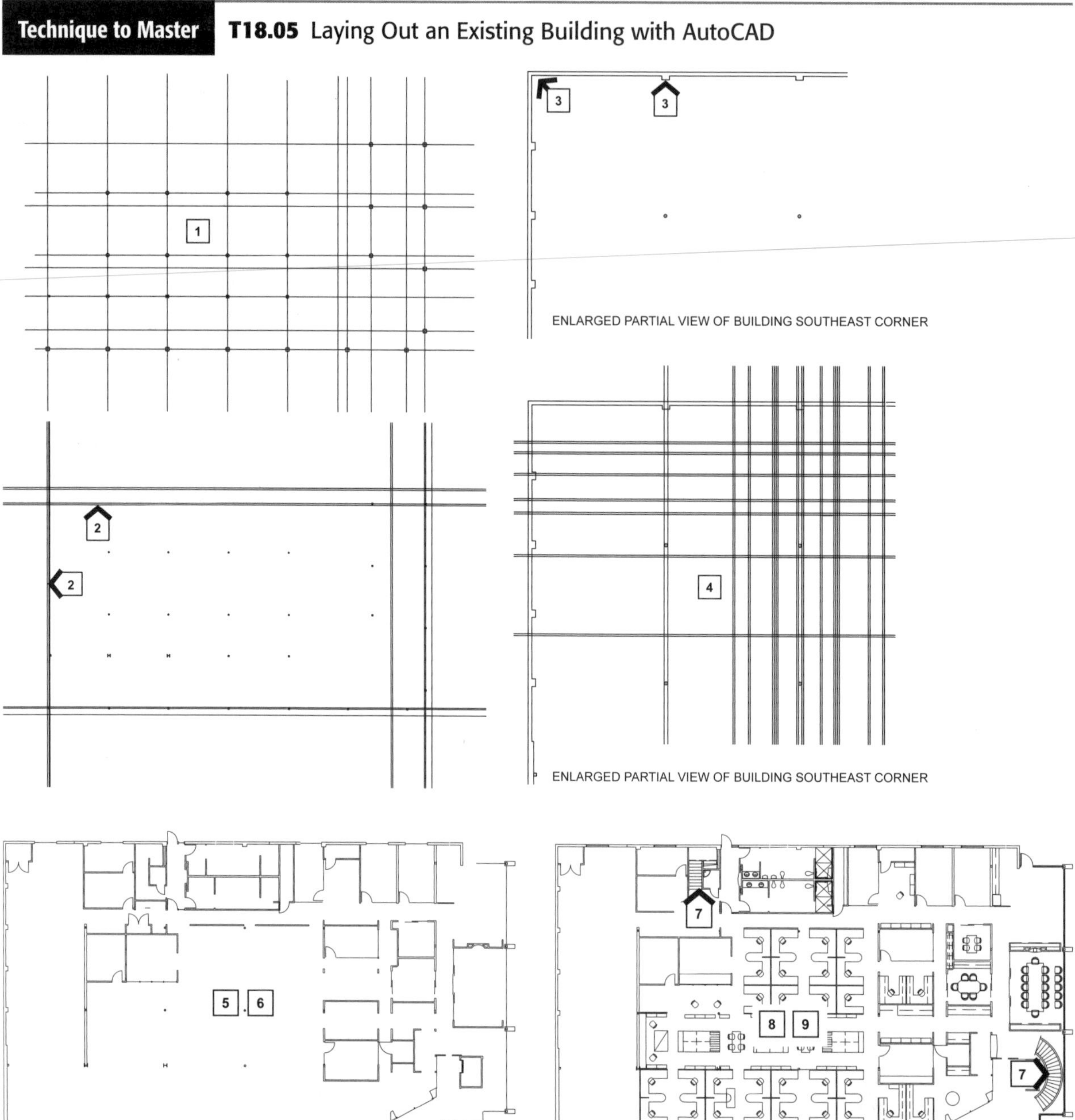

Figure 18.5

1	If there are columns, lay out the column grid structure, then draw/insert the columns. Columns are always centered within the grid structure.
2	If using AutoCAD, use construction lines to lay out exterior walls in order of massing priority. If using ADT, use a combination of rectangles and lines to create these shapes. If using ADT, continue by converting this linework to walls and/or curtain walls.
3	Clean up exterior wall corners.
4	Lay out all interior walls.
5	Clean up interior wall corners.
6	Locate the position of all openings. Draw all doors and windows.
7	Draw stairs, if applicable.
8	Draw/insert all casework, fixtures, appliances, equipment, and furniture.
9	Finally, add any additional detail including symbols, notes, and floor hatching. Refer to the Floor Plan Visual checklist later in this chapter.

Floor Plans and Their Common Scales

For most small projects, floor plans are plotted at 1/4" scale since they can easily fit on the standard sheet sizes. Residential and a limited amount of commercial and retail projects fit neatly within this category. With larger building footprints, floor plans are plotted at 1/8" scale with 1/4" scale enlargements of important areas. Building footprints that exceed the 30 × 42-inch plot sheet size at 1/8" scale are plotted at 1/16" = 1'-0". Most smaller-scaled drawings at 1/16" scale reference enlarged partial floor plan sheets. Figure 18.6 illustrates the matrix of how the various scales relate to the size of the building's overall footprint.

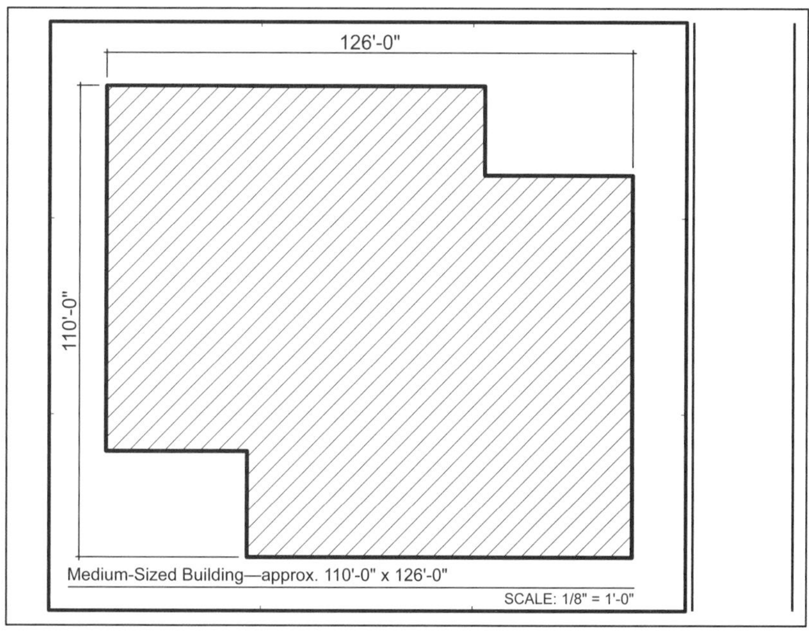

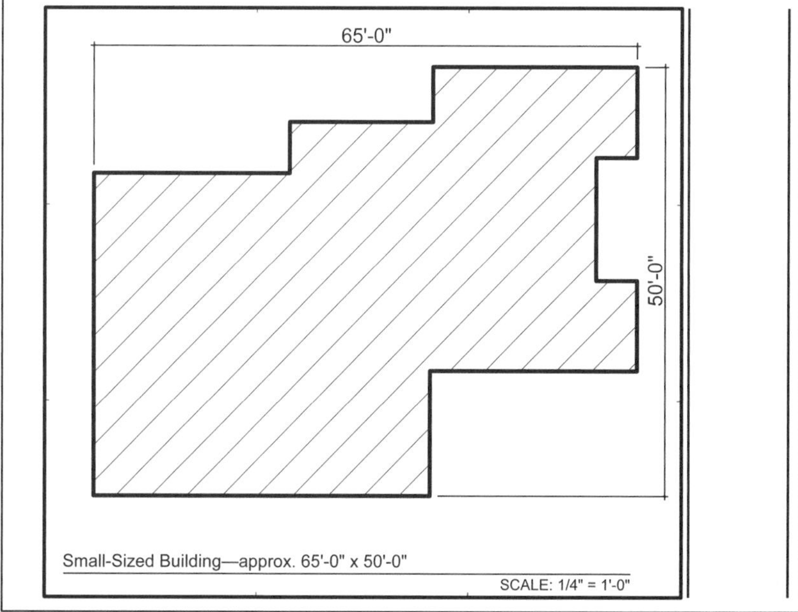

Building footprints scaled at 1/4" = 1'-0" and 1/8" = 1'-0" (24" x 18" sized borders).

Figure 18.6a Scales and their relationship to building footprint. The example shows a 24" × 18" border. The upper border includes a building footprint drawn at 1/8" = 1'-0". The lower border includes a building footprint drawn at 1/4" = 1'-0". Notice the building's maximum footprint size changes based on the scale of the drawing–approximately 110' × 126' for the 1/8" scale building and approximately 50' × 65' for the 1/4" scale building.

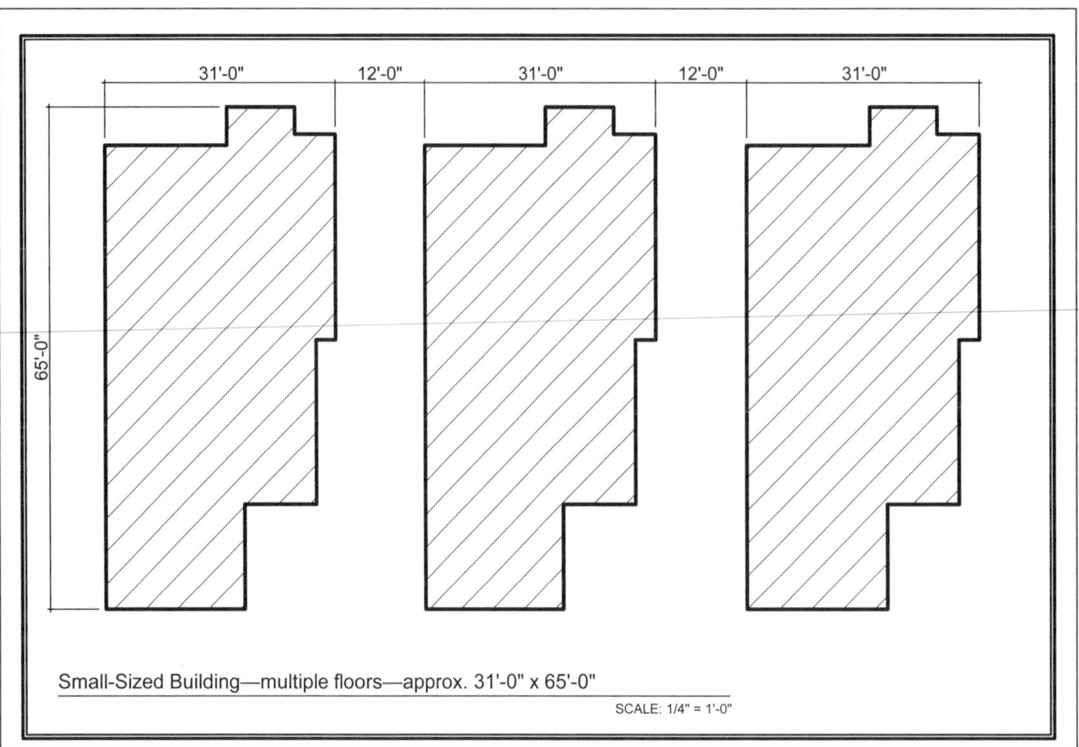

Building footprints scaled at 1/4" = 1'-0" (36" x 24" sized border).

Figure 18.6b Scales and their relationship to building footprint. This example shows a 36" × 24" border that includes a building footprint drawn at 1/4" = 1'-0". Notice that the border can contain multiple floor levels of a small-size building that is approximately 65' × 31'.

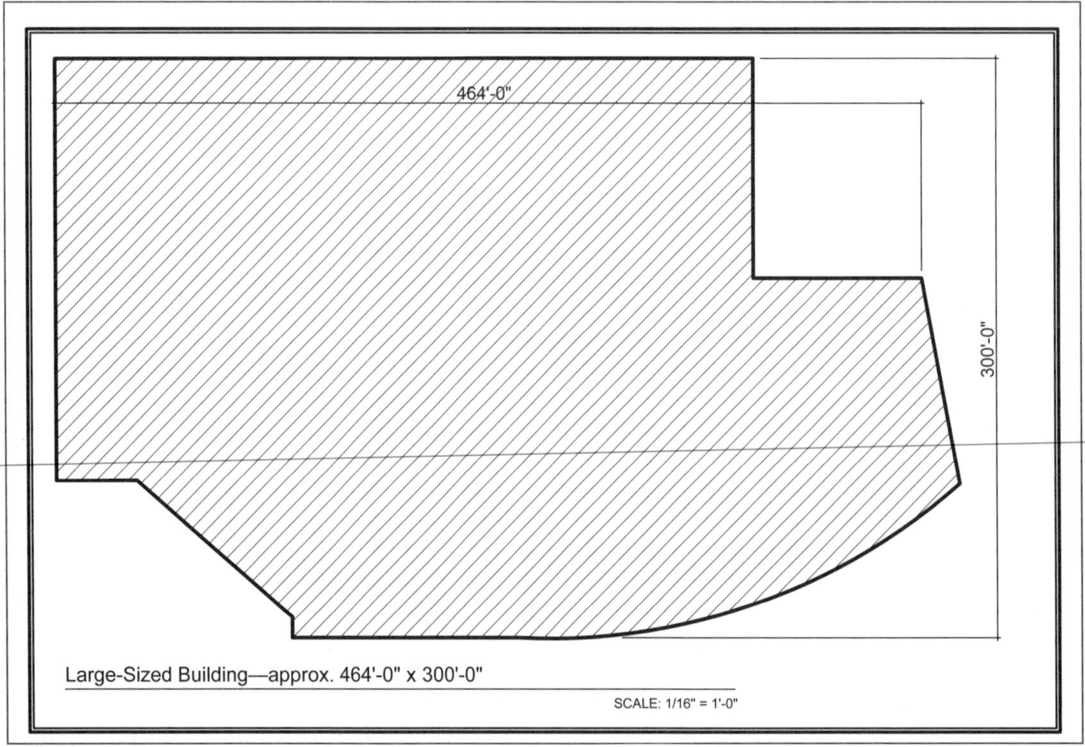

Building footprint scaled at 1/16" = 1'-0" (36" x 24" sized border).

Figure 18.6c Scales and their relationship to building footprint. This example shows a 36" × 24" border that includes one building footprint drawn at 1/16" = 1'-0". Notice that the border can contain a maximum footprint size that is approximately 300' × 464'.

Apply the Drawing Conventions in Floor Plans

Summarized in Chapter 17, drawing conventions not only add legibility to drawings but also create a language that professionals in design and construction related fields can all understand. While it is important to incorporate proper drawing conventions in all orthographic drawing types, the floor plan is probably the most critical. Drawing conventions always vary with plotting scale; therefore, it is important to become familiar with how scale influences conventions. Figures 18.7 and 18.8 provide examples of drawing conventions and annotation symbols used at the various scales.

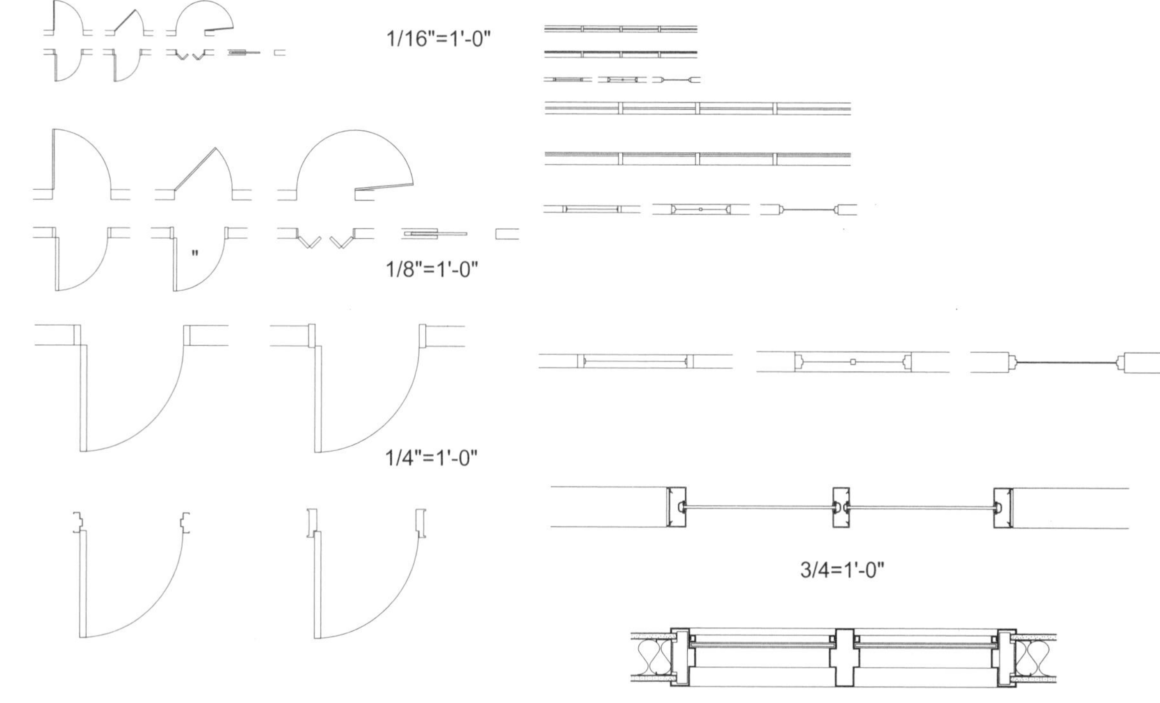

Figure 18.7a Getting to know floor plan objects and their typical drawing representations. The example shows how the amount of detail changes for doors and window symbols when plotting scale changes.

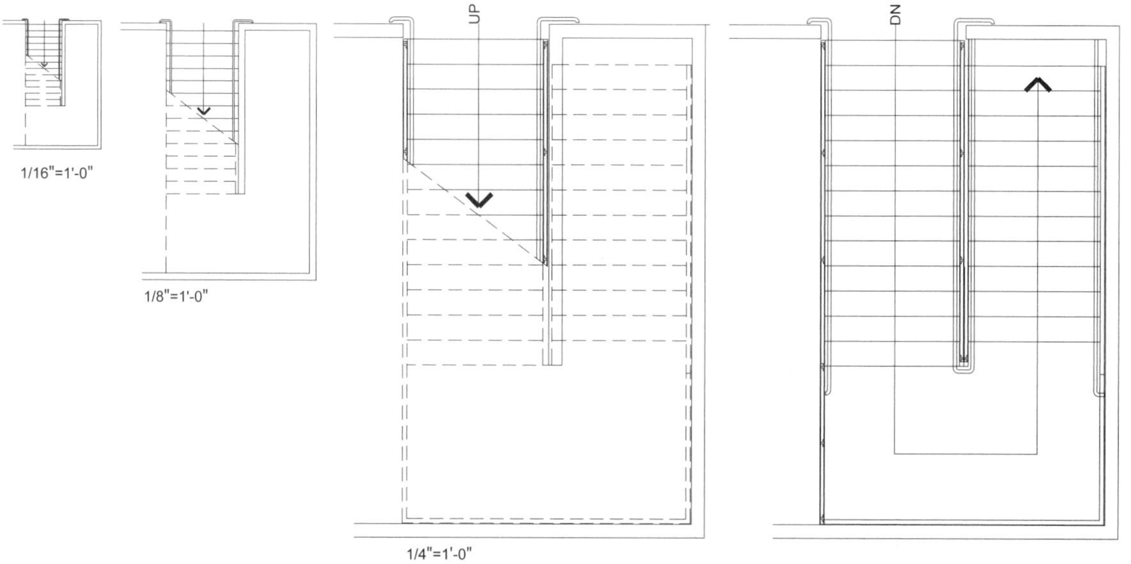

Figure 18.7b Getting to know floor plan objects and their typical drawing representations. The example shows a U-shaped stair at 1/16" = 1'-0", 1/8" = 1'-0", and 1/4" = 1'-0" scales.

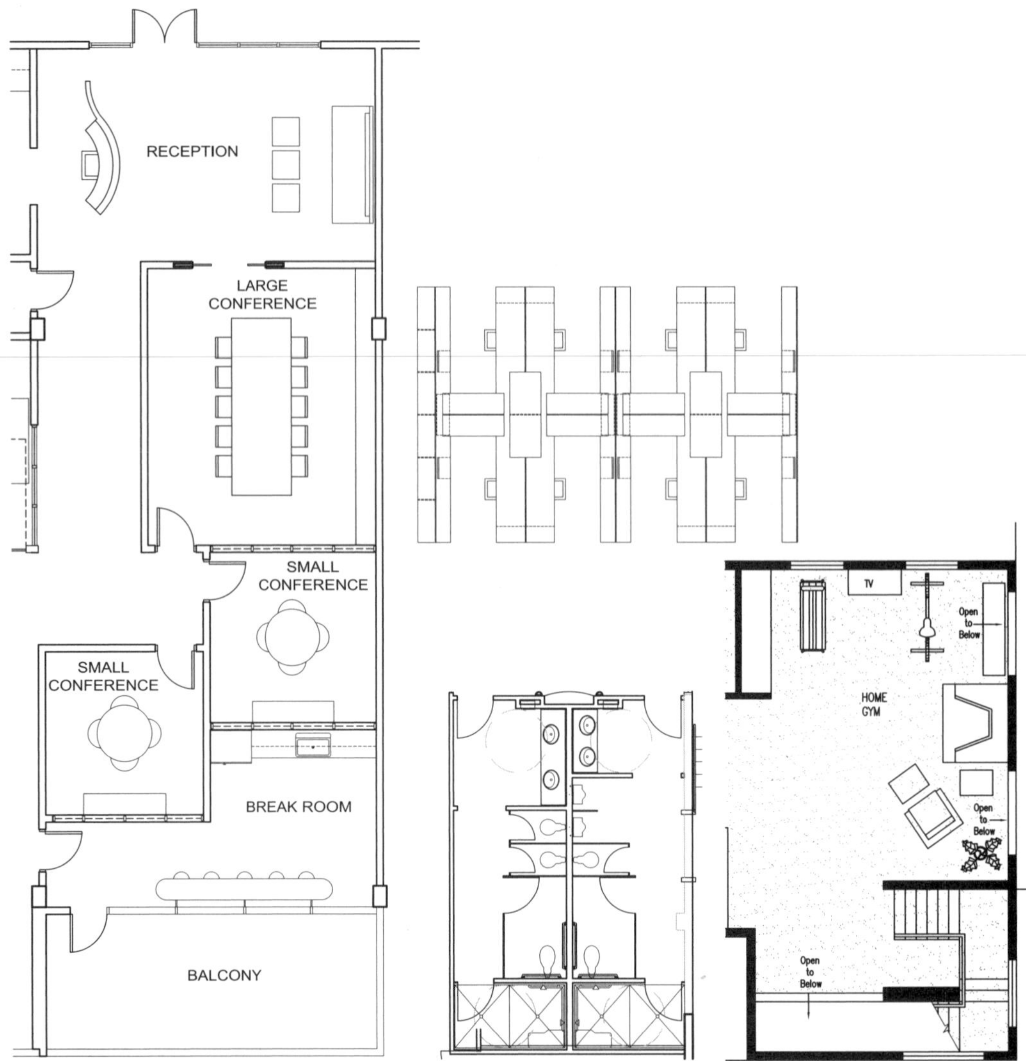

Figure 18.8 The Floor Plan Visual Checklist

Walls

1. Full-height walls should differentiate with lineweights from low or partial height walls.
2. Low or partial height walls do not clean up to full height walls.
3. Make sure lines at walls cut by any type of opening are assigned the wall layer.

Doors

4. At 1/16" and 1/8" scales, most doors and windows are drawn very generically—many times leaving out detail like type and jamb frame condition.
5. Draw doors with correct swinging direction, jamb condition, and lineweight. Door swing directions for residential and commercial buildings are established by a combination of code regulations and custom. Show correct door symbol based on plotting scale.

Windows

6. In plan view, window jambs and glazing are assigned the heavier lineweight. Window sills are the lightest lineweight.
7. Windows located above the floor plan's cut plane are dashed.

Stairs and ramps

8. Stairs going up have different conventions from stairs going down. Show ramps using correct drawing conventions.
9. Correctly draw all handrails and/or guardrails. Most stair flights, at a minimum, require handrails.

Casework

10. Casework located above the cutting plane is always dashed. Casework below work surfaces or counters are assigned a hidden linetype. Refer to Chapter 3 for a review of linetypes.
11. Before drawing, research casework's form, materials, and joinery so that drawings show greater accuracy.

Accessories

12. At scales greater than 1/16", draw accessory items.

Systems furniture

13. Before drawing, research the manufacturer and product lines to find systems that best match what you want to accomplish. Systems furniture accessories should be shown. This includes file cabinets, shelving, and fixtures.

Significant changes in ceiling planes

14. Draw important ceiling relationships, which should be dashed. These might include ceiling soffits and skylights.

Floor material and floor level changes

15. Show all changes in level with a light lineweight.
16. Show floor materials as hatches using correct scaling.

Fireplaces

17. Before drawing, research fireplace types so that drawings show greater accuracy.

Entourage

18. Entourage, for the most part (people, plants, vehicles) should only be used at scales greater than 1/16".

Drawing with Confidence: The Floor Plan Checklist

A beginning design student often has trouble memorizing all of the various drawing do's and don'ts and lineweights and linetypes. The amount of information is often overwhelming and confusing. Beginning students are therefore encouraged to buy or create a small pocket reference where information can be stored and retrieved easily. Checklists are another type of organizational method that provide priceless reminders to beginning and advanced students alike. In fact, professional designers use checklists regularly to control information accuracy and as reminders for task-related procedures.

Visual checklists in interior design and architecture often refer to drawing sets of completed projects that are used for reference in future projects. When used properly, these drawing sets provide visual examples for the type and layout of drawings for a specific building type.

A checklist for the floor plan drawing type has been created in Appendix P to help start your own personal reference notebook. Items prefixed with a * symbol are typically not found in presentation-oriented floor plans. This checklist is by no means exhaustive. Additional blank lines are provided for you to add your own reminders. Refer to the topic Apply the Drawing Conventions in Floor Plans for a visual reference to the drawing conventions associated with objects listed.

Scenario #1

Figures 18.9a and 18.9b use several technical pen widths to quickly practice the concept of lineweight conventions at several scales. Assess your results by printing the drawings 180101.pdf through 180103.pdf found on the CD-ROM.

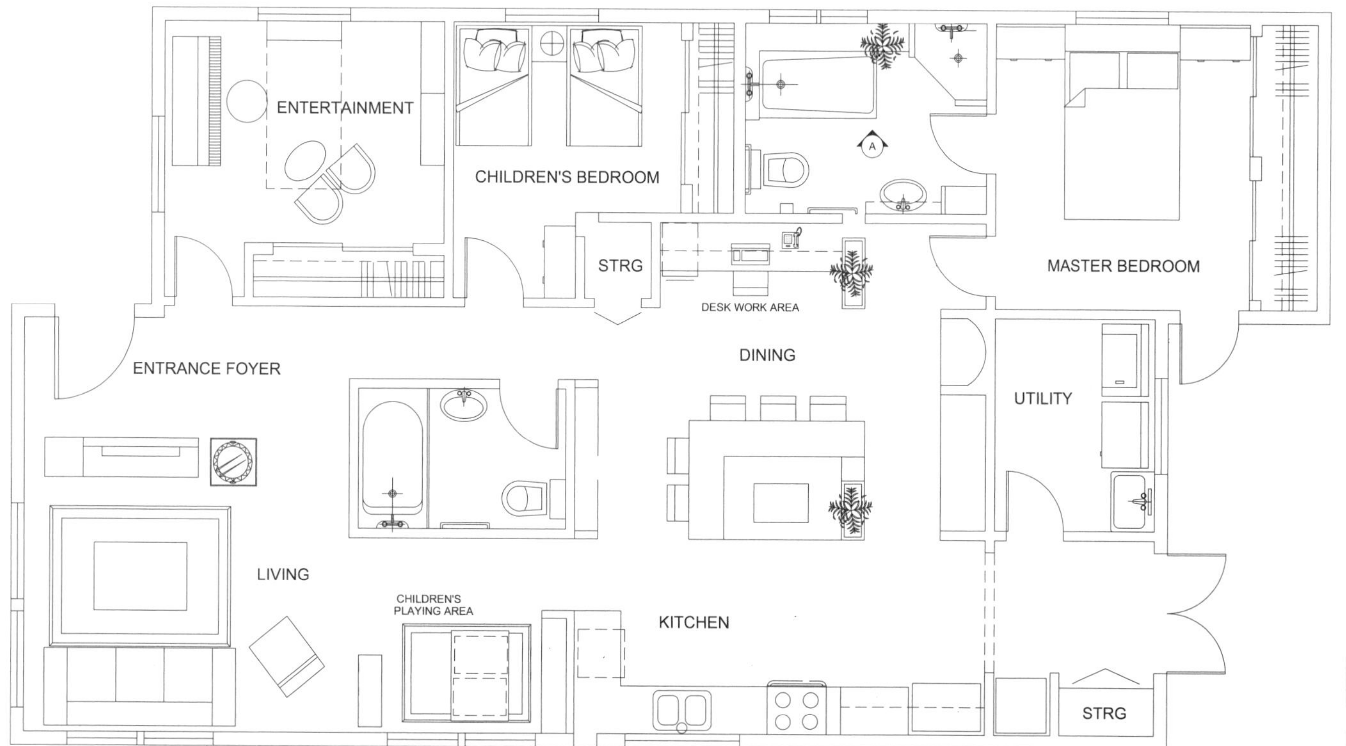

Figure 18.9a Floor plan scenario.
Make several copies of the drawings shown here (full size, half size, and double size).
Student Project: Smith House Renovation, courtesy of Tomoko Shibamoto.

Figure 18.9b Floor plan scenario.

Make several copies of the drawing shown (full size, half size, and double size). A variety of multi-thickness technical pens or markers will be needed to complete this exercise. Place the copied drawings from Figure 18.9a underneath these copies. Using only your own knowledge, quickly trace each object at the three different scales using the appropriate pen thickness. Erase extraneous detail with correction fluid or tape. Assess your results by printing the drawings 180101.pdf through 180103.pdf found on the CD-ROM.

Student Project: Smith House Renovation, courtesy of Tomoko Shibamoto.

Drawing Craft in Ceiling Plans

Like floor plan views, ceiling plans show the exterior and interior plan relationships of all ceiling elements. Drawing conventions for ceiling plan cut planes are typically around 6 to 7 feet above the finish floor (Figure 18.10). For each building level, a ceiling plan is usually drawn. Ceiling plans are rarely drawn in the beginning of the design process. Instead, at early stages of the design process, designers usually rely on sections to convey ceiling related design intentions and ideas.

Ceiling plans are difficult to visualize since they are not a mirror image of the floor plan. Similar to the floor plan view, the ceiling plan also looks downward, drawing all ceiling elements in the top view orientation. This allows the floor plan to be used as a template for the ceiling plan view (Figure 18.11).

Knowing How to Draw Ceiling Plans

Discipline-specific drawing conventions greatly influence the type of information shown on ceiling plans. In general, architectural ceiling plans show the following:

- Ceiling systems and materials, and any ceiling-mounted lighting and/or equipment
- Exposed HVAC ductwork and/or diffusers
- Sprinkler systems
- Other ceiling-related equipment, including audiovisual, motion, smoke, and/or security detection devices
- Wall or ceiling mounted upper casework
- Door and opening headers

Typically ceilings plans do not show the following:

- Low walls
- Doors, sills, and/or thresholds
- Any floor equipment or furniture

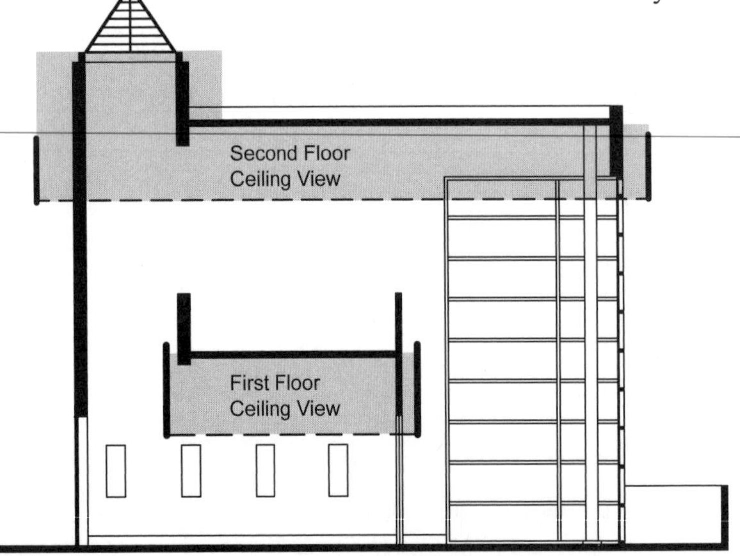

Figure 18.10 Drawing conventions for ceiling plan cut planes are typically around 6 to 7 feet above finish floor.

Figure 18.11 Floor plans are typically used as templates for ceiling plans. In this example, the doors, furniture, plumbing fixtures, and lower cabinetry layers are turned so that the walls, fireplace, windows, and upper casework can be reused (without redrawing) for the ceiling plan view.

Student Project: Parker Residence, courtesy of Lauren Baez.

Technique to Master **T18.12** Drawing the Ceiling Plan View

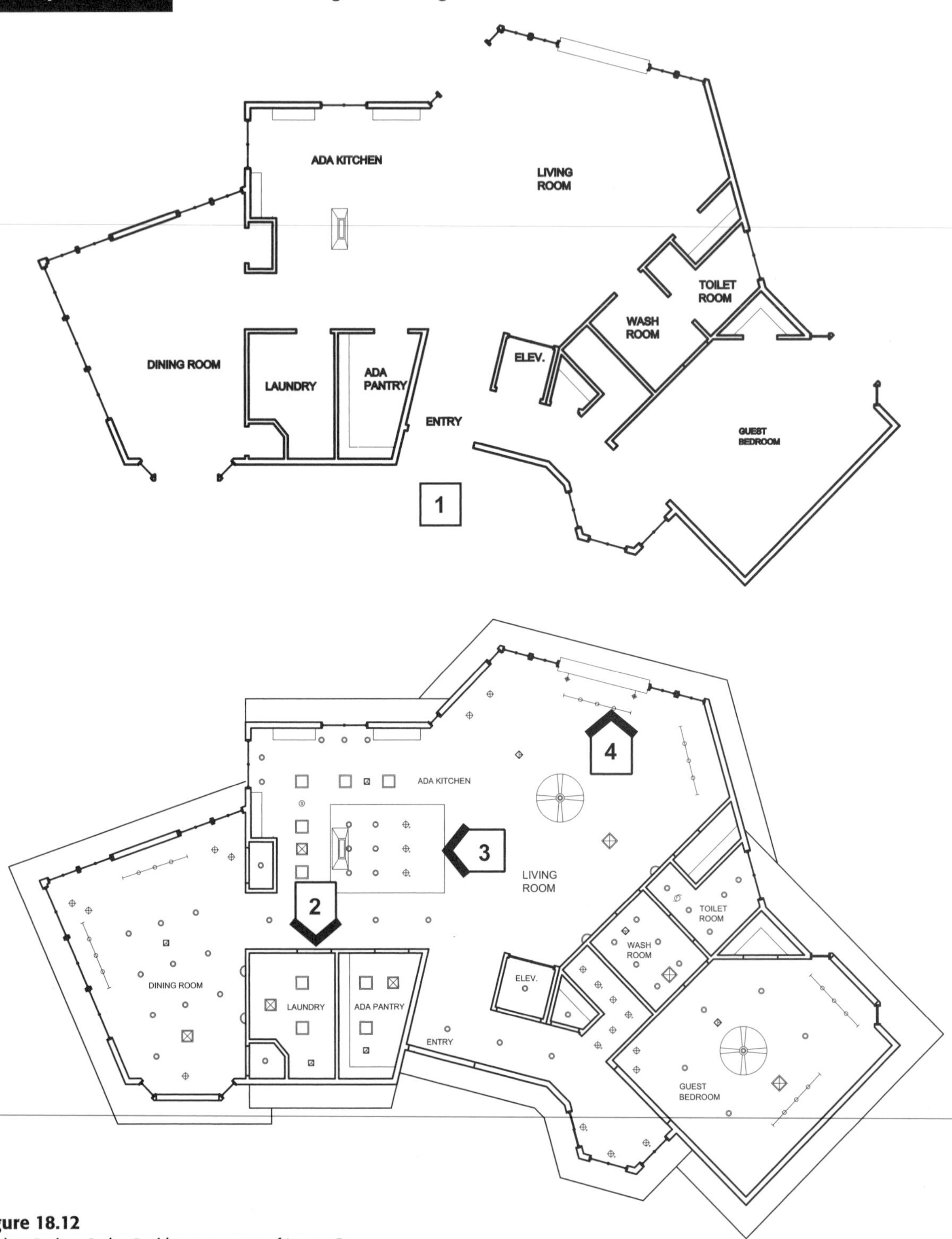

Figure 18.12
Student Project: Parker Residence, courtesy of Lauren Baez.

1	Freeze (turn off) all layers that have floor related information drawn on them. These might include furniture, lower casework, plumbing fixtures, appliances, low walls, systems furniture, and floor material hatches. Doors and stairs are typically, by convention, also turned off.
2	Add additional linework to represent door, window, and opening headers.
3	Add representative linework for skylights or ceiling/roof penetrations.
4	Add representative linework for lighting fixtures, HVAC equipment, and fire-protective devices.

(continued)

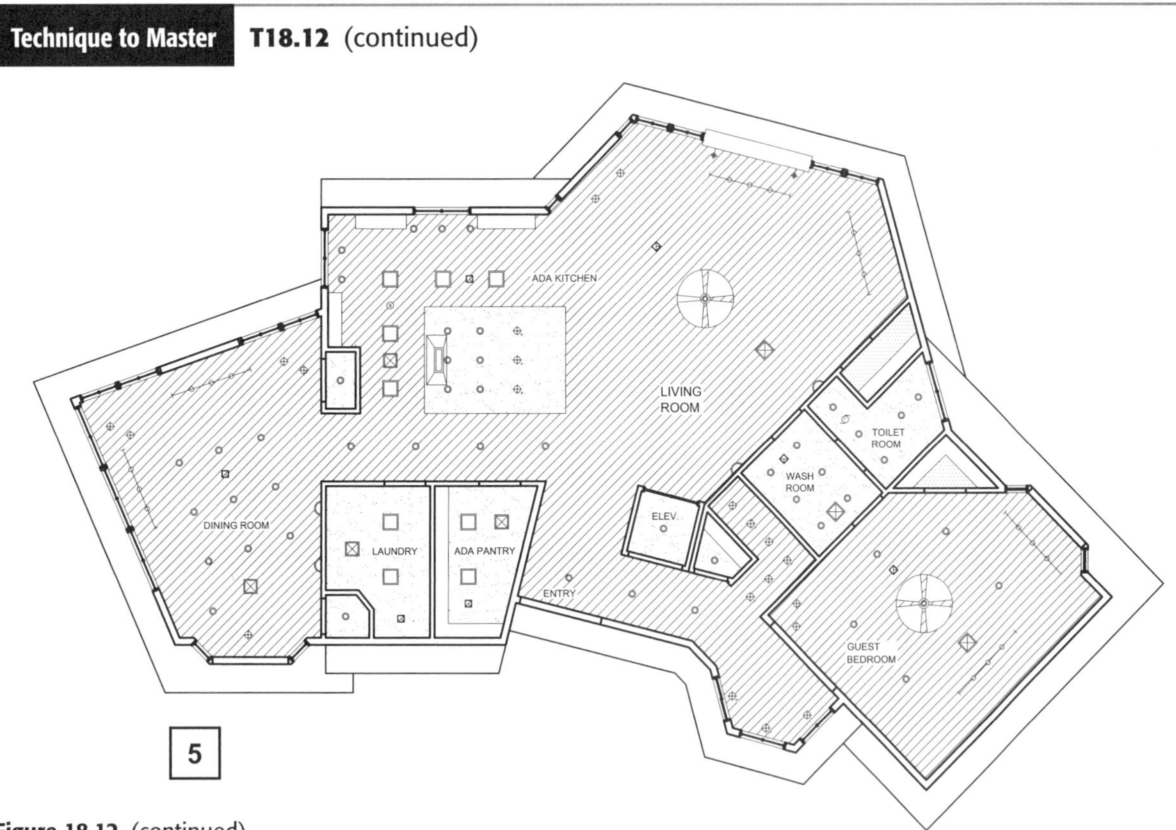

Figure 18.12 (continued)
Student Project: Parker Residence, courtesy of Lauren Baez.

5	Add representative linework and hatching for ceiling finish materials and exposed structural framing systems.

Drawing Ceiling Plans Efficiently

Figure 18.12 outlines one possible process for drawing ceiling plans.

Apply the Drawing Conventions in Ceiling Plans

Summarized in Chapter 17, drawing conventions add legibility to drawings and create a language that all professionals in design and construction related fields understand. Drawing conventions always vary with plotting scale; therefore, it is important to become familiar with how scale influences conventions. Figures 18.13 through 18.15 illustrate some examples of the drawing conventions used in ceiling plans.

Drawing with Confidence: The Ceiling Plan Checklist

The ceiling plan checklist located in Appendix P lists drawing content, labeling, and annotation reminders for ceiling plan drawings. Additional blank lines are provided for you to add your own reminders. Items prefixed with a * symbol are typically not found in presentation-oriented ceiling plans. Refer to the topic Apply the Drawing Conventions in Ceiling Plans for an illustrated summary.

Drawing Craft in Roof Plans

Roof plans are used to show the shape and slope direction for buildings. Roof plan views are the true top view of a building since the

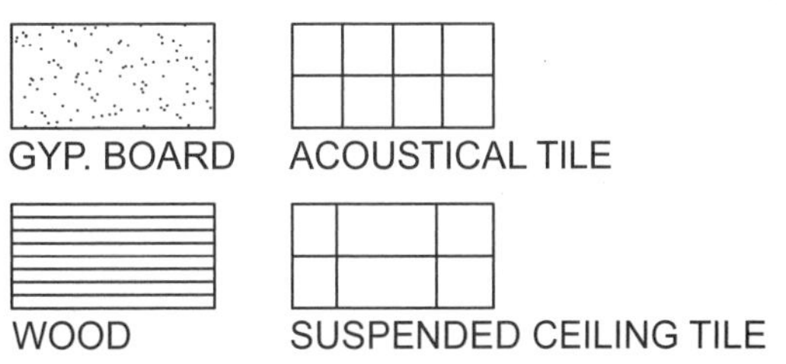

Figure 18.13 Material and hatching conventions used in ceiling plans

REFLECTED CEILING PLAN LEGEND

HVAC SUPPLY
HVAC RETURN
HVAC RETURN
LINEAR DIFFUSER
FIRE EXIT SIGN
PROJECTOR EQUIPMENT
RECESSED CAN LIGHTING
RECESSED DOWNLIGHT
SUSPENDED LIGHTING FIXTURE
HANGING CYLINDER LIGHTING FIXTURE
SURFACED MOUNTED FLOURESCENT STRIP
2X4 TRAUFFER

REFLECTED CEILING PLAN LEGEND

2'X2' RECESSED FLUORESCENT LIGHT FIXTURE
CEILING MOUNTED PENDANT LIGHT FIXTURE
CEILING MOUNTED LIGHT FIXTURE
RECESSED LIGHT FIXTURE
WALL-MOUNTED LIGHT FIXTURE
CEILING-MOUNTED TRACK LIGHTING
AIR SUPPLY DUCT INSTALLED IN CEILING
RETURN DUCT
SMOKE DETECTOR
CEILING FAN W/ INTEGRAL LIGHTS
EXHAUST FAN
WALL-MOUNTED UP-LIGHT
RANGE HOOD (COMPLIANT WITH SPECIALTY STOVE)

Figure 18.14 Lighting and equipment symbols used in ceiling plans

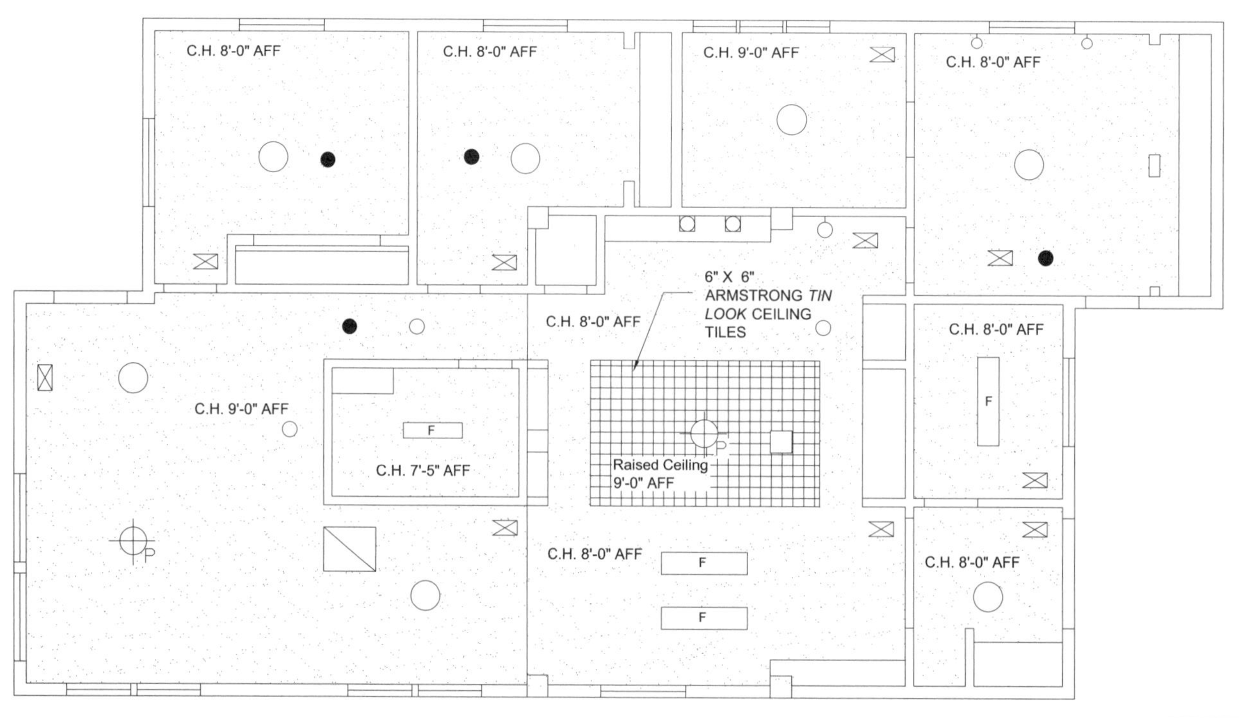

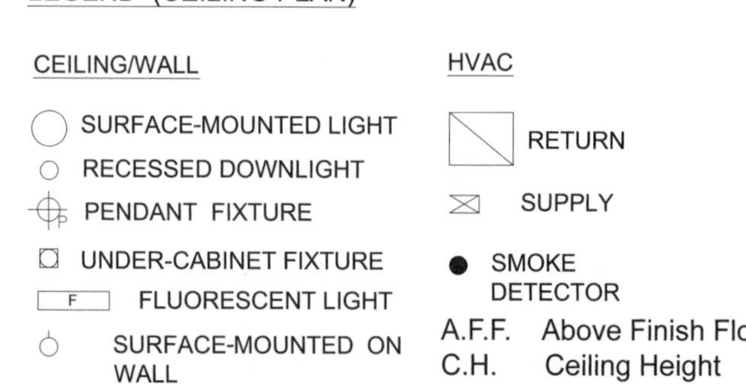

Figure 18.15 The ceiling plan visual checklist

orthographic view is looking down on the building from the outside. Unlike the floor plans, only one roof plan is used for a multi-story building.

Most interior designers will never actually design or draw a roof plan in their professional careers; however, understanding how a roof plan is drawn is still critical to an interior designer's education. Knowing how sloped roofs work and how they are drawn will inevitably transfer into your overall understanding of building construction. This topic focuses on the drawing methodology and drawing conventions related to the roof plan view. It also utilizes roofing vocabulary introduced in Chapter 16.

Know How to Draw Roof Plans

The ability to draw complex roof plans is directly tied to a student's ability to visualize the roof three-dimensionally. Sloped roof visualization is another aspect of buildings that many beginning and intermediate design students have difficulty mastering. Developing the skill usually requires an approach that simultaneously models the roof while drawing its front, side, and back views. The following approaches demonstrate how the orthographic views of a roof can be derived from its other views.

Drawing a Roof Plan by First Choosing the Roof Type

Sometimes complex sloped roofs are designed by choosing the individual roof shapes for the various parts of the building (Figure 18.16). Using this approach, elevations are related to the floor plan and then quickly diagrammed out. Figure 18.17 demonstrates this approach.

Drawing a Roof Plan Using a Floor Plan

In most design timelines, floor plans have already been developed before a roof plan is attempted. When floor plan drawings are available, roof plans can be easily constructed from these drawings (see CD-ROM).

Drawing a Roof Plan Using Exterior Elevations or Building Sections

When you have access to elevation or building section drawings, you can construct roof plans based on these drawings, as illustrated on the CD-ROM.

Drawing with Confidence: The Roof Plan Checklist

The roof plan checklist located in Appendix P lists drawing content, labeling, and annotation reminders for roof plan drawings.

Drawing Craft in Sections and Elevations

Sections and elevations are an important extension to the plan drawings. In combination with floor and ceiling plans, sections and elevations assist in describing the whole design intention. Although interior designers

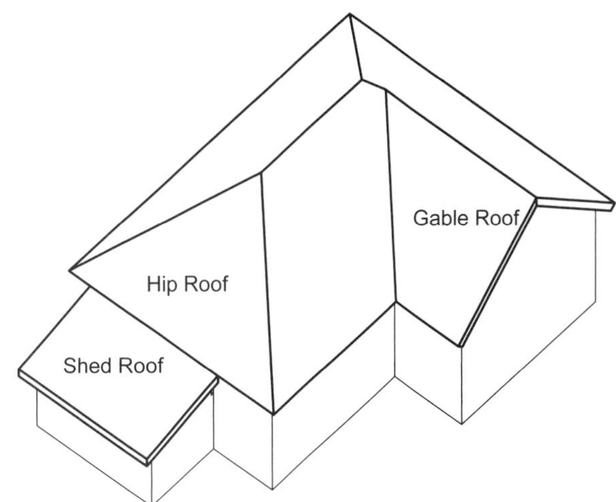

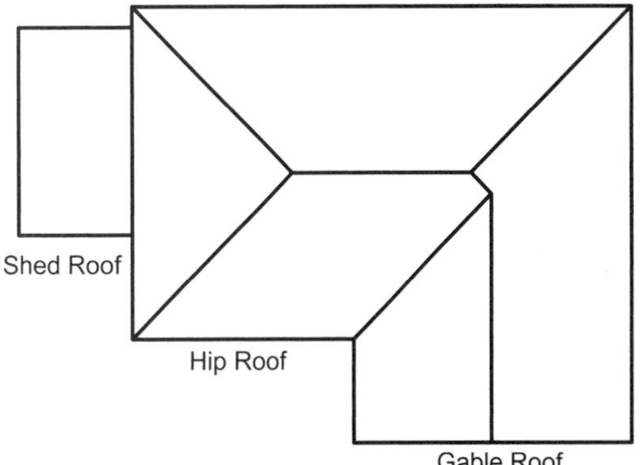

Figure 18.16 Complex sloped roofs can be designed by choosing the individual roof shapes for the various parts of the building.

Technique to Master **T18.17** Drawing a Roof Plan by First Choosing the Roof Type

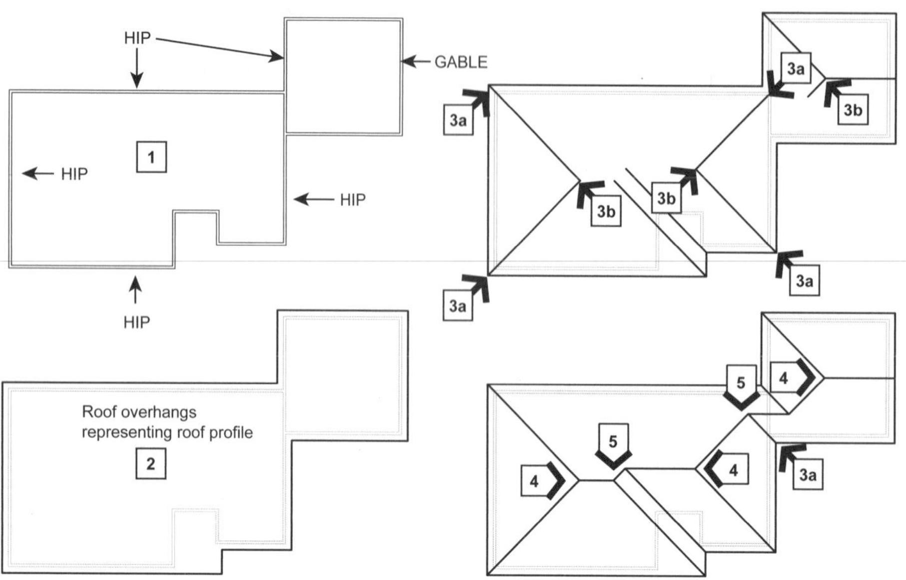

Figure 18.17 The following example shows a residence that integrates three hip roof forms and one gable roof form. Each roof form is centered over its respective floor plate, thus creating four distinct ridge lines.

1	Decide which areas of the building will receive which building form.
2	Using the building's outline, create the roof's profile.
3	Create the hip boundaries by extending a line from the roof profile corners through the building corner. Extend hip boundaries until they intersect.
4	Draw ridge lines where hip boundaries intersect.
5	Complete roof plan by connecting ridges.

typically only use interior elevations as their primary sectional/elevational type, expanding your understanding of all the drawings will help you understand drawings from the other disciplines.

Section Types

Types of sections include building sections, sectional perspectives, wall sections, stair and ramp sections, and casework sections.

The vertical cut plane that creates a building section slices through the entire building—showing all the building systems and how they connect to one another (Figure 18.18). Critical building relationships that cannot be seen in plan are exposed—the relationships of outside ground to floor levels, floor levels to ceilings, and walls to ceilings and roofs.

Building sections are typically drawn at a scale of 1/16", 1/8", and 1/4". Because of the smallness of the scale, the actual detailing of building sections is limited (Figure 18.19). Instead, to illustrate additional detail, areas of

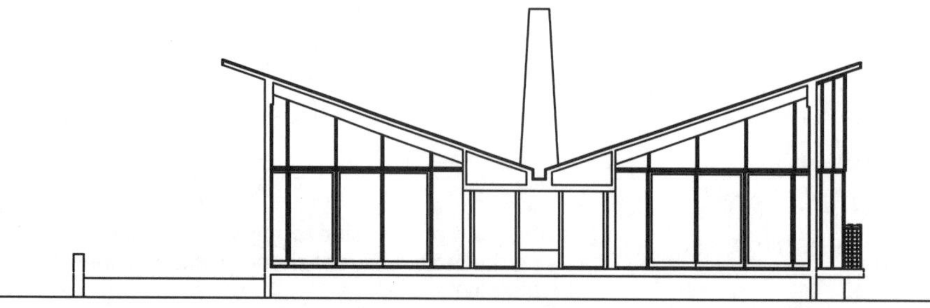

Figure 18.18 Building sections are vertical slices through a building showing all the building systems and how they connect to one another.

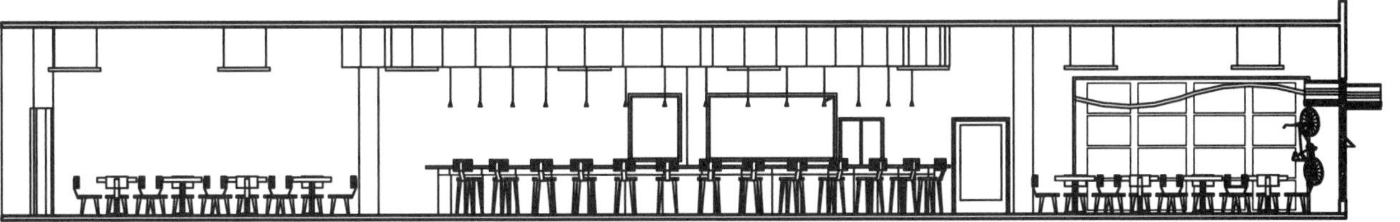

Building Section at 1/16"=1'-0"

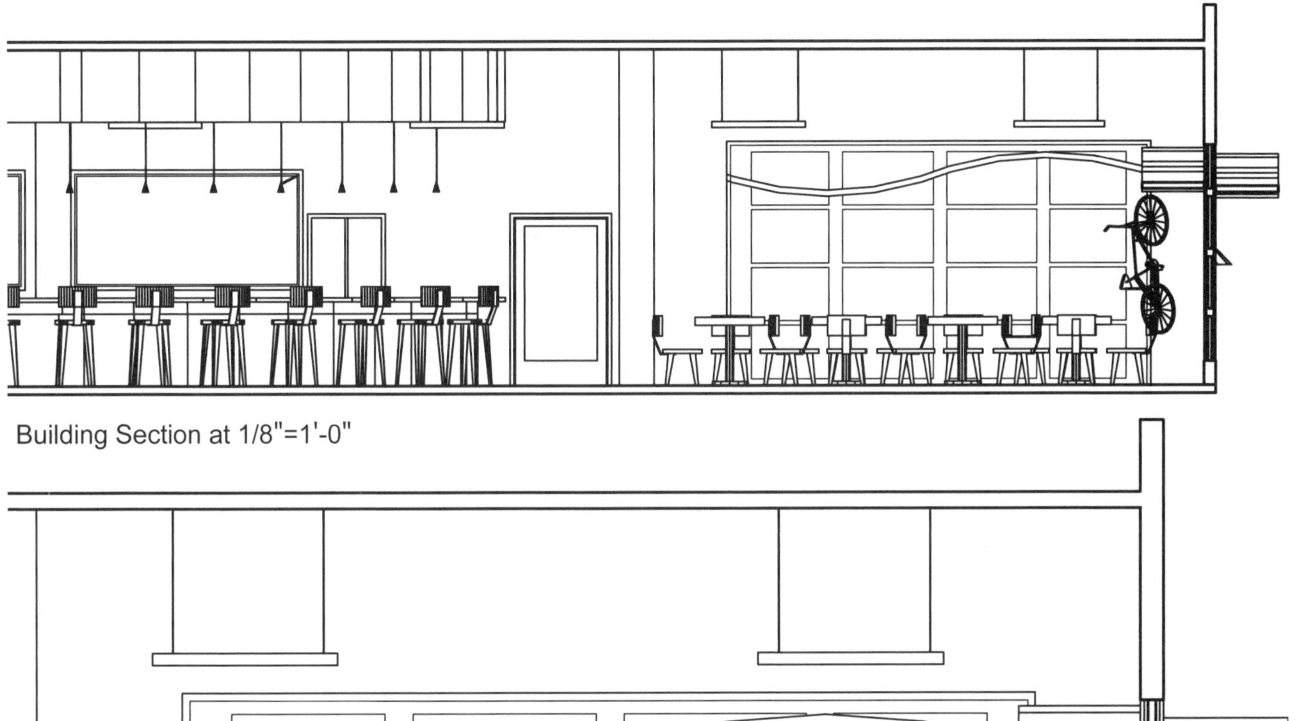

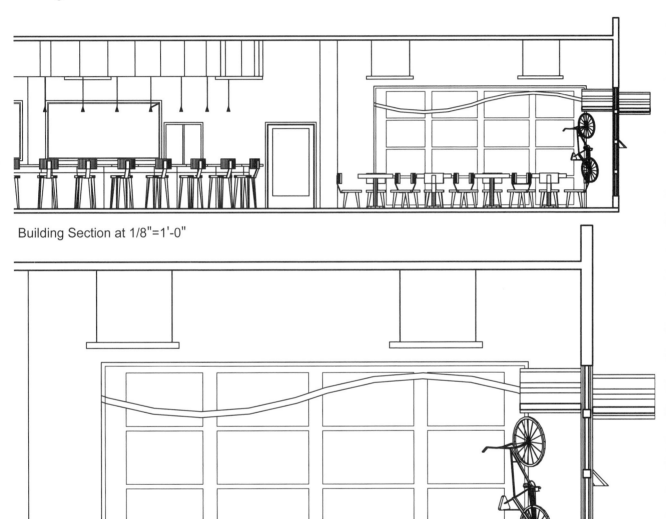

Building Section at 1/8"=1'-0"

Building Section at 1/4"=1'-0"

Figure 18.19 Because of the smallness of the scale, the actual detailing of building sections is limited. The example shows the same section drawing plotted at three different scales—$^{1}/_{16}$", $^{1}/_{8}$", and $^{1}/_{4}$". Notice that detail level in the chairs, bike, and window canopy cannot be the same for all scales.

Student Project: Restaurant design, courtesy of Andrea Pabon.

the building section are referenced to other enlarged drawings using symbol callouts.

Wall sections communicate how a wall is constructed—its materials, finishes, and assembly. Most wall sections are cut at building exterior conditions. However, partition schedules often use sectional drawings of walls to identify and label the interior partitions within a building (Figure 18.20). Wall sections are usually plotted at 1" = 1'-0" or 3/4" = 1'-0".

> **Box 18.1**
> A partition schedule or wall legend is a list of all the wall assemblies that are used in the design. Partition schedules are typically included in all renovation projects.

Elevation Types

Elevations are used to show the materials and finishes of vertical surfaces. The two common types of elevations are the interior elevation and the exterior elevation. Other variations include casework and cabinetry elevations.

Exterior elevations delineate the exterior facades of a building from a frontal view. It includes the major massing forms of the building, its roof forms (if visible), its fenestration, as well as the materials and finishes (Figure 18.21). Exterior elevations also show how the building relates to the ground at the location of the facade. They are usually plotted at 1/8" and 1/4" scales.

> **Box 18.2**
> Fenestration refers to the design and location of windows, doors, and curtain walls on the exterior of a building.

An interior elevation is a drawing of the frontal view of an interior wall within a room or space. Included in the drawing are the wall's materials and finishes, its openings and other penetrations, as well as the objects that are attached to the wall (Figure 18.22). Interior elevations are great for delineating special ornamentation or architectural detailing of a wall. Most construction sets include interior elevations of toilet rooms, custom casework, kitchens, and lobbies. Most interior elevations are plotted at 1/4" scale.

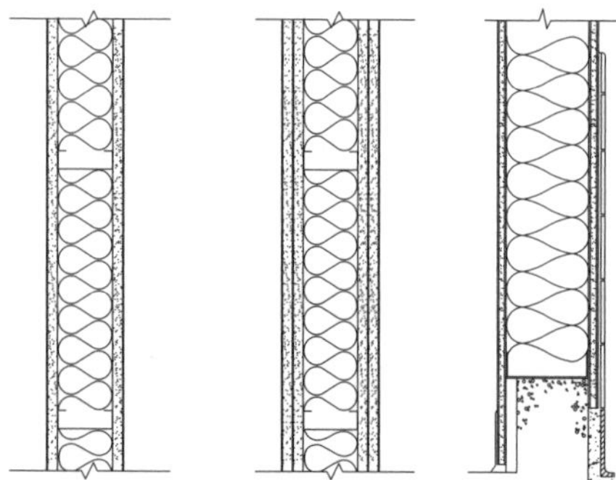

Figure 18.20 Partition schedules often use sectional drawings of walls to identify and label the interior partitions within a building.

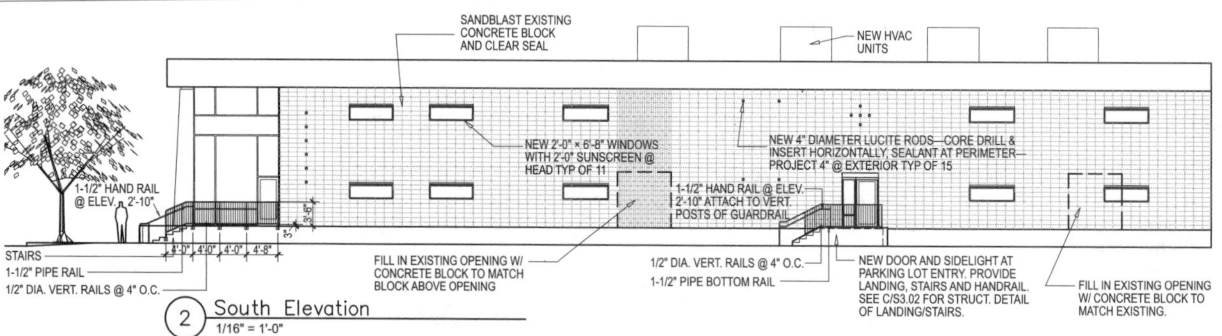

Figure 18.21 Exterior elevations delineate the exterior facades of a building from a frontal view.
Drawing: Front exterior elevation. NLA Office Renovation, courtesy of Nacht & Lewis Architects, Sacramento, CA.

Know How to Draw Sections and Elevations

The beginning steps of laying out sections and elevations are similar. When available, the floor plan is used to establish the positional relationships of the objects that will appear in the section or elevation. See Chapter 18 files on the supplementary CD-ROM for the basics of section and elevation construction. See Figure 18.23a–c for elevation and section drawings. Figures 18.24 through 18.26 illustrate some of the common mistakes prevalent in section and elevation drawings, including drawing objects not parallel to the drawing plane and drawing wall corners not cleaning up.

KITCHEN/DINING

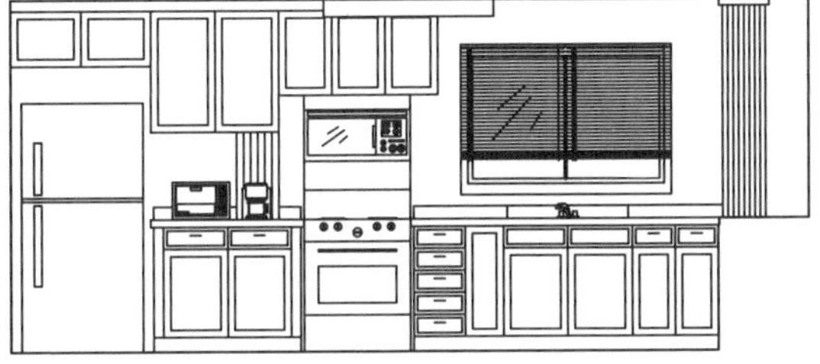

KITCHEN

Figure 18.22 An interior elevation is a drawing of the frontal view of an interior wall within a room or space.

Student Project: Smith House Renovation, courtesy of Tomoko Shibamoto.

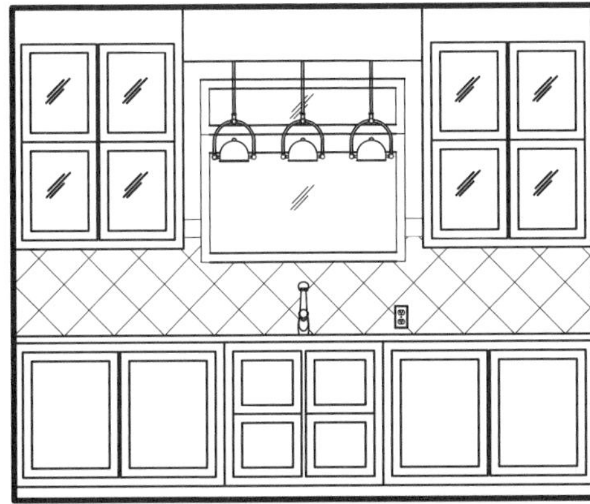

Figure 18.23a Cabinetry in elevation. The example shows the elevation of residential kitchen cabinetry. Glass cabinet panels are conveyed using three parallel lines at 45-degree angles.

Student Project: Smith House Renovation, courtesy of Brianna Bennett.

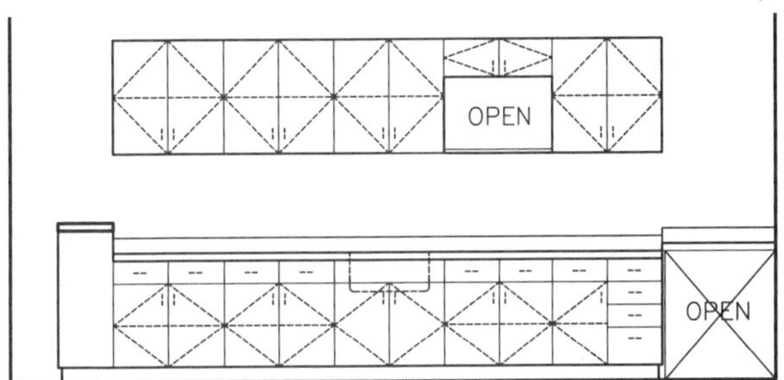

Figure 18.23b Casework in elevation. The example shows a typical commercial elevation drawing for upper and lower casework. Notice the detailing of the casework is less. Instead, information like shelving locations and panel swings are important to convey.

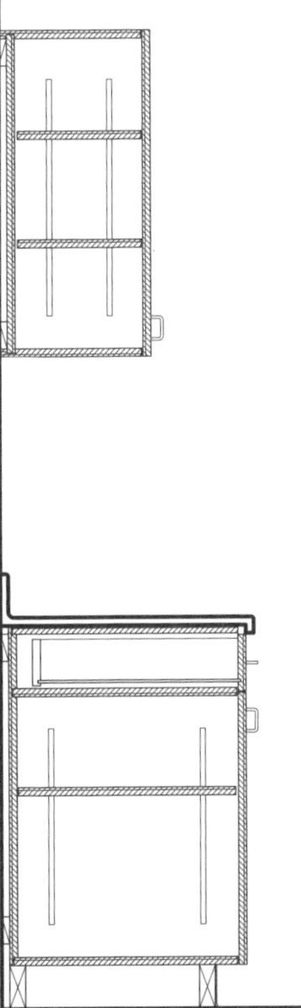

Figure 18.23c Casework and cabinetry in section. Both upper and lower casework are shown. Shelving location and attachment as well as countertop and base information are communicated.

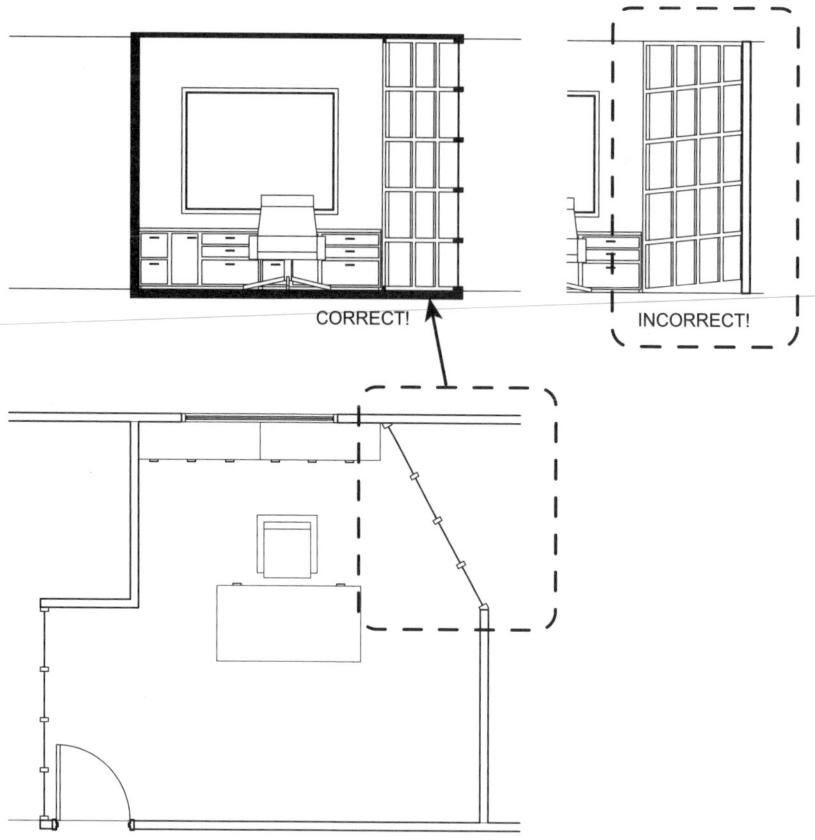

Figure 18.24 Objects in elevation that are not parallel to the drawing plane.

Objects that are at an angle in plan view will still remain horizontal in section and elevation view. Notice that the horizontal mullions in the above section remain parallel to the floor and ceiling planes, not angled like shown in the incorrect drawing.

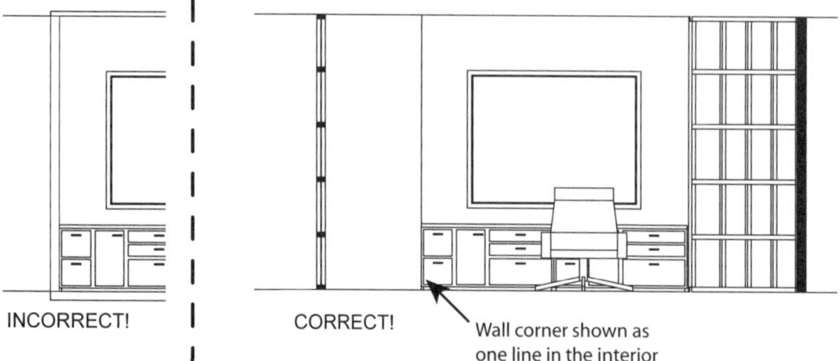

Figure 18.25 Wall corners should be delineated as one line not two (as drawn in the upper left).

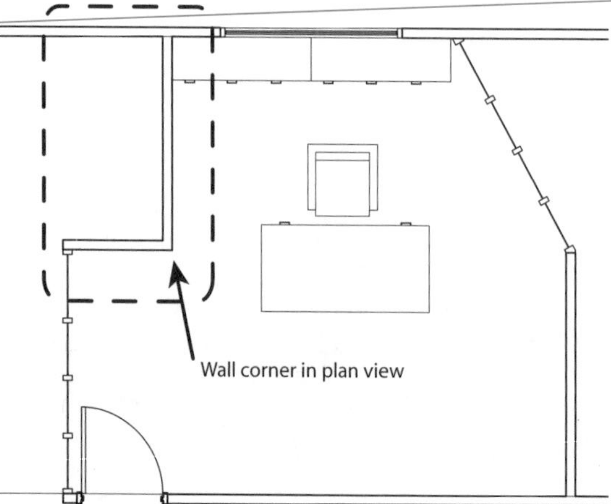

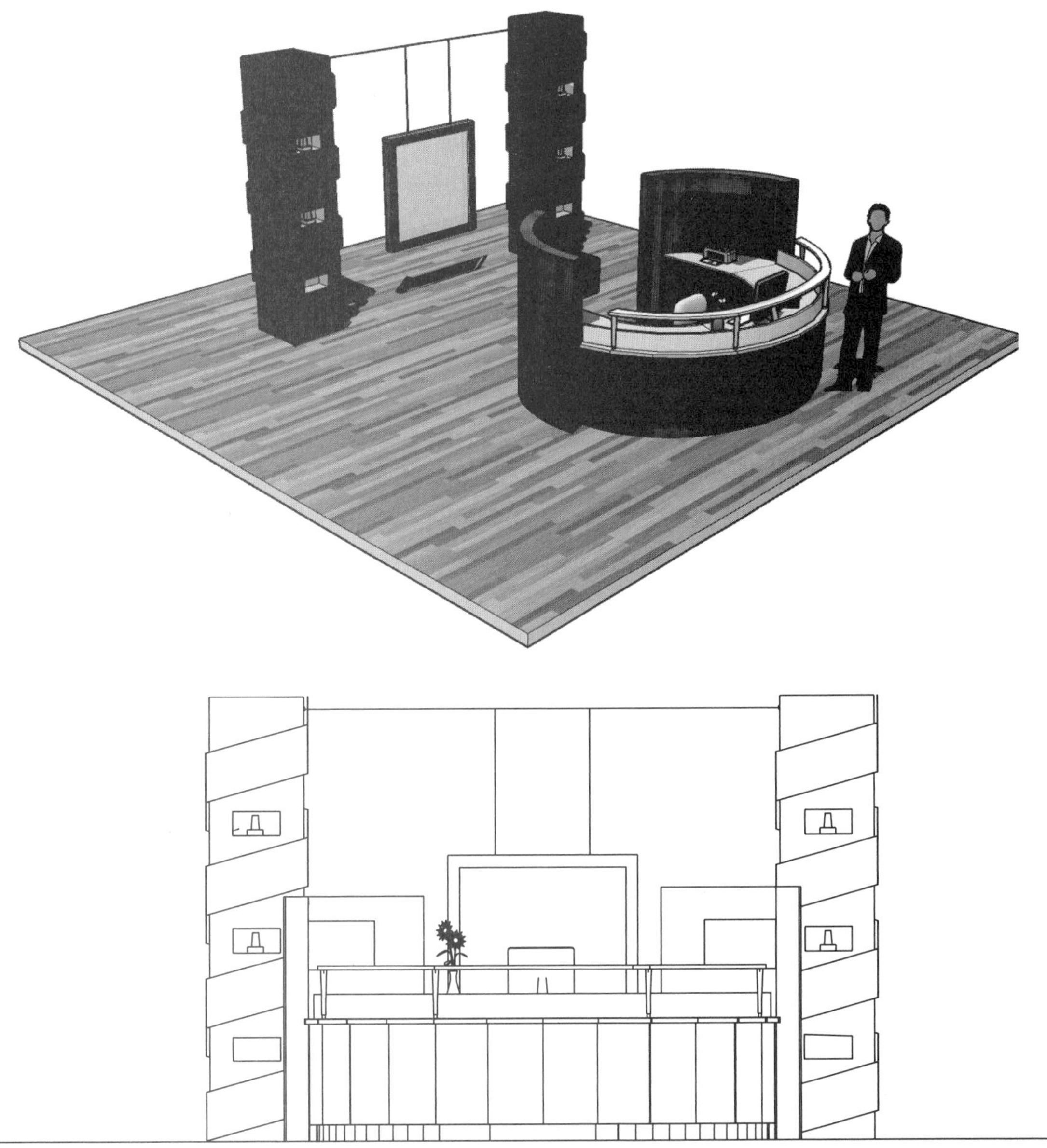

Figure 18.26 When drawing curves correctly in section and elevation, vertical lines are spaced further apart at the bump, or apex, of the curve. The interior elevation shows how the vertical parallel lines in the curved reception desk change as the curve moves away from its apex.

Student Project: Reception Desk Design, courtesy of Tiffany White.

Draw with Confidence: The Section and Elevation Checklist

The checklist located in Appendix P lists the drawing content and annotation reminders for the various section and elevation drawing types. Refer to the topic Apply the Drawing Conventions in Sections and Elevations for an illustrated summary.

Drawing Craft in Space Planning Studies

This section illustrates how to create some of the standard programming diagrams used at the beginning of the design process. The act of space planning is customarily linked to the earlier stages of the design process where project research and analysis takes place. Many space planning documents are a result of this initial programming process. However, space planning is a design process that spans several of the distinct design phases. Space planning starts in the programming phase, where diagrams and drawings are made to analyze and graphically represent zonal relationships, room adjacencies, and circulation patterns (Figure 18.27). Space planning continues into the conceptual and schematic design phases where area requirements, room adjacencies, and circulation systems are clarified (Figure 18.28). Finally, space planning also includes the planning and arrangement of furniture and workspaces, which are often refined in later stages of the design process (Figure 18.29).

Examples of space planning skills include the following:

- Arranging abstract representations of rooms and spaces to understand their proximity requirements
- Creating abstract polygonal representations of rooms and spaces to understand their square footage requirements
- Creating abstract representations of furniture, casework, and equipment arrangements within spaces to understand functional room-size issues

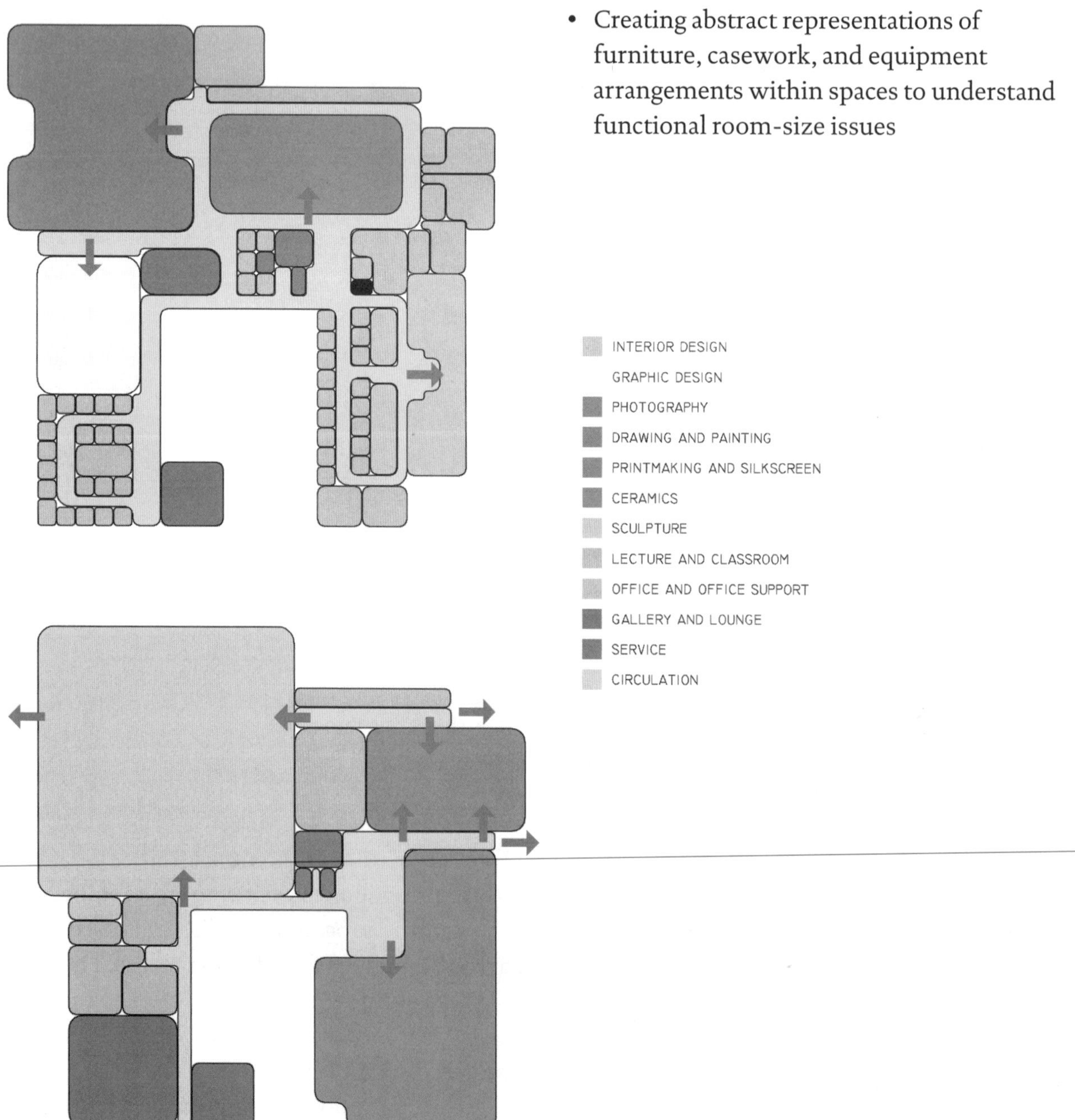

Figure 18.27 Space planning drawings in the programming phase include zonal relationships, room adjacencies, and circulation patterns. (See image in color on the CD-ROM.)

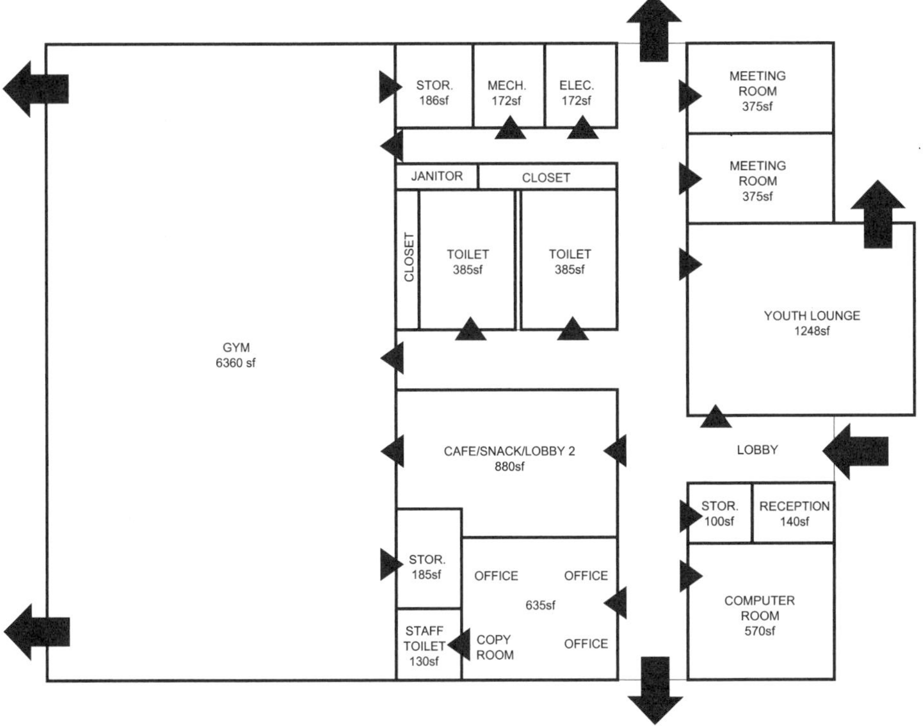

Figure 18.28 Space planning in the conceptual and schematic design phases show area requirements, room adjacencies, and circulation systems.

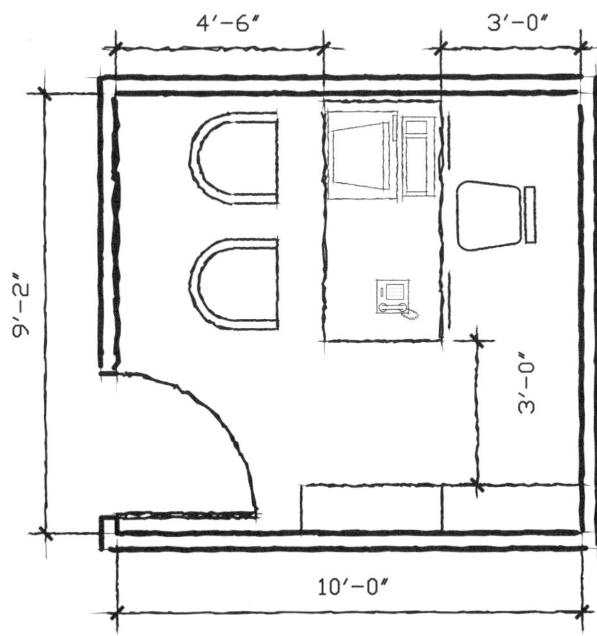

Figure 18.29 Space planning drawings can also include the planning and arrangement of furniture and workspaces.

- Creating representations of workspace arrangements
- Arranging interior building elements such as walls, doors, and windows to meet programmatic, functional, aesthetic, and regulatory requirements

Since there are many different kinds of space planning problems, this text does not attempt, in any way, to define the parameters of space planning nor does it cover the space planning process in depth. Instead, this topic focuses on using the AutoCAD and Architectural Desktop tools to aid in the development of space planning drawings. It introduces some of the types of drawings that are used in space planning studies and demonstrates how to achieve similar drawings using the AutoCAD/ADT toolset.

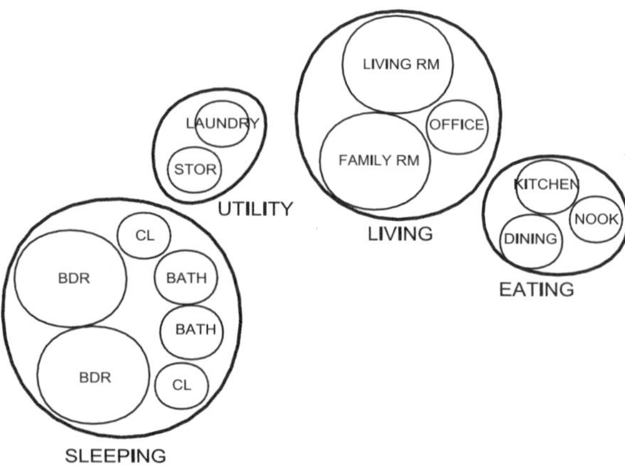

Figure 18.30 The zones of a residential program might include sleeping, eating, utility, and living.

Drawings Used in the Space Planning Process

Zonal diagrams help to classify programmatic spaces into more general categories. The zones of a residential program might include sleeping, eating, utility, and living (Figure 18.30). Types of zonal diagrams might include private/public, noisy/quiet, programmatic space/auxiliary space, and so on.

Bubble diagrams visually represent room and/or activity proximity relationships through heavy lines and arrow symbols. Additional information like circulation, view, light, and entry are also sometimes included. Bubble diagrams can be created with or without site context (Figure 18.31).

Block diagrams are always room and building area specific. Although room shapes remain undefined, block diagrams still provide an accurate visual representation of square footages for each programmatic space. Each room or function in a space is represented as a diagrammatic shape in the block diagram. The shapes are then organized and arranged based on program requirements, adjacencies, and other research that impacts room placement. Block diagrams also help relate circulation systems with the rooms/spaces they are serving (Figure 18.32).

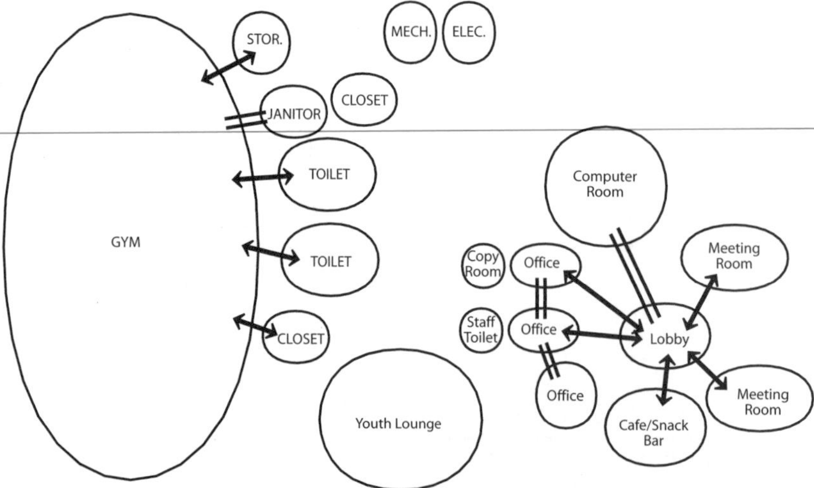

Figure 18.31 Bubble diagrams visually represent room and/or activity proximity relationships.

Plan prototype diagrams evaluate room sizes against room function. Furniture and equipment arrangements along with their individual clearances are laid out within the speculative room to determine the practicality of its size and shape (Figure 18.33). Plan prototype diagrams are excellent ways of learning how to functionally furnish rooms and spaces. They are also used as a method for approximating the room's square footage for block diagrams.

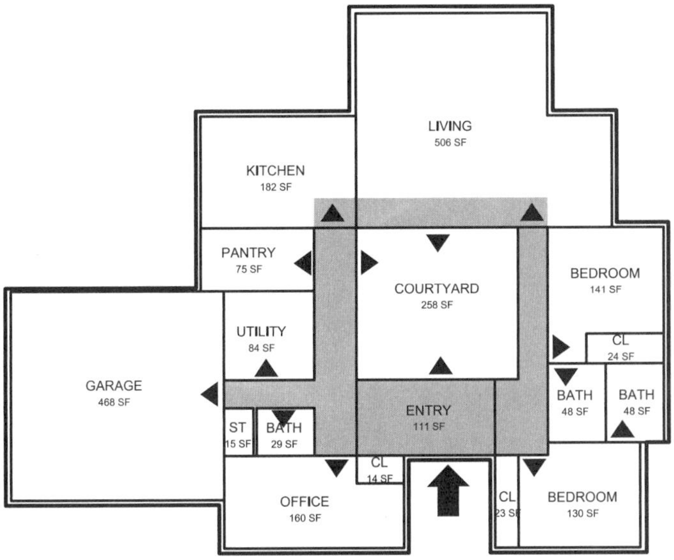

Figure 18.32 Block diagrams also relate circulation systems with the rooms/spaces they are serving.

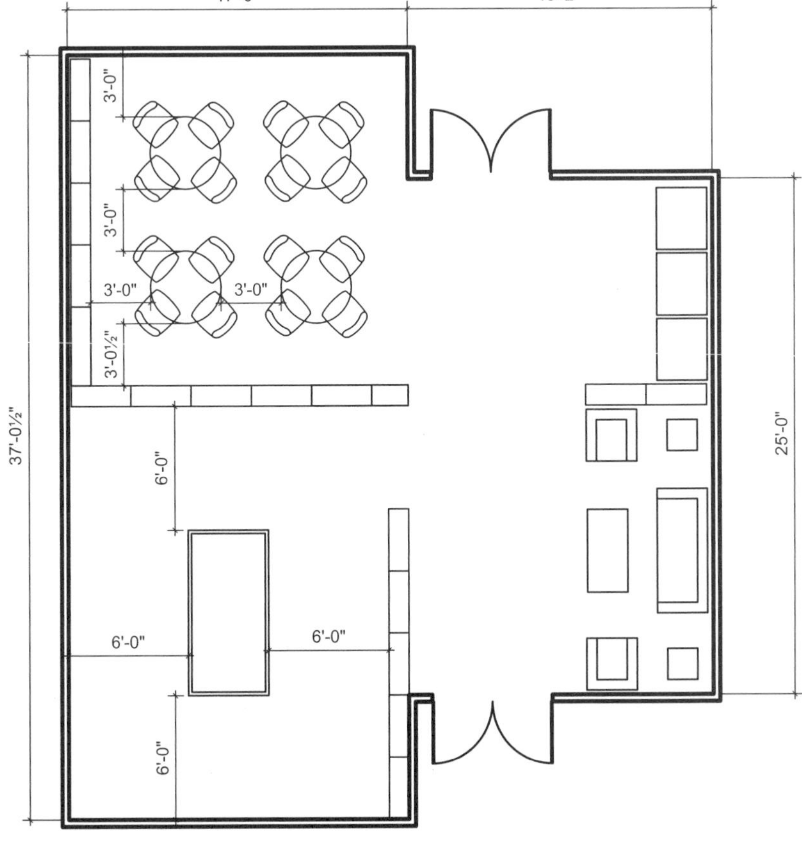

Figure 18.33 Furniture and equipment arrangements along with their individual clearances are laid out within the speculative room to determine the practicality of its size and shape.

Space utilization studies use color and hatching techniques to graphically categorize spaces into types of functions. These types of programming diagrams can be plan or section generated (Figure 18.34). Plan-generated space utilization diagrams resemble block diagrams.

Creating Space Planning Drawings

Most students learn to create space planning diagrams manually. The following techniques demonstrate digital alternatives using AutoCAD.

Creating Bubble Diagrams

In bubble diagrams, circular shapes are sized proportionally to represent rooms. Their proximity is represented visually through room adjacency requirements. Other symbols can be added to clarify proximity relationships, circulation, as well as view, light, and acoustical privacy requirements. See Chapter 18 on the CD-ROM for one approach to creating bubble diagrams digitally.

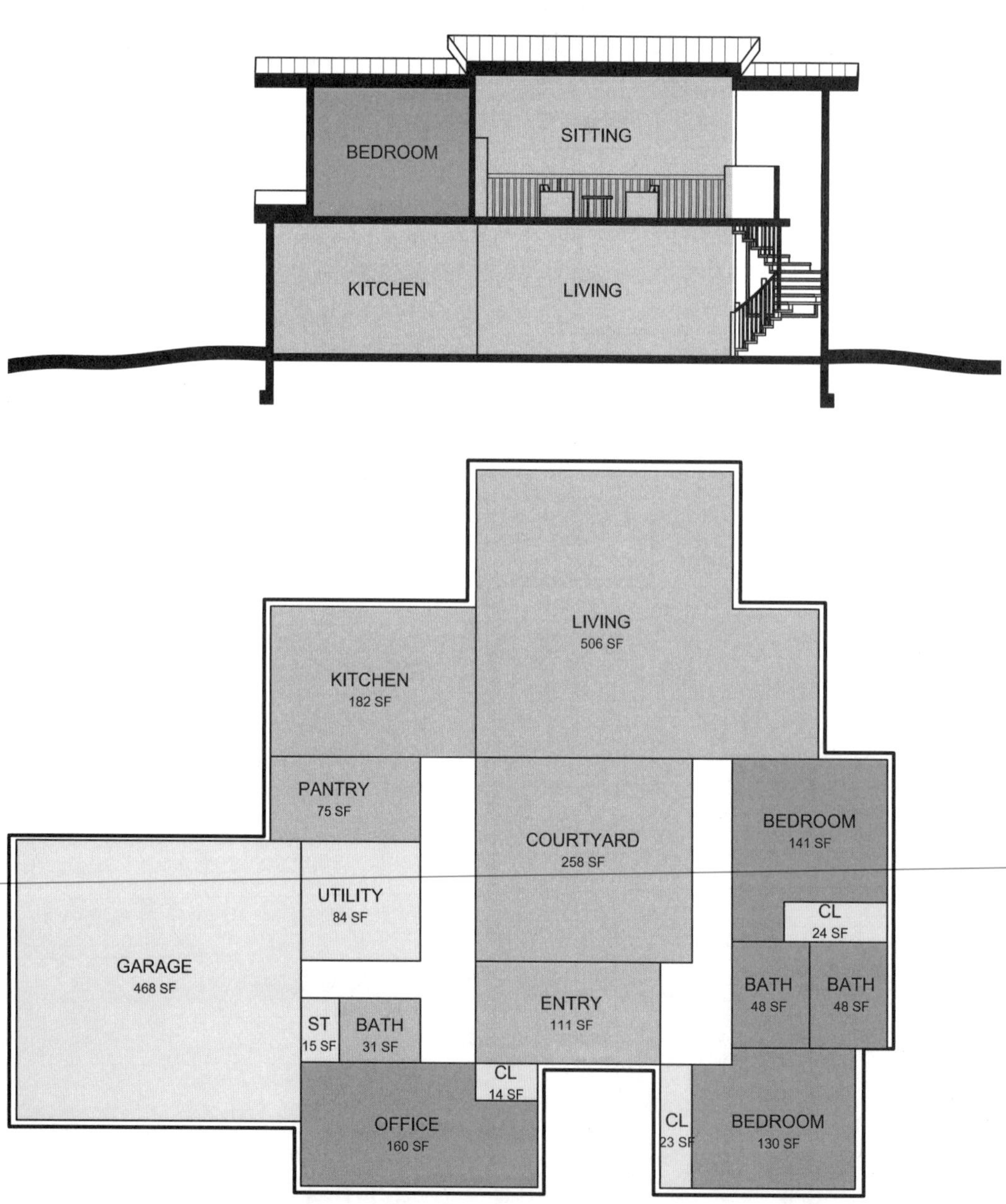

Figure 18.34 Space utilization diagrams can be plan or section generated. (See this image in color on the CD-ROM.)

Student Project: Parker Residence, courtesy of Megan Kreitzberg.

Technique to Master **T18.35** Creating Digital Block Diagrams

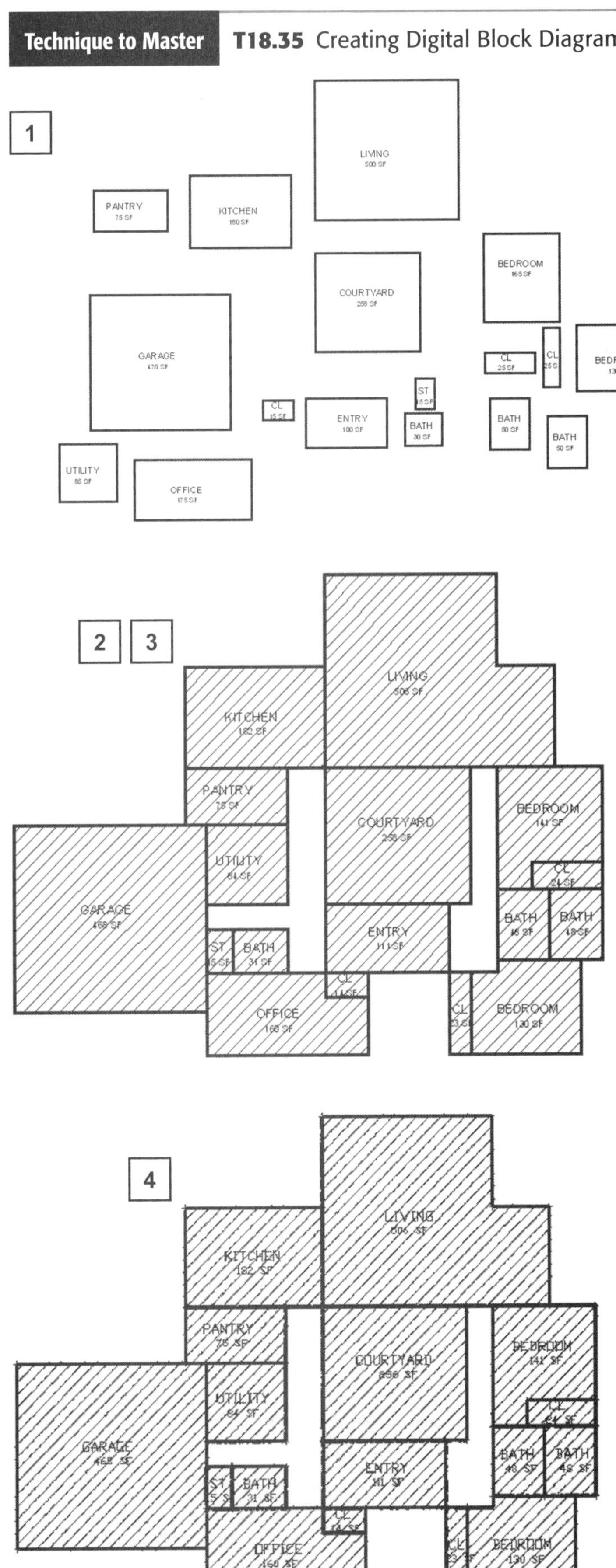

Figure 18.35

1	Create rectangles and/or polygonal shapes at the accurate room size for each room/space (shapes should be rectangles or closed polyline objects when completed—refer to Techniques T05.15 and T05.16 to review polyline creation).
2	Arrange and modify shapes to conform to space planning, programmatic, and creative requirements.
3	Convert polylines to 2-D space objects—see Technique T16.92.
4	(optional) Use Visual Styles to soften the drawing. Refer to Technique T20.24.

Creating Block Diagrams and Area Calculations

In block diagrams, rectangular and polygonal shapes are used to create accurate representations of the square footages for each programmatic space. Shapes are arranged in the building site to reflect a preliminary layout for the design. Figure 18.35 (on the previous page) demonstrates a digital approach for creating block diagrams.

Creating Room Prototypes

Room prototype diagrams should be created as separate drawing files with dashed lines representing the interior side of the boundary walls (Figure 18.36). This allows the diagram to integrate well into the schematic design phase without replicating work. Figures 18.37 and 18.38 demonstrate two digital approaches for creating plan prototype diagrams.

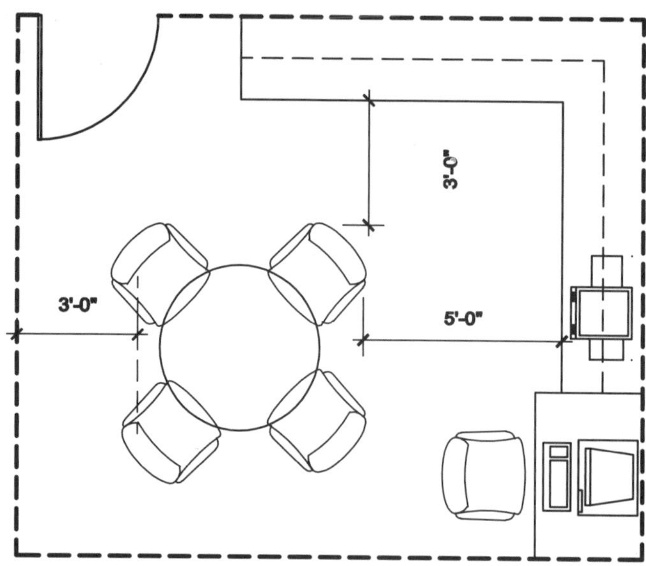

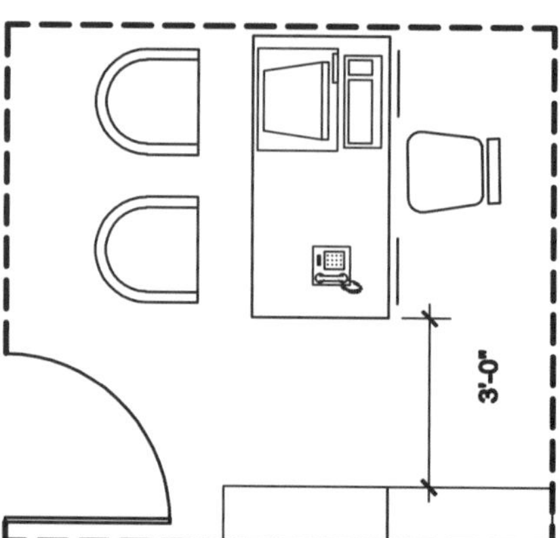

Figure 18.36 Room prototype diagram

Technique to Master **T18.37** Creating Digital Room Prototype Diagrams Using Xrefs

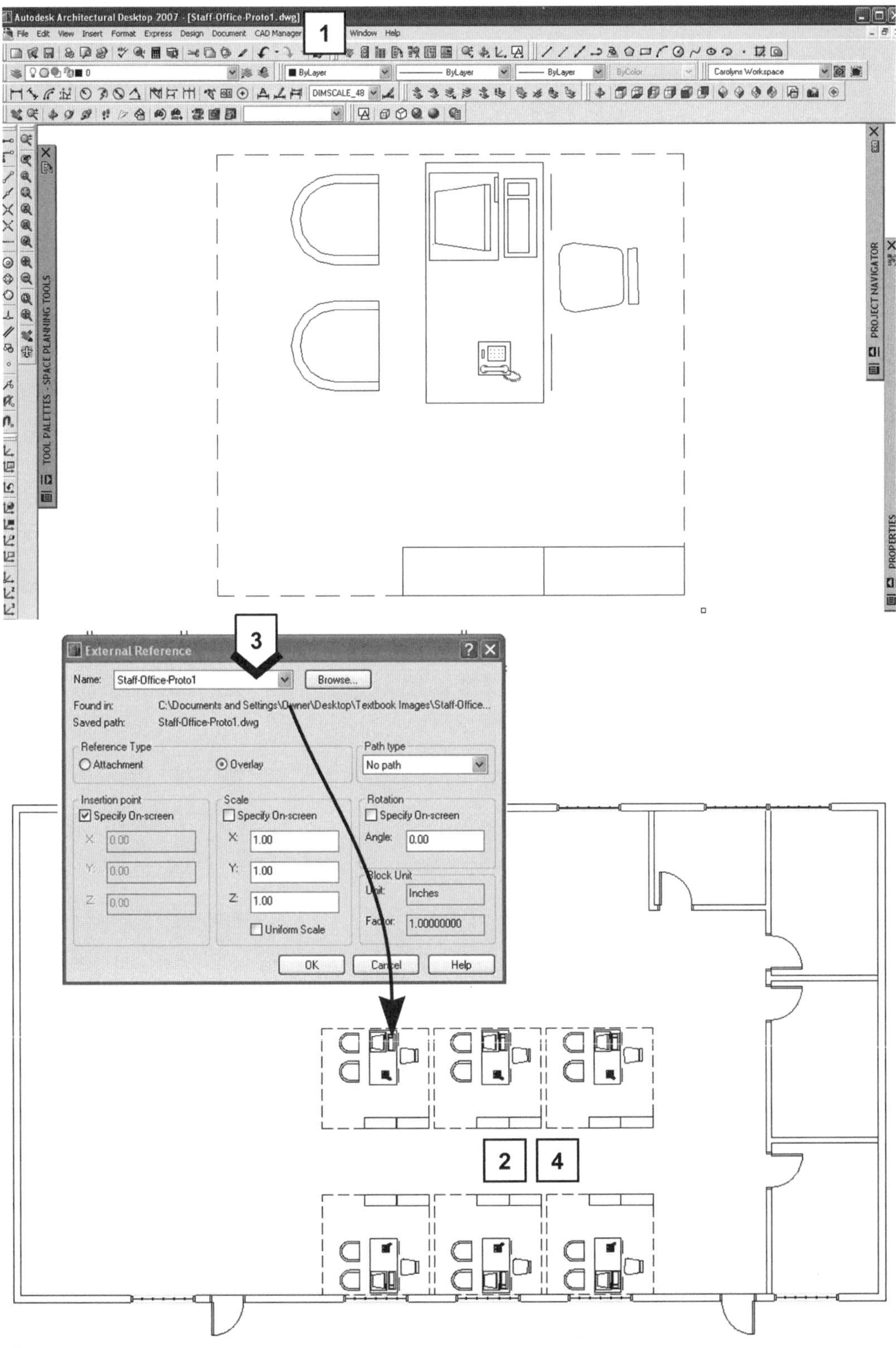

Figure 18.37

1	Create plan prototype for room in its own drawing.
2	Open floor plan or block diagram where room prototypes will be tested.
3	Xref room prototypes into drawing.
4	Duplicate as necessary to create desired space plan.

Technique to Master **T18.38** Creating Digital Room Prototype Diagrams Using Elements

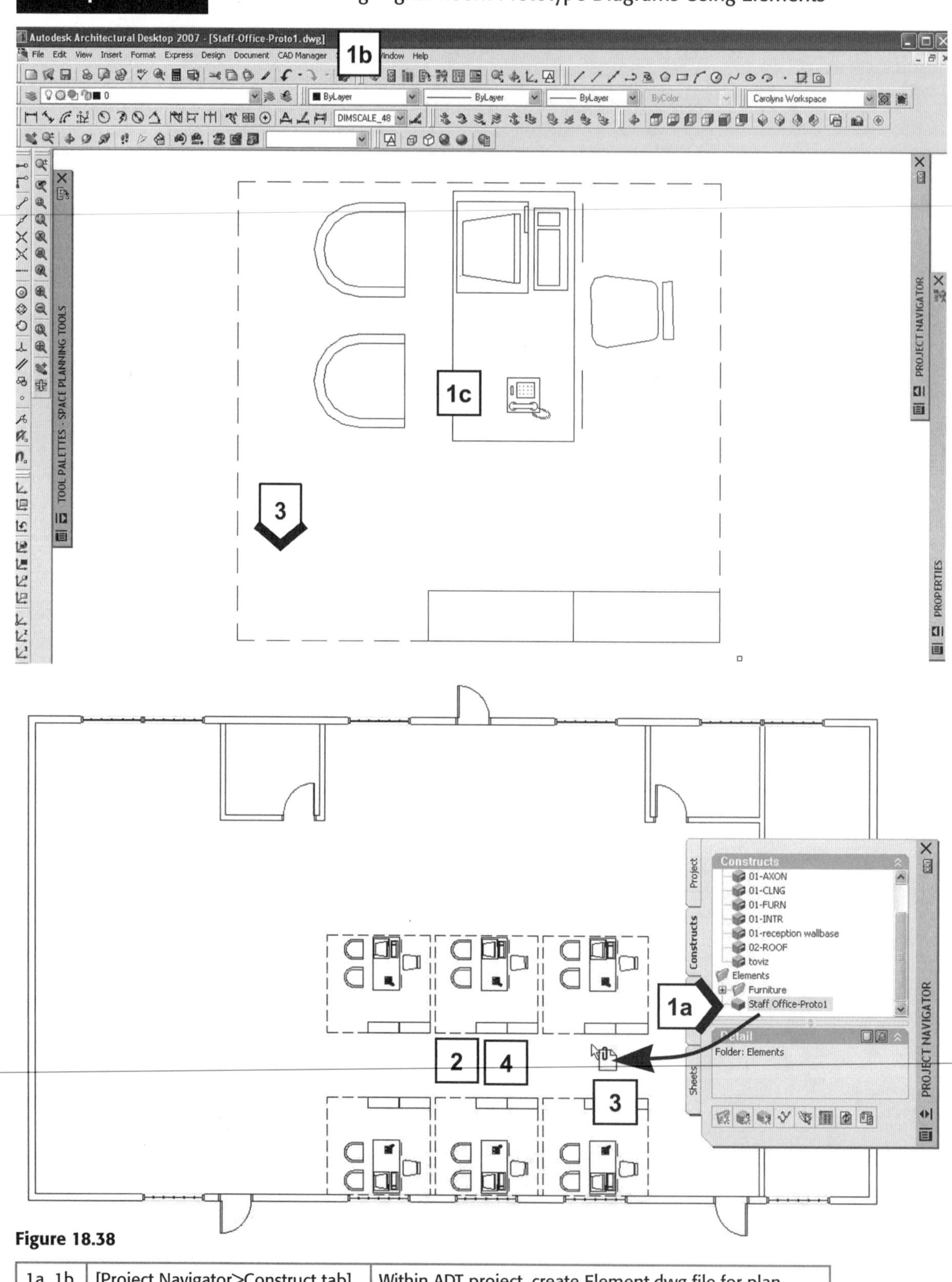

Figure 18.38

1a, 1b, 1c	[Project Navigator>Construct tab]	Within ADT project, create Element.dwg file for plan prototype. Draw plan prototype within element.
2	Open floor plan or block diagram where room prototypes will be tested.	
3	Drag and drop the room prototype Element.dwg file into drawing.	
4	Duplicate elements as necessary to create desired space plan.	

Technique to Master **T18.39** Creating Digital Space Utilization Diagrams Using Polylines

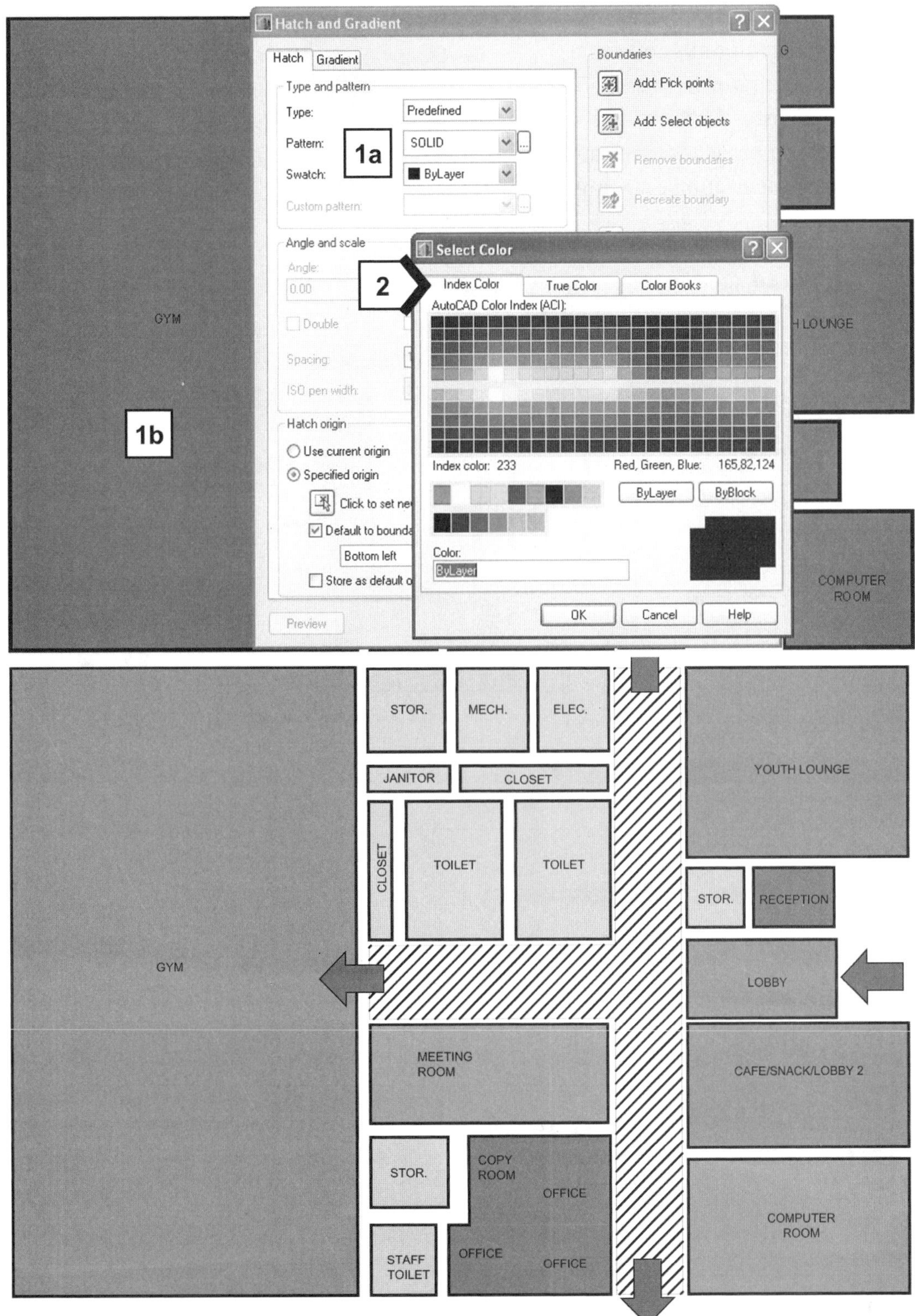

Figure 18.39

1a, 1b	Using block diagram or schematic design floor plan, hatch each closed polyline with the solid hatch type. Refer to Techniques T05.07 and T05.08 for hatching review.
2	AutoCAD's index color, true color, or color books can be used to assign color fills. Color typing is distinguished by space type and usage. Examples include building support, office, and circulation.

Creating Space Utilization Studies

Plan-generated space utilization diagrams use the block diagram as an underlay for the drawing. AutoCAD solid color fills and other patterns are then added to categorize each space in the building. Figures 18.39 and 18.40 demonstrate two digital approaches for creating plan-generated space utilization diagrams.

Chapter Exercises

Open the Chapter 18 folder located on the CD-ROM to access the exercises related to this chapter. Exercises and Drawing Technique Problems for this chapter help students practice conceptualizing spaces and communicating their ideas with digital drawings.

Technique to Master **T18.40** Creating Digital Space Utilization Diagrams Using Space Objects

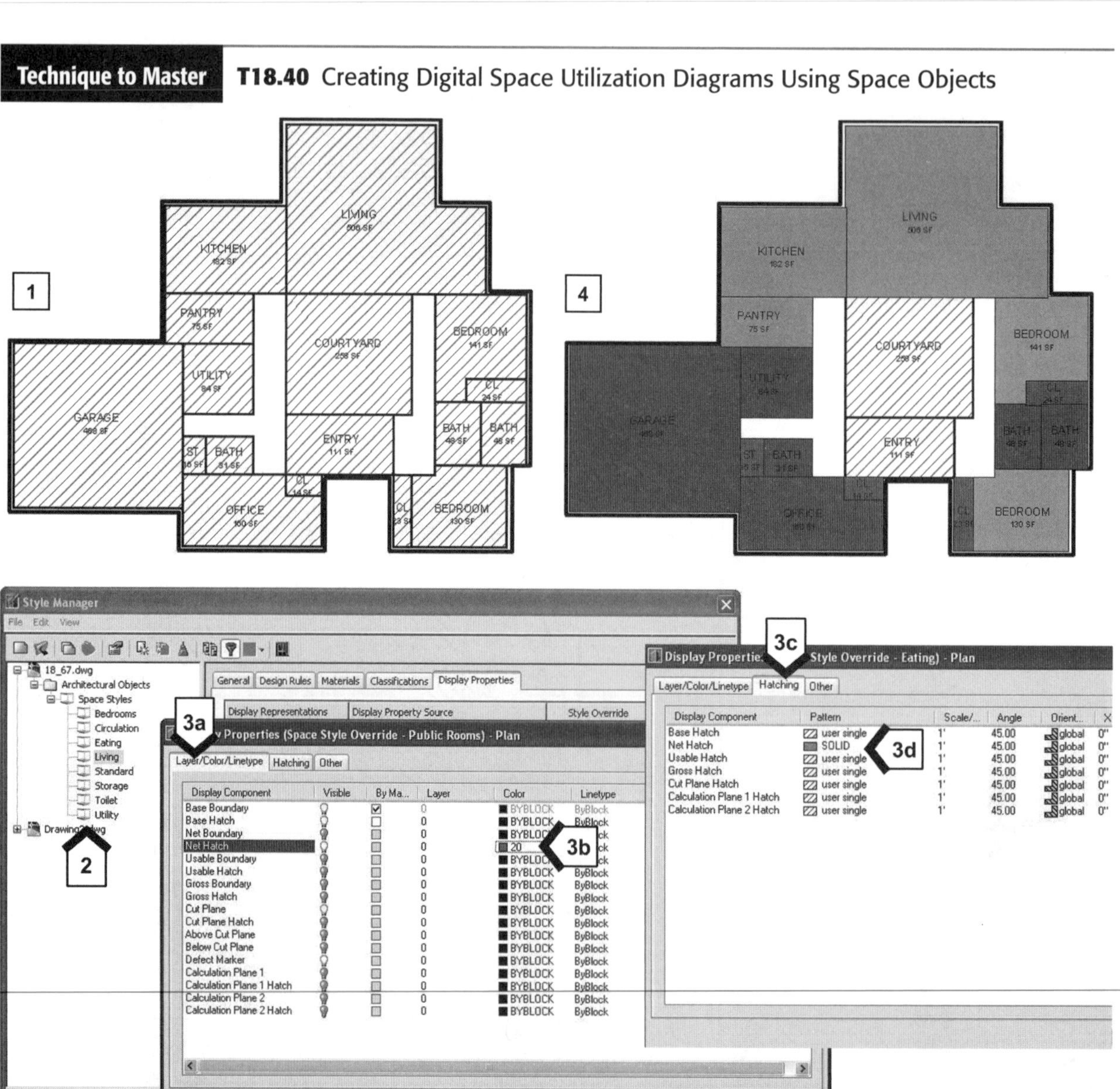

Figure 18.40 (See this image in color on the CD-ROM.)

1	Spaces are by default hatched with an angled line.
2	To create space utilization diagrams, first distinguish each space using ADT's styles. Refer to Technique T13.10.
3a, 3b, 3c, 3d	Next, create style overrides for each space style (refer to Technique T13.50). For the most part, only color and hatch type changes need to be made to each space style override.
4	Complete space utilization diagram using ADT space styles.

Drawing Techniques II: Approaches to 3-D Modeling Craft

19

Objectives

This chapter continues to build on your knowledge of the practice of drawing craft within the digital context. It emphasizes drawing craft in 3-D modeling practices specifically using Architectural Desktop. It ties the various characteristics of digital craft to the virtual model's organization, design process, and presentation. The end-of-chapter exercises and Drawing Technique Problems help students master these approaches quickly.

Drawing Craft in the 3-D Modeling Process

The conventional design process of interior designers and architects has been going through many changes in the past decade. New technology, construction time compression, environmental ethics, and more have forced a reevaluation of the way professionals in these disciplines plan and implement projects. The two-dimensional paradigm that has served the profession in the past is being questioned and replaced by practices that correspond more faithfully to the business-oriented approaches of the field.

This chapter encourages the same replacement of practice within the classroom. The two-dimensional paradigm that subscribes to a process where each drawing is worked on separately discourages volumetric skill development in many students. When designing two-dimensionally, there is a tendency for students to design in only plan view and then extrude the plan to create the sections and elevations. Three-dimensional modeling, however, requires the reaction to the third dimension very early in the design process.

New challenges—both good and bad—will arise from this paradigm shift. Connections and details that are not always resolved when only working in plan and section suddenly have to be addressed in the virtual model (Figure 19.1). Furthermore, drawing imbalances often occur because of the amount of

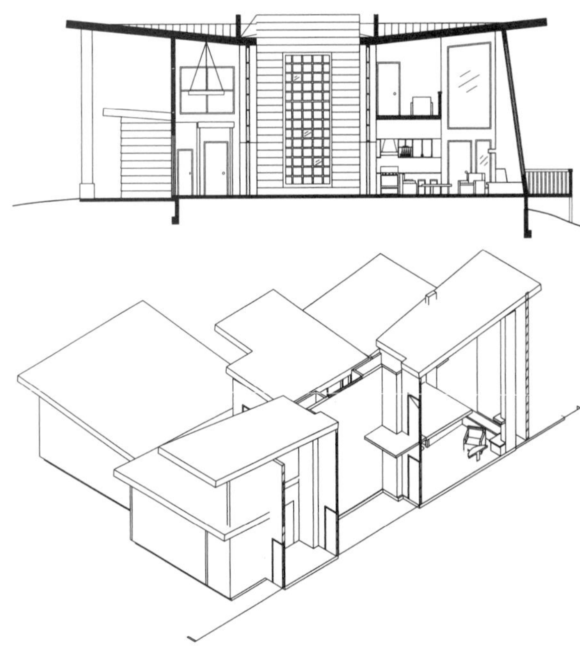

Figure 19.1 Designing and developing a project in 3-D often requires areas of the design to be worked out in much earlier stages of the design process. In the example, the fenestration of the curtain wall located in the center courtyard needs to be resolved with the floor slab on the second floor extending outside to create the balcony.
Student Project: Parker Residence, courtesy of Megan Kreitzberg.

detail included in most 3-D objects found in the pre-built libraries. It sets up a danger of adding excessive detail to some areas while other areas of the virtual model remain noticeably underdeveloped.

All of the above challenges create a need to structure the methods in which 3-D models are built in Architectural Desktop. This chapter suggests a few possible approaches to virtual model development. The pedagogy behind this structure reinforces the importance of using *all* drawings to inform design development. This is not necessarily used in professional practice. Our reasoning stems from the belief that beginning and intermediate design students need this type of approach to reinforce the relationship of building systems in design.

This chapter is divided differently from previous chapters. The first section, Drawing Craft in Creating the View Slices, teaches the view creation process within the Project Navigator and demonstrates section and elevation view creation. Drawing Craft in the Virtual Model suggests possible approaches to virtual model creation and development. The final section, Approaches to Efficient Modeling Practices, reinforces good three-dimensional drawing practices and habits.

Drawing Craft in Creating the View Slices

View drawings were first introduced in Chapter 9. As a part of Architectural Desktop's project organization system, they create the conventional orthographic view drawings for the virtual model (Figure 19.2). Typical view examples might include the following:

- Floor plans
- Reflected ceiling plans
- Exterior elevations
- Building sections
- Three-dimensional isometrics or perspectives

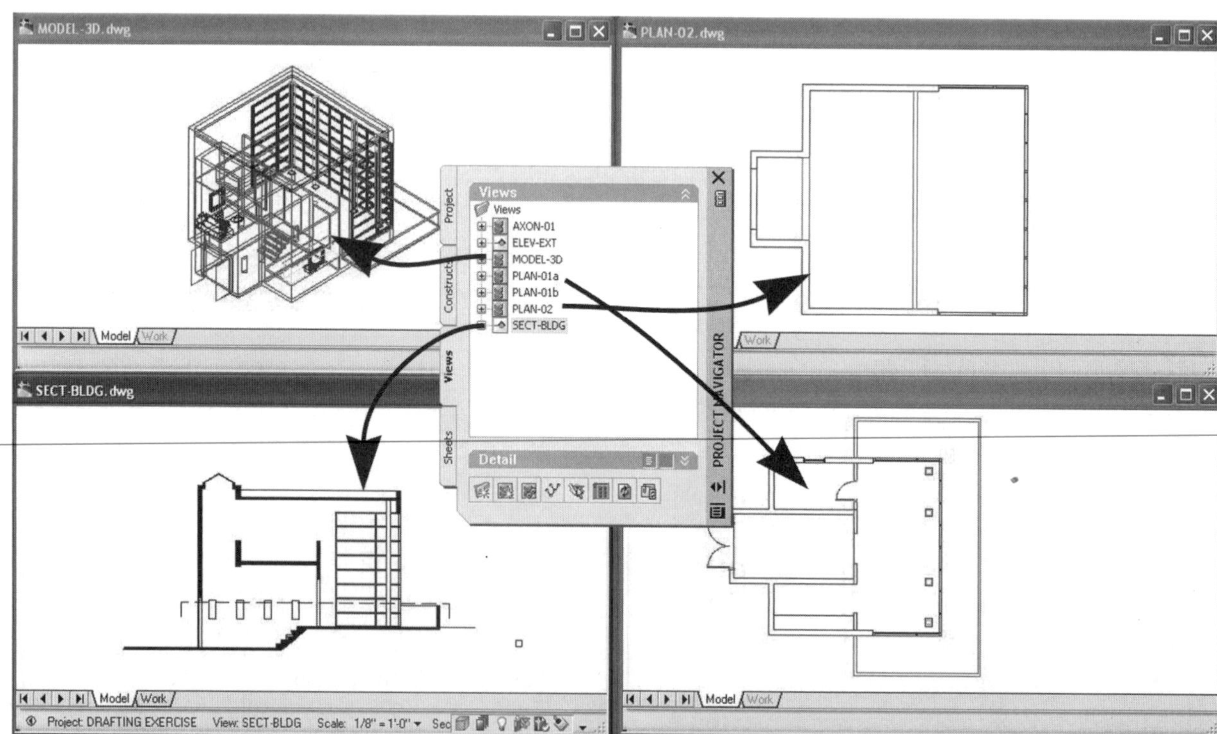

Figure 19.2 Each view drawing is representative of conventional orthographic views.

Understanding How ADT Creates View Drawings

View drawings use the virtual model's constructs to generate the conventional orthographic views used in presentation and construction drawings. These constructs are automatically referenced (Xrefed) during the view creation process.

Architectural Desktop, however, is not consistent in the way the orthographic views are created within the view creation process. Views created for floor and ceiling plans use referenced constructs and remain three-dimensional in nature (Figure 19.3). To achieve the correct orthographic display for the view, floor plans and ceiling plans rely on Display Configurations (Figure 19.4).

This method is inconsistent with how ADT creates its sections and elevations. First, the New View Dwg command for section/elevations only creates the .dwg file with the appropriate constructs referenced into this drawing file; the view creation process does not actually create the section or elevation slices through the virtual model. Secondly, Display Configurations, while helpful for controlling the level of detail, are not needed for the display of the section/elevation object. This inconsistency may cause confusion in students who are learning about views and view creation.

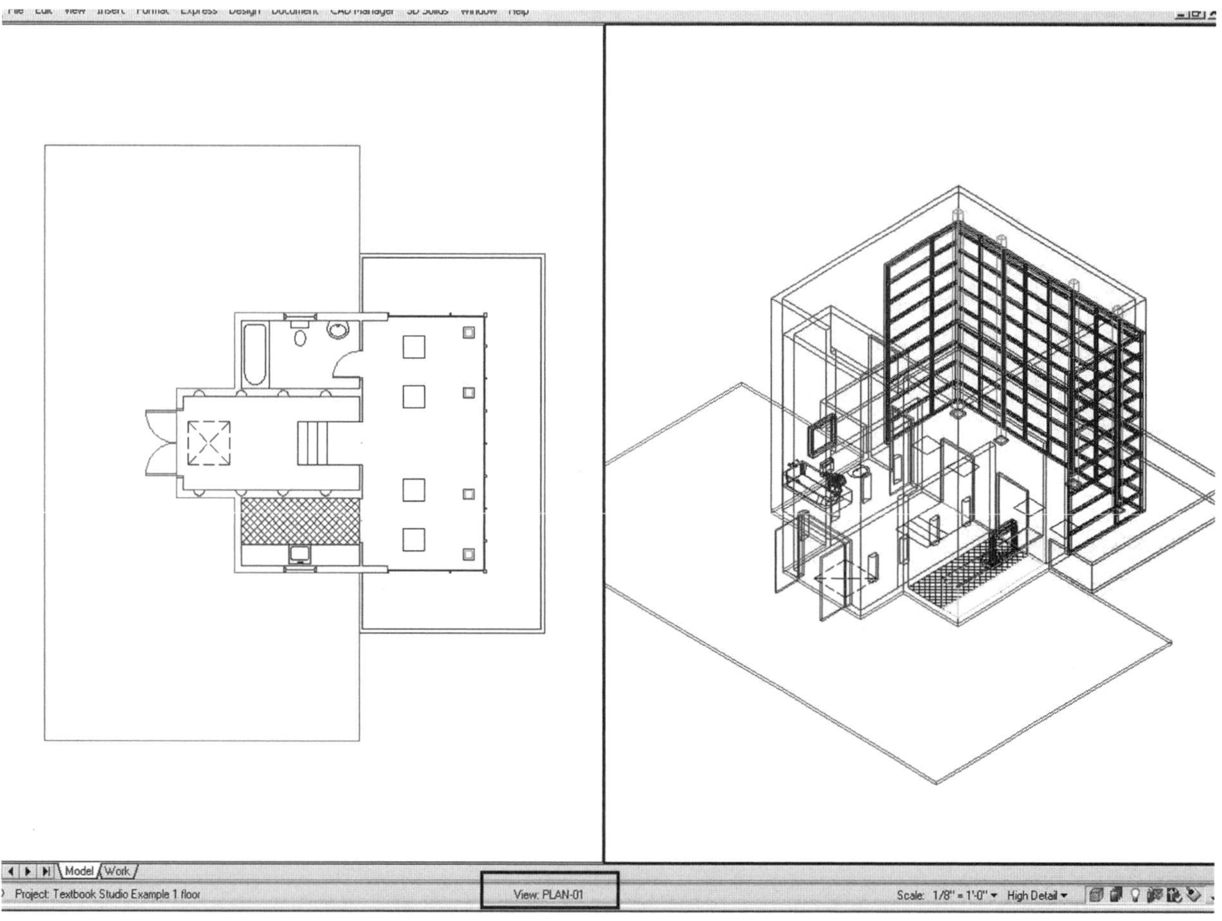

Figure 19.3 Though view drawings are used to create the conventional orthographic floor plans, these plan views are actually three-dimensional in nature.

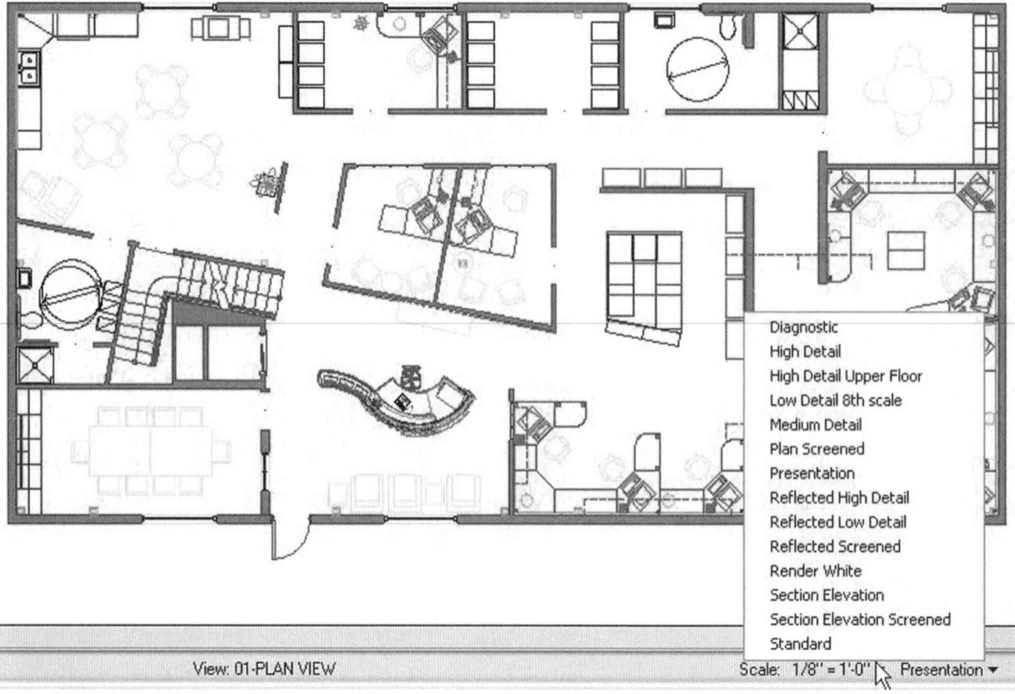

Figure 19.4 The use of Display Configurations will easily change a floor plan view to a ceiling plan view.

Student Project: Office Renovation, courtesy of Lauren Baez.

Creating View Drawings

Technique T09.26 in Chapter 9 demonstrated the view creation process for plans and other general drawings. Figures 19.5 through 19.7 demonstrate view creation techniques for isometrics and perspectives. See these figures in the Chapter 19 folder on the CD-ROM. Section/elevation view creation is introduced in the paragraphs that follow.

Section/Elevation Objects and Their Associative Capabilities

The actual section/elevation generation process uses the linked constructs to create separate, unique object types that are the generated results of the specified slice. These object types can be either two-dimensional or three-dimensional representations of the section/elevation (Figure 19.8).

Generated section and elevation objects retain an associative link to their building section (or elevation) lines (Figure 19.9). This link allows these objects to be updated when design changes are made to the virtual model. Associative links are one-way only—that is, changes made to the section or elevation object will not update the virtual model.

Technique to Master T19.05 Creating Floor Plan Views

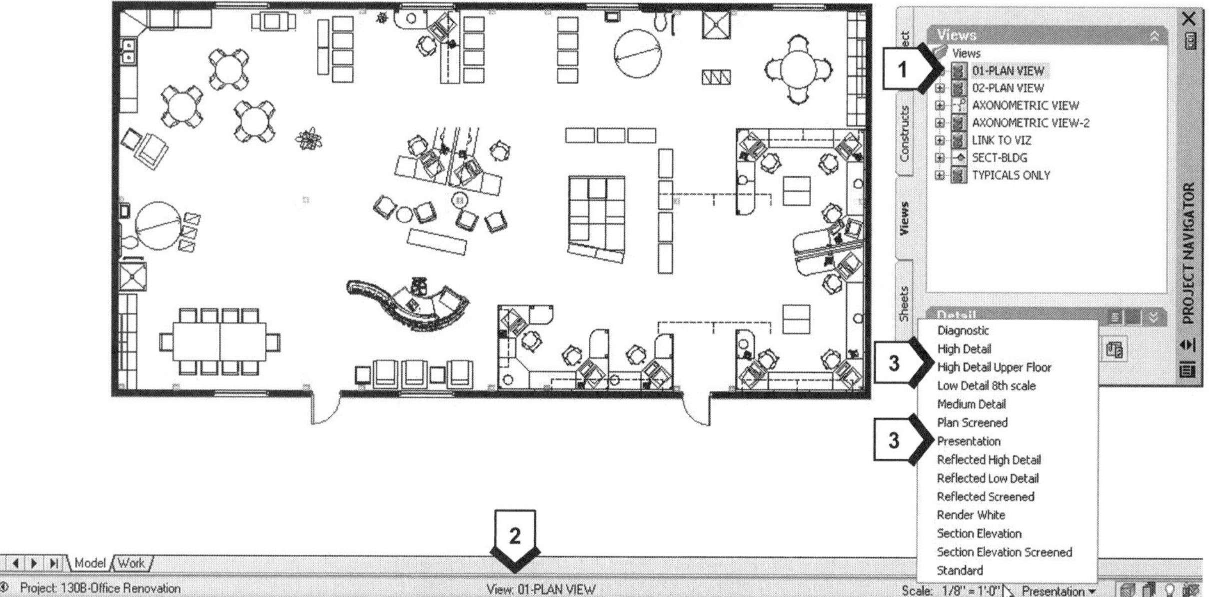

Figure 19.5

1	Create a plan view drawing using Technique T09.26.
2	Open the plan view drawing.
3	Select desired Display Configuration. High Detail and High Detail Upper Floor will display full height walls as lines while the Presentation display will display a solid fill for all full-height walls.

Technique to Master T19.06 Creating Ceiling Plan Views

Figure 19.6

1	Create a plan view drawing using Technique T09.26.
2	Open the plan view drawing.
3	Select desired Reflected Display Configuration.

Technique to Master **T19.07** Creating Roof Plan Views

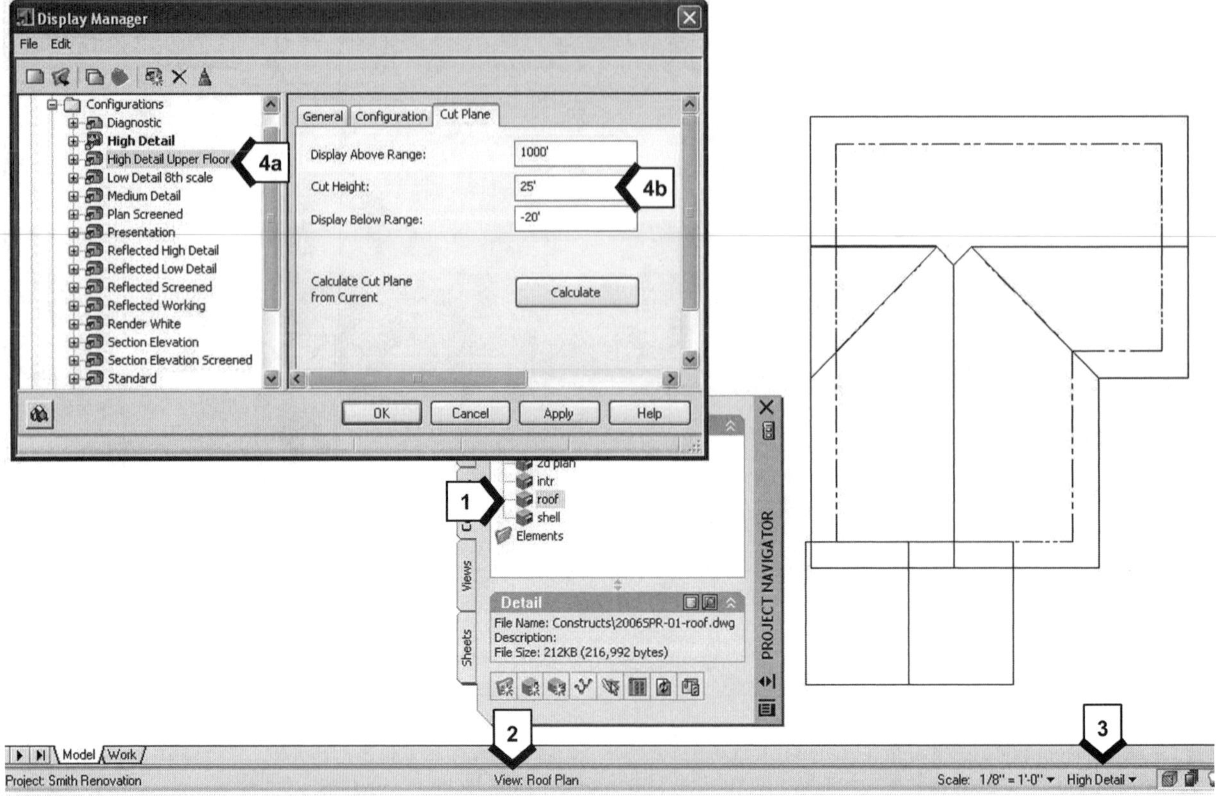

Figure 19.7

1	Create a plan view drawing using Technique T09.26.
2	Open the plan view drawing.
3	Either select the High Detail or High Detail Upper Floor Display Configuration.
4a, 4b	Change the global cut plane for the chosen Display Configuration so that it is higher than the tallest roof.

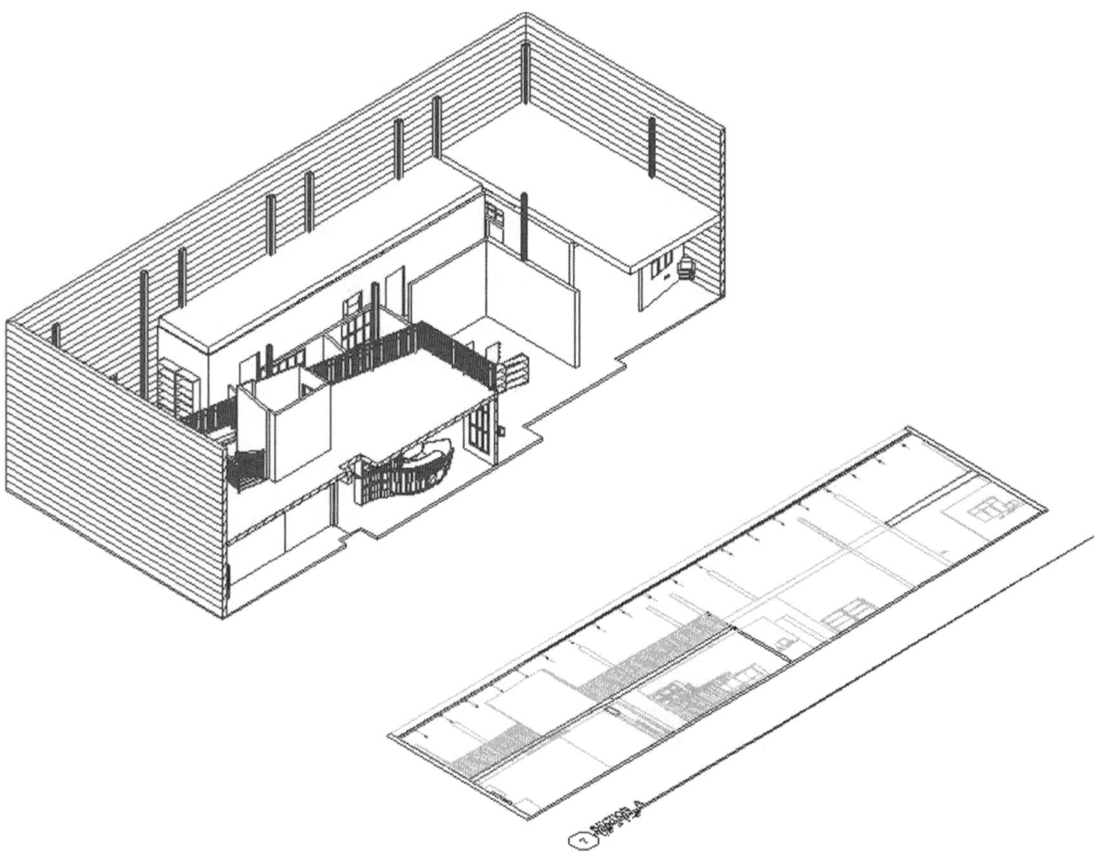

Figure 19.8 Generated sections can be two-dimensional or three-dimensional.

Student Project: Office Renovation, courtesy of Lauren Baez.

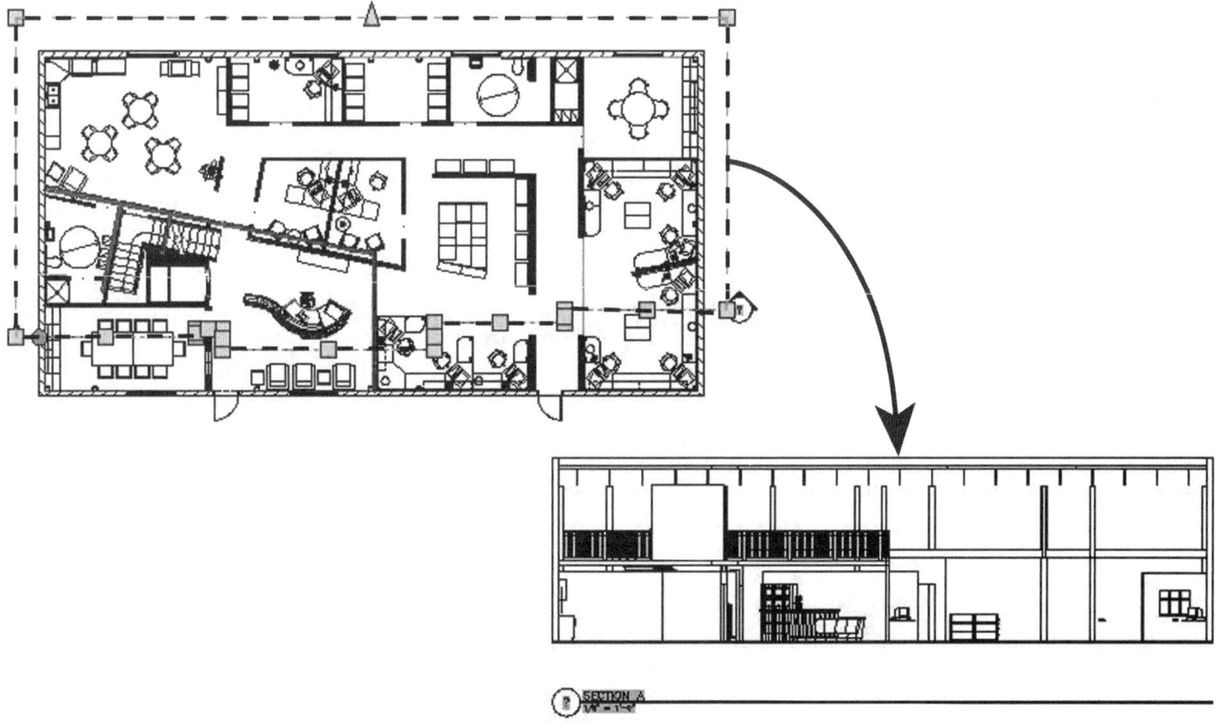

Figure 19.9 Generated section and elevation objects will always retain an associative link to their section (or elevation) lines. Updates to the generated section or elevation can be made through the regenerate tool.

Student Project: Office Renovation, courtesy of Lauren Baez.

Creating Sections and Elevations in ADT–The Workflow Process

Figures 19.10 through 19.14 summarize the steps needed to create a section or an elevation in ADT using a 3-D virtual model as its source.

1. Create a view drawing where the section (or elevation) will be generated. Refer to Technique T19.10.
2. Open Plan View drawing. Refer to Technique T19.05 for Floor Plan View creation.
3. Use symbol callouts to identify section slice (or elevation direction). Refer to Techniques T19.11 through T19.13.

(continued on page 472)

Technique to Master **T19.10** Creating a Section/Elevation View Drawing

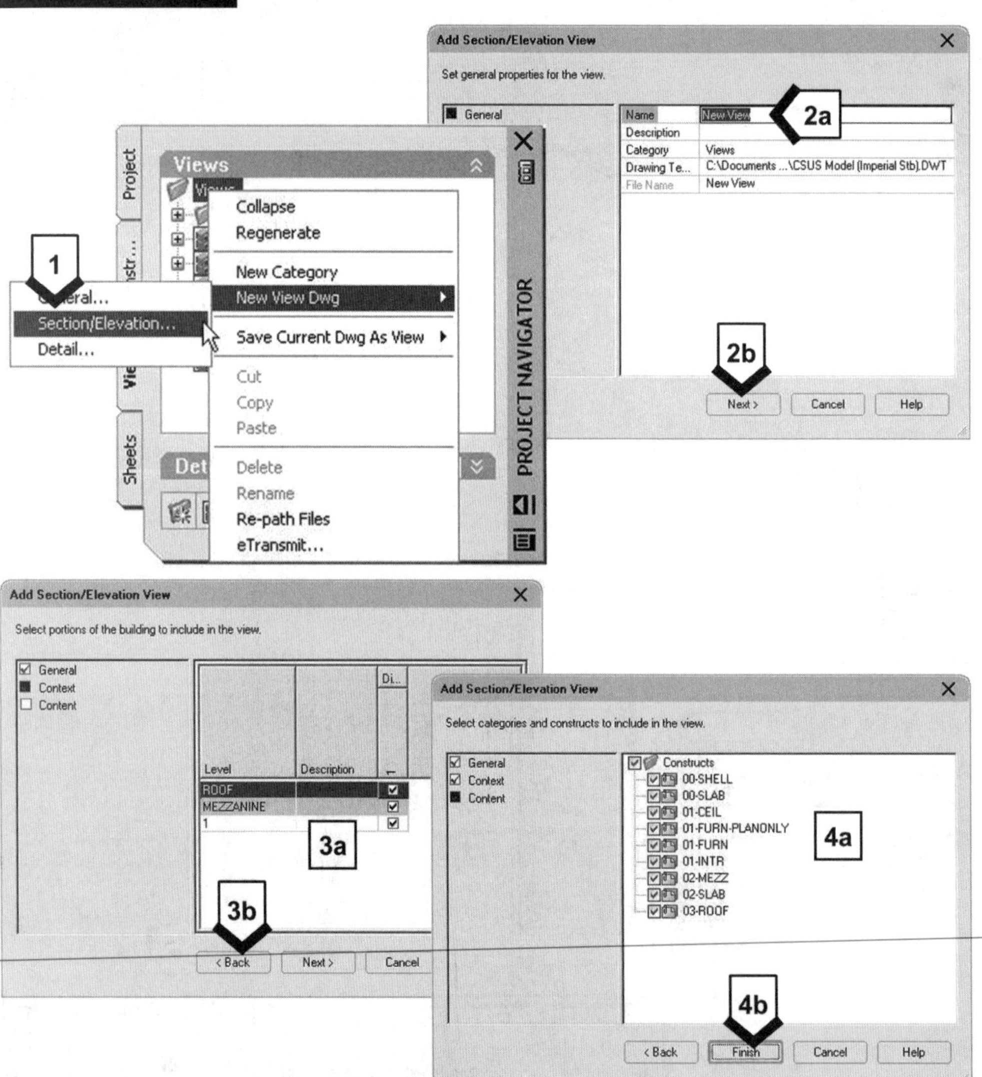

Figure 19.10

1	Create a new view drawing using the Section/Elevation command option.	
2a, 2b	[Add Section/Elevation View dialogue box]	Name the drawing using file naming standards for view drawings. Click the Next button.
3a, 3b	[Add Section/Elevation View dialogue box]	Check all levels that will be included in building sections. (This is normally all of them including the roof.) Click the Next button.
4a, 4b	[Add Section/Elevation View dialogue box]	Check all constructs to be included in building sections. Click the Finish Button.

Technique to Master **T19.11** Using a Section Callout to Generate a Building Section

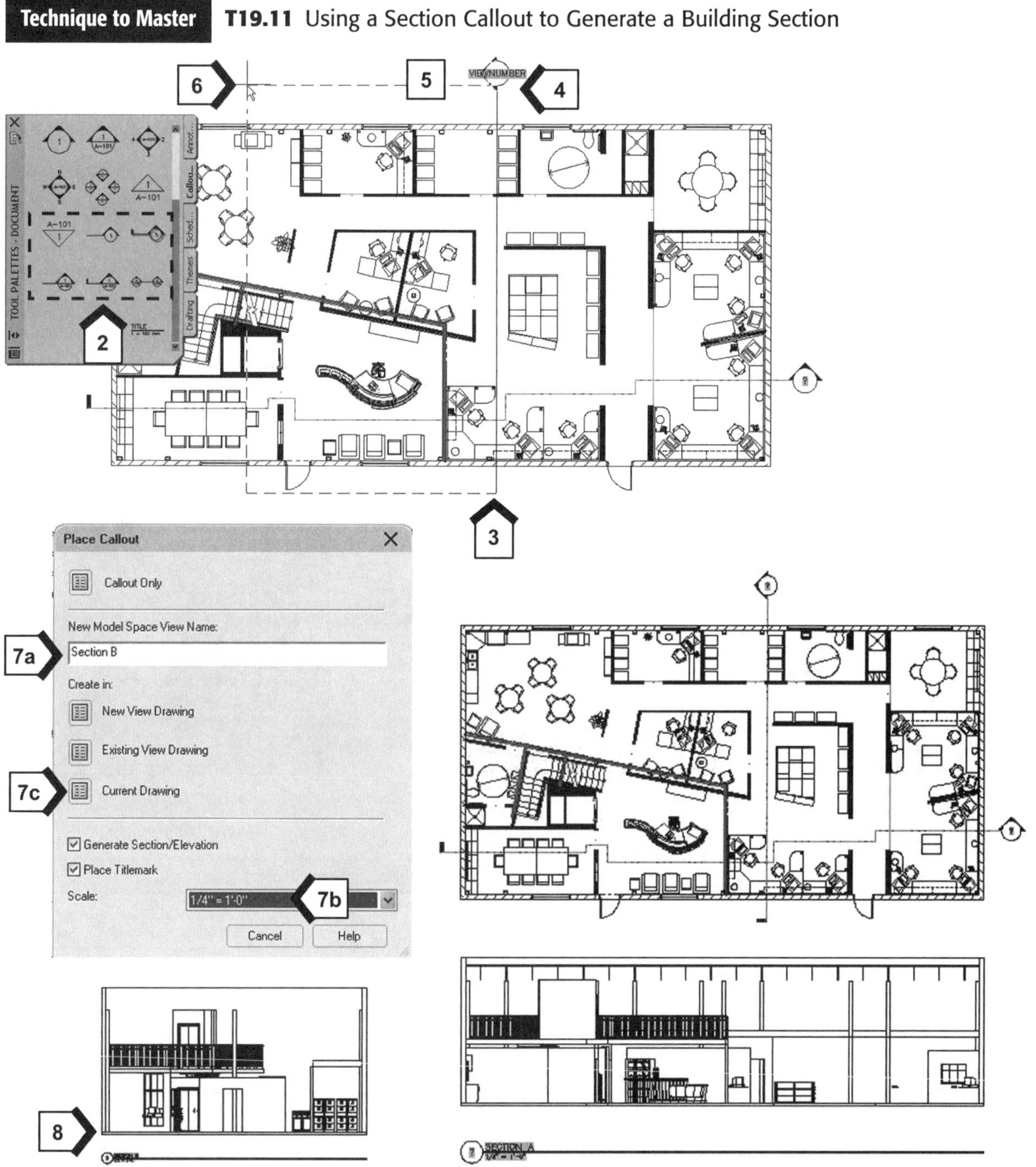

Figure 19.11

Student Project: Office Renovation, courtesy of Lauren Baez.

1	[Project Navigator>View tab]	Open the section view drawing through the Project Navigator.
2	[Document Tool palette>Callouts tab]	Select any section tag.
3	[Drawing Screen]	With Ortho on, specify first point of section line.
4	[Drawing Screen]	Specify last point. Press Enter.
5	[Drawing Screen]	Specify arrow direction.
6	[Drawing Screen]	Specify extents of section rectangle.
7a, 7b, 7c	[Place Callout dialogue box]	Name the building section. Make sure the scale is correct and then click the Current Drawing button.
8	[Drawing Screen]	Specify insertion point for section.

Technique to Master **T19.12** Using an Elevation Callout to Generate a Building Elevation

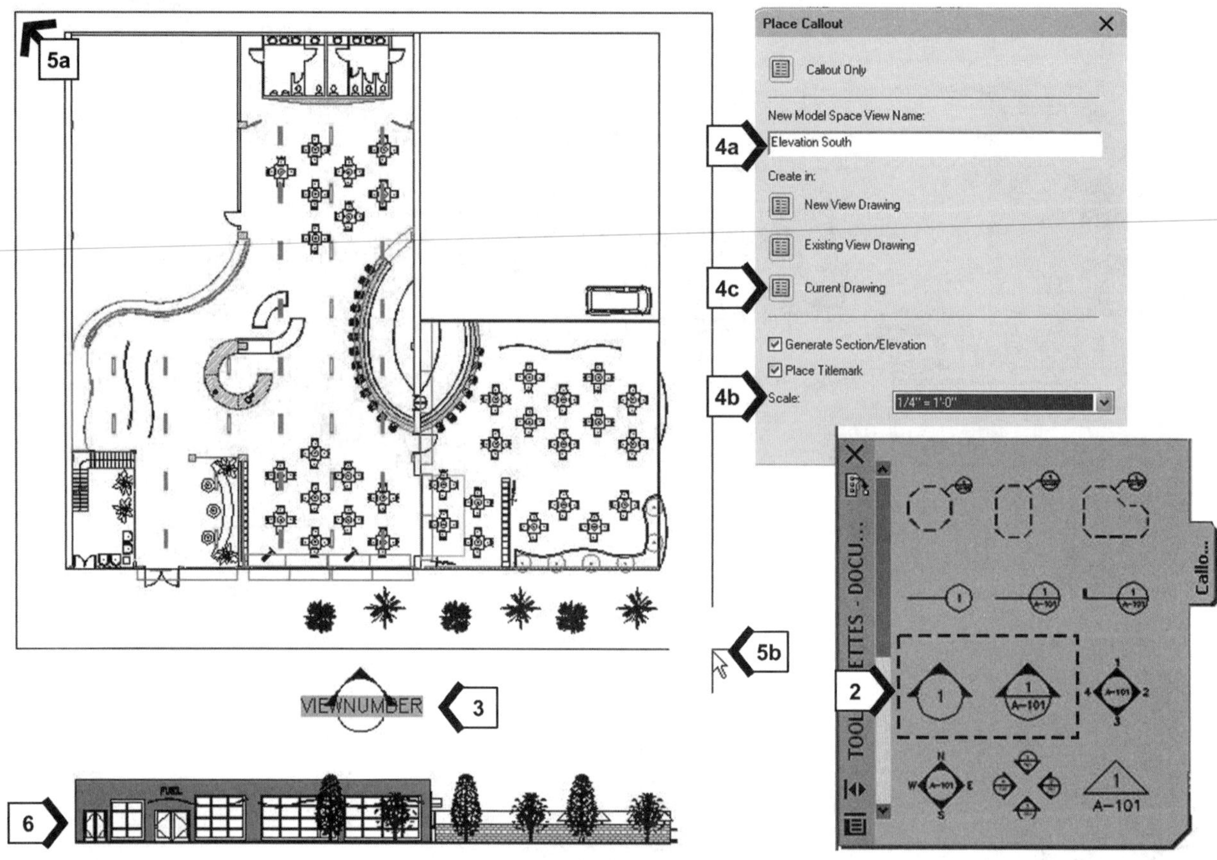

Figure 19.12

Student Project: Restaurant Design, courtesy of Andrea Pabon.

1	[Project Navigator>View tab]	Open the elevation view drawing through the Project Navigator.
2	[Document Tool palette> Callouts tab]	Select any elevation tag.
3	[Drawing Screen]	Place the elevation tag. Specify arrow direction.
4a, 4b, 4c	[Place Callout dialogue box]	Name the elevation (north, south, east, west, etc.). Make sure the scale is correct and then click the Current Drawing button.
5a, 5b	[Drawing Screen]	Create a rectangle around the building and site that you want to include within your elevation.
6	[Drawing Screen]	Specify the insertion point for your elevation.

4. Place generated sections (or elevations) in the appropriate view drawing. Refer to Technique T19.14.
5. Open section (or elevation) view drawing.
6. Refine section line (or elevation line) extents. Refer to Technique T19.25.
7. Refine sections (or elevations) keeping the associative link. Refer to Techniques T19.30 through T19.33.

Technique to Master T19.13 Using an Elevation Callout to Generate a Interior Elevation

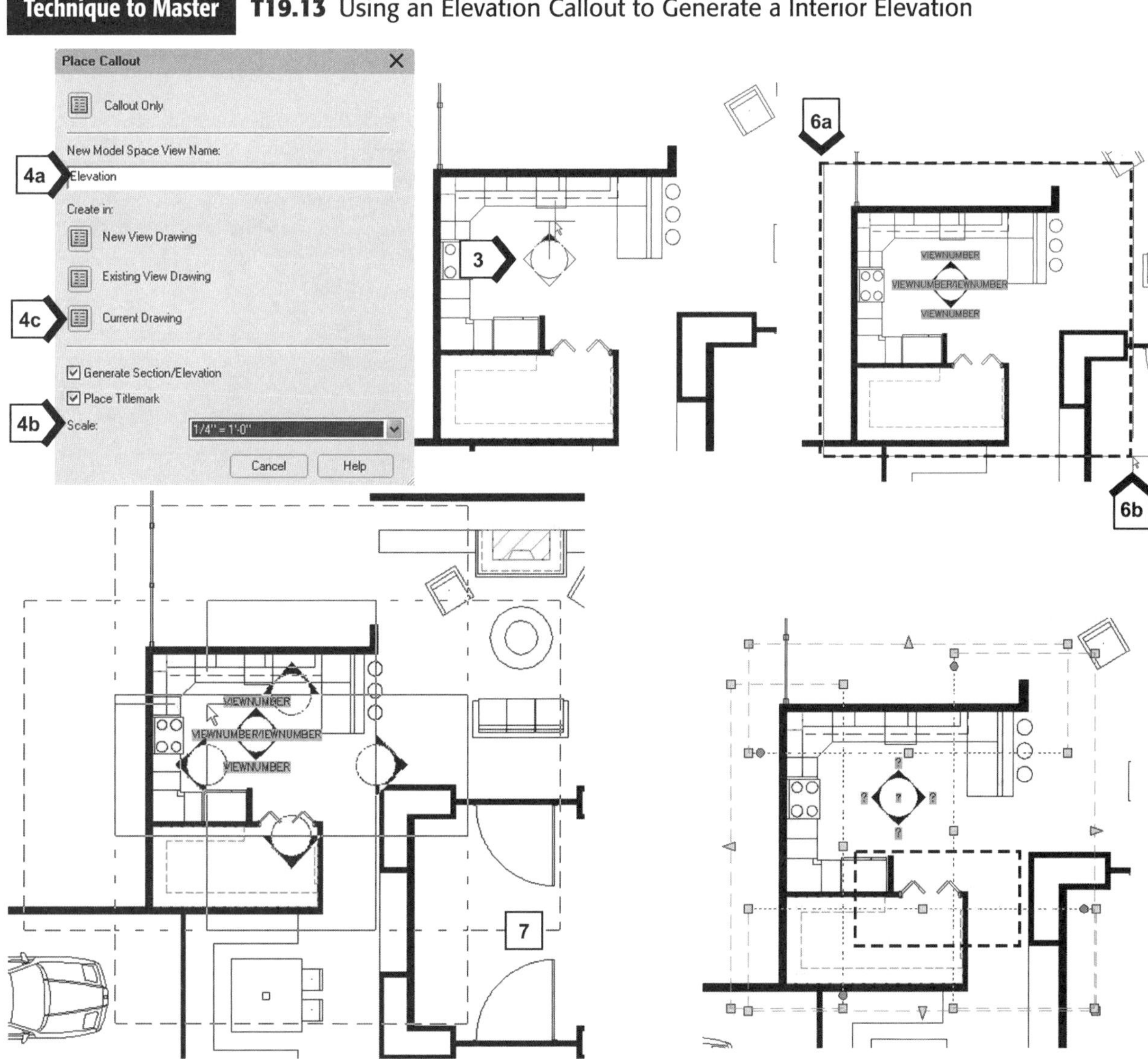

Figure 19.13

Student Project: Parker Residence, courtesy of Megan Kreitzberg.

1	[Project Navigator>View tab]	Open the elevation view drawing through the Project Navigator.
2	[Document Tool palette> Callouts tab]	Select any interior elevation tag.
3	[Drawing Screen]	Place the elevation tag. Specify the first elevation's direction.
4a, 4b, 4c	[Place Callout dialogue box]	Name the interior elevation. Make sure the scale is correct and then select the Current Drawing button.
5	[Drawing Screen]	Press Enter.
6a, 6b	[Drawing Screen]	Create a rectangle around the room or space to include in the elevation.
7	[Drawing Screen]	Move mouse to specify the depth of the elevation rectangle.
8	[Command Line]	Specify the extent of the elevation's height.
9	[Drawing Screen]	Specify the insertion point for the interior elevations.
10	[Drawing Screen]	Specify distance between elevations.

Technique to Master **T19.14** Placing Generated Sections (or Elevations) in the Appropriate View Drawing

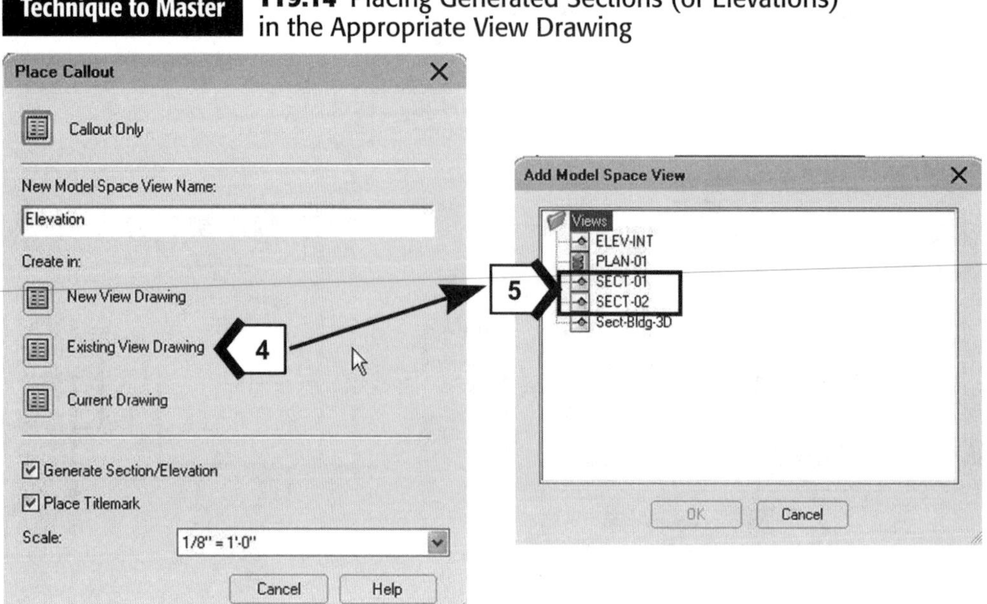

Figure 19.14 This procedure demonstrates how to place the callout symbol in the plan view while generating the section or elevation their respective view drawings. Make sure the section or elevation view drawing has been created first. Refer to Technique T19.10.

1	Open the plan view drawing.	
2	[Drawing Screen]	Use the symbol callouts to identify the section slice (or elevation direction). Refer to Techniques T19.11 through T19.13 for placing symbols correctly.
3	[Place Callout dialogue box]	Name the elevation or section. Make sure the scale is correct.
4	[Place Callout dialogue box]	Select the Existing View Drawing button.
5	[Add Model Space View]	Select the section or elevation view drawing.
6	[Drawing Screen]	Continue completing prompts for completing section or elevation generation.

View Drawing Refinement

View drawing refinement refers to the additional development that has to occur to make the drawing print-ready. In most cases, some adjustment will need to take place for the orthographic drawings that are created by views. These adjustments could be anything from lineweight and plot style adjustments to object detail adjustments (Figure 19.15).

Drawing refinement for views, in general, can be accomplished in two ways. The primary method keeps the associative link between the view and its constructs. This is the preferred method since this associative link is critical during further design development. The second method breaks the link and essentially converts the view drawing to a normal AutoCAD 2-D line drawing. This method can be used during the later stages of the design process when the desired drawing refinement can be achieved only using two-dimensional modification techniques.

Figures 19.16 through 19.22 illustrate some of the more common issues and solutions regarding view refinement.

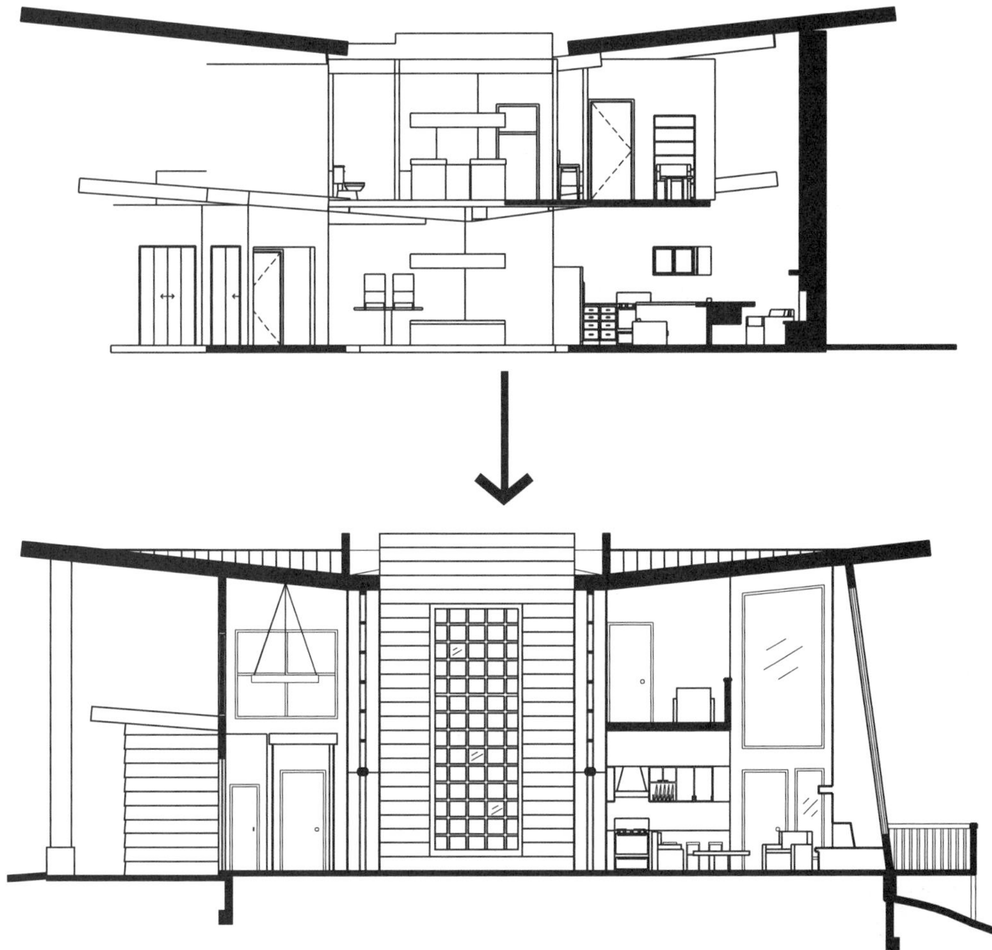

Figure 19.15 View drawing refinement refers to the additional development that has to occur to make the drawing print-ready. The top example shows a generated section that needs additional refinement (bottom).

Student Project: Parker Residence, courtesy of Megan Kreitzberg.

Technique to Master **T19.16** ADT Objects in Plan View Are Not Displaying

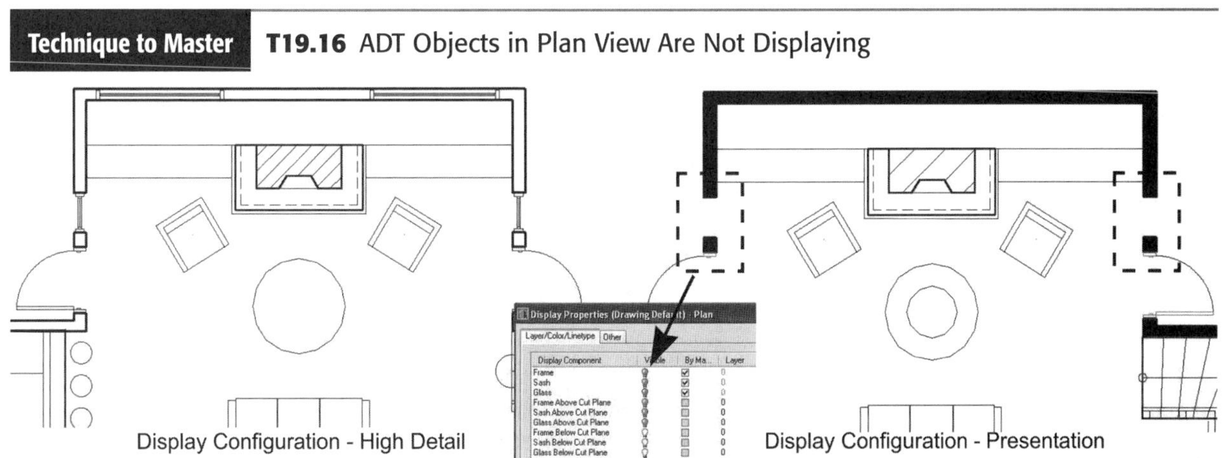

Figure 19.16

A typical problem is when ADT objects do not display at all in plan view. If the layer of the object (in the Layer Manager) is On and Thawed, this is most likely a display problem. Check the Display Properties for the ADT object style in question. Many times the visibility settings have been turned off through the object itself or the material definition to which the object is assigned. Refer to Technique T13.51 for object style override techniques.

Technique to Master **T19.17** ADT Objects in Plan View Display Unwanted Hatching

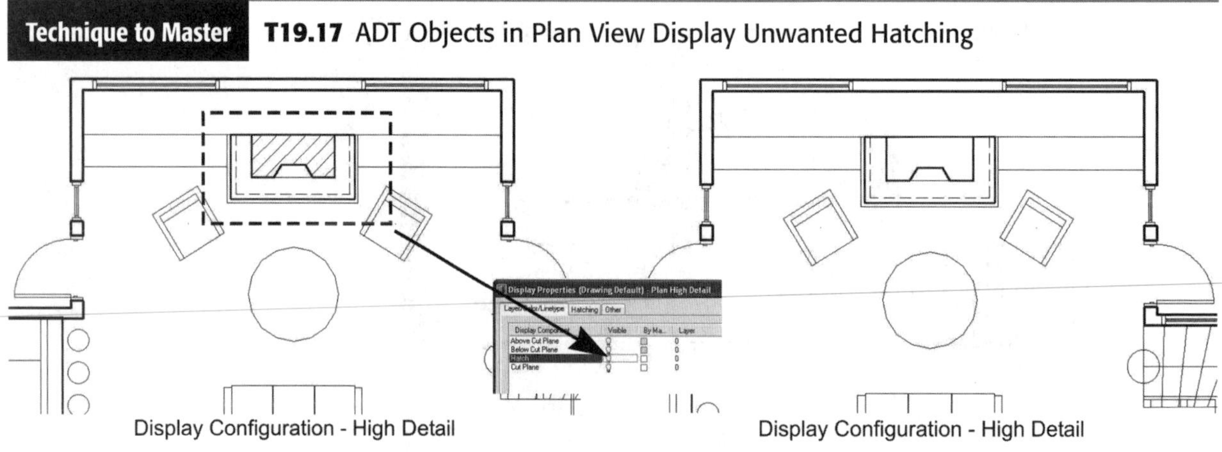

Figure 19.17

By default, mass elements and structural objects display hatching in the plan view. This may be undesirable for furniture or equipment objects inserted in your design. Hatch visibility can be easily turned off in the Display Properties of any ADT object.

Technique to Master **T19.18** ADT Objects in Plan View Have Too Much Detail

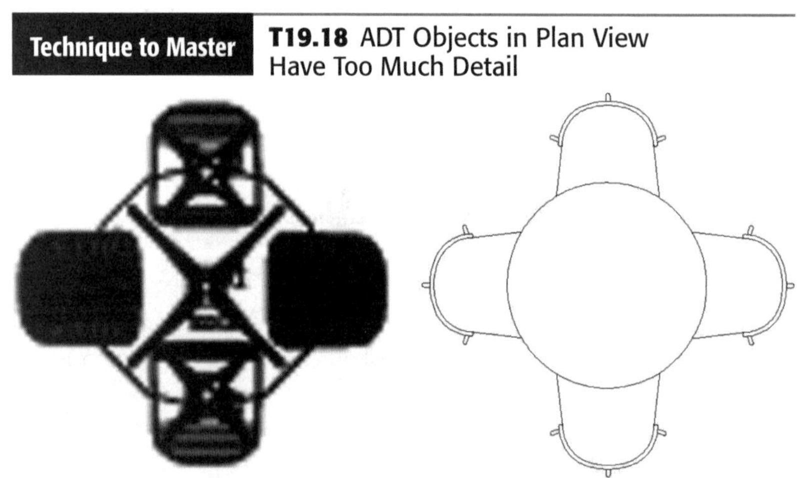

Figure 19.18

This is a common problem when using premade 3-D libraries found from sources other than the Design Center. To resolve the problem, create multi-view blocks for all problematic furniture, fixtures, and equipment. Multi-view blocks allow you to assign 2-D blocks to a specific view direction. This allows you to simplify plan, elevation, and side views of 3-D objects.

Technique to Master **T19.19** ADT Objects in Plan View Display the Wrong Linetype

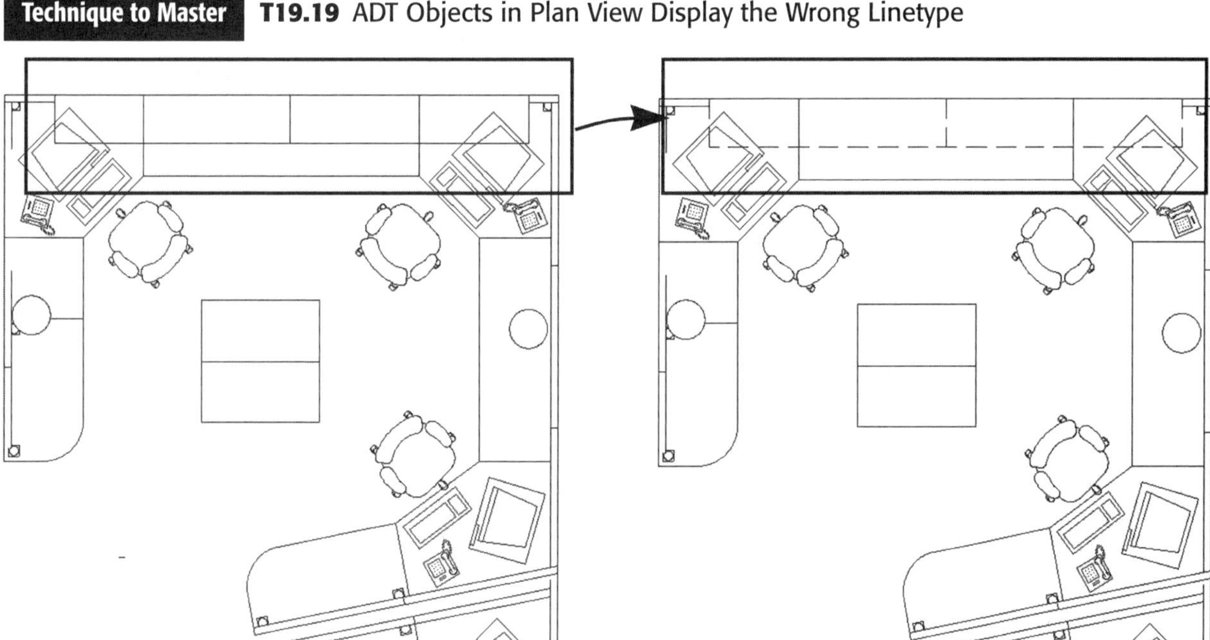

Figure 19.19

First, check to make sure the drawing's Ltscale is set correctly. Refer to Chapter 3 for more information on linetype scaling.

If the Ltscale is correct, try changing the linetype property within the Display Properties for the object in question. This may be done through a style override (Technique T13.50) or object overrides (Technique T13.51).

Technique to Master **T19.20** ADT Object Type Should Be Hidden in Display Configuration

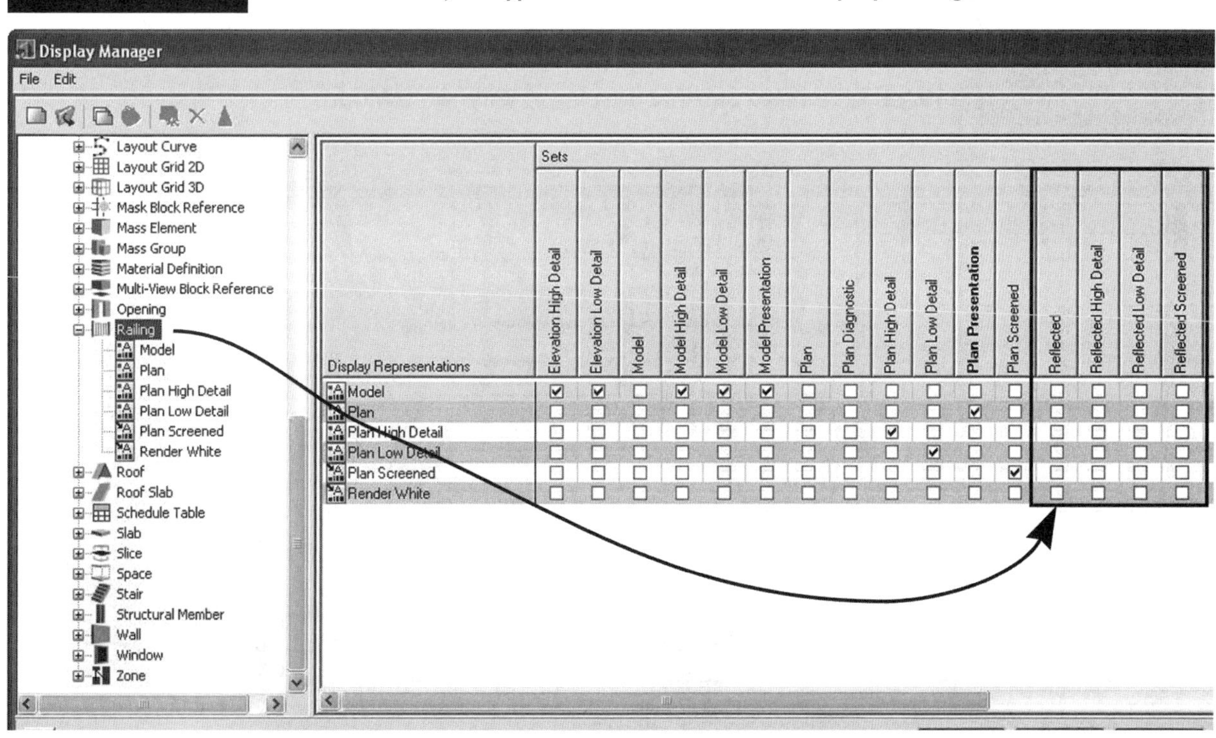

Figure 19.20

ADT objects like railings should not display in reflected ceiling plans. All boxes below the Reflected Display Sets remain unchecked as a result. Object Representations in the Display Manager help to resolve visibility issues by object type.

Technique to Master **T19.21** ADT Object Type Is Not Visible in Display Configuration

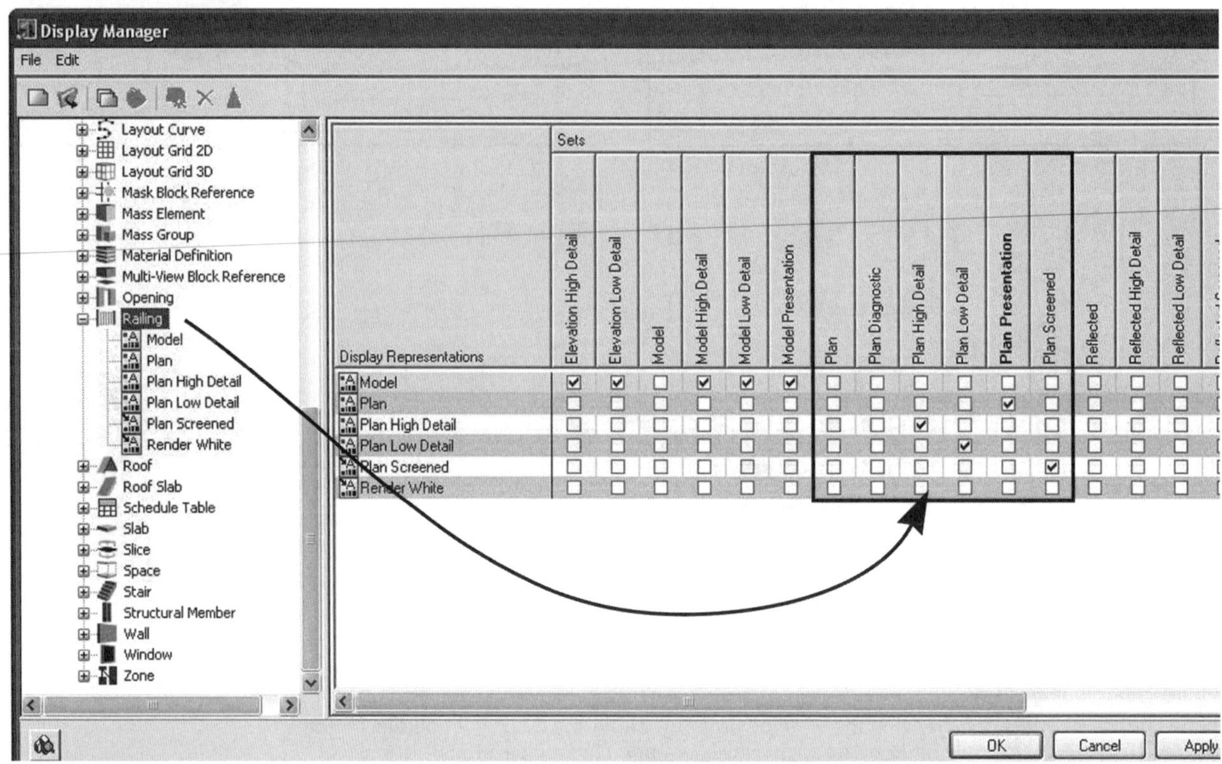

Figure 19.21

ADT objects like railings should, however, display in all floor plans. Boxes below the Plan Display Sets are matched with their Display Representation as a result. Object Representations in the Display Manager help to resolve visibility issues by object type.

Technique to Master **T19.22** Generated Sections Display in Wireframe Mode

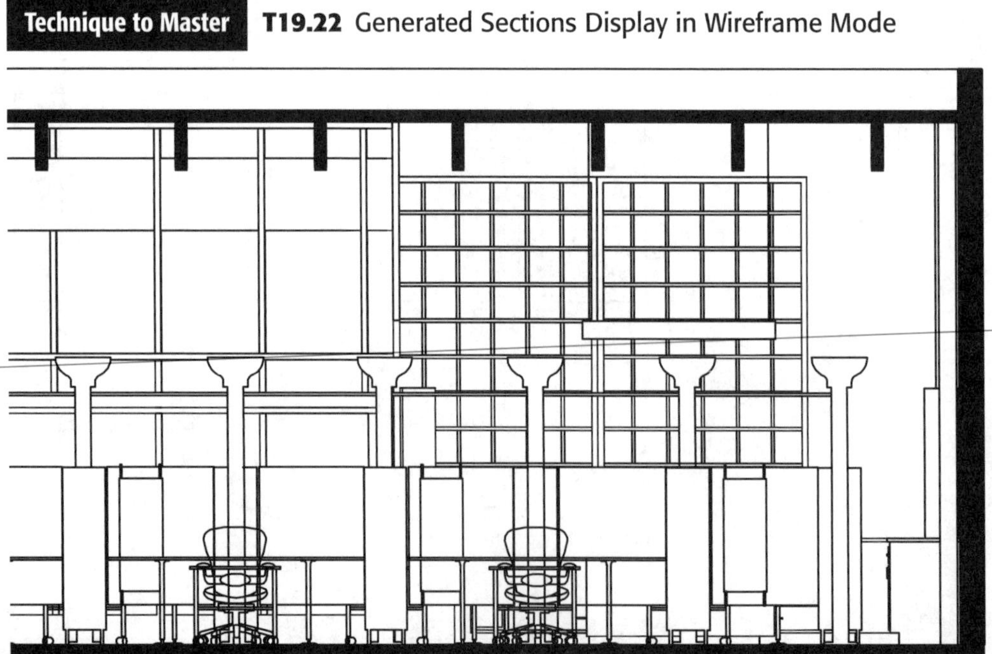

Figure 19.22

After creating a 2-D section, the generated result did hide objects beyond the cut plane correctly. This is usually a problem when the section line is placed non-orthogonally to the drawing. Relocate section line and update section.

Refining Floor and Ceiling View Drawings While Maintaining the Associative Link

Most floor and ceiling plan refinement is associated with the modification of display representations for the object in question. These typically include layer, lineweight, visibility, and hatching issues. For the most part, all modifications to Object Display Representations should take place in the construct not the view drawing.

Other refinements, like global cut planes and object type visibility issues are controlled through the Display Manager in all the drawings—construct, view, and sheet, as shown in Figures 19.23 and 19.24.

Refining the Extents of Section/Elevation Lines

When sections and elevations are generated, they are directly linked by their building section (or elevation) lines. These section and elevation lines (along with their symbol marks) can be manipulated like any other CAD entity. They can be moved and/or stretched to correspond to the desired section or elevation result. Figure 19.25 demonstrates the modification of section/elevation lines through the use of grips.

Technique to Master **T19.23** Global Cut Plane Is Inappropriate for View

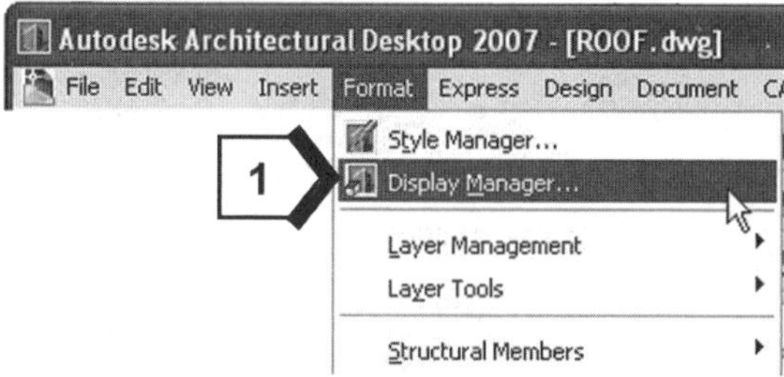

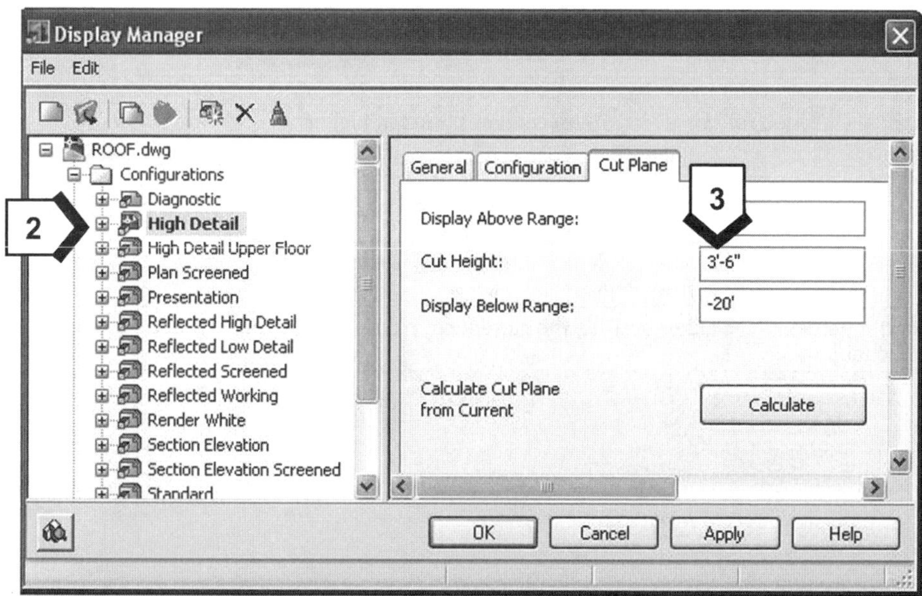

Figure 19.23

1	[Format menu>Display Manager]	Open the Display Manager.
2	[Display Manager>Left Pane]	Choose the Display Configuration (High Detail).
3	[Display Manager>Cut Plane tab]	Change the cut plane.

Technique to Master **T19.24** Object Cut Plane Needs to Be Different from the Global Cut Plane

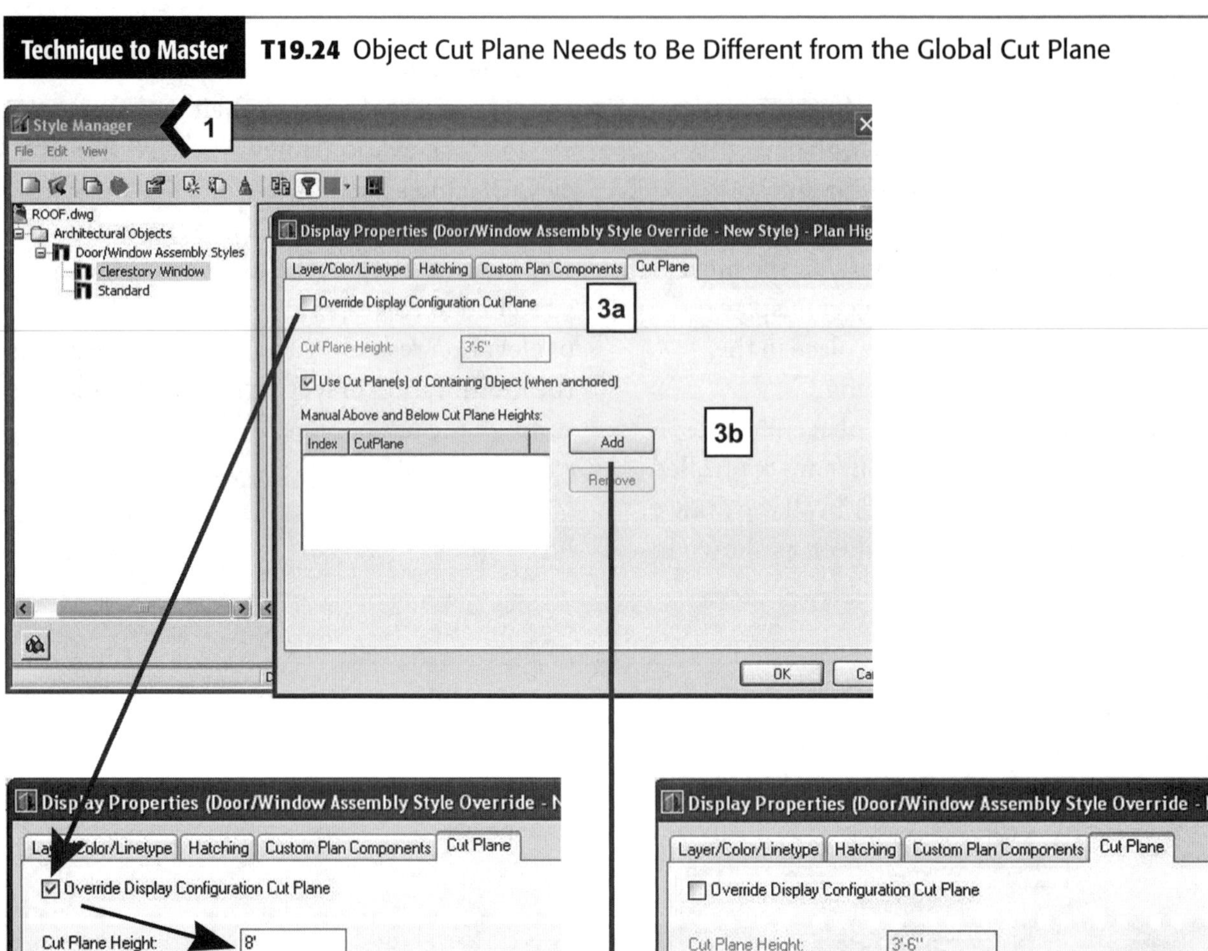

Figure 19.24 This technique is usually needed for door/window assemblies placed at higher or lower elevations.

1	[Style Manager]	Open the Style Manager for the ADT object. Only walls, door/window assemblies, and curtain walls have additional cut plane control.
2	[Style Manager>Display Properties tab]	Create a style override or edit the existing style override for the desired Display Representation.
3a, 3b	[Style Manager>Display Properties Style Override>Cut Plane tab]	Either override the current cut plane or create additional cut planes.

Technique to Master T19.25 Using Grips for Section and Elevation Line

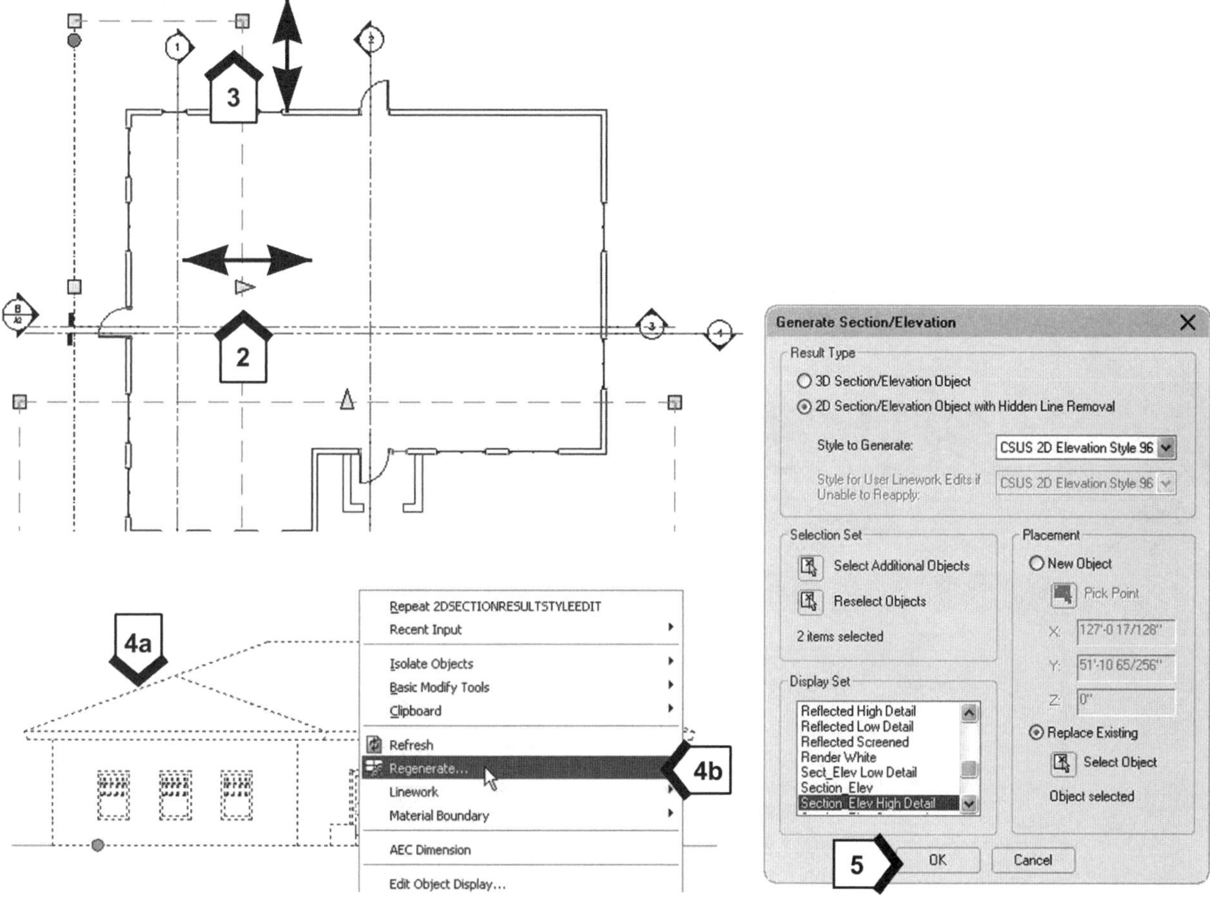

Figure 19.25

1	[Drawing Screen]	Select Section or Elevation Line to modify.
2	[Drawing Screen]	Use the triangular grip to increase or decrease the depth of the section or elevation line.
3	[Drawing Screen]	Use the square grips to alter the width of the section or elevation line.
Regenerate the section (or elevation).		
4a, 4b	[Drawing Screen]	Select the section (or elevation), right-click, and choose Regenerate.
5	[Generate Section/ Elevation dialogue box]	Left click OK to regenerate.

Why Generated Sections and Elevations Display in the Color and Lineweight That They Do

All generated sections and elevations are style-based like the other ADT object types. The 2-D Section/Elevation Style Properties are used to control how you see the section/elevation. Generated sections and elevations display (or hide) linework based on Design Rules and Display Properties settings in the 2-D Section/Elevation Style Properties (Figure 19.26). You will also notice that the 2-D Section/Elevation Style Properties makes use of categories called subdivisions. Subdivisions break up the section (elevation) line rectangle into smaller units (Figure 19.27). Special rules are then set up to relate the linework to its appropriate subdivision category (Figure 19.28). Figure 19.29 demonstrates subdivision creation for sections and elevations. Figure 19.30 demonstrates how to adjust the Design Rules and Display Properties of 2-D Section/Elevation Style Properties.

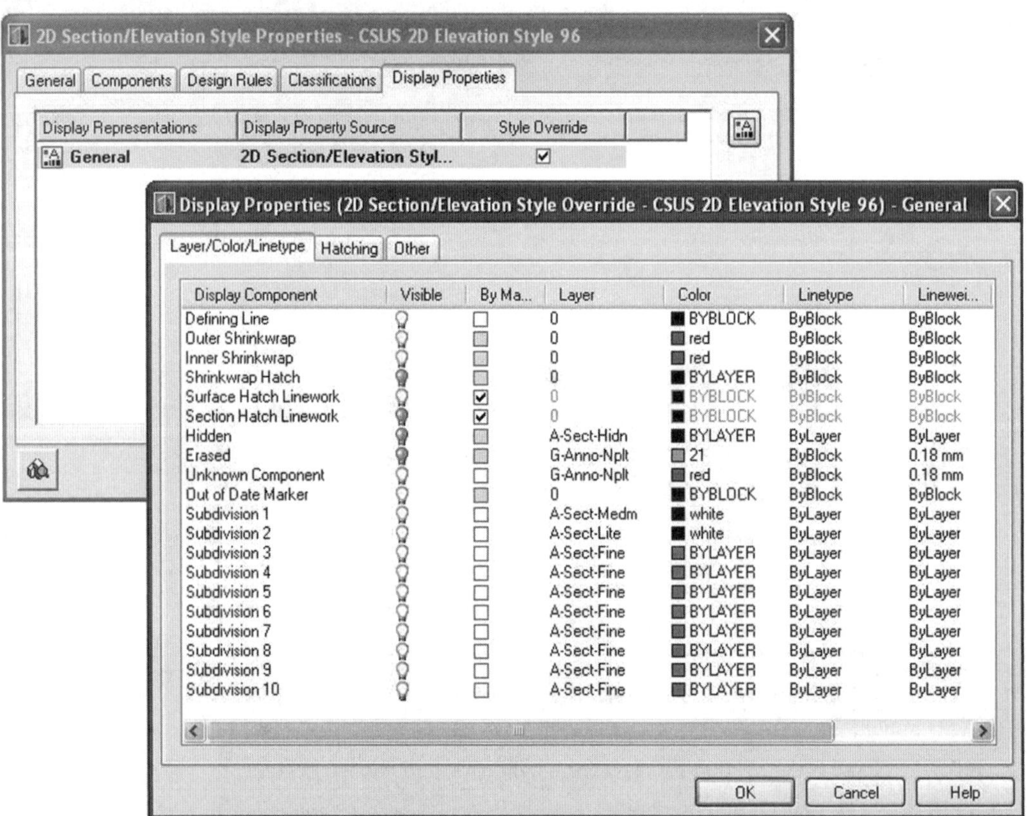

Figure 19.26 The Display Properties for the 2-D Section/Elevation Style control how a section or elevation is displayed and printed. It allows you to adjust the visibility, layer, lineweight, and linetype for each of the subdivisions and hatching in the generated sections and elevations.

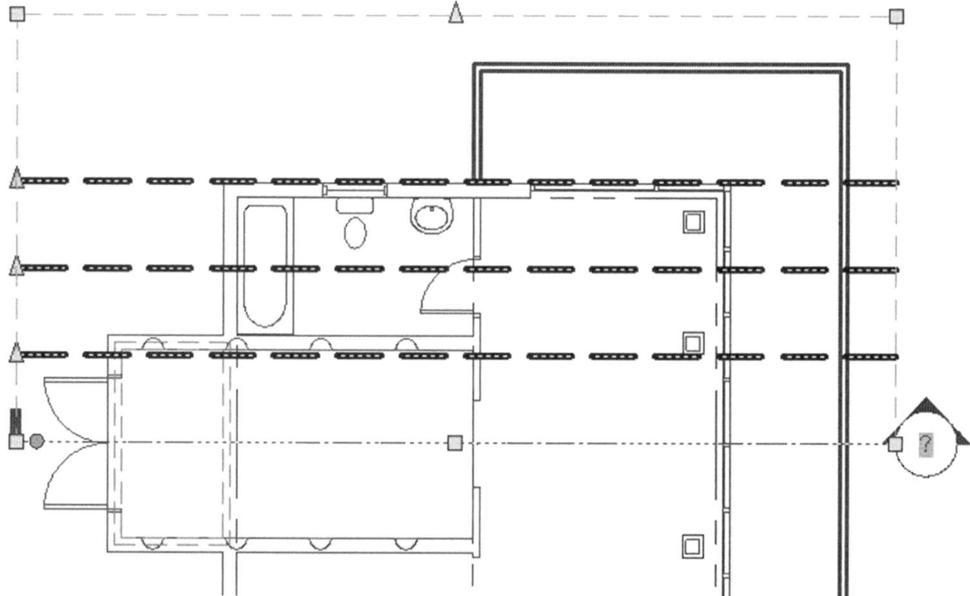

Figure 19.27 Subdivisions

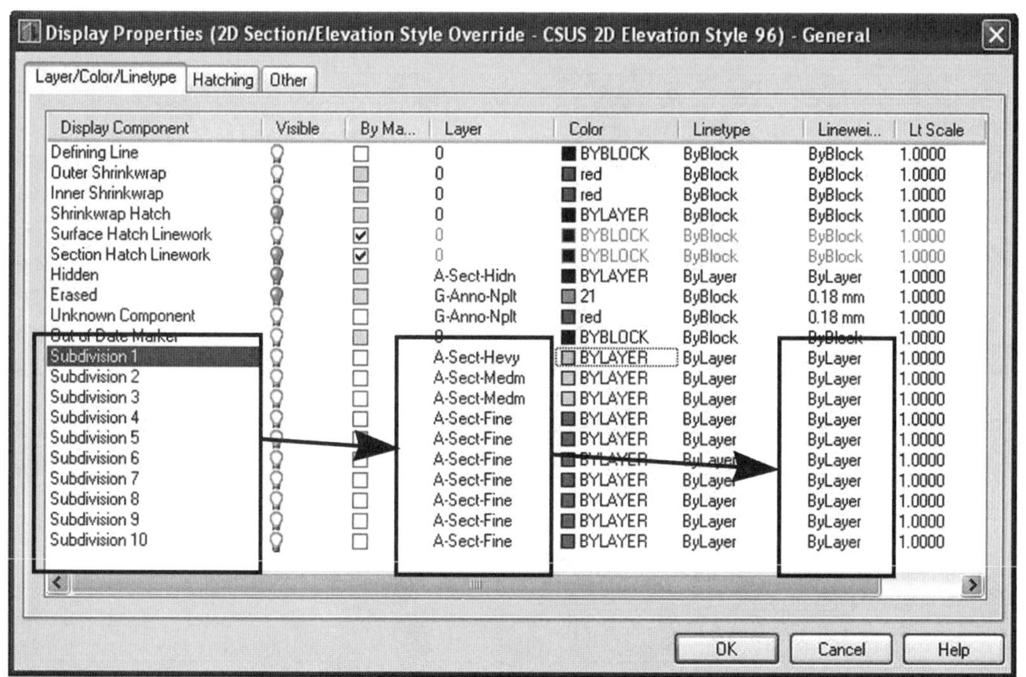

Figure 19.28 Subdivisions are assigned layers and lineweights to control how they print. The example shows the Display Properties dialogue box where the subdivisions are assigned to specific layers.

Technique to Master **T19.29** To Refine the Appearance of the Section, Create Subdivisions

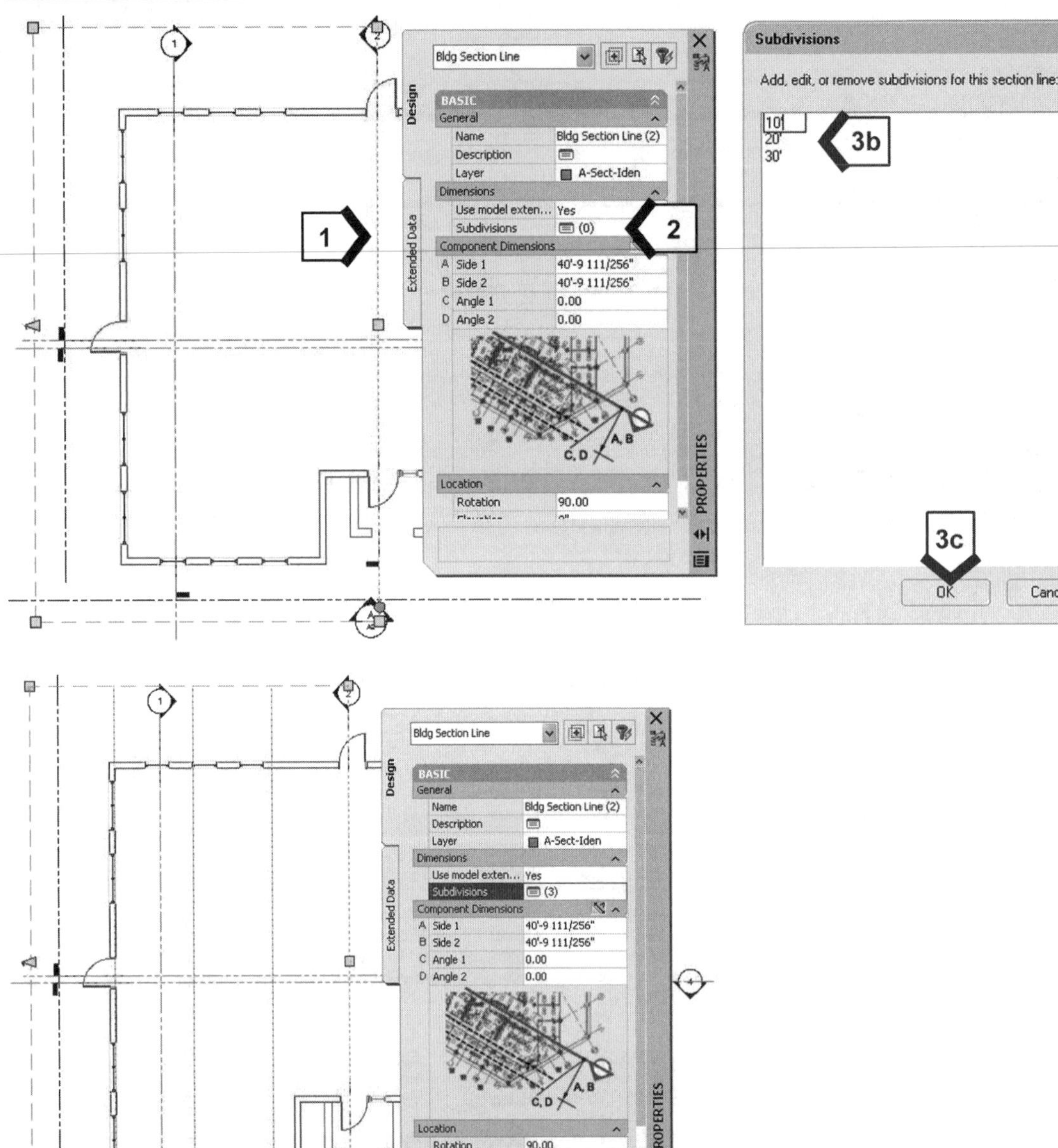

Figure 19.29

1	[Drawing Screen]	Select section or elevation line.
2	[Properties palette>Dimensions]	Left-click on icon next to subdivisions.
3a, 3b, 3c	[Subdivisions dialogue box]	Add subdivisions by clicking the Add button and modifying subdivision distance. (Subdivision depths can be visually modified on the drawing screen after they are added.) Click OK to apply changes.
4	Regenerate the building section to apply subdivisions.	

Technique to Master **T19.30** Adjusting the Design Rules and Display Properties of 2-D Section/Elevation Styles

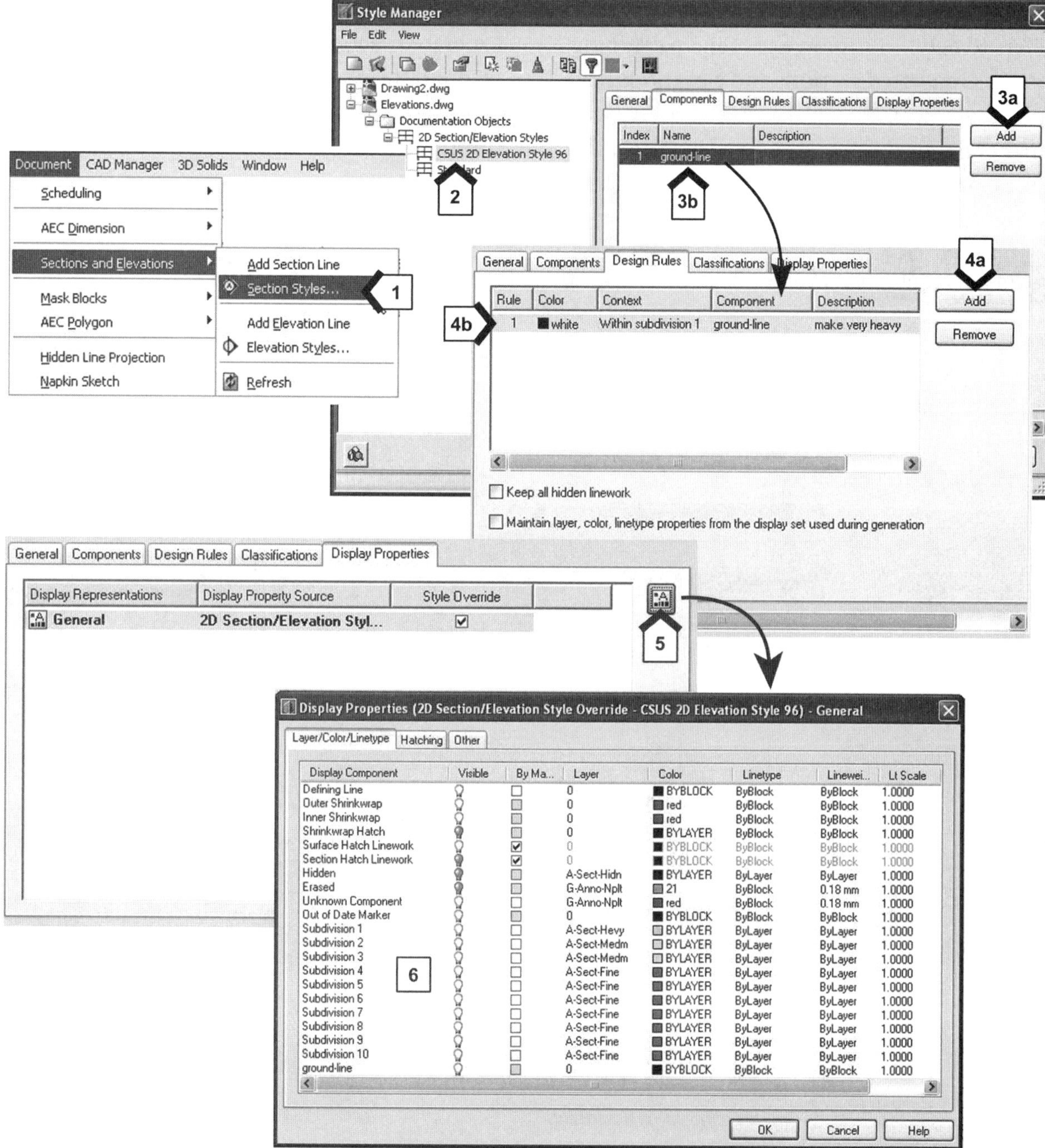

Figure 19.30

1	[Document menu>Sections and Elevations> Section Styles (or Elevation Styles)]	Open the Section/Elevation Style Manager.
2	[Section/Elevation Style Manager>Left Pane]	Select Section/Elevation Style to modify.
3a, 3b	[Section/Elevation Style Manager>Components]	Add additional special components that might be needed for the section or elevation. These might include a ground line or an elevation outline.
4a, 4b	[Section/Elevation Style Manager>Design Rules]	Rules can then be set up for any created components.
5	[Section/Elevation Style Manager>Display Properties]	Select the Edit Display Properties button.
6	[Section/Elevation Style Manager>Display Properties Style Override>Layer/Color/Linetype tab]	Verify/change visibility, layer, lineweight, and linetype settings for subdivisions and components.

Refining Generated Section/Elevation Content While Maintaining the Associative Link

Refinement in sections and elevations typically refers to detailing, lineweight, and patterning issues. Generated sections and elevations have their own specialty commands that allow for further drawing refinement without breaking the associative links. Editing techniques for generated sections and elevations include linework edits, hatch edits, and section/elevation updating. Specialty commands for generated sections and elevations are found through the object's right-click menu. Each technique is demonstrated in Figures 19.31 through 19.33.

Technique to Master **T19.31** Editing Linework in a 2-D Generated Section or Elevation

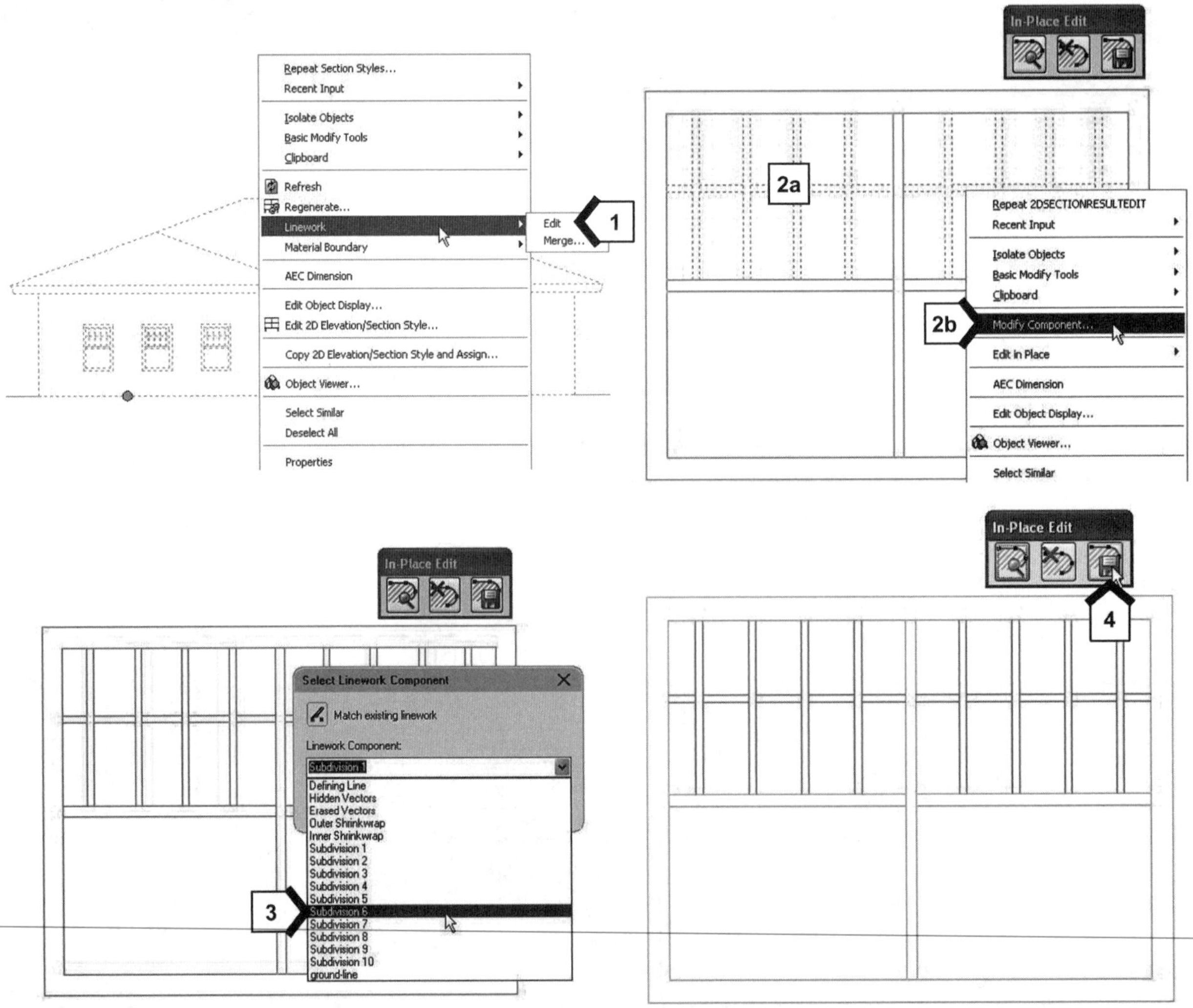

Figure 19.31

1	[Drawing Screen]	Select section or elevation, right click, and choose Linework>Edit.
2a, 2b	[Drawing Screen]	Select all lines that will be assigned a similar lineweight. Right-click and choose Modify Component.
3	[Select Linework Component dialogue box]	Choose the appropriate component to assign selected linework.
4	[In-Place Edit toolbar]	Save changes.

Technique to Master T19.32 Merging Linework into a 2-D Generated Section or Elevation

Figure 19.32

1	[Drawing Screen]	Select section or elevation, right-click, and choose Linework>Merge.
2	[Drawing Screen]	Select the linework to merge into section or elevation. Press Enter to complete selection. (This procedure is perfect for the heavy ground lines in exterior elevation drawings.)
3	[Select Linework Component dialogue box]	Choose the appropriate component to assign selected linework.

Technique to Master **T19.33** Changing How Patterns Are Shown in a 2-D Generated Section or an Elevation

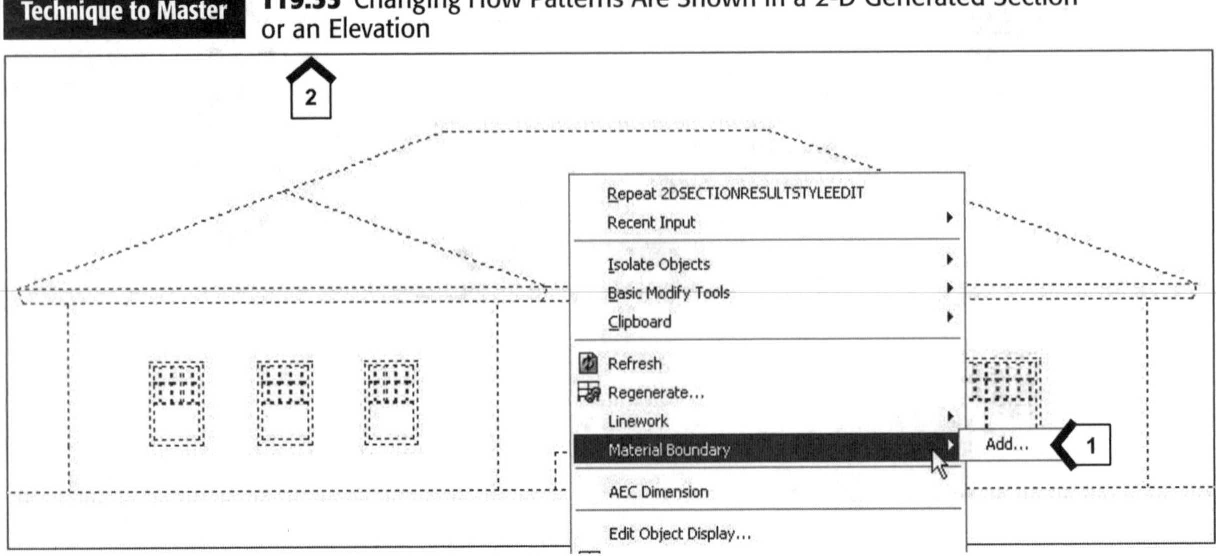

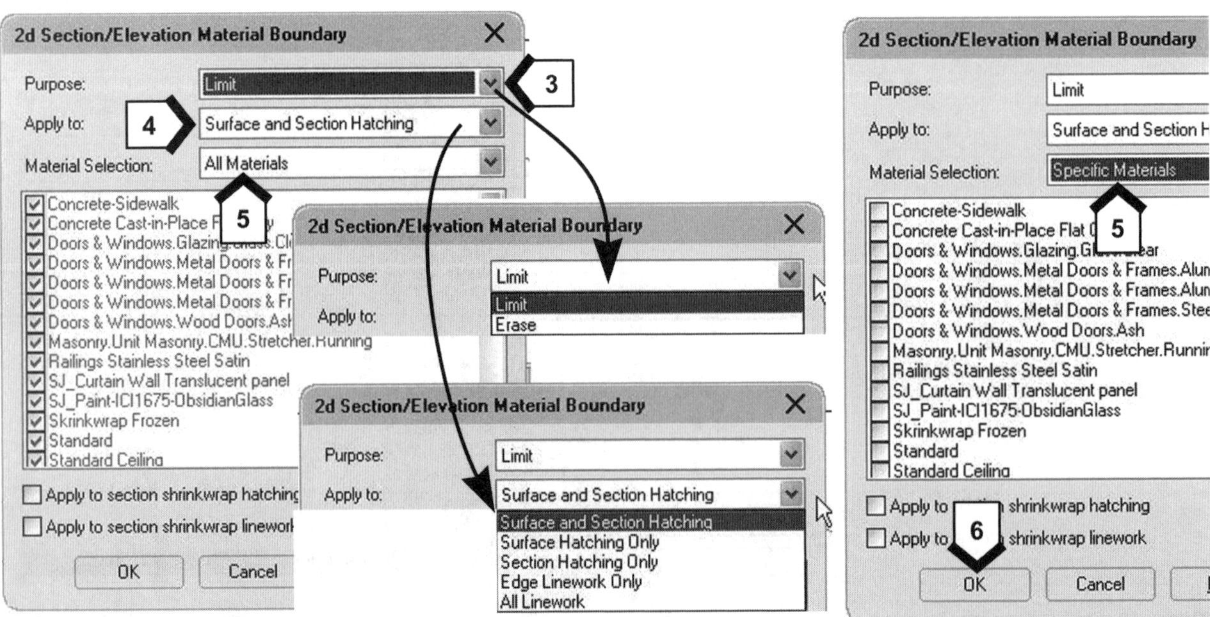

Figure 19.33 Surface and section hatching can be turned on and off on an elevation by elevation basis through the Material Boundary>Add command.

1	[Drawing Screen]	Select section or elevation, right-click, and choose Material Boundary>Add.
2	[Drawing Screen]	Select closed polyline boundary. This boundary will represent the extents of the display of the surface and/or sectional hatching.
3	[2-D Section/Elevation Material Boundary dialogue box]	Specify whether to erase or display specified materials.
4	[2-D Section/Elevation Material Boundary dialogue box]	Specify which type of hatching the command will apply to.
5	[2-D Section/Elevation Material Boundary dialogue box]	Specify whether to apply the command to all materials or specific materials.
6	[2-D Section/Elevation Material Boundary dialogue box]	Click OK to apply changes.

Refining View Drawings by Breaking the Associative Link

Controlling the display of orthographic drawings created through the view process is not always possible. This may be a result of software knowledge, software experience, project complexity, or a combination of the three. Architectural Desktop has a variety of techniques designed to convert view drawings to 2-D AutoCAD linework. Drawings can then be manipulated through traditional layer, lineweight, line style, and plot style methods. The primary advantage is obvious. In the beginning stages of learning, student frustrations due to the inability to control software can be eliminated at the time of project deadlines. This, however, is counterbalanced by the resultant associative break between view drawings and the virtual model.

There are two techniques for converting ADT View slices to traditional 2-D AutoCAD linework. The first is through the export process where the entire drawing is converted (Figure 19.34). The second method uses the Hidden Line Projection command and creates a block entity made up of 2-D linework within the current drawing. Figures 19.35 and 19.36 demonstrate these conversion techniques.

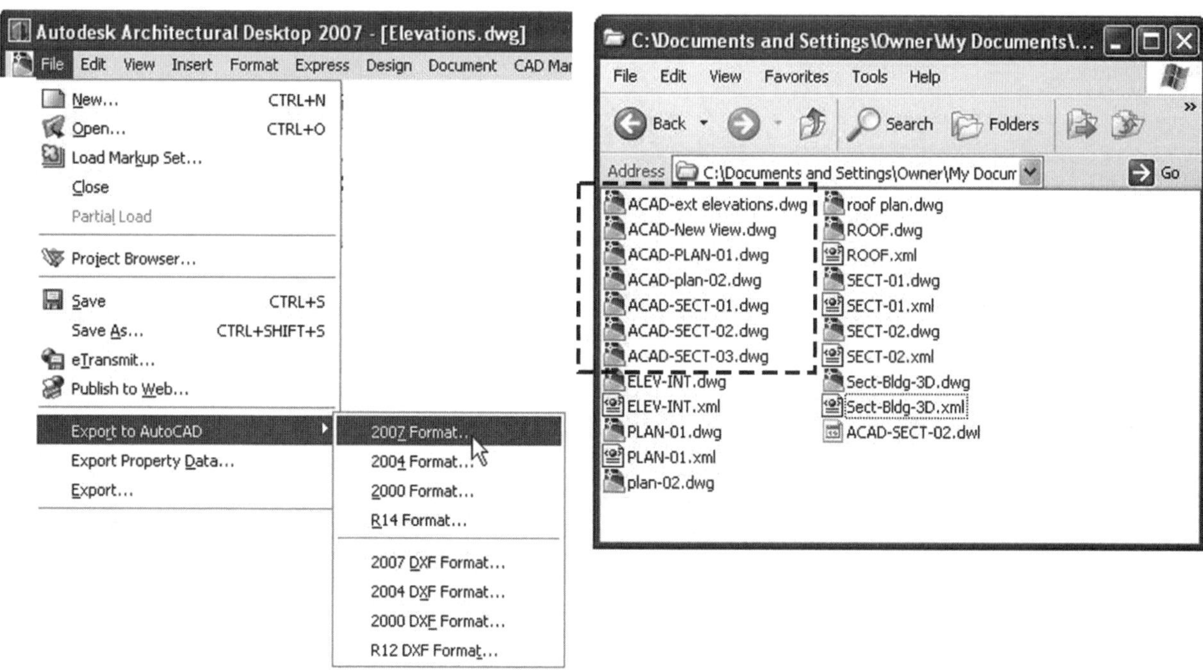

Figure 19.34 The Export to AutoCAD commands will create a duplicate of the current drawing and then explode all ADT objects into 2-D linework.

Technique to Master **T19.35** Creating 2-D Linework from Perspective Views Using the Hidden Line Projection Command

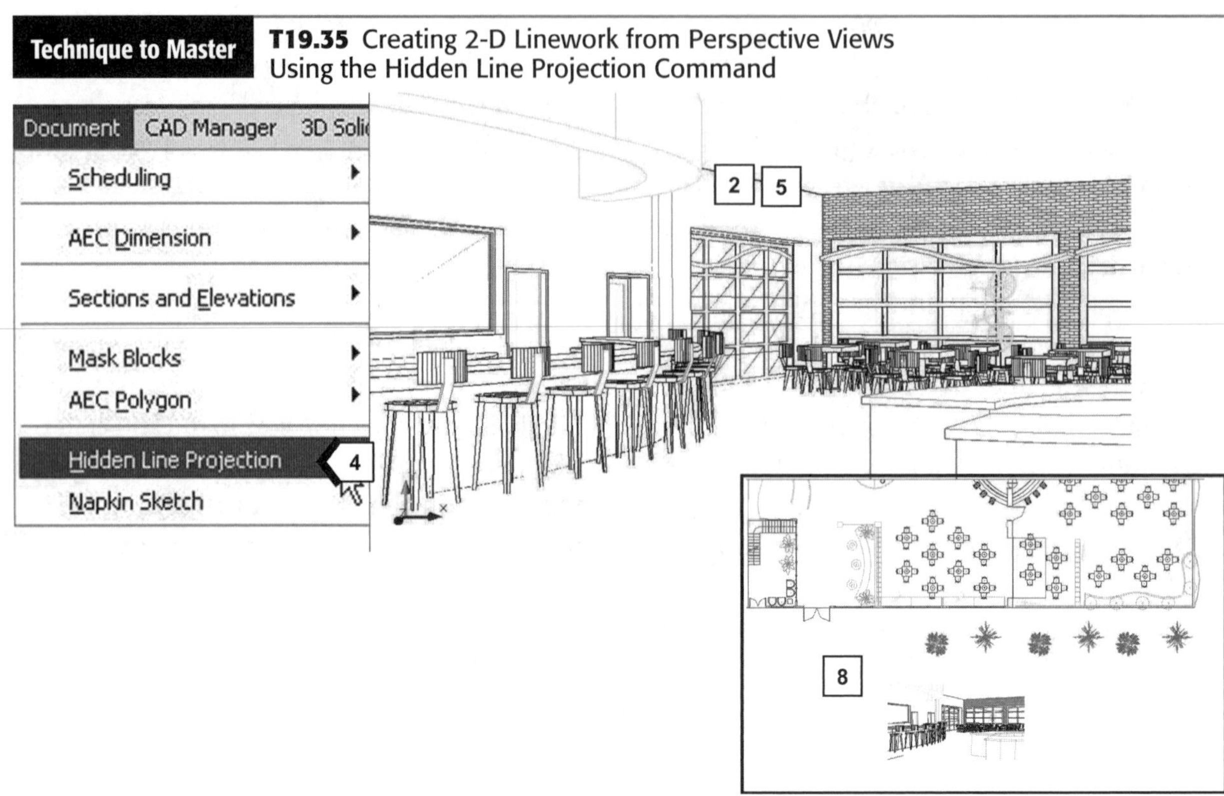

Figure 19.35

Student Project: Restaurant Design, courtesy of Andrea Pabon.

1	Open appropriate view drawing.	
2	[Drawing Screen]	Change view to desired perspective using the Orbit or Dview commands.
3	[Command Line]	Use the Hide command.
4	[Document Menu]	Select Hidden Line Projection command.
5	[Drawing Screen]	Select 3-D objects.
6	[Command Line]	Type Y and press Enter to insert the 2-D result in plan view.
7	[Drawing Screen]	Specify location for 2-D projection result in any free drawing area.
8	[Drawing Screen]	Switch to plan view to view 2-D projection result.
9	[Drawing Screen]	Wblock the 2-D projection result to its own drawing. Refer to Technique T04.11.

Technique to Master **T19.36** Refining Linework in Exported Drawings

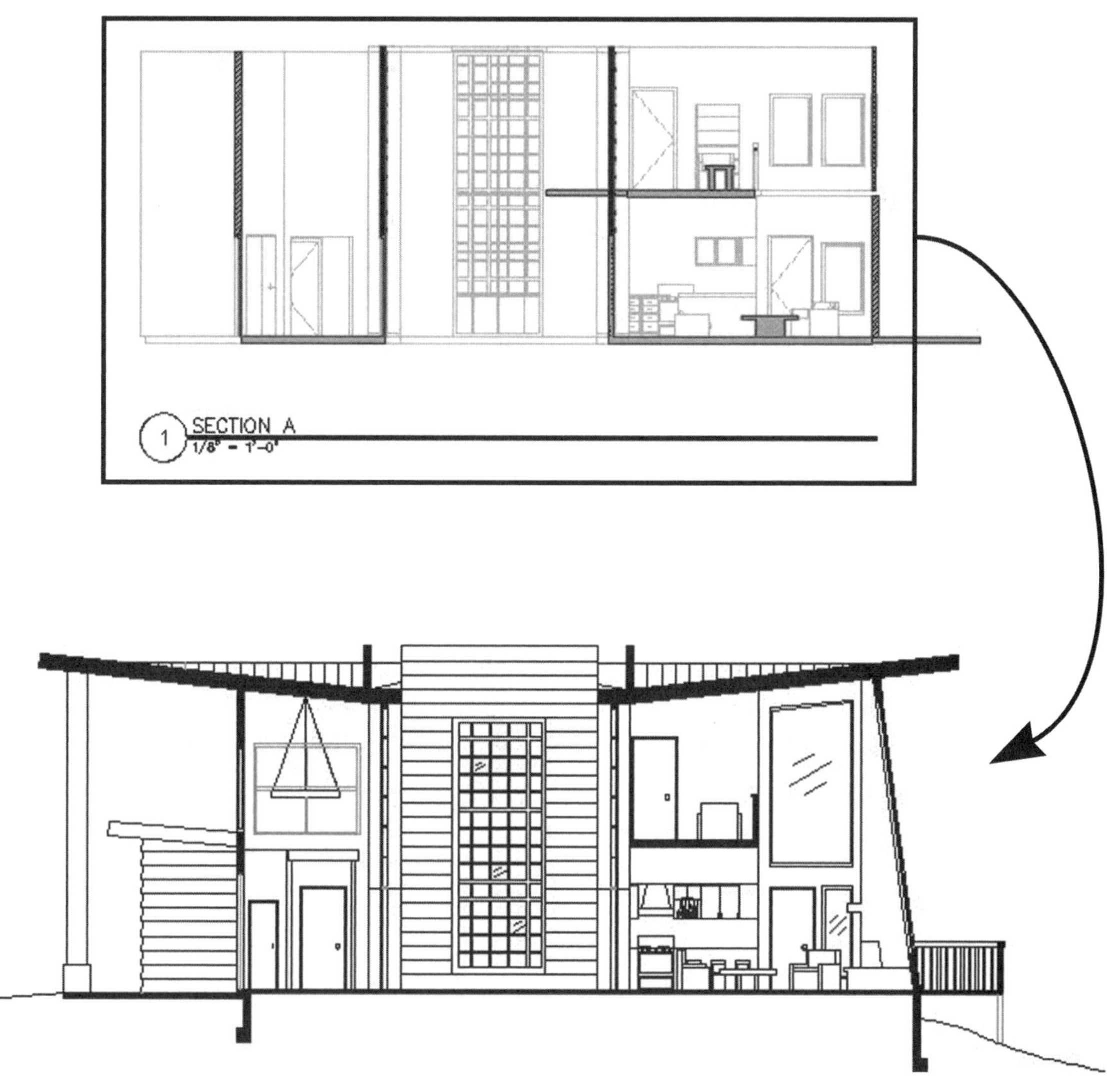

Figure 19.36

The 2-D results of exported drawings are grouped into blocks. To refine, explode blocks first. Make desired linework modifications to clean up drawing.

Student Project: Parker Residence, courtesy of Megan Kreitzberg.

Drawing Craft in the Virtual Model

As a beginner designer, you will find that juggling design development when learning software techniques can be overwhelming. This topic attempts to provide a framework for your first few design projects using Architectural Desktop. The first section, Drawing Craft and Drawing Organization, provides a few strategies for setting up various types of projects in ADT. Drawing Craft and the Design Process continues the theme by describing two approaches for using ADT within a design project. You will find that as your technical mastery increases, other strategies and approaches will become evident.

Drawing Craft and Drawing Organization

Chapter 9 introduced you to Architectural Desktop's Project Navigator and its organizational concepts and procedures. This topic applies these concepts and procedures by showing how different project phases and project types are implemented within the Project Navigator, including setting up multistory and split-level building types and using the Project Navigator for the programming and conceptual massing phases of design.

Using the Project Navigator to Set Up Multistory Design Projects

Multistory buildings differentiate themselves from single-story buildings through their vertical circulation. The stairs, elevators, and double-height spaces that occur in this building type will always need to show up in two or more floor plans—that is, two or more view drawings. Because of this, stairs, elevators, and double-height spaces will need to be placed within their own distinct constructs.

Figure 19.37 provides an example construct and view structure for multistory projects. During the construct drawing creation for these types of building elements, multiple levels are assigned (Figure 19.38).

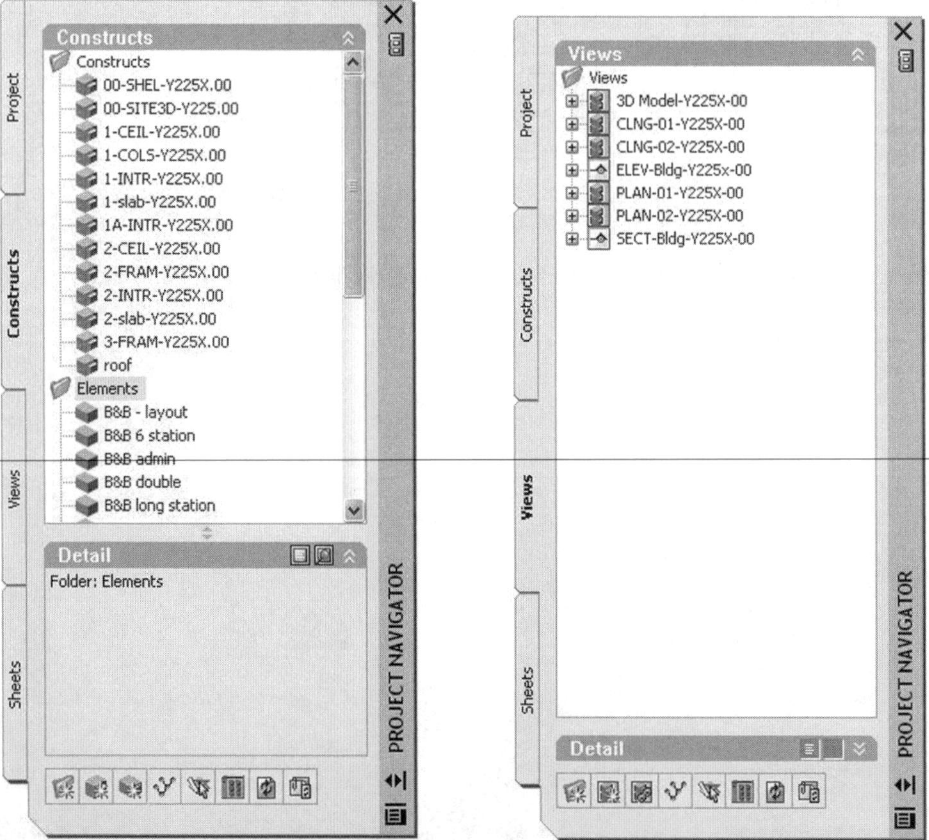

Figure 19.37 Examples of the construct and view file-naming structure

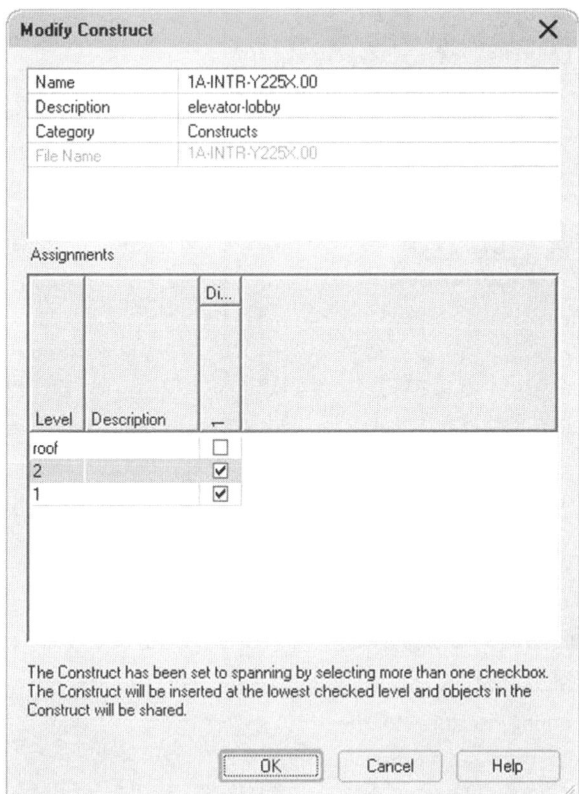

Figure 19.38 Objects that are shown on multiple floors are placed within their own construct. Notice the 1A-INTR construct references multiple levels.

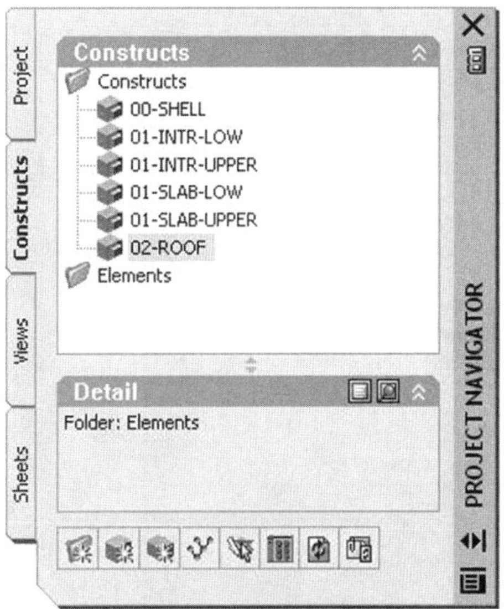

Figure 19.39 Split-level projects should use separate Constructs for each level to provide for maximum flexibility. Refer to Technique T09.25 to review Construct creation within an ADT project.

Using the Project Navigator to Set Up Split-Level Design Projects

Split-level projects are best organized by creating separate Constructs for each level change (Figure 19.39). This allows cut planes to remain true to each individual floor level.

Using the Project Navigator to Set Up the Programming Phase of a Design Project

Traditional programming drawings include zonal diagrams, bubble diagrams, block diagrams, and plan prototypes. Utilizing the advantages of the Project Navigator, the space objects in these diagrams can easily bridge the transitory phase from programming to schematics, which in turn reinforces the cyclical nature of the design process. Figure 19.40 shows sample Construct, Element, and View structures for the programming phase of a design project.

Using the Project Navigator to Set Up the Three-Dimensional Massing Phase of a Design Project

During the three-dimensional massing phase, project levels and Views are used to create the building level slices that are needed to refine the buildings interior spaces (Figure 19.41). Figure 19.42 shows sample windows where project levels, Constructs, and Views are organized for the massing phase of design projects.

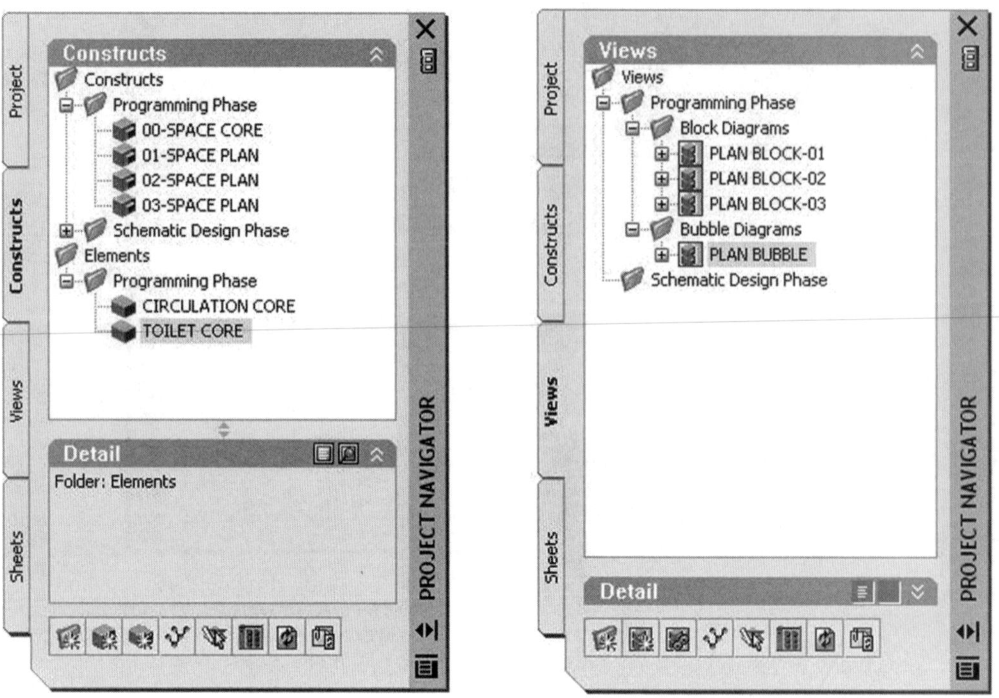

Figure 19.40 Examples of the Construct, Element, and View file-naming structures for the Programming Phase of a project

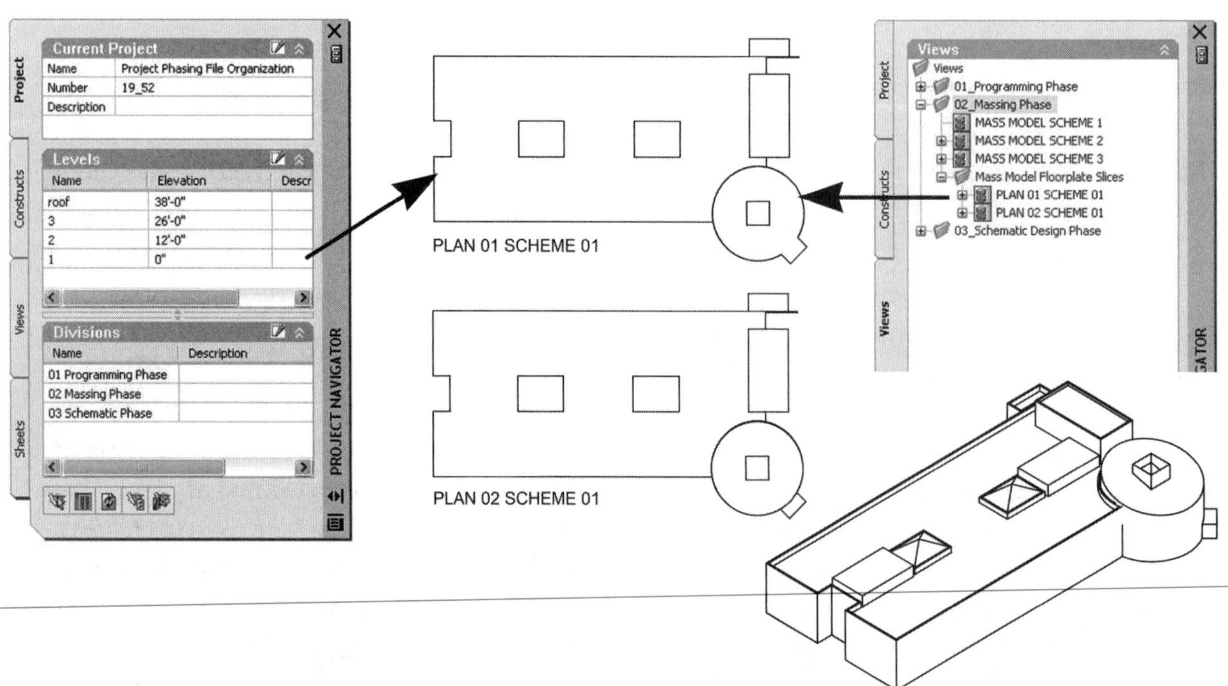

Figure 19.41 During the three-dimensional massing phase, project levels and Views are used to create the building level slices that are needed to refine the building's interior spaces.

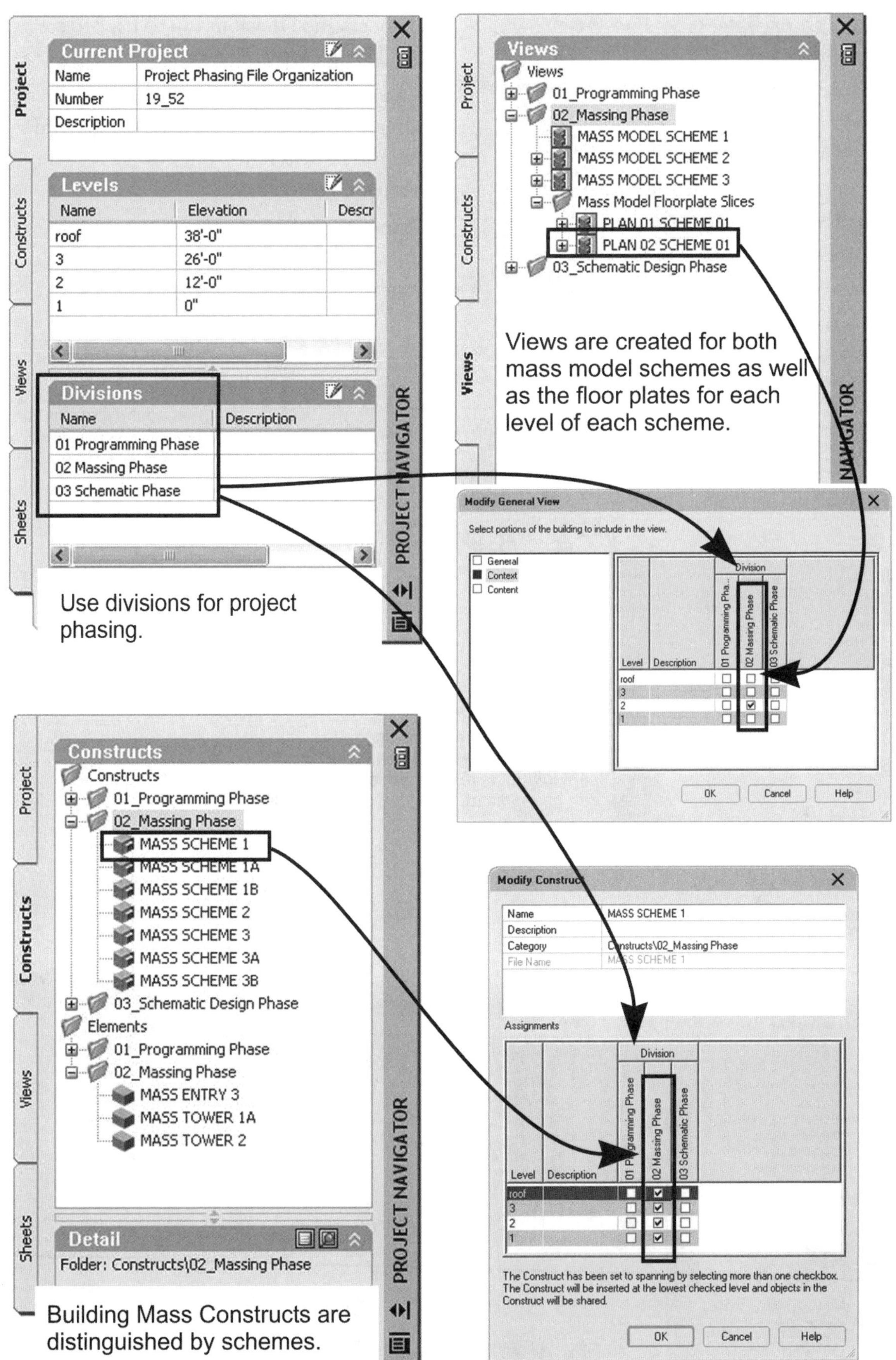

Figure 19.42 Examples of project levels, Construct, and View structure for the massing phase of design projects

Using the Project Navigator to Set Up a Project for Design Alternatives

The benefits of using the Project Navigator to organize design alternative schemes are many and are listed as follows:

- Constructs and Construct folders can be used to distinguish the various major design schemes during the programming and schematic phases of the design process.
- Elements and Divisions can be used to create smaller alternative changes to a scheme.
- Views help to present (and organize) the scheme and scheme alternatives in an order that can be different from how they were created (Figure 19.43).

Figure 19.44 provides an example of the organization structure for design alternative schemes.

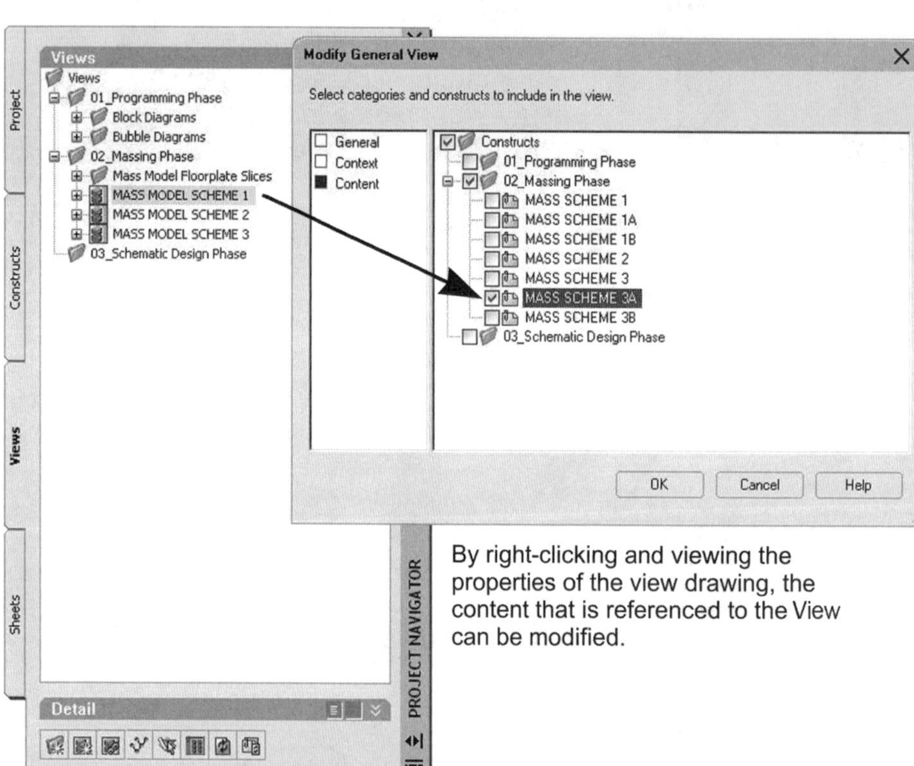

By right-clicking and viewing the properties of the view drawing, the content that is referenced to the View can be modified.

Figure 19.43 Views help present (and organize) the scheme and scheme alternatives in an order that can be different from how they were created.

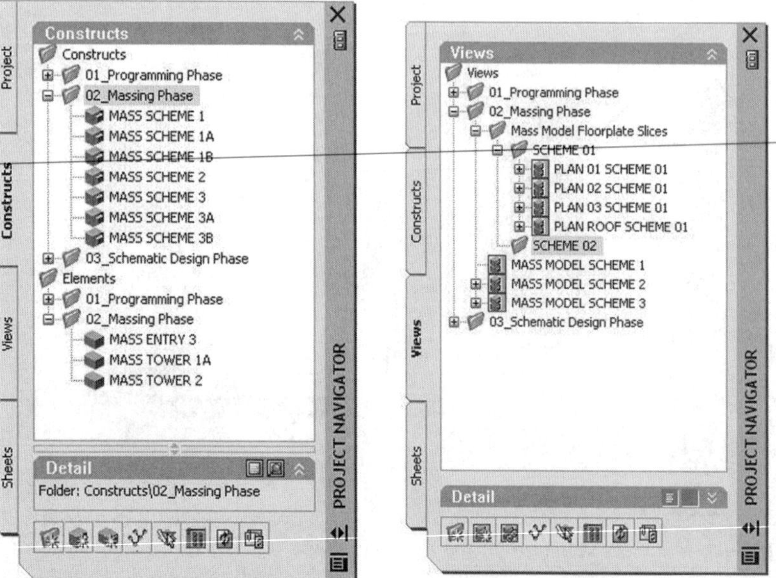

Figure 19.44 Example of an organization structure for using Views for design alternative schemes

Drawing Craft and the Design Process

The following are suggested approaches to structuring a design process within the ADT environment. Generally, the two approaches describe an iterative process that breaks the design/drawing cycle into smaller increments. A somewhat linear approach is prescribed to help you minimize Architectural Desktop's vast learning curve when applied to a design project. The first approach emphasizes the development of space planning skills, while the second approach, the three-dimensional massing emphasis, builds off many of the design exploration ideas in Chapter 21. Figures 19.45 through 19.50 illustrate each approach in detail.

Space Plan Emphasis–Stage 1

The goals of this stage in the design process are to do the following:

- Use ADT's space objects to develop Plan View space relationships that meet functional and adjacency requirements. Use ADT's space objects to develop circulation systems that are efficient.
- Use ADT's space objects to create digital versions of traditional programming diagrams.
- Use ADT's Project Navigator to organize programming source files and programming presentation drawings.

Space Plan Emphasis–Stage 2

The goals of this stage in the design process are to do the following:

- Use Constructs to set up and organize the parts of the virtual model.
- Use conversion techniques to transform space objects into walls and openings of the virtual model.
- Use Views to create floor plans, ceiling plans, and building sections.
- Use Elements in ADT's Project Navigator to test and develop furniture arrangements that support room function and size.
- Use learned strategies to troubleshoot display and/or drawing conventions within drawings.
- Use the additional building systems to further refine the virtual model.

Space Plan Emphasis–Stage 3

The goals of this stage in the design process are to do the following:

- Develop a final presentation strategy for the project.
- Use sheet set manager to organize and print presentation.

Three-Dimensional Massing Emphasis–Stage 1

The goals of this stage in the design process are to do the following:

- Use Constructs and Divisions to set up and organize the massing model, including its alternative schemes.
- Use mass elements and solids to develop form studies and massing models.
- Use ADT's Project Navigator to organize and present massing alternatives.
- Use Views with massing and space objects to relate the project's form to its function.
- Use Views with massing objects to explore vertical relationships.
- Use ADT's space objects to develop Plan View space relationships that meet functional and adjacency requirements. Use ADT's space objects to develop circulation systems that are efficient.

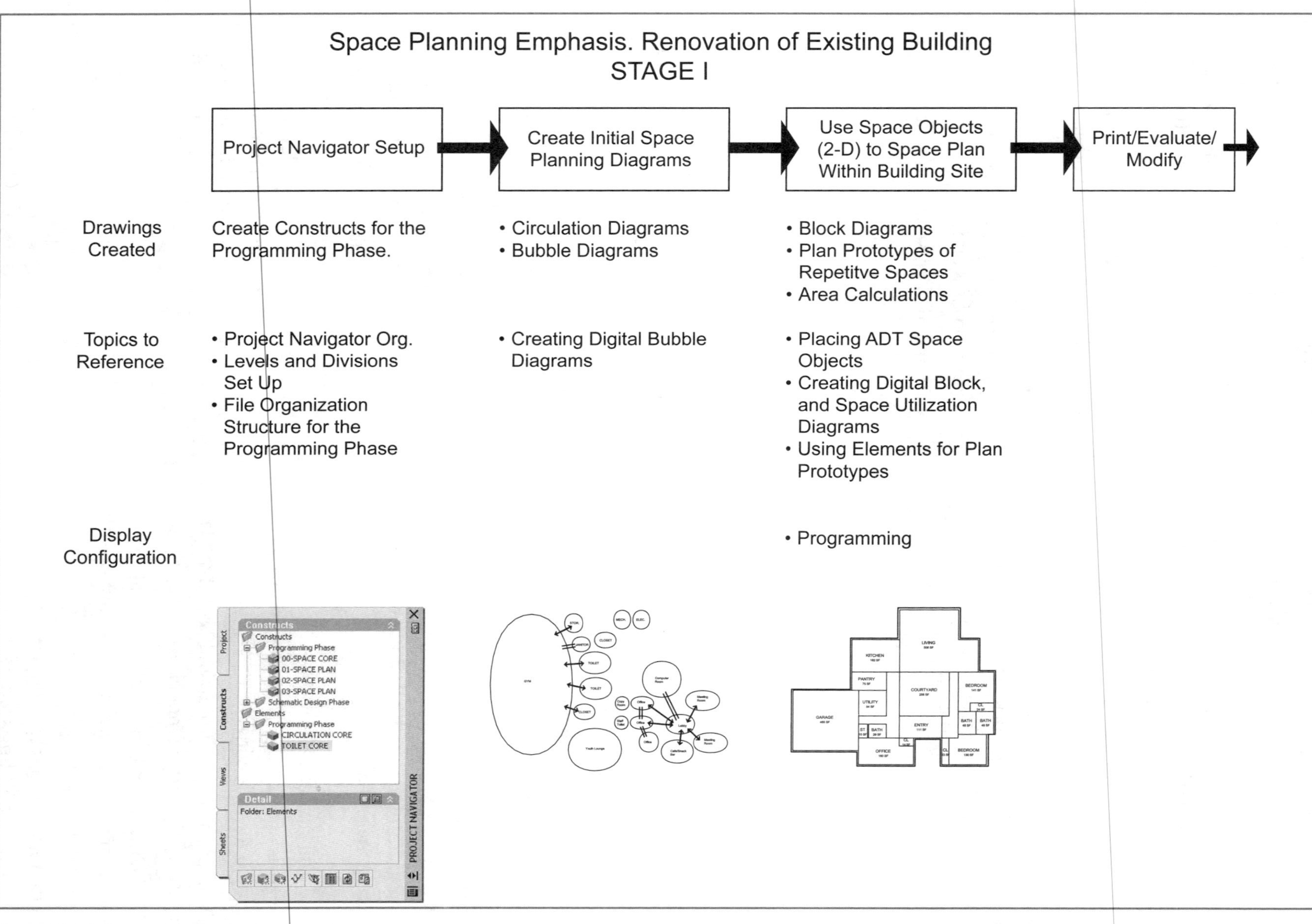
Space Planning Emphasis. Renovation of Existing Building
STAGE I
Project Navigator Setup
Create Initial Space Planning Diagrams
Use Space Objects (2-D) to Space Plan Within Building Site
Print/Evaluate/ Modify
Drawings Created
Create Constructs for the Programming Phase.
• Circulation Diagrams
• Bubble Diagrams
• Block Diagrams
• Plan Prototypes of Repetitve Spaces
• Area Calculations
Topics to Reference
• Project Navigator Org.
• Levels and Divisions Set Up
• File Organization Structure for the Programming Phase
• Creating Digital Bubble Diagrams
• Placing ADT Space Objects
• Creating Digital Block, and Space Utilization Diagrams
• Using Elements for Plan Prototypes
Display Configuration
• Programming
Constructs
Programming Phase
00-SPACE CORE
01-SPACE PLAN
02-SPACE PLAN
03-SPACE PLAN
Schematic Design Phase
Elements
CIRCULATION CORE
TOILET CORE
Detail
Folder: Elements
PROJECT NAVIGATOR
Project
Views
Sheets
LIVING
KITCHEN
PANTRY
UTILITY
COURTYARD
BEDROOM
GARAGE
ENTRY
BATH
OFFICE

Figure 19.45 Space plan emphasis—Stage 1

Space Planning Emphasis. Renovation of Existing Building STAGE 2

	Project Navigator Setup →	Convert Spaces to Walls. Add Windows, Doors, etc. →	Create Views →	Print/Evaluate/ Modify
Drawings Created	Create Constructs for the Building Shell, Interior Walls, and Furniture.		Plan Views for Each Level Multiple Section Views to Initially Evaluate Connections Between Systems	
Topics to Reference	• Project Navigator Org. • File Organization Structure for the Schematic Design Phase	• Placing ADT Walls, Windows, Doors, and Openings	• Creating Floor Plan and Section Views Using the Project Navigator	
		Display Representation—Schematic	Display Representation—Schematic	

Project
Constructs
PROJECT NAVIGATOR
Constructs
00-SHEL-Y225X.00
00-SITE3D-Y225.00
1-CEIL-Y225X.00
1-COLS-Y225X.00
1-INTR-Y225X.00
1-slab-Y225X.00
1A-INTR-Y225X.00
2-CEIL-Y225X.00
2-FRAM-Y225X.00
2-INTR-Y225X.00
2-slab-Y225X.00
3-FRAM-Y225X.00
roof
Elements

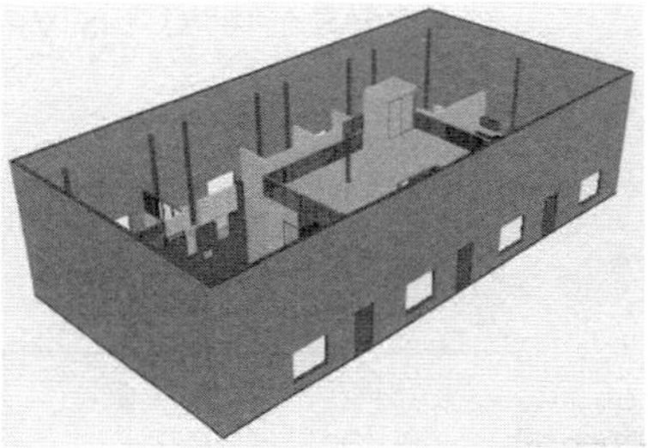

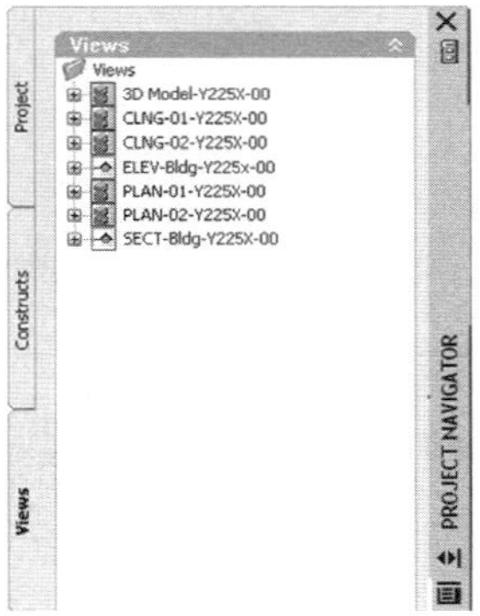

Project
Constructs
Views
PROJECT NAVIGATOR
Views
3D Model-Y225X-00
CLNG-01-Y225X-00
CLNG-02-Y225X-00
ELEV-Bldg-Y225x-00
PLAN-01-Y225X-00
PLAN-02-Y225X-00
SECT-Bldg-Y225X-00

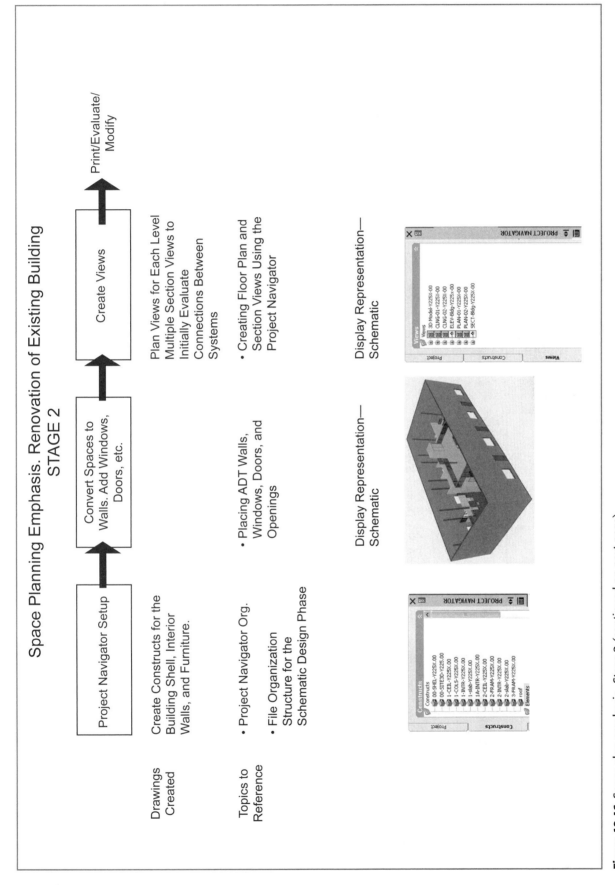

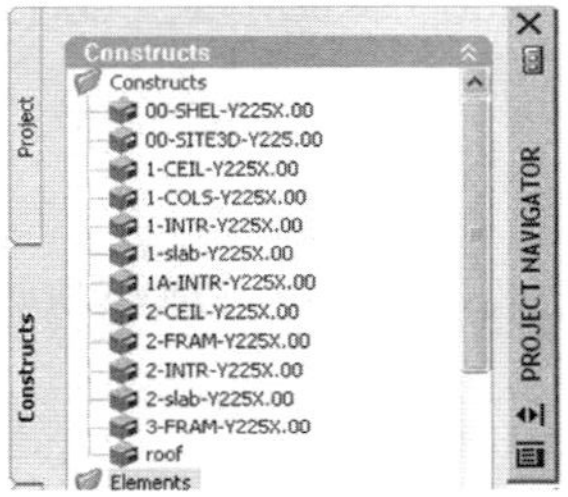

Figure 19.46 Space plan emphasis–Stage 2 (continued on next page)

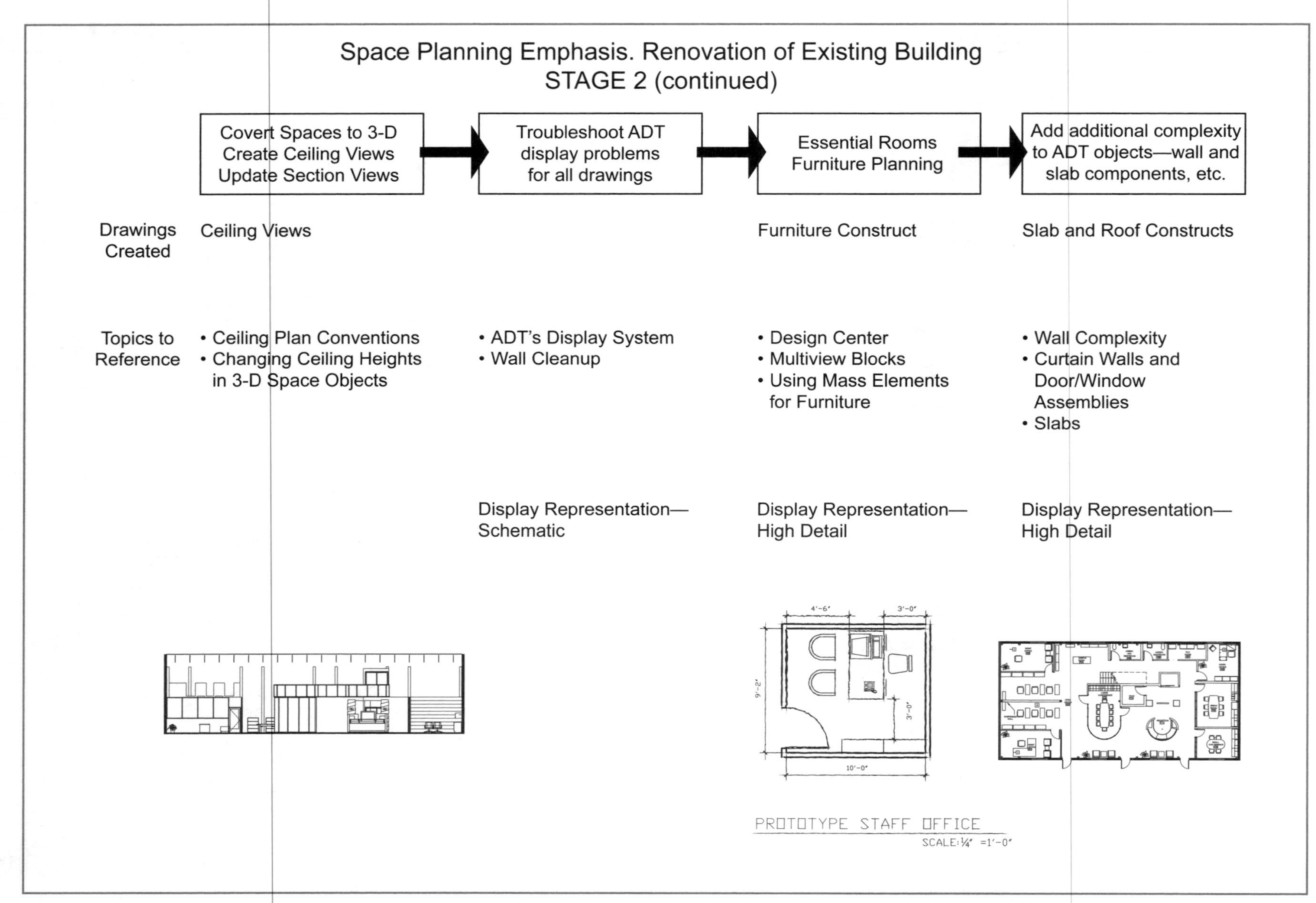
Space Planning Emphasis. Renovation of Existing Building
STAGE 2 (continued)
Covert Spaces to 3-D
Create Ceiling Views
Update Section Views
Troubleshoot ADT
display problems
for all drawings
Essential Rooms
Furniture Planning
Add additional complexity
to ADT objects—wall and
slab components, etc.
Drawings Created
Ceiling Views
Furniture Construct
Slab and Roof Constructs
Topics to Reference
• Ceiling Plan Conventions
• Changing Ceiling Heights in 3-D Space Objects
• ADT's Display System
• Wall Cleanup
• Design Center
• Multiview Blocks
• Using Mass Elements for Furniture
• Wall Complexity
• Curtain Walls and Door/Window Assemblies
• Slabs
Display Representation—Schematic
Display Representation—High Detail
Display Representation—High Detail
4'-6"
3'-0"
9'-2"
3'-0"
10'-0"
PROTOTYPE STAFF OFFICE
SCALE:¼" =1'-0"

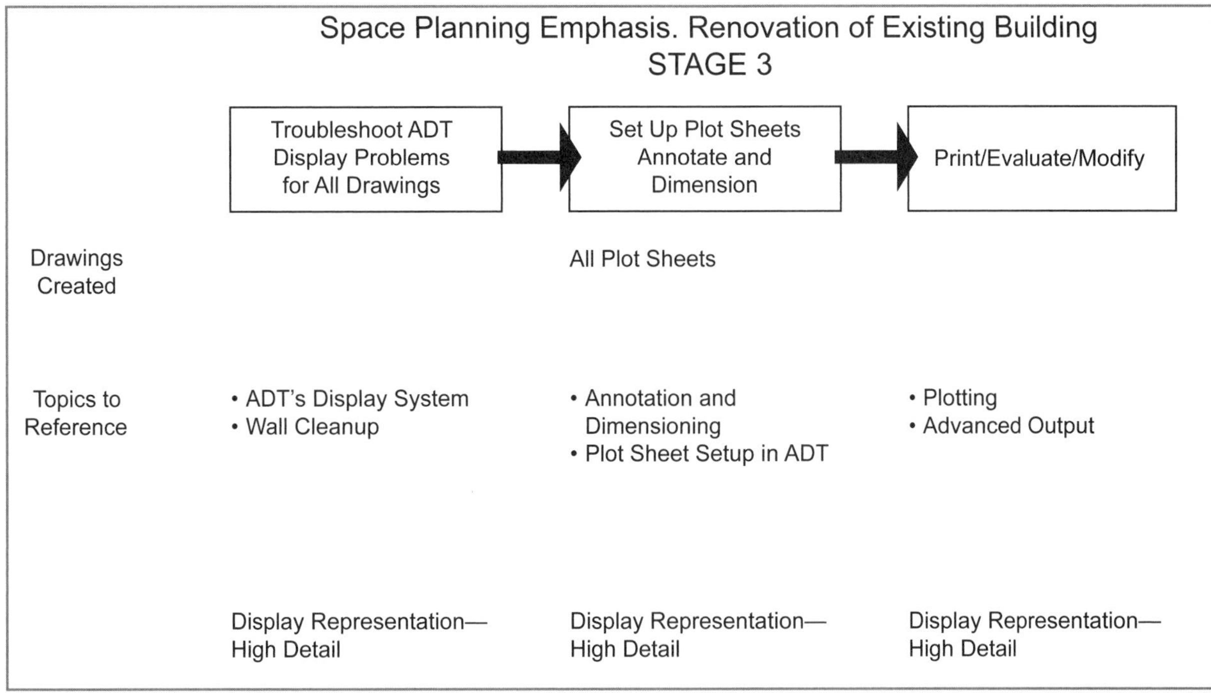

Figure 19.47 Space plan emphasis–Stage 3

Three-Dimensional Massing Emphasis–Stage 2

The goals of this stage in the design process are to do the following:

- Use Constructs to set up and organize the parts of the virtual model.
- Use conversion techniques to transform massing objects into the floor levels of the virtual model.
- Use conversion techniques to transform space objects into walls and openings of the virtual model.
- Use Views to create floor plans, building sections, isometrics, and perspectives.

Three-Dimensional Massing Emphasis–Stage 3

The goals of this stage in the design process are to do the following:

- Use Elements in ADT's Project Navigator to test and develop furniture arrangements that support room function and size.
- Use learned strategies to troubleshoot display and/or drawing conventions within drawings.
- Use the additional building systems to further refine the virtual model.
- Develop final presentation strategy for the project.
- Use sheet set manager to organize and print presentation.

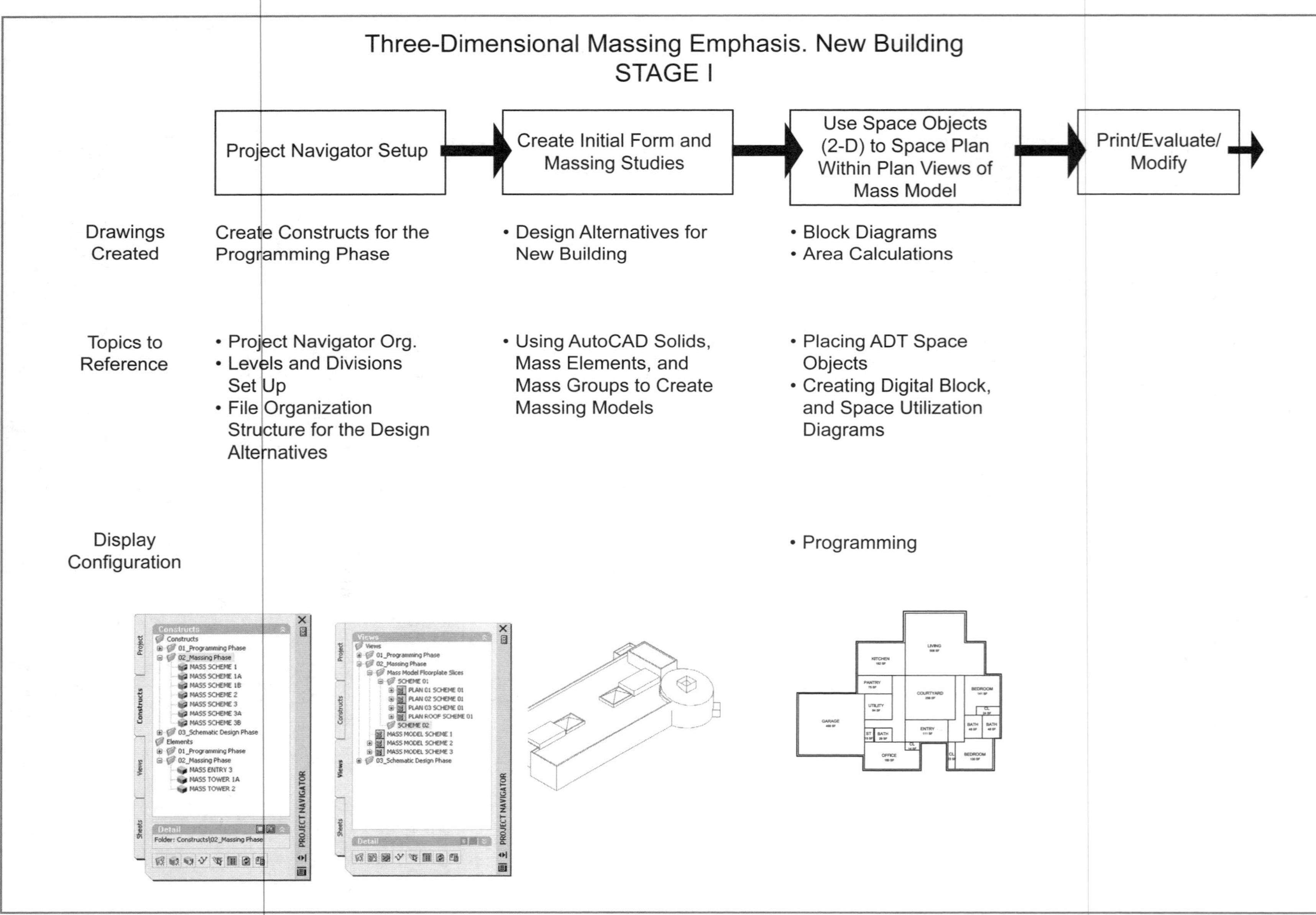

Figure 19.48 Three-dimensional massing emphasis—Stage 1

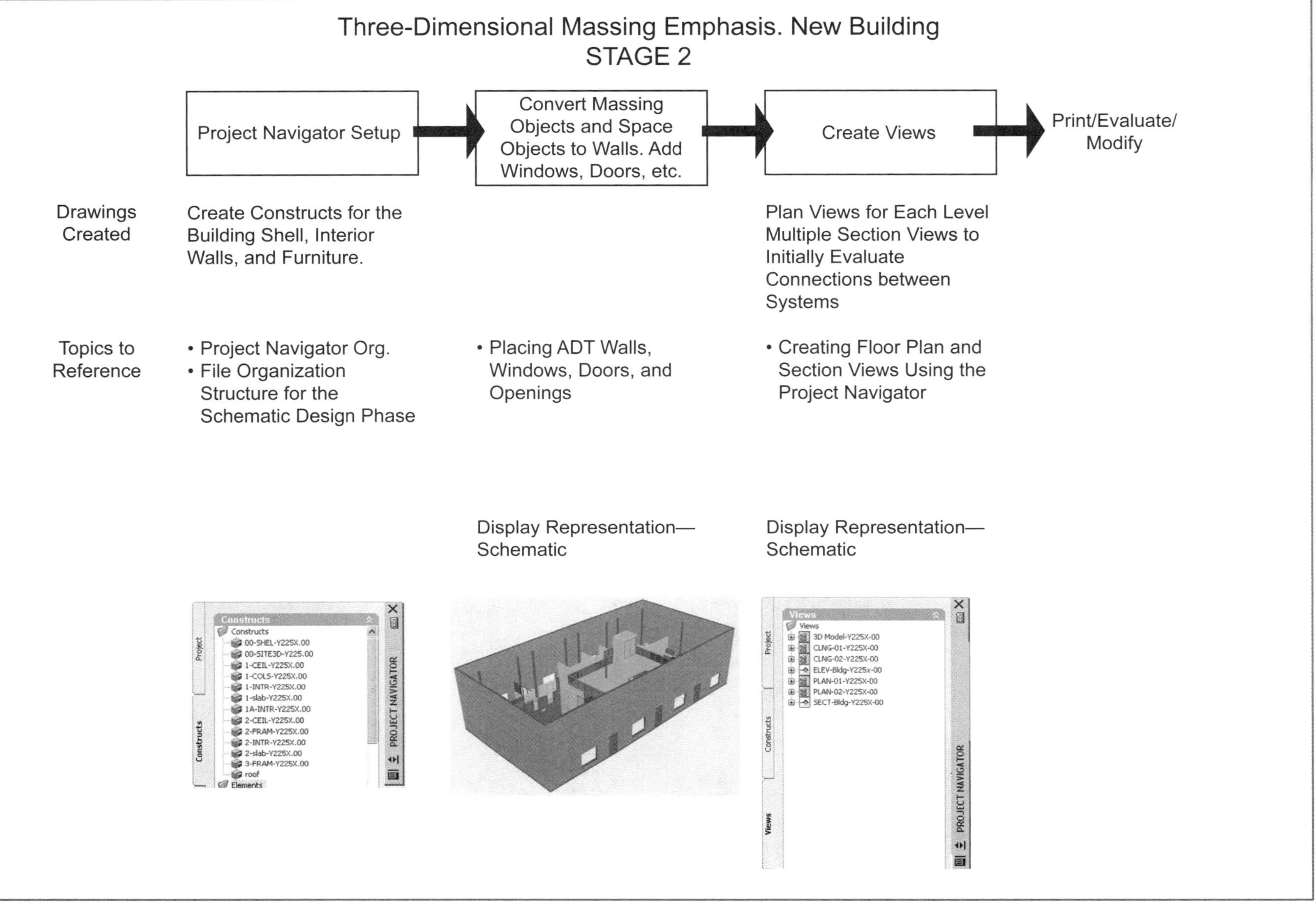

Figure 19.49 Three-dimensional massing emphasis—Stage 2

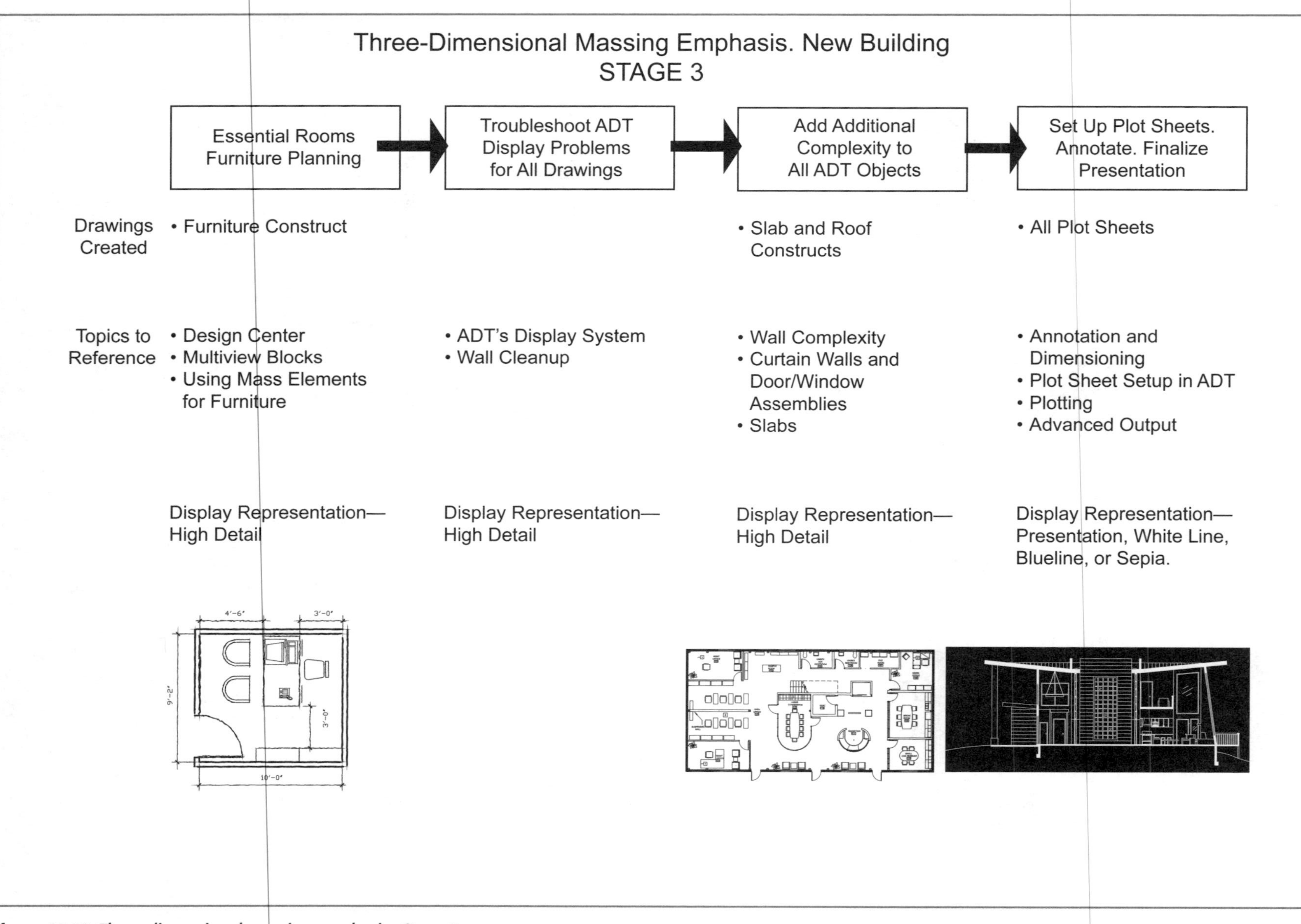
Three-Dimensional Massing Emphasis. New Building
STAGE 3
Essential Rooms Furniture Planning
Troubleshoot ADT Display Problems for All Drawings
Add Additional Complexity to All ADT Objects
Set Up Plot Sheets. Annotate. Finalize Presentation
Drawings Created
• Furniture Construct
• Slab and Roof Constructs
• All Plot Sheets
Topics to Reference
• Design Center
• Multiview Blocks
• Using Mass Elements for Furniture
• ADT's Display System
• Wall Cleanup
• Wall Complexity
• Curtain Walls and Door/Window Assemblies
• Slabs
• Annotation and Dimensioning
• Plot Sheet Setup in ADT
• Plotting
• Advanced Output
Display Representation—High Detail
Display Representation—High Detail
Display Representation—High Detail
Display Representation—Presentation, White Line, Blueline, or Sepia.
4'-6"
3'-0"
9'-2"
3'-0"
10'-0"

Figure 19.50 Three-dimensional massing emphasis—Stage 3

Approaches to Efficient Modeling Practices

Modeling a virtual building that has any type of complexity requires strategic planning. ADT includes many built-in mechanisms that help guide the overall process. However, these same mechanisms sometimes cause disorientation and loss of control in a project's development and presentation. Efficiency in modeling practices, therefore, requires knowing the correct modeling strategy and/or technique to implement, as well as knowing the best method of implementation. Much of this comes from experience. Nevertheless, there are a few tips that will accelerate the learning curve.

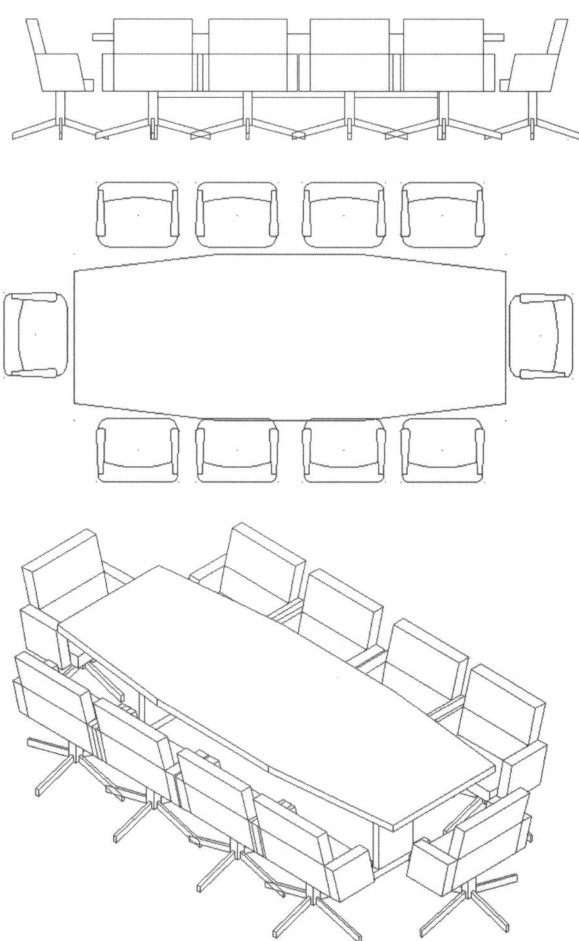

Figure 19.51 Always use multiview blocks for complicated furniture, casework, and equipment.

1. Use the Project Navigator to organize your virtual model. The Project Navigator in ADT makes virtual model creation and organization much easier. Refer to the section Drawing Craft and Drawing Organization in this chapter for the various organizational strategies.
2. It is much more efficient to create all the Constructs and View drawings at once, immediately after project setup.
3. Start all projects with a minimum amount of detail. Starting generically then adding detail as the design develops ensures that your focus is on the important issues of that stage. Worrying about gypboard wall cleanups during the early stages of the space planning process wastes valuable time and energy.
4. Similarly, at each stage within the design process, make sure all objects within the virtual model are at the same level of detail. Placing a well-detailed chair when the custom cabinets remain as boxes is noticeable to the eye and creates an unbalanced presentation.
5. Always use multiview blocks for complicated furniture, casework, and equipment (Figure 19.51).
6. Keep models healthy and small. Do regular audits and purges to prevent file corruption. Virtual models—even the simplest ones—have a tendency to grow in file size and every once in a while become corrupt. Regular drawing audits help to fix small problems before they become larger (Figure 19.52). In addition, having the patience to let a drawing properly close (or open) will also ensure against potential drawing corruption. Purging ADT drawings is a two-phase process. It first requires a purge of all unused AEC object styles, which is followed by an AutoCAD purge. Figures 19.53 and 19.54 illustrate the two processes.

```
Command: audit
Fix any errors detected? [Yes/No]
<N>: y
Auditing Header
Auditing Tables
Auditing Entities Pass 1
Pass 1 6100    objects audited
Object Z offset is an invalid number.
  Set to zero.
Object Z offset is an invalid number.
  Set to zero.
Object Z offset is an invalid number.
  Set to zero.
Object Z offset is an invalid number.
  Set to zero.
Object Z offset is an invalid number.
  Set to zero.
Pass 1 44000   objects audited
Auditing Entities Pass 2
Pass 2 44000   objects audited
Auditing Blocks
 258     Blocks audited
Total errors found 5 fixed 5
Erased 0 objects
```

Figure 19.52 Regular drawing audits help to fix small problems before they become larger.

Technique to Master **T19.53** Purging Unused ADT Styles

Figure 19.53

1	[Format menu]	Open the Style Manager.
2	[Style Manager> Left Pane]	Left-click on drawing name.
3	[Style Manager]	Left-click on Purge button.
4	[Style Manager]	Click Apply to finalize changes.

Technique to Master **T19.54** Purging Unused AutoCAD Layers, Blocks, Styles, and so on

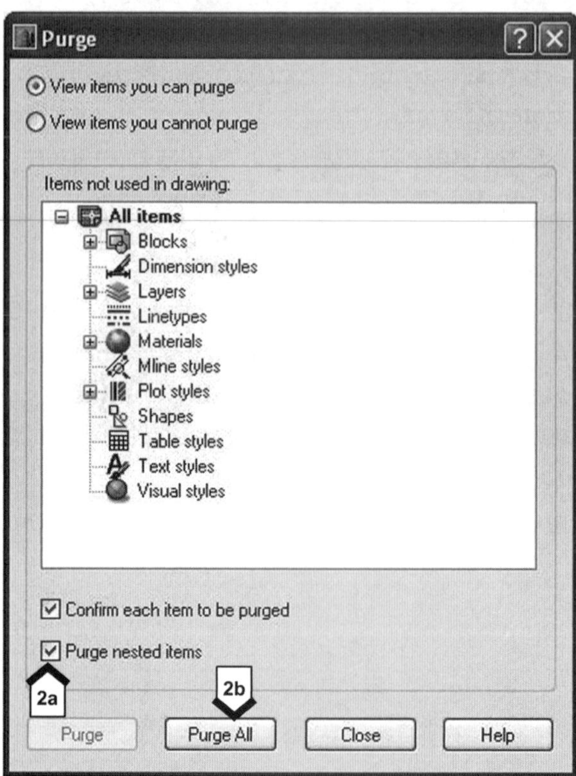

Figure 19.54 This procedure purges all unused AutoCAD items from the current drawing. To purge individual items, expand the plus signs next to each item type and purge manually.

1	[Command Line]	Type the Purge command, then press Enter.
2a 2b	[Purge dialogue box]	Check the Purge nested items box. Left-click on the Purge All button.

Chapter Exercises

Open the Chapter 19 folder located on the CD-ROM to access the exercises related to this chapter. The exercises and Drawing Technique Problems help students master using the Project Navigator and its associated concepts and techniques.

Controlling Output: Drawing Presentation Techniques 20

Objectives

This chapter exposes beginning students to the various output methods and graphic presentation techniques using AutoCAD and Architectural Desktop.

Controlling Output

Sometimes the most difficult part of the digital design process is getting the printed results you want. This is true from the beginner level all the way to advanced users. The reason is that even with the advancement of what-you-see-is-what-you-get (WYSIWYG) technology, the monitor screen never accurately represents its plotted counterpart. This is especially true with CAD software. In this chapter we look at some of the variables in AutoCAD and ADT that affect printed output. We also explore graphic and presentation techniques that expand on conventional practice.

Conventional Output with AutoCAD and ADT

Most output techniques require an underlying knowledge of how line thickness, line styling, and color correlate to their output representation. In the AutoCAD and Architectural Desktop environments, this means knowing about the plotting process (Chapter 1) and understanding object properties (Chapter 3). Conventional output in AutoCAD and ADT usually refers to the print/plot process that is accomplished through the Plot command. Figures 20.1a and b illustrate how the drawing attributes relate to the output.

AutoCAD objects are assigned properties.

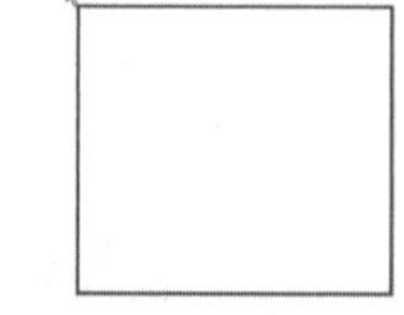

either by object

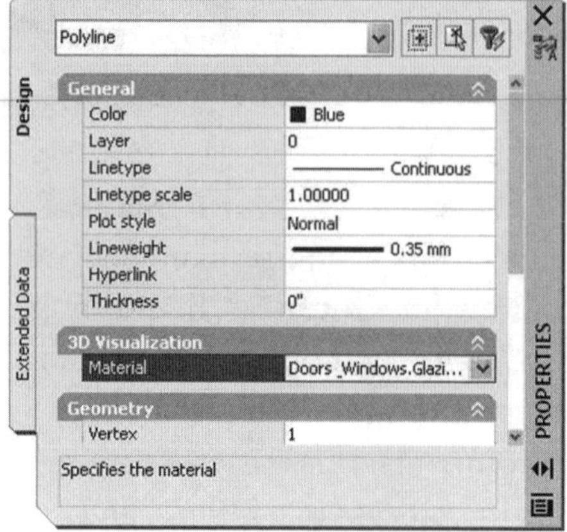

or by layer

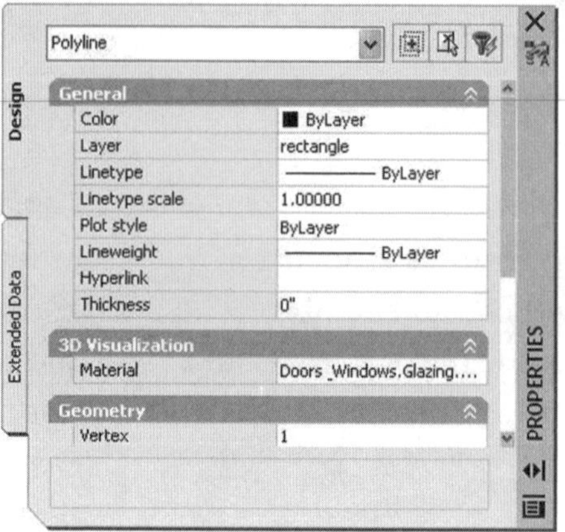

Plot styles will then determine if objects will print based on their assigned properties.

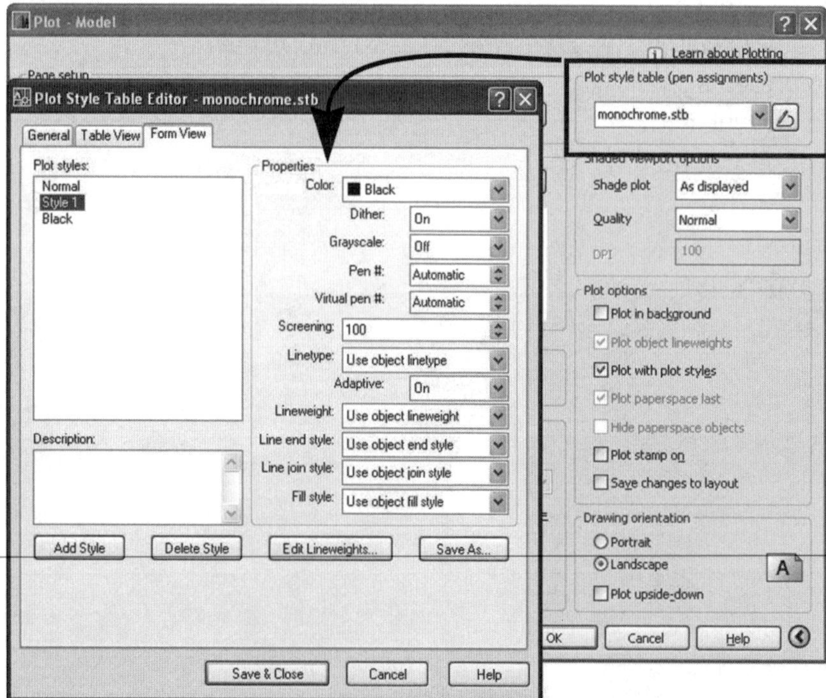

Figure 20.1a Object properties and the plotting process within AutoCAD

ADT objects are assigned properties.

either by object

or by layer

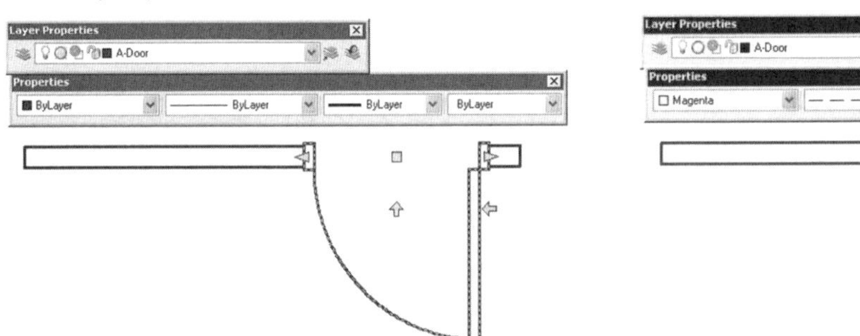

or by Object Style where each component is assigned its own properties

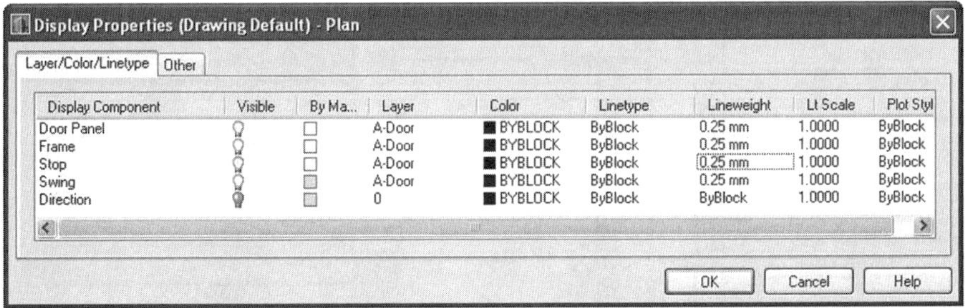

or by Material Definition where each material is assigned its own properties

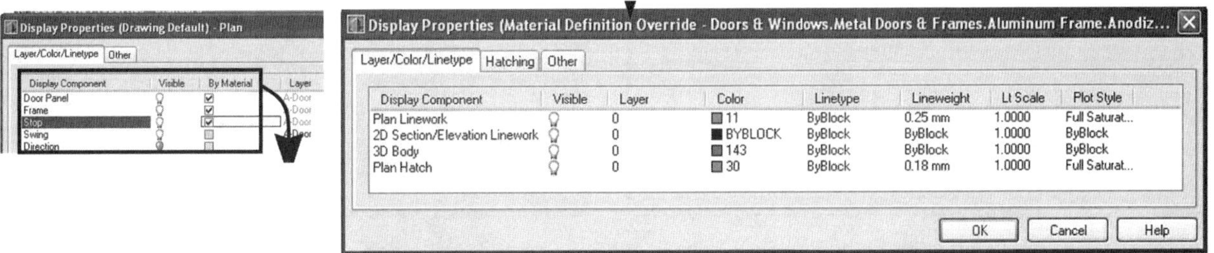

Plot styles will then determine if objects will print based on their assigned properties.

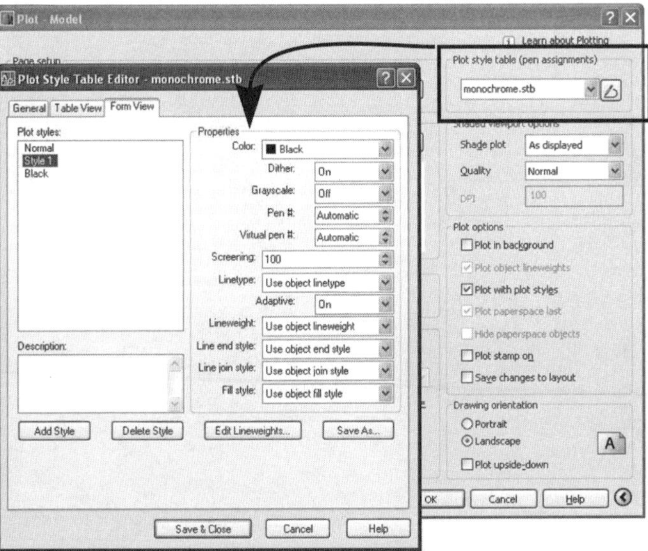

Figure 20.1b Object properties and the plotting process within Architectural Desktop

The Plot Style Table Editor

Plot style tables save settings that control how objects look when printed. This includes control of color, line thickness, line styling, screening, joins, and fills. When objects are printed/plotted, AutoCAD or ADT will first read the instructions of the plot style (Figure 20.2). If the plot style says use the object's color and lineweight, then whatever color and lineweight the object is assigned will be printed.

There are two plot style table types—color dependent and named. The color dependent table uses the old method of plotting where the object's color controls how it gets printed (Figure 20.3). This usually requires memorization of color to lineweight assignments (Table 20.1).

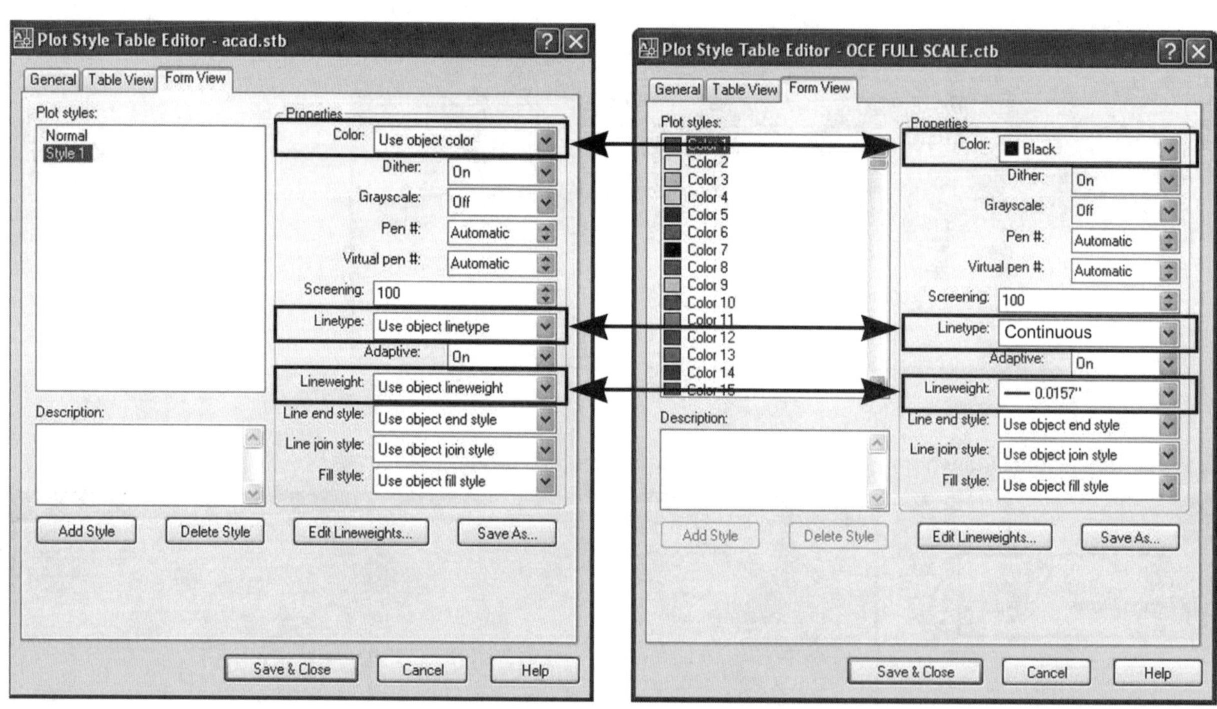

Figure 20.2 The important fields in the Plot Style Table Editor

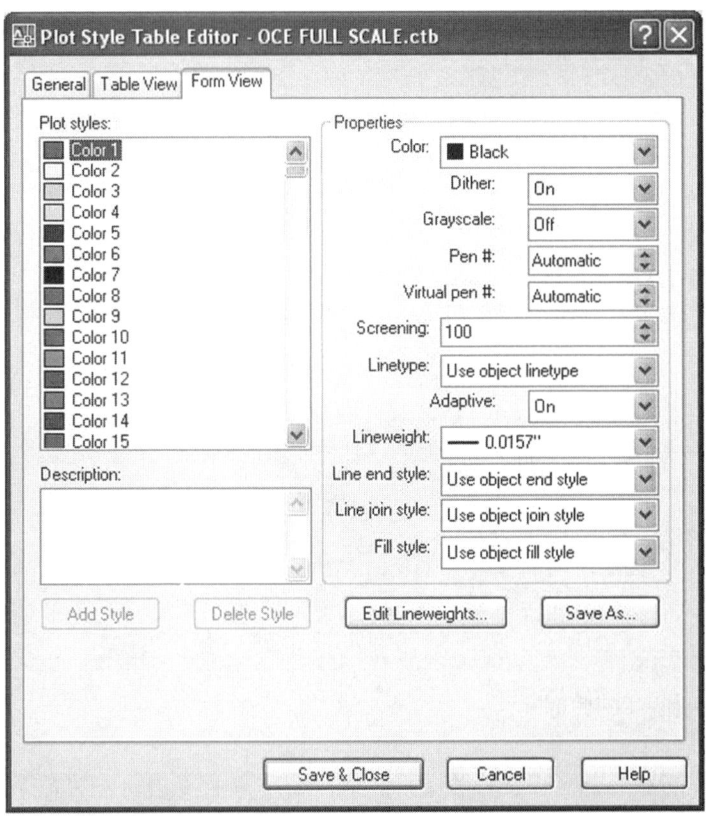

Figure 20.3 The color-dependent plot style table uses the old method of plotting where the object's color controls how it gets printed.

Table 20.1 Color to Lineweight Assignments for Color-Dependent Plot Styles

Color Number	Color Description	Lineweight Assigned
1	Red	.50mm
2	Yellow	.35mm
3	Green	.25mm
4	Cyan	.13mm
5	Blue	.70mm
6	Magenta	.05mm
7	White	.25mm
8	Gray	.13mm

Named plot styles frees the color property of these duties and allows each layer (regardless of color) to be assigned to a plot style. Named plot styles are assigned specific output properties (Figure 20.4).

Plot Resolution and Shading Parameters

The shaded viewport plotting options provide additional control over how drawings will output (Figure 20.5). These options are mostly relevant for three-dimensional views of drawings where shading and resolution settings are important. For the most part, the shaded viewport options area of the Plot dialogue box can be left at its default settings—As displayed and Normal.

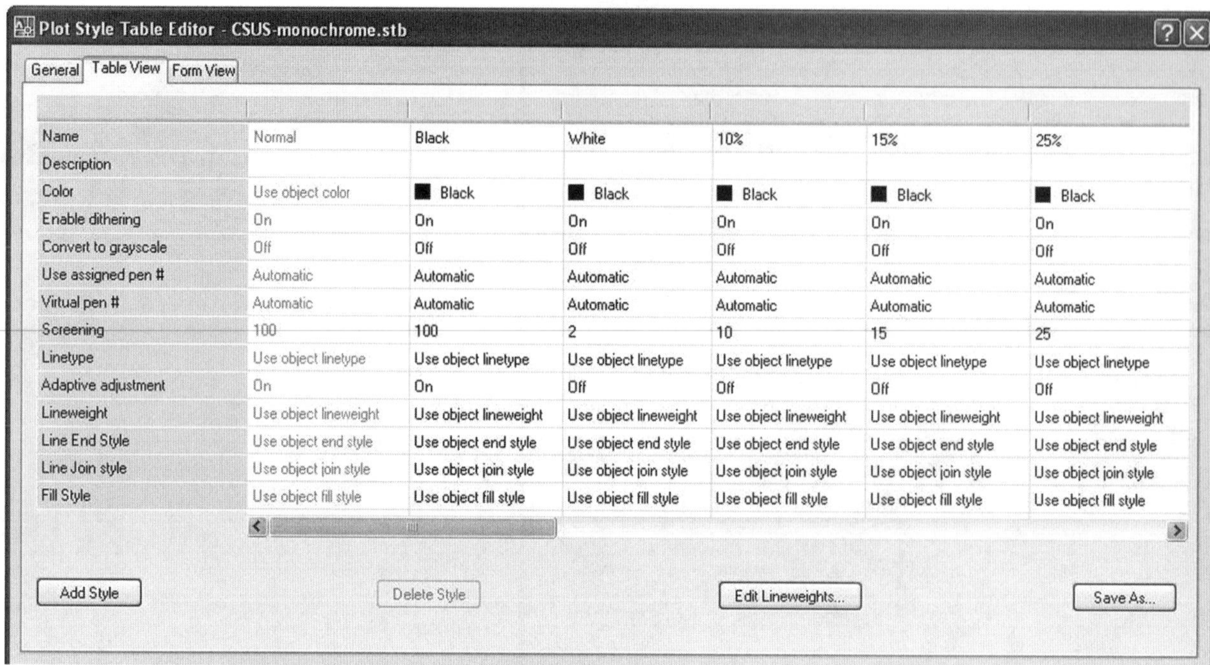

Plot Style Table Editor - CSUS-monochrome.stb

General | Table View | Form View

Name	Normal	Black	White	10%	15%	25%
Description						
Color	Use object color	Black	Black	Black	Black	Black
Enable dithering	On	On	On	On	On	On
Convert to grayscale	Off	Off	Off	Off	Off	Off
Use assigned pen #	Automatic	Automatic	Automatic	Automatic	Automatic	Automatic
Virtual pen #	Automatic	Automatic	Automatic	Automatic	Automatic	Automatic
Screening	100	100	2	10	15	25
Linetype	Use object linetype	Use object linetype	Use object linetype	Use object linetype	Use object linetype	Use object linetype
Adaptive adjustment	On	On	Off	Off	Off	Off
Lineweight	Use object lineweight	Use object lineweight	Use object lineweight	Use object lineweight	Use object lineweight	Use object lineweight
Line End Style	Use object end style	Use object end style	Use object end style	Use object end style	Use object end style	Use object end style
Line Join style	Use object join style	Use object join style	Use object join style	Use object join style	Use object join style	Use object join style
Fill Style	Use object fill style	Use object fill style	Use object fill style	Use object fill style	Use object fill style	Use object fill style

Add Style | Delete Style | Edit Lineweights... | Save As...

Figure 20.4 Named plot styles are assigned specific output properties.

Plot - Model

Learn about Plotting

Page setup
Name: <None> | Add...

Printer/plotter
Name: DWF6 ePlot.pc3 | Properties...
Plotter: DWF6 ePlot - DWF ePlot - by Autodesk
Where: File
Description:
Plot to file
36.0″
24.0″

Paper size
ARCH D (36.00 x 24.00 Inches)

Number of copies
1

Plot area
What to plot:
Display

Plot offset (origin set to printable area)
X: 0.000000 inch
Y: 0.000000 inch
Center the plot

Plot scale
Fit to paper
Scale: Custom
1 inches =
6.273 units
Scale lineweights

Plot style table (pen assignments)
CSUS-monochrome.stb

Shaded viewport options
Shade plot: As displayed
Quality
DPI
As displayed
Wireframe
Hidden
3D Hidden
3D Wireframe
Conceptual
Realistic
Rendered
Draft
Low
Medium
High
Presentation

Plot options
Plot in backg
Plot object l
Plot with plo
Plot papers
Hide paperspace objects
Plot stamp on
Save changes to layout

Drawing orientation
Portrait
Landscape
Plot upside-down

Preview... | Apply to Layout | OK | Cancel | Help

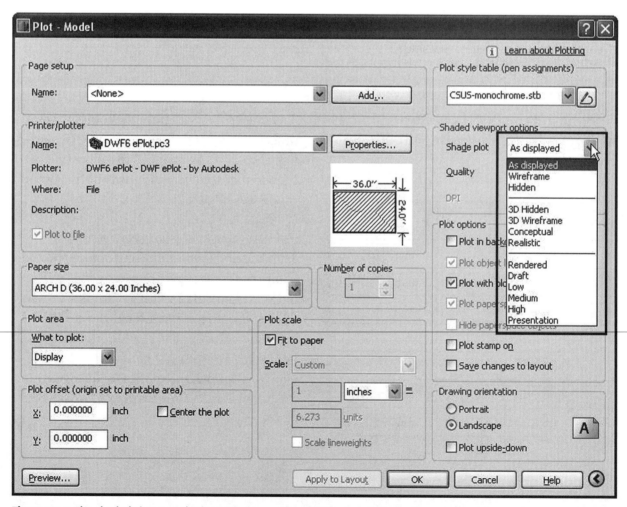

Figure 20.5 The shaded viewport plotting options provide additional control over how drawings will output.

Managing Output Efficiency

Plotting can be time-consuming, especially when there are multiple drawings involved. AutoCAD and ADT have several built-in mechanisms to automate the plotting process. In this section we look at three workflow changes that could help you speed up the plotting process.

Page Setups

Page setups are saved plotting parameters that can be recalled at any time. Though they are only saved within the current drawing file, page setups can be easily imported from other drawings. Page setups save valuable time during the plotting process. Rather than adjusting and verifying plot parameters each time you print, page setups will automatically assign the parameters based on its saved settings. Chapter 20 files on the supplementary CD-ROM demonstrate how to create a page setup using the Page Setup Manager. The same technique can be executed within the Plot dialogue box. The CD-ROM lessons also demonstrate how to import page setups from other drawings.

Using Views in Page Setups

Chapters 8 and 19 introduced the use of views for saving specific zoom magnifications and drawing area frames (Figure 20.6). These same saved views can also be used as view setups for printing and plotting. Once established within page setups, plot areas no longer need to be verified through the plot preview, thus improving plot accuracy and efficiency.

Using the Publish Command

The Publish command provides the ability to output multiple drawings to a printer, plotter, or Design Web Format (DWF) device. The publish command, however, only works if page setups are available for the model or layout views to be plotted. You can refer to Chapter 20 on the CD-ROM for a demonstration of how to publish multiple drawings to a printer using this command.

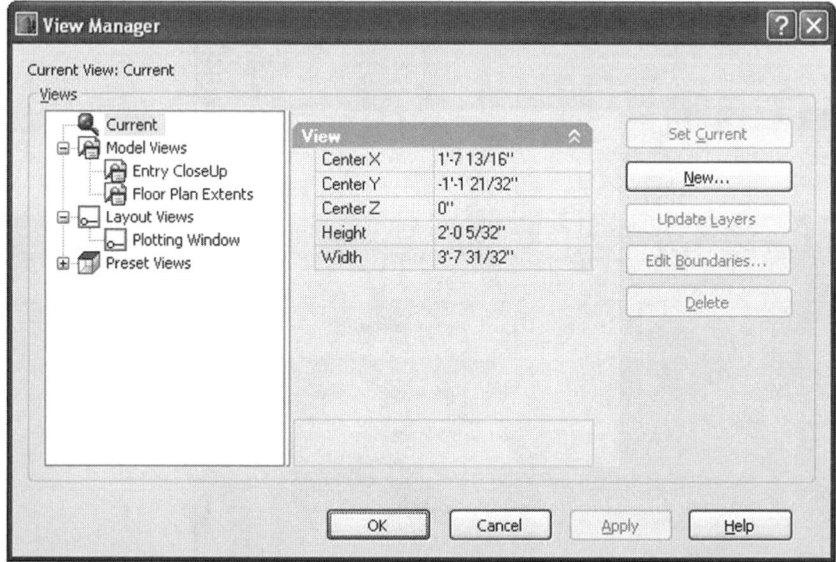

Figure 20.6 By using saved views within page setups, plot areas no longer need to be verified through the plot preview, thus improving plot accuracy and efficiency.

A Brief Look at Other Types of Output

Besides conventional printing and plotting, other types of output are possible within the AutoCAD and ADT environments. This section introduces four useful output options that are available.

DWF Outputs

The Design Web Format (DWF) output type was designed by the makers of Autodesk so that drawings could be viewed over the Internet and Intranet with Microsoft Internet Explorer. Autodesk offers two free downloadable viewer programs—Autodesk DWF Viewer and Autodesk DWG TrueView. Both viewers allow you to open, view, and print .dwf and .dwg files without AutoCAD or ADT. The Autodesk Design Review (formerly called DWF Composer) is the retail version available for purchase. In addition to the viewer's capabilities, it has tools for adding notes, dimensions, and other types of markups to drawings without changing the original. Figure 20.7 demonstrates outputting to the DWF file format. This technique is also outlined on your CD-ROM.

PDF Outputs

The PDF format (Adobe Portable Document Format) was invented by Abobe as a means to open, print, and share all types of documents electronically without needing the specific software. The versatility of the PDF format makes outputting to PDF a huge advantage. PDF drawings are created through the Plot command using the PDF device driver. To view created PDF files, a free downloadable Adobe Reader is available at www.adobe.com/downloads.

Technique to Master **T20.07** Plotting to the DWF Format Using the Plot Command

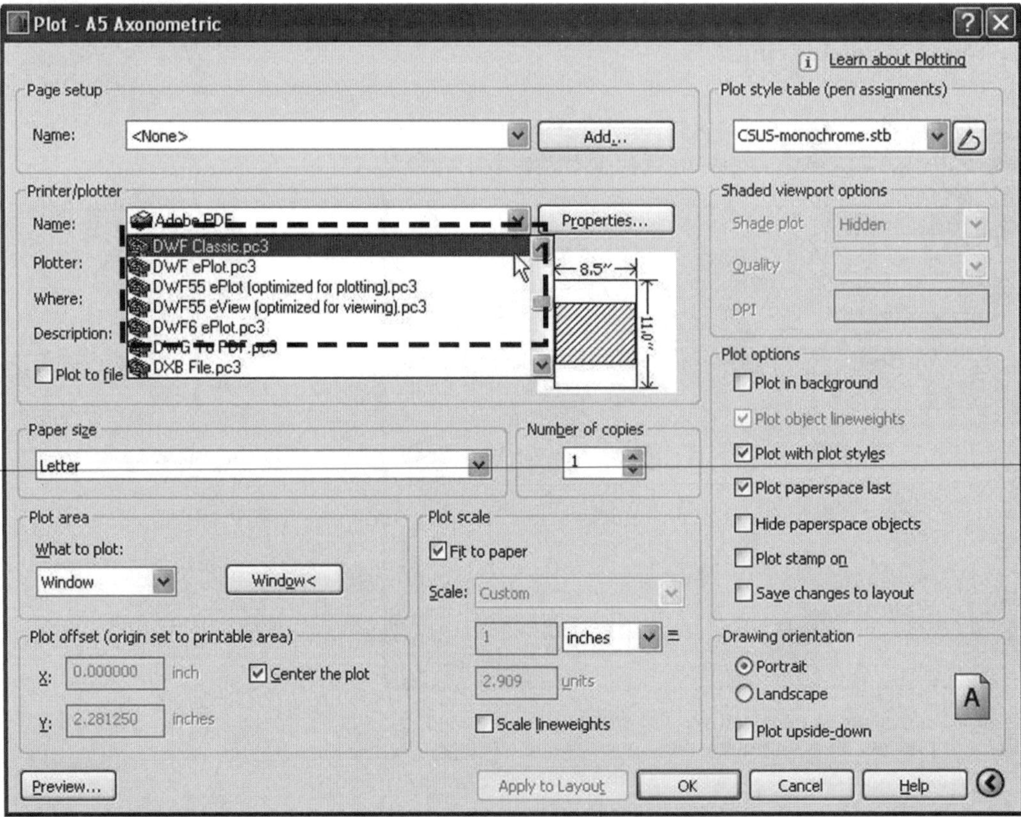

Figure 20.7
Using the Plot command, choose any of the DWF printer drivers shown above.

Rasterized Output

Rasterized output converts the AutoCAD and ADT drawings into raster images such as bitmap, JPEG, TIFF, and PNG formats that can be opened in photo-editing software. Raster images are created based on how objects are displayed on-screen. Note that this type of output should be used for presentation purposes only—not to output scalable drawings. Figure 20.8 demonstrates the technique using the Export command, Figure 20.9 using the Plot command.

Exporting ADT Drawings to AutoCAD

The three-dimensional characteristics of Architectural Desktop drawings can be flattened to a two-dimensional drawing using the Export To AutoCAD command. There are two Export command types located in the File menu. The Export To AutoCAD will convert the current ADT drawing into an AutoCAD .dwg or .dxf format with a choice of release types—R2007, R2004, R2000, and R14.

The Export command will covert the convert drawing to other graphic format types including .eps, .wmf, .dwf, and .bmp.

Technique to Master **T20.08** Creating Raster Images Using the Export Command

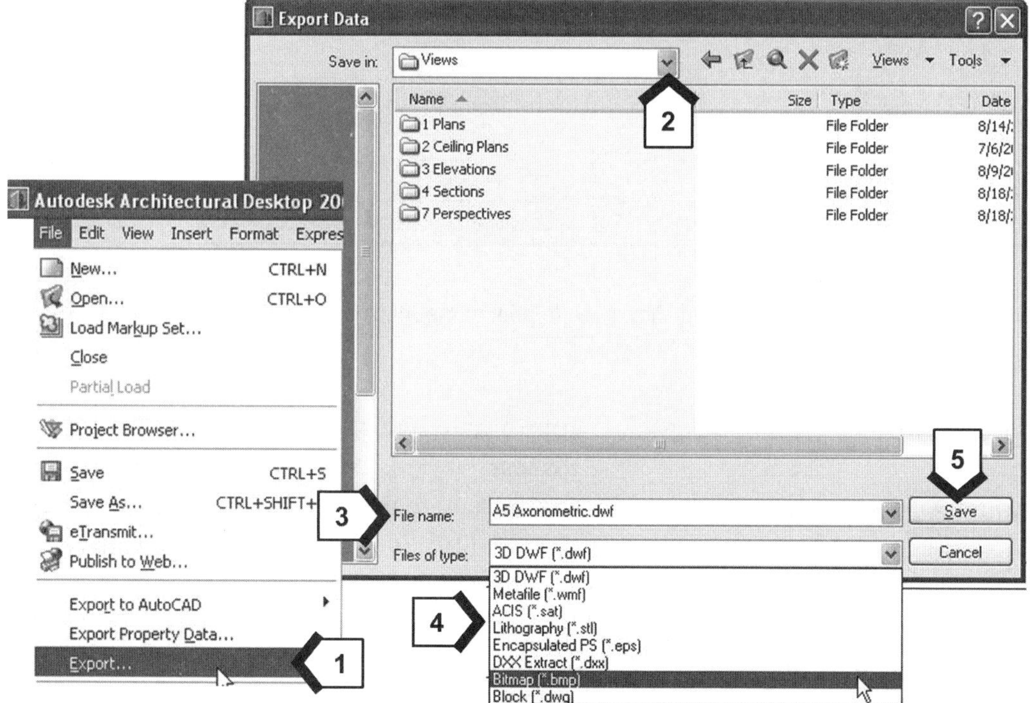

Figure 20.8 The Export command provides Bitmap and Metafile raster outputs.

1	[File Menu]	Choose Export command.
2	[Export Data dialogue box]	Specify location for exported file.
3	[Export Data dialogue box]	Name exported file.
4	[Export Data dialogue box]	Select file type.
5	[Export Data dialogue box]	Left-click Save button.

Technique to Master **T20.09** Creating Raster Images Using the Plot Command

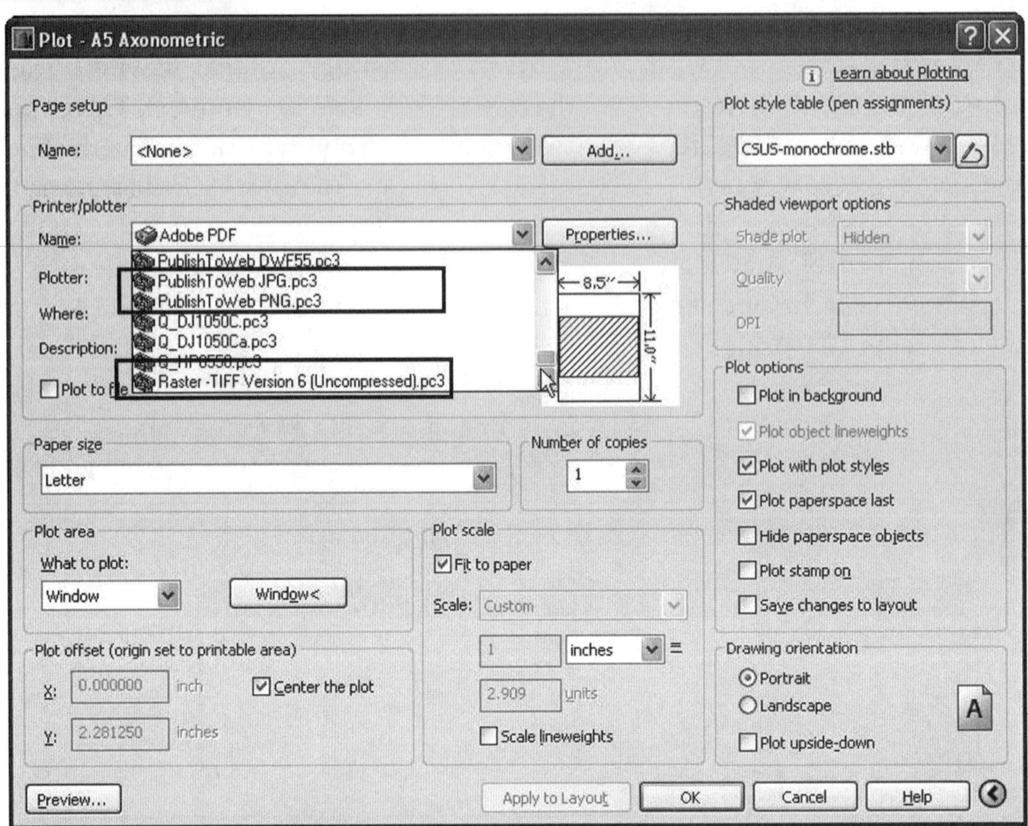

Figure 20.9

The printer/plotter selections within the Plot command allows you to print to the JPEG, PNG, and TIFF raster file formats. Refer to Chapter 1 to review plotting procedures.

Trouble-Shooting Conventional Output Problems

Most beginner AutoCAD and Architectural Desktop users have problems that are associated with plot output because of the numerous variables that affect the plotting process. As a result, sometimes it can be difficult to isolate the problem. The following offers some trouble-shooting suggestions.

Lineweights Are All the Same

Lineweights are typically controlled through layers. First, make sure you are utilizing layer organization techniques—that is, all objects within a drawing should be assigned to their appropriate layers (Chapter 3). Next, verify that each layer is assigned a lineweight that is appropriate to its convention. Finally, verify that the plot style is using the object's layer assignment. Figure 20.10a illustrates each of the possible problems.

Plotted Output Has a Lot of Undesired Gray Lines and Hatches

This is a typical problem for students who forget to verify plot style assignments. See Figure 20.10b for an example of lineweights plotting as gray lines.

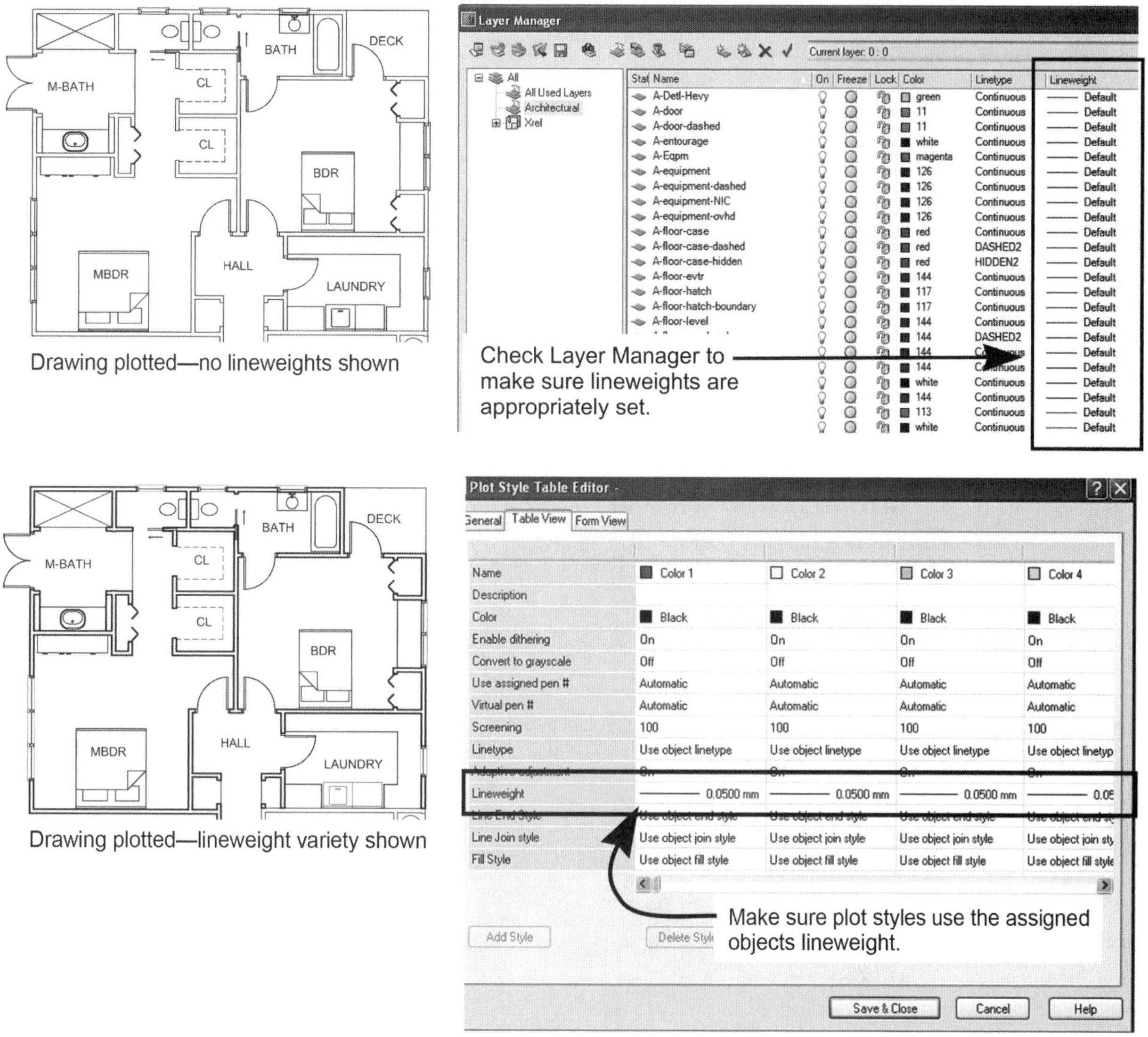

M-BATH
BATH
DECK
CL
CL
BDR
MBDR
HALL
LAUNDRY

Drawing plotted—no lineweights shown

Layer Manager

Current layer: 0 : 0

All
All Used Layers
Architectural
Xref

Name	Color	Linetype	Lineweight
A-Detl-Hevy	green	Continuous	Default
A-door	11	Continuous	Default
A-door-dashed	11	Continuous	Default
A-entourage	white	Continuous	Default
A-Eqpm	magenta	Continuous	Default
A-equipment	126	Continuous	Default
A-equipment-dashed	126	Continuous	Default
A-equipment-NIC	126	Continuous	Default
A-equipment-ovhd	126	Continuous	Default
A-floor-case	red	Continuous	Default
A-floor-case-dashed	red	DASHED2	Default
A-floor-case-hidden	red	HIDDEN2	Default
A-floor-evtr	144	Continuous	Default
A-floor-hatch	117	Continuous	Default
A-floor-hatch-boundary	117	Continuous	Default
A-floor-level	144	Continuous	Default

Check Layer Manager to make sure lineweights are appropriately set.

M-BATH
BATH
DECK
CL
CL
BDR
MBDR
HALL
LAUNDRY

Drawing plotted—lineweight variety shown

Plot Style Table Editor

General | Table View | Form View

Name	Color 1	Color 2	Color 3	Color 4
Description				
Color	Black	Black	Black	Black
Enable dithering	On	On	On	On
Convert to grayscale	Off	Off	Off	Off
Use assigned pen #	Automatic	Automatic	Automatic	Automatic
Virtual pen #	Automatic	Automatic	Automatic	Automatic
Screening	100	100	100	100
Linetype	Use object linetype	Use object linetype	Use object linetype	Use object linetyp
Lineweight	0.0500 mm	0.0500 mm	0.0500 mm	0.05
Line Join style	Use object join style	Use object join style	Use object join style	Use object join sty
Fill Style	Use object fill style	Use object fill style	Use object fill style	Use object fill style

Add Style | Delete Style | Save & Close | Cancel | Help

Make sure plot styles use the assigned objects lineweight.

Figure 20.10a Output problems: Lineweights are all plotting the same.

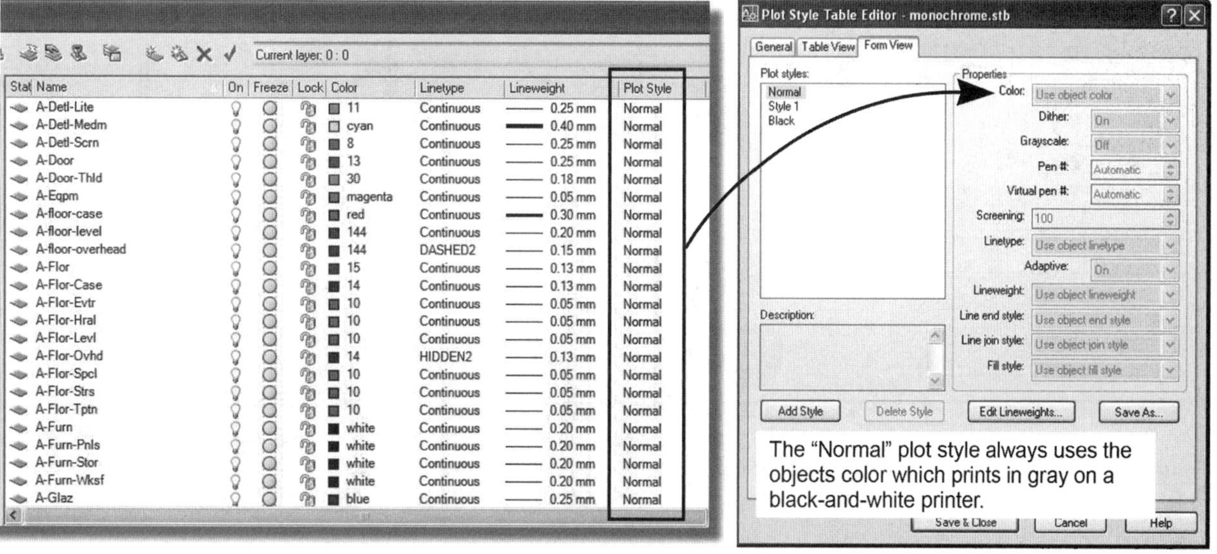

Figure 20.10b Output problems: Lineweights are plotting as gray lines.

Plotted Output Has Black Blobs

The black blob problem is a result of too much detail plotted at too small a scale (Figure 20.11). The first step is to reduce the amount of detail in the object. If the object is three-dimensional, it might mean converting the 3-D view to a 2-D projection and then deleting extra linework. Review Chapters 17 through 19 for help resolving this issue.

Dashed and Hidden Lines Are Displaying as Continuous

This is a classic Ltscale issue (Figure 20.12a). Ltscale is a drawing variable that affects the scale of noncontinuous line types in AutoCAD and ADT (Figure 20.12b). Review Chapter 3 for more information on linetype properties.

Curved Objects Are Not Printing Curved

Since displaying curved objects takes a lot of processing power, AutoCAD and ADT by default will display curves as faceted. There are three drawing variables that can be changed to resolve the problem—AecFacetDev, Viewres, and Facetres. The AecFacetDev variable controls the smoothness of ADT curved objects (Figure 20.13). The Viewres variable controls the smoothness of 2-D curves and the Facetres controls the smoothness of mesh and solid geometry. The Facetres variable has a direct relationship to the Viewres variable—that is, when the Viewres is raised or lowered, Facetres is affected proportionately. All of these variables can be changed through the Command Line or through the Options dialogue box (Figure 20.14).

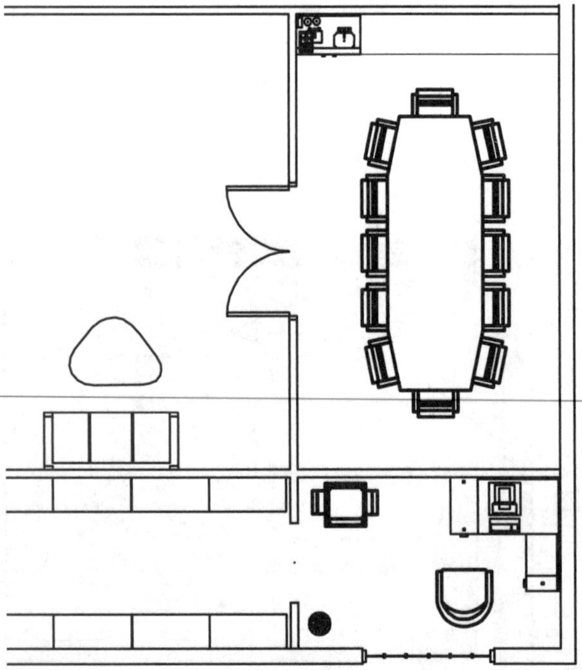

Figure 20.11 Output problems: Plotted output has black blobs.

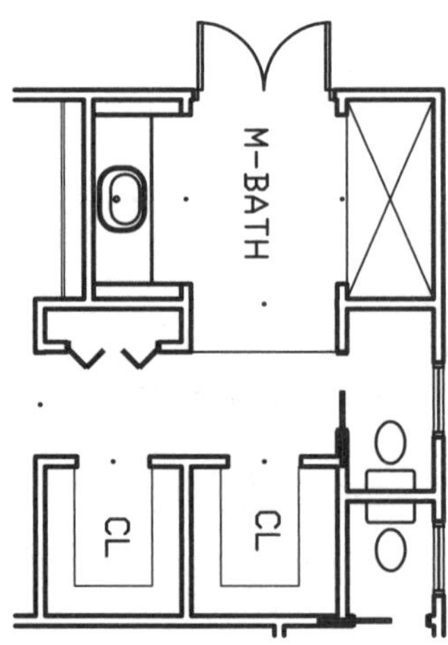

Figure 20.12a Output problems: Dashed and hidden lines are displaying as continuous.

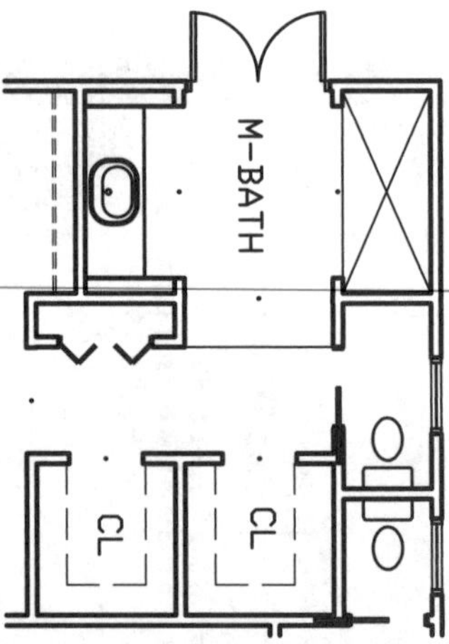

Figure 20.12b Ltscale is a drawing variable that affects the scale of noncontinuous line types in AutoCAD and ADT. Refer to Appendix J for appropriate Ltscale scaling settings.

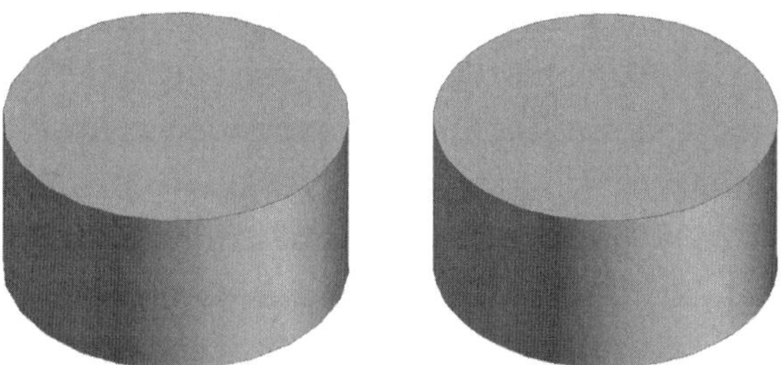

Figure 20.13 The AecFacetDev variable controls the smoothness of ADT curved objects.

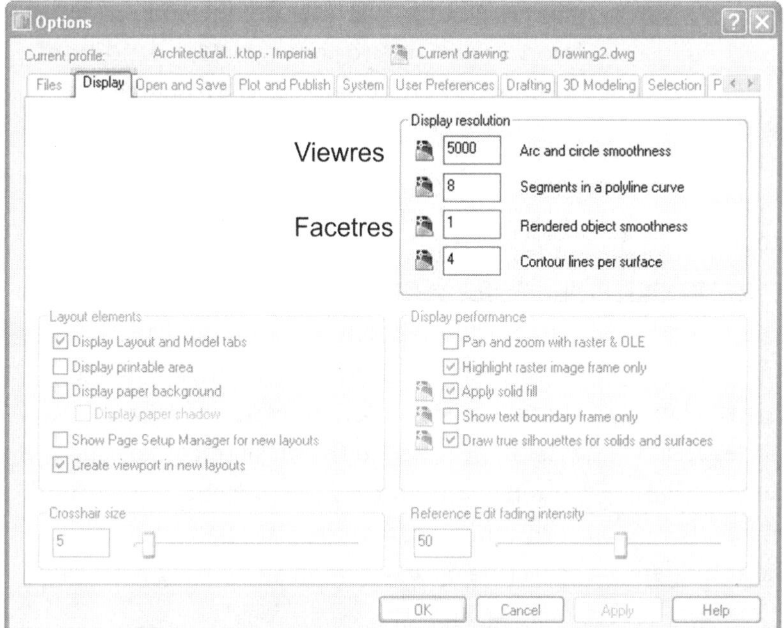

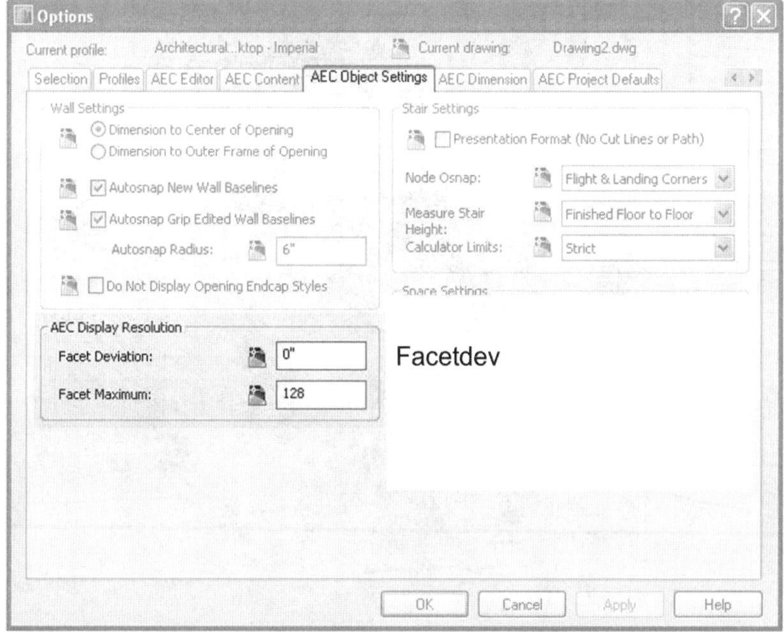

Figure 20.14 Output problems: Curved objects are not printing curved.

Graphic Presentation Techniques

Once the control of output is mastered in AutoCAD and ADT, other graphic presentation techniques can be explored. This topic introduces some of the graphic approaches that have evolved from the computer as a medium. It also demonstrates how to achieve some of the graphic techniques that were previously accomplished either by hand or through diazo, blueline, and blackline processes.

> **Box 20.1**
> Diazo, blueline, and blackline are printing processes used for large format printing. They were widely used prior to computer and xerographic printing.

The Chaos of Wireframe Views

The complexity of the wireframe view can be contrasted with hidden or shaded modes as a graphic presentation technique. In perspective and isometric views, all three-dimensional objects are described by edges. Without hidden line or shaded mode on, the edges create a complex graphic that is often used in presentations (Figure 20.15). Wireframe views can be outputted using any of the previous techniques learned thus far. The supplementary CD-ROM demonstrates how to setup viewports that contrast hidden and shaded views with wireframe views for plotting.

Creating Screened Drawings

Screened drawings are often used in construction documents to show existing conditions (Figure 20.16). They reduce the percentage intensity of the black (or color) ink. As a graphic presentation technique, screened areas of drawings are a great way to keep graphic information without taking away compositional focus (Figure 20.17). While screened construction documents are typically screened to around 50 percent, any range between 10 and 85 percent will create a visible contrast to the black ink at its full intensity. Reducing the percentage to 1 will print in white. Figures 20.18a and 20.18b describe how to screen an existing drawing.

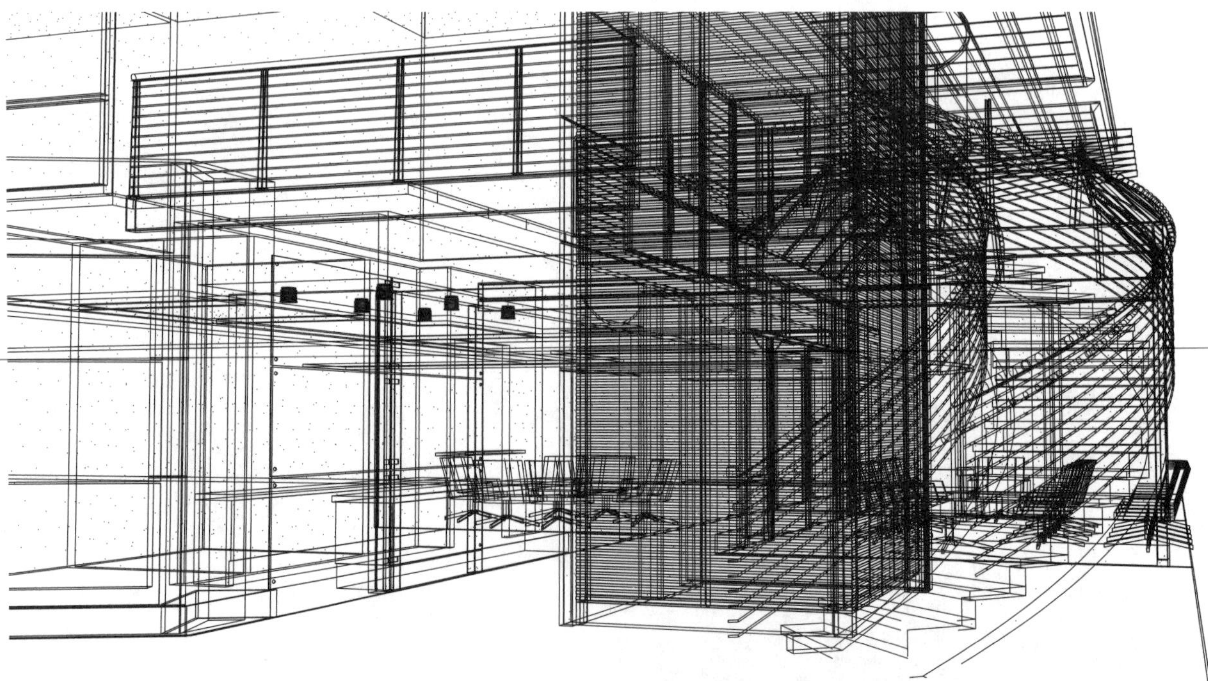

Figure 20.15 Presentation graphic

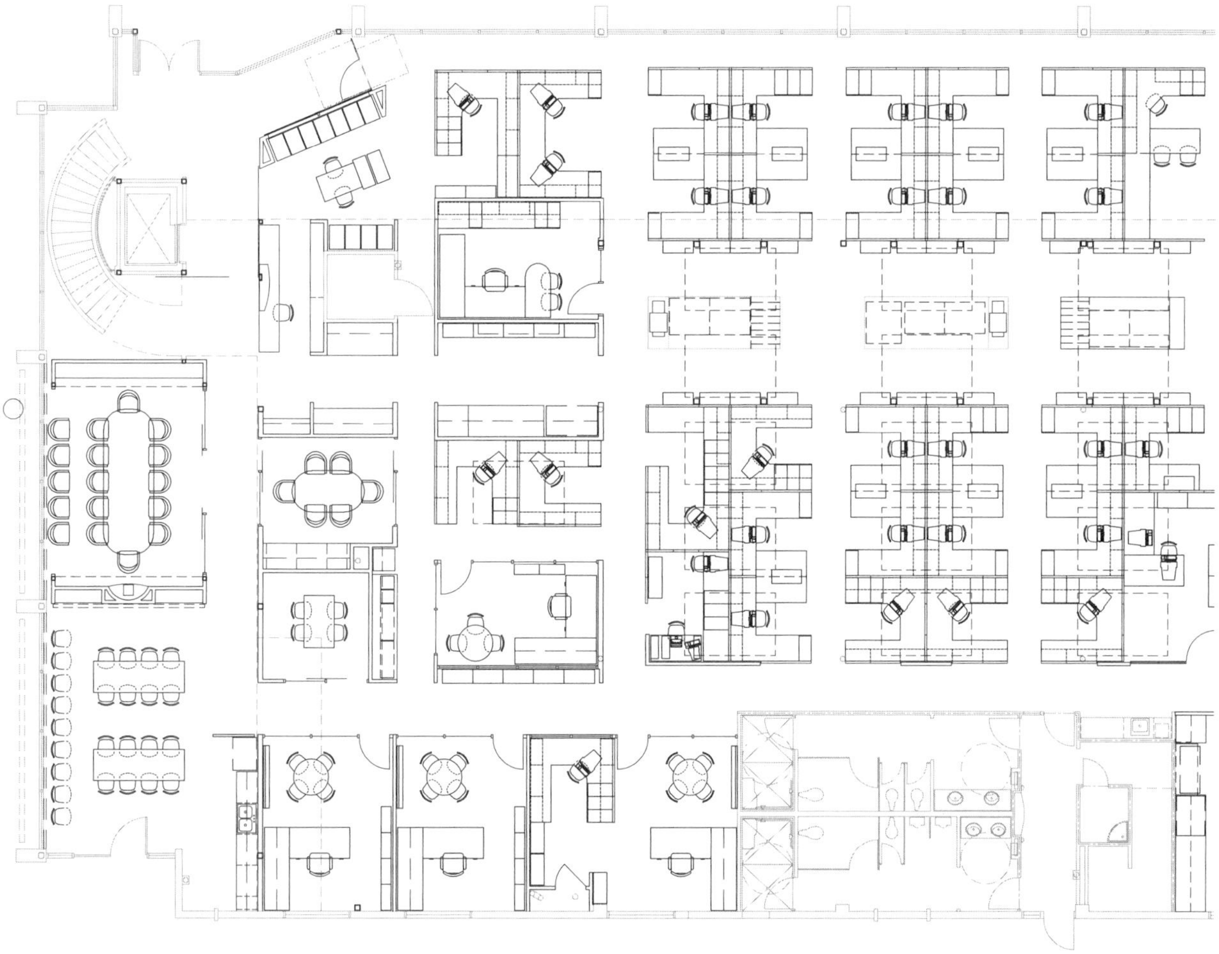

Figure 20.16 Screened drawing

Drawing: First Floor Plan. NLA Office Renovation, courtesy of Nacht & Lewis Architects, Sacramento, CA.

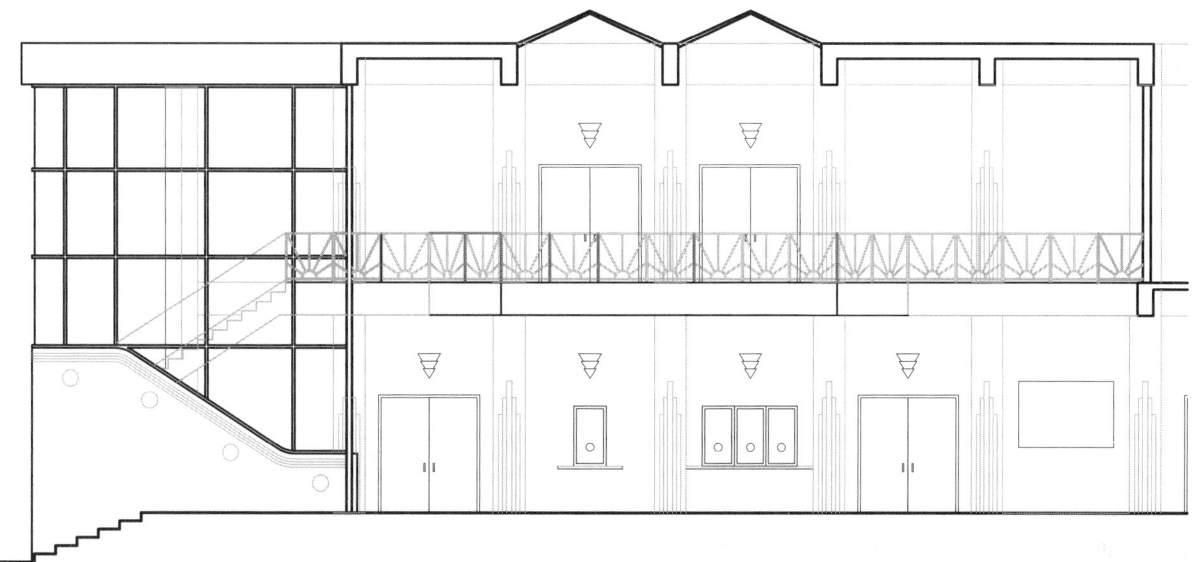

Figure 20.17 Screened areas of a drawing

Student Project: Music Hall Lobby Renovation, courtesy of Darci Drawbert.

Technique to Master T20.18a Creating a Screened Drawing Using a Color Dependent Template

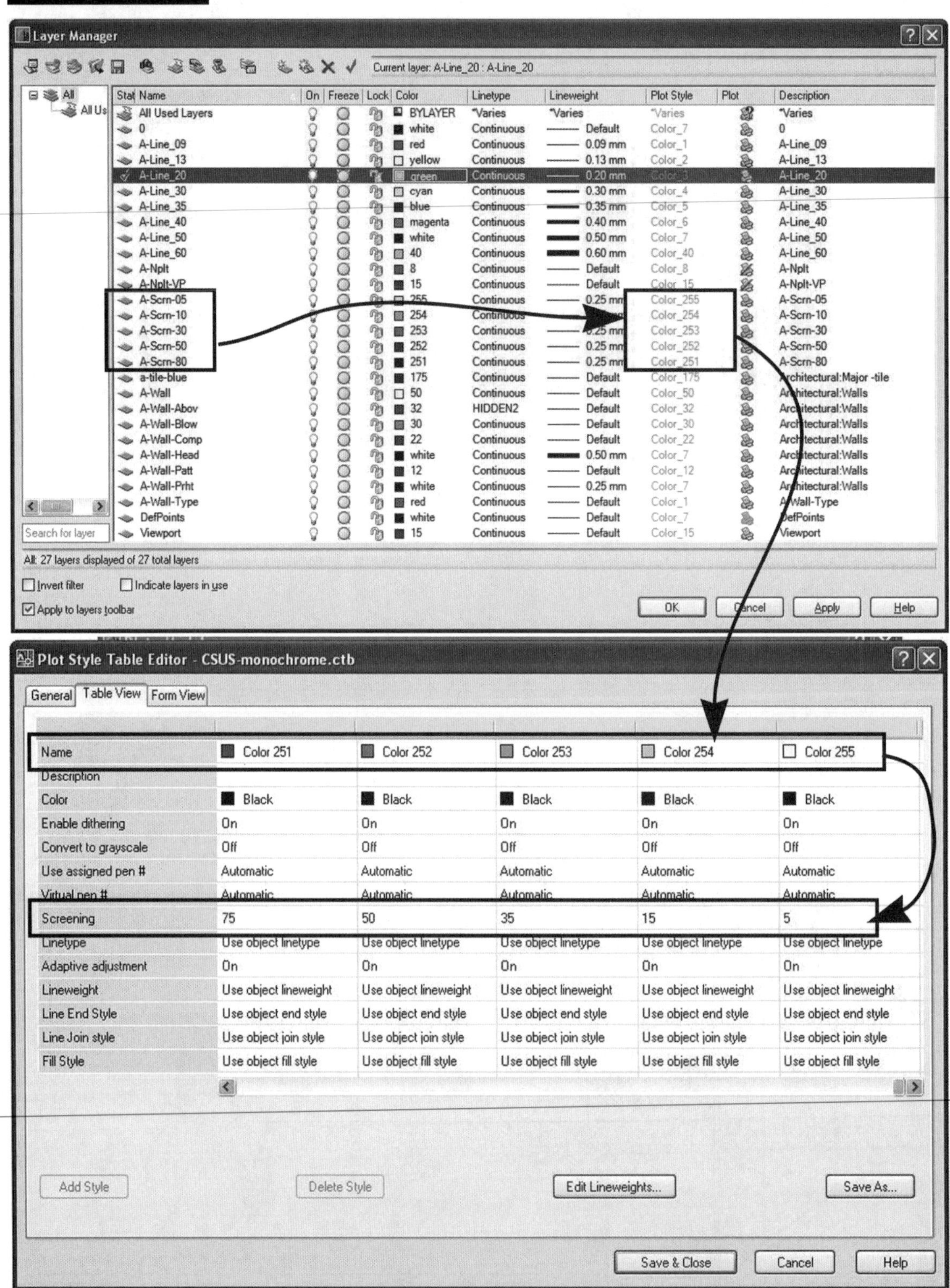

Figure 20.18a Screened drawings are best created by referencing (Xref) drawings into a new drawing. This allows you to change layer colors and plot styles without changing the original file.

1	Color dependent drawing templates use color dependent plot style tables for plotting. Using this type of template, the screened effect is achieved by assigning the AutoCAD gray colors to percentage screens of black.
2	All objects to be screened can then be placed on their associated screened layers.

Technique to Master **T20.18b** Creating a Screened Drawing Using a Named Dependent Template

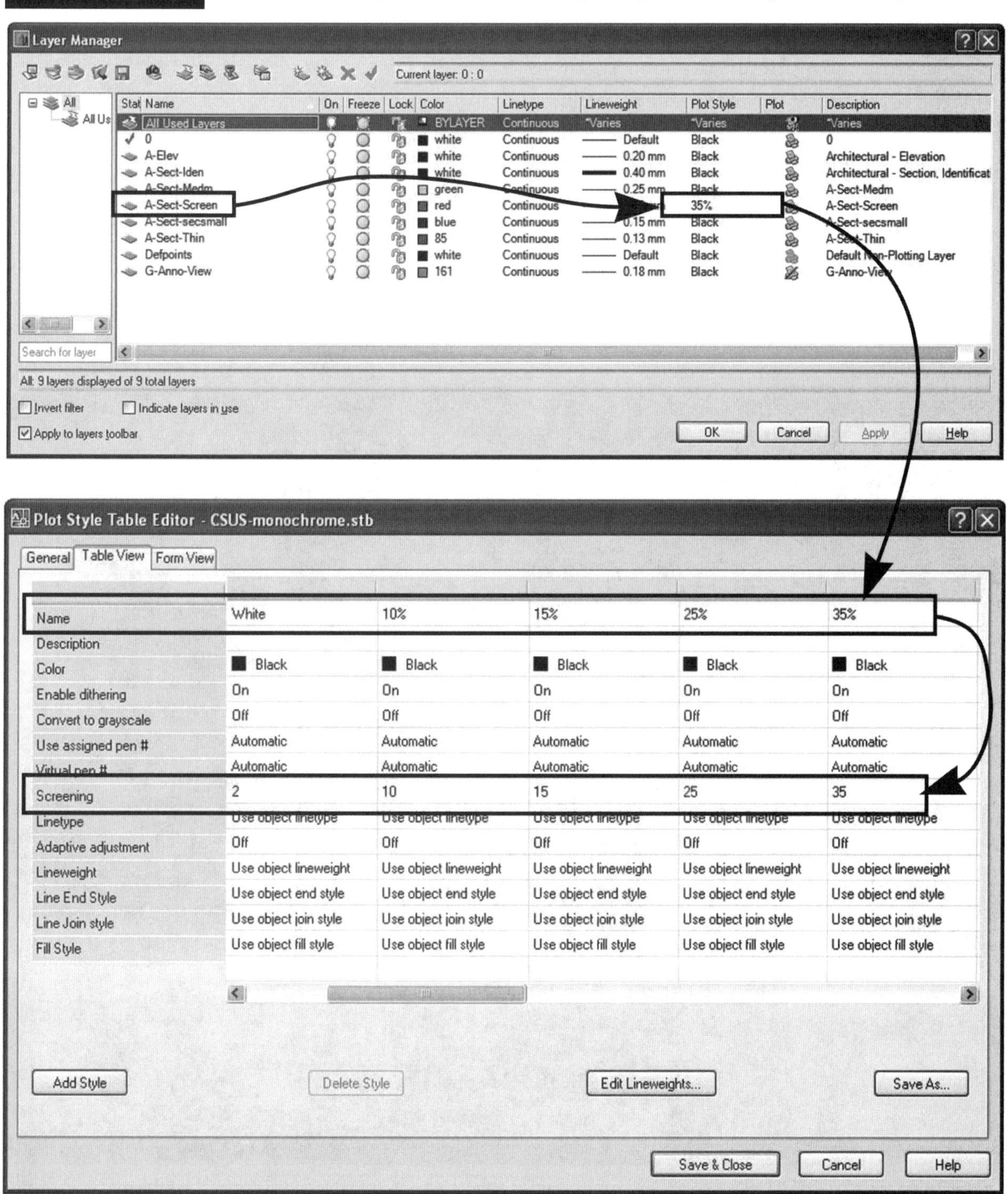

Figure 20.18b

Screened drawings are best created by referencing (Xref) drawings into a new drawing. This allows you to change layer colors and plot styles without changing the original file. Name dependent drawing templates use name dependent plot style tables for plotting. Using this type of template, the screened effect is achieved by assigning specific screened plot styles to objects or layers.

Creating White Drawings

White drawings are reverse plots that have black backgrounds and white lines, patterns, and fills. Since most printers cannot actually print the color white, the technique actually uses a 1 percent screening of the color black (a very, very light gray) to imitate the color white. White drawings are great for emphasizing the spatial qualities of a drawing (Figure 20.19). The technique requires you to set your plot style screening to 1 percent as demonstrated in Figure 20.20.

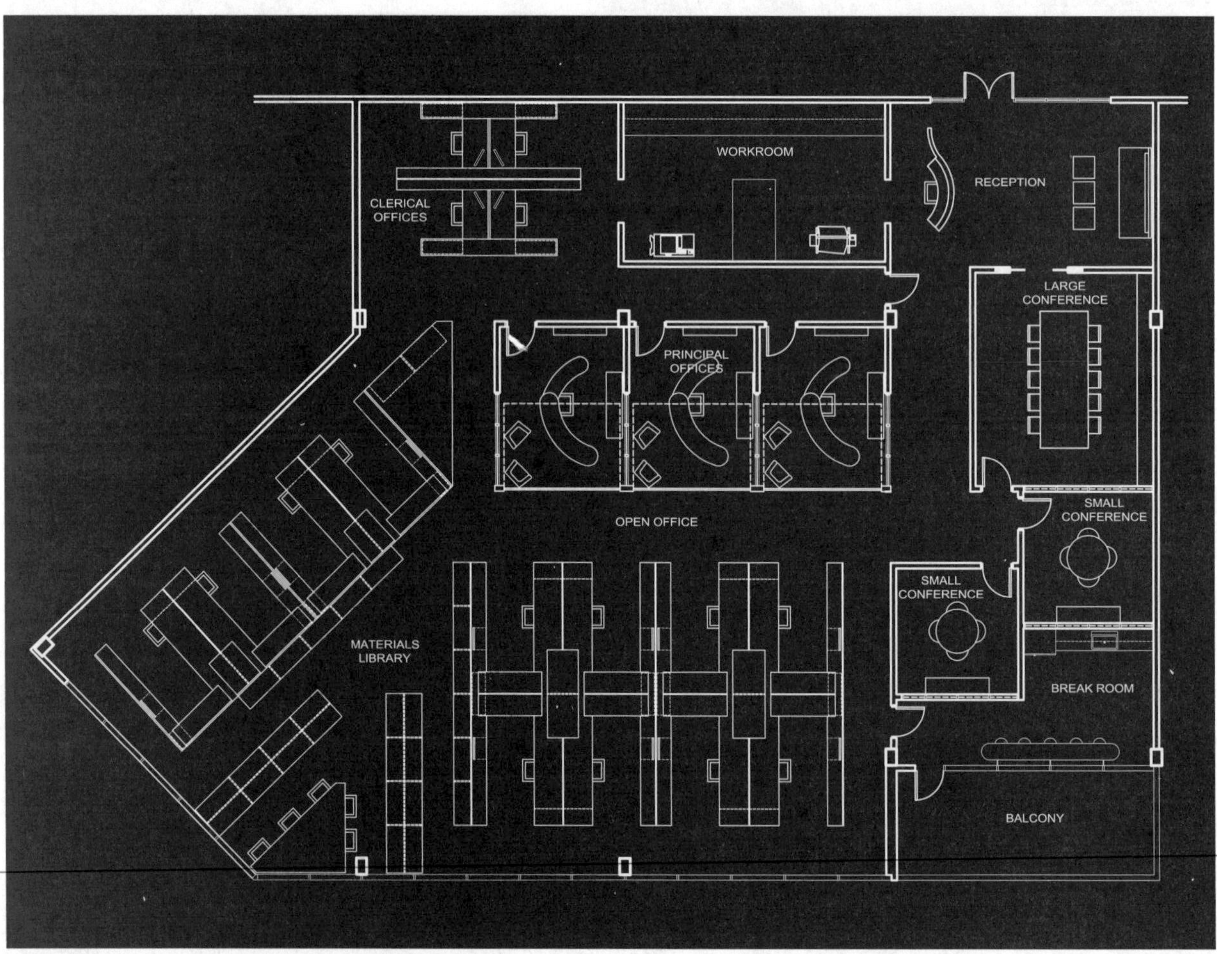

Figure 20.19 White drawings are great for emphasizing the spatial qualities of a drawing.
Student Project: Coursesy of Barbara Rhinehart.

Technique to Master **T20.20** Creating White Line Presentations

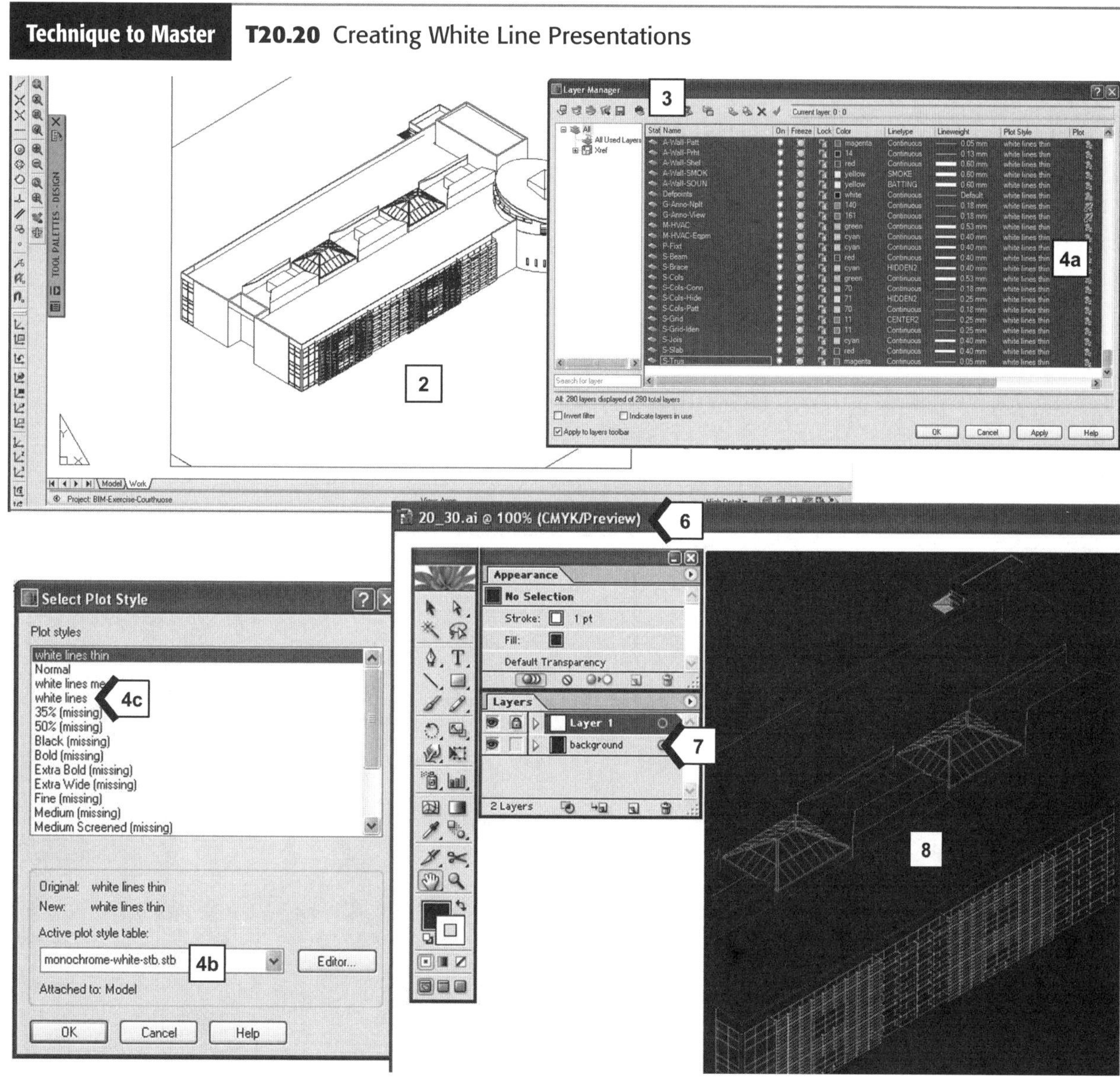

Figure 20.20 With this technique, you will create a white line drawing using plot style assignments. The plotted PDF file will then be opened in Illustrator so that the black background can be applied.

1	Create or open the drawing to be printed with white lines.	
2	Change to the desired view (plan, axonometric, perspective, and so on).	
3	Open the Layer Manager.	
4a, 4b, 4c	[Layer Manager dialogue box]	Select all layers and change plot style property to one of the plot styles in the Monochrome White-stb Plot Style Table. This is a custom plot style table that can be retrieved from the CD-ROM.
5	[Plot dialogue box]	Plot the drawing to a PDF file format. Make sure the Monochrome White-stb Plot Style Table is assigned. Refer to Chapter 1 to review plotting procedures. Notice that when plot previews, the drawing will not display. This is because all lines would print white on a white background.
6	Open the plotted PDF file in Adobe Illustrator.	
7	[Adobe Illustrator]	Create a new layer and move it below the existing line drawing layer.
8	[Adobe Illustrator]	With the new layer current, create a black filled rectangle surrounding the drawing.
9	[Adobe Illustrator]	Print/Plot drawing.

Mimicking Brownline and Blueline

The diazo, bluelines, and brownlines processes used in the past to reproduce drawings in design and construction practice is another graphic technique that has become popular in presentations (Figures 20.21). This technique requires utilizing AutoCAD's true color palette. Figures 20.22 and 20.23 demonstrate the technique within the 2-D and 3-D environments.

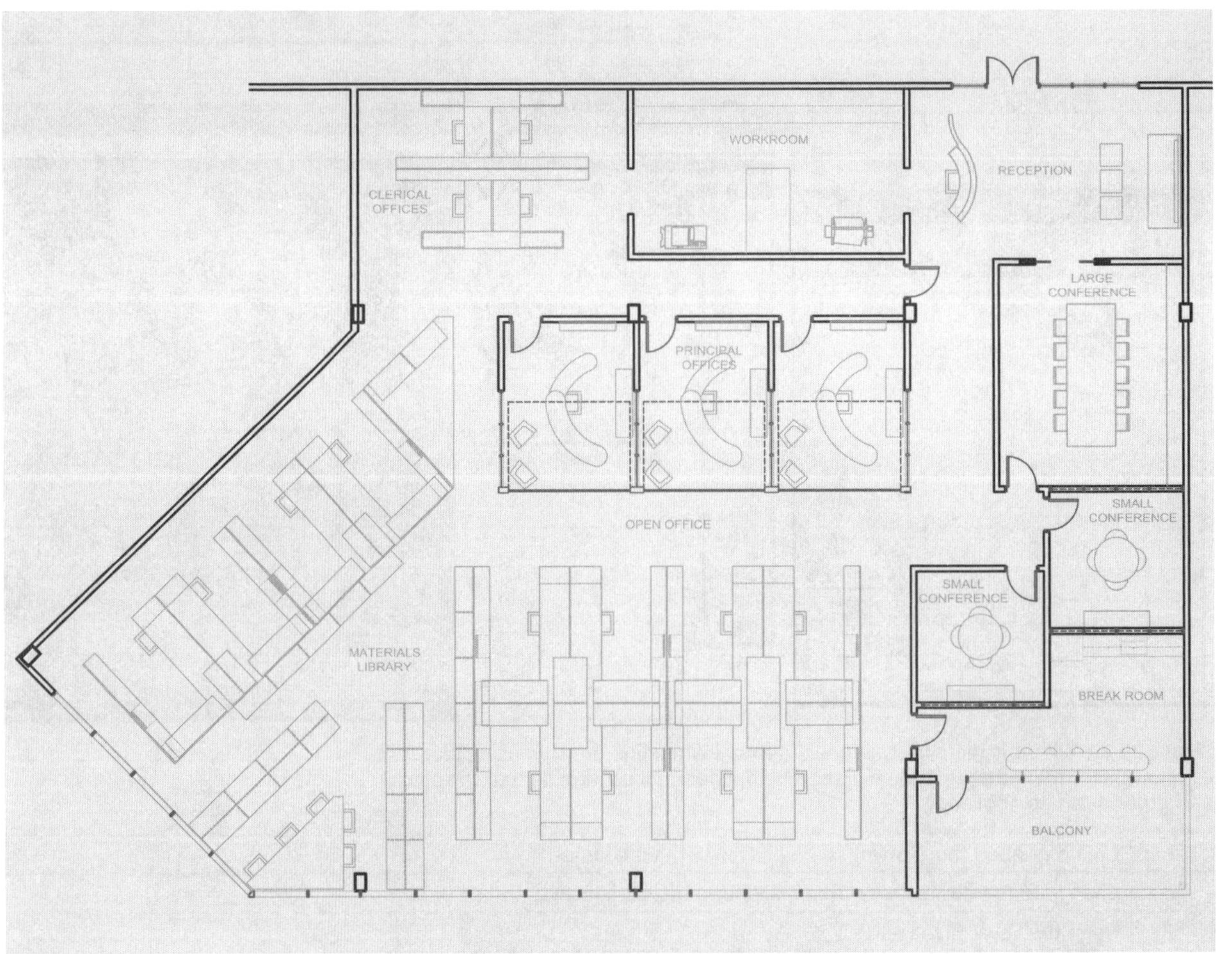

Figure 20.21 Brownline and blueline prints look like this. (See the CD-ROM for this image in color.)

Technique to Master

T20.22 Reproducing the Brownline and Blueline Look with 2-D AutoCAD Drawings

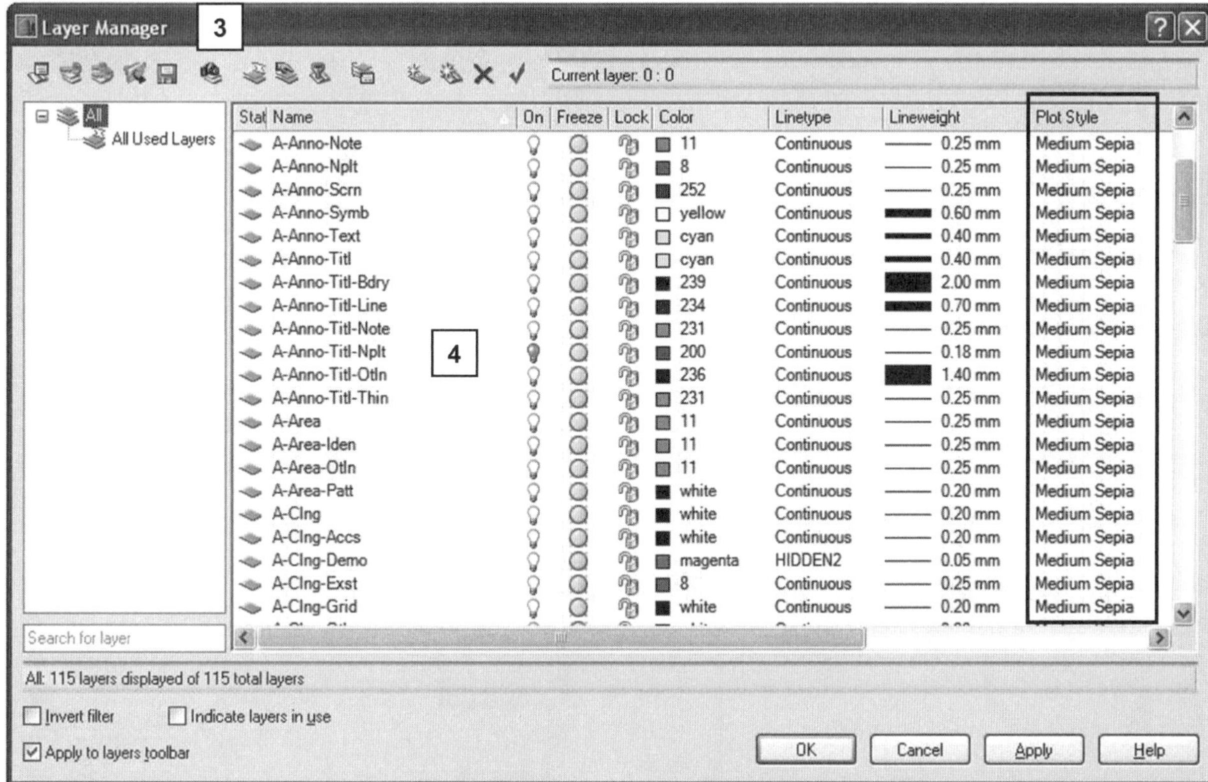

Figure 20.22 With this technique you will create the brownline and blueline look using plot style assignments. The sepia toned drawing and bluelined toned drawing plot style tables are available on the CD-ROM to complete this technique. The associated color dependent plot style converts all colors to a single toned brownline.

1	Create a new plot sheet drawing. Refer to Technique T07.34.	
2	Xref drawings into plot sheet. Refer to Technique T07.09.	
3	If using a named plot style dependent drawing, open the Layer Manager. (Color plot style dependent drawings can skip to Step 5.)	
4	[Layer Manager dialogue box]	Select all layers and change plot style property to one of the plot styles in the sepia toned or blueline toned plot style table. This is a custom plot style table that can be retrieved from the CD-ROM.
5	Print/Plot composition using the appropriate plot style table.	

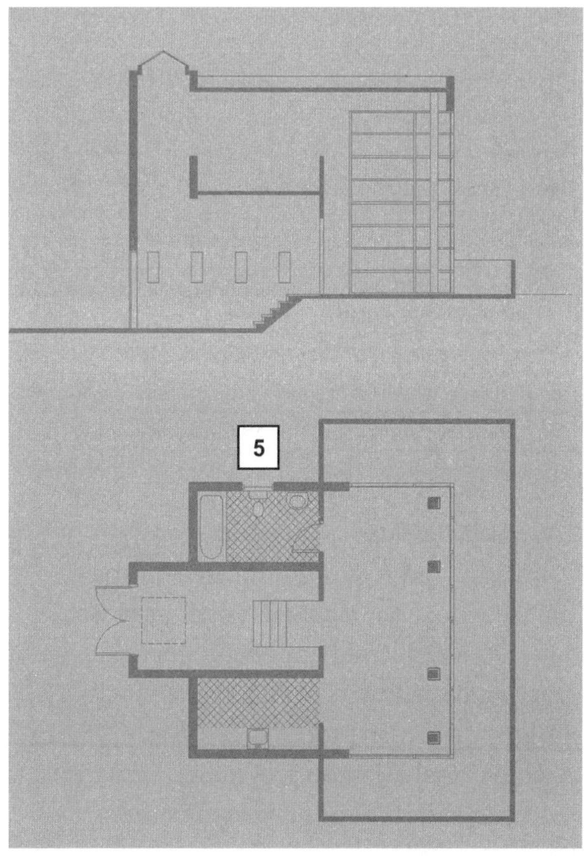

Technique to Master **T20.23** Reproducing the Brownline and Blueline Look with ADT Plan, Isometric, and Perspective Views

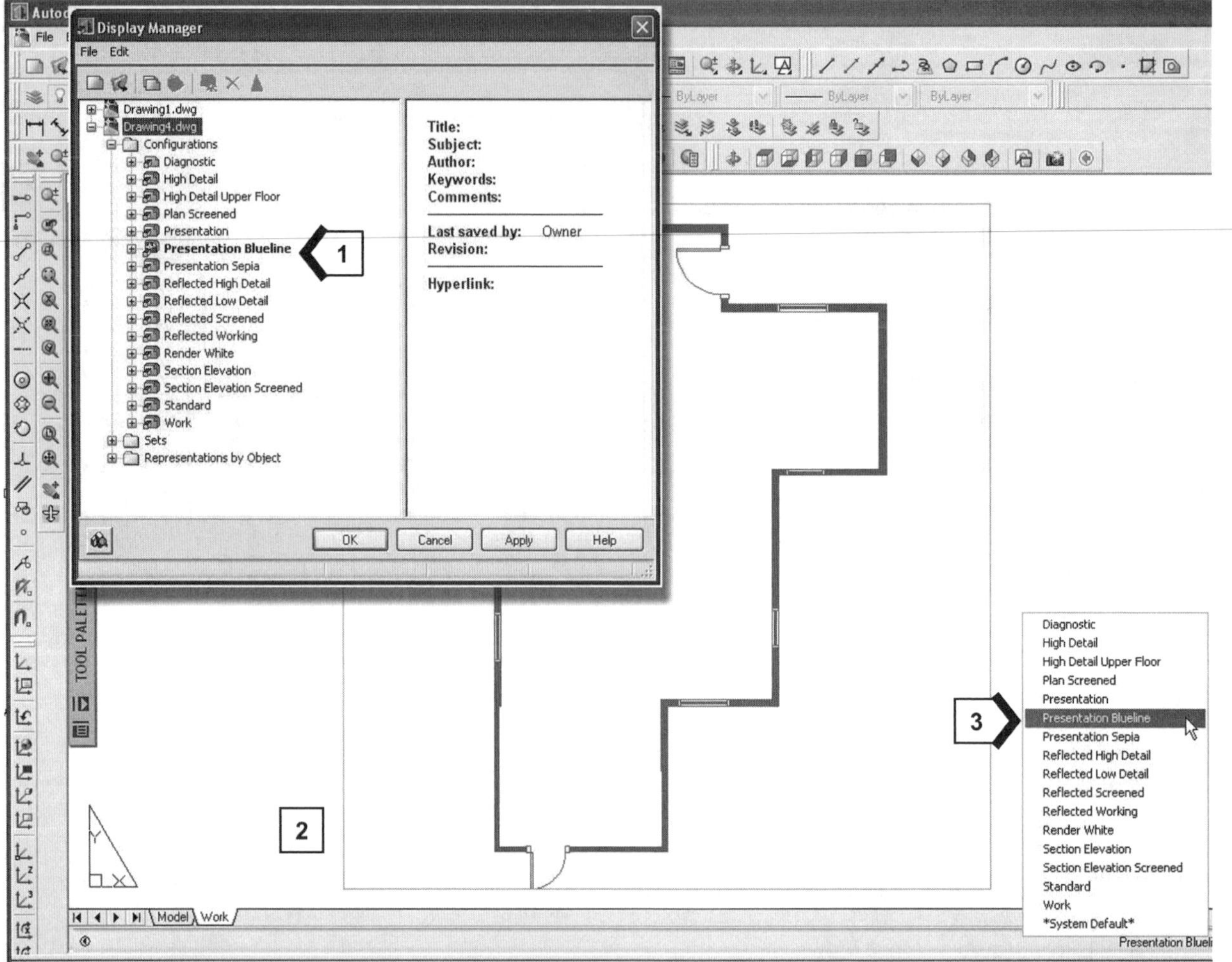

Figure 20.23 With this technique you will create the brownline and blueline look using the Display System. The Presentation Sepia and Presentation Blueline Display Configurations are available on the CD-ROM to complete this technique.

1	Open each Construct and View drawing. Import Display Configuration Presentation Sepia or Presentation Blueline.
2	Create a new plot sheet drawing and place View drawings.
3	Change Viewport Display Configuration to appropriate brownline and blueline look.
4	Print/Plot composition using the appropriate plot style table.

The Sketched Look

AutoCAD and ADT are criticized for the finished look that is characteristic of most computer-generated drawings. Since sketched graphics have always been associated with designs that are in process, both AutoCAD and Architectural Desktop provide a command to soften drawings by approximating the stroke technique and look of a freehand sketch.

AutoCAD's Visual Styles

AutoCAD uses Visual Styles—a new feature in AutoCAD 2007—to control how objects are displayed within a viewport. A visual style has several settings that manage the shading and edge display of 2-D and 3-D geometry. Default visual styles include 2D Wireframe, 3D Wireframe, 3D Hidden, Realistic, and Conceptual. To create new visual styles, use the Visual Style Manager.

Visual Styles can also be used to create a sketched look for 2-D and 3-D geometry as shown in Figure 20.24.

Architectural Desktop's Napkin Sketch

The Napkin Sketch command generates random jagged and/or wavy line segments that replace the original tight graphic treatment. However, to achieve this sketched look, each object is replaced with several wavy objects. As a result, complex drawings that are converted can result in significant file size increases.

There are three freehand styles to choose from—tight line, loose line, and messy line. The tight line style produces the most accurate trace of the original object or drawing. It gives the appearance of a refined freehand illustration (Figure 20.25). The loose and messy line styles produce a more relaxed portrayal of the original drawing owing to the number of trace iterations.

Technique to Master **T20.24** Creating the Sketched Look with Visual Styles

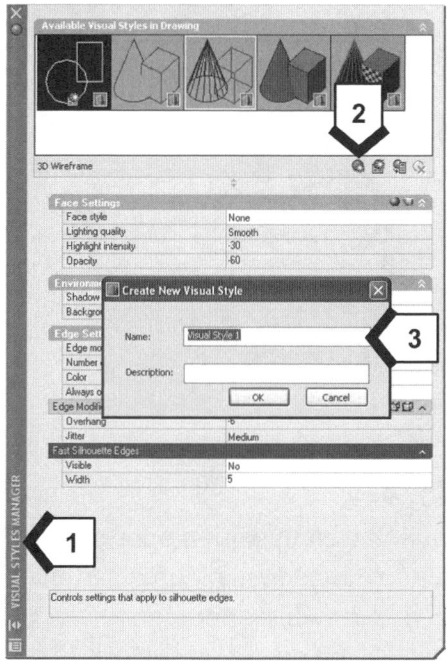

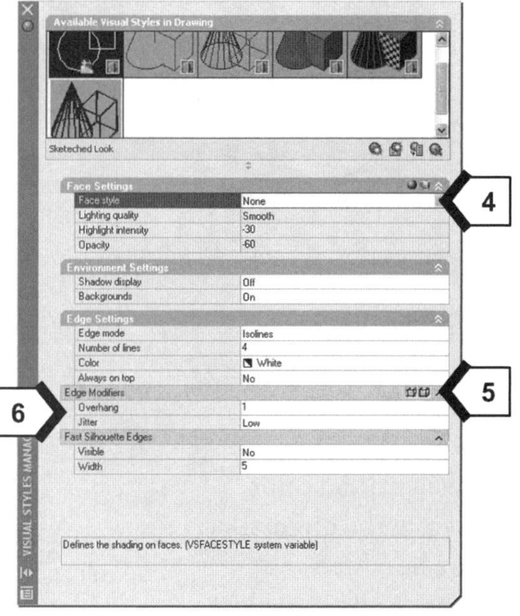

Figure 20.24

1	[View menu]	Open Visual Styles Manager.
2	[Visual Styles Manager palette]	Create new Visual Style by left-clicking Create New Visual Style button.
3	[Create New Visual Style dialogue box]	Name the Visual Style.
4	[Visual Styles Manager palette]	Change Face style to None.
5	[Visual Styles Manager palette]	Toggle Overhanging edges button ON. Toggle Jitter edges button ON.
6	[Visual Styles Manager palette]	Adjust Overhang and Jitter settings as desired.

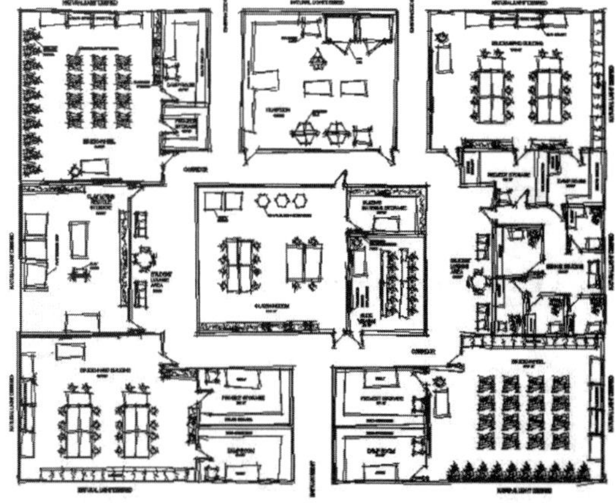

Resulting sketched plan

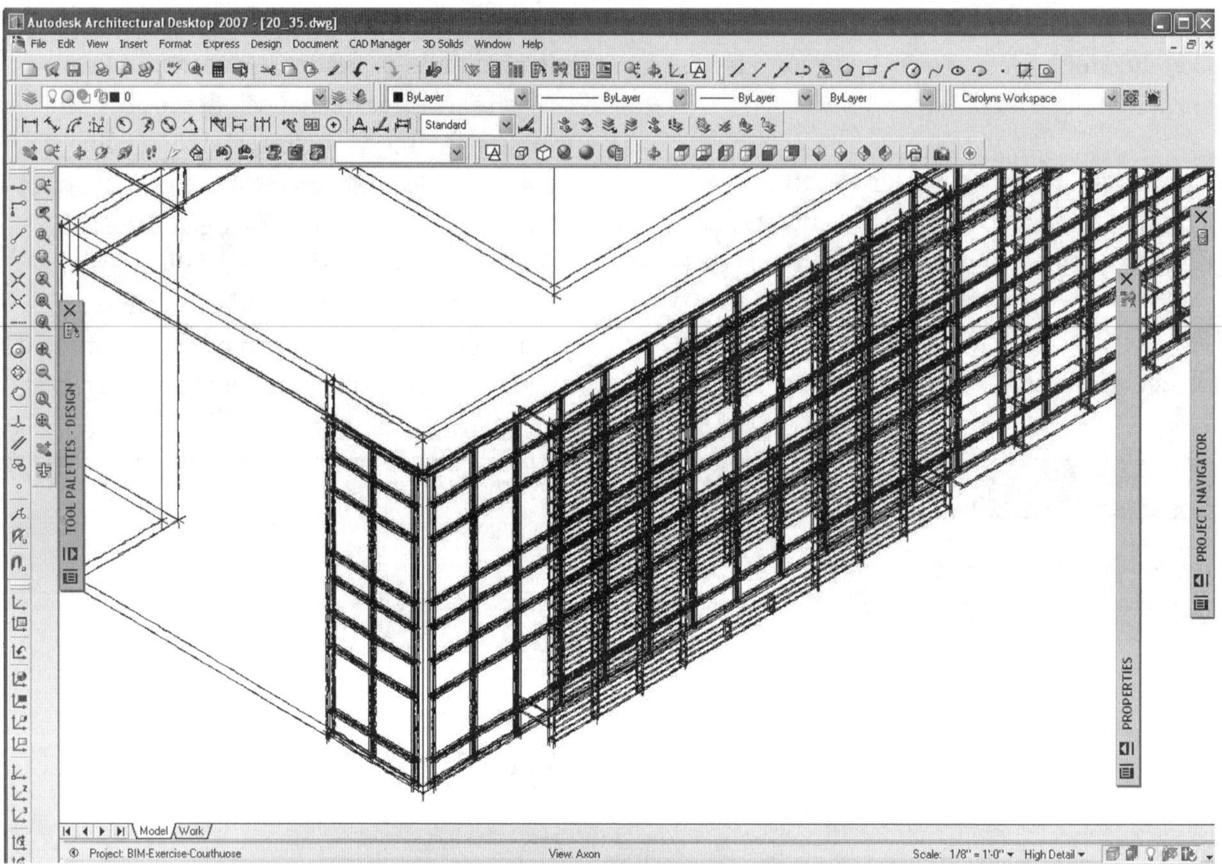

Figure 20.25 The tight line style gives the appearance of a refined freehand illustration.

The end result of this command is an AutoCAD block that overlays the original drawing. All layer, lineweight, and color information is retained from the original. Napkin sketch blocks can be edited and manipulated like any other AutoCAD block.

Using the Napkin Sketch on Objects

All AutoCAD and ADT objects, including objects linked through the Xref Manager, can be used in the napkin sketch selection set. Autodesk, however, first recommends converting all three-dimensional drawings to two-dimensional projections before invoking the command. Figures 20.26 and 20.27 demonstrate the workflow process.

Advanced Techniques in Board Presentations

Presentation Board composition refers to the organizing and arrangement of informational elements such as drawings, photographs, text, renderings, and so on onto large format presentations for display. Presentation Board compositions can be manually pasted onto boards or laid out digitally as an integrated whole with various software programs. Here we review some basic compositional concepts surrounding board composition. We also illustrate some of the current composite board presentation techniques used in graphic presentations.

Technique to Master **T20.26** Using the Sketched Look on Plans, Elevations, and Sections in ADT

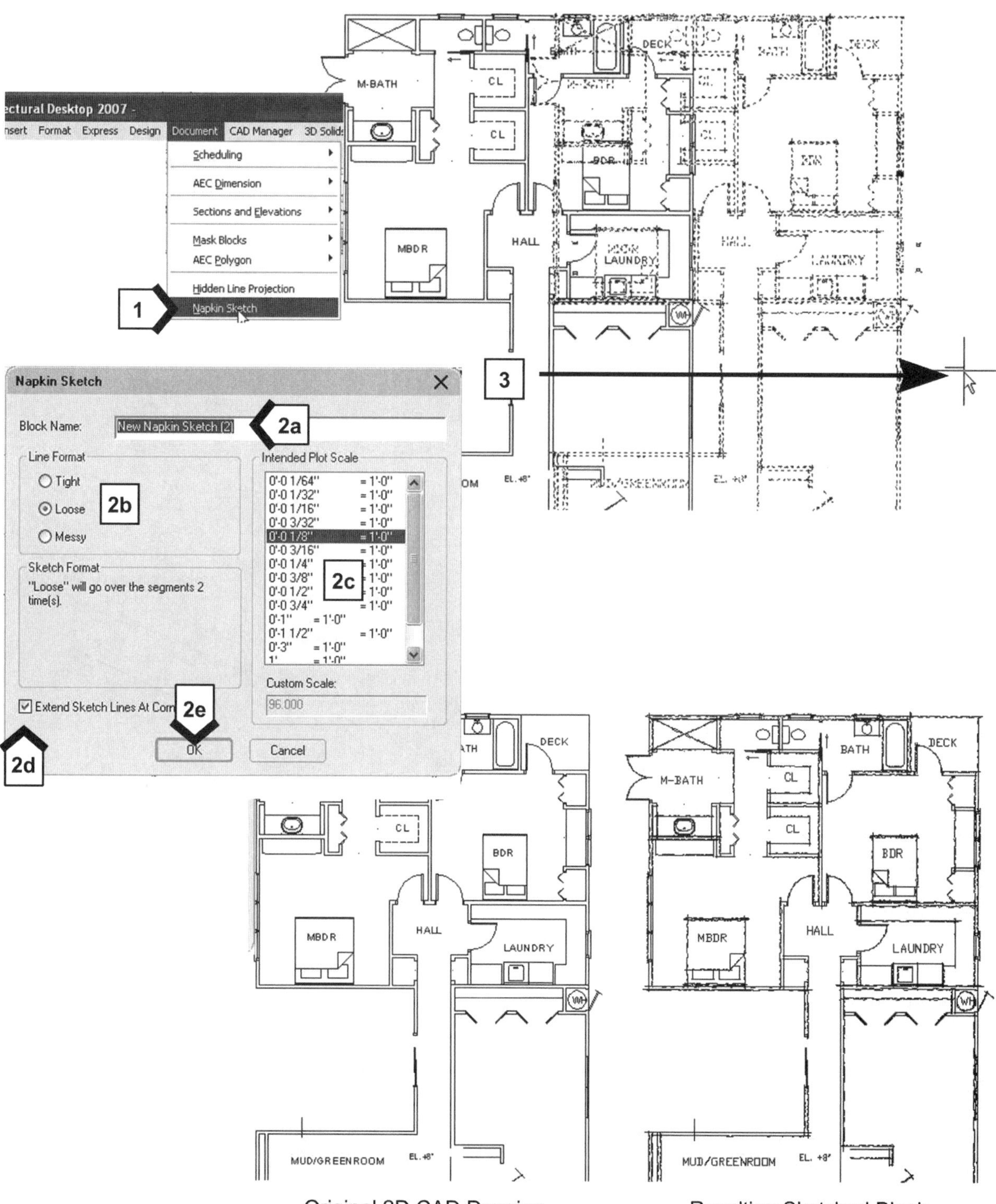

Figure 20.26

1	[Document Menu]	Invoke Napkin Sketch command.
2a–2e	[Napkin Sketch dialogue box]	Name the sketch block. Specify line format and intended plot scale for the sketch drawing. Check the box to Extend Sketch Lines At Corners. Left-click OK to complete the command.
3	[Drawing Screen]	Move the sketch block. To export the sketch to its own distinct drawing, use the Wblock command. Refer to Technique T04.11.

Technique to Master **T20.27** Using the Sketched Look on ADT Generated Drawings

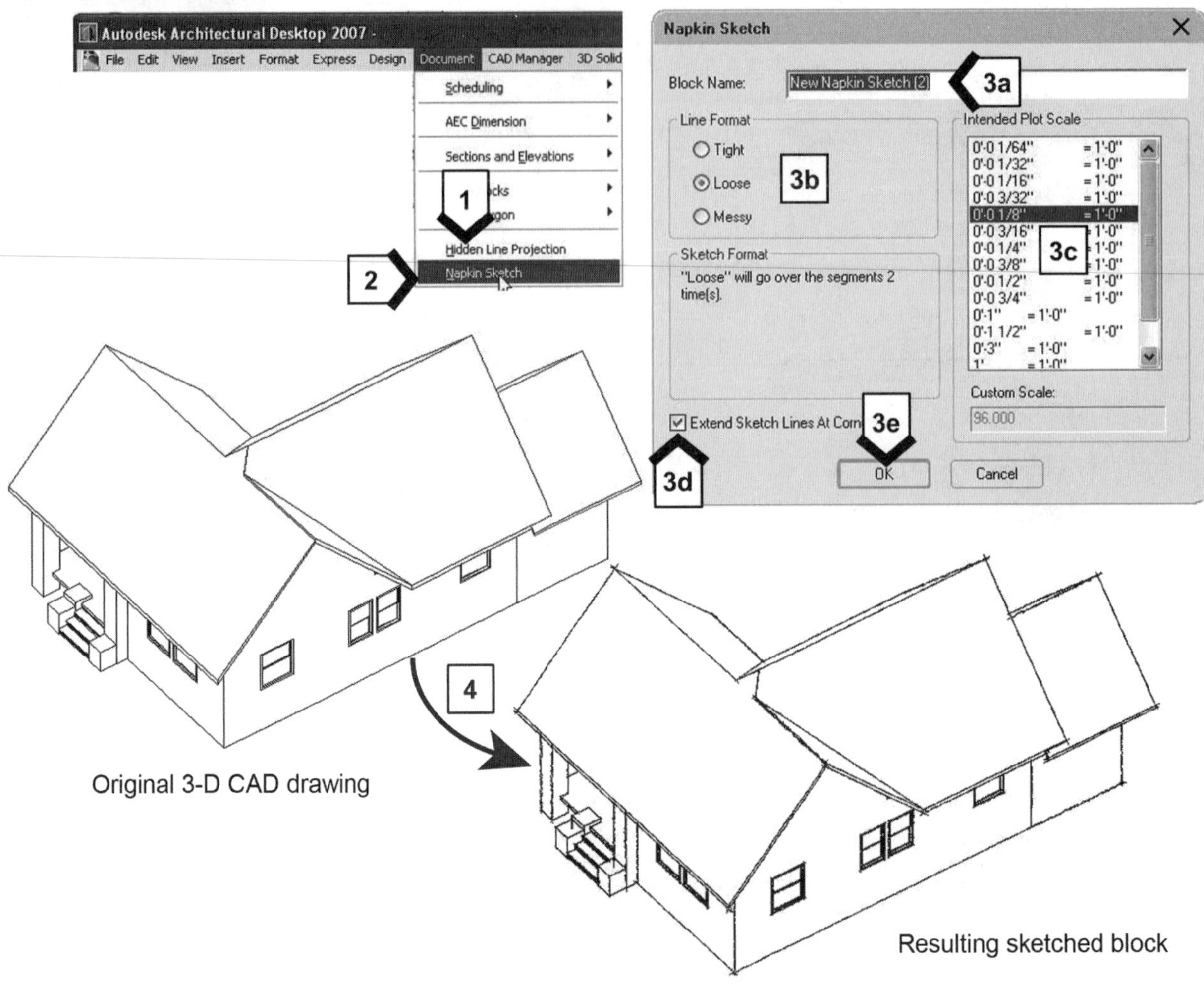

Figure 20.27 Three-dimensional drawings created with ADT first need to be converted to two-dimensional projections before invoking the Napkin Sketch command.

1	Convert isometric or perspective drawing to 2-D. Refer to Technique T19.35	
2	[Document Menu]	Invoke Napkin Sketch command.
3a–3e	[Napkin Sketch dialogue box]	Name the sketch block. Specify line format and intended plot scale for the sketch drawing. Check the box to Extend Sketch Lines At Corners. Left-click OK to complete the command.
4	[Drawing Screen]	Move the sketch block. To export sketch to its own distinct drawing, use the Wblock command. Refer to Technique T04.11.

The Elements of Board Layouts

The design and arrangement of digital boards involves the same compositional techniques that manual boards use. Moreover, while there are no specific right answers when it comes to creating good compositions, all presentations take board content, size, and orientation into consideration when structuring the layout of information.

Board Shape, Size, and Orientation

Board content refers to the drawings, photos, text, and other graphic items that will be included on the board (Figure 20.28). The decisions on the presentation board's shape and orientation will be determined by the amount and size of the graphic content that will be placed on the board as well as the maximum paper size of your plotting device.

The Board's Structure or Composition

Layout grids provide guides for how all content is placed and organized. This underlying structure should attempt to support each of the graphics that are used. Good layout grids will help you organize all of the content on the board into a coherent and legible composition. Good layout grids have established areas for graphic image emphasis (Figure 20.29). With multiple-board compositions, grids should allow for a great deal of flexibility to add variety to image and text placement while still maintaining a consistency between multiple boards.

Digital board layouts have the advantage since many layout ideas can be tested before committing. A good approach is to adopt the storyboarding method that is used in the graphics and film disciplines (Figure 20.30).

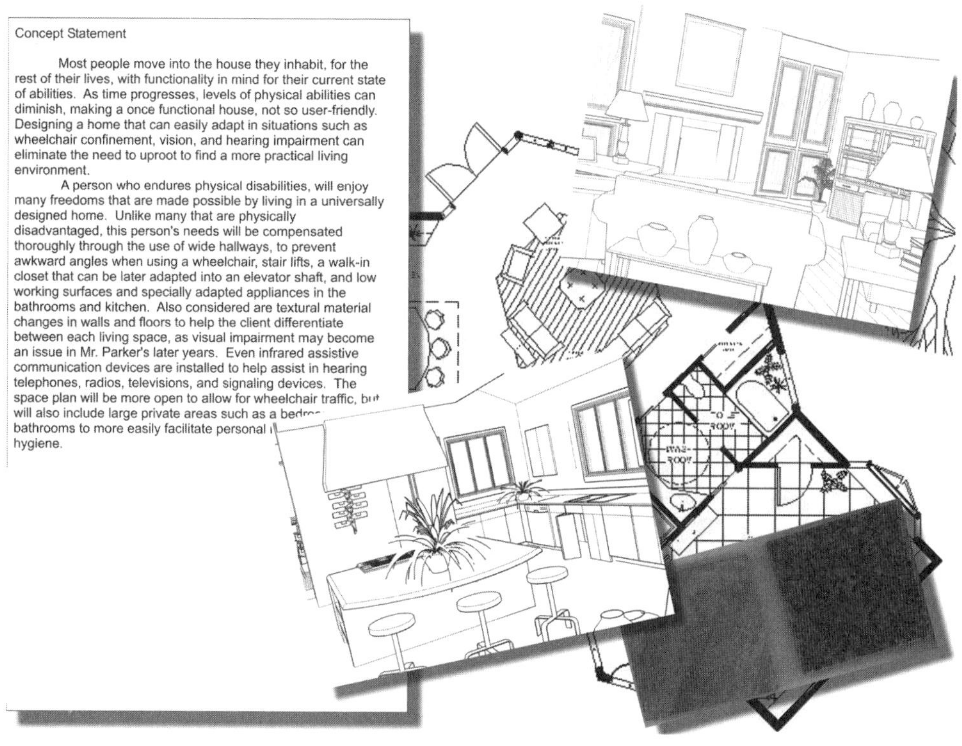

Figure 20.28 Drawings, photos, text, and other graphic items are included in this board.

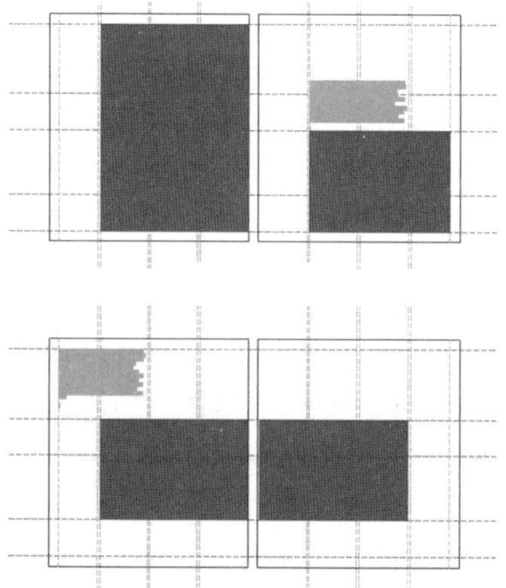

Figure 20.29 Layout grids

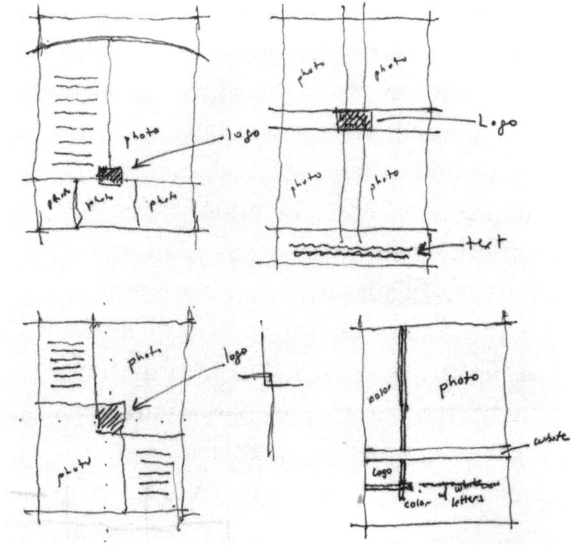

Figure 20.30 Storyboard

A Few Compositional Ideas

1. Text: Use font size, style, letter spacing, word spacing, and line spacing as graphic devices to add visual interest to the layout.
2. Borders and frames: Use line thickness, line color, and frame color to group content, emphasize content, and/or direct movement within the layout.
3. Empty areas of the layout (called white space) can be an effective compositional element. Don't feel the need to fill up every blank area.

A Few Do's and Don'ts to Remember

1. Remember, the drawings and renderings are generally the most important part of the presentation. Keep all other graphic and text content subordinate.
2. Try to establish focal points or areas of visual emphasis in layouts that have a lot of content.
3. With multiple-board compositions, keep orientation of the boards, borders, and text labeling consistent.
4. Although a board may have different types of text (titles, body text, notes, and so forth), all text of the same type should remain consistent in design, size, and placement.
5. All subordinate content—text, rules, borders, and frames—should harmonize with the main images and not distract the viewer.

Composite Board Presentation Techniques

Composite drawings use an approach that brings together several drawings into one board presentation. Usually drawings are created and presented as independent from one another using only symbol callouts to create their relationships. Similar to print media in graphic design, composite drawings treat the board layout and its informational elements (text, drawings, photographs) as one integrated graphic. Using this process, advance thought must be given to the relationship and hierarchy of the informational elements as well as the graphic techniques used to present them.

Approaches in Composite Drawing

The examples below represent just a few approaches for composite drawing techniques. While not the most appropriate software tools for accomplishing the examples below, an improvised version of each can be undertaken in AutoCAD and ADT.

Traditional Collage

This composite drawing technique composes several drawings into one composition (Figure 20.31). Drawings maybe overlapped, combined, or cropped to produce the collage effect. Collages tend to be difficult to compose because of the complexity of all the images colliding together. Therefore, a simple background color or graphic is used to create the unifying element for the entire composition.

Traditional collage techniques are best designed in a page layout program like Adobe InDesign or QuarkXPress. Simplified collage techniques, however, can be accomplished in AutoCAD or ADT using layouts and viewports. Figure 20.32 illustrates an example.

Photomontage

Photomontage utilizes several photographic images (or renderings) to create the collage effect (Figure 20.33). This is best carried out in a photo-editing program like Photoshop or a combination of AutoCAD and the image-editing program.

Composite Montage

The composite montage technique combines photographic images with drawings and other types of graphics. Often these types of drawings are used to superimpose existing conditions with new design proposals. Figure 20.34 illustrates an example.

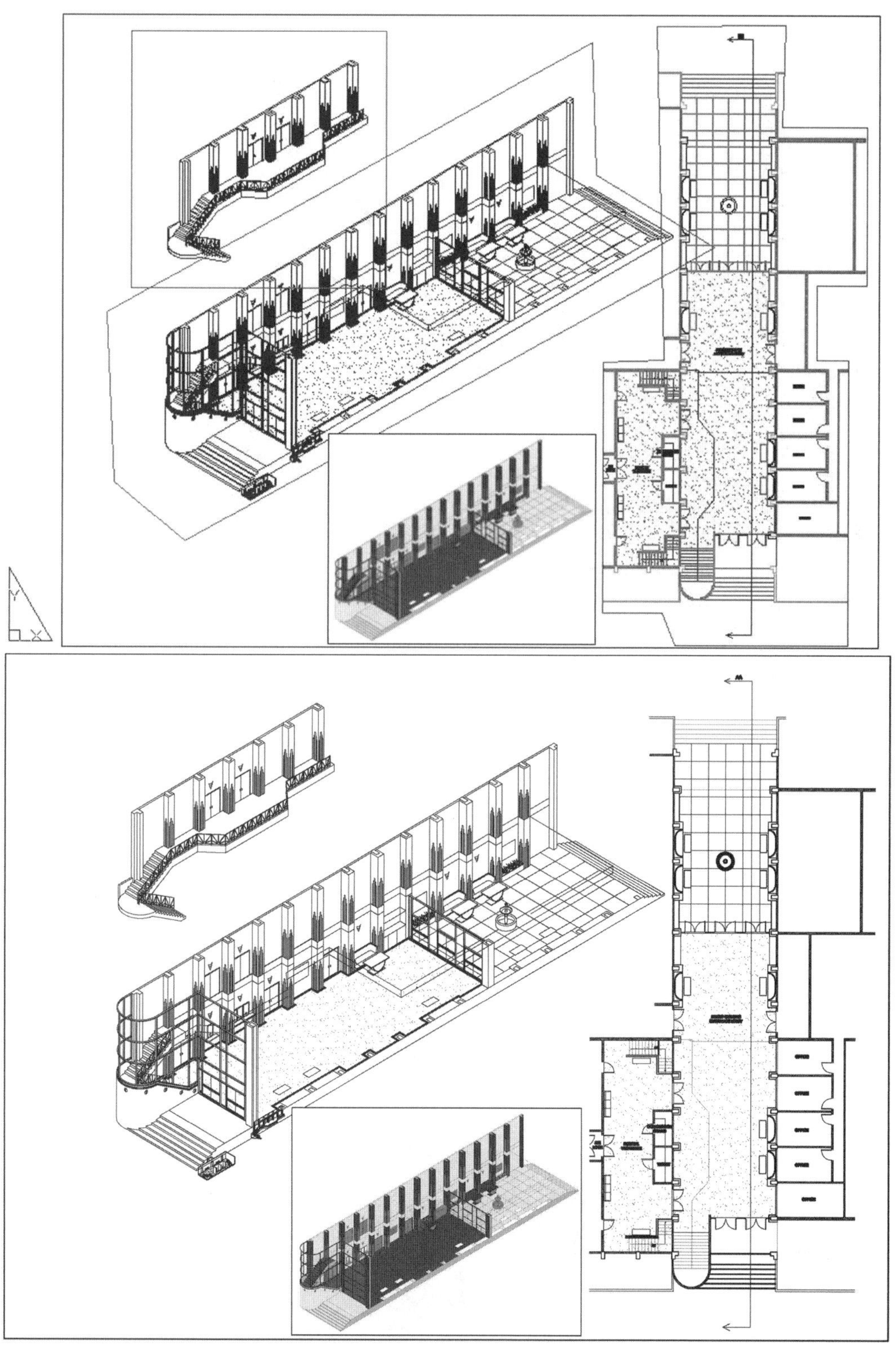

Figure 20.31 A composite drawing

Student Project: Courtesy of Darci Drawbert.

Technique to Master **T20.32** Using Layouts and Viewports to Create Traditional Collage Compositions

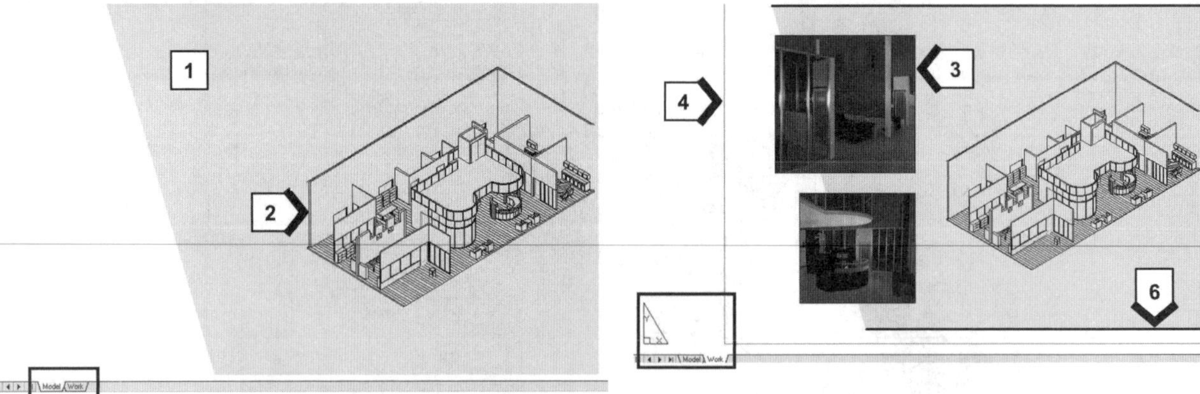

Figure 20.32

1	[Model Space Drawing Screen]	Create a background for images using a solid hatch.
2	[Model Space Drawing Screen]	Xref drawings to be used in collage composition. Refer to Technique T07.09.
3	[Paper Space Drawing Screen]	Xref images into AutoCAD. Refer to Technique T20.37.
4	[Paper Space Drawing Screen]	Create viewport for Xrefed drawings. Refer to Techniques T07.23 and T07.24.
5	[Paper Space Drawing Screen]	Compose collage by moving photos and viewports to desired composition.
6	[Paper Space Drawing Screen]	Add text and other graphic devices.

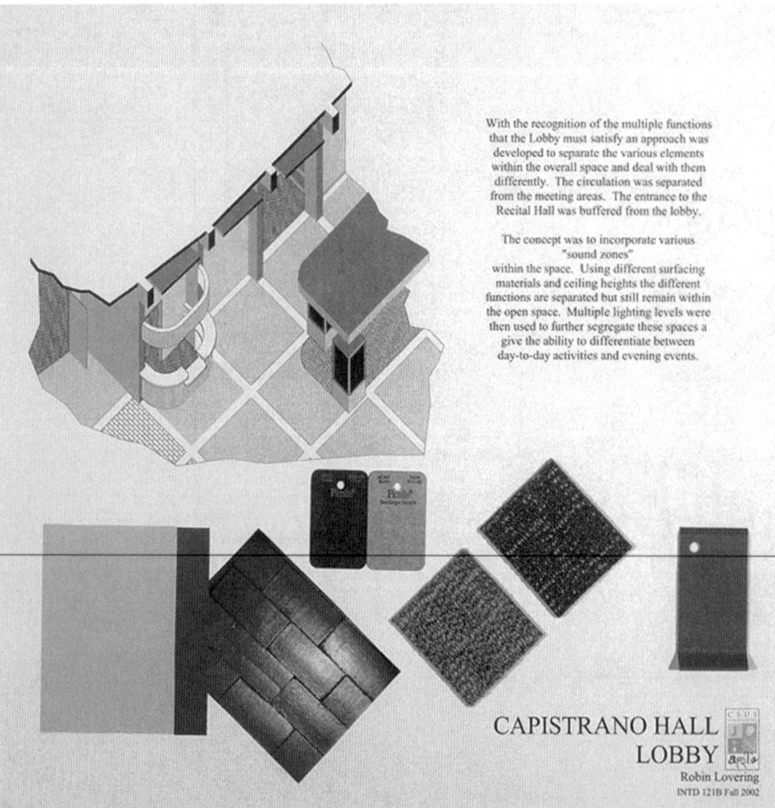

Figure 20.33 Photomontage utilizes several photographic images (or renderings) to create the collage effect.

Student project: Capistrano Hall Lobby Renovation, courtesy of Robin Lovering.

Technique to Master **T20.34** Using Layouts and Viewports to Create Montage Compositions

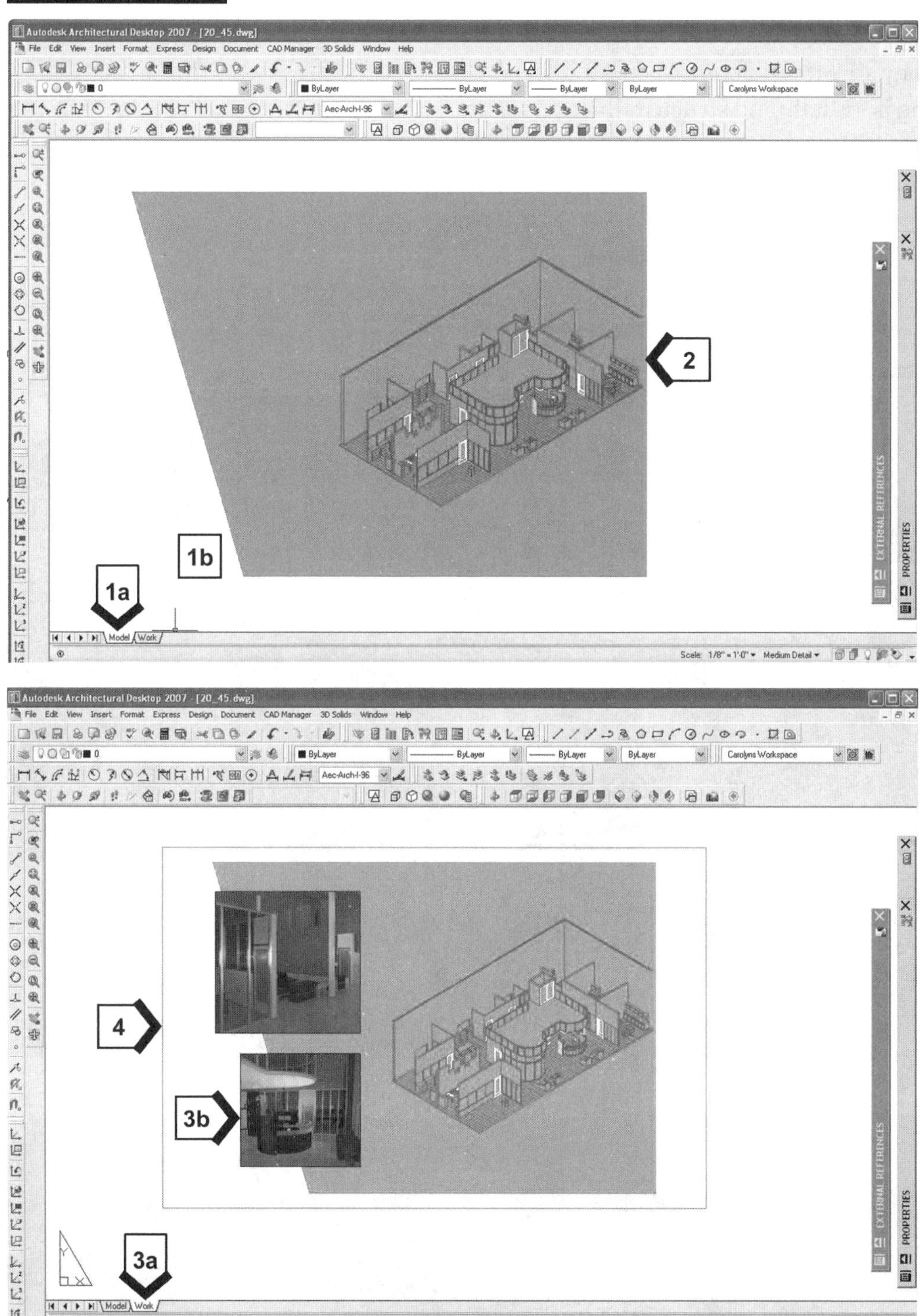

Figure 20.34

1a, 1b	[Model Space Drawing Screen]	Create background for images using a solid hatch.
2	[Model Space Drawing Screen]	Xref drawings to be used in collage composition. Refer to Technique T07.09.
3a, 3b	[Paper Space Drawing Screen]	Xref images into AutoCAD. Refer to Technique T20.37.
4	[Paper Space Drawing Screen]	Create viewport for Xrefed drawings. Refer to Techniques T07.23 and T07.24.
5	[Paper Space Drawing Screen]	Compose collage by moving photos and viewports to desired composition.
6	[Paper Space Drawing Screen]	Add text and other graphic devices.

Figure/Ground Composites

Figure/ground composites use contrasting line and color as their main graphic device (Figure 20.35). They are often referential—where one drawing is visually and structurally related to its adjacent drawings. Figure 20.36 illustrates an example.

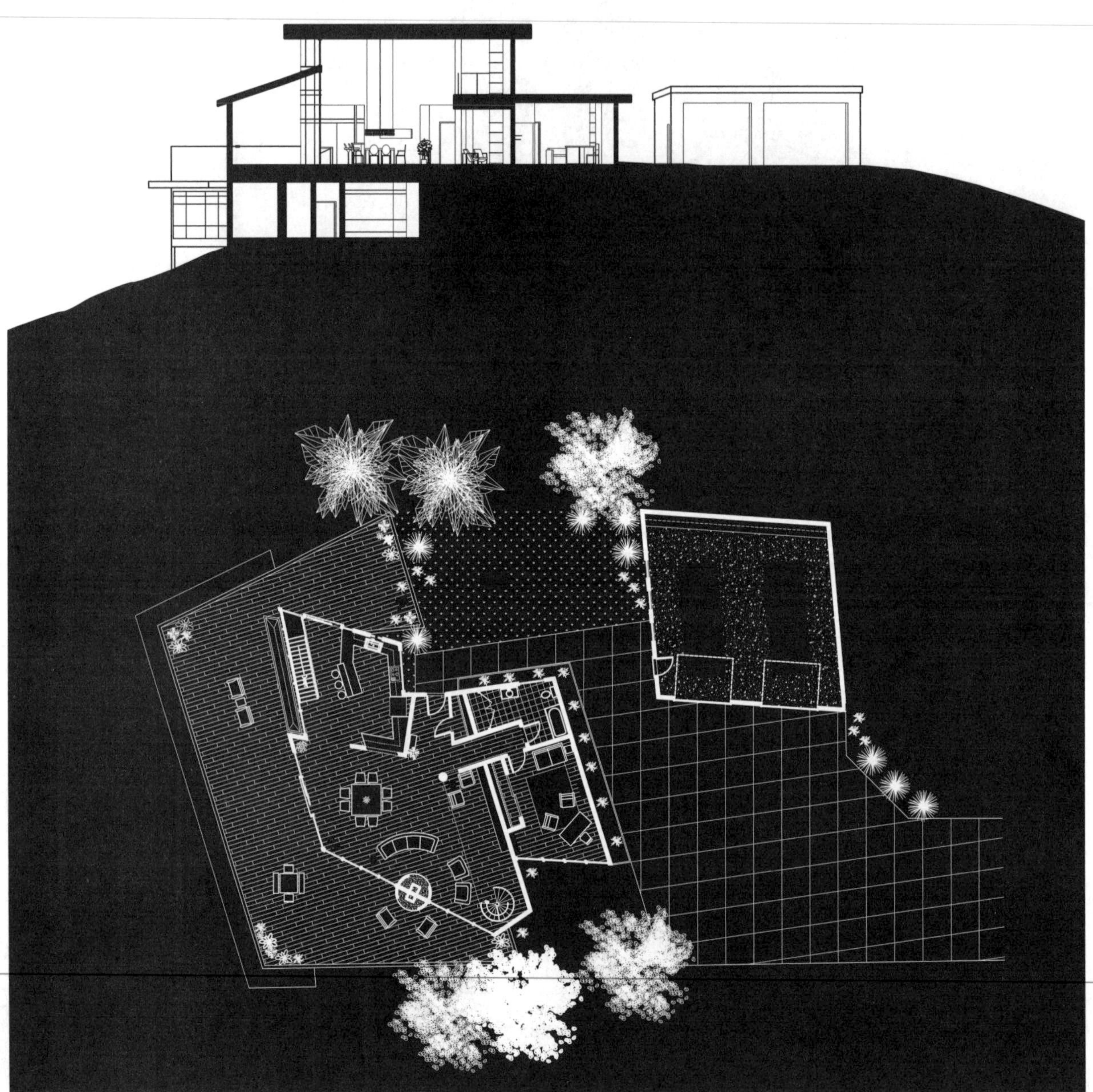

Figure 20.35 Figure/ground composites use contrasting line and color as their main graphic device.

Drawings courtesy of Elizabeth Butler.

Technique to Master T20.36 Using Xrefs to Create Figure/Ground Compositions

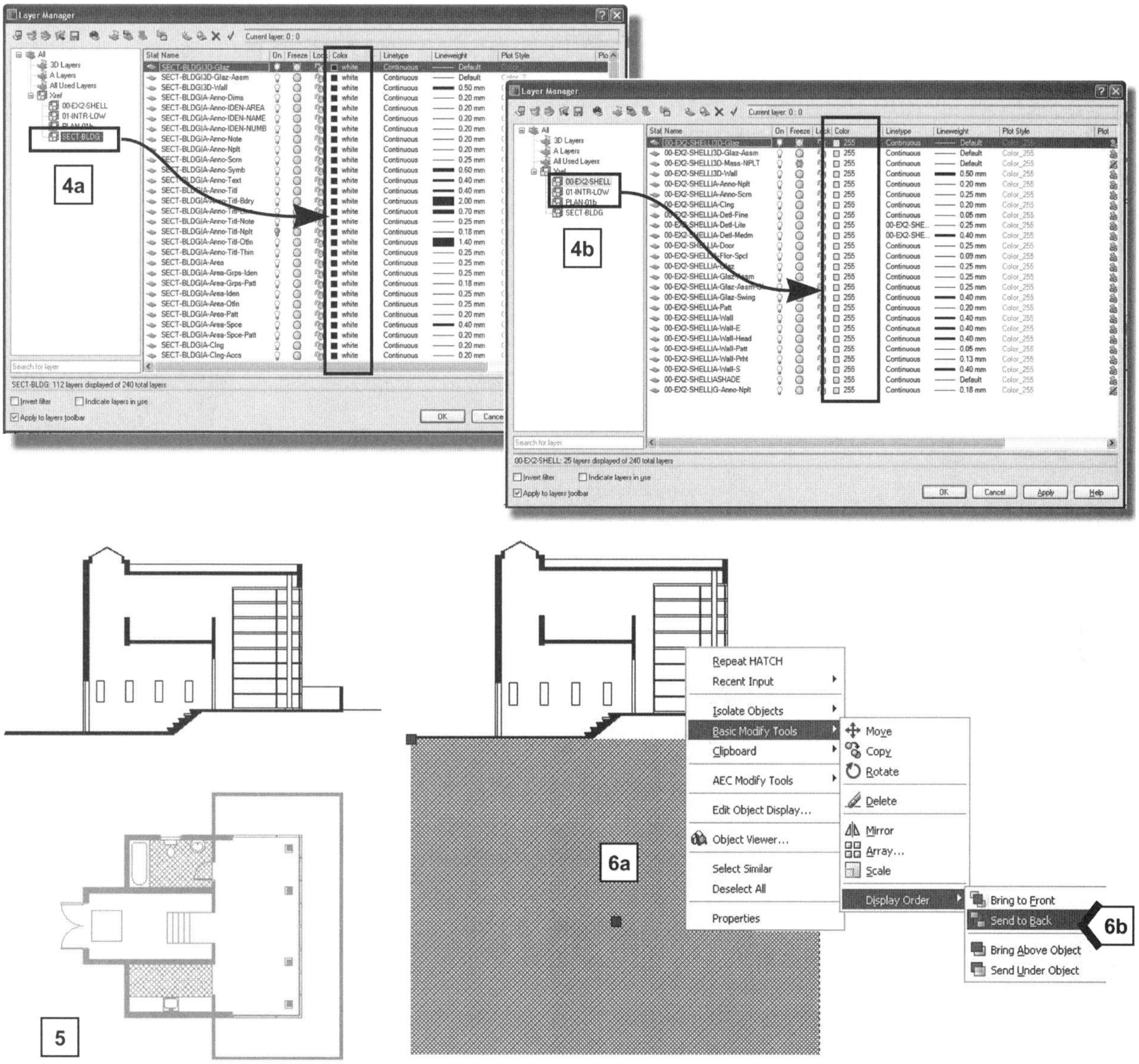

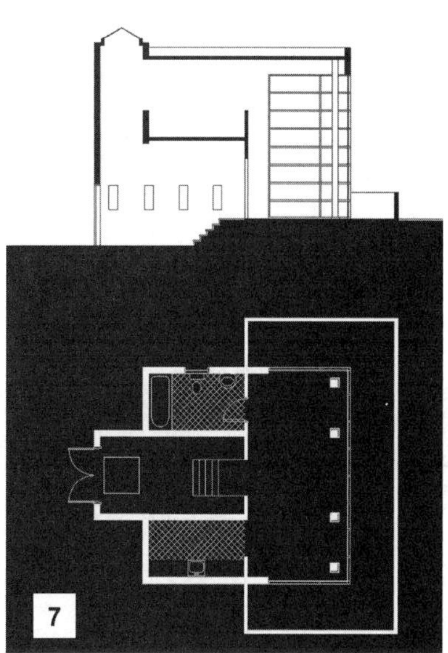

Figure 20.36

1	Create a new plot sheet drawing.	
2	Xref drawings into plot sheet.	
3	Open the Layer Manager.	
4a 4b	[Layer Manager dialogue box]	Using the Xref Layer Filtering in the left pane, select all layers for the first reference, and change their color (for color dependent drawings) or plot style (for name-dependent drawings).
5	[Drawing Screen]	Drawings should appear as light gray and black.
6a 6b	[Drawing Screen]	Create a 2-D solid hatch beneath the white-lined drawing. Make sure the hatch's display order is below all objects.
7	Print/Plot composition using the Monochrome White Plot Style Table. This is a custom plot style table that can be retrieved from the CD-ROM.	

Importing Photographs and Other Artwork

Raster and vector artwork including .gif, .jpg, .png, .pict, .tiff, and .bmp can be imported into AutoCAD and ADT for a variety of uses. Logos are often imported for title-blocks and borders. Photos can become a part of the construction set showing existing conditions. The option to import these types of artwork allows AutoCAD and ADT to perform many of the tasks of page layout programs. Figure 20.37 demonstrates the import process.

Technique to Master **T20.37** Importing Photographs in AutoCAD and ADT

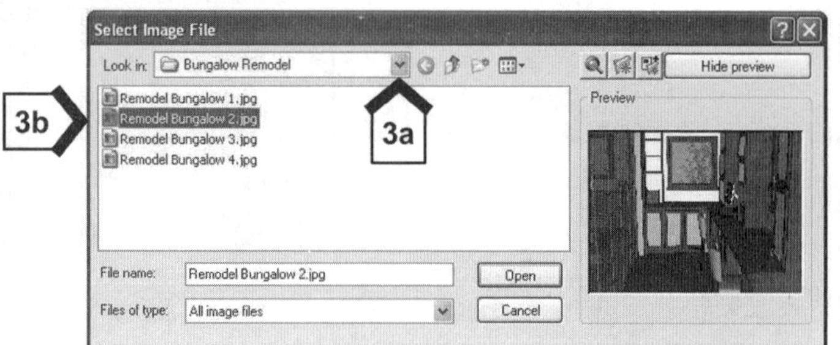

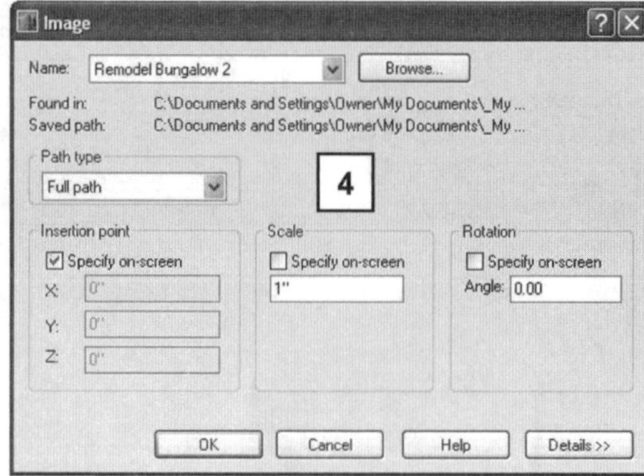

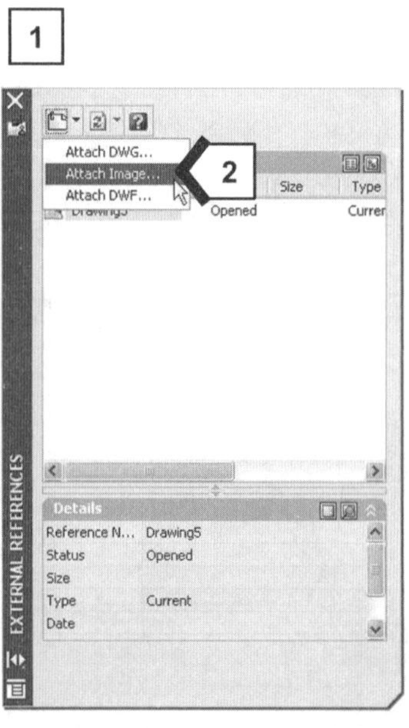

File References

Referen...	Status	Size	Type
20_54	Opened	216 KB	Currer
Remodel Bung...	Loaded	702 KB	JPG
Remodel Bung...	Loaded	606 KB	JPG
Remodel Bung...	Loaded	650 KB	JPG

Details
Reference N...
Status
Size
Type
Date
EXTERNAL REFERENCES

Figure 20.37

Student Project: Courtesy of Andrea Pabon.

1	Open External References palette.	
2	[External Reference palette]	Select Attach Image command.
3a, 3b	[Select Image File dialogue box]	Locate and select image to attach. Readable file formats include .gif, .jpg, .png, .tif, .tga, and .bmp.
4	[Image dialogue box]	Specify path type, insertion point, scale, and rotation. Illustration shows typical specifications.
5	[Drawing Screen]	Specify insertion point for image.

Adding Entourage

Entourage refers to the added people, plants, and other elements that give a drawing a sense of scale and realism. The AutoCAD and ADT design library and content library provides a comprehensive collection of entourage elements that can be used in all of your drawings. Two-dimensional plan and elevation as well as three-dimensional models of automobiles, trees, plants, and people are available.

Due to the complexity of most 3-D entourage models, material assignments are difficult and time-consuming. Therefore, it is recommended that other entourage libraries are used for your rendering needs. Many third-party software applications work with AutoCAD, Architectural Desktop, and VIZ Render to provide entourage models that are photorealistic. Archvision's RPC (Rich Photorealistic Content) technology and product line contains libraries of photorealistic entourage objects (trees, people, cars, and other objects) that can be used in 3-D models. These objects are prerendered solutions to the material assignment problem. They also render faster and better than the geometry-based blocks.

The plug-in software for Architectural Desktop and VIZ Render can be downloaded at www.archvision.com. Entourage libraries are sold at various prices.

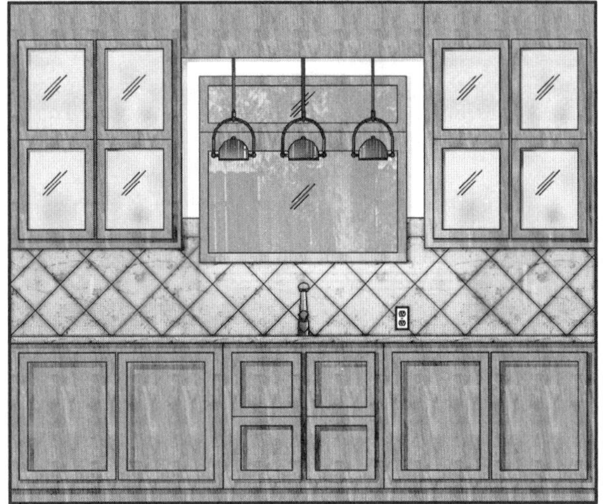

Figure 20.38 Example of using CAD drawing files in photo-editing programs

Student Project: Courtesy of Elizabeth Butler.

Using CAD Drawings in Image Editing Programs

Once line drawings are exported from AutoCAD or ADT, they can be imported into any photo-editing or illustration program for further enhancements. Figure 20.38 shows an example of how these programs provide additional presentation capabilities. Figure 20.39 demonstrates the step-by-step instructions for reproducing some of these examples in Photoshop.

Chapter Exercises

Open the Chapter 20 folder located on the CD-ROM to access the exercises related to this chapter. The exercises allow you to practice using the various output methods and composition concepts.

Technique to Master T20.39 Adding Color and Texture to AutoCAD Drawings in Photoshop

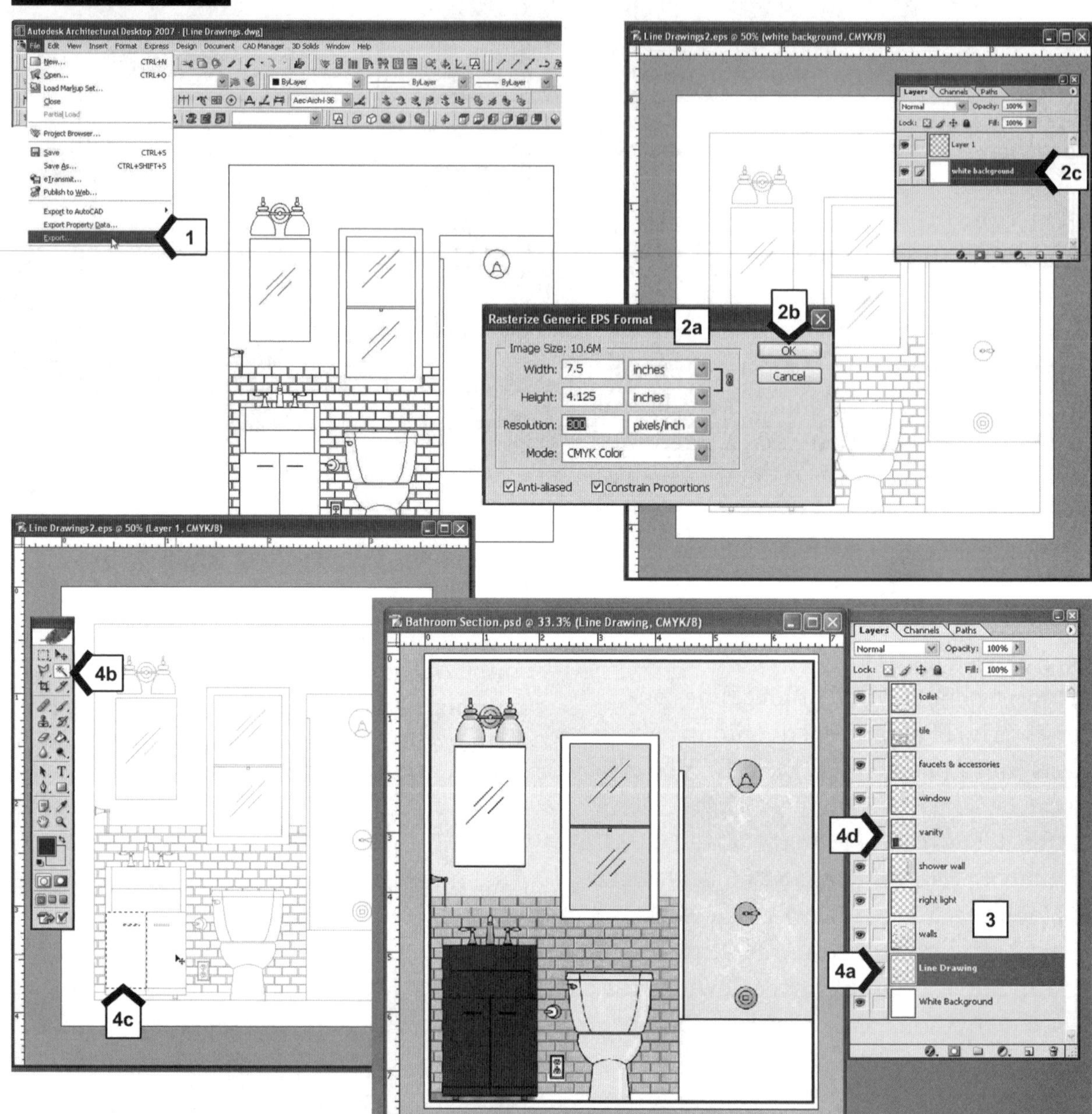

Figure 20.39 This technique uses an AutoCAD drawing as a background to render floor plans, and elevations, as well as perspectives. Some familiarity with Photoshop is necessary to complete this technique successfully.

1	Within AutoCAD, export the line drawing using the File>Export command. Export to the .eps file format.
2a–2c	In Photoshop, open the exported file. Make sure the resolution is set between 150 and 300 for a good quality image. The image will have a transparent background. To see the image better, create a new layer with a white fill. Place the layer below the line drawing.
3	Add new layers as appropriate for each material and/or texture.
4a–4d	The repeatable procedure is as follows: a. Make the line drawing current. b. Select Photoshop's Magic Wand tool. c. Select a section of the image. d. Make the material layer current. Apply color and/or texture to selected area using the Edit Menu> Fill command or the Paint bucket, Gradient, and/or Rubber stamp tool. e. Shade and shadow can be added by darkening selected areas with Image Menu>Adjustments> Levels command. f. Repeat until image is completely rendered.

Part IV

Linking Drawing Technique to Design Exploration

Linking CAD Skills Learning to Design Vocabulary Building

21

Objectives

This chapter examines how CAD, through its toolset, can extend the ways in which beginning design students learn about design vocabulary. It introduces some of the visual mechanisms used by designers to analyze and generate form. Visual examples illustrate how the vocabulary of design can be applied within design projects. The end-of-chapter exercises and Design Expression Problems provide additional practice solving several types of creative conditions.

Learning About Design Using CAD

There is a certain practicality about the integration of CAD learning and design learning. First, it is parallel to the current pedagogy using manual drawing methods where design skills depend on the development of drawings skills and vice versa. Moreover, since digital drawing is the current common method of design communication, the logical progression would be the linking of the two curricula.

Second, architecture and interior design are form-making and space-making endeavors. On a fundamental level, the functions of all CAD systems are essentially the same. They explore geometry and form in a similar fashion. Analogous relationships can be made between the CAD editing tools and the methods designers use to shape and express form. From the basic principles of design learned in general art and design classes to the proportional and ordering systems in architecture, all can be expressed and expanded on within the medium, thus broadening the traditional roles of CAD software.

This chapter explores the derivation of form and space in the context of AutoCAD and ADT. It looks at some of the various sources of form generation that can be easily incorporated into CAD skill development. Because the chapter's focus is on this partnership between design vocabulary and CAD, each topic encourages the use of additional reference material to further your knowledge of the subject matter.

Learning About Design Problems Using CAD

Since the text encourages the integration of the computer and CAD into most every aspect of the design process, it is appropriate that a discussion of design problems is included.

Design is about solving problems. The problems may vary in size and complexity, function and aesthetics, but the essence of a designed thing is its purpose. The design problem, an integral component to all design students' education, is the verbal expression of the question or situation. In his book *How Designers Think* (2001), Bryan Lawson describes design problems as "multi-dimensional and highly interactive" since they always introduce additional problems that must be researched, analyzed, and responded to. In his description, solving one problem many times creates others. The interconnectedness and ambiguity surrounding these types of problems characterizes them, according to Lawson.

These traits also set up the potential for failure in design projects. Lawson describes the superficial handling of design problems among students that results in a lack of understanding of the problem in detail. This, in turn, becomes evident within the project's final solution.

This section looks at how diagrammatic drawings—both digital and manual—can be used to unveil the multidimensionality of design problems. By developing the skills of visual expression in the areas of design problem research and understanding, inherent biases and reactions to the problem can be revealed.

Facilitating Learning About Design Problems in CAD

Easy methods to facilitate design-problem learning within the design studio is to create diagrams of increasing difficulty that visually represents one or more underlying problems or program requirements. An example might be the underlying problem of summer heat that coincides with the best views of a building site (Figure 21.1). Another example might visually express the need for privacy zoning within floor levels. Diagrams offer excellent methods to practice the functions of lineweight, line style, and line color while trying to work through all the parameters of the problem.

While sketch diagramming offers the looseness and spontaneity in expression and thought, when combined with digital diagramming, graphic language, graphic style, and graphic content can all be quickly evaluated and substituted during development (Figure 21.2). Digital diagrams can be superimposed, simplified, or complicated—all without retracing or damaging the original. Used in combination with virtual printing techniques, results can be evaluated.

Although design problems are typically researched in the early phases of the design process, it is always a good idea to revisit design problems at the beginning of each new phase. Since each design phase examines the design problem with an increased level of detail, it follows that additional levels of understanding will also occur.

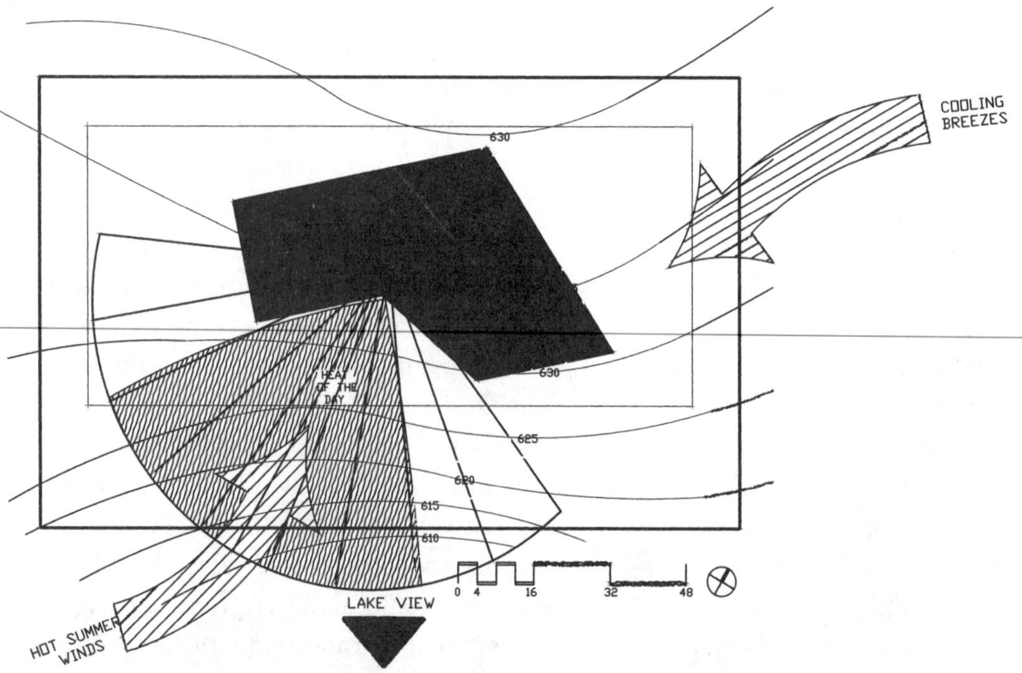

Figure 21.1 Visual representations of the different parts of a design problem will help to uncover previously unnoticed underlying problems.

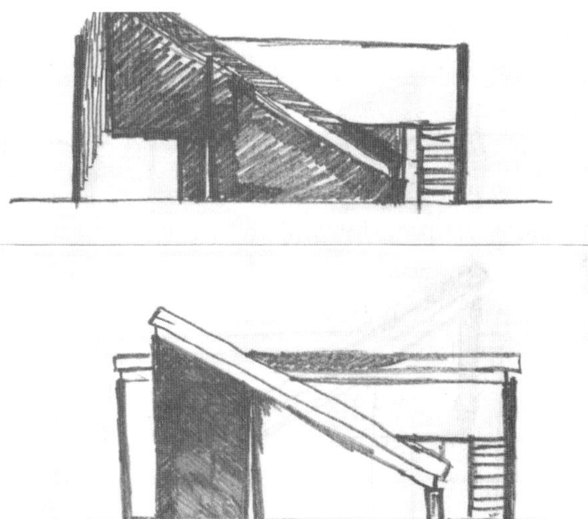

Figure 21.2 Sketch diagramming offers the looseness and spontaneity in expression and thought.

Making Digital Diagramming More Intuitive

While fluency with CAD is important to all the phases of the drawing process, it is especially key during the early stages of design. The need for the simultaneous connection between eye, hand, and brain is what spurs continuous thought and creativity in these early stages. The immediacy of manual diagrams can be somewhat replicated in CAD with planning and experience. Nevertheless, as long as keyboards and mice remain the intermediary instrument, it will always be at a disadvantage. Diagrams started at the beginning of a design problem can be continuously developed as the design strategy changes and develops.

Learning About Design Relationships Using CAD

There are many directions that are currently being pursued when it comes to form and space-making within the digital realm. Daniela Bertol's *Visualizing with CAD* (1994) was one of the first reference books for correlating geometry and geometric transformations with the shape and shape modification commands in most CAD programs (Figure 21.3). Her book not only ties these design principles and

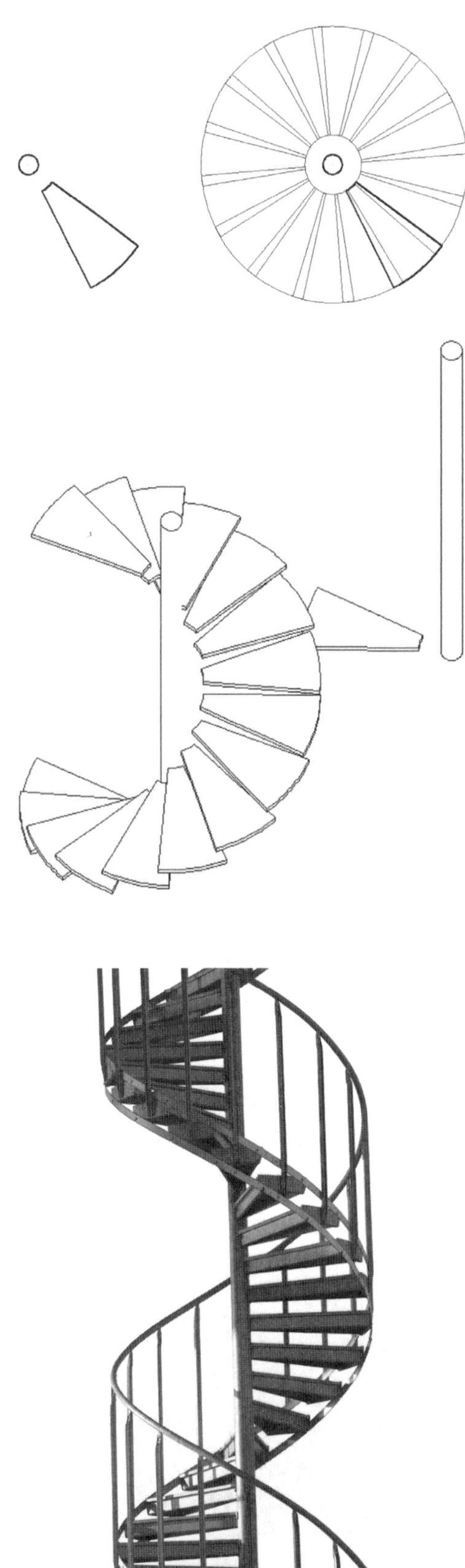

Figure 21.3 A wedge-shaped extrusion is duplicated while arrayed around a cylinder. The result is a spiral staircase.

organizational systems to the logic and geometric manipulations of the CAD environment but also explores how the computational methodology could ultimately direct a design's formal expression. As demonstrated in the following section, implementing these concepts is well within the limits of AutoCAD and ADT.

Form and Spatial Transformations

Within the context of design, form and spatial transformations refer to the deliberate physical changes made to an object or objects. There are four types of transformations that will be discussed—compositional, relational, perceptual, and metamorphic. Compositional transformations start with the primary shapes (geometries) that are combined and edited to create more complex and irregular forms. Relational transformations keep the integrity of the object or space and instead use orientation, multiplication, and proximity to change how it is perceived. Perceptual transformations use compositional transformations to explore the more perceptual qualities of how we experience form and space (Figure 21.4).

Figure 21.4 The Chapel designed by Le Corbusier was designed to be experienced from within the chapel.

Chapol de Notre-Dame-du-Haut Ronohamp, France. Project date: 1950–54. Digital Image © The Museum of Modern Art/Licensed by SCALA / Art Resource, NY.

Metamorphic transformations change the original object by applying external actions (Figure 21.5).

Compositional Transformations

In the interior design and architectural disciplines, compositional transformations form the foundation for all design work. Exterior buildings as well as interior spaces all rely on the shape of its boundaries to give it form. In AutoCAD and ADT, compositional transformations occur through shape and object modifications learned in Parts I and II. There are four types of compositional transformations—dimensional, additive, subtractive, and intersectional (exemplified by the shapes you see in Figure 21.6). Each type can be directly linked to an AutoCAD or ADT editing procedure.

Dimensional transformations modify objects by changing their physical dimensions. Height, width, depth, and length changes are affected by dimensional transformations. AutoCAD and Architectural Desktop's stretch,

Figure 21.5 The leaning glass tower in Frank Gehry's Nationale-Nederlande Building in Prague 1992–1996 is an example how a cylindrical object gets transformed using a bending and twisting action.

scale, and grip editing tools are common for this type of transformation (Figure 21.7).

Additive transformations are modifications made to a primary shape by the addition of other shapes, often referred to as shape combining (Figure 21.8).

Subtractive transformations are modifications made to a primary shape by the subtraction of other shapes (Figure 21.9).

Intersectional transformations are modifications from the coincident parts of overlapping shapes (Figure 21.10).

Although compositional transformations are found in the design of everyday objects and buildings, they have no meaning in the design world. They are essentially the raw ingredients that artists and designers use to create the recipe. They require intention. What about the object are you choosing to emphasize? What parts will be deleted? While arbitrary form generation using compositional transformations has been encourages in many design programs, it becomes difficult to use this type of method for further design development. When compositional transformations are combined with the principles and ordering systems of design, a strategy toward form is created.

Figure 21.6 There are four types of compositional transformations: dimensional, additive, subtractive, and intersectional.

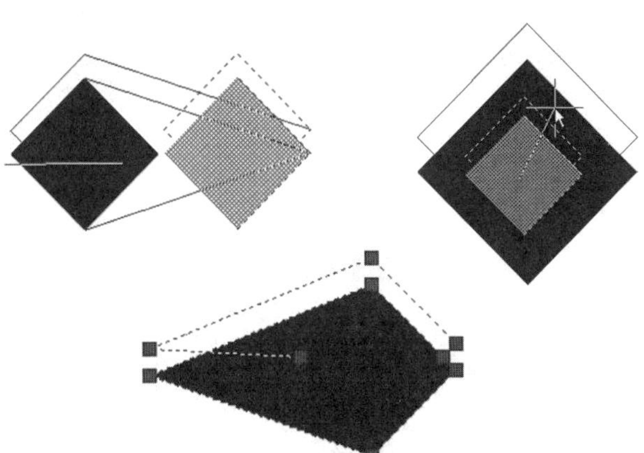

Figure 21.7 AutoCAD and Architectural Desktop's stretch, scale, and grip editing tools are common for dimensional transformations.

Figure 21.8 Additive transformations

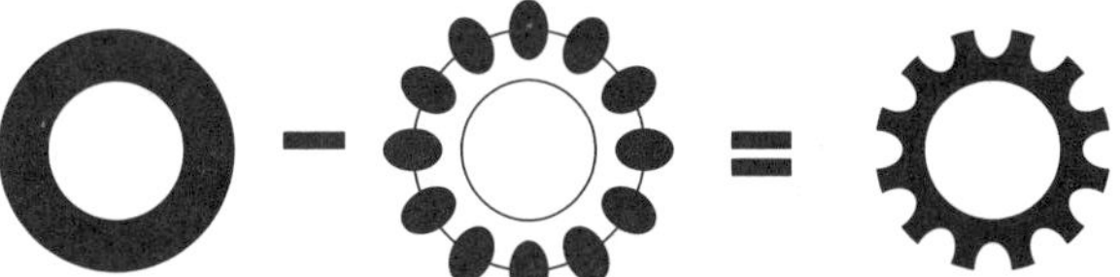

Figure 21.9 Subtractive transformations

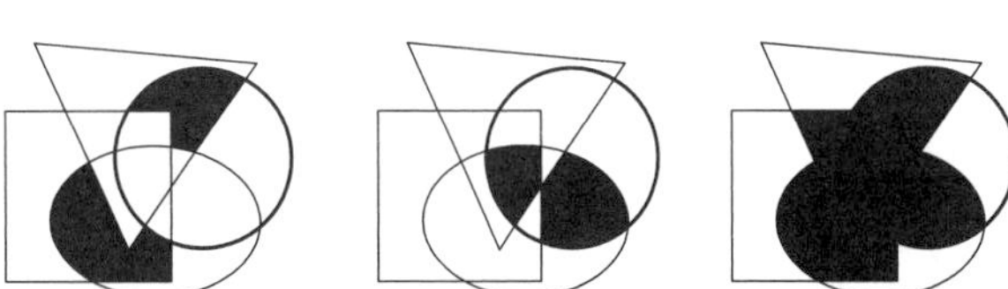

Figure 21.10 Intersectional transformations

Exploring the Compositional Transformations in AutoCAD and ADT

Figures 21.11 through 21.16 provide some examples of how two-dimensional shapes and three-dimensional objects can create complex compositional transformations. Try using these same objects to create shapes and objects that are familiar.

Exploring Relational Transformations in AutoCAD and ADT

Most of the AutoCAD and ADT modification commands are examples of relational transformations. The Copy, Array, and Offset commands imply alteration through duplication and proximity, while the Mirror and Rotate commands use orientation.

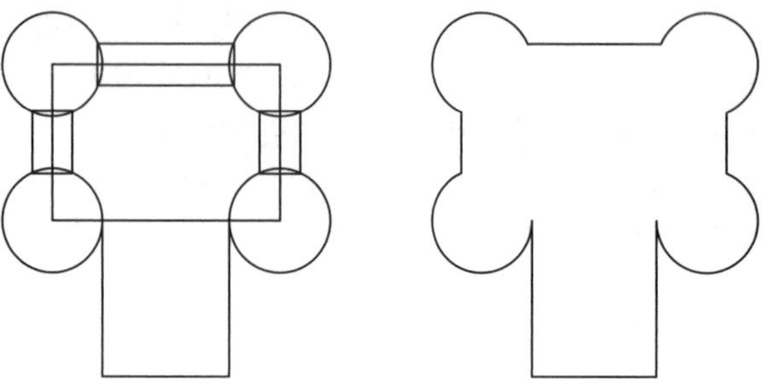

Figure 21.11 Example of additive transformation in a two-dimensional shape.

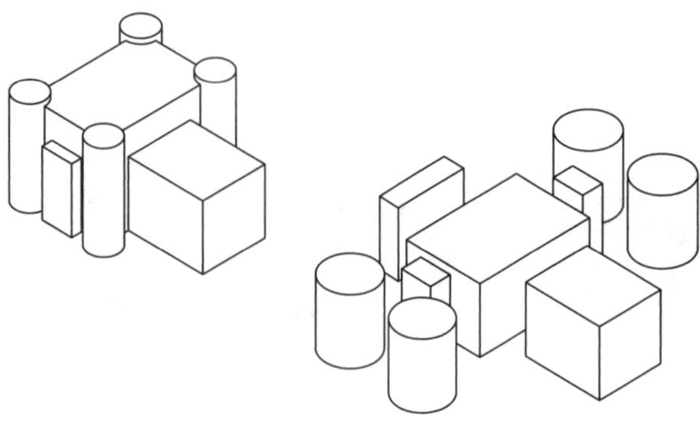

Figure 21.12 Example of additive transformation in a three-dimensional shape.

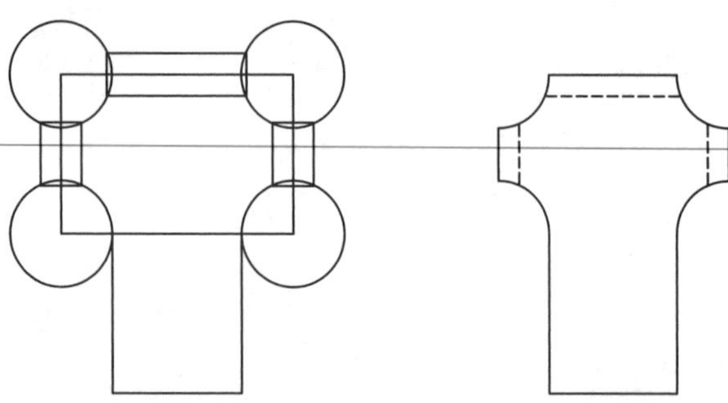

Figure 21.13 Example of subtractive transformation in a two-dimensional shape.

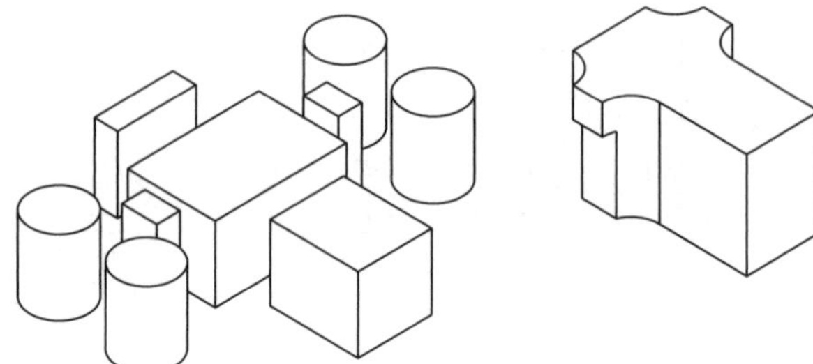

Figure 21.14 Example of subtractive transformation in a three-dimensional shape.

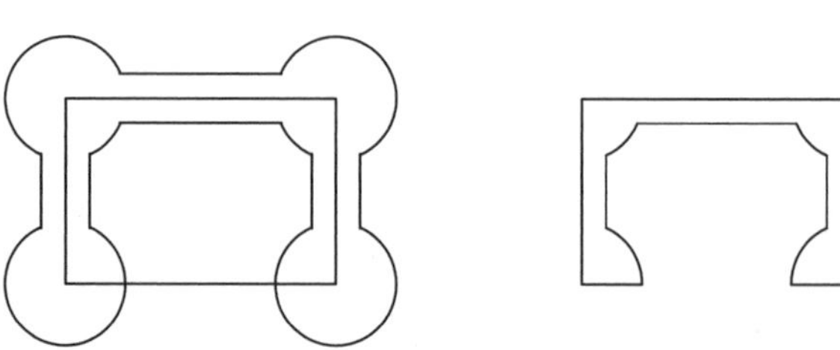

Figure 21.15 Example of intersectional transformation in a two-dimensional shape.

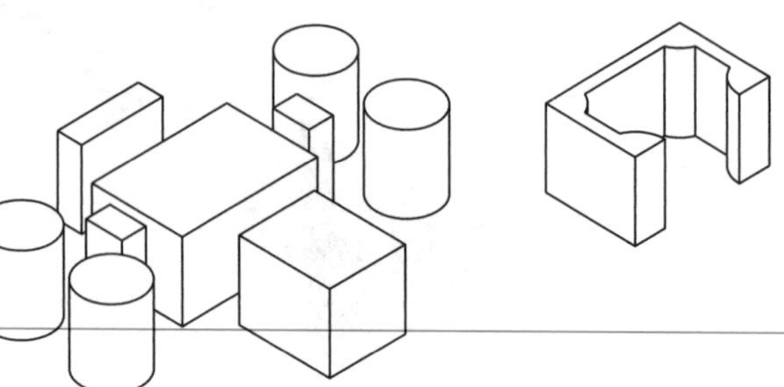

Figure 21.16 Example of intersectional transformation in a three-dimensional shape.

Exploring Perceptual Transformations in AutoCAD and ADT

Perceptual transformations give significance to how we perceive our world experientially. They rely on the direct feedback of your senses for design direction. Compositional transformations can be used divisively to create experiences like spatial allusion, spatial extension, inside/outside, and solid/void contrasts (Figure 21.17). The automatic feedback that perspective views and motion sequencing provides allows for this kind of direct feedback in AutoCAD and ADT.

One approach for creating these kinds of transformations uses AutoCAD solids and ADT mass elements. The approach starts with a large rectangle that is carved into to create and explore space. Perspectives and dynamic real-time sections provide the automatic perceptual feedback required for additional design decisions. Further design studies that explore daylight and shade-and-shadow are also possible using this approach. Figure 21.18 illustrates the approach using AutoCAD solids and mass elements.

Figure 21.17 Solid/void contrasts are created with the stair form hovering in space.

Stadthaus Scharnhauser Park, Ostfildern, Germany. Interior. Photo date: 2002. Digital Image © The Museum of Modern Art/Licensed by SCALA/Art Resource, NY.

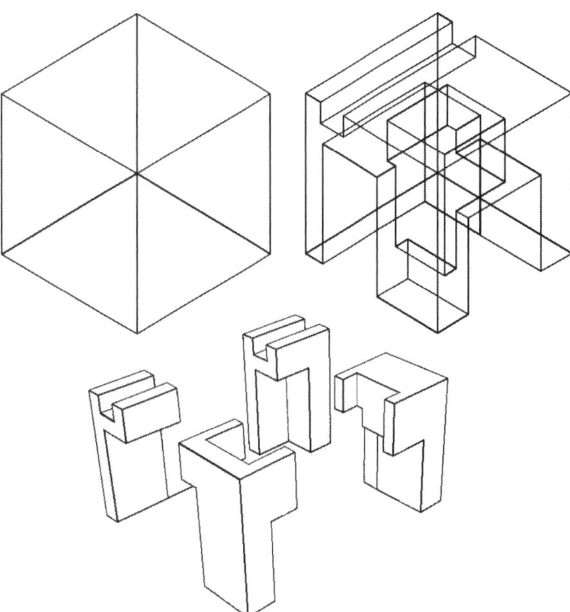

Figure 21.18 One approach for creating perceptual transformations uses AutoCAD solids and ADT mass elements. The approach starts with a large rectangle that is carved into to create and explore space. Perspectives and dynamic real-time sections provide the automatic perceptual feedback required for additional design decisions.

Exploring Metamorphic Transformations in AutoCAD and ADT

Metamorphic transformations distort objects as a result of external forces that are applied to the object. They include transformations like folding, twisting, curling, and rippling. For the most part AutoCAD and ADT do not have the tools to apply these kinds of transformations automatically. Figures 21.19 through 21.21 demonstrate these transformations using a combination of tools.

Form and Spatial Organizations

Design principles and ordering systems help satisfy our need for order in the world. As a visual syntax, they offer rules for formulating and structuring how objects relate in space. Most design principles and ordering systems are deeply rooted in human perception. In our search for visual solutions, they are useful as guidelines for how buildings and interior spaces are organized.

Figure 21.19 Folding metamorphic transformations seen in the folding planes of the glass

To create the transformation, a polyline representing the plan profile of the glass walls is created. A curtainwall is placed using the Reference Base Curve method. Refer to Technique T14.15.

This topic concentrates on how the design principles and ordering systems can be explored within the constraints of AutoCAD and ADT's toolsets. Before moving forward in the chapter, take the time to understand each of the design principles and ordering systems using one of the suggested reference books in Appendix N.

Figure 21.20 Twisting metamorphic transformations found in the handrail

To create the transformation, a 3-D polyline is created using several vertices that are smoothed into a spline. The 3-D polyline represents the twisting path of the handrail. Using the AutoCAD 3-D Sweep tool, a circular profile of the handrail is sweeped along the path.

Figure 21.21 Rippling metamorphic transformations found in the shape of the roof

To create the transformation, a sectional profile of the roof is lofted using the AutoCAD 3-D Loft tool.

Exploring the Design Principles in AutoCAD and ADT

Symmetry and reflection suggest an equality that exists between two sides. In AutoCAD and ADT, these design principles are tied to the Mirror command (Figure 21.22).

Balance and harmony are two very similar design principles that also are expressions of visual equality. Objects and spaces do not need to be alike to establish the awareness of balance and harmony. For many people, balance and harmony are often not consciously perceived in the everyday use of spaces. Because these principles rely more on our perceptual experience of a space than specific rules of organization, balance and harmony are best explored in perspective views.

Hierarchy, emphasis, dominance, and focal point are all design principles that imply prominence of one object over others. In architecture and interior design, this can be translated to a hierarchy of spaces and forms, as wells as the building objects themselves. Since prominence can be established in multiple ways—through scale, height, complexity, or proximity—it is difficult to establish specific CAD commands that relate. An obvious answer is the Scale command; however, any of the transformations can be used.

Rhythm and repetition of objects can be completed using the Array and Copy commands. In architecture and interior design, rhythm and repetition are often used to imply direction and visual unity. Repetitive patterns can be organized in linear, radial, rectangular, or circular fashions (Figure 21.23). Path-oriented and gradational organizations are also possible (Figure 21.24).

Proportioning systems have been around since man quantified the study of geometry.

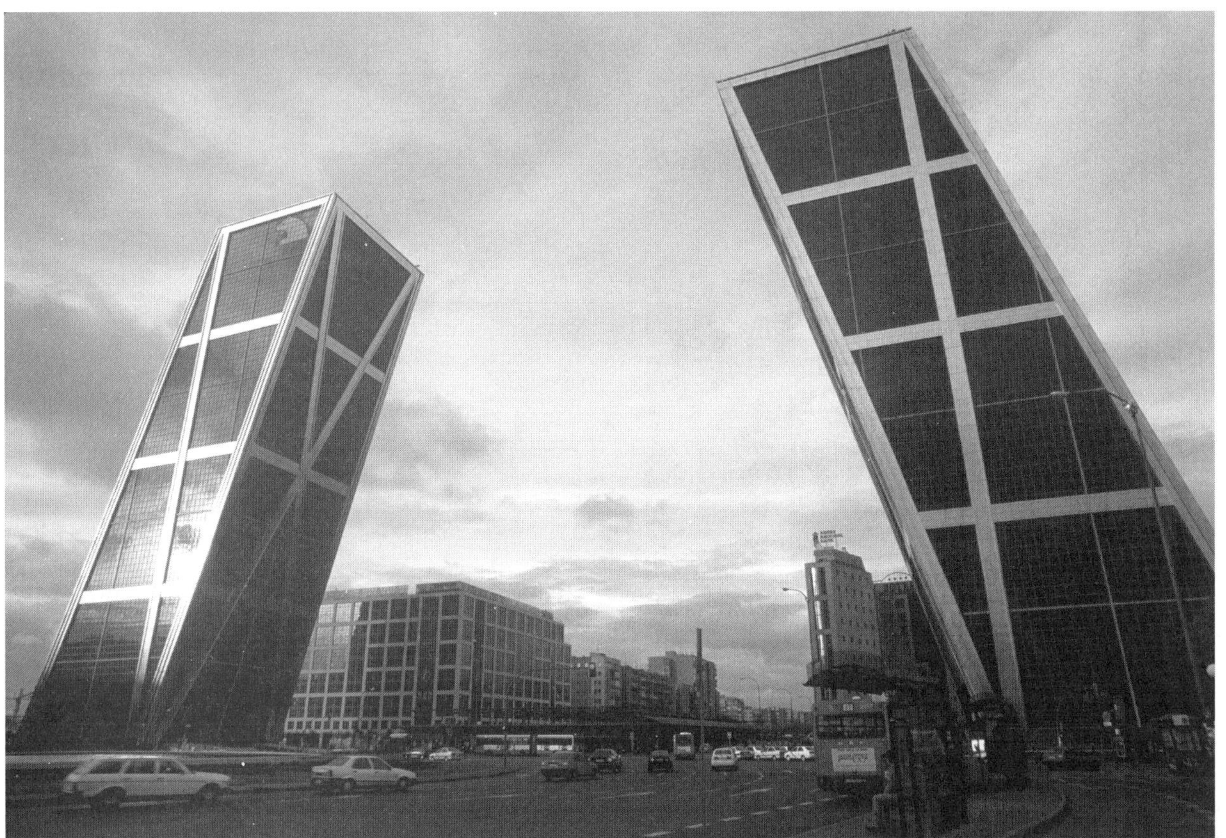

Figure 21.22 Symmetry and reflection can be tied to the Mirror command.

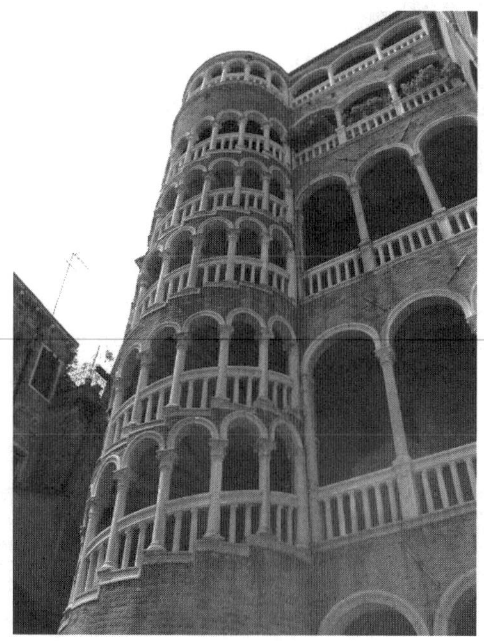

Figure 21.23 Rhythm and repetition can be expressed in a linear, radial, rectangular, or circular fashion.

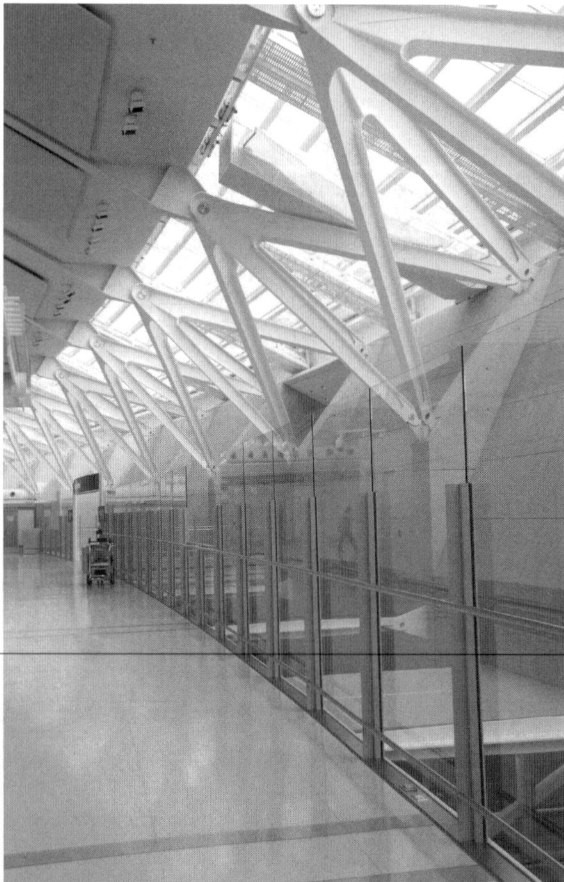

Figure 21.24 Path-oriented and gradational organizations are also possible.

They use a ratio system to establish specific dimensional relationships between one object and another. Figures 21.25 through 21.28 demonstrate the construction of the golden section rectangle, ellipse, and triangle, as well as the root 2 rectangle in AutoCAD.

Technique to Master **T21.25** Constructing the Golden Section Rectangle in CAD

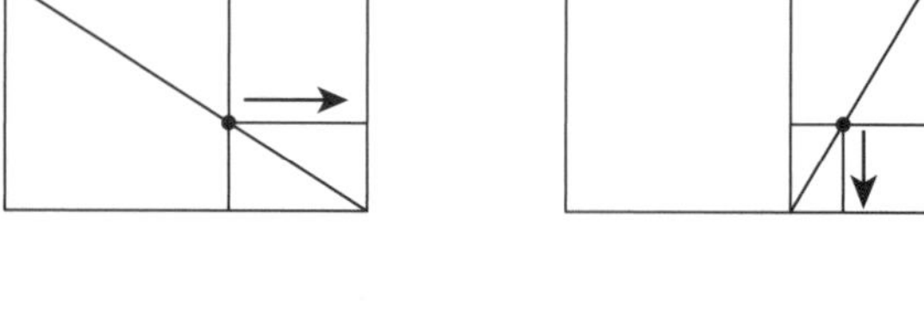

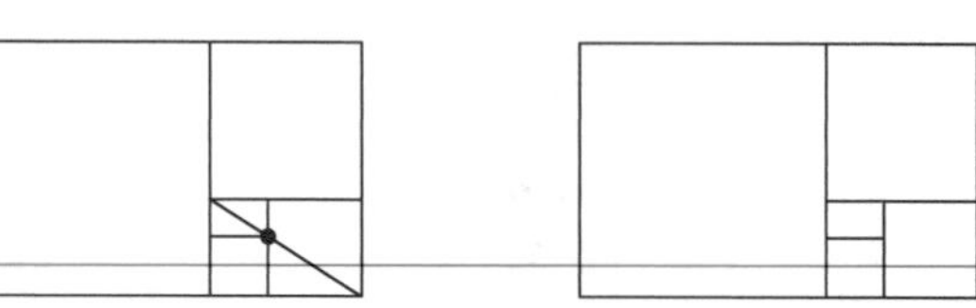

Figure 21.25

1	Create a rectangle.
2	Draw a circle with a center located at point A and radius at point B.
3	The intersection of the circle when the ground line is extended creates point C.
4	Draw another rectangle from points B and C.
5	The golden rectangle can be infinitely divided into smaller golden rectangles.

Technique to Master

T21.26 Constructing the Golden Section Ellipse in CAD

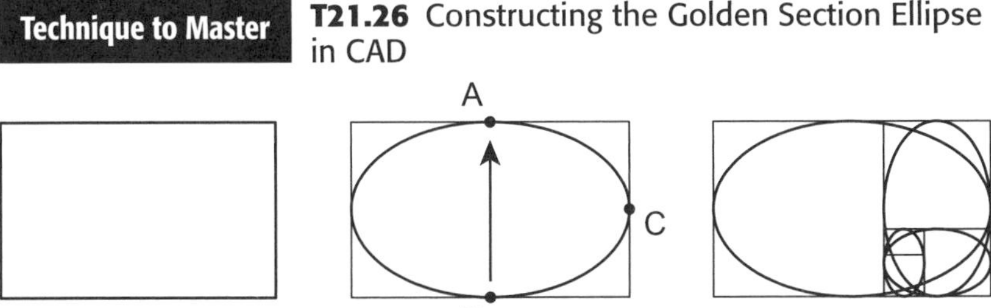

Figure 21.26 Using a golden rectangle, create the ellipse by first specifying the width of the minor axis (points A and B), then specifying the radius of the major axis (point C).

Technique to Master

T21.27 Constructing the Golden Section Triangle in CAD

C
C
A B A B

Figure 21.27

1	Create a five-sided polygon (pentagon) using the Polygon command.
2	Connect opposite points to create the golden triangle.
3	The golden triangle can be infinitely divided into smaller golden triangles.

Technique to Master

T21.28 Constructing the Root 2 Rectangle in CAD

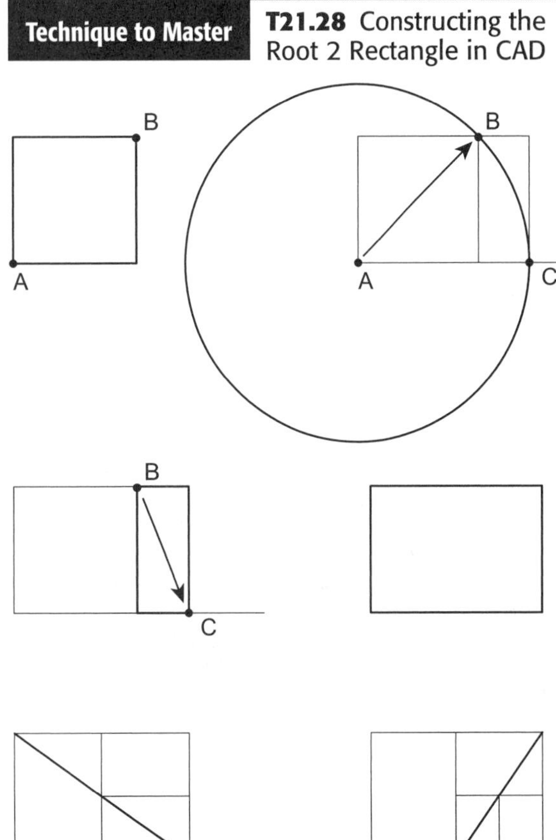

Figure 21.28

1	Create a rectangle.
2	Draw a circle with a center located at point A and radius at point B.
3	The intersection of the circle when the ground line is extended creates point C.
4	Draw another rectangle from points B and C.
5	The root 2 rectangle can also be infinitely divided.

Figures 21.29a–e provide additional examples of how each design principle can be explored using interior design and architecture.

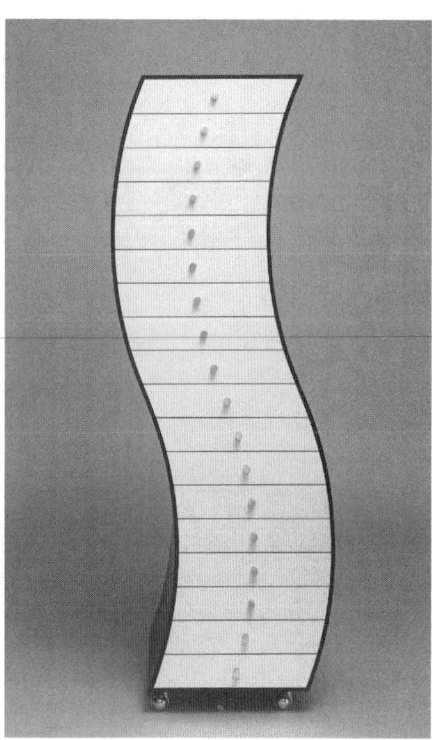

Figure 21.29a Using the design principles in interior space

Lacquered wood and aluminum. 1970. Shiro Kuramata. Digital Image © The Museum of Modern Art/Licensed by SCALA / Art Resource, NY. The Museum of Modern Art, New York, NY.

Figure 21.29b

Figure 21.29c

Figure 21.29d

Katsura Imperial Villa. Interior of the formal tea house. Kyoto, Japan. 1590. Kyoto, Japan. Photo Credit: Werner Forman/Art Resource, NY

Figure 21.29e Using the design principles in interior space

Nineteenth century CE. Changing rooms. 1821. Frauenbad (Women's bath). Thermal Baths, Baden, Austria. Photo Credit: Erich Lessing / Art Resource, NY.

Exploring the Organizational Systems in AutoCAD and ADT

Linear organizations use the design and placement of objects, rooms, and building systems to emphasize a visible linear path. Similar to linear organizations, axial, and bi-axial organizations use imaginary lines to establish how rooms and objects are arranged (Figure 21.30). Centralized and concentric organizations can use the Array and Offset commands to transpose emphasis to the center (Figure 21.31). Radial organizations radiate outward from an established center using the Offset and Scale commands. The Rotate command is easily tied to rotational organizations. Shifting, overlapping, clustered, and linked organizations explore proximity relationships through implied touching. The formal expression of these organizational systems relies on the positional relationship that the Copy command produces.

Figures 21.32 and 21.33 provide additional examples of how the above organizational systems can be explored using interior design and architecture.

Figure 21.30 Axial and bi-axial organizations use imaginary lines to establish how rooms and objects are arranged.

Figure 21.31 Centralized and concentric organizations can use the Array and Offset commands to transpose emphasis to the center.

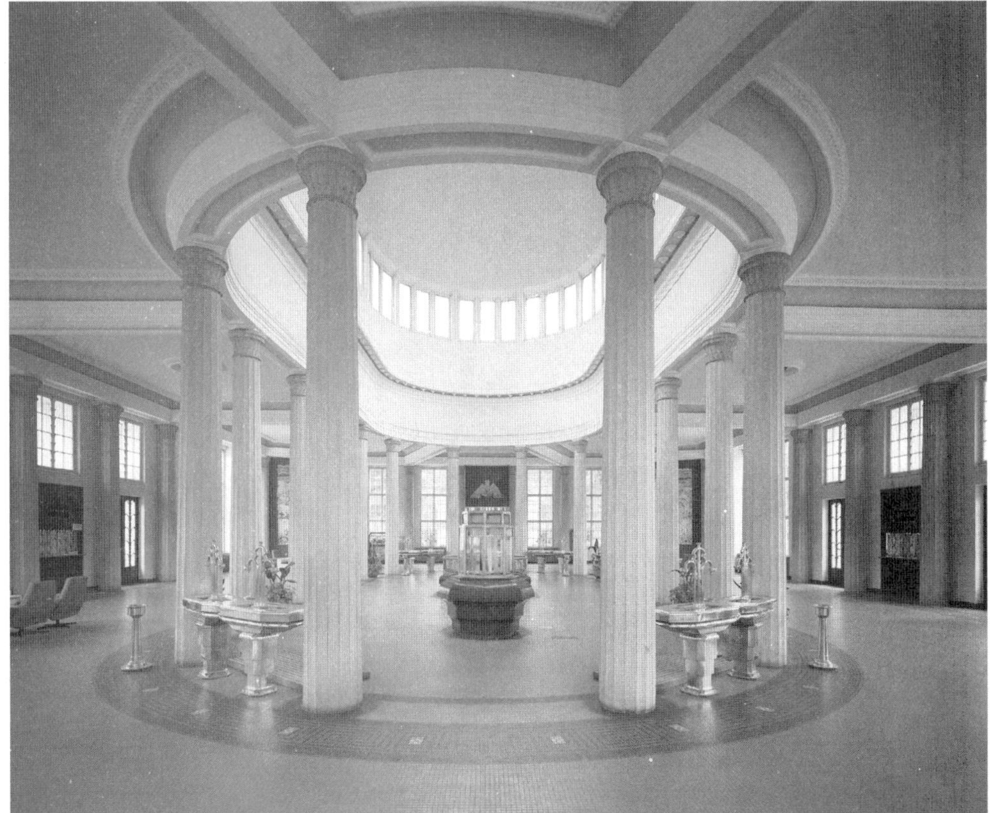

Figure 21.32 Using the organizational principles in exterior and interior space

Nineteenth century CE. Franzensbad Spa: Interior of the Glauber-source pump room. Thermal Baths, Frantiskovy Lazne (Franzensbad), Czech Republic. Photo Credit: Erich Lessing / Art Resource, NY.

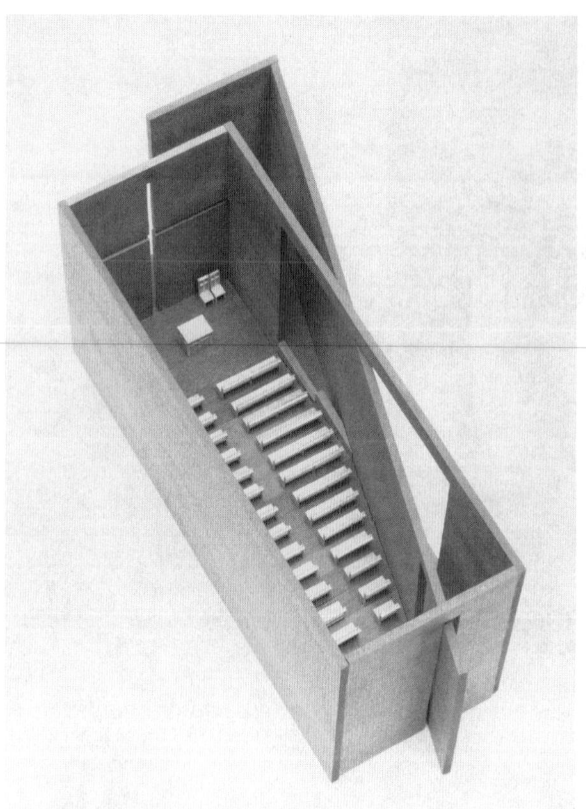

Figure 21.33 Using the organizational principles in exterior and interior space

Church of the Light, Ibaraki, Osaka, Japan. Project Date: 1984–89. Digital Image © The Museum of Modern Art/Licensed by SCALA / Art Resource, NY. The Museum of Modern Art, New York, NY.

Chapter Exercises

Open the Chapter 21 folder located on the CD-ROM to access the exercises related to this chapter. Exercises and Design Expression Problems provide practice using the design principles and compositional transformations within AutoCAD and ADT.

Appendices

Appendix A: Templates Shipped with AutoCAD and Architectural Desktop

The templates listed here represent the most often used ones for interior designers and architects for imperial units, that is, feet and inches. Notice that the naming of the templates categorize them into types—templates for 3-D drawing, templates using named plot style tables, and templates using color-dependent plot style tables. Templates with an ANSI prefix refer to the size of the title block drawn in paper space that complies with the standards set by the American National Standards Institute (ANSI). Refer to Appendix R for a table of all standard architectural and ANSI standard title block sizes.

While templates can save any type and amount of information for reuse in future projects, most templates at a minimum save the following:

- Unit type and level of accuracy for the drawing
- Grid spacing and limits
- Layer names with assigned color, lineweights, linetypes, and plot styles
- Loaded linetypes
- Dimension styles
- Text styles
- Visual styles
- Title blocks

The AutoCAD 2007 Templates

Templates for AutoCAD 2007 are located in the following folder: C:\Documents and Settings\ *{your computer login}* \Local Settings\Application Data\Autodesk\ AutoCAD 2007\R17.0\enu\Template. Substitute *{your computer login}* with the login name used for your computer.

- acad3D.dwt
- acad Named Plot Styles3D.dwt
- acad Named Plot Styles.dwt
- acad.dwt
- acadiso3D.dwt
- ANSI A (portrait) Color Dependent Plot Styles.dwt
- ANSI A (portrait) Named Plot Styles.dwt
- ANSI A Color Dependent Plot Styles.dwt
- ANSI A Named Plot Styles.dwt
- ANSI B Color Dependent Plot Styles.dwt
- ANSI B Named Plot Styles.dwt
- ANSI C Color Dependent Plot Styles.dwt
- ANSI C Named Plot Styles.dwt
- ANSI D Color Dependent Plot Styles.dwt
- ANSI D Named Plot Styles.dwt
- ANSI E Color Dependent Plot Styles.dwt
- ANSI E Named Plot Styles.dwt
- ANSI Layout templates.dwt
- Architectural, English units Color Dependent Plot Styles.dwt

- Architectural, English units Named Plot Styles.dwt
- Generic 24in × 32in Title Block Color Dependent Plot Styles.dwt
- Generic 24in × 32in Title Block Named Plot Styles.dwt

Sheetsets

Sheetset templates are used with the Sheetset Manager (refer to Chapter 7).

- Architectural Imperial.dwt

The Architectural Desktop 2007 Templates

Templates for Architectural Desktop 2007 are located in the following folder: C:\Documents and Settings\All Users\Application Data\Autodesk\ADT 2007\enu\Template

- acad.dwt
- Aec Model (Imperial Ctb).dwt
- Aec Model (Imperial Stb).dwt
- Aec Sheet (Imperial Ctb).dwt
- Aec Sheet (Imperial Stb).dwt

Appendix B: Creating New Drawings from the CD-ROM Templates

The following AutoCAD and Architectural Desktop templates are created with additional customizations. Notice that there are AutoCAD templates specifically for floor plans, ceiling plans, elevations, and plot sheets. These templates have layer assignments specific to the orthographic view saved within the template. The customized Architectural Desktop templates provided on the CD-ROM contain additional display configurations that might be helpful for during a project's development. To use the templates, copy the contents of each template folder located on the CD-ROM to the appropriate template folders on your computer. See Appendix A for these locations.

The CD-ROM AutoCAD Templates

- Sheetset Plot Sheet.dwt
- Source Border—18 × 24 Presentation Stb.dwt
- Source Border—24 × 36 Working Stb.dwt
- Source Border—24 × 36 Presentation Stb.dwt
- Source Border—Letter Working Stb.dwt
- Source Border—Letter Presentation Stb.dwt
- Source Border—Legal Working Stb.dwt
- Source Border—Tabloid Presentation Stb.dwt
- Source Border—Tabloid Working Stb.dwt
- Source Floor Plan Stb.dwt
- Source Ceiling Plan Stb.dwt
- Source Section—Elevation Stb.dwt

The CD-ROM Architectural Desktop Templates

- CDS Model (Imperial Stb).DWT
- CDS Presentation Sheet (Imperial Stb).dwt
- CDS Sheet (Imperial Stb).dwt
- CDS Model (Imperial Ctb).DWT
- CDS Presentation Sheet (Imperial Ctb).dwt
- CDS Sheet (Imperial Ctb).dwt

Appendix C: Menus Screen Shots for AutoCAD and Architectural Desktop

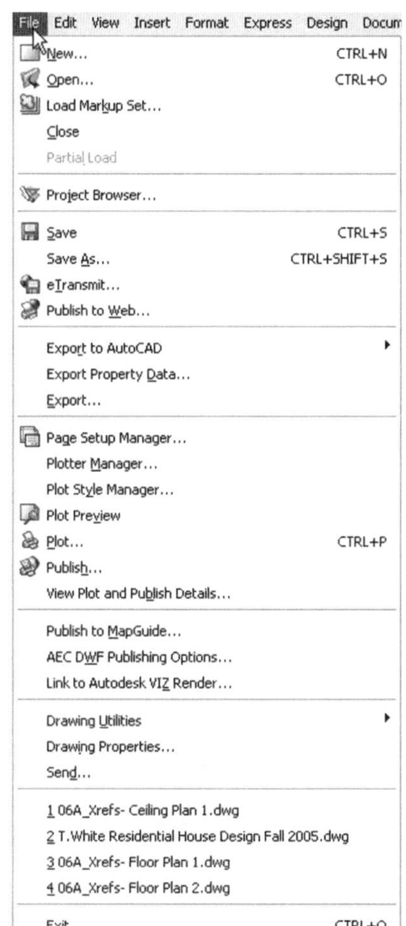

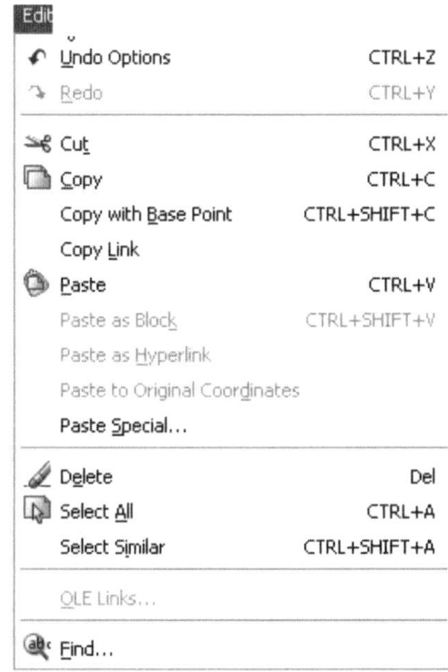

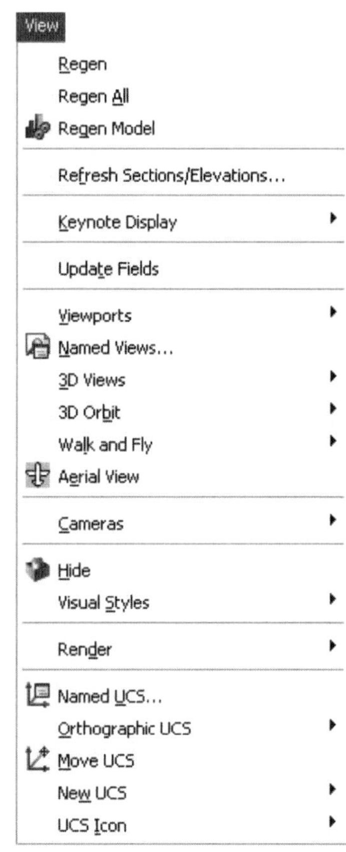

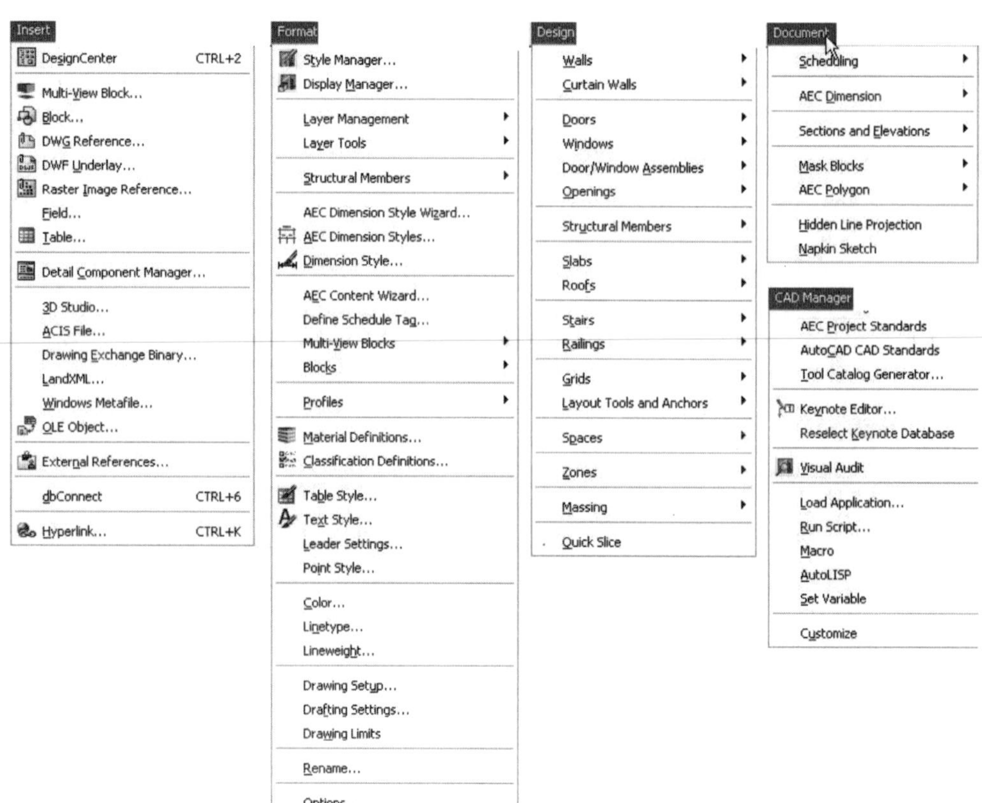
Insert
DesignCenter CTRL+2
Multi-View Block...
Block...
DWG Reference...
DWF Underlay...
Raster Image Reference...
Field...
Table...
Detail Component Manager...
3D Studio...
ACIS File...
Drawing Exchange Binary...
LandXML...
Windows Metafile...
OLE Object...
External References...
dbConnect CTRL+6
Hyperlink... CTRL+K
Format
Style Manager...
Display Manager...
Layer Management
Layer Tools
Structural Members
AEC Dimension Style Wizard...
AEC Dimension Styles...
Dimension Style...
AEC Content Wizard...
Define Schedule Tag...
Multi-View Blocks
Blocks
Profiles
Material Definitions...
Classification Definitions...
Table Style...
Text Style...
Leader Settings...
Point Style...
Color...
Linetype...
Lineweight...
Drawing Setup...
Drafting Settings...
Drawing Limits
Rename...
Options...
Design
Walls
Curtain Walls
Doors
Windows
Door/Window Assemblies
Openings
Structural Members
Slabs
Roofs
Stairs
Railings
Grids
Layout Tools and Anchors
Spaces
Zones
Massing
Quick Slice
Document
Scheduling
AEC Dimension
Sections and Elevations
Mask Blocks
AEC Polygon
Hidden Line Projection
Napkin Sketch
CAD Manager
AEC Project Standards
AutoCAD CAD Standards
Tool Catalog Generator...
Keynote Editor...
Reselect Keynote Database
Visual Audit
Load Application...
Run Script...
Macro
AutoLISP
Set Variable
Customize

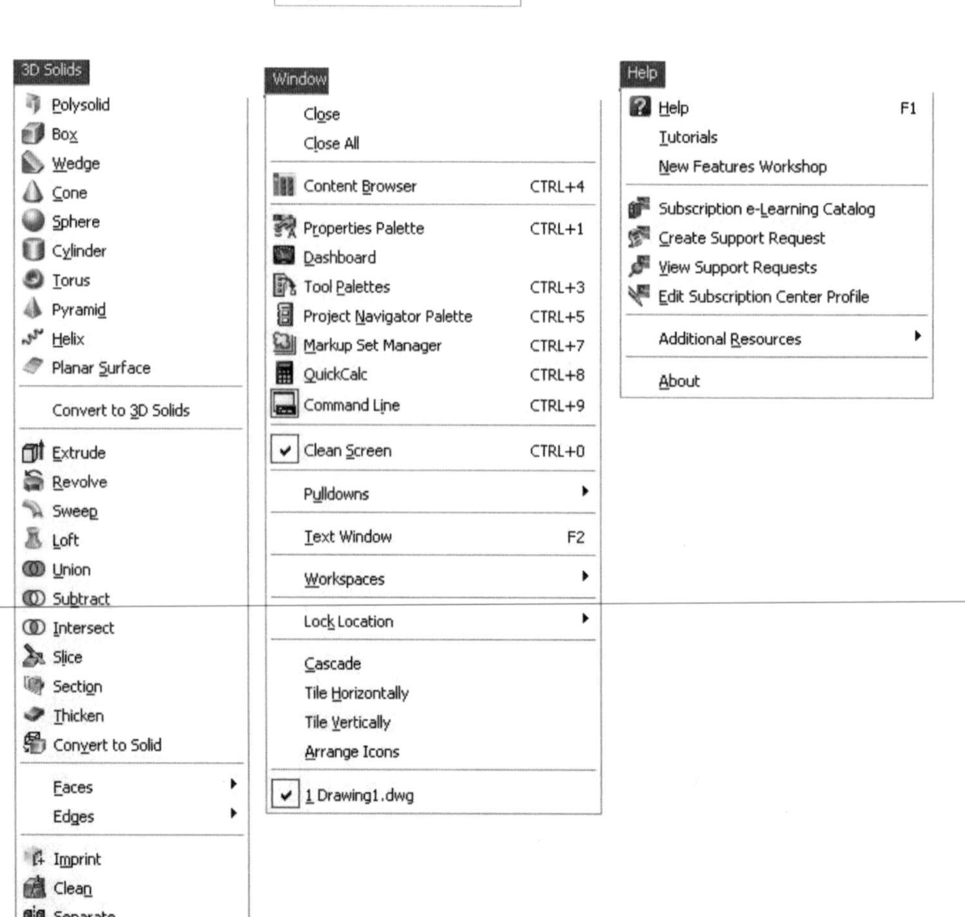
3D Solids
Polysolid
Box
Wedge
Cone
Sphere
Cylinder
Torus
Pyramid
Helix
Planar Surface
Convert to 3D Solids
Extrude
Revolve
Sweep
Loft
Union
Subtract
Intersect
Slice
Section
Thicken
Convert to Solid
Faces
Edges
Imprint
Clean
Separate
Shell
Check
Setup
Window
Close
Close All
Content Browser CTRL+4
Properties Palette CTRL+1
Dashboard
Tool Palettes CTRL+3
Project Navigator Palette CTRL+5
Markup Set Manager CTRL+7
QuickCalc CTRL+8
Command Line CTRL+9
Clean Screen CTRL+0
Pulldowns
Text Window F2
Workspaces
Lock Location
Cascade
Tile Horizontally
Tile Vertically
Arrange Icons
1 Drawing1.dwg
Help
Help F1
Tutorials
New Features Workshop
Subscription e-Learning Catalog
Create Support Request
View Support Requests
Edit Subscription Center Profile
Additional Resources
About

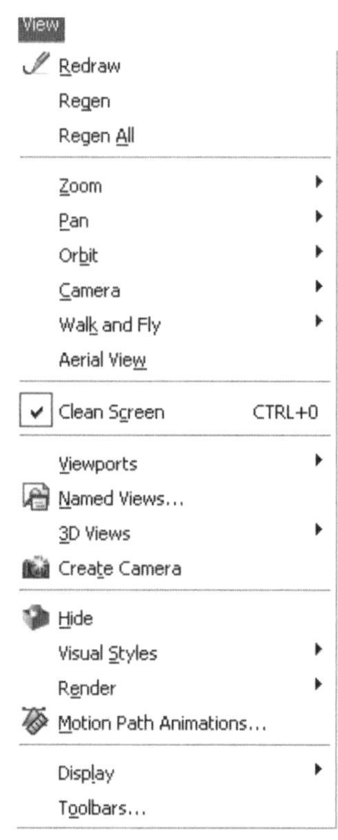

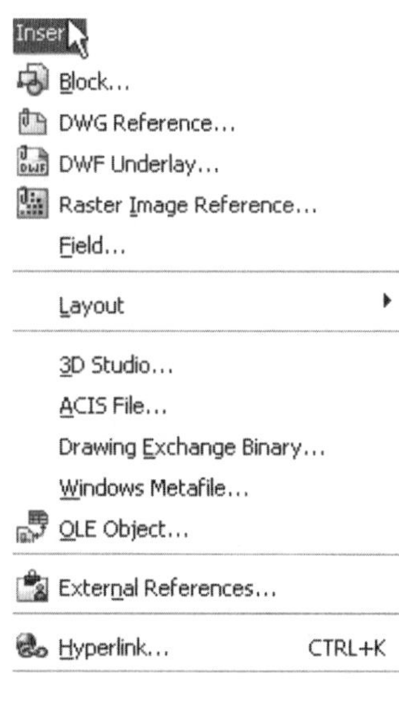

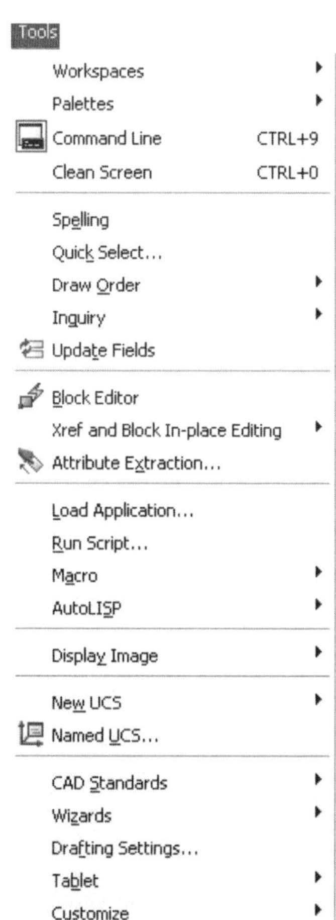

Modify
Properties
Match Properties
Object
Clip
Erase
Copy
Mirror
Offset
Array...
Move
Rotate
Scale
Stretch
Lengthen
Trim
Extend
Break
Join
Chamfer
Fillet
3D Operations
Solid Editing
Change Space
Explode

Appendix D: Essential Drawing and System Variables

Helpful Drawing and System Variables to Take Note of

Facetratio	Controls the mesh density for 3-D AutoCAD cylindrical and conic solids
Facetres	(drawing) In shaded modes, controls the smoothness of objects
Fillmode	(drawing) Controls whether hatch solids are filled in. Setting of 1 = filled.
Hidetext	(drawing) Controls how text objects are displayed during the Hide command. Off = Text is not hidden.
Ltscale	(drawing) Controls the global linetype scale, which sizes the dashes and spaces.
Mirrtext	(drawing) Specifies whether the text is mirrored during the Mirror command.
Osoptions	(system) If set to 1, object snaps will ignore hatch patterns. A setting of 3 allows object snaps to snap to hatches.
Pdmode	(drawing) Controls what point objects look like. 0 = dot, 2 = cross, 3 = x. Refer to Point command for a complete list.
Pdsize	(drawing) Controls the display size of points.
Pellipse	(drawing) When set to a value of 1, ellipses are converted to polylines. Default = 0.

Appendix E: User Workspace Customization

Loading Menus and Lisp Routines

Add-on programs and Lisp routines (small macro programs made for AutoCAD) can add additional tools and command shortcuts to the main AutoCAD toolset. Load the programs using the Appload command.

Toolbar Changes

Toolbar changes, including moving, docking, refloating, altering content, showing, hiding, and creating.

Palette Changes

Palette changes, including moving, docking, refloating, altering content, showing, and hiding.

AutoCAD Housekeeping

Below is a reminder of the basic rules for communicating with AutoCAD and Architectural Desktop.

- The mouse is used to select an object on-screen or select a tool to invoke a command.
- The command line displays the command in progress along with prompts for input. Prompts can be answered with a typed entry (followed by pressing the Enter key) and/or a mouse selection or location.
- The Enter key and spacebar are interchangeable except in the text editor.
- The Escape key cancels any command in progress.
- When specifying a coordinate, it must have an x-value and a y-value. When specifying a distance, it only needs one value.
- Use the Clean Screen (Ctrl + 0) toggle to increase your drawing area.

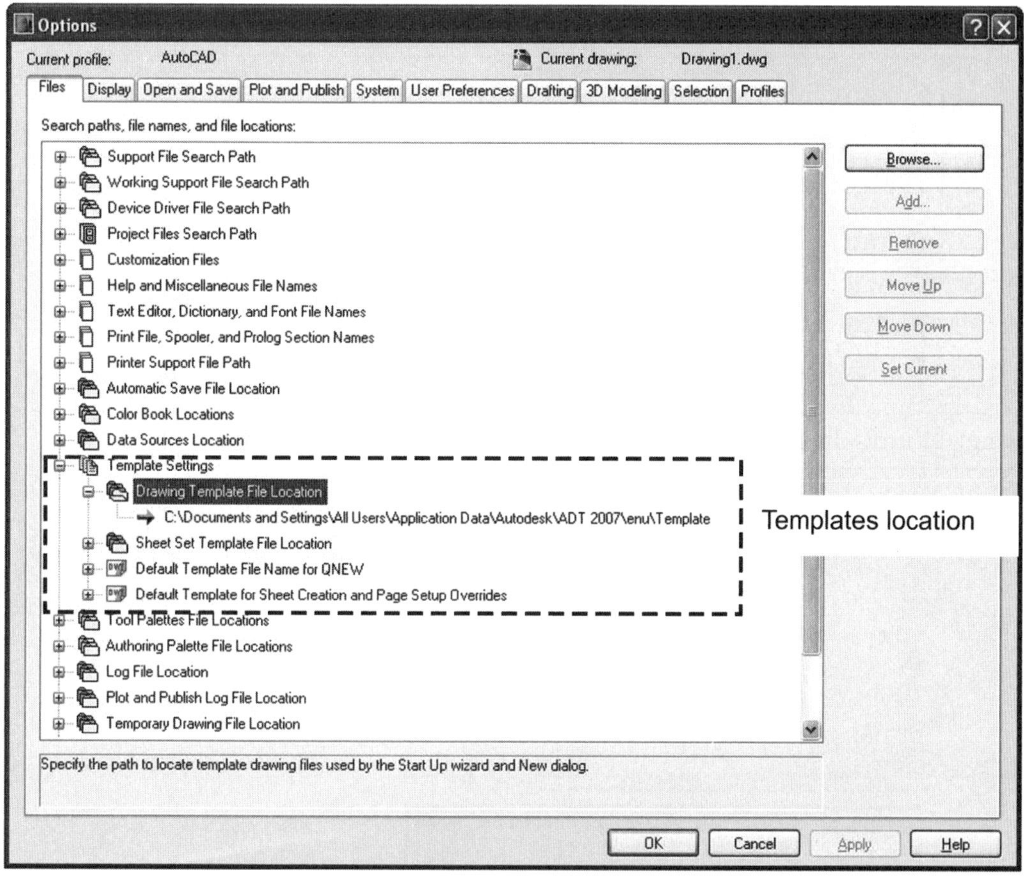

Figure E.1

Appendices

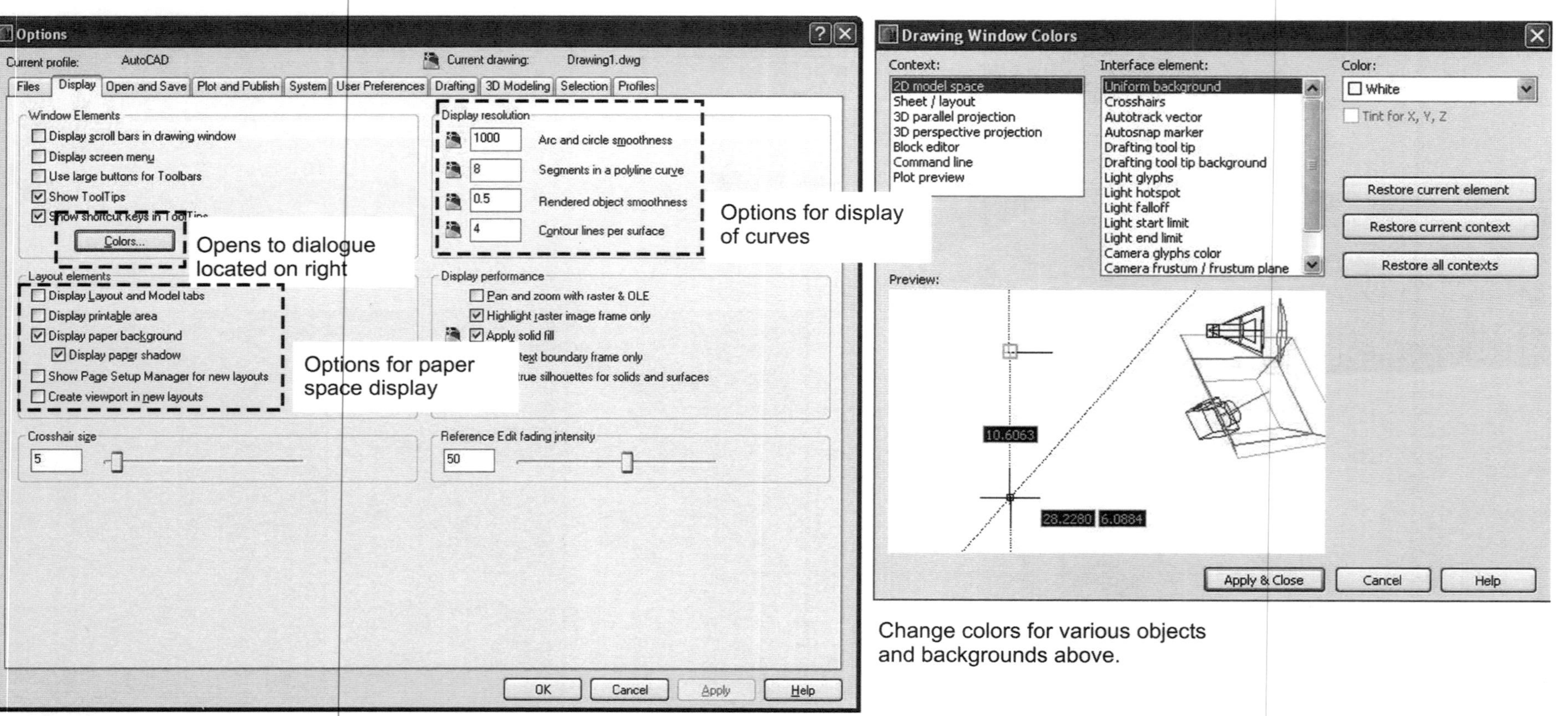
Options
Current profile: AutoCAD
Current drawing: Drawing1.dwg
Files
Display
Open and Save
Plot and Publish
System
User Preferences
Drafting
3D Modeling
Selection
Profiles
Window Elements
Display scroll bars in drawing window
Display screen menu
Use large buttons for Toolbars
Show ToolTips
Colors...
Opens to dialogue located on right
Display resolution
1000 Arc and circle smoothness
8 Segments in a polyline curve
0.5 Rendered object smoothness
4 Contour lines per surface
Options for display of curves
Layout elements
Display Layout and Model tabs
Display printable area
Display paper background
Display paper shadow
Show Page Setup Manager for new layouts
Create viewport in new layouts
Options for paper space display
Display performance
Pan and zoom with raster & OLE
Highlight raster image frame only
Apply solid fill
text boundary frame only
true silhouettes for solids and surfaces
Crosshair size
5
Reference Edit fading intensity
50
OK
Cancel
Apply
Help
Drawing Window Colors
Context:
2D model space
Sheet / layout
3D parallel projection
3D perspective projection
Block editor
Command line
Plot preview
Interface element:
Uniform background
Crosshairs
Autotrack vector
Autosnap marker
Drafting tool tip
Drafting tool tip background
Light glyphs
Light hotspot
Light falloff
Light start limit
Light end limit
Camera glyphs color
Camera frustum / frustum plane
Color:
White
Tint for X, Y, Z
Restore current element
Restore current context
Restore all contexts
Preview:
10.6063
28.2280
6.0884
Apply & Close
Cancel
Help
Change colors for various objects and backgrounds above.

Figure E.2

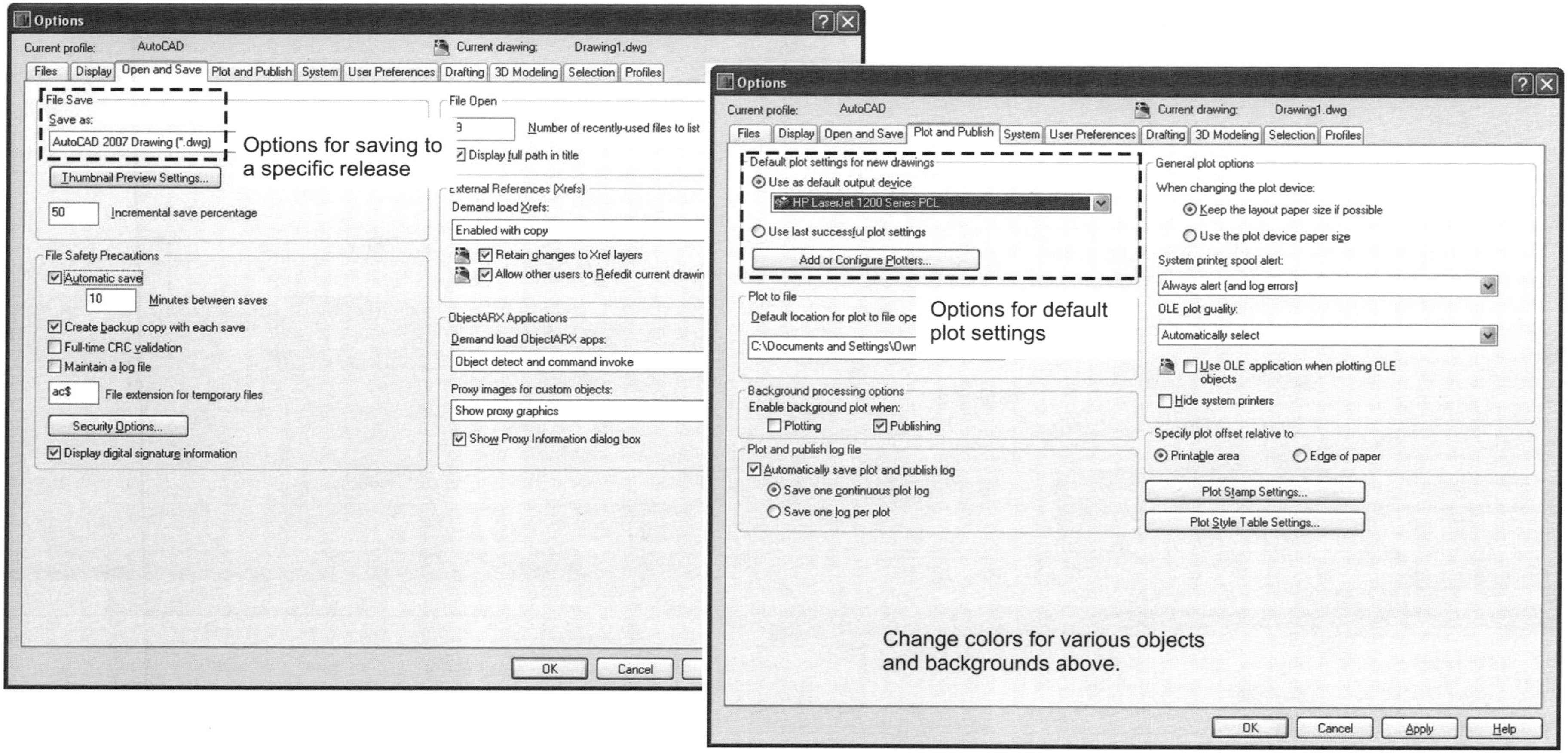

Options for saving to a specific release
Options for default plot settings
Change colors for various objects and backgrounds above.

Figure E.3

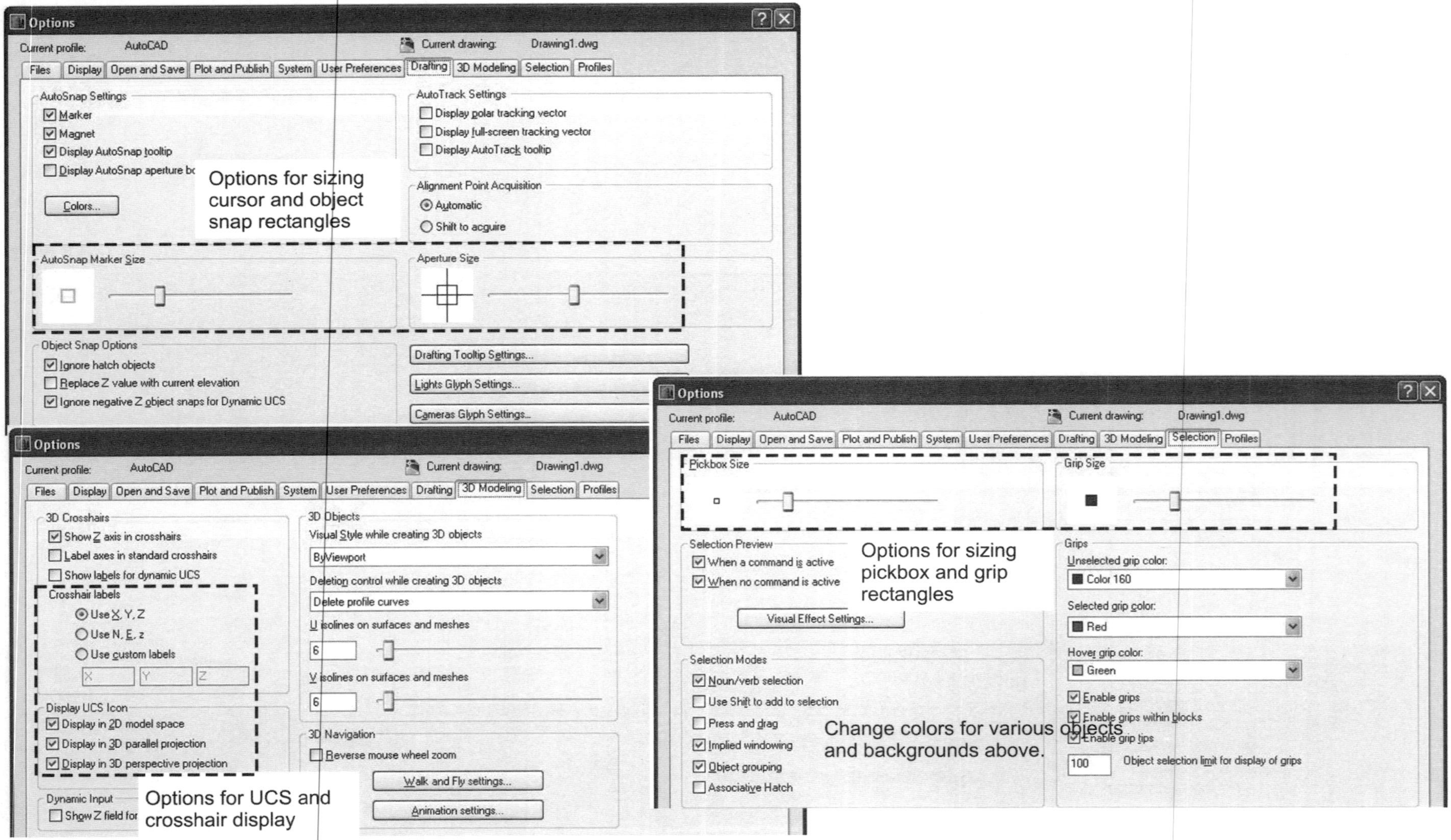

Options for sizing cursor and object snap rectangles
Options for UCS and crosshair display
Options for sizing pickbox and grip rectangles
Change colors for various objects and backgrounds above.

Figure E.4

Appendix F: AutoCAD Shortcuts

3A	3DARRAY
3DO	3DORBIT
3DW	3DWALK
3F	3DFACE
3M	3DMOVE
3P	3DPOLY
3R	3DROTATE
A	ARC
AC	BACTION
ADC	ADCENTER
AA	AREA
AL	ALIGN
3AL	3DALIGN
AP	APPLOAD
AR	ARRAY
ATT	ATTDEF
ATE	ATTEDIT
AT	ATTEDIT
ATTE	-ATTEDIT
B	BLOCK
BC	BCLOSE
BO	BOUNDARY
BR	BREAK
BS	BSAVE
BVS	BVSTATE
C	CIRCLE
CAM	CAMERA
CH	PROPERTIES
CF	CHAMFER
COL	COLOR
CO	COPY
CP	COPY
CYL	CYLINDER
D	DIST
DAL	DIMALIGNED
DAN	DIMANGULAR
DAR	DIMARC
JOG	DIMJOGGED
DBA	DIMBASELINE
DCE	DIMCENTER
DDI	DIMDIAMETER
DED	DIMEDIT
DI	DIST
DIV	DIVIDE
DLI	DIMLINEAR

DO	DONUT
DOR	DIMORDINATE
DOV	DIMOVERRIDE
DR	DRAWORDER
DRD	DIMRADIUS
DRM	DRAWINGRECOVERY
DS	DSETTINGS
DST	DIMSTYLE
DT	DTEXT
DV	DVIEW
E	ERASE
ED	DDEDIT
EL	ELLIPSE
ER	EXTERNALREFERENCES
EX	EXTEND
EXIT	QUIT
EXP	EXPORT
F	FILLET
FI	FILTER
G	GROUP
GD	GRADIENT
GR	DDGRIPS
H	BHATCH
HE	HATCHEDIT
HI	HIDE
I	INSERT
IAD	IMAGEADJUST
IAT	IMAGEATTACH
ICL	IMAGECLIP
IM	IMAGE
IMP	IMPORT
IN	INTERSECT
INF	INTERFERE
IO	INSEROBJ
J	JOIN
L	LINE
LA	LAYER
LE	QLEADER
LEN	LENGTHEN
LI	LIST
LO	LAYOUT
LT	LINETYPE
LTS	LTSCALE
LW	LWEIGHT
M	MOVE

MA	MATCHPROP
MAT	MATERIALS
ME	MEASURE
MI	MIRROR
ML	MLINE
MS	MSPACE
MT	MTEXT
MV	MVIEW
O	OFFSET
OP	OPTIONS
OS	OSNAP
P	PAN
PA	PASTESPEC
PE	PEDIT
PL	PLINE
PO	POINT
POL	POLYGON
PR	PROPERTIES
PS	PSPACE
PU	PURGE
PYR	PYRAMID
QC	QUICKCALC
R	REDRAW
RA	REDRAWALL
REC	RECTANG
RE	REGEN
REA	REGENALL
REG	REGION
REN	RENAME
REV	REVOLVE
RM	DDRMODES
RO	ROTATE
RPR	RPREF
RR	RENDER
S	STRETCH
SC	SCALE
SCR	SCRIPT
SE	DSETTINGS
SEC	SECTION
SET	SETVAR
SHA	SHADE
SL	SLICE
SN	SNAP
SO	SOLID
SP	SPELL

SPL	SPLINE
SPE	SPLINEDIT
SSM	SHEETSET
ST	STYLE
SU	SUBTRACT
T	MTEXT
TA	TASKBAR
TB	TABLE
TH	THICKNESS
TI	TILEMODE
TO	TOOLBAR
TOR	TORUS
TP	TOOLPALETTES
TR	TRIM
TS	TABLESTYLE
UC	UCSMAN
UN	UNITS
V	VIEW
VP	DDVPOINT
VS	VSCURRENT
VSM	VISUALSTYLES
W	WBLOCK
WE	WEDGE
X	EXPLODE
XA	XATTACH
XB	XBIND
XC	XCLIP
XL	XLINE
XR	XREF
Z	ZOOM

F1	HELP
F2	COMMAND LINE DISPLAY
F3	RUNNING OSNAO ON/OFF
F4	TABLET ON/OFF
F5	ISOPLANE TOGGLE
F6	DYNAMIC UCS TOGGLE
F7	GRID ON/OFF
F8	ORTHO ON/OFF
F9	SNAP ON/OFF
F10	POLAR ON/OFF
F11	OBJECT SNAP TRACKING ON/OFF
F12	DYNAMIC INPUT ON/OFF

Appendix G: Example Layer Naming Guidelines

Example Naming for Floor Plan Layers

Layer Name	Description
A_accessory	Toilet accessories, fire extinguishers, etc.
A_accessory-dashed	Toilet accessories, fire extinguishers, etc. above cut plane
A_appliances	Residential appliances
A_bldg-outline	Outline of building boundary
A_casework	Casework visible on floor plan
A_casework-dashed	Casework above cut plane
A_clg-penetration	Ceiling access panels
A_door	Door and swing symbol
A_door-dashed	Special doors to be dashed
A_equipment	Elevators, lifts, escalators, and commercial kitchen equipment
A_equipment-dashed	Equipment above cut plane
A_floor-hatch	Floor hatches and floor patterns
A_floor-hatch-boundary	Hatch boundary lines
A_floor-penetration	Floor penetrations
A_floor-slab	Lines designating change in slab height
A_furniture	Any type of furniture that is a part of the contract
A_header	Door and window headers
A_mech-equipment	Mechanical equipment
A_note-dimension	Dimension lines and associated text
A_note	Annotations and keynotes
A_plumbing-fixture	Plumbing fixtures (toilet, janitorial, and kitchen)
A_railing	Handrails and guardrails
A_railing-dashed	Handrails and guardrails: dashed elements
A_ramp	Ramps

Layer Name	Description
A_roof-outline	Outline of roof below (for multistory building)
A_roof-outline-dashed	Outline of roof above
A_roof-penetration	Skylights and roof hatches
A_soffit	Soffit shown dashed on floor plan
A_stair	Stairs and landings
A_stair-dashed	Stairs and landings: dashed elements
A_struct-column	Columns
A_struct-footing	Structural footings (hidden)
A_tag-HC	Handicap clear width designations
A_threshold	Door thresholds
A_toilet-partition	Toilet partitions and urinal screens
A_wall	All walls
A_wall-folding	Folding walls and movable partitions
A_wall-furring	Plaster, gypsum board, and other interior wall furring
A_wall-hatch	Wall hatches
A_wall-hatch-boundary	Wall hatch boundary lines (nonplotting)
A_wall-low	Low walls
A_wall-ratings	Rated linetypes for walls
A_window-jamb	Windows
A_window-dashed	Clerestory windows and other windows to be dashed
A_window-glass	Window glazing
A_window-sill	Window sill
A_Xref	All Xrefs
X_nonplotting	Items that are not plotted
X_viewport	All viewports (not plotted)

Example Naming for Ceiling Plan Layers

Layer Name	Description
A_clg-grid	Suspended ceiling grids
A_clg-hatch-gyp	Gypsum board ceiling hatch
A_clg-hatch-plaster	Plaster ceiling hatch
A_clg-joist	Exposed ceiling joists
A_clg-penetration	Ceiling access panels
A_soffit	Soffits and changes in ceiling heights
A_elect-fan	Ceiling fans
A_elect-lights	Lights
A_header	Miscellaneous headers
A_mech-duct	Visible mechanical ducts
A_mech-grille	Mechanical supply and return grilles and exhaust
A_misc	
A_roof-outline	
A_roof-overhang	Canopies and shade devices
A_roof-penetration	Skylights and roof hatches
A_soffit	Soffits
A_soffit-dashed	Hidden soffits
A_wall-hatch	Infill wall hatches for header areas
A_wall-hatch-boundary	Wall hatch boundaries
A_wall-rating	Infill wall rating lines for header areas

Example Naming for Plot Sheet Layers

Layer Name	Description
A_keynote	General keynotes and keynote leaders
A_note-dimension	Dimension lines and associated text
A_note-heavy	Note titles and notes > 3/32" height
A_note-thin	Small text < 3/32" height
A_note	Notes 1/8" to 3/32" in height
A_pen-005	.005 mm lineweight (.002")
A_pen-015	.015 mm lineweight (.006")
A_pen-025	.025 mm lineweight (.010")
A_pen-035	.035 mm lineweight (.014")
A_pen-053	.053 mm lineweight (.021")
A_pen-070	.070 mm lineweight (.028")
A_pen-100	1.00 mm lineweight (.039" or 1/32")
A_pen-140	1.40 mm lineweight (.055" or 1/16")
A_pen-211	2.11 mm lineweight (.083" or 5/64")
A_symbols	All other symbols
A_tag-ceiling	Ceiling height and type tags
A_tag-equipment	Equipment type tags
A_tag-openings	Door and window tags
A_tag-roomname	Room name tag
A_tag-roomnum	Room number tag
A_tag-wall	Wall type tag
A_Xref	All Xrefs

Example Naming for Section and Elevation Layers

Layer Name	Description
A_pen-005	.005 mm lineweight (.002")
A_pen-015	.015 mm lineweight (.006")
A_pen-025	.025 mm lineweight (.010")
A_pen-035	.035 mm lineweight (.014")
A_pen-053	.053 mm lineweight (.021")
A_pen-070	.070 mm lineweight (.028")
A_pen-100	1.00 mm lineweight (.039" or 1/32")
A_pen-140	1.40 mm lineweight (.055" or 1/16")
A_pen-211	2.11 mm lineweight (.083" or 5/64")

Example Naming for Roof Layers

Layer Name	Description
A_equipment	Miscellaneous roof equipment
A_mech-equip	Mechanical roof equipment and ducts
A_misc	
A_roof-fascia	
A_roof-gutter	
A_roof-heavy	
A_roof-medium	
A_roof-penetrations	
A_roof-thin	

Appendix H: Commonly Used Patterns in Interior Design and Architecture

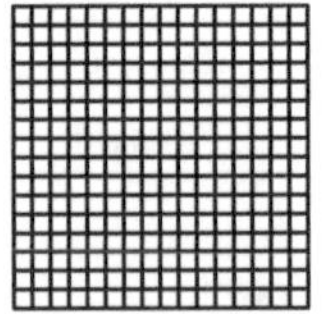
6 IN. SQ. TILE FLOOR

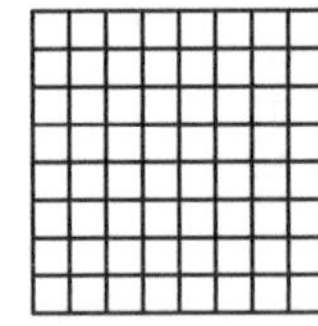
12 IN. SQ. TILE FLOOR

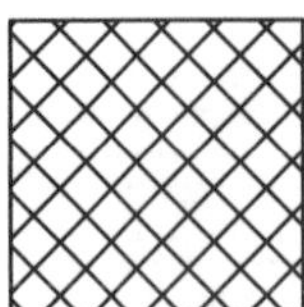
12 IN. SQ. TILE FLOOR

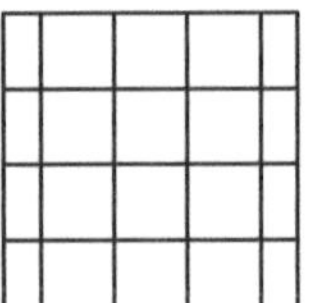
24 IN. SQ. STONE FLOOR

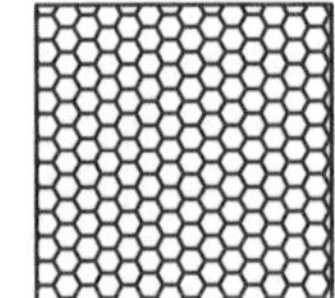
CERAMIC TILE

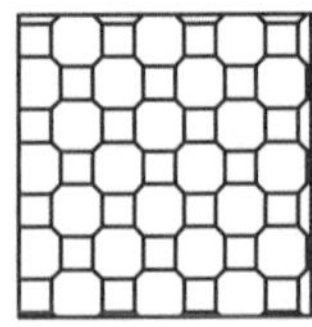
FLOOR PAVERS

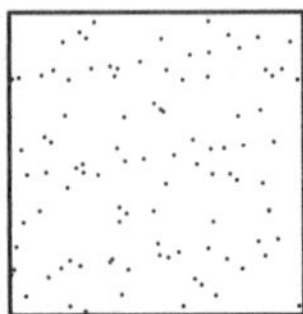
CARPET

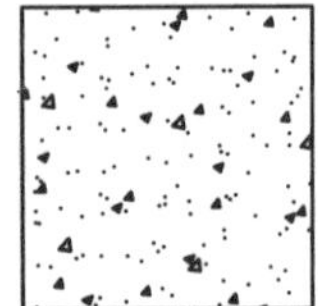
CONCRETE FLOOR

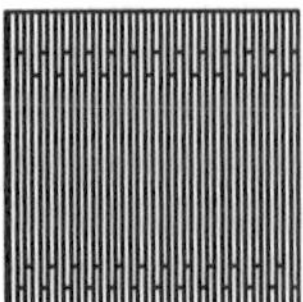
WOOD FLOORING

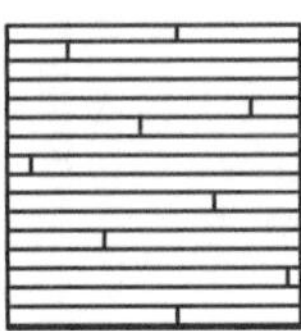
WOOD FLOORING

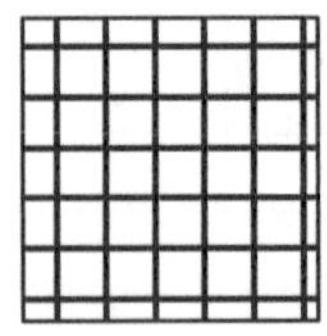
GLASS BLOCK

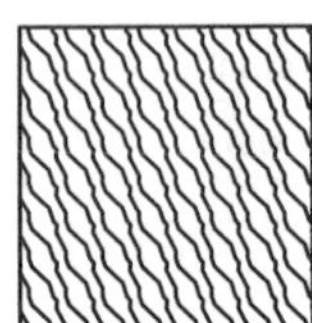
WOOD FLOORING

BRICK FLOOR

WOOD FLOORING

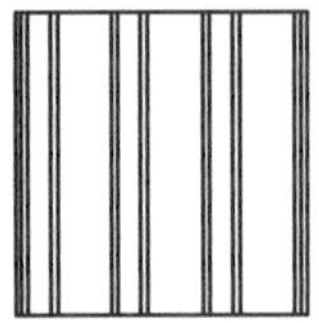
METAL SIDING/ROOFING

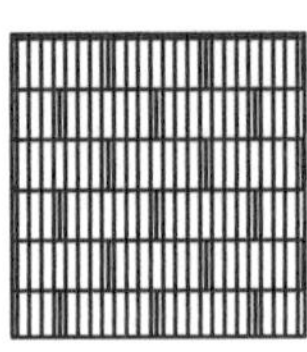
CMU RIBBED

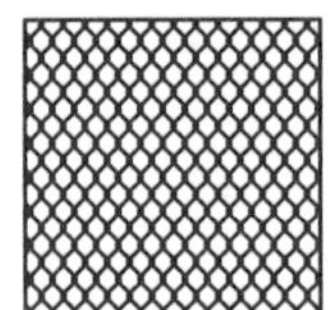
FENCING

ASPHALT PAVEMENT

Appendix I: Common Annotation and Callout Symbols Used in Floor Plans and Elevations

SYMBOLS FOR FLOOR PLANS INCLUDE:

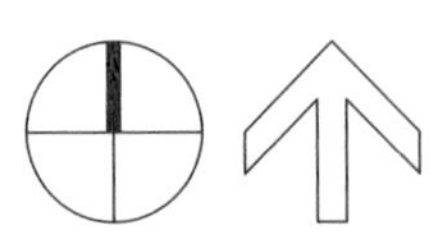
NORTH ARROWS

A A

SECTION SYMBOLS

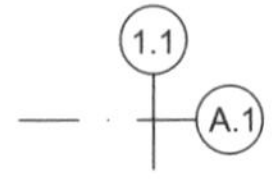

COLUMN GRID IDENTIFICATION

WINDOW TAG

DOOR TAG

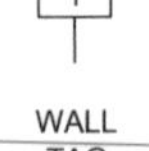

WALL TAG

KEYNOTE TAG

ROOMNAME
1301

ROOM NAMES AND NUMBERS

INTERIOR ELEVATION SYMBOLS

SYMBOLS FOR SECTIONS AND ELEVATIONS INCLUDE:

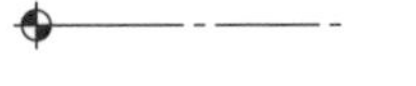
DATUM OR ELEVATION LINE

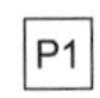

FINISH TAG

KEYNOTE TAG

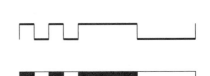

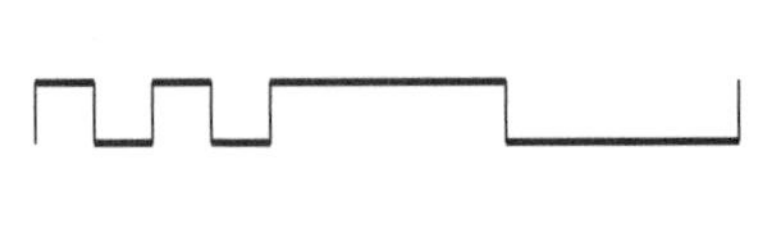
GRAPHIC SCALES

Appendix J: AutoCAD Scaling Table for Linetype Scaling, Text Sizes, and Dimscale Settings

Scaling in AutoCAD: Model Space Scaling

OUTPUT PLOT SCALE	XREF RATIOS (FOR GEOMETRY DWGS TO FIT BORDER DWGS)	DIMSCALE SETTINGS	LTSCALE SETTINGS (FOR SCALING LINETYPES IN MODEL SPACE)	PLOTTED SCALE FRACTION CONVERTED TO DECIMAL	TEXT HEIGHT IN MODEL SPACE FOR 1/16"	TEXT HEIGHT IN MODEL SPACE FOR 3/32"	TEXT HEIGHT IN MODEL SPACE FOR 1/8"	TEXT HEIGHT IN MODEL SPACE FOR 3/16"	TEXT HEIGHT IN MODEL SPACE FOR 1/4"	TEXT HEIGHT IN MODEL SPACE FOR 3/8"
1/32" = 1'-0"	.002604	384	192	.03125	2'-0"	3'-0"	4'-0"	6'-0"	8'-0"	12'-0"
1/16" = 1'-0"	.005208	192	96	.0625	1'-0"	1'-6"	2'-0"	3'-0"	4'-0"	6'-0"
1/8" = 1'-0"	.0104166	96	48	.125	6"	9"	1'-0"	1'-6"	2'-0"	3'-0"
1/4" = 1'-0"	.0208333	48	24	.25	3"	4.5"	6"	9"	1'-0"	1'-6"
3/8" = 1'-0"	.03125	32	16	.375	2"	3"	4"	6"	8"	12"
1/2" = 1'-0"	.041667	24	12	.5	1.5"	2.25"	3"	4.5"	6"	9"
1" = 1'-0"	.083333	12	6	1	3/4"	1.125"	1.5"	2.25"	3"	4.5"
3/4" = 1'-0"	.0625	16	8	.75	1"	1.5"	2"	3"	4"	6"
1 1/2" = 1'-0"	.125	8	4	1.5	1/2"	.75"	1"	1.5"	2"	3"
3" = 1'-0"	.25	4	2	3	1/4"	3/8"	1/2"	3/4"	1"	1.5"
6" = 1'-0"	.5	2	1	6	1/8"	3/16"	1/4"	3/8"	1/2"	3/4"

Appendix K: Category Organizational Structures for Constructs, Views, and Elements

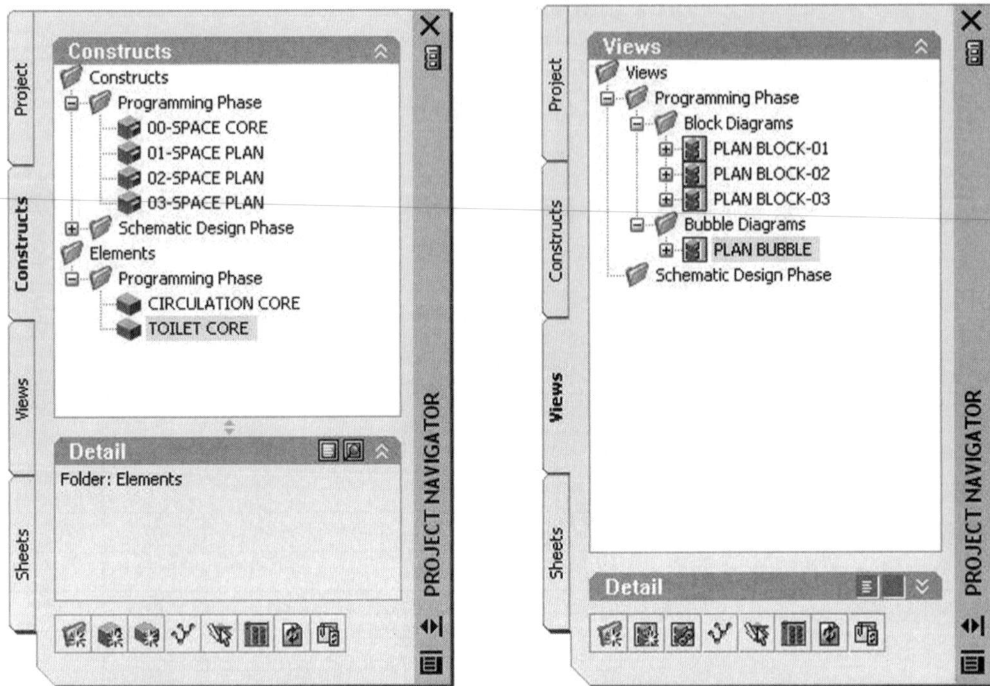

Figure K1 File naming standards for constructs and views in programming phase

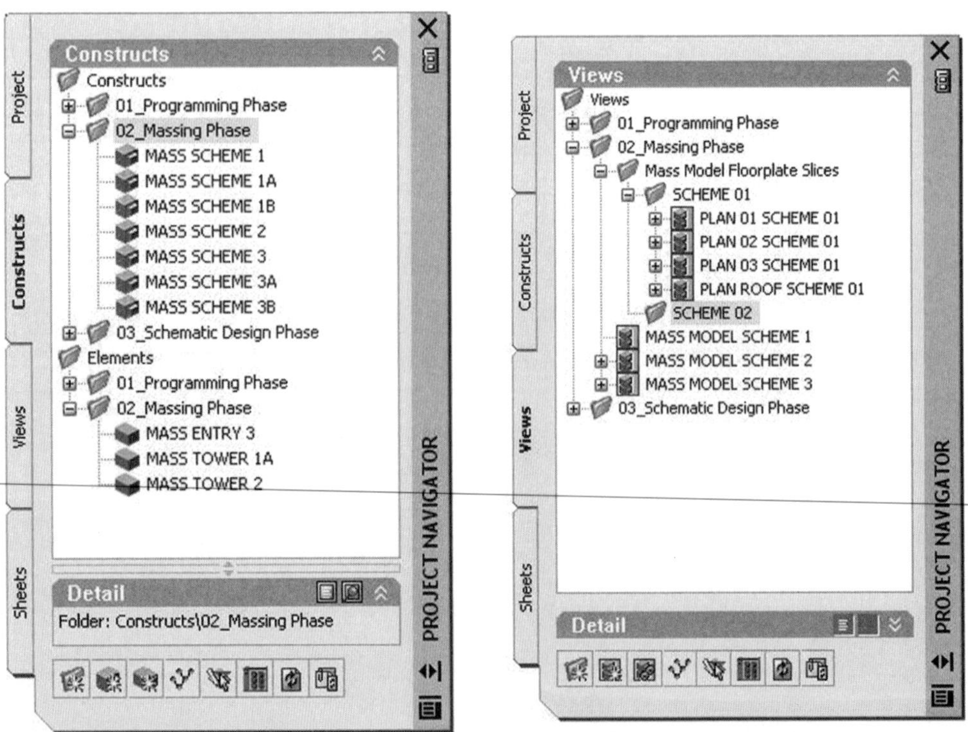

Figure K2 File naming standards for constructs and views in mass modeling phase

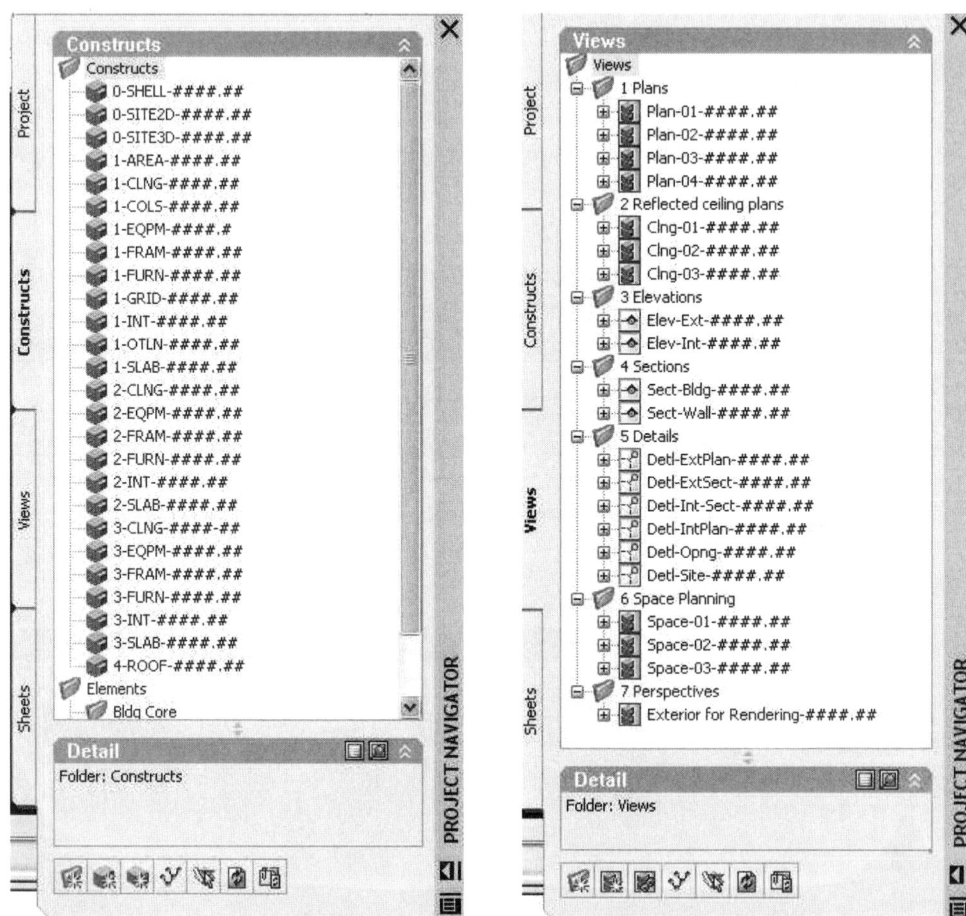

Figure K.3 File naming standards for constructs and views in schematic design and design development phases

Appendix L: References to Learn More About the Design and Construction Industries

Interior Design and Architecture

www.asid.org American Society of Interior Designers

www.iida.org International Interior Design Association

www.nbm.org National Building Museum

http://en.structurae.de International Database of Built Structures

www.aias.org Student organization of American Institute of Architects

Construction

http://library.nevada.edu/arch/rsrce/webrsrce/contents.html#contents UNLV Libraries Architecture and Building Resources

www.jlconline.com/cgi-bin/jlconline.storefront The Journal of Light Construction

www.jlconline.com/cgi-bin/jlconline.storefront/453d0ba00014391127177f0000010531/UserTemplate/88 The Journal of Light Construction Dictionary

www.efficientwindows.org Efficient Windows Collaborative (EWC)

www.transformitdesign.com Tension Fabric Architecture

www.maconline.org/tech/tech.html Masonry Advisory Council's Technical Library

Environmental and Sustainable Design Focused Websites

www.edcmag.com Environmental Design + Construction magazine

www.daylighting.org Daylighting Collaborative

www.greenbuilder.com Sourcebook for Green and Sustainable Building

www.edra.org Environmental Design Research Association (EDRA)

Miscellaneous

www.reedfirstsource.com/codes/index.asp First Source national codes resource (requires membership)

Appendix M: Mass Element Style Display Examples for Various Furniture and Fixture Types

The following screen shots illustrate the High Detail settings for viewing various mass element style conditions in plan view, including casework, furniture, and workstation elements both below and above the cut planes.

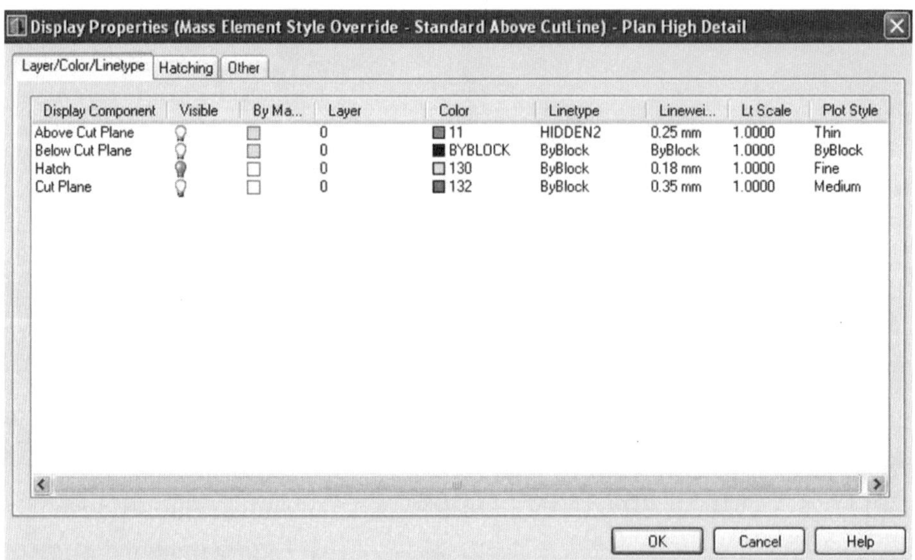

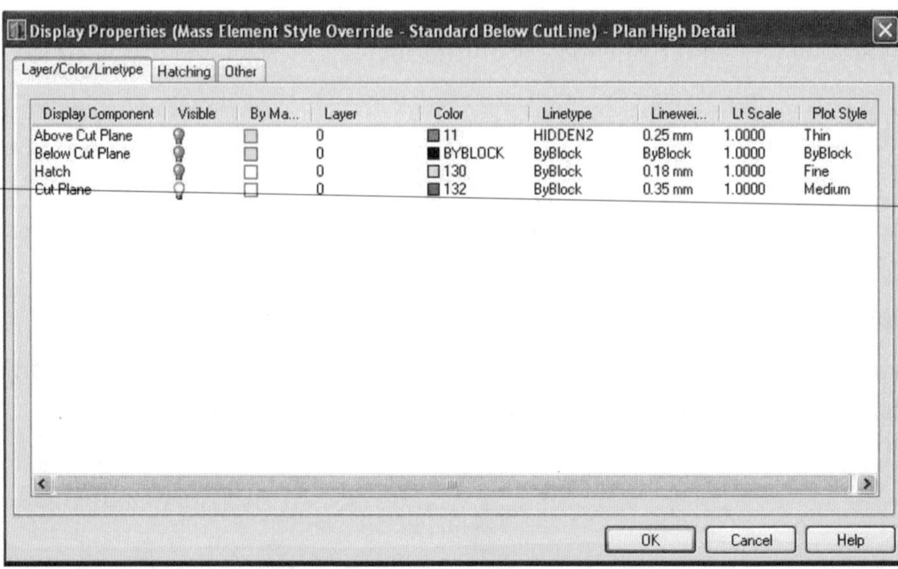

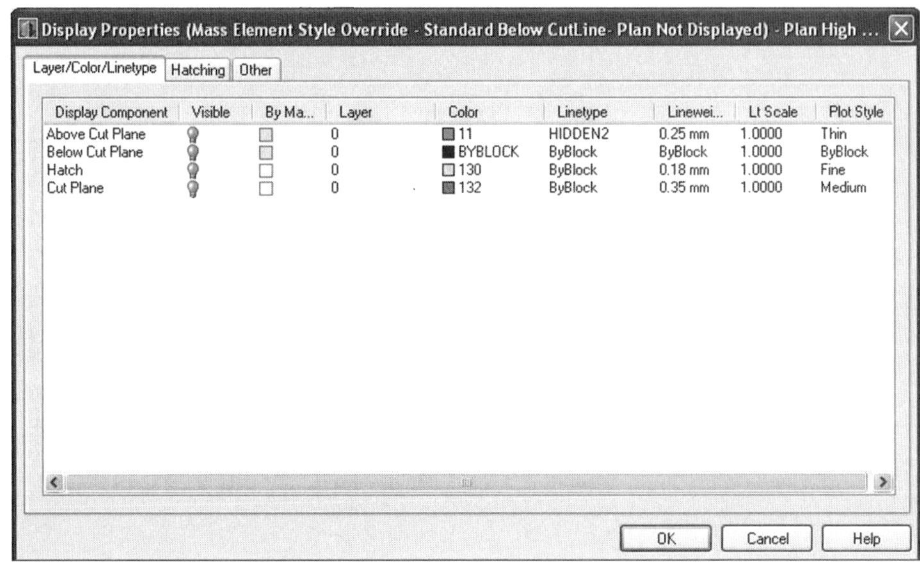
Display Properties (Mass Element Style Override - Standard Below CutLine- Plan Not Displayed) - Plan High ...
Layer/Color/Linetype
Hatching
Other
Display Component | Visible | By Ma... | Layer | Color | Linetype | Linewei... | Lt Scale | Plot Style
Above Cut Plane | 0 | 11 | HIDDEN2 | 0.25 mm | 1.0000 | Thin
Below Cut Plane | 0 | BYBLOCK | ByBlock | ByBlock | 1.0000 | ByBlock
Hatch | 0 | 130 | ByBlock | 0.18 mm | 1.0000 | Fine
Cut Plane | 0 | 132 | ByBlock | 0.35 mm | 1.0000 | Medium
OK
Cancel
Help

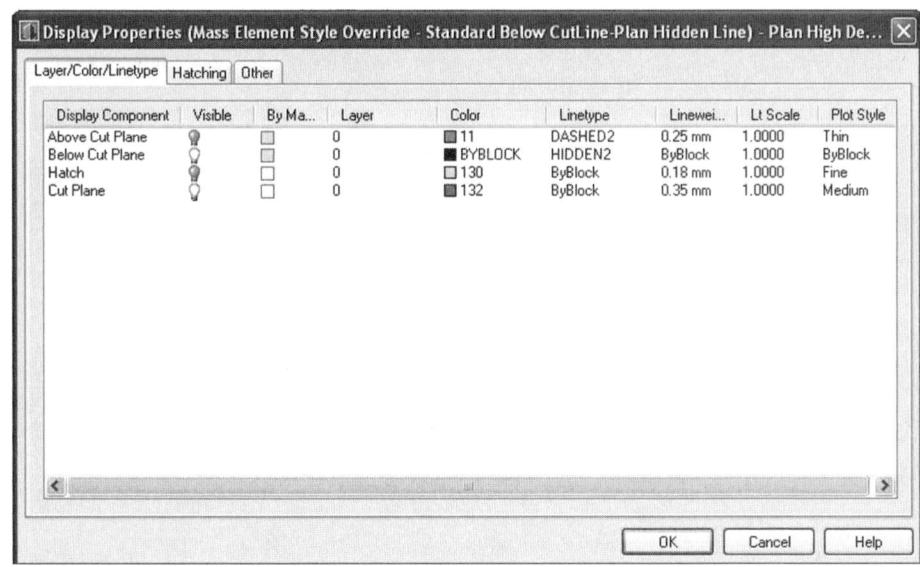
Display Properties (Mass Element Style Override - Standard Below CutLine-Plan Hidden Line) - Plan High De...
Layer/Color/Linetype
Hatching
Other
Display Component | Visible | By Ma... | Layer | Color | Linetype | Linewei... | Lt Scale | Plot Style
Above Cut Plane | 0 | 11 | DASHED2 | 0.25 mm | 1.0000 | Thin
Below Cut Plane | 0 | BYBLOCK | HIDDEN2 | ByBlock | 1.0000 | ByBlock
Hatch | 0 | 130 | ByBlock | 0.18 mm | 1.0000 | Fine
Cut Plane | 0 | 132 | ByBlock | 0.35 mm | 1.0000 | Medium
OK
Cancel
Help

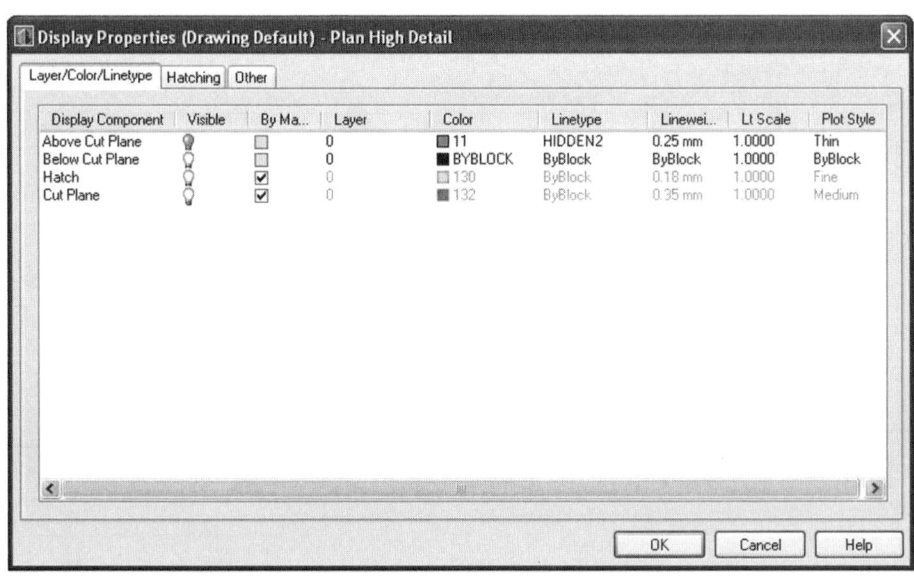
Display Properties (Drawing Default) - Plan High Detail
Layer/Color/Linetype
Hatching
Other
Display Component | Visible | By Ma... | Layer | Color | Linetype | Linewei... | Lt Scale | Plot Style
Above Cut Plane | 0 | 11 | HIDDEN2 | 0.25 mm | 1.0000 | Thin
Below Cut Plane | 0 | BYBLOCK | ByBlock | ByBlock | 1.0000 | ByBlock
Hatch | 0 | 130 | ByBlock | 0.18 mm | 1.0000 | Fine
Cut Plane | 0 | 132 | ByBlock | 0.35 mm | 1.0000 | Medium
OK
Cancel
Help

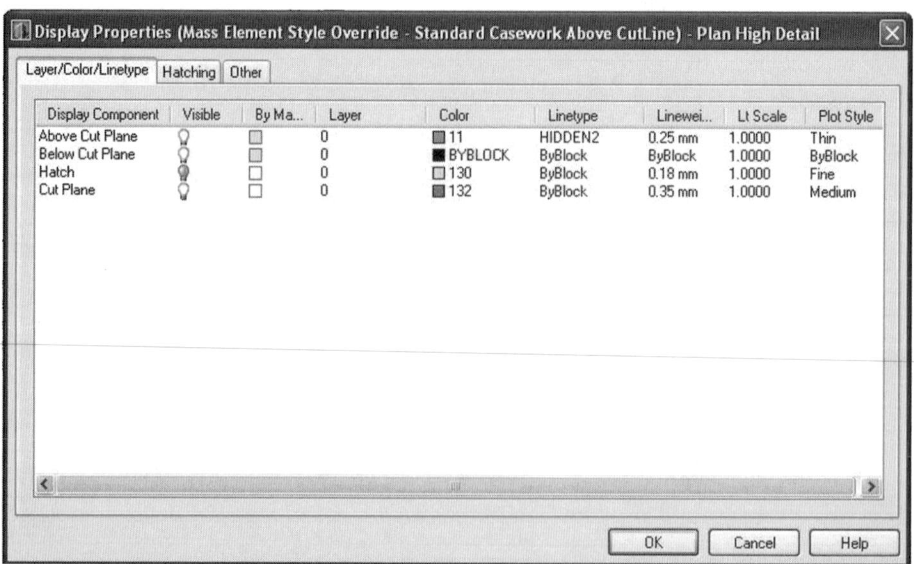
Display Properties (Mass Element Style Override - Standard Casework Above CutLine) - Plan High Detail
Layer/Color/Linetype
Hatching
Other
Display Component | Visible | By Ma... | Layer | Color | Linetype | Linewei... | Lt Scale | Plot Style
Above Cut Plane | 0 | 11 | HIDDEN2 | 0.25 mm | 1.0000 | Thin
Below Cut Plane | 0 | BYBLOCK | ByBlock | ByBlock | 1.0000 | ByBlock
Hatch | 0 | 130 | ByBlock | 0.18 mm | 1.0000 | Fine
Cut Plane | 0 | 132 | ByBlock | 0.35 mm | 1.0000 | Medium
OK
Cancel
Help

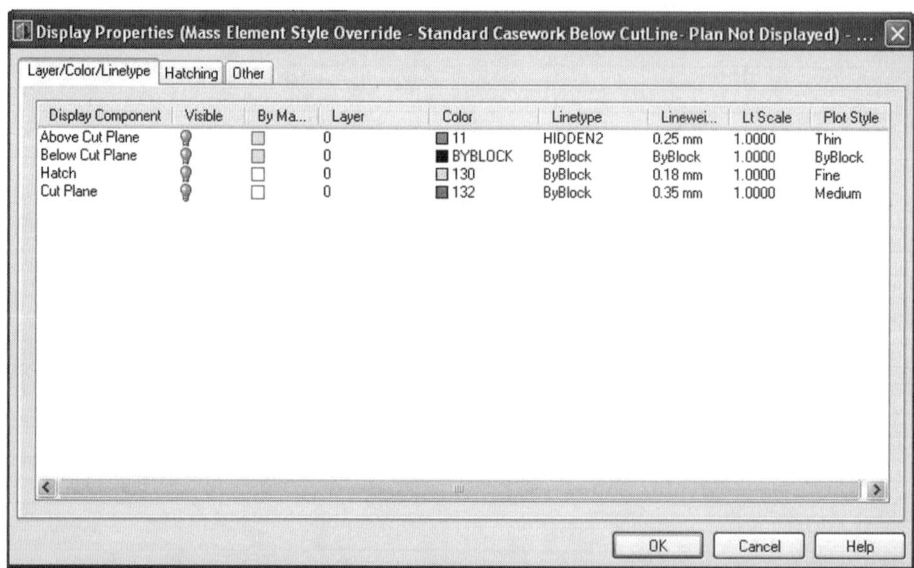
Display Properties (Mass Element Style Override - Standard Casework Below CutLine- Plan Not Displayed) - ...
Layer/Color/Linetype
Hatching
Other
Display Component | Visible | By Ma... | Layer | Color | Linetype | Linewei... | Lt Scale | Plot Style
Above Cut Plane | 0 | 11 | HIDDEN2 | 0.25 mm | 1.0000 | Thin
Below Cut Plane | 0 | BYBLOCK | ByBlock | ByBlock | 1.0000 | ByBlock
Hatch | 0 | 130 | ByBlock | 0.18 mm | 1.0000 | Fine
Cut Plane | 0 | 132 | ByBlock | 0.35 mm | 1.0000 | Medium
OK
Cancel
Help

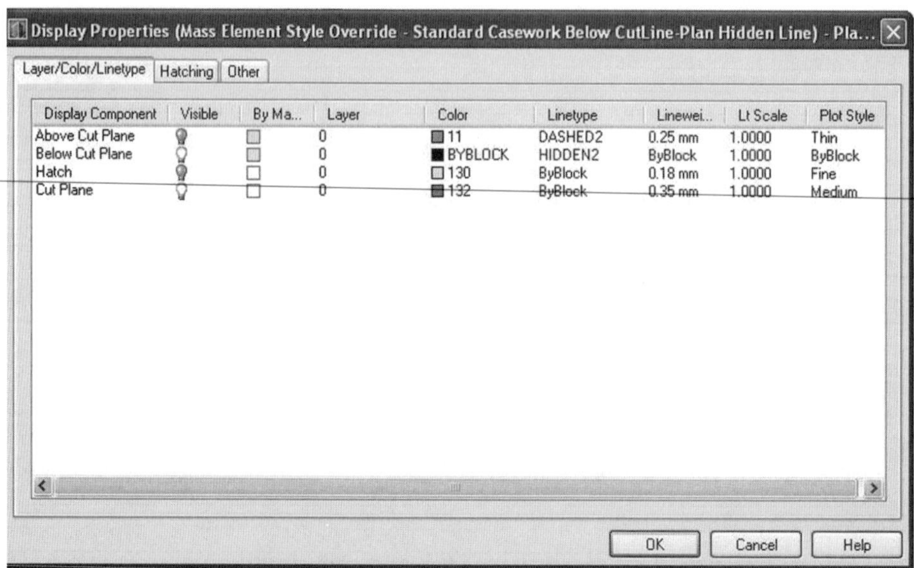
Display Properties (Mass Element Style Override - Standard Casework Below CutLine-Plan Hidden Line) - Pla...
Layer/Color/Linetype
Hatching
Other
Display Component | Visible | By Ma... | Layer | Color | Linetype | Linewei... | Lt Scale | Plot Style
Above Cut Plane | 0 | 11 | DASHED2 | 0.25 mm | 1.0000 | Thin
Below Cut Plane | 0 | BYBLOCK | HIDDEN2 | ByBlock | 1.0000 | ByBlock
Hatch | 0 | 130 | ByBlock | 0.18 mm | 1.0000 | Fine
Cut Plane | 0 | 132 | ByBlock | 0.35 mm | 1.0000 | Medium
OK
Cancel
Help

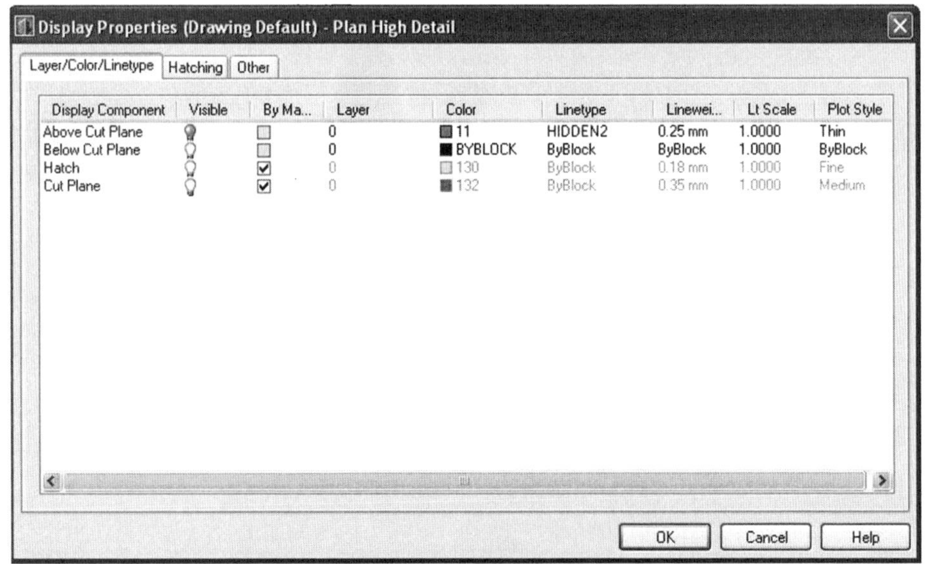

Display Properties (Drawing Default) - Plan High Detail

Layer/Color/Linetype | Hatching | Other

Display Component	Visible	By Ma...	Layer	Color	Linetype	Linewei...	Lt Scale	Plot Style
Above Cut Plane		☐	0	11	HIDDEN2	0.25 mm	1.0000	Thin
Below Cut Plane		☐	0	BYBLOCK	ByBlock	ByBlock	1.0000	ByBlock
Hatch		☑	0	130	ByBlock	0.18 mm	1.0000	Fine
Cut Plane		☑	0	132	ByBlock	0.35 mm	1.0000	Medium

OK | Cancel | Help

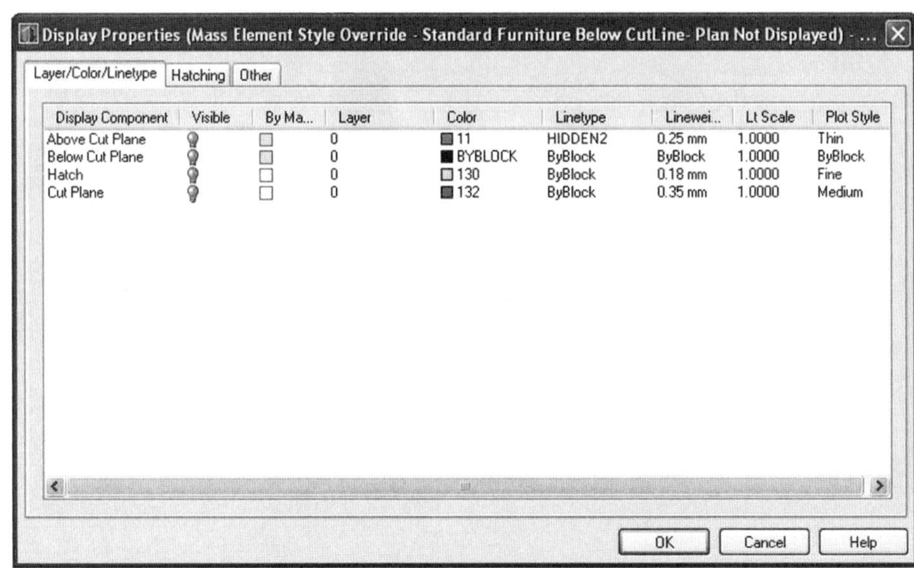

Display Properties (Mass Element Style Override - Standard Furniture Below CutLine- Plan Not Displayed) - ...

Layer/Color/Linetype | Hatching | Other

Display Component	Visible	By Ma...	Layer	Color	Linetype	Linewei...	Lt Scale	Plot Style
Above Cut Plane		☐	0	11	HIDDEN2	0.25 mm	1.0000	Thin
Below Cut Plane		☐	0	BYBLOCK	ByBlock	ByBlock	1.0000	ByBlock
Hatch		☐	0	130	ByBlock	0.18 mm	1.0000	Fine
Cut Plane		☐	0	132	ByBlock	0.35 mm	1.0000	Medium

OK | Cancel | Help

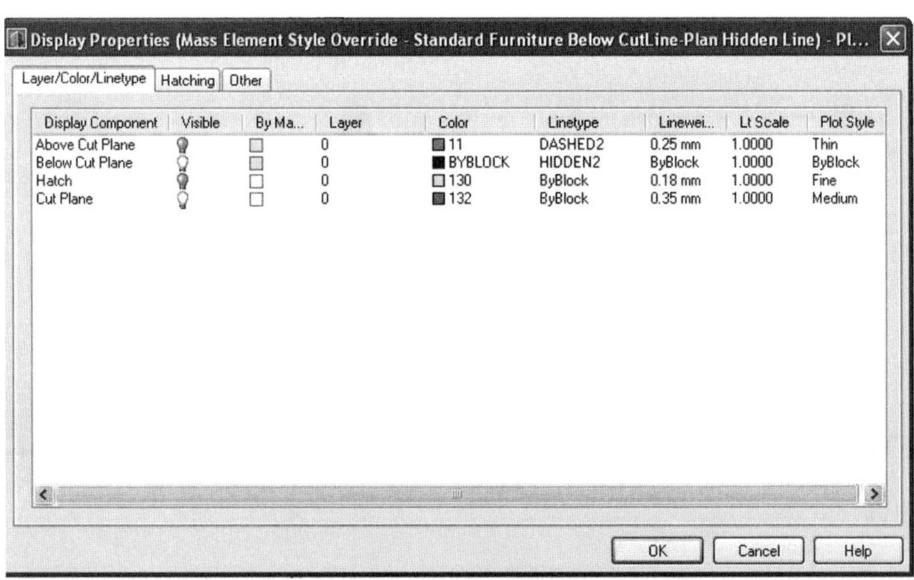

Display Properties (Mass Element Style Override - Standard Furniture Below CutLine-Plan Hidden Line) - Pl...

Layer/Color/Linetype | Hatching | Other

Display Component	Visible	By Ma...	Layer	Color	Linetype	Linewei...	Lt Scale	Plot Style
Above Cut Plane		☐	0	11	DASHED2	0.25 mm	1.0000	Thin
Below Cut Plane		☐	0	BYBLOCK	HIDDEN2	ByBlock	1.0000	ByBlock
Hatch		☐	0	130	ByBlock	0.18 mm	1.0000	Fine
Cut Plane		☐	0	132	ByBlock	0.35 mm	1.0000	Medium

OK | Cancel | Help

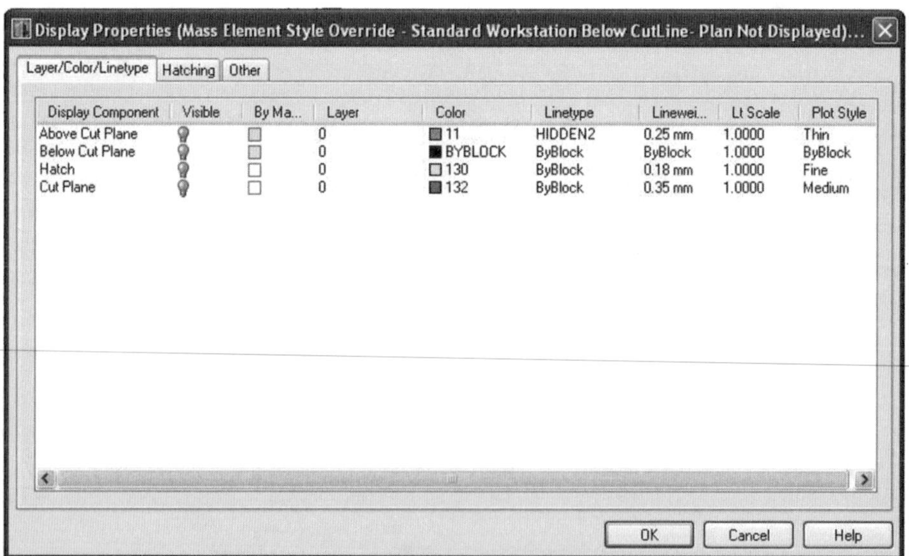

Display Properties (Mass Element Style Override - Standard Workstation Below CutLine- Plan Not Displayed)...
Layer/Color/Linetype
Hatching
Other
Display Component
Visible
By Ma...
Layer
Color
Linetype
Linewei...
Lt Scale
Plot Style
Above Cut Plane 0 11 HIDDEN2 0.25 mm 1.0000 Thin
Below Cut Plane 0 BYBLOCK ByBlock ByBlock 1.0000 ByBlock
Hatch 0 130 ByBlock 0.18 mm 1.0000 Fine
Cut Plane 0 132 ByBlock 0.35 mm 1.0000 Medium
OK
Cancel
Help

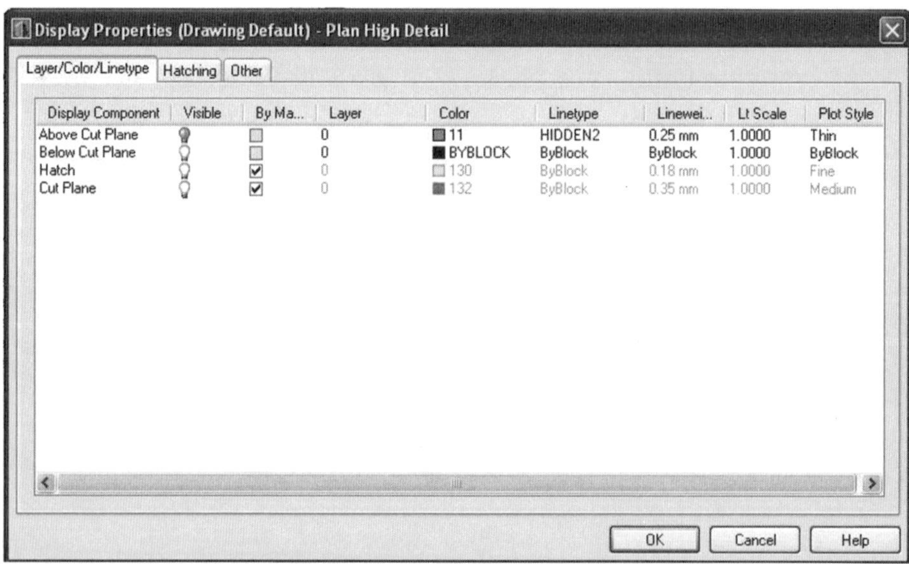

Display Properties (Drawing Default) - Plan High Detail
Layer/Color/Linetype
Hatching
Other
Display Component
Visible
By Ma...
Layer
Color
Linetype
Linewei...
Lt Scale
Plot Style
Above Cut Plane 0 11 HIDDEN2 0.25 mm 1.0000 Thin
Below Cut Plane 0 BYBLOCK ByBlock ByBlock 1.0000 ByBlock
Hatch 0 130 ByBlock 0.18 mm 1.0000 Fine
Cut Plane 0 132 ByBlock 0.35 mm 1.0000 Medium
OK
Cancel
Help

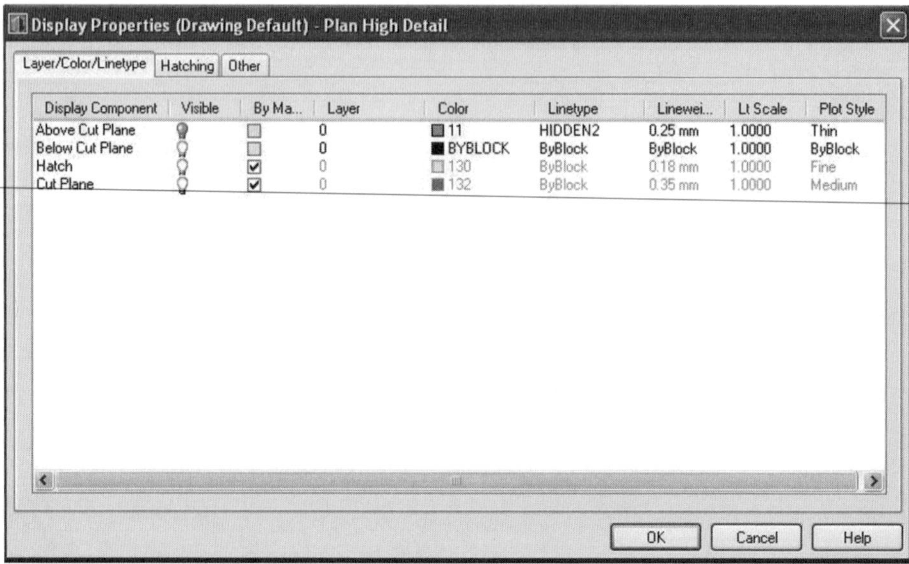

Display Properties (Drawing Default) - Plan High Detail
Layer/Color/Linetype
Hatching
Other
Display Component
Visible
By Ma...
Layer
Color
Linetype
Linewei...
Lt Scale
Plot Style
Above Cut Plane 0 11 HIDDEN2 0.25 mm 1.0000 Thin
Below Cut Plane 0 BYBLOCK ByBlock ByBlock 1.0000 ByBlock
Hatch 0 130 ByBlock 0.18 mm 1.0000 Fine
Cut Plane 0 132 ByBlock 0.35 mm 1.0000 Medium
OK
Cancel
Help

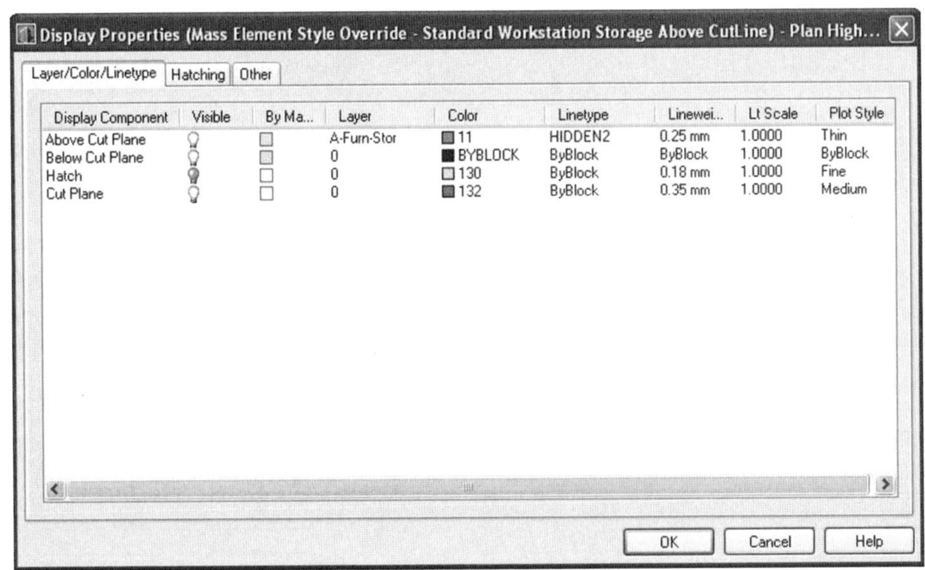
Display Properties (Mass Element Style Override - Standard Workstation Storage Above CutLine) - Plan High...
Layer/Color/Linetype
Hatching
Other
Display Component | Visible | By Ma... | Layer | Color | Linetype | Linewei... | Lt Scale | Plot Style
Above Cut Plane | A-Furn-Stor | 11 | HIDDEN2 | 0.25 mm | 1.0000 | Thin
Below Cut Plane | 0 | BYBLOCK | ByBlock | ByBlock | 1.0000 | ByBlock
Hatch | 0 | 130 | ByBlock | 0.18 mm | 1.0000 | Fine
Cut Plane | 0 | 132 | ByBlock | 0.35 mm | 1.0000 | Medium
OK
Cancel
Help

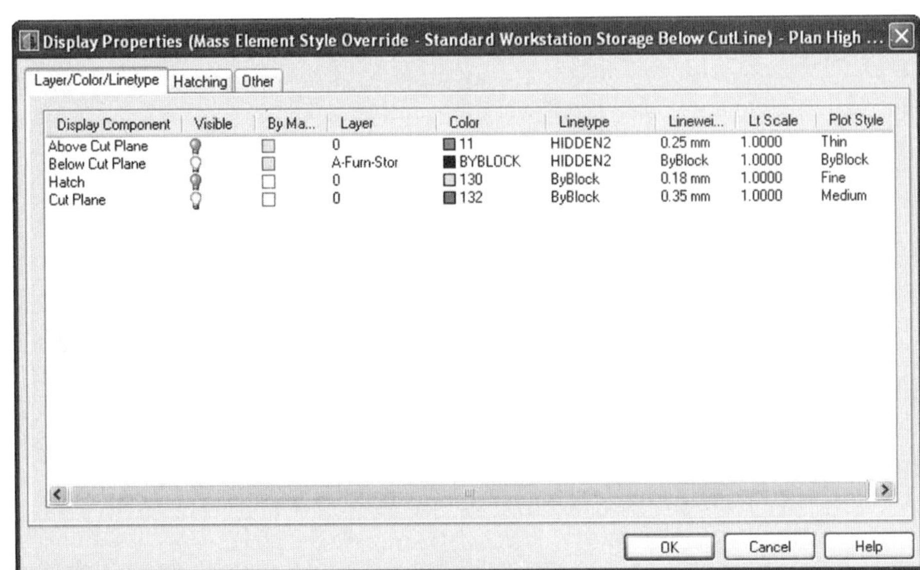
Display Properties (Mass Element Style Override - Standard Workstation Storage Below CutLine) - Plan High ...
Layer/Color/Linetype
Hatching
Other
Display Component | Visible | By Ma... | Layer | Color | Linetype | Linewei... | Lt Scale | Plot Style
Above Cut Plane | 0 | 11 | HIDDEN2 | 0.25 mm | 1.0000 | Thin
Below Cut Plane | A-Furn-Stor | BYBLOCK | HIDDEN2 | ByBlock | 1.0000 | ByBlock
Hatch | 0 | 130 | ByBlock | 0.18 mm | 1.0000 | Fine
Cut Plane | 0 | 132 | ByBlock | 0.35 mm | 1.0000 | Medium
OK
Cancel
Help

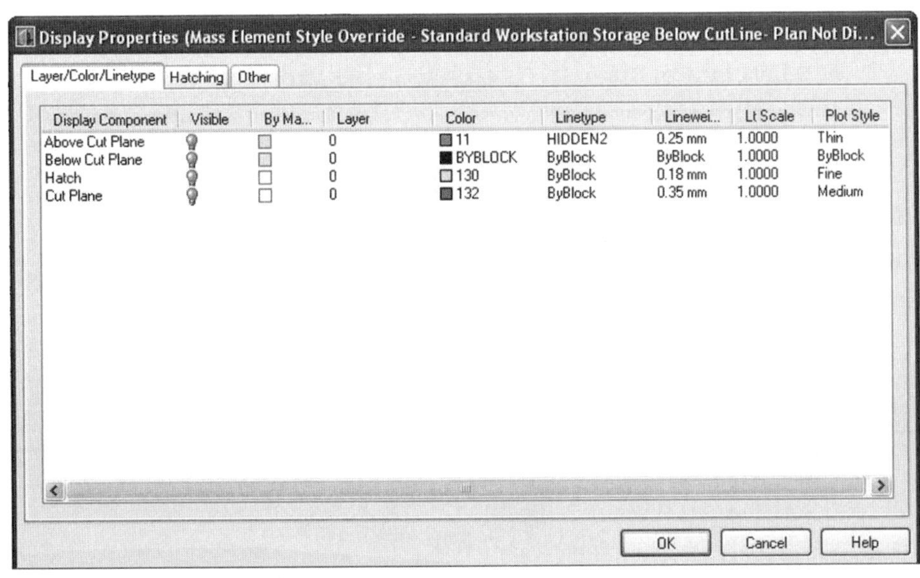
Display Properties (Mass Element Style Override - Standard Workstation Storage Below CutLine- Plan Not Di...
Layer/Color/Linetype
Hatching
Other
Display Component | Visible | By Ma... | Layer | Color | Linetype | Linewei... | Lt Scale | Plot Style
Above Cut Plane | 0 | 11 | HIDDEN2 | 0.25 mm | 1.0000 | Thin
Below Cut Plane | 0 | BYBLOCK | ByBlock | ByBlock | 1.0000 | ByBlock
Hatch | 0 | 130 | ByBlock | 0.18 mm | 1.0000 | Fine
Cut Plane | 0 | 132 | ByBlock | 0.35 mm | 1.0000 | Medium
OK
Cancel
Help

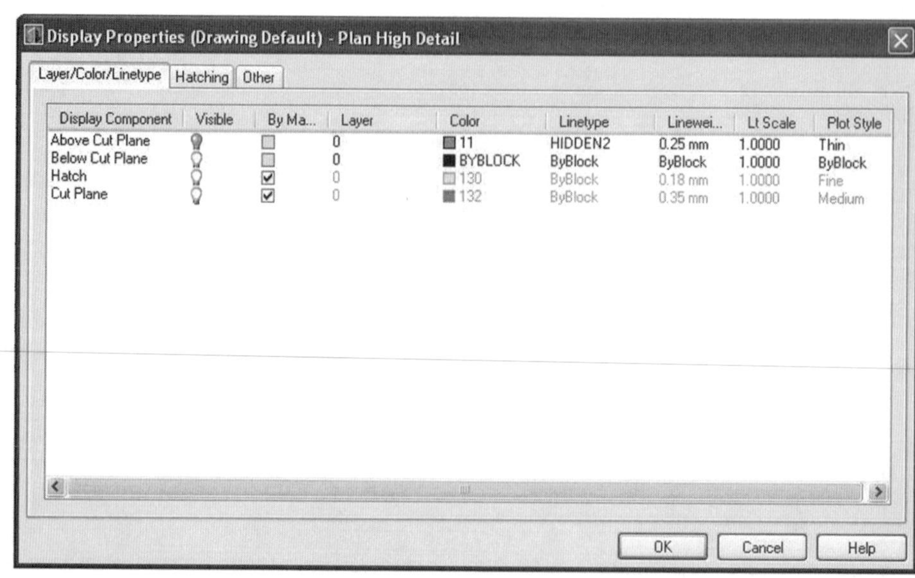

Appendices

Appendix N: Design References

Architects and Designers

Alvar Aalto
Tadao Ando
Edward Larabee Barnes
Luis Barragan
Mario Botta
Marcel Breuer
Santiago Calatrava
Cambridge Seven
Le Corbusier
Charles and Ray Eames
Peter Eisenman
Norman Foster
Antonio Gaudí
Bruce Goff
Michael Graves
Greene and Greene
Walter Gropius
Guarino Guarini
Gwathmey-Siegel
Zaha Hadid
Hans Hollein
Hardy Holzman Pfeiffer
Helmut Jahn
Philip Johnson
Fay Jones
Louis Kahn
Rem Koolhaas
Daniel Libeskind
Maya Lin
Richard Meier
Julia Morgan
Morphosis
Glen Murcutt
Andrew Palladio
I.M. Pei
Cesar Pelli
Aldo Rossi
Eero Saarinen
Moshe Safdie
Carlo Scarpa
Rudolf Schindler
Louis Sullivan
Stanley Tigerman
Mies van der Rohe
Frank Lloyd Wright

Book References

Ching, Frank. 1996. *Architecture: Form, Space, and Order.* Second ed. New York: John Wiley & Sons.

— 1998. *Design Drawing.* New York: John Wiley & Sons.

— 1987. *Interior Design Illustrated.* New York: John Wiley & Sons.

Laseau, Paul. 1991. *Architectural Drawing: Options for Design.* First ed. New York: Design Press.

Mitton, Maureen. 1999. *Interior Design Visual Presentation.* New York: John Wiley & Sons.

Yee, Rendow. 1997. *Architectural Drawing: A Complete Compendium of Types and Methods.* New York: John Wiley & Sons.

Appendix O: AutoCAD Lineweight and Linetype Examples

AutoCAD Lineweights

.05 MM

.09 MM

.13 MM

.15 MM

.18 MM

.20 MM

.25 MM

.30 MM

.35 MM

.40 MM

.50 MM

.60 MM

1.00 MM

1.20 MM

AutoCAD Linetypes

CONTINUOUS

DASHED

HIDDEN

CENTER

BATTING

BORDER

DIVIDE

DOTS

PHANTOM

TRACKS

ZIGZAG

Appendix P: Checklists for Floor Plans, Ceiling Plans, Roof Plans, and Sections and Elevations

Note: Items preceded by an asterisk (*) are usually found only in construction related drawings

Floor Plan Checklist

Architectural Objects

1. Full-height walls
2. Low or partial height walls do not clean up to full height walls.
3. Doors: Reference codes on door sizes and approach requirements for residential and commercial buildings.
4. Windows: Reference codes on window requirements for residential and commercial buildings.
5. Stairs with handrail and/or guardrails: Review code restrictions for residential and commercial buildings.
6. Lower cabinetry or casework
7. Upper cabinetry or casework
8. Upper shelving and rods in closets
9. Appliances
10. Toilet partitions
11. Plumbing fixtures
12. Systems furniture and equipment (file cabinets, shelving, and bookcases)
13. Furniture
14. Accessories, including mirror, medicine cabinet, toilet paper, sanitary napkin, toilet cover, grab bar, soap holder, soap dispenser, paper napkin dispenser, drinking fountains, hand dryer, and towel bar
15. (optional) Entourage accessories, including computers, televisions, plants, sculpture, and wall hangings
16. Significant changes in ceiling planes and double-height spaces
17. Skylights overhead
18. Floor material and floor level changes
19. Fireplaces
20. *Hose bib and fire extinguisher locations

Annotation and Labeling

1. Drawing title, scale, and north arrow for each floor plan drawing
2. Leadered notes that explain special floor plan features
3. Changes in floor level, including ramp slopes
4. Stair directions
5. Room names or room legend
6. Applicable circles and rectangles to indicate ADA compliance (if required)
7. *Wall types legend
8. Section callout symbols
9. Exterior elevation callouts (if new building)
10. Detail callouts
11. *Exterior dimensions
12. *Interior dimensions

Ceiling Plan Checklist

Architectural Objects

1. Full-height walls
2. Columns
3. Door headers instead of doors
4. Exposed beams, joists, and/or girders
5. *Unistrut systems
6. Exposed ductwork
7. Exposed roofs
8. Ceiling-hung toilet partitions
9. Ceiling soffits, light coves, and ceiling changes in height
10. Ceiling-mounted equipment, including projection screens
11. Ceiling mounted tracks for doors or movable partitions
12. *Curtain tracks
13. Ceiling penetrations, including skylights
14. Catwalks
15. Exterior overhangs, trellises, and/or canopies
16. *Exterior venting/soffit ventilation
17. Hatching to represent ceiling materials—gypsum board, acoustical tile, plaster, metal panels, and more
18. *Expansion and/or control joints
19. Ceiling light fixtures—surface mounted, recessed, track, and pendant
20. Ceiling fans
21. Mechanical diffusers and grilles
22. *Fire sprinklers piping and heads (if required)

Annotation and Labeling

1. Drawing title, scale, and north arrow for each ceiling plan drawing
2. Leadered notes that explain special ceiling features
3. Ceiling height tags
4. Room names or room legend
5. Ceiling symbols legend
6. Open to above labels
7. Section callout symbols
8. Exterior elevation callouts (if new building)
9. Detail callouts
10. Exterior dimensions (if new building and required)
11. Interior dimensions to locate soffits (if required)

Roof Plan Checklist

Architectural Objects

1. Roof plan shape
2. Changes in roof elevation
3. Ridge lines, valley lines, and crickets
4. Exposed parapets and walls
5. Gutters, scuppers, and downspouts
6. Skylights and solar panels
7. *Roof hatches
8. *Traffic pads
9. *Mechanical units
10. Exterior freestanding columns
11. Hatching to represent roofing materials

Annotation and Labeling

1. Drawing title, scale, and north arrow for each roof plan drawing
2. Leadered notes that explain special roof features
3. Arrows identifying roof slopes with pitch identification
4. Section callout symbols

5. Exterior elevation callouts (if new building)
6. *Exterior dimensions
7. *Exterior vertical dimensions of floor levels, soffits, canopies, balconies, top plate heights, roof lines, and parapet framing

Section and Elevation Checklist

Architectural Objects–Exterior Elevations

In general, draw exterior elevations in a north, east, south, west sequence. Building entrance elevations should, however, be at the top of the plot sheet.

- Ground Line (finish grade)
- Building outline and all setbacks and building shape changes
- Roof shape/outline, *ridge vents, and attic vents (if visible)
- *Downspouts, scuppers, and splash blocks
- Doors, windows, openings, louvers, and garage doors
- Trim, moldings, and flashing for doors, windows, openings, and so on
- Wall material patterns and finishes, including joints and scoring
- Canopies, sunscreens, and trellises
- *Below grade footings and stairs
- Signage and plaques
- Mailboxes, standpipes, and/or other mechanical equipment
- Exterior stairs, ramps, and ladders
- Exterior handrails and guardrails
- Loading docks with truck bumpers and restrainers
- Exterior wall-mounted lighting
- Retaining walls, fences, gates, and planters

Annotation and Labeling–Exterior Elevations

1. Drawing title and scale for each elevation drawing
2. Leadered notes that identify exterior materials, finishes, and/or colors
3. *Window and louver identification tags
4. *Column lines and column bubbles that coordinate with floor plans
5. *Section callout symbols
6. Indicate slope ratios for all pitched roofs that are visible

Architectural Objects–Interior Elevations

In general, draw exterior elevations in a north, east, south, west sequence in numerical order of room numbers.

- Wall materials, finishes, and wall treatments
- Wainscot, chair rails, and other wall trim
- Doors and windows, including door swing and window opening indicators
- Casework including counters, shelving, and other built-in furniture
- Casework hardware
- Plumbing fixtures, including lavatories, toilets, bathtubs, showers, and drinking fountains
- Appliances, including stoves, dishwashers, and refrigerators
- Accessories, including mirrors, medicine cabinets, toilet paper dispensers, sanitary napkin dispensers, toilet covers, grab bars, soap holders, soap dispensers, paper napkin dispensers, drinking fountains, hand dryers, and towel bars
- Wall-mounted light fixtures
- Chalkboards, tackboards, wipeboards, and display and trophy cases
- Wall outlets, phone jacks, speakers, thermostats, and motion-sensor equipment
- Vending machines

Annotation and Labeling–Interior Elevations

1. Drawing title and scale for each elevation drawing
2. Room numbers and room names
3. Leadered notes or symbols that label materials
4. *Dimensions—floor to ceiling, counter heights, toilet accessories, and drinking fountains

Architectural Objects–Building Sections

Since the building section is a combination of a sectional and elevation drawing, many of the same items in the interior and exterior elevations might also be visible in the building section.

- Ground line (finish grade)
- Wall system components, including sound-proofing and thermal insulation
- Ceilings
- Roof shape/outline, *ridge vents, and attic vents (if visible)
- Skylights
- *Downspouts, scuppers, and splash blocks (if visible)
- Doors, windows, openings, louvers, and garage doors
- Trim, moldings, and flashing for doors, windows, openings, and so on
- Wall material patterns and finishes, including joints and scoring
- Canopies, sunscreens, and trellises
- Below-grade footings, walls, and stairs
- Stairs, ramps, and ladders
- Handrails and guardrails
- Structural framing
- *Fireproofing symbols, including fire-rated walls, structural protection, fire blocking, and draft stops
- *Mechanical equipment

Annotation and Labeling–Building Sections

- Drawing title and scale for each building section drawing
- Room numbers and room names
- Leadered notes that label parts of the section
- *Column lines and column bubbles that coordinate with floor plans
- Indicate slope ratios for all pitched roofs that are visible
- Section callout symbols
- *Exterior vertical dimensions of floor levels, soffits, canopies, balconies, top plate heights, roof lines, and parapet framing

Appendix Q: Additional Website Resources for AutoCAD and ADT

The following Web sites offer additional resources for learning and using AutoCAD and Architectural Desktop.

Hatch Patterns, Linetypes, and AutoCAD fonts

www.autocadhatchpatterns.com

2-D and 3-D Objects and Symbols

www.3dcadbrowser.com/browse.aspx
www.mr-cad.com
www.vizdepot.com
www.3dmodelsharing.com

Tutorials

www.scottonstott.com
www.autocadcentral.com
www.caddigest.com/subjects/autocad/TIPS.htm
http://usa.autodesk.com
www.hyperpics.com/tipsandtricks/index.asp
www.dotsoft.com/acadtips.htm

Software Add-ons

www.archvision.com
www.bluebeam.com/web03/?src=99
www.motivesys.com

Online CAD-related Stores, Magazines, Informational Web sites

www.cadalog.com
www.cadopolis.com
www.caddigest.com/subjects/autocad
www.caddepot.com
www.cadalyst.com/cadalyst
www.geocities.com/cadgurucool
www.activedwg.com

Appendix R: Standard Paper Sizes

ANSI Paper Sizes

ANSI A	11 × 8.5	Letter
ANSI B	17 × 11	Tabloid
ANSI C	22 × 17	
ANSI D	34 × 22	
ANSI E	44 × 34	

Architectural Sizes

ARCH A	12 × 9
ARCH B	18 × 12
ARCH C	24 × 18
ARCH D	36 × 24
ARCH E	48 × 36

Index